# Data Structures and Abstractions with Java™

*Fourth Edition*

*Global Edition*

## Frank M. Carrano
*University of Rhode Island*

## Timothy M. Henry
*New England Institute of Technology*

Global Edition contributions by

Mohit P. Tahiliani
*National Institute of Technology Karnataka*

**PEARSON**

Boston   Columbus   Indianpolis   New York   San Francisco   Amsterdam
Cape Town   Dubai   London   Madrid   Milan   Munich   Paris   Montréal   Toronto
Delhi   Mexico City   São Paulo   Sydney   Hong Kong   Seoul   Singapore   Taipei   Tokyo

*Editorial Director, ECS:* Marcia Horton
*Executive Editor:* Tracy Johnson (Dunkelberger)
*Editorial Assistant:* Kelsey Loanes
*Director of Marketing:* Christy Lesko
*Product Marketing Manager:* Bram van Kempen
*Field Marketing Manager:* Demetrius Hall
*Marketing Assistant:* Jon Bryant
*Director of Program Management:* Erin Gregg
*Program Management-Team Lead:* Scott Disanno
*Program Manager:* Carole Snyder
*Project Manager:* Robert Engelhardt
*Procurement Specialist:* Maura Zaldivar-Garcia
*Assistant Acquisitions Editor, Global Edition:*
   Aditee Agarwal

*Project Editor, Global Edition:*
   Amrita Naskar
*Manager, Media Production, Global Edition:*
   Vikram Kumar
*Senior Manufacturing Controller, Production,*
   *Global Edition:* Trudy Kimber
*Senior Art Director:* Kathryn Foot
*Cover Designer:* Lumina Datamatics Ltd.
*Cover Art:* Kris Leov/Shutterstock
*Permissions Supervisor:* Rachel Youdelman
*Permissions Administrator:* William Opaluch
*Web Development, Senior Manager:*
   Steve Wright
*Associate Web Developer:* Barry Offringa

Credits and acknowledgments borrowed from other sources and reproduced, with permission, in this textbook appear on the appropriate page within text.

Oracle and Java are registered trademarks of Oracle and/or its affiliates. Other names may be trademarks of their respective owners.

Pearson Education Limited
Edinburgh Gate
Harlow
Essex CM20 2JE
England

and Associated Companies throughout the world

Visit us on the World Wide Web at:
www.pearsonglobaleditions.com

© Pearson Education Limited 2016

ISBN 10: 1-292-07718-2
ISBN 13: 978-1-292-07718-5

British Library Cataloguing-in-Publication Data
A catalogue record for this book is available from the British Library

10 9 8 7 6 5 4 3 2 1

Typeset by GEX Publishing Services

Printed by Ashford Colour Press Ltd, Gosport

Welcome to the fourth edition of *Data Structures and Abstractions with Java*, a book for an introductory course in data structures, typically known as CS-2.

I wrote this book with you in mind—whether you are an instructor or a student—based upon my experiences during more than three decades of teaching undergraduate computer science. I wanted my book to be reader friendly so that students could learn more easily and instructors could teach more effectively. To this end, you will find the material covered in small pieces—I call them "segments"—that are easy to digest and facilitate learning. Numerous examples that mimic real-world situations provide a context for the new material and help to make it easier for students to learn and retain abstract concepts. Many simple figures illustrate and clarify complicated ideas. Included are over 60 video tutorials to supplement the instruction and help students when their instructor is unavailable.

I am pleased and excited to welcome my co-author and colleague, Dr. Timothy Henry, to this edition. Together we have given a fresh update to this work, while retaining the topics and order of the previous edition. You will find a greater emphasis on our design decisions for both specifications and implementations of the various data structures, as well as a new introduction to safe and secure programming practices. The new features in this edition are given on the next page.

We hope that you enjoy reading this book. Like many others before you, you can learn—or teach—data structures in an effective and sustainable way.

Warm regards,

*Frank M. Carrano*

## Organization and Structure

This book's organization, sequencing, and pace of topic coverage make learning and teaching easier by focusing your attention on one concept at a time, by providing flexibility in the order in which you can cover topics, and by clearly distinguishing between the specification and implementation of abstract data types, or ADTs. To accomplish these goals, we have organized the material into 29 chapters, composed of small, numbered segments that deal with one concept at a time. Each chapter focuses on either the specification and use of an ADT or its various implementations. You can choose to cover the specification of an ADT followed by its implementations, or you can treat the specification and use of several ADTs before you consider any implementation issues. The book's organization makes it easy for you to choose the topic order that you prefer.

## Table of Contents at a Glance

The following brief table of contents shows the overall composition of the book. Notice the new Prelude and nine Java Interludes. Further details—including a chapter-by-chapter description—are given later in this preface. Note that some of the appendixes and the glossary are available online.

## What's New?

While the chapters are in the same order and cover the same topics as in the previous edition, reader feedback convinced us to move some material from the appendixes or online into the main portion of the book. Other changes are motivated by reader suggestions and our own desire to improve the presentation. Here are the significant changes in this edition:

- A new Prelude follows the Introduction and precedes Chapter 1 to discuss how to design classes. This material was in Appendix D of the previous edition.
- Relevant aspects of Java have been extracted from either the appendixes or the chapters themselves and placed into new Java Interludes that occur throughout the book and as needed. By doing so, we increase the distinction and separation between concepts and Java-specific issues. The titles of these interludes follow, and you can see their placement between chapters on the previous page:

Java Interlude 1  Generics
Java Interlude 2  Exceptions
Java Interlude 3  More About Generics
Java Interlude 4  More About Exceptions
Java Interlude 5  Iterators
Java Interlude 6  Mutable and Immutable Objects
Java Interlude 7  Inheritance
Java Interlude 8  Generics Once Again
Java Interlude 9  Cloning

- Safe and secure programming is a new topic that is introduced in Chapter 2, discussed in new Security Notes, and reflected in the Java code that implements the ADTs.
- Beginning with stacks in Chapter 5, most ADT methods now indicate failure by throwing an exception. Methods only return null when it cannot be a data value within a collection.
- Expanded coverage of generics treats generic methods and bounded types.
- Immutable, mutable, and cloneable objects are covered in Java Interludes instead of the online Chapter 30 of the previous edition.
- Additional Design Decisions continue to present the options one has when specifying and implementing particular ADTs and provide the rationale behind our choices.
- Illustrations have been revised to show objects specifically instead of as values within nodes or array elements.
- Vector-based implementations of the ADT list and queue are no longer covered, but are left as programming projects.
- Line numbers appear in program listings.
- Java code is Java 8 compliant.
- Supplements now include a test bank.

Here are the significant changes to specific chapters:

- Chapter 1 introduces the ADT set in addition to the bag.
- Chapter 2 introduces safe and secure programming. The code changes suggested here are integrated into all ADT implementations in subsequent chapters.
- Chapters 5 and 6 use exceptions in the specification and implementations of the ADT stack.
- Chapters 8 and 9 replace some Java code for sorting methods with pseudocode.

- Chapters 10 and 11 use exceptions in the specification and implementations of the ADTs queue, deque, and priority queue.
- Chapter 11 no longer covers the vector-based implementation of the ADT queue; it is left as a programming project.
- Chapters 12, 13, and 14 use exceptions in the specification and implementations of the ADT list.
- Chapter 13 changes the array-based implementation of the ADT list by ignoring the array element at index 0. The vector-based implementation of the ADT list is no longer covered, but is left as a programming project.
- Chapter 15 covers only iterators for the ADT list. The concepts of an iterator in Java are treated in the preceding Java Interlude 5 instead of in this chapter.
- Chapter 20 no longer covers the vector-based implementation of the ADT dictionary; it is left as a programming project.
- Chapter 23 defines balanced binary trees, which previously was in Chapter 25.
- Chapter 24 no longer defines an interface for a binary node, and the class `BinaryNode` no longer implements one.

The topics that we cover in this book deal with the various ways of organizing data so that a given application can access and manipulate data in an efficient way. These topics are fundamental to your future study of computer science, as they provide you with the foundation of knowledge required to create complex and reliable software. Whether you are interested in designing video games or software for robotic controlled surgery, the study of data structures is vital to your success. Even if you do not study all of the topics in this book now, you are likely to encounter them later. We hope that you will enjoy reading the book, and that it will serve as a useful reference tool for your future courses.

After looking over this preface, you should read the Introduction. There you will quickly see what this book is about and what you need to know about Java before you begin. The Prelude discusses class design and the use of Java interfaces. We use interfaces throughout the book. Appendixes A through E review javadoc comments, Java basics, classes, inheritance, and files. New Java Interludes occur throughout the book and cover advanced aspects of Java as they are needed. Note that at the end of the book you will find Java's reserved words, its primitive data types, the precedence of its operators, and a list of Unicode characters.

Please be sure to browse the rest of this preface to see the features that will help you in your studies.

A Note to Students

# Features to Enhance Learning

Each chapter begins with a table of contents, a list of prerequisite portions of the book that you should have read, and the learning objectives for the material to be covered. Other pedagogical elements appear throughout the book, as follows:

 **Notes** Important ideas are presented or summarized in highlighted paragraphs and are meant to be read in line with the surrounding text.

 **Security Notes** Aspects of safe and secure programming are introduced and highlighted in this new feature.

 **A Problem Solved** Large examples are presented in the form of "A Problem Solved," in which a problem is posed and its solution is discussed, designed, and implemented.

 **Design Decisions** To give readers insight into the design choices that one could make when formulating a solution, "Design Decision" elements lay out such options, along with the rationale behind the choice made for a particular example. These discussions are often in the context of one of the "A Problem Solved" examples.

 **Examples** Numerous examples illuminate new concepts.

 **Programming Tips** Suggestions to improve or facilitate programming are presented as soon as they become relevant.

 **Self-Test Questions** Questions are posed throughout each chapter, integrated within the text, that reinforce the concept just presented. These "self-test" questions help readers to understand the material, since answering them requires pause and reflection. Solutions to these questions are provided at the end of each chapter.

 **VideoNotes** Online tutorials are a Pearson feature that provides visual and audio support to the presentation given throughout the book. They offer students another way to recap and reinforce key concepts. VideoNotes allow for self-paced instruction with easy navigation, including the ability to select, play, rewind, fast-forward, and stop within each video. Unique VideoNote icons appear throughout this book whenever a video is available for a particular concept or problem. A detailed list of the VideoNotes for this text and their associated locations in the book can be found on page 26. VideoNotes are free with the purchase of a new textbook. To purchase access to VideoNotes, please go to

www.pearsonglobaleditions.com/Carrano

**Exercises and Programming Projects** Further practice is available by solving the exercises and programming projects at the end of each chapter. Unfortunately, we cannot give readers the answers to these exercises and programming projects, even if they are not enrolled in a class. Only instructors who adopt the book can receive selected answers from the publisher. For help with these exercises and projects, you will have to contact your instructor.

# Accessing Instructor and Student Resource Materials

The following items are available on the publisher's website at www.pearsonglobaleditions.com/Carrano:

- Java code as it appears in the book
- A link to any misprints that have been discovered since the book was published
- Links to additional online content, which is described next

## Instructor Resources

The following protected material is available to instructors who adopt this book by logging onto Pearson's Instructor Resource Center, accessible from www.pearsonglobaleditions.com/Carrano:

- PowerPoint lecture slides
- Instructor solutions manual
- Figures from the book
- Test bank

Additionally, instructors can access the book's Companion Website for the following online premium content, also accessible from www.pearsonglobaleditions.com/Carrano:

- Instructional VideoNotes
- Appendixes B, C, and E
- A glossary of terms

## Student Resources

The following material is available to students by logging onto the Companion Website accessible from www.pearsonglobaleditions.com/Carrano:

- Instructional VideoNotes
- Appendixes B, C, and E
- A glossary of terms

Students must use the access card located in the front of the book to register for and then enter the Companion Website.

Note that the Java Class Library is available at docs.oracle.com/javase/8/docs/api/.

# Content Overview

**R**eaders of this book should have completed a programming course, preferably in Java. The appendixes cover the essentials of Java that we assume readers will know. You can use these appendixes as a review or as the basis for making the transition to Java from another programming language. The book itself begins with the Introduction, which sets the stage for the data organizations that we will study.

- **Prelude:** At the request of readers of the previous edition, we have moved the introduction to class design from the appendix to the beginning of the book. Most of the material that was in Appendix D of the third edition is now in the Prelude, which follows the Introduction.
- **Chapters 1 through 3:** We introduce the bag as an abstract data type (ADT). By dividing the material across several chapters, we clearly separate the specification, use, and implementation of the bag. For example, Chapter 1 specifies the bag and provides several examples of its use. This chapter also introduces the ADT set. Chapter 2 covers implementations that use arrays, while Chapter 3 introduces chains of linked nodes and uses one in the definition of a class of bags.

  In a similar fashion, we separate specification from implementation throughout the book when we discuss various other ADTs. You can choose to cover the chapters that specify and use the ADTs and then later cover the chapters that implement them. Or you can cover the chapters as they appear, implementing each ADT right after studying its specification and use. A list of chapter prerequisites appears later in this preface to help you plan your path through the book.

  Chapter 2 does more than simply implement the ADT bag. It shows how to approach the implementation of a class by initially focusing on core methods. When defining a class, it is often useful to implement and test these core methods first and to leave definitions of the other methods for later. Chapter 2 also introduces the concept of safe and secure programming, and shows how to add this protection to your code.
- **Java Interludes 1 and 2:** The first Java interlude introduces generics, so that we can use it with our first ADT, the bag. This interlude immediately follows Chapter 1. Java Interlude 2 introduces exceptions and follows Chapter 2. We apply this material, which was formerly in an appendix, to the implementations of the ADT bag.
- **Chapter 4:** Here we introduce the complexity of algorithms, a topic that we integrate into future chapters.
- **Chapters 5 and 6:** Chapter 5 discusses stacks, giving examples of their use, and Chapter 6 implements the stack using an array, a vector, and a chain.
- **Chapter 7:** Next, we present recursion as a problem-solving tool and its relationship to stacks. Recursion, along with algorithm efficiency, is a topic that is revisited throughout the book.
- **Java Interlude 3:** This interlude provides the Java concepts needed for the sorting methods that we are about to present. It introduces the standard interface `Comparable`, generic methods, bounded type parameters, and wildcards.
- **Chapters 8 and 9:** The next two chapters discuss various sorting techniques and their relative complexities. We consider both iterative and recursive versions of these algorithms.
- **Java Interlude 4:** This Java interlude shows how the programmer can write new exception classes. In doing so, it shows how to extend an existing class of exceptions. It also introduces the `finally` block.
- **Chapters 10 and 11:** Chapter 10 discusses queues, deques, and priority queues, and Chapter 11 considers their implementations. It is in this latter chapter that we introduce circularly linked and doubly linked chains. Chapter 11 also uses the programmer-defined class `EmptyQueueException`.
- **Chapters 12, 13, and 14:** The next three chapters introduce the ADT list. We discuss this collection abstractly and then implement it by using an array and a chain of linked nodes.
- **Java Interlude 5 and Chapter 15:** The coverage of Java iterators that was formerly in Chapter 15 now appears before the chapter in Java Interlude 5. Included are the standard interfaces `Iterator`,

`Iterable`, and `ListIterator`. Chapter 15 then shows ways to implement an iterator for the ADT list. It considers and implements Java's iterator interfaces `Iterator` and `ListIterator`.

- **Java Interlude 6**: This interlude discusses mutable and immutable objects, material that previously was in the online Chapter 30.
- **Chapters 16 and 17 and Java Interlude 7:** Continuing the discussion of a list, Chapter 16 introduces the sorted list, looking at two possible implementations and their efficiencies. Chapter 17 shows how to use the list as a superclass for the sorted list and discusses the general design of a superclass. Although inheritance is reviewed in Appendix D, the relevant particulars of inheritance—including protected access, abstract classes, and abstract methods—are presented in Java Interlude 7 just before Chapter 17.
- **Chapter 18:** We then examine some strategies for searching an array or a chain in the context of a list or a sorted list. This discussion is a good basis for the sequence of chapters that follows.
- **Java Interlude 8:** Before we get to the next chapter, we quickly cover in this interlude situations where more than one generic data type is necessary.
- **Chapters 19 through 22:** Chapter 19 covers the specification and use of the ADT dictionary. Chapter 20 presents implementations of the dictionary that are linked or that use arrays. Chapter 21 introduces hashing, and Chapter 22 uses hashing as a dictionary implementation.
- **Chapters 23 and 24 and Java Interlude 9:** Chapter 23 discusses trees and their possible uses. Included among the several examples of trees is an introduction to the binary search tree and the heap. Chapter 24 considers implementations of the binary tree and the general tree. Java Interlude 9 discusses cloning, a topic that was previously online. We clone an array, a chain of linked nodes, and a binary node. We also investigate a sorted list of clones. Although this material is important, you can treat it as optional, as it is not required in the following chapters.
- **Chapters 25 through 27:** Chapter 25 focuses on the implementation of the binary search tree. Chapter 26 shows how to use an array to implement the heap. Chapter 27 introduces balanced search trees. Included in this chapter are the AVL, 2-3, 2-4, and red-black trees, as well as B-trees.
- **Chapters 28 and 29:** Finally, we discuss graphs and look at several applications and two implementations.
- **Appendixes A through E:** The appendixes provide supplemental coverage of Java. As we mentioned earlier. Appendix A considers programming style and comments. It introduces `javadoc` comments and defines the tags that we use in this book. Appendix B reviews Java up to but not including classes. However, this appendix also covers the `Scanner` class, enumerations, boxing and unboxing, and the for-each loop. Appendix C discusses Java classes, Appendix D expands this topic by looking at composition and inheritance, and Appendix E discusses files.

# Acknowledgments

O ur sincere appreciation and thanks go to the following reviewers for carefully reading the previous edition and making candid comments and suggestions that greatly improved the work:

Tony Allevato—*Virginia Polytechnic Institute and State University*
Mary Boelk—*Marquette University*
Suzanne Buchele—*Southwestern University*
Kevin Buffardi—*Virginia Polytechnic Institute and State University*
Jose Cordova—*University of Louisiana at Monroe*
Greg Gagne—*Westminster College*
Victoria Hilford—*University of Houston*
Jim Huggins—*Kettering University*
Shamim Kahn—*Columbus State University*
Kathy Liszka—*University of Akron*
Eli Tilevich—*Virginia Polytechnic Institute and State University*
Jianhua Yang—*Columbus State University*
Michelle Zhu—*Southern Illinois University*

Special thanks go to our support team at Pearson Education Computer Science during the lengthy process of revising this book: Executive Editor Tracy Dunkelberger, Program Manager Carole Snyder, Program Management-Team Leader Scott Disanno, and Project Manager Bob Engelhardt have always been a great help to us in completing our projects. Our long-time copy editor, Rebecca Pepper, ensured that the presentation is clear, correct, and grammatical. Thank you so much!

Our gratitude for the previously mentioned people does not diminish our appreciation for the help provided by many others. Steve Armstrong produced the lecture slides for this edition and previous editions of the book. Professor Charles Hoot of the Oklahoma City University created the lab manual, Professor Kathy Liszka from the University of Akron created the new collection of test questions, and Jesse Grabowski provided the solutions to many of the programming projects. Thank you again to the reviewers of the previous editions of the book:

**Reviewers for the third edition:**

Steven Andrianoff—*St. Bonaventure University*
Brent Baas—*LeTourneau University*
Timothy Henry—*New England Institute of Technology*
Ken Martin—*University of North Florida*
Bill Siever—*Northwest Missouri State University*
Lydia Sinapova—*Simpson College*
Lubomir Stanchev—*Indiana University*
Judy Walters—*North Central College*
Xiaohui Yuan—*University of North Texas*

**Reviewers for the second edition:**

Harold Anderson—*Marist College*
Razvan Andonie—*Central Washington University*
Tom Blough—*Rensselaer Polytechnic Institute*
Chris Brooks—*University of San Francisco*
Adrienne Decker—*University at Buffalo, SUNY*

Henry Etlinger—*Rochester Institute of Technology*
Derek Harter—*Texas A&M University*
Timothy Henry—*New England Institute of Technology*
Robert Holloway—*University of Wisconsin, Madison*
Charles Hoot—*Oklahoma City University*
Teresa Leyk—*Texas A&M University*
Robert McGlinn—*Southern Illinois University, Carbondale*
Edward Medvid—*Marymount University*
Charles Metzler—*City College of San Francisco*
Daniel Zeng—*University of Arizona*

**Reviewers for the first edition:**

David Boyd—*Valdosta State University*
Dennis Brylow—*Purdue University*
Michael Croswell—*Industry trainer/consultant*
Matthew Dickerson—*Middlebury College*
Robert Holloway—*University of Wisconsin, Madison*
John Motil—*California State University, Northridge*
Bina Ramamurthy—*University at Buffalo, SUNY*
David Surma—*Valparaiso University*

We continue to appreciate the many others who helped during previous editions. They include Alan Apt, James Blanding, Lianne Dunn, Mike Giacobbe, Toni Holm, Charles Hoot, Brian Jepson, Rose Kernan, Christianna Lee, Patrick Lindner, John Lovell, Vince O'Brien, Patty Roy, Walt Savitch, Ben Schomp, Heather Scott, Carole Snyder, Chirag Thakkar, Camille Trentacoste, Nate Walker, and Xiaohong Zhu.

Finally, we thank our families and friends—Doug, Joanne, Tita, Bobby, Ted, Nancy, Sue, Tom, Maybeth, Marge, and Lorraine—for giving us lives away from computers.

Thank you, everyone, for your expertise and good cheer.

**Frank M. Carrano**
**Timothy M. Henry**

The publishers would like to thank the following for reviewing the content of the Global Edition:
S. H. Chung, *Wawasan Open University*
Shaligram Prajapat, *Devi Ahilya University*
Holger Eichelberger, *University of Hildesheim*

Acknowledgments

# Contents

Table of Contents

Table of Contents

Table of Contents

18

Table of Contents

Table of Contents

Table of Contents

# VideoNotes Directory

**VideoNote**

This table lists the VideoNotes that are available online. The page numbers indicate where in the book each VideoNote has relevance.

VideoNotes

**VideoNotes**

# Chapter Prerequisites

Each chapter and appendix assumes that the reader has studied certain previous material. This list indicates those prerequisites. Numbers represent chapter numbers, letters reference appendixes, and "JI" precedes each interlude number. You can use this information to plan a path through the book.

| | | Prerequisites |
|---|---|---|
| **Prelude** | Designing Classes | A, B, C, D |
| **Chapter 1** | Bags | Prelude, D |
| **Java Interlude 1** | Generics | Prelude |
| **Chapter 2** | Bag Implementations That Use Arrays | Prelude, 1 |
| **Java Interlude 2** | Exceptions | B, C, D |
| **Chapter 3** | A Bag Implementation That Links Data | 1, 2, JI2 |
| **Chapter 4** | The Efficiency of Algorithms | 2, 3, C |
| **Chapter 5** | Stacks | Prelude, 1, JI2 |
| **Chapter 6** | Stack Implementations | 2, 3, 4, 5 |
| **Chapter 7** | Recursion | 2, 3, 4, 5, C |
| **Java Interlude 3** | More About Generics | JI1 |
| **Chapter 8** | An Introduction to Sorting | 3, 4, 7, JI3 |
| **Chapter 9** | Faster Sorting Methods | 4, 7, 8, JI3 |
| **Java Interlude 4** | More About Exception | D, JI2 |
| **Chapter 10** | Queues, Deques, and Priority Queues | Prelude, 5, 8 |
| **Chapter 11** | Queue, Deque, and Priority Queue Implementations | 2, 3, 6, 10 |
| **Chapter 12** | Lists | Prelude, 6, C, JI2, JI3 |
| **Chapter 13** | List Implementations That Use Arrays | Prelude, 2, 4, 12 |
| **Chapter 14** | A List Implementation That Links Data | 3, 11, 12, 13 |
| **Java Interlude 5** | Iterators | 12, JI2 |
| **Chapter 15** | Iterators | 13, 14, JI5 |
| **Java Interlude 6** | Mutable and Immutable Objects | 12, D |
| **Chapter 16** | Sorted Lists | 4, 7, 12, 14 |
| **Java Interlude 7** | Inheritance and Polymorphism | Prelude, 6, D |
| **Chapter 17** | Inheritance and Lists | 12, 13, 14, 16, D, JI7 |
| **Chapter 18** | Searching | 4, 7, 12, 13, 14, 16 |
| **Java Interlude 8** | Generics Once Again | C, JI3 |
| **Chapter 19** | Dictionaries | 12, 15, 18, JI5, JI8 |
| **Chapter 20** | Dictionary Implementations | 3, 4, 12, 13, 14, 18, 19, JI5 |
| **Chapter 21** | Introducing Hashing | 19, 20 |

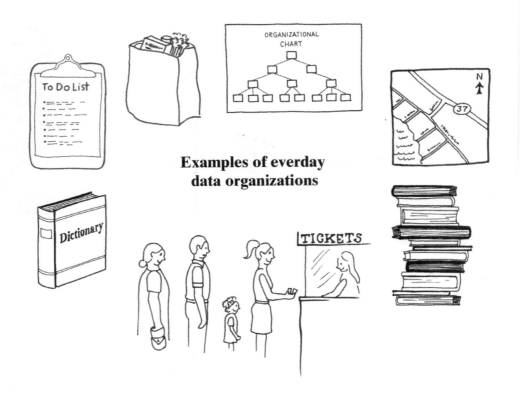

**Examples of everday data organizations**

Computer programs also need to organize their data. They do so in ways that parallel the examples we just cited. That is, programs can use a stack, a list, a dictionary, and so on. These ways of organizing data are represented by abstract data types. An **abstract data type**, or **ADT**, is a specification that describes a data set and the operations on that data. Each ADT specifies what data is stored and what the operations on the data do. Since an ADT does not indicate how to store the data or how to implement the operations, we can talk about ADTs independently of any programming language. In contrast, a **data structure** is an implementation of an ADT within a programming language.

A **collection** is a general term for an ADT that contains a group of objects. Some collections allow duplicate items, some do not. Some collections arrange their contents in a certain order, while others do not.

We might create an ADT **bag** consisting of an unordered collection that allows duplicates. It is like a grocery bag, a lunch bag, or a bag of potato chips. Suppose you remove one chip from a bag of chips. You don't know when the chip was placed into the bag. You don't know whether the bag contains another chip shaped exactly like the one you just removed. But you don't really care. If you did, you wouldn't store your chips in a bag!

A bag does not order its contents, but sometimes you do want to order things. ADTs can order their items in a variety of ways. The ADT **list**, for example, simply numbers its items. A list, then, has a first item, a second item, and so on. Although you can add an item to the end of a list, you can also insert an item at the beginning of the list or between existing items. Doing so renumbers the items after the new item. Additionally, you can remove an item at a particular position within a list. Thus, the position of an item in the list does not necessarily indicate when it was added. Notice that the list does not decide where an item is placed; you make this decision.

In contrast, the ADTs **stack** and **queue** order their items chronologically. When you remove an item from a stack, you remove the one that was added most recently. When you remove an item from a queue, you remove the one that was added the earliest. Thus, a stack is like a pile of books. You can remove the top book or add another book to the top of the pile. A queue is like a line of people. People leave a line from its front and join it at its end.

Some ADTs maintain their entries in sorted order, if the items can be compared. For instance, strings can be organized in alphabetical order. When you add an item to the ADT **sorted list**, for example, the ADT determines where to place the item in the list. You do not indicate a position for the item, as you would with the ADT list.

The ADT **dictionary** contains pairs of items, much as a language dictionary contains a word and its definition. In this example, the word serves as a **key** that is used to locate the entries. Some dictionaries sort their entries and some do not.

The ADT **tree** organizes its entries according to some hierarchy. For example, in a family tree, people are associated with their children and their parents. The ADT **binary search tree** has a combined hierarchical and sorted organization that makes locating a particular entry easier.

The ADT **graph** is a generalization of the ADT tree that focuses on the relationship among its entries instead of any hierarchical organization. For example, a road map is a graph that shows the existing roads and distances between towns.

This book shows you how to use and implement these data organizations. Throughout the book, we've assumed that you already know Java. If you need a refresher, you will find the appendixes helpful. Appendix A gives an overview of writing comments suitable for javadoc. Appendix B reviews the basic statements in Java. Appendix C discusses the fundamental construction of classes and methods, and Appendix D covers the essentials of composition and inheritance. Finally, Appendix E presents reading and writing external files. Appendixes B, C, and E are on the book's website (see page 9 of the Preface). You can download them and refer to the material as needed. Special sections throughout the book, called Java Interludes, focus on relevant aspects of Java that might be new to you, including how to handle exceptions. The Prelude, which follows, discusses how to design classes, specify methods, and write Java interfaces. Using interfaces and writing comments to specify methods are essential to our presentation of ADTs.

# Designing Classes

## Contents

## Prerequisites

Object-oriented programming embodies three design concepts: encapsulation, inheritance, and polymorphism. If you are not familiar with inheritance and polymorphism, please review Appendixes B, C, and D. Here we will discuss encapsulation as a way to hide the details of an implementation during the design of a class. We emphasize the importance both of specifying how a method should behave before you implement it and of expressing your specifications as comments in your program.

We introduce Java interfaces as a way to separate the declarations of a class's behavior from its implementation. Finally, we present, at an elementary level, some techniques for identifying the classes necessary for a particular solution.

# Encapsulation

**P.1** What is the most useful description of an automobile, if you want to learn to drive one? It clearly is not a description of how its engine goes through a cycle of taking in air and gasoline, igniting the gasoline/air mixture, and expelling exhaust. Such details are unnecessary when you want to learn to drive. In fact, such details can get in your way. If you want to learn to drive an automobile, the most useful description of an automobile has such features as the following:

- If you press your foot on the accelerator pedal, the automobile will move faster.
- If you press your foot on the brake pedal, the automobile will slow down and eventually stop.
- If you turn the steering wheel to the right, the automobile will turn to the right.
- If you turn the steering wheel to the left, the automobile will turn to the left.

Just as you need not tell somebody who wants to drive a car how the engine works, you need not tell somebody who uses a piece of software all the fine details of its Java implementation. Likewise, suppose that you create a software component for another programmer to use in a program. You should describe the component in a way that tells the other programmer how to use it but that spares the programmer all the details of how you wrote the software.

**P.2** **Encapsulation** is one of the design principles of object-oriented programming. The word "encapsulation" sounds as though it means putting things into a capsule, and that image is indeed correct. Encapsulation hides the fine detail of what is inside the "capsule." For this reason, encapsulation is often called **information hiding**. But not everything should be hidden. In an automobile, certain things are visible—like the pedals and steering wheel—and others are hidden under the hood. In other words, the automobile is encapsulated so that the details are hidden, and only the controls needed to drive the automobile are visible, as Figure P-1 shows. Similarly, you should encapsulate your Java code so that details are hidden and only the necessary controls are visible.

Encapsulation encloses data and methods within a class and hides the implementation details that are not necessary for using the class. If a class is well designed, its use does not require an understanding of its implementation. A programmer can use the class's methods without knowing the details of how they are coded. The programmer must know only how to provide a method with appropriate arguments, leaving the method to perform the right action. Stated simply, the programmer need not worry about the internal details of the class definition. The programmer who uses encapsulated software to write more software has a simpler task. As a result, software is produced more quickly and with fewer errors.

 **Note:** **Encapsulation** is a design principle of object-oriented programming that encloses data and methods within a class, thereby hiding the details of a class's implementation. A programmer receives only enough information to be able to use the class. A well-designed class can be used as though the body of every method was hidden from view.

FIGURE P-1    An automobile's controls are visible to the driver, but its inner
workings are hidden

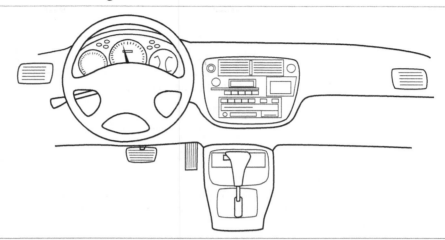

**P.3**    **Abstraction** is a process that asks you to focus on *what* instead of *how*. When you design a class, you practice **data abstraction**. You focus on what you want to do with or to the data without worrying about how you will accomplish these tasks and how you will represent the data. Abstraction asks you to focus on what data and operations are important. When you abstract something, you identify the central ideas. For example, an abstract of a book is a brief description of the book, as opposed to the entire book.

When designing a class, you should not think about any method's implementation. That is, you should not worry about *how* the class's methods will accomplish their goals. This separation of specification from implementation allows you to concentrate on fewer details, thereby making your task easier and less error-prone. Detailed, well-planned specifications facilitate an implementation that is more likely to be successful.

 **Note:** The process of abstraction asks you to focus on *what* instead of *how*.

**P.4**    When done correctly, encapsulation divides a class definition into two parts, which we will call the **client interface** and the **implementation**. The client interface describes everything a programmer needs to know to use the class. It consists of the headers for the public methods of the class, the comments that tell a programmer how to use these public methods, and any publicly defined constants of the class. The client interface part of the class definition should be all you need to know to use the class in your program.

The implementation consists of all data fields and the definitions of all methods, including those that are public, private, and protected. Although you need the implementation to run a client (a program that uses the class), you should not need to know anything about the implementation to write the client. Figure P-2 illustrates an encapsulated implementation of a class and the client interface. Although the implementation is hidden from the client, the interface is visible and provides a well-regulated means for the client to communicate with the implementation.

FIGURE P-2    An interface provides well-regulated communication between
a hidden implementation and a client

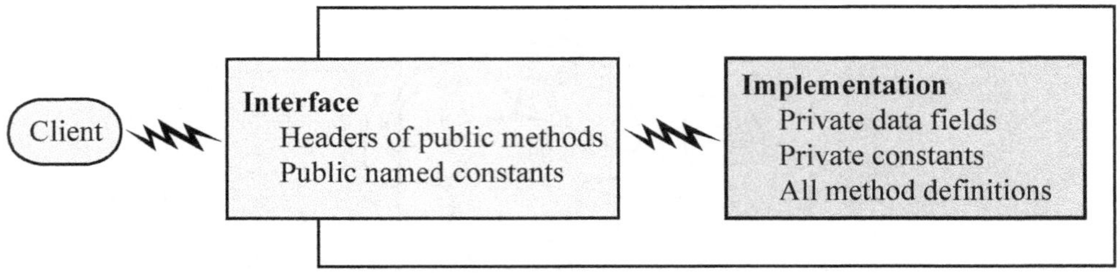

The client interface and implementation are not separated in the definition of a Java class. They are mixed together. You can, however, create a separate Java interface as a companion to your class. A later section of this prelude describes how to write such an interface, and we will write several of them in this book.

**Question 1** How does a client interface differ from a class implementation?

**Question 2** Think of an example, other than an automobile, that illustrates encapsulation. What part of your example corresponds to a client interface and what part to an implementation?

## Specifying Methods

Separating the purpose of a class and its methods from their implementations is vital to a successful software project. You should specify what each class and method does without concern for its implementation. Writing descriptions enables you to capture your ideas initially and to develop them so that they are clear enough to implement. Your written descriptions should reach the point where they are useful as comments in your program. You need to go beyond a view that sees comments as something you add after you write the program to satisfy an instructor or boss.

### Comments

Let's focus on comments that you write for a class's methods. Although organizations tend to have their own style for comments, the developers of Java have specified a commenting style that you should follow. If you include comments written in this style in your program, you can run a utility program called javadoc to produce documents that describe your classes. This documentation tells people what they need to know to use your class but omits all the implementation details, including the bodies of all method definitions.

The program javadoc extracts the header for your class, the headers for all public methods, and comments that are written in a certain form. Each such comment must appear immediately before a public class definition or the header of a public method and must begin with /** and end with */. Certain **tags** that begin with the symbol @ appear within the comments to identify various aspects of the method. For example, you use @param to identify a parameter, @return to identify a return value, and @throws to indicate an exception that the method throws. You will see some examples of these tags within the comments in this prelude. Appendix A provides the details for writing comments acceptable to javadoc.

Rather than talk further about the rules for javadoc here, we want to discuss some important aspects of specifying a method. First, you need to write a concise statement of the method's purpose or task. Beginning this statement with a verb will help you to avoid many extra words that you really do not need.

In thinking about a method's purpose, you should consider its input parameters, if any, and describe them. You also need to describe the method's results. Does it return a value, does it cause some action, or does it affect the state of an argument? In writing such descriptions, you should keep in mind the following ideas.

## Preconditions and Postconditions

**P.5**   A **precondition** is a statement of the conditions that must be true before a method begins execution. The method should not be used, and cannot be expected to perform correctly, unless the precondition is satisfied. A precondition can be related to the description of a method's parameters. For example, a method that computes the square root of $x$ can have $x \geq 0$ as a precondition.

A **postcondition** is a statement of what is true after a method completes its execution, assuming that the precondition was met. For a valued method, the postcondition will describe the value returned by the method. For a void method, the postcondition will describe actions taken and any changes to the calling object. In general, the postcondition describes all the effects produced by a method invocation.

Thinking in terms of a postcondition can help you to clarify a method's purpose. Notice that going from precondition to postcondition leaves out the *how*—that is, we separate the method's specification from its implementation.

 **Programming Tip:**  A method that cannot satisfy its postcondition, even though its precondition is met, can throw an exception. (See Java Interludes 2 and 4 for a discussion of exceptions.)

**P.6**   **Responsibility.** A precondition implies responsibility for guaranteeing that certain conditions are met. If the client is responsible for meeting the conditions before calling the method, the method need not check the conditions. On the other hand, if the method is responsible for enforcing the conditions, the client does not check them. A clear statement of who must check a given set of conditions increases the probability that someone will do so and avoids duplication of effort.

For example, you could specify the square root method that we mentioned in the previous segment by writing the following comments before its header:

```
/** Computes the square root of a number.
    @param x  A real number >= 0.
    @return  The square root of x.
*/
```

In this case, the method assumes that the client will provide a nonnegative number as an argument.

A safer technique is to make the method assume responsibility for checking the argument. In that case, its comments could read as follows:

```
/** Computes the square root of a number.
    @param x  A real number.
    @return  The square root of x if x >= 0.
    @throws  ArithmeticException if x < 0.
*/
```

Although we've integrated the precondition and postcondition into the previous comments, we could instead identify them separately.

> **Programming Tip:** Specify each public method fully in comments placed before the method's header. State whether a method or its client is responsible for ensuring that the necessary conditions are met for the successful execution of the method. In this way, checking is done but not duplicated. During debugging, however, a method should check that its precondition has been met.

**P.7**    When you use inheritance and polymorphism to override a method in a superclass, the method in the subclass could be inconsistent with the method in the superclass. Preconditions and postconditions will help you, as programmer, to avoid this problem. A postcondition must apply to all versions of a method throughout the subclasses. An overriding method can add to a postcondition—that is, it can do more—but it should not do less. However, an overriding method cannot augment its precondition. In other words, it cannot require more than a version of the method in a base class requires.

 **Question 3** Assume that the class `Square` has a data field `side` and the method `setSide` to set the value of `side`. What header and comments can you write for this method? Keep in mind a precondition and postcondition as you do this.

## Assertions

**P.8**    An **assertion** is a statement of truth about some aspect of your program's logic. You can think of it as a boolean expression that is true, or that at least should be true, at a certain point. Preconditions and postconditions, for example, are assertions made about conditions at the beginning and end of a method. If one of these assertions is false, something is wrong with your program.

You can state assertions as comments within your code. For example, if at some point in a method's definition, you know that the variable `sum` should be positive, you could write the following comment:

```
// Assertion: sum > 0
```

Such comments point out aspects of the logic that might not be clear. Additionally, they provide places for you to check the accuracy of your code during debugging.

 **Question 4** Suppose that you have an array of positive integers. The following statements find the largest integer in the array. What assertion can you write as a comment after the `if` statement in the following loop?

```
int max = 0;
for (int index = 0; index < array.length; index++)
{
   if (array[index] > max)
      max = array[index];
   // Assertion:
} // end for
```

**P.9**    **The assert statement.** Java enables you to do more than simply write a comment to make an assertion. You can enforce the assertion by using an `assert` statement, such as

```
assert sum > 0;
```

If the boolean expression that follows the reserved word `assert` is true, the statement does nothing. If it is false, an **assertion error** occurs and program execution terminates. An error message such as the following is displayed:

```
Exception in thread "main" java.lang.AssertionError
```

You can clarify this error message by adding a second expression to the `assert` statement. The second expression must represent a value, since its representation as a string is displayed within the error message. For example, the statement

```
assert sum > 0 : sum;
```

adds the value of `sum` to the error message in case $sum \leq 0$. For example, the error message might be

```
Exception in thread "main" java.lang.AssertionError: -5
```

By default, `assert` statements are disabled at execution time. Thus, you can leave `assert` statements in your program after you have finished it without wasting execution time. When you run a program, you must enable the `assert` statements if you want them to execute. Exactly how you enable them depends on your programming environment.[1]

**Note:** Assertions within a program identify aspects of your logic that must be true. In Java, you can use an `assert` statement to make an assertion. It has the following form:

> **assert** *boolean_expression* : *valued_expression*;

The value of the optional second expression appears in the error message that occurs if the first expression is false.

**Programming Tip:** Using the `assert` statement is a simple but effective way to find errors in your program's logic. After serving this purpose, assertions left in your program document its logic for those who want to revise or expand its capability. Remember, Java ignores `assert` statements unless the user of your program specifies otherwise.

**Programming Tip:** Use an `assert` statement during debugging to enforce that a method's precondition has been met. However, an `assert` statement is not a substitute for an `if` statement. You should use `assert` statements as a programming aid, not as part of a program's logic.

## Java Interfaces

**P.10**    Earlier in this prelude, we spoke in general terms about the client interface, which tells you all you need to know to use a particular class in your program. Although a Java class intermixes its interface with its implementation, you can write a separate interface.

A **Java interface** is a program component that declares a number of public methods and can define public named constants. Such an interface should include comments that specify the methods, in order to provide a programmer with the necessary information to implement them. Some interfaces describe all the public methods in a class, while others specify only certain methods.

When you write a class that defines the methods declared in an interface, we say that the class **implements** the interface. A class that implements an interface must define a body for every method that the interface specifies. The interface, however, might not declare every method defined in the class.

---

1. If you use the Java Development Kit (JDK) from Oracle, the command `java -ea MyProgram` executes `MyProgram` with assertions enabled. Further details about enabling assertions when using the JDK are available at the following URL: `docs.oracle.com/javase/8/docs/technotes/guides/language/assert.html`

You can write your own interfaces, and you can use those that are in the Java Class Library. When you write a Java interface, you place it in its own file. That is, the interface and the class that implements it are in two separate files.

## Writing an Interface

**P.11**   A Java interface begins like a class definition, except that you use the word `interface` instead of `class`. That is, an interface begins with the statement

> **public interface** *interface-name*

rather than

> **public class** *class-name*

The interface can contain any number of public method headers, each followed by a semicolon. An interface does not declare the constructors for a class and cannot declare static or final methods. Note that methods within an interface are public by default, so you can omit `public` from their headers. The interface can also define any number of public named constants.

**P.12**   **Example.** Imagine objects such as circles, squares, or plots of land that have both a perimeter  and an area. Suppose that we want the classes of these objects to have get methods that return these quantities. If various programmers implemented these classes, they likely would not name or specify these get methods in the same way. To ensure that these classes define our methods in a uniform way, we write the interface shown in Listing P-1. This interface provides a programmer with a handy summary of the methods' specifications. The programmer should be able to use these methods without looking at the class that implements them.

```
LISTING P-1   An interface Measurable
1  /** An interface for methods that return
2      the perimeter and area of an object.
3  */
4  public interface Measurable
5  {
6     /** Gets the perimeter.
7         @return  The perimeter. */
8     public double getPerimeter();
9
10    /** Gets the area.
11        @return  The area. */
12    public double getArea();
13 } // end Measurable
```

You store an interface definition in a file with the same name as the interface, followed by `.java`. For example, the previous interface is in the file `Measurable.java`.

 **Programming Tip:** A Java interface is a good place to provide comments that specify each method's purpose, parameters, precondition, and postcondition. In this way, you can specify a class in one file and implement it in another.

 **Note:** An interface can declare data fields, but they must be public. By convention, a class's data fields are private, so any data fields in an interface should represent named constants. Thus, they should be public, final, and static.

**Note:**  Methods declared within an interface cannot be static and cannot be final. However, such methods can be declared as final within a class that implements the interface.

**P.13**    **Example.** Suppose that you eventually want to define a class of people's names. You might begin by writing the Java interface given in Listing P-2 to specify the methods for such a class. We have included comments for only the first two methods, to save space. This interface provides specifications of the desired methods for an entire class. You could use it when implementing a class such as Name, as shown in Listing D-1 of Appendix D. Additionally, you should be able to write a client for the class just by looking at the interface.

---

**LISTING P-2**   The interface NameInterface

```
1  /** An interface for a class of names. */
2  public interface NameInterface
3  {
4     /** Sets the first and last names.
5        @param firstName  A string that is the desired first name.
6        @param lastName   A string that is the desired last name. */
7     public void setName(String firstName, String lastName);
8
9     /** Gets the full name.
10        @return  A string containing the first and last names. */
11    public String getName();
12
13    public void setFirst(String firstName);
14    public String getFirst();
15
16    public void setLast(String lastName);
17    public String getLast();
18
19    public void giveLastNameTo(NameInterface aName);
20
21    public String toString();
22 } // end NameInterface
```

---

Notice that the parameter of the method giveLastNameTo has NameInterface as its data type instead of Name. We will talk about interfaces as data types beginning with Segment P.17. For now, simply be aware that an interface should not restrict the name of the class or classes that might implement it.

**Note:**  **Naming an interface**
Interface names, particularly those that are standard in Java, often end in "able," such as Measurable. That ending does not always provide a good name, so endings such as "er" or "Interface" are also used. Just as Java's exception names end in "Exception," we will usually end our interface names with "Interface."

## Implementing an Interface

**P.14**  Any class that implements an interface must state this at the beginning of its definition by using an implements clause. For example, if a class Circle implemented the interface Measurable, it would begin as follows:

```
public class Circle implements Measurable
```

The class then must provide a definition for each method declared in the interface. In this example, the class Circle must implement at least the methods getPerimeter and getArea.

If we wrote a class `Square` that implemented `Measurable`, the class would begin as

**public class** Square **implements** Measurable

and would define at least the methods `getPerimeter` and `getArea`. Clearly, the definitions of these two methods would differ from those in the class `Circle`.

Figure P-3 illustrates the files that contain `Measurable`, `Circle`, `Square`, and their client.

---

**FIGURE P-3**     The files for an interface, a class that implements the interface, and the client

---

**The interface**

```
public interface Measurable
{
    . . .



}
```
Measurable.java

**The classes**

```
public class Circle implements
                        Measurable
{
    . . .
}
```
Circle.java

```
public class Square implements
                        Measurable
{
    . . .
}
```
Square.java

**The client**

```
public class Client
{
    Measurable aCircle;
    Measurable aSquare;

    aCircle = new Circle();
    aSquare = new Square();
    . . .

}
```
Client.java

---

**Note:** Writing an interface is a way for a class designer to specify methods for another programmer. Implementing an interface is a way for a programmer to guarantee that a class has defined certain methods.

**Note:** Several classes can implement the same interface, perhaps in different ways. For example, many classes can implement the interface `Measurable` and provide their own version of the methods `getPerimeter` and `getArea`.

**P.15**

**Example.** Imagine classes for various geometric forms like circles, spheres, and cylinders. Each of these forms has a radius. We could define the following interface that our classes would implement:

```
public interface Circular
{
    public void setRadius(double newRadius);
    public double getRadius();
} // end Circular
```

This interface recognizes that a radius will exist, and so declares both set and get methods for it. However, it cannot declare a field for the radius. The class that implements the interface will do that.

A class `Circle` that implements this interface could appear as follows:

```
public class Circle implements Circular
{
    private double radius;
```

```
    public void setRadius(double newRadius)
    {
        radius = newRadius;
    } // end setRadius
    public double getRadius()
    {
        return radius;
    } // end getRadius
    public double getArea()
    {
        return Math.PI * radius * radius;
    } // end getArea
} // end Circle
```

The class defines a private data field `radius`, and implements the methods `setRadius` and `getRadius` that the interface `Circular` declares. An interface cannot contain a data field like `radius`, since it is private.

**Note:** A class can define more methods than are declared in the interfaces it implements. For example, the class `Circle` defines the method `getArea`, which is not in the interface `Circular`.

P.16    **Multiple interfaces.** A class can implement more than one interface. If it does, you simply list all the interface names, separated by commas. If the class is derived from another class, the `implements` clause always follows the `extends` clause. Thus, you could write

   `public class C extends B implements Measurable, AnotherInterface`

To remember this order, note that the reserved words `extends` and `implements` appear alphabetically in the heading of the class.

A class that implements several interfaces must define each method declared in the interfaces. If the same method header appears in more than one interface that a class implements, the class defines only one corresponding method.

You cannot derive a class from more than one base class. This restriction avoids the possibility of inheriting conflicting implementations. But a Java interface contains method specifications, not implementations. A class can implement these specifications regardless of whether they appear in one interface or are spread among several interfaces. By allowing a class to implement any number of interfaces, Java approximates multiple inheritance without the complications it can cause.

**Question 5** Write a Java interface that specifies and declares methods for a class of students.

**Question 6** Begin the definition of a class that implements the interface that you wrote in answer to the previous question. Include data fields, a constructor, and at least one method definition.

## An Interface as a Data Type

P.17    You can use a Java interface as you would a data type when you declare a variable, a data field, or a method's parameter. For example, the method `giveLastNameTo` in Segment P.13 has a parameter whose type is `NameInterface`:

   `public void giveLastNameTo(NameInterface aName);`

Any argument that you pass to this method must be an object of a class that implements `NameInterface`.

Why didn't we declare aName's type to be a class type such as Name? We want the interface to be independent of any class that implements it, since more than one class can implement an interface. By using NameInterface as the parameter's type, you ensure that the method's argument will have all of the methods declared in NameInterface. In general, you can be sure that a method's parameter will have particular methods, namely those declared in an interface, if its data type is the interface. Additionally, the parameter will have only those methods.

What if the header of a class C does not contain the phrase implements NameInterface, yet still implements the methods in the interface? You could not pass an instance of C to giveLastNameTo.

**Note:** By using an interface as a variable's type, you indicate that the variable can reference an object that has a certain set of methods and only those methods.

**Note:** An **interface type** is a reference type.

**P.18** A variable declaration such as

```
NameInterface myName;
```

makes myName a reference variable. Now myName can reference any object of any class that implements NameInterface. So if Name implements NameInterface, and you have

```
myName = new Name("Coco", "Puffs");
```

then myName.getFirst() returns a reference to the string "Coco". If the class AnotherName also implements NameInterface, and you later write

```
myName = new AnotherName("April", "MacIntosh");
```

then myName.getFirst() returns a reference to the string "April".

**Question 7** What revision(s) should you make to both the interface you wrote for Question 5 and the class Student that implements it to make use of NameInterface?

## Extending an Interface

**P.19** Once you have an interface, you can derive another interface from it by using inheritance. In fact, you can derive an interface from several interfaces, even though you cannot derive a class from several classes.

When an interface extends another interface, it has all the methods of the inherited interface. Thus, you can create an interface that consists of the methods in an existing interface plus some new methods. For example, consider classes of pets and the following interface:

```
public interface Nameable
{
    public void setName(String petName);
    public String getName();
} // end Nameable
```

We can extend `Nameable` to create the interface `Callable`:

```java
public interface Callable extends Nameable
{
   public void come(String petName);
} // end Callable
```

A class that implements `Callable` must implement the methods `come`, `setName`, and `getName`.

**P.20** You also can combine several interfaces into a new interface and add even more methods if you like. For example, suppose that in addition to the previous two interfaces, we define the following interfaces:

```java
public interface Capable
{
   public void hear();
   public void respond();
} // end Capable
```

```java
public interface Trainable extends Callable, Capable
{
   public void sit();
   public void speak();
   public void lieDown();
} // end Trainable
```

A class that implements `Trainable` must implement the methods `setName`, `getName`, `come`, `hear`, and `respond`, as well as the methods `sit`, `speak`, and `lieDown`.

 **Note:** A Java interface can be derived from several interfaces, even though you cannot derive a class from several classes.

 **Question 8** Imagine a class `Pet` that contains the method `setName`, yet does not implement the interface `Nameable` of Segment P.19. Could you pass an instance of `Pet` as the argument of the method with the following header?

```java
void enterShow(Nameable petName)
```

## Named Constants Within an Interface

An interface can contain named constants, that is, public data fields that you initialize and declare as final. If you want to implement several classes that share a common set of named constants, you can define the constants in an interface that the classes implement. You also could define your constants in a separate class instead of an interface. We will look at both ways in this section. Whichever way you choose, you have only one set of constants to keep current.

Imagine several classes that must convert measurements to the metric system. We can define conversion factors as constants that these classes can share. Let's place the constants in an interface.

**P.21** **An interface of constants.** The following interface defines three named constants:

```java
public interface ConstantsInterface
{
   public static final double INCHES_PER_CENTIMETER = 0.39370079;
   public static final double FEET_PER_METER = 3.2808399;
   public static final double MILES_PER_KILOMETER = 0.62137119;
} // end ConstantsInterface
```

Any interface can define constants in addition to declaring methods, but this interface contains only constants.

To use these constants in a class, you write an `implements` clause in the class definition. The constants then will be available by name throughout the class. For example, consider the following simple class:

```
public class Demo implements ConstantsInterface
{
   public static void main(String[] args)
   {
      System.out.println(FEET_PER_METER);
      System.out.println(ConstantsInterface.MILES_PER_KILOMETER);
   } // end main
} // end Demo
```

Qualifying the constants with the name of the interface is optional. However, if the same named constant is defined in more than one interface that a class implements, the class must qualify the constant with the name of the interface.

**P.22**    **A class of constants.** Instead of defining constants in an interface, you can define them in a class just for that purpose:

```
public class Constants
{
   private Constants()
   {
   } // end private default constructor

   public static final double INCHES_PER_CENTIMETER = 0.39370079;
   public static final double FEET_PER_METER = 3.2808399;
   public static final double MILES_PER_KILOMETER = 0.62137119;
} // end Constants
```

Notice the private constructor. Since we provide a constructor, Java will not. And since our constructor is private, a client cannot create instances of the class.

Using this class is simple, as the following example shows:

```
public class Demo
{
   public static void main(String[] args)
   {
      System.out.println(Constants.FEET_PER_METER);
      System.out.println(Constants.MILES_PER_KILOMETER);
   } // end main
} // end Demo
```

Since the constants are static, you must precede their names with the name of the class and a period. This can be an advantage, as readers of your program will see immediately the source of the constant. If doing so becomes an annoyance, you can always define a local copy of the constant, such as

```
final double FEET_PER_METER = Constants.FEET_PER_METER;
```

and use it instead.

**Design Decision:** **Should you define constants in an interface or in a class?**
Programmers seem to disagree about the answer to this question. Even the Java Class Library contains examples of both techniques. Generally, constant definitions are an implementation detail that should appear within a class. Interfaces declare methods and so are in the realm of specification, not implementation. Reserving interfaces solely for methods is a reasonable guideline.

# Choosing Classes

We have talked about specifying classes and implementing classes, but up to now, we have described the class to specify or implement. If you must design an application from scratch, how will you choose the classes you need? In this section, we introduce you to some techniques that software designers use in choosing and designing classes. Although we will mention these techniques from time to time throughout the book, our intent is simply to expose you to these ideas. Future courses will cover ways to select and design classes in more depth.

**P.23**   Imagine that we are designing a registration system for your school. Where should we begin? A useful way to start would be to look at the system from a functional point of view, as follows:

- **Who or what will use the system?** A human user or a software component that interacts with the system is called an **actor**. So a first step is to list the possible actors. For a registration system, two of the actors could be a student and the registrar.
- **What can each actor do with the system?** A **scenario** is a description of the interaction between an actor and the system. For example, a student can add a course. This basic scenario has variations that give rise to other scenarios. For instance, what happens when the student attempts to add a course that is closed? Our second step, therefore, is to identify scenarios. One way to do this is to complete the question that begins "What happens when...".
- **Which scenarios involve common goals?** For example, the two scenarios we just described are related to the common goal of adding a course. A collection of such related scenarios is called a **use case**. Our third step, then, is to identify the use cases.

You can get an overall picture of the use cases involved in a system you are designing by drawing a **use case diagram**. Figure P-4 is a use case diagram for our simple registration system. Each actor— the student and the registrar—appears as a stick figure. The box represents the registration system, and the ovals within the box are the use cases. A line joins an actor and a use case if an interaction exists between the two.

---

**FIGURE P-4**      A use case diagram for a registration system

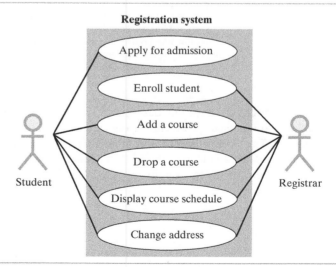

Registration system

Apply for admission

Enroll student

Add a course

Drop a course

Display course schedule

Change address

Student

Registrar

Some use cases in this example involve one actor, and some involve both. For example, only the student applies for admission, and only the registrar enrolls a student. However, both the student and the registrar can add a course to a student's schedule.

 **Note:** Use cases depict a system from the actors' points of view. They do not necessarily suggest classes within the system.

## Identifying Classes

**P.24**    Although drawing a use case diagram is a step in the right direction, it does not identify the classes that are needed for your system. Several techniques are possible, and you will probably need to use more than one.

One simple technique is to describe the system and then identify the nouns and verbs in the description. The nouns can suggest classes, and the verbs can suggest appropriate methods within the classes. Given the imprecision of natural language, this technique is not foolproof, but it can be useful.

For example, we could write a sequence of steps to describe each use case in Figure P-4. Figure P-5 gives a description of the use case for adding a course from the point of view of a student. Notice the alternative actions taken in Steps 2a and 4a when the system does not recognize the student or when a requested course is closed.

**FIGURE P-5**    A description of a use case for adding a course

```
System:    Registration
Use case:  Add a course
Actor:     Student
Steps:
      1. Student enters identifying data.
      2. System confirms eligibility to register.
         a. If ineligible to register, ask student to enter identification data again.
      3. Student chooses a particular section of a course from a list of course offerings.
      4. System confirms availability of the course.
         a. If course is closed, allow student to return to Step 3 or quit.
      5. System adds course to student's schedule.
      6. System displays student's revised schedule of courses.
```

What classes does this description suggest? Looking at the nouns, we could decide to have classes to represent a student, a course, a list of all courses offered, and a student's schedule of courses. The verbs suggest actions that include confirming whether a student is eligible to register, seeing whether a course is closed, and adding a course to a student's schedule. One way to assign these actions to classes is to use CRC cards, which we describe next.

## CRC Cards

**P.25**   A simple technique for exploring the purpose of a class uses index cards. Each card represents one class. You begin by choosing a descriptive name for a class and writing it at the top of a card. You then list the actions that represent the class's **responsibilities**. You do this for each class in the system. Finally, you indicate the interactions, or **collaborations**, among the classes. That is, you write on each class's card the names of other classes that have some sort of interaction with the class. Because of their content, these cards are called **class-responsibility-collaboration**, or **CRC, cards**.

For example, Figure P-6 shows a CRC card for the class `CourseSchedule` that represents the courses in which a student has enrolled. Notice that the small size of each card forces you to write brief notes. The number of responsibilities must be small, which suggests that you think at a high level and consider small classes. The size of the cards also lets you arrange them on a table and move them around easily while you search for collaborations.

**Question 9** Write a CRC card for the class `Student` given in Appendix D.

**FIGURE P-6**      A class-responsibility-collaboration (CRC) card

| CourseSchedule |
| --- |
| *Responsibilities* |
| *Add a course* |
| *Remove a course* |
| *Check for time conflict* |
| *List course schedule* |
| |
| *Collaborations* |
| *Course* |
| *Student* |

## The Unified Modeling Language

**P.26**   The use case diagram in Figure P-4 is part of a larger notation known as the **Unified Modeling Language**, or **UML**. Designers use the UML to illustrate a software system's necessary classes and their relationships. The UML gives people an overall view of a complex system more effectively than either a natural language or a programming language can. English, for example, can be ambiguous, and Java code provides too much detail. Providing a clear picture of the interactions among classes is one of the strengths of the UML.

Besides the use case diagram, the UML provides a **class diagram** that places each class description in a box analogous to a CRC card. The box contains a class's name, its **attributes** (data fields), and **operations** (methods). For example, Figure P-7 shows a box for the class `CourseSchedule`. Typically, you omit from the box such common operations as constructors, get methods, and set methods.

FIGURE P-7        A class representation that can be a part of a class diagram

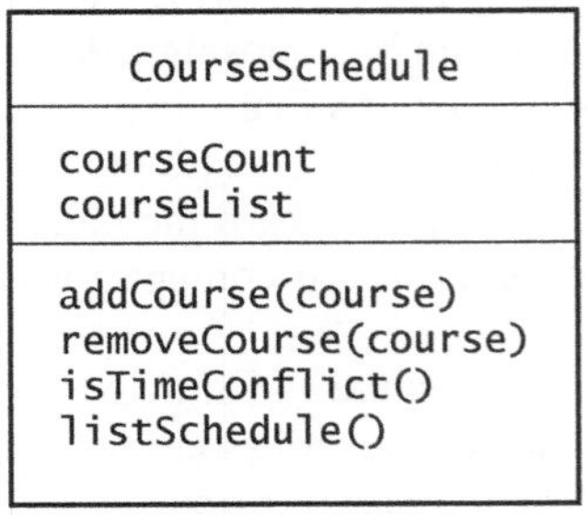

| CourseSchedule |
| --- |
| courseCount<br>courseList |
| addCourse(course)<br>removeCourse(course)<br>isTimeConflict()<br>listSchedule() |

As your design progresses, you can provide more detail when you describe a class. You can indicate the visibility of a field or method by preceding its name with + for public, - for private, and # for protected. You also can write the data type of a field, parameter, or return value after a colon that follows the particular item. Thus, in Figure P-7 you can write the data fields as

```
-courseCount: integer
-courseList: List
```

and the methods as

```
+addCourse(course: Course): void
+removeCourse(course: Course): void
+isTimeConflict(): boolean
+listSchedule(): void
```

You represent an interface in UML much as you represent a class, but you precede its name with <<interface>>. Figure P-8 shows the notation for the interface Measurable that appears in Segment P.12.

FIGURE P-8        UML notation for the interface Measurable

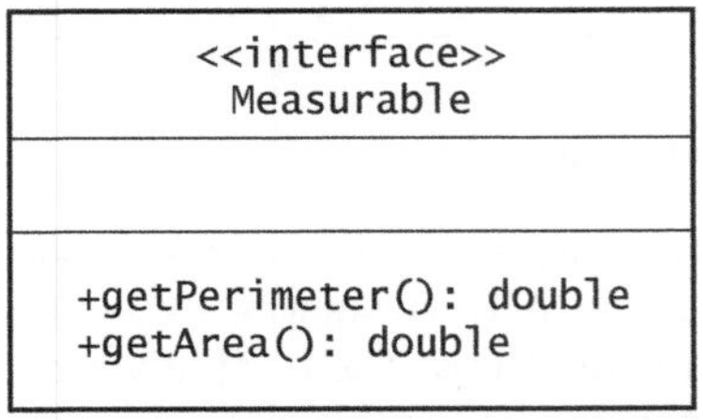

| <<interface>><br>Measurable |
| --- |
|  |
| +getPerimeter(): double<br>+getArea(): double |

**Question 10** How would the class Name, given in Appendix C, appear in a class diagram of the UML?

P.27    In a class diagram, lines join the class boxes to show the relationships among the classes, including any inheritance hierarchy. For example, the class diagram in Figure P-9 shows that the classes UndergradStudent and GradStudent are each derived from the class Student. An arrow with a hollow head points to the superclass. Within the UML, the superclass `Student` is said to be a **generalization** of `UndergradStudent` and `GradStudent`. If a class implements an interface, you draw an arrow having a dotted shaft and hollow head from the class to the interface.

**FIGURE P-9**   A class diagram showing the base class `Student` and two subclasses

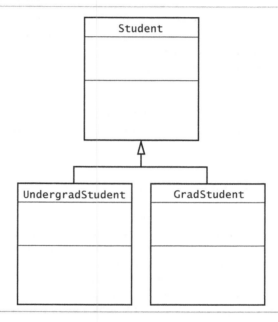

An **association** is a relationship between two objects of different classes. Basically, an association is what a CRC card calls a collaboration. For example, relationships exist among the classes `Student`, `CourseSchedule`, and `Course`. Figure P-10 shows how the UML pictures these relationships as arrows. The arrow between the classes `CourseSchedule` and `Course`, for example, indicates a relationship between objects of the class `CourseSchedule` and objects of the class `Course`. This arrow points toward `Course` and indicates responsibilities. Thus, a `CourseSchedule` object should be able to tell us the courses it contains, but a `Course` object need not be able to tell us to which schedules it belongs. The UML calls this aspect of the notation the **navigability**.

**FIGURE P-10**   Part of a UML class diagram with associations

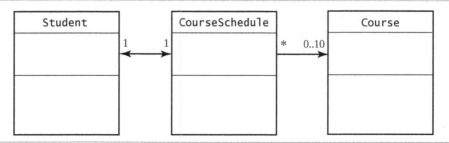

This particular association is said to be **unidirectional**, since its arrow points in one direction. An association indicated by a line with arrowheads on both ends is called **bidirectional**. For example, a `Student` object can find its course schedule, and a `CourseSchedule` object can discover the student to which it belongs. You can assume that the navigability of an association represented by a line without arrowheads is unspecified at the present stage of the design.

At the ends of each arrow are numbers. At the head of the arrow between `CourseSchedule` and `Course`, you see the notation 0..10. This notation indicates that each `CourseSchedule` object is associated with between zero and ten courses. At the other end of this arrow is an asterisk. It has the same meaning as the notation 0..infinity. Each `Course` object can be associated with many, many course schedules—or with none at all. The class diagram also indicates a relationship between one `Student` object and one `CourseSchedule` object. This notation on the ends of an arrow is called the association's **cardinality** or **multiplicity**.

**Question 11** Combine Figures P-9 and P-10 into one class diagram. Then add a class `AllCourses` that represents all courses offered this semester. What new association(s) do you need to add?

# Reusing Classes

**P.28**    When you first start to write programs, you can easily get the impression that each program is designed and written from scratch. On the contrary, most software is created by combining already existing components with new components. This approach saves time and money. In addition, the existing components have been used many times and so are better tested and more reliable.

For example, a highway simulation program might include a new highway object to model a new highway design, but it would probably model automobiles by using an automobile class that had already been designed for some other program. As you identify the classes that you need for your project, you should see whether any of the classes exist already. Can you use them as is, or would they serve as a good base class for a new class?

**P.29**    As you design new classes, you should take steps to ensure that they are easily reusable in the future. You must specify exactly how objects of that class interact with other objects. This is the principle of encapsulation that we discussed in the first section of this prelude. But encapsulation is not the only principle you must follow. You must also design your class so that the objects are general and not tailored too much for one particular program. For example, if your program requires that all simulated automobiles move only forward, you should still include a reverse in your automobile class. Some other simulation may require automobiles to back up.

Admittedly, you cannot foresee all the future uses of your class. But you can and should avoid dependencies that will restrict its use later. Chapter 17 describes the design of a class with its future use in mind.

Using the principles that this prelude discusses to design a reusable class with an interface that has comments suitable for `javadoc` takes work. Hacking together a solution to your specific problem would take less time. But the payback for your effort will come later on, when you or another programmer needs to reuse an interface or a class. If you planned for the future when you wrote those components, every use of them will be faster and easier. Actual software developers use these principles to save time over the long term, because saving time saves them money. You should use them, too.

1. Consider the interface `NameInterface` defined in Segment P.13. We provided comments for only two of the methods. Write comments in `javadoc` style for each of the other methods.

2. Consider the interface `Circular` and the class `Circle`, as given in Segment P.15.

   a. Is the client or the method `setRadius` responsible for ensuring that the circle's radius is positive?
   b. Write a precondition and a postcondition for the method `setRadius`.
   c. Write comments for the method `setRadius` in a style suitable for `javadoc`.
   d. Revise the method `setRadius` and its precondition and postcondition to change the responsibility mentioned in your answer to Part *a*.

3. Write a CRC card and a class diagram for a proposed class called `Counter`. An object of this class will be used to count things, so it will record a count that is a nonnegative whole number. Include methods to set the counter to a given integer, to increase the count by 1, and to decrease the count by 1. Also include a method that returns the current count as an integer, a method `toString` that returns the current count as a string suitable for display on the screen, and a method that tests whether the current count is zero.

4. Suppose you want to design software for a pharmacy. Give use cases for purchasing medicines and settling the bill. Identify a list of possible classes. Pick two of these classes, and write CRC cards for them.

PROJECTS

1. Create an interface for the class `Counter` that you designed in Exercise 3. Include comments, suitable for `javadoc`, that specify the methods of the class. No method allows the value of the counter to become negative.

2. a. Write a Java interface for the class `CollegeStudent` given in Listing D-3 of Appendix D.
   b. What revision(s) should you make to the class `CollegeStudent` so that it implements the interface that you wrote in Part *a*?

3. Suppose you want to design a class that is given numbers one at a time. The class computes the smallest, second smallest, and average of the numbers that have been seen so far. Create an interface for the class. Include comments, suitable for `javadoc`, that specify the methods of the class.

4. Consider a class `Fraction` of fractions. Each fraction is signed and has a numerator and a denominator that are integers. Your class should be able to add, subtract, multiply, and divide two fractions. These methods should have a fraction as a parameter and should return the result of the operation as a fraction. The class should also be able to find the reciprocal of a fraction, compare two fractions, decide whether two fractions are equal, and convert a fraction to a string.

   Your class should handle denominators that are zero. Fractions should always occur in lowest terms, and the class should be responsible for this requirement. For example, if the user tries to create a fraction such as 4/8, the class should set the fraction to 1/2. Likewise, the results of all arithmetic operations should be in lowest terms. Note that a fraction can be improper—that is, have a numerator that is larger than its denominator. Such a fraction, however, should be in lowest terms.

   Design, but do not implement, the class `Fraction`. Begin by writing a CRC card for this class. Then write a Java interface that declares each public method. Include `javadoc`-style comments to specify each method.

5. Write a Java class `Fraction` that implements the interface you designed in the previous project. Begin with reasonable constructors. Design and implement useful private methods, and include comments that specify them.

To reduce a fraction such as 4/8 to lowest terms, you need to divide both the numerator and the denominator by their greatest common denominator. The greatest common denominator of 4 and 8 is 4, so when you divide the numerator and denominator of 4/8 by 4, you get the fraction 1/2. The following recursive algorithm finds the greatest common denominator of two positive integers:

*Algorithm* `gcd(integerOne, integerTwo)`
```
if (integerOne % integerTwo == 0)
    result = integerTwo
else
    result = gcd(integerTwo, integerOne % integerTwo)
return result
```

It will be easier to determine the correct sign of a fraction if you force the fraction's denominator to be positive. However, your implementation must handle negative denominators that the client might provide.

Write a program that adequately demonstrates your class.

6. A mixed number contains both an integer portion and a fractional portion. Design a class `MixedNumber` of mixed numbers that uses the class `Fraction` that you designed in the previous project. Provide operations for `MixedNumber` that are analogous to those of `Fraction`. That is, provide operations to set, retrieve, add, subtract, multiply, and divide mixed numbers. The fractional portion of any mixed number should be in lowest terms and have a numerator that is strictly less than its denominator.

Write a Java interface, including `javadoc` comments, for this class.

7. Implement the class `MixedNumber` that you designed in the previous project. Use the operations in `Fraction` whenever possible. For example, to add two mixed numbers, convert them to fractions, add the fractions by using `Fraction`'s add operation, and then convert the resulting fraction to mixed form. Use analogous techniques for the other arithmetic operations.

Handling the sign of a mixed number can be a messy problem if you are not careful. Mathematically, it makes sense for the sign of the integer part to match the sign of the fraction. But if you have a negative fraction, for example, the `toString` method for the mixed number could give you the string `"-5 -1/2"`, instead of `"-5 1/2"`, which is what you would normally expect. Here is a possible solution that will greatly simplify computations.

Represent the sign of a mixed number as a character data field. Once this sign is set, make the integer and fractional parts positive. When a mixed number is created, if the given integer part is not zero, take the sign of the integer part as the sign of the mixed number and ignore the signs of the fraction's numerator and denominator. However, if the given integer part is zero, take the sign of the given fraction as the sign of the mixed number.

8. Consider two identical pails. One pail hangs from a hook on the ceiling and contains a liquid. The other pail is empty and rests on the floor directly below the first pail. Suddenly a small hole develops in the bottom of the full pail. Liquid streams from the full pail and falls into the empty pail on the floor, as the following figure illustrates:

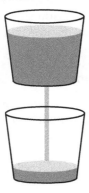

Liquid continues to fall until the upper pail is empty.

Design classes for a program that illustrates this action. When the program begins execution, it should display both pails in their original condition before the leak occurs. Decide whether the leak will occur spontaneously or at a user signal, such as pressing the Return key or clicking the mouse. If the latter, you could have the user position the cursor on the pail bottom to indicate where the leak will occur.

Write CRC cards and Java interfaces that include comments in `javadoc` style.

**9.** Implement your design for the leaking pail, as described in the previous project.

**10.** An odometer records a car's mileage. A mechanical odometer contains a number of wheels that turn as the car travels. Each wheel shows a digit from 0 to 9. The rightmost wheel turns the fastest and increases by 1 for every mile traveled. Once a wheel reaches 9, it rolls over to 0 on the next mile and increases by 1 the value on the wheel to its left. You can generalize the behavior of such wheels by giving them symbols other than the digits from 0 to 9. Examples of such wheel counters include

- A binary odometer whose wheels each show either 0 or 1
- A desktop date display with three wheels, one each for year, month, and day
- A dice roll display whose wheels each show the spots for a single die

Write a Java interface for a general wheel counter that has up to four wheels. Also, write a Java interface for any class that represents a wheel. Include comments in `javadoc` style.

**11.** Implement your design for a general wheel counter, as described in the previous project. Write a program to compute the probability that the sum of the values shown on four dice will be greater than 12. (Divide the number of configurations of the dice where the sum is greater than 12 by the total number of possible configurations of the dice.) Use an instance of the wheel counter to get all the possible configurations of four six-sided dice. For example, if the wheels start at [1, 1, 1, 1], the wheel counter will advance as follows: [1, 1, 1, 2], [1, 1, 1, 3], [1, 1, 1, 4], [1, 1, 1, 5], [1, 1, 1, 6], [1, 1, 2, 1], and so on.

**12.** Using your design and implementation of a general wheel counter, as described in the previous two projects, write a class to represent a desktop date display with four wheels, one each for the day of the week, the month, the day, and the year. Note that the name and number of the day increment at the same rate, but roll over at different points. They are not part of the same wheel counter.

## Answers to Self-Test Questions

**1.** A client interface describes how to use the class. It contains the headers for the class's public methods, the comments that tell you how to use these methods, and any publicly defined constants of the class. The implementation consists of all data fields and the definitions of all methods, including those that are public, private, and protected.

**2.** A television is one example. The remote control and the controls on the TV form the client interface. The implementation is inside the TV itself.

**3.** Here are three possibilities:

```
/** Sets the side of the square to a new value.
    @param newSide  A real number >= 0. */
public void setSide(double newSide)

/** Sets the side of the square to a new value.
    @param newSide  A real number.
    @return  True if the side is set, or
             false if newSide is < 0. */
public boolean setSide(double newSide)

/** Sets the side of the square to a new value.
    @param newSide  A real number.
    @throws  IllegalArgumentException if newSide is < 0. */
public void setSide(double newSide)
```

**4.** `// Assertion: max is the largest of array[0],..., array[index]`

**5.**
```
public interface StudentInterface
{
    public void setStudent(Name studentName, String studentId);
    public void setName(Name studentName);
    public Name getName();
    public void setId(String studentId);
    public String getId();
    public String toString();
} // end StudentInterface
```

**6.**
```
public class Student implements StudentInterface
{
    private Name   fullName;
    private String id;       // Identification number

    public Student()
    {
        fullName = new Name();
        id = "";
    } // end default constructor

    public Student(Name studentName, String studentId)
    {
        fullName = studentName;
        id = studentId;
    } // end constructor

    public void setStudent(Name studentName, String studentId)
    {
        setName(studentName); // Or fullName = studentName;
        setId(studentId);     // Or id = studentId;
    } // end setStudent
```

```
    public void setName(Name studentName)
    {
        fullName = studentName;
    } // end setName
    public Name getName()
    {
        return fullName;
    } // end getName
    public void setId(String studentId)
    {
        id = studentId;
    } // end setId
    public String getId()
    {
        return id;
    } // end getId
    public String toString()
    {
        return id + " " + fullName.toString();
    } // end toString
} // end Student
```

7. In the interface and in the class, replace `Name` with `NameInterface` in the methods `setStudent`, `setName`, and `getName`. Additionally in the class, replace `Name` with `NameInterface` in the declaration of the data field `fullName` and in the parameterized constructor.

8. No. The class `Pet` must state that it implements `Nameable` in an `implements` clause.

9.

| Student |
|---|
| **Responsibilities** |
|     Set name and ID |
|     Set name |
|     Set ID |
|     Get name |
|     Get ID |
|     Get a string that represents a student |
| **Collaborations** |
|     String |
|     Name |

**10.**

| Name |
|---|
| -first: String<br>-last: String |
| +setName(firstName: String, lastName: String): void<br>+getName(): String<br>+setFirst(firstName: String): void<br>+getFirst(): String<br>+setLast(lastName: String): void<br>+getLast(): String<br>+giveLastNameTo(aName: Name): void<br>+toString(): String |

**11.** Add a unidirectional association (arrow) from AllCourses to Course with a cardinality of 1 on its tail and * on its head.

# Bags

## Contents

## Prerequisites

## Objectives

After studying this chapter, you should be able to

- Describe the concept of an abstract data type (ADT)
- Describe the ADT bag
- Use the ADT bag in a Java program

This chapter builds on the concepts of encapsulation and data abstraction presented in the prelude, and it develops the notion of an abstract data type. As you probably know, a **data type** such as int or double is a group of values and operations on those values that is defined within a specific programming language. In contrast, an **abstract data type**, or **ADT**, is a specification for a group of values and the operations on those values that is defined conceptually and independently of any programming language. A **data structure** is an implementation of an ADT within a programming language.

This chapter also begins to generalize the idea of grouping objects. A **collection** is an object that groups other objects and provides various services to its client. In particular, a typical collection enables a client to add, remove, retrieve, and query the objects it represents. Various collections exist for different purposes. Their behaviors are specified abstractly and can differ in purpose according to the collection. Thus, a collection is an abstraction and is an abstract data type. However, an ADT is not necessarily a collection.

To provide an example of a collection and of an abstract data type, we will specify and use the ADT bag. In doing so we will provide a Java interface for our bag. Knowing just this interface, you will be able to use a bag in a Java program. You do not need to know how the entries in the bag are stored or how the bag operations are implemented. Indeed, your program will not depend on these specifics. As you will see, this important program characteristic is what data abstraction is all about.

# The Bag

1.1 Imagine a paper bag, a reusable cloth bag, or even a plastic bag. People use bags when they shop, pack a lunch, or eat potato chips. Bags contain things. In everyday language, a bag is a kind of container. In Java, however, a **container** is an object whose class extends the standard class `Container`. Such containers are used in graphics programs. Rather than being considered a container, a **bag** in Java is a kind of collection.

What distinguishes a bag from other collections? A bag doesn't do much more than contain its items. It doesn't order them in a particular way, nor does it prevent duplicate items. Most of its behaviors could be performed by other kinds of collections. While describing the behaviors for the collection that we'll design in this chapter, let's keep in mind that we are specifying an abstraction inspired by an actual physical bag. For example, a paper bag holds things of various dimensions and shapes in no particular order and without regard for duplicates. Our abstract bag will hold unordered and possibly duplicate objects, but let's insist that these objects have the same or related data types.

 **Note:** A bag is a finite collection of objects in no particular order. These objects have the same or related data types. A bag can contain duplicate items.

## A Bag's Behaviors

1.2 Since a bag contains a finite number of objects, reporting how many objects it contains could be one of a bag's behaviors:

> *Get the number of items currently in the bag*

A related behavior detects whether a bag is empty:

> *See whether the bag is empty*

1.3 We should be able to add and remove objects:

> *Add a given object to the bag*
> *Remove an unspecified object from the bag*
> *Remove an occurrence of a particular object from the bag, if possible*
> *Remove all objects from the bag*

While you hope that the bagger at the grocery store does not toss six cans of soup into a bag on top of your bread and eggs, our add operation does not indicate where in the bag an object should go. Remember that a bag does not order its contents. Likewise, the first remove operation just removes any object it can. This operation is like reaching into a grab bag and pulling something out. On the other hand, the second remove operation looks for a particular item in the bag. If you find it, you take it out. If the bag contains several equal objects that satisfy your search, you remove any one of them. If you can't find the object in the bag, you can't remove it, and you just say so. Finally, the last remove operation simply empties the bag of all objects.

1.4    How many cans of dog food did you buy? Did you remember to get anchovy paste? Just what is in that bag? The answers to these questions can be answered by the following operations:

*Count the number of times a certain object occurs in the bag*
*Test whether the bag contains a particular object*
*Look at all objects that are in the bag*

We have enough behaviors for now. At this point, we would have written all behaviors on a piece of paper or on the class-responsibility-collaboration (CRC) card pictured in Figure 1-1, as suggested in the prelude.

---

**FIGURE 1-1**      A CRC card for a class Bag

| *Bag* |
|---|
| *Responsibilities* |
|    *Get the number of items currently in the bag* |
|    *See whether the bag is empty* |
|    *Add a given object to the bag* |
|    *Remove an unspecified object from the bag* |
|    *Remove an occurrence of a particular object from* |
|      *the bag, if possible* |
|    *Remove all objects from the bag* |
|    *Count the number of times a certain object occurs in the bag* |
|    *Test whether the bag contains a particular object* |
|    *Look at all objects that are in the bag* |
|   |
| *Collaborations* |
|    *The class of objects that the bag can contain* |

---

1.5    Since a bag is an abstract data type, we only describe its data and specify its operations. We do not indicate how to store the data or how to implement its operations. Don't think about arrays, for example. You first need to clearly know what the bag operations do: Focus on *what* the operations do, not on *how* they do them. That is, you need a detailed set of specifications before you can use a bag in a program. In fact, you should specify the bag operations before you even decide on a programming language.

> **Note:** Since an abstract data type, or ADT, describes a data organization independently of a programming language, you have a choice of programming languages for its implementation.

## Specifying a Bag

**VideoNote**
**Designing an ADT**

Before we can implement a bag in Java, we need to describe its data and specify in detail the methods that correspond to the bag's behaviors. We'll name the methods, choose their parameters, decide their return types, and write comments to fully describe their effect on the bag's data. Our eventual goal, of course, is to write a Java header and comments for each method, but first we will express the methods in pseudocode and then in Unified Modeling Language (UML) notation.

**1.6**    The first behavior on our CRC card gives rise to a method that returns a count of the current number of entries in the bag. The corresponding method has no parameters and returns an integer. In pseudocode, we have the following specification:

> *// Returns the current number of entries in the bag.*
> `getCurrentSize()`

We can express this method using UML as

> `+getCurrentSize(): integer`

and add this line to a class diagram.

We can test whether the bag is empty by using a boolean-valued method, again without parameters. Its specification in pseudocode and UML is

> *// Returns true if the bag is empty.*
> `isEmpty()`

and

> `+isEmpty(): boolean`

We add this line to our class diagram.

 **Note:** Because we can detect when a bag is empty by seeing whether `getCurrentSize` returns zero, the operation `isEmpty` is not really needed. However, it is a so-called **convenience method**, and many collections provide such an operation.

**1.7**    We now want to add a given object to the bag. We can name the method add and give it a parameter to represent the new entry. We could write the following pseudocode:

> *// Adds a new entry to the bag.*
> `add(newEntry)`

We might be tempted to make add a void method, but if the bag is full, for example, we cannot add a new entry to it. What should we do in this case?

 **Design Decision:**  **What should the method add do when it cannot add a new entry?**
Here are two options that we can take when add cannot complete its task:

- Do nothing. We cannot add another item, so we ignore it and leave the bag unchanged.
- Leave the bag unchanged, but signal the client that the addition is impossible.

The first option is easy, but it leaves the client wondering what happened. Of course, we could state as a precondition of add that the bag must not already be full. Then the client has the responsibility to avoid adding a new entry to a full bag.

The second option is the better one, and it is not too hard to specify or implement. How can we indicate to the client whether the addition was successful? The standard Java interface `Collection` specifies that an exception should occur if the addition was not successful. We will leave this approach for later and use another way. Displaying an error message is not a good choice, as you should let the client dictate all written output. Since the addition is either successful or not, we can simply have the method add return a boolean value.

Thus, we can specify the method add in UML as

> `+add(newEntry: T): boolean`

where `T` represents `newEntry`'s data type.

**Question 1** Suppose aBag represents an empty bag that has a finite capacity. Write some pseudocode statements to add user-supplied strings to the bag until the operation fails.

1.8    Three behaviors involve removing entries from a bag: remove all entries, remove any one entry, and remove a particular entry. Suppose we name the methods and any parameters and specify them in pseudocode as follows:

```
// Removes all entries from the bag.
clear()

// Removes one unspecified entry from the bag.
remove()

// Removes one occurrence of a particular entry from the bag, if possible.
remove(anEntry)
```

What return types are these methods?

1.9    The method clear can be a void method: We just want to empty the bag, not retrieve any of its contents. Thus, we write

```
+clear(): void
```

in UML.

If the first remove method removes an entry from the bag, the method can easily return the object it has removed. Its return type is then T, the data type of the entries in the bag. In UML, we have

```
+remove(): T
```

For now, we can respond to an attempt to remove an object from an empty bag by returning null.

The second remove method won't be able to remove a particular entry from the bag if the bag does not contain that entry. We could have the method return a boolean value, much as add does, so it can indicate success or not. Or the method could return either the removed object or null if it can't remove the object. Here are the specifications for these two possible versions of the method in UML—we must choose one:

```
+remove(anEntry: T): boolean
```

or

```
+remove(anEntry: T): T
```

If anEntry equals an entry in the bag, the first version of this method would remove that entry and return true. Even though the method would not return the removed entry, the client would have the method's argument, anEntry, which is equal to the removed entry. We will choose this first version, to be consistent with the interface Collection.

**Question 2** Is it legal to have both versions of remove(anEntry), which were just described, in one class? Explain.

**Question 3** Is it legal to have two versions of remove, one that has no parameter and one that has a parameter, in the same class? Explain.

**Question 4** Given the full bag aBag that you created in Question 1, write some pseudocode statements that remove and display all of the strings in the bag.

**1.10**    The remaining behaviors do not change the contents of the bag. One of these behaviors counts the number of times a given object occurs within the bag. We specify it first in pseudocode and then in UML, as follows:

> *// Counts the number of times a given entry appears in the bag.*
> getFrequencyOf(anEntry)
>
> +getFrequencyOf(anEntry: T): integer

Another method tests whether the bag contains a given object. Its specifications in pseudocode and UML are

> *// Tests whether the bag contains a given entry.*
> contains(anEntry)
>
> +contains(anEntry: T): boolean

**Question 5** Given the full bag aBag that you created in Question 1, write some pseudocode statements to find the number of times, if any, that the string "Hello" occurs in aBag.

**1.11**    Finally, we want to look at the contents of the bag. Rather than providing a method that displays the entries in the bag, we will define one that returns an array of these entries. The client is then free to display any or all of them in any way desired. Here are the specifications for our last method:

> *// Looks at all entries in the bag.*
> toArray()
>
> +toArray(): T[]

When a method returns an array, it usually should define a new one to return. We will note that detail for this method.

**1.12**    As we developed the previous specifications for the bag's methods, we represented them using UML notation. Figure 1-2 shows the result of doing so.

**FIGURE 1-2**    UML notation for the class Bag

```
┌─────────────────────────────────────────────┐
│                     Bag                       │
├─────────────────────────────────────────────┤
│                                               │
├─────────────────────────────────────────────┤
│ +getCurrentSize(): integer                    │
│ +isEmpty(): boolean                           │
│ +add(newEntry: T): boolean                    │
│ +remove(): T                                  │
│ +remove(anEntry: T): boolean                  │
│ +clear(): void                                │
│ +getFrequencyOf(anEntry: T): integer          │
│ +contains(anEntry: T): boolean                │
│ +toArray(): T[]                               │
└─────────────────────────────────────────────┘
```

Notice that the CRC card and the UML do not reflect all of the details, such as assumptions and unusual circumstances, that we mentioned in our previous discussion. However, after you have identified such conditions, you should specify how your methods will behave under each one.

You should write down your decisions about how you want your methods to behave, as we have done in the following table. Later, you can incorporate these informal descriptions into the Java comments that document your methods.

| ABSTRACT DATA TYPE: BAG | | |
| --- | --- | --- |

**DATA**

- A finite number of objects, not necessarily distinct, in no particular order, and having the same data type
- The number of objects in this collection

**OPERATIONS**

| PSEUDOCODE | UML | DESCRIPTION |
| --- | --- | --- |
| getCurrentSize() | +getCurrentSize(): integer | Task: Reports the current number of objects in the bag.<br>Input: None.<br>Output: The number of objects currently in the bag. |
| isEmpty() | +isEmpty(): boolean | Task: Sees whether the bag is empty.<br>Input: None.<br>Output: True or false according to whether the bag is empty. |
| add(newEntry) | +add(newEntry: T): boolean | Task: Adds a given object to the bag.<br>Input: newEntry is an object.<br>Output: True or false according to whether the addition succeeds. |
| remove() | +remove(): T | Task: Removes an unspecified object from the bag, if possible.<br>Input: None.<br>Output: Either the removed object, if the removal was successful, or null. |
| remove(anEntry) | +remove(anEntry: T): boolean | Task: Removes an occurrence of a particular object from the bag, if possible.<br>Input: anEntry is an object.<br>Output: True or false according to whether the removal succeeds. |

| clear() | +clear(): void | Task: Removes all objects from the bag.<br>Input: None.<br>Output: None. |
| getFrequencyOf(anEntry) | +getFrequencyOf(anEntry: T):<br>       integer | Task: Counts the number of times an object<br> occurs in the bag.<br>Input: anEntry is an object.<br>Output: The number of times anEntry<br> occurs in the bag. |
| contains(anEntry) | +contains(anEntry: T): boolean | Task: Tests whether the bag contains a<br> particular object.<br>Input: anEntry is an object.<br>Output: True or false according to whether<br> anEntry occurs in the bag. |
| toArray() | +toArray(): T[] | Task: Looks at all objects in the bag.<br>Input: None.<br>Output: A new array of entries currently in<br> the bag. |

**Design Decision: What should happen when an unusual condition occurs?**

As class designer, you need to make decisions about how to treat unusual conditions and include these decisions in your specifications. The documentation for the ADT bag should reflect both these decisions and the details in the previous discussion.

In general, you can address unusual situations in several ways. Your method could

- Assume that the invalid situations will not occur. This assumption is not as naive as it might sound. A method could state as an assumption—that is, a precondition—restrictions to which a client must adhere. It is then up to the client to check that the precondition is satisfied before invoking the method. For example, a precondition for the method remove might be that the bag is not empty. Notice that the client can use other methods of the ADT bag, such as isEmpty and getCurrentSize, to help with this task. As long as the client obeys the restriction, the invalid situation will not occur.
- Ignore the invalid situations. A method could simply do nothing when given invalid data. Doing absolutely nothing, however, leaves the client without knowledge of what happened.
- Guess at the client's intention. Like the previous option, this choice can cause problems for the client.
- Return a value that signals a problem. For example, if a client tries to remove an entry from an empty bag, the remove method could return null. The value returned must be something that cannot be in the bag.
- Return a boolean value that indicates the success or failure of an operation.
- Throw an exception.

**Note:** Throwing an exception is often a desirable way for a Java method to react to unusual events that occur during its execution. The method can simply report a problem without deciding what to do about it. The exception enables each client to do what is needed in its own particular situation. Java Interlude 2 will review the basic mechanics of exceptions.

**Note:** A first draft of an ADT's specifications often overlooks or ignores situations that you really need to consider. You might intentionally make these omissions to simplify this first draft. Once you have written the major portions of the specifications, you can concentrate on the details that make the specifications complete.

## An Interface

**1.13**   As your specifications become more detailed, they increasingly should reflect your choice of programming language. Ultimately, you can write Java headers for the bag's methods and organize them into a Java interface for the class that will implement the ADT. The Java interface in Listing 1-1 contains the methods for an ADT bag and detailed comments that describe their behaviors. Recall that a class interface does not include data fields, constructors, private methods, or protected methods.

For now, the items in the bag will be objects of the same class. For example, we could have a bag of strings. To accommodate entries of a class type, the bag methods use a **generic data type** T for each entry. To give meaning to the identifier T, we must write <T> after the name of the interface. Once the actual data type is chosen within a client, the compiler will use that data type wherever T appears. Java Interlude 1, which follows this chapter, will discuss the use of generic data types to give us flexibility in the type of data our ADTs can hold.

As you examine the interface, notice the decisions that were made to address the unusual situations mentioned in the previous segment. In particular, each of the methods add, remove, and contains returns a value. Since our programming language is Java, notice that one of the remove methods returns a reference to an entry, not the entry itself.

Although writing an interface before implementing a class is certainly not required, doing so enables you to document your specifications in a concise way. You then can use the code in the interface as an outline for the actual class. Having an interface also provides a data type for a bag that is independent of a particular class definition. The next two chapters will develop different implementations of a class of bags. Code written with respect to an interface allows us to more easily replace one implementation of a bag with another.

**LISTING 1-1   A Java interface for a class of bags**

```java
1  /**
2      An interface that describes the operations of a bag of objects.
3      @author Frank M. Carrano
4  */
5  public interface BagInterface<T>
6  {
7      /** Gets the current number of entries in this bag.
8          @return  The integer number of entries currently in the bag. */
9      public int getCurrentSize();
10
```

```
11     /** Sees whether this bag is empty.
12         @return  True if the bag is empty, or false if not. */
13     public boolean isEmpty();
14
15     /** Adds a new entry to this bag.
16         @param newEntry  The object to be added as a new entry.
17         @return  True if the addition is successful, or false if not. */
18     public boolean add(T newEntry);
19
20     /** Removes one unspecified entry from this bag, if possible.
21         @return  Either the removed entry, if the removal
22                  was successful, or null. */
23     public T remove();
24
25     /** Removes one occurrence of a given entry from this bag, if possible.
26         @param anEntry  The entry to be removed.
27         @return  True if the removal was successful, or false if not. */
28     public boolean remove (T anEntry);
29
30     /** Removes all entries from this bag. */
31     public void clear();
32
33     /** Counts the number of times a given entry appears in this bag.
34         @param anEntry  The entry to be counted.
35         @return  The number of times anEntry appears in the bag. */
36     public int getFrequencyOf(T anEntry);
37
38     /** Tests whether this bag contains a given entry.
39         @param anEntry  The entry to locate.
40         @return  True if the bag contains anEntry, or false if not. */
41     public boolean contains(T anEntry);
42
43     /** Retrieves all entries that are in this bag.
44         @return  A newly allocated array of all the entries in the bag.
45                  Note: If the bag is empty, the returned array is empty. */
46     public T[] toArray();
47 } // end BagInterface
```

1.14   After specifying an ADT and writing a Java interface for its operations, you should write some Java statements that use the ADT. Although we cannot execute these statements yet—after all, we have not written a class that implements BagInterface—we can use them to confirm or revise both our decisions about the design of the methods and the accompanying documentation. In this way, you check both the suitability and your understanding of the specifications. It is better to revise the design or documentation of the ADT now, instead of after you have written its implementation. An added benefit of doing this task carefully is that you can use these same Java statements later to test your implementation.

**Question 6** Given the bag aBag that you created in Question 1, write some Java statements that display all of the strings in aBag. Do not alter the contents of aBag.

**Programming Tip:** **Write a test program before you implement a class**
Writing Java statements that test a class's methods will help you to fully understand the specifications for the methods. Obviously, you must understand a method before you can implement it correctly. If you are also the class designer, your use of the class might help you see desirable changes to your design or its documentation. You will save time if you make these revisions before you have implemented the class. Since you must write a program that tests your implementation sometime, why not get additional benefits from the task by writing it now instead of later?

**Note:** Although we said that the entries in a bag belong to the same class, those entries can also belong to classes related by inheritance. For example, assume Bag is a class that implements the interface BagInterface. If we create a bag of class C objects by writing

```
BagInterface<C> aBag = new Bag<>();
```

aBag can contain objects of class C, as well as objects of any subclass of C.

The following section looks at two examples that use a bag. Later, these examples can be part of a test of your implementation.

## Using the ADT Bag

**VideoNote**
**Designing a test for an ADT**

**1.15**   Imagine that we hire a programmer to implement the ADT bag in Java, given the interface and specifications that we have developed so far. If we assume that these specifications are clear enough for the programmer to complete the implementation, we can use the ADT's operations in a program without knowing the details of the implementation. That is, we do not need to know *how* the programmer implemented the bag to be able to use it. We only need to know *what* the ADT bag does. This section assumes that we have a Java class, Bag, that implements the Java interface BagInterface given in Listing 1-1. The simple examples demonstrate how we can use Bag.

In Line 13 of Listing 1-2, notice that once we choose the data type of the objects to be in a bag—Item in this case—that data type is enclosed in brackets that follow the interface name. Also notice that empty brackets follow the class name. All entries in the bag then must have either that data type or a subtype of that data type. The compiler will enforce this restriction for us. For primitive types, you can place instances of an appropriate wrapper class into a bag. For example, instead of instances of the primitive type int, you could use instances of the wrapper class Integer.

**1.16**   **Example: Shopping online.** When you shop online, your selections are saved in a shopping cart, or bag, until you are ready to check out. The program that implements the shopping website can use the class Bag to maintain the shopping cart. After all, the order in which you choose items to purchase is not important. Listing 1-2 shows a simple example of such a program.

---

LISTING 1-2    A program that maintains a bag for online shopping

```java
1  /**
2      A class that maintains a shopping cart for an online store.
3      @author Frank M. Carrano
4  */
5  public class OnlineShopper
6  {
7      public static void main(String[] args)
```

```
8    {
9        Item[] items = {new Item("Bird feeder", 2050),
10                       new Item("Squirrel guard", 1547),
11                       new Item("Bird bath", 4499),
12                       new Item("Sunflower seeds", 1295)};
13       BagInterface<Item> shoppingCart = new Bag<>();
14       int totalCost = 0;
15
16       // Statements that add selected items to the shopping cart:
17       for (int index = 0; index < items.length; index++)
18       {
19           Item nextItem = items[index]; // Simulate getting item from shopper
20           shoppingCart.add(nextItem);
21           totalCost = totalCost + nextItem.getPrice();
22       } // end for
23
24       // Simulate checkout
25       while (!shoppingCart.isEmpty())
26           System.out.println(shoppingCart.remove());
27
28       System.out.println("Total cost: " + "\t$" + totalCost / 100 + "." +
29                           totalCost % 100);
30   } // end main
31 } // end OnlineShopper
```

**Output**
```
Sunflower seeds $12.95
Bird bath       $44.99
Squirrel guard  $15.47
Bird feeder     $20.50
Total cost:     $93.91
```

To keep the example simple, we create an array of Item objects to represent the choices made by the shopper. The class Item, which is available to you in this book's online resources, defines data fields for an item's description and price, accessor methods for these fields, and the method toString.

Initially, we create an empty bag for Item objects by using Bag's default constructor. Notice that the data type of shoppingCart is BagInterface<Item>. This declaration obliges shoppingCart to receive only calls to methods declared in BagInterface. Moreover, we could replace the class Bag with another class that also implements BagInterface without modifying the subsequent statements in the program.

Notice the loop that adds the chosen items to the bag and the loop that removes them one at a time during checkout.

**Question 7** In the previous example, a while loop executes during the checkout process until the bag is empty. What for statement could replace the while statement? Use only the existence of shoppingCart, not the array items.

**1.17** **Example: A piggy bank**. You might have a piggy bank, jar, or some other receptacle to hold your spare coins. The piggy bank holds the coins but gives them no other organization. And certainly the bank can contain duplicate coins. A piggy bank is like a bag, but it is simpler, as it has only three operations: You can add a coin to the bank, remove one (you shake the bank, so you have no control over what coin falls out), or see whether the bank is empty.

Assuming that we have the class `Coin` to represent coins, we can create the class `PiggyBank` given in Listing 1-3. A `PiggyBank` object stores its coins in a bag, that is, in an instance of a class that implements the interface `BagInterface`. The `add`, `remove`, and `isEmpty` methods of `PiggyBank` each call the respective bag method to achieve their results. The class `PiggyBank` is an example of an adapter class. See Appendix D for more on adapter classes.

---

**LISTING 1-3    A class of piggy banks**

```java
/**
    A class that implements a piggy bank by using a bag.
    @author Frank M. Carrano
*/
public class PiggyBank
{
    private BagInterface<Coin> coins;

    public PiggyBank()
    {
        coins = new Bag<>();
    } // end default constructor

    public boolean add(Coin aCoin)
    {
        return coins.add(aCoin);
    } // end add

    public Coin remove()
    {
        return coins.remove();
    } // end remove

    public boolean isEmpty()
    {
        return coins.isEmpty();
    } // end isEmpty
} // end PiggyBank
```

---

**1.18** Listing 1-4 provides a brief demonstration of the class `PiggyBank`. The program adds some coins to the bank and then removes all of them. Since the program does not keep a record of the coins it adds to the bank, it has no control over which coins are removed. Although the output indicates that the coins leave the bank in the opposite order from how they entered it, that order depends on the bag's implementation. We'll consider these implementations in the next chapters.

Notice that, in addition to the `main` method, the program defines another method, `addCoin`. Since `main` is static and calls `addCoin`, it must be static as well. The method `addCoin` accepts as its arguments a `Coin` object and a `PiggyBank` object. The method then adds the coin to the bank.

**LISTING 1-4    A demonstration of the class** `PiggyBank`

```java
/**
    A class that demonstrates the class PiggyBank.
    @author Frank M. Carrano
*/
public class PiggyBankExample
{
   public static void main(String[] args)
   {
      PiggyBank myBank = new PiggyBank();

      addCoin(new Coin(1, 2010), myBank);
      addCoin(new Coin(5, 2011), myBank);
      addCoin(new Coin(10, 2000), myBank);
      addCoin(new Coin(25, 2012), myBank);

      System.out.println("Removing all the coins:");
      int amountRemoved = 0;

      while (!myBank.isEmpty())
      {
         Coin removedCoin = myBank.remove();
         System.out.println("Removed a " + removedCoin.getCoinName() + ".");
         amountRemoved = amountRemoved + removedCoin.getValue();
      } // end while
      System.out.println("All done. Removed " + amountRemoved + " cents.");
   } // end main

   private static void addCoin(Coin aCoin, PiggyBank aBank)
   {
      if (aBank.add(aCoin))
         System.out.println("Added a " + aCoin.getCoinName() + ".");
      else
         System.out.println("Tried to add a " + aCoin.getCoinName() +
                            ", but couldn't");
   } // end addCoin
} // end PiggyBankExample
```

**Output**

```
Added a PENNY.
Added a NICKEL.
Added a DIME.
Added a QUARTER.
Removing all the coins:
Removed a QUARTER.
Removed a DIME.
Removed a NICKEL.
Removed a PENNY.
All done. Removed 41 cents.
```

**Note:  A method can change the state of an object passed to it as an argument**
You pass two arguments to the method addCoin: a coin and a piggy bank. Both of these arguments are references to objects that exist in the main method. The method addCoin stores copies of these references in its parameters, which, as you will recall, behave as local variables. Although addCoin cannot change the references, because they exist in the main method, it can alter the state of the referenced objects. In particular, it changes the piggy bank—that is, the PiggyBank object—by adding coins to it. That bank, remember, is local to main and is outside of addCoin.

**Note:**  As soon as we implement a class of bags in the next chapters, you can actually run the programs shown in the previous listings. You just need to replace the class name Bag that these examples use with the name of one of the classes in the next chapters.

**Question 8** Consider the program in Listing 1-4. After creating the instance myBank of the class PiggyBank, suppose that we add several unknown coins to myBank. Write some code that will remove coins from the bank until either you remove a penny or the bank becomes empty.

## Using an ADT Is Like Using a Vending Machine

**1.19**   Imagine that you are in front of a vending machine, as Figure 1-3 depicts; or better yet, take a break and go buy something from one!

FIGURE 1-3      A vending machine

When you look at the front of a vending machine, you see its interface. By inserting coins and pressing buttons, you are able to make a purchase. Here are some observations that we can make about the vending machine:

- You can perform only the specific tasks that the machine's interface presents to you.
- You must understand these tasks—that is, you must know what to do to buy a soda.
- You cannot access the inside of the machine, because a locked shell encapsulates it.
- You can use the machine even though you do not know what happens inside.
- If someone replaced the machine's inner mechanism with an improved version, leaving the interface unchanged, you could still use the machine in the same way.

You, as the user of a vending machine, are like the client of the ADT bag that you saw earlier in this chapter. The observations that we just made about the user of a vending machine are similar to the following observations about a bag's client:

- The client can perform only the operations specific to the ADT bag. These operations often are declared within a Java interface.
- The client must adhere to the specifications of the operations that the ADT bag provides. That is, the programmer of the client must understand how to use these operations.
- The client cannot access the data within the bag without using an ADT operation. The principle of encapsulation hides the data representation within the ADT.
- The client can use the bag, even though the programmer does not know how the data is stored.
- If someone changed the implementation of the bag's operations, the client could still use the bag in the same way, as long as the interface did not change.

**1.20**    In the examples of the previous section, each bag is an instance of a class that implements the ADT bag. That is, each bag is an object whose behaviors are the operations of the ADT bag. You can think of each such object as being like the vending machine we just described. Each object encapsulates the bag's data and operations, just as the vending machine encapsulates its product (soda cans) and delivery system.

Some ADT operations have inputs analogous to the coins you insert into a vending machine. Some ADT operations have outputs analogous to the change, soda cans, messages, and warning lights that a vending machine provides.

Now imagine that you are the designer of the front, or interface, of the vending machine. What can the machine do, and what should a person do to use the machine? Will it help you or hinder you to think about how the soda cans will be stored and transported within the machine? We maintain that you should ignore these aspects and focus solely on how someone will use the machine—that is, you focus on designing the interface. Ignoring extraneous details makes your task easier and increases the quality of your design.

Recall that abstraction as a design principle asks you to focus on *what* instead of *how*. When you design an ADT, and ultimately a class, you use data abstraction to focus on what you want to do with or to the data, without worrying about how you will accomplish these tasks. We practiced data abstraction at the beginning of this chapter when we designed the ADT bag. As we chose the methods that a bag would have, we did not consider how we would represent the bag. Instead, we focused on what each method should do.

Ultimately, we wrote a Java interface that specified the methods in detail. We were then able to write a client that used the bag, again without knowledge of its implementation. If someone wrote the implementation for us, our program would presumably run correctly. If someone else gave us a better implementation, we could use it without changing our already-written client. This feature of the client is a major advantage of abstraction.

# The ADT Set

**1.21**  A **set** is a special kind of bag, one that does not allow repeated, or duplicate, entries. Whenever you must process an item in a data collection only once, you can use a set. For example, a compiler must find the identifiers in a program and ensure that each one has been defined only once. It could add each identifier encountered to a set. If this addition is unsuccessful, the compiler will have detected an identifier previously found.

To specify this ADT, we look back at the interface for a bag. Most of the bag's operations are the same for the ADT set; however, we need to modify the specifications of add and remove. Moreover, we really do not need the operation getFrequencyOf, since it would return either 0 or 1 for a set. Although the result would give us an indication of whether the set contains a given entry, we can use the contains method instead. Listing 1-5 contains an interface for the ADT set. Methods without comments have the same specifications as given for BagInterface in Listing 1-1.

---

**LISTING 1-5    A Java interface for a class of sets**

```java
/** An interface that describes the operations of a set of objects. */
public interface SetInterface<T>
{
    public int getCurrentSize();
    public boolean isEmpty();

    /** Adds a new entry to this set, avoiding duplicates.
        @param newEntry  The object to be added as a new entry.
        @return   True if the addition is successful, or
                  false if the item already is in the set. */
    public boolean add(T newEntry);

    /** Removes a specific entry from this set, if possible.
        @param anEntry  The entry to be removed.
        @return   True if the removal was successful, or false if not. */
    public boolean remove(T anEntry);

    public T remove();
    public void clear();
    public boolean contains(T anEntry);
    public T[] toArray();
} // end SetInterface
```

---

# Java Class Library: The Interface Set

As we mention at the end of Appendix C, the Java Class Library is a collection of classes and interfaces that Java programmers use as a matter of course. From time to time, we will present members of the Java Class Library that are like or relevant to our current discussion. The **Java Collections Framework** is a subset of this library that provides us with a uniform way of representing and working with collections. Many of the classes and interfaces in the Java Class Library that we will note are a part of this framework, although we usually will not point out this fact.

**1.22**  Finally, we present the standard interface Set, which belongs to the package java.util within the Java Class Library. Sets that adhere to the specifications of this interface do not contain a pair of objects x and y such that x.equals(y) is true.

The following method headers declared in the interface Set are similar to the methods within our SetInterface. The differences between a method in Set and a corresponding method in SetInterface are highlighted.

```
public boolean add(T newEntry)
public boolean remove(Object anEntry)
public void clear()
public boolean contains(Object anEntry)
public boolean isEmpty()
public int size()
public Object[] toArray()
```

Each of the interfaces Set and SetInterface declares additional methods that are not in the other.

## CHAPTER SUMMARY

- An abstract data type, or ADT, is a specification of a data set and the operations on that data. This specification does not indicate how to store the data or how to implement the operations, and it is independent of any programming language.

- When you use data abstraction to design an ADT, you focus on what you want to do with or to the data without worrying about how you will accomplish these tasks. That is, you ignore the details of how you represent data and how you manipulate it.

- The manifestation of the ADT in a programming language encapsulates the data and operations. As a result, the particular data representations and method implementations are hidden from the client.

- A collection is an object that holds a group of other objects.

- A bag is a finite collection whose entries are in no particular order.

- A client manipulates or accesses a bag's entries by using only the operations defined for the ADT bag.

- When you add an object to a bag, you cannot indicate where in the bag it will be placed.

- You can remove from a bag an object having either a given value or one that is unspecified. You also can remove all objects from a bag.

- A bag can report whether it contains a given object. It can also report the number of times a given object occurs within its contents.

- A bag can tell you the number of objects it currently contains and can provide an array of those objects.

- A set is a bag that does not contain duplicate entries.

- Carefully specify the methods for a proposed class before you begin to implement them, using tools such as CRC cards and UML notation.

- After designing a draft of an ADT, confirm your understanding of the operations and their design by writing some pseudocode that uses the ADT.

- You should specify the action a method should take if it encounters an unusual situation.

- Writing a Java interface is a way to organize a specification for an ADT.

- Writing a program that tests a class before it is defined is a way to see whether you fully understand and are satisfied with the specification of the class's methods.

## EXERCISES

1. Identify each method used by the class OnlineShopper, as given in Listing 1-2, by stating the method's purpose; by describing its parameters; and by writing preconditions, postconditions, and a pseudocode version of its header. Then write a Java interface for these methods that includes javadoc-style comments.

2. Suppose that groceryBag is a bag filled to its capacity with 10 strings that name various groceries. Write Java statements that remove and count all occurrences of "soup" in groceryBag. Do not remove any other strings from the bag. Report the number of times that "soup" occurred in the bag. Accommodate the possibility that groceryBag does not contain any occurrence of "soup".

3. Given groceryBag, as described in Exercise 2, what effect does the operation groceryBag.toArray() have on groceryBag?

4. Given groceryBag, as described in Exercise 2, write some Java statements that create an array of the distinct strings that are in this bag. That is, if "soup" occurs three times in groceryBag, it should appear only once in your array. After you have finished creating this array, the contents of groceryBag should be unchanged.

5. The *union* of two collections consists of their contents combined into a new collection. Add a method union to the interface BagInterface for the ADT bag that returns as a new bag the union of the bag receiving the call to the method and the bag that is the method's one argument. Include sufficient comments to fully specify the method.

   Note that the union of two bags might contain duplicate items. For example, if object x occurs five times in one bag and twice in another, the union of these bags contains x seven times. Specifically, suppose that bag1 and bag2 are Bag objects, where Bag implements BagInterface; bag1 contains the String objects a, b, and c; and bag2 contains the String objects b, b, d, and e. After the statement

   ```
   BagInterface<String> everything = bag1.union(bag2);
   ```

   executes, the bag everything contains the strings a, b, b, b, c, d, and e. Note that union does not affect the contents of bag1 and bag2.

6. The *intersection* of two collections is a new collection of the entries that occur in both collections. That is, it contains the overlapping entries. Add a method intersection to the interface BagInterface for the ADT bag that returns as a new bag the intersection of the bag receiving the call to the method and the bag that is the method's one argument. Include sufficient comments to fully specify the method.

   Note that the intersection of two bags might contain duplicate items. For example, if object x occurs five times in one bag and twice in another, the intersection of these bags contains x twice. Specifically, suppose that bag1 and bag2 are Bag objects, where Bag implements BagInterface; bag1 contains the String objects a, b, and c; and bag2 contains the String objects b, b, d, and e. After the statement

   ```
   BagInterface<String> commonItems = bag1.intersection(bag2);
   ```

   executes, the bag commonItems contains only the string b. If b had occurred in bag1 twice, commonItems would have contained two occurrences of b, since bag2 also contains two occurrences of b. Note that intersection does not affect the contents of bag1 and bag2.

7. The *difference* of two collections is a new collection of the entries that would be left in one collection after removing those that also occur in the second. Add a method `difference` to the interface `BagInterface` for the ADT bag that returns as a new bag the difference of the bag receiving the call to the method and the bag that is the method's one argument. Include sufficient comments to fully specify the method.

    Note that the difference of two bags might contain duplicate items. For example, if object $x$ occurs five times in one bag and twice in another, the difference of these bags contains $x$ three times. Specifically, suppose that `bag1` and `bag2` are `Bag` objects, where `Bag` implements `BagInterface`; `bag1` contains the `String` objects a, b, and c; and `bag2` contains the `String` objects b, b, d, and e. After the statement

    ```
    BagInterface leftOver1 = bag1.difference(bag2);
    ```

    executes, the bag `leftOver1` contains the strings a and c. After the statement

    ```
    BagInterface leftOver2 = bag2.difference(bag1);
    ```

    executes, the bag `leftOver2` contains the strings b, d, and e. Note that `difference` does not affect the contents of `bag1` and `bag2`.

8. Write a code that accomplishes the following tasks: Consider two bags that can hold integers. One bag is named `numbers` and contains several integers between 1 and 10. The other bag is empty and is named `evens`. One at a time, remove an integer from `numbers`. If the integer is even, place it into the bag `evens`; otherwise, discard the integer. After you have checked all of the integers in `numbers`, report the number of evens in the bag `evens` and the number of times each even number appears in the bag.

9. Write code that accomplishes the following tasks: Consider three bags that can hold integers. One bag is named `numbers` and contains several integers from 1 to 10. Another bag is named `evens` and contains five even integers from 1 to 10. The third bag is empty and is named `odds`. One at a time, remove an integer from `numbers`. Check whether the integer is in the bag `evens`. If it is, discard the integer. Otherwise, place it into the bag `odds`. After you have checked all of the integers in `numbers`, report the number of odd integers in the bag `odds` and the number of times each odd integer appears in the bag.

## PROJECTS

1. As we stated in Segment 1.21, a set is a special bag that does not allow duplicates. Suppose the class `Set<T>` implements `SetInterface<T>`. Given an empty set that is an object of `Set<String>` and given an object of the class `Bag<String>` that contains several strings, write statements at the client level that create a set from the given bag.

2. Imagine a pile of books on your desk. Each book is so large and heavy that you can remove only the top one from the pile. You cannot remove a book from under another one. Likewise, you can add another book to the pile only by placing it on the top of the pile. You cannot add a book beneath another one.

    If you represent books by their titles alone, design a class that you can use to track the books in the pile on your desk. Specify each operation by stating its purpose, by describing its parameters, and by writing a pseudocode version of its header. Then write a Java interface for the pile's methods. Include `javadoc`-style comments in your code.

3. A *ring* is a collection of items that has a reference to a current item. An operation—let's call it `advance`—moves the reference to the next item in the collection. When the reference reaches the last item, the next `advance` operation will move the reference back to the first item. A ring also has operations to get the current item, add an item, and remove an item. The details of where an item is added and which one is removed are up to you.

    Design an ADT to represent a ring of objects. Specify each operation by stating its purpose, by describing its parameters, and by writing a pseudocode version of its header. Then write a Java interface for a ring's methods. Include `javadoc`-style comments in your code.

4. A *shoe* of playing cards contains some number of standard decks of cards. Cards in the shoe can be shuffled together and dealt one at a time. The number of cards in the shoe can also be calculated.

   After a hand is complete, you should be able to return all cards to the shoe and shuffle them. Some card games require that the discard pile be returned to the shoe when the shoe becomes empty. Then the cards in the shoe can be shuffled. In this case, not all cards are in the shoe; some are held by the players.

   Design an ADT for a shoe, assuming that you have the class `PlayingCard`, which you should specify, too. You do not need an ADT deck, since a deck is a shoe whose number of decks is 1.

   Specify each ADT operation by stating its purpose, by describing its parameters, and by writing a pseudocode version of its header. Then write a Java interface for a shoe's methods. Include `javadoc`-style comments in your code.

5. A bid for installing an air conditioner consists of the name of the company, a description of the unit, the performance of the unit, the cost of the unit, and the cost of installation.

   Design an ADT that represents any bid. Then design another ADT to represent a collection of bids. The second ADT should include methods to search for bids based on price and performance. Also note that a single company could make multiple bids, each with a different unit.

   Specify each ADT operation by stating its purpose, by describing its parameters, and by writing a pseudocode version of its header. Then write a Java interface for a bid's methods. Include `javadoc`-style comments in your code.

6. A *matrix* is a rectangular array of numerical values. You can add or multiply two matrices to form a third matrix. You can multiply a matrix by a scalar, and you can transpose a matrix. Design an ADT that represents a matrix that has these operations.

   Specify each ADT operation by stating its purpose, by describing its parameters, and by writing a pseudocode version of its header. Then write a Java interface for the methods of a matrix. Include `javadoc`-style comments in your code.

## ANSWERS TO SELF-TEST QUESTIONS

1.
```
// aBag is empty
entry = next string read from user
while (aBag.add(entry))
{
    entry = next string read from user
}
// aBag is full
```

2. No. The two methods have identical signatures. Recall that a method's return type is not a part of its signature. These methods have the same name and parameter list.

3. Yes. The two methods have different signatures. They are overloaded methods.

4.
```
// aBag is full
while (!aBag.isEmpty())
{
    entry = aBag.remove()
    Display entry
}
// aBag is empty
```

5. Display "The string Hello occurs in aBag " + aBag.getFrequencyOf("Hello") + " times."

**6.**
```java
String[] contents = aBag.toArray();
for (int index = 0; index < contents.length; index++)
    System.out.print(contents[index] + " ");
System.out.println();
```

**7.**
```java
int itemCount = shoppingCart.getCurrentSize();
for (int counter = 0; counter < itemCount; counter++)
    System.out.println(shoppingCart.remove());
```

**8.**
```java
boolean lookingForPenny = true;
while (!myBank.isEmpty() && lookingForPenny)
{
    Coin removedCoin = myBank.remove();
    System.out.println("Removed a " + removedCoin.getCoinName() + ".");
    if (removedCoin.getCoinName() == CoinName.PENNY)
//  if (removedCoin.getValue() == 1) // ALTERNATE
    {
        System.out.println("Found a penny. All done!");
        lookingForPenny = false; // Penny is found
    } // end if
} // end while

if (lookingForPenny)
    System.out.println("No penny was found. Sorry!");
```

# Generics

## Contents

## Prerequisite

This book is about designing and building classes whose instances contain collections of data. The data items in any one collection have the same or related—by inheritance—data types. For example, we might have a collection of strings, a collection of Name objects, a collection of Student objects, and so on. Instead of writing a different class for each of these collections, Java enables you to write a placeholder instead of an actual class type within the definition of a class or interface. This is possible because of a feature known as **generics**. By using generics, you can define a class of objects whose data type is determined later by the client of your class. This technique is important to our study of data structures, and this interlude will show you what you need to know right now.

## Generic Data Types

**JI1.1**  Generics enable you to write a placeholder instead of an actual class type within the definition of a class or interface. The placeholder is a **generic data type**, or simply a **generic type** or a **type parameter**. When you define a class whose instances hold various data collections, you need not give a specific data type for the objects in these collections. Instead, by using a generic data type instead of an actual data type, you define a **generic class** whose client chooses the data type of the objects in the collection.

As Appendix B mentions, the class Object is the ultimate ancestor of all other classes. Given a reference to an object of any type, you can assign the reference to a variable whose type is Object. Although you might be tempted to use Object as a general class, you should not do so. Instead, you should use a generic data type to represent any class type.

Imagine an array A of objects. If the data type of A was declared as Object[], you could place strings, for example, into the array. Nothing, however, would stop you from placing objects of several other classes into the array along with the strings. While this might sound attractive, you likely would have a problem using such an array. For example, if you removed an object from the array, you would not know its dynamic type. Is it a string or some other object? Methods are available to retrieve an object's dynamic type, however, so such an array can have a use.

In contrast, an array or any other group whose entries are referenced by variables of a generic type can contain only objects of classes related by inheritance. Thus, by using generics, you can restrict the types of entries in your collections. This restriction is not unusual, as it makes these collections easier to use.

## Generic Types Within an Interface

**VideoNote**
Generics

**JI1.2**    In mathematics, an *ordered pair* is a pair of values, *a* and *b*, denoted as (*a*, *b*). We say that the values in (*a*, *b*) are ordered because (*a*, *b*) does not equal (*b*, *a*) unless *a* equals *b*. For example, a point in a two-dimensional space is described by its *x*-coordinate and *y*-coordinate, that is, the ordered pair (*x*, *y*).

Imagine objects that pair other objects whose data types are the same class type. We can define an interface to describe the behavior of such pairs and use a generic type in its definition. For example, Listing JI1-1 defines the interface Pairable that specifies these pairs. A Pairable object contains two objects of the same generic type T.

---

**LISTING JI1-1    The interface Pairable**

```
1  public interface Pairable<T>
2  {
3     public T getFirst();
4     public T getSecond();
5     public void changeOrder();
6  }  // end Pairable
```

---

**JI1.3**    A class that implements this interface could begin with the statement

```
public class OrderedPair<T> implements Pairable<T>
```

In this example, the data type that we pass to the interface in the implements clause is the generic type T declared for the class. In general, one could pass the name of an actual class to the interface that appears in an implements clause. You will see an example of this situation in Java Interlude 3.

**Note:** To establish a generic type when you define an interface or a class, you write an identifier—T for example—enclosed in angle brackets after the name of the interface or class in its header. The identifier T can be any identifier but usually is a single capital letter. It represents a reference type—not a primitive type—within the definition of the interface or class.

## Generic Classes

**JI1.4**   Listing JI1-2 shows the class OrderedPair that we began in the previous segment. The class assumes that we care about the order in which the objects appear in the pair. The notation <T> follows the identifier *name* in the class's header. Within the definition, T represents the data type of the two private data fields, the data type of the two parameters of the constructor, the return type of the methods getFirst and getSecond, and the data type of the local variable temp in the method changeOrder.

---

**LISTING JI1-2**   The class OrderedPair

```java
1  /**
2      A class of ordered pairs of objects having the same data type.
3      @author Frank M. Carrano
4  */
5  public class OrderedPair<T> implements Pairable<T>
6  {
7      private T first, second;
8
9      public OrderedPair(T firstItem, T secondItem) // NOTE: no <T> after
10     {                                             // constructor name
11         first = firstItem;
12         second = secondItem;
13     } // end constructor
14
15     /** Returns the first object in this pair. */
16     public T getFirst()
17     {
18         return first;
19     } // end getFirst
20
21     /** Returns the second object in this pair. */
22     public T getSecond()
23     {
24         return second;
25     } // end getSecond
26
27     /** Returns a string representation of this pair. */
28     public String toString()
29     {
30         return "(" + first + ", " + second + ")";
31     } // end toString
32
33     /** Interchanges the objects in this pair. */
34     public void changeOrder()
35     {
36         T temp = first;
37         first = second;
38         second = temp;
39     } // changeOrder
40 } // end OrderedPair
```

**Note:** Within the definition of a class *name*<T>, where T is a generic type parameter,
- <T> follows the identifier *name* in the class's header
- <T> does not follow the names of the constructors in their definitions
- T—not <T>—can be a data type of data fields, method parameters, and local variables, and it can be a return type of methods

**JI1.5**   **Example: Creating `OrderedPair` objects**. To create an ordered pair of `String` objects, for example, you can write a statement such as

```
OrderedPair<String> fruit = new OrderedPair<>("apple", "banana");
```

Now, wherever T appears as a data type in the definition of `OrderedPair`, `String` is used.

**Programming Tip:** Prior to Java 7, the previous Java statement would need to repeat the data type `String` as follows:

```
OrderedPair<String> aPair = new OrderedPair<String>("apple", "banana");
```
Now, doing so is optional.

The following statements are an example of how you could use the object `fruit`:

```
System.out.println(fruit);
fruit.changeOrder();
System.out.println(fruit);
String firstFruit = fruit.getFirst();
System.out.println(firstFruit + " has length " + firstFruit.length());
```

The output from these statements is

```
(apple, banana)
(banana, apple)
banana has length 6
```

Note that the ordered pair `fruit` has the `OrderedPair` methods `changeOrder` and `getFirst`. Moreover, the object returned by `getFirst` is a `String` object that has the method `length`.

Let's also note something that is illegal. You cannot assign a pair of objects that are not strings to the object `fruit`:

```
fruit = new OrderedPair<Integer>(1, 2); // ERROR! Incompatible types
```

The problem is that you cannot convert `OrderedPair<Integer>` to `OrderedPair<String>`. You can, however, create a pair of `Integer` objects, as follows:

```
OrderedPair<Integer> intPair = new OrderedPair<>(1, 2);
System.out.println(intPair);
intPair.changeOrder();
System.out.println(intPair);
```

The output is as you would expect:

```
(1, 2)
(2, 1)
```

Now consider the class Name, as given in Listing B-1 of Appendix B. If the variable namePair has the type OrderedPair<Name>, you can create pairs of objects of any class that uses inheritance to extend Name. For example, if the class FormalName extends Name and adds a title, such as Mr. or Ms., namePair could contain objects of both Name and FormalName.

**Note:** Within the client of a generic class *name<class-type>*,
- An expression of the form

  **new** *name<class-type>*(...)

  creates an object of the class. As of Java 7, if this expression is assigned to a variable whose data type is *name<class-type>*, you can omit *class-type* in the expression. That is, you can write a statement such as

  *name<class-type>* var = **new** *name*<>(...)

- The data type of objects of the class is *name<class-type>*, not *name*

**Question 1** What method must a class such as String or Name define so that OrderedPair's method toString works correctly?

**Question 2** Consider the class OrderedPair, as given in Listing JI1-2. Suppose that we did not use a generic type, but instead omitted <T> and declared the data types of the private fields, method parameters, and local variable to be Object instead of T. What would the effect of these changes be on the use of the class?

**Question 3** Can you use the class OrderedPair, as defined in Listing JI1-2, to pair two objects having different and unrelated data types? Why or why not?

**Question 4** Using the class Name, as defined in Listing C-1 of Appendix C, write statements that pair two students as lab partners.

## ANSWERS TO SELF-TEST QUESTIONS

1. `toString`

2. The statements given in Segment JI1.5, for example, would begin with

   ```
   OrderedPair fruit = new OrderedPair("apple", "banana");
   ```

   The disadvantage to this version of `OrderedPair` is that the compiler cannot warn you if you pair objects of different and unrelated types. Thus, you would be able to write

   ```
   Name joe = new Name("Joe", "Java");
   String joePhone = "(401) 555-1234";
   OrderedPair joeEntry = new OrderedPair();
   joeEntry.setPair(joe, joePhone);
   ```

3. No. The class defines only one generic type.

4. 
   ```
   Name kristen = new Name("Kristen", "Doe");
   Name luci = new Name("Luci", "Lei");
   OrderedPair<Name> labPartners = new OrderedPair<>(kristen, luci);
   ```

# Bag Implementations That Use Arrays

## Chapter

## 2

## Contents

## Prerequisites

Prelude      Designing Classes
Chapter   1   Bags

## Objectives

After studying this chapter, you should be able to

- Implement the ADT bag by using a fixed-size array or an array that you expand dynamically
- Discuss the advantages and disadvantages of the two implementations presented

$Y$ou have seen several examples of how to use the ADT bag in a program. This chapter presents two different ways—each involving an array—to implement a bag in Java. When you use an array to organize data, the implementation is said to be **array based**. You will see a completely different approach in the next chapter.

We begin by using an ordinary Java array to represent the entries in a bag. With this implementation, your bag could become full, just as a grocery bag does. We then offer another implementation that does not suffer from this problem. With this second implementation, when you use all of the space in an array, you move the data to a larger array. The effect is to have an array that apparently expands to meet your needs. Thus, we can have a bag that is never full.

# Using a Fixed-Size Array to Implement the ADT Bag

Our task is to define the methods we specified in the previous chapter when we wrote the interface `BagInterface`. We begin by using an analogy to describe how a fixed-size array could contain the entries in a bag. In doing so, we show how the add and remove methods would work. Subsequently, we present a corresponding Java implementation for the bag.

## An Analogy

**2.1**    Imagine a classroom—call it room A—containing 40 desks in fixed positions. If a course is restricted to 30 students, 10 desks are idle and wasted. If we lift the enrollment restriction, we can accommodate only 10 more students, even if 20 more want to take the course.

An array is like this classroom, and each desk is like one array location. Suppose that we number the 40 desks in the room sequentially, beginning with zero, as Figure 2-1 illustrates. Although desks are arranged in rows in typical classrooms, we will ignore this detail and treat the desks as a one-dimensional array.

FIGURE 2-1    A classroom that contains desks in fixed positions

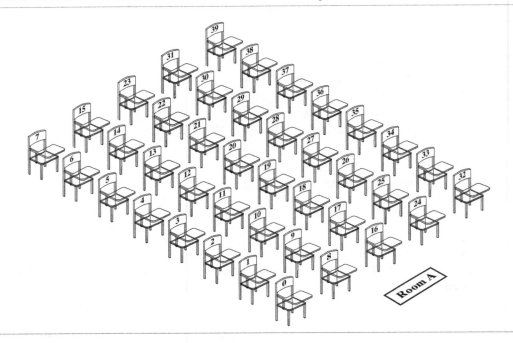

**2.2**    **Adding a new student.** Suppose that the instructor asks arriving students to occupy consecutively numbered desks. Thus, the first student who arrives at the classroom sits at desk 0, the second student sits at desk 1, and so on. The instructor's request that consecutively numbered desks be occupied is arbitrary and simply for his or her convenience. As you will see, we will fill an array of bag entries in an analogous way.

Imagine that 30 students in room A occupy the desks numbered sequentially from 0 to 29, and a new student wants to join those students. Since 40 desks are in the room, the desk numbered 30 is available. We can simply assign the new student to desk 30. When all 40 desks are occupied, we can no longer accommodate more students. The room is full.

**2.3**    **Removing a particular student.** Now imagine that the student in desk 5 of room A drops the course. Desk 5 stays in its fixed location within the room and will be vacant. If we still want students to sit in consecutively numbered desks, however, one student will need to move to desk 5. Since the students are not in any particular order, if the student in the highest-numbered desk moves to desk 5, no one else need move. For example, if 30 students are seated in the room in desks 0 to 29, the student in desk 29 would move to desk 5. Desks 29 and above would be vacant.

**Question 1** What is an advantage of moving a student as just described so that the vacated desk does not remain vacant?

**Question 2** What is an advantage of leaving the vacated desk vacant?

**Question 3** If a student were to drop the course, which one could do so without forcing another to change desks?

## A Group of Core Methods

VideoNote
An array-based bag

**2.4**    The Java array-based implementation for the ADT bag incorporates some of the ideas that our classroom example illustrates. The result is the class `ArrayBag`, which implements the interface `BagInterface` that you saw in Listing 1-1 of Chapter 1. Each public method within the interface corresponds to an ADT bag operation. Recall that the interface defines a generic type `T` for the objects in a bag. We use this same generic type in the definition of `ArrayBag`.

The definition for the class `ArrayBag` could be fairly involved. The class certainly will have quite a few methods. For such classes, you should not define the entire class and then attempt to test it. Instead, you should identify a group of **core methods** to both implement and test before continuing with the rest of the class definition. By leaving the definitions of the other methods for later, you can focus your attention and simplify your task. But what methods should be part of this group? In general, such methods should be central to the purpose of the class and allow reasonable testing. We sometimes will call a group of core methods a **core group**.

When dealing with a collection such as a bag, you cannot test most methods until you have created the collection. Thus, adding objects to the collection is a fundamental operation. If the method `add` does not work correctly, testing other methods such as `remove` would be pointless. Thus, the bag's add method is part of the group of core methods that we implement first.

To test whether `add` works correctly, we need a method that allows us to see the bag's contents. The method `toArray` serves this purpose, and so it is a core method. The constructors are also fundamental and are in the core group. Similarly, any methods that a core method might call are part of the core group as well. For example, since we cannot add an entry to a full bag, the method add can detect a full array by calling a private method `isArrayFull`.

**2.5**    **The core methods.** We have identified the following core methods to be a part of the first draft of the class `ArrayBag`:

- Constructors
- **public boolean** add(T newEntry)
- **public T[]** toArray()
- **private boolean** isArrayFull()

With this core, we will be able to construct a bag, add objects to it, and look at the result. We will not implement the remaining methods until these core methods work correctly.

 **Note:** Methods such as add and remove that can alter the underlying structure of a collection are likely to have the most involved implementations. In general, you should define such methods before the others in the class. But since we can't test remove before add is correct, we will delay implementing it until after add is completed and thoroughly tested.

 **Programming Tip:** When defining a class, implement and test a group of core methods. Begin with methods that add to a collection of objects and/or have involved implementations.

## Implementing the Core Methods

**2.6**    **The data fields.** Before we define any of the core methods, we need to consider the class's data fields. Since the bag will hold a group of objects, one field can be an array of these objects. The length of the array defines the bag's capacity. We can let the client specify this capacity, and we can also provide a default capacity. In addition, we will want to track the current number of entries in the bag. Thus, we can define the following data fields for our class,

```
private final T[] bag;
private int numberOfEntries;
private static final int DEFAULT_CAPACITY = 25;
```

and add them to our earlier UML representation of the class in Figure 1-2 of the previous chapter. The resulting notation appears in Figure 2-2.

FIGURE 2-2    UML notation for the class ArrayBag, including the class's data fields

```
                    ArrayBag
-bag: T[]
-numberOfEntries: integer
-DEFAULT_CAPACITY: integer
+getCurrentSize(): integer
+isEmpty(): boolean
+add(newEntry: T): boolean
+remove(): T
+remove(anEntry: T): boolean
+clear(): void
+getFrequencyOf(anEntry: T): integer
+contains(anEntry: T): boolean
+toArray(): T[]
-isArrayFull(): boolean
```

 **Programming Tip: Final Arrays**
By declaring the array bag as a final data member of the class ArrayBag, we know that the reference in the variable bag cannot change. Although declaring the array in this way is a good practice, realize that the values in the elements bag[0], bag[1], ... in the array can change. Such change is necessary, but we must prevent the client from obtaining the reference in bag to the array. Such an event would make the contents of the array vulnerable to malicious damage. We will discuss this further when we define the method toArray in Segment 2.12.

**2.7** **About the constructors.** A constructor for this class must create the array bag. Notice that the declaration of the data field bag in the previous segment does not create an array. Forgetting to create an array in a constructor is a common mistake. To create the array, the constructor must specify the array's length, which is the bag's capacity. And since we are creating an empty bag, the constructor should also initialize the field numberOfEntries to zero.

The decision to use a generic data type in the declaration of the array bag affects how we allocate this array within the constructor. A statement such as

```
bag = new T[capacity]; // SYNTAX ERROR
```

is syntactically incorrect. You cannot use a generic type when allocating an array. Instead, we allocate an array of objects of type Object, as follows:

```
new Object[capacity];
```

However, problems arise when we try to assign this array to the data field bag. The statement

```
bag = new Object[capacity]; // SYNTAX ERROR: incompatible types
```

causes a syntax error because you cannot assign an array of type Object[] to an array of type T[]. That is, the types of the two arrays are not compatible.

A cast is necessary but creates its own problem. The statement

```
bag = (T[])new Object[capacity];
```

produces the compiler warning

```
ArrayBag.java uses unchecked or unsafe operations.
Note: Recompile with -Xlint:unchecked for details.
```

If you compile the class again and use the option -Xlint, the messages will be more detailed, beginning as follows:

```
ArrayBag.java:24: warning: [unchecked] unchecked cast¹
bag = (T[])new Object[capacity]
      ^
required: T[]
found:    Object[]
where T is a type-variable:
T extends Object declared in class ArrayBag
```

The compiler wants you to ensure that casting each entry in the array from type Object to the generic type T is safe. Since the array has just been allocated, it contains null entries. Thus, the cast is safe, and so we instruct the compiler to ignore the warning by writing the annotation

```
@SuppressWarnings("unchecked")
```

before the offending statement. This instruction to the compiler can precede only a method definition or a variable declaration. Since the assignment

```
bag = (T[])new Object[capacity];
```

does not declare bag—bag has already been declared—we revise it as follows:

```
// The cast is safe because the new array contains null entries.
@SuppressWarnings("unchecked")
T[] tempBag = (T[])new Object[capacity]; // Unchecked cast
bag = tempBag;
```

**Note: Suppressing compiler warnings**
To suppress an unchecked-cast warning from the compiler, you precede the flagged statements with the instruction

```
@SuppressWarnings("unchecked")
```

Note that this instruction can precede only a method definition or a variable declaration. You should always include a comment that justifies your suppression of compiler warnings.

---

1. 24 is the line number of the statement that causes the problem.

**2.8** **The constructors.** The following constructor performs the previous steps, using a capacity given as an argument:

```
/** Creates an empty bag having a given capacity.
    @param capacity  The integer capacity desired. */
public ArrayBag(int capacity)
{
    // The cast is safe because the new array contains null entries.
    @SuppressWarnings("unchecked")
    T[] tempBag = (T[])new Object[capacity]; // Unchecked cast
    bag = tempBag;
    numberOfEntries = 0;
} // end constructor
```

The default constructor can invoke the previous one, passing it the default capacity as an argument, as follows:

```
/** Creates an empty bag whose capacity is 25. */
public ArrayBag()
{
    this(DEFAULT_CAPACITY);
} // end default constructor
```

Recall that a constructor can invoke another constructor in the same class by using the keyword this as a method name.

**2.9** **An outline of the class.** Let's look at the class as we have defined it so far. After you complete the initial portion of the class—that is, the header, data fields, and constructors—you can add the comments and headers for the public methods simply by copying them from BagInterface. You then write empty bodies after each of those headers. Listing 2-1 shows the result of these steps. Our next task is to implement our three core methods.

---

**LISTING 2-1** An outline of the class Arraybag

```
1  /**
2      A class of bags whose entries are stored in a fixed-size array.
3      @author Frank M. Carrano
4  */
5  public final class ArrayBag<T> implements BagInterface<T>
6  {
7      private final T[] bag;
8      private int numberOfEntries;
9      private static final int DEFAULT_CAPACITY = 25;
10
11     /** Creates an empty bag whose initial capacity is 25. */
12     public ArrayBag()
13     {
14         this(DEFAULT_CAPACITY);
15     } // end default constructor
16
17     /** Creates an empty bag having a given initial capacity.
18         @param capacity  The integer capacity desired. */
19     public ArrayBag(int capacity)
20     {
21         // The cast is safe because the new array contains null entries.
22         @SuppressWarnings("unchecked")
23         T[] tempBag = (T[])new Object[capacity]; // Unchecked cast
24         bag = tempBag;
25         numberOfEntries = 0;
26     } // end constructor
27
```

```
28    /** Adds a new entry to this bag.
29        @param newEntry  The object to be added as a new entry.
30        @return  True if the addition is successful, or false if not. */
31    public boolean add(T newEntry)
32    {
33        < Body to be defined >
34    } // end add
35
36    /** Retrieves all entries that are in this bag.
37        @return  A newly allocated array of all the entries in the bag. */
38    public T[] toArray()
39    {
40        < Body to be defined >
41    } // end toArray
42
43    // Returns true if the arraybag is full, or false if not.
44    private boolean isArrayFull()
45    {
46        < Body to be defined >
47    } // end isArrayFull
48
49    < Similar partial definitions are here for the remaining methods
50      declared in BagInterface. >
51
52        . . .
53 } // end ArrayBag
```

 **Programming Tip:** When defining a class that implements an interface, add the comments and headers of the public methods to the class by copying them from the interface. In this way, it is easy for you to check each method's specifications as you implement it. Moreover, anyone who maintains your code later has easy access to these specifications.

 **Design Decision:** **When the array bag is partially full, which array elements should contain the bag's entries?**

When you add a first entry to an array, you typically place it in the array's first element, that is, the element whose index is 0. Doing so, however, is not a requirement, especially for arrays that implement collections. For example, some collection implementations can benefit by ignoring the array element whose index is 0 and using index 1 as the first element in the array. Sometimes you might want to use the elements at the end of the array before the ones at its beginning. For the bag, we have no reason to be atypical, and so the objects in our bag will begin at index 0 of the array.

Another consideration is whether the bag's objects should occupy consecutive elements of the array. Requiring the add method to place objects into the array bag consecutively is certainly reasonable, but why should we care, and is this really a concern? We need to establish certain truths, or assertions, about our planned implementation so that the action of each method is not detrimental to other methods. For example, the method toArray must "know" where add has placed the bag's entries. Our decision now also will affect what must happen later when we remove an entry from the bag. Will the method remove ensure that the array entries remain in consecutive elements? It must, because for now at least, we will insist that bag entries occupy consecutive array elements.

2.10    **The method add.** If the bag is full, we cannot add anything to it. In that case, the method add should return false. Otherwise, we simply add newEntry immediately after the last entry in the array bag by writing the following statement:

```
bag[numberOfEntries] = newEntry;
```

If we are adding to an empty bag, numberOfEntries would be zero, and the assignment would be to bag[0]. If the bag contained one entry, an additional entry would be assigned to bag[1], and so on. After each addition to the bag, we increase the counter numberOfEntries. These steps are illustrated in Figure 2-3 and accomplished by the definition of the method add that follows the figure.

FIGURE 2-3    Adding entries to an array that represents a bag, whose capacity is six, until it becomes full

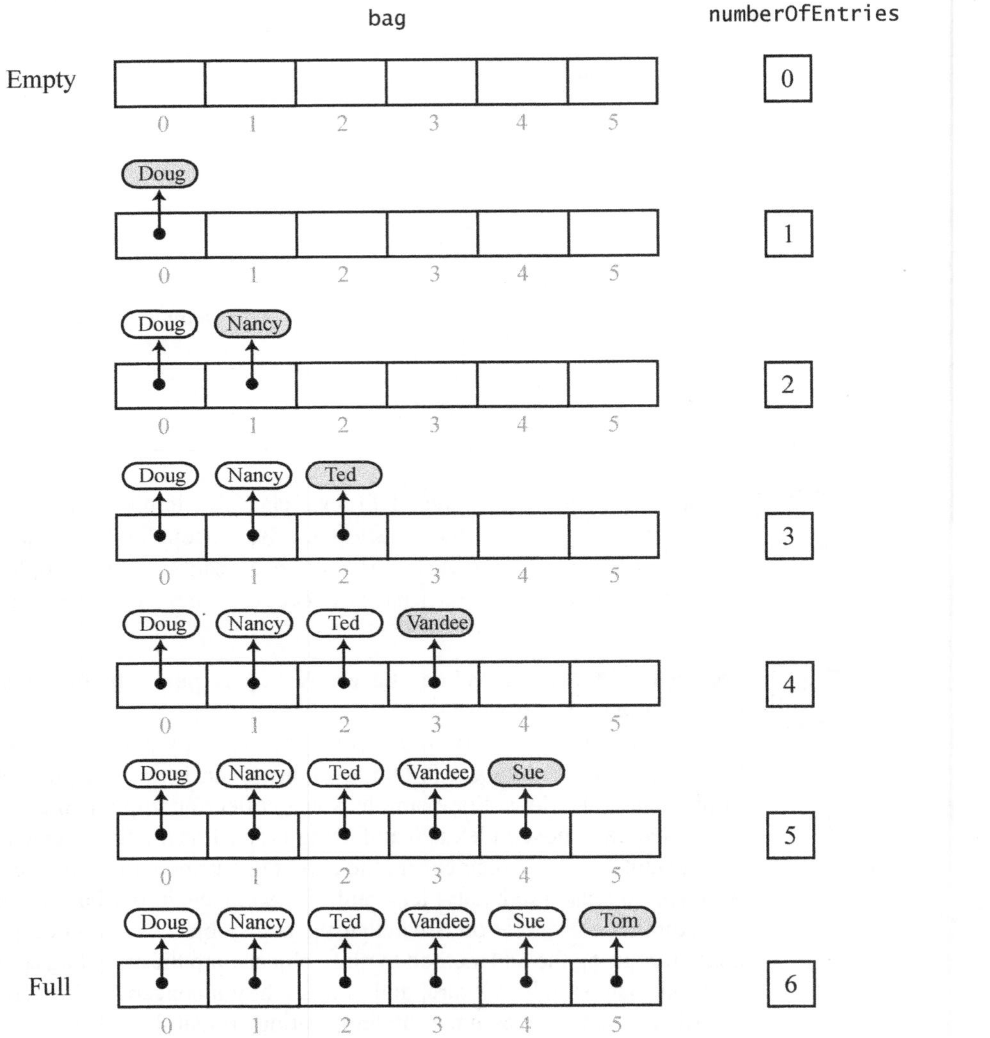

```
/** Adds a new entry to this bag.
    @param newEntry  The object to be added as a new entry.
    @return  True if the addition is successful, or false if not. */
public boolean add(T newEntry)
{
    boolean result = true;
    if (isArrayFull())
    {
```

```
         result = false;
      }
      else
      {  // Assertion: result is true here
         bag[numberOfEntries] = newEntry;
         numberOfEntries++;
      } // end if

      return result;
   } // end add
```

Notice that we call isArrayFull as if it has been defined already. Had we not considered isArrayFull as a core method earlier, its use now would indicate to us that it should be in the core group.

**Note:** The entries in a bag have no particular order. Thus, the method add can place a new entry into a convenient element of the array bag. In the previous definition of add, that element is the one immediately after the last element used.

**Note:** Often, our discussions portray arrays as if they actually contained objects. In reality, Java arrays contain references to objects, as in the array in Figure 2-3.

**2.11**   **The method isArrayFull.** A bag is full when it contains as many objects as the array bag can accommodate. That situation occurs when numberOfEntries is equal to the capacity of the array. Thus, isArrayFull has the following straightforward definition:

```
      // Returns true if the bag is full, or false if not.
      private boolean isArrayFull()
      {
         return numberOfEntries >= bag.length;
      } // end isArrayFull
```

**2.12**   **The method toArray.** The last method, toArray, in our initial core group retrieves the entries that are in a bag and returns them to the client within a newly allocated array. The length of this new array can equal the number of entries in the bag—that is, numberOfEntries—rather than the length of the array bag. However, we have the same problems in allocating an array that we had in defining the constructor, so we take the same steps as for the constructor.

After toArray creates the new array, a simple loop can copy the references in the array bag to this new array before returning it. Thus, the definition of toArray can appear as follows:

```
      /** Retrieves all entries that are in this bag.
          @return  A newly allocated array of all the entries in the bag. */
      public T[] toArray()
      {
         // The cast is safe because the new array contains null entries.
         @SuppressWarnings("unchecked")
         T[] result = (T[])new Object[numberOfEntries]; // Unchecked cast
         for (int index = 0; index < numberOfEntries; index++)
         {
            result[index] = bag[index];
         } // end for
         return result;
      } // end toArray
```

**Design Decision:**   **Should the method `toArray` return the array bag instead of a copy?**
Suppose that we define `toArray` as follows:

```
public String[] toArray()
{
    return bag;
} // end toArray
```

This simple definition would certainly return an array of the bag's contents to a client. For example, the statement

```
String[] bagArray = myBag.toArray();
```

provides a reference to an array of the entries in `myBag`. A client could use the variable `bagArray` to display the contents of `myBag`.

The reference `bagArray`, however, is to the array `bag` itself. That is, `bagArray` is an alias for the private instance variable `bag` within the object `myBag`, and therefore it gives the client direct access to this private data. Thus, a client could change the contents of the bag without calling the class's public methods. For instance, if `myBag` is the full bag pictured in Figure 2-3, the statement

```
bagArray[2] = null;
```

would change the entry Ted to `null`. Although this approach might sound good to you if the intent is to remove Ted from the bag, doing so would destroy the integrity of the bag. In particular, the entries in the array `bag` would no longer be consecutive, and the count of the number of entries in the bag would be incorrect.

**Security Note:**   A class should not return a reference to an array that is a private data field.

**Note:**   By using generics, you can restrict the data types of the entries in your collections, because

- A variable whose declared data type is `Object` can reference an object of any data type, but a variable having a generic data type can reference only an object of specific data types.
- A collection whose entries are referenced by variables of type `Object` can contain objects of various unrelated classes, but a collection whose entries are referenced by variables of a generic type can contain only objects of classes related by inheritance.

**Question 4** In the previous method `toArray`, does the value of `numberOfEntries` equal `bag.length` in general?

**Question 5** Suppose that the previous method `toArray` gave the new array `result` the same length as the array `bag`. How would a client get the number of entries in the returned array?

**Question 6** Suppose that the previous method `toArray` returned the array `bag` instead of returning a new array such as `result`. If `myBag` is a bag of five entries, what effect would the following statements have on the array `bag` and the field `numberOfEntries`?

```
Object[] bagArray = myBag.toArray();
bagArray[0] = null;
```

**Question 7** The body of the method `toArray` could consist of one `return` statement if you call the method `Arrays.copyOf`. Make this change to `toArray`.

## Making the Implementation Secure

**2.13**   Given the present-day reality of hackers and unauthorized intrusions into vital software systems, programmers must include fail-safe measures in their code to make programs safe and secure for their users. Although Java manages memory for you, checks the validity of array indices, and is type-safe, a mistake could make your code vulnerable to attack. You should be mindful of security as you implement ADTs, as adding secure measures to existing code can be difficult.

 **Note:** You can practice **fail-safe programming** by including checks for anticipated errors within your programs. **Safe and secure programming** extends the notion of fail-safe programming by validating any input data and arguments to a method, by eliminating a method's side effects, and by making no assumptions about the actions of clients and users.

 **Security Note: Protect the integrity of ADT implementations**
When implementing an ADT, two of the questions we need to ask ourselves are

- What might happen if a constructor does not execute completely? For example, a constructor could throw an exception or error before it completes its initialization. An intruder, however, could catch the exception or error and try to use the partially initialized object.
- What might happen if a client tries to create a bag whose capacity exceeds a given limit?

If either action could lead to a problem, we need to prevent it.

**2.14**   For the class `ArrayBag`, we want to guard against both situations that the previous security note describes. We can begin to refine the incomplete implementation of `ArrayBag` to make the code more secure by adding the following two data fields to the class:

```
private boolean initialized = false;
private static final int MAX_CAPACITY = 10000;
```

Both changes involve the constructors. Since the default constructor invokes the parameterized constructor, it is sufficient to modify only the latter one. To ensure that the client cannot create a bag that is too large, the constructor should check the client's desired bag capacity against MAX_CAPACITY. If the requested capacity is too large, the constructor can throw an exception.

If the requested capacity is within range, why wouldn't the `ArrayBag` constructor complete normally? The allocation of the array might fail due to insufficient memory. Such an event would cause the error `OutOfMemoryError`. Normally, a client treats this error as a fatal event. A hacker, however, could catch the error as you would catch an exception and try to use the partially initialized object. To prevent this, each vital method of the class can check the status of the field `initialized` before it performs its operation. In this way, we can disable its action for malformed objects. For correctly initialized objects, the constructor would set the field `initialized` to true.

Here is the revised constructor:

```
public ArrayBag(int desiredCapacity)
{
   if (desiredCapacity <= MAX_CAPACITY)
   {
      // The cast is safe because the new array contains null entries
      @SuppressWarnings("unchecked")
      T[] tempBag = (T[])new Object[desiredCapacity]; // Unchecked cast
      bag = tempBag;
      numberOfEntries = 0;
      initialized = true;                             // Last action
   }
```

```
      else
         throw new IllegalStateException("Attempt to create a bag " +
                                         "whose capacity exceeds " +
                                         "allowed maximum.");
   } // end constructor
```

Note that the constructor sets initialized to true as its last action after it has successfully completed its other tasks. Also note that IllegalStateException is a standard runtime exception. Let's see how to use initialized.

**2.15** Any public methods of ArrayBag that depend on the successful allocation of the array bag should ensure that the field initialized is true before continuing to execute. If initialized is false, such methods can throw an exception. For example, we can revise the method add as follows:

```
public boolean add(T newEntry)
{
   if (initialized)
   {
      boolean result = true;
      if (isArrayFull())
      {
         result = false;
      }
      else
      {  // Assertion: result is true here
         bag[numberOfEntries] = newEntry;
         numberOfEntries++;
      } // end if

      return result;
   }
   else
      throw new SecurityException("ArrayBag object is not initialized " +
                                  "properly.");
} // end add
```

 **Note:** The exceptions SecurityException and IllegalStateException are standard runtime exceptions in the package java.lang. As such, no import statement is needed.

Since we will check initialized in several methods, we can avoid repetitive code by defining the following private method:

```
// Throws an exception if this object is not initialized.
private void checkInitialization()
{
   if (!initialized)
      throw new SecurityException("ArrayBag object is not initialized " +
                                  "properly.");
} // end checkInitialization
```

The method add can then be revised as follows:

```
public boolean add(T newEntry)
{
   checkInitialization();
   boolean result = true;
   if (isArrayFull())
   {
      result = false;
   }
   else
```

```
  { // Assertion: result is true here
    bag[numberOfEntries] = newEntry;
    numberOfEntries++;
  } // end if
  return result;
} // end add
```

You should modify the core method toArray in the same way, since it involves ArrayBag's data field bag.

**Security Note:** Some common guidelines for writing Java code, which are likely familiar to you, actually increase the security of your code. They are

- Declare most, if not all, data fields of a class as private. Any public data fields should be static and final and have constant values.
- Avoid clever logic if it obscures the fact that your code is safe.
- Avoid duplicate code. Instead, encapsulate such code into a private method that other methods can call.
- When a constructor calls a method, ensure that the method cannot be overridden.

**Security Note: Final Classes** Notice that we declared ArrayBag as a final class. As such, no other class can extend ArrayBag. That is, ArrayBag cannot be the superclass, or base class, of another class. A final class is more secure than one that is not final, because a programmer cannot use inheritance to change its behavior. Later, we will refine this approach by defining final methods instead of entire classes.

## Testing the Core Methods

**2.16** **Getting ready.** Now that we have defined the three core methods, we can test them. But what about the other methods in BagInterface? Since ArrayBag—as given in Listing 2-1—implements BagInterface, Java's syntax checker will look for a definition of each method declared in this interface. Should we wait until we complete their definitions to begin testing? Absolutely not! Testing methods as you write them makes finding logical errors easier. However, instead of writing a complete implementation of each method in BagInterface, we can provide incomplete definitions of the methods we choose to temporarily ignore.

An incomplete definition of a method is called a **stub**. The stub needs only to keep the syntax checker happy. For example, for each method that returns a value, you can avoid syntax errors by adding a return statement that returns a dummy value. Methods that return a boolean value could return false. Methods that return an object could return null. On the other hand, void methods can simply have an empty body.

For instance, the method remove ultimately will return the removed entry, so its stub must contain a return statement and could appear as follows:

```
public T remove()
{
   return null; // STUB
} // end remove
```

A stub for the void method clear could be

```
public void clear()
{
   // STUB
} // end clear
```

Note that if you plan to call a stub within your test program, the stub should report that it was invoked by displaying a message.

 **Programming Tip:** Do not wait until you complete the implementation of an ADT before testing it. By writing stubs, which are incomplete definitions of required methods, you can begin testing early in the process.

**2.17**    **A test program.** Listing 2-2 shows a program to test the core methods add and toArray of the class ArrayBag[2] at this stage of its development. Initially, the main method creates an empty bag by using the default constructor. Since the capacity of this bag is 25, the array should not get full if you add fewer than 25 entries to it. Thus, add should return true after each of these additions. The program's descriptive output, in fact, indicates that the tested methods are correct.

Next in the main method, we consider a bag whose capacity is seven and then add seven strings to it. This time, add should return false if an eighth addition is attempted. Again, the program's output shows that our methods are correct.

---

**LISTING 2-2    A program that tests the core methods of the class ArrayBag**

```
1  /**
2     A test of the constructors and the methods add and toArray,
3     as defined in the first draft of the class ArrayBag.
4     @author Frank M. Carrano
5  */
6  public class ArrayBagDemo1
7  {
8     public static void main(String[] args)
9     {
10       // Adding to an initially empty bag with sufficient capacity
11       System.out.println("Testing an initially empty bag with" +
12                          " the capacity to hold at least 6 strings:");
13       BagInterface<String> aBag = new ArrayBag<> ();
14       String[] contentsOfBag1 = {"A", "A", "B", "A", "C", "A"};
15       testAdd(aBag, contentsOfBag1);
16
17       // Filling an initially empty bag to capacity
18       System.out.println("\nTesting an initially empty bag that " +
19                          " will be filled to capacity:");
20       aBag = new ArrayBag<>(7);
21       String[] contentsOfBag2 = {"A", "B", "A", "C", "B", "C", "D",
22                                  "another string"};
23       testAdd(aBag, contentsOfBag2);
24    } // end main
25
26    // Tests the method add.
27    private static void testAdd(BagInterface<String> aBag,
28                                String[] content)
29    {
30       System.out.print("Adding the following " + content.length +
31                        " strings to the bag: ");
32       for (int index = 0; index < content.length; index++)
33       {
34          if (aBag.add(content[index]))
35             System.out.print(content[index] + " ");
36          else
```

---

2. Note that this version of the class ArrayBag is available online at the book's website and is named ArrayBag1.

```
37                    System.out.print("\nUnable to add " + content[index] +
38                                      " to the bag.");
39          } // end for
40          System.out.println();
41
42          displayBag(aBag);
43       } // end testAdd
44
45       // Tests the method toArray while displaying the bag.
46       private static void displayBag(BagInterface<String> aBag)
47       {
48          System.out.println("The bag contains the following string(s):");
49          Object[] bagArray = aBag.toArray();
50          for (int index = 0; index < bagArray.length; index++)
51          {
52             System.out.print(bagArray[index] + " ");
53          } // end for
54
55          System.out.println();
56       } // end displayBag
57 } // end ArrayBagDemo1
```

**Output**

```
Testing an initially empty bag with sufficient capacity:
Adding the following 6 strings to the bag: A A B A C A
The bag contains the following string(s):
A A B A C A

Testing an initially empty bag that will be filled to capacity:
Adding the following 8 strings to the bag: A B A C B C D
Unable to add another string to the bag.
The bag contains the following string(s):
A B A C B C D
```

**Programming Tip:** Thorough testing of a method should include arguments that lie within and outside of the legal range of their corresponding parameter.

**2.18**   Notice that, in addition to the main method, ArrayBagDemo1 has two other methods. Since main is static and calls these other methods, they must be static as well. The method testAdd accepts as its arguments a bag and an array of strings. The method uses a loop to add each string in the array to the bag. It also tests the return value of the add method. Finally, the method displayBag takes a bag as its argument and uses the bag's method toArray to access its contents. Once we have an array of the bag's entries, a simple loop can display them.

**Question 8** What is the result of executing the following statements within the main method of ArrayBagDemo1?

```
ArrayBag<String> aBag = new ArrayBag<>();
displayBag(aBag);
```

## Implementing More Methods

Now that we can add objects to a bag, we can implement the remaining methods, beginning with the easiest ones. We will postpone the definitions of remove momentarily until we see how to search a bag.

**2.19** **The methods isEmpty and getCurrentSize.** The methods isEmpty and getCurrentSize have straightforward definitions, as you can see:

```java
public boolean isEmpty()
{
    return numberOfEntries == 0;
} // end isEmpty

public int getCurrentSize()
{
    return numberOfEntries;
} // end getCurrentSize
```

**Security Note:** **When should a method call checkInitialization?**
The methods isEmpty and getCurrentSize do not call checkInitialization. Although they could, we do not want to burden the client with a degradation of performance due to unnecessary security checks. Both methods involve the data field numberOfEntries. Even if the constructor does not complete its initialization, and so does not set this field to zero, Java will have initialized it to zero by default. Thus, any use of a partially initialized bag will appear empty. For ArrayBag, methods that access the array bag should ensure that it exists.

**Note:** The definitions of some methods are almost as simple as the stubs you might use to define them in an early version of a class. Such is the case for the bag methods isEmpty and getCurrentSize. Although these two methods are not in our first group of core methods, they could have been. That is, we could have defined them earlier instead of writing stubs.

**2.20** **The method getFrequencyOf.** To count the number of times a given object occurs in a bag, we count the number of times the object occurs in the array bag. Using a for loop to cycle through the array's indices from 0 to numberOfEntries - 1, we compare the given object to every object in the array. Each time we find a match, we increment a counter. When the loop ends, we simply return the value of the counter. Note that we must use the method equals instead of the equality operator == to compare objects. That is, we must write

```java
anEntry.equals(bag[index]) // Compares values
```

and not

```java
anEntry == bag[index] // WRONG! Compares locations (addresses)
```

We assume that the class to which the objects belong defines its own version of equals.

The method definition follows:

```java
public int getFrequencyOf(T anEntry)
{
    checkInitialization();
    int counter = 0;
    for (int index = 0; index < numberOfEntries; index++)
    {
        if (anEntry.equals(bag[index]))
        {
            counter++;
        } // end if
    } // end for

    return counter;
} // end getFrequencyOf
```

**2.21**    **The method `contains`.** To see whether a bag contains a given object, we once again search the array bag. The loop we need here is similar to the one in the method `getFrequencyOf`, but it should stop as soon as it finds the first occurrence of the desired entry. The following pseudocode describes this logic:

```
while (anEntry is not found and we have more array elements to check)
{
    if (anEntry equals the next array entry)
    anEntry is found in the array
}
```

This loop terminates under one of two conditions: Either `anEntry` has been found in the array or the entire array has been searched without success.

Here, then, is our definition of the method `contains`:

```
public boolean contains(T anEntry)
{
    checkInitialization();
    boolean found = false;
    int index = 0;
    while (!found && (index < numberOfEntries))
    {
        if (anEntry.equals(bag[index]))
        {
            found = true;
        } // end if
        index++;
    } // end while

    return found;
} // end contains
```

**Note:  Two kinds of loops**
To count how many times an entry occurs in an array, the method `getFrequencyOf` uses a loop that cycles through all of the array's entries. In fact, the body of the loop executes `numberOfEntries` times. In contrast, to indicate whether a given entry occurs in an array, the loop in the method `contains` ends as soon as the desired entry is discovered. The body of this loop executes between one and `numberOfEntries` times. You should be comfortable writing loops that execute either a definitive or a variable number of times.

**Question 9** The method `contains` could call `getFrequencyOf` instead of executing a loop. That is, you could define the method as follows:

```
public boolean contains(T anEntry)
{
    return getFrequencyOf(anEntry) > 0;
} // end contains
```

What is an advantage and a disadvantage of this definition as compared to the one given in the previous segment?

**2.22**    **Testing the additional methods.** As you define additional methods for the class `ArrayBag`, you should test them. The program `ArrayBagDemo2`, which is available online from the book's website, focuses only on these additional methods. However, you should form a test program incrementally so that it tests all the methods you have defined so far. The version of the class `ArrayBag` to date is named `ArrayBag2` within the source code available online.

## Methods That Remove Entries

We have postponed the three methods that remove entries from a bag until now because one of them is somewhat difficult and involves a search much like the one we performed in the method `contains`. We begin with the two methods that are easier to define.

**2.23**    **The method `clear`.** The method `clear` removes all entries from a bag, one at a time. The following definition of `clear` calls the method `remove` until the bag is empty:

```java
/** Removes all entries from this bag. */
public void clear()
{
    while (!isEmpty())
        remove();
} // end clear
```

Exactly which entry is removed by each cycle of the loop is unimportant. Thus, we call the `remove` method that removes an unspecified entry. Moreover, we do not save the entry that the method returns.

Note that since `remove` will call `checkInitialization`, `clear` need not call it explicitly.

 **Note:**  We can write the definition of the method `clear` in terms of the as yet undefined method `remove`. However, we cannot test `clear` completely until `remove` is defined.

 **Question 10** Revise the definition of the method `clear` so that it does not call `isEmpty`. *Hint:* The `while` statement should have an empty body.

**Question 11** What is a disadvantage of replacing the loop shown in Segment 2.23 within the definition of `clear` with the following statement?
`numberOfEntries = 0;`

**2.24**    **Removing an unspecified entry.** The method `remove` that has no parameter removes an unspecified entry from a bag, as long as the bag is not empty. Recall from the method's specification given in the interface in Listing 1-1 of the previous chapter that the method returns the entry it removes:

```java
/** Removes one unspecified entry from this bag, if possible.
    @return  Either the removed entry, if the removal was successful,
             or null otherwise. */
public T remove()
```

If the bag is empty before the method executes, `null` is returned.

Removing an entry from a bag involves removing it from an array. Although we can access any entry in the array `bag`, the last one is easy to remove. To do so, we

- Access the last entry so it can be returned
- Set the entry's array element to `null`
- Decrement `numberOfEntries`

Decrementing `numberOfEntries` causes the last entry to be ignored, meaning that it is effectively removed, even if we did not set its location in the array to `null`. Do not, however, skip this step.

A literal translation of the previous steps into Java leads to the following definition of the method:

```java
public T remove()
{
    checkInitialization();
    T result = null;
    if (numberOfEntries > 0)
    {
        result = bag[numberOfEntries - 1];
        bag[numberOfEntries - 1] = null;
        numberOfEntries--;
    } // end if

    return result;
} // end remove
```

**Security Note:** By setting the array element bag[numberOfEntries - 1] to null, we flag the removed object for garbage collection and prevent malicious code from accessing it.

**Security Note:** **Update counters after the activity they count has successfully completed.** In our previous code, we incremented `numberOfEntries` after removing the last entry in the array, even though we computed `numberOfEntries - 1` three times. Although the following refinement avoids this repetition, the small savings in time is not worth the insecurity of decrementing the counter too soon:

```java
numberOfEntries--;
result = bag[numberOfEntries];
bag[numberOfEntries] = null;
```

Admittedly, in this case there is little chance that the array and the counter will become out of sync. If the logic were more complex, however, an exception could occur during array processing. This interruption would cause the already updated counter to be inaccurate.

**Question 12** Why does the method `remove` replace the entry removed from the array bag with `null`?

**Question 13** The previous `remove` method removes the last entry in the array bag. Why might removing a different entry be more difficult to accomplish?

**2.25**    **Removing a given entry.** Our third method that removes an entry from the bag involves removing a given entry —call it `anEntry`. If the entry occurs more than once in the bag, we will remove only one occurrence. Exactly which occurrence is removed is unspecified. We will simply remove the first occurrence of `anEntry` that we encounter while searching for it. As we discussed in Segment 1.9 of Chapter 1, we will return either true or false, according to whether we find the entry in the bag.

Assuming that the bag is not empty, we search the array bag much as the method `contains` did in Segment 2.21. If anEntry equals bag[index], we note the value of index. Figure 2-4 illustrates the array after a successful search.

**FIGURE 2-4**    The array bag after a successful search for the string "Nancy"

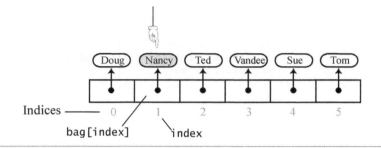

We now need to remove the entry in bag[index]. If we simply write

bag[index] = **null**;

the reference in bag[index] to the entry will be removed, but we will have a gap in the array. That is, the contents of the bag will no longer be in consecutive array locations, as Figure 2-5a illustrates. We could get rid of that gap by shifting the subsequent entries, as shown in Figure 2-5b, and replacing the duplicate reference to the last entry with null, as Figure 2-5c indicates. This time-consuming approach is not necessary, however.

**FIGURE 2-5**    (a) A gap in the array bag after setting the entry in bag[index] to null; (b) the array after shifting subsequent entries to avoid a gap; (c) after replacing the duplicate reference to the last entry with null

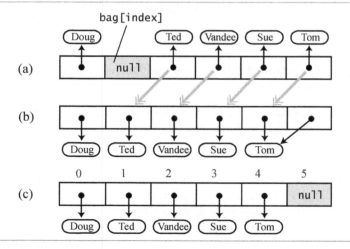

Remember that we are not required to maintain any particular order for a bag's entries. So instead of shifting array entries after removing an entry, we can replace the entry being removed with the last entry in the array, as follows. After locating anEntry in bag[index], as Figure 2-6a indicates, we copy the entry in bag[numberOfEntries - 1] to bag[index] (Figure 2-6b). We then replace the entry in bag[numberOfEntries - 1] with null, as Figure 2-6c illustrates, and finally we decrement numberOfEntries.

**FIGURE 2-6**   Avoiding a gap in the array while removing an entry

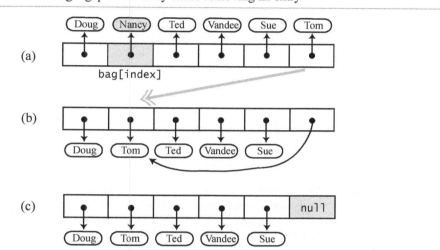

2.26   **Pseudocode for removing a given entry.** Let's organize our discussion by writing some pseudocode to remove the given entry, anEntry, from a bag that contains it:

```
Locate anEntry in the array bag; assume it occurs at bag[index]
bag[index] = bag[numberOfEntries - 1]
bag[numberOfEntries - 1] = null
Decrement the counter numberOfEntries
return true
```

This pseudocode assumes that the bag contains anEntry.

After we add some details to the pseudocode to accommodate the situation in which anEntry is not in the bag, the pseudocode appears as follows:

```
Search the array bag for anEntry
if (anEntry is in the bag at bag[index])
{
    bag[index] = bag[numberOfEntries - 1]
    bag[numberOfEntries - 1] = null
    Decrement the counter numberOfEntries
    return true
}
else
    return false
```

2.27   **Avoiding duplicate effort.** We can easily translate this pseudocode into the Java method remove. However, if we were to do so, we would see much similarity between our new method and the remove method we wrote earlier in Segment 2.24. In fact, if anEntry occurs in bag[numberOfEntries - 1], both `remove` methods will have exactly the same effect. To avoid this duplicate effort, both `remove` methods can call a private method that performs the removal. We can specify such a method as follows:

```
// Removes and returns the entry at a given array index.
// If no such entry exists, returns null.
private T removeEntry(int givenIndex)
```

Since this is a private method, other methods within the class can pass it an index as an argument and still keep the index—an implementation detail—hidden from the class's client.

Before we implement this private method, let's see if we can use it by revising the `remove` method in Segment 2.24. Since that method removes and returns the last entry in the array bag, that is, `bag[numberOfEntries - 1]`, its definition can make the call `removeEntry(numberOfEntries - 1)`. Proceeding as if `removeEntry` were defined and tested, we can define `remove` as follows:

```
/** Removes one unspecified entry from this bag, if possible.
    @return  Either the removed entry, if the removal was successful,
             or null otherwise */
public T remove()
{
   checkInitialization();
   T result = removeEntry(numberOfEntries - 1);
   return result;
} // end remove
```

This definition looks good; let's implement the second `remove` method.

**2.28**   **The second `remove` method.** The first `remove` method does not search for the entry to remove, as it removes the last entry in the array. The second `remove` method, however, does need to perform a search. Rather than thinking about the details of locating an entry in an array right now, let's delegate that task to another private method, which we specify as follows:

```
// Locates a given entry within the array bag.
// Returns the index of the entry, if located, or -1 otherwise.
private int getIndexOf(T anEntry)
```

Assuming that this private method is defined and tested, we call it in the second `remove` method as follows:

```
/** Removes one occurrence of a given entry from this bag.
    @param anEntry  The entry to be removed.
    @return  True if the removal was successful, or false if not. */
public boolean remove(T anEntry)
{
   checkInitialization();
   int index = getIndexOf(anEntry);
   T result = removeEntry(index);
   return anEntry.equals(result);
} // end remove
```

Notice that `removeEntry` returns either the entry it removes or `null`. That is exactly what the first `remove` method needs, but the second `remove` method has to return a boolean value. Thus, in the second method we need to compare the entry we want to remove with the one `removeEntry` returns to get the desired boolean value.

**Question 14** Can the `return` statement in the previous definition of `remove` be written as follows?

  a.  `return result.equals(anEntry);`
  b.  `return result != null;`

**Question 15** The array bag in `ArrayBag` contains the entries in the bag aBag. If the array contains the strings "A", "A", "B", "A", "C", why does `aBag.remove("B")` change the array's contents to "A", "A", "C", "A", null instead of either "A", "A", "A", "C", null or "A", "A", null, "A", "C"?

**2.29** **The definition of the private method removeEntry.** Let's look back at the pseudocode we wrote in Segment 2.26 for removing a particular entry from the bag. The private method removeEntry assumes that the search for the entry is done already, so we can ignore the first step of the pseudocode. The rest of the pseudocode, however, gives the basic logic for removing an entry. We can revise the pseudocode as follows:

```
// Removes and returns the entry at a given index within the array bag.
// If no such entry exists, returns null.
if (the bag is not empty and the given index is not negative)
{
    result = bag[givenIndex]
    bag[givenIndex] = bag[numberOfEntries - 1]
    bag[numberOfEntries - 1] = null
    Decrement the counter numberOfEntries
    return result
}
else
    return null
```

The definition of the method remove given in the previous segment passes the integer returned by getIndexOf to removeEntry. Since getIndexOf can return −1, removeEntry must watch for such an argument. Thus, if the bag is not empty—that is, if numberOfEntries is greater than zero—and givenIndex is greater than or equal to zero, removeEntry removes the array entry at givenIndex by replacing it with the last entry and decrementing numberOfEntries. The method then returns the removed entry. If, however, the bag is empty, the method returns null.

The code for the method is

```
// Removes and returns the entry at a given index within the array bag.
// If no such entry exists, returns null.
// Preconditions: 0 <= givenIndex < numberOfEntries;
//                checkInitialization has been called.
private T removeEntry(int givenIndex)
{
    T result = null;
    if (!isEmpty() && (givenIndex >= 0))
    {
        result = bag[givenIndex];                    // Entry to remove
        bag[givenIndex] = bag[numberOfEntries - 1];  // Replace entry with last
                                                     // entry
        bag[numberOfEntries - 1] = null;             // Remove last entry
        numberOfEntries--;
    } // end if

    return result;
} // end removeEntry
```

**2.30** **Locating the entry to remove.** We now need to think about locating the entry to remove from the bag, so we can pass its index to removeEntry. The method contains performs the same search that we will use to locate anEntry within the definition of remove. Unfortunately, contains returns true or false; it does not return the index of the entry it locates in the array. Thus, we cannot simply call that method within our method definition.

**Design Decision: Should the method contains return the index of a located entry?** Should we change the definition of contains so that it returns an index instead of a boolean value? No. As a public method, contains should not provide a client with such implementation details. The client should have no expectation that a bag's entries are in an array, since they are in no particular order. Instead of changing the specifications for contains, we will follow our original plan to define a private method to search for an entry and return its index.

**2.31**  **The definition of `getIndexOf`.** The definition of `getIndexOf` will be like the definition of `contains`, whose loop we recall from Segment 2.21:

```
boolean found = false;
int index = 0;
while (!found && (index < numberOfEntries))
{
   if (anEntry.equals(bag[index]))
   {
      found = true;
   } // end if
   index++;
} // end while
```

The structure of the loop is suitable for the method `getIndexOf`, but we must save the value of `index` when the entry is found. The method will return this index instead of a boolean value.

To revise the previous loop for use in `getIndexOf`, we define an integer variable `where` to record the value of `index` when `anEntry` equals `bag[index]`. Thus, the definition of `getIndexOf` looks like this:

```
// Locates a given entry within the array bag.
// Returns the index of the entry, if located, or -1 otherwise.
// Precondition: checkInitialization has been called.
private int getIndexOf(T anEntry)
{
   int where = -1;
   boolean found = false;
   int index = 0;
   while (!found && (index < numberOfEntries))
   {
      if (anEntry.equals(bag[index]))
      {
         found = true;
         where = index;
      } // end if
      index++;
   } // end while

   // Assertion: If where > -1, anEntry is in the array bag, and it
   // equals bag[where]; otherwise, anEntry is not in the array

   return where;
} // end getIndexOf
```

The method `getIndexOf` returns the value of `where`. Notice that we initialize `where` to −1, which is the value to return if `anEntry` is not found.

---

**Question 16** What `assert` statement can you add to the definition of the method `getIndexOf` just before the `return` statement to indicate the possible values that the method can return?

**Question 17** Revise the definition of the method `getIndexOf` so that it does not use a boolean variable.

---

**Aside:    Thinking positively**

Unlike the method `contains`, the method `getIndexOf` uses the boolean variable `found` only to control the loop and not as a return value. Thus, we can modify the logic somewhat to avoid the use of the not operator `!`.

Let's use a variable `stillLooking` instead of `found` and initialize it to true. Then we can replace the boolean expression `!found` with `stillLooking`, as you can see in the following definition of the method `getIndexOf`:

```java
// Locates a given entry within the array bag.
// Returns the index of the entry, if located, or -1 otherwise.
private int getIndexOf(T anEntry)
{
    int where = -1;
    boolean stillLooking = true;

    int index = 0;
    while (stillLooking && (index < numberOfEntries))
    {
        if (anEntry.equals(bag[index]))
        {
            stillLooking = false;
            where = index;
        } // end if
        index++;
    } // end while

    return where;
} // end getIndexOf
```

If `anEntry` is found within the array, `stillLooking` is set to false to end the loop. Some programmers prefer to think positively, as in this revision, while others find `!found` to be perfectly clear.

**2.32**    **A revised definition for the method `contains`.** Having completed the definitions of `remove` and the private methods they call, we realize that the method `contains` can call the private method `getIndexOf`, resulting in a simpler definition than the one given in Segment 2.21. Recall that the expression `getIndexOf(anEntry)` returns an integer between 0 and `numberOfEntries` − 1 if `anEntry` is in the bag, or −1 otherwise. That is, `getIndexOf(anEntry)` is greater than −1 if `anEntry` is in the bag. Thus, we can define `contains` as follows:

```java
public boolean contains(T anEntry)
{
    checkInitialization();
    return getIndexOf(anEntry) > -1;
} // end contains
```

Since we have changed the definition of `contains`, we should test it again. By doing so, we are also testing the private method `getIndexOf`.

**Note:** Both the method `contains` and the second `remove` method must perform similar searches for an entry. By isolating the search in a private method that both `contains` and `remove` can call, we make our code easier to debug and to maintain. This strategy is the same one we used when we defined the removal operation in the private method `removeEntry` that both `remove` methods call.

**Design Decision: What methods should call `checkInitialization`?**

The critical aspect of the class `ArrayBag` is the allocation of the array `bag`. You have seen that methods, such as `add`, that depend on this array begin by calling `checkInitialization` to ensure that the constructor has completely initialized the `ArrayBag` object, including the allocation of the array. While we could insist that we call `checkInitialization` in each method that directly involves the array `bag`, we chose to be more flexible. For example, the private methods `getIndexOf` and `removeEntry` directly access `bag`, but they do not call `checkInitialization`. Why? The `remove` method that removes a given entry calls both `getIndexOf` and `removeEntry`. If both of these private methods called `checkInitialization`, it would be invoked twice by the public method. Thus, for this particular implementation, we call `checkInitialization` in the public methods and add a precondition to the two private methods to document that `checkInitialization` must be called first. Since they are private methods, such a precondition is for us, the implementors and maintainers of this code. Once we have made this decision, the other `remove` method and the method `contains` must call `checkInitialization`, since they each call one of these two private methods.

Note that the private methods `getIndexOf` and `removeEntry` each perform one well-defined task. They no longer are responsible for a second task, checking initialization.

**Programming Tip:** Even though you might have written a correct definition of a method, do not hesitate to revise it if you think of a better implementation. Be sure to test the method again!

**2.33**   **Testing.** Our class `ArrayBag` is essentially complete. We can use the previously tested methods—which we assume are correct—in the tests for `remove` and `clear`. Starting with a bag that is not full, the online program `ArrayBagDemo3` removes the bag's entries until it is empty. It also includes similar tests beginning with a full bag. Finally, we should consolidate our previous tests and run them again. The source code available on the book's website identifies our test program as `ArrayBagDemo` and the complete version of the class as `ArrayBag`.

# Using Array Resizing to Implement the ADT Bag

**2.34**   An array has a fixed size, which is chosen by either the programmer or the user before the array is created. A fixed-size array is like a classroom. If the room contains 40 desks but only 30 students, we waste 10 desks. If 40 students are taking the course, the room is full and cannot accommodate anyone else. Likewise, if we do not use all of the locations in an array, we waste memory. If we need more, we are out of luck.

Using a fixed-size array to implement the ADT bag, therefore, limits the size of the bag. When the array, and hence the bag, becomes full, subsequent calls to the `add` method return false. Some applications can use a bag or other collection that has a limited capacity. For other applications, however, we need the size of a collection to grow without bound. We will now show you how a group of items can be as large as you want—within the limits of your computer's memory—but still be in an array.

## Resizing an Array

**2.35**   **The strategy.** When a classroom is full, one way to accommodate additional students is to move to a larger room. In a similar manner, when an array becomes full, you can move its contents to a larger array. This process is called **resizing** an array. Figure 2-7 shows two arrays: an original array of five consecutive memory locations and another array—twice the size of the original array—that is in another part of the computer's memory. If you copy the data from the original smaller array to the beginning of the new larger array, the result will be like expanding the original array. The only glitch in this scheme is the name of the new array: You want it to be the same as the name of the old array. You will see how to accomplish this momentarily.

FIGURE 2-7      Resizing an array copies its contents to a larger second array

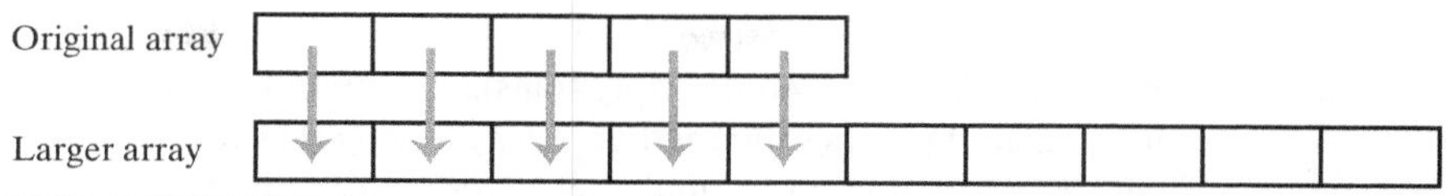

Original array

Larger array

**2.36**   **The details.** Suppose we have an array that myArray references, as Figure 2-8a illustrates. We first define an alias oldArray that also references the array, as Figure 2-8b shows. The next step is to create a new array that is larger than the original array and let myArray reference this new array. As pictured in Figure 2-8c, the new array typically doubles the size of the original array. The final step copies the contents of the original array to the new array (Figure 2-8d) and then discards the original array (Figure 2-8e). The following pseudocode summarizes these steps:

```
oldArray = myArray
myArray = a new array whose length is 2 * oldArray.length
Copy entries from the original array—oldArray—to the new array—myArray
oldArray = null  // Discard old array
```

FIGURE 2-8      (a) An array; (b) two references to the same array; (c) the original array variable
                now references a new, larger array; (d) the entries in the original array are
                copied to the new array; (e) the original array is discarded

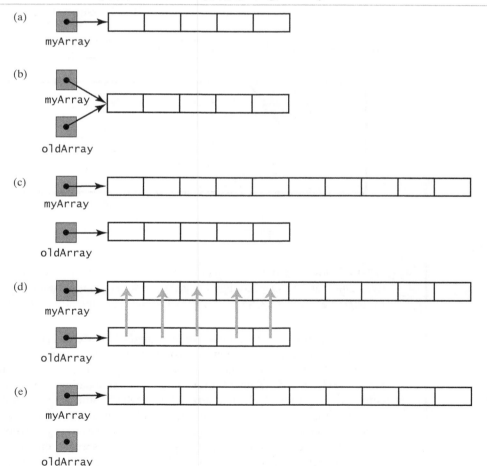

**Note:** When an array is no longer referenced, its memory is recycled during garbage collection, just as occurs with any other object.

**2.37**   **The code.** While we could simply translate the previous pseudocode into Java, much of the work can be done by using the method `Arrays.copyOf(sourceArray, newLength)`, which is in the Java Class Library. For example, let's work with a simple array of integers:

```
int[] myArray = {10, 20, 30, 40, 50};
```

At this point, `myArray` references the array, as Figure 2-9a shows. Next, we'll call `Arrays.copyOf`. The method's first parameter, `sourceArray`, is assigned the reference in the variable `myArray`, as Figure 2-9b implies. Next the method creates a new, larger array and copies the entries in the argument array to it (Figure 2-9c). Finally, the method returns a reference (Figure 2-9d) to the new array, and we assign this reference to `myArray` (Figure 2-9e). The following statement performs these steps:

```
myArray = Arrays.copyOf(myArray, 2 * myArray.length);
```

---

**FIGURE 2-9**   The effect of the statement

```
myArray = Arrays.copyOf(myArray, 2 * myArray.length);
```

(a) The argument array; (b) the parameter that references the argument array; (c) a new, larger array that gets the contents of the argument array; (d) the return value that references the new array; (e) the argument variable is assigned the return value

---

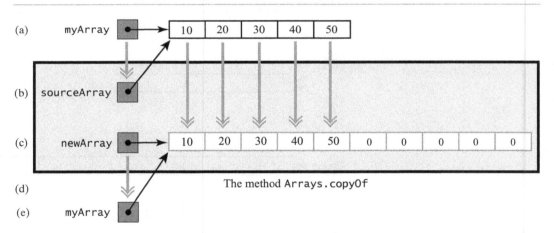

 **Note:** Notice that the array pictured in Figure 2-9 contains integers. These integers are primitive values, and as such, occupy the locations in the array. In contrast, the array in Figure 2-6, for example, contains references to objects instead of the objects themselves.

**2.38**   Resizing an array is not as attractive as it might first seem. Each time you expand the size of an array, you must copy its contents. If you were to expand an array by one element each time you needed additional space in the array, the process would be expensive in terms of computing time. For example, if a 50-element array is full, accommodating another entry would require you to copy the array to a 51-element array. Adding yet another entry would require that you copy the 51-element array to a 52-element array, and so on. Each addition would cause the array to be copied. If you added 100 entries to the original 50-entry array, you would copy the array 100 times.

However, expanding the array by *m* elements spreads the copying cost over *m* additions instead of just one. Doubling the size of an array each time it becomes full is a typical approach.

For example, when you add an entry to a full array of 50 entries, you copy the 50-element array to a 100-element array before completing the addition. The next 49 additions then can be made quickly without copying the array. Thus, you will have copied the array only once.

 **Programming Tip:** When increasing the size of an array, you copy its entries to a larger array. You should expand the array sufficiently to reduce the impact of the cost of copying. A common practice is to double the size of the array.

 **Note:** To say that we "resize" an array is really a misnomer, since an array's length cannot be changed. The process of resizing an array involves creating a completely new array that contains the entries of the original array. The new array is given the name of the original array—in other words, a reference to the new array is assigned to the variable that had referenced the original array. The original array is then discarded.

 **Note:  Importing a class**
The definition of a class that uses a class from the Java Class Library must be preceded by an `import` statement. For example, to use the class `Arrays`, you would write the following statement prior to your class definition and its descriptive comments:

```
import java.util.Arrays;
```

Some programmers replace `Arrays` in this statement with an asterisk to make all classes in the package `java.util` available to their program.

 **Question 18** Consider the array of strings that the following statement defines:

```
String[] text = {"cat", "dog", "bird", "snake"};
```

What Java statements will increase the capacity of the array `text` by five elements without altering its current contents?

**Question 19** Consider an array `text` of strings. If the number of strings placed into this array is less than its length (capacity), how could you decrease the array's length without altering its current contents? Assume that the number of strings is in the variable `size`.

## A New Implementation of a Bag

2.39.   **The approach.** We can revise the previous implementation of the ADT bag by resizing the array bag so that the bag's capacity is limited only by the amount of memory available on your computer. If we look at the outline of the class `ArrayBag` in Listing 2-1, we can see what we need to revise. Let's itemize these tasks:

VideoNote
A resizable bag

- Change the name of the class to `ResizableArrayBag` so we can distinguish between our two implementations.
- Remove the modifier `final` from the declaration of the array bag to enable it to be resized.
- Change the names of the constructors to match the new class name.
- Revise the definition of the method `add` to always accommodate a new entry. The method will never return false as a bag will never become full.

Revising the method add is the only substantial task in this list. The rest of the class will remain unchanged.

**2.40** **The method add.** Here is the definition of the method add, as it appears at the end of Segment 2.15:

```
public boolean add(T newEntry)
{
    checkInitialization();
    boolean result = true;
    if (isArrayFull())
    {
        result = false;
    }
    else
    { // Assertion: result is true here
        bag[numberOfEntries] = newEntry;
        numberOfEntries++;
    } // end if
    return result;
} // end add
```

Since the bag will never be full, add should always return true. To accomplish this goal, we double the size of the array bag when isArrayFull returns true rather than setting result to false. To resize the array, we will define and call another private method, doubleCapacity, and specify it as follows:

```
// Doubles the size of the array bag.
private void doubleCapacity()
```

Assuming the we have defined this private method, we can revise the method add as follows:

```
/** Adds a new entry to this bag.
    @param newEntry  The object to be added as a new entry.
    @return  True. */
public boolean add(T newEntry)
{
    checkInitialization();
    if (isArrayFull())
    {
        doubleCapacity();
    } // end if

    bag[numberOfEntries] = newEntry;
    numberOfEntries++;

    return true;
} // end add
```

**2.41** **The private method doubleCapacity.** We resize the array bag using the technique described earlier in Segment 2.37. Because we are increasing the bag's capacity, we must check that the new capacity does not exceed MAX_CAPACITY. We made the same check in the constructor, but instead of duplicating that code, we will define another private method that both the constructor and doubleCapacity can call to enforce the limit on the bag's capacity:

```
// Throws an exception if the client requests a capacity that is too large.
private void checkCapacity(int capacity)
{
    if (capacity > MAX_CAPACITY)
    throw new IllegalStateException("Attempt to create a bag whose " +
                                    "capacity exeeds allowed " +
                                    "maximum of " + MAX_CAPACITY);
} // end checkCapacity
```

The method `doubleCapacity` now has the following definition:

```java
// Doubles the size of the array bag.
// Precondition: checkInitialization has been called.
private void doubleCapacity()
{
    int newLength = 2 * bag.length;
    checkCapacity(newLength);
    bag = Arrays.copyOf(bag, newLength);
} // end doubleCapacity
```

**2.42**   **The class `ResizableArrayBag`.** Our new class is available online from the book's website. You should examine its details.

---

**Design Decision:**  You might wonder about some of the decisions we made while defining the class `ResizableArrayBag`, with questions such as the following:

- Why is the method add a boolean method and not a void method? It always returns true!
- Why did we define the private method `doubleCapacity`? Only one method, add, calls it!

The class implements the interface `BagInterface`, so we followed its specifications when defining add. As a result, we have two different implementations, `ArrayBag` and `ResizableArrayBag`, each of which can be used by the same client. Our answer to the second question reflects our approach to problem solving. To implement add, we first need to resize the array if it is full. Rather than risking the distraction of performing this task within the method add, we chose to specify a private method to expand the array. Admittedly, the definition of this private method turned out to be short. We could now integrate the body of the private method into that of add, but we have no pressing reason to do so. Moreover, by retaining the private method, we adhere to the philosophy that a method should perform one action.

---

**Question 20** What is the definition of a constructor that you could add to the class `ResizableArrayBag` to initialize the bag to the contents of a given array?

**Question 21** In the definition of the constructor described in the previous question, is it necessary to copy the entries from the argument array to the array bag, or would a simple assignment (bag = contents) be sufficient?

**Question 22** What is an advantage of using an array to organize data? What is a disadvantage?

---

**2.43**   **Testing the class.** A program that tests the class `ResizableArrayBag` can create a bag whose initial capacity is small—3, for example. This choice allows us to easily test the bag's ability to increase its capacity. For instance, when the fourth item is added, the bag's capacity is doubled to 6. At the seventh addition, the capacity is doubled again, this time to 12. Such a program, `ResizableArrayBagDemo`, is available online at the book's website.

**Programming Tip:**  A class implementing a single interface that declares the operations of an ADT should define the methods declared in the interface as its only public methods. However, the class can also define private methods and protected methods.

## The Pros and Cons of Using an Array to Implement the ADT Bag

**2.44**   This chapter discussed two implementations of the ADT bag that use an array to store a bag's entries. An array is simple to use and enables you to access any element immediately, if you know its index. Since we know the index of the last entry in the array, removing it is easy and fast. Similarly, adding an entry at the end of the array is equally easy and fast. On the other hand, removing a particular entry, if it occurs between other entries, requires us to avoid a gap within the array. To do so, we replace the removed entry with the last entry in the array. This is an insignificant increase in execution time, as it is overshadowed by the time it takes to locate the desired entry. We will talk more about such a search later in this book.

Using a fixed-size array limits the capacity of a bag, which is usually a disadvantage. Resizing an array dynamically enables you to increase the array's size but requires copying data. You should realize that the array entries that we copy are references, and so do not occupy much space nor take much time to move. Some languages other than Java store the data itself within the array. In such cases, moving large, complex objects can be quite time-consuming.

**Note:**  When you use an array to implement the ADT bag,
- Adding an entry to the bag is fast
- Removing an unspecified entry is fast
- Removing a particular entry requires time to locate the entry
- Increasing the size of the array requires time to copy its entries

## CHAPTER SUMMARY

- You can use a Java array to define a relatively simple implementation of the ADT bag, but other implementations are possible.

- Adding an entry right after the last entry in an array does not disturb the position of existing entries. Likewise, deleting the last entry from an array does not disturb the position of existing entries.

- Because a bag does not maintain its entries in a specific order, deleting an entry does not require you to move all subsequent array entries to the next lower position. Instead, you can replace the entry that you want to delete with the last entry in the array and replace the last entry with null.

- Identifying and implementing a class's central, or core, methods before any others is a good strategy to use when you expect the class to be lengthy or complex. Use stubs for the remaining methods.

- Test a class at each stage of its development, particularly after adding a significant method.

- Using a fixed-size array can result in a full bag.

- Resizing an array makes it appear to change size. To do so, you allocate a new array, copy the entries from the original array to the new array, and use the original variable to reference the new array.

- Resizing an array enables you to implement collections whose contents are limited in number only by the size of the computer's memory.

- You should practice safe and secure programming. For example, our implementations of the ADT bag check that a bag has been completely initialized before use and that its capacity does not exceed a given limit.

## PROGRAMMING TIPS

- When defining a class, implement and test a group of core methods. Begin with methods that add to a collection of objects and/or have involved implementations.

- A class should not return a reference to an array that is a private data field.

- Do not wait until you complete the implementation of an ADT before testing it. By writing stubs, which are incomplete definitions of required methods, you can begin testing early in the process.

- Even though you might have written a correct definition of a method, do not hesitate to revise it if you think of a better implementation. Be sure to test the method again!

- When increasing the size of an array, you copy its entries to a larger array. You should expand the array sufficiently to reduce the impact of the cost of copying. A common practice is to double the size of the array.

- A class implementing a single interface that declares the operations of an ADT should define the methods declared in the interface as its only public methods. However, the class can also define private methods and protected methods.

## EXERCISES

1. What is the significance of the methods `doubleCapacity` and `checkCapacity` in the class `ResizableArrayBag`?

2. Implement a method `replace` for the ADT bag that replaces and returns any object currently in a bag with a given object.

3. Revise the definition of the method `clear`, as given in Segment 2.23, so that it is more efficient and calls only the method `checkInitialization`.

4. Revise the definition of the method `remove`, as given in Segment 2.27, so that it removes a random entry from a bag. Would this change affect any other method within the class `ArrayBag`?

5. Is a method such as `isArrayHalfFull`, which checks whether the array is half full, required for the class `ResizableArrayBag`?

6. Both the classes `ArrayBag` and `ResizableArrayBag` make use of `MAX_CAPACITY` as the upperbound while fixing the size of the array. State the difference in the usage of `MAX_CAPACITY` between these two classes.

7. Suppose that you wanted to define a class `PileOfBooks` that implements the interface described in Project 2 of the previous chapter. Would a bag be a reasonable collection to represent the pile of books? Explain.

8. Consider an instance `myBag` of the class `ResizableArrayBag`, as discussed in Segments 2.39 to 2.43. Suppose that the initial capacity of `myBag` is 10. What is the length of the array `bag` after
   a. Adding 145 entries to `myBag`?
   b. Adding an additional 20 entries to `myBag`?

9. Modify the methods `isEmpty` and `getCurrentSize` to include a call to the method `checkInitialization` as a measure of security check. Is such a call to `checkInitialization` needed from the method `clear`?

10. Suppose that a bag contains `Comparable` objects such as strings. A `Comparable` object belongs to a class that implements the standard interface `Comparable<T>`, and so has the method `compareTo`. Implement the following methods for the class `ArrayBag`:

    - The method `getMin` that returns the smallest object in a bag
    - The method `getMax` that returns the largest object in a bag
    - The method `removeMin` that removes and returns the smallest object in a bag
    - The method `removeMax` that removes and returns the largest object in a bag

11. Suppose that a bag contains `Comparable` objects, as described in the previous exercise. Define a method for the class `ArrayBag` that returns a new bag of items that are less than some given item. The header of the method could be as follows:

    **public** BagInterface<T> getAllLessThan(Comparable<T> anObject)

    Make sure that your method does not affect the state of the original bag.

12. Define an `equals` method for the class `ArrayBag` that returns true when the contents of two bags are the same. Note that two equal bags contain the same number of entries, and each entry occurs in each bag the same number of times. The order of the entries in each array is irrelevant.

13. The class `ResizableArrayBag` has an array that can grow in size as objects are added to the bag. Revise the class so that its array also can shrink in size as objects are removed from the bag. Accomplishing this task will require two new private methods, as follows:

   - The first new method checks whether we should reduce the size of the array:

     **private boolean** isTooBig()

     This method returns true if the number of entries in the bag is less than half the size of the array and the size of the array is greater than 20.

   - The second new method creates a new array that is three quarters the size of the current array and then copies the objects in the bag to the new array:

     **private void** reduceArray()

   Implement each of these two methods, and then use them in the definitions of the two remove methods.

14. Consider the two private methods described in the previous exercise.

   a. The method isTooBig requires the size of the array to be greater than 20. What problem could occur if this requirement is dropped?

   b. The method reduceArray is not analogous to the method doubleCapacity in that it does not reduce the size of the array by one half. What problem could occur if the size of the array is reduced by one half instead of three quarters?

15. Define the method union, as described in Exercise 5 of the previous chapter, for the class ResizableArrayBag.

16. Define the method intersection, as described in Exercise 6 of Chapter 1, for the class ResizableArrayBag.

17. Define the method difference, as described in Exercise 7 of Chapter 1, for the class ResizableArrayBag.

## PROJECTS

1. Design and implement a one-person guessing game that chooses $n$ random integers in the range from 1 to $m$ and asks the user to guess them. The same integer might be chosen more than once. For example, the game might choose the following four integers that range from 1 to 10: 4, 6, 1, 6. The following interaction could occur between the user and the game:

   ```
   Enter your guesses for the 4 integers in the range from 1 to 10 that have been selected:
   1 2 3 4
   2 of your guesses are correct. Guess again.
   Enter your guesses for the 4 integers in the range from 1 to 10 that have been selected:
   2 4 6 8
   2 of your guesses are correct. Guess again.
   1 4 6 6
   You are correct! Play again? No
   Good-bye!
   ```

   Design the game as an ADT. Use a bag to contain the integers chosen by the game. The integers $m$ and $n$ are specified by the client.

2. Define a class ArraySet that represents a set and implements the interface described in Segment 1.21 of the previous chapter. Use the class ResizableArrayBag in your implementation. Then write a program that adequately demonstrates your implementation.

3. Repeat the previous project, but use a resizable array instead of the class ResizableArrayBag.

4. Define a class PileOfBooks that implements the interface described in Project 2 of the previous chapter. Use a resizable array in your implementation. Then write a program that adequately demonstrates your implementation.

5. Define a class Ring that implements the interface described in Project 3 of the previous chapter. Use a resizable array in your implementation. Then write a program that adequately demonstrates your implementation.

**6.** You can use either a set or a bag to create a spell checker. The set or bag serves as a dictionary and contains a collection of correctly spelled words. To see whether a word is spelled correctly, you see whether it is contained in the dictionary. Use this scheme to create a spell checker for the words in an external file. To simplify your task, restrict your dictionary to a manageable size.

**7.** Repeat the previous project to create a spell checker, but instead place the words whose spelling you want to check into a bag. The difference between the dictionary (the set or bag containing the correctly spelled words) and the bag of words to be checked is a bag of incorrectly spelled words.

## ANSWERS TO SELF-TEST QUESTIONS

**1.** The students remain in consecutively numbered desks. You do not have to keep track of the locations of the empty desks.

**2.** Time is saved by not moving a student.

**3.** The student in the highest-numbered desk.

**4.** No. The two values are equal only when a bag is full.

**5.** If the client contained a statement such as

```
Object[] bagContents = myBag.toArray();
```

myBag.getCurrentSize() would be the number of entries in the array bagContents. With the proposed design, bagContents.length could be larger than the number of entries in the bag.

**6.** The statements set the first element of bag to null. The value of numberOfEntries does not change, so it is 5.

**7.**
```
public T[] toArray()
{
   return Arrays.copyOf(bag, bag.length);
} // end toArray
```

**8.** The bag aBag is empty. When displayBag is called, the statement

```
Object[] bagArray = aBag.toArray();
```

executes. When toArray is called, the statement

```
T[] result = (T[])new Object[numberOfEntries];
```

executes. Since aBag is empty, numberOfEntries is zero. Thus, the new array, result, is empty. The loop in toArray is skipped and the empty array is returned and assigned to bagArray. Since bagArray.length is zero, the loop in displayBag is skipped. The result of the call displayBag(aBag) is simply the line

```
The bag contains the following string(s):
```

**9.** Advantage: This definition is easier to write, so you are less likely to make a mistake.
Disadvantage: This definition takes more time to execute, if the bag contains more than one occurrence of anEntry. Note that the loop in the method getFrequencyOf cycles through all of the entries in the bag, whereas the loop in the method contains, as given in Segment 2.21, ends as soon as the desired entry is found.

**10.**
```
public void clear()
{
   while (remove() != null)
   {
   } // end while
} // end clear
```

**11.** Although the bag will appear empty to both the client and the other methods in ArrayBag, the references to the removed objects will remain in the array bag. Even if the client does not retain references to these objects, the memory associated with them will not be deallocated.

**12.** By setting bag[numberOfEntries] to null, the method causes the memory assigned to the deleted entry to be recycled, unless another reference to that entry exists in the client.

**13.** An entry in the array bag, other than the last one, would be set to null. The remaining entries would no longer be in consecutive elements of the array. We could either rearrange the entries to get rid of the null entry or modify other methods to skip any null entry.

**14.** **a.** No. If result were null—and that is quite possible—a NullPointerException would occur.

**b.** Yes.

**15.** After locating "B" in the bag, the remove method replaces it with the last relevant entry in the array bag, which is "C". It then replaces that last entry with null. Although we could define remove to result in either of the two other possibilities given in the question, both choices are inferior. For example, to get "A", "A", "A", "C", null, remove would shift the array elements, requiring more execution time. Leaving a gap in the array, such as "A", "A", null, "A", "C", is easy for remove to do but complicates the logic of the remaining methods.

**16.**
```
assert ((where >= 0) && (where < numberOfEntries)) || (where == -1);
```

**17.**
```
private int getIndexOf(T anEntry)
{
    int where = -1;
    for (int index = 0; (where == -1) && (index < numberOfEntries); index++)
    {
        if (anEntry.equals(bag[index]))
            where = index;
    } // end for
    return where;
} // end getIndexOf
```
or
```
private int getIndexOf(T anEntry)
{
    int where = numberOfEntries - 1;
    while ((where > -1) && !anEntry.equals(bag[where]))
        where--;
    return where;
} // end getIndexOf
```

**18.**
```
text = Arrays.copyOf(text, text.length + 5);
```
or
```
String[] origText = text;
text = new String[text.length + 5];
System.arraycopy(origText, 0, text, 0, origText.length);
```

**19.**
```
text = Arrays.copyOf(text, size);
```

**20.**
```
/** Creates a bag containing the given array of entries.
    @param contents  An Array of objects. */
public ResizableArrayBag(T[] contents)
{
    checkCapacity(contents.length);
    bag = Arrays.copyOf(contents, contents.length);
    numberOfEntries = contents.length;
    initialized = true;
} // end constructor
```

**21.** A simple assignment statement would be a poor choice, since then the client could corrupt the bag's data by using the reference to the array that it passes to the constructor as an argument. Copying the argument array to the array bag is necessary to protect the integrity of the bag's data.

**22.** Advantage: You can access any array location directly if you know its index.
Disadvantages: The array has a fixed size, so you will either waste space or run out of room. Resizing the array avoids the latter disadvantage, but requires you to copy the contents of the original array to a larger array.

# Exceptions

## Contents

The Basics
Handling an Exception
- Postpone Handling: The throws Clause
- Handle It Now: The try-catch Blocks
- Multiple catch Blocks
Throwing an Exception

## Prerequisites

An **exception** is an unusual circumstance or event that occurs during the execution of a method, thereby interrupting program execution. Some exceptions indicate mistakes in your code. By correcting those mistakes, you avoid the exceptions and no longer have to worry about them. In fact, your final code gives no indication that an exception could occur. Furthermore, if your code is entirely correct, an exception will not occur.

On the other hand, a programmer can intentionally cause an exception to occur under certain conditions. In fact, the programmers who wrote the code for the Java Class Library did so. If you peruse the documentation for this library, you will see names of the exceptions that might occur during the execution of certain methods. We need to know about exceptions so we can use these methods. What should we do when such an exception occurs? Should we ever intentionally cause an exception in our own programs, and if so, how would we do so? These are some of the questions that this interlude will answer. This knowledge is particularly important to us as we discuss ADT operations that fail.

# The Basics

**JI2.1**   When an exception occurs within a method, the method creates an exception object and gives it to the Java runtime system. We say that the method **throws** the exception. A thrown exception is a signal to the rest of the program that something unexpected has happened. Our code can react appropriately to the exception based on its class type and what the exception, as an object, can tell us via its methods. We **handle** the exception when we detect and react to it.

Exceptions belong to various classes, but all of these classes have the standard class Throwable as an ancestor. Throwable is in the Java Class Library and is available to us without an import statement. Exceptions are classified into three groups:

- Checked exceptions, which must be handled
- Runtime exceptions, which need not be handled
- Errors, which need not be handled

**JI2.2**   **Checked exceptions** are the result of a serious occurrence during program execution. For example, if a program is reading data from a disk and the system cannot find the file that contains the data, a checked exception will occur. The name of the class to which this exception belongs is FileNotFoundException. Maybe the user gave the program the wrong file name. A well-written program should anticipate this event and recover gracefully from it, perhaps by asking the user to enter the file name again. This name, like the names of all exception classes in the Java Class Library, is meant to describe the cause of the exception. A common practice is to describe an exception by its class name. For example, we might say that a FileNotFoundException has occurred. All classes of checked exceptions are subclasses of the class Exception, which is a descendant of Throwable.

> **Note:   Checked exceptions in the Java Class Library**
> The following classes in the Java Class Library represent some of the checked exceptions that you might encounter:
>
> ```
> ClassNotFoundException
> FileNotFoundException
> IOException
> NoSuchMethodException
> WriteAbortedException
> ```

**JI2.3**   **Runtime exceptions** usually are the result of a logical error in the program. For example, an out-of-bounds array index causes an exception of the class ArrayIndexOutOfBounds. A division by zero causes an ArithmeticException. Although we could add code that would handle a runtime exception, we usually just need to fix the mistakes in our program. All classes of runtime exceptions are subclasses of the class RuntimeException, which is a descendant of Exception.

> **Note:   Runtime exceptions in the Java Class Library**
> The following classes in the Java Class Library represent some of the runtime exceptions that you are likely to encounter:
>
> ```
> ArithmeticException
> ArrayIndexOutOfBoundsException
> ClassCastException
> EmptyStackException
> IllegalArgumentException
> IllegalStateException
> IndexOutOfBoundsException
> NoSuchElementException
> NullPointerException
> UnsupportedOperationException
> ```

**JI2.4**   An **error** is an object of either the standard class Error or one of its descendant classes. We will refer to such classes as **error classes**. Note that Error is a descendant of Throwable. In general, an error indicates the occurrence of an abnormal situation, such as running out of memory. If your program uses more memory than is available, you must either revise your program to make it more efficient in its use of memory, change a setting to let Java access more memory, or buy more memory for your computer. These situations are too serious for a typical program to handle. Hence, errors need not be handled, even though doing so is legal.

**JI2.5**   Figure JI2-1 shows the hierarchy of some exception and error classes. Runtime exceptions, such as ArithmeticException, are descended from RuntimeException. Checked exceptions, such as

**FIGURE JI2-1**    The hierarchy of some standard exception and error classes

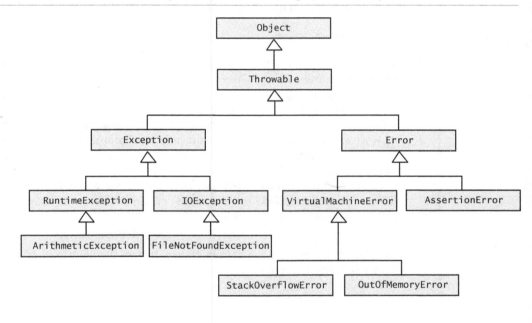

IOException, are descended from Exception but not from RuntimeException. An assertion error, which Segment P.9 of the prelude defined, is an object of the class AssertionError, which has the class Error as its superclass. When we discuss recursion in Chapter 7, we will mention a stack overflow error. This error belongs to the class StackOverflowError. Both StackOverflowError and OutOfMemoryError are derived from the abstract class VirtualMachineError, which has Error as its superclass. Right now, all that is important to us is knowing that StackOverflowError, OutOfMemoryError, and AssertionError have Error, instead of Exception, as an ancestor class, although all exceptions and errors derive from Throwable.

**Note: The hierarchy of exceptions**
Classes of checked exceptions, runtime exceptions, and errors—collectively known as **exception classes**—have the standard class Throwable as an ancestor. All classes for runtime exceptions extend RuntimeException, which extends Exception. Checked exceptions are objects of classes that descend from Exception, but do not have RuntimeException as an ancestor. Runtime exceptions and errors are described as **unchecked exceptions**.

**Note:** Many exception classes are in the package java.lang, and so do not need to be imported. Some exception classes, however, are in another package, and these do need to be imported. For example, when we use the class IOException in a program, we will need the import statement

> **import** java.io.IOException;

We will encounter this exception in Appendix E.

# Handling an Exception

When a checked exception might occur, it must be handled somewhere. For a method that might cause a checked exception, you have two choices: Handle the exception within the method or postpone handling it by telling the method's client to do so.

## Postpone Handling: The throws Clause

**JI2.6**   Imagine a method that returns the string it reads from a disk. Since we will learn how to write such a method in Appendix E, let's not worry about how this method accomplishes its task. However, something might go wrong while reading from the disk. That something could generate an IOException. Since an IOException is a checked exception, it must be handled. We could handle the exception within the method's body. Sometimes, however, a programmer is not sure what action is best for a client when an exception occurs. Should execution end, or would another action make more sense? When you're not sure what action to take, you can leave the handling of the exception to the method's client. As long as the exception is handled at some point, you need not handle it within the method itself.

A method that can cause but does not handle a checked exception must declare that fact in its header. For example, if the method readString might throw an IOException but does not handle it, its header would look like this:

> **public** String readString(. . .) **throws** IOException

The highlighted portion is a **throws clause**. It frees the method readString of the responsibility of handling any exceptions of type IOException that might occur during its execution. If, however, another method calls readString, it must deal with the exception. That invoking method can either handle the IOException itself or tell its client to handle the exception by including it in a throws clause in its header. Eventually, every thrown, checked exception should be handled somewhere in the program.

You can list more than one checked exception in a throws clause by separating the exceptions with commas.

 **Syntax: The throws clause**
A method's header can contain a throws clause that lists the possible exceptions the method can throw but will not handle. The clause has the following syntax:

**throws** *exception-list*

The exception names listed in *exception-list* are separated by commas. Their order here is unimportant.

 **Note:** If a method can throw a checked exception, you must either declare the exception in the method's header by writing a throws clause or handle the exception within the method. Failure to do so will cause a syntax error.

If a method can throw an unchecked exception, you can declare it in a throws clause or handle it, but neither action is required.

**Note:** The `javadoc` tag `@throws`
A javadoc comment that precedes a method's header should contain a separate line for each exception the method might throw. Each of these lines begins with the tag `@throws`, and they should be ordered alphabetically by the names of the exceptions. All checked exceptions must be documented.

Documenting runtime exceptions is optional and is generally not done. However, a designer can document those runtime exceptions that a client might reasonably want to handle. In fact, you will encounter some documented runtime exceptions in the Java Class Library. Realize, however, that your use of a method might cause a runtime exception that is undocumented. If you decide to document runtime exceptions, they must not depend on how the method is defined. Thus, identifying the exceptions a method might throw should be done as part of its design and specification, and not its implementation.

**Note:** **A method's execution ends if it throws but does not handle an exception**
If a method throws an exception but does not handle it, the method's execution ends. For example, if the previous method `readString` throws an `IOException`, its execution ends immediately. Program execution continues, however, and the exception is passed to `readString`'s client.

**Programming Tip:** When defining a method that can throw a checked exception, if you cannot provide a reasonable reaction to the exception, pass it on to the method's client by writing a `throws` clause in the method's header. Avoid using `Exception` in a `throws` clause, as doing so provides another programmer with little if any useful information about calling the method. Instead, use as specific an exception as you can.

## Handle It Now: The `try-catch` Blocks

**JI2.7**     To handle an exception, we first must identify the Java statements that can cause it. We also must decide which exception to look for. A method's documentation and `throws` clause will tell us which checked exceptions might occur. It is those exceptions that we will handle.

The code to handle an exception consists of two pieces. The first piece, the **try block**, contains the statements that might throw an exception. The second piece consists of one or more catch blocks. Each **catch block** contains code to react to, or **catch**, a particular type of exception. Thus, the code to handle an `IOException` as a result of invoking the method `readString` would have the following form:

```
try
{
    < Possibly some code >
    anObject.readString(. . .); // Might throw an IOException
    < Possibly some more code >
}
catch (IOException e)
{
    < Code to react to the exception, probably including the following statement: >
    System.out.println(e.getMessage());
}
```

**JI2.8**  The statements within the `try` block execute just as they would if the block was not there. If no exception occurs and the `try` block completes execution, execution continues with the statement after the `catch` block. However, if an `IOException` occurs within the `try` block, execution immediately transfers to the `catch` block. The exception now has been caught.

The syntax for a `catch` block resembles that of a method definition. The identifier e is called a **catch block parameter**; it represents the object of `IOException` that the `catch` block will handle. Although a `catch` block is not a method definition, throwing an exception within a `try` block is like calling a `catch` block, in that the parameter e represents an actual exception.

As an object, every exception has the accessor method `getMessage`, which returns a descriptive string created when the exception is thrown. By displaying this string, we provide a programmer with an indication of the nature of the exception.

**JI2.9**  After the `catch` block executes, the statements after it execute. But what if the problem is serious, and the best reaction to it is to terminate the program? The `catch` block can end the program by calling the `exit` method as follows:

```
System.exit(0);
```

The number 0 given as the argument to `System.exit` indicates a normal termination of the program. Although we have encountered a serious problem, we intentionally terminate the program, which, in the view of the operating system, is normal.

**Note:**  If you do not handle a checked exception or declare it in a `throws` clause, the compiler will complain. You can handle some of a method's exceptions within its definition and declare some in its `throws` clause. Generally, you do not handle or declare runtime (unchecked) exceptions, since they indicate a bug in your program. Such exceptions terminate program execution when they are thrown.

**Note:**  A `catch` block whose parameter has the type C can catch exceptions of the class C and any of C's descendant classes.

## Multiple catch Blocks

**JI2.10**  The statements within a single `try` block can throw any one of a number of different types of exceptions. For example, suppose that the code within the `try` block in Segment JI2.7 could throw more than one type of checked exception. The `catch` block after this `try` block can catch exceptions of the class `IOException` and any class derived from `IOException`. To catch exceptions of other types, we can write more than one `catch` block after the `try` block. When an exception is thrown, the order in which `catch` blocks appear is significant. Execution continues with the first `catch` block—in order of appearance—whose parameter matches the exception in type.

**JI2.11**  **A poor order for catch blocks.** For example, the following sequence of `catch` blocks is poor, because the `catch` block for `FileNotFoundException` never executes:

```
catch (IOException e)
{
    . . .
}
catch (FileNotFoundException e)
{
    . . .
}
```

With this ordering, any I/O exception will be caught by the first catch block. Because FileNot-FoundException extends IOException, a FileNotFoundException is a kind of IOException and will match the parameter of the first catch block. Fortunately, this ordering likely will receive a warning from the compiler.

**JI2.12** **A good order for catch blocks.** The correct ordering places the more specific exception before its ancestor class, as follows:

```
catch (FileNotFoundException e)
{
   . . .
}
catch (IOException e) // Handle all other IOExceptions
{
   . . .
}
```

**Programming Tip:** Since classes of checked exceptions and runtime exceptions have Exception as an ancestor, avoid using Exception in a catch block. Instead, catch as specific an exception as you can, and catch the most specific one first.

**Java**

**Syntax:** The try-catch blocks have the following syntax:

```
try
{
   < Statements that can cause an exception >
}
catch (exceptionType e)
{
   < Code to react to the exception, probably including the following: >
   System.out.println(e.getMessage());
}
< Possibly other catch blocks >
```

**Programming Tip:** **Avoid nested try-catch blocks, if possible**
Although nesting try-catch blocks within either a try block or a catch block is legal, you should avoid doing so if possible. First see whether you can organize your logic differently to avoid the nesting. Failing that, move the inner blocks to a new method that you call within what was an outer block.

If you must nest try-catch blocks, the following guidelines apply. When a catch block appears within another catch block, they must use different identifiers for their parameters. If you plan to nest try-catch blocks within a try block, you could omit the inner catch blocks if the outer catch blocks deal with the relevant exceptions appropriately. In such a case, an exception thrown within an inner try block is caught in the outer try block.

## Throwing an Exception

Although the ability to handle an exception is quite useful, knowing how to throw an exception is also important. This section looks at how exceptions are thrown. You should throw an exception within a method only in unusual or unexpected situations that you cannot resolve within the method in a reasonable way.

**JI2.13 The throw statement.** A method intentionally throws an exception by executing a throw statement. Its general form is

**throw** *exception_object;*

Rather than creating the exception object in a separate step, programmers usually create the object within the throw statement, as in the following example:

**throw new** IOException();

This statement creates a new object of the class IOException and throws it. Just as we should catch as specific an exception as possible, the exceptions we throw should be as specific as possible.

Although we can invoke the default constructor of the exception class, as in the previous example, we also can provide the constructor with a string as an argument. The resulting object will contain that string in a data field, and both the object and this string will be available to the catch block that handles the exception. The catch block then can use the exception's method getMessage to retrieve the string, as you saw earlier. The default constructor provides a default value for such a string.

---

**Syntax:** The throw statement has the following syntax:

**throw** *exception_object*;

where *exception_object* is an instance of a class of exceptions, typically created by one of the following invocations of the class's constructor:

**new** *class_name*()

or

**new** *class_name*(*message*)

Either the string provided by the default constructor or the string *message* is available, via the exception's method getMessage, to the code that catches the exception.

---

**Design Decision:** **If an unusual situation occurs, should I throw an exception?**

- If you can resolve the unusual situation in a reasonable manner, you likely can use a decision statement instead of throwing an exception.
- If several resolutions to an abnormal occurrence are possible, and you want the client to choose one, you should throw a checked exception.
- If a programmer makes a coding mistake by using your method incorrectly, you can throw a runtime exception. However, you should not throw a runtime exception simply to enable a client to avoid handling it.

---

**Programming Tip:** If a method contains a throw statement to throw an exception, add a throws clause to its header rather than catching the exception within the method's body. In general, throwing an exception and catching one should occur in separate methods.

---

**Programming Tip:** **Do not confuse the keywords** throw **and** throws
You use the Java reserved word throws in a method's header to declare the exceptions that the method might throw. The reserved word throw is used within the body of a method to actually throw an exception.

# A Bag Implementation That Links Data

## Contents

## Prerequisites

## Objectives

After studying this chapter, you should be able to

- Describe a linked organization of data
- Describe how to add a new node to the beginning of a chain of linked nodes
- Describe how to remove the first node in a chain of linked nodes
- Describe how to locate a particular piece of data within a chain of linked nodes
- Implement the ADT bag by using a chain of linked nodes
- Describe the differences between the array-based and linked implementations of the ADT bag

Using an array to implement the ADT bag has both advantages and disadvantages, as you saw in Chapter 2. An array has a fixed size, and so it can either become full or have several unused elements. You can resize an array when it becomes full by moving its entries to a larger array. Although resizing an array can provide as much space as a bag needs, you must move data each time you expand the array.

This chapter introduces a data organization that uses memory only as needed for a new entry and returns the unneeded memory to the system after an entry is removed. By linking data, this new organization avoids moving data when adding or removing bag entries. These features make this way of implementing a bag an important alternative to array-based approaches.

# Linked Data

VideoNote
Linked data

**3.1**    In Chapter 2, we used the analogy of a classroom to describe how data is stored in an array. Here we use a classroom to show you another way to organize data.

Imagine an empty classroom—room L—that is assigned to a course. All available desks are in the hallway. Any student who registers for the course receives a desk, takes it into the room, and sits at it. The room can accommodate all of the desks that are in the hall.

Each desk in the hallway has a number stamped on its back. This number—called an **address**— never changes and is not considered when desks are given to students. Thus, the room will eventually contain desks whose addresses are not sequential.

Now imagine that Jill is among 30 students who are seated in room L at exactly 30 desks. Taped to each desktop is a blank piece of paper. As Jill entered the room, we wrote on her paper the desk number (address) of another desk in the room. For example, the paper on Jill's desk might contain the number 20. If her desk is desk 15, we say that desk 15 **references** desk 20 and that desks 15 and 20 are **linked**. Since all of the desks are linked to one another in this way, we say that they form a **chain** of desks.

Figure 3-1 shows a chain of five desks. No desk references the first desk in the chain, but the instructor knows its desk number, 22. Notice that the last desk in the chain does not reference another desk; the piece of paper on this desk is blank.

**FIGURE 3-1**    A chain of five desks

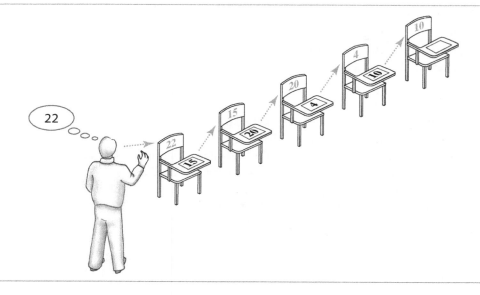

**3.2**    The chain of desks provides an order for the desks. Suppose that first in the chain is the student who arrived most recently. Written on this student's desk is the desk number of the student who arrived just before. With one exception, everyone's desk references the desk of the student who arrived just before. The exception is the person who arrived first. That person sits at the last desk, which does not reference another desk.

The instructor knows the address of the first desk in the chain and so can ask questions of the student at that first desk. Then, by looking at the address, or desk number, that is written on the paper on the first desk, the instructor can locate the second desk in the chain and can question its occupant. Continuing in this way, the instructor can visit every desk in the order in which it appears in the chain. Ultimately, the instructor reaches the last desk in the chain, which references no other desk. Note that the only way the instructor can locate the student in this last desk is to begin at the first desk. Also note that the instructor can traverse this chain in only one order. In our similar example in Chapter 2, the instructor in room A was able to ask questions of any student in any order.

## Forming a Chain by Adding to Its Beginning

**3.3**    How did we form the chain of desks in the first place? Let's return to the time when room L was empty and all available desks were in the hallway.

Suppose that Matt arrives first. He gets a desk from the hallway and enters the room. The instructor notes Matt's desk number (address), and we leave the paper on his desk blank to indicate that no other student has arrived. The room appears as in Figure 3-2.

---

**FIGURE 3-2**    One desk in the room

---

**3.4**    When the second student arrives, we write Matt's desk number on the new desk's paper and give the instructor the number of the new desk to remember. Let's assume that the instructor can remember only one desk number at a time. The room now appears as in Figure 3-3. The new desk is at the beginning of the chain.

When the third student arrives, we write the instructor's memorized desk number, which is that of the desk at the beginning of the chain, on the new desk's paper. We then tell the instructor to remember the number of the new desk, which is now at the beginning of the chain. The room now appears as in Figure 3-4.

After all the students have arrived, the instructor knows only the desk number of the student who arrived most recently. On that student's desk is the desk number of the student who arrived just previously. In general, written on each student's desk is the number of the desk that belongs to the previous student who arrived. Since Matt was the first student to arrive, the paper on his desk is still blank. In Figures 3-1 through 3-4, desk 10 belongs to Matt.

**FIGURE 3-3**     Two linked desks, with the newest desk first

**FIGURE 3-4**     Three linked desks, with the newest desk first

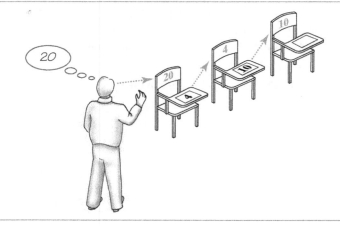

**Question 1** The instructor knows the address of only one desk.

    **a.** Where in the chain is that desk: first, last, or somewhere else?
    **b.** Who is sitting at that desk: the student who arrived first, the student who arrived last, or someone else?

**Question 2** Where in the chain of desks is a new desk added: at the beginning, at the end, or somewhere else?

**3.5** The following pseudocode details the steps taken to form a chain of desks by adding new desks to the beginning of the chain:

```
// Process the first student
newDesk represents the new student's desk
New student sits at newDesk
Instructor memorizes the address of newDesk
```

```
// Process the remaining students
while (students arrive)
{

    newDesk represents the new student's desk
    New student sits at newDesk
    Write the instructor's memorized address on newDesk
    Instructor memorizes the address of newDesk

}
```

# A Linked Implementation of the ADT Bag

The previous section described how you can organize data by linking it together. This section expresses these ideas in Java by beginning the implementation of the ADT bag.

## The Private Class Node

**3.6**   We begin by defining the Java equivalent of a desk, called a **node**. Nodes are objects that you typically link together to form a data structure. Our particular nodes have two data fields each: one to reference a piece of data—presently, an entry in a bag—and one to reference another node. An entry in a bag is analogous to a person who sits at a desk. The reference to another node is analogous to the address written on the paper that is on each desk.

The class that represents these nodes can have the following form:

```
class Node
{
    private T    data; // Entry in bag
    private Node next; // Link to next node
    < Constructors >
    . . .
    < Accessor and mutator methods: getData, setData, getNextNode, setNextNode >
    . . .
} // end Node
```

**3.7**   Let's focus on the data fields. The field data contains a reference to one of the objects in the bag. Sometimes we will call this field the **data portion** of the node. The data type of data is represented here by the generic type T. Soon, you will see that T is the same generic type that the class of bags will declare.

The field next contains a reference to another node. Notice that its data type is Node, which is the class that we are currently defining! Such a circular definition might surprise you, but it is perfectly legal in Java. It also enables one node to reference another node, just as one desk references another desk in our example. Notice that a desk does not reference a student in another desk. Likewise, a node does not reference the data in another node, but rather references the entire other node. Sometimes we will call the field next the **link portion** of the node. Figure 3-5 illustrates two nodes that are linked and contain references to objects in the bag.

---

FIGURE 3-5        Two linked nodes that each reference object data

---

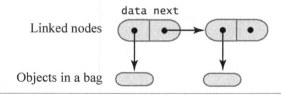

**3.8**   The rest of the definition of the class Node is uneventful. Constructors to initialize the node are useful, and since the data fields are private, methods to access and alter their contents are provided. But are they really necessary? If we intend Node to be for public use, like our other classes, such methods are necessary; however, Node is a detail of this implementation of the ADT bag that should be hidden from the bag's client. One way to hide Node from the world is to define it within a package that also contains the class that implements the bag. Another way— the way we will use here— is to define Node within an **outer class**, the one that implements the bag. Because of its placement within another class, Node is an example of an **inner class**. We declare it to be private. An outer class can access the data fields of an inner class directly by name without the need for accessor and mutator methods. Thus, we write the simpler definition of Node shown in Listing 3-1.

---

LISTING 3-1    The private inner class Node

```
 1  private class Node
 2  {
 3     private T    data; // Entry in bag
 4     private Node next; // Link to next node
 5
 6     private Node(T dataPortion)
 7     {
 8        this(dataPortion, null);
 9     } // end constructor
10
11     private Node(T dataPortion, Node nextNode)
12     {
13        data = dataPortion;
14        next = nextNode;
15     } // end constructor
16  } // end Node
```

---

We did not include a default constructor because we will not need one.

Because Node will be an inner class, the generic type T will be the same as the generic type declared by the outer class that contains Node. Thus, we do not write <T> after Node. If, however, Node was not an inner class but instead had package access or public access, you would write Node<T>. In that case, Node would also require set and get methods for its data fields.

**Note: Terminology**
A **nested class** is defined entirely within another class definition. Nested classes can be static, although we will not encounter any in this book. An inner class is a nested class that is not static. An outer class, or **enclosing class**, contains a nested class. A **top-level class** is one that is not nested.

## An Outline of the Class LinkedBag

**3.9**   For this implementation of the ADT bag, we will use a chain of linked nodes to contain the bag's entries. In our earlier classroom example, the instructor remembered the address of the first desk in a chain of desks. Similarly, our implementation must "remember" the address of the first node in the chain of nodes. We use a data field called the **head reference** to record a reference to this first node. A second data field can track the number of entries in the bag, that is, the number of nodes in the chain.

Listing 3-2 contains an outline of the class LinkedBag that implements the ADT bag and contains the class Node as an inner class. Recall that Chapter 1 introduced the interface BagInterface in Listing 1-1. It and the classes that implement it define a generic type for the objects in a bag. The identifier T that we use for this generic type must match the one that we use within the inner class Node.

VideoNote

Beginning the class
LinkedBag

---

LISTING 3-2    An outline of the class LinkedBag

```java
 1  /**
 2      A class of bags whose entries are stored in a chain of linked nodes.
 3      The bag is never full.
 4      @author Frank M. Carrano
 5  */
 6  public final class LinkedBag<T> implements BagInterface<T>
 7  {
 8      private Node firstNode;          // Reference to first node
 9      private int  numberOfEntries;
10
11      public LinkedBag()
12      {
13         firstNode = null;
14         numberOfEntries = 0;
15      } // end default constructor
16
17      < Implementations of the public methods declared in BagInterface go here. >
18
19      . . .
20
21      private class Node // Private inner class
22      {
23         < See Listing 3-1. >
24      } // end Node
25  } // end LinkedBag
```

---

The data field firstNode is the head reference of the chain of nodes. Just like the instructor who knew the address of the first desk in the chain of desks, firstNode references the first node in the chain of nodes. Another data field, numberOfEntries, records the number of entries in the current bag. This number is also the number of nodes in the chain. Initially, a bag is empty, so the default constructor simply initializes the data fields firstNode to null and numberOfEntries to zero.

Notice that we did not define a boolean field initialized, as we did for the class ArrayBag in Chapter 2. We will explain why later in this chapter.

## Defining Some Core Methods

As we stated in the previous chapter, implementing and testing a core group of methods often is advantageous when you write a class. Any method that adds an entry to a collection typically is a core method for a class that implements a collection, such as a bag. Moreover, to verify that additions to a collection are made correctly, we need a way to look at the collection's entries. The method toArray can serve this purpose, and so it also is a core method. Such was the case for the class ArrayBag in the previous chapter, and it is true of our present class LinkedBag. Before we do anything else, let's define the bag's methods add and toArray.

**3.10**    **The method add: Beginning a chain of nodes.** In Segment 3.3, the room was empty when the first student arrived. As we noted in Segment 3.5, we took the following steps to begin a chain of desks:

> newDesk *represents the new student's desk*
> *New student sits at* newDesk
> *Instructor memorizes the address of* newDesk

Here are the analogous steps that the method add must take to add the first entry to an initially empty bag. Note that the desk in the previous pseudocode is analogous to a node defined within LinkedBag, the student is analogous to a bag entry—that is, the data within the node—and the instructor is analogous to firstNode.

> newNode *references a new instance of* Node
> *Place data in* newNode
> firstNode = *address of* newNode

Thus, when the method add adds the first entry to an initially empty bag, it creates a new node and makes it a one-node chain.

In Java, these steps appear as follows, where newEntry references the entry to be added to the bag:

```
Node newNode = new Node(newEntry);
firstNode = newNode;
```

Figure 3-6 illustrates these two steps. Part *a* of this figure shows the empty chain and the node created by the first statement. Part *b* shows the result of the second statement. Notice that in Part *b*, both firstNode and newNode reference the same node. After the insertion of the new node is complete, only firstNode should reference it. We could set newNode to null, but as you will see shortly, newNode is a local variable of the method add. As such, newNode will not exist after add ends its execution. The same is true of the parameter newEntry, which behaves like a local variable.

**FIGURE 3-6**    (a) An empty chain and a new node; (b) after adding a new node to a chain that was empty

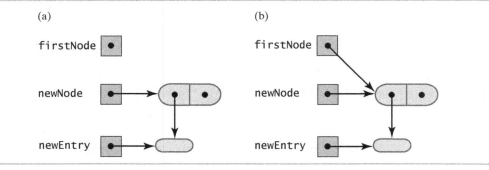

**3.11**    **The method add: Adding to the chain of nodes.** Just as we added new desks to the beginning of an existing chain in Segment 3.5, the method add will add new nodes to the beginning of its chain. In the context of desks in a room, the necessary steps are

> newDesk *represents the new student's desk*
> *New student sits at* newDesk
> *Write the instructor's memorized address on* newDesk
> *Instructor memorizes the address of* newDesk

As a result of these steps, the new desk references the current first desk in the chain and becomes the new first desk.

Here are the analogous steps that add takes:

newNode *references a new instance of* Node
*Place data in* newNode
*Set* newNode*'s link to* firstNode
*Set* firstNode *to* newNode

That is, we make the new node reference the first node in the chain, making it the new first node. Figure 3-7 illustrates these steps, and the following Java statements implement them:

```
Node newNode = new Node(newEntry);
newNode.next = firstNode;
firstNode = newNode;
```

---

FIGURE 3-7      A chain of nodes (a) just prior to adding a node at the beginning; (b) just after adding a node at the beginning

---

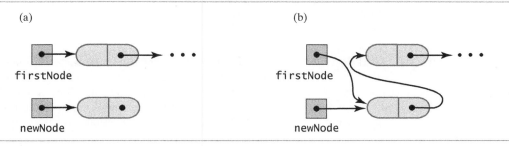

---

Adding a node to an empty chain, as Figure 3-6 depicts, is actually the same as adding a node to the beginning of a chain. Question 3 asks you to think about this fact.

---

**Question 3** The code that we developed in Segment 3.10 to add a node to an empty chain is

```
Node newNode = new Node(newEntry);
firstNode = newNode;
```

The code that we just developed to add to the beginning of a chain is

```
Node newNode = new Node(newEntry);
newNode.next = firstNode;
firstNode = newNode;
```

Why do these three statements also work correctly when the chain is empty?

---

3.12    **The method add.** As you have seen, although it might appear that an empty bag is a special case when adding a new entry to a bag, it really is not. The following definition of the method add uses this conclusion:

```
/** Adds a new entry to this bag.
    @param newEntry  The object to be added as a new entry.
    @return  True. */
public boolean add(T newEntry) // OutOfMemoryError possible
{
   // Add to beginning of chain:
   Node newNode = new Node(newEntry);
   newNode.next = firstNode;   // Make new node reference rest of chain
                               // (firstNode is null if chain is empty)
```

```
            firstNode = newNode;    // New node is at beginning of chain
            numberOfEntries++;

            return true;
    } // end add
```

**3.13**   **An out-of-memory error.** With a linked implementation, the bag cannot become full. Anytime you add a new entry, you create a new node for that entry. Thus, the method add always returns true. It is possible, however, for your program to use all of your computer's memory. If this occurs, your request for a new node will cause the error OutOfMemoryError. You might interpret this condition as a full bag, but there is little the client can do to recover from this error.

**Note:  Allocating memory**
When you use the new operator, you create, or instantiate, an object. At that time, the Java run-time environment **allocates**, or assigns, memory to the object. When you create a node for a linked chain, we sometimes say that you have allocated the node.

**Security Note:  Should the inner class Node perform security checks?**
Because Node is a private inner class, we will treat it as an implementation detail of the outer class LinkedBag. As such, we will make LinkedBag responsible for any security checking. Moreover, notice that Node's constructors make simple assignments that will not throw an exception. Even if that were not the case, and Node could throw an exception, LinkedBag would be able to handle it.

**Security Note:  Should the class LinkedBag perform security checks?**
We mentioned at the end of Segment 3.9 that LinkedBag does not need a boolean data field initialized to check that the constructor executed completely. As you can see in Listing 3-2, LinkedBag's default constructor makes two simple assignments. In fact, the values assigned are the same values that would be assigned by default if we omitted the constructor. These assignments will not fail.

The method add allocates a new node. As we noted, this allocation could fail, if sufficient memory is not available. If an OutOfMemoryError occurs, the chain would be intact and unchanged. It might either be empty or contain nodes that were assigned during previous calls to add. If a client caught the OutOfMemoryError and proceeded to operate on the bag, those operations would behave appropriately.

Since the integrity of any LinkedBag object is maintained, we do not need the security checks that we added to the class ArrayBag.

**3.14**   **The method toArray.** The method toArray returns an array of the entries currently in a bag. By implementing this method, we will be able to test whether the add method works before we complete the rest of the class LinkedBag. To access the bag's entries, we need to access each node in a chain, beginning with the first one. This action is called a **traversal**, and it is analogous to visiting each desk in a chain of desks, as we described in Segment 3.2.

The data field firstNode contains a reference to the first node in the chain. That node contains a reference to the second node in the chain, the second node contains a reference to the third node, and so on. To traverse the chain, the method toArray needs a temporary, local variable currentNode to reference each node in turn. When currentNode references the node whose data we want to access, that data is at currentNode.data.

Initially, we want `currentNode` to reference the first node in the chain, so we set it to `firstNode`. After accessing the data at `currentNode.data`, we move to the next node by executing

```
currentNode = currentNode.next;
```

We again access the data at `currentNode.data` and then move to the next node by executing

```
currentNode = currentNode.next;
```

once again. We continue in this manner until we reach the last node and `currentNode` becomes `null`. The following method `toArray` uses these ideas:

```java
/** Retrieves all entries that are in this bag.
    @return  A newly allocated array of all the entries in the bag. */
public T[] toArray()
{
    // The cast is safe because the new array contains null entries
    @SuppressWarnings("unchecked")
    T[] result = (T[])new Object[numberOfEntries]; // Unchecked cast

    int index = 0;
    Node currentNode = firstNode;
    while ((index < numberOfEntries) && (currentNode != null))
    {
        result[index] = currentNode.data;
        index++;
        currentNode = currentNode.next;
    } // end while

    return result;
} // end toArray
```

 **Programming Tip:** If `ref` is a reference to a node in a chain, be sure that `ref` is not `null` before you use it to access `ref.data` or `ref.next`. Otherwise, if `ref` is `null`, a `NullPointerException` will occur.

 **Question 4** In the previous definition of `toArray`, the `while` statement uses the boolean expression (`index < numberOfEntries`) && (`currentNode != null`) to control the loop. Is it necessary to test the values of both `index` and `currentNode`? Explain your answer.

## Testing the Core Methods

**3.15** Earlier, we realized that the add method is fundamental to our class, so it is one of the core methods that we implement and test first. The method `toArray` lets us see whether add works correctly, so it too is in our core group. But what about the methods that are not in our core group? Because `LinkedBag` implements the interface `BagInterface`, it must define every method in the interface. As the previous chapter described, we write stubs for methods that are declared in the interface but are not a part of our core group. Since the methods `getCurrentSize` and `isEmpty` have simple definitions, we will write them instead of stubs in this first draft of the class `LinkedBag`.

A test program for `LinkedBag`[1] could be similar to the one for `ArrayBag`, as given in Listing 2-2 of the previous chapter, except for its name, the class used to create a bag, and one other significant distinction: Although an instance of `ArrayBag` can become full, an instance of `LinkedBag` will not. Listing 3-3 outlines such a test program. Notice that the private static methods here are exactly the same as those given in Listing 2-2 of the previous chapter. This is possible because the methods use `BagInterface` as the data type of a bag.

---

1. Note that this version of the class `LinkedBag` is available online at the book's website and is named `LinkedBag1`.

---

**LISTING 3-3    A sample program that tests some methods in the class** `LinkedBag`

```
1   /** A test of the methods add, toArray, isEmpty, and getCurrentSize,
2       as defined in the first draft of the class LinkedBag.
3       @author Frank M. Carrano
4   */
5   public class LinkedBagDemo1
6   {
7      public static void main(String[] args)
8      {
9         System.out.println("Creating an empty bag.");
10        BagInterface<String> aBag = new LinkedBag<>();
11        testIsEmpty(aBag, true);
12        displayBag(aBag);
13
14        String[] contentsOfBag = {"A", "D", "B", "A", "C", "A", "D"};
15        testAdd(aBag, contentsOfBag);
16        testIsEmpty(aBag, false);
17     } // end main
18
19     // Tests the method isEmpty.
20     // Precondition: If the bag is empty, the parameter empty should be true;
21     // otherwise, it should be false.
22     private static void testIsEmpty(BagInterface<String> bag, boolean empty)
23     {
24     System.out.print("\nTesting isEmpty with ");
25     if (empty)
26        System.out.println("an empty bag:");
27     else
28        System.out.println("a bag that is not empty:");
29
30     System.out.print("isEmpty finds the bag ");
31     if (empty && bag.isEmpty())
32        System.out.println("empty: OK.");
33     else if (empty)
34        System.out.println("not empty, but it is: ERROR.");
35     else if (!empty && bag.isEmpty())
36        System.out.println("empty, but it is not empty: ERROR.");
37     else
38        System.out.println("not empty: OK.");
39     } // end testIsEmpty
40     < The static methods testAdd and displayBag from Listing 2-2 are here. >
41  } // end LinkedBagDemo1
```

## The Method getFrequencyOf

**3.16**    To count the number of times a given entry appears in a bag, we must traverse the chain of nodes and look at the entry in each one. The traversal is much like the one we used in the method `toArray`. Thus, if `currentNode` will reference the node that we want to examine, we set it initially to `firstNode`—the first node in the chain—and then use the statement

```
currentNode = currentNode.next;
```

to advance it to the next node. Using this technique, we can write a loop like the following one:

```
int loopCounter = 0;
Node currentNode = firstNode;
while ((loopCounter < numberOfEntries) && (currentNode != null))
{
   . . .
```

**VideoNote**

**Completing the class**
**LinkedBag**

```
        loopCounter++;
        currentNode = currentNode.next;
    } // end while
```

Although the method `toArray` uses the variable `index`, since it deals with an array, we use the variable `loopCounter` here, as we do not have an array. You should note that `loopCounter` is counting nodes for loop control; it is not counting how many times a given entry occurs in a bag. Moreover, we could omit `loopCounter` entirely, but we retain it as a check on our logic.

Within the body of the loop, we access the data in the current node and compare it with the entry passed to the method as its argument. Each time we find a match, we increment a frequency count. Thus, we have the following definition for the method `getFrequencyOf`:

```java
/** Counts the number of times a given entry appears in this bag.
    @param anEntry  The entry to be counted.
    @return  The number of times anEntry appears in the bag. */
public int getFrequencyOf(T anEntry)
{
    int frequency = 0;
    int loopCounter = 0;
    Node currentNode = firstNode;

    while ((loopCounter < numberOfEntries) && (currentNode != null))
    {
        if (anEntry.equals(currentNode.data))
            frequency++;

        loopCounter++;
        currentNode = currentNode.next;
    } // end while

    return frequency;
} // end getFrequencyOf
```

## The Method contains

**3.17**    In the previous chapter—where we used an array to represent the bag's entries—we determined whether a bag contained a given entry by examining each array element—starting at index zero— until we either found the desired entry or discovered that it was not in the array. We use an analogous approach here to search a chain for a particular piece of data by looking at the chain's nodes, one at a time. We begin at the first node, and if that does not contain the entry we are seeking, we look at the second node, and so on.

When searching an array, we use an index. To search a chain, we use a reference to a node. So, just as in the method `getFrequencyOf`, we use a local variable `currentNode` to reference the node that we want to examine. Initially, we set `currentNode` to `firstNode` and then to `currentNode.next` as we traverse the chain. However, instead of traversing the entire chain like `getFrequencyOf` does, our loop iterates until either we find the desired entry or `currentNode` becomes `null`—in which case the entry is not in the bag.

Thus, the method `contains` has the following implementation:

```java
public boolean contains(T anEntry)
{
    boolean found = false;
    Node currentNode = firstNode;

    while (!found && (currentNode != null))
    {
        if (anEntry.equals(currentNode.data))
            found = true;
        else
            currentNode = currentNode.next;
    } // end while

    return found;
} // end contains
```

**Question 5** If currentNode in the previous method contains becomes null, what value does the method return when the bag is not empty?

**Question 6** Trace the execution of the method contains when the bag is empty. What is the result?

## Removing an Item from a Linked Chain

**3.18**   Earlier in this chapter, we used the analogy of a classroom to describe how to form a linked chain of data. Available desks are in the hallway outside of the classroom. Each desk has a number (address) stamped on its back and a blank piece of paper taped to its desktop. As students enter the room, they take a desk from the hall. The number of another desk already in the room is written on the new desk's piece of paper, and the instructor is given the new desk's number. In this way, the desks are linked to one another, forming a chain of desks. As you saw in Figure 3-1, no desk references the first desk in the chain, but the instructor knows its address. The last desk does not reference another desk; its paper is blank.

Students who leave our classroom—room L—return their desks to the hall. Such desks can be reassigned to other students who enter either room L or other rooms that share this hallway. Suppose that you are a student in room L but you want to drop the course. If you simply move your desk to the hallway, you will not actually remove yourself from the chain of desks in the room: Either another desk or the instructor will still reference your desk. We need to disconnect your desk from the chain. The details of how we do this depend on where your desk is in the chain. Here are the possible cases:

- Case 1: Your desk is first in the chain of desks.
- Case 2: Your desk is not first in the chain of desks.

**3.19**   **Case 1.** Figure 3-8 illustrates Case 1 before we remove the first desk from the chain. The following steps are necessary to remove the first desk:

1. Locate the first desk by asking the instructor for its address.
2. Give the address that is written on the first desk to the instructor. This is the address of the second desk in the chain.
3. Return the first desk to the hallway.

FIGURE 3-8      A chain of desks just prior to removing its first desk

Figure 3-9 shows the chain after the first two steps take place. Notice that the first desk is no longer a part of the chain. Technically, it still references the second desk. But if this desk is ever used again, a new address will be written on its paper.

---

FIGURE 3-9    A chain of desks just after removing its first desk

---

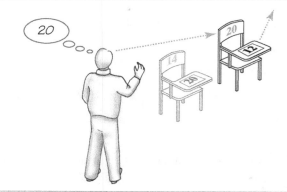

---

**3.20**    **Case 2.** Remember that a bag does not order its entries in any particular way. Thus, in our analogous classroom, we assume that the students are seated in no particular order. If you want to drop the course and are not seated at the first desk in the chain, we do not have to remove your desk. Instead, we take the following steps:

1. Move the student in the first desk to your former desk.
2. Remove the first desk using the steps described for Case 1.

In effect, we have changed Case 2 into Case 1, which we know how to handle.

---

**Question 7** What steps are necessary to remove the first desk in a chain of five desks?

**Question 8** What steps are necessary to remove the third desk in a chain of five desks?

---

## The Methods remove and clear

**3.21**    **Removing an unspecified entry.** The method remove without a parameter removes an unspecified entry from a bag that is not empty. According to the method's specification, as given in the interface in Listing 1-1 of Chapter 1, the method returns the entry it removes:

```
/** Removes one unspecified entry from this bag, if possible.
    @return  Either the removed object, if the removal was successful,
             or null. */
public T remove()
```

If the bag is empty before the method executes, null is returned.

Removing an entry from a bag involves removing it from a chain of linked nodes. Since the first node is easy to remove from the chain, we can define remove so that it removes the entry in this first node. To do so, we take the following steps:

- Access the entry in the first node so it can be returned.
- Set firstNode to reference the second node, as Figure 3-10 indicates. If a second node does not exist, set firstNode to null.
- Decrement numberOfEntries.

FIGURE 3-10    A chain of nodes (a) just prior to removing the first node;
(b) just after removing the first node

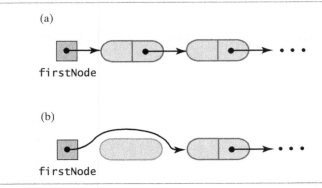

Notice how we implement these steps in the following Java definition of remove:

```
public T remove()
{
    T result = null;
    if (firstNode != null)
    {
        result = firstNode.data;
        firstNode = firstNode.next; // Remove first node from chain
        numberOfEntries--;
    } // end if

    return result;
} // end remove
```

We first check whether the chain is empty by comparing firstNode with null. Note that we could have called isEmpty instead. While accessing the data in the first node and decrementing the number of entries have straightforward expressions in Java, the entire effect of the statement

```
firstNode = firstNode.next;
```

might not be obvious. It should be clear by now that this statement makes firstNode reference the second node in the chain, if such a node exists. But what if it doesn't? That is, what happens when the chain contains only one node? In that case, firstNode.next is null, so the statement sets firstNode to null, as required.

**3.22**    **Removing a given entry.** As the interface in Listing 1-1 of Chapter 1 specifies, a second method remove removes a given entry and returns true or false according to the success of the operation:

```
/** Removes one occurrence of a given entry from this bag, if possible.
    @param anEntry  The entry to be removed.
    @return  True if the removal was successful, or false otherwise. */
public boolean remove(T anEntry)
```

If the bag is empty before the method executes, or if anEntry is not in the bag, the method returns false.

To remove a specific entry that is in a chain of linked nodes, we first must locate the entry. That is, we must traverse the chain and examine the entries in the nodes. Suppose that we find the desired entry in node N. From our previous discussion in Segment 3.20 about a classroom, we can see that if node N is not first in the chain, we can remove its entry by taking the following steps:

1. Replace the entry in node N with the entry in the first node.
2. Remove the first node from the chain.

What if node *N* is first in the chain? If we do not treat this situation separately, the previous steps will replace the entry in the first node with itself. It will be easier to let this happen than to add logic that asks whether node *N* is the first one.

Thus, we have the following pseudocode for the method `remove`:

*Locate a node N that contains* `anEntry`
**if** (*node N exists*)
{
    *Replace the entry in node N with the entry in the first node*
    *Remove the first node from the chain*
}
**return** *true or false according to whether the operation succeeds*

**3.23** **Removing a given entry, continued.** The search to locate a node that contains a given entry is the same one done by the method `contains` in Segment 3.17. Rather than repeating this code in the method `remove`, we can place it into a new private method that both `remove` and `contains` can call. The definition of this private method follows:

```java
// Locates a given entry within this bag.
// Returns a reference to the node containing the entry, if located,
// or null otherwise.
private Node getReferenceTo(T anEntry)
{
   boolean found = false;
   Node currentNode = firstNode;

   while (!found && (currentNode != null))
   {
      if (anEntry.equals(currentNode.data))
         found = true;
      else
         currentNode = currentNode.next;
   } // end while

   return currentNode;
} // end getReferenceTo
```

The pseudocode given in the previous segment for the method `remove` now translates into Java as follows:

```java
public boolean remove(T anEntry)
{
   boolean result = false;
   Node nodeN = getReferenceTo(anEntry);

   if (nodeN != null)
   {
      nodeN.data = firstNode.data; // Replace located entry with entry
                                   // in first node
      firstNode = firstNode.next;  // Remove first node
      numberOfEntries--;
      result = true;
   } // end if

   return result;
} // end remove
```

**Question 9** Instead of calling the method `getReferenceTo`, could the method `remove` have called the original definition of `contains`, as given in Segment 3.17? Explain.

**Question 10** Revise the definition of the method `contains` so that it calls the private method `getReferenceTo`.

**Question 11** Revise the definition of the method `getReferenceTo` so that it controls its loop by using a counter and `numberOfEntries` instead of `currentNode`.

**Question 12** What is an advantage of the definition of `getReferenceTo`, as given in the previous segment, over the one that the previous question describes?

3.24   **The method `clear`.** In the class `ArrayBag`, as given in the previous chapter, the method `clear` called the methods `remove` and `isEmpty` to remove all entries from the bag. Since this definition does not depend on how we represent the bag, we can use the same definition here in `LinkedBag`. Thus, `clear`'s definition is

```java
public void clear()
{
   while (!isEmpty())
      remove();
} // end clear
```

**Question 13** Does the following version of the method `clear` deallocate all of the nodes in the chain, thereby resulting in an empty bag? Explain.

```java
public void clear()
{
   firstNode = null;
} // end clear
```

**Note: Deallocating memory**
After the method `remove` removes a node from a chain, you have no way to reference the removed node, so you cannot use it. Moreover, as Segment C.20 in Appendix C notes, the Java runtime environment automatically deallocates and recycles the memory associated with such nodes. No explicit instruction from the programmer is necessary or, in fact, possible to cause deallocation to occur.

**Design Decision:  Should `LinkedBag` limit the capacity of a bag?**
Although the array-based implementations of the ADT bag presented in Chapter 2 prevented the bag's capacity from exceeding a set limit, `LinkedBag` does not. Unlike `ArrayBag`, `LinkedBag` does not allocate an array as a data field large enough to contain the expected bag entries. The chain of these entries grows one node at a time on demand. If an addition fails, the existing chain remains intact.

Although we chose to let a `LinkedBag` object have an unrestricted capacity, you could make `LinkedBag` limit the capacity, if you expect to use `LinkedBag` in a restricted memory situation.

## A Class **Node** That Has Set and Get Methods

Because Node is an inner class of the class LinkedBag, LinkedBag can access Node's private data fields directly by name. Doing so makes the implementation somewhat easier to write, read, and understand, particularly for novice Java programmers. However, you really should access a class's data fields only by calling accessor and mutator (set and get) methods. In fact, we will do so in the rest of the book. This section adds these methods to Node and explores three ways to define this class.

**3.25**    **As an inner class.** Suppose that we add the methods getData, setData, getNextNode, and setNextNode to the inner class Node, as it appears in Listing 3-1. The class would then appear as given in Listing 3-4.

---

LISTING 3-4    The inner class Node with set and get methods

```
1  private class Node
2  {
3     private T    data; // Entry in bag
4     private Node next; // Link to next node
5
6     private Node(T dataPortion)
7     {
8        this(dataPortion, null);
9     } // end constructor
10
11    private Node(T dataPortion, Node nextNode)
12    {
13       data = dataPortion;
14       next = nextNode;
15    } // end constructors
16
17    private T getData()
18    {
19       return data;
20    } // end getData
21
22    private void setData(T newData)
23    {
24       data = newData;
25    } // end setData
26
27    private Node getNextNode()
28    {
29       return next;
30    } // end getNextNode
31
32    private void setNextNode(Node nextNode)
33    {
34       next = nextNode;
35    } // end setNextNode
36 } // end Node
```

**3.26**   With these additions to Node, we could revise the implementation of LinkedBag by making changes such as the following:

- Change

  ```
  newNode.next = firstNode;
  ```

  to

  ```
  newNode.setNextNode(firstNode);
  ```

- Change

  ```
  currentNode = currentNode.next;
  ```

  to

  ```
  currentNode = currentNode.getNextNode();
  ```

- Change

  ```
  result = firstNode.data;
  ```

  to

  ```
  result = firstNode.getData();
  ```

- Change

  ```
  entryNode.data = firstNode.data;
  ```

  to

  ```
  entryNode.setData(firstNode.getData());
  ```

Project 2 at the end of this chapter asks you to complete these revisions to LinkedBag.

**3.27**   **As a class within a package.** After we modify Node and LinkedBag as just described, Node could remain as a private inner class. Since Node is an implementation detail that we want to hide, making it an inner class is appropriate. But if we ever changed our minds and wanted to define Node outside of LinkedBag, we could do so while retaining the modifications to LinkedBag made in the previous segment. We could—with a few changes—make Node accessible only within a package, or we could even make it a public class.

To transform Node, as given in Listing 3-4, into a class accessible only by other classes in its package, you first omit all the access modifiers except the ones for the data fields. You then add <T> after each occurrence of Node within the class definition, except when it is used as a constructor name. The revised class appears in Listing 3-5.

**LISTING 3-5**   The class Node with package access

```
1  package BagPackage;
2  class Node<T>
3  {
4     private T       data;
5     private Node<T> next;
6
7     Node(T dataPortion) // The constructor's name is Node, not Node<T>
8     {
9        this(dataPortion, null);
10    } // end constructor
11
```

```
12      Node(T dataPortion, Node<T> nextNode)
13      {
14         data = dataPortion;
15         next = nextNode;
16      } // end constructor
17
18      T getData()
19      {
20         return data;
21      } // end getData
22
23      void setData(T newData)
24      {
25         data = newData;
26      } // end setData
27
28      Node<T> getNextNode()
29      {
30         return next;
31      } // end getNextNode
32
33      void setNextNode(Node<T> nextNode)
34      {
35         next = nextNode;
36      } // end setNextNode
37   } // end Node
```

**3.28**   The class `LinkedBag` can access `Node`, as just given in Listing 3-5, if both classes are in the same package and we modify `LinkedBag` slightly. Each occurrence of `Node` within `LinkedBag` must now appear as `Node<T>`. We begin to make these changes to `LinkedBag` and highlight them in Listing 3-6.

---

**LISTING 3-6**   The class `LinkedBag` when `Node` is in the same package

```
1  package BagPackage;
2  public class LinkedBag<T> implements BagInterface<T>
3  {
4     private Node<T> firstNode;
5     . . .
6
7     public boolean add(T newEntry)          This occurrence of T is optional
8     {
9        Node<T> newNode = new Node<T>(newEntry);
10       newNode.setNextNode(firstNode);
11       firstNode = newNode;
12       numberOfEntries++;
13
14       return true;
15    } // end add
16    . . .
17 } // end LinkedBag
```

---

Project 3 at the end of this chapter asks you to complete this revision of `LinkedBag`.

**3.29**   **As an inner class with a declared generic type.** The version of LinkedBag just described in Listing 3-6 could define Node as an inner class. Node would be similar to the class given in Listing 3-5, but would require the following changes:

- Omit the package statement.
- Make the class, constructors, and methods private.
- Replace the generic type T with another identifier, such as S.

Since both LinkedBag and Node declare generic types, they must use different identifiers to represent them.

Project 4 at the end of the chapter asks you to revise Node and LinkedBag as described here.

# The Pros and Cons of Using a Chain to Implement the ADT Bag

**3.30**   You have seen how to use a chain in the implementation of the ADT bag. One of the greatest advantages of this approach is that the chain, and therefore the bag, can grow and shrink in size as necessary. As long as memory is available, you can add as many nodes to a chain as you wish. Moreover, you can remove and recycle nodes that are no longer needed. Although you can resize an array to allow a bag to grow in size—as the previous chapter describes—each time a larger array is necessary, you must copy the entries from the full array to the new array. No such copying is required when you use a chain.

Adding a new entry to the end of an array or to the beginning of a chain are both relatively simple tasks. Both operations are fast, unless the array needs to be resized. Likewise, removing the entry at the end of an array or the beginning of a chain takes about the same effort. However, removing a specific entry requires a search of the array or chain.

Lastly, a chain requires more memory than an array of the same length. Although both data structures contain references to data objects, each node in a chain also contains a reference to another node. However, an array is often larger than necessary, so memory is wasted. A chain uses memory only as needed.

**Question 14** Compare the efforts made by the contains methods in the classes LinkedBag in this chapter and ResizableArrayBag in Chapter 2. Does one take more time to perform its task? Explain.

## CHAPTER SUMMARY

- You can form a chain of linked data by using objects called nodes. Each node has two parts. One part contains a reference to a data object, and the second part references the next node in the chain. The last node, however, references no other node and contains null. A head reference external to the chain references the first node.

- You can add a node to the beginning of a chain of linked nodes by changing two references: the one within the node to be added and the chain's head reference.

- You can remove the first node in a chain of linked nodes by setting the chain's head reference to the reference within the first node.

- Locating a particular node in a chain of linked nodes requires a traversal of the chain. Beginning at the first node, you move from node to node sequentially until you reach the desired node.

- The class Node can be an inner class of LinkedBag or a class within a package that contains LinkedBag. In the latter case, Node must define set and get methods to provide access to its data fields.

## PROGRAMMING TIP

- If ref is a reference to a node in a chain, be sure that ref is not null before you use it to access ref.data or ref.next.

## EXERCISES

1. Add a boolean data field called initialized to the class LinkedBag, and define a method that uses it.

2. Consider the definition of LinkedBag's add method that appears in Segment 3.12. Interchange the second and third statements in the method's body, as follows:

   ```
   firstNode = newNode;
   newNode.next = firstNode;
   ```

   a. What is displayed by the following statements in a client of the modified LinkedBag?

   ```
   BagInterface<String> myBag = new LinkedBag<>();
   myBag.add("30");
   myBag.add("40");
   myBag.add("50");
   myBag.add("10");
   myBag.add("60");
   myBag.add("20");
   int numberOfEntries = myBag.getCurrentSize();
   Object[] entries = myBag.toArray();
   for (int index = 0; index < numberOfEntries; index++)
      System.out.print(entries[index] + " ");
   ```

   b. What methods, if any, in LinkedBag could be affected by the change to the method add when they execute? Why?

3. Repeat Exercise 2 in the previous chapter for the class LinkedBag.

4. Revise the definition of the method remove, as given in Segment 3.21, so that it removes a random entry from a bag. Would this change affect any other method within the class LinkedBag?

5. Modify the method remove for the class LinkedBag by using isEmpty() to check whether the chain is empty.

6. Repeat Exercise 10 in Chapter 2 for the class LinkedBag.

7. Repeat Exercise 11 in Chapter 2 for the class LinkedBag.

8. Define an equals method for the class LinkedBag. Consult Exercise 12 in Chapter 2 for details about this method.

9. Define the method union, as described in Exercise 5 of Chapter 1, for the class LinkedBag.

10. Define the method intersection, as described in Exercise 6 of Chapter 1, for the class LinkedBag.

11. Define the method difference, as described in Exercise 7 of Chapter 1, for the class LinkedBag.

**12.** In a **doubly linked chain**, each node can reference the previous node as well as the next node. Figure 3-11 shows a doubly linked chain and its head reference. Define a class to represent a node in a doubly linked chain. Write the class as an inner class of a class that implements the ADT bag. You can omit set and get methods.

**FIGURE 3-11**    A doubly linked chain for Exercises 12, 13, 14, and 15, and Project 7

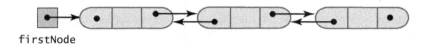

firstNode

**13.** Repeat Exercise 12, but instead write the class within a package that contains an implementation of the ADT bag. Set and get methods will be necessary.

**14.** List the steps necessary to add a node to the beginning of the doubly linked chain shown in Figure 3-11.

**15.** List the steps necessary to remove the first node from the beginning of the doubly linked chain shown in Figure 3-11.

## PROJECTS

**1.** Write a program that thoroughly tests the class LinkedBag.

**2.** Listing 3-4 shows the inner class Node with set and get methods. Revise the class LinkedBag so that it invokes these set and get methods instead of accessing the private data fields data and next directly by name.

**3.** Listing 3-5 shows Node as a class within a package that also contains LinkedBag. Revise LinkedBag to use this version of Node.

**4.** Revise Node and LinkedBag as described in Segment 3.29.

**5.** Define a class LinkedSet that represents a set and implements the interface given in Listing 1-5 of Chapter 1. Use the class LinkedBag in your implementation. Then write a program that adequately demonstrates your implementation.

**6.** Repeat the previous project, but use a chain of linked nodes instead of the class LinkedBag.

**7.** Define a class DoublyLinkedBag that implements the ADT bag by using a doubly linked chain, as shown in Figure 3-11. Use the inner class of nodes that Exercise 12 defines.

**8.** Repeat the previous project, but define set and get methods in the inner class of nodes.

**9.** Use the classes for a set or a bag, as defined in this chapter or described in the previous projects, to create a spell checker. Consult the details given in Projects 6 and 7 of Chapter 2.

## ANSWERS TO SELF-TEST QUESTIONS

1. **a.** First.
   **b.** The student who arrived last (most recently).

2. At the beginning.

3. When the chain is empty, `firstNode` is `null`. Setting `newNode.next` to `firstNode` sets it to `null`. Since `newNode.next` already is `null`, no harm is done by the additional assignment.

4. Testing the values of both `index` and `currentNode` is not necessary. Although testing either one of these values is sufficient, testing both values provides a check against mistakes in your code.

5. The method returns false. If `currentNode` becomes `null`, the entire chain has been searched without success.

6. Since the bag is empty, `firstNode`—and hence `currentNode`—is `null`. The `while` loop ends immediately and the method returns false.

7. 
   - Locate the first desk by asking the instructor for its address.
   - Give the address that is written on the first desk's paper to the instructor. This is the address of the second desk in the chain.
   - Return the first desk to the hallway.

8. 
   - The student in the first desk moves to the third desk.
   - Remove the first desk using the three steps given as the answer to the previous question.

9. No. The method `contains` returns either true or false. Although `remove` would be able to tell whether `anEntry` is in the bag, it would not have a reference to `anEntry`. Thus, it would not be able to remove `anEntry` without doing its own search.

10. 
```
public boolean contains(T anEntry)
{
    return getReferenceTo(anEntry) != null;
} // end contains
```

11. 
```
private Node getReferenceTo(T anEntry)
{
    boolean found = false;
    Node currentNode = firstNode;
    int counter = 0;
    while (!found && (counter < numberOfEntries))
    {
        if (anEntry.equals(currentNode.data))
            found = true;
        else
        {
            currentNode = currentNode.next;
            counter++;
        } // end if
    } // end while
    return currentNode;
} // end getReferenceTo
```

12. The original definition of `getReferenceTo` ensures that `currentNode` is not `null`, and thus avoids a `NullPointerException`.

**13.** The variable firstNode references the first node in the chain. The first node references the second node, and so on. If we set firstNode to null, the first node in the chain is no longer referenced. Thus, the system deallocates the first node. As a result, the second node is no longer referenced, and so the system deallocates it. This process continues one node at a time until the entire chain is deallocated.

**14.** The effort expended by each of these two methods is about the same. Each method calls a private method that searches for the desired entry. In LinkedBag, contains calls getReferenceTo, which searches at most numberOfEntries nodes for the desired entry. In ResizableArrayBag, contains calls getIndexOf, which searches at most numberOfEntries array elements for the desired entry. The next chapter will discuss these methods and analyze their time requirements in more detail.

# The Efficiency of Algorithms

## Contents

## Prerequisites

## Objectives

After studying this chapter, you should be able to

- Assess the efficiency of a given algorithm
- Compare the expected execution times of two methods, given the efficiencies of their algorithms

With amazing frequency, manufacturers introduce new computers that are faster and have larger memories than their recent predecessors. Yet we—and likely your computer science professors—ask you to write code that is efficient in its use of time and space (memory). Admittedly, such efficiency is not as pressing an issue as it was fifty years ago, when computers were much slower and their memory size was much smaller than they are now.

(Computers had small memories, but they were physically huge, occupying entire rooms.) Even so, efficiency remains an issue—in some circumstances, a critical issue.

This chapter will introduce you to the terminology and ways that computer scientists use to measure the efficiency of an algorithm. With this background, not only will you have an intuitive feel for efficiency, but you also will be able to talk about efficiency in a quantitative way.

# Motivation

**4.1**　**Example.** Perhaps you think that you are not likely to write a program in the near future whose execution time is noticeably long. You might be right, but we are about to show you some simple Java code that does take a long time to perform its computations.

Consider the problem of computing the sum $1 + 2 + \ldots + n$ for any positive integer $n$. Figure 4-1 contains pseudocode showing three ways to solve this problem. Algorithm A computes the sum $0 + 1 + 2 + \ldots + n$ from left to right. Algorithm B computes $0 + (1) + (1 + 1) + (1 + 1 + 1) + \ldots + (1 + 1 + \ldots + 1)$. Finally, Algorithm C uses an algebraic identity to compute the sum.

FIGURE 4-1　　Three algorithms for computing the sum $1 + 2 + \ldots + n$ for
　　　　　　　　an integer $n > 0$

| Algorithm A | Algorithm B | Algorithm C |
|---|---|---|
| ```
sum = 0
for i = 1 to n
    sum = sum + i
``` | ```
sum = 0
for i = 1 to n
{
    for j = 1 to i
        sum = sum + 1
}
``` | ```
sum = n * (n + 1) / 2
``` |

**4.2**　Let's translate these algorithms into Java code. If we use `long` integers, we could write the following statements:

```
// Computing the sum of the consecutive integers from 1 to n:
long n = 10000; // Ten thousand
// Algorithm A
long sum = 0;
for (long i = 1; i <= n; i++)
    sum = sum + i;
System.out.println(sum);
// Algorithm B
sum = 0;
for (long i = 1; i <= n; i++)
{
    for (long j = 1; j <= i; j++)
        sum = sum + 1;
} // end for
System.out.println(sum);
// Algorithm C
sum = n * (n + 1) / 2;
System.out.println(sum);
```
```

If you execute this code with n equal to ten thousand (10000), you will get the right answer of 50005000 for each of the algorithms. Now change the value of n to one hundred thousand (100000), and execute the code again. Once more, you will get the correct answer, which this time is 5000050000. However, you should notice a delay in seeing the result for Algorithm B. Now try one million (1000000) for the value of n. Again you will get the correct answer—500000500000— but you will have to wait even longer for the result from Algorithm B. The wait might be long enough for you to suspect that something is broken. If not, try a larger value of n.

The previous simple code for Algorithm B takes a noticeably long time to execute, much longer than either of the other two algorithms. If it were the only algorithm you tried, what should you do? Use a faster computer? While that might be a solution, it's clear that we should use a different algorithm.

 **Note:** As the previous example shows, even a simple program can be noticeably inefficient.

 **Note:** If an algorithm takes longer to execute than is practical, try to reformulate it to make it more efficient of time.

# Measuring an Algorithm's Efficiency

**4.3**    The previous section should have convinced you that a program's efficiency matters. How can we measure efficiency so that we can compare various approaches to solving a problem? In the previous section, we computed the sum of the first *n* consecutive integers in three different ways. We then observed that one was noticeably slower than the others as the value of *n* increased. In general, however, implementing several ideas before you choose one requires too much work to be practical. Besides, a program's execution time depends in part on the particular computer and the programming language used. It would be much better to measure an *algorithm's* efficiency before you implement it.

**VideoNote**
**Measuring efficiency**

For example, suppose that you want to go to a store downtown. Your options are to walk, drive your car, ask a friend to take you, or take a bus. What is the best way? First, what is your concept of best? Is it the way that saves money, your time, your friend's time, or the environment? Let's say that the best option for you is the fastest one. After defining your criterion, how do you evaluate your options? You certainly do not want to try all four options so you can discover which is fastest. That would be like writing four different programs that perform the same task so you can measure which one is fastest. Instead you would investigate the "cost" of each option, considering the distance, the speed at which you can travel, the amount of other traffic, the number of stops at traffic lights, the weather, and so on. That is, you would consider the factors that have the most impact on the cost.

**4.4**    The same considerations apply when deciding what algorithm is best. Again, we need to define what we mean by best. An algorithm has both time and space requirements, called its **complexity**, that we can measure. When we assess an algorithm's complexity, we are not measuring how involved or difficult it is. Instead, we measure an algorithm's **time complexity**—the time it takes to execute—or its **space complexity**—the memory it needs to execute. Typically we analyze these requirements separately. So a "best" algorithm might be the fastest one or the one that uses the least memory.

**Note: What's best?**
Usually the "best" solution to a problem balances various criteria such as time, space, generality, programming effort, and so on.

The process of measuring the complexity of algorithms is called the **analysis of algorithms**. We will concentrate on the time complexity of algorithms, because it is usually more important than the space complexity. You should realize that an inverse relationship often exists between an algorithm's time complexity and its space complexity. If you revise an algorithm to save execution time, you usually will need more space. If you reduce an algorithm's space requirement, it likely will require more time to execute. Sometimes, however, you will be able to save both time and space.

Your measure of the complexity of an algorithm should be easy to compute, certainly easier than implementing the algorithm. You should express this measure in terms of the size of the problem. This **problem size** is the number of items that an algorithm processes. For example, if you are searching a collection of data, the problem size is the number of items in the collection. Such a measure enables you to compare the relative cost of algorithms as a function of the size of the problem. Typically, we are interested in large problems; a small problem is likely to take little time, even if the algorithm is inefficient.

**4.5**   Realize that you cannot compute the actual time requirement of an algorithm. After all, you have not implemented the algorithm in Java and you have not chosen the computer. Instead, you find a function of the problem size that behaves like the algorithm's actual time requirement. Therefore, as the time requirement increases by some factor, the value of the function increases by the same factor, and vice versa. The value of the function is said to be **directly proportional** to the time requirement. Such a function is called a **growth-rate function** because it measures how an algorithm's time requirement grows as the problem size grows. Because they measure time requirements, growth-rate functions have positive values. By comparing the growth-rate functions of two algorithms, you can see whether one algorithm is faster than the other for large-size problems.

**4.6**   **Example.** Consider again the problem of computing the sum $1 + 2 + \ldots + n$ for any positive integer $n$. Figure 4-1 gives three algorithms—A, B, and C— to perform this computation. Algorithm A computes the sum $0 + 1 + 2 + \ldots + n$ from left to right. Algorithm B computes $0 + (1) + (1 + 1) + (1 + 1 + 1) + \ldots + (1 + 1 + \ldots + 1)$, and Algorithm C uses an algebraic identity to compute the sum. By executing the Java code in Segment 4.2, we found that Algorithm B is the slowest. We now want to predict this behavior without actually running the code.

So how can we tell which algorithm is slowest and which is fastest? We can begin to answer these questions by considering both the size of the problem and the effort involved. The integer $n$ is a measure of the problem size: As $n$ increases, the sum involves more terms. To measure the effort, or time requirement, of an algorithm, we must find an appropriate growth-rate function. To do so, we might begin by counting the number of operations required by the algorithm.

For example, Algorithm A in Figure 4-1 contains the pseudocode statement

```
for i = 1 to n
```

This statement represents the following loop-control logic:

```
i = 1
while (i <= n)
{
   ...
   i = i + 1
}
```

This logic requires an assignment to $i$, $n + 1$ comparisons between $i$ and $n$, $n$ additions to $i$, and $n$ more assignments to $i$. In total, the loop-control logic requires $n + 1$ assignments, $n + 1$ comparisons, and $n$ additions. Furthermore, Algorithm A requires for its initialization and loop body another $n + 1$ assignments and $n$ additions. All together, Algorithm A requires $2n + 2$ assignments, $2n$ additions, and $n + 1$ comparisons.

These various operations probably take different amounts of time to execute. For example, if each assignment takes no more than $t_=$ time units, each addition takes no more than $t_+$ time units, and each comparison takes no more than $t_c$ time units, Algorithm A would require no more than

$$(2n + 2) \, t_= + (2n) \, t_+ + (n + 1) \, t_c \text{ time units}$$

If we replace $t_=$, $t_+$, and $t_c$ with the largest of the three values and call it $t$, Algorithm A requires no more than $(5n + 3) \, t$ time units. We conclude that Algorithm A requires time directly proportional to $5n + 3$.

What is important, however, is not the exact count of operations, but the general behavior of the algorithm. The function $5n + 3$ is directly proportional to $n$. As you are about to see, we do not have to count every operation to see that Algorithm A requires time that increases linearly with $n$.

## Counting Basic Operations

**4.7**   An algorithm's **basic operation** is the most significant contributor to its total time requirement. For example, Algorithms A and B in Figure 4-1 have addition as their basic operation. An algorithm that sees whether an array contains a particular object has comparison as its basic operation. Realize that the most frequent operation is not necessarily the basic operation. For example, assignments are often the most frequent operation in an algorithm, but they rarely are basic.

Ignoring operations that are not basic, such as initializations of variables, the operations that control loops and so on will not affect our final conclusion about algorithm speed. For example, Algorithm A requires $n$ additions of $i$ to sum in the body of the loop. We can conclude that Algorithm A requires time that increases linearly with $n$, even though we ignored operations that are not basic to the algorithm.

Whether we look at the number, $n$, of basic operations or the total number of operations, $5n + 3$, we can draw the same conclusion: Algorithm A requires time directly proportional to $n$. Thus, Algorithm A's growth-rate function is $n$.

**4.8**    **Example continued.** Now let's count the number of basic operations required by Algorithms B and C. The basic operation for Algorithm B is addition; for Algorithm C, the basic operations are addition, multiplication, and division. Figure 4-2 tabulates the number of basic operations that Algorithms A, B, and C require. Remember, these counts do not include assignments and the operations that control the loops. Our discussion in the previous segment should have convinced you that we can ignore these operations.

FIGURE 4-2   The number of basic operations required by the algorithms in Figure 4-1

|  | Algorithm A | Algorithm B | Algorithm C |
|---|---|---|---|
| Additions | $n$ | $n(n+1)/2$ | 1 |
| Multiplications |  |  | 1 |
| Divisions |  |  | 1 |
| **Total basic operations** | $n$ | $(n^2 + n)/2$ | **3** |

Algorithm B requires time directly proportional to $(n^2 + n) / 2$, and Algorithm C requires time that is constant and independent of the value of $n$. Figure 4-3 plots these time requirements as a function of $n$. You can see from this figure that as $n$ grows, Algorithm B requires the most time.

---

FIGURE 4-3     The number of basic operations required by the algorithms
                in Figure 4-1 as a function of $n$

---

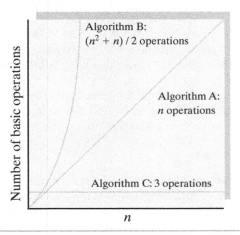

---

**Question 1** For any positive integer $n$, the identity

$$1 + 2 + \ldots + n = n\,(n + 1) / 2$$

is one that you will encounter while analyzing algorithms. Can you derive it? If you can, you will not need to memorize it. *Hint*: Write $1 + 2 + \ldots + n$. Under it write $n + (n - 1) + \ldots + 1$. Then add the terms from left to right.

**Question 2** Can you derive the values in Figure 4-2? *Hint*: For Algorithm B, use the identity given in Question 1.

---

**Note: Useful identities**
$1 + 2 + \ldots + n = n\,(n + 1) / 2$
$1 + 2 + \ldots + (n - 1) = n\,(n - 1) / 2$

**4.9**     Typical growth-rate functions are algebraically simple. Why? Recall that since you are not likely to notice the effect of an inefficient algorithm when the problem is small, you should focus on large problems. Thus, if we care only about large values of $n$ when comparing the algorithms, we can consider only the dominant term in each growth-rate function.

For example, $(n^2 + n) / 2$ behaves like $n^2$ when $n$ is large. First, $n^2$ is much larger than $n$ for large values of $n$, so $(n^2 + n) / 2$ behaves like $n^2 / 2$. Moreover, $n^2 / 2$ behaves like $n^2$ when $n$ is large. In other words, for large $n$, the difference between the value of $(n^2 + n) / 2$ and that of $n^2$ is relatively small and can be ignored. So instead of using $(n^2 + n) / 2$ as Algorithm B's growth-rate function, we can use $n^2$—the term with the largest exponent—and say that Algorithm B requires time proportional to $n^2$. On the other hand, Algorithm C requires time that is independent of $n$, and we saw earlier that Algorithm A requires time proportional to $n$. We conclude that Algorithm C is the fastest and Algorithm B is the slowest.

**Note: The relative magnitudes of common growth-rate functions**
The growth-rate functions that you are likely to encounter grow in magnitude as follows when $n > 10$:

$$1 < \log(\log n) < \log n < \log^2 n < n < n \log n < n^2 < n^3 < 2^n < n!$$

The logarithms given here are base 2. As you will see later in Segment 4.16, the choice of base does not matter.

Figure 4-4 tabulates the magnitudes of these functions for increasing values of the problem size $n$. From this data you can see that algorithms whose growth-rate functions are $\log(\log n)$, $\log n$, or $\log^2 n$ take much less time than algorithms whose growth-rate function is $n$. Although the value of $n \log n$ is significantly larger than $n$, either of those functions describes a growth rate that is markedly faster than $n^2$.

**FIGURE 4-4**    Typical growth-rate functions evaluated at increasing values of $n$

| $n$ | $\log(\log n)$ | $\log n$ | $\log^2 n$ | $n$ | $n \log n$ | $n^2$ | $n^3$ | $2^n$ | $n!$ |
|---|---|---|---|---|---|---|---|---|---|
| 10 | 2 | 3 | 11 | 10 | 33 | $10^2$ | $10^3$ | $10^3$ | $10^5$ |
| $10^2$ | 3 | 7 | 44 | 100 | 664 | $10^4$ | $10^6$ | $10^{30}$ | $10^{94}$ |
| $10^3$ | 3 | 10 | 99 | 1000 | 9966 | $10^6$ | $10^9$ | $10^{301}$ | $10^{1435}$ |
| $10^4$ | 4 | 13 | 177 | 10,000 | 132,877 | $10^8$ | $10^{12}$ | $10^{3010}$ | $10^{19,335}$ |
| $10^5$ | 4 | 17 | 276 | 100,000 | 1,660,964 | $10^{10}$ | $10^{15}$ | $10^{30,103}$ | $10^{243,338}$ |
| $10^6$ | 4 | 20 | 397 | 1,000,000 | 19,931,569 | $10^{12}$ | $10^{18}$ | $10^{301,030}$ | $10^{2,933,369}$ |

**Note:** When analyzing the time efficiency of an algorithm, consider large problems. For small problems, the difference between the execution times of two solutions to the same problem is usually insignificant.

## Best, Worst, and Average Cases

**4.10**    For some algorithms that operate on a data set, the execution time depends only on the size of the data set. For example, the time needed to find the smallest integer in an array of integers depends only on the number of integers, not on the integers themselves. Finding the smallest of 100 integers takes the same amount of time regardless of the values of the integers.

Other algorithms, however, have time requirements that depend not only on the size of the data set, but also on the data itself. For example, imagine that an array contains a certain value, and we want to know where in the array it occurs. Suppose our search algorithm examines each value in the array until it finds the desired one. If the algorithm finds this desired value in the first array element it examines, it makes only one comparison. In this **best case**, the algorithm takes the least time. The algorithm can do no better than its best-case time. If the best-case time is still too slow, you need another algorithm.

Now suppose that the algorithm locates the desired value after comparing it to every value in the array. This would be the algorithm's **worst case**, since it requires the most time. If you can tolerate this worst-case time, your algorithm is acceptable. For many algorithms, the worst and best cases rarely occur. Thus, we consider an algorithm's **average case**, when it processes a typical data set. The average-case time requirement of an algorithm is more useful, but harder to estimate. Note that the average-case time is not the average of the best-case and worst-case times.

**Note:** The time requirements of some algorithms depend on the data values given to them. Those times range from a minimum, or best-case, time to a maximum, or worst-case, time. Typically, the best and worst cases do not occur. A more useful measure of such an algorithm's time requirement is its average-case time.

Some algorithms, however, do not have a best, worst, and average case. Their time requirements depend only on the number of data items given them, not on the values of that data.

# Big Oh Notation

**4.11**   Computer scientists use a notation to represent an algorithm's complexity. For example, consider Algorithms A, B, and C given in Figure 4-1 and the number of basic operations that each requires, as shown in Figure 4-2. Instead of saying that Algorithm A has a time requirement proportional to $n$, we say that A is **O($n$)**. We call this notation **Big Oh** since it uses the capital letter O. We read O($n$) as either "Big Oh of $n$" or "order of at most $n$." Similarly, since Algorithm B has a time requirement proportional to $n^2$, we say that B is O($n^2$). Algorithm C always requires three basic operations. Regardless of the problem size $n$, this algorithm requires the same time. We say that Algorithm C is O(1).

**4.12**   **Example.** Imagine that you are at a wedding reception, seated at a table of $n$ people. In preparation  for the toast, the waiter pours champagne into each of $n$ glasses. That task is O($n$). Someone makes a toast. It is O(1), even if the toast seems to last forever, because it is independent of the number of guests. If you clink your glass with everyone at your table, you perform an O($n$) operation. If everyone at your table does likewise, a total of O($n^2$) clinks are performed.

**4.13**   Big Oh notation has a formal mathematical meaning that can justify our discussion in the previous sections. You saw that an algorithm's actual time requirement is directly proportional to a function $f$ of the problem size $n$. For example, $f(n)$ might be $n^2 + n + 1$. In this case, we would conclude that the algorithm is of order at most $n^2$—that is, O($n^2$). We essentially have replaced $f(n)$ with a simpler function—let's call it $g(n)$. In this example, $g(n)$ is $n^2$.

What does it really mean to say that a function $f(n)$ is of order at most $g(n)$—that is, $f(n)$ is O($g(n)$), or $f(n) = $O($g(n)$)? Formally, its meaning is described by the following mathematical definition:

**Note: Formal definition of Big Oh**
A function $f(n)$ is of order at most $g(n)$—that is, $f(n)$ is O($g(n)$)—if

- A positive real number $c$ and positive integer $N$ exist such that $f(n) \leq c \times g(n)$ for all $n \geq N$. That is, $c \times g(n)$ is an upper bound on $f(n)$ when $n$ is sufficiently large.

In simple terms, $f(n)$ is $O(g(n))$ means that $c \times g(n)$ provides an **upper bound** on $f(n)$'s growth rate when $n$ is large enough. For all data sets of a sufficient size, the algorithm will always require fewer than $c \times g(n)$ basic operations.

Figure 4-5 illustrates the formal definition of Big Oh. You can see that when $n$ is large enough—that is, when $n \geq N$—$f(n)$ does not exceed $c \times g(n)$. The opposite is true for smaller values of $n$. That is unimportant, since we can ignore these values of $n$.

**FIGURE 4-5** An illustration of the definition of Big Oh

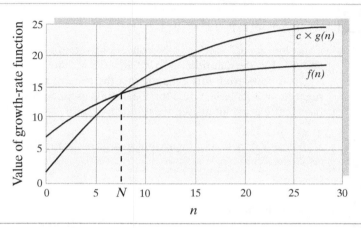

**4.14**  **Example.** In Segment 4.6, we said that if an algorithm uses $5n + 3$ operations, it requires time proportional to $n$. We now can show that $5n + 3$ is $O(n)$ by using the formal definition of Big Oh.

When $n \geq 3$, $5n + 3 \leq 5n + n = 6n$. Thus, if we let $f(n) = 5n + 3$, $g(n) = n$, $c = 6$, and $N = 3$, we have shown that $f(n) \leq 6 \, g(n)$ for $n \geq 3$, or $5n + 3 = O(n)$. That is, if an algorithm requires time directly proportional to $5n + 3$, it is $O(n)$.

Other values for the constants $c$ and $N$ will also work. For example, $5n + 3 \leq 5n + 3n = 8n$ when $n \geq 1$. Thus, by choosing $c = 8$ and $N = 1$, we have shown that $5n + 3$ is $O(n)$.

You need to be careful when choosing $g(n)$. For example, we just found that $5n + 3 \leq 8n$ when $n \geq 1$. But $8n < n^2$ when $n \geq 9$. So why wouldn't we let $g(n) = n^2$ and conclude that our algorithm is $O(n^2)$? Although this conclusion is correct, it is not as good—or **tight**—as it could be. You want the upper bound on $f(n)$ to be as small as possible.

 **Note:** The upper bound on an algorithm's time requirement should be as small as possible and should involve simple functions like the ones given in Figure 4-4.

**4.15**  **Example.** Let's show that $4n^2 + 50n - 10$ is $O(n^2)$. It is easy to see that

$$4n^2 + 50n - 10 \leq 4n^2 + 50n \text{ for any } n$$

Since $50n \leq 50n^2$ for $n \geq 50$,

$$4n^2 + 50n - 10 \leq 4n^2 + 50n^2 = 54n^2 \text{ for } n \geq 50$$

Thus, with $c = 54$ and $N = 50$, we have shown that $4n^2 + 50n - 10$ is $O(n^2)$.

**Note:** To show that $f(n)$ is $O(g(n))$, replace the smaller terms in $f(n)$ with larger terms until only one term is left.

**Question 3** Show that $3n^2 + 2^n$ is $O(2^n)$. What values of $c$ and $N$ did you use?

**4.16**

**Example: Show that $\log_b n$ is $O(\log_2 n)$.** Let $L = \log_b n$ and $B = \log_2 b$. From the meaning of a logarithm, we can conclude that $n = b^L$ and $b = 2^B$. Combining these two conclusions, we have

$$n = b^L = (2^B)^L = 2^{BL}$$

Thus, $\log_2 n = BL = B \log_b n$ or, equivalently, $\log_b n = (1 / B) \log_2 n$ for any $n \geq 1$. Taking $c = 1 / B$ and $N = 1$ in the definition of Big Oh, we reach the desired conclusion.

It follows from this example that the general behavior of a logarithmic function is the same regardless of its base. Often the logarithms used in growth-rate functions are base 2. But since the base really does not matter, we typically omit it.

**Note:** The base of a logarithm in a growth-rate function is usually omitted, since $O(\log_a n)$ is $O(\log_b n)$.

**Note:  Identities**
The following identities hold for Big Oh notation:

$O(k \, g(n)) = O(g(n))$ for a constant $k$

$O(g_1(n)) + O(g_2(n)) = O(g_1(n) + g_2(n))$

$O(g_1(n)) \times O(g_2(n)) = O(g_1(n) \times g_2(n))$

$O(g_1(n) + g_2(n) + \ldots + g_m(n)) = O(\max(g_1(n), g_2(n), \ldots, g_m(n)))$

$O(\max(g_1(n), g_2(n), \ldots, g_m(n))) = \max(O(g_1(n)), O(g_2(n)), \ldots, O(g_m(n)))$

By using these identities and ignoring smaller terms in a growth-rate function, you can usually find the order of an algorithm's time requirement with little effort. For example, if the growth-rate function is $4n^2 + 50n - 10$,

$O(4n^2 + 50n - 10) = O(4n^2)$    by ignoring the smaller terms

$\qquad\qquad\qquad\quad = O(n^2)$    by ignoring the constant multiplier

**Question 4** If $P_k(n) = a_0 n^k + a_1 n^{k-1} + \ldots + a_k$ for $k > 0$ and $n > 0$, what is $O(P_k(n))$?

## The Complexities of Program Constructs

**4.17**

The time complexity of a sequence of statements in an algorithm or program is the sum of the statements' individual complexities. However, it is sufficient to take instead the largest of these complexities. In general, if $S_1, S_2, \ldots, S_k$ is a sequence of program segments, and if $g_i$ is the growth-rate function for segment $S_i$, the time complexity of the sequence would be $O(\max(g_1, g_2, \ldots, g_k))$, which is equivalent to $\max(O(g_1), O(g_2), \ldots, O(g_k))$.

The time complexity of the `if` statement

```
if (condition)
    S₁
else
    S₂
```

is the sum of the complexity of the condition and the complexity of $S_1$ or $S_2$, whichever is largest.

The time complexity of a loop is the complexity of its body times the number of times the body executes. Thus, the complexity of a loop such as

```
for i = 1 to m
    S
```

is $O(m \times g(n))$, or $m \times O(g(n))$, where $g(n)$ is the growth-rate function for $S$. Note that the loop variable $i$ in this example increments by 1. In the following loop, $i$ is doubled at each iteration:

```
for i = 1 to m, i = 2 * i
    S
```

The complexity of this loop is $O(\log(m) \times g(n))$, or $O(\log(m)) \times O(g(n))$.

**Note:** **The complexities of program constructs**

| Construct | Time Complexity |
|---|---|
| Consecutive program segments $S_1, S_2, \ldots, S_k$ whose growth-rate functions are $g_1, \ldots, g_k$, respectively | $\max(O(g_1), O(g_2), \ldots, O(g_k))$ |
| An `if` statement that chooses between program segments $S_1$ and $S_2$ whose growth-rate functions are $g_1$ and $g_2$, respectively | $O(condition) + \max(O(g_1), O(g_2))$ |
| A loop that iterates $m$ times and has a body whose growth-rate function is $g$ | $m \times O(g(n))$ |

**Note:** **Other notations**

Although we will use Big Oh notation most often in this book, other notations are sometimes useful when describing an algorithm's time requirement $f(n)$. We mention them here primarily to expose you to them. Beginning with the definition of Big Oh that you saw earlier, we define **Big Omega** and **Big Theta**.

- **Big Oh.** $f(n)$ is of order at most $g(n)$—that is, $f(n)$ is $O(g(n))$—if positive constants $c$ and $N$ exist such that $f(n) \leq c \times g(n)$ for all $n \geq N$. That is, $c \times g(n)$ is an upper bound on the time requirement $f(n)$. In other words, $f(n)$ is no larger than $c \times g(n)$. Thus, an analysis that uses Big Oh produces a maximum time requirement for an algorithm.

- **Big Omega.** $f(n)$ is of order at least $g(n)$—that is, $f(n)$ is $\Omega(g(n))$—if $g(n)$ is $O(f(n))$. In other words, $f(n)$ is $\Omega(g(n))$ if positive constants $c$ and $N$ exist such that $f(n) \geq c \times g(n)$ for all $n \geq N$. The time requirement $f(n)$ is not smaller than $c \times g(n)$, its **lower bound**. Thus, a Big Omega analysis produces a minimum time requirement for an algorithm.

- **Big Theta.** $f(n)$ is of order $g(n)$—that is, $f(n)$ is $\Theta(g(n))$—if $f(n)$ is $O(g(n))$ and $g(n)$ is $O(f(n))$. Alternatively, we could say that $f(n)$ is $O(g(n))$ and $f(n)$ is $\Omega(g(n))$. The time requirement $f(n)$ is the same as $g(n)$. That is, $c \times g(n)$ is both a lower bound and an upper bound on $f(n)$. A Big Theta analysis assures us that the time estimate is as good as possible. Even so, Big Oh is the more common notation.

## Picturing Efficiency

**4.18**   Much of an algorithm's work occurs during its repetitive phases, that is, during the execution of loops or—as you will see in Chapter 7—as a result of recursive calls. In this section, we will illustrate the time efficiency of several examples.

We begin with the loop in Algorithm A of Figure 4-1, which appears in pseudocode as follows:

```
for i = 1 to n
    sum = sum + i
```

The body of this loop requires a constant amount of execution time, and so it is O(1). Figure 4-6 represents that time with one icon, and so a row of $n$ icons represents the loop's total execution time. This algorithm is O($n$): Its time requirement grows as $n$ grows.

---

**FIGURE 4-6**      An O($n$) algorithm

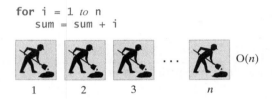

**4.19**   Algorithm B in Figure 4-1 contains nested loops, as follows:

```
for i = 1 to n
{
    for j = 1 to i
        sum = sum + 1
}
```

When loops are nested, you examine the innermost loop first. Here, the body of the inner loop requires a constant amount of execution time, and so it is O(1). If we again represent that time with an icon, a row of $i$ icons represents the time requirement for the inner loop. Since the inner loop is the body of the outer loop, it executes $n$ times. Figure 4-7 illustrates the time requirement for these nested loops, which is proportional to $1 + 2 + \ldots + n$. Question 1 asked you to show that

$$1 + 2 + \ldots + n = n(n+1)/2$$

which is $n^2/2 + n/2$. Thus, the computation is O($n^2$).

**4.20**   The body of the inner loop in the previous segment executes a variable number of times that depends on the outer loop. Suppose we change the inner loop so that it executes the same number of times for each repetition of the outer loop, as follows:

```
for i = 1 to n
{
    for j = 1 to n
        sum = sum + 1
}
```

Figure 4-8 illustrates these nested loops and shows that the computation is O($n^2$).

**FIGURE 4-7** An O($n^2$) algorithm

```
for i = 1 to n
{   for j = 1 to i
        sum = sum + 1
}
```

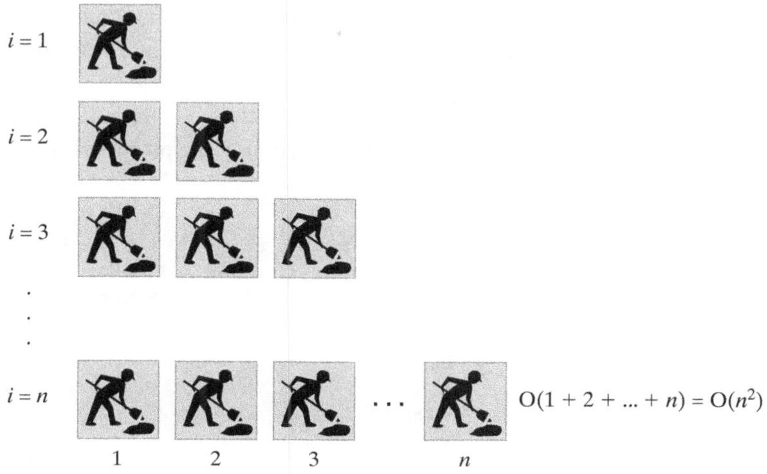

$i = 1$

$i = 2$

$i = 3$

 .
 .
 .

$i = n$     ...  O($1 + 2 + ... + n$) = O($n^2$)

    1  2  3   $n$

**FIGURE 4-8** Another O($n^2$) algorithm

```
for i = 1 to n
{   for j = 1 to n
        sum = sum + 1
}
```

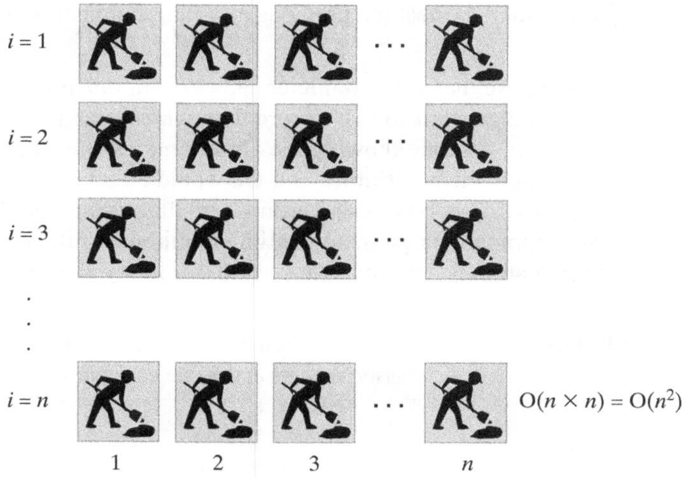

$i = 1$     ...

$i = 2$     ...

$i = 3$     ...

 .
 .
 .

$i = n$   ...  O($n \times n$) = O($n^2$)

    1  2  3   $n$

**Question 5** Using Big Oh notation, what is the order of the following computation's time requirement?

```
for i = 1 to n
{
    for j = 1 to 5
        sum = sum + 1
}
```

**4.21**   Let's get a feel for the growth-rate functions in Figure 4-4. As we mentioned, the time requirement for an O(1) algorithm is independent of the problem size $n$. We can apply such an algorithm to larger and larger problems without affecting the execution time. This situation is ideal, but not typical.

For other orders, what happens if we double the problem size? The time requirement for an O(log $n$) algorithm will change, but not by much. An O($n$) algorithm will need twice the time, an O($n^2$) algorithm will need four times the time, and an O($n^3$) algorithm will need eight times the time. Doubling the problem size for an O($2n$) algorithm squares the time requirement. Figure 4-9 tabulates these observations.

**FIGURE 4-9**   The effect of doubling the problem size on an algorithm's time requirement

| Growth-Rate Function for Size $n$ Problems | Growth-Rate Function for Size $2n$ Problems | Effect on Time Requirement |
|---|---|---|
| 1 | 1 | None |
| log $n$ | 1 + log $n$ | Negligible |
| $n$ | $2n$ | Doubles |
| $n$ log $n$ | $2n$ log $n$ + $2n$ | Doubles and then adds $2n$ |
| $n^2$ | $(2n)^2$ | Quadruples |
| $n^3$ | $(2n)^3$ | Multiplies by 8 |
| $2^n$ | $2^{2n}$ | Squares |

**Question 6**  Suppose that you can solve a problem of a certain size on a given computer in time $t$ by using an O($n$) algorithm. If you double the size of the problem, how fast must your computer be to solve the problem in the same time?

**Question 7**  Repeat the previous question, but instead use an O($n^2$) algorithm.

**4.22**   Now suppose that your computer can perform one million operations per second. How long will it take an algorithm to solve a problem whose size is one million? We cannot answer this question exactly without knowing the algorithm, but the computations in Figure 4-10 will give you a sense of how the algorithm's Big Oh would affect our answer. An O(log $n$) algorithm would take a fraction of a second, whereas an O($2n$) algorithm would take many trillions of years! Note that these computations estimate the time requirement of an O($g(n)$) algorithm as $g(n)$. Although this approximation is not universally valid, for many algorithms it is reasonable.

**FIGURE 4-10**   The time required to process one million items by algorithms of various orders at the rate of one million operations per second

| Growth-Rate Function $g$ | $g(10^6) / 10^6$ |
|---|---|
| log $n$ | 0.0000199 seconds |
| $n$ | 1 second |
| $n$ log $n$ | 19.9 seconds |
| $n^2$ | 11.6 days |
| $n^3$ | 31,709.8 years |
| $2^n$ | $10^{301,016}$ years |

**Note:**  You can use $O(n^2)$, $O(n^3)$, or even $O(2^n)$ algorithms as long as your problem size is small. For example, at the rate of one million operations per second, an $O(n^2)$ algorithm would take one second to solve a problem whose size is 1000. An $O(n^3)$ algorithm would take one second to solve a problem whose size is 100. And an $O(2^n)$ algorithm would take about one second to solve a problem whose size is 20.

**Question 8** The following algorithm discovers whether an array contains duplicate entries within its first $n$ elements. What is the Big Oh of this algorithm in the worst case?

*Algorithm* hasDuplicates(array, n)
for index = 0 *to* n - 2
    for rest = index + 1 *to* n - 1
        if (array[index] *equals* array[rest])
            return true
return false

# The Efficiency of Implementations of the ADT Bag

We now consider the time efficiency of two of the implementations of the ADT bag that we discussed in previous chapters.

## An Array-Based Implementation

One of the implementations of the ADT bag given in Chapter 2 used a fixed-size array to represent the bag's entries. We can now assess the efficiency of the bag operations when implemented in this way.

**4.23**    **Adding an entry to a bag.** Let's begin with the operation that adds a new entry to a bag. Segment 2.15 in Chapter 2 provided the following implementation for this operation:

VideoNote

Comparing ADT bag
implementations

```
public boolean add(T newEntry)
{
    checkInitialization();
    boolean result = true;
    if (isArrayFull())
    {
        result = false;
    }
    else
    {  // Assertion: result is true here
        bag[numberOfEntries] = newEntry;
        numberOfEntries++;
    } // end if

    return result;
} // end add
```

Each step in this method—checking whether initialization is complete, detecting whether the bag is full, assigning a new entry to an array element, and incrementing the length—is an $O(1)$ operation. It follows then that this method is $O(1)$. Intuitively, since the method adds the new entry right after the last entry in the array, we know the index of the array element that will contain the new entry. Thus, we can make this assignment independently of any other entries in the bag.

4.24   **Searching a bag for a given entry.** The ADT bag has a method `contains` that detects whether a bag contains a given entry. The array-based implementation of the method, as given in Segment 2.32 of Chapter 2, is:

```java
public boolean contains(T anEntry)
{
   checkInitialization();
   return getIndexOf(anEntry) > -1;
} // end contains
```

The execution time of `checkInitialization` is independent of the number of entries in the bag, and so is O(1). By calling the private method `getIndexOf`, the method locates the first array element, if any, that contains the entry we seek. Let's examine `getIndexOf`, as described in Segment 2.31 of Chapter 2:

```java
private int getIndexOf(T anEntry)
{
   int where = -1;
   boolean found = false;
   int index = 0;
   while (!found && (index < numberOfEntries))
   {
      if (anEntry.equals(bag[index]))
      {
         found = true;
         where = index;
      } // end if
      index++;
   } // end while
   return where;
} // end getIndexOf
```

This method searches the array bag for the given entry `anEntry`. The basic operation for the method is comparison. As we described earlier in Segment 4.10, the method would make one comparison in the best case and *n* comparisons in the worst case, assuming that the bag contains *n* entries. Typically, the method would make about *n* / 2 comparisons. We can conclude that the method `contains` is O(1) in the best case and O(*n*) in both the worst and average cases.

 **Note:** To simplify our example, we have considered a fixed-size array. Typically, an array-based bag resizes the array as needed. Doubling the size of an array is an O(*n*) operation. As Segment 2.38 of Chapter 2 noted, the next *n* additions would share the cost of this doubling.

 **Question 9** What is the Big Oh of the bag's `remove` methods? Assume that a fixed-size array represents the bag, and use an argument similar to the one we just made for `contains`.

**Question 10** Repeat Question 9, but instead analyze the method `getFrequencyOf`.

**Question 11** Repeat Question 9, but instead analyze the method `toArray`.

## A Linked Implementation

**4.25**    **Adding an entry to a bag.** Now consider a linked implementation of the ADT bag as given in Chapter 3. Let's begin with Segment 3.12 and the method add that adds an entry to a bag:

```java
public boolean add(T newEntry) // OutOfMemoryError possible
{
    // Add to beginning of chain:
    Node newNode = new Node(newEntry);
    newNode.next = firstNode;     // Make new node reference rest of chain
                                  // (firstNode is null if chain is empty)
    firstNode = newNode;          // New node is at beginning of chain
    numberOfEntries++;

    return true;
} // end add
```

All of the statements in this method represent $O(1)$ operations, and so the method is $O(1)$.

**4.26**    **Searching a bag for a given entry.** The method contains, given in Segment 3.17 of Chapter 3, searches a chain of nodes for a given entry:

```java
public boolean contains(T anEntry)
{
    boolean found = false;
    Node currentNode = firstNode;

    while (!found && (currentNode != null))
    {
        if (anEntry.equals(currentNode.data))
            found = true;
        else
            currentNode = currentNode.next;
    } // end while

    return found;
} // end contains
```

The best case occurs when the desired entry is in the first node of the chain of nodes. Since the method has a reference to the chain's first node, no traversal is needed. Thus, the method is $O(1)$ in this case.

In the worst case, the traversal of the chain continues to the last node. The operation is $O(n)$ in this case. Finally, in the typical, or average, case, the traversal would examine $n / 2$ nodes, making it an $O(n)$ operation.

**Note: Searching a bag that has a linked implementation**
Searching for an item that is at the beginning of a chain of nodes is an $O(1)$ operation. It takes the least time of any search of the chain, making this case the best case. If the item is in the last node of the chain, searching for it is $O(n)$. This search takes the most time among the searches for an item that is in one of the nodes, and so this is the worst case. The actual time required to find an entry in a chain of nodes depends on which node contains it.

**Question 12** What is the Big Oh of the method `contains` when it searches for an entry that is not in the bag? Assume that a chain of linked nodes represents the bag.

**Question 13** What is the Big Oh of the bag's `remove` methods? Assume that a chain of linked nodes represents the bag, and use an argument similar to the one you just made for `contains`.

**Question 14** Repeat Question 13, but instead analyze the method `getFrequencyOf`.

**Question 15** Repeat Question 13, but instead analyze the method `toArray`.

## Comparing the Implementations

4.27    Using Big Oh notation, Figure 4-11 summarizes the time complexities of the operations of the ADT bag for the implementations that use a fixed-size array and a chain of linked nodes. For some operations, multiple time requirements indicate the best, worst, and average cases.

**FIGURE 4-11**    The time efficiencies of the ADT bag operations for two implementations, expressed in Big Oh notation

| Operation | Fixed-Size Array | Linked |
|---|---|---|
| add(newEntry) | O(1) | O(1) |
| remove() | O(1) | O(1) |
| remove(anEntry) | O(1), O(n), O(n) | O(1), O(n), O(n) |
| clear() | O(n) | O(n) |
| getFrequencyOf(anEntry) | O(n) | O(n) |
| contains(anEntry) | O(1), O(n), O(n) | O(1), O(n), O(n) |
| toArray() | O(n) | O(n) |
| getCurrentSize(), isEmpty() | O(1) | O(1) |

As you can see, all of the operations have the same Big Oh for both implementations. This phenomenon is unusual, but it reflects the simplicity of the ADT bag. Subsequent ADTs will have at least some operations whose time efficiencies differ according to their implementations.

## CHAPTER SUMMARY

- An algorithm's complexity is described in terms of the time and space required to execute it.

- An algorithm's time requirement $f(n)$ is of order at most $g(n)$—that is, $f(n)$ is $O(g(n))$—if positive constants $c$ and $N$ exist such that $f(n) \leq c \times g(n)$ for all $n \geq N$.

- The relationships among typical growth-rate functions are as follows:
  $1 < \log(\log n) < \log n < \log^2 n < n < n \log n < n^2 < n^3 < 2n < n!$

- The time complexity of an ADT bag operation is the same for the fixed-size array implementation and the linked implementation. This situation is atypical of ADTs but reflects the details of the implementations that are possible due to the nature of a bag.

EXERCISES

1. Using Big Oh notation, indicate the time requirement of each of the following tasks in the worst case. Describe any assumptions that you make.

    a. After entering the classroom, you give chocolates to every student there.
    b. Every student in the classroom gifts a pencil to every other student.
    c. You visit all the classrooms in the school.
    d. You jump from a wall.
    e. After entering a room, you press a switch to turn on the fan.
    f. You turn on the fans of all the rooms in a house.
    g. You read an article thrice.

2. Describe a way to visit each classroom in a line of classrooms in time that is no better than $O(n)$.

3. Using Big Oh notation, indicate the time requirement of each of the following tasks in the worst case.

    a. Display all the characters in an array-based bag of characters.
    b. Display all the characters in an array-based bag in the reverse order.
    c. Display the $n^{th}$ character in an array-based bag of characters.
    d. Compute the product of the first $n$ odd integers in an array-based bag of integers.

4. By using the definition of Big Oh, show that

    a. $7n^4 + 2$ is $O(n^4)$
    b. $9^n + 2n^4$ is $O(9^n)$
    c. $n^5 + 5n^3 + 1$ is $O(n^5)$
    d. $12n^2 + 6$ is $O(n^2)$

5. Algorithm 1 requires $3n^2 + 9$ operations, and Algorithm 2 requires $n^2 + 2n$ operations. What can you conclude about the time requirements for these algorithms when $n$ is small and when $n$ is large? Which is the slower algorithm in these two cases?

6. By using appropriate identities, show that $7n^4 + 2n^3 + n^2 + 11$ is $O(n^4)$.

7. If $f(n)$ is $\Omega(g(n))$ and $g(n)$ is $\Omega(h(n))$, use the definition of Big Omega to show that $f(n)$ is $\Omega(h(n))$.

8. Segment 4.9 and the chapter summary showed the relationships among typical growth-rate functions. Indicate where the following growth-rate functions belong in this ordering:

    a. $n^2 \log n$
    b. $\sqrt{n}$
    c. $n^2 / \log n$
    d. $3^n$

9. Show that $15n^2 + 9n^4 + 3n^8$ is not $O(n^4)$.

10. What is the Big Oh of the following computation?
```
int product = 1;
for (int counter = n; counter > 0; counter = counter / 2)
        product = product * counter;
```

11. What is the Big Oh of the following computation?
```
int product = 1;
for (int counter = 1; counter < n - 1; counter = counter * 5)
        product = product * counter;
```

**12.** Suppose that your implementation of a particular algorithm appears in Java as follows:

```java
for (int pass = 100; pass >= 5; pass--)
{
   for (int index = 1; index < 2n; index++)
   {
      for (int count = 1000; count > 2; count = count / 2)
      {
         . . .
      } // end for
   } // end for
} // end for
```

The algorithm involves an array of *n* items. The previous code shows the only repetition in the algorithm, but it does not show the computations that occur within the loops. These computations, however, are independent of *n*. What is the order of the algorithm?

**13.** Repeat the previous exercise, but replace 100 with *n* in the outer loop.

**14.** What is the Big Oh of method1? Is there a best case and a worst case?

```java
public static void method1(int[] array, int n)
{
   for (int index = 0; index < n - 1; index--)
   {
      int mark = privateMethod1(array, index, n - 1);
      int temp = array[index];
      array[index] = array[mark];
      array[mark] = temp;
   } // end for
} // end method1

public static int privateMethod1(int[] array, int first, int last)
{
   int max = array[first];
   int indexOfMax = first;
   for (int index = last; index > first; index--)
   {
      if (array[index] > max)
      {
         max = array[index];
         indexOfMax = index;
      } // end if
   } // end for

   return indexOfMax;
} // end privateMethod1
```

**15.** What is the Big Oh of method2? Is there a best case and a worst case?

```java
public static boolean method2(int[] array, int n, int key)
{
   int indexOfKey = -1;
   for (int index = 1; index <= n - 1; index++)
   {
      if (array[index] == key)
         indexOfKey = index;
   }
   if (indexOfKey ≥ 0)
         return true;
   else
         return false;
} // end privateMethod2
```

**16.** Consider two programs, 1 and 2. Program 1 requires $9n + 50$ operations and Program 2 requires $n^3$ operations. For which values of $n$ will Program 1 execute faster than Program 2?

**17.** Consider four programs—A, B, C, and D—that have the following performances:

A: $O(n)$
B: $O(n^3)$
C: $O(nm)$
D: $O(n^4)$

If each program requires 50 seconds to solve a problem of size 10000, estimate the time required by each program for a problem of size 20000.

**18.** Suppose that you have a dictionary whose words are not sorted in alphabetical order. As a function of the number, $n$, of words, what is the time complexity of searching for a particular word in this dictionary?

**19.** Repeat the previous exercise for a dictionary whose words are sorted alphabetically. Compare your results with those for the previous exercise.

**20.** Consider a principal who goes the rounds in the school everyday. He starts from his office and walks to the first classroom and then back to his office, then he walks to the second classroom and back to his office, then to the third classroom and back to his office, and so on until he has visited all the 12 classrooms of the school and returned to his office. Assume that the distances between the classrooms are uniform.

   **a.** What is the total distance that he walks?
   **b.** What is the total distance that he walks if he visits $n$ classrooms instead of 12 classrooms?
   **c.** How does the total distance he walks compare to that of a teacher who simply starts from the office and walks directly to the twelfth classroom?

**21.** Consider the following definition of a sequence $A$ of positive integers:

$$A_{i+1} = \begin{cases} A_i/2 \text{ if } A_i \text{ is even} \\ 3A_i - 1 \text{ if } A_i \text{ is odd} \end{cases}$$

If $A_0$ has some value $v$, give a Big Oh expression for the

   **a.** Minimum value
   **b.** Maximum value

that $A_k$ can have in terms of $k$ and $v$.

**22.** Chapter 3 describes an implementation of the ADT bag that uses a chain of linked nodes. Of the following operations, which ones have a constant growth-rate function: `add`, `remove`, `contains`?

**23.** Exercise 13 of Chapter 2 describes an implementation of the ADT bag that shrinks an array as objects are removed from the bag. Using Big Oh notation, derive the time complexity of the method `isTooBig`.

**24.** Consider an array of length $n$ containing unique integers in random order and in the range 1 to $n + 1$. For example, an array of length 5 would contain 5 unique integers selected randomly from the integers 1 through 6. Thus, the array might contain 3 6 5 1 4. Of the integers 1 through 6, notice that the 2 was not chosen and is not in the array. Write Java code that finds the integer that does not appear in such an array. Your solution should use

   **a.** $O(n^2)$ operations
   **b.** $O(n)$ operations

**25.** Consider an array of length $n$ containing positive and negative integers in random order. Write Java code that rearranges the integers so that the negative integers appear before the positive integers. Your solution should use

   **a.** $O(n^2)$ operations
   **b.** $O(n)$ operations

## PROJECTS

For the following projects, you should know how to time a section of code in Java. One approach is to use the class `java.util.Date`. A `Date` object contains the time at which it was constructed. This time is stored as a `long` integer equal to the number of milliseconds that have passed since 00:00:00.000 GMT on January 1, 1970. By subtracting the starting time in milliseconds from the ending time in milliseconds, you get the run time—in milliseconds—of a section of code.

For example, suppose that `thisMethod` is the name of a method you wish to time. The following statements will compute the number of milliseconds that `thisMethod` requires to execute:

```
Date current = new Date();          // Get current time
long startTime = current.getTime();
thisMethod();                        // Code to be timed
current = new Date();                // Get current time
long stopTime = current.getTime();
long elapsedTime = stopTime - startTime;   // Milliseconds
```

1. Write a Java program that implements the three algorithms in Figure 4-1 and times them for various values of *n*. The program should display a table of the run times of each algorithm for various values of *n*.

2. Consider the following two loops:

```
// Loop A
for (i = 1; i <= n; i++)
    for (j = 1; j <= 10000; j++)
        sum = sum + j;

// Loop B
for (i = 1; i <= n; i++)
    for (j = 1; j <= n; j++)
        sum = sum + j;
```

Although Loop A is $O(n)$ and Loop B is $O(n^2)$, Loop B can be faster than Loop A for small values of *n*. Design and implement an experiment to find a value of *n* for which Loop B is faster.

3. Repeat the previous project, but use the following for Loop B:

```
// Loop B
for (i = 1; i <= n; i++)
    for (j = 1; j <= n; j++)
        for (k = 1; k <= n; k++)
            sum = sum + k;
```

4. Segment 2.12 of Chapter 2 gave the definition of the method `toArray` for the ADT bag, as follows:

```
public T[] toArray()
{
    // The cast is safe because the new array contains null entries.
    @SuppressWarnings("unchecked")
    T[] result = (T[])new Object[numberOfEntries]; // Unchecked cast
    for (int index = 0; index < numberOfEntries; index++)
    {
        result[index] = bag[index];
    } // end for

    return result;
} // end toArray
```

An alternate definition calls the method `Arrays.copyOf` and appears as follows:

```java
public T[] toArray()
{
   return Arrays.copyOf(bag, bag.length);
} // end toArray
```

Compare the execution times of these two methods for bags of various sizes.

5.  Suppose that you have several numbered billiard balls on a pool table. At each step you remove a billiard ball from the table. If the ball removed is numbered $n$, you replace it with $n$ balls whose number is $n / 2$, where the division is truncated to an integer. For example, if you remove the 5 ball, you replace it with five 2 balls. Write a program that simulates this process. Use a bag of positive integers to represent the balls on the pool table.

    Using Big Oh notation, predict the time requirement for this algorithm when the initial bag contains only the value $n$. Then time the actual execution of the program for various values of $n$ and plot its performance as a function of $n$.

6.  Repeat the previous project, but instead replace the $n$ ball with $n$ balls randomly numbered less than $n$.

7.  In mythology, the Hydra was a monster with many heads. Every time the hero chopped off a head, two smaller heads would grow in its place. Fortunately for the hero, if the head was small enough, he could chop it off without two more growing in its place. To kill the Hydra, all our hero needed to do was to chop off all the heads.

    Write a program that simulates the Hydra. Instead of heads, we will use strings. A bag of strings, then, represents the Hydra. Every time you remove a string from the bag, delete the first letter of the string and put two copies of the remaining string back into the bag. For example, if you remove *HYDRA*, you add two copies of *YDRA* to the bag. If you remove a one-letter word, you add nothing to the bag. To begin, read one word from the keyboard and place it into an empty bag. The Hydra dies when the bag becomes empty.

    Using Big Oh notation, predict the time requirement for this algorithm in terms of the number $n$ of characters in the initial string. Then time the actual execution of the program for various values of $n$ and plot its performance as a function of $n$.

## ANSWERS TO SELF-TEST QUESTIONS

1.  If you follow the hint given in the question, you will get the sum of $n$ occurrences of $n + 1$, which is $(n + 1) + (n + 1) + \ldots + (n + 1)$. This sum is simply the product $n (n + 1)$. To get this sum, we added $1 + 2 + \ldots + n$ to itself. Thus, $n(n + 1)$ is $2 (1 + 2 + \ldots + n)$. The desired conclusion follows immediately from this fact.

2.  Algorithm A: The loop iterates $n$ times, so there are $n$ additions and a total of $n + 1$ assignments. We ignore the assignments.
    Algorithm B: For each value of $i$, the inner loop iterates $i$ times, and so performs $i$ additions and $i$ assignments. The outer loop iterates $n$ times. Together, the loops perform $1 + 2 + \ldots + n$ additions and the same number of assignments. Using the identity given in Question 1, the number of additions is $n (n + 1) / 2$. The additional assignment to set `sum` to zero makes the total number of assignments equal to $1 + n (n + 1) / 2$, which we ignore.

3.  $3n^2 + 2n < 2n + 2n = 2 \times 2n$ when $n \geq 8$. So $3n^2 + 2n = O(2n)$, using $c = 2$ and $N = 8$.

4.  $n^k$.

5.  The inner loop requires a constant amount of time, and so it is $O(1)$. The outer loop is $O(n)$, and so the entire computation is $O(n)$.

**6.** Twice as fast.

**7.** Four times as fast.

**8.** Let's tabulate the maximum number of times the inner loop executes for various values of index:

| index | Inner Loop Iterations |
|-------|----------------------|
| 0 | $n - 1$ |
| 1 | $n - 2$ |
| 2 | $n - 3$ |
| . . . | . . . |
| $n - 2$ | 1 |

As you can see, the maximum number of times the inner loop executes is $1 + 2 + \ldots + n - 1$, which is $n(n-1)/2$. Thus, the algorithm is $O(n^2)$ in the worst case.

**9.** Removing an unspecified entry is $O(1)$. Removing a particular entry is $O(1)$ in the best case and $O(n)$ in the worst and average cases.

**10.** $O(n)$.

**11.** $O(n)$.

**12.** $O(n)$.

**13.** Removing an unspecified entry is $O(1)$. Removing a particular entry is $O(1)$ in the best case and $O(n)$ in the worst and average cases.

**14.** $O(n)$.

**15.** $O(n)$.

# Stacks

## Contents

## Prerequisites

## Objectives

After studying this chapter, you should be able to
- Describe the operations of the ADT stack
- Use a stack to decide whether the delimiters in an algebraic expression are paired correctly
- Use a stack to convert an infix expression to a postfix expression
- Use a stack to evaluate a postfix expression
- Use a stack to evaluate an infix expression
- Use a stack in a program
- Describe how the Java run-time environment uses a stack to track the execution of methods

In everyday life, a stack is a familiar thing. You might see a stack of books on your desk, a stack of dishes in the cafeteria, a stack of towels in the linen closet, or a stack of boxes in the attic. When you add an item to a stack, you place it on top of the stack. When you remove an item, you take the topmost one. This topmost item is the last one that was added to the stack. So when you remove an item, you remove the item added most recently. That is, the last item added to the stack is the first one removed.

VideoNote
The ADT stack

In spite of our examples of a stack, everyday life usually does not follow this **last-in, first-out**, or **LIFO**, behavior. Although the employee hired most recently is often the first one fired during a layoff, we live in a first-come, first-served society. In the computer science world, however, last-in, first-out is exactly the behavior required by many important algorithms. These algorithms often use the abstract data type stack, which is an ADT that exhibits a last-in, first-out behavior. For example, a compiler uses a stack to interpret the meaning of an algebraic expression, and a run-time environment uses a stack when executing a recursive method.

This chapter describes the ADT stack and provides several examples of its use.

## Specifications of the ADT Stack

**5.1**    The ADT **stack** organizes its entries according to the order in which they were added. All additions are to one end of the stack called the **top**. The **top entry**—that is, the entry at the top—is thus the newest item among the items currently in a stack. Figure 5-1 shows some stacks that should be familiar to you.

FIGURE 5-1        Some familiar stacks

 **Note:** Among the items currently in a stack, the one added most recently is at the top of the stack. (Other items might have been added to the stack more recently and then removed.)

The stack restricts access to its entries. A client can look at or remove only the top entry. The only way to look at an entry that is not at the top of the stack is to repeatedly remove items from the stack until the desired item reaches the top. If you were to remove all of a stack's entries, one by one, you would get them in reverse chronological order, beginning with the most recent and ending with the first item added to the stack.

**5.2**    The operation that adds an entry to a stack is traditionally called push. The remove operation is pop. The operation that retrieves the top entry without removing it is named peek. Typically, you cannot search a stack[1] for a particular entry. The following specifications define a set of operations for the ADT stack.

---

1. However, the Java Class Library has a class of stacks that does define a search method, as you will see later in this chapter.

| ABSTRACT DATA TYPE: STACK | | |
|---|---|---|

**DATA**

- A collection of objects in reverse chronological order and having the same data type

**OPERATIONS**

| PSEUDOCODE | UML | DESCRIPTION |
|---|---|---|
| push(newEntry) | +push(newEntry: T): void | Task: Adds a new entry to the top of the stack.<br>Input: newEntry is the new entry.<br>Output: None. |
| pop() | +pop(): T | Task: Removes and returns the stack's top entry.<br>Input: None.<br>Output: Returns the stack's top entry. Throws an exception if the stack is empty before the operation. |
| peek() | +peek(): T | Task: Retrieves the stack's top entry without changing the stack in any way.<br>Input: None.<br>Output: Returns the stack's top entry. Throws an exception if the stack is empty. |
| isEmpty() | +isEmpty(): boolean | Task: Detects whether the stack is empty.<br>Input: None.<br>Output: Returns true if the stack is empty. |
| clear() | +clear(): void | Task: Removes all entries from the stack.<br>Input: None.<br>Output: None. |

**Design Decision: What should pop and peek do when the stack is empty?**

Clients really should not call methods, such as pop and peek, that attempt to remove or retrieve entries from an ADT when the ADT is empty. Even so, these methods must behave reasonably in this case. We consider three possible actions by such methods:

- Assume that the ADT is not empty; that is, honor a precondition making this assumption.
- Return null.
- Throw an exception.

The first option is reasonable for private methods, since they are invoked only by other methods within the same class. Thus, you—as the programmer of the class—can ensure that a private method's preconditions are met before calling it. The private method in turn is called by code it can trust—that is, by another method from the same class—and so it can assume its preconditions have been met.

The stack methods pop and peek are public; we cannot trust the client to honor any preconditions required by these methods. Therefore, the first option is not a viable choice. Instead, these methods must assume that the stack might be empty and guard against this situation.

If we want that method to return a value that signals a problem, such as an empty ADT, the value must have the return type of the method. Since there is no entry to remove from the ADT, it is natural to return null. This choice is fine as long as the ADT does not permit null entries, since null must clearly indicate a lack of anything in the ADT to return. However, we want the ADT stack to permit null values as valid entries. Therefore, the meaning of null as a return value is ambiguous: A client would not know whether null is a data entry in the ADT or an indication of an empty ADT without the extra work of calling isEmpty. Requiring a client to call a second method to interpret another method's actions either can lead to misinterpretation of a method's actions or exposes the code to the same situation as a precondition. Note that most of the ADTs in this textbook permit null values as valid entries in a data collection.

We are left with throwing an exception when a stack is empty. For this design, a return value of null will be considered valid data.

**Security Note: Trust**

The previous design decision talked about trust. Can you trust a piece of code? No, unless you prove that it behaves correctly and securely, in which case it becomes **trusted code**. Can you trust a client to use your software in a certain manner, thereby honoring any and all preconditions and correctly interpreting return codes? No. However, a private method in a class can reliably assume, or trust, that its precondition will be honored and its return value will be treated correctly.

**Design Decision: What kind of exception should pop and peek throw when the stack is empty: checked or runtime?**

In general, a method should throw a checked exception if its client can reasonably recover from the exception at execution time. In this case, the client can either deal with the exception directly or propagate it to another method. On the other hand, if you consider the exception to indicate a misuse of your method—that is, a mistake by the programmer using your method—the method should throw a runtime exception. A runtime exception need not —but could—be declared in a throws clause and need not—but could—be caught by the client.

We consider calling pop or peek when a stack is empty to be a mistake by the client. Thus, we throw a runtime exception. If, however, an application can recover from this occurrence, it can catch the exception and deal with it.

**Note: Alternate names for methods**

It is not unusual for a class designer to include aliases for certain methods. For example, you could include the additional methods add and remove (or insert and delete) in the ADT stack to mean push and pop. Moreover, pull is sometimes used to mean pop, and getTop can mean peek, so including them as aliases is reasonable.

**5.3**   The Java interface in Listing 5-1 specifies a stack of objects. The generic type T—which represents any class type—is the data type of the items in the stack. Note that `EmptyStackException` is a runtime exception that is in the package `java.util` of the Java Class Library.

---

**LISTING 5-1   An interface for the ADT stack**

```java
public interface StackInterface<T>
{
   /** Adds a new entry to the top of this stack.
       @param newEntry  An object to be added to the stack. */
   public void push(T newEntry);

   /** Removes and returns this stack's top entry.
       @return  The object at the top of the stack.
       @throws  EmptyStackException if the stack is empty before
       the operation. */
   public T pop();

   /** Retrieves this stack's top entry.
       @return  The object at the top of the stack.
       @throws  EmptyStackException if the stack is empty. */
   public T peek();

   /** Detects whether this stack is empty.
       @return  True if the stack is empty. */
   public boolean isEmpty();

   /** Removes all entries from this stack. */
   public void clear();
} // end StackInterface
```

---

**5.4**   **Example: Demonstrating the stack methods.** The following statements add, retrieve, and remove strings from a stack. We assume that the class `OurStack` implements `StackInterface` and is available for our use.

```java
StackInterface<String> stringStack = new OurStack<>();
stringStack.push("Jim");
stringStack.push("Jess");
stringStack.push("Jill");
stringStack.push("Jane");
stringStack.push("Joe");

String top = stringStack.peek(); // Returns "Joe"
System.out.println(top + " is at the top of the stack.");

top = stringStack.pop();         // Removes and returns "Joe"
System.out.println(top + " is removed from the stack.");

top = stringStack.peek();        // Returns "Jane"
System.out.println(top + " is at the top of the stack.");

top = stringStack.pop();         // Removes and returns "Jane"
System.out.println(top + " is removed from the stack.");
```

Parts *a* through *e* of Figure 5-2 show five additions to the stack. At this point, the stack contains—from top to bottom—the strings *Joe, Jane, Jill, Jess*, and *Jim*. The string at the top of the stack is *Joe*; peek retrieves it. The method pop retrieves *Joe* again and then removes it (Figure 5-2f). A subsequent call to peek retrieves *Jane*. Then pop retrieves *Jane* and removes it (Figure 5-2g).

Three more calls to pop would remove *Jill*, *Jess*, and *Jim*, leaving the stack empty. A subsequent call to either pop or peek would throw an EmptyStackException.

---

**FIGURE 5-2**    A stack of strings after (a) push adds *Jim*; (b) push adds *Jess*; (c) push adds *Jill*; (d) push adds *Jane*; (e) push adds *Joe*; (f) pop retrieves and removes *Joe*; (g) pop retrieves and removes *Jane*

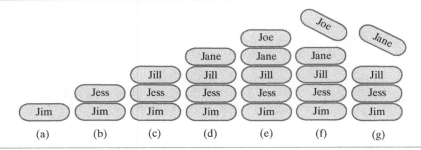

**Security Note:  Design guidelines**

- Use preconditions and postconditions to document assumptions.
- Do not trust that a client will use public methods correctly.
- Avoid ambiguous return values.
- Prefer throwing exceptions instead of returning values to signal a problem.

---

**Question 1** After the following statements execute, what string is at the top of the stack and what string is at the bottom?

```
StackInterface<String> stringStack = new OurStack<>();
stringStack.push("Jim");
stringStack.push("Jess");
stringStack.pop();
stringStack.push("Jill");
stringStack.push("Jane");
stringStack.pop();
```

**Question 2** Consider the stack that was created in Question 1, and define a new empty stack nameStack.

a. Write a loop that pops the strings from stringStack and pushes them onto nameStack.
b. Describe the contents of the stacks stringStack and nameStack when the loop that you just wrote completes its execution.

---

# Using a Stack to Process Algebraic Expressions

5.5    In mathematics, an algebraic expression is composed of operands that are variables or constants and operators, such as + and *. We will use the Java notation +, -, *, and / to indicate addition, subtraction, multiplication, and division. We will use ∧ to indicate exponentiation, with the warning that Java has no operator for exponentiation; in Java ∧ is the exclusive-or operator.

Operators generally have two operands, and so are called **binary operators**. For example, the + in $a + b$ is a binary operator. The operators + and - can also be **unary operators** when they have one operand. For example, the minus sign in -5 is a unary operator.

When an algebraic expression has no parentheses, operations occur in a certain order. Exponentiations occur first; they take **precedence** over the other operations. Next, multiplications and divisions occur, and then additions and subtractions. For example, the expression

20 - 2 * 2 ∧ 3

evaluates as 20 - 2 * 8, then as 20 - 16, and finally as 4.

But what happens when two or more adjacent operators have the same precedence? Exponentiations, such as those in $a ∧ b ∧ c$, occur right to left. Thus, $2 ∧ 2 ∧ 3$ means $2 ∧ (2 ∧ 3)$, or $2^8$, instead of $(2 ∧ 2) ∧ 3$, which is $4^3$. Other operations occur from left to right, such as the multiplication and division in $a * b / c$ or the addition and subtraction in $a - b + c$. Therefore, 8 - 4 + 2 means (8 - 4) + 2, or 6, instead of 8 - (4 + 2), which is 2. Parentheses in an expression override the normal operator precedence.

Ordinarily, we place a binary operator between its operands, as in $a + b$. An expression in this familiar notation is called an **infix expression**. Other notations are possible. For example, you could write a binary operator before its two operands. Thus, $a + b$ becomes + $a$ $b$. This expression is called a **prefix expression**. Or you could write a binary operator after its two operands, so $a + b$ becomes $a$ $b$ +. This expression is a **postfix expression**. Although infix expressions are more familiar to us, both prefix and postfix expressions are simpler to process because they do not use precedence rules or parentheses. The precedence of an operator in either a prefix expression or a postfix expression is implied by the order in which the operators and operands occur in the expression. We will learn more about these types of expressions later in this chapter.

Our first example looks at ordinary infix expressions.

**Note:  Algebraic expressions**
In an infix expression, each binary operator appears between its operands, as in $a + b$.
In a prefix expression, each binary operator appears before its operands, as in + $a$ $b$.
In a postfix expression, each binary operator appears after its operands, as in $a$ $b$ +.

**Note:**  The notation in a prefix expression is sometimes called **Polish notation**, because it was invented by the Polish mathematician Jan Lukasiewicz in the 1920s. The notation in a postfix expression is sometimes called **reverse Polish notation**.

## A Problem Solved: Checking for Balanced Delimiters in an Infix Algebraic Expression

Although programmers use parentheses when writing arithmetic expressions in Java, mathematicians use parentheses, square brackets, and braces for the same purpose. These delimiters must be paired correctly. For example, an open parenthesis must correspond to a close parenthesis. In addition, pairs of delimiters must not intersect. Thus, an expression can contain a sequence of delimiters such as

{ [ ( ) ( ) ] ( ) }

but not

[ ( ] )

For convenience, we will say that a **balanced expression** contains delimiters that are paired correctly, or are **balanced**.

We want an algorithm that detects whether an infix expression is balanced.

**5.6   Example: A balanced expression.** Let's see whether the expression

$$a \, \{b \, [c \, (d + e)/2 - f] + 1\}$$

is balanced. We scan the expression from left to right, looking for delimiters and ignoring any characters that are not delimiters. When we encounter an open delimiter, we must save it. When we find a close delimiter, we must see whether it corresponds to the most recently encountered open delimiter. If it does, we discard the open delimiter and continue scanning the expression. If we are able to scan the entire expression without a mismatch, the delimiters in the expression are balanced.

The ADT that enables us to store objects and then retrieve or remove the most recent one is a stack. Figure 5-3 shows the contents of a stack as we scan the previous expression. Since we ignore all characters that are not delimiters, it is sufficient for us to represent the expression here as

$$\{ \, [ \, ( \, ) \, ] \, \}$$

**FIGURE 5-3**   The contents of a stack during the scan of an expression that contains the balanced delimiters $\{ \, [ \, ( \, ) \, ] \, \}$

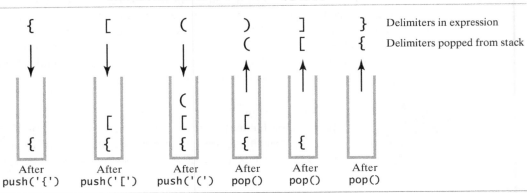

After pushing the first three open delimiters onto the stack, the open parenthesis is at the top of the stack. The next delimiter, the close parenthesis, pairs with the open parenthesis at the top of the stack. We pop the stack and continue by comparing the close bracket with the delimiter now at the top of the stack. They correspond, so we pop the stack again and continue by comparing the close brace with the top entry of the stack. These delimiters correspond, so we pop the stack. We have reached the end of the expression, and the stack is empty. Each open delimiter correctly corresponds to a close delimiter, so the delimiters are balanced.

**5.7   Examples: Unbalanced expressions.** Let's examine some expressions that contain unbalanced delimiters. Figure 5-4 shows a stack during the scan of an expression that contains the delimiters $\{ \, [ \, ( \, ] \, ) \, \}$. This is an example of intersecting pairs of delimiters. After we push the first three open delimiters onto the stack, the open parenthesis at the top of the stack does not correspond to the close bracket that comes next in the expression.

**FIGURE 5-4**    The contents of a stack during the scan of an expression that contains the unbalanced delimiters { [ ( ] ) }

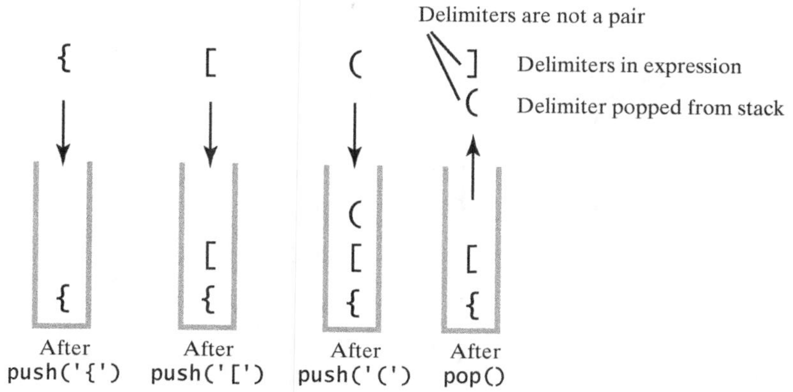

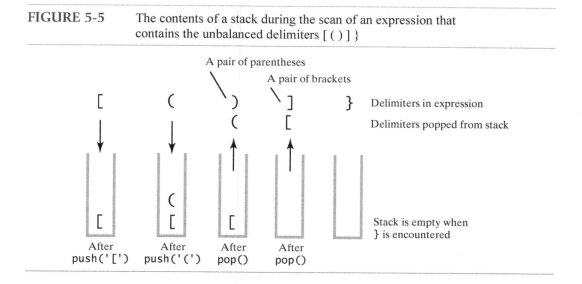

Figure 5-5 shows a stack during the scan of an expression that contains the unbalanced delimiters [ ( ) ] }. The close brace does not have a corresponding open brace. When we finally reach the close brace, the stack is empty. Since the stack does not contain an open brace, the delimiters are unbalanced.

**FIGURE 5-5**    The contents of a stack during the scan of an expression that contains the unbalanced delimiters [ ( ) ] }

Figure 5-6 shows a stack during the scan of an expression that contains the unbalanced delimiters { [ ( ) ]. The open brace does not have a corresponding close brace. When you reach the end of the expression, having processed the brackets and parentheses, the stack still contains the open brace. Since this delimiter is left over, the expression contains unbalanced delimiters.

FIGURE 5-6    The contents of a stack during the scan of an expression that
contains the unbalanced delimiters { [ ( ) ]

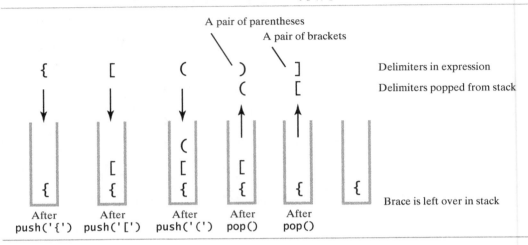

**5.8**    **The algorithm.** The previous discussion and figures reveal the paths that our algorithm must take. We formalize these observations in the following pseudocode:

*Algorithm* **checkBalance(expression)**
*// Returns true if the parentheses, brackets, and braces in an expression are paired correctly.*

```
isBalanced = true // The absence of delimiters is balanced
while ((isBalanced == true) and not at end of expression)
{
    nextCharacter = next character in expression
    switch (nextCharacter)
    {
        case '(': case '[': case '{':
            Push nextCharacter onto stack
            break
        case ')': case ']': case '}':
            if (stack is empty)
                isBalanced = false
            else
            {
                openDelimiter = top entry of stack
                Pop stack
                isBalanced = true or false according to whether openDelimiter and
                             nextCharacter are a pair of delimiters
            }
            break
    }
}

if (stack is not empty)
    isBalanced = false
return isBalanced
```

**5.9**    Let's examine this algorithm for each of the examples given in the previous figures. For the balanced expression in Figure 5-3, the while loop ends when the end of the expression is reached. The stack is empty, and isBalanced is true. For the expression in Figure 5-4, the loop ends when it finds that the close bracket does not correspond to the open parenthesis and sets the flag isBalanced to false. The fact that the stack is not empty does not affect the outcome of the algorithm.

With the expression in Figure 5-5, the loop ends at the close brace because the stack is empty and the flag isBalanced is set to false. Finally, with the expression in Figure 5-6, the loop ends at the end of the expression with isBalanced set to true. But the stack is not empty—it contains an open brace—so after the loop, isBalanced becomes false.

**Question 3** Show the contents of the stack as you trace the algorithm checkBalance, as given in Segment 5.8, for each of the following expressions. What does checkBalance return in each case?

    **a.**  $[a \{b / (c - d) + e/(f + g)\} - h]$
    **b.**  $\{a [b + (c + 2)/d] + e) + f\}$
    **c.**  $[a \{b + [c (d + e) - f] + g\}$

**5.10**  **Java implementation.** The class BalanceChecker, shown in Listing 5-2, implements our algorithm as the static method checkBalance. The method has one parameter, the expression as a string. We assume that the class OurStack implements StackInterface and is available. Since StackInterface specifies a stack of objects, but the previous algorithm uses a stack of characters, checkBalance uses the wrapper class Character to create objects suitable for the stack.

LISTING 5-2    The class BalanceChecker

```java
public class BalanceChecker
{
    /** Decides whether the parentheses, brackets, and braces
        in a string occur in left/right pairs.
        @param expression  A string to be checked.
        @return  True if the delimiters are paired correctly. */
    public static boolean checkBalance(String expression)
    {
        StackInterface<Character> openDelimiterStack = new OurStack<>();

        int characterCount = expression.length();
        boolean isBalanced = true;
        int index = 0;
        char nextCharacter = ' ';

        while (isBalanced && (index < characterCount))
        {
            nextCharacter = expression.charAt(index);
            switch (nextCharacter)
            {
                case '(': case '[': case '{':
                    openDelimiterStack.push(nextCharacter);
                    break;
                case ')': case ']': case '}':
                    if (openDelimiterStack.isEmpty())
                        isBalanced = false;
                    else
                    {
                        char openDelimiter = openDelimiterStack.pop();
                        isBalanced = isPaired(openDelimiter, nextCharacter);
                    } // end if
                    break;
```

```
33              default: break; // Ignore unexpected characters
34          } // end switch
35          index++;
36       } // end while
37
38       if (!openDelimiterStack.isEmpty())
39          isBalanced = false;
40       return isBalanced;
41    } // end checkBalance
42
43    // Returns true if the given characters, open and close, form a pair
44    // of parentheses, brackets, or braces.
45    private static boolean isPaired(char open, char close)
46    {
47       return (open == '(' && close == ')') ||
48              (open == '[' && close == ']') ||
49              (open == '{' && close == '}');
50    } // end isPaired
51 } // end BalanceChecker
```

The following statements provide an example of how you might use this class:

```
String expression = "a {b [c (d + e)/2 - f] + 1}";
boolean isBalanced = BalanceChecker.checkBalance(expression);
if (isBalanced)
   System.out.println(expression + " is balanced");
else
   System.out.println(expression + " is not balanced");
```

## A Problem Solved: Transforming an Infix Expression to a Postfix Expression

 Our ultimate goal is to show you how to evaluate infix algebraic expressions, but postfix expressions are easier to evaluate. So we first look at how to represent an infix expression by using postfix notation.

**5.11**   Recall that in a postfix expression, a binary operator follows its two operands. Here are a few examples of infix expressions and their corresponding postfix forms:

| Infix | Postfix |
|-------|---------|
| $a + b$ | $a\,b +$ |
| $(a + b) * c$ | $a\,b + c *$ |
| $a + b * c$ | $a\,b\,c * +$ |

Notice that the order of the operands $a$, $b$, and $c$ in an infix expression is the same in the corresponding postfix expression. However, the order of the operators might change. This order depends on the precedence of the operators and the existence of parentheses. As we mentioned, parentheses do not appear in a postfix expression.

**5.12**   **A pencil and paper scheme.** One way to determine where the operators should appear in a postfix expression begins with a fully parenthesized infix expression. For example, we write the infix expression $(a + b) * c$ as $((a + b) * c)$. By adding parentheses, we remove the expression's dependence on the rules of operator precedence. Each operator is now associated with a pair of parentheses. We now move each operator to the right so that it appears immediately before its associated close parenthesis to get $((a\ b\ +)\ c\ *)$. Finally, we remove the parentheses to obtain the postfix expression $a\ b + c\ *$.

This scheme should give you some understanding of the order of the operators in a postfix expression. It also can be useful when checking the results of a conversion algorithm. However, the algorithm that we will develop next is not based on this approach.

**Question 4** Using the previous scheme, convert each of the following infix expressions to postfix expressions:

   **a.**   $a + b * c$
   **b.**   $a * b\ /\ (c - d)$
   **c.**   $a\ /\ b + (c - d)$
   **d.**   $a\ /\ b + c - d$

**5.13**   **The basics of a conversion algorithm.** To convert an infix expression to postfix form, we scan the infix expression from left to right. When we encounter an operand, we place it at the end of the new expression that we are creating. Recall that operands in an infix expression remain in the same order in the corresponding postfix expression. When we encounter an operator, we must save it until we determine where in the output expression it belongs. For example, to convert the infix expression $a + b$, we append $a$ to the initially empty output expression, save +, and append $b$ to the output expression. We now need to retrieve the + and put it at the end of the output expression to get the postfix expression $a\ b +$. Retrieving the operator saved most recently is easy if we have saved it in a stack.

In this example, we saved the operator until we processed its second operand. In general, we hold the operator in a stack at least until we compare its precedence with that of the next operator. For example, to convert the expression $a + b * c$, we append $a$ to the output expression, push + onto a stack, and then append $b$ to the output. What we do now depends on the relative precedences of the next operator, *, and the + at the top of the stack. Since * has a greater precedence than +, $b$ is not the addition's second operand. Instead, the addition waits for the result of the multiplication. Thus, we push * onto the stack and append $c$ to the output expression. Having reached the end of the input expression, we now pop each operator from the stack and append it to the end of the output expression, getting the postfix expression $a\ b\ c * +$. Figure 5-7 illustrates these steps. The stack is shown horizontally; the leftmost element is at the bottom of the stack.

FIGURE 5-7      Converting the infix expression $a + b * c$ to postfix form

| Next Character in Infix Expression | Postfix Form | Operator Stack (bottom to top) |
|:---:|:---:|:---:|
| $a$ | $a$ | |
| + | $a$ | + |
| $b$ | $a\ b$ | + |
| * | $a\ b$ | + * |
| $c$ | $a\ b\ c$ | + * |
| | $a\ b\ c *$ | + |
| | $a\ b\ c * +$ | |

**5.14**   **Successive operators with the same precedence.** What if two successive operators have the same precedence? We need to distinguish between operators that have a left-to-right association—namely +, -, *, and /—and exponentiation, which has a right-to-left association. For example, consider the expression $a - b + c$. When we encounter the +, the stack will contain the operator - and the incomplete postfix expression will be $ab$. The subtraction operator belongs to the operands $a$ and $b$, so we pop the stack and append - to the end of the expression $ab$. Since the stack is empty, we push the + onto the stack. We then append $c$ to the result, and finally we pop the stack and append the +. The result is $a\ b - c +$. Figure 5-8a illustrates these steps.

Now consider the expression $a \wedge b \wedge c$. By the time we encounter the second exponentiation operator, the stack contains ∧, and the result so far is $ab$. As before, the current operator has the same precedence as the top entry of the stack. But since $a \wedge b \wedge c$ means $a \wedge (b \wedge c)$, we must push the second ∧ onto the stack, as Figure 5-8b shows.

---

**FIGURE 5-8**       Converting an infix expression to postfix form:
(a) $a - b + c$; (b) $a \wedge b \wedge c$

---

(a)

| Next Character in Infix Expression | Postfix Form | Operator Stack (bottom to top) |
|:---:|:---:|:---:|
| $a$ | $a$ | |
| $-$ | $a$ | $-$ |
| $b$ | $a\ b$ | $-$ |
| $+$ | $a\ b -$ | |
| | $a\ b -$ | $+$ |
| $c$ | $a\ b - c$ | $+$ |
| | $a\ b - c +$ | |

(b)

| Next Character in Infix Expression | Postfix Form | Operator Stack (bottom to top) |
|:---:|:---:|:---:|
| $a$ | $a$ | |
| $\wedge$ | $a$ | $\wedge$ |
| $b$ | $a\ b$ | $\wedge$ |
| $\wedge$ | $a\ b$ | $\wedge\ \wedge$ |
| $c$ | $a\ b\ c$ | $\wedge\ \wedge$ |
| | $a\ b\ c\ \wedge$ | $\wedge$ |
| | $a\ b\ c\ \wedge\ \wedge$ | |

---

**Question 5**  In general, when should you push an exponentiation operator ∧ onto the stack?

---

**5.15**   **Parentheses.** Parentheses override the rules of operator precedence. We always push an open parenthesis onto the stack. Once it is in the stack, we treat an open parenthesis as an operator with the lowest precedence. That is, any subsequent operator will get pushed onto the stack. When we encounter a close parenthesis, we pop operators from the stack and append them to the forming postfix expression until we pop an open parenthesis. The algorithm continues with no parentheses added to the postfix expression.

**Note:** **Infix-to-postfix conversion**
To convert an infix expression to postfix form, you take the following actions, according to the symbols you encounter, as you process the infix expression from left to right:

- Operand — Append each operand to the end of the output expression.
- Operator ∧ — Push ∧ onto the stack.
- Operator +, -, *, or / — Pop operators from the stack, appending them to the output expression, until the stack is empty or its top entry has a lower precedence than the new operator. Then push the new operator onto the stack.
- Open parenthesis — Push ( onto the stack.
- Close parenthesis — Pop operators from the stack and append them to the output expression until an open parenthesis is popped. Discard both parentheses.

**5.16** **The infix-to-postfix algorithm.** The following algorithm encompasses the previous observations about the conversion process. For simplicity, all operands in our expression are single-letter variables.

```
Algorithm convertToPostfix(infix)
// Converts an infix expression to an equivalent postfix expression.

operatorStack = a new empty stack
postfix = a new empty string
while (infix has characters left to parse)
{
    nextCharacter = next nonblank character of infix
    switch (nextCharacter)
    {
        case variable:
            Append nextCharacter to postfix
            break

        case '∧' :
            operatorStack.push(nextCharacter)
            break

        case '+' : case '-' : case '*' : case '/' :
            while (!operatorStack.isEmpty() and
                    precedence of nextCharacter <= precedence of operatorStack.peek())
            {
                Append operatorStack.peek() to postfix
                operatorStack.pop()
            }
            operatorStack.push(nextCharacter)
            break

        case '(' :
            operatorStack.push(nextCharacter)
            break

        case ')' :  // Stack is not empty if infix expression is valid
            topOperator = operatorStack.pop()
            while (topOperator != '(')
            {
```

```
                    Append topOperator to postfix
                    topOperator = operatorStack.pop()
                }
                break
            default: break  // Ignore unexpected characters
        }
    }
    while (!operatorStack.isEmpty())
    {
        topOperator = operatorStack.pop()
        Append topOperator to postfix
    }
    return postfix
```

Figure 5-9 traces this algorithm for the infix expression $a \ / \ b * (c + (d - e))$. The resulting postfix expression is $a \ b \ / \ c \ d \ e \ - \ + \ *$.

---

**FIGURE 5-9**    The steps in converting the infix expression $a \ / \ b * (c + (d - e))$
to postfix form

| Next Character from Infix Expression | Postfix Form | Operator Stack (bottom to top) |
|---|---|---|
| $a$ | $a$ | |
| $/$ | $a$ | $/$ |
| $b$ | $a \ b$ | $/$ |
| $*$ | $a \ b \ /$ | |
|  | $a \ b \ /$ | $*$ |
| $($ | $a \ b \ /$ | $* \ ($ |
| $c$ | $a \ b \ / \ c$ | $* \ ($ |
| $+$ | $a \ b \ / \ c$ | $* \ ( +$ |
| $($ | $a \ b \ / \ c$ | $* \ ( + \ ($ |
| $d$ | $a \ b \ / \ c \ d$ | $* \ ( + \ ($ |
| $-$ | $a \ b \ / \ c \ d$ | $* \ ( + \ (-$ |
| $e$ | $a \ b \ / \ c \ d \ e$ | $* \ ( + \ (-$ |
| $)$ | $a \ b \ / \ c \ d \ e \ -$ | $* \ ( + \ ($ |
|  | $a \ b \ / \ c \ d \ e \ -$ | $* \ ( +$ |
| $)$ | $a \ b \ / \ c \ d \ e \ - \ +$ | $* \ ($ |
|  | $a \ b \ / \ c \ d \ e \ - \ +$ | $*$ |
|  | $a \ b \ / \ c \ d \ e \ - \ + \ *$ | |

---

**Question 6**  Using the previous algorithm, represent each of the following infix expressions as a postfix expression:

a. $(a + b) \ / \ (c - d)$
b. $a \ / \ (b - c) * d$
c. $a - (b \ / \ (c - d) * e + f) \wedge g$
d. $(a - b * c) \ / \ (d * e \wedge f * g + h)$

## A Problem Solved: Evaluating Postfix Expressions

> Evaluate a postfix expression that uses the operators +, -, *, /, and ^ to indicate addition, subtraction, multiplication, division, and exponentiation.

**VideoNote**

**Using the ADT stack**

**5.17**   Evaluating a postfix expression requires no rules of operator precedence, since the order of its operators and operands dictates the order of the operations. Additionally, a postfix expression contains no parentheses to complicate the evaluation.

As we scan the postfix expression, we must save operands until we find the operators that apply to them. For example, to evaluate the postfix expression *a b /*, we locate the variables *a* and *b* and save their values.[2] When we identify the operator /, its second operand is the most recently saved value—that is, *b*'s value. The value saved before that—*a*'s value—is the operator's first operand. Storing values in a stack enables us to access the necessary operands for an operator. Figure 5-10 traces the evaluation of *a b /* when *a* is 2 and *b* is 4. The result of 0 assumes integer division.

---

**FIGURE 5-10**   The stack during the evaluation of the postfix expression
*a b /* when *a* is 2 and *b* is 4

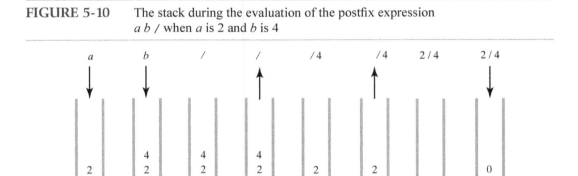

---

Now consider the postfix expression *a b + c /*, where *a* is 2, *b* is 4, and *c* is 3. The expression corresponds to the infix expression (*a* + *b*) / *c*, so its value should be 2. After finding the variable *a*, we push its value 2 onto a stack. Likewise, we push *b*'s value 4 onto the stack. The + operator is next, so we pop two values from the stack, add them, and push their sum 6 onto the stack. Notice that this sum will be the first operand of the / operator. The variable *c* is next in the postfix expression, so we push its value 3 onto the stack. Finally, we encounter the operator /, so we pop two values from the stack and form their quotient, 6 / 3. We push this result onto the stack. We are at the end of the expression, and one value, 2, is in the stack. This value is the value of the expression. Figure 5-11 traces the evaluation of this postfix expression.

---

2. Finding the value of a variable is not an easy task, but we will not explore this detail in this book.

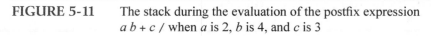

FIGURE 5-11    The stack during the evaluation of the postfix expression
$a\ b + c\ /$ when $a$ is 2, $b$ is 4, and $c$ is 3

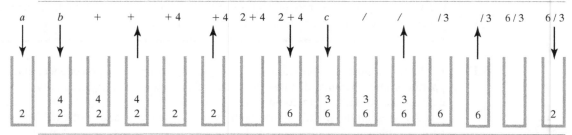

**5.18**    The evaluation algorithm follows directly from these examples:

*Algorithm* **evaluatePostfix(postfix)**
// *Evaluates a postfix expression.*

```
valueStack = a new empty stack
while (postfix has characters left to parse)
{
    nextCharacter = next nonblank character of postfix
    switch (nextCharacter)
    {
      case variable:
        valueStack.push(value of the variable nextCharacter)
        break

      case '+' : case '-' : case '*' : case '/' : case '^' :
        operandTwo = valueStack.pop()
        operandOne = valueStack.pop()
        result = the result of the operation in nextCharacter and its operands
                       operandOne and operandTwo
        valueStack.push(result)
        break

      default: break // Ignore unexpected characters
    }
}

return valueStack.peek()
```

We can implement this algorithm and the algorithm `convertToPostfix` given in Segment 5.16 as static methods of a class `Postfix`. The implementations are left as an exercise.

**Question 7**  Using the previous algorithm, evaluate each of the following postfix expressions. Assume that $a = 2$, $b = 3$, $c = 4$, $d = 5$, and $e = 6$.

    **a.** $a\ e + b\ d - /$
    **b.** $a\ b\ c * d * -$
    **c.** $a\ b\ c - / d *$
    **d.** $e\ b\ c\ a \wedge * + d -$

## A Problem Solved: Evaluating Infix Expressions

Evaluate an infix expression that uses the operators +, -, *, /, and ∧ to indicate addition, subtraction, multiplication, division, and exponentiation.

**5.19**    Using the two algorithms in Segments 5.16 and 5.18, we could evaluate an infix expression by converting it to an equivalent postfix expression and then evaluating it. We can save some intermediate work, however, by combining the two algorithms into one that evaluates an infix expression directly by using two stacks. This combined algorithm maintains a stack of operators according to the algorithm that converts an infix expression to postfix form. But instead of appending operands to the end of an expression, the new algorithm pushes the value of an operand onto a second stack according to the algorithm that evaluates a postfix expression.

**5.20**    **Example.** Consider the infix expression $a + b * c$. When $a$ is 2, $b$ is 3, and $c$ is 4, the expression's value is 14. To compute this result, we push the value of the variable $a$ onto a stack of values, push the + onto a stack of operators, and push the value of $b$ onto the stack of values. Since * has a higher precedence than the + at the top of the operator stack, we push it onto the stack. Finally, we push the value of $c$ onto the stack of values. Figure 5-12a shows the state of the two stacks at this point.

---

FIGURE 5-12    Two stacks during the evaluation of $a + b * c$ when $a$ is 2, $b$ is 3, and $c$ is 4:
    (a) after reaching the end of the expression
    (b) while performing the multiplication
    (c) while performing the addition

---

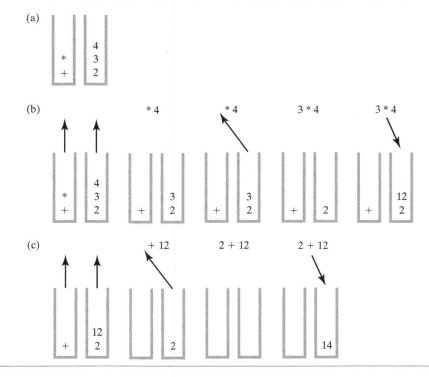

We now pop the operator stack and get the *. We get this operator's second and first operands, respectively, by popping the stack of values twice. After computing the product 3 * 4, we push the result 12 onto the stack of values, as Figure 5-12b shows. In a similar fashion, we pop the operator stack once and the value stack twice, compute 2 + 12, and push the result, 14, onto the stack of values. Since the operator stack is now empty, the value of the expression—14—is at the top of the stack of values. Figure 5-12c shows these final steps.

**5.21**    **The algorithm.** The algorithm to evaluate an infix expression follows. You should recognize aspects of its logic from the previous algorithms.

```
Algorithm evaluateInfix(infix)
// Evaluates an infix expression.

operatorStack = a new empty stack
valueStack = a new empty stack
while (infix has characters left to process)
{
    nextCharacter = next nonblank character of infix
    switch (nextCharacter)
    {
    case variable:
        valueStack.push(value of the variable nextCharacter)
        break

    case '^' :
        operatorStack.push(nextCharacter)
        break

    case '+' : case '-' : case '*' : case '/' :
        while (!operatorStack.isEmpty() and
                precedence of nextCharacter <= precedence of operatorStack.peek())
        {
            // Execute operator at top of operatorStack
            topOperator = operatorStack.pop()
            operandTwo = valueStack.pop()
            operandOne = valueStack.pop()
            result = the result of the operation in topOperator and its operands
                        operandOne and operandTwo
            valueStack.push(result)
        }
        operatorStack.push(nextCharacter)
        break

    case '(' :
        operatorStack.push(nextCharacter)
        break

    case ')' :  // Stack is not empty if infix expression is valid
        topOperator = operatorStack.pop()
        while (topOperator != '(')
        {
            operandTwo = valueStack.pop()
            operandOne = valueStack.pop()
            result = the result of the operation in topOperator and its operands
                        operandOne and operandTwo
            valueStack.push(result)
            topOperator = operatorStack.pop()
        }
        break
```

```
            default: break // Ignore unexpected characters
        }
    }
    while (!operatorStack.isEmpty())
    {
        topOperator = operatorStack.pop()
        operandTwo = valueStack.pop()
        operandOne = valueStack.pop()
        result = the result of the operation in topOperator and its operands
                operandOne and operandTwo
        valueStack.push(result)
    }
    return valueStack.peek()
```

**Question 8** Using the previous algorithm, evaluate each of the following infix expressions. Assume that $a = 2$, $b = 3$, $c = 4$, $d = 5$, and $e = 6$.

    **a.**  $a + b * c - 9$
    **b.**  $(a + e) / (b - d)$
    **c.**  $a + (b + c * d) - e / 2$
    **d.**  $e - b * c ^ a + d$

# The Program Stack

**5.22**    When a program executes, a special location called the **program counter** references the current instruction. The program counter might be part of an actual computer or, in the case of Java, part of a virtual computer.[3]

When a method is called, the program's run-time environment creates an object called an **activation record**, or **frame**, for the method. The activation record shows the method's state during its execution. In particular, the activation record contains the method's arguments, local variables, and a reference to the current instruction—that is, a copy of the program counter. At the time the method is called, the activation record is pushed onto a stack called the **program stack** or, in Java, the **Java stack**. Since one method can call another, the program stack often contains more than one activation record. The record at the top of the stack belongs to the method that is currently executing. The record just beneath the top record belongs to the method that called the current method, and so on.

Figure 5-13 illustrates a program stack for a main method that calls methodA, which then calls methodB. When main begins execution, its activation record is at the top of the program stack (Figure 5-13a). When main calls methodA, a new record is pushed onto the stack. The program counter is 50 at that time. Figure 5-13b shows the updated record for main and the new record for methodA just as the method begins execution. When methodA calls methodB, the program counter is 120. A new activation record is pushed onto the stack. Figure 5-13c shows the unchanged record for main, the updated record for methodA, and the new record for methodB just as it begins execution.

---

3. To maintain computer independence, Java runs on a virtual computer called the **Java Virtual Machine (JVM)**.

FIGURE 5-13     The program stack at three points in time: (a) when `main`
                begins execution; (b) when `methodA` begins execution; (c)
                when `methodB` begins execution

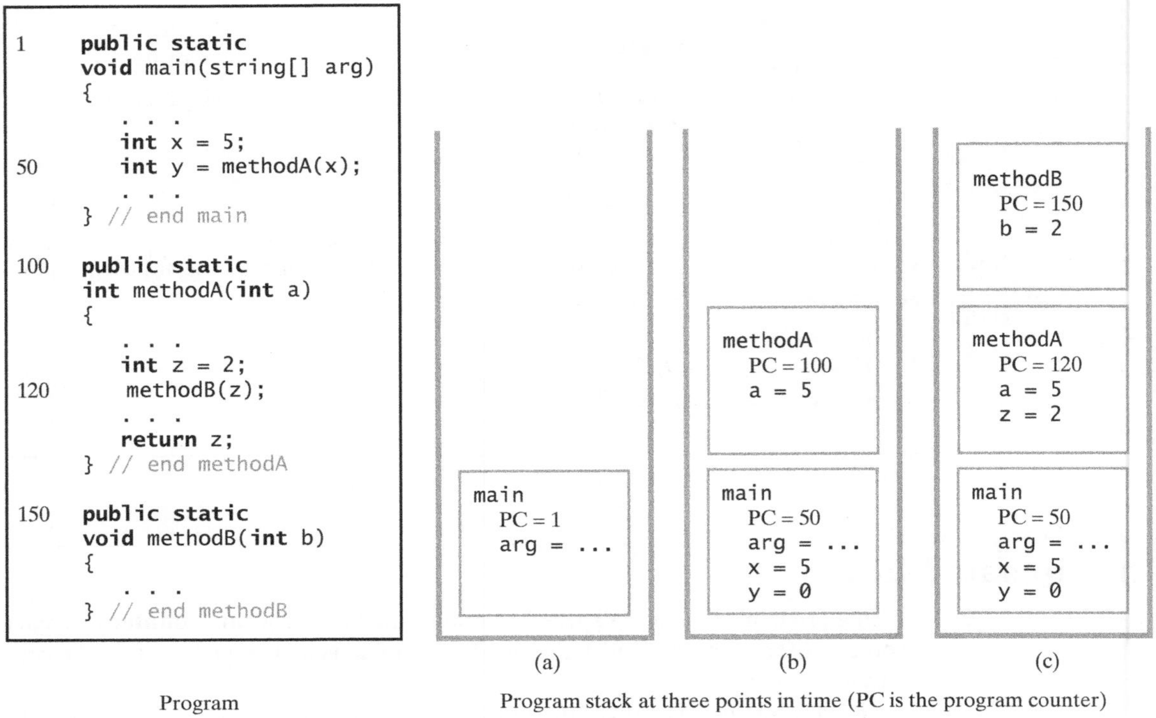

```
1    public static
     void main(string[] arg)
     {
        . . .
        int x = 5;
50      int y = methodA(x);
        . . .
     } // end main

100  public static
     int methodA(int a)
     {
        . . .
        int z = 2;
120     methodB(z);
        . . .
        return z;
     } // end methodA

150  public static
     void methodB(int b)
     {
        . . .
     } // end methodB
```

```
                                          methodB
                                          PC = 150
                                          b = 2

                       methodA            methodA
                       PC = 100           PC = 120
                       a = 5              a = 5
                                          z = 2

     main              main               main
     PC = 1            PC = 50            PC = 50
     arg = ...         arg = ...          arg = ...
                       x = 5              x = 5
                       y = 0              y = 0

       (a)               (b)                (c)
```

Program                          Program stack at three points in time (PC is the program counter)

As `methodB` executes, its activation record is updated, but the records for `main` and `methodA`
remain unchanged. The record for `methodA`, for example, represents the method's state at the time
it called `methodB`. When `methodB` completes its execution, its record is popped from the stack. The
program counter is reset to 120 and then advanced to the next instruction. Thus, `methodA` resumes
execution with the values of its argument and local variable as given in its activation record.
Ultimately, `methodA` completes its execution, its activation record is popped from the program
stack, and `main` continues its execution to completion.

## Java Class Library: The Class Stack

**5.23**     The Java Class Library contains the class `Stack`, which is an implementation of the ADT stack,
within the package `java.util`. This class has only one constructor—a default constructor that
creates an empty stack. In addition, the following four methods in this class are similar to
methods in our `StackInterface`. We have highlighted where they differ from our methods.

```
public T push(T item);
public T pop();
public T peek();
public boolean empty();
```

Stack also defines methods that enable you to search or traverse the entries in the stack, as well as other methods not supported by a traditional stack ADT.

 **Note:** The standard class java.util.Stack provides a slower implementation of a stack than do some newer standard classes. As you will see in Chapter 10, you instead should use a class—such as ArrayDeque—that implements the interface java.util.Deque when you do not want to define your own class of stacks. However, you can use Stack for now, and we will define our own stack classes in the next chapter.

## CHAPTER SUMMARY

- The ADT stack organizes its entries on a last-in, first-out basis. The entry at the top of the stack is the one added most recently.

- A stack's major operations—push, pop, and peek—deal only with the top of the stack. The method push adds an entry to the top of the stack; pop removes and returns the top entry, and peek just returns it.

- Arithmetic operators that have two operands are binary operators. When an operator such as + or - has one operand, it is a unary operator.

- An algebraic expression often contains parentheses, square brackets, and braces. You can use a stack to discover whether these delimiters are paired correctly.

- Ordinary algebraic expressions are called infix expressions, because each binary operator appears between its two operands. An infix expression requires rules of operator precedence and can use parentheses to override these rules.

- In a postfix expression, each binary operator appears after its two operands. In a prefix expression, each binary operator appears before its two operands. Postfix and prefix expressions use no parentheses and have no rules of operator precedence.

- You can use a stack of operators when forming a postfix expression that is equivalent to a given infix expression.

- You can use a stack of values to evaluate a postfix expression.

- You can use two stacks—one for operators and one for values—to evaluate an infix expression.

- When a method is called, the Java run-time environment creates an activation record, or frame, to record the status of the method. The record contains the method's arguments and local variables, along with the address of the current instruction. The record is placed in a stack called the program stack.

## PROGRAMMING TIP

- Methods such as peek and pop must behave reasonably when the stack is empty. For example, they could return null or throw an exception.

## EXERCISES

1. If you push the objects 1, 2, and 3 onto a stack that has numbers from 11 to 20, in what order will the pop operations remove them from the stack?

**2.** What pseudocode statements create a stack of the three integers 1234, 5678, and 9101, in that order with 1234 at the top?

**3.** Suppose that a, b, and c are empty stacks and 1, 2, 3, and 4 are objects. What do the stacks contain after the following sequence of operations executes?

```
a.push(1);
b.push(a.pop());
c.push(2);
a.push(3);
b.push(c.pop());
c.push(4);
b.push(a.pop());
b.push(c.pop());
```

**4.** What are the contents of the stack num after the following statements execute? Assume that NumStack is a class that implements the interface StackInterface.

```
StackInterface<Integer> num = new NumStack<>();
num.push(111);
num.push(num.pop());
num.push(222);
num.push(333);
num.push(444);
num.push(num.pop());
int n = num.pop();
num.push(num.peek());
```

**5.** Consider the following Java statements, assuming that NumStack is a class that implements the interface StackInterface:

```
int a = 3;
StackInterface<Integer> m = new NumStack<>();
while (a > 0)
{
   m.push(a);
   a--;
} // end while

int sum = 0;
while (!m.isEmpty())
{
   int integer = m.pop();
   sum = sum + integer;
} // end while
System.out.println("sum = " + sum);
```

    **a.** What value is displayed when this code executes?
    **b.** What mathematical function does the code evaluate?

**6.** Show the contents of the stack as you trace the algorithm checkBalance, given in Segment 5.8, for each of the following expressions:

    **a.** $a \{ b [c * (d + e)] - f \}$
    **b.** $\{ a (b * c) / [d + e] / f) - g \}$
    **c.** $a \{ b [c - d] e]) f$

7. Using the algorithm `convertToPostfix`, given in Segment 5.16, convert each of the following infix expressions to postfix expressions:

   a. $a * b / (c - d)$
   b. $(a - b * c) / (d * e * f + g)$
   c. $a / b * (c + (d - e))$
   d. $(a \wedge b * c - d) \wedge e + f \wedge g \wedge h$

8. Using the algorithm `evaluatePostfix`, given in Segment 5.18, evaluate each of the following postfix expressions. Assume that $a = 2$, $b = 3$, $c = 4$, $d = 5$, and $e = 6$.

   a. $a\, b + c * d -$
   b. $a\, b * c\, a - / d\, e * +$
   c. $a\, c - b \wedge d +$

9. What prefix expressions are represented by the postfix expressions given in the previous exercise?

10. Show the contents of the two stacks as you trace the algorithm `evaluateInfix`, given in Segment 5.21, to evaluate each of the following infix expressions. Assume that $m = 5$, $n = 4$, $o = 3$, $p = 2$, $q = 1$, and $r = 10$.

    a. $((m * n) + (r \wedge q) - o)$
    b. $((o + 2) - (n * m) / (r \wedge q))$
    c. $m + n - o * p / q \wedge r$

11. A *palindrome* is a string of characters (a word, phrase, or sentence) that is the same regardless of whether you read it forward or backward—assuming that you ignore spaces, punctuation, and case. For example, *Race car* is a palindrome. So is *A man, a plan, a canal: Panama*. Describe how you could use a stack to test whether a string is a palindrome.

12. Suppose that you read a binary string—that is, a string of 0s and 1s—one character at a time. Describe how you could use a stack but no arithmetic to see whether the number of 0s is equal to the number of 1s. When these counts are not equal, state how you could tell which character—0 or 1—occurs most frequently and by how much its count exceeds the other's.

13. Write Java code that displays all the objects in a stack in the reverse order in which they were pushed onto it. After all the objects are displayed, the stack should have the same contents as when you started but in the reverse order.

## PROJECTS

1. Using the class `java.util.Stack`, define a class `OurStack` that implements the interface `StackInterface`, as given in Listing 5-1.

2. Use the class `OurStack` from the previous project in a program that demonstrates the class `BalanceChecker`, as given in Listing 5-2.

   *Whenever you need a stack for any of the following projects, use the class `OurStack` that Project 1 asks you to define.*

3. Write a Java program that uses a stack to test whether an input string is a palindrome. Exercise 11 defines "palindrome" and asks you to describe a solution to this problem.

4. Define a class `Postfix` that includes the static methods `convertToPostfix` and `evaluatePostfix`. These methods should implement the algorithms given in Segments 5.16 and 5.18, respectively. Assume that the given algebraic expressions are syntactically correct. The standard class `StringBuilder`, which is in the Java Class Library and is described in Segment B.79 of Appendix B, will be helpful.

**5.** Define and demonstrate a method that evaluates infix expressions using the algorithm given in Segment 5.21. Assume that expressions are syntactically correct and use single-letter operands.

**6.** Repeat the previous project, but remove the assumption that the expressions are syntactically correct.

**7.** In the language Lisp, each of the four basic arithmetic operators appears before an arbitrary number of operands, which are separated by spaces. The resulting expression is enclosed in parentheses. The operators behave as follows:

- (+ a b c ...) returns the sum of all the operands, and (+) returns 0.
- (- a b c ...) returns a - b - c - ..., and (- a) returns -a. The minus operator must have at least one operand.
- (* a b c ...) returns the product of all the operands, and (*) returns 1.
- (/ a b c ...) returns a / b / c / ..., and (/ a) returns 1 / a. The divide operator must have at least one operand.

You can form larger arithmetic expressions by combining these basic expressions using a fully parenthesized prefix notation. For example, the following is a valid Lisp expression:

```
(+ (- 6) (* 2 3 4) (/ (+ 3) (*) (- 2 3 1)))
```

This expression is evaluated successively as follows:

```
(+ (- 6) (* 2 3 4) (/ 3 1 -2))
(+ -6 24 -1.5)
16.5
```

Design and implement an algorithm that uses a stack to evaluate a legal Lisp expression composed of the four basic operators and integer values. Write a program that reads such expressions and demonstrates your algorithm.

**8.** Consider arithmetic expressions like the ones described in the previous project. Allow operands to be either integer values or variable names that are strings of letters. Design and implement an iterative algorithm that uses a stack to test whether an expression is legal in Lisp. Write a program that reads potential expressions and demonstrates your algorithm.

Each expression that your program reads can be split across several lines, which is the style used by typical Lisp programmers. For example, the following expression is legal in Lisp:

```
(+ (- height)
   (* 3 3 4)
   (/ 3 width length)
   (* radius radius)
)
```

In contrast, the following expressions are illegal in Lisp:

```
(+ (-)                   (+ (- height)          (+ (- height)          (+ (- height)
   (* 3 3 4)                (* 3 3 4) )s            (* 3 3 4)              (* 3 3 4)
   (/ 3 width length)    (* (/ 3 width length)    (/ 3 width length))    ((/ 3 width length))
   (* radius radius)        (* radius radius)       (* radius radius)      (* radius radius)
)                        )                      )                      )
```

9. Write a program that graphically displays a working calculator for simple infix expressions that consist of single-digit operands; the operators +, -, *, and /; and parentheses. Make the following assumptions:

- Unary operators (as in -2) are illegal.
- All operations, including division, are integer operations.
- The input expression contains no embedded spaces and no illegal characters, since it is entered by using a keypad.
- The input expression is a syntactically correct infix expression.
- Division by zero will not occur. (Consider how you can remove this restriction.)

The calculator has a display and a keypad of 20 keys, which are arranged as follows:

```
C < Q /
7 8 9 *
4 5 6 -
1 2 3 +
0 ( ) =
```

As the user presses keys to enter an infix expression, the corresponding characters appear in the display. The C (Clear) key erases all input entered so far; the < (Backspace) key erases the last character entered. When the user presses the = key, the expression is evaluated and the result replaces the expression in the display window. The user can then press C and enter another expression. If the user presses the Q (Quit) key, the calculator ceases operation and is erased from the screen.

10. Consider a maze made up of a rectangular array of squares, such as the following one:

```
X X X X X X X X X X X X
      X       X X X X      X
X X       X           X   X
X X     X X  X    X    X   X
X X       X      X         X
X X     X X X X X
X X X X X X X X X X X X
```

The Xs represent a blocked square and form the walls of the maze. Let's consider mazes that have only one entrance and one exit on opposite sides of the maze, as in our example. Beginning at the entrance at the top left side of the maze, find a path to the exit at the bottom right side. You can move only up, down, left, or right.

Each square in the maze can be in one of four states: clear, blocked, path, or visited. Initially, each square is either clear or blocked. If a square lies on a successful path, mark it with a period. If you enter a square but it does not lead to a successful path, mark the square as visited.

Let a two-dimensional array represent the maze. Use a stack-based algorithm to find a path through the maze. Some mazes might have more than one successful path, while others have no path.

## ANSWERS TO SELF-TEST QUESTIONS

1. *Jill* is at the top, and *Jim* is at the bottom.

2. a. StackInterface<String> nameStack = **new** OurStack<>();
      **while** (!stringStack.isEmpty())
          nameStack.push(stringStack.pop());
   b. stringStack is empty, and nameStack contains the strings that were in stringStack but in reverse order (*Jim* is at the top, and *Jill* is at the bottom).

**3.** The following stacks are shown bottom to top when read from left to right:

|  | **a.** [ | **b.** { | **c.** [ |
|---|---|---|---|
|  | [ { | { [ | [ { |
|  | [ { ( | { [ ( | [ { [ |
|  | [ { | { [ | [ { [ ( |
|  | { { ( | { | [ { [ |
|  | [ { |  | [ { |
|  | [ |  | [ |
|  | *empty* |  |  |

The algorithm `checkBalance` returns true for the expression in Part *a* and false for the other two.

**4.**  **a.** *a b c * +*
 **b.** *a b * c d - /*
 **c.** *a b / c d - +*
 **d.** *a b / c + d -*

**5.** Always. Segment 5.14 showed that you push ^ onto the stack if another ^ is already at the top of the stack. But if a different operator is at the top, ^ has a higher precedence, so you push it onto the stack in that situation as well.

**6.**  **a.** *a b + c d - /*
 **b.** *a b c - / d **
 **c.** *a b c d - / e * f + g ^ -*
 **d.** *a b c * - d e f ^ * g * h + /*

**7.**  **a.** -4.
 **b.** -58.
 **c.** -10.
 **d.** 49.

**8.**  **a.** 5.
 **b.** -4.
 **c.** 22.
 **d.** -37.

# Stack Implementations

## Contents

## Prerequisites

## Objectives

After studying this chapter, you should be able to

- Implement the ADT stack by using either a linked chain, an array, or a vector
- Compare and contrast the various implementations and their performance

$T$wo of the implementations of the ADT stack described in this chapter use techniques like the ones we used to implement the ADT bag. We will use, in turn, a chain of linked nodes and an array to store the stack's entries. We also will introduce the standard class Vector as a part of the Java Class Library and use an instance of Vector to represent a stack. You should be pleasantly surprised by the simplicity and efficiency of these implementations.

## A Linked Implementation

**6.1** Each of the operations push, pop, and peek of the ADT stack involve the top of the stack. If we use a chain of linked nodes to implement a stack, where in the chain should we place the stack's top entry? If we have only the chain's head reference, we can add, remove, or access its first node faster than any other node. Thus, the stack operations will execute fastest if the first node in the chain references the top entry in the stack, as Figure 6-1 illustrates.

Also note in the figure that each node in the chain references one entry in the stack. Nodes are allocated—that is, created—only when needed for a new entry. They are deallocated when an entry is removed. Recall from the note in Segment 3.24 of Chapter 3 that the Java run-time environment automatically reclaims, or deallocates, memory that a program no longer references, without explicit instruction from the programmer.

**VideoNote**

**The Class LinkedStack**

---

**FIGURE 6-1** A chain of linked nodes that implements a stack

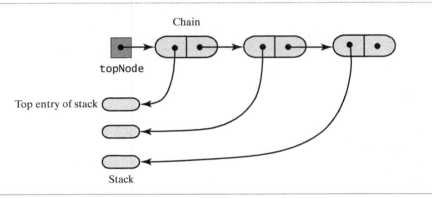

---

 **Note:** If you use a chain of linked nodes to implement a stack, the first node should reference the stack's top entry.

**6.2** **An outline of the class.** The linked implementation of the stack has a data field `topNode`, which is the head reference of the chain of nodes. The default constructor sets this field to `null`. An outline of our class appears in Listing 6-1.

Each node in the chain is an instance of the private class `Node` that is defined within the class `LinkedStack`. This class has set and get methods and is like the one you saw in Listing 3-4 of Chapter 3.

**LISTING 6-1** An outline of a linked implementation of the ADT stack

```
1  /**
2      A class of stacks whose entries are stored in a chain of nodes.
3      @author Frank M. Carrano
4  */
5  public final class LinkedStack<T> implements StackInterface<T>
6  {
7      private Node topNode; // References the first node in the chain
8
9      public LinkedStack()
10     {
11        topNode = null;
12     } // end default constructor
13     < Implementations of the stack operations go here. >
14     . . .
15
16     private class Node
17     {
18
```

```
19        private T    data; // Entry in stack
20        private Node next; // Link to next node
21
22        < Constructors and the methods getData, setData, getNextNode, and setNextNode
23          are here. >
24    } // end Node
25 } // end LinkedStack
```

**6.3**  **Adding to the top.** We push an entry onto the stack by first allocating a new node that references the stack's existing chain, as Figure 6-2a illustrates. This reference is in topNode, the head reference to the chain. We then set topNode to reference the new node, as in Figure 6-2b. Thus, the method push has the following definition:

```
public void push(T newEntry)
{
    Node newNode = new Node(newEntry, topNode);
    topNode = newNode;
} // end push
```

Note that you can replace the two statements in the body of this method with

```
        topNode = new Node(newEntry, topNode);
```

This operation is independent of the other entries in the stack. Its performance is thus O(1).

---

**FIGURE 6-2**      (a) A new node that references the node at the top of the stack;
                    (b) the new node is now at the top of the stack

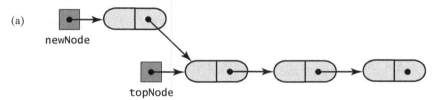

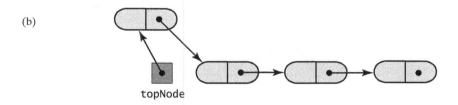

---

**6.4**  **Retrieving the top.** We get the top entry in the stack by accessing the data portion of the first node in the chain. Thus, peek, like push, is an O(1) operation. Note that if the stack is empty, peek throws an exception.

```
public T peek()
{
    if (isEmpty())
        throw new EmptyStackException();
    else
        return topNode.getData();
} // end peek
```

**6.5**    **Removing the top.** We pop, or remove, the top entry in the stack by setting `topNode` to the reference in the first node. Thus, `topNode` will reference what was the second node in the chain, as Figure 6-3 shows. Moreover, the original first node will no longer be referenced, so it will be deallocated. Since we also want the operation to return the stack's top entry before it is removed, the method pop has the following implementation:

```
public T pop()
{
    T top = peek(); // Might throw EmptyStackException

    assert topNode != null;
    topNode = topNode.getNextNode();

    return top;
} // end pop
```

This operation also is O(1).

---

**FIGURE 6-3**    The stack (a) before and (b) after the first node in the chain is deleted

---

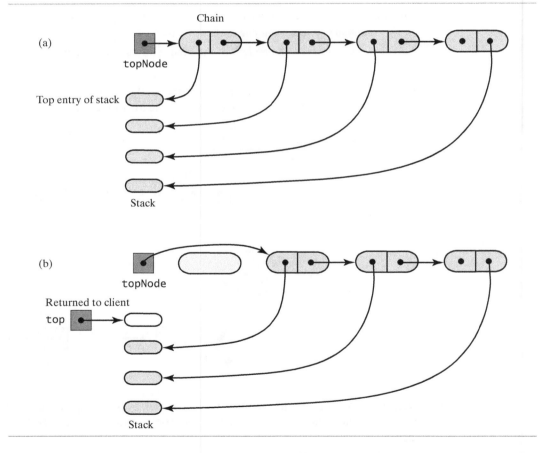

---

 **Security Note:  Implementation guidelines**
  ● Use assertions to verify assumptions.
  ● When verifying data, check that it is valid instead of invalid.
  ● Verify return values given to you, especially those provided by code you did not write.

**Question 1** Revise the previous implementation of pop so that it does not call peek.

**6.6** **The rest of the class.** The remaining public methods isEmpty and clear involve only topNode:

```java
public boolean isEmpty()
{
   return topNode == null;
} // end isEmpty

public void clear()
{
   topNode = null;
} // end clear
```

**Question 2** Is an implementation of the ADT stack reasonable if the top of the stack is at the end of a chain of linked nodes instead of its beginning? Explain.

## An Array-Based Implementation

**6.7** If we use an array to implement the stack, where should we place the stack's top entry? If the first location of the array references the top entry, as shown in Figure 6-4a, we must move all the entries in the array any time we add or remove a stack entry. We can have more efficient stack operations if the first array location references the bottom entry of the stack. The top entry of the stack is then referenced by the last occupied location in the array, as Figure 6-4b shows. This configuration allows us to add or remove stack entries without moving other items in the array. Thus, one disadvantage of a typical array-based implementation does not apply here. The exercises at the end of this chapter consider other ways to place a stack's entries in an array.

Resizing the array avoids a stack that is too full to accept another entry. However, unlike the linked chain in the previous section, the array in Figure 6-4 contains locations that are unused. If we eventually fill the array with additional stack entries, we can expand the size of the array—but then we will have more unused locations. The chain has its downside as well, in that it uses additional memory for the link portions of its nodes.

VideoNote
The Class ArrayStack

**Note:** If you use an array to implement a stack, the array's first location is the bottom of the stack. The last occupied location in the array, then, references the stack's top entry.

**FIGURE 6-4**    An array that implements a stack; its first location references
(a) the top entry in the stack; (b) the bottom entry in the stack

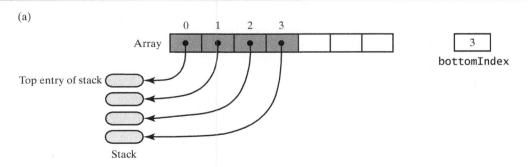

**(Figure 6-4 continued)**

(b)

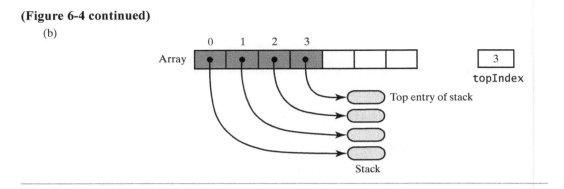

6.8   **An outline of the class.** The array-based implementation of the stack has as data fields an array of stack entries and an index to the top entry. The default constructor creates a stack with a default capacity; another constructor lets the client choose the stack's capacity. Listing 6-2 outlines our class.

**LISTING 6-2    An outline of an array-based implementation of the ADT stack**

```java
/**
    A class of stacks whose entries are stored in an array.
    @author Frank M. Carrano
*/
public final class ArrayStack<T> implements StackInterface<T>
{
   private T[] stack;     // Array of stack entries
   private int topIndex;  // Index of top entry
   private boolean initialized = false;
   private static final int DEFAULT_CAPACITY = 50;
   private static final int MAX_CAPACITY = 10000;

   public ArrayStack()
   {
      this(DEFAULT_CAPACITY);
   } // end default constructor

   public ArrayStack(int initialCapacity)
   {
      checkCapacity(initialCapacity);

      // The cast is safe because the new array contains null entries
      @SuppressWarnings("unchecked")
      T[] tempStack = (T[])new Object[initialCapacity];
      stack = tempStack;
      topIndex = -1;
      initialized = true;
   } // end constructor

   < Implementations of the stack operations go here. >
   < Implementations of the private methods go here; checkCapacity and checkInitialization
     are analogous to those in Chapter 2. >
   . . .
} // end ArrayStack
```

To indicate an empty stack, we have assigned -1 to topIndex as its initial value. This choice allows push to simply increment topIndex before using it when placing a new entry in the array.

**6.9** **Adding to the top.** The push method checks whether the array has room for a new entry by calling the private method ensureCapacity. It then places the new entry immediately after the last occupied location in the array:

```
public void push(T newEntry)
{
   checkInitialization();
   ensureCapacity();
   stack[topIndex + 1] = newEntry;
   topIndex++;
} // end push

private void ensureCapacity()
{
   if (topIndex == stack.length - 1) // If array is full, double its size
   {
      int newLength = 2 * stack.length;
      checkCapacity(newLength);
      stack = Arrays.copyOf(stack, newLength);
   } // end if
} // end ensureCapacity
```

Note that ensureCapacity is similar to the ensureCapacity method in the class Resizable-ArrayBag, which we encountered in Chapter 2. Both private methods double the size of an array after it becomes full.

When ensureCapacity does not resize the array stack, push is an O(1) operation, since its performance is independent of the size of the stack. However, resizing the array is an O($n$) operation, so when the array is full, the performance of push degrades to O($n$). If this happens, however, the very next push is O(1) again. To be fair, all push operations should share the cost of the occasional resize of the array. That is, we **amortize** the cost of doubling the array size over all additions to the stack. Unless we must resize the array many times, each push is almost O(1).

**6.10** **Retrieving the top.** The operation peek either returns the array entry at topIndex or throws an exception if the stack is empty:

```
public T peek()
{
   checkInitialization();
   if (isEmpty())
      throw new EmptyStackException();
   else
      return stack[topIndex];
} // end peek
```

This operation is O(1).

**6.11** **Removing the top.** The pop operation, like peek, retrieves the top entry in the stack, but then removes it. To remove the stack's top entry in Figure 6-4b, we could simply decrement topIndex, as Figure 6-5a illustrates. This simple step would be sufficient, since the other methods would behave correctly. For example, given the stack pictured in Figure 6-5a, peek would return the item that stack[2] references. However, the object that previously was the top entry and has now been returned to the client would still be referenced by the array. No harm will come from this situation if our implementation is correct. To be safe, pop can set stack[topIndex] to null before decrementing topIndex. Figure 6-5b illustrates the stack in this case.

FIGURE 6-5    An array-based stack after its top entry is removed by
(a) decrementing `topIndex`; (b) setting `stack[topIndex]` to
`null` and then decrementing `topIndex`

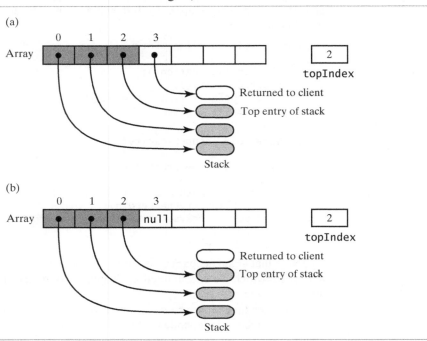

The following implementation of pop reflects these comments:

```java
public T pop()
{
  checkInitialization();
  if (isEmpty())
    throw new EmptyStackException();
  else
  {
    T top = stack[topIndex];
    stack[topIndex] = null;
    topIndex--;
    return top;
  } // end if
} // end pop
```

Like peek, pop is an O(1) operation.

**Question 3** Revise the previous implementation of pop so that it calls peek.

**Question 4** If we were to implement a stack of primitives instead of a stack of objects, what changes should we make to the method pop?

**6.12**   **The methods `isEmpty` and `clear`.** The method `isEmpty` involves only `topIndex`:

```
public boolean isEmpty()
{
   return topIndex < 0;
} // end isEmpty
```

The method `clear` could simply set `topIndex` to -1, because the stack methods would behave correctly as though the stack were empty. However, the objects that were in the stack would remain allocated. Just as `pop` sets `stack[topIndex]` to `null`, `clear` should set to `null` each array location that was used for the stack. Alternatively, `clear` could call `pop` repeatedly until the stack is empty. We leave the implementation of `clear` as an exercise.

**Question 5**   If `stack` is an array that contains the entries in a stack, what is a disadvantage of maintaining the top entry of the stack in `stack[0]`?

**Question 6**   If you use the locations at the end of an array `stack` for a stack's entries before you use the array's first locations, should the stack's top entry or its bottom entry be in `stack[stack.length - 1]`? Why?

**Question 7**   Write an implementation of `clear` that sets to `null` each array location that was used for the stack.

**Question 8**   Write an implementation of `clear` that repeatedly calls `pop` until the stack is empty.

# A Vector-Based Implementation

**6.13**   One way to let a stack grow as needed is to store its entries in an array that you resize, as we did in the implementation of `ArrayStack`. Another way is to use a **vector** instead of an array. A vector is an object that behaves like a high-level array. A vector's entries are indexed beginning with 0, just like an array's entries. But unlike an array, a vector has methods to set or access its entries. You can create a vector of a given size, and it will grow in size as needed. The details of this process are hidden from the client.

If we store a stack's entries in a vector, we can use the vector's methods to manipulate the stack's entries. Figure 6-6 shows a client interacting with a stack by using the methods in `StackInterface`. The implementations of these methods in turn interact with the vector's methods to produce the desired effects on the stack.

A vector is an instance of the standard class `Vector`, which we describe next.

**FIGURE 6-6**   A client using the methods given in `StackInterface`; these methods interact with a vector's methods to perform stack operations

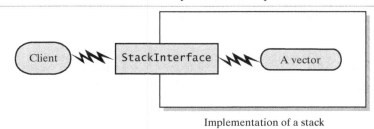

Implementation of a stack

## Java Class Library: The Class Vector

**6.14** The Java Class Library contains a class `Vector`, whose instances—called vectors—behave like a resizable array. Here are some constructors and methods of `Vector` that we will use to implement the ADT stack:

**public** `Vector()`
Creates an empty vector, or arraylike container, with an initial capacity of 10. When the vector needs to increase its capacity, the capacity doubles.

**public** `Vector(int initialCapacity)`
Creates an empty vector with the specified initial capacity. When the vector needs to increase its capacity, the capacity doubles.

**public boolean** `add(T newEntry)`
Adds a new entry to the end of this vector.

**public** T `remove(int index)`
Removes and returns the entry at the given index in this vector.

**public void** `clear()`
Removes all entries from this vector.

**public** T `lastElement()`
Returns the entry at the end of this vector.

**public boolean** `isEmpty()`
Returns true if this vector is empty.

**public int** `size()`
Returns the number of entries currently in this vector.

You can learn more about `Vector` at docs.oracle.com/javase/8/docs/api/.

**Note: Java Class Library: The class Vector**
The Java Class Library has the class `Vector` in the package java.util. A vector is analogous to a resizable array in that its elements are indexed beginning with 0. You work with a vector by using its methods.

## Using a Vector to Implement the ADT Stack

**6.15** Using a vector to contain a stack's entries is like using an array, but easier. We let the first element of the vector reference the bottom entry of the stack. Thus, the vector looks like the array in Figure 6-4b. We do not need to maintain an index to the top entry of the stack, however, as we can infer this index from the vector's size, which is readily available. Also, the vector expands as necessary, so we do not have to worry about this detail.

Since the implementation of `Vector` is based on an array that can be resized dynamically, the performance of this implementation of the stack is like that of the array-based implementation given in the previous section.

**Note:** If you use a vector to implement a stack, the vector's first element should reference the stack's bottom entry. Then the last occupied location in the vector references the stack's top entry.

**6.16**  **An outline of the class.** The class that implements the stack begins by declaring a vector as a data field and allocating the vector in its constructors. Thus, we must provide an `import` statement prior to the class definition. Listing 6-3 outlines our class.

---

**LISTING 6-3**     An outline of a vector-based implementation of the Adt stack

```
1  /**
2     A class of stacks whose entries are stored in a vector.
3     @author Frank M. Carrano
4  */
5  public final class VectorStack<T> implements StackInterface<T>
6  {
7     private Vector<T> stack; // Last element is the top entry in stack
8     private boolean initialized = false;
9     private static final int DEFAULT_CAPACITY = 50;
10    private static final int MAX_CAPACITY = 10000;
11
12    public VectorStack()
13    {
14       this(DEFAULT_CAPACITY);
15    } // end default constructor
16
17    public VectorStack(int initialCapacity)
18    {
19       checkCapacity(initialCapacity);
20       stack = new Vector<>(initialCapacity); // Size doubles as needed
21       initialized = true;
22    } // end constructor
23
24    < Implementations of checkInitialization, checkCapacity, and the stack operations go here. >
25       . . .
26  } // end VectorStack
```

---

**6.17**  **Adding to the top.** We use `Vector`'s method add to add an entry to the end of the vector, that is, to the top of the stack.

```
public void push(T newEntry)
{
   checkInitialization();
   stack.add(newEntry);
} // end push
```

**6.18**  **Retrieving the top.** We retrieve the stack's top entry by using `Vector`'s method `lastElement`.

```
public T peek()
{
   checkInitialization();
   if (isEmpty())
      throw new EmptyStackException();
   else
      return stack.lastElement();
} // end peek
```

**6.19** **Removing the top.** We can remove the stack's top entry by using Vector's method remove. The argument to this method is the index of the last entry in the vector, since that entry is at the top of the stack. This index is 1 less than the vector's current size stack.size().

```
public T pop()
{
    checkInitialization();
    if (isEmpty())
        throw new EmptyStackException();
    else
        return stack.remove(stack.size() - 1);
} // end pop
```

**6.20** **The rest of the class.** The remaining public methods isEmpty and clear invoke analogous Vector methods:

```
public boolean isEmpty()
{
    return stack.isEmpty();
} // end isEmpty

public void clear()
{
    stack.clear();
} // end clear
```

**Question 9** If a vector contains the entries in a stack, is it reasonable to maintain the stack's top entry in the vector's first element?

**Note:** Since Java's class Vector uses an array in its implementation, VectorStack is an array-based implementation of the ADT stack. It uses a resizable array to contain the stack's entries, and so the stack can grow in size as needed.

**Note:** Writing VectorStack is certainly easier than writing the array-based implementation that this chapter describes. Since the methods of VectorStack invoke the methods of Vector, they can require more execution time than those of ArrayStack. However, this time increase typically is insignificant.

## CHAPTER SUMMARY

- You can implement a stack by using a chain of linked nodes that has only a head reference. The stack operations execute fastest if the first node in the chain references the stack's top entry. This is true because you can add, remove, or access a chain's first node faster than any other node.

- The stack operations are O(1) for a linked implementation.

- You can implement a stack by using an array. If the first location in the array contains the stack's bottom entry, no array elements will be moved when you add or remove stack entries.

- Resizing an array avoids a stack that is too full to accept another entry. However, the array generally contains locations that are unused.

- The stack operations are O(1) for an array-based implementation. However, when the array is full, push doubles the size of the array. In that case, push is O($n$). If you spread this extra cost over all other pushes, and if doubling the array is not frequent, push is almost O(1).

- You can implement a stack by using a vector. You maintain the stack's bottom entry at the beginning of the vector.

- Since the implementation of Vector is based on an array that can be resized dynamically, the performance of a vector-based implementation is like that of the array-based implementation.

## EXERCISES

1. What are the similarities between a vector-based implementation and an array-based implementation of the ADT stack?

2. Consider the ADT bag, as described in Chapters 1 through 3.

   a. Can a compiler make use of the ADT bag to interpret the meaning of an algebraic expression? Justify your answer.
   b. Would you prefer to use a stack to implement the shopping cart for an online-shopping website? Justify your answer.

3. Suppose that the ADT stack included the void method display, which displays the entries in a stack. Implement this method for each of the following classes:

   a. LinkedStack, as outlined in Listing 6-1.
   b. ArrayStack, as outlined in Listing 6-2.
   c. VectorStack, as outlined in Listing 6-3.
   d. Any client of LinkedStack, ArrayStack, or VectorStack.

4. Repeat the previous exercise, but define the method toArray instead of the method display.

5. Suppose that the ADT stack included a void method remove(n) that removes the topmost n entries from a stack. Specify this method by writing comments and a header. Consider the possible outcomes for stacks that do not contain at least n entries.

6. Repeat Exercise 3, but define the method remove(n), as described in the previous exercise, instead of the method display.

7. Imagine a linked implementation of the ADT stack that places the top entry of the stack at the end of a chain of linked nodes. Describe how you can define the stack operations push, pop, and peek so that they do not traverse the chain.

8. Segment 6.9 noted that an array-based push method is normally O(1), but when a stack needs to be doubled in size, push is O($n$). This observation is not as bad as it seems, however. Suppose that you double the size of a stack from $n$ elements to $2n$ elements.

 a. How many calls to push can you make before the stack must double in size again?
 b. Remembering that each of these calls to push is O(1), what is the average cost of all the push operations? (The average cost is the total cost of all calls to push divided by the number of calls to push.)

9. Suppose that instead of doubling the size of an array-based stack when it becomes full, you just increase the size of the array by some positive constant $k$.

 a. If you have an empty stack that uses an array whose initial size is $k$, and you perform $n$ pushes, how many resize operations will be performed? Assume that $n > k$.
 b. What is the average cost of the $n$ push operations?

10. Suppose that instead of doubling the size of an array-based stack when it becomes full, you increase the size of the array by the following sequence $3k$, $5k$, $7k$, $9k$, ... for some positive constant $k$.

 a. If you have an empty stack that uses an array whose initial size is $k$, and you perform $n$ pushes, how many resize operations will be performed? Assume that $n > k$.
 b. What is the average cost of the $n$ push operations?

11. When an array becomes full, you can double its size or use one of the schemes described in Exercises 9 and 10. What are the advantages and disadvantages of each of these three schemes?

12. Imagine several stack operations on a vector-based stack. Suppose that the vector increases in size, but later fewer than half of the vector's locations are actually used by the stack. Describe an implementation that halves the size of the vector in this case. What are the advantages and disadvantages of such an implementation?

## PROJECTS

1. Implement the ADT stack by using an array stack to contain its entries. Expand the array dynamically, as necessary. Maintain the stack's bottom entry in stack[stack.length - 1].

2. Repeat Project 1, but maintain the stack's top entry in stack[stack.length - 1].

3. Repeat Project 1, but maintain the stack's top entry in stack[0].

4. Write the implementation of the ADT stack that Exercise 7 describes.

5. The ADT stack lets you peek at its top entry without removing it. For some applications of stacks, you also need to peek at the entry beneath the top entry without removing it. We will call such an operation peek2. If the stack has more than one entry, peek2 returns the second entry from the top without altering the stack. If the stack has fewer than two entries, peek2 throws an exception. Write a linked implementation of a stack that includes a method peek2.

6. When the client attempts to either retrieve or remove an item from an empty stack, our stacks throw an exception. An alternative action is to return null.

 a. Modify the interface StackInterface so that null is returned in these cases.
 b. Modify the array-based implementation of the stack to conform to your changes to StackInterface. Write a program that demonstrates the modifications.
 c. Repeat Part b for the linked implementation of the stack.

7. Suppose that we wish to implement the resizing schemes described in Exercises 9 and 10 in addition to the doubling scheme.

    **a.** Write a new version of the array-based stack that lets the client specify the resizing scheme and the associated constant when a stack is created.

    **b.** Write a program that demonstrates the modifications.

    **c.** Discuss the advantages and disadvantages of adding methods that allow the client to change the resize scheme and associated constant after the stack has been created.

8. Implement the ADT bag by using a vector to contain its entries.

## ANSWERS TO SELF-TEST QUESTIONS

1.
```java
public T pop()
{
    if (topNode != null)
    {
        T top = topNode.getData();
        topNode = topNode.getNextNode();
        return top;
    }
    else
        throw new EmptyStackException();
} // end pop
```

2. No. Although maintaining an external reference to the chain's last node, in addition to the chain's head reference, would enable you to either access the stack's top entry or push a new entry onto the stack efficiently, it is not enough to pop the stack. You need a reference to the next-to-last node to remove the chain's last node. To get that reference, you could either traverse the chain or maintain a reference to the next-to-last node in addition to references to the first and last nodes. Thus, placing the stack's top entry at the end of the chain is not as efficient or easy to implement as placing it at the beginning.

3.
```java
public T pop()
{
    T top = peek(); // Might throw EmptyStackException

    assert !isEmpty();
    stack[topIndex] = null;
    topIndex--;

    return top;
} // end pop
```

4. Change T to the primitive type and do not assign null to stack[topIndex].

5. Each push or pop would need to move all of the entries currently in the stack.

6. The bottom entry. You can then push entries onto the stack without moving the other entries already in the array.

7.
```java
public void clear()
{
    while (topIndex > -1)
    {
        stack[topIndex] = null;
        topIndex--;
    } // end while
    // Assertion: topIndex is -1
} // end clear
```

8. 
```java
public void clear()
{
    while (!isEmpty())
        pop();
// Assertion: topIndex is -1
} // end clear
```

9. No. Since Vector uses an array to store a vector's entries, each push would need to move all of the entries in the vector to vacate its first location, thus making room for the addition to the stack. Although Vector, not your code, would take care of the details, your code would execute slower than if you had maintained the stack's bottom entry in the vector's first element.

# Chapter

# 7

# Recursion

## Contents

## Prerequisites

## Objectives

After studying this chapter, you should be able to

- Decide whether a given recursive method will end successfully in a finite amount of time
- Write a recursive method
- Estimate the time efficiency of a recursive method
- Identify tail recursion and replace it with iteration

Repetition is a major feature of many algorithms. In fact, repeating actions rapidly is a key ability of computers. Two problem-solving processes involve repetition; they are called iteration and recursion. In fact, most programming languages provide two kinds of repetitive constructs, iterative and recursive.

You know about iteration because you know how to write a loop. Regardless of the loop construct you use—for, while, or do—your loop contains the statements that you want to repeat and a mechanism for controlling the number of repetitions. You might have a counted loop that counts repetitions as 1, 2, 3, 4, 5, or 5, 4, 3, 2, 1. Or the loop might execute repeatedly while a boolean variable or expression is true. Iteration often provides a straightforward and efficient way to implement a repetitive process.

At times, iterative solutions are elusive or hopelessly complex. For some problems, discovering or verifying such solutions is not a simple task. In these cases, recursion can provide an elegant alternative. Some recursive solutions can be the best choice, some provide insight for finding a better iterative solution, and some should not be used at all because they are grossly inefficient. Recursion, however, remains an important problem-solving strategy, especially in the areas of cryptography and image processing.

This chapter will show you how to think recursively.

## What Is Recursion?

7.1    You can build a house by hiring a contractor. The contractor in turn hires several subcontractors to complete portions of the house. Each subcontractor might hire other subcontractors to help. You use the same approach when you solve a problem by breaking it into smaller problems. In one special variation of this problem-solving process, the smaller problems are identical except for their size. This special process is called **recursion**.

VideoNote
Introducing recursion

Suppose that you can solve a problem by solving an identical but smaller problem. How will you solve the smaller problem? If you use recursion again, you will need to solve an even smaller problem that is just like the original problem in every other respect. How will replacing a problem with another one ever lead to a solution? One key to the success of recursion is that eventually you will reach a smaller problem whose solution you know because either it is obvious or it is given. The solution to this smallest problem is probably not the solution to your original problem, but it can help you reach it. Either just before or just after you solve a smaller problem, you usually contribute a portion of the solution. This portion, together with the solutions to the other, smaller problems, provides the solution to the larger problem.

Let's look at an example.

7.2    **Example: The countdown.** It's New Year's Eve and the giant ball is falling in Times Square. The crowd counts down the last 10 seconds: "10, 9, 8, . . ." Suppose that I ask you to count down to 1 beginning at some positive integer like 10. You could shout "10" and then ask a friend to count down from 9. Counting down from 9 is a problem that is exactly like counting down from 10, except that there is less to do. It is a smaller problem.

To count down from 9, your friend shouts "9" and asks a friend to count down from 8. This sequence of events continues until eventually someone's friend is asked to count down from 1. That friend simply shouts "1." No other friend is needed. You can see these events in Figure 7-1.

In this example, I've asked you to complete a task. You saw that you could contribute a part of the task and then ask a friend to do the rest. You know that your friend's task is just like the original task, but it is smaller. You also know that when your friend completes this smaller task, your job will be done. What is missing from the process just described is the signal that each friend gives to the previous person at the completion of a task.

**FIGURE 7-1**      Counting down from 10

To provide this signal, when you count down from 10, I need you to tell me when you are done. I don't care how—or who—does the job, as long as you tell me when it is done. I can take a nap until I hear from you. Likewise, when you ask a friend to count down from 9, you do not care how your friend finishes the job. You just want to know when it is done so you can tell me that you are done. You can take a nap while you are waiting.

 **Note:** Recursion is a problem-solving process that breaks a problem into identical but smaller problems.

Ultimately, we have a group of napping people waiting for someone to say "I'm done." The first person to make that claim is the person who shouts "1," as Figure 7-1 illustrates, since that person needs no help in counting down from 1. At this time in this particular example, the problem is solved, but I don't know that because I'm still asleep. The person who shouted "1" says "I'm done"

to the person who shouted "2." The person who shouted "2" says "I'm done" to the person who shouted "3," and so on, until you say "I'm done" to me. The job is done; thanks for your help; I have no idea how you did it, and I don't need to know!

**7.3**　What does any of this have to do with Java? In the previous example, you play the role of a Java method. I, the client, have asked you, the recursive method, to count down from 10. When you ask a friend for help, you are invoking a method to count down from 9. But you do not invoke another method; you invoke yourself!

**Note:** A method that calls itself is a **recursive method**. The invocation is a **recursive call** or **recursive invocation**.

The following Java method counts down from a given positive integer, displaying one integer per line.

```
/** Counts down from a given positive integer.
   @param integer  An integer > 0. */
public static void countDown(int integer)
{
   System.out.println(integer);
   if (integer > 1)
      countDown(integer - 1);
} // end countDown
```

Since the given integer is positive, the method can display it immediately. This step is analogous to you shouting "10" in the previous example. Next the method asks whether it is finished. If the given integer is 1, there is nothing left to do. But if the given integer is larger than 1, we need to count down from integer - 1. We've already noted that this task is smaller but otherwise identical to the original problem. How do we solve this new problem? We invoke a method, but countDown is such a method. It does not matter that we have not finished writing it at this point!

**7.4**　Will the method countDown actually work? Shortly we will trace the execution of countDown both to convince you that it works and to show you how it works. But traces of recursive methods are messy, and you usually do not have to trace them. If you follow certain guidelines when writing a recursive method, you can be assured that it will work.

In designing a recursive solution, you need to answer certain questions:

**Note:**　**Questions to answer when designing a recursive solution**
- What part of the solution can you contribute directly?
- What smaller but identical problem has a solution that, when taken with your contribution, provides the solution to the original problem?
- When does the process end? That is, what smaller but identical problem has a known solution, and have you reached this problem, or **base case**?

For the method countDown, we have the following answers to these questions:

- The method countDown displays the given integer as the part of the solution that it contributes directly. This happens to occur first here, but it need not always occur first.
- The smaller problem is counting down from integer - 1. The method solves the smaller problem when it calls itself recursively.
- The if statement asks if the process has reached the base case. Here the base case occurs when integer is 1. Because the method displays integer before checking it, nothing is left to do once the base case is identified.

**Note:  Design guidelines for successful recursion**
To write a recursive method that behaves correctly, you generally should adhere to the following design guidelines:

- The method must be given an input value, usually as an argument.
- The method definition must contain logic that involves this input value and leads to different cases. Typically, such logic includes an `if` statement or a `switch` statement.
- One or more of these cases should provide a solution that does not require recursion. These are the base cases, or **stopping cases**.
- One or more cases must include a recursive invocation of the method. These recursive invocations should in some sense take a step toward a base case by using "smaller" arguments or solving "smaller" versions of the task performed by the method.

**Programming Tip:  Infinite recursion**
A recursive method that does not check for a base case, or that misses the base case, will execute "forever." This situation is known as infinite recursion.

**7.5**    Before we trace the method `countDown`, we should note that we could have written it in other ways. For example, a first draft of this method might have looked like this:

```java
public static void countDown(int integer)
{
   if (integer == 1)
      System.out.println(integer);
   else
   {
      System.out.println(integer);
      countDown(integer - 1);
   } // end if
} // end countDown
```

Here, the programmer considered the base case first. The solution is clear and perfectly acceptable, but you might want to avoid the redundant `println` statement that occurs in both cases.

**7.6**    Removing the redundancy just mentioned could result in either the version given earlier in Segment 7.3 or the following one:

```java
public static void countDown(int integer)
{
   if (integer >= 1)
   {
      System.out.println(integer);
      countDown(integer - 1);
   } // end if
} // end countDown
```

When `integer` is 1, this method will produce the recursive call `countDown(0)`. This turns out to be the base case for this method, and nothing is displayed.

All three versions of `countDown` produce correct results; there are probably others as well. Choose the one that is clearest to you.

**7.7**    The version of countDown just given in Segment 7.6 provides us an opportunity to compare it with the following iterative version:

```
// Iterative version.
public static void countDown(int integer)
{
   while (integer >= 1)
   {
      System.out.println(integer);
      integer--;
   } // end while
} // end countDown
```

The two methods have a similar appearance. Both compare integer with 1, but the recursive version uses an if, and the iterative version uses a while. Both methods display integer. Both compute integer - 1.

---

**Programming Tip:** An iterative method contains a loop. A recursive method calls itself. Although some recursive methods contain a loop *and* call themselves, if you have written a while statement within a recursive method, be sure that you did not mean to write an if statement.

---

**Question 1** Write a recursive void method that skips *n* lines of output, where *n* is a positive integer. Use System.out.println() to skip one line.

**Question 2** Describe a recursive algorithm that draws a given number of concentric circles. The innermost circle should have a given diameter. The diameter of each of the other circles should be four-thirds the diameter of the circle just inside it.

---

## Tracing a Recursive Method

**7.8**    Now let's trace the method countDown given in Segment 7.3:

```
public static void countDown(int integer)
{
   System.out.println(integer);
   if (integer > 1)
      countDown(integer - 1);
} // end countDown
```

For simplicity, suppose that we invoke this method with the statement

```
countDown(3);
```

from within a main method of the class that defines countDown. This call behaves like any other call to a nonrecursive method. The argument 3 is copied into the parameter integer and the following statements are executed:

```
System.out.println(3);
if (3 > 1)
   countDown(3 - 1); // First recursive call
```

A line containing 3 is displayed, and the recursive call countDown(2) occurs, as Figure 7-2a shows.

Execution of the call to countDown(3) is suspended until the results of countDown(2) are known. In this particular method definition, no statements appear after the recursive call. So although it appears that nothing will happen when execution resumes, it is here that the method returns to the client.

FIGURE 7-2    The effect of the method call countDown(3)

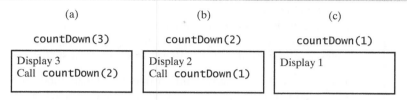

(a)                          (b)                          (c)

countDown(3)              countDown(2)              countDown(1)

| Display 3<br>Call countDown(2) | Display 2<br>Call countDown(1) | Display 1 |

**7.9**    Continuing our trace, countDown(2) causes the following statements to execute:

```
System.out.println(2);
if (2 > 1)
    countDown(2 - 1); // Second recursive call
```

A line containing 2 is displayed, and the recursive call countDown(1) occurs, as shown in Figure 7-2b. Execution of the call to countDown(2) is suspended until the results of countDown(1) are known.

The call countDown(1) causes the following statements to execute:

```
System.out.println(1);
if (1 > 1)
```

A line containing 1 is displayed, as Figure 7-2c shows, and no other recursive call occurs.

Figure 7-3 illustrates the sequence of events from the time that countDown is first called. The numbered arrows indicate the order of the recursive calls and the returns from the method. After 1 is displayed, the method completes execution and returns to the point (arrow 4) after the call

FIGURE 7-3    Tracing the recursive call countDown(3)

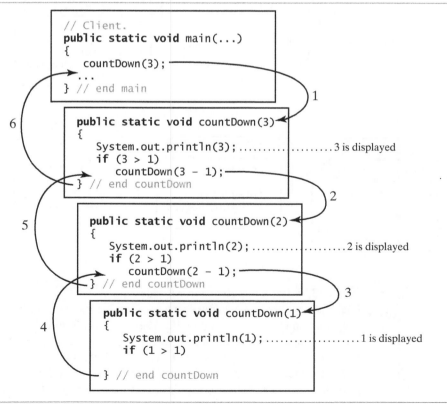

countDown(2 - 1). Execution continues from there and the method returns to the point (arrow 5) after the call countDown(3 - 1). Ultimately, a return to the point (arrow 6) after the initial recursive call in main occurs.

Although tracking these method returns seems like a formality that has gained us nothing, it is an important part of any trace because some recursive methods will do more than simply return to their calling method. You will see an example of such a method shortly.

**7.10**   Figure 7-3 appears to show multiple copies of the method countDown. In reality, however, multiple copies do not exist. Instead, for each call to a method—be it recursive or not—Java records the current state of the method's execution, including the values of its parameters and local variables as well as the location of the current instruction. As Segment 5.22 of Chapter 5 described, each record is called an activation record and provides a snapshot of a method's state during its execution. The records are placed into the program stack. The stack organizes the records chronologically, so that the record of the currently executing method is on top. In this way, Java can suspend the execution of a recursive method and invoke it again with new argument values. The boxes in Figure 7-3 correspond roughly to activation records, although the figure does not show them in the order in which they would appear in a stack. Figure 7-4 illustrates the stack of activation records as a result of the call countDown(3) in a main method.

**FIGURE 7-4**   The stack of activation records during the execution of the call
countDown(3)

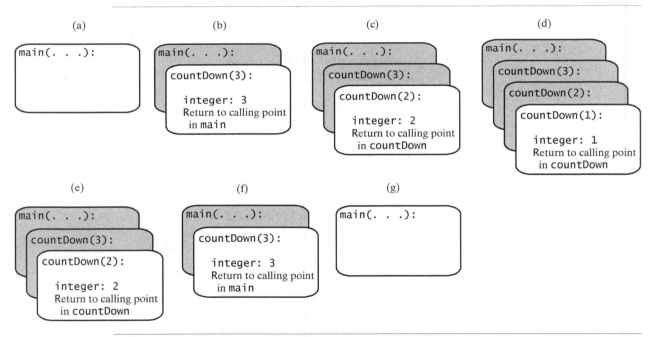

**Note:  The stack of activation records**
Each call to a method generates an activation record that captures the state of the method's execution and that is placed into the program stack. Figure 5-13 in Chapter 5 illustrated the program stack when methodA calls the distinct method methodB. However, these methods need not be distinct. That is, the program stack enables a run-time environment to execute recursive methods. Each invocation of any method produces an activation record that is pushed onto the program stack. The activation record of a recursive method is not special in any way.

**Note:** A recursive method uses more memory than an iterative method, in general, because each recursive call generates an activation record.

 **Programming Tip: Stack overflow**
A recursive method that makes many recursive calls will place many activation records in the program stack. Too many recursive calls can use all the memory available for the program stack, making it full. As a result, the error message "stack overflow" occurs. Infinite recursion or large-size problems are the likely causes of this error.

 **Question 3** Write a recursive void method countUp(n) that counts up from 1 to *n*, where *n* is a positive integer. *Hint*: A recursive call will occur before you display anything.

## Recursive Methods That Return a Value

**7.11**   The recursive method countDown in the previous sections is a void method. Valued methods can also be recursive. The guidelines for successful recursion given in Segment 7.4 apply to valued methods as well, with an additional note. Recall that a recursive method must contain a statement such as an if that chooses among several cases. Some of these cases lead to a recursive call, but at least one case has no recursive call. For a valued method, each of these cases must provide a value for the method to return.

**7.12**   **Example: Compute the sum $1 + 2 + \ldots + n$ for any integer $n > 0$.** The given input value for this problem is the integer *n*. Beginning with this fact will help us to find the smaller problem because its input will also be a single integer. The sum always starts at 1, so that can be assumed.

So suppose that I have given you a positive integer *n* and asked you to compute the sum of the first *n* integers. You need to ask a friend to compute the sum of the first *m* integers for some positive integer *m*. What should *m* be? Well, if your friend computes $1 + \ldots + (n - 1)$, you can simply add *n* to that sum to get your sum. Thus, if sumOf(n) is the method call that returns the sum of the first *n* integers, adding *n* to your friend's sum occurs in the expression sumOf(n-1) + n.

What small problem can be the base case? That is, what value of *n* results in a sum that you know immediately? One possible answer is 1. If *n* is 1, the desired sum is 1.

With these thoughts in mind, we can write the following method:

```
/** @param n  An integer > 0.
    @return  The sum 1 + 2 + ... + n. */
public static int sumOf(int n)
{
   int sum;
   if (n == 1)
      sum = 1;                   // Base case
   else
      sum = sumOf(n - 1) + n; // Recursive call

   return sum;
} // end sumOf
```

**7.13**   The definition of the method sumOf satisfies the design guidelines for successful recursion. Therefore, you should be confident that the method will work correctly without tracing its execution. However, a trace will be instructive here because it will not only show you how a valued recursive method works, but also demonstrate actions that occur after a recursive call is complete.

Suppose that we invoke this method with the statement

System.out.println(sumOf(3));

The computation occurs as follows:

1. sumOf(3) is sumOf(2) + 3; sumOf(3) suspends execution, and sumOf(2) begins.
2. sumOf(2) is sumOf(1) + 2; sumOf(2) suspends execution, and sumOf(1) begins.
3. sumOf(1) returns 1.

Once the base case is reached, the suspended executions resume, beginning with the most recent. Thus, sumOf(2) returns 1 + 2, or 3; then sumOf(3) returns 3 + 3, or 6. Figure 7-5 illustrates this computation.

**Question 4** Write a recursive valued method that computes the product of the integers from 1 to *n*, where *n* > 0.

**Note:  Should you trace a recursive method?**
We have shown you how to trace the execution of a recursive method primarily to show you how recursion works and to give you some insight into how a typical compiler implements recursion. Should you ever trace a recursive method? Usually no. You certainly should not trace a recursive method while you are writing it. If the method is incomplete, your trace will be, too, and you are likely to become confused. If a recursive method does not work, follow the suggestions given in the next programming tip. You should trace a recursive method only as a last resort.

**FIGURE 7-5**      Tracing the execution of sumOf(3)

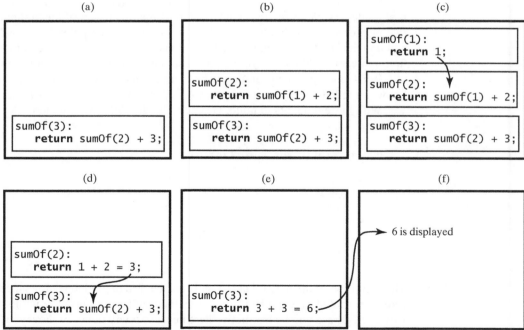

> **Programming Tip: Debugging a recursive method**
> If a recursive method does not work, answer the following questions. Any "no" answers should guide you to the error.
>
> - Does the method have at least one input value?
> - Does the method contain a statement that tests an input value and leads to different cases?
> - Did you consider all possible cases?
> - Does at least one of these cases cause at least one recursive call?
> - Do these recursive calls involve smaller arguments, smaller tasks, or tasks that get closer to the solution?
> - If these recursive calls produce or return correct results, will the method produce or return a correct result?
> - Is at least one of the cases a base case that has no recursive call?
> - Are there enough base cases?
> - Does each base case produce a result that is correct for that case?
> - If the method returns a value, does each of the cases return a value?

**7.14**    Our previous examples were simple so that you could study the construction of recursive methods. Since you could have solved these problems iteratively with ease, should you actually use their recursive solutions? Nothing is inherently wrong with these recursive methods. However, given the way that typical present-day systems execute recursive methods, a stack overflow is likely for large values of *n*. Iterative solutions to these simple examples would not have this difficulty and are easy to write. Realize, however, that future computing systems might be able to execute these recursive methods without difficulty.

## Recursively Processing an Array

**VideoNote**

Using recursion to solve problems

Later in this book we will talk about searching an array for a particular item. We will also look at algorithms that **sort**, or arrange, the items in an array into either ascending or descending order. Some of the more powerful searching and sorting algorithms often are stated recursively. In this section, we will process arrays recursively in ways that will be useful to us later. We have chosen a simple task—displaying the integers in an array—for our examples so that you can focus on the recursion without the distraction of the task. We will consider more-complex tasks later in this book and in the exercises at the end of this chapter.

**7.15**    Suppose that we have an array of integers and we want a method that displays it. So that we can display all or part of the array, the method will display the integers in the array elements whose indices range from `first` through `last`. Thus, we can declare the method as follows:

```
/** Displays the integers in an array.
    @param array  An array of integers.
    @param first  The index of the first element displayed.
    @param last   The index of the last element displayed,
                  0 <= first <= last < array.length. */
public static void displayArray(int[] array, int first, int last)
```

This task is simple and could readily be implemented using iteration. You might not imagine, however, that we could also implement it recursively in a variety of ways. But we can and will.

**7.16**    **Starting with array[first].** An iterative solution would certainly start at the first element, `array[first]`, so it is natural to have our first recursive method begin there also. If I ask you to display the array, you could display `array[first]` and then ask a friend to display the rest of the array. Displaying the rest of the array is a smaller problem than displaying the entire array.

You wouldn't have to ask a friend for help if you had to display only one element—that is, if `first` and `last` were equal. This is the base case. Thus, we could write the method `displayArray` as follows:

```java
public static void displayArray(int array[], int first, int last)
{
   System.out.print(array[first] + " ");
   if (first < last)
      displayArray(array, first + 1, last);
} // end displayArray
```

For simplicity, we assume that the integers will fit on one line. Notice that the client would follow a call to `displayArray` with `System.out.println()` to get to the next line.

**7.17**   **Starting with `array[last]`.** Strange as it might seem, we can begin with the last element in the array and still display the array from its beginning. Rather than displaying the last element right away, you would ask a friend to display the rest of the array. After the elements `array[first]` through `array[last - 1]` had been displayed, you would display `array[last]`. The resulting output would be the same as in the previous segment.

The method that implements this plan follows:

```java
public static void displayArray(int array[], int first, int last)
{
   if (first <= last)
   {
      displayArray(array, first, last - 1);
      System.out.print (array[last] + " ");
   } // end if
} // end displayArray
```

**7.18**   **Dividing the array in half.** A common way to process an array recursively divides the array into two pieces. You then process each of the pieces separately. Since each of these pieces is an array that is smaller than the original array, each defines the smaller problem necessary for recursion. Our first two examples also divided the array into two pieces, but one of the pieces contained only one element. Here we divide the array into two approximately equal pieces. To divide the array, we find the element at or near the middle of the array. The index of this element is

```java
int mid = (first + last) / 2;
```

Figure 7–6 shows two arrays and their middle elements. Suppose that we include `array[mid]` in the left "half" of the array, as the figure shows. In Part $b$, the two pieces of the array are equal in length; in Part $a$ they are not. This slight difference in length doesn't matter.

**FIGURE 7-6**   Two arrays with their middle elements within their left halves

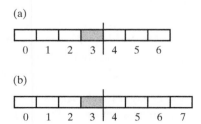

Once again, the base case is an array of one element. You can display it without help. But if the array contains more than one element, you divide it into halves. You then ask a friend to display one half and another friend to display the other half. These two friends, of course, represent two recursive calls in the following method:

```java
public static void displayArray(int array[], int first, int last)
{
   if (first == last)
      System.out.print(array[first] + " ");
   else
   {
      int mid = (first + last) / 2;
      displayArray(array, first, mid);
      displayArray(array, mid + 1, last);
   } // end if
} // end displayArray
```

**Question 5** Suppose that the array's middle element is not in either half of the array. Instead you can recursively display the left half, display the middle element, and then recursively display the right half. What is the implementation of displayArray if you make these changes?

**Note:** When you process an array recursively, you can divide it into two pieces. For example, the first or last element could be one piece, and the rest of the array could be the other piece. Or you could divide the array into halves or in some other way.

**Note:  Finding an array's midpoint**

To compute the index of an array's middle element, we should use the statement

```java
int mid = first + (last - first) / 2;
```

instead of

```java
int mid = (first + last) / 2;
```

If we were to search an array of at least $2^{30}$, or about one billion, elements, the sum of first and last could exceed the largest possible int value of $2^{31} - 1$. Thus, the computation first + last would overflow to a negative integer and result in a negative value for mid. If this negative value of mid was used as an array index, an ArrayIndexOutOfBoundsException would occur. The computation first + (last - first)/2, which is algebraically equivalent to (first + last)/2, avoids this error.

**7.19**   **Displaying a bag.** In Chapter 2, we used an array to implement the ADT bag. Suppose that a bag had a method display to display its contents. Although we could define this method iteratively, we'll use recursion instead. Since display has no parameters, it must call another method—displayArray— that has parameters and displays the array of bag entries. The arguments in the call to displayArray would be zero for the first index and numberOfEntries - 1 for the last index, where numberOfEntries is a data field of the bag's class. Since the array, bag, of bag entries is a data field of the class that implements the bag, it need not be a parameter of displayArray. Finally, since display is not a static method, displayArray is not static.

We can use the approach of any version of `displayArray` given previously. However, we will display objects, one per line, instead of integers on one line. Using the technique shown in Segment 7.16, we revised the methods as follows:

```java
public void display()
{
    displayArray(0, numberOfEntries - 1);
} // end display

private void displayArray(int first, int last)
{
    System.out.println(bag[first]);
    if (first < last)
        displayArray(first + 1, last);
} // end displayArray
```

**Note:** A recursive method that is part of an implementation of an ADT often is private, because its use requires knowledge of the underlying data structure. Such a method is unsuitable as an ADT operation.

## Recursively Processing a Linked Chain

**7.20**    We can illustrate the recursive processing of a chain of linked nodes by performing a simple task such as displaying the data in the chain. Once again, we'll implement the method `display` for the ADT bag, but this time let's use the linked implementation introduced in Chapter 3. That implementation defines the field `firstNode` as a reference to the first node in the chain.

Dividing a linked chain into pieces is not as easy as dividing an array, since we cannot access any particular node without traversing the chain from its beginning. Hence, our first approach displays the data in the first node and then recursively displays the data in the rest of the chain. Thus, as it did in Segment 7.19, `display` will call a private recursive method. We will name that method `displayChain`. As a recursive method, `displayChain` needs an input value. That input should represent the chain, so we give `displayChain` a parameter that references the first node in the chain.

Suppose that we name `displayChain`'s parameter `nodeOne`. Then `nodeOne.getData()` is the data in the first node, and `nodeOne.getNextNode()` is a reference to the rest of the chain. What about the base case? Although a one-element array was a fine base case for `displayArray`, using an empty chain as the base case is easier here because we can simply compare `nodeOne` to `null`. Thus, we have the following implementations for the methods `display` and `displayChain`:

```java
public void display()
{
    displayChain(firstNode);
} // end display

private void displayChain(Node nodeOne)
{
    if (nodeOne != null)
    {
        System.out.println(nodeOne.getData()); // Display first node
        displayChain(nodeOne.getNextNode());   // Display rest of chain
    } // end if
} // end displayChain
```

**Note:** When you write a method that processes a chain of linked nodes recursively,

- You use a reference to the chain's first node as the method's parameter.
- You process the first node followed by the rest of the chain.
- You stop when the value of the parameter is `null`.

**7.21** **Displaying a chain backwards.** Suppose that you want to traverse a chain of linked nodes in reverse order. In particular, suppose that you want to display the object in the last node, then the one in the next-to-last node, and so on, working your way toward the beginning of the chain. Since each node references the next node but not the previous one, using iteration for this task would be difficult. You could traverse to the last node, display its contents, go back to the beginning and traverse to the next-to-last node, and so on. Clearly, however, this is a tedious and time-consuming approach. Alternatively, you could traverse the chain once and save a reference to each node. You could then use these references to display the objects in the chain's nodes in reverse order. A recursive solution would do this for you.

If a friend could display the nodes in reverse order, beginning with the second node, you could display the first node and complete the task. The following recursive solution implements this idea:

```java
public void displayBackward()
{
   displayChainBackward(firstNode);
} // end displayBackward
private void displayChainBackward(Node nodeOne)
{
   if (nodeOne != null)
   {
      displayChainBackward(nodeOne.getNextNode());
      System.out.println(nodeOne.getData());
   } // end if
} // end displayChainBackward
```

 **Note:** Traversing a chain of linked nodes in reverse order is easier when done recursively rather than iteratively.

 **Question 6** Trace the previous method `displayBackward` for a chain of three nodes.

# The Time Efficiency of Recursive Methods

Chapter 4 showed you how to measure an algorithm's time requirement by using Big Oh notation. We used a count of the algorithm's major operations as a first step in selecting an appropriate growth-rate function. For the iterative examples we examined, that process was straightforward. We will use a more formal technique here to measure the time requirement of a recursive algorithm and thereby choose the right growth-rate function.

## The Time Efficiency of countDown

**7.22**   As a first example, consider the countDown method given in Segment 7.3. The size of the problem of counting down to 1 from a given integer is directly related to the size of that integer. Since Chapter 4 used $n$ to represent the size of the problem, we will rename the parameter integer in countDown to n to simplify our discussion. Here is the revised method:

```
public static void countDown(int n)
{
   System.out.println(n);
   if (n > 1)
      countDown(n - 1);
} // end countDown
```

When $n$ is 1, countDown displays 1. This is the base case and requires a constant amount of time. When $n > 1$, the method requires a constant amount of time for both the println statement and the comparison. In addition, it needs time to solve the smaller problem represented by the recursive call. If we let $t(n)$ represent the time requirement of countDown(n), we can express these observations by writing

$t(1) = 1$
$t(n) = 1 + t(n - 1)$ for $n > 1$

The equation for $t(n)$ is called a **recurrence relation**, since the definition of the function $t$ contains an occurrence of itself—that is, a recurrence. What we need is an expression for $t(n)$ that is not given in terms of itself. One way to find such an expression is to pick a value for $n$ and to write out the equations for $t(n)$, $t(n - 1)$, and so on, until we reach $t(1)$. From these equations, we should be able to guess at an appropriate expression to represent $t(n)$. We then need only to prove that we are right. This is actually easier than it sounds.

**7.23**   **Solving a recurrence relation.** To solve the previous recurrence relation for $t(n)$, let's begin with $n = 4$. We get the following sequence of equations:

$t(4) = 1 + t(3)$
$t(3) = 1 + t(2)$
$t(2) = 1 + t(1) = 1 + 1 = 2$

Substituting 2 for $t(2)$ in the equation for $t(3)$ results in

$t(3) = 1 + 2 = 3$

Substituting 3 for $t(3)$ in the equation for $t(4)$ results in

$t(4) = 1 + 3 = 4$

It appears that

$t(n) = n$ for $n \geq 1$

We can start with a larger value of $n$, get the same result, and convince ourselves that it is true. But we need to *prove* that this result is true for every $n \geq 1$. This is not hard to do.

**7.24**   **Proving that $t(n) = n$.** To prove that $t(n) = n$ for $n \geq 1$, we begin with the recurrence relation for $t(n)$, since we know it is true:

$t(n) = 1 + t(n - 1)$ for $n > 1$

We need to replace $t(n - 1)$ on the right side of the equation. Now if $t(n - 1) = n - 1$ when $n > 1$, the following would be true for $n > 1$:

$t(n) = 1 + n - 1 = n$

Thus, if we can find an integer $k$ that satisfies the equation $t(k) = k$, the next larger integer will also satisfy it. By a similar chain of reasoning, the equation is true for all integers larger than $k$. Since we are given that $t(1) = 1$, all integers larger than 1 will satisfy the equation. This proof is an example of a **proof by induction**.

To conclude, we now know that countDown's time requirement is given by the function $t(n) = n$. Thus, the method is $O(n)$.

**Question 7** What is the Big Oh of the method sumOf given in Segment 7.12?

**Question 8** Computing $x^n$ for some real number $x$ and an integral power $n \geq 0$ has a simple recursive solution:

$$x^n = x \ x^{n-1}$$
$$x^0 = 1$$

**a.** What recurrence relation describes this algorithm's time requirement?
**b.** By solving this recurrence relation, find the Big Oh of this algorithm.

## The Time Efficiency of Computing $x^n$

**7.25** We can compute $x^n$ for some real number $x$ and an integral power $n \geq 0$ more efficiently than the approach that Question 8 suggests. To reduce the number of recursive calls and therefore the number of multiplications, we can express $x^n$ as follows:

$$x^n = (x^{n/2})^2 \text{ when } n \text{ is even and positive}$$
$$x^n = x \ (x^{(n-1)/2})^2 \text{ when } n \text{ is odd and positive}$$
$$x^0 = 1$$

This computation could be implemented by a method power(x, n) that contains the recursive call power(x, n/2). Since integer division in Java truncates its result, this call is appropriate regardless of whether $n$ is even or odd. Thus, power(x, n) would invoke power(x, n/2) once, square the result, and, if $n$ is odd, multiply the square by $x$. These multiplications are $O(1)$ operations. Thus, the execution time for power(x, n) is proportional to the number of recursive calls.

The recurrence relation that represents the number of recursive calls and, therefore, the method's time requirement to compute $x^n$ is then

$$t(n) = 1 + t(n/2) \text{ when } n \geq 2$$
$$t(1) = 1$$
$$t(0) = 1$$

Again, $n/2$ truncates to an integer.

**7.26** Since the recurrence relation involves $n/2$, let's choose a power of 2—such as 16—as $n$'s initial value. We then write the following sequence of equations:

$$t(16) = 1 + t(8)$$
$$t(8) = 1 + t(4)$$
$$t(4) = 1 + t(2)$$
$$t(2) = 1 + t(1)$$

By substituting repeatedly, we get the following:

$$t(16) = 1 + t(8) = 1 + (1 + t(4)) = 2 + (1 + t(2)) = 3 + (1 + t(1)) = 4 + t(1)$$

Since $16 = 2^4$, $4 = \log_2 16$. This fact, together with the base case $t(1) = 1$, leads us to guess that

$$t(n) = 1 + \log_2 n$$

**7.27** Now we need to prove that this guess is, in fact, true for $n \geq 1$. It is true for $n = 1$, because

$$t(1) = 1 + \log_2 1 = 1$$

For $n > 1$, we know that the recurrence relation for $t(n)$

$$t(n) = 1 + t(n/2)$$

is true. Remember that $n/2$ truncates to an integer.

We need to replace $t(n/2)$. If our guess $t(n) = 1 + \log_2 n$ were true for all values of $n < k$, we would have $t(k/2) = 1 + \log_2 (k/2)$, since $k/2 < k$. Thus,

$$
\begin{aligned}
t(k) &= 1 + t(k/2) \\
&= 1 + (1 + \log_2 (k/2)) \\
&= 2 + \log_2 (k/2) \\
&= \log_2 4 + \log_2 (k/2) \\
&= \log_2 (4k/2) \\
&= \log_2 (2k) \\
&= \log_2 2 + \log_2 k \\
&= 1 + \log_2 k
\end{aligned}
$$

To summarize, we assumed that $t(n) = 1 + \log_2 n$ for all values of $n < k$ and showed that $t(k) = 1 + \log_2 k$. Thus, $t(n) = 1 + \log_2 n$ for all $n \geq 1$. Since power's time requirement is given by $t(n)$, the method is $O(\log n)$.

## A Simple Solution to a Difficult Problem

**7.28**    The Towers of Hanoi is a classic problem in computer science whose solution is not obvious. Imagine three poles and a number of disks of varying diameters. Each disk has a hole in its center so that it can fit over each of the poles. Suppose that the disks have been placed on the first pole in order from largest to smallest, with the smallest disk on top. Figure 7-7 illustrates this initial configuration for three disks.

**FIGURE 7-7**    The initial configuration of the Towers of Hanoi for three disks.

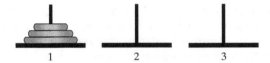

The problem is to move the disks from the first pole to the third pole so that they remain piled in their original order. But you must adhere to the following rules:

1. Move one disk at a time. Each disk you move must be a topmost disk.
2. No disk may rest on top of a disk smaller than itself.
3. You can store disks on the second pole temporarily, as long as you observe the previous two rules.

**7.29**    The solution is a sequence of moves. For example, if three disks are on pole 1, the following sequence of seven moves will move the disks to pole 3, using pole 2 temporarily:

Move a disk from pole 1 to pole 3
Move a disk from pole 1 to pole 2
Move a disk from pole 3 to pole 2
Move a disk from pole 1 to pole 3
Move a disk from pole 2 to pole 1
Move a disk from pole 2 to pole 3
Move a disk from pole 1 to pole 3

Figure 7-8 illustrates these moves.

FIGURE 7-8    The sequence of moves for solving the Towers of Hanoi problem
with three disks

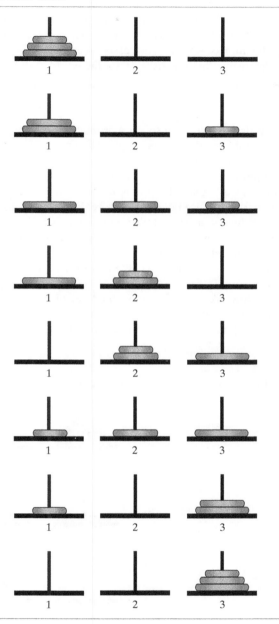

**Question 9** We discovered the previous solution for three disks by trial and error. Using the same approach, find a sequence of moves that solves the problem for four disks.

With four disks, the problem's solution requires 15 moves, so it is somewhat difficult to find by trial and error. With more than four disks, the solution is much more difficult to discover. What we need is an algorithm that produces a solution for any number of disks. Even though discovering a solution by trial and error is hard, finding a recursive algorithm to produce the solution is fairly easy.

> **Aside**
>
> Invented in the late 1800s, the Towers of Hanoi problem was accompanied by this legend. A group of monks was said to have begun moving 64 disks from one tower to another. When they finish, the world will end. When you finish reading this section, you will realize that the monks—or their successors—could not have finished yet. By the time they do, it is quite plausible that the disks, if not the world, will have worn out!

**7.30**   A recursive algorithm solves a problem by solving one or more smaller problems of the same type. The problem size here is simply the number of disks. So imagine that the first pole has four disks, as in Figure 7-9a, and that I ask you to solve the problem. Eventually, you will need to move the bottom disk, but first you need to move the three disks on top of it. Ask a friend to move these three disks—a smaller problem—according to our rules, but make pole 2 the destination. Allow your friend to use pole 3 as a spare. Figure 7-9b shows the final result of your friend's work.

When your friend tells you that the task is complete, you move the one disk left on pole 1 to pole 3. Moving one disk is a simple task. You don't need help—or recursion—to do it. This disk is the largest one, so it cannot rest on top of any other disk. Thus, pole 3 must be empty before this move. After the move, the largest disk will be first on pole 3. Figure 7-9c shows the result of your work.

Now ask a friend to move the three disks on pole 2 to pole 3, adhering to the rules. Allow your friend to use pole 1 as a spare. When your friend tells you that the task is complete, you can tell me that your task is complete as well. Figure 7-9d shows the final results.

**FIGURE 7-9**   The smaller problems in a recursive solution for four disks

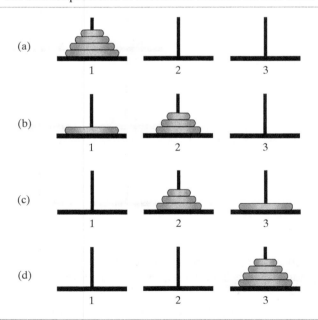

**7.31** Before we write some pseudocode to describe the algorithm, we need to identify a base case. If only one disk is on pole 1, we can move it directly to pole 3 without using recursion. With this as the base case, the algorithm is as follows:

*Algorithm to move* `numberOfDisks` *disks from* `startPole` *to* `endPole` *using* `tempPole`
*as a spare according to the rules of the Towers of Hanoi problem*
```
if (numberOfDisks == 1)
```
    *Move disk from* `startPole` *to* `endPole`
```
else
{
```
    *Move all but the bottom disk from* `startPole` *to* `tempPole`
    *Move disk from* `startPole` *to* `endPole`
    *Move all disks from* `tempPole` *to* `endPole`
```
}
```

At this point, we can develop the algorithm further by writing

*Algorithm* `solveTowers(numberOfDisks, startPole, tempPole, endPole)`
```
if (numberOfDisks == 1)
```
    *Move disk from* `startPole` *to* `endPole`
```
else
{
    solveTowers(numberOfDisks - 1, startPole, endPole, tempPole)
```
    *Move disk from* `startPole` *to* `endPole`
```
    solveTowers(numberOfDisks - 1, tempPole, startPole, endPole)
}
```

If we choose zero disks as the base case instead of one disk, we can simplify the algorithm a bit, as follows:

*Algorithm* `solveTowers(numberOfDisks, startPole, tempPole, endPole)`
```
// Version 2.
if (numberOfDisks > 0)
{
    solveTowers(numberOfDisks - 1, startPole, endPole, tempPole)
```
    *Move disk from* `startPole` *to* `endPole`
```
    solveTowers(numberOfDisks - 1, tempPole, startPole, endPole)
}
```

Although somewhat easier to write, the second version of the algorithm executes many more recursive calls. Both versions, however, make the same moves.

---

 **Question 10** For two disks, how many recursive calls are made by each version of the algorithm just given?

---

Your knowledge of recursion should convince you that both forms of the algorithm are correct. Recursion has enabled us to solve a problem that appeared to be difficult. But is this algorithm efficient? Could we do better if we used iteration?

**7.32** **Efficiency.** Let's look at the efficiency of our algorithm. How many moves occur when we begin with *n* disks? Let $m(n)$ denote the number of moves that `solveTowers` needs to solve the problem for *n* disks. Clearly,

$$m(1) = 1$$

For $n > 1$, the algorithm uses two recursive calls to solve problems that have $n - 1$ disks each. The required number of moves in each case is $m(n - 1)$. Thus, you can see from the algorithm that

$$m(n) = m(n - 1) + 1 + m(n - 1) = 2 \times m(n - 1) + 1$$

From this equation, you can see that $m(n) > 2 \times m(n - 1)$. That is, solving the problem with $n$ disks requires more than twice as many moves as solving the problem with $n - 1$ disks.

It appears that $m(n)$ is related to a power of 2. Let's evaluate the recurrence for $m(n)$ for a few values of $n$:

$$m(1) = 1, \ m(2) = 3, \ m(3) = 7, \ m(4) = 15, \ m(5) = 31, \ m(6) = 63$$

It seems that

$$m(n) = 2^n - 1$$

We can prove this conjecture by using mathematical induction, as follows.

**7.33**   **Proof by induction that $m(n) = 2^n - 1$.** We know that $m(1) = 1$ and $2^1 - 1 = 1$, so the conjecture is true for $n = 1$. Now assume that it is true for $n = 1, 2, \ldots, k$, and consider $m(k + 1)$.

$$
\begin{aligned}
m(k + 1) &= 2 \times m(k) + 1 &&\text{(use the recurrence relation)}\\
&= 2 \times (2^k - 1) + 1 &&\text{(we assumed that } m(k) = 2^k - 1)\\
&= 2^{k+1} - 1
\end{aligned}
$$

Since the conjecture is true for $n = k + 1$, it is true for all $n \geq 1$.

**7.34**   **Exponential growth.** The number of moves required to solve the Towers of Hanoi problem grows exponentially with the number of disks $n$. That is, $m(n) = O(2^n)$. This rate of growth is alarming, as you can see from the following values of $2^n$:

$$
\begin{aligned}
2^5 &= 32\\
2^{10} &= 1024\\
2^{20} &= 1,048,576\\
2^{30} &= 1,073,741,824\\
2^{40} &= 1,099,511,627,776\\
2^{50} &= 1,125,899,906,842,624\\
2^{60} &= 1,152,921,504,606,846,976
\end{aligned}
$$

Remember the monks mentioned at the end of Segment 7.29? They are making $2^{64} - 1$ moves. It should be clear that you can use this exponential algorithm only for small values of $n$, if you want to live to see the results.

Before you condemn recursion and discard our algorithm, you need to know that you cannot do any better. Not you, not the monks, not anyone. We demonstrate this observation next by using mathematical induction.

**7.35**   **Proof that Towers of Hanoi cannot be solved in fewer than $2^n - 1$ moves.** We have shown that our algorithm for the Towers of Hanoi problem requires $m(n) = 2^n - 1$ moves. Since we know that at least one algorithm exists—we found one—there must be a fastest one. Let $M(n)$ represent the number of moves that this optimal algorithm requires for $n$ disks. We need to show that $M(n) = m(n)$ for $n \geq 1$.

When the problem has one disk, our algorithm solves it in one move. We cannot do better, so we have that $M(1) = m(1) = 1$. If we assume that $M(n - 1) = m(n - 1)$, consider $n$ disks. Looking back at Figure 7-9b, you can see that at one point in our algorithm the largest disk is isolated on one pole and $n - 1$ disks are on another. This configuration would have to be true of an optimal algorithm as well, for there is no other way to move the largest disk. Thus, the optimal algorithm must have moved these $n - 1$ disks from pole 1 to pole 2 in $M(n - 1) = m(n - 1)$ moves.

After moving the largest disk (Figure 7-9c), the optimal algorithm moves $n - 1$ disks from pole 2 to pole 3 in another $M(n - 1) = m(n - 1)$ moves. Altogether, the optimal algorithm makes at least $2 \times M(n - 1) + 1$ moves. Thus,

$$M(n) \geq 2 \times M(n - 1) + 1$$

Now apply the assumption that $M(n - 1) = m(n - 1)$ and then the recurrence for $m(n)$ given in Segment 7.32 to get

$$M(n) \geq 2 \times m(n - 1) + 1 = m(n)$$

We have just shown that $M(n) \geq m(n)$. But since the optimal algorithm cannot require more moves than our algorithm, the expression $M(n) > m(n)$ cannot be true. Thus, we must have $M(n) = m(n)$ for all $n \geq 1$.

**7.36**   Finding an iterative algorithm to solve the Towers of Hanoi problem is not as easy as finding a recursive algorithm. We now know that any iterative algorithm will require at least as many moves as the recursive algorithm. An iterative algorithm will save the overhead—space and time—of tracking the recursive calls, but it will not really be more efficient than `solveTowers`. An algorithm that uses both iteration and recursion to solve the Towers of Hanoi problem is discussed in the section "Tail Recursion," and an entirely iterative algorithm is the subject of Project 7 at the end of this chapter.

## A Poor Solution to a Simple Problem

Some recursive solutions are so inefficient that you should avoid them. The problem that we will look at now is simple, occurs frequently in mathematical computations, and has a recursive solution that is so natural that you are likely to be tempted to use it. Don't!

**7.37**    **Example: Fibonacci numbers.** Early in the 13th century, the mathematician Leonardo Fibonacci proposed a sequence of integers to model the number of descendants of a pair of rabbits. Later named the *Fibonacci sequence*, these numbers occur in surprisingly many applications.

The first two terms in the Fibonacci sequence are 1 and 1. Each subsequent term is the sum of the preceding two terms. Thus, the sequence begins as 1, 1, 2, 3, 5, 8, 13, . . . Typically, the sequence is defined by the equations

$$F_0 = 1$$
$$F_1 = 1$$
$$F_n = F_{n-1} + F_{n-2} \text{ when } n \geq 2$$

You can see why the following recursive algorithm would be a tempting way to generate the sequence:

```
Algorithm Fibonacci(n)
if (n <= 1)
    return 1
else
    return Fibonacci(n - 1) + Fibonacci(n - 2)
```

**7.38**   This algorithm makes two recursive calls. That fact in itself is not the difficulty. Earlier, you saw perfectly good algorithms—`displayArray` in Segment 7.18 and `solveTowers` in Segment 7.31—that make several recursive calls. The trouble here is that the same recursive calls are made repeatedly. A call to `Fibonacci(n)` invokes `Fibonacci(n - 1)` and then `Fibonacci(n - 2)`. But the call to `Fibonacci(n - 1)` has to compute `Fibonacci(n - 2)`, so the same Fibonacci number is computed twice.

Things get worse. The call to `Fibonacci(n - 1)` calls `Fibonacci(n - 3)` as well. The two previous calls to `Fibonacci(n - 2)` each invoke `Fibonacci(n - 3)`, so `Fibonacci(n - 3)` is computed three times. Figure 7-10a illustrates the dependency of $F_6$ on previous Fibonacci numbers and so indicates the number of times a particular number is computed repeatedly by the method `Fibonacci`. In contrast, Figure 7-10b shows that an iterative computation of $F_6$ computes each prior term once. The recursive solution is clearly less efficient. The next segments will show you just how inefficient it is.

**FIGURE 7-10**   The computation of the Fibonacci number $F_6$ using (a) recursion; (b) iteration

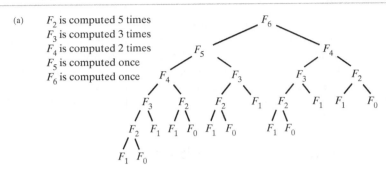

(a)   $F_2$ is computed 5 times
$F_3$ is computed 3 times
$F_4$ is computed 2 times
$F_5$ is computed once
$F_6$ is computed once

(b)   $F_0 = 1$
$F_1 = 1$
$F_2 = F_1 + F_0 = 2$
$F_3 = F_2 + F_1 = 3$
$F_4 = F_3 + F_2 = 5$
$F_5 = F_4 + F_3 = 8$
$F_6 = F_5 + F_4 = 13$

**7.39**   **The time efficiency of the algorithm Fibonacci.** We can investigate the efficiency of the Fibonacci algorithm by using a recurrence relation, as we did in Segments 7.22 through Segment 7.27. First, notice that $F_n$ requires one add operation plus the operations that $F_{n-1}$ and $F_{n-2}$ require. So if $t(n)$ represents the time requirement of the algorithm in computing $F_n$, we have

$t(n) = 1 + t(n - 1) + t(n - 2)$ for $n \geq 2$
$t(1) = 1$
$t(0) = 1$

This recurrence relation looks like the recurrence for the Fibonacci numbers themselves. It should not surprise you then that $t(n)$ is related to the Fibonacci numbers. In fact, if you look at Figure 7-10a and count the occurrences of the Fibonacci numbers $F_2$ through $F_6$, you will discover a Fibonacci sequence.

To find a relationship between $t(n)$ and $F_n$, let's expand $t(n)$ for a few values of $n$:

$t(2) = 1 + t(1) + t(0) = 1 + F_1 + F_0 = 1 + F_2 > F_2$
$t(3) = 1 + t(2) + t(1) > 1 + F_2 + F_1 = 1 + F_3 > F_3$
$t(4) = 1 + t(3) + t(2) > 1 + F_3 + F_2 = 1 + F_4 > F_4$

We guess that $t(n) > F_n$ for $n \geq 2$. Notice that $t(0) = 1 = F_0$ and $t(1) = 1 = F_1$. These do not satisfy the strict inequality of our guess.

We now prove that our guess is indeed fact. (You can skip the proof on your first reading.)

**7.40**   **Proof by induction that $t(n) > F_n$ for $n \geq 2$.** Since the recurrence relation for $t(n)$ involves two recursive terms, we need two base cases. In the previous segment, we already showed that $t(2) > F_2$ and $t(3) > F_3$. Now if $t(n) > F_n$ for $n = 2, 3, \ldots, k$, we need to show that $t(k + 1) > F_{k+1}$. We can do this as follows:

$t(k + 1) = 1 + t(k) + t(k - 1) > 1 + F_k + F_{k-1} = 1 + F_{k+1} > F_{k+1}$

We can conclude that $t(n) > F_n$ for all $n \geq 2$.

Since we know that $t(n) > F_n$ for all $n \geq 2$, we can say that $t(n) = \Omega(F_n)$. Recall from Chapter 4 that the Big Omega notation means that $t(n)$ is at least as large as the Fibonacci number $F_n$. It turns out that we can compute $F_n$ directly without using the recurrence relation given in Segment 7.37. It can be shown that

$$F_n = (a^n - b^n)/\sqrt{5}$$

where $a = (1 + \sqrt{5})/2$ and $b = (1 - \sqrt{5})/2$. Since $|1 - \sqrt{5}| < 2$, we have $|b| < 1$ and $|b^n| < 1$. Therefore, we have

$$F_n > (a^n - 1)/\sqrt{5}$$

Thus, $F_n = \Omega(a^n)$, and since we know that $t(n) = \Omega(F_n)$, we have $t(n) = \Omega(a^n)$. Some arithmetic shows that the previous expression for $a$ equals approximately 1.6. We conclude that $t(n)$ grows exponentially with $n$. That is, the time required to compute $F_n$ recursively increases exponentially as $n$ increases.

**7.41**    At the beginning of this section, we observed that each Fibonacci number is the sum of the preceding two Fibonacci numbers in the sequence. This observation should lead us to an iterative solution that is $O(n)$. (See Exercise 9 at the end of this chapter.) Although the clarity and simplicity of the recursive solution make it a tempting choice, it is much too inefficient to use.

**Programming Tip:** Do not use a recursive solution that repeatedly solves the same problem in its recursive calls.

**Question 11** If you compute the Fibonnaci number $F_6$ recursively, how many recursive calls are made, and how many additions are performed?

**Question 12** If you compute the Fibonnaci number $F_6$ iteratively, how many additions are performed?

# Tail Recursion

**7.42**    **Tail recursion** occurs when the last action performed by a recursive method is a recursive call. For example, the following method `countDown` from Segment 7.6 is tail recursive:

```java
public static void countDown(int integer)
{
    if (integer >= 1)
    {
        System.out.println(integer);
        countDown(integer - 1);
    } // end if
} // end countDown
```

A method that implements the algorithm `Fibonacci` given in Segment 7.37 will not be tail recursive, even though a recursive call *appears* last in the method. A closer look reveals that the last *action* is an addition.

The tail recursion in a method simply repeats the method's logic with changes to parameters and variables. Thus, you can perform the same repetition by using iteration. Converting a tail-recursive method to an iterative one is usually a straightforward process. For example, let's see how to convert the recursive method `countDown` just given. First we replace the `if` statement with a `while` statement. Then, instead of the recursive call, we assign its argument integer - 1 to the method's formal parameter integer. Doing so gives us the following iterative version of the method:

```
public static void countDown(int integer)
{
   while (integer >= 1)
   {
      System.out.println(integer);
      integer = integer - 1;
   } // end while
} // end countDown
```

This method is essentially the same as the iterative method given in Segment 7.7.

Because converting tail recursion to iteration is often uncomplicated, some languages other than Java automatically convert tail-recursive methods to iterative methods to save the overhead involved with recursion. Most of this overhead involves memory, not time. If you need to save space, you should consider replacing tail recursion with iteration.

**7.43** **Example.** Let's replace the tail recursion in the second version of the algorithm solveTowers given in Segment 7.31:

```
Algorithm solveTowers(numberOfDisks, startPole, tempPole, endPole)
if (numberOfDisks > 0)
{
   solveTowers(numberOfDisks - 1, startPole, endPole, tempPole)
   Move disk from startPole to endPole
   solveTowers(numberOfDisks - 1, tempPole, startPole, endPole)
}
```

This algorithm contains two recursive calls. The second one is tail recursive, since it is the algorithm's last action. Thus, we could try replacing the second recursive call with appropriate assignment statements and use a loop to repeat the method's logic, including the first recursive call, as follows:

```
Algorithm solveTowers(numberOfDisks, startPole, tempPole, endPole)
while (numberOfDisks > 0)
{
   solveTowers(numberOfDisks - 1, startPole, endPole, tempPole)
   Move disk from startPole to endPole
   numberOfDisks = numberOfDisks - 1
   startPole = tempPole
   tempPole = startPole
   endPole = endPole
}
```

This isn't quite right, however. Obviously, assigning endPole to itself is superfluous. Assigning tempPole to startPole and then assigning startPole to tempPole destroys startPole but leaves tempPole unchanged. What we need to do is exchange tempPole and startPole. Let's look at what is really happening here.

The only instruction that actually moves disks is *Move disk from* startPole *to* endPole. This instruction moves the largest disk that is not already on endPole. The disk to be moved is at the bottom of a pole, so any disks that are on top of it need to be moved first. Those disks are moved by the first recursive call. If we want to omit the second recursive call, what would we need to do instead before repeating the first recursive call? We must make sure that startPole contains the disks that have not been moved to endPole. Those disks are on tempPole as a result of the first recursive call. Thus, we need to exchange the contents of tempPole and startPole.

Making these changes results in the following revised algorithm:

*Algorithm* `solveTowers(numberOfDisks, startPole, tempPole, endPole)`

```
while (numberOfDisks > 0)
{
    solveTowers(numberOfDisks - 1, startPole, endPole, tempPole)
    Move disk from startPole to endPole
    numberOfDisks--
    Exchange the contents of tempPole and startPole
}
```

This revised algorithm is unusual in that its loop contains a recursive call. The base case for this recursion occurs when `numberOfDisks` is zero. Even though the method does not contain an `if` statement, it does detect the base case, ending the recursive calls.

 **Note:** In a tail-recursive method, the last action is a recursive call. This call performs a repetition that can be done by using iteration. Converting a tail-recursive method to an iterative one is usually a straightforward process.

# Indirect Recursion

**7.44**    Some recursive algorithms make their recursive calls indirectly. For example, we might have the following chain of events: Method A calls Method B, Method B calls Method C, and Method C calls Method A. Such recursion—called **indirect recursion**—is more difficult to understand and trace, but it does arise naturally in certain applications.

For example, the following rules describe strings that are valid algebraic expressions:

- An algebraic expression is either a term or two terms separated by a + or - operator.
- A term is either a factor or two factors separated by a * or / operator.
- A factor is either a variable or an algebraic expression enclosed in parentheses.
- A variable is a single letter.

Suppose that the methods `isExpression`, `isTerm`, `isFactor`, and `isVariable` detect whether a string is, respectively, an expression, a term, a factor, or a variable. The method `isExpression` calls `isTerm`, which in turn calls `isFactor`, which then calls `isVariable` and `isExpression`. Figure 7-11 illustrates these calls.

A special case of indirect recursion, where Method A calls Method B, and Method B calls Method A, is called **mutual recursion**. Project 10 at the end of this chapter describes an example of mutual recursion.

**FIGURE 7-11**    An example of indirect recursion

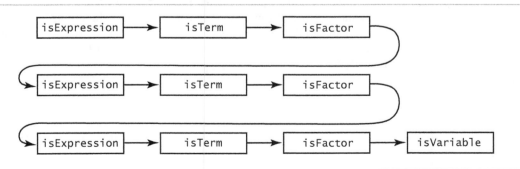

# Using a Stack Instead of Recursion

**7.45** One way to replace recursion with iteration is to simulate the program stack. In fact, we can implement a recursive algorithm by using a stack instead of recursion. As an example of converting a recursive method to an iterative one, we will consider the method `displayArray`, as given in Segment 7.18. For this demonstration, we will revise `displayArray` to be a nonstatic method in a class that has an array as a data field. With these changes, the method appears as follows:

```java
public void displayArray(int first, int last)
{
    if (first == last)
        System.out.println(array[first] + " ");
    else
    {
        int mid = first + (last - first) / 2; // Improved calculation of midpoint
        displayArray(first, mid);
        displayArray(mid + 1, last);
    } // end if
} // end displayArray
```

**7.46** We can replace the recursive method `displayArray` given in the previous segment with an iterative version by using a stack that mimics the program stack. To do so, we create a stack that is local to the method. We push objects onto this stack that are like the activation records described in Segment 7.10. An activation record in Java's program stack contains the method's arguments, its local variables, and a reference to the current instruction. Since both recursive calls to the method `displayArray` are consecutive, there is no need for our activation records to distinguish between them by storing a representation of the program counter in the record. This simplification is not true in general, however.

To represent a record, we define a class that, in this case, has data fields for the method's arguments `first` and `last`. The following simple class is sufficient if we make it internal to our class containing `displayArray`:

```java
private class Record
{
    private int first, last;
    private Record(int firstIndex, int lastIndex)
    {
        first = firstIndex;
        last = lastIndex;
    } // end constructor
} // end Record
```

**7.47** In general, when a method begins execution, it pushes an activation record onto a program stack. At its return, a record is popped from this stack. We want an iterative `displayArray` to maintain its own stack. When the method begins execution, it should push a record onto this stack. Each recursive call should do likewise. As long as the stack is not empty, the method should remove a record from the stack and act according to the contents of the record. The method ends its execution when the stack becomes empty.

Here is an iterative version of displayArray that uses a stack as we just described:

```
private void displayArray(int first, int last)
{
    boolean done = false;
    StackInterface<Record> programStack = new LinkedStack<>();
    programStack.push(new Record(first, last));
    while (!done && !programStack.isEmpty())
    {
        Record topRecord = programStack.pop();
        first = topRecord.first;
        last = topRecord.last;
        if (first == last)
            System.out.println(array[first] + " ");
        else
        {
            int mid = first + (last - first) / 2;
            // Note the order of the records pushed onto the stack
            programStack.push(new Record(mid + 1, last));
            programStack.push(new Record(first, mid));
        } // end if
    } // end while
} // end displayArray
```

This approach does not always produce an elegant solution. We certainly could write an iterative version of displayArray that was easier to understand than this version and did not require a stack. But sometimes a simple iterative solution is not apparent; in such cases, the stack approach offers a possible solution. You will see a more useful example of a stack-based iteration in Segment 24.13 of Chapter 24.

## CHAPTER SUMMARY

- Recursion is a problem-solving process that breaks a problem into identical but smaller problems.

- The definition of a recursive method must contain logic that involves an input—often a parameter—to the method and leads to different cases. One or more of these cases are base cases, or stopping cases, because they provide a solution that does not require recursion. One or more cases include a recursive invocation of the method that takes a step toward a base case by solving a "smaller" version of the task performed by the method.

- For each call to a method, Java records the values of the method's parameters and local variables in an activation record. The records are placed into a stack, which organizes them chronologically. The record most recently added to the stack is of the currently executing method. In this way, Java can suspend the execution of a recursive method and invoke it again with new argument values.

- A recursive method that processes an array often divides the array into portions. Recursive calls to the method work on each of these array portions.

- A recursive method that processes a chain of linked nodes needs a reference to the chain's first node as its parameter.

- A recursive method that is part of an implementation of an ADT often is private, because its use requires knowledge of the underlying data structure. Although such a method is unsuitable as an ADT operation, it can be called by a public method that implements the operation.

- A recurrence relation expresses a function in terms of itself. You can use a recurrence relation to describe the work done by a recursive method.

- Any solution to the Towers of Hanoi problem with $n$ disks requires at least $2^n - 1$ moves. A recursive solution to this problem is clear and as efficient as possible. As an $O(2^n)$ algorithm, however, it is practical for small values of $n$.

- Each number in the Fibonacci sequence—after the first two—is the sum of the previous two numbers. Computing a Fibonacci number recursively is quite inefficient, as the required previous numbers are computed several times each.

- Tail recursion occurs when the last action of a recursive method is a recursive call. This recursive call performs a repetition that can be done by using iteration. Converting a tail-recursive method to an iterative one is usually a straightforward process.

- Indirect recursion results when a method calls a method that calls a method, and so on until the first method is called again.

- You can use a stack instead of recursion to implement a recursive algorithm. This stack mimics the behavior of the program stack.

## PROGRAMMING TIPS

- An iterative method contains a loop. A recursive method calls itself. Although some recursive methods contain a loop *and* call themselves, if you have written a `while` statement within a recursive method, be sure that you did not mean to write an `if` statement.

- A recursive method that does not check for a base case, or that misses the base case, will not terminate normally. This situation is known as infinite recursion.

- Too many recursive calls can cause the error message "stack overflow." This means that the stack of activation records has become full. In essence, the method uses too much memory. Infinite recursion or large-size problems are the likely causes of this error.

- Do not use a recursive solution that repeatedly solves the same problem in its recursive calls.

- If a recursive method does not work, answer the following questions. Any "no" answers should guide you to the error.

  - Does the method have at least one parameter or input value?
  - Does the method contain a statement that tests a parameter or input value, leading to different cases?
  - Did you consider all possible cases?
  - Does at least one of these cases cause at least one recursive call?
  - Do these recursive calls involve smaller arguments, smaller tasks, or tasks that get closer to the solution?
  - If these recursive calls produce or return correct results, will the method produce or return a correct result?
  - Is at least one of the cases a base case that has no recursive call?
  - Are there enough base cases?
  - Does each base case produce a result that is correct for that case?
  - If the method returns a value, does each of the cases return a value?

## EXERCISES

1. Consider the method `displayRowOfIntegers` that displays any given integer twice the specified number of times on one line. For example, the call

   ```
   displayRowOfIntegers(9, 3);
   ```

   produces the line

   ```
   999999
   ```

   Implement this method in Java by using recursion.

2. Describe a recursive algorithm that draws concentric squares, given the height of the outermost square. The height of each inner square should be two-thirds the height of the square that encloses it. The height of the innermost square should exceed 2 inches.

3. Write a method that asks the user to input an even integer between 10 and 100, inclusive. If the input is odd or out of range, the method should recursively ask the user to enter a new input value.

4. Suppose that a program is required to calculate the sum of the first $n$ natural numbers, that is, the positive integers such as 1, 2, and 3. Suggest two different recursive methods to implement this program.

5. Write a recursive method that writes a given array backward. Consider the last element of the array first.

6. Repeat Exercise 5, but instead consider the first element of the array first.

7. Repeat Exercises 5 and 6, but write a string backward instead of an array.

8. A palindrome is a string that reads the same forward and backward. For example *deed* and *level* are palindromes. Write an algorithm in pseudocode that tests whether a string is a palindrome. Implement your algorithm as a static method in Java. Exercise 11 and Project 3 in Chapter 5 asked you to describe how to do this using a stack.

9. Segment 7.37 introduced the Fibonacci sequence. Computing this sequence recursively is inefficient and takes too much time. Write two methods that each compute the $n^{th}$ term in the Fibonacci sequence by using iteration instead of recursion. One method should use an array to store the Fibonacci numbers. The other method should use three variables to contain the current term in the sequence and the two terms before it.

   What is the Big Oh for each of your iterative methods? Compare these results with the performance of the recursive algorithm.

10. For three disks, how many recursive calls are made by each of the two `solveTowers` algorithms given in Segment 7.31?

11. Write a recursive method that counts the number of odd integers in a given array.

12. If n is a positive integer in Java, n % 10 is its rightmost digit and n/10 is the integer obtained by dropping the rightmost digit from n. Using these facts, write a recursive method that calculates the sum of the digits of a given integer. For example, if the given integer is 138, the method should return the sum of the digits 1, 3, and 8.

13. Consider the method `getFrequencyOf` in the class `ArrayBag`, as given in Segment 2.20 of Chapter 2. Write a private recursive method that `getFrequencyOf` can call, and revise the definition of `getFrequencyOf` accordingly.

14. Repeat Exercise 13, but instead use the class `LinkedBag` and the method `getFrequencyOf` in Segment 3.16 of Chapter 3.

15. Write four different recursive methods that each compute the sum of integers in an array of integers. Model your methods after the `displayArray` methods given in Segments 7.15 through 7.18 and described in Question 5.

16.  Write a recursive method that returns the smallest integer in an array of integers. If you divide the array into two pieces— halves, for example—and find the smallest integer in each of the two pieces, the smallest integer in the entire array will be the smaller of the these two integers. Since you will be searching a portion of the array—for example, the elements `array[first]` through `array[last]`—it will be convenient for your method to have three parameters: the array and two indices, `first` and `last`. You can refer to the method `displayArray` in Segment 7.18 for inspiration.

17.  Trace the call `f(16)` to the following method by showing a stack of activation records:

```
public int f(int n)
{
   int result = 0;
   if (f <= 4)
      result = 1;
   else
      result = f(n / 2) + f(n / 4);
   return result;
} // end f
```

18.  Write a recursive algorithm in pseudocode that finds the second largest object in an array of `Comparable` objects. Implement your algorithm as a static method in Java.

19.  Consider the class `ArrayBag`, as given in Chapter 2. Implement the method `sumOfIntegers` for `ArrayBag` to calculate the sum of the integers in the bag recursively.

20.  If
$$t(1) = 2$$
$$t(n) = 2 * t(n - 1) \text{ for } n > 1$$
find an expression for  $t(n)$ that is not given in terms of itself. Prove that your result is correct by using induction.

21.  If
$$t(1) = 0$$
$$t(n) = 1 + t(n - 1) \text{ for } n > 1$$
find an expression for $t(n)$ that is not given in terms of itself. Prove that your result is correct by using induction.

22.  Consider a checkerboard that has a dollar amount printed on each of its squares. You can place a checker on the board anywhere you want and then move it across the board with standard diagonal moves. Once you reach the other side, you are finished. You will collect an amount of money equal to the sum of the values written on the squares that your checker traveled over.

   a.  Give a recursive algorithm that will compute the maximum amount you can collect.
   b.  Give an iterative algorithm that uses a stack to compute the maximum amount you can collect.

23.  Consider the recursive method given in Segment 7.21 that displays the contents of a chain of linked nodes in backward order. Also consider the recursive method described in Exercise 5 that displays the contents of an array in backward order.

   a.  What is the time complexity of each of these two methods, and how do they compare?
   b.  Write an iterative method that displays the contents of a chain of linked nodes in backward order. What is this method's time complexity, and how does it compare to the complexities that you computed in Part *a*?

**24.** Write a static recursive method that displays all of the permutations of the digits in a string passed to the method as its argument. For example, the string *396* has the following permutations: *369, 936, 963, 639, 693.*

## PROJECTS

**1.** The following algorithm finds the square root of a positive number:

```
Algorithm squareRoot(number, lowGuess, highGuess, tolerance)
newGuess = (lowGuess + highGuess) / 2
if ((highGuess - newGuess) / newGuess < tolerance)
   return newGuess
else if (newGuess * newGuess > number)
   return squareRoot(number, lowGuess, newGuess, tolerance)
else if (newGuess * newGuess < number)
   return squareRoot(number, newGuess, highGuess, tolerance)
else
   return newGuess
```

To begin the computation, you need a value `lowGuess` less than the square root of the number and a value `highGuess` that is larger. You can use zero as `lowGuess` and the number itself as `highGuess`. The parameter `tolerance` controls the precision of the result independently of the magnitude of `number`. For example, computing the square root of 250 with `tolerance` equal to 0.00005 results in 15.81. This result has four digits of accuracy.

Implement this algorithm.

**2.** Implement the two versions of the `solveTower` algorithm given in Segment 7.31. Represent the towers by either single characters or strings. Each method should display directions that indicate the moves that must be made. Insert counters into each method to count the number of times it is called. These counters can be data fields of the class that contains these methods. Compare the number of recursive calls made by each method for various numbers of disks.

**3.** Consider the following algorithm to sort the entries in a stack $S_1$. First create two empty stacks, $S_2$ and $S_3$. At any given time, stack $S_2$ will hold the entries in sorted order, with the smallest at the top of the stack. Move the top entry of $S_1$ to $S_2$. Pop and consider the top entry $t$ of $S_1$. Pop entries of stack $S_2$ and push them onto stack $S_3$ until you reach the correct place to put $t$. Then push $t$ onto $S_2$. Next move all the entries from $S_3$ to $S_2$.

Write a recursive implementation of this algorithm.

**4.** Implement the algorithms that Exercise 22 describes.

**5.** Imagine an array of $n$ items from which you can choose. You will place the items you choose into a knapsack of size $k$. Each item has a size and a value. Of course, you cannot take more items than you have space for in the knapsack. Your goal is to maximize the total value of the items you take.

  **a.** Design a recursive algorithm `maxKnapsack` to solve this knapsack problem. The parameters to the algorithm are the knapsack, the array of items, and the position within the array of the next item to consider. The algorithm chooses the items for the knapsack and returns a knapsack containing the chosen items. A knapsack can report its size, its contents, the value of its contents, and the size of its contents.

  *Hint*: If any items in the array have not yet been considered, retrieve the next item in the array. You can either ignore the item or, if it fits, put it in the knapsack. To decide, make a recursive call for each of these two cases. Compare the knapsacks returned by these calls to see which one has the most valuable contents. Then return that knapsack.

**b.** Write the classes `Knapsack` and `KnapsackItem`. Then write a program that defines the method `maxKnapsack`. The program should read the size of the knapsack and then the size, value, and name of each available item. Here is some sample input data for a knapsack of size 10:

| Size | Value | Name |
|---|---|---|
| 1 | 50000 | rare coin |
| 2 | 7000 | small gold coin |
| 4 | 10000 | packet of stamps |
| 4 | 11000 | pearl necklace |
| 5 | 12000 | silver bar |
| 10 | 60000 | painting |

After displaying the items, call `maxKnapsack`. Then display the chosen items, their values, and their total value.

6. Suppose that you are scheduling a room. You are given a group of activities each of which has a start time and stop time. Two activities are compatible if they do not overlap. For example, in the following activities, activity A is compatible with activities B and D, but not activity C:

| Activity | Start Time | Stop Time |
|---|---|---|
| A | 1 | 2 |
| B | 2 | 5 |
| C | 1 | 3 |
| D | 5 | 6 |

Your goal is to schedule compatible activities that result in a maximum usage of the room.

**a.** Design a recursive algorithm to solve this room-scheduling problem. The method whose signature is

```
maxRoomUse(int startTime, int stopTime, Activity[] activities)
```

returns a pair consisting of the maximum usage in hours and an array of activities scheduled. Note that `startTime` is the first time that an activity can be scheduled, `stopTime` is the final time, and `activities` is an array of possible activities.

**b.** Write the class `Activity` and a class `Schedule` that represents the pair that `maxRoomUse` returns. Then write a program that defines the method `maxRoomUse`. The program should read the start time and stop time for the room followed by the start and stop times for each activity (one activity per line). After displaying the given activities, display the maximum usage in hours of the room along with a list of the scheduled activities.

7. You can get a solution to the Towers of Hanoi problem by using the following iterative algorithm. Beginning with pole 1 and moving from pole to pole in the order pole 1, pole 3, pole 2, pole 1, and so on, make at most one move per pole according to the following rules:

- Move the topmost disk from a pole to the next possible pole in the specified order. Remember that you cannot place a disk on top of a smaller one.
- If the disk that you are about to move is the smallest of all the disks and you just moved it to the present pole, do not move it. Instead, consider the next pole.

This algorithm should make the same moves as the recursive algorithms given in Segment 7.31 and pictured in Figure 7-8. Thus, this iterative algorithm is $O(2^n)$ as well.

Implement this algorithm.

8. Write an application or applet that animates the solution to the Towers of Hanoi problem. The problem asks you to move *n* disks from one pole to another, one at a time. You move only the top disk on a pole, and you place a disk only on top of larger disks on a pole. Since each disk has certain characteristics, such as its size, it is natural to define a class of disks.

Design and implement an ADT tower that includes the following operations:

- Add a disk to the top of the disks on the pole
- Remove the topmost disk

Also, design and implement a class that includes a recursive method to solve the problem.

9. Java's class Graphics has the following method to draw a line between two given points:

```
/** Draws a line between the points (x1, y1) and (x2, y2). */
public void drawLine(int x1, int y1, int x2, int y2)
```

Graphics uses a coordinate system that measures points from the top left corner of a window.

Write a recursive method that draws a picture of a 12-inch ruler. Mark inches, half inches, quarter inches, and eighth inches. Mark the half inches with marks that are smaller than those that mark the inches. Mark the quarter inches with marks that are smaller than those that mark the half inches, and so on. Your picture need not be full size. *Hint*: Draw a mark in the middle of the ruler and then draw rulers to the left and right of this mark.

10. Imagine a row of *n* lights that can be turned on or off only under certain conditions, as follows. The first light can be turned on or off anytime. Each of the other lights can be turned on or off only when the preceding light is on and all other lights before it are off. If all the lights are on initially, how can you turn them off? For three lights numbered 1 to 3, you can take the following steps, where 1 is a light that is on and 0 is a light that is off:

| | |
|---|---|
| 1 1 1 | All on initially |
| 0 1 1 | Turn off light 1 |
| 0 1 0 | Turn off light 3 |
| 1 1 0 | Turn on light 1 |
| 1 0 0 | Turn off light 2 |
| 0 0 0 | Turn off light 1 |

You can solve this problem in general by using mutual recursion, as follows:

*Algorithm* turnOff(n)
*// Turns off n lights that are initially on.*
```
if (n == 1)
    Turn off light 1
else
{
    if (n > 2)
        turnOff(n - 2)
    Turn off light n
    if (n > 2)
        turnOn(n - 2)
    turnOff(n - 1)
}
```

*Algorithm* turnOn(n)
*// Turns on n lights that are initially off.*
```
if (n == 1)
    Turn on light 1
```

```
        else
        {
           turnOn(n - 1)
           if (n > 2)
              turnOff(n - 2)
           Turn on light n
           if (n > 2)
              turnOn(n - 2)
        }
```

**a.** Implement these algorithms in Java. Use the results in a program to display directions to turn off *n* lights that initially are on.

**b.** What recurrence relation expresses the number of times that lights are switched on or off during the course of solving this problem for *n* lights?

**11.** Repeat Project 10 in Chapter 5, using a recursive algorithm instead of a stack-based one.

**12.** Define a static recursive method that returns the arabic integer equivalent of a roman numeral given to the method as a string argument.

## ANSWERS TO SELF-TEST QUESTIONS

**1.**
```java
public static void skipLines(int givenNumber)
{
   if (givenNumber >= 1)
   {
      System.out.println();
      skipLines(givenNumber - 1);
   } // end if
} // end skipLines
```

**2.**
```
Algorithm drawConcentricCircles(givenNumber, givenDiameter, givenPoint)
if (givenNumber >= 1)
{
   Draw a circle whose diameter is givenDiameter and whose center is at givenPoint
   givenDiameter = 4 * givenDiameter / 3
   drawConcentricCircles(givenNumber - 1, givenDiameter, givenPoint)
}
```

**3.**
```java
public static void countUp(int n)
{
   if (n >= 1)
   {
      countUp(n - 1);
      System.out.println(n);
   } // end if
} // end countUp
```

**4.** 
```java
public static int productOf(int n)
{
   int result = 1;
   if (n > 1)
      result = n * productOf(n - 1);
   return result;
} // end productOf
```

**5.** 
```java
public static void displayArray(int[] array, int first, int last)
{
   if (first == last)
      System.out.print(array[first] + " ");
   else
   {
      int mid = (first + last) / 2;
      displayArray(array, first, mid - 1);
      System.out.print(array[mid] + " ");
      displayArray(array, mid + 1, last);
   } // end if
} // end displayArray
```

**6.** The order of events is as follows:

```
displayBackward()
displayChainBackward(firstNode)
displayChainBackward(a reference to the second node)
displayChainBackward(a reference to the third node)
displayChainBackward(null)
Print the data in the third node
Print the data in the second node
Print the data in the first node
```

Activation records for the calls to displayChainBackward appear in a stack, as follows (dCB is an abbreviation for displayChainBackward; the stack is shown top to bottom):

```
dCB(firstNode)
dCB(reference to second node)  dCB(firstNode)
dCB(reference to third node)  dCB(reference to second node)  dCB(firstNode)
dCB(null)  dCB(reference to third node)  dCB(reference to second node)  dCB(firstNode)
dCB(reference to third node)  dCB(reference to second node)  dCB(firstNode)
Print the data in the third node
dCB(reference to second node)  dCB(firstNode)
Print the data in the second node
dCB(firstNode)
Print the data in the first node
```

**7.** $O(n)$. You can use the same recurrence relation that was shown in Segments 7.22 and 7.23 for the method countDown.

**8.** **a.** $t(n) = 1 + t(n - 1)$ for $n > 0$, $t(0) = 1$.
   **b.** Since $t(n) = n + 1$, the algorithm is $O(n)$.

9.  Move a disk from pole 1 to pole 2
    Move a disk from pole 1 to pole 3
    Move a disk from pole 2 to pole 3
    Move a disk from pole 1 to pole 2
    Move a disk from pole 3 to pole 1
    Move a disk from pole 3 to pole 2
    Move a disk from pole 1 to pole 2
    Move a disk from pole 1 to pole 3
    Move a disk from pole 2 to pole 3
    Move a disk from pole 2 to pole 1
    Move a disk from pole 3 to pole 1
    Move a disk from pole 2 to pole 3
    Move a disk from pole 1 to pole 2
    Move a disk from pole 1 to pole 3
    Move a disk from pole 2 to pole 3

10. 2 and 6, respectively.

11. 24 recursive calls and 12 additions.

12. 5 additions.

# More About Generics

## Contents

## Prerequisites

This interlude continues our discussion of generics and interfaces that we began in Java Interlude 1. We will use these aspects of Java in the next two chapters, which introduce ways to place objects into ascending or descending order.

## The Interface Comparable

**JI3.1**    **The method compareTo.** Appendix B describes the method compareTo for the class String. This method returns an integer as a result of comparing two strings. For example, if s and t are strings, s.compareTo(t) is

- Negative if s comes before t
- Zero if s and t are equal
- Positive if s comes after t

Other classes can have their own compareTo method that behaves in an analogous way.

 **Note:** The method compareTo compares two objects and returns a signed integer that indicates the result of the comparison. For example, if x and y are two instances of the same class that implements the interface Comparable, x.compareTo(y) returns

- A negative integer if x is less than y
- Zero if x equals y
- A positive integer if x is greater than y

If x and y have different types, x.compareTo(y) throws the exception ClassCastException.

**Note:** Enumerations have a compareTo method. The order in which the enumerated objects appear in the enumeration determines the result of a comparison. For example, if we have

    `enum Coin {PENNY, NICKEL, DIME, QUARTER}`

and myCoin is an instance of Coin, myCoin.compareTo(Coin.DIME) decides whether myCoin is before, after, or equal to Coin.DIME. In particular, if myCoin has the value Coin.PENNY, the result of the comparison with Coin.DIME is a negative integer.

**JI3.2**    All classes that define the method compareTo implement the standard interface Comparable, which is in the Java Class Library in the package java.lang. This interface, which is shown in Listing JI3-1, uses a generic type T to represent the class that implements the interface. Thus, by invoking compareTo, you compare two objects of the class T.

---

**LISTING JI3-1**  The interface java.lang.Comparable

```
1  package java.lang;
2  public interface Comparable<T>
3  {
4     public int compareTo(T other);
5  } // end Comparable
```

---

**JI3.3**    Let's create the class Circle, giving it the methods equals and compareTo, and the methods in the interface Measurable, as given in Listing P-1 of the Prelude. The class implements two interfaces, so we begin it as follows:

```
public class Circle implements Comparable<Circle>, Measurable
{
    private double radius;

    < Definitions of constructors and methods are here >
    . . .
```

The name of the class appears in brackets after the interface name Comparable. Thus, Circle corresponds to T in the interface and is therefore the data type of compareTo's parameter.

The method compareTo has the following implementation within the class:

```
public int compareTo(Circle other)
{
    int result;
    if (this.equals(other))
        result = 0;
    else if (radius < other.radius)
        result = -1;
    else
        result = 1;

    return result;
} // end compareTo
```

This version of compareTo compares circles by comparing their radii and assumes that Circle has its own equals method. While compareTo need not invoke equals, these two methods usually should return consistent results. That is, if object1.equals(object2) is true, object1.compareTo(object2) should return zero.

**JI3.4**    Although the previous version of compareTo returns either -1 or +1 for unequal objects, the specification of compareTo does not insist on these values. Only the sign of the result must be correct. Thus, when the comparison involves integers, a simple subtraction often produces a suitable return value. For example, if the data field `radius` in the class `Circle` were an integer instead of a real value, `compareTo` could have had the following simple definition:

```java
// Assumes radius is an integer
public int compareTo(Circle other)
{
   return radius - other.radius;
} // end compareTo
```

**JI3.5**   You might wonder why `compareTo` does not belong to the class `Object`. The reason is that not all classes should have a `compareTo` method. Classes of objects without a natural ordering are possible and not at all unusual. For example, consider a class of mailing addresses. Deciding whether two addresses are equal should be simple, but what does it mean for one address to be less than another?

**Note:** Not all classes should implement the interface `Comparable`.

**Question 1** Define a class `Name` that implements the interface `NameInterface`, as given in Listing P-2, and the interface `Comparable`.

## Generic Methods

VideoNote

Generic classes
and methods

**JI3.6**   Suppose that you have a class that does not define a type parameter in its header, but you want to use a generic data type in a method of that class. For example, you might have a class of static methods that perform various utility functions. The class `Math` in the Java Class Library is one such class. You would take the following steps in writing such a **generic method:**

- Write a type parameter enclosed in angle brackets in the method's header just before its return type.
- Use the type parameter within the method as you would if it were in a generic class, that is, as either a return type, the data type of the method's parameters, or the data type of a variable within the body of the method.

Listing JI3-2 provides an example of a generic method `displayArray` that displays the contents of an array whose entries have generic types. The `main` method calls `displayArray`, passing it an array of strings and then an array of characters.

---

LISTING JI3-2   An example of a generic method

```java
1 public class Example
2 {
3    public static <T> void displayArray(T[] anArray)
4    {
5       for (T arrayEntry : anArray)
6       {
7          System.out.print(arrayEntry);
8          System.out.print(' ');
9       } // end for
10       System.out.println();
11    } // end displayArray
12
```

```
13    public static void main(String args[])
14    {
15       String[] stringArray = {"apple", "banana", "carrot", "dandelion"};
16       System.out.print("stringArray contains ");
17       displayArray(stringArray);
18
19       Character[] characterArray = {'a', 'b', 'c', 'd'};
20       System.out.print("characterArray contains ");
21       displayArray(characterArray);
22    } // end main
23 } // end Example
```

**Output**
```
stringArray contains apple banana carrot dandelion
characterArray contains a b c d
```

**Question 2**  Define a generic method swap that exchanges the objects at two given positions in a given array.

## Bounded Type Parameters

**JI3.7**  In the previous listing, a generic data type represents any class type that the client chooses. Some situations, however, require that you limit, or control, the client's choices. For example, consider the following simple class of squares:

```
public class Square<T>
{
   private T side;

   public Square(T initialSide)
   {
      side = initialSide;
   } // end constructor

   public T getSide()
   {
      return side;
   } // end getSide
} // end Square
```

We can create a Square<Integer> object and a Square<Double> object by writing statements such as

```
Square<Integer> intSquare = new Square<>(5);
Square<Double> realSquare = new Square<>(2.1);
```

We also can create a square whose side is not a numeric value:

```
Square<String> stringSquare= new Square<>("25");
```

This flexibility is a problem, however.

**JI3.8**  Had the class Square included a method to return its area, such as,

```
public double getArea()
{
   double s = side.doubleValue();
   return s * s;
} // end getArea
```

the compiler would complain by giving the following error message:

```
error: cannot find symbol
double s = side.doubleValue();
           ^
symbol:   method doubleValue()
location: variable side of type T
where T is a type-variable:
T extends Object declared in class Square
```

Because T represents any class type, and all classes are derived from Object, the compiler cannot tell whether side has the method doubleValue. If side references a string, for example, it does not have this method.

**JI3.9**   We want the side of a square to be a numeric value. We can impose this restriction by making T represent a class that is derived from Number, the base class (superclass) of the classes Byte, Double, Float, Integer, Long, and Short. Thus, we **bound** T by writing T extends Number in Square's header:

**public class** Square<T **extends** Number>

Here, Number is said to be an **upper bound** on T. Now Square can include the previous method getArea. Moreover, the compiler will reject any attempt to create a square whose side is a string. For example, the statement

Square<String> stringSquare = **new** Square<>("25");

causes the following message from the compiler:

```
error: type argument String is not within bounds of type-variable T
Square<String> stringSquare = new Square<>("25");
               ^
where T is a type-variable:
T extends Number declared in class Square
```

**JI3.10**   **Example.** Imagine that we want to write a static method that returns the smallest object in an array. The objects in the array might be strings, Integer objects, or any objects that can be compared. That is, the class of these objects must implement the interface Comparable. We need the client to give us an array of objects that can be compared.

Suppose that we wrote our method as follows:

```
public MyClass
{
   // First draft and INCORRECT:
   public static <T> T arrayMinimum(T[] anArray)
   {
      T minimum = anArray[0];
      for (T arrayEntry : anArray)
      {
         if (arrayEntry.compareTo(minimum) < 0)
            minimum = arrayEntry;
      } // end for

      return minimum;
   } // end arrayMinimum
   . . .
```

Because the generic type T can represent any class type, the client could pass to this method an array of objects that do not have a compareTo method. For this reason, the compiler will issue a syntax error.

To correct this method, we must bound T so that it represents class types that provide the method compareTo. To do so, we replace <T> in the method's header with <T extends Comparable<T>>. Thus, the header becomes

**public static** <T **extends** Comparable<T>> T arrayMinimum(T[] anArray) // CORRECT

If the class Gadget implements Comparable, and if myArray is an array of Gadget objects, a client could call arrayMinimum as follows:

```
Gadget smallestGadget = MyClass.arrayMinimum(myArray);
```

The compiler will discover that myArray contains Gadget objects. However, if myArray contains objects whose class does not implement Comparable, the compiler will complain.

> **Note:** **The types that can bound a type parameter**
> Any class, interface, or enumerated type—even if parameterized—can be a bound for a type parameter. Primitive types and array types cannot be bounds.

> **Security Note:** The use of generics provides a way for the compiler to detect invalid data types, giving our code another degree of safety.

**Question 3** What, if anything, is wrong with the following class?

```
public final class Min
{
    public static T smallerOf(T x, T y)
    {
        if (x < y)
            return x;
        else
            return y;
    } // end smallerOf
} // end Min
```

# Wildcards

**JI3.11** The question mark, ?, is used to represent an unknown class type and is referred to as a **wildcard**. To demonstrate its meaning, let's look at some statements in a client of the class OrderedPair, as given in Listing JI1-2 of Java Interlude 1. First, let's create a variable of type OrderedPair<?> by writing

```
OrderedPair<?> aPair;
```

We now could assign to this variable either a pair of strings—by writing

```
aPair = new OrderedPair<>("apple", "banana"); // A pair of String objects
```

or a pair of Integer objects—by writing

```
aPair = new OrderedPair<>(1, 2);              // A pair of Integer objects
```

or a pair of objects of any other one class.

**JI3.12** Now consider the static method

```
public static void displayPair(OrderedPair<?> pair)
{
    System.out.println(pair);
} // end displayPair
```

and the following objects:

```
OrderedPair<String> aPair = new OrderedPair<>("apple", "banana");
OrderedPair<Integer> anotherPair = new OrderedPair<>(1, 2);
```

The method displayPair will accept as an argument a pair of objects whose data type is any one class, as the following statements indicate:

```
displayPair(aPair);
displayPair(anotherPair);
```

However, if we replace the wildcard in the method with Object, so that the method's header is

```
public static void displayPair(OrderedPair<Object> pair)
```

both of the previous calls to displayPair are illegal and cause the compiler to issue the following messages:

```
error: incompatible types: OrderedPair<String> cannot be converted to
       OrderedPair<Object>
error: incompatible types: OrderedPair<Integer> cannot be converted to
       OrderedPair<Object>
```

## Bounded Wildcards

**JI3.13**  Recall the method arrayMinimum, as discussed in Segment JI3.10:

```
public MyClass
{
    public static <T extends Comparable<T>> T arrayMinimum(T[] anArray)
    {
        T minimum = anArray[0];
        for (T arrayEntry : anArray)
        {
            if (arrayEntry.compareTo(minimum) < 0)
                minimum = arrayEntry;
        } // end for

        return minimum;
    } // end arrayMinimum
    . . .
```

We called this method with the statement

```
Gadget smallestGadget = MyClass.arrayMinimum(myArray);
```

where myArray is an array of Gadget objects. Because the expression T extends Comparable<T> in the definition of arrayMinimum bounds the generic data type T, Gadget must implement the interface Comparable<Gadget>. But insisting that a Gadget object be compared only to another Gadget object is more restrictive than we really need to be. What would happen if we had derived Gadget from Widget, where Widget implements Comparable<Widget>, as Figure JI3-1 shows? If gadgets and widgets are similar enough to have the same basis for comparison, Gadget could use the method compareTo it inherits from Widget without defining its own. But then a call to the method arrayMinimum with an array of gadgets and widgets as an argument would not compile.

Instead of comparing an object of T only with other objects of T, we can allow comparisons to objects of a superclass of T. So instead of writing T extends Comparable<T>, we write

```
T extends Comparable<? super T>
```

The wildcard ? represents any class type, but the notation ? super T means any superclass of T. Thus, the header for the method arrayMinimum would be

```
public static <T extends Comparable<? super T>> void arrayMinimum(T[] a, int n)
```

**Programming Tip:** To use Comparable with arbitrary types, write Comparable<? super T> instead of Comparable<T>.

FIGURE JI3-1    The class Gadget is derived from the class Widget, which implements the interface Comparable

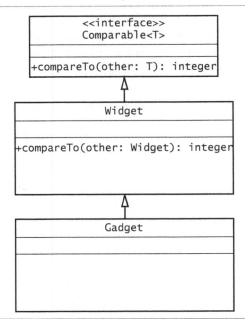

> **Note: Bounded wildcards**
> When using generic types, the wild card ? represents any class. You can bound, or limit, the wildcard in one of two ways. For example, ? super Gizmo means any superclass of Gizmo. We say that Gizmo is the **lower bound** of the wildcard. Analogously, ? extends Gizmo means any subclass of Gizmo. Here, Gizmo is the **upper bound** of the wildcard. In Chapter 4, Segments 4.13 and 4.17, respectively, provide other meanings for the terms "upper bound" and "lower bound."

> **Note: Generic classes and interfaces**
> Any class or interface that defines a generic data type can bound the type using the notation that we have described in this interlude beginning with Segment JI3.9.

## ANSWERS TO SELF-TEST QUESTIONS

```java
1.  /**
        A class that represents a person's name.
        @author Frank M. Carrano
    */
    public class Name implements NameInterface, Comparable<Name>
    {
        private String first; // First name
        private String last;  // Last name

        public Name()
        {
            this("", "");
        } // end default constructor
```

```java
public Name(String firstName, String lastName)
{
   first = firstName;
   last = lastName;
} // end constructor

public void setName(String firstName, String lastName)
{
   setFirst(firstName);
   setLast(lastName);
} // end setName

public String getName()
{
   return toString();
} // end getName

public void setFirst(String firstName)
{
   first = firstName;
} // end setFirst

public String getFirst()
{
   return first;
} // end getFirst

public void setLast(String lastName)
{
   last = lastName;
} // end setLast

public String getLast()
{
   return last;
} // end getLast

public void giveLastNameTo(NameInterface aName)
{
   aName.setLast(last);
} // end giveLastNameTo

public String toString()
{
   return first + " " + last;
} // end toString
```

```
    public int compareTo(Name other)
    {
        int result = last.compareTo(other.last);
        // If last names are equal, check first names
        if (result == 0)
            result = first.compareTo(other.first);
        return result;
    } // end compareTo
} // end Name
```

2. 
```
/** Interchanges two entries at given position within a given array.
    @param a  An array of objects.
    @param i  An integer >= 0 and < a.length.
    @param j  An integer >= 0 and < a.length. */
public static <T> void swap(T[] a, int i, int j)
{
    T temp = a[i];
    a[i] = a[j];
    a[j] = temp;
} // end swap
```

3. T is undefined, so as a first attempt at correcting the code, change

```
    public static T smallerOf(T x, T y)
```

to

```
    public static <T> T smallerOf(T x, T y)
```

The operator < is undefined for objects, so we must use the compareTo method in the if statement:

```
    if (x.compareTo(y) < 0)
```

But to use compareTo, we must bound T by changing the method's header, as follows:

```
    public static <T extends Comparable<T>> T smallerOf(T x, T y)
```

# An Introduction to Sorting

## Contents

## Prerequisites

## Objectives

After studying this chapter, you should be able to

- Sort an array into ascending order by using the following methods: selection sort, insertion sort, and Shell sort
- Sort a chain of linked nodes into ascending order by using an insertion sort
- Assess the efficiency of a sort and discuss the relative efficiencies of the various methods

We are all familiar with arranging objects in order from smallest to largest or from largest to smallest. Not only do we order numbers this way, but we also can arrange people by height, age, or name; music by title, artist, or album; and so on. Arranging things into either ascending or descending order is called **sorting**. You can sort any collection of items that can be compared with one another. Exactly how you compare two objects depends on the nature of the objects. For example, you can arrange a row of books on your bookshelf in several ways: by title, by author, by height, by color, and so on. The designer of a class of book objects would choose one of these ways when implementing the method compareTo.

Suppose you have a collection of items that need to be sorted in some way. For example, you might want to arrange a group of numbers from lowest to highest or from highest to lowest, or you might want to place some strings in alphabetical order. This chapter discusses and implements a few simple algorithms that sort items into ascending order. That is, our algorithms rearrange the first $n$ entries in a collection so that

entry $1 \le$ entry $2 \le \ldots \le$ entry $n$

With only small changes to our algorithms, you will be able to sort entries into descending order.

Sorting an array is usually easier than sorting a chain of linked nodes. For this reason, typical sorting algorithms sort an array. In particular, our algorithms will rearrange the first $n$ values in an array a so that

a[0] $\le$ a[1] $\le$ a[2] $\le$ . . . $\le$ a[n - 1]

However, we also will use one of our algorithms to sort a chain of linked nodes.

Sorting is such a common and important task that many sorting algorithms exist. This chapter examines some basic algorithms for sorting data. Although most of our examples will sort integers, the Java implementations given will sort any Comparable objects—that is, objects of any class that implements the interface Comparable and, therefore, defines the method compareTo.

The efficiency of a sorting algorithm is significant, particularly when large amounts of data are involved. We will examine the performance of the algorithms in this chapter and find that they are relatively slow. The next chapter will present sorting algorithms that usually are much faster.

## Organizing Java Methods That Sort an Array

**8.1**    One way to organize methods that sort an array is to create a class of static methods that perform the various sorts. The methods define a generic type T for the objects in the array. For example, we could write the header of such a method as follows:

**public static** <T> **void** sort(T[] a, **int** n)

Here, the array a can contain objects of any one class, and n is the number of entries in the array that we want to sort.

For an array to be sortable, the objects in that array must be Comparable. Thus, the class that T represents must implement the interface Comparable. To ensure this requirement, we write

<T **extends** Comparable<T>>

instead of simply <T> before the return type in the headers of the sort methods. We then can use T as the data type of the parameters and local variables within the methods. For example, our class could begin as follows:

```
public class SortArray
{
    public static <T extends Comparable<T>> void sort(T[] a, int n)
    { . . .
```

However, as described at the end of the previous Java interlude, we can allow comparisons of objects of a superclass of T by writing

T **extends** Comparable<? **super** T>

Thus, the header for the method sort would be

**public static** <T **extends** Comparable<? **super** T>> **void** sort(T[] a, **int** n)

We now turn our attention to several ways of sorting an array.

# Selection Sort

**8.2**   Imagine that you want to rearrange the books on your bookshelf by height, with the shortest book on the left. You might begin by tossing all of the books onto the floor. You then could return them to the shelf one by one, in their proper order. If you first return the shortest book to the shelf, and then the next shortest, and so on, you would perform a kind of **selection sort**. But using the floor—or another shelf—to store your books temporarily uses extra space needlessly.

**VideoNote**
Selection sort

Instead, approach your intact bookshelf and *select* the shortest book. Since you want it to be first on the shelf, you remove the first book on the shelf and put the shortest book in its place. You still have a book in your hand, so you put it into the space formerly occupied by the shortest book. That is, the shortest book has traded places with the first book, as Figure 8-1 illustrates. You now ignore the shortest book and repeat the process for the rest of the bookshelf.

---

**FIGURE 8-1**   Before and after exchanging the shortest book and the first book

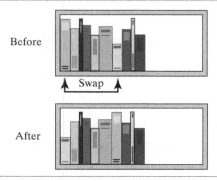

---

In terms of an array a, the selection sort finds the smallest entry in the array and exchanges it with a[0]. Then, ignoring a[0], the sort finds the next smallest entry and swaps it with a[1], and so on. Notice that we use only one array. We sort it by making entries trade places with other entries.

We could have copied the array into a second array and then moved the entries back to the original array in their proper order. But that would be like using the floor to store books temporarily. Fortunately, all of that extra space is unnecessary.

**8.3**   Figure 8-2 shows how a selection sort rearranges an array of integers by interchanging values. Beginning with the original array, the sort locates the smallest value in the array, that is, the 2 in a[3]. The value in a[3] is interchanged with the value in a[0]. After that interchange, the smallest value is in a[0] where it belongs.

The next smallest value is the 5 in a[4]. The sort then interchanges the value in a[4] with the value in a[1]. So far, the values in a[0] and a[1] are the smallest in the array and are in their correct position within the final sorted array. The algorithm then interchanges the next smallest entry—the 8—with a[2], and so on until the entire array is sorted.

FIGURE 8-2      A selection sort of an array of integers into ascending order

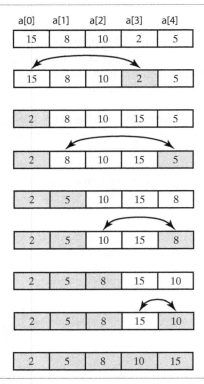

## Iterative Selection Sort

**8.4**   The following pseudocode describes an iterative algorithm for the selection sort:

*Algorithm* `selectionSort(a, n)`
*// Sorts the first* `n` *entries of an array* `a`.

```
for (index = 0; index < n - 1; index++)
{
    indexOfNextSmallest = the index of the smallest value among
                          a[index], a[index + 1], . . . , a[n - 1]
    Interchange the values of a[index] and a[indexOfNextSmallest]
    // Assertion: a[0] ≤ a[1] ≤ . . . ≤ a[index], and these are the smallest
    // of the original array entries. The remaining array entries begin  at a[index + 1].
}
```

Notice that during the last iteration of the `for` loop, the value of `index` is `n - 2`, even though the last array entry is `a[n - 1]`. Once the entries `a[0]` through `a[n - 2]` are in their correct places, only the one entry `a[n - 1]` remains to be positioned. But since the other entries are correctly positioned, it must already be in the correct place as well.

> **♪ Note: Notation**
>
> In mathematics, one-letter variable names are common. Recognizing this, and seeking to save some space, we use a and n within the text and pseudocode to represent, respectively, an array and its number of entries. Within Java code elsewhere, we have tried to avoid one-letter identifiers, using them only sparingly. However, the code that you will see in this chapter and the next uses a and n simply to maintain consistency with the text.

**8.5**   The class in Listing 8-1 contains the public method selectionSort and two private methods that assist in sorting. We can add other sorting methods as we develop them.

It is easy to see that the definition of selectionSort is a direct translation of the previous pseudocode into Java code. The method getIndexOfSmallest searches the array entries a[first] through a[last] and returns the index of the smallest among them. The method uses two local variables, min and indexOfMin. At any point in the search, min references the smallest value found so far. That value occurs at a[indexOfMin]. At the end of the search, the method returns indexOfMin. Notice that for our purposes here, we could have assumed that last is always n - 1 and omitted it as a parameter. However, this general version will be useful in other settings.

Since exchanging entries in an array does not involve the method compareTo, the method swap can simply use Object as the type of these entries.

---

**LISTING 8-1     A class for sorting an array using selection sort**

```java
/**
   Class for sorting an array of Comparable objects from smallest to largest.
*/
public class SortArray
{
   /** Sorts the first n objects in an array into ascending order.
       @param a  An array of Comparable objects.
       @param n  An integer > 0. */
   public static <T extends Comparable<? super T>>
         void selectionSort(T[] a, int n)
   {
      for (int index = 0; index < n - 1; index++)
      {
         int indexOfNextSmallest = getIndexOfSmallest(a, index, n - 1);
         swap(a, index, indexOfNextSmallest);
         // Assertion: a[0] <= a[1] <= . . . <= a[index] <= all other a[i].
      } // end for
   } // end selectionSort

   // Finds the index of the smallest value in a portion of an array a.
   // Precondition: a.length > last >= first >= 0.
   // Returns the index of the smallest value among
   // a[first], a[first + 1], . . . , a[last].
   private static <T extends Comparable<? super T>>
         int getIndexOfSmallest(T[] a, int first, int last)
   {
      T min = a[first];
```

```
28        int indexOfMin = first;
29        for (int index = first + 1; index <= last; index++)
30        {
31           if (a[index].compareTo(min) < 0)
32           {
33              min = a[index];
34              indexOfMin = index;
35           } // end if
36           // Assertion: min is the smallest of a[first] through a[index].
37        } // end for
38
39        return indexOfMin;
40     } // end getIndexOfSmallest
41
42     // Swaps the array entries a[i] and a[j].
43     private static void swap(Object[] a, int i, int j)
44     {
45        Object temp = a[i];
46        a[i] = a[j];
47        a[j] = temp;
48     } // end swap
49  } // end SortArray
```

**Question 1** Trace the steps that a selection sort takes when sorting the following array into ascending order: 9 6 2 4 8.

## Recursive Selection Sort

**8.6**    Selection sort also has a natural recursive form. Often recursive algorithms that involve arrays operate on a portion of the array. Such algorithms use two parameters, first and last, to designate the portion of the array containing the entries a[first] through a[last]. The method getIndexOfSmallest in Listing 8-1 illustrates this technique. The recursive selection sort algorithm uses this notation as well:

> *Algorithm* selectionSort(a, first, last)
> *// Sorts the array entries* a[first] *through* a[last] *recursively.*
>
> if (first < last)
> {
>     indexOfNextSmallest = *the index of the smallest value among*
>                                 a[first], a[first + 1], . . . , a[last]
>     *Interchange the values of* a[first] *and* a[indexOfNextSmallest]
>     *// Assertion:* a[0] ≤ a[1] ≤ . . . ≤ a[first] *and these are the smallest*
>     *// of the original array entries. The remaining array entries begin at* a[first + 1].
>     selectionSort(a, first + 1, last)
> }

After we place the smallest entry into the first position of the array, we ignore it and sort the rest of the array by using a selection sort. If the array has only one entry, sorting is unnecessary. In this case, first and last are equal, so the algorithm leaves the array unchanged.

**8.7**   When we implement the previous recursive algorithm in Java, the resulting method will have first and last as parameters. Thus, its header will differ from the header of the iterative method selectionSort given in Segment 8.5. We could, however, provide the following method to simply invoke the recursive method:

```
public static <T extends Comparable<? super T>>
        void selectionSort(T[] a, int n)
{
    selectionSort(a, 0, n - 1); // Invoke recursive method
} // end selectionSort
```

Whether you make the recursive method selectionSort private or public is up to you, but making it public provides the client with a choice of two ways in which to invoke the sort. In a similar fashion, you could revise the iterative selection sort given in Segment 8.5 to use the parameters first and last (see Exercise 6) and then provide the method just given to invoke it.

With these observations in mind, we will make the subsequent sorting algorithms more general by giving them three parameters—a, first, and last—so that they sort the entries a[first] through a[last].

### The Efficiency of Selection Sort

**8.8**   In the iterative method selectionSort, the for loop executes $n - 1$ times, so it invokes the methods getIndexOfSmallest and swap $n - 1$ times each. In the $n - 1$ calls to getIndexOfSmallest, last is $n - 1$ and first ranges from 0 to $n - 2$. Each time getIndexOfSmallest is invoked, its loop executes last - first times. Since last - first ranges from $(n - 1) - 0$, or $n - 1$, to $(n - 1) - (n - 2)$, or 1, this loop executes a total of

$$(n - 1) + (n - 2) + \ldots + 1$$

times. This sum is $n (n - 1)/2$. Therefore, since each operation in the loop is O(1), the selection sort is O($n^2$). Notice that our discussion does not depend on the nature of the data in the array. It could be wildly out of order, nearly sorted, or completely sorted; in any case, selection sort would be O($n^2$).

The recursive selection sort performs the same operations as the iterative selection sort, and so it is also O($n^2$).

**Note:  The time efficiency of selection sort**
Selection sort is O($n^2$) regardless of the initial order of the entries in an array. Although the sort requires O($n^2$) comparisons, it performs only O($n$) swaps. Thus, the selection sort requires little data movement.

## Insertion Sort

**8.9**   Another intuitive sorting algorithm is the **insertion sort**. Suppose again that you want to rearrange the books on your bookshelf by height, with the shortest book on the left. If the leftmost book on the shelf were the only book, your shelf would be sorted. But you also have all the other books to sort. Consider the second book. If it is taller than the first book, you now

VideoNote
Insertion sort

have two sorted books. If not, you remove the second book, slide the first book to the right, and *insert* the book you just removed into the first position on the shelf. The first two books are now sorted.

Now consider the third book. If it is taller than the second book, you now have three sorted books. If not, remove the third book and slide the second book to the right, as Parts *a* through *c* of Figure 8-3 illustrate. Now see whether the book in your hand is taller than the first book. If so, insert the book into the second position on the shelf, as shown in Figure 8-3d. If not, slide the first book to the right, and insert the book in your hand into the first position on the shelf. If you repeat this process for each of the remaining books, your bookshelf will be arranged by the heights of the books.

**FIGURE 8-3**      The placement of the third book during an insertion sort

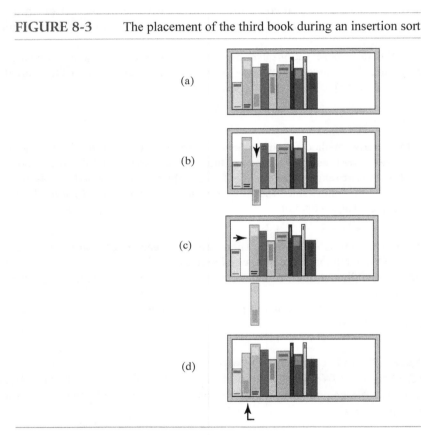

(a)

(b)

(c)

(d)

Figure 8-4 shows the bookshelf after several steps of the insertion sort. The books on the left side of the shelf are sorted. You remove the next unsorted book from the shelf and slide sorted books to the right, one at a time, until you find the right place for the book in your hand. You then insert this book into its new sorted location.

FIGURE 8-4        An insertion sort of books

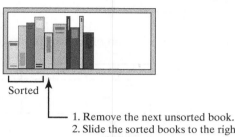

Sorted

1. Remove the next unsorted book.
2. Slide the sorted books to the right one by one until
   you find the right spot for the removed book.
3. Insert the book into its new position.

## Iterative Insertion Sort

**8.10**    An insertion sort of an array **partitions**—that is, divides—the array into two parts. One part is sorted and initially contains just the first entry in the array. The second part contains the remaining entries. The algorithm removes the first entry from the unsorted part and inserts it into its proper sorted position within the sorted part. Just as you did with the bookshelf, you choose the proper position by comparing the unsorted entry with the sorted entries, beginning at the end of the sorted part and continuing toward its beginning. As you compare, you shift array entries in the sorted part to make room for the insertion.

Figure 8-5 illustrates these steps for a sort that has already positioned the first three entries of the array. The 3 is the next entry that must be placed into its proper position within the sorted region. Since 3 is less than 8 and 5 but greater than 2, the 8 and 5 are shifted to make room for the 3.

FIGURE 8-5        Inserting the next unsorted entry into its proper location
                  within the sorted portion of an array during an insertion sort

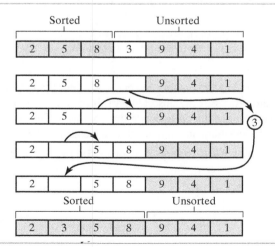

Figure 8-6 illustrates an entire insertion sort of an array of integers. At each pass of the algorithm, the sorted part expands by one entry as the unsorted part shrinks by one entry. Eventually, the unsorted part is empty and the array is sorted.

---

**FIGURE 8-6**      An insertion sort of an array of integers into ascending order

---

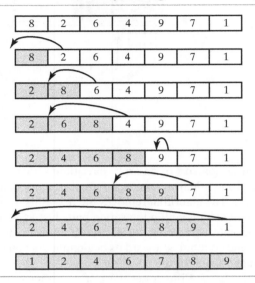

The following iterative algorithm describes an insertion sort of the entries at indices `first` through `last` of the array a. To sort the first n entries in the array, the call to the algorithm would be `insertionSort(a, 0, n - 1)`.

*Algorithm* `insertionSort(a, first, last)`
*// Sorts the array entries* `a[first]` *through* `a[last]` *iteratively.*

```
for (unsorted = first + 1 through last)
{
    nextToInsert = a[unsorted]
    insertInOrder(nextToInsert, a, first, unsorted - 1)
}
```

The sorted part contains one entry, a[`first`], and so the loop in the algorithm begins at index `first` + 1 and processes the unsorted part. It then invokes another method—`insertInOrder`—to perform the insertions. In the pseudocode that follows for this method, `anEntry` is the value to be inserted into its proper position, and `begin` and `end` are array indices.

*Algorithm* `insertInOrder(anEntry, a, begin, end)`
*// Inserts* `anEntry` *into the sorted entries* `a[begin]` *through* `a[end]`.

```
index = end                    // Index of last entry in the sorted portion
// Make room, if needed, in sorted portion for another entry
while ( (index >= begin) and (anEntry < a[index]) )
{
    a[index + 1] = a[index] // Make room
    index--
}
// Assertion: a[index + 1] is available.
a[index + 1] = anEntry     // Insert
```

**Question 2** Trace the steps that an insertion sort takes when sorting the following array into ascending order: 9 6 2 4 8.

## Recursive Insertion Sort

**8.11**    You can describe an insertion sort recursively as follows. If you sort all but the last item in the array— a smaller problem than sorting the entire array—you then can insert the last item into its proper position within the rest of the array. The following pseudocode describes a recursive insertion sort:

*Algorithm* `insertionSort(a, first, last)`
*// Sorts the array entries* `a[first]` *through* `a[last]` *recursively.*

**if** *(the array contains more than one entry)*
{
    *Sort the array entries* `a[first]` *through* `a[last - 1]`
    *Insert the last entry* `a[last]` *into its correct sorted position within the rest of the array*
}

We can implement this algorithm in Java as follows:

```java
public static <T extends Comparable<? super T>>
       void insertionSort(T[] a, int first, int last)
{
    if (first < last)
    {
        // Sort all but the last entry
        insertionSort(a, first, last - 1);

        // Insert the last entry in sorted order
        insertInOrder(a[last], a, first, last - 1);
    } // end if
} // end insertionSort
```

**8.12**    **The algorithm `insertInOrder`: first draft.** The previous method can call the iterative version of `insertInOrder`, given earlier, or the recursive version that we now describe. If the entry to insert is greater than or equal to the last item in the sorted portion of the array, the entry belongs immediately after this last item, as Figure 8-7a illustrates. Otherwise, we move the last sorted item to the next higher position in the array and insert the entry into the remaining portion, as shown in Figure 8-7b.

We can describe these steps more carefully as follows:

*Algorithm* `insertInOrder(anEntry, a, begin, end)`
*// Inserts* `anEntry` *into the sorted array entries* `a[begin]` *through* `a[end]`.
*// First draft.*

```java
if (anEntry >= a[end])
    a[end + 1] = anEntry
else
{
    a[end + 1] = a[end]
    insertInOrder(anEntry, a, begin, end - 1)
}
```

**FIGURE 8-7**   Inserting the first unsorted entry into the sorted portion of the array. (a) The entry is greater than or equal to the last sorted entry; (b) the entry is smaller than the last sorted entry

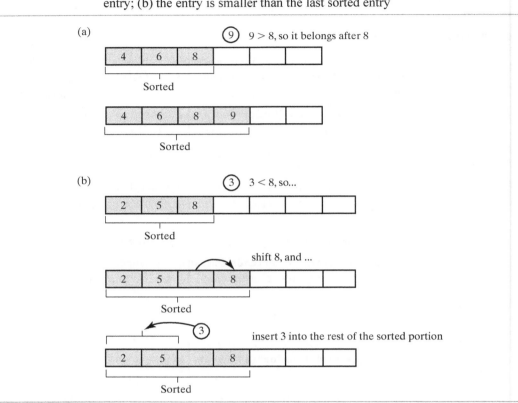

**8.13**   **The algorithm `insertInOrder`: final draft.** This algorithm is not quite right. The `else` clause will work only if we have more than one entry in the remaining portion of the array—that is, if `begin < end`. If `begin` and `end` were equal, for example, the recursive call would be equivalent to

```
insertInOrder(anEntry, a, begin, begin - 1);
```

which is incorrect.

Will `end` ever equal `begin`, if they were not equal initially? Yes. When `anEntry` is less than all entries `a[begin], ..., a[end]`, each recursive call decreases `end` by 1 until eventually `end` equals `begin`. What should we do when this happens? Since the sorted portion consists of one entry `a[end]`, we will move `a[end]` to the next higher position and place `anEntry` in `a[end]`.

The following revised algorithm reflects these changes:

*Algorithm* `insertInOrder(anEntry, a, begin, end)`
*// Inserts anEntry into the sorted array entries* `a[begin]` *through* `a[end]`.
*// Revised draft.*

```
if (anEntry >= a[end])
   a[end + 1] = anEntry
else if (begin < end)
{
   a[end + 1] = a[end]
   insertInOrder(anEntry, a, begin, end - 1)
}
```

```
else // begin == end and anEntry < a[end]
{
   a[end + 1] = a[end]
   a[end] = anEntry
}
```

## The Efficiency of Insertion Sort

**8.14** Look back at the iterative algorithm insertionSort given in Segment 8.10. For an array of $n$ entries, first is 0 and last is $n - 1$. The for loop then executes $n - 1$ times, and so the method insertInOrder is invoked $n - 1$ times. Thus, within insertInOrder, begin is 0 and end ranges from 0 to $n - 2$. The loop within insertInOrder executes at most end - begin + 1 times each time the method is invoked. Thus, this loop executes at most a total of

$$1 + 2 + \ldots + (n - 1)$$

times. This sum is $n(n-1)/2$, so the insertion sort is $O(n^2)$. The recursive insertion sort performs the same operations as the iterative insertion sort, so it is also $O(n^2)$.

This analysis provides a worst-case scenario. In the best case, the loop in insertInOrder would exit immediately. Such is the case if the array is sorted already. In the best case, then, insertion sort is $O(n)$. In general, the more sorted an array is, the less work insertInOrder needs to do. This fact and its relatively simple implementation make the insertion sort popular for applications in which the array does not change much. For example, some customer databases add only a small percentage of new customers each day.

The next chapter will use the insertion sort when the array size is small.

 **Note: The time efficiency of insertion sort**
Insertion sort is at best $O(n)$ and at worst $O(n^2)$. The closer an array is to sorted order, the less work an insertion sort does.

## Insertion Sort of a Chain of Linked Nodes

**8.15** Usually you will sort arrays, but sometimes you might need to sort a chain of linked nodes. When you do, the insertion sort is one that is easy to understand.

Figure 8-8 shows a chain whose nodes contain integers that are sorted into ascending order. To begin to see how we can construct an insertion sort for a chain, imagine that we want to insert a node into this chain so that the integers in the nodes remain in sorted order.

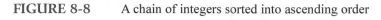

**FIGURE 8-8**     A chain of integers sorted into ascending order

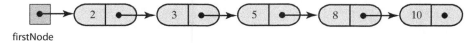

firstNode

Suppose that the node to be inserted into the chain contains the integer 6. We need to locate where in the chain the new node belongs. Since we have a reference, firsNode, to the first node in the chain, we can start there. We make comparisons as we move toward the end of the chain until we find the correct insertion point. Thus, we would compare 6 with 2, then with 3, with 5, and finally with 8 to see that 6 belongs between 5 and 8.

To insert a node into a chain, we need a reference to the node prior to the point of insertion. Thus, during the traversal of the chain, we save a reference to the node before the current one, as Figure 8-9 illustrates. Note that inserting at the beginning of the chain differs somewhat from inserting anywhere else in the chain.

**FIGURE 8-9**   During the traversal of a chain to locate the insertion point, save a reference to the node before the current one

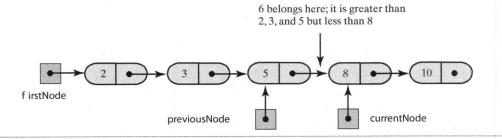

**8.16**   Now imagine that we have a method `insertInOrder(nodeToInsert)` that inserts a node into its correct sorted position within a chain, as just described. We can use this method to implement an insertion sort by adopting the same strategy that we used to sort an array: Divide the chain into two parts. The first part is sorted, and it initially contains only the first node. The second part is unsorted and initially is the rest of the chain. Figure 8-10 illustrates how to make this division. We first make the variable `unsortedPart` reference the second node and then set the link portion of the first node to `null`.

**FIGURE 8-10**   Breaking a chain of nodes into two pieces as the first step in an insertion sort: (a) the original chain; (b) the two pieces

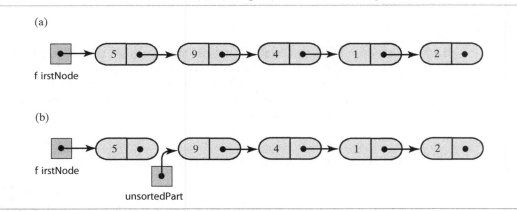

To sort the nodes, we use the method `insertInOrder` to take each node from the unsorted part and insert it into the sorted part. Notice that our plan relinks existing nodes instead of creating new ones.

**8.17**   To give this discussion some context, suppose that we plan to add a sort method to a class LinkedGroup that uses a linked chain to represent a certain collection. As sorting requires us to compare the objects in the collection, they must belong to a class that implements the interface Comparable. Thus, the class definition begins as follows:

```java
public class LinkedGroup<T extends Comparable<? super T>>
{
    private Node firstNode;
    int length; // Number of objects in the group
    . . .
```

Recall from the previous Java interlude that you can bound a generic data type in the header of a class definition.

This class has an inner class Node that has set and get methods for its private data fields. The following private method inserts the node that nodeToInsert references into the sorted chain that firstNode references.

```java
private void insertInOrder(Node nodeToInsert)
{
    T item = nodeToInsert.getData();
    Node currentNode = firstNode;
    Node previousNode = null;
    // Locate insertion point
    while ( (currentNode != null) &&
            (item.compareTo(currentNode.getData()) > 0) )
    {
        previousNode = currentNode;
        currentNode = currentNode.getNextNode();
    } // end while
    // Make the insertion
    if (previousNode != null)
    { // Insert between previousNode and currentNode
        previousNode.setNextNode(nodeToInsert);
        nodeToInsert.setNextNode(currentNode);
    }
    else // Insert at beginning
    {
        nodeToInsert.setNextNode(firstNode);
        firstNode = nodeToInsert;
    } // end if
} // end insertInOrder
```

The value of local variable item will be the data portion of the node to be inserted. The while loop compares item to the data in each node in the chain until either item is less than or equal to a data value or the end of the chain is reached. The references previousNode and currentNode are then used to insert the given node into its proper position.

**8.18**   The method to perform the insertion sort appears as follows. The local variable unsortedPart starts at the second node and then references each node in the rest of the chain as the loop executes. Each of these nodes is inserted in turn into the sorted part of the chain. Note that length is the number of nodes in the chain.

```java
public void insertionSort()
{
    // If zero or one item is in the chain, there is nothing to do
    if (length > 1)
    {
        assert firstNode != null;
```

```
                    // Break chain into 2 pieces: sorted and unsorted
                    Node unsortedPart = firstNode.getNextNode();
                    assert unsortedPart != null;
                    firstNode.setNextNode(null);

                    while (unsortedPart != null)
                    {
                        Node nodeToInsert = unsortedPart;
                        unsortedPart = unsortedPart.getNextNode();
                        insertInOrder(nodeToInsert);
                    } // end while
                } // end if
            } // end insertionSort
```

**Question 3**  In the previous method `insertionSort`, if you move the line

        unsortedPart = unsortedPart.getNextNode();

after the call to `insertInOrder`, will the method still work? Explain.

**Question 4**  The previous method `insertionSort` is not a static method. Why?

**8.19**  **The efficiency of an insertion sort of a chain**. For a chain of *n* nodes, the number of comparisons that the method `insertInOrder` makes is at most the number of nodes in the sorted portion of the chain. The method `insertionSort` calls `insertInOrder` *n* - 1 times. The first time it does so, the sorted portion contains one item, so one comparison is made. The second time, the sorted portion contains two items, so at most two comparisons are made. Continuing in this fashion, you can see that the maximum number of comparisons is

$$1 + 2 + \ldots + (n - 1)$$

This sum is $n\,(n - 1)/2$, so this insertion sort is O($n^2$).

**Note:**  Sorting a chain of linked nodes can be difficult. The insertion sort, however, provides a reasonable way to perform this task.

# Shell Sort

**8.20**  The sorting algorithms that we have discussed so far are simple and often useful, but they are too inefficient to use on large arrays. The Shell sort is a variation of the insertion sort that is faster than O($n^2$).

During an insertion sort, an array entry moves to an adjacent location. When an entry is far from its correct sorted position, it must make many such moves. So when an array is completely scrambled, an insertion sort takes a good deal of time. But when an array is almost sorted, an insertion sort is more efficient. In fact, Segment 8.14 showed that the more sorted an array is, the less work the method `insertInOrder` needs to do.

By capitalizing on these observations, Donald Shell devised in 1959 an improved insertion sort, now called the **Shell sort**. Shell wanted entries to move beyond their adjacent locations. To do so, he sorted subarrays of entries at equally spaced indices. Instead of moving to an adjacent location, an entry moves several locations away. The result is an array that is almost sorted—one that can be sorted efficiently by using an ordinary insertion sort.

**8.21**  For example, Figure 8-11 shows an array and the subarrays obtained by considering every sixth entry. The first subarray contains the integers 10, 9, and 7; the second subarray contains 16 and 6; and so on. There happen to be six of these subarrays.

Now we sort each of the six subarrays separately by using an insertion sort. Figure 8-12 shows the sorted subarrays and the state of the original array as a result. Notice that the array is "more sorted" than it was originally.

**FIGURE 8-11** An array and the subarrays formed by grouping entries whose indices are 6 apart

0 1 2 3 4 5 6 7 8 9 10 11 12
10 16 11 4 15 3 9 6 1 17 8 12 7
10 - 9 - 7
16 - 6
11 - 1
4 - 17
15 - 8
3 - 12

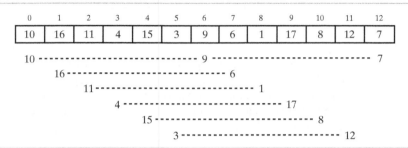

**FIGURE 8-12** The subarrays of Figure 8-11 after each is sorted, and the array that contains them

7 - 9 - 10
6 - 16
1 - 11
4 - 17
8 - 15
3 - 12
7 6 1 4 8 3 9 16 11 17 15 12 10
0 1 2 3 4 5 6 7 8 9 10 11 12

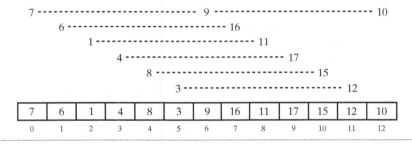

**8.22** Now we form new subarrays, but this time we reduce the separation between indices. Shell suggested that the initial separation between indices be $n/2$ and that you halve this value at each pass until it is 1. The array in our example has 13 entries, so we began with a separation of 6. We now reduce the separation to 3. Figure 8-13 shows the resulting subarrays, and Figure 8-14 shows the subarrays after they are sorted.

**FIGURE 8-13** The subarrays of the array in Figure 8-12 formed by grouping entries whose indices are 3 apart

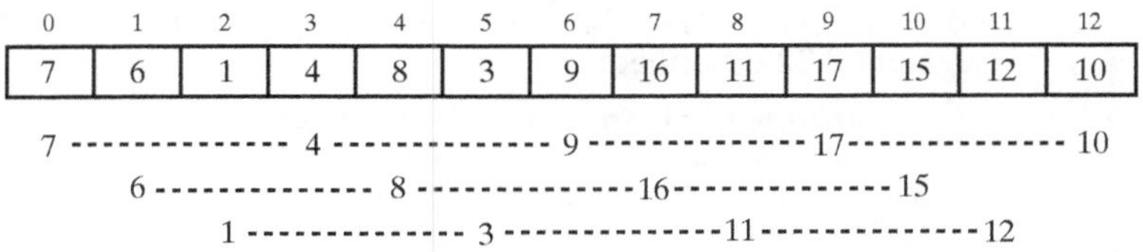

0 1 2 3 4 5 6 7 8 9 10 11 12
7 6 1 4 8 3 9 16 11 17 15 12 10
7 - 4 - 9 - 17 - 10
6 - 8 - 16 - 15
1 - 3 - 11 - 12

FIGURE 8-14     The subarrays of Figure 8-13 after each is sorted, and the
                array that contains them

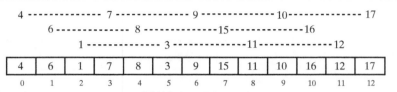

| 4 | 6 | 1 | 7 | 8 | 3 | 9 | 15 | 11 | 10 | 16 | 12 | 17 |
|---|---|---|---|---|---|---|----|----|----|----|----|----|
| 0 | 1 | 2 | 3 | 4 | 5 | 6 | 7  | 8  | 9  | 10 | 11 | 12 |

Dividing the current separation, 3, by 2 results in 1. Therefore, the final step is simply an ordinary insertion sort of the entire array. This last step will sort the array regardless of what we have done to it beforehand. Thus, Shell sort will work if you use any sequence of index separations, as long as the last one is 1. But not just any sequence will make the Shell sort efficient, as you will see in Segment 8.24.

**Question 5** Apply the Shell sort to the array of letters *I H B G E D F C A*, with index separations of 4, 2, and 1. What are the intermediate steps?

## The Algorithm

**8.23**    The heart of the Shell sort is the adaptation of the insertion sort to work on a subarray of equally spaced entries. By combining and modifying the two algorithms that describe the insertion sort, as given in Segment 8.10, we obtain the following algorithm that sorts array entries whose indices are separated by an increment of space.

*Algorithm* `incrementalInsertionSort(a, first, last, space)`
*// Sorts equally spaced entries of an array* `a[first..last]` *into ascending order.*
*//* `first >= 0` *and* `< a.length;` `last >= first` *and* `< a.length;`
*//* `space` *is the difference between the indices of the entries to sort.*

```
for (unsorted = first + space through last at increments of space)
{
   nextToInsert = a[unsorted]
   index = unsorted - space
   while ( (index >= first) and (nextToInsert.compareTo(a[index]) < 0) )
   {
      a[index + space] = a[index]
      index = index - space
   }
   a[index + space] = nextToInsert
}
```

A method to perform a Shell sort will invoke `incrementalInsertionSort` and supply any sequence of spacing factors. For example, the following algorithm uses the spacing that Segment 8.22 described:

*Algorithm* `shellSort(a, first, last)`
*// Sorts the entries of an array* `a[first..last]` *into ascending order.*
*//* `first >= 0` *and* `< a.length;` `last >= first` *and* `< a.length.`

```
n = number of array entries
space = n / 2
```

```
while (space > 0)
{
   for (begin = first through first + space - 1)
   {
      incrementalInsertionSort(a, begin, last, space)
   }
   space = space / 2
}
```

**Question 6** Trace the steps that a Shell sort takes when sorting the following array into ascending order: 9 6 2 4 8 7 5 3.

## The Efficiency of Shell Sort

**8.24**  Since the Shell sort uses an insertion sort repeatedly, it certainly seems like much more work than using only one insertion sort. Actually, however, it is not. Although we used an insertion sort several times instead of just once, the initial sorts are of arrays that are much smaller than the original one, the later sorts are on arrays that are partially sorted, and the final sort is on an array that is almost entirely sorted. Intuitively, this seems good. But even though the Shell sort is not very complicated, its analysis is.

Since incrementalInsertionSort involves a loop and is called from within nested loops, the Shell sort uses three nested loops. Often such algorithms are $O(n^3)$, but it turns out that the worstcase behavior of the Shell sort is still $O(n^2)$. If $n$ is a power of 2, the average-case behavior is $O(n^{1.5})$. And if you tweak the spacing a bit, you can make the Shell sort even more efficient.

One improvement is to avoid even values of space. Figure 8-11 provided an example of the subarrays when space was 6. The first subarray contained 10, 9, and 7, for instance. Later, after we halved space, the first subarrray contained 7, 4, 9, 17, and 10, as Figure 8-13 shows. Notice that these two subarrays have entries in common, namely the 10, 9, and 7. Thus, the comparisons that you make when space is even will be repeated on the next pass when the increment is space/2.

To avoid this inefficiency, simply add 1 to space whenever it is even. This simple change results in consecutive increments that have no factor in common. The worst-case behavior of the Shell sort is then $O(n^{1.5})$. Other sequences for space result in even greater efficiencies, although the proof that this is the case remains elusive. An improved Shell sort can be a reasonable choice for moderately large arrays.

 **Note: The time efficiency of Shell sort**
The Shell sort, as implemented in this chapter, is $O(n^2)$ in the worst case. By adding 1 to space anytime that it is even, you can improve the worst-case behavior to $O(n^{1.5})$.

# Comparing the Algorithms

**8.25**  Figure 8-15 summarizes the time efficiencies of the three sorting algorithms presented in this chapter. Generally, the selection sort is the slowest algorithm. The Shell sort, by capitalizing on the best-case behavior of the insertion sort, is the fastest.

FIGURE 8-15    The time efficiencies of three sorting algorithms, expressed
in Big Oh notation

| | Best Case | Average Case | Worst Case |
|---|---|---|---|
| Selection sort | $O(n^2)$ | $O(n^2)$ | $O(n^2)$ |
| Insertion sort | $O(n)$ | $O(n^2)$ | $O(n^2)$ |
| Shell sort | $O(n)$ | $O(n^{1.5})$ | $O(n^{1.5})$ |

## CHAPTER SUMMARY

- A selection sort of an array selects the smallest entry and swaps it with the first one. Ignoring the new first entry, the sort then finds the smallest entry in the rest of the array and swaps it with the second entry, and so on.

- Typically, you perform a selection sort iteratively, although a simple recursive form is possible.

- A selection sort is $O(n^2)$ in all cases.

- An insertion sort divides an array into two portions, sorted and unsorted. Initially, the array's first entry is in the sorted portion. The sort takes the next unsorted entry and compares it with entries in the sorted portion. As the comparisons continue, each sorted entry is shifted by one position toward the end of the array until the unsorted entry's correct position is located. The sort then inserts the entry into its correct position, which has been vacated by the shifts.

- You can perform an insertion sort either iteratively or recursively.

- An insertion sort is $O(n^2)$ in the worst case but is $O(n)$ in the best case. The more sorted an array is, the less work an insertion sort does.

- You can use an insertion sort to sort a chain of linked nodes, a task that typically is difficult.

- The Shell sort is a modification of the insertion sort that sorts subarrays of entries that are equally spaced within the array. The strategy efficiently arranges the array so that it is almost sorted, enabling an ordinary insertion sort to quickly finish the job.

- The worst-case behavior of Shell sort, as implemented in this chapter, is $O(n^2)$. With a simple change, its worst-case behavior can be improved to at least $O(n^{1.5})$.

## PROGRAMMING TIPS

- To use `Comparable` with arbitrary types, write `Comparable<? super T>` instead of `Comparable<T>`.

## EXERCISES

1. Show the contents of the array of integers 5 7 4 9 8 5 6 3 each time a selection sort changes it while sorting the array into ascending order.

2. Repeat Exercise 1, but use an insertion sort instead.

3. Repeat Exercise 1, but use a Shell sort instead.

4. **a.** Write pseudocode for a selection sort algorithm that selects the largest, instead of the smallest, entry in the array and sorts the array into descending order.
   **b.** Using your algorithm, repeat Exercise 1.
   **c.** Revise the iterative method `selectionSort`, as given in Segment 8.5, so that it implements your algorithm.

5. Repeat Exercise 4, but this time sort the array into ascending order.

6. Revise the iterative method `selectionSort`, as given in Segment 8.5, so that it has `first` and `last` as parameters instead of `n`.

7. Consider a revised selection sort algorithm so that on each pass it finds the largest and the second largest values in the unsorted portion of the array. The sort then moves each of these values into its correct location by swapping array entries.
   **a.** How many comparisons are necessary to sort 10 values?
   **b.** Is the answer to Part *a* greater than, less than, or equal to the number of comparisons required by the original version of selection sort?

8. A **bubble sort** can sort an array of *n* entries into ascending order by making $n - 1$ passes through the array. On each pass, it compares adjacent entries and swaps them if they are out of order. For example, on the first pass, it compares the first and second entries, then the second and third entries, and so on. At the end of the first pass, the largest entry is in its proper position at the end of the array. We say that it has bubbled to its correct spot. Each subsequent pass ignores the entries at the end of the array, since they are sorted and are larger than any of the remaining entries. Thus, each pass makes one fewer comparison than the previous pass. Figure 8-16 gives an example of a bubble sort.
   Implement the bubble sort
   **a.** Iteratively
   **b.** Recursively

FIGURE 8-16    A bubble sort of an array (see Exercise 8)

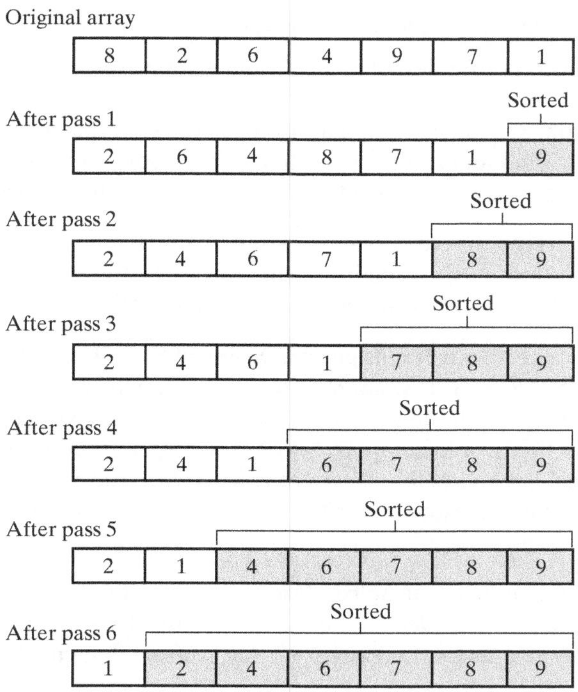

9. What is the most significant difference between bubble sort and selection sort?

10. The bubble sort in Exercise 8 always makes *n* passes. However, it is possible for the array to become sorted before all *n* passes are complete. For example, a bubble sort of the array

    9 2 1 6 4 7 8

    is sorted after only two passes:

    2 1 6 4 7 8 9 (end of pass 1)
    1 2 4 6 7 8 9 (end of pass 2)

    But since a swap occurred during the second pass, the sort needs to make one more pass to check that the array is in order. Additional passes, such as the ones that the algorithm in Exercise 8 would make, are unnecessary.

    You can skip these unnecessary passes and even do less work by remembering where the last swap occurred. During the first pass, the last swap is of the 9 and 8. The second pass checks up to the 8. But during the second pass, the last swap is of the 6 and 4. You now know that 6, 7, 8, and 9 are sorted. The third pass needs only to check up to the 4, instead of the 7, as an ordinary bubble sort would do. No swaps occur during the third pass, so the index of the last swap during this pass is taken as zero, indicating that no further passes are necessary. Implement this revised bubble sort.

11. Devise an algorithm that detects whether a given array is sorted into non-descending order. Write a Java method that implements your algorithm. You can use your method to test whether a sort method has executed correctly.

12. Imagine wanting to perform an insertion sort on a collection of Comparable objects. The collection is an instance of the class Group.

    a. What methods would you need?
    b. Implement a method to perform an insertion sort on the objects in an instance of Group.
    c. Using Big Oh notation, describe the time efficiency of your method.

13. Why is Shell sort considered to be an improved insertion sort?

14. As Segment 8.24 suggests, you can improve the efficiency of the Shell sort by adding 1 to space any time it is even.

    a. By looking at several examples, convince yourself that consecutive increments do not have a common factor.
    b. Subtracting 1 from space any time that it is even does not produce consecutive increments without common factors. Find an example of *n* that demonstrates this phenomenon.
    c. Revise the Shell sort algorithm given in Segment 8.23 so that space is not even.

15. Suppose you want to develop an online sorting application that keeps sorting the integers that are inserted by the user. This application needs a sorting algorithm that can sort a continuous stream of numbers and keep the sequence sorted at any point of time. Which sorting algorithm will you use? Justify your answer.

16. Consider the algorithm insertInOrder, as given in Segment 8.10, that inserts an object into its correct position within a sorted portion of an array. If we were to use a similar algorithm to insert a node into a sorted chain of linked nodes, we would begin at the end of the chain. For example, to insert a node containing 6 into the chain shown in Figure 8-8, we first would compare 6 with the integer 10. Since 6 belongs before 10, we would then compare 6 with 8. Since 6 belongs before 8, we compare 6 with 5 and discover that 6 belongs between 5 and 8.

    Describe how you could use this algorithm to define a method insertInOrder for a sorted chain of linked nodes.

17. Consider a class Student that has a string rollNumber as a private data field. Roll numbers have the following format: the year of admission, three letters indicating the branch of the institution, and the serial number. For example, 2014CSE20. Write a method compareTo() for Student that enables an array of Student objects to be sorted by roll number.

18. Consider a class `Employee` that has private data fields for name, department, employee ID, and gross salary per annum. Imagine an array of `Employee` objects that you want to sort according to any one of the previously given fields.

   a. What would be the challenges in implementing such a sort?
   b. One solution to this problem defines a new class for each criterion for sorting. Each of these classes encapsulates an `Employee` object. In this way, you can use the sorting methods given in this chapter. Provide the details necessary for another programmer to implement this solution.
   c. Another solution to this problem changes the signature and definition of the sorting method. One parameter of the method is an object that can compare two `Employee` objects according to a certain criterion. This parameter belongs to one of the several new classes that correspond to the sorting criteria. Provide the details necessary for another programmer to implement this solution.

## PROJECTS

1. Graphical demonstrations of various sorting algorithms are instructive, as they provide insight into how an algorithm behaves. Consider a collection of vertical lines of varying lengths, such as the ones in Figure 8-17a. Create a sorting demonstration that sorts the lines by length, as shown in Figure 8-17b. You should draw the configuration of lines after every swap or move that a given sorting algorithm makes. If you delay execution very briefly after each redraw, the result will be an animation of the sort.

   You could begin by drawing 256 lines, each one pixel wide but of different lengths—and perhaps different colors—arranged from shortest to longest so that they appear as a triangle. The user then should exercise an option to scramble the lines. At a user signal, your sorting algorithm should sort the lines.

   You can provide individual demonstrations, perhaps as applets, for each sort algorithm. Or you can include all the algorithms in one program that asks the user to choose an algorithm. Each sort should start with the same scrambled lines so the user can compare methods. You might also choose a sort algorithm at random and see whether the user can guess which one it is.

FIGURE 8-17     Initial and final images of an animated sorting demonstration that sorts vertical lines

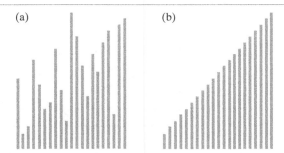

2. Implement the insertion sort and the Shell sort so that they count the number of comparisons made during a sort. Use your implementations to compare the two sorts on arrays of random `Integer` objects of various sizes. Also, compare the Shell sort as implemented in Segment 8.23 with a revised Shell sort that adds 1 to `space` any time it is even. For what array size does the difference in the number of comparisons become significant? Is the size consistent with the size predicted by the algorithm's Big Oh?

3. Complete the implementations of the sorting algorithms given in this chapter. Use your implementations to compare the run times of the sorts on various arrays of 50,000 random `Integer` objects. See the projects at the end of Chapter 4 for a description of how to time a block of Java code. Write a summary of which algorithm you find to be more efficient and why.

4. Consider an *n* by *n* array of integer values.

    **a.** Write an algorithm to sort the rows of the array by their first value.

    **b.** Using Big Oh notation, describe the efficiency of your algorithm.

    **c.** Implement your algorithm.

5. Suppose that you want to perform a Shell sort on a linked chain.

    **a.** Revise the algorithm `incrementalInsertionSort` to work with a linked chain instead of an array.

    **b.** Compare the performance of `incrementalInsertionSort` on an array with its performance on a linked chain.

    **c.** Using the revised algorithm, implement a Shell sort for a linked chain.

    **d.** Find the run time required to sort *n* values in a linked chain for different values of *n*. (See the projects at the end of Chapter 4 for a description of how to time a block of Java code.) Graph the run time versus *n*.

    **e.** Assuming that the performance of your sort is $O(n^k)$, make an estimate for the value of *k*.

6. A **counting sort** is a simple way to sort an array of *n* positive integers that lie between 0 and *m*, inclusive. You need *m* + 1 counters. Then, making only one pass through the array, you count the number of times each integer occurs in the array. For example, Figure 8-18 shows an array of integers that lie between 0 and 4 and the five counters after a counting sort has made its pass through the array. From the counters, you can see that the array contains one 0, three 1s, two 2s, one 3, and three 4s. These counts enable you to determine that the sorted array should contain 0 1 1 1 2 2 3 4 4 4.

    **a.** Write a method that performs a counting sort.

    **b.** Using Big Oh notation, describe the efficiency of this algorithm.

    **c.** How does the efficiency of a counting sort compare to that of an insertion sort?

    **d.** Is this algorithm useful as a general sorting algorithm? Explain.

---

**FIGURE 8-18**    A counting sort of an array (see Project 6)

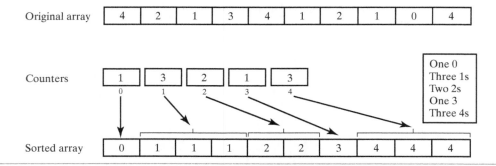

---

7.    **a.** Repeat Project 3 in Chapter 7, using an iterative stack-based implementation of the algorithm instead of a recursive one.

    **b.** Consider the following revision of the algorithm. After moving the top entry of $S_1$ to $S_2$, compare the new top entry *t* of $S_1$ with the top entry of $S_2$ and the top entry of $S_3$. Then either move entries from $S_2$ to $S_3$ or from $S_3$ to $S_2$ until you locate the correct position for *t*. Push *t* onto $S_2$. Continue until $S_1$ is empty. Finally, move any entries remaining in $S_3$ to $S_2$. Implement this revised algorithm iteratively using a stack-based approach.

ANSWERS TO SELF-TEST QUESTIONS

1.  9 6 2 4 8
    2 6 9 4 8
    2 4 9 6 8
    2 4 6 9 8
    2 4 6 8 9

2.  9 6 2 4 8
    6 9 2 4 8
    2 6 9 4 8
    2 4 6 9 8
    2 4 6 8 9

3.  No; `insertInOrder` links the node to be inserted into the sorted part of the chain so that the node no longer references the rest of the unsorted part. Since `unsortedPart` still references the inserted node, executing the line in question next would make `unsortedPart` either reference a node in the sorted part or be `null`.

4.  The public method `insertionSort` is to be invoked by using an object of `LinkedGroup`, which is the class that defines this method. Thus, the method should not be static.

5.  First, you consider the subarray of equally spaced letters at the indices 0, 4, and 8 (they appear in bold):

    *I  H  B  G  E  D  F  C  A*

    Now sort them to get

    *A  H  B  G  E  D  F  C  I*

    The indices 0, 4, and 8 have a separation of 4. Next, consider the letters at indices 1 and 5:

    *A  H  B  G  E  D  F  C  I*

    Sort them to get

    *A  D  B  G  E  H  F  C  I*

    Then sort the letters at indices 2 and 6; they already are in order:

    *A  D  B  G  E  H  F  C  I*

    Next, consider the letters at indices 3 and 7. Sort them to get

    *A  D  B  C  E  H  F  G  I*

    Now decrease the separation between indices to 2. You consider the letters at the indices 0, 2, 4, 6, and 8:

    *A  D  B  C  E  H  F  G  I*

    You find that they are sorted. Then consider the letters at indices 1, 3, 5, and 7:

    *A  D  B  C  E  H  F  G  I*

Sort them to get

*A* *C* *B* *D* *E* *G* *F* *H* *I*

Decreasing the separation to 1 results in an ordinary insertion sort of an array that is almost sorted.

6. **9** 6 2 4 **8** 7 5 3
**8** 6 2 4 **9** 7 5 3
8 **6** 2 4 9 **7** 5 3
8 6 **2** 4 9 7 **5** 3
8 6 2 **4** 9 7 5 **3**
8 6 2 **3** 9 7 5 **4**
**8** 6 **2** 3 9 **7** 5 **4**
**2** 6 **5** 3 8 **7** 9 4
2 **6** 5 3 8 **7** 9 **4**
2 **3** 5 **4** 8 **6** 9 **7**

Now apply a regular insertion sort.

# Faster Sorting Methods

## Contents

## Prerequisites

## Objectives

After studying this chapter, you should be able to

- Sort an array into ascending order by using the following methods: merge sort, quick sort, and radix sort
- Assess the efficiency of a sort and discuss the relative efficiencies of the various methods

The sorting algorithms that you saw in the previous chapter often are sufficient when you want to sort small arrays. They even can be a reasonable choice if you need to sort a larger array once. Additionally, the insertion sort is a good way to sort a chain of linked nodes. However, when you need to sort very large arrays frequently, those methods take too much time. This chapter presents sorting algorithms that are much faster in general than the methods in Chapter 8.

# Merge Sort

**9.1**   The **merge sort** divides an array into halves, sorts the two halves, and then merges them into one sorted array. The algorithm for merge sort is usually stated recursively. Recall that a recursive algorithm expresses the solution to a problem in terms of a smaller version of the same problem. When you divide a problem into two or more smaller but *distinct* problems, solve *each* new problem, and then combine their solutions to solve the original problem, the strategy is said to be a **divide and conquer** algorithm. That is, you divide the problem into pieces and conquer each piece to reach a solution. Although divide and conquer algorithms often are expressed recursively, this is not a requirement.

When expressed recursively, a divide and conquer algorithm contains two or more recursive calls. Most of the recursive solutions that you have seen so far do not use the divide and conquer strategy. For example, Segment 8.6 gave a recursive version of the selection sort. Even though that algorithm considers smaller and smaller arrays, it does not divide the problem into two sorting problems.

The real effort during the execution of a merge sort occurs during the merge step, and this is also the step that involves most of the programming effort, so we will begin there.

VideoNote
Merge sort

## Merging Arrays

**9.2**   Imagine that you have two distinct arrays that are sorted. Merging two sorted arrays is not difficult, but it does require an additional array. Processing both arrays from beginning to end, you compare an entry in one array with an entry in the other and copy the smaller entry to a new third array, as Figure 9-1 shows. After reaching the end of one array, you simply copy the remaining entries from the other array to the new third array.

---

**FIGURE 9-1**      Merging two sorted arrays into one sorted array

First array

| 3 | 5 | 7 | 9 |

Second array

| 0 | 2 | 4 | 6 |

3 > 0, so copy 0 to new array

| 3 | 5 | 7 | 9 |    | 0 | 2 | 4 | 6 |

3 > 2, so copy 2 to new array

| 3 | 5 | 7 | 9 |    | 0 | 2 | 4 | 6 |

3 < 4, so copy 3 to new array

| 3 | 5 | 7 | 9 |    | 0 | 2 | 4 | 6 |

5 > 4, so copy 4 to new array

| 3 | 5 | 7 | 9 |    | 0 | 2 | 4 | 6 |

5 < 6, so copy 5 to new array

| 3 | 5 | 7 | 9 |    | 0 | 2 | 4 | 6 |

7 > 6, so copy 6 to new array

| 3 | 5 | 7 | 9 |    | 0 | 2 | 4 | 6 |

New merged array:

| 0 |
| 2 |
| 3 |
| 4 |
| 5 |
| 6 |
| 7 |
| 9 |

The entire second array has been copied to the new array
Copy the rest of the first array to the new array

## Recursive Merge Sort

**9.3**    **The algorithm.** In a merge sort, you merge two sorted arrays that are actually halves of the original array. That is, you divide the array into halves, sort each half, and merge the sorted halves into a second temporary array, as Figure 9-2 shows. You then copy the temporary array back to the original array.

**FIGURE 9-2**    The major steps in a merge sort

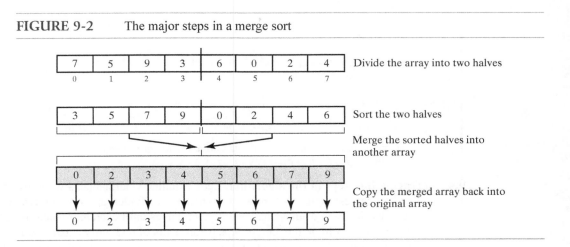

This sounds like a simple plan, but how did we sort the two halves of the array? By using a merge sort, of course! If mid is the index of the approximate midpoint of an array of $n$ entries, we need to sort the entries indexed by 0 through mid, and then the entries indexed by mid + 1 through $n - 1$. Since we perform these sorts by making recursive calls to the merge sort algorithm, the algorithm needs two parameters—first and last—to specify the first and last indices of the sub-range of the array to be sorted. We will use the notation a[first..last] to mean the array entries a[first], a[first + 1], ..., a[last].

Merge sort has the following recursive formulation:

*Algorithm* **mergeSort(a, tempArray, first, last)**
*// Sorts the array entries* a[first] *through* a[last] *recursively.*

```
if (first < last)
{
    mid = approximate midpoint between first and last
    mergeSort(a, tempArray, first, mid)
    mergeSort(a, tempArray, mid + 1,last)
    Merge the sorted halves a[first..mid] and a[mid + 1..last] using the array tempArray
}
```

Notice that the algorithm ignores arrays of one or fewer entries.

The following pseudocode describes the merge step:

*Algorithm* **merge(a, tempArray, first, mid, last)**
*// Merges the adjacent subarrays* a[first..mid] *and* a[mid + 1..last].

```
beginHalf1 = first
endHalf1 = mid
beginHalf2 = mid + 1
endHalf2 = last
```

```
// While both subarrays are not empty, compare an entry in one subarray with
// an entry in the other; then copy the smaller item into the temporary array
index = 0 // Next available location in tempArray
while ( (beginHalf1 <= endHalf1) and (beginHalf2 <= endHalf2) )
{
    if (a[beginHalf1] <= a[beginHalf2])
    {
        tempArray[index] = a[beginHalf1]
        beginHalf1++
    }
    else
    {
        tempArray[index] = a[beginHalf2]
        beginHalf2++
    }
    index++
}
// Assertion: One subarray has been completely copied to tempArray.

Copy remaining entries from other subarray to tempArray
Copy entries from tempArray to array a
```

**9.4** **Tracing the steps in the algorithm.** Let's examine what happens when we invoke mergeSort on the array halves. Figure 9-3 shows that mergeSort divides an array into two halves and then recursively divides each of those halves into two halves until each half contains only one entry. At this point in the algorithm, the merge steps begin. Pairs of one-entry subarrays are merged to form two-entry subarrays. Pairs of two-entry subarrays are merged to form four-entry subarrays, and so on.

FIGURE 9-3    The effect of the recursive calls and the merges during a merge sort

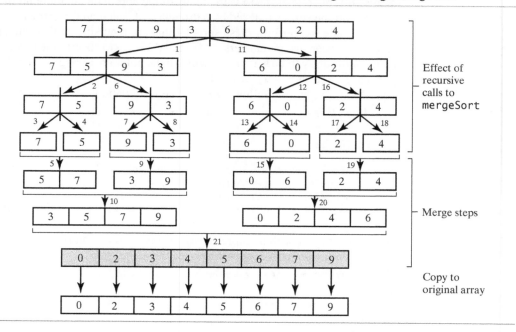

Numbers on the arrows in the figure indicate the order in which the recursive calls and the merges occur. Notice that the first merge occurs after four recursive calls to mergeSort and before other recursive calls to mergeSort. Thus, the recursive calls to mergeSort are interwoven with calls to merge. The actual sorting takes place during the merge steps and not during the recursive calls.

As you will see, we can use these observations in two ways. First, we can ascertain the algorithm's efficiency. Second, we can formulate the mergeSort algorithm iteratively.

**Note:** Merge sort rearranges the entries in an array during its merge steps.

**Question 1** Trace the steps that a merge sort takes when sorting the following array into ascending order: 9 6 2 4 8 7 5 3.

**9.5**    **Implementation note.** Although the implementation of the recursive mergesort is straightforward, you should be careful to allocate the temporary array only once. Since the array is an implementation detail, you might be tempted to hide its allocation in the method merge. But since merge is called each time mergesort is called recursively, this approach would cause a temporary array to be allocated and initialized many times. Instead, we can allocate a temporary array in the following public version of mergesort and pass it to a private mergesort that implements the pseudocode given previously:

```java
public static <T extends Comparable<? super T>>
        void mergeSort(T[] a, int first, int last)
{
    // The cast is safe because the new array contains null entries
    @SuppressWarnings("unchecked")
    T[] tempArray = (T[])new Comparable<?>[a.length]; // Unchecked cast
    mergeSort(a, tempArray, first, last);
} // end mergeSort
```

Java Interlude 3 introduced the notation ? super T to mean any superclass of T. When we allocate an array of Comparable objects, we use a wildcard ? to represent any object. We then cast the array to an array of type T objects.

## The Efficiency of Merge Sort

**9.6**    Assume for now that $n$ is a power of 2, so that we can divide $n$ by 2 evenly. The array in Figure 9-3 has $n = 8$ entries. The initial call to mergeSort makes two recursive calls to mergeSort, dividing the array into two subarrays of $n/2$, or 4, entries each. Each of the two recursive calls to mergeSort makes two recursive calls to mergeSort, dividing the two subarrays into four subarrays of $n/2^2$, or 2, entries each. Finally, recursive calls to mergeSort divide the four subarrays into eight subarrays of $n/2^3$, or 1, entry each. It takes three levels of recursive calls to obtain subarrays of one entry each. Notice that the original array contained $2^3$ entries. The exponent 3 is the number of levels of recursive calls. In general, if $n$ is $2^k$, $k$ levels of recursive calls occur.

Now consider the merge steps, because that is where the real work occurs. The merge step makes at most $n - 1$ comparisons among the $n$ entries in the two subarrays. Figure 9-4 provides an example of a merge that requires $n - 1$ comparisons, while Figure 9-1 shows an example where fewer than $n - 1$ comparisons occur. Each merge also requires $n$ moves to a temporary array and $n$ moves back to the original array. In total, each merge requires at most $3n - 1$ operations.

Each call to mergeSort calls merge once. The merge operation as a result of the original call to mergeSort requires at most $3n - 1$ operations. It is $O(n)$. An example of this merge appears as step 21 in Figure 9-3. The two recursive calls to mergeSort result in two calls to merge. Each call merges $n/2$ entries in at most $3n/2 - 1$ operations. The two merges then require at most $3n - 2$ operations. They are $O(n)$. The next level of recursion involves $2^2$ calls to mergeSort resulting in four calls to merge. Each call to merge merges $n/2^2$ entries in at most $3n/2^2 - 1$ operations. Together these four merges use at most $3n - 2^2$ operations, and so are $O(n)$.

**FIGURE 9-4**    A worst-case merge of two sorted arrays

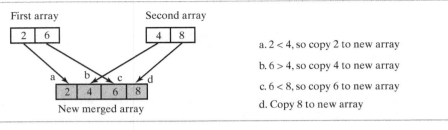

a. 2 < 4, so copy 2 to new array

b. 6 > 4, so copy 4 to new array

c. 6 < 8, so copy 6 to new array

d. Copy 8 to new array

If $n$ is $2^k$, the $k$ levels of recursive calls to mergeSort result in $k$ levels of merges. The merges at each level are O($n$). Since $k$ is $\log_2 n$, mergeSort is O($n \log n$). When $n$ is not a power of 2, we can find an integer $k$ so that $2^{k-1} < n < 2^k$. For example, when $n$ is 15, $k$ is 4. Thus,

$k - 1 < \log_2 n < k$

so if we round $\log_2 n$ up, we will get $k$. Therefore, the merge sort is O($n \log n$) in this case as well. Notice that the merge steps are O($n$) regardless of the initial order of the array. Merge sort is then O($n \log n$) in the worst, best, and average cases.

A disadvantage of merge sort is the need for the temporary array during the merge step. At the beginning of Chapter 8, we spoke of sorting the books on your bookshelf by height. We were able to do so without the extra space that another shelf or the floor would provide. You can see now that the merge sort would require this extra space. Later in this chapter, you will see another algorithm that sorts in O($n \log n$) time without a second array.

 **Note:  The time efficiency of merge sort**
Merge sort is O($n \log n$) in all cases. Its need for a temporary array is a disadvantage.

9.7    **Assessing efficiency another way.** In Chapter 7, we used a recurrence relation to estimate the time efficiency of recursive algorithms. We can use the same technique here. If $t(n)$ represents the time requirement of mergeSort in the worst case, the two recursive calls each require time $t(n/2)$. The merge step is O($n$). Thus, we have the following:

$t(n) = t(n/2) + t(n/2) + n$
$\quad\quad = 2 \times t(n/2) + n$ when $n > 1$
$t(1) = 0$

As a first step in solving this recurrence relation, we evaluate it for a specific value of $n$. Since $t(n)$ involves $n/2$, choosing $n$ to be a power of 2—8, for example—is convenient. We then have

$t(8) = 2 \times t(4) + 8$
$t(4) = 2 \times t(2) + 4$
$t(2) = 2 \times t(1) + 2 = 2$

By substituting repeatedly, we get the following for $t(8)$:

$t(8) = 2 \times t(4) + 8$
$\quad\quad = 2 \times [2 \times t(2) + 4] + 8$
$\quad\quad = 4 \times t(2) + 8 + 8$
$\quad\quad = 4 \times 2 + 8 + 8$
$\quad\quad = 8 + 8 + 8$
$\quad\quad = 8 \times 3$

Since $8 = 2^3$, $3 = \log_2 8$, so we guess that

$$t(n) = n \log_2 n$$

Just as we did in Chapter 7, we now need to prove that our guess is in fact true. We leave this proof as an exercise.

## Iterative Merge Sort

**9.8**   Once we have the merge algorithm, developing the recursive merge sort is easy. Developing an iterative merge sort is not as simple. We begin by making some observations about the recursive solution.

The recursive calls simply divide the array into $n$ one-entry subarrays, as you can see in Figure 9-3. Although we do not need recursion to isolate the entries in an array, the recursion controls the merging process. To replace the recursion with iteration, we will need to control the merges. Such an algorithm will be more efficient of both time and space than the recursive algorithm, since it will eliminate the recursive calls and, therefore, the stack of activation records. But an iterative merge sort will be trickier to code without error.

Basically, an iterative merge sort starts at the beginning of the array and merges pairs of individual entries to form two-entry subarrays. Then it returns to the beginning of the array and merges pairs of the two-entry subarrays to form four-entry subarrays, and so on. However, after merging all pairs of subarrays of a particular length, we might have entries left over. Merging these requires some care. Project 2 at the end of this chapter asks you to develop an iterative merge sort. You will see there that you can save much of the time necessary to copy the temporary array back to the original array during the merges.

## Merge Sort in the Java Class Library

**9.9**   The class `Arrays` in the package `java.util` defines several versions of a static method `sort` to sort an array into ascending order. For an array of objects, `sort` uses a merge sort. The method

```java
public static void sort(Object[] a)
```

sorts an entire array a of objects, while the method

```java
public static void sort(Object[] a, int first, int after)
```

sorts the objects in a[`first`] through a[`after` - 1]. For both methods, objects in the array must define the `Comparable` interface.

The merge sort used by these methods skips the merge step if none of the entries in the left half of the array are greater than the entries in the right half. Since both halves are sorted already, the merge step is unnecessary in this case.

**Question 2** Modify the merge sort algorithm given in Segment 9.3 so that it skips any unnecessary merges, as just described.

**Note:  Stable sorts**
A sorting algorithm is **stable** if it does not change the relative order of objects that are equal. For example, if object x appears before object y in a collection of data, and x.compareTo(y) is zero, a stable sorting algorithm will leave object x before object y after sorting the data. Stability is important to certain applications. For example, suppose that you sort a group of people, first by name and then by age. A stable sorting algorithm will ensure that people of the same age will remain in alphabetical order.

The merge sorts in the Java Class Library are stable. Exercise 9 at the end of this chapter asks you to identify the stable sorting algorithms presented in this chapter and the previous one.

# Quick Sort

**9.10**   We now look at another divide and conquer strategy for sorting an array. The **quick sort** divides an array into two pieces, but unlike merge sort, these pieces are not necessarily halves of the array. Instead, quick sort chooses one entry in the array—called the **pivot**—and rearranges the array entries so that

- The pivot is in the position that it will occupy in the final sorted array
- Entries in positions before the pivot are less than or equal to the pivot
- Entries in positions after the pivot are greater than or equal to the pivot

**VideoNote**

**Quick sort**

This arrangement is called a **partition** of the array.

Creating the partition divides the array into two pieces, which we will call *Smaller* and *Larger*, separated by the pivot, as Figure 9-5 illustrates. Since the entries in *Smaller* are less than or equal to the pivot, and the entries in *Larger* are greater than or equal to the pivot, the pivot is in its correct and final position within the sorted array. If we now sort the two subarrays *Smaller* and *Larger*—by using quick sort, of course—the original array will be sorted. The following algorithm describes our sorting strategy:

*Algorithm* `quickSort(a, first, last)`
*// Sorts the array entries* `a[first]` *through* `a[last]` *recursively.*

```
if (first < last)
{

    Choose a pivot
    Partition the array about the pivot
    pivotIndex = index of pivot
    quickSort(a, first, pivotIndex - 1)  // Sort Smaller
    quickSort(a, pivotIndex + 1, last)   // Sort Larger

}
```

**FIGURE 9-5**   A partition of an array during a quick sort

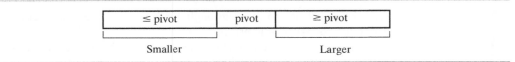

## The Efficiency of Quick Sort

**9.11**   Notice that creating the partition—which accounts for most of `quickSort`'s work—occurs before the recursive calls to `quickSort`. Contrast this with merge sort, where most of the work occurs during the merge phase *after* the recursive calls to `mergeSort`. Partitioning will require no more than $n$ comparisons, and so, like merging, it will be an $O(n)$ task. Thus, we can assess the efficiency of quick sort, even though we have not yet developed a partitioning strategy.

The ideal situation occurs when the pivot moves to the center of the array, so the two subarrays that the partition forms are the same size. If every recursive call to `quickSort` forms a partition with equal-sized subarrays, the quick sort will be like merge sort in that the recursive calls halve the array. Thus, quick sort would be $O(n \log n)$, and this would be its best case.

This ideal situation might not always occur, however. In the worst case, each partition has one empty subarray. Although one recursive call will have nothing to do, the other call must sort $n - 1$ entries instead of $n/2$. The result is $n$ levels of recursive calls instead of $\log n$. Thus, in the worst case, quick sort is $O(n^2)$.

The choice of pivots, then, affects quick sort's efficiency. Some pivot-selection schemes can lead to worst-case behavior if the array is already sorted or nearly sorted. In practice, nearly sorted arrays can occur more frequently than you might imagine. As you will see later, our pivot-selection scheme will avoid worst-case behavior for sorted arrays.

Although we will not prove it, quick sort is O($n \log n$) in the average case. While merge sort is always O($n \log n$), quick sort can be faster than merge sort in practice and does not require the additional memory that merge sort needs for merging.

**Note: The time efficiency of quick sort**
Quick sort is O($n \log n$) in the average case but O($n^2$) in the worst case. The choice of pivots affects its behavior.

## Creating the Partition

**9.12**   Various strategies are possible for choosing a pivot and for creating the partition in Figure 9-5. For now, we will assume that you have chosen a pivot, and so we will describe how to create a partition independently of your pivot-selection strategy. Later, our actual pivot-selection scheme will suggest minor changes to this partitioning process.

After choosing a pivot, swap it with the last entry in the array so that the pivot is not in your way while you create the partition. Figure 9-6a on the next page shows an array after this step. Starting at the beginning of the array and moving toward the end (left to right in the figure), look for the first entry that is greater than or equal to the pivot. In Figure 9-6b, that entry is 5 and occurs at the index `indexFromLeft`. In a similar fashion, starting at the next-to-last entry and moving toward the beginning of the array (right to left in the figure), look for the first entry that is less than or equal to the pivot. In Figure 9-6b, that entry is 2 and occurs at the index `indexFromRight`. Now, if `indexFromLeft` is less than `indexFromRight`, swap the two entries at those indices. Figure 9-6c shows the result of this step. The 2, which is less than the pivot, has moved toward the beginning of the array while the 5, which is greater than the pivot, has moved in the opposite direction.

Continue the searches from the left and from the right. Figure 9-6d shows that the search from the left stops at 4 and the search from the right stops at 1. Since `indexFromLeft` is less than `indexFromRight`, swap 4 and 1. The array now appears as in Figure 9-6e. Entries equal to the pivot are allowed in either piece of the partition.

Continue the searches again. Figure 9-6f shows that the search from the left stops at 6 while the search from the right goes beyond the 6 to stop at 1. Since `indexFromLeft` is not less than `indexFromRight`, no swap is necessary and the searches end. The only remaining step is to place the pivot between the subarrays *Smaller* and *Larger* by swapping a[`indexFromLeft`] and a[`last`], as Figure 9-6g shows. The completed partition appears in Figure 9-6h.

Note that the previous searches must not go beyond the ends of the array. Soon, in Segment 9.15, you will see a convenient way to implement this requirement.

**9.13**   **Entries equal to the pivot.** Notice that both of the subarrays *Smaller* and *Larger* can contain entries equal to the pivot. This might seem a bit strange to you. Why not always place any entries that equal the pivot into the same subarray? Such a strategy would tend to make one subarray larger than the other. However, to enhance quick sort's performance, we want the subarrays to be as nearly equal in size as possible.

Notice that both the search from the left and the search from the right stop when they encounter an entry that equals the pivot. This means that rather than being left in place, such entries are swapped. It also means that such an entry has a chance of landing in each of the subarrays.

FIGURE 9-6    A partitioning strategy for quick sort

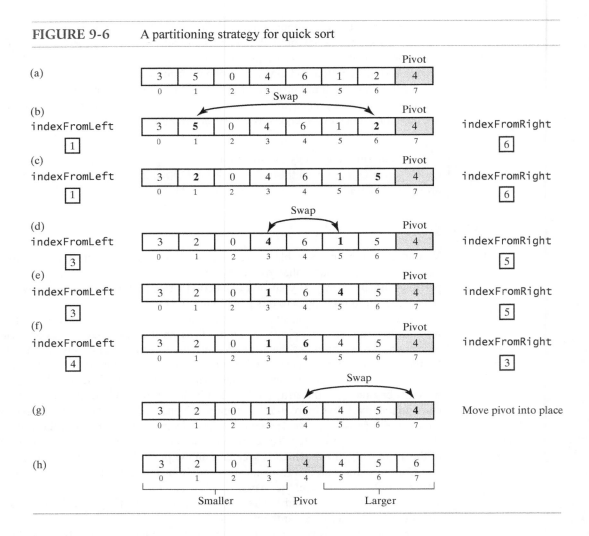

**9.14**   **Pivot selection.** Ideally, the pivot should be the median value in the array, so that the subarrays *Smaller* and *Larger* each have the same—or nearly the same—number of entries. One way to find the median value is to sort the array and then get the value in the middle. But sorting the array is the original problem, so this circular logic is doomed. Other ways to find the median are too slow to use.

Since choosing the best pivot takes too much time, we should at least try to avoid a bad pivot. So instead of finding the median of all values in the array, we will take as our pivot the median of three entries in the array: the first entry, the middle entry, and the last entry. One way to accomplish this task is to sort only those three entries and use the middle entry of the three as the pivot. Figure 9-7 shows an array both before and after its first, middle, and last entries are sorted. The pivot is the 5. This pivot selection strategy is called **median-of-three pivot selection**.

FIGURE 9-7    Median-of-three pivot selection: (a) The original array;
(b) the array with its first, middle, and last entries sorted

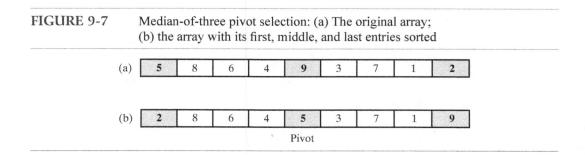

 **Note:** Median-of-three pivot selection avoids worst-case performance by quick sort when the given array is already sorted or nearly sorted. While it theoretically does not avoid worstcase performance for other arrays, such performance is unlikely in practice.

**9.15**  **Adjusting the partition algorithm.** Median-of-three pivot selection suggests some minor adjustments to our partitioning scheme. Previously, we swapped the pivot with the last entry in the array prior to partitioning. But here, the first, middle, and last entries in the array are sorted, so we know that the last entry is at least as large as the pivot. Thus, the last entry belongs in the subarray *Larger*. We can simply leave the last entry in place. To get the pivot out of the way, we can swap it with the next-to-last entry, a[last - 1], as Figure 9-8 shows. Thus, the partition algorithm can begin its search from the right at index last - 2.

FIGURE 9-8    (a) The array with its first, middle, and last entries sorted;
(b) the array after positioning the pivot and just before partitioning

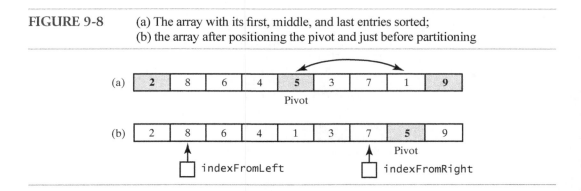

Also notice that the first entry is at least as small as the pivot, and so it belongs in the subarray *Smaller*. Thus, we can leave the first entry in place and have the partition algorithm begin its search from the left at index first + 1. Figure 9-8b shows the status of the array at this point, just prior to partitioning.

This scheme provides a side benefit that simplifies the loops for the two searches. The search from the left looks for an entry that is greater than or equal to the pivot. That search will terminate because, at worst, it will stop at the pivot. The search from the right looks for an entry that is less than or equal to the pivot. That search will terminate because, at worst, it will stop at the first entry. Thus, the loops need not do anything special to prevent the searches from going beyond the ends of the array.

After the search loops end, we need to position the pivot between the subarrays *Smaller* and *Larger*. We do this by swapping the entries a[indexFromLeft] and a[last - 1].

**Note:** Quick sort rearranges the entries in an array during the partitioning process. Each partition places one entry—the pivot—in its correct sorted position. The entries in each of the two subarrays that are before and after the pivot will remain in their respective subarrays.

## Implementing Quick Sort

**9.16** **Pivot selection.** Median-of-three pivot selection requires us to sort three entries: the first, middle, and last entries of the array. We can specify the following private method to accomplish this task by using simple comparisons and swaps:

```
// Sorts the first, middle, and last entries of an array into ascending order.
private static <T extends Comparable<? super T>>
        void sortFirstMiddleLast(T[] a, int first, int mid, int last)
```

After passing the indices of the first, middle, and last entries of the array to this method, we will have the pivot at the middle index.

**9.17** **Partitioning.** Median-of-three pivot selection assumes that the array has at least three entries. If you have only three entries, the pivot selection sorts them, so there is no need for the partition method or for quick sort. Thus, the following partition algorithm assumes that the array contains at least four entries:

*Algorithm* `partition(a, first, last)`
```
// Partitions an array a[first..last] as part of quick sort into two subarrays named
// Smaller and Larger that are separated by a single entry—the pivot—named pivotValue.
// Entries in Smaller are <= pivotValue and appear before pivotValue in the array.
// Entries in Larger are >= pivotValue and appear after pivotValue in the array.
// first >= 0; first < a.length; last – first >= 3; last < a.length.
// Returns the index of the pivot.

mid = index of the array's middle entry
sortFirstMiddleLast(a, first, mid, last)
// Assertion: a[mid] is the pivot, that is, pivotValue;
// a[first] <= pivotValue and a[last] >= pivotValue, so do not compare these two
// array entries with pivotValue.

// Move pivotValue to next-to-last position in array
Exchange a[mid] and a[last – 1]
pivotIndex = last – 1
pivotValue = a[pivotIndex]

// Determine two subarrays:
//    Smaller = a[first..endSmaller] and
//    Larger = a[endSmaller+1..last-1]
// such that entries in Smaller are <= pivotValue and
// entries in Larger are >= pivotValue.
// Initially, these subarrays are empty.
indexFromLeft = first + 1
indexFromRight = last – 2
done = false
while (!done)
{
    // Starting at the beginning of the array, leave entries that are < pivotValue and
    // locate the first entry that is >= pivotValue. You will find one, since the last
    // entry is >= pivotValue.
    while (a[indexFromLeft] < pivotValue)
        indexFromLeft++
```

```
// Starting at the end of the array, leave entries that are > pivotValue and
// locate the first entry that is <= pivotValue. You will find one, since the first
// entry is <= pivotValue.
while (a[indexFromRight] > pivotValue)
    indexFromRight--

// Assertion: a[indexFromLeft] >= pivotValue and
//            a[indexFromRight] <= pivotValue
if (indexFromLeft < indexFromRight)
{

    Exchange a[indexFromLeft] and a[indexFromRight]
    indexFromLeft++
    indexFromRight--

}
else
    done = true
}
// Place pivotValue between the subarrays Smaller and Larger
Exchange a[pivotIndex] and a[indexFromLeft]
pivotIndex = indexFromLeft

// Assertion:  Smaller = a[first..pivotIndex-1]
//             pivotValue = a[pivotIndex]
//             Larger = a[pivotIndex+1..last]
return pivotIndex
```

**9.18**    **The quick sort method.** Before completing the Java code for quick sort, we need to think about small arrays. You have seen that the array should contain at least four entries before you call the partition method. But simply agreeing to use quick sort only on large arrays is not enough. The pseudocode given for quick sort in Segment 9.10 shows that partitioning even a very large array will eventually lead to a recursive call that involves an array as small as two entries. The code for quick sort needs to screen out these small arrays and use another way to sort them. An insertion sort is a good choice for small arrays. In fact, using it instead of quick sort on arrays of as many as ten entries is reasonable. The following method implements quick sort with these observations in mind. The method assumes a constant MIN_SIZE that specifies the size of the smallest array on which we will use a quick sort.

```
/** Sorts an array into ascending order. Uses quick sort with
    median-of-three pivot selection for arrays of at least
    MIN_SIZE entries, and uses insertion sort for smaller arrays. */
public static <T extends Comparable<? super T>>
    void quickSort(T[] a, int first, int last)
{
    if (last - first + 1 < MIN_SIZE)
    {
        insertionSort(a, first, last);
    }
    else
    {
        // Create the partition: Smaller | Pivot | Larger
        int pivotIndex = partition(a, first, last);

        // Sort subarrays Smaller and Larger
        quickSort(a, first, pivotIndex - 1);
        quickSort(a, pivotIndex + 1, last);
    } // end if
} // end quickSort
```

**Question 3** Trace the steps that the method quickSort takes when sorting the following array into ascending order: 9 6 2 4 8 7 5 3. Assume that MIN_SIZE is 4.

## Quick Sort in the Java Class Library

**9.19** The class `Arrays` in the package `java.util` uses a quick sort to sort arrays of primitive types into ascending order. The method

```
public static void sort(type[] a)
```

sorts an entire array a, while the method

```
public static void sort(type[] a, int first, int after)
```

sorts the entries in a[first] through a[after - 1]. Note that *type* is either `byte`, `char`, `double`, `float`, `int`, `long`, or `short`.

# Radix Sort

**9.20** The sorting algorithms that you have seen so far sort objects that can be compared. The **radix sort** does not use comparison, but to work, it must restrict the data that it sorts. For this restricted data, the radix sort is $O(n)$, and so it is faster than any other sort in this chapter. However, it is not suitable as a general-purpose sorting algorithm, because it treats array entries as if they were strings that have the same length.

Let's look at an example of a radix sort of the following three-digit positive integers:

123 398 210 019 528 003 513 129 220 294

Notice that 19 and 3 are padded with zeros to make them three-digit integers. The radix sort begins by grouping the integers according to their rightmost digits. Since a digit can have one of 10 values, we need 10 groups, or **buckets**. If bucket *d* corresponds to the digit *d*, we place 123 into bucket 3, 398 into bucket 8, and so on. Figure 9-9a shows the result of this process. Notice that each bucket must retain the order in which it receives the integers.

Looking at the buckets sequentially, we see that the integers are now in the following order:

210 220 123 003 513 294 398 528 019 129

We move these integers from the buckets to the original array. We then group the integers by their middle digits, using the now empty buckets. Thus, 210 goes into bucket 1, 220 goes into bucket 2, 123 goes into bucket 2, and so on. Figure 9-9b shows the result of this pass.

The integers in the buckets are now in this order:

003 210 513 019 220 123 528 129 294 398

After moving these integers from the buckets back to the array, we group them by their leftmost digits. Thus, 003 goes into bucket 0, 210 goes into bucket 2, 513 goes into bucket 5, and so on. Figure 9-9c shows the result of this pass.

The integers in the buckets are now in their final sorted order:

003 019 123 129 210 220 294 398 513 528

---

**Aside: Origin of the radix sort**

During the early days of computing, data was stored on punched cards. Each card had 80 columns in which to store 80 characters. Each column had 12 rows that were the possible positions for holes. A machine called a card sorter distributed the cards among 12 bins according to the row punched in the column chosen by the machine's operator. These bins are analogous to the buckets in a radix sort. After running a stack of cards through the card sorter, the operator would gather the cards a bin at a time to create a new stack. The cards would be run through the sorter again to sort the next column of holes. By repeating this process, the operator could sort the cards.

FIGURE 9-9    Radix sort: (a) Original array and buckets after first distribution;
(b) reordered array and buckets after second distribution;
(c) reordered array and buckets after third distribution;
(d) sorted array

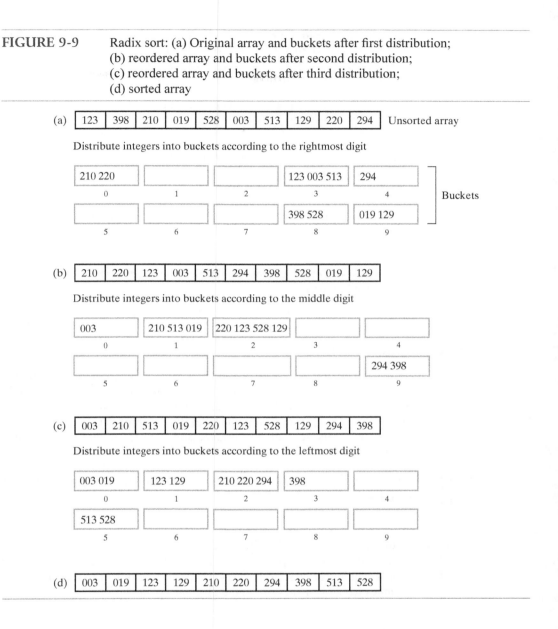

## Pseudocode for Radix Sort

**9.21**   Our previous description of radix sort assumed that the integers to be sorted each contain the same number of digits. Actually, this requirement is unnecessary as long as you get 0 when you ask for a digit that does not exist. For example, if you ask for the hundreds digit of a two-digit integer, you should get 0.

The following algorithm describes a radix sort of an array of positive decimal integers. We number the digits in each integer from the right beginning at 0. Thus, the units digit is digit 0, the tens digit is digit 1, and so on.

*Algorithm* radixSort(a, first, last, maxDigits)
*// Sorts the array of positive decimal integers* a[first..last] *into ascending order;*
*//* maxDigits *is the number of digits in the longest integer.*

```
for (i = 0 to maxDigits - 1)
{
    Clear bucket[0], bucket[1], ... , bucket[9]
    for (index = first to last)
    {
        digit = digit i of a[index]
        Place a[index] at end of bucket[digit]
    }
    Place contents of bucket[0], bucket[1], ... , bucket[9] into the array a
}
```

This algorithm uses an array of buckets. The nature of a bucket is unspecified, but after you read Chapter 10, you will see that a bucket can be an instance of the ADT queue.

 **Question 4** Trace the steps that the algorithm radixSort takes when sorting the following array into ascending order:

6340 1234 291 3 6325 68 5227 1638

### The Efficiency of Radix Sort

**9.22**   If an array contains $n$ integers, the inner loop in the previous algorithm iterates $n$ times. If each integer contains $d$ digits, the outer loop iterates $d$ times. Thus, the radix sort is $O(d \times n)$. The $d$ in this expression tells us that the actual running time for a radix sort depends on the size of the integers. But on a computer, the typical integer is restricted in size to about 10 decimal digits, or 32 bits. As long as $d$ is fixed and is much smaller than $n$, radix sort is simply an $O(n)$ algorithm.

 **Note:** Although radix sort is an $O(n)$ algorithm for certain data, it is not appropriate for all data.

 **Question 5** One of the difficulties with the radix sort is that the number of buckets depends on the kind of strings you are sorting. You saw that sorting integers requires 10 buckets; sorting words requires at least 26 buckets. If you use radix sort to alphabetize an array of words, what changes would be necessary to the given algorithm?

## Comparing the Algorithms

**9.23**   Figure 9-10 summarizes the efficiencies of the sorting algorithms presented in this chapter and the previous chapter. Although a radix sort is fastest, it is not always applicable. The merge sort and quick sort are generally faster than any of the other algorithms.

To give you an idea of how the problem size affects time efficiency, Figure 9-11 tabulates the four growth-rate functions that appear in Figure 9-10 for several values of $n$. You certainly could use an $O(n^2)$ sort algorithm when $n$ is 10. When $n$ is 100, a Shell sort is almost as fast as a quick sort in the average case. But when $n$ is one million, an average-case quick sort is much faster than a Shell sort and much, much faster than an insertion sort.

FIGURE 9-10    The time efficiency of various sorting algorithms, expressed in
Big Oh notation

|  | Average Case | Best Case | Worst Case |
| --- | --- | --- | --- |
| Radix sort | $O(n)$ | $O(n)$ | $O(n)$ |
| Merge sort | $O(n \log n)$ | $O(n \log n)$ | $O(n \log n)$ |
| Quick sort | $O(n \log n)$ | $O(n \log n)$ | $O(n^2)$ |
| Shell sort | $O(n^{1.5})$ | $O(n)$ | $O(n^2)$ or $O(n^{1.5})$ |
| Insertion sort | $O(n^2)$ | $O(n)$ | $O(n^2)$ |
| Selection sort | $O(n^2)$ | $O(n^2)$ | $O(n^2)$ |

If your array has relatively few entries, or if it is nearly sorted, the insertion sort is a good choice. Otherwise, the quick sort is generally preferable. Note that merge sort is useful when the data collection is too large to reside entirely in main memory and so is in an external file.

We will discuss another sorting algorithm, the heap sort, in Chapter 26. This technique is also $O(n \log n)$, but the quick sort is usually preferable.

FIGURE 9-11    A comparison of growth-rate functions as $n$ increases

| $n$ | 10 | $10^2$ | $10^3$ | $10^4$ | $10^5$ | $10^6$ |
| --- | --- | --- | --- | --- | --- | --- |
| $n \log_2 n$ | 33 | 664 | 9966 | 132,877 | 1,660,964 | 19,931,569 |
| $n^{1.5}$ | 32 | $10^3$ | 31,623 | $10^6$ | 31,622,777 | $10^9$ |
| $n^2$ | $10^2$ | $10^4$ | $10^6$ | $10^8$ | $10^{10}$ | $10^{12}$ |

## CHAPTER SUMMARY

- Merge sort is a divide and conquer algorithm that halves an array, recursively sorts the two halves, and then merges them into one sorted array.

- Merge sort is $O(n \log n)$. However, it does use additional memory to perform the merge step.

- Quick sort is another divide and conquer algorithm that partitions an array into two subarrays that are separated by one entry, the pivot. The pivot is in its correct sorted position. The entries in one subarray are less than or equal to the pivot, while the entries in the second subarray are greater than or equal to the pivot. Quick sort recursively sorts the two subarrays.

- Quick sort is $O(n \log n)$ most of the time. Although it is $O(n^2)$ in its worst case, you usually can avoid this case by choosing appropriate pivots.

- Even though merge sort and quick sort are $O(n \log n)$ algorithms, quick sort is usually faster in practice and does not require additional memory.

- Radix sort treats array entries as if they were strings that have the same length. Initially radix sort distributes the entries into buckets according to the character (digit) at one end of the strings. The sort then collects the strings and distributes them again among the buckets according to the character or digit in the next position. The sort continues this process until all character positions are considered.

- Radix sort does not compare array entries. Although it is $O(n)$, it cannot sort all types of data. Thus, it is not appropriate as a general-purpose sorting algorithm.

## EXERCISES

1. Suppose that 85  90  75  80  65  95  50  45 represents an array of Integer objects, and is to be sorted using merge sort. Show the steps that this sort takes using recursion.

2. Consider the method quickSort, as given in Segment 9.18, that sorts an array of objects into ascending order by using a quick sort. Suppose that 80  90  70  85  60  40  50  95 represents an array of Integer objects.

   a. What does the array look like after quickSort partitions it for the first time? (Show all intermediate results.)
   b. How many comparisons did this partition process require?
   c. The pivot is now between two subarrays called *Smaller* and *Larger*. Will the position of this particular entry change during subsequent steps of the sort? Why or why not?
   d. What recursive call to quickSort occurs next?

3. Consider the merge step of the merge sort.

   a. What is the maximum number of comparisons needed to merge two subarrays each of size *n*/2?
   b. Give a recurrence relation that counts the number of comparisons made in the worst case.
   c. Make an educated guess at the solution to the recurrence relation.

4. It has been observed that the performances of quick sort and selection sort are similar in worst cases. What are the reasons?

5. Show the steps that a quick sort takes when sorting the following array of Integer objects:

   38  25  78  83  62  59  40  95

6. Show the steps that a radix sort takes when sorting the following array of strings into alphabetical order:

   page   case   dot   bow   cab   fad   cat   sack   face   city   fact   door

7. Explain with the help of an example how a radix sort that selects digits from left to right works.

8. Consider a collection of Comparable objects that is represented by a chain of linked nodes. Suppose that you want to provide a sort operation for this collection.

   a. Assuming that merge sort has been used, how would you divide the chain into two?
   b. One way of merging two chains of linked nodes is to create a new chain. Can you think of any other way of doing this?

9. Recall that a sorting algorithm is stable if it does not change the relative order of objects that are equal. What sorting algorithms in this chapter and the previous one are stable?

10. Segment 9.7 showed that you can compute the efficiency of merge sort by solving the recurrence relation

    $t(n) = 2 \times t(n/2) + n$ when $n > 1$
    $t(1) = 0$
    Prove by induction that $t(n) = n \log_2 n$.

11. Recall that a sorting algorithm is stable if it does not change the relative order of objects that are equal. Give one example where an algorithm's stability is important.

## PROJECTS

1. **a.** Implement the recursive algorithm for merge sort.
   **b.** Complete the implementation of quick sort by implementing the method `partition`.

2. Segment 9.8 introduced you to an iterative merge sort. This project continues that discussion by providing more details about the merge steps.

   **a.** If $n$ is a power of 2, as it is in Figure 9-3, you would merge pairs of individual entries, starting at the beginning of the array. Then you would return to the beginning of the array and merge pairs of two-entry subarrays. Finally, you would merge one pair of four-entry subarrays. Notice that the subarrays in each pair of subarrays contain the same number of entries.

   In general, $n$ might not be a power of 2. After merging a certain number of pairs of subarrays, you might have too few entries left to make up a complete pair of subarrays. In Figure 9-12a (on the next page), after merging pairs of single entries, one entry is left over. You then merge one pair of two-entry subarrays, and merge the leftover two-entry subarray with the leftover single entry. Parts $b$ and $c$ of Figure 9-12 show two other possibilities.

   Implement an iterative merge sort. Use the algorithm `merge` that was given in Segment 9.3. A private method that uses `merge` to merge the pairs of subarrays is useful. After the method completes its task, you can handle the leftovers that we just described.

   **b.** Merging two subarrays requires an additional temporary array. Although you need to use this extra space, you can save much of the time that our earlier merge algorithm spends in copying entries from the temporary array back to the original array. If $a$ is the original array and $t$ is the temporary array, you first merge subarrays of $a$ into the array $t$. Instead of copying $t$ back to $a$ and continuing the merge, you determine subarrays of $t$ and merge them into $a$. If you can do this an even number of times, no additional copying is necessary. Make these changes to the iterative merge sort that you wrote in Part $a$.

3. Consider the following implementation of an iterative merge sort. Scan the array from its beginning and partition it into segments that are each sorted. As you find each segment, represent it as a pair of indices and place the pair at the end of an initially empty vector.

   Next, remove the first two pairs from the vector and merge the array segments they represent. Notice that these segments are adjacent in the array. The merge results in a larger segment that is sorted. Place the pair of indices that represents the resulting segment at the end of the vector. Repeat the steps in this paragraph until only one entry remains in the vector.

   Sometimes during the process, the two pairs at the beginning of the vector will represent segments that are not adjacent. In this case, move the first pair to the end of the vector and continue.

   **a.** What is the best-case performance of this algorithm?
   **b.** What is the worst-case performance of this algorithm?
   **c.** Implement the algorithm.

**FIGURE 9-12**     Special cases in an iterative merge sort after merging one-entry subarrays

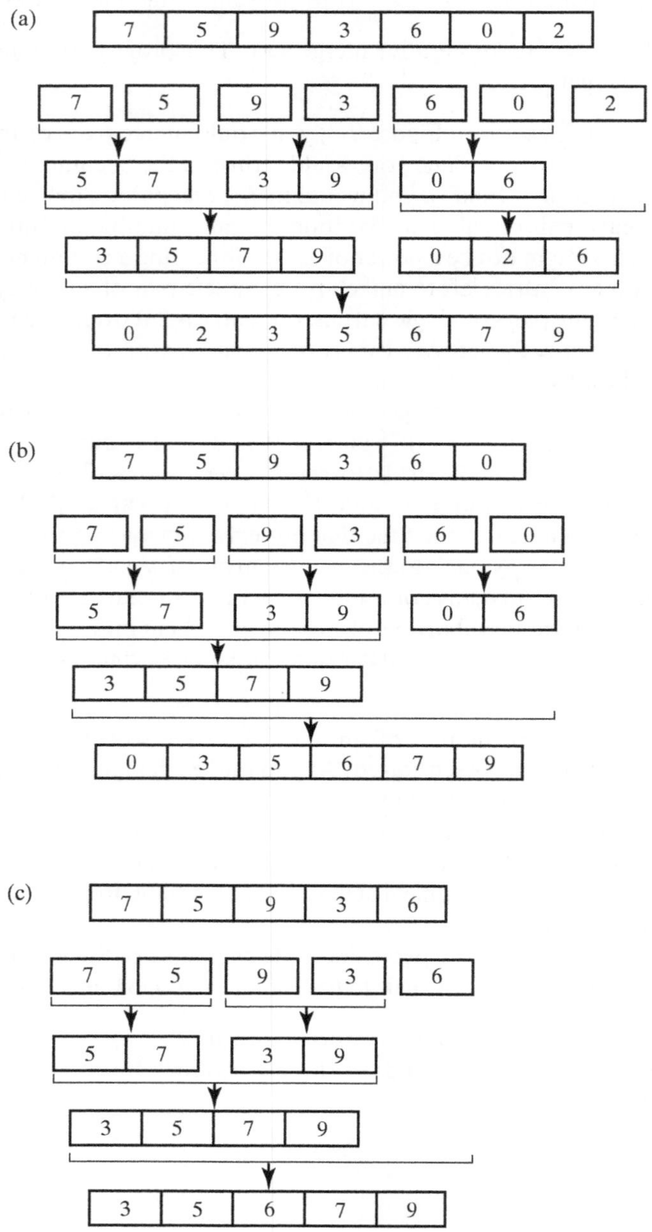

(a)

(b)

(c)

**4.** Revise the implementation of quick sort as follows. If the array has 7 entries, choose the middle entry as the pivot. For arrays of between 8 and 40 entries, use the median-of-three pivot-selection scheme described in Segments 9.14 and 9.16. For larger arrays, the pivot is the median of 9 entries that are about equally spaced, including the first, last, and middle entries. For arrays of fewer than 7 entries, use insertion sort instead of quick sort.

**5.** Extend Project 1 of the previous chapter to provide graphical demonstrations of the merge sort and quick sort algorithms introduced in this chapter.

6. The *median* of a collection of data is the middle value. One way to find the median is to sort the data and take the value that is at—or nearly at—the center of the collection. But sorting does more than necessary to find the median. You need to find only the $k^{th}$ smallest entry in the collection for an appropriate value of $k$. To find the median of $n$ items, you would take $k$ as $n/2$ rounded up—that is, $[n / 2]$.

You can use the partitioning strategy of quick sort to find the $k^{th}$ smallest entry in an array. After choosing a pivot and forming the subarrays *Smaller* and *Larger*, as described in Segment 9.10, you can draw one of the following conclusions:

- If *Smaller* contains $k$ or more entries, it must contain the $k^{th}$ smallest entry.
- If *Smaller* contains $k - 1$ entries, the $k^{th}$ smallest entry is the pivot.
- If *Smaller* contains fewer than $k - 1$ entries, the $k^{th}$ smallest entry is in *Larger*.

You now can develop a recursive solution to finding the $k^{th}$ smallest entry. The first and last conclusions correspond to the recursive calls. The remaining one is the base case.

Implement a recursive method that finds the $k^{th}$ smallest entry in an unsorted array. Use your method to find the median in the array.

7. A binary radix sort will sort an array $a$ of $n$ integer values based on their binary bits instead of their decimal digits. This sort will need only two buckets. Represent the buckets as a 2 by $n$ array. You can avoid some work by not copying the contents of the buckets back into the array $a$ at the end of each pass. Instead just add the values from the second bucket to the end of the first bucket.

Implement this algorithm.

8. Repeat Project 3 of the previous chapter, but instead compare the merge sort and the quick sort.

9. Implement a merge sort of the objects in a chain of linked nodes. Compare the run times of this version of merge sort and a quick sort of the same data in an array. See the projects at the end of Chapter 4 for a description of how to time a block of Java code.

10. Implement a radix sort of the strings in a chain of linked nodes.

## ANSWERS TO SELF-TEST QUESTIONS

```
1.          9 6 2 4 8 7 5 3
        9 6 2 4           8 7 5 3
        9 6     2 4       8 7     5 3
        9 6     2 4       8 7     5 3
        6 9     2 4       7 8     3 5
        2 4 6 9             3 5 7 8
            2 3 4 5 6 7 8 9

2. Algorithm mergeSort(a, tempArray, first, last)
   if (first < last)
   {
      mid = first + (last - first) / 2
      mergeSort(a, first, mid)
      mergeSort(a, mid + 1, last)
      if (array[mid] > array[mid + 1]))
         Merge the sorted halves a[first..mid] and a[mid+1..last] using the array tempArray
   }
```

**3.** 
```
quickSort(array, 0, 7)
partition(array, 0, 7)
```
    9 6 2 4 8 7 5 3
    3 6 2 4 8 7 5 9
    3 6 2 5 8 7 4 9
    3 2 6 5 8 7 4 9
    3 2 4 5 8 7 6 9

```
quickSort(array, 0, 1)
insertionSort(array, 0, 1)
```
    2 3 4 5 8 7 6 9

```
quickSort(array, 3, 7)
partition(array, 3, 7)
```
    2 3 4 5 8 7 6 9
    2 3 4 5 8 6 7 9
    2 3 4 5 6 8 7 9
    2 3 4 5 6 7 8 9

```
quickSort(array, 3, 4)
insertionSort(array, 3, 4)
```
    2 3 4 5 6 7 8 9

```
quickSort(array, 6, 7)
insertionSort(array, 6, 7)
```
    2 3 4 5 6 7 8 9

**4.**
    6340  1234  0291  0003  6325  0068  5227  1638

    6340  0291  0003  1234  6325  5227  0068  1638

    0003  6325  5227  1234  1638  6340  0068  0291

    0003  0068  5227  1234  0291  6325  6340  1638

    0003  0068  0291  1234  1638  5227  6325  6340

    0003  0068  0291  1234  1638  5227  6325  6340

**5.** *Algorithm* `radixSort(a, first, last, wordLength)`
*// Sorts the array of lowercase words* `a[first..last]` *into ascending order;*
*// treats each word as if it was padded on the right with blanks to make all words have*
*// the same length,* `wordLength`.

```
for (i = 1 to wordlength)
{
    Clear bucket['a'], bucket['b'], ... , bucket['z'], bucket[' ']
    for (index = first to last)
    {
        letter = iᵗʰ letter from the right of a[index]
        Place a[index] at end of bucket[letter]
    }
    Place contents of bucket['a'], bucket['b'], ... , bucket['z'], bucket[' ']
        into the array a
}
```

# More About Exceptions

## Contents

## Prerequisites

**I**n this interlude, we continue our study of exceptions that we began in Java Interlude 2.

## Programmer-Defined Exception Classes

You can define your own exception classes by extending existing exception classes. An existing superclass could be one in the Java Class Library or one of your own. The constructors in an exception subclass are the most important—and often the only—methods you need to define. Other methods are inherited from the superclass.

**JI4.1**

**A sample definition.** For example, consider the method `sqrt` provided by Java's class `Math` to compute the square root of a real number. Since `sqrt` returns a `double` value, it computes the square root of only nonnegative numbers. If we give the method a negative number, it returns the special value `NaN`, which stands for "not a number." If displayed, this value appears as `NaN`. If it is involved in arithmetic, the result is `NaN`.

Imagine, instead, a square root method that requires a nonnegative argument. Let's treat the passing of a negative number to the method as a programming mistake and throw a runtime exception. The method certainly could throw an instance of `RuntimeException`, but a more specific exception would be better. So let's define our own class, `SquareRootException`, as shown in Listing JI4-1. Because we want a runtime exception, our class extends `RuntimeException`. Each of the two constructors for this class uses `super` to invoke `RuntimeException`'s constructor, passing it a string as a message. The default constructor passes a default message, but the second constructor passes the message provided as its argument when it is called. Most programmer-defined exception classes are as straightforward as `SquareRootException`.

**VideoNote**
Creating your own exceptions

---

**LISTING JI4-1** The exception class `SquareRootException`

```
1  /**
2      A class of runtime exceptions thrown when an attempt
3      is made to find the square root of a negative number.
4      @author Frank M. Carrano
5  */
6  public class SquareRootException extends RuntimeException
7  {
8     public SquareRootException()
9     {
10       super("Attempted square root of a negative number.");
11    } // end default constructor
12
13    public SquareRootException(String message)
14    {
15       super(message);
16    } // end constructor
17 } // end SquareRootException
```

---

**JI4.2** Note that `SquareRootException`'s default constructor could use `this` instead of `super`, as follows:

```
public SquareRootException()
{
   this("Attempted square root of a negative number.");
} // end default constructor
```

By using `this`, the constructor calls the second constructor, which in turn calls `RuntimeException`'s constructor. In contrast, the default constructor shown in Listing JI4-1 uses `super` to call `RuntimeException`'s constructor directly. Although the version in Listing JI4-1 is more direct and might seem better, using `this` to link one constructor to another is usually preferable, as the technique tends to reduce mistakes.

**JI4.3**  **Using our own exception class.** We have imagined a square root method that throws a runtime exception when given a negative number as its argument. Now that we have an appropriate class of exceptions, let's define this method within a class of static methods, as shown in Listing JI4-2, that is much like the class `Math`.

The header for the method `squareRoot` is similar to the header of `Math.sqrt` but also includes a `throws` clause to indicate that the method might throw a `SquareRootException`. Notice the tag `@throws` in the `javadoc` comment preceding the header. Recall from Java Interlude 2 that it labels a description of the exception that might occur. Since `SquareRootException` is a runtime exception, listing it in a `throws` clause and documenting it in `javadoc` are optional.

Within the body of the method `squareRoot` is a `throw` statement. It throws a `SquareRootException` if the method's argument is negative. If the argument is not negative, the method simply returns the square root as computed by the method `Math.sqrt`.

---

**LISTING JI4-2** The class `OurMath` and its static method `squareRoot`

```
1  /**
2      A class of static methods to perform various mathematical
3      computations, including the square root.
4      @author Frank M. Carrano
5  */
6  public class OurMath
7  {
8     /** Computes the square root of a nonnegative real number.
9         @param value   A  real value whose square root is desired.
```

```
10          @return  The square root of the given value.
11          @throws  SquareRootException if value < 0. */
12     public static double squareRoot(double value)
13          throws SquareRootException
14     {
15        if (value < 0)
16           throw new SquareRootException();
17        else
18           return Math.sqrt(value);
19     } // end squareRoot
20
21     < Other methods not relevant to this discussion are here. >
22
23  } // end OurMath
```

**JI4.4**  A demonstration of the class `OurMath` is given in Listing JI4-3. Note the message displayed as a result of the exception. Also note that execution stops when the exception occurs.

**LISTING JI4-3   A driver for the class `OurMath`**

```
1  /**
2      A demonstration of a runtime exception using the class OurMath.
3  */
4  public class OurMathDriver
5  {
6     public static void main(String[] args)
7     {
8        System.out.print("The square root of 9 is ");
9        System.out.println(OurMath.squareRoot(9.0));
10
11        System.out.print("The square root of -9 is ");
12        System.out.println(OurMath.squareRoot(-9.0));
13
14        System.out.print("The square root of 16 is ");
15        System.out.println(OurMath.squareRoot(16.0));
16     } // end main
17  } // end OurMathDriver
```

**Output**

```
The square root of 9 is 3.0
The square root of -9 is Exception in thread "main" SquareRootException:
Attempted square root of a negative number.
        at OurMath.squareRoot(OurMath.java:16)
        at OurMathDriver.main(OurMathDriver.java:12)
```

**JI4.5**   Imagine that our class `OurMath` is widely available to other programmers. Joe wants to use our class to compute the square root, but he doesn't want to receive an error message when `squareRoot` encounters a negative argument. Instead, he wants the method to return a complex[1] number involving $i$, which is an abbreviation for the square root of $-1$. For example, the square root of $-9$ is $3i$, because

$$\sqrt{-9} = \sqrt{9(-1)} = \sqrt{9}\sqrt{-1} = 3i$$

---

1. Only a rudimentary knowledge of complex numbers is needed here. Complex numbers build on real numbers by adding an imaginary part involving $i$. Every complex number has the form $a + b\,i$, where $a$ and $b$ are real numbers. To represent a real number in this notation, you would have $b$ be zero.

To accommodate results that involve *i* and those that do not, Joe has his method return a string. Thus, Joe envisions a method that would return the string "3i" as the square root of −9 and would return the string "3" as the square root of 9.

Joe's method will invoke `OurMath.squareRoot`. As this invocation must appear within a `try` block, Joe writes

```
String result = "";
try
{
   Double temp = OurMath.squareRoot(value);
   result = temp.toString();
}
```

All is fine, as long as `value` is not negative, but if it is negative, a `SquareRootException` is thrown. Instead of displaying an error message, as the driver in Listing JI4-3 does, Joe wants his method to return the correct value for a negative argument. He writes the following pseudocode to get his ideas on paper:

```
// Assume value is negative
catch (SquareRootException e)
{
   Double temp = the square root of -value
   result = temp.toString() followed by "i"
}
```

Joe then translates this pseudocode into the following catch block:

```
catch (SquareRootException e)
{  // Assertion: value is negative
   Double temp = OurMath.squareRoot(-value);
   result = temp.toString() + "i";
}
```

**JI4.6** Listing JI4-4 shows Joe's method `squareRoot` within his class `JoeMath`, and Listing JI4-5 provides a demonstration of the class.

**LISTING JI4-4**   The class `JoeMath`

```
1  /**
2      A class of static methods to perform various mathematical
3      computations, including the square root.
4  */
5  public class JoeMath
6  {
7     /** Computes the square root of a real number.
8         @param value  A  real value whose square root is desired.
9         @return  A string containing the square root. */
10    public static String squareRoot(double value)
11    {
12       String result = "";
13       try
14       {
15          Double temp = OurMath.squareRoot(value);
16          result = temp.toString();
17       }
18       catch (SquareRootException e)
19       {
20          Double temp = OurMath.squareRoot(-value);
21          result = temp.toString() + "i";
22       }
```

```
23
24        return result;
25     } // end squareRoot
26
27     < Other methods not relevant to this discussion could be here. >
28
29 } // end JoeMath
```

---

**LISTING JI4-5   A driver for the class `JoeMath`**

```
1  /**
2      A demonstration of a runtime exception using the class JoeMath.
3  */
4  public class JoeMathDriver
5  {
6     public static void main(String[] args)
7     {
8        System.out.print("The square root of 9 is ");
9        System.out.println(JoeMath.squareRoot(9.0));
10
11       System.out.print("The square root of -9 is ");
12       System.out.println(JoeMath.squareRoot(-9.0));
13
14       System.out.print("The square root of 16 is ");
15       System.out.println(JoeMath.squareRoot(16.0));
16
17       System.out.print("The square root of -16 is ");
18       System.out.println(JoeMath.squareRoot(-16.0));
19    } // end main
20 } // end JoeMathDriver
```

**Output**
```
The square root of 9 is 3.0
The square root of -9 is 3.0i
The square root of 16 is 4.0
The square root of -16 is 4.0i
```

## Inheritance and Exceptions

JI4.7   Imagine a class whose method `someMethod` has a `throws` clause in its header. If we override `some-Method` in a subclass, can we list additional checked exceptions in its `throws` clause? No, Java will not let us; we will get a syntax error if we do.

For example, consider the following superclass and subclass:

```
public class SuperClass
{
   public void someMethod() throws Exception1
   { . . .
   } // end someMethod
} // end SuperClass

public class SubClass extends SuperClass
{
   public void someMethod() throws Exception1, Exception2 // ERROR!
   { . . .
   } // end someMethod
} // end SubClass
```

The throws clause in the overriding method will be flagged as syntactically incorrect. Let's think about why this is an error.

Suppose a program creates an instance of SubClass, assigns the object to a variable of SuperClass—let's call it superObject—and places the call superObject.someMethod() within a try block, as follows:

```
public class Driver
{
   public static void main(String[] args)
   {
      SuperClass superObject = new SubClass();
      try
      {
         superObject.someMethod();
      }
      catch (Exception1 e)
      {
         System.out.println(e.getMessage());
      }
   } // end main
} // end Driver
```

Since superObject references an instance of SubClass, SubClass's version of someMethod is called. But since superObject's static type is SuperClass, the compiler sees only SuperClass's definition for someMethod. Thus, it checks only that Exception1 is caught. If the throws clause in SubClass was legal, we could call SubClass's someMethod without catching Exception2.

**JI4.8**  The rule governing which exceptions can appear in a throws clause of an overriding method is relaxed somewhat if the exceptions are related by inheritance. For example, if Exception2 extends Exception1, the following is legal:

```
public class SuperClass
{
   public void someMethod() throws Exception1
   { . . .
   } // end someMethod
} // end SuperClass

public class SubClass extends SuperClass
{
   public void someMethod() throws Exception2 // OK, assuming Exception2
   { . . .                                     //      extends Exception1
   } // end someMethod
} // end SubClass
```

**Note:**  An overriding method in a subclass cannot list exceptions in a throws clause that aren't listed in a throws clause of the overridden method in the superclass, unless they are derived from the exception classes listed in the overridden method. However, an overriding method can list fewer exceptions in its throws clause or none at all.

# The finally Block

**JI4.9**  If you have code that must execute regardless of whether an exception occurs, you could place it at the end of the try block and at the end of each catch block. An easier way to accomplish this, however, is to place one copy of the code in question within a finally block that follows the last catch block. Code within a finally block executes after either the try block or an executing catch block ends. Although optional, the finally block is a good way to provide cleanup services, such as closing a file or releasing system resources.

The following code shows the placement of the `finally` block:

```
try
{
    < Code that might throw an exception, either by executing a throw statement or by calling a
      method that throws an exception >
}
catch (AnException e)
{
    < Code that handles exceptions of type AnException or a subclass of AnException >
}

< Possibly other catch blocks to handle other types of exceptions >

finally
{
    < Code that executes after either the try block or an executing catch block ends >
}
```

> **Note:** Statements within a `finally` block execute regardless of whether an exception occurs, but they do not execute if either the `try` block or a `catch` block calls `System.exit`. If no exception takes place, the `finally` block executes after its corresponding `try` block completes its execution. (If the `try` block contains a `return` statement, the `finally` block executes before the `return`.) However, if an exception occurs, and it is caught by one of the `catch` blocks, the `finally` block executes after that `catch` block executes.

**JI4.10**  **Example.** Imagine that you open the refrigerator door and reach for the milk. Whether you find milk or not, you should close the door. In the following code, the method `takeOutMilk` will throw an exception if no milk is found. Whether an exception occurs or not, `closeRefrigerator` is called within the `finally` block.

```
try
{
    openRefrigerator();
    takeOutMilk();
    pourMilk();
    putBackMilk();
}
catch (NoMilkException e)
{
    System.out.println(e.getMessage());
}
finally
{
    closeRefrigerator();
}
```

**JI4.11** Let's explicitly demonstrate the behavior of a `finally` block by executing the code given in the previous example. The program in Listing JI4-6 provides simple definitions for the methods called in this example. All but `takeOutMilk` simply display an appropriate message. The method `take-OutMilk`, however, displays a message some of the time at random but throws a `NoMilkException` the rest of the time.

In the first sample output shown in Listing JI4-6, no exception occurs. Each method within the `try` block executes in turn, as the output indicates. Lastly, the method `closeRefrigerator` within the `finally` block executes. In the second sample output, `openRefrigerator` executes normally, but then `takeOutMilk` throws an exception. After the exception is caught by the `catch` block, the `finally` block executes as expected.

**LISTING JI4-6** A demonstration of a `finally` block

```java
/**
    Demonstrates the behavior of a finally block.
*/
public class GetMilk
{
    public static void main(String[] args)
    {
        try
        {
            openRefrigerator();
            takeOutMilk();
            pourMilk();
            putBackMilk();
        }
        catch (NoMilkException e)
        {
            System.out.println(e.getMessage());
        }
        finally
        {
            closeRefrigerator();
        }
    } // end main

    public static void openRefrigerator()
    {
        System.out.println("Open the refrigerator door.");
    } // end openRefrigerator

    public static void takeOutMilk() throws NoMilkException
    {
        if (Math.random() < 0.5)
            System.out.println("Take out the milk. ");
        else
            throw new NoMilkException("Out of Milk!");
    } // end openRefrigerator

    < The methods pourMilk, putBackMilk, and closeRefrigerator are analogous to
      openRefrigerator and are here. >
    . . .
} // end GetMilk
```

**Sample Output 1 (no exception is thrown)**

```
Open the refrigerator door.
Take out the milk.
Pour the milk.
Put the milk back.
Close the refrigerator door.
```

**Sample Output 2 (exception is thrown)**

```
Open the refrigerator door.
Out of milk!
Close the refrigerator door.
```

# Queues, Deques, and Priority Queues

**Chapter**

# 10

## Contents

## Prerequisites

## Objectives

After studying this chapter, you should be able to

- Describe the operations of the ADT queue
- Use a queue to simulate a waiting line
- Use a queue in a program that organizes data in a first-in, first-out manner
- Describe the operations of the ADT deque
- Use a deque in a program that organizes data chronologically and can operate on both the oldest and newest entries
- Describe the operations of the ADT priority queue
- Use a priority queue in a program that organizes data objects according to their priorities

W aiting for your turn is a fact of life. Most people have spent much time standing in lines at stores, banks, or movie theaters. You have probably waited on the telephone for an airline representative or a technical support person, and you may have waited for your printed output to finally reach the printer in the computer lab. In each of these examples, people wait with the expectation that they will be served before everyone who has come after them. That is, first come, first served.

A queue is another name for a waiting line, and it is the name of one of the ADTs that we will investigate in this chapter. Queues are used within operating systems and to simulate real-world events—that is, they come into play whenever processes or events must wait.

Sometimes you need more flexibility than a queue permits. A double-ended queue, or deque, organizes data like a queue but enables you to operate on both its oldest and newest entries. And when the importance of an object depends on criteria other than its arrival time, you can assign it a priority. You can organize such objects within a priority queue according to their priorities instead of chronologically.

The queue, deque, and priority queue are three ADTs that this chapter will explore.

## The ADT Queue

**10.1**  Like a stack, the ADT **queue** organizes its entries according to the order in which they were added. But while a stack has a last-in, first-out behavior, a queue exhibits a **first-in**, **first-out**, or **FIFO**, behavior. To achieve this behavior, all additions to a queue are at its **back**. The item added most recently, then, is at the back of a queue. The item that was added earliest is at the **front** of a queue. Figure 10-1 provides examples of some common queues.

FIGURE 10-1     Some everyday queues

**Note:** Among the items in a queue, the one added first, or earliest, is at the **front** of the queue, and the one added most recently is at the **back** of the queue.

VideoNote
The ADT queue

A queue, like a stack, restricts access to its entries. Although someone might cut into a line of people, additions to a software queue must occur at its back. A client can look at or remove only the entry at the front of the queue. The only way to look at an entry that is not at the front of a queue is to repeatedly remove items from the queue until the desired item reaches the front. If you were to remove all of a queue's entries one by one, you would get them in chronological order, beginning with the first item added to the queue.

The queue has no search operation. An entry's value is not relevant to the queue or to the entry's position within the queue.

**10.2**   The operation that adds an entry to a queue is traditionally called enqueue (pronounced "N-Q"). The operation to remove an entry is dequeue (pronounced "D-Q"). The operation that retrieves the queue's front entry is called getFront. The following specifications define a set of operations for the ADT queue:

| ABSTRACT DATA TYPE: QUEUE | | |
|---|---|---|
| **DATA** | | |
| • A collection of objects in chronological order and having the same data type | | |
| **OPERATIONS** | | |
| PSEUDOCODE | UML | DESCRIPTION |
| enqueue(newEntry) | +enqueue(newEntry: integer): void | Task: Adds a new entry to the back of the queue.<br>Input: newEntry is the new entry.<br>Output: None. |
| dequeue() | +dequeue(): T | Task: Removes and returns the entry at the front of the queue.<br>Input: None.<br>Output: Returns the queue's front entry. Throws an exception if the queue is empty before the operation. |
| getFront() | +getFront(): T | Task: Retrieves the queue's front entry without changing the queue in any way.<br>Input: None.<br>Output: Returns the queue's front entry. Throws an exception if the queue is empty. |
| isEmpty() | +isEmpty(): boolean | Task: Detects whether the queue is empty.<br>Input: None.<br>Output: Returns true if the queue is empty. |
| clear() | +clear(): void | Task: Removes all entries from the queue.<br>Input: None.<br>Output: None. |

**Note: Alternate names for methods**
As we mentioned in Chapter 5, class designers often include aliases for certain methods. For a queue, you could include the additional methods put and get to mean enqueue and dequeue. The names add, insert, remove, and delete are also reasonable aliases. Likewise, you could provide a method peek to mean getFront.

**10.3** The Java interface in Listing 10-1 specifies a queue of objects. The generic type T—which can be any class type—represents the data type of the items in the queue. Note that we must define EmptyQueueException. We leave its definition as a runtime exception to you as an exercise.

---

**LISTING 10-1    An interface for the ADT queue**

```java
1  public interface QueueInterface<T>
2  {
3      /** Adds a new entry to the back of this queue.
4          @param newEntry  An object to be added. */
5      public void enqueue(T newEntry);
6
7      /** Removes and returns the entry at the front of this queue.
8          @return  The object at the front of the queue.
9          @throws  EmptyQueueException if the queue is empty before the operation.
10     public T dequeue();
11
12     /** Retrieves the entry at the front of this queue.
13         @return  The object at the front of the queue.
14         @throws  EmptyQueueException if the queue is empty. */
15     public T getFront();
16
17     /** Detects whether this queue is empty.
18         @return  True if the queue is empty, or false otherwise. */
19     public boolean isEmpty();
20
21     /** Removes all entries from this queue. */
22     public void clear();
23 } // end QueueInterface
```

---

**10.4**    **Example: Demonstrating the queue methods.** The following statements add, retrieve, and remove strings from a queue. We assume that the class LinkedQueue implements QueueInterface and is available.

```java
QueueInterface<String> myQueue = new LinkedQueue<>();
myQueue.enqueue("Jim");
myQueue.enqueue("Jess");
myQueue.enqueue("Jill");
myQueue.enqueue("Jane");
myQueue.enqueue("Joe");

String front = myQueue.getFront();   // Returns "Jim"
System.out.println(front + " is at the front of the queue.");

front = myQueue.dequeue();           // Removes and returns "Jim"
System.out.println(front + " is removed from the queue.");

myQueue.enqueue("Jerry");
front = myQueue.getFront();          // Returns "Jess"
System.out.println(front + " is at the front of the queue.");

front = myQueue.dequeue();           // Removes and returns "Jess"
System.out.println(front + " is removed from the queue.");
```

Parts *a* through *e* of Figure 10-2 illustrate the five additions to the queue. Following these additions, the queue contains—from front to back—the strings *Jim*, *Jess*, *Jill*, *Jane*, and *Joe*. The string at the front of the queue is *Jim*; getFront retrieves it. The method dequeue retrieves *Jim* again and then removes it from the queue (Figure 10-2f). A subsequent call to enqueue adds *Jerry* to the back of the queue but does not affect the front (Figure 10-2g). Thus, getFront retrieves *Jess*, and dequeue retrieves *Jess* and then removes it (Figure 10-2h).

If we now were to execute dequeue repeatedly until the queue was empty, an additional call to either dequeue or getFront would throw an EmptyQueueException.

**FIGURE 10-2**    A queue of strings after (a) enqueue adds *Jim*; (b) enqueue adds *Jess*; (c) enqueue adds *Jill*; (d) enqueue adds *Jane*; (e) enqueue adds *Joe*; (f) dequeue retrieves and removes *Jim*; (g) enqueue adds *Jerry*; (h) dequeue retrieves and removes *Jess*

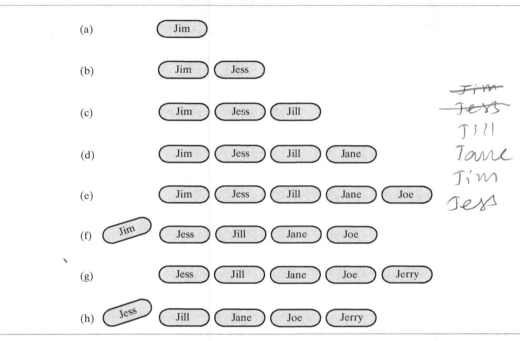

**Question 1** After the following nine statements execute, what string is at the front of the queue and what string is at the back?

```
QueueInterface<String> myQueue = new LinkedQueue<>();
myQueue.enqueue("Jim");
myQueue.enqueue("Jess");
myQueue.enqueue("Jill");
myQueue.enqueue("Jane");
String name = myQueue.dequeue();
myQueue.enqueue(name);
myQueue.enqueue(myQueue.getFront());
name = myQueue.dequeue();
```

**Question 2** Define the class EmptyQueueException as a class of runtime exceptions.

**Programming Tip:** Methods such as getFront and dequeue must behave reasonably when the queue is empty. Here, we specify that they throw an exception. Just as we discussed in Chapter 5 in the context of the ADT stack, other possibilities include returning null or giving these methods the precondition that the queue is not empty.

## A Problem Solved: Simulating a Waiting Line

 In many everyday situations, you will wait in a line. Whether the line is at a store, a ticket window, or a car wash, a line behaves like the ADT queue. The person at the front of the line is served first; newcomers go to the back of the line, as Figure 10-3 shows. In this problem, we will perform a computer simulation of a waiting line.

FIGURE 10-3     A line, or queue, of people

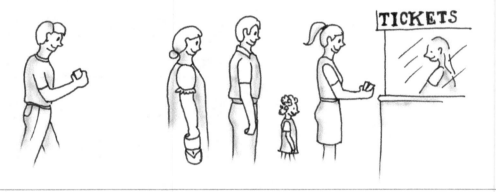

10.5     Most businesses are concerned with the time that their customers must wait for service. A short wait time enables an organization to increase customer satisfaction, serve more people, and make more money. If two agents serve one line, you will wait less time than if only one agent is on duty. A business, however, does not want to employ more people than necessary. And a car wash certainly would not build an additional service bay to test its effect on the time its customers wait in a single line.

Computer simulation of a real-world situation is a common way to test various business scenarios. In this example, we will simulate one line of people waiting for service from one agent. Customers arrive at different intervals and require various times to complete their transactions. One way to achieve this variety is to assume that the events are random.

In a **time-driven simulation**, a counter enumerates simulated units of time—minutes, for example. Customers arrive at random times during the simulation and enter the queue. Each customer is assigned a random transaction time—that is, the amount of time required for the customer's transaction—that does not exceed some arbitrary upper bound. During the simulation, the time that each customer waits in the queue is recorded. At the conclusion of the simulation, summary statistics are generated, including the number of customers served and the average time that each waited.

10.6     **Solution design.** Two kinds of objects occur in the description of this problem: the waiting line and the customers. We can design a class for each of these.

The class WaitLine simulates the waiting line for a given period of time. During this time, customers enter the line at random intervals and leave it after being served. At the conclusion of the simulation, the class computes the summary statistics. Figure 10-4 shows a CRC card for this class.

The class Customer records and makes available the customer's arrival time, transaction time, and customer number. Figure 10-5 contains a class diagram for WaitLine and Customer.

FIGURE 10-4    A CRC card for the class WaitLine

| WaitLine |
| --- |
| Responsibilities |
|    Simulate customers entering and leaving a<br>     waiting line<br>   Display number served, total wait time,<br>     average wait time, and number left in line |
| Collaborations |
|    Customer |

FIGURE 10-5    A diagram of the classes WaitLine and Customer

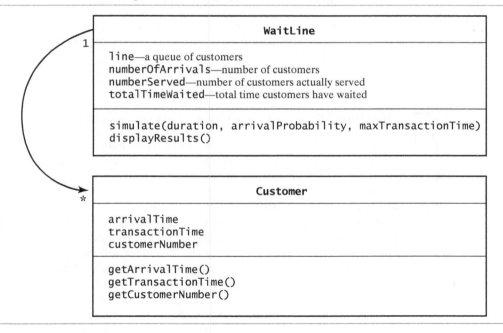

```
                            WaitLine
      ─────────────────────────────────────────────────────
  1   line—a queue of customers
      numberOfArrivals—number of customers
      numberServed—number of customers actually served
      totalTimeWaited—total time customers have waited
      ─────────────────────────────────────────────────────
      simulate(duration, arrivalProbability, maxTransactionTime)
      displayResults()


                            Customer
      ─────────────────────────────────────────────────────
  *   arrivalTime
      transactionTime
      customerNumber
      ─────────────────────────────────────────────────────
      getArrivalTime()
      getTransactionTime()
      getCustomerNumber()
```

**10.7**   **The method simulate.** The method simulate is the heart of this example and of the class WaitLine. To maintain the clock for this time-driven simulation, simulate contains a loop that counts up to a given duration. For example, the clock could simulate one hour by counting minutes, beginning at 0 and continuing to 60.

At each value of the clock, the method sees whether the current customer is still being served and whether a new customer has arrived. If a new customer arrives, the method creates a new customer object, assigns it a random transaction time, and places the customer into the queue. If a customer is still being served, the clock advances; if not, a customer leaves the front of the queue and begins service. At this point, the time the customer waited is noted. Figure 10-6 provides an example of the queue for a portion of the simulation.

The following pseudocode describes the method `simulate`. It assumes that the class `WaitLine` has initialized its data fields as follows: `line` is an empty queue, and `numberOfArrivals`, `numberServed`, and `totalTimeWaited` are each zero.

*Algorithm* `simulate(duration, arrivalProbability, maxTransactionTime)`

```
transactionTimeLeft = 0
for (clock = 0; clock < duration; clock++)
{
    if (a new customer arrives)
    {
        numberOfArrivals++
        transactionTime = a random time that does not exceed maxTransactionTime
        nextArrival = a new customer containing clock, transactionTime, and
                         a customer number that is numberOfArrivals
        line.enqueue(nextArrival)
    }
    if (transactionTimeLeft > 0) // If present customer is still being served
        transactionTimeLeft--
    else if (!line.isEmpty())
    {
        nextCustomer = line.dequeue()
        transactionTimeLeft = nextCustomer.getTransactionTime() - 1
        timeWaited = clock - nextCustomer.getArrivalTime()
        totalTimeWaited = totalTimeWaited + timeWaited
        numberServed++
    }
}
```

**Question 3** Consider the simulation begun in Figure 10-6.

    **a.** At what time does Customer 4 finish and depart?

    **b.** How long does Customer 5 wait before beginning the transaction?

**10.8**    **Implementation details for `simulate`.** At each value of the clock, `simulate` must determine whether a new customer has arrived. To do so, it needs the probability that a customer will arrive. This arrival probability is a parameter of the method and has a value between 0 and 1. For example, if there is a 65 percent chance that a customer will arrive at any given time, the arrival probability is 0.65. We then generate a random number between 0 and 1 by using the method `random` in Java's class `Math`. If the value returned by `Math.random()` is less than the given arrival probability, `simulate` creates a new customer and places it into the queue.

The method assigns to each new customer a random transaction time. Given a maximum value for the transaction time, we can multiply it by `Math.random()` to get a random time. Adding 1 to the result ensures that the transaction time is never 0 but allows a small chance that the transaction time will exceed the given maximum value by 1. For simplicity, we will tolerate this small imprecision.

FIGURE 10-6    A simulated waiting line

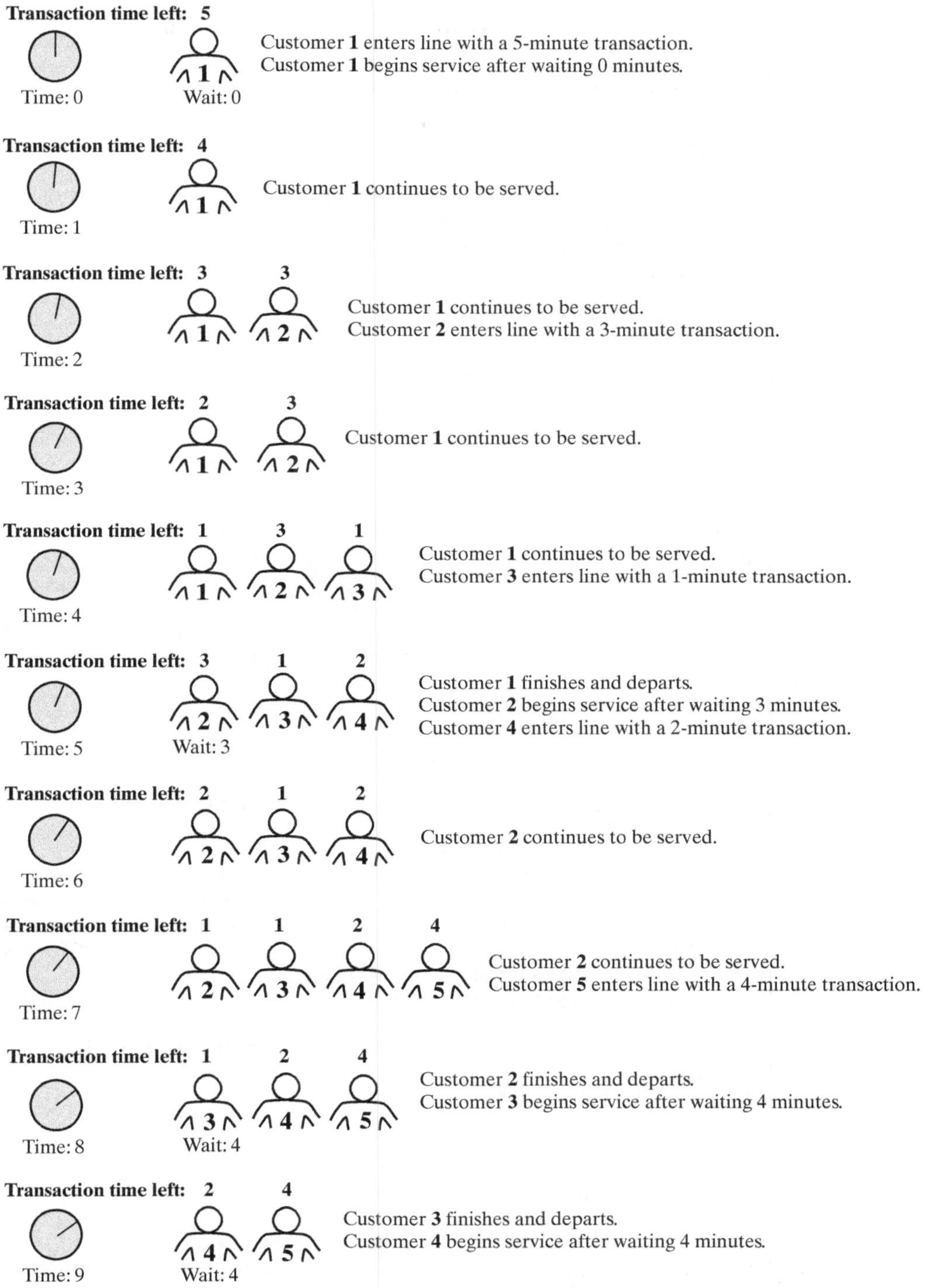

**Transaction time left:  5**

Time: 0        Wait: 0

Customer **1** enters line with a 5-minute transaction.
Customer **1** begins service after waiting 0 minutes.

**Transaction time left:  4**

Time: 1

Customer **1** continues to be served.

**Transaction time left:  3        3**

Time: 2

Customer **1** continues to be served.
Customer **2** enters line with a 3-minute transaction.

**Transaction time left:  2        3**

Time: 3

Customer **1** continues to be served.

**Transaction time left:  1        3        1**

Time: 4

Customer **1** continues to be served.
Customer **3** enters line with a 1-minute transaction.

**Transaction time left:  3        1        2**

Time: 5        Wait: 3

Customer **1** finishes and departs.
Customer **2** begins service after waiting 3 minutes.
Customer **4** enters line with a 2-minute transaction.

**Transaction time left:  2        1        2**

Time: 6

Customer **2** continues to be served.

**Transaction time left:  1        1        2        4**

Time: 7

Customer **2** continues to be served.
Customer **5** enters line with a 4-minute transaction.

**Transaction time left:  1        2        4**

Time: 8        Wait: 4

Customer **2** finishes and departs.
Customer **3** begins service after waiting 4 minutes.

**Transaction time left:  2        4**

Time: 9        Wait: 4

Customer **3** finishes and departs.
Customer **4** begins service after waiting 4 minutes.

An implementation of the class WaitList appears in Listing 10-2. The definition of the method simulate contains print statements to help you follow the simulation. The other methods in the class are straightforward.

LISTING 10-2     The class WaitLine

```
1   /** Simulates a waiting line. */
2   public class WaitLine
3   {
4      private QueueInterface<Customer> line;
5      private int numberOfArrivals;
6      private int numberServed;
7      private int totalTimeWaited;
8
9      public WaitLine()
10     {
11        line = new LinkedQueue<>();
12        reset();
13     } // end default constructor
14
15     /** Simulates a waiting line with one serving agent.
16         @param duration  The number of simulated minutes.
17         @param arrivalProbability  A real number between 0 and 1, and the
18                                    probability that a customer arrives at
19                                    a given time.
20         @param maxTransactionTime  The longest transaction time for a
21                                    customer. */
22     public void simulate(int duration, double arrivalProbability,
23                      int maxTransactionTime)
24     {
25        int transactionTimeLeft = 0;
26
27        for (int clock = 0; clock < duration; clock++)
28        {
29           if (Math.random() < arrivalProbability)
30           {
31              numberOfArrivals++;
32              int transactionTime = (int)(Math.random()
33                                     * maxTransactionTime + 1);
34              Customer nextArrival = new Customer(clock, transactionTime,
35                                           numberOfArrivals);
36              line.enqueue(nextArrival);
37              System.out.println("Customer " + numberOfArrivals
38                              + " enters line at time " + clock
39                              + ". Transaction time is "
40                              + transactionTime);
41           } // end if
42
43           if (transactionTimeLeft > 0)
44              transactionTimeLeft--;
45           else if (!line.isEmpty())
46           {
47              Customer nextCustomer = line.dequeue();
48              transactionTimeLeft = nextCustomer.getTransactionTime() - 1;
49              int timeWaited = clock - nextCustomer.getArrivalTime();
50              totalTimeWaited = totalTimeWaited + timeWaited;
51              numberServed++;
```

```
52              System.out.println("Customer " + nextCustomer.getCustomerNumber()
53                               + " begins service at time " + clock
54                               + ". Time waited is " + timeWaited);
55          } // end if
56       } // end for
57    } // end simulate
58
59    /** Displays summary results of the simulation. */
60    public void displayResults()
61    {
62       System.out.println();
63       System.out.println("Number served = " + numberServed);
64       System.out.println("Total time waited = " + totalTimeWaited);
65       double averageTimeWaited = ((double)totalTimeWaited) / numberServed;
66       System.out.println("Average time waited = " + averageTimeWaited);
67       int leftInLine = numberOfArrivals - numberServed;
68       System.out.println("Number left in line = " + leftInLine);
69    } // end displayResults
70
71    /** Initializes the simulation. */
72    public final void reset()
73    {
74       line.clear();
75       numberOfArrivals = 0;
76       numberServed = 0;
77       totalTimeWaited = 0;
78    } // end reset
79 } // end WaitLine
```

**10.9    Sample output.** The Java statements

```
WaitLine customerLine = new WaitLine();
customerLine.simulate(20, 0.5, 5);
customerLine.displayResults();
```

simulate the line for 20 minutes with a 50 percent arrival probability and a 5-minute maximum transaction time. They produce the following results:

```
Customer 1 enters line at time 0. Transaction time is 4
Customer 1 begins service at time 0. Time waited is 0
Customer 2 enters line at time 2. Transaction time is 2
Customer 3 enters line at time 4. Transaction time is 1
Customer 2 begins service at time 4. Time waited is 2
Customer 4 enters line at time 6. Transaction time is 4
Customer 3 begins service at time 6. Time waited is 2
Customer 4 begins service at time 7. Time waited is 1
Customer 5 enters line at time 9. Transaction time is 1
Customer 6 enters line at time 10. Transaction time is 3
Customer 5 begins service at time 11. Time waited is 2
Customer 7 enters line at time 12. Transaction time is 4
Customer 6 begins service at time 12. Time waited is 2
Customer 8 enters line at time 15. Transaction time is 3
Customer 7 begins service at time 15. Time waited is 3
Customer 9 enters line at time 16. Transaction time is 3
```

```
Customer 10 enters line at time 19. Transaction time is 5
Customer 8 begins service at time 19. Time waited is 4

Number served = 8
Total time waited = 16
Average time waited = 2.0
Number left in line = 2
```

Since this example uses random numbers, another execution of the Java statements likely will have different results.

> **Note: Pseudo-random numbers**
> Java's method `Math.random` generates numbers that are uniformly distributed over the interval from 0 to 1. Actual times for processing customer transactions, however, are not uniformly distributed. They are close together, and few times are far from the average transaction time. One such distribution is called a *Poisson distribution*. Ideally, this simulation should use a different pseudo-random number generator. Since our maximum transaction time is small, however, using `Math.random` probably has little effect on the average wait time.

## A Problem Solved: Computing the Capital Gain in a Sale of Stock

> Suppose that you buy *n* shares of a stock or mutual fund for *d* dollars each. Later you sell some of these shares. If the sale price exceeds the purchase price, you have made a profit—a *capital gain*. On the other hand, if the sale price is lower than the purchase price, you experience a loss. We will designate a loss as a negative capital gain.
>
> Typically, investors buy shares in a particular company or fund over a period of time. For example, suppose that last year you bought 20 shares of Presto Pizza at $45 per share. Last month, you bought 20 additional shares at $75 per share, and today you sold 30 shares at $65 per share. What is your capital gain? Well, which of your 40 shares did you actually sell? Unfortunately, you cannot pick and choose. When computing capital gains, you must assume that you sell shares in the order in which you purchased them (meaning that stock sales are a first-in, first-out application). So in our example, you sold the 20 shares that you bought at $45 each and 10 of the shares that you bought at $75 each. Your cost for the 30 shares is $1650. You sold them for $1950, a profit of $300.
>
> Design a way to record your investment transactions chronologically and to compute the capital gain of any stock sale.

**10.10  Solution design.** To simplify the example, we assume that all transactions are for stocks of a single company and that there is no commission charge for the transactions. The class `StockPurchase` records the cost of a single share of stock.

Figure 10-7 shows a CRC card for the class `StockLedger`. The class enables us to record stock purchases in chronological order. At the time of sale, the class computes the capital gain and updates the record of stocks owned. These last two steps are related, so we combine them into one method. Thus, the class has two methods, `buy` and `sell`, as Figure 10-8 illustrates.

FIGURE 10-7    A CRC card for the class StockLedger

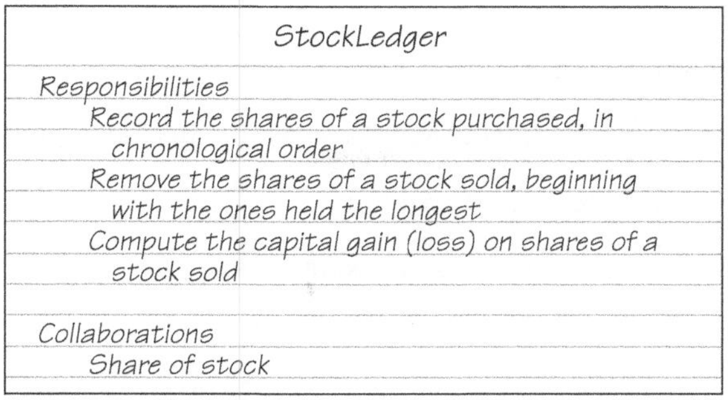

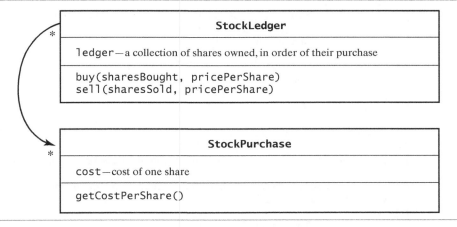

StockLedger

Responsibilities
  Record the shares of a stock purchased, in
    chronological order
  Remove the shares of a stock sold, beginning
    with the ones held the longest
  Compute the capital gain (loss) on shares of a
    stock sold

Collaborations
  Share of stock

FIGURE 10-8    A diagram of the classes StockLedger and StockPurchase

**StockLedger**

`ledger`—a collection of shares owned, in order of their purchase

```
buy(sharesBought, pricePerShare)
sell(sharesSold, pricePerShare)
```

**StockPurchase**

`cost`—cost of one share

```
getCostPerShare()
```

The following statements demonstrate how we could use StockLedger to record the transactions given in the problem description:

```
StockLedger myStocks = new StockLedger();
myStocks.buy(20, 45);                       // Buy  20 shares at $45
myStocks.buy(20, 75);                       // Buy  20 shares at $75
double capGain = myStocks.sell(30, 65); // Sell 30 shares at $65
```

**10.11  Implementation.** In this example, StockLedger records instances of StockPurchase—which represent the shares we own—in a queue. A queue orders the shares chronologically, so we can sell them in the order in which we purchased them. The method buy then just enqueues each share that is bought.

The method sell removes from the queue as many shares as are sold. As it does this, it computes the total capital gain from the sale and returns it. The class StockLedger is given in Listing 10-3.

LISTING 10-3  The class StockLedger

```java
1  /** A class that records the purchase and sale of stocks, and provides the
2       capital gain or loss. */
3  public class StockLedger
4  {
5     private QueueInterface<StockPurchase> ledger;
6
7     public StockLedger()
8     {
9        ledger = new LinkedQueue<>();
10    } // end default constructor
11
12    /** Records a stock purchase in this ledger.
13        @param sharesBought   The number of shares purchased.
14        @param pricePerShare  The price per share. */
15    public void buy (int sharesBought, double pricePerShare)
16    {
17       while (sharesBought > 0)
18       {
19          StockPurchase purchase = new StockPurchase(pricePerShare);
20          ledger.enqueue(purchase);
21          sharesBought--;
22       } // end while
23    } // end buy
24
25    /** Removes from this ledger any shares that were sold
26        and computes the capital gain or loss.
27        @param sharesSold     The number of shares sold.
28        @param pricePerShare  The price per share.
29        @return  The capital gain (loss). */
30    public double sell(int sharesSold, double pricePerShare)
31    {
32       double saleAmount = sharesSold * pricePerShare;
33       double totalCost = 0;
34
35       while (sharesSold > 0)
36       {
37          StockPurchase share = ledger.dequeue();
38          double shareCost = share.getCostPerShare();
39          totalCost = totalCost + shareCost;
40          sharesSold--;
41       } // end while
42
43       return saleAmount - totalCost; // Gain or loss
44    } // end sell
45  } // end StockLedger
```

**10.12**  **An observation about this solution.** A typical stock transaction involves multiple shares, and the two methods buy and sell reflect this reality in their parameters. For example, the invocation myStocks.buy(30, 45) indicates a purchase of 30 shares at $45 per share. However, notice that the implementation of buy adds each of the 30 shares to a queue. Figure 10-9a shows such a queue. The advantage of this approach is that sell can remove as many or as few shares as necessary.

Suppose that we instead encapsulate the purchase of 30 shares into one object and add it to the queue, as Figure 10-9b illustrates. If we then sell 20 of those shares, we would remove the object from the queue and learn the shares' purchase price. But we would have 10 shares that must remain in the queue. Since these are the oldest shares, we could not simply add them to the back of the queue; they must remain at the front. The ADT queue has no operation that modifies its front entry, nor does it have one to add an object to its front. If each entry has set methods, however, Java will allow the client to modify the entry at the front by using the reference that getFront returns. In this case, you would not remove the front entry until you have sold all of the shares it represents. Exercise 10 at the end of this chapter asks you to explore this approach.

On the other hand, if each entry does not have set methods, you would not be able to modify it. If, in addition, each entry represents more than one share of stock, the queue would not be the right ADT to use. Segment 10.14 explores another ADT that you can use instead.

FIGURE 10-9     A queue of (a) individual shares of stock; (b) grouped shares

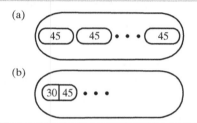

 **Note:** A class that has set methods is a class of **mutable objects**. A class without set methods is a class of **immutable objects**. Java Interlude 6 talks about such classes in more detail.

## Java Class Library: The Interface Queue

**10.13**     The standard package java.util in the Java Class Library contains an interface Queue that is similar to our QueueInterface but specifies more methods. We list here a selection of method headers similar to the ones you have seen in this chapter. We have highlighted where they differ from our methods. A header that is highlighted completely means that our interface does not specify a similar method. Once again, T is the generic type. The methods that either add, remove, or retrieve entries occur in pairs.

> **public boolean** add(T newEntry)
> Adds a new entry to the back of this queue, returning true if successful and throwing an exception if not.
>
> **public boolean** offer(T newEntry)
> Adds a new entry to the back of this queue, returning true or false according to the success of the operation.

**public** T remove()
Retrieves and removes the entry at the front of this queue, but throws NoSuchElementException if the queue is empty prior to the operation.

**public** T poll()
Retrieves and removes the entry at the front of this queue, but returns null if the queue is empty prior to the operation.

**public** T element()
Retrieves the entry at the front of this queue, but throws NoSuchElementException if the queue is empty. Our method getFront throws an EmptyQueueException instead of a NoSuchElementException.

**public** T peek()
Retrieves the entry at the front of this queue, but returns null if the queue is empty.

**public boolean** isEmpty()
Detects whether this queue is empty.

**public void** clear()
Removes all entries from this queue.

**public int** size()
Gets the number of elements currently in this queue.

Some of these methods occur in pairs. Both add and offer add a new entry to the queue. If the operation is unsuccessful, add throws an exception but offer returns false. Likewise, each of the methods remove and poll removes and returns the entry at the front of the queue. If the queue is empty before the operation, remove throws an exception but poll returns null. Finally, peek and element each retrieve the entry at the front of the queue. If the queue is empty, element throws an exception but peek returns null.

You can learn more about Queue and the other components of the Java Class Library at docs.oracle.com/javase/8/docs/api/.

## The ADT Deque

10.14    Imagine that you are in a line at the post office. When it is finally your turn, the postal agent asks you to fill out a form. You step aside to do so and let the agent serve the next person in the line. After you complete the form, the agent will serve you next. Essentially, you go to the front of the line, rather than waiting in line twice.

Similarly, suppose that you join a line at its end but then decide it is too long, so you leave it. To simulate both of these examples, you want an ADT whose operations enable you to add, remove, or retrieve entries at both the front and back of a queue. Such an ADT is called a **double-ended queue**, or **deque** (pronounced "deck").

A deque has both queuelike operations and stacklike operations. For example, the deque operations addToBack and removeFront resemble the queue operations enqueue and dequeue, respectively. And addToBack and removeBack are like the stack operations push and pop, respectively. In addition, a deque has the operations getFront, getBack, and addToFront. Figure 10-10 illustrates a deque and these methods.

**Note:** Although the ADT deque is called a double-ended queue, it actually behaves like a double-ended stack. As Figure 10-10 shows, you can push, pop, or get items at either of its ends.

FIGURE 10-10    An instance d of a deque

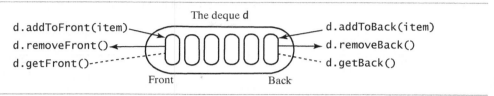

Since the specifications for the deque operations are like those you have already seen for a queue and a stack, we condensed the comments in the Java interface in Listing 10-4.

LISTING 10-4    An interface for the ADT deque

```java
/**
   An interface for the ADT deque.
   @author Frank M. Carrano
*/
public interface DequeInterface<T>
{
   /** Adds a new entry to the front/back of this deque.
       @param newEntry  An object to be added. */
   public void addToFront(T newEntry);
   public void addToBack(T newEntry);

   /** Removes and returns the front/back entry of this deque.
       @return  The object at the front/back of the deque.
       @throws  EmptyQueueException if the deque is empty before the
                operation. */
   public T removeFront();
   public T removeBack();

   /** Retrieves the front/back entry of this deque.
       @return  The object at the front/back of the deque.
       @throws  EmptyQueueException if the deque is empty. */
   public T getFront();
   public T getBack();

   /** Detects whether this deque is empty.
       @return  True if the deque is empty, or false otherwise. */
   public boolean isEmpty();

   /* Removes all entries from this deque. */
   public void clear();
} // end DequeInterface
```

A comparison of the operations that add, remove, and retrieve the entries of a stack, queue, and deque is provided in Figure 10-11.

FIGURE 10-11    A comparison of operations for a stack s, a queue q, and
a deque d: (a) add; (b) remove; (c) retrieve

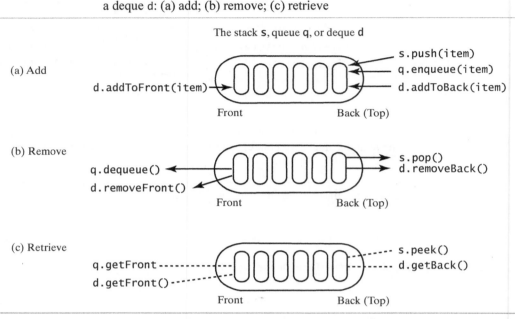

**Question 4** After the following nine statements execute, what string is at the front of the deque and what string is at the back?

```
DequeInterface<String> myDeque = new LinkedDeque<>();
myDeque.addToFront("Jim");
myDeque.addToBack("Jess");
myDeque.addToFront("Jill");
myDeque.addToBack("Jane");
String name = myDeque.getFront();
myDeque.addToBack(name);
myDeque.removeFront();
myDeque.addToFront(myDeque.removeBack());
```

**10.15    Example.** When typing at your keyboard, you might make a mistake. If you backspace to correct your mistake, what logic is used to decipher your intention? For example, if the symbol ← represents a backspace, and you type

cm←ompte←←utr←er

the result should be

computer

Each backspace erases the previous character entered.

To replicate this process, as characters are entered, we retain them in an ADT. We want this ADT to be stacklike so we can access the most recently entered character. But since we ultimately want the corrected characters to be in the order in which they were entered, we want the ADT to also behave like a queue. The ADT deque can satisfy these requirements.

The following pseudocode uses a deque to read and display a line of keyboard input:

```
// Read a line
d = a new empty deque
while (not end of line)
{
    character = next character read
    if (character == ←)
        d.removeBack()
    else
        d.addToBack(character)
}
// Display the corrected line
while (!d.isEmpty())
    System.out.print(d.removeFront())
System.out.println()
```

## A Problem Solved: Computing the Capital Gain in a Sale of Stock

When we concluded the capital gain example, Segment 10.12 noted that our queue contained individual shares of stock. Since a typical stock transaction involves more than one share, representing a transaction as one object is more natural. But you saw that the transaction object must have set methods if we use a queue. That would not be the case if we used a deque instead.

**10.16** In this section, we revise the implementation, but not the design, of the class StockLedger that was introduced in Segment 10.10. We also revise the class StockPurchase so that it represents the purchase of *n* shares of stock at *d* dollars per share, as Segment 10.12 suggests. The revised class has the data fields shares and cost, a constructor, and the accessor methods getNumberOfShares and getCostPerShare.

We can revise the implementation of the class StockLedger given in Segment 10.11 as follows. The data field ledger is now an instance of a deque instead of a queue. The method buy creates an instance of StockPurchase and places it at the back of the deque, as follows:

```
public void buy(int sharesBought, double pricePerShare)
{
    StockPurchase purchase = new StockPurchase(sharesBought, pricePerShare);
    ledger.addToBack(purchase);
} // end buy
```

The method sell is more involved. It must remove a StockPurchase object from the front of the deque and decide whether that object represents more shares than the number sold. If it does, the method creates a new instance of StockPurchase to represent the shares that remain in the portfolio. It then adds that instance to the front of the deque, since it is these shares that would be sold next.

```
public double sell(int sharesSold, double pricePerShare)
{
    double saleAmount = sharesSold * pricePerShare;
    double totalCost = 0;

    while (sharesSold > 0)
    {
        StockPurchase transaction = ledger.removeFront();
        double shareCost = transaction.getCostPerShare();
        int numberOfShares = transaction.getNumberOfShares();
```

```
                    if (numberOfShares > sharesSold)
                    {
                        totalCost = totalCost + sharesSold * shareCost;
                        int numberToPutBack = numberOfShares - sharesSold;
                        StockPurchase leftOver = new StockPurchase(numberToPutBack,
                                                                   shareCost);
                        ledger.addToFront(leftOver); // Return leftover shares
                        // Note: loop will exit since sharesSold will be <= 0 later
                    }
                    else
                        totalCost = totalCost + numberOfShares * shareCost;
                    sharesSold = sharesSold - numberOfShares;
                } // end while
                return saleAmount - totalCost; // Gain or loss
            } // end sell
```

## Java Class Library: The Interface Deque

**10.17** The standard package java.util in the Java Class Library contains an interface Deque that is similar to our DequeInterface but specifies more methods. Here is a selection of the method headers that this interface declares. The methods that either add, remove, or retrieve entries occur in pairs. One method in a pair throws an exception if the operation is unsuccessful, while the other method returns either null or false. T is the generic type of the entries in a deque.

**public void** addFirst(T newEntry)
Adds a new entry to the front of this deque, but throws one of several exceptions if it cannot.

**public boolean** offerFirst(T newEntry)
Adds a new entry to the front of this deque, returning true or false according to the success of the operation.

**public void** addLast(T newEntry)
Adds a new entry to the back of this deque, but throws one of several exceptions if it cannot.

**public boolean** offerLast(T newEntry)
Adds a new entry to the back of this deque, returning true or false according to the success of the operation.

**public** T removeFirst()
Retrieves and removes the entry at the front of this deque, but throws NoSuchElementException if the deque is empty prior to the operation.

**public** T pollFirst()
Retrieves and removes the entry at the front of this deque, but returns null if the deque is empty prior to the operation.

**public** T removeLast()
Retrieves and removes the entry at the back of this deque, but throws NoSuchElementException if the deque is empty prior to the operation.

**public** T pollLast()
Retrieves and removes the entry at the back of this deque, but returns null if the deque is empty prior to the operation.

**public** T getFirst()
Retrieves the entry at the front of this deque, but throws NoSuchElementException if the deque is empty.

**public** T peekFirst()
Retrieves the entry at the front of this deque, but returns null if the deque is empty.

```
public T getLast()
```
Retrieves the entry at the back of this deque, but throws NoSuchElementException if the deque is empty.

```
public T peekLast()
```
Retrieves the entry at the back of this deque, but returns null if the deque is empty.

```
public boolean isEmpty()
```
Detects whether this deque is empty.

```
public void clear()
```
Removes all entries from this deque.

```
public int size()
```
Gets the number of entries currently in this deque.

The interface Deque extends the interface Queue, so it also has the methods add, offer, remove, poll, element, and peek that were described earlier in Segment 10.13. In addition, Deque declares the following two stack methods:

```
public void push(T newEntry)
public T pop()
```

These methods are like the ones defined in the class java.util.Stack, which we encountered earlier in Segment 5.23 of Chapter 5, except that push is a void method in Deque. As we mentioned in Chapter 5, you should no longer use the standard class Stack. The following segment describes an alternate class for you to use.

The online documentation for the interface Deque, as given at docs.oracle.com/javase/8/ docs/api, tabulates the correspondence between deque methods and both queue and stack methods.

### Java Class Library: The Class ArrayDeque

**10.18**   The standard package java.util in the Java Class Library contains the class ArrayDeque, which implements the interface Deque that we just described. Since Deque declares methods appropriate for a deque, a queue, and a stack, you can use ArrayDeque to create instances of any of these data collections.

The following two constructors are defined by this class:

```
public ArrayDeque()
```
Creates an empty deque whose initial capacity is 16 entries.

```
public ArrayDeque(int initialCapacity)
```
Creates an empty deque having a given initial capacity.

Instances of ArrayDeque grow in size as needed by a client.

**Note:** As indicated in the Note at the end of Chapter 5, if you want to use a standard class instead of your own to create a stack, you should use an instance of the standard class ArrayDeque, but not the standard class Stack. ArrayDeque is a newer class that provides a faster implementation of a stack than does Stack. Stack is retained in the Java Class Library to support previously written Java programs.

## The ADT Priority Queue

**10.19**   Although a bank serves its customers in the order in which they arrive, an emergency room treats patients according to the urgency of their malady. The bank organizes its customers into chronological order by using a queue. A hospital assigns a **priority** to each patient that overrides the time at which the patient arrived.

The ADT **priority queue** organizes objects according to their priorities. Exactly what form a priority takes depends on the nature of the object. Priorities can be integers, for example. A priority of 1 can be the highest priority, or it can be the lowest. By making the objects Comparable, we can hide this detail in the objects' method compareTo. The priority queue then can use compareTo to compare objects by their priorities. Thus, the priority queue can have the Java interface given in Listing 10-5. We use the notation ? super T, which Segment JI3.13 of Java Interlude 3 introduced, to mean any superclass of the generic type T.

---

**LISTING 10-5    An interface for the ADT priority queue**

```java
public interface PriorityQueueInterface<T extends Comparable<? super T>>
{
    /** Adds a new entry to this priority queue.
        @param newEntry  An object to be added. */
    public void add(T newEntry);

    /** Removes and returns the entry having the highest priority.
        @return  Either the object having the highest priority or, if the
                 priority queue is empty before the operation, null. */
    public T remove();

    /** Retrieves the entry having the highest priority.
        @return  Either the object having the highest priority or, if the
                 priority queue is empty, null. */
    public T peek();

    /** Detects whether this priority queue is empty.
        @return  True if the priority queue is empty, or false otherwise. */
    public boolean isEmpty();

    /** Gets the size of this priority queue.
        @return  The number of entries currently in the priority queue. */
    public int getSize();

    /** Removes all entries from this priority queue. */
    public void clear();
} // end PriorityQueueInterface
```

---

**Design Decision:** **Which ADTs can have null data?**

In the Design Decision in Segment 5.2 of Chapter 5, we decided that a return value of null can either indicate a failure of the method or be a valid entry in the collection, but not both. It also stated that most ADTs in this book permit null values as valid data entries. The stack, queue, and deque are such ADTs. Their methods throw an exception if they attempt to retrieve or remove an entry from an empty data collection. Any ADT whose entries are either unordered or ordered by a criterion independent of the entry's value can be null. For example, the data in a bag is unordered, the data in a stack or queue is ordered by when it is added to the ADT, and the data in a deque is ordered by when and to which end it is added. Each of these ADTs can have null entries.

A priority queue, however, orders its entries by comparing them based on their priority values. It cannot have null entries. Thus, null can signal the failure to remove or retrieve an entry from a priority queue.

**Question 5** After the following statements execute, what string is at the front of the priority queue and what string is at the back? Let the alphabetic order of the strings determine their priority. Note that "z" has a higher priority than "a".

```
PriorityQueueInterface<String> myPriorityQueue = new LinkedPriorityQueue<>();
myPriorityQueue.add("Jane");
myPriorityQueue.add("Jim");
myPriorityQueue.add("Jill");
String name = myPriorityQueue.remove();
myPriorityQueue.add(name);
myPriorityQueue.add("Jess");
```

## A Problem Solved: Tracking Your Assignments

Professors and bosses like to assign tasks for us to do by certain dates. Using a priority queue, organize these assignments in the order in which we should complete them.

**10.20**   To keep our example simple, we will order the assignments by their due dates. A task with the earliest due date will have the highest priority.

We can define a class `Assignment` of tasks that includes a data field `date` representing a task's due date. Figure 10-12 shows a diagram of such a class. We assume that `date` is an instance of a `Comparable` class such as `java.sql.Date` in the Java Class Library. Thus, the expression `date.compareTo(otherDate)` is negative, for example, if `date` occurs before `otherDate`. The `compareTo` method for `Assignment` is then

```
public int compareTo(Assignment other)
{
   return -date.compareTo(other.date);
} // end compareTo
```

A more sophisticated version of `Assignment` could include other criteria in `compareTo` to assess priority.

FIGURE 10-12    A diagram of the class `Assignment`

| Assignment |
|---|
| course—the course code<br>task—a description of the assignment<br>date—the due date |
| getCourseCode()<br>getTask()<br>getDueDate()<br>compareTo() |

**Note: The class `java.sql.Date`**
The class `Date` in the package `java.sql` of the Java Class Library has a constructor whose parameter specifies the date as the number of milliseconds since midnight GMT on January 1, 1970. A more convenient way for us to construct a `Date` object is to use the following static method `valueOf`:

**public static** Date valueOf(String s)
Returns a `Date` object whose value is given by a string s in the form *yyyy-mm-dd*.

For example, the expression `Date.valueOf("2016-02-29")` returns a `Date` object representing February 29, 2016.

Date implements the interface `Comparable<Date>` and overrides `toString`.

**10.21**   We can either add instances of `Assignment` directly to a priority queue or write a simple wrapper class `AssignmentLog` to organize our assignments. As Figure 10-13 shows, `AssignmentLog` has a data field `log`, which is an instance of a priority queue that contains the assignments in priority order. The methods `addProject`, `getNextProject`, and `removeNextProject` manipulate the priority queue indirectly.

FIGURE 10-13    A diagram of the class `AssignmentLog`

| **AssignmentLog** |
|---|
| `log`—a priority queue of assignments |
| addProject(newAssignment)<br>addProject(courseCode, task, dueDate)<br>getNextProject()<br>removeNextProject() |

An implementation of `AssignmentLog` appears in Listing 10-6.

LISTING 10-6    The class `AssignmentLog`

```java
1  import java.sql.Date;
2  public class AssignmentLog
3  {
4     private PriorityQueueInterface<Assignment> log;
5
6     public AssignmentLog()
7     {
8        log = new PriorityQueue<>();
9     } // end constructor
10
11    public void addProject(Assignment newAssignment)
12    {
13       log.add(newAssignment);
14    } // end addProject
15
```

```
16    public void addProject(String courseCode, String task, Date dueDate)
17    {
18       Assignment newAssignment = new Assignment(courseCode, task, dueDate);
19       addProject(newAssignment);
20    } // end addProject
21
22    public Assignment getNextProject()
23    {
24       return log.peek();
25    } // end getNextProject
26
27    public Assignment removeNextProject()
28    {
29       return log.remove();
30    } // end removeNextProject
31 } // end AssignmentLog
```

**10.22** The following statements could appear in a client of `AssignmentLog`:

```
AssignmentLog myHomework = new AssignmentLog();
myHomework.addProject("CSC211", "Pg 50, Ex 2", Date.valueOf("2015-2-20"));
Assignment pg75Ex8 = new Assignment("CSC215", "Pg 75, Ex 8",
                                    Date.valueOf("2015-3-14"));
myHomework.addProject(pg75Ex8);

. . .

System.out.println("The following assignment is due next:");
System.out.println(myHomework.getNextProject());
```

The assignment with the earliest due date is displayed but is not removed from the assignment log.

## Java Class Library: The Class `PriorityQueue`

**10.23** The standard package `java.util` in the Java Class Library contains the class `PriorityQueue`. This class implements the interface `Queue` that we described earlier in this chapter. An instance of `PriorityQueue` behaves like a priority queue, not a queue, in that its entries are ordered, with the entry having the smallest value, and therefore the highest priority, at the front of the priority queue. Since `PriorityQueue` uses the method `compareTo` to order its entries, the entries must belong to a class that implements the interface `Comparable`. In addition, the entries cannot be `null`.

Here are the basic constructors and methods of the class `PriorityQueue`:

**public** `PriorityQueue()`
Creates an empty priority queue whose initial capacity is 11 entries.

**public** `PriorityQueue(int initialCapacity)`
Creates an empty priority queue having a given initial capacity.

**public boolean** `add(T newEntry)`
Adds a new entry to this priority queue, returning true if successful and throwing an exception if not.

**public boolean** `offer(T newEntry)`
Adds a new entry to this priority queue, returning true or false according to the success of the operation.

**public** T remove()
Retrieves and removes the entry at the front of this priority queue, but throws NoSuchElementException if the priority queue is empty prior to the operation.

**public** T poll()
Retrieves and removes the entry at the front of this priority queue, but returns null if the priority queue is empty prior to the operation.

**public** T element()
Retrieves the entry at the front of this priority queue, but throws NoSuchElementException if the priority queue is empty.

**public** T peek()
Retrieves the entry at the front of this priority queue, but returns null if the priority queue is empty.

**public boolean** isEmpty()
Detects whether this priority queue is empty.

**public void** clear()
Removes all entries from this priority queue.

**public int** size()
Gets the number of elements currently in this priority queue.

Instances of PriorityQueue grow in size as needed by a client.

## Chapter Summary

- The ADT queue organizes its entries on a first-in, first-out basis. Among its items, the one added first, or earliest, is at the front of the queue, and the one added most recently is at the back of the queue.

- A queue's major operations—enqueue, dequeue, and getFront—deal only with the ends of the queue. The method enqueue adds an entry to the back of the queue; dequeue removes and returns the entry at the front of the queue, and getFront just returns it.

- You can use a queue to simulate a waiting line. A time-driven simulation counts simulated units of time. Customers arrive at random times, are assigned a random transaction time, and enter a queue.

- When computing the capital gain from a sale of stock, you must sell shares in the order in which you purchased them. If you record your purchases of individual shares in a queue, they will be in the order in which they must be sold.

- A double-ended queue, or deque, has operations that add, remove, or retrieve entries at both its front and back. As such, it combines and expands the operations of a queue and a stack. The deque's major operations are addToFront, removeFront, getFront, addToBack, removeBack, and getBack.

- A priority queue organizes its entries according to their priorities, as determined by the entries' compareTo method. Besides adding entries to a priority queue, you can retrieve and remove the entry with the highest priority.

- A mutable object has set methods; an immutable object does not.

- Methods such as `getFront` and `dequeue` must behave reasonably when the queue is empty. Here, we specify that they throw an exception. Just as we discussed in Chapter 5 in the context of the ADT stack, other possibilities include returning `null` or giving these methods the precondition that the queue is not empty.

## EXERCISES

1. If you add the objects a and b to a queue that has c and d as its first and last objects, respectively, in what order will four `dequeue` operations remove a and b from the queue?

2. If you add the objects a and b to a queue that has c and d as its first and last objects, respectively, in what order will four `removeBack` operations remove a and b from the queue?

3. After the following statements execute, what are the contents of the queue?

```
QueueInterface<String> myQueue = new LinkedQueue<>();
myQueue.enqueue("June");
myQueue.enqueue("January");
myQueue.enqueue("July");
myQueue.enqueue("May");
myQueue.enqueue(myQueue.getFront());
myQueue.enqueue(myQueue.dequeue());
String name = myQueue.dequeue();
myQueue.enqueue(myQueue.getFront());
```

4. After the following statements execute, what are the contents of the deque?

```
DequeInterface<String> myDeque = new LinkedDeque<>();
myDeque.addToFront("July");
myDeque.addToFront("January");
String name = myDeque.removeFront();
myDeque.addToBack(name);
myDeque.addToFront(myDeque.removeBack());
myDeque.addToFront("May");
myDeque.addToBack("June");
myDeque.addToFront(myDeque.getBack());
myDeque.addToBack(myDeque.removeFront());
```

5. After the following statements execute, what are the contents of the priority queue? Assume that the alphabetically earliest string has the highest priority.

```
PriorityQueueInterface<String> myPriorityQueue = new LinkedPriorityQueue<>();
myPriorityQueue.add("January");
myPriorityQueue.add("June");
String name = myPriorityQueue.remove();
myPriorityQueue.add("July");
myPriorityQueue.add(name);
myPriorityQueue.add(myPriorityQueue.peek());
myPriorityQueue.add("May");
myPriorityQueue.add("August");
myPriorityQueue.remove();
```

6. Consider strings that read the same when read from either side (ignoring spaces, punctuation, and case). For example, the string *madam* when read from either side reads the same. Such strings, as discussed in Chapter 5, are known as palindromes. However, the string *book* is not a palindrome. Describe how you could use a queue to test whether a string has this property.

7. Complete the simulation begun in Figure 10-6. Let Customer 6 enter the line at time 10 with a transaction time of 2.

8. Assume that `customerLine` is an instance of the class `WaitLine`, as given in Segment 10.8. The invocation `CustomerLine.simulate(15, 0.5, 5)` produces the following random events:

   Customer 1 enters the line at time 6 with a transaction time of 3.
   Customer 2 enters the line at time 8 with a transaction time of 3.
   Customer 3 enters the line at time 10 with a transaction time of 1.
   Customer 4 enters the line at time 11 with a transaction time of 5.

   During the simulation, how many customers are served, and what is their average waiting time?

9. Repeat Exercise 8, but instead use the following random events:

   Customer 1 enters the line at time 0 with a transaction time of 4.
   Customer 2 enters the line at time 1 with a transaction time of 4.
   Customer 3 enters the line at time 3 with a transaction time of 1.
   Customer 4 enters the line at time 4 with a transaction time of 4.
   Customer 5 enters the line at time 9 with a transaction time of 3.
   Customer 6 enters the line at time 12 with a transaction time of 2.
   Customer 7 enters the line at time 13 with a transaction time of 1.

10. When using a queue to compute capital gains, we observed in Segment 10.12 that each of the queue's entries could represent more than one share of stock if each entry has set methods. Revise the class `StockPurchase` so that each of its instances has set methods and represents the purchase of multiple shares of one company's stock. Then revise the class `StockLedger`, using a queue to contain the `StockPurchase` objects.

11. Segment 9.21 in Chapter 9 provided the pseudocode for a radix sort of an array. Each bucket in that algorithm is actually a queue. Describe why you can use a queue but not a stack for a radix sort.

12. Exercise 11 of Chapter 5 describes a palindrome. Can you use one of the ADTs described in this chapter instead of a stack to see whether a string is a palindrome? If so, develop an algorithm to do so for each applicable ADT.

13. Consider a special kind of queue that has a finite size but allows an unlimited number of `enqueue` operations. If the queue is full when an `enqueue` occurs, the queue makes room for the new entry by deleting the entry at its back. A page replacement algorithm in an operating system, such as "`Most Recently Used`", can use this kind of queue. Implement this queue as a deque.

## PROJECTS

1. Project 3 of Chapter 9 used a vector in the implementation of an iterative merge sort. In that project, the vector was used as if it were a queue. Repeat the project, but use a queue instead of a vector.

2. Implement the radix sort, as given in Segment 9.21 of Chapter 9, by using a queue for each bucket.

3. Expand the capital gains example described in this chapter to allow more than one type of stock in the portfolio. Identify different stocks by using a string for the stock's symbol. Record the shares of each company in a separate queue, deque, or priority queue. Maintain the collection of these ADTs in a vector.

4. Simulate a small airport with one runway. Airplanes waiting to take off join a queue on the ground. Planes waiting to land join a queue in the air. Only one plane can use the runway at any given time. All planes in the air must land before any plane can take off.

5. Repeat Project 4, but use a priority queue for the planes waiting to land. Develop a priority schedule for situations such as low fuel or mechanical problems.

6. When each object in a collection has a priority, how should you organize several objects that have the same priority? One way is to order the objects with the same priority in chronological order. Thus, you can create a priority queue of queues. Design such an ADT.

7. Write a program to simulate a train route. A train route consists of a number of stations, starting and ending with a terminal station. The time that the train needs to travel between a pair of consecutive stations on the route is given. Associated with each station is a queue of passengers. Passengers are generated at random times, assigned to entry stations randomly, and given random destination stations. Trains leave a terminal at regular intervals and visit the stations on the route. When a train stops at a station, all passengers for that station exit first. Then any passengers waiting in the queue at the station board the train until either the queue is empty or the train is full.

8. Write a program to simulate job scheduling in an operating system. Jobs are generated at random times. Each job is given both a random priority from 1 to 4—where 1 is the highest priority—and a random amount of time to complete its execution.

   Jobs do not begin execution and run to completion, but instead share the processor. The operating system executes a job for a fixed unit of time called a *time slice*. At the end of the time slice, the current job's execution is suspended. The job is then placed in a priority queue, where it waits for its next share of processor time. The job having the highest priority is then removed from the priority queue and executed for a time slice.

   When a job is first generated, it will begin executing immediately if the processor is free. Otherwise it will be placed in the priority queue.

9. The largest positive integer of type int is 2,147,483,647. Another integer type, long, represents integers up to 9,223,372,036,854,775,807. Imagine that you want to represent even larger integers. For example, cryptography uses integers having more than 100 digits. Design and implement a class Huge of very large nonnegative integers. The largest integer should contain at least 30 digits. Use a deque to represent the value of an integer.

   Provide operations for the class that

   - Set the value of a nonnegative integer (provide both set methods and constructors)
   - Return the value of a nonnegative integer as a string
   - Read a large nonnegative integer (skip leading zeros, but remember that zero is a valid number)
   - Display a large nonnegative integer (do not display leading zeros, but if the integer is zero, display a single zero)
   - Add two nonnegative integers to produce the sum as a third integer
   - Multiply two nonnegative integers to produce the product as a third integer

   You should handle overflow when reading, adding, or multiplying integers. An integer is too large if it exceeds MAX_SIZE digits, where MAX_SIZE is a named constant that you define. Write a test program that demonstrates each method.

10. One way to shuffle playing cards is to use a *perfect shuffle*. First, you divide a deck of 52 cards into two halves of 26 cards each. Next, you merge the halves by interleaving the cards as follows. Beginning with the top half and alternating halves, you take the bottom card from a half and place it on top of a new deck.

    For example, if our deck contains the six cards 1 2 3 4 5 6, the top half is 1 2 3, and the bottom half is 4 5 6. The 3 at the bottom of the top half becomes the bottom card in the shuffled deck. We then place the 6, which is at the bottom of the bottom half, on top of the shuffled deck. Next, we place 2 on top, then 5, 1, and finally 4. The shuffled deck is then 4 1 5 2 6 3. Notice that the card that was on top of the original deck is now second in the shuffled result, and the bottom card in the original deck is now second from the bottom in the shuffled deck. This shuffle is called an *in-shuffle* and is achieved by beginning with the top half when you move cards into the shuffled result. If you begin with the bottom half, you get an *out-shuffle*, whereby the original top card and bottom card remain in their positions in the shuffled deck.

Define a class of playing-card decks by using a deque to contain the cards. Your class should define methods to perform perfect in-shuffles and perfect out-shuffles. Using your class,

**a.** Determine the number of perfect out-shuffles needed to return a deck of $n$ cards to its original order.

**b.** Determine the number of perfect in-shuffles needed to return a deck of $n$ cards to its original order.

**c.** You can move a deck's top card, which is at position 0, to any desired position $m$ by performing a sequence of in-shuffles and out-shuffles, as follows. You write $m$ in binary. Beginning with the leftmost 1 and proceeding to the right, you perform an in-shuffle for each 1 encountered and an out-shuffle for each 0. For example, if $m$ is 8, we have 1000 for its binary equivalent. We would perform one in-shuffle followed by three out-shuffles to move the original top card to position 8, that is, so it is the ninth card from the top of the deck. Define a method to perform this card trick.

## ANSWERS TO SELF-TEST QUESTIONS

**1.** *Jill* is at the front, *Jess* is at the back.

**2.**
```
/**
   A class of runtime exceptions thrown when an attempt
   is made to access or remove the front of a queue.
   @author Frank M. Carrano
*/
public class EmptyQueueException extends RuntimeException
{
    public EmptyQueueException()
    {
        this (null);
    } // end default constructor

    public EmptyQueueException(String message)
    {
        super (message);
    } // end constructor
} // end EmptyQueueException
```

**3.** **a.** 11.
   **b.** 4.

**4.** *Jill* is at the front, *Jane* is at the back.

**5.** *Jim* is at the front, *Jane* is at the back.

# Queue, Deque, and Priority Queue Implementations

## Contents

## Prerequisites

## Objectives

After studying this chapter, you should be able to

- Implement the ADT queue by using either a chain of linked nodes or an array
- Add or delete nodes at either end of a chain of doubly linked nodes
- Implement the ADT deque by using a chain of doubly linked nodes
- Implement the ADT priority queue by using either an array or a chain of linked nodes

The implementations of the ADT queue that are in this chapter use techniques like the ones we used to implement the ADT bag and the ADT stack. We will use either a chain of linked nodes or an array to store the queue's entries. Although the stack implementations we saw in Chapter 6 were quite simple, the implementations of a queue are a bit more involved.

We also present a linked implementation of the double-ended queue, or deque. Since the deque allows access to both its front and its back, an ordinary chain of linked nodes is not sufficient. For example, deleting the last node in a chain is not possible without a reference to the preceding node. Thus, we use a new kind of chain, one that links its nodes in both directions. That is, a node in this chain references both the next node and the one that precedes it. Such a chain provides an efficient implementation of the deque.

Finally, we suggest some implementations of the ADT priority queue. We note, however, that a more efficient implementation will be possible when we encounter the ADT heap in Chapters 23 and 26.

# A Linked Implementation of a Queue

**11.1**    If we use a chain of linked nodes to implement a queue, the two ends of the queue will be at opposite ends of the chain. If we have only a head reference to the chain, accessing the chain's last node will require a traversal of the entire chain, making the access inefficient. Adding a **tail reference**—an external reference to the last node in the chain—is one approach to this problem and is the one we will take here.

VideoNote
The class LinkedQueue

With both head and tail references, which node should be the front of the queue and which node should be the back? We must be able to remove the entry at the front of the queue. If it is at the beginning of the chain, we will be able to remove it easily. If it is at the end of the chain, removing it will require a reference to the preceding node. To get such a reference, we must traverse the chain. Thus, we reject this option and make the chain's first node contain the queue's front entry.

Placing the front of the queue at the beginning of the chain obviously forces the back of the queue to the chain's end. Since we add entries only to the back of the queue, and since we have a tail reference for the chain, this arrangement will work well.

Figure 11-1 illustrates a chain of linked nodes with both head and tail references. The chain contains one node for each entry in the queue. Nodes are allocated only when needed for a new entry and are deallocated when an entry is removed.

FIGURE 11-1    A chain of linked nodes that implements a queue

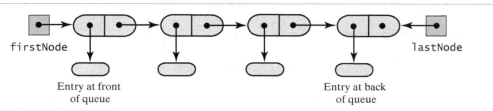

**11.2**    **An outline of the class.** The linked implementation of the queue has two data fields. The field firstNode references the chain's first node, which contains the queue's front entry. And lastNode references the chain's last node, which contains the entry at the back of the queue. Since both of these fields are null when the queue is empty, the default constructor sets them to null. An outline of our class appears in Listing 11-1.

The class also contains the private class Node, like the one you saw in Listing 3-4 of Chapter 3. We also used this class in Chapter 6 for an implementation of the ADT stack.

LISTING 11-1    An outline of a linked implementation of the ADT queue

```
1  /**
2     A class that implements a queue of objects by using
3     a chain of linked nodes.
4     @author Frank M. Carrano
5  */
6  public final class LinkedQueue<T> implements QueueInterface<T>
7  {
8     private Node firstNode; // References node at front of queue
9     private Node lastNode;  // References node at back of queue
10
11    public LinkedQueue()
12    {
13       firstNode = null;
14       lastNode = null;
15    } // end default constructor
16
17    < Implementations of the queue operations go here. >
18    . . .
19
20    private class Node
21    {
22       private T    data; // Entry in queue
23       private Node next; // Link to next node
24
25       < Constructors and the methods getData, setData, getNextNode, and setNextNode
26         are here. >
27
28       . . .
29    } // end Node
30  } // end LinkedQueue
```

**11.3    Adding to the back.** To add an entry to the back of the queue, we allocate a new node and add it to the end of the chain. If the queue—and therefore the chain—is empty, we make both data fields, firstNode and lastNode, reference the new node, as Figure 11-2 illustrates. Otherwise, both the last node in the chain and the data field lastNode must reference the new node, as shown in Figure 11-3.

FIGURE 11-2    (a) Before adding a new node to an empty chain; (b) after adding it

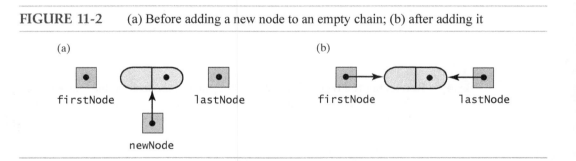

Thus, the definition of enqueue appears as follows:

```java
public void enqueue(T newEntry)
{
    Node newNode = new Node(newEntry, null);

    if (isEmpty())
        firstNode = newNode;
    else
        lastNode.setNextNode(newNode);

    lastNode = newNode;
} // end enqueue
```

This operation requires no search and is independent of the other entries in the queue. Its performance is thus O(1).

---

**FIGURE 11-3**   (a) Before, (b) during, and (c) after adding a new node to the end of a nonempty chain that has a tail reference

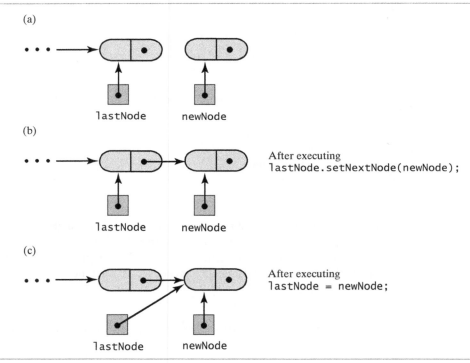

(a)

lastNode   newNode

(b)

After executing
`lastNode.setNextNode(newNode);`

lastNode   newNode

(c)

After executing
`lastNode = newNode;`

lastNode   newNode

---

**11.4**   **Retrieving the front entry.** We get the entry at the front of the queue by accessing the data portion of the first node in the chain. Like enqueue, getFront is an O(1) operation.

```java
public T getFront()
{
    if (isEmpty())
        throw new EmptyQueueException();
    else
        return firstNode.getData();
} // end getFront
```

**11.5**    **Removing the front entry.** The method dequeue retrieves the entry at the front of the queue and then removes the chain's first node by making firstNode reference the second node in the chain, as shown in Figure 11-4. If the chain had only one node, dequeue would make the chain empty by setting both firstNode and lastNode to null, as Figure 11-5 illustrates.

```java
public T dequeue()
{
    T front = getFront(); // Might throw EmptyQueueException
    assert firstNode != null;
    firstNode.setData(null);
    firstNode = firstNode.getNextNode();

    if (firstNode == null)
        lastNode = null;

    return front;
} // end dequeue
```

Like enqueue, dequeue requires no search and is independent of the other entries in the queue. Its performance is thus O(1).

FIGURE 11-4      (a) A queue of more than one entry; (b) after removing the entry at the front of the queue

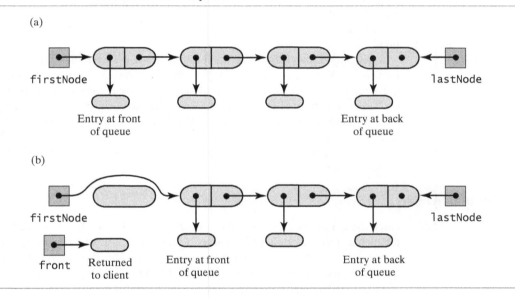

FIGURE 11-5      (a) A queue of one entry; (b) after removing the entry at the front of the queue

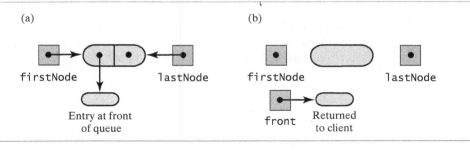

**11.6**    **The rest of the class.** The remaining public methods isEmpty and clear are straightforward:

```
public boolean isEmpty()
{
    return (firstNode == null) && (lastNode == null);
} // end isEmpty

public void clear()
{
    firstNode = null;
    lastNode = null;
} // end clear
```

**Question 1** Why is a tail reference desirable when you use a chain of linked nodes to implement a queue?

## An Array-Based Implementation of a Queue

**11.7**    If we use an array queue to contain the entries in a queue, we could let queue[0] be the queue's front, as Figure 11-6a shows. Here, frontIndex and backIndex are the indices of the entries at the queue's front and back, respectively. But what happens when we remove the front entry? If we insist that the new front entry be in queue[0], we would need to shift each array entry by one position toward the beginning of the array. This arrangement would make the operation dequeue inefficient.

Instead, we can leave other array entries in their current positions when we remove the queue's front entry. For example, if we begin with the array in Figure 11-6a and execute dequeue twice, the array will be as shown in Figure 11-6b. Not moving array entries is attractive, but after several additions and removals, the array can look like the one pictured in Figure 11-6c. The queue entries have migrated to the end of the array. The last available array location is allocated to the last entry added to the queue. We could expand the array, but the queue has only three entries. Since most of the array is unoccupied, why not use this space for future additions? In fact, that is just what we will do next.

### A Circular Array

**11.8**    Once the queue reaches the end of the array, as in Figure 11-6c, we can add subsequent entries to the queue at the beginning of the array. Figure 11-6d shows the array after two such additions to the queue. We make the array behave as though it were **circular**, so that its first location follows its last one. To do this, we use modulo arithmetic on the indices. Specifically, when we add an entry to the queue, we increment backIndex modulo the size of the array. For example, if queue is the name of the array, we increment backIndex with the statement

```
backIndex = (backIndex + 1) % queue.length;
```

To remove an entry, we increment frontIndex modulo the size of the array in a similar fashion.

**Question 2** When we removed an entry from an array-based bag in Chapter 2, we replaced the removed entry with the last one in the array. Yet the implementation of the queue just described does not do so. Explain this difference in implementations.

FIGURE 11-6    An array that represents a queue without moving any entries:
                (a) initially; (b) after removing the entry at the front twice;
                (c) after several more additions and removals; (d) after two
                additions that wrap around to the beginning of the array

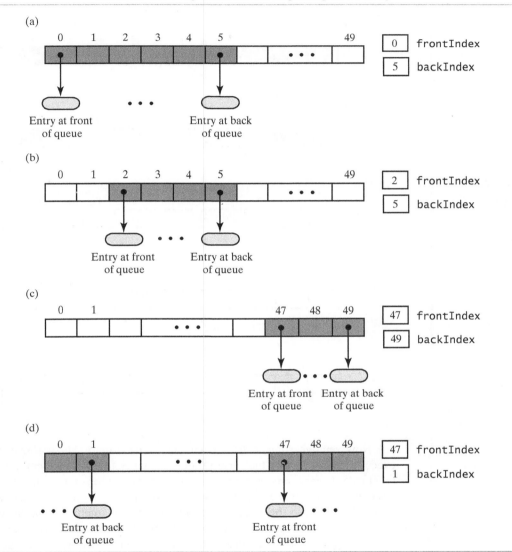

**11.9    Complications.** Using a circular array complicates the implementation somewhat. For example, how can we detect when the array is full? Clearly the array in Figure 11-7a is full. This array is the result of several additions to the queue pictured in Figure 11-6d. So it appears that the queue is full when frontIndex is backIndex + 1.

**FIGURE 11-7**    A circular array that represents a queue: (a) when full;
(b) after removing two entries; (c) after removing three more
entries; (d) after removing all but one entry; (e) after removing the remaining entry

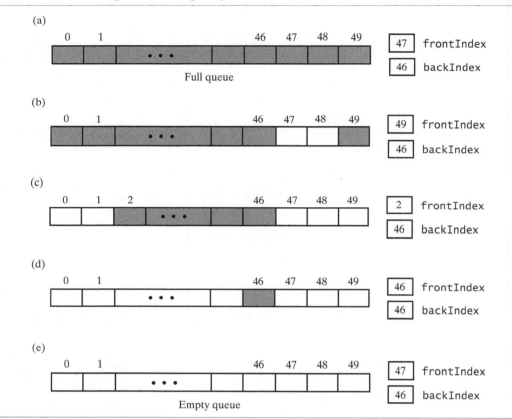

Now remove some entries from the queue. Figure 11-7b shows the array after `dequeue` executes twice. Notice that `frontIndex` advances to 49. If we continue to remove items from the queue, `frontIndex` will wrap around to zero and beyond. Figure 11-7c shows the array after three more items are removed. As we remove more items from the queue, `frontIndex` advances. Figure 11-7d shows the array after all but one item is removed from the queue. Now let's remove that one item. In Figure 11-7e, we see that this last removal has caused `frontIndex` to advance so that it is 1 more than `backIndex`. Although the queue is empty, `frontIndex` is `backIndex` + 1. This is exactly the same condition we encountered in Figure 11-7a when the queue was full.

**Note:** With a circular array, `frontIndex` equals `backIndex` + 1 both when the queue is empty and when it is full.

As you can see, we cannot test whether the queue is empty or full by using `frontIndex` and `backIndex`. One solution is to maintain a count of queue items. If the count is zero, the queue is empty; if the count equals the array's capacity, the queue is full. When the queue is full, the next `enqueue` operation can double the array's size before adding a new entry.

Having a counter as a data field leads to a reasonable implementation, but each `enqueue` and `dequeue` must update the count. We can avoid this extra work by leaving one array location unused. We develop this approach next.

## A Circular Array with One Unused Location

**VideoNote**

The class ArrayQueue

**11.10**  Not using one array location allows us to distinguish between an empty queue and a full queue by examining only `frontIndex` and `backIndex`. In Java, each array location contains only a reference, so we waste little memory by having an unused location. Here we will leave unused the array location that follows the back of the queue. Project 3 at the end of this chapter considers a different location.

Figure 11-8 illustrates a seven-element circular array that represents a queue of at most six entries. As we add and remove entries, you should observe the effect on the indices `frontIndex` and `backIndex`. Part *a* of the figure shows the array initially, when the queue is empty. Notice that `frontIndex` is zero and `backIndex` contains the index of the array's last location. Adding an entry to this queue increments the initial value of `backIndex` so that it becomes zero, as shown in Part *b*. Part *c* illustrates the queue after five more additions, making it full. Now remove the front entry and add an entry to the back, as Parts *d* and *e* show. The queue is full once again. Repeating this pair of operations leads to the queues shown in Parts *f* and *g*. Now repeatedly remove the entry at the front until the queue is empty. Part *h* shows the queue after the first of these dequeue operations, Part *i* shows it after all but one entry is removed, and Part *j* shows the empty queue.

To summarize, the queue is full in Parts *c*, *e*, and *g* of this figure. In each of these examples, the index of the unused location is 1 more than `backIndex` and 1 less than `frontIndex`, if we treat the array as circular. That is, `frontIndex` is 2 more than `backIndex`. Thus, the queue is full when

`frontIndex equals (backIndex + 2) % queue.length`

The queue is empty in Parts *a* and *j*. In those cases, `frontIndex` is 1 more than `backIndex`. Thus, the queue is empty when

`frontIndex equals (backIndex + 1) % queue.length`

Admittedly, these criteria are more involved than checking a counter of the number of entries in the queue. However, once we have them, the rest of the implementation is simpler and more efficient because there is no counter to maintain.

**11.11**  **An outline of the class.** This array-based implementation of a queue begins with four data fields and two constructors. The fields are the array of queue entries, indices to the front and back of the queue, and an initial capacity for the queue that the default constructor creates. Another constructor lets the client choose the initial queue capacity. The initial size of the array is one more than the queue's initial capacity. Listing 11-2 outlines the class.

---

**LISTING 11-2**  An outline of an array-based implementation of the ADT queue

```java
1  /**
2      A class that implements a queue of objects by using an array.
3      @author Frank M. Carrano
4  */
5  public final class ArrayQueue<T> implements QueueInterface<T>
6  {
7      private T[] queue; // Circular array of queue entries and one unused
8                         // location
9      private int frontIndex;
10     private int backIndex;
11     private boolean initialized = false;
12     private static final int DEFAULT_CAPACITY = 50;
```

```
13      private static final int MAX_CAPACITY = 10000;
14
15      public ArrayQueue()
16      {
17         this(DEFAULT_CAPACITY);
18      } // end default constructor
19
20      public ArrayQueue(int initialCapacity)
21      {
22         checkCapacity(initialCapacity);
23
24         // The cast is safe because the new array contains null entries
25         @SuppressWarnings("unchecked")
26         T[] tempQueue = (T[]) new Object[initialCapacity + 1];
27         queue = tempQueue;
28         frontIndex = 0;
29         backIndex = initialCapacity;
30         initialized = true;
31      } // end constructor
32      < Implementations of the queue operations go here. >
33         . . .
34   } // end ArrayQueue
```

11.12   **Adding to the back.** The method enqueue calls the private method ensureCapacity, which doubles the size of the array if it is full, and then places the new entry immediately after the last occupied location in the array. To determine the index of this location, we increment backIndex. But since the array is circular, we use the operator % to make backIndex zero after it reaches its maximum value.

```
public void enqueue(T newEntry)
{
   checkInitialization();
   ensureCapacity();
   backIndex = (backIndex + 1) % queue.length;
   queue[backIndex] = newEntry;
} // end enqueue
```

The implementation of ensureCapacity differs from the one given in Chapter 6 because the array here is circular. We will see how to implement it shortly.

The performance of enqueue when it does not resize the array is independent of the number of entries in the queue. Thus, it is $O(1)$ in this case. However, its performance degrades to $O(n)$ when the array is full, because resizing the array is an $O(n)$ operation. If this happens, however, the very next enqueue is $O(1)$ again. As we mentioned in Segment 6.9, we could amortize the cost of doubling the array over all additions to the queue. That is, we let all enqueue operations share the cost of resizing the array. Unless the array is resized many times, each enqueue is almost $O(1)$.

11.13   **Retrieving the front entry.** The method getFront either returns the array entry at frontIndex or throws an exception if the queue is empty:

```
public T getFront()
{
   checkInitialization();
   if (isEmpty())
      throw new EmptyQueueException();
   else
      return queue[frontIndex];
} // end getFront
```

This operation is $O(1)$.

FIGURE 11-8     A seven-location circular array that contains at most six entries
                of a queue

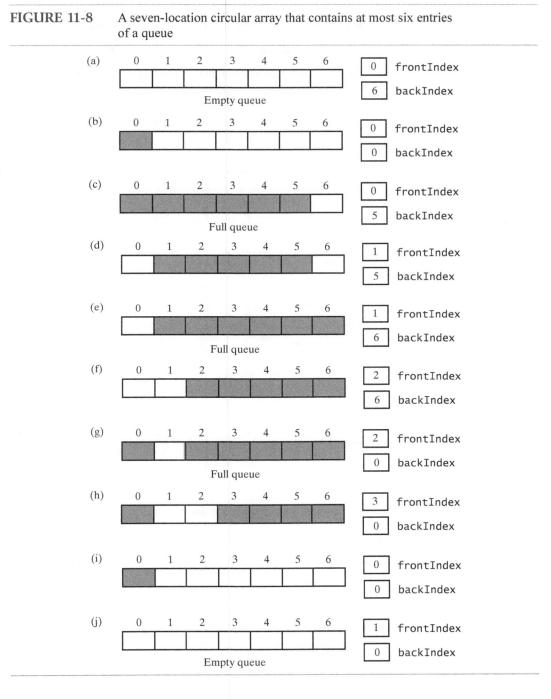

**11.14 Removing the front entry.** The method dequeue, like getFront, retrieves the entry at the front of the queue, but then it removes it. To remove the front entry of the queue shown in Figure 11-9a, we could simply increment frontIndex, as Figure 11-9b illustrates. This step would suffice because the other methods would behave correctly. For example, getFront would return the item that queue[6] references. However, the object that previously was the front of the queue and is returned to the client would still be referenced by the array. This fact is of no real concern if our implementation is correct. To be safe, dequeue can set queue[frontIndex] to null before incrementing frontIndex. Figure 11-9c illustrates the queue in this case.

**FIGURE 11-9**     An array-based queue: (a) initially; (b) after removing its front entry by incrementing frontIndex; (c) after removing its front entry by setting queue[frontIndex] to null and then incrementing frontIndex

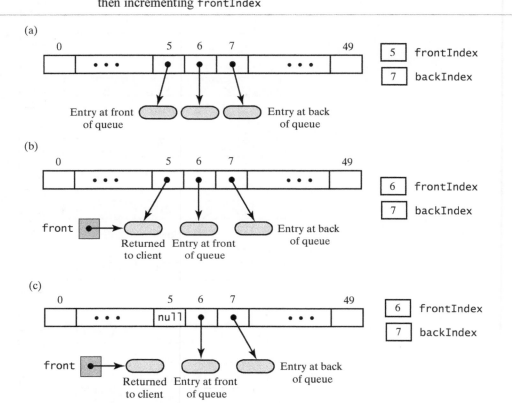

The following implementation of dequeue reflects these comments:

```java
public T dequeue()
{
    checkInitialization();
    if (isEmpty())
        throw new EmptyQueueException();
    else
    {
        T front = queue[frontIndex];
        queue[frontIndex] = null;
        frontIndex = (frontIndex + 1) % queue.length;
        return front;
    } // end if
} // end dequeue
```

Like getFront, dequeue is an O(1) operation.

**11.15** **The private method ensureCapacity.** As you saw in Segment 2.35 of Chapter 2, when we increase the size of an array, we must copy its entries into the newly allocated space. We need to be careful, though, because here the array is circular. We must copy entries in the order in which they appear in the queue.

For example, the seven-element array in Figure 11-8g is full and appears again in Figure 11-10. Call this array oldQueue. After allocating a new array queue of 14 locations, we copy the front of the queue from oldQueue[frontIndex] to queue[0]. We continue copying elements from the old array to the new array, proceeding to the end of the old array and wrapping around to its beginning, as the figure shows. In addition, we must set frontIndex and backIndex to reflect the reorganized array.

**FIGURE 11-10**    Doubling the size of an array-based queue

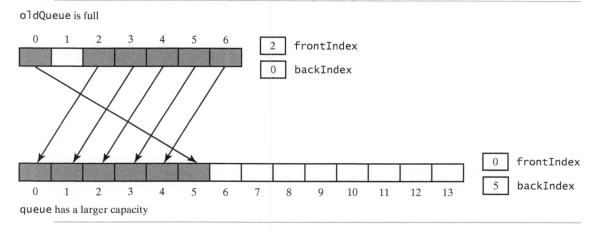

The following definition of ensureCapacity detects when the array is full by using the criterion given in Segment 11.10:

```
// Doubles the size of the array queue if it is full.
// Precondition: checkInitialization has been called.
private void ensureCapacity()
{
    if (frontIndex == ((backIndex + 2) % queue.length)) // If array is full,
    {                                                    // double size of array
        T[] oldQueue = queue;
        int oldSize = oldQueue.length;
        int newSize = 2 * oldSize;
        checkCapacity(newSize);
        // The cast is safe because the new array contains null entries
        @SuppressWarnings("unchecked")
        T[] tempQueue = (T[]) new Object[newSize];
        queue = tempQueue;
        for (int index = 0; index < oldSize - 1; index++)
        {
            queue[index] = oldQueue[frontIndex];
            frontIndex = (frontIndex + 1) % oldSize;
        } // end for

        frontIndex = 0;
        backIndex = oldSize - 2;
    } // end if
} // end ensureCapacity
```

You can use the method System.arraycopy to copy the array. However, since the array is circular, you will need two calls to this method. Exercise 1 at the end of this chapter asks you to revise ensureCapacity in this way.

**11.16** **The rest of the class.** The public method isEmpty has the following implementation, based on our comments at the end of Segment 11.10:

```java
public boolean isEmpty()
{
    return frontIndex == ((backIndex + 1) % queue.length);
} // end isEmpty
```

The method clear could simply set frontIndex to 0 and backIndex to queue.length − 1. The other queue methods would behave as expected for an empty queue. However, the objects that were in the queue would then remain allocated. To deallocate them, clear should set to null each array location that was used for the queue. Alternatively, clear could call dequeue repeatedly until the queue is empty, if dequeue sets queue[frontIndex] to null. We leave the implementation of clear as an exercise.

**Question 3** Write an implementation of clear that sets to null each array location that was used for the queue.

**Question 4** Write an implementation of clear that repeatedly calls dequeue until the queue is empty. How does this implementation compare to the one you wrote for Question 3?

**Question 5** If queue is an array that contains the entries in a queue, and queue is not treated as a circular array, what is a disadvantage of maintaining the back of the queue at queue[0]?

**Note:** In some languages other than Java, leaving an array location empty wastes memory because the location contains an object instead of a reference to an object. Project 4 at the end of this chapter considers an array-based implementation of a queue that does not have an unused location and does not maintain a counter.

# Circular Linked Implementations of a Queue

**11.17** Figure 11-1 in Segment 11.1 shows a chain of linked nodes that implements the ADT queue. This chain has two external references—one to the first node and one to the last node in the chain. Recall that these references are particularly useful for a queue implementation, since a queue's operations affect both of its ends. Like the chains you have seen before, the last node in this chain contains null. Such chains are sometimes called **linear linked chains**, regardless of whether they have a tail reference in addition to a head reference.

VideoNote

Other queue implementations

In a **circular linked chain**, the last node references the first node, so no node contains null in its next field. Despite the fact that each node references the next node, a circular linked chain has a beginning and an end. We could have an external reference to the chain's first node, but then a traversal of the chain would be necessary to locate the last node. Having both a reference to the first node and a reference to the last node is usually more than is necessary. Since the chain's last node references its first node, we can have a solitary reference to the last node and still locate the first node quickly. Figure 11-11 illustrates such a chain.

When a class uses a circular linked chain to represent a queue, its only data field is the reference lastNode to the chain's last node. The implementation therefore does not have the overhead of maintaining a data field that references the first node. Any time such a reference is needed, the expression lastNode.getNextNode() provides it. Despite this simplification, this approach is not necessarily better than the one used in the first section of this chapter. It is mostly just different, as you will see if you complete Project 5 at the end of this chapter.

We now investigate another way to use a circular linked chain to represent a queue.

FIGURE 11-11    A circular linked chain with an external reference to its last node that (a) has
more than one node; (b) has one node; (c) is empty

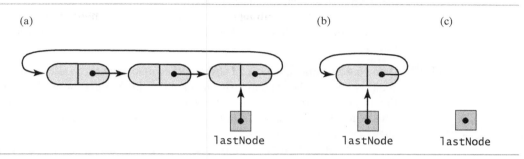

## A Two-Part Circular Linked Chain

**11.18**    When a linked chain—whether it is linear or circular—represents a queue, it has one node for each
entry in the queue. When we add an entry to the queue, we allocate a new node for the chain. When
we remove an entry from the queue, a node is deallocated.

In the circular array implementation, the queue uses a subset of the fixed number of array
locations available. When we add an entry to the queue, we use the next unoccupied location in
the array. When we remove an entry from the queue, we make its array location available for the
queue's later use. Since additions and removals are at the ends of a queue, the queue occupies contiguous locations in the circular array. The available locations also are contiguous, again because
the array is circular. Thus, the circular array has two parts: One part contains the queue and the
other part is available for the queue.

Suppose that we had two parts in a circular linked chain. The linked nodes that form the queue
are followed by linked nodes that are available for use in the queue, as Figure 11-12 illustrates. Here
queueNode references the node assigned to the front of the queue; freeNode references the first available node that follows the end of the queue. You could think of this configuration as two chains—one
for the queue and one for the available nodes—that are joined at their ends to form a circle.

FIGURE 11-12    A two-part circular linked chain that represents both a queue
and the nodes available to the queue

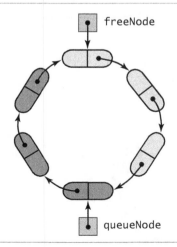

The available nodes are not allocated all at once the way locations are allocated for an array. Initially there are no available nodes; we allocate a node each time we add a new entry to the queue. However, when we remove an entry from the queue, we keep its node in the circle of nodes rather than deallocating it. Thus, a subsequent addition to the queue uses a node from the chain of available nodes. But if no such node is available, we allocate a new one and link it into the chain.

**11.19**   Detecting an empty queue or an absence of available nodes is easier if one node in the circular linked chain is unused. The situation is analogous to the circular array that we used in Segment 11.10. Figure 11-13a shows the queue when it is empty. Both `queueNode` and `freeNode` reference the same unused node. Notice that the node references itself. We can tell that the queue is empty because `queueNode` equals `freeNode`.

To add an entry to this empty queue, we allocate a new node and link it into the circular chain. Figure 11-13b shows the resulting chain for a queue of one entry. To simplify the figure, we have not illustrated the actual object in the queue. Although a node in the chain references an object in the queue, we will sometimes say that the node is in the queue.

While `queueNode` references the node assigned to the queue, `freeNode` still references the unused node. After three more additions to the queue, three more nodes are allocated and linked into the chain. Segment 11.21 will describe exactly how to accomplish this. The chain is now as shown in Figure 11-13c. Again, `freeNode` references the unused node. Since `queueNode` references the node at the front of the queue, retrieving the front entry is easy.

**FIGURE 11-13**   A two-part circular linked chain that represents a queue: (a) when it is empty; (b) after adding one entry; (c) after adding three more entries; (d) after removing the front entry; (e) after adding one more entry

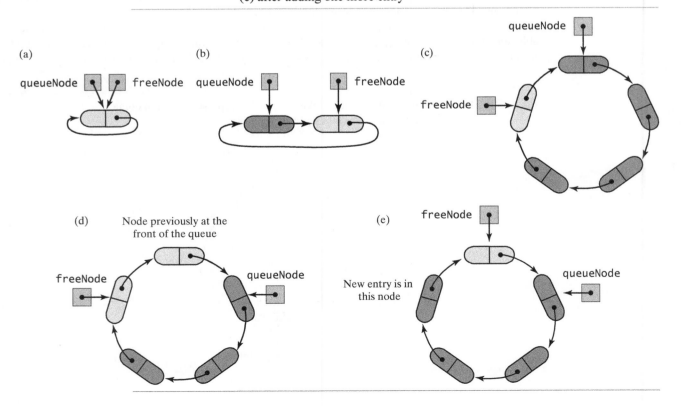

Now if we remove the entry at the front of the queue, we advance queueNode so the chain is as pictured in Figure 11-13d. The node that was at the front of the queue is not deallocated. A subsequent addition—since it is at the back of the queue—uses the node that freeNode references. We then advance freeNode. Figure 11-13e shows the chain at this point. Notice that we did not allocate a new node for the additional entry in this case.

How can we tell whether we must allocate a new node when we add to the queue? We must do so if queueNode equals freeNode.getNextNode(), as shown in Figure 11-13e. That was not the case when we added an entry to the queue in Figure 11-13d; a node was available without allocating a new one. But notice in Figure 11-13a that queueNode also equals freeNode.getNextNode() when the queue is empty. This makes sense, because to add to an empty queue, we need to allocate a new node.

 **Note:** In a two-part circular linked implementation of a queue, one node is unused. Two external references partition the chain into two parts: queueNode references the front node of the queue and freeNode references the node that follows the queue. The queue is empty if queueNode equals freeNode. You use the node at freeNode for a new entry. This node is either the first available node or the unused node. You must allocate a new unused node if queueNode equals freeNode.getNextNode().

**11.20   An outline of the class.** The class that implements the queue by using a two-part circular linked chain has the references queueNode and freeNode as data fields. Since the chain must always contain at least one node, the default constructor allocates a node, makes the node reference itself, and sets queueNode and freeNode to reference this new node. Thus, the class appears as outlined in Listing 11-3.

**LISTING 11-3**   An outline of a two-part circular linked implementation of the ADT queue

```
1  /**
2     A class that implements a queue of objects by using
3     a two-part circular chain of linked nodes.
4     @author Frank M. Carrano
5  */
6  public final class TwoPartCircularLinkedQueue<T> implements QueueInterface<T>
7  {
8     private Node queueNode; // References first node in queue
9     private Node freeNode;  // References node after back of queue
10
11    public TwoPartCircularLinkedQueue()
12    {
13       freeNode = new Node(null, null);
14       freeNode.setNextNode(freeNode);
15       queueNode = freeNode;
16    } // end default constructor
17
18    < Implementations of the queue operations go here. >
19    . . .
20    private class Node
21    {
22       private T    data; // Queue entry
23       private Node next; // Link to next node
24
25       < Constructors and the methods getData, setData, getNextNode, and setNextNode
26         are here. >
27       . . .
28    } // end Node
29 } // end TwoPartCircularLinkedQueue
```

**Programming Tip:** When a circular linked chain has one node, the node must reference itself. Forgetting this step is easy to do and leads to an error during execution.

**11.21** **Adding to the back.** Before adding an entry to the queue, we see whether a node is available in the chain. If one is not, we must allocate a new one and link it into the chain. We insert a new node into the chain *after* the node that `freeNode` references, as we are about to do in Figure 11-14a. We do not insert it before this node, because we would need a reference to the previous node to do so. Getting such a reference would take time. The node that `freeNode` references joins the queue and will contain the new entry. The new node becomes the unused node, and we make `freeNode` reference it, as Figure 11-14b shows.

FIGURE 11-14    A chain that requires a new node for an addition to a queue:
(a) before the addition; (b) after the addition

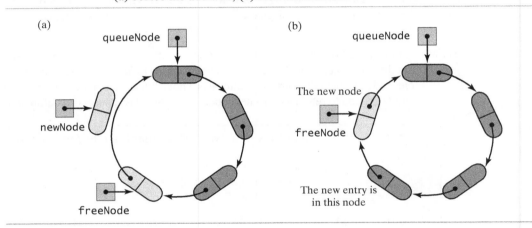

If a node is available in the chain, we use the node that `freeNode` references for the new entry. Figure 11-15 shows the chain before and after two existing nodes become part of the queue. After each addition, `freeNode` references the node that follows the back of the queue. In Figure 11-15b, this node is available for another addition, but in Figure 11-15c, it is unused.

The method `enqueue` is easier to write and to understand if we hide the detail of seeing whether to allocate a new node within the private method `isChainFull`. It returns true if the chain has no nodes available for use in the queue. The implementation of `isChainFull` is not difficult and appears later in Segment 11.24.

The following implementation of `enqueue` is an O(1) operation:

```java
public void enqueue(T newEntry)
{
   freeNode.setData(newEntry);

   if (isChainFull())
   {
      // Allocate a new node and insert it after the node that
      // freeNode references
      Node newNode = new Node(null, freeNode.getNextNode());
      freeNode.setNextNode(newNode);
   } // end if

   freeNode = freeNode.getNextNode();
} // end enqueue
```

**FIGURE 11-15**    (a) A chain with nodes available for additions to a queue;
(b) the chain after one addition; (c) the chain after another addition

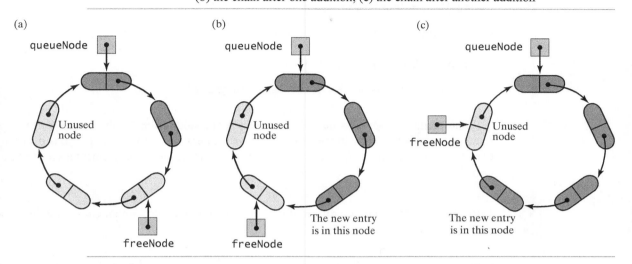

**Question 6** Adding an entry to the queue pictured in Figure 11-15c requires the creation of a new node. Where in the chain would you insert the new node? Which node would contain the new entry?

**11.22    Retrieving the front.** If the queue is not empty, queueNode references its front node. The method getFront is therefore straightforward:

```
public T getFront()
{
    if (isEmpty())
        throw new EmptyQueueException();
    else
        return queueNode.getData();
} // end getFront
```

This method is O(1).

**11.23    Removing the front.** The method dequeue returns the entry at the front of the queue. It then moves the node at the front from the queue's part of the chain to the available part simply by advancing queueNode. Parts *c* and *d* of Figure 11-13 show a chain before and after this step. Since the node that contained the removed entry is not deallocated, it still references the removed entry. Thus, we set the node's data portion to null.

Like getFront, dequeue is an O(1) operation:

```
public T dequeue()
{
    T front = getFront(); // Might throw EmptyQueueException
    assert !isEmpty();
    queueNode.setData(null);
    queueNode = queueNode.getNextNode();

    return front;
} // end dequeue
```

**11.24** **The rest of the class.** The methods `isEmpty` and `isChainFull` follow from the discussion in Segment 11.19:

```java
public boolean isEmpty()
{
   return queueNode == freeNode;
} // end isEmpty

private boolean isChainFull()
{
   return queueNode == freeNode.getNextNode();
} // end isChainFull
```

The method `clear` sets `queueNode` equal to `freeNode` to make the queue appear empty. It retains all nodes currently in the chain. However, unless you set the data portions of these nodes to `null`, the objects in the queue are not deallocated. We leave the implementation of `clear` as an exercise.

**Question 7** Describe two different ways in which you could implement the method `clear`.

**11.25** **Choosing a linked implementation.** So far, we have discussed several possible linked implementations of the ADT queue. You can use a linear chain with both head and tail references, as shown in Figure 11-1, or an equivalent circular chain with one external reference, as shown in Figure 11-11. In both of these implementations, removing an entry from the queue disconnects and deallocates a node in the chain. If, after removing entries from the queue, you seldom add entries, these implementations are fine. But if you frequently add an entry after removing one, the two-part circular chain saves the time of deallocating and reallocating nodes.

# Java Class Library: The Class **AbstractQueue**

**11.26** The standard package `java.util` in the Java Class Library contains the abstract class `AbstractQueue`. This class implements the interface `java.util.Queue` and does not allow `null` entries in the queue. Recall from Segment 10.13 of the previous chapter the following methods in this interface:

```java
public boolean add(T newEntry)
public boolean offer(T newEntry)
public T remove()
public T poll()
public T element()
public T peek()
public boolean isEmpty()
public void clear()
public int size()
```

`AbstractQueue` provides implementations of the methods `add`, `remove`, and `element` that invoke `offer`, `poll`, and `peek`, respectively.

You can define a class of queues by using inheritance to extend `AbstractQueue`. Your class must override at least the following methods: `offer`, `poll`, `peek`, and `size`. Note that the class `java.util.PriorityQueue`, which we mentioned in the previous chapter, extends `AbstractQueue` and, thereby, implements the methods declared in the interface `java.util.Queue`.

To learn more about `AbstractQueue`, consult the online documentation for the Java Class Library.

# A Doubly Linked Implementation of a Deque

**11.27** Earlier, in Segment 11.1, we planned the linked implementation of the queue and noticed that the front of the queue should not be at the tail of the chain of linked nodes. If it were, we would have to traverse the chain to get a reference to the preceding node so that we could remove the queue's front entry.

Although placing the front of the queue at the head of the chain solved our problem, such is not the case for a deque. We must be able to remove both the front *and* the back of a deque. So even if the deque's front is at the head of the chain, the deque's back will be at the chain's tail—and therein lies the problem.

Each node in a chain references only the next node. Thus, a chain, with its head reference, permits us to begin at the first node and move ahead from node to node. Having a tail reference lets us access the last node in the chain, but not the next-to-last node. That is, we cannot move backward from a node, and this is just what we need to do to remove the back of a deque.

**11.28** What we need is a node that can reference the previous node as well as the next node in a chain. We call a chain of such nodes a **doubly linked chain**. We sometimes will call an ordinary chain a **singly linked chain** when a distinction is necessary. Figure 11-16 illustrates a doubly linked chain with its head and tail references. While an interior node references both the next node and the previous node, the first and last nodes each contain one `null` reference. Thus, when traversing the chain from the first node to the last, we will encounter `null` when we reach the last node. Likewise, when traversing the chain from the last node to the first, we will encounter `null` when we reach the first node.

**FIGURE 11-16** A doubly linked chain with head and tail references

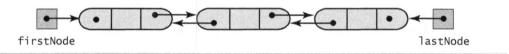

firstNode                                                                    lastNode

The node in a doubly linked chain is an instance of an inner class similar to the class `Node`. We will call this inner class `DLNode` and give it three data fields: `next` and `previous` are references to two other nodes, and `data` is a reference to the node's data. `DLNode` also has the methods `getData`, `setData`, `getNextNode`, `setNextNode`, `getPreviousNode`, and `setPreviousNode`.

**11.29** **An outline of the class.** The doubly linked implementation of the deque begins much like the linked implementation of the queue given in Segment 11.2. The class has two data fields—`firstNode` and `lastNode`—that the default constructor sets to `null`, as you can see in Listing 11-4.

---

**LISTING 11-4   An outline of a linked implementation of the ADT deque**

```
1  /**
2     A class that implements a deque of objects by using
3     a chain of doubly linked nodes.
4     @author Frank M. Carrano
5  */
6  public final class LinkedDeque<T> implements DequeInterface<T>
7  {
8     private DLNode firstNode; // References node at front of deque
9     private DLNode lastNode;  // References node at back of deque
10
11    public LinkedDeque()
12    {
13       firstNode = null;
14       lastNode = null;
15    } // end default constructor
16
17    < Implementations of the deque operations go here. >
18    . . .
19    private class DLNode
20    {
21       private T      data;      // Deque entry
22       private DLNode next;      // Link to next node
23       private DLNode previous;  // Link to previous node
24
25       < Constructors and the methods getData, setData, getNextNode, setNextNode,
26         getPreviousNode, and setPreviousNode are here. >
27       . . .
28    } // end DLNode
29  } // end LinkedDeque
```

---

**11.30**   **Adding an entry.** The implementation of the method `addToBack` is like the implementation of enqueue given in Segment 11.3. Both methods add a node to the end of a chain so that the chain's current last node references the new node. Here, we also make the new node reference the current last node by passing the deque's data field `lastNode` to the node's constructor. The addition to the back of a chain that is not empty is illustrated in Figure 11-17. An implementation of the method follows:

```
public void addToBack(T newEntry)
{
   DLNode newNode = new DLNode(lastNode, newEntry, null);

   if (isEmpty())
      firstNode = newNode;
   else
      lastNode.setNextNode(newNode);

   lastNode = newNode;
} // end addToBack
```

Aside from its name, this method differs from enqueue only in the statement that allocates a new node. Note that the constructor for `DLNode` has the parameters `previousNode`, `nodeData`, and `nextNode` in that order.

FIGURE 11-17    Adding to the back of a nonempty deque: (a) after the new
node is allocated; (b) after the addition is complete

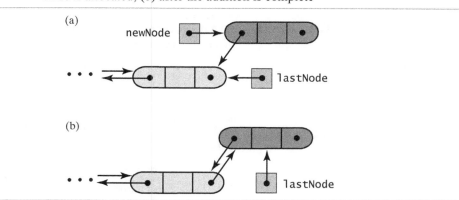

The method addToFront has an analogous implementation. When adding a node to the beginning of a doubly linked chain, we must make the chain's current first node reference the new node
by passing the deque's data field firstNode to the node's constructor. Compare the following
definition for addToFront with the one just given for addToBack:

```java
public void addToFront(T newEntry)
{
    DLNode newNode = new DLNode(null, newEntry, firstNode);

    if (isEmpty())
        lastNode = newNode;
    else
        firstNode.setPreviousNode(newNode);

    firstNode = newNode;
} // end addToFront
```

As given here, both addToFront and addToBack are O(1) operations.

**11.31**    **Removing an entry.** The method removeFront has an implementation much like that of dequeue
given in Segment 11.5, but it must perform one other step. After detaching the first node, if the
deque is not empty, removeFront must set the field previous in the new first node to null. This
step occurs in the else clause of the following definition:

```java
public T removeFront()
{
    T front = getFront(); // Might throw EmptyQueueException

    assert firstNode != null;

    firstNode = firstNode.getNextNode();

    if (firstNode == null)
        lastNode = null;
    else
        firstNode.setPreviousNode(null);

    return front;
} // end removeFront
```

Aside from its name, this method differs from dequeue only in the addition of the else clause. Figure 11-18 illustrates the effect of removeFront for a deque of at least two entries.

FIGURE 11-18     (a) A deque containing at least two entries; (b) after removing the first node and obtaining a reference to the deque's new first entry

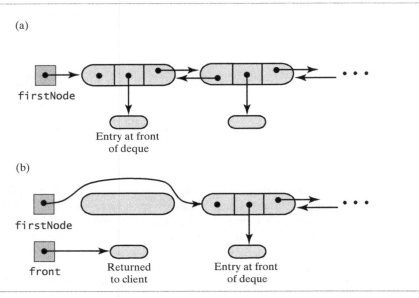

(a)

firstNode

Entry at front
of deque

(b)

firstNode

front          Returned          Entry at front
               to client         of deque

The method removeBack has an analogous definition:

```
public T removeBack()
{
    T back = getBack(); // Might throw EmptyQueueException;
    assert lastNode != null;
    lastNode = lastNode.getPreviousNode();

    if (lastNode == null)
        firstNode = null;
    else
        lastNode.setNextNode(null);
    return back;
} // end removeBack
```

The implementations of removeFront and removeBack are each O(1).

**11.32**  **Retrieving an entry.** The method getFront has the same implementation as given in Segment 11.4 for a queue. The method getBack is analogous to getFront and is left as an exercise. Both getFront and getBack are O(1) operations.

**Question 8** Implement the method getBack for the ADT deque when a doubly linked chain contains the deque's entries.

**11.33**  **Reusing this implementation.** Once you have implemented the ADT deque, you can use it to implement other ADTs such as the queue and the stack. These implementations are straightforward and are left as exercises.

**Note:** In a doubly linked chain, the first and last nodes each contain one `null` reference, since the first node has no previous node and the last node has no node after it. In a **circular doubly linked chain**, the first node references the last node, and the last node references the first. Only one external reference is necessary—a reference to the first node—since you can quickly get to the last node from the first node. You can use a circular doubly linked chain in an implementation of the ADT deque. Project 9 asks you to do this.

## Possible Implementations of a Priority Queue

**11.34**   We can use an array, a linked chain, or a vector to implement the ADT priority queue. In each of these cases, we would maintain the entries in sorted order by their priorities. With an array, the entry with the highest priority should occur at the end of the array, so removing it would leave the other entries in their present places. Figure 11-19a illustrates this implementation.

If a linked chain contains the entries in a priority queue, the entry with the highest priority should occur at the beginning of the chain, where it is easy to remove. Figure 11-19b shows such a chain.

The next chapter will introduce the ADT list, and Chapter 16 will discuss a kind of list called the sorted list. A sorted list can maintain a priority queue's entries in priority order, doing much of the work for us. Project 10 at the end of Chapter 16 asks you to complete such an implementation.

Chapter 23 describes a more efficient implementation of a priority queue that uses an ADT called a heap.

**FIGURE 11-19**   Two possible implementations of a priority queue using (a) an array; (b) a chain of linked nodes

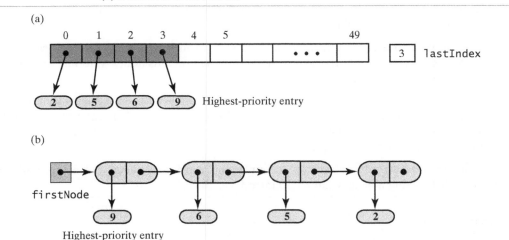

## CHAPTER SUMMARY

- You can implement a queue by using a chain of linked nodes that has both a head reference and a tail reference. The first node in the chain represents the front of the queue, because you can remove or access a chain's first node faster than any other node. The tail reference allows you to quickly add a node to the end of the chain, which is the queue's back.

- The queue operations are O(1) for a linked implementation.

- You can implement a queue by using an array. Once a queue entry is added to the array, it does not move. After many additions, the last array location will be used. Removals, however, will free locations at the beginning of the array. Thus, the array can appear full even when it is not. To solve this problem, you treat the array as if it were circular.

- The queue operations are O(1) for an array-based implementation. However, when the array is full, enqueue doubles the size of the array. In that case, enqueue is O(n). Typically, we amortize the cost of resizing the array over all additions to the queue. If the array is resized occasionally, each enqueue is almost O(1).

- In a circular linked chain, every node references the next node in the chain. No node contains null in its next field. A circular linked chain can have a beginning and an end. Since the last node references the first node in the chain, one external reference to the last node provides convenient access to both the chain's last node and its first node.

- You can use a circular linked chain to implement a queue in much the same way that you use a linear linked chain that has both head and tail references. With both kinds of chain, dequeue removes a node and deallocates it.

- Another implementation of a queue uses a circular linked chain that has two parts. One part is used for the queue and the other part contains one unused node and any nodes that are available for use. In this implementation, dequeue removes an entry from the queue but does not remove a node from the chain. Instead, the node joins the available part of the chain.

- Since a deque has operations that add and remove entries at both ends, you can use a doubly linked chain whose nodes reference both the next node and the previous node. A doubly linked chain with head and tail references provides O(1) implementations of the deque operations.

- In a circular doubly linked chain, every node references the next node as well as the previous node in the chain. No node contains null in its next and previous fields. One external reference to the first node provides fast access to both the chain's last node and its first node. You can use a circular doubly linked chain in the implementation of a deque.

- You can use an array or a chain to implement a priority queue, but a more efficient implementation is possible by using a heap. Chapter 23 introduces the ADT heap.

## PROGRAMMING TIP

- When a circular linked chain has one node, the node must reference itself. Forgetting this step is easy to do and leads to an error during execution.

## EXERCISES

1. Segment 11.15 defines the private method `ensureCapacity` for an array-based implementation of the ADT queue. Revise that method to use the method `System.arraycopy` to copy the old array to a new expanded array.

2. Segment 11.24 describes an implementation of the queue's method `clear` when a two-part circular linked chain represents the queue. Write two different implementations of `clear`. One version should repeatedly invoke `dequeue`. The other version should set the data portion of each node in the queue to `null`.

3. Suppose that we want to add a method to a class of queues that will splice two queues together. This method adds to the end of a queue all items that are in a second queue. The header of the method could be as follows:

   ```
   public void splice(QueueInterface<T> anotherQueue)
   ```

   Write this method in such a way that it will work in any class that implements `QueueInterface<T>`.

4. Consider the method `splice` that Exercise 3 describes. Implement this method specifically for the class `ArrayQueue`. Take advantage of your ability to manipulate the array representation of the queue.

5. Consider a method similar to the method `splice` that Exercise 3 describes. Implement this method for a class of deque that will splice two deques together by adding to the front of one deque all items of the second deque.

6. Using Big Oh notation, describe the time complexity of each queue operation in the class `LinkedQueue`. Briefly explain your answers.

7. Using Big Oh notation, describe the time complexity of each operation in the class `TwoPartCircularLinkedQueue`. Briefly explain your answers.

8. Implement the `addToBack` and `removeFront` methods of deque by using an ADT queue to contain the entries.

9. Implement the ADT stack by using an ADT queue to contain its entries.

10. Implement the `addToBack` and `removeFront` methods of deque that use two stacks, and comment on their efficiency.

11. Implement the ADT queue by using a vector to contain its entries.

12. Consider an application that uses a priority queue. You have two implementations available. One implementation uses an array to maintain the entries in the priority queue, while the other uses a linked chain. Compare the performances of these implementations for each of the following sequences of operations on a priority queue.

    **a.** Insert 100 objects having the priorities 1, 2, 3,..., 99, 100.
    **b.** Insert 100 objects having priorities 100, 99, 98,...., 2, 1.
    **c.** Add 100 objects having random priorities within the range 1 to 100.
    **d.** Starting with 100 objects in the priority queue having priorities 1 through 100, remove them all.
    **e.** Starting with 100 objects in the priority queue having priorities 1 through 100, repeat the following pair of operations 1000 times:
    - Add an item having a random priority within the range 1 to 100.
    - Remove an item.

## PROJECTS

1. Use an instance of the standard class `Vector` to implement the queue. How does this implementation compare with the array-based approach given in this chapter?

2. Use a circular array, as described in Segments 11.8 and 11.9, to implement the queue. Count entries to ascertain whether the queue is empty or full.

**3.** The implementation of the ADT queue that was introduced in Segment 11.10 uses a circular array with one unused location. Revise that implementation so that the unused location is always before the front of the queue, with `frontIndex` as the index of this unused location. Let `backIndex` be the index of the entry at the back of the queue. Initially, both `frontIndex` and `backIndex` are set to the maximum size of the queue (the array will be 1 larger than this number). You can distinguish an empty queue from a full queue by examining these indices. What tests should you perform to do so?

**4.** The array-based implementations of the ADT queue in this chapter used a circular array. One implementation counted the entries in the queue, while the other left one location in the array unused. We used these strategies to tell when the queue was empty and when it was full.

A third strategy is possible. It does not count and does not have an unused location in the circular array. After initializing `frontIndex` to 0 and `backIndex` to −1, you do not use modulo arithmetic when you increment these fields. Instead, you use modulo arithmetic when you index the array, but without changing `frontIndex` and `backIndex`. Thus, if queue is the array, `queue[frontIndex % queue.length]` is the front entry, and the entry at the back of the queue is `queue[backIndex % queue.length]`.

Now if `backIndex` is less than `frontIndex`, the queue is empty. The number of entries in the queue is `backIndex - frontIndex + 1`. You can compare this number with the size of the array to see whether the array is full.

Since `frontIndex` and `backIndex` can continue to grow, they might become too large to represent. To reduce the chance of this happening, set `frontIndex` to 0 and `backIndex` to −1 whenever the implementation detects an empty queue. Note that adding to a full queue invokes `ensureCapacity`, which sets `frontIndex` to 0 and `backIndex` to the index of the entry at the back of the queue.

Complete this array-based implementation of the ADT queue.

**5.** Implement the ADT queue by using a circular linked chain, as shown in Figure 11-11. Recall that this chain has only an external reference to its last node.

**6.** Consider a new kind of queue that allows only a single copy of an object in the queue. If an object is added to the queue, but it is already there, leave the queue unchanged. This queue has another operation `moveToBack` that takes an object in the queue and moves it to the back. If an object is not in the queue, the operation adds it at the back of the queue.

Create an interface `NoDuplicatesQueueInterface` that extends `QueueInterface`. Then write an array-based implementation of `NoDuplicatesQueueInterface`. Finally, write a program that adequately demonstrates your new class.

**7.** Implement the ADT deque by using an array to contain its entries. Expand the array dynamically when necessary.

**8.** One difficulty with implementing the doubly linked chain described in Segment 11.28 is the number of special cases that occur at the beginning and end of the chain. You can eliminate these cases if the chain is never empty. Thus, you begin each chain with a **dummy node** that you do not use for data.

Revise the implementation of the deque given in this chapter by using a dummy node.

**9.** Use a circular doubly linked chain (see the note at the end of Segment 11.33) to implement the ADT deque.

**10.** Repeat the previous project, but add a dummy node to the chain, as Project 8 describes.

**11.** In Project 6 you created a queue that does not allow duplicates. In this project you will create a deque that does not allow duplicates. The function of the deque's operations `addToBack` and `addToFront` should be analogous to the changed `enqueue` method in Project 6. Add two operations, `moveToBack` and `moveToFront`.

Create an interface `NoDuplicatesDequeInterface` that extends `DequeInterface`. Then write a linked implementation of `NoDuplicatesDequeInterface`. Finally, write a program that adequately demonstrates your new class.

**12.** Implement the ADT priority queue by using an array, as pictured in Figure 11-19a.

**13.** Implement the ADT priority queue by using a chain of linked nodes, as pictured in Figure 11-19b.

**14.** Revise the interface for the ADT priority queue, as given in Segment 10.19 of the previous chapter, by replacing the method add with the following method:

```
public void add(T newEntry, Comparable<? super T> priorityValue)
```

The client provides an entry and its priority value to this method. The priority queue does not use newEntry's compareTo method to assess its priority. Implement this version of the priority queue.

**15.** In Project 6 you created a queue that does not allow duplicates. In this project you will create a priority queue that does not allow duplicates. The function of the add operation should be analogous to the changed enqueue method in Project 6. In this case, the test for equals should not include the priority, so the header of the add method should be changed to the one given in the previous project. A new operation move will change the priority of a given item, if it is already in the priority queue. If the item is not in the priority queue, move will add it with the given priority.

Create an interface for a priority queue that does not allow duplicates. Then write a class that implements this interface. Finally, write a program that adequately demonstrates your new class.

**16.** Implement a priority queue of queues, as described in Project 6 of the previous chapter.

**17.** The ADT *randomized queue* is like a queue, but the removal and retrieval operations involve an entry chosen at random instead of the entry at the beginning of the queue. These operations should return null if they encounter an empty randomized queue.

    **a.** Write a Java interface that specifies the methods for a randomized queue. Name the retrieval operation get instead of getFront.

    **b.** Define a class of randomized queues, named RandomizedQueue, that implements the interface you created in Part *a*.

## ANSWERS TO SELF-TEST QUESTIONS

**1.** The back of the queue is at the end of the chain. Since you add to the back of a queue, you need to add a node to the end of the chain. A tail reference allows you to do this without first traversing the chain to locate its last node. Thus, a tail reference enables an efficient enqueue operation.

**2.** Entries in a bag are in no particular order within the bag and, thus, the array. Queue entries have an order relative to one another that must be maintained.

**3.**
```
public void clear()
{
    checkInitialization();
    if (!isEmpty())
    {
        for (int index = frontIndex; index != backIndex;
            index = (index + 1) % queue.length)
        {
            queue[index] = null;
        } // end for

        queue[backIndex] = null;
    } // end if

    frontIndex = 0;
    backIndex = queue.length - 1;
} // end clear
```

4. 
```java
public void clear()
{
    while (!isEmpty())
        dequeue();
} // end clear
```

This version of `clear` is easier to write than the version given in Question 3.

5. Each `enqueue` operation needs to move all of the entries in the queue to vacate `queue[0]` before it adds a new entry.

6. You place the new entry into the node that `freeNode` currently references. You then insert a new node after that node and make `freeNode` reference the new node. The new node is now the unused node.

7. You can repeatedly call `dequeue` until the queue is empty, as in the answer to Question 4. Or you can set the data fields of each node in the queue to `null` and then set `queueNode` equal to `freeNode`.

8. 
```java
public T getBack()
{
    if (isEmpty())
        throw new EmptyQueueException();
    else
        return lastNode.getData();
} // end getBack
```

## Contents

## Prerequisites

## Objectives

After studying this chapter, you should be able to

- Describe the ADT list
- Use the ADT list in a Java program

$\mathbf{A}$ list provides a way to organize data. We can have to-do lists, gift lists, address lists, grocery lists, even lists of lists. These lists provide a useful way for us to organize our lives, as illustrated in Figure 12-1. Each list has a first item, a last item, and usually items in between. That is, the items in a list have a position: first, second, and so on. An item's position might be important to you, or it might not. When adding an item to your list, you might always add it at the end, or you might insert it between two other items already in the list.

A **list** is a collection, and this chapter formalizes it as an ADT.

---

**FIGURE 12-1**    A to-do list

---

## Specifications for the ADT List

**12.1**   Everyday lists such as to-do lists, gift lists, address lists, and grocery lists have entries that are strings. What can you do to such lists?

- Typically, you **add** a new entry **at the end** of the list.
- Actually, you can **add** a new entry **anywhere**: at the beginning, at the end, or in between items.
- You can cross out an entry—that is, **remove** it.
- You can **remove all** entries.
- You can **replace** an entry.
- You can **look at** any entry.
- You can **look at all** of the entries.
- You can find out whether the list **contains** a particular entry.
- You can **count** the number of entries in the list.
- You can see whether the list is **empty**.

When you work with a list, you determine where an entry is or should be. You probably are not conscious of its exact position: Is it tenth? Fourteenth? However, when your program uses a list, a convenient way to identify a particular entry is by the entry's position within the list. It could be first, that is, at position 1, or second (position 2), and so on. This convention allows you to describe, or specify, the operations on a list more precisely.

**VideoNote**
**The ADT list**

**12.2**   To specify the ADT list, we describe its data and specify the operations on that data. Unlike common lists whose entries are strings, the ADT list is more general and has entries that are objects of the same type. The following is an initial specification of the ADT list:

add(newEntry): Adds a new entry to the end of a list.
add(newPosition, newEntry): Adds a new entry at a given position in a list.
remove(givenPosition): Removes the entry at a given position from a list.
clear(): Removes all entries from a list.
replace(givenPosition, newEntry): Replaces the entry at a given position in a list with a given entry.

getEntry(givenPosition): Retrieves the entry at a given position in a list.
toArray(): Retrieves all entries in a list in their current order.
contains(anEntry): Sees whether a list contains a given entry.
getLength(): Gets the number of entries in a list.
isEmpty(): Sees whether a list is empty.

We have only begun to specify the behaviors of these list operations, as the descriptions just given leave some details to the imagination. Some examples will help us to better understand these operations so that we can improve the specifications. We'll need precise specifications before we implement the operations.

**12.3**

**Example.** When you first declare a new list, it is empty and its length is zero. If you add three objects—a, b, and c—one at a time and in the order given, to the end of the list, the list will appear as

a

b

c

The object a is first, at position 1, b is at position 2, and c is last at position 3.[1] To save space here, we will sometimes write a list's contents on one line. For example, we might write

a  b  c

to represent this list.

The following pseudocode represents the previous three additions to the specific list myList:

```
myList.add(a)
myList.add(b)
myList.add(c)
```

At this point, myList is not empty, so myList.isEmpty() is false. Since the list contains three entries, myList.getLength() is 3. Notice that adding entries to the end of a list does not change the positions of entries already in the list. Figure 12-2 illustrates these add operations as well as the operations that we describe next.

---

**FIGURE 12-2**    The effect of ADT list operations on an initially empty list

---

myList.add(a)

a

myList.add(b)

a
b

myList.add(c)

a
b
c

myList.add(2,d)

a
d
b
c

myList.add(1,e)

e
a
d
b
c

myList.remove(3)

e
a
b
c

---

1. Some people number the entries in a list beginning with 0 instead of 1.

**12.4**    Now suppose that we add entries at various positions within the list a b c. For example,

    myList.add(2, d)

places d second—that is, at position 2—within the list. Doing so, however, moves b to position 3 and c to position 4, so that the list now contains

    a d b c

If we add e to the beginning of the list by writing

    myList.add(1, e)

the current entries in the list move to the next higher position. The list then contains

    e a d b c

Look at Figure 12-2 again to see the effect of these operations.

**12.5**    We can get the second entry in this list by writing

    entry2 = myList.getEntry(2)

Remember that we are writing pseudocode here and ignoring details such as semicolons.
        What happens when we remove an entry? For example,

    myList.remove(3)

removes the third entry—d in the previous example—from the list. The list then contains

    e a b c

Notice that entries after the one that was removed move to the next lower position within the list. Figure 12-2 on the previous page illustrates this change to the list.

**12.6**    What if an application requires us to remove an entry from a list but retain the entry for another purpose? Our specification of remove would force us to first use getEntry to obtain the entry and then use remove to remove it from the list. We could refine the specification of remove to return the object removed from the list. To use this revised version of remove, we would write a pseudocode statement such as

    oldEntry3 = myList.remove(3)

This change makes remove more versatile, as the client could either save or ignore the returned entry.
        We can replace the third entry b of our list with f by writing

    myList.replace(3, f)

No other entries move or change. We could refine the specification of replace to return the object that was replaced. So if we wrote

    ref = myList.replace(3, f)

ref would reference the former entry b.

 **Note:** The objects in an ADT list have an order determined by the client of the list. To add, remove, or retrieve an entry, you must specify the entry's position within the list. The first entry in the list is at position 1.

**12.7**    The previous specifications and examples ignore some difficulties that might arise during the use of the ADT list:

- The operations add, remove, replace, and getEntry are well behaved when the given position is valid for the current list. What happens when one of these operations receives an invalid position number?
- The methods remove, replace, and getEntry are not meaningful for empty lists. What happens when an empty list executes one of these operations?

As usual, we must decide how to handle these conditions and refine our specifications. The documentation for the ADT list should reflect both these decisions and the detail that the previous examples demonstrate.

As a reminder, we repeat the following note from Chapter 1.

 **Note:** A first draft of an ADT's specifications often overlooks or ignores situations that you really need to consider. You might intentionally make these omissions to simplify this first draft. Once you have written the major portions of the specifications, you can concentrate on the details that make the specifications complete.

**12.8**   We now summarize and refine our description of the ADT list in light of our previous discussion.

| ABSTRACT DATA TYPE: LIST | | |
| --- | --- | --- |
| **DATA** | | |
| • A collection of objects in a specific order and having the same data type<br>• The number of objects in the collection | | |
| **OPERATIONS** | | |
| **PSEUDOCODE** | **UML** | **DESCRIPTION** |
| add(newEntry) | +add(newEntry: T): void | Task: Adds newEntry to the end of the list.<br>Input: newEntry is an object.<br>Output: None. |
| add(newPosition, newEntry) | +add(newPosition: integer, newEntry: T): void | Task: Adds newEntry at position newPosition within the list. Position 1 indicates the first entry in the list.<br>Input: newPosition is an integer, newEntry is an object.<br>Output: Throws an exception if newPosition is invalid for this list before the operation. |
| remove(givenPosition) | +remove(givenPosition: integer): T | Task: Removes and returns the entry at position givenPosition.<br>Input: givenPosition is an integer.<br>Output: Either returns the removed entry or throws an exception if givenPosition is invalid for this list. Note that any value of givenPosition is invalid if the list is empty before the operation. |

| clear() | +clear(): void | Task: Removes all entries from the list.<br>Input: None.<br>Output: None. |
|---|---|---|
| replace(givenPosition,<br>        newEntry) | +replace(givenPosition: integer,<br>        newEntry: T): T | Task: Replaces the entry at position givenPosition with newEntry.<br>Input: givenPosition is an integer, newEntry is an object.<br>Output: Either returns the replaced entry or throws an exception if givenPosition is invalid for this list. Note that any value of givenPosition is invalid if the list is empty before the operation. |
| getEntry(givenPosition) | +getEntry(givenPosition: integer): T | Task: Retrieves the entry at position givenPosition.<br>Input: givenPosition is an integer.<br>Output: Either returns the entry at position givenPosition or throws an exception if givenPosition is invalid for this list. Note that any value of givenPosition is invalid if the list is empty before the operation. |
| toArray() | +toArray: T[] | Task: Retrieves all entries that are in the list in the order in which they occur.<br>Input: None.<br>Output: Returns a new array of the entries currently in the list. |
| contains(anEntry) | +contains(anEntry: T): boolean | Task: Sees whether the list contains anEntry.<br>Input: anEntry is an object.<br>Output: Returns true if anEntry is in the list, or false if not. |
| getLength() | +getLength(): integer | Task: Gets the number of entries currently in the list.<br>Input: None.<br>Output: Returns the number of entries currently in the list. |
| isEmpty() | +isEmpty(): boolean | Task: Sees whether the list is empty.<br>Input: None.<br>Output: Returns true if the list is empty, or false if not. |

**12.9**   The Java interface in Listing 12-1 contains the methods for an ADT list and detailed comments that describe their behaviors. These comments refine the specifications given in the previous segment. The items in the list will be objects of the same class or classes related by inheritance.

---

LISTING 12-1   The interface `ListInterface`

```
 1  /** An interface for the ADT list.
 2      Entries in a list have positions that begin with 1.
 3      @author Frank M. Carrano
 4  */
 5  public interface ListInterface<T>
 6  {
 7      /** Adds a new entry to the end of this list.
 8          Entries currently in the list are unaffected.
 9          The list's size is increased by 1.
10          @param newEntry  The object to be added as a new entry. */
11      public void add(T newEntry);
12
13      /** Adds a new entry at a specified position within this list.
14          Entries originally at and above the specified position
15          are at the next higher position within the list.
16          The list's size is increased by 1.
17          @param newPosition  An integer that specifies the desired
18                              position of the new entry.
19          @param newEntry     The object to be added as a new entry.
20          @throws  IndexOutOfBoundsException if either
21                   newPosition < 1 or newPosition > getLength() + 1. */
22      public void add(int newPosition, T newEntry);
23
24      /** Removes the entry at a given position from this list.
25          Entries originally at positions higher than the given
26          position are at the next lower position within the list,
27          and the list's size is decreased by 1.
28          @param givenPosition  An integer that indicates the position of
29                                the entry to be removed.
30          @return  A reference to the removed entry.
31          @throws  IndexOutOfBoundsException if either
32                   givenPosition < 1 or givenPosition > getLength(). */
33      public T remove(int givenPosition);
34
35      /** Removes all entries from this list. */
36      public void clear();
37
38      /** Replaces the entry at a given position in this list.
39          @param givenPosition  An integer that indicates the position of
40                                the entry to be replaced.
41          @param newEntry  The object that will replace the entry at the
42                           position givenPosition.
43          @return  The original entry that was replaced.
44          @throws  IndexOutOfBoundsException if either
45                   givenPosition < 1 or givenPosition > getLength(). */
46      public T replace(int givenPosition, T newEntry);
47
```

```
48    /** Retrieves the entry at a given position in this list.
49        @param givenPosition  An integer that indicates the position of
50                               the desired entry.
51        @return  A reference to the indicated entry.
52        @throws  IndexOutOfBoundsException if either
53                 givenPosition < 1 or givenPosition > getLength(). */
54    public T getEntry(int givenPosition);
55
56    /** Retrieves all entries that are in this list in the order in which
57        they occur in the list.
58        @return  A newly allocated array of all the entries in the list.
59                 If the list is empty, the returned array is empty. */
60    public T[] toArray();
61
62    /** Sees whether this list contains a given entry.
63        @param anEntry  The object that is the desired entry.
64        @return  True if the list contains anEntry, or false if not. */
65    public boolean contains(T anEntry);
66
67    /** Gets the length of this list.
68        @return  The integer number of entries currently in the list. */
69    public int getLength();
70
71    /** Sees whether this list is empty.
72        @return  True if the list is empty, or false if not. */
73    public boolean isEmpty();
74 } // end ListInterface
```

**Design Decision:** Who should decide what **toArray** does when the collection is empty?
The method toArray returns a newly allocated array that contains the entries in a collection.
When the collection is empty, the method could either

- Return an empty array, or
- Throw an exception

While either behavior can be reasonable, should the ADT's designer make the choice and document it in the interface, or should the designer ignore the situation and let the implementor of the interface make the decision?

When we wrote ListInterface in Listing 12-1, for example, we decided that toArray should return an empty array if the list is empty. Thus, any class that implements ListInterface must adhere to this decision. The result is that any client of such a class can be written with the knowledge of toArray's behavior. We can use any one of the classes in the client and get the same behavior.

Now suppose that toArray in ListInterface does not mention what happens when the list is empty. The programmer who writes a class that implements ListInterface can decide what toArray does in that case. Such implementations can behave differently from one another. For example, toArray in the class XList could throw an exception, while toArray in YList could return an empty array. Even if we clearly document the behavior of toArray within these classes, the client could not substitute one class for another without changing the use of toArray.

Our decision is to completely specify each method in an interface so that its implementations produce the same behaviors.

**Question 1** Write pseudocode statements that add some objects to a list, as follows. First add c, then a, then b, and then d, such that the order of the objects in the list will be a, b, c, d.

**Question 2** Write pseudocode statements that exchange the third and seventh entries in a list of 10 objects.

**Note:** The entries in a list of $n$ entries are numbered from 1 to $n$. Although you cannot add a new entry at position 0, you can add one at position $n + 1$.

## Using the ADT List

**VideoNote**
**Using the ADT list**

Imagine that we hire a programmer to implement the ADT list in Java, given the interface and specifications that we have developed so far. If we assume that these specifications are clear enough for the programmer to complete the implementation, we can use the ADT's operations in a program without knowing the details of the implementation. That is, we do not need to know *how* the programmer implemented the list to be able to use it. We only need to know *what* the ADT list does.

This section assumes that we have an implementation for the list and demonstrates how we can use a list in our program. The examples here can be part of a program that tests your implementation.

12.10     **Example.** Imagine that we are organizing a local road race. Our job is to note the order in which the runners finish the race. Since each runner wears a distinct identifying number, we can add each runner's number to the end of a list as the runners cross the finish line. Figure 12-3 illustrates such a list.

FIGURE 12-3    A list of numbers that identify runners in the order in which they finished a race

The Java program in Listing 12-2 shows how we can perform this task by using the ADT list. It assumes that the class AList implements the Java interface ListInterface that you saw in the previous section. Since ListInterface assumes that the items in the list are objects, we will treat each runner's identifying number as a string.

---

**LISTING 12-2    A client of a class that implements ListInterface**

```
1  public class ListClient
2  {
3     public static void main(String[] args)
4     {
5        testList();
6     } // end main
7
8     public static void testList()
9     {
10       ListInterface<String> runnerList = new AList<>();
11    // runnerList has only methods in ListInterface
12
13       runnerList.add("16"); // Winner
14       runnerList.add(" 4"); // Second place
15       runnerList.add("33"); // Third place
16       runnerList.add("27"); // Fourth place
17       displayList(runnerList);
18    } // end testList
19
20    public static void displayList(ListInterface<String> list)
21    {
22       int numberOfEntries = list.getLength();
23       System.out.println("The list contains " + numberOfEntries +
24                        " entries, as follows:");
25
26       for (int position = 1; position <= numberOfEntries; position++)
27          System.out.println(list.getEntry(position) +
28                          " is entry " + position);
29
30       System.out.println();
31    } // end displayList
32 } // end ListClient
```

**Output**

```
The list contains 4 entries, as follows:
16 is entry 1
 4 is entry 2
33 is entry 3
27 is entry 4
```

---

The data type of displayList's input parameter list is ListInterface<String>. Thus, the argument of the method must be an object that satisfies both of the following conditions:

- The object's class must implement ListInterface.
- The object must be instantiated as a list of strings.

Although the method works for any implementation of the ADT list, it works only for lists of strings. You could remove the latter restriction by revising the header of the method as follows:

**public static** <T> **void** displayList(ListInterface<T> list)

Now the list passed to the method can contain objects of any one class.

> **Note: A reminder**
> Notice that the data type of runnerList is ListInterface<String>. This declaration obliges runnerList to call only methods in the interface and to add only strings to the list. If the data type was AList<String> instead, runnerList would be able to call any public methods in AList even if they were not declared in ListInterface.

**Question 3** In the previous example, what changes to the method testList are necessary to represent the runner's numbers as Integer objects instead of strings? Use Java's auto-boxing feature, as described in Segment B.99 of Appendix B.

---

**12.11**

**Example.** A professor wants an alphabetical list of the names of the students who arrive for class today. As each student enters the room, the professor adds the student's name to a list. It is up to the professor to place each name into its correct position in the list so that the names will be in alphabetical order. The ADT list does *not* choose the order of its entries.

The following Java statements place the names Amy, Ellen, Bob, Drew, Aaron, and Carol in an alphabetical list. The comment at the end of each statement shows the list after the statement executes.

```
// Make an alphabetical list of names as students enter a room
ListInterface<String> alphaList = new AList<>();
alphaList.add(1, "Amy");     // Amy
alphaList.add(2, "Ellen");   // Amy Ellen
alphaList.add(2, "Bob");     // Amy Bob Ellen
alphaList.add(3, "Drew");    // Amy Bob Drew Ellen
alphaList.add(1, "Aaron");   // Aaron Amy Bob Drew Ellen
alphaList.add(4, "Carol");   // Aaron Amy Bob Carol Drew Ellen
```

After initially adding Amy to the beginning of the list and Ellen to the end of the list (at position 2), the professor inserts

- Bob between Amy and Ellen at position 2
- Drew between Bob and Ellen at position 3
- Aaron before Amy at position 1
- Carol between Bob and Drew at position 4

Recall from Chapter 8 that this technique of inserting each name into a collection of alphabetized names is called an insertion sort.

If we now remove the entry at position 4—Carol—by writing

```
alphaList.remove(4);
```

Drew and Ellen will then be at positions 4 and 5, respectively. Thus, alphaList.getEntry(4) would return a reference to Drew.

Finally, suppose that we want to replace a name in this list. We cannot replace a name with just any name and expect that the list will remain in alphabetical order. Replacing Bob with Ben by writing

```
alphaList.replace(3, "Ben");
```

would maintain alphabetical order, but replacing Bob with Nancy would not. The list's alphabetical order resulted from our original decisions about where to add names to the list. The order did not come about automatically as a result of list operations. That is, the client, not the list, maintained the order. We could, however, design an ADT that maintains its data in alphabetical order. You will see an example of such an ADT in Chapter 16.

**Question 4** Suppose that `alphaList` contains a list of the four names Amy, Ellen, Bob, and Drew as strings. Write Java statements that swap Ellen and Bob and that then swap Ellen and Drew so that the list will be in alphabetical order.

**12.12**  **Example.** Let's look at a list of objects that are not strings. Suppose that we have the class `Name` from Listing C-1 in Appendix C that represents a person's first and last names. The following statements indicate how we could make a list of the names Amy Smith, Tina Drexel, and Robert Jones:

```
// Make a list of names as you think of them
ListInterface<Name> nameList = new AList<>();
Name amy = new Name("Amy", "Smith");
nameList.add(amy);
nameList.add(new Name("Tina", "Drexel"));
nameList.add(new Name("Robert", "Jones"));
```

Now let's retrieve the name that is second in the list, Tina Drexel:

```
Name secondName = nameList.getEntry(2);
```

The definition of `getEntry` declares its return type as `T`, the generic type of the entries in the list. This type for `nameList` is `Name`, so `getEntry` returns a `Name` object.

**Question 5** Suppose that the return type of `getEntry` was `Object` instead of a generic type. Would this change affect how you use the method? In particular, would the statement in the previous example that retrieved the second name in `nameList` be correct? Why?

**12.13**  **Example.** Let's talk a bit more about the previous example. The variable `secondName` is a reference to the second object in the list. Using this reference, we can modify the object. For example, we could change its last name by writing

```
secondName.setLast("Doe");
```

If the class `Name` did not have set methods like `setLast`, we would be unable to modify the objects in this list. For instance, if we had a list of strings, we would not be able to alter one of the strings in this way. The class `String` has no set methods, so once we create a `String` object, we cannot alter it. We could, however, replace an entire object in the list—regardless of its type—by using the ADT list operation `replace`.

Recall that Chapter 10 mentioned mutable and immutable objects. Since the class Name has set methods, its objects are mutable. The class String, on the other hand, does not define set methods, so its objects are immutable.

## Java Class Library: The Interface List

**12.14**  The standard package java.util contains an interface List for an ADT list that is similar to the list that our interface describes. One difference between a list in the Java Class Library and our ADT list is the numbering of a list's entries. A list in the Java Class Library uses the same numbering scheme as a Java array: The first entry is at position, or index, 0. In contrast, we begin our list at position 1. The interface List also declares more methods than our interface does. You'll see a few of those additional methods in Java Interlude 5.

The following method headers from the interface List are for a selection of methods that are similar to the ones you have seen in this chapter. We have highlighted where they differ from our methods. Once again, T is the generic type of the entries in the list.

```java
public boolean add(T newEntry)
public void add(int index, T newEntry)
public T remove(int index)
public void clear()
public T set(int index, T anEntry) // Like replace
public T get(int index)           // Like getEntry
public boolean contains(Object anEntry)
public int size()                 // Like getLength
public boolean isEmpty()
```

The first add method, which adds an entry to the end of a list, returns a boolean value, whereas our analogous method is a void method. The method set is like our replace method, and the method get is like our method getEntry. The data type of contains' parameter is Object instead of a generic type. In practice, this difference has little consequence. Lastly, the method size is like our getLength.

You can learn more about the interface List in the online documentation for the Java Class Library.

## Java Class Library: The Class ArrayList

**12.15**  The Java Class Library contains an implementation of the ADT list that uses a resizable array. This class, called ArrayList, implements the interface java.util.List, that we just discussed. The class also is in the package java.util.

Two of the constructors available for ArrayList are as follows:

```java
public ArrayList()
```
Creates an empty list with an initial capacity of 10. The list increases its capacity as needed by an unspecified amount.

```java
public ArrayList(int initialCapacity)
```
Creates an empty list with the specified initial capacity. The list increases its capacity as needed by an unspecified amount.

**12.16** The class java.util.Vector, which we described in Chapter 6, is similar to ArrayList. Both classes implement the same interfaces: java.util.List, as well as others. Even so, Vector contains a few more methods than ArrayList. We will ignore these extra methods, as they mostly are redundant.

You can use either ArrayList or Vector as an implementation of the interface List. For example, you could write the following statement to define a list of strings:

```java
List<String> myList = new ArrayList<>();
```

Now myList has only the methods declared in the interface List.

Our ListInterface is somewhat simpler than Java's List, since it has fewer methods. We can retain the simplicity of our interface and still make use of an existing class by using either ArrayList or Vector in an implementation of ListInterface. The approach is like the one we used in Chapter 6 to implement the ADT stack. We leave the details for you as a programming project.

## CHAPTER SUMMARY

- A list is an object whose data consists of ordered entries. Each entry is identified by its position within the list.

- The ADT list specifies operations that add an entry either to the end of a list or at a given position within the list. Among its other operations are those that retrieve, remove, or replace the entry at a given position.

- A client manipulates or accesses a list's entries by using only the operations defined for the ADT list.

- The entries in a bag are unordered, whereas the entries in a list, a stack, a queue, a deque, or a priority queue do have an order. A list, unlike these other collections, enables you to add, retrieve, remove, or replace an entry at any given position.

## EXERCISES

1. If myList is an empty list of strings, what does it contain after the following statements execute?

```java
myList.add(1, "ten");
myList.add(1, "nine");
myList.add(1, "eight");
myList.add(1, "seven");
myList.add("W");
myList.add("X");
myList.add("Y");
myList.add("Z");
```

2. If myList is an empty list of strings, what does it contain after the following statements execute?

```java
myList.add("apple");
myList.add("mango");
myList.add(2, "banana");
myList.add(3, "orange");
myList.add(1, "kiwi");
myList.replace(3, "kiwi");
myList.remove(1);
myList.replace(1, "banana");
```

3. Revise the method displayList in Listing 12-2 so that it uses the list method replace to replace the string in the third position with "ABC" (assuming that there are at least three entries in the list).

**4.** Suppose that you want an operation for the ADT list that returns an object at a given position in the list. The header of the method could be as follows:

```
public T getObject(T aPos)
```

Write comments that specify this method.

**5.** Suppose that you want an operation for the ADT list that deletes the last occurrence of a given object from the list. The header of the method could be as follows:

```
public boolean delete(T anObject)
```

Write comments that specify this method.

**6.** Suppose that you want an operation for the ADT list that moves the third item in the list to the beginning of the list. The header of the method could be as follows:

```
public void moveToBeginning()
```

Write comments that specify this method.

**7.** Write Java statements at the client level that return the position of the second element from a given object in the list myList. Assume that the object is in the list.

**8.** Suppose that the ADT list did not have a method replace. Write Java statements at the client level that replace an object in the list nameList. The object's position in the list is givenPosition and the replacement object is newObject.

**9.** Suppose further that nameList is a list of Name objects, where Name is as defined in Listing C-1 of Appendix C. Write a Java method at the client level that checks whether the Name object myName is the first object in the list nameList.

**10.** Suppose that you have a list that is created by the following statement:

```
ListInterface<Student> studentList = new AList<>();
```

Imagine that someone has added to the list several instances of the class Student that Appendix D defined in Segment D.2.

    **a.** Write Java statements that display the last names of the students in the list in the same order in which the students appear in the list. Do not alter the list.

    **b.** Write Java statements that interchange the first and last students in the list.

**11.** Suppose that you have a list that is created by the following statement:

```
ListInterface<Double> assignmentScores = new AList<>();
```

Imagine that someone has added to this list the assignment scores received by a student throughout a course. The professor would like to know the sum of these assignment scores, ignoring the highest score.

    **a.** Write Java statements at the client level that will find and remove the highest score in the list.

    **b.** Write Java statements at the client level that will compute the sum of the scores remaining in the list.

**12.** Consider a class Coin that represents a coin. The class has methods such as getValue, toss, and isHeads. The method getValue returns the value, or denomination, of a coin. The method toss simulates a coin toss in which the coin lands either heads up or tails up. The method isHeads returns true if a coin is heads up.

Suppose that coinList is an ADT list of coins that have randomly selected denominations. Toss each of these coins. If the result of a coin toss is heads, move the coin to a second list called headsList; if it is tails, leave the coin in the original list. When you are finished tossing coins, compute the total value of the coins that came up heads. Assume that the list headsList has been created for you and is empty initially.

## PROJECTS

1. Using the standard class Vector, define a class of lists that implements the interface ListInterface, as defined in Listing 12-1 of this chapter.

2. Repeat the previous project, but use the class ArrayList instead of Vector.

3. Define a class of bags that implements the interface BagInterface, as defined in Listing 1-1 in Chapter 1. Use an instance of the class ArrayList to contain a bag's entries. Then write a program that adequately demonstrates your new class. Note that you might have to handle exceptions thrown by methods of ArrayList.

4. Repeat Project 3, but instead define a class of stacks that implements the interface StackInterface, as defined in Listing 5-1 in Chapter 5.

5. Repeat Project 3, but instead define a class of queues that implements the interface QueueInterface, as defined in Listing 10-1 in Chapter 10.

6. Repeat Project 3, but instead define a class of deques that implements the interface DequeInterface, as defined in Listing 10-4 in Chapter 10.

7. Repeat Project 3, but instead define a class of sets that implements the interface SetInterface, as defined in Listing 1-5 in Chapter 1. Recall that a set is a bag whose entries are distinct.

8. Santa Claus allegedly keeps lists of those who are naughty and those who are nice. On the naughty list are the names of those who will get coal in their stockings. On the nice list are those who will receive gifts. Each object in this list contains a name (an instance of Name, as defined in Listing C-1 of Appendix C) and a list of that person's gifts (an instance of an ADT list).

   Design an ADT for the objects in the nice list. Specify each ADT operation by stating its purpose, by describing its parameters, and by writing preconditions, postconditions, and a pseudocode version of its header. Then write a Java interface for the ADT that includes javadoc-style comments.

9. A recipe contains a title, a list of ingredients, and a list of directions. An entry in the list of ingredients contains an amount, a unit, and a description. For example, an object that represents *2 cups of flour* could be an entry in this list. An entry in the list of directions is a string.

   Design an ADT that represents any entry in a list of ingredients, assuming that you have the class MixedNumber, which was described in Project 6 of the Prelude. Then design another ADT to represent any recipe. Specify each ADT operation by stating its purpose, by describing its parameters, and by writing preconditions, postconditions, and a pseudocode version of its header. Then write a Java interface for the ADT that includes javadoc-style comments.

10. Define and test a class that implements the interface for the ADT recipe that the previous project describes. Use an instance of ArrayList for each list that you need. Using a text editor, create a text file of recipes for your demonstration program to read.

11. Repeat Project 7 of Chapter 4, but use an instance of ArrayList instead of a bag.

**12.** As early as the tenth century, mathematicians studied the following triangular pattern of integers, now known as *Pascal's Triangle*:

```
            1
          1   1
        1   2   1
      1   3   3   1
    1   4   6   4   1
            . . .
```

Despite the early advent of this pattern, it was named after the 17th-century mathematician Blaise Pascal.

Staggering the entries, as we have here, is traditional. Each row begins and ends with 1. Each interior entry is the sum of the two entries above it. For example, in the last row given here, 4 is the sum of 1 and 3, 6 is the sum of 3 and 3, and 4 is the sum of 3 and 1.

If we number both the rows and the entries in each row beginning with 0, the entry in position $k$ of row $n$ is often denoted as $C(n, k)$. For example, the 6 in the last row is $C(4, 2)$. Given $n$ items, $C(n, k)$ turns out to be the number of ways that you can select $k$ of the $n$ items. Thus, $C(4, 2)$, which is 6, is the number of ways that you can select two of four given items. So if A, B, C, and D are the four items, here are the six possible choices:

A B, A C, A D, B C, B D, C D

Note that the order of the items in each pair is irrelevant. For instance, the choice A B is the same as the choice B A.

Design and implement the class `PascalTriangle`. Represent each row in a triangle as a list and the entire triangle as a list of these lists. Use the class `ArrayList` for these lists. Include constructors in your class and at least the method `getChoices(n, k)`, which returns the integer value of $C(n, k)$.

## ANSWERS TO SELF-TEST QUESTIONS

**1.**
```
myList.add(c)
myList.add(1, a)
myList.add(2, b)
myList.add(4, d) or myList.add(d)
```

**2.**
```
seven = myList.remove(7)
three = myList.remove(3)
myList.add(3, seven)
myList.add(7, three)
```

Another solution:
```
seven = myList.getEntry(7)
three = myList.getEntry(3)
myList.replace(3, seven)
myList.replace(7, three)
```

**3.**
```
ListInterface<Integer> rList = new AList<>();
rList.add(16);
rList.add(4);
rList.add(33);
rList.add(27);
rList.displayList();
```

4.
```
bob = alphaList.remove(3);
ellen = alphaList.remove(2);
alphaList.add(2, bob);
alphaList.add(3, ellen);
drew = alphaList.remove(4);
ellen = alphaList.remove(3);
alphaList.add(3, drew);
alphaList.add(4, ellen);
```

Another solution uses getEntry and replace, much like the second solution to Question 2.

5. The change to getEntry would affect its use by requiring a cast to the type of entry retrieved. Thus, you would write

```
Name secondName = (Name)nameList.getEntry(2);
```

A similar statement without the type cast would be incorrect. A reference to Object cannot be assigned to a Name variable without a cast.

# A List Implementation That Uses an Array

## Chapter

# 13

## Contents

## Prerequisites

## Objectives

After studying this chapter, you should be able to

- Implement the ADT list by using an array that you can resize
- Discuss the advantages and disadvantages of the implementation presented

You have seen several examples of how to use the ADT list in a program. We now discuss different ways that you can implement a list in Java. This chapter uses an array to represent the entries in a list. As in earlier implementations of other ADTs, when you use all of the space in an array, you can move the data to a larger array. Although we leave it as a project, you could also use an instance of either of the Java classes ArrayList or Vector to represent the list entries. The result is like using an array that can expand, since the underlying implementations of ArrayList and Vector use such an array. Finally, the next chapter uses a chain of linked nodes. Because you can insert and remove entries at any position within a list, the array-based and linked implementations are a bit more challenging than the ADT implementations we have encountered previously.

**Question 2** What is an advantage of moving students as just described so that the vacated desk does not remain vacant?

**Question 3** What is an advantage of leaving the vacated desk vacant?

## The Java Implementation

**13.4** The Java array-based implementation for the ADT list incorporates some of the ideas that our classroom example illustrates. The implementation is a class `AList`[1] that implements the interface `ListInterface` that you saw in Chapter 12. Each public method within the class corresponds to an ADT list operation. The private data fields are

- An array of objects
- An integer that counts the number of entries in the list
- An integer constant that defines the default capacity of the list
- An integer constant that defines the maximum capacity of the list
- A boolean flag that indicates whether the list is properly initialized

We can describe the class using the UML notation shown in Figure 13-3, where T represents the data type of the entries in the list. We have added the data fields `MAX_CAPACITY` and `initialized` to assist with the class's security, as we have done with other classes in previous chapters.

**FIGURE 13-3** UML notation for the class `AList`

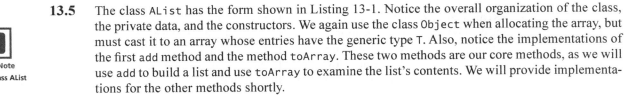

```
                        AList
─────────────────────────────────────────────────────
-list: T[]
-numberOfEntries: integer
-DEFAULT_CAPACITY: integer
-MAX_CAPACITY: integer
-initialized: boolean
─────────────────────────────────────────────────────
+add(newEntry: T): void
+add(newPosition: integer, newEntry: T): void
+remove(givenPosition: integer): T
+clear(): void
+replace(givenPosition: integer, newEntry: T): T
+getEntry(givenPosition: integer): T
+toArray(): T[]
+contains(anEntry: T): boolean
+getLength(): integer
+isEmpty(): boolean
```

**VideoNote**
**The class AList**

**13.5** The class `AList` has the form shown in Listing 13-1. Notice the overall organization of the class, the private data, and the constructors. We again use the class `Object` when allocating the array, but must cast it to an array whose entries have the generic type T. Also, notice the implementations of the first add method and the method `toArray`. These two methods are our core methods, as we will use add to build a list and use `toArray` to examine the list's contents. We will provide implementations for the other methods shortly.

---

1. Ordinarily we would name this class `ArrayList`. But as you saw in the previous chapter, Java already provides a class with that name. Although we certainly could have named our class `ArrayList` as well, we chose a different name to avoid confusion.

**Note:** The class AList will not be a final class, to allow its use as a base class in Chapter 17 when we discuss inheritance. The same will be true of the class LList that we will define in the next chapter.

**LISTING 13-1    The class AList**

```java
import java.util.Arrays;
/**
    A class that implements a list of objects by using an array.
    Entries in a list have positions that begin with 1.
    Duplicate entries are allowed.
    @author Frank M. Carrano
*/
public class AList<T> implements ListInterface<T>
{
    private T[] list;    // Array of list entries; ignore list[0]
    private int numberOfEntries;
    private boolean initialized = false;
    private static final int DEFAULT_CAPACITY = 25;
    private static final int MAX_CAPACITY = 10000;

    public AList()
    {
        this(DEFAULT_CAPACITY); // Call next constructor
    } // end default constructor

    public AList(int initialCapacity)
    {
        // Is initialCapacity too small?
        if (initialCapacity < DEFAULT_CAPACITY)
            initialCapacity = DEFAULT_CAPACITY;
        else // Is initialCapacity too big?
            checkCapacity(initialCapacity);

        // The cast is safe because the new array contains null entries
        @SuppressWarnings("unchecked")
        T[] tempList = (T[])new Object[initialCapacity + 1];
        list = tempList;
        numberOfEntries = 0;
        initialized = true;
    } // end constructor

    public void add(T newEntry)
    {
        checkInitialization();
        list[numberOfEntries + 1] = newEntry;
        numberOfEntries++;
        ensureCapacity();
    } // end add

    public void add(int newPosition, T newEntry)
    { < Implementation deferred >
    } // end add

    public T remove(int givenPosition)
    { < Implementation deferred >
    } // end remove
```

```
81
82      public void clear()
83      { < Implementation deferred >
91      } // end clear
92
93      public T replace(int givenPosition, T newEntry)
94      { < Implementation deferred >
106     } // end replace
107
108     public T getEntry(int givenPosition)
109     { < Implementation deferred >
119     } // end getEntry
120
121     public T[] toArray()
122     {
123        checkInitialization();
124
125        // The cast is safe because the new array contains null entries
126        @SuppressWarnings("unchecked")
127        T[] result = (T[])new Object[numberOfEntries];
128        for (int index = 0; index < numberOfEntries; index++)
129        {
130           result[index] = list[index + 1];
131        } // end for
132
133        return result;
134     } // end toArray
135
136     public boolean contains(T anEntry)
137     { < Implementation deferred >
149     } // end contains
150
151     public int getLength()
152     {
153        return numberOfEntries;
154     } // end getLength
155
156     public boolean isEmpty()
157     {
158        return numberOfEntries == 0; // Or getLength() == 0
159     } // end isEmpty
160
161     // Doubles the capacity of the array list if it is full.
162     // Precondition: checkInitialization has been called.
163     private void ensureCapacity()
164     {
165        int capacity = list.length - 1;
166        if (numberOfEntries >= capacity)
167        {
168           int newCapacity = 2 * capacity;
169           checkCapacity(newCapacity); // Is capacity too big?
170           list = Arrays.copyOf(list, newCapacity + 1);
171        } // end if
172     } // end ensureCapacity
173     < This class will define checkCapacity, checkInitialization, and two more private
174       methods that will be discussed later. >
175  } // end AList
```

**13.6**    **The core methods.** As we just mentioned, we have chosen to implement the first add method and the method toArray before the others, as they are central, or core, to our class. Adding a new entry to the end of the list is easy; we simply add the entry to the array immediately after its last occupied location. Of course, adding a new entry is possible only if the array has available space.

To guarantee this space for at least the first addition, the constructors now create lists whose capacities are at least DEFAULT_CAPACITY. Following each addition, the add method calls the private method ensureCapacity to resize the array if necessary. Thus, except for the point at which the array's capacity is checked, the first add method has an implementation much like the one you saw in Segment 2.40 of Chapter 2 for the class ResizableArrayBag. Moreover, the definition of ensureCapacity, which appears at the end of Listing 13-1, as well as the definition of the method toArray, are analogous to the corresponding methods in ResizableArrayBag.

**Design Decision:** **When should the method add call ensureCapacity?**
The methods that add entries to array-based bags and stacks, as defined earlier in the classes ArrayBag and ArrayStack given in Chapters 2 and 6, respectively, ensure that the array has sufficient capacity before adding another entry to the array. Thus, the addition to the array might have to wait until a larger array has become available. However, if the addition fills the array, the array will not be expanded until the next call to add.

For the list, we take the opposite approach. We have chosen to verify the array's capacity—by calling ensureCapacity—after the addition of another entry to the array. Assuming sufficient space in the array for at least the first addition, we enlarge the array as soon as an addition fills it. Thus, the array will always be ready to accept another entry. If, however, another addition does not occur, the array expansion will have been unnecessary.

In our present context, the point at which you call ensureCapacity is irrelevant. However, performing certain tasks at the same time, or in **parallel**, is possible and common with today's technology. By calling ensureCapacity last, you can have the array expansion occur in the background as a separate **thread**. This allows add to return so the client can continue execution while the array is expanded. In this way, we ensure sufficient array capacity without delay for when the client needs to add an entry. Creating a separate thread, however, is beyond our present scope.

**Note:**   Because each of AList's constructors creates a list whose capacity is at least DEFAULT_CAPACITY, the method add can now assume that the array has sufficient space for at least the first addition to the list.

**13.7**    **Testing the partial implementation.** You should now write a main method to test what you have completed at this point. Testing a class should begin well before its implementation is complete. To avoid syntax errors in the incomplete class in Listing 13-1, make the incomplete methods stubs as Chapter 2 describes in Segment 2.16. You can provide the actual definitions of methods, such as getLength and isEmpty, as they are just as simple as their stubs would be.

As you define more methods, test them by adding statements to main. As Appendix C notes, you can include your method main in the definition of AList for future use and reference.

**Question 4** Write the method displayList that displays all entries in a list. This method should be a part of the driver that tests the core methods.

**13.8** **Adding to a list at a given position.** The ADT list has another method that adds a new entry to a list, adding it at a position that the client specifies. Adding a new entry at an arbitrary position within the list is like adding a student to room A in our example in Segment 13.2. Although that example positions students alphabetically by their names, remember that the list's client—not the list itself—determines the desired position of each entry. Thus, if that position is before the end of the list, we need to shift existing entries in the array to vacate the desired location so that it can accommodate the new entry. If the addition is to the end of the list, no such shift is necessary. In either case, space must be available in the array to accommodate a new entry.

The following implementation of add uses a private method makeRoom to handle the details of moving data within the array. Remember that we can add to the list at positions that range from 1 to the length of the list plus 1. According to the method's specifications given in Segment 12.8 of the previous chapter, we must throw an exception if the given position is invalid.

```java
// Precondition: The array list has room for another entry.
public void add(int newPosition, T newEntry)
{
    checkInitialization();
    if ((newPosition >= 1) && (newPosition <= numberOfEntries + 1))
    {
        if (newPosition <= numberOfEntries)
            makeRoom(newPosition);
        list[newPosition] = newEntry;
        numberOfEntries++;
        ensureCapacity(); // Ensure enough room for next add
    }
    else
        throw new IndexOutOfBoundsException(
                "Given position of add's new entry is out of bounds.");
} // end add
```

**13.9** **The private method makeRoom.** Now we must implement the private method makeRoom. Typically, the method shifts list entries toward the end of the array, beginning with the last entry, as Figure 13-4 illustrates. However, if newPosition is numberOfEntries + 1, the addition is at the end of the list, so no shift is necessary. In this case, makeRoom does nothing, since its for statement exits immediately.

```java
// Makes room for a new entry at newPosition.
// Precondition: 1 <= newPosition <= numberOfEntries + 1;
//               numberOfEntries is list's length before addition;
//               checkInitialization has been called.
private void makeRoom(int newPosition)
{
    assert (newPosition >= 1) && (newPosition <= numberOfEntries + 1);

    int newIndex = newPosition;
    int lastIndex = numberOfEntries;

    // Move each entry to next higher index, starting at end of
    // list and continuing until the entry at newIndex is moved
    for (int index = lastIndex; index >= newIndex; index--)
        list[index + 1] = list[index];
} // end makeRoom
```

Notice that the add method enforces the preconditions of makeRoom. While testing makeRoom, however, we can enable the assertion to be sure that newPosition is valid.

FIGURE 13-4   Making room to insert Carla as the third entry in an array

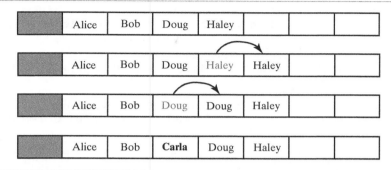

**Question 5** You could implement the first add method, which adds an entry to the end of the list, by invoking the second add method, as follows:

```
public void add(T newEntry)
{
    add(numberOfEntries + 1, newEntry);
} // end add
```

Discuss the pros and cons of this revised approach.

**Question 6** Suppose that myList is a list that contains the five entries a b c d e.

    **a.** What does myList contain after executing myList.add(5, w)?

    **b.** Starting with the original five entries, what does myList contain after executing myList.add(6, w)?

    **c.** Which of the operations in Parts *a* and *b* of this question require entries in the array to shift?

**Question 7** If myList is a list of five entries, each of the following statements adds a new entry to the end of the list:

```
myList.add(newEntry);
myList.add(6, newEntry);
```

Which way requires fewer operations?

13.10   **The method remove.** After thoroughly testing the two add methods and toArray, we begin to define the remaining methods. Removing a list entry at an arbitrary position is like the response when a student leaves room A in our example in Segment 13.3. We need to shift existing entries to avoid a gap in the array, except when removing the list's last entry. The following implementation uses a private method removeGap to handle the details of moving data within the array. Like the method add, remove is responsible for checking the validity of the given position. Note how this check also ensures that the list is not empty.

```
public T remove(int givenPosition)
{
    checkInitialization();
    if ((givenPosition >= 1) && (givenPosition <= numberOfEntries))
    {
        assert !isEmpty();
```

VideoNote
Completing the class AList

```
            T result = list[givenPosition]; // Get entry to be removed
            // Move subsequent entries toward entry to be removed,
            // unless it is last in list
            if (givenPosition < numberOfEntries)
               removeGap(givenPosition);

            numberOfEntries--;
            return result; // Return reference to removed entry
         }
         else
            throw new IndexOutOfBoundsException(
                     "Illegal position given to remove operation.");
      } // end remove
```

**Question 8** Since the method `remove` does not explicitly check for an empty list, why is the assertion given in the method true?

**Question 9** When a list is empty, how does `remove` throw an exception?

13.11    **The private method `removeGap`.** The following private method `removeGap` shifts list entries within the array, as Figure 13-5 illustrates. Beginning with the entry after the one to be removed and continuing until the end of the list, `removeGap` moves each entry to its next lower position.

```
      // Shifts entries that are beyond the entry to be removed to the
      // next lower position.
      // Precondition: 1 <= givenPosition < numberOfEntries;
      //               numberOfEntries is list's length before removal;
      //               checkInitialization has been called.
      private void removeGap(int givenPosition)
      {
         assert (givenPosition >= 1) && (givenPosition < numberOfEntries);

         int removedIndex = givenPosition;
         int lastIndex = numberOfEntries;

         for (int index = removedIndex; index < lastIndex; index++)

            list[index] = list[index + 1];
      } // end removeGap
```

FIGURE 13-5    Removing Bob by shifting array entries

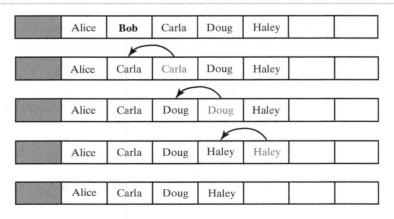

Note that no shift is necessary if the deletion is at the end of the list. In that case, the last entry in the list is at position numberOfEntries, since the first entry is at position 1. If givenPosition equals numberOfEntries, the for statement in removeGap will exit immediately. Even so, remove will not call removeGap in this case. Notice that removeGap's precondition requires givenPosition to be less than numberOfEntries, and the remove method enforces this precondition. You can enable the assert statement in removeGap to verify this enforcement.

This precondition of removeGap implies that the method should not be called if a list is empty. In fact, remove ensures that this requirement is followed.

**Question 10** Figure 13-5 shows Haley shifted toward the beginning of the array. Actually, the reference to Haley is copied, not moved, to its new location. Should we assign null to Haley's original location?

**Question 11** The method clear could simply set the data field numberOfEntries to zero. Although the list methods would correctly behave as though the list was empty, the objects that were in the list would remain allocated. Suggest at least two ways that clear could deallocate these objects.

**13.12** **The methods replace and getEntry.** Replacing a list entry and retrieving a list entry are two straightforward operations when an array is used to represent the entries. You simply replace or retrieve the object that is in the indicated array location. Like earlier methods, replace and getEntry are responsible for validating the given position. Like remove, these methods do not need an explicit test for an empty list to behave correctly. The assert statement is available to verify this claim during testing.

The following methods implement these two operations:

```
public T replace(int givenPosition, T newEntry)
{
    checkInitialization();
    if ((givenPosition >= 1) && (givenPosition <= numberOfEntries))
    {
        assert !isEmpty();
        T originalEntry = list[givenPosition];
        list[givenPosition] = newEntry;
        return originalEntry;
    }
    else
        throw new IndexOutOfBoundsException(
                "Illegal position given to replace operation.");
} // end replace

public T getEntry(int givenPosition)
{
    checkInitialization();
    if ((givenPosition >= 1) && (givenPosition <= numberOfEntries))
    {
        assert !isEmpty();
        return list[givenPosition];
    }
    else
        throw new IndexOutOfBoundsException(
                "Illegal position given to getEntry operation.");
} // end getEntry
```

**13.13**   **The method** `contains`**.** The method `getEntry` locates the entry at a given position by going directly to the appropriate array element. In contrast, the method `contains` is given an entry, not its position, and so must search the array for the entry. Beginning at index 1, the method examines each array entry until it either locates the desired one or reaches the end of the list without success. In the following implementation, we use a local boolean variable to terminate the loop when we find the desired entry:

```java
public boolean contains(T anEntry)
{
   checkInitialization();
   boolean found = false;
   int index = 1;
   while (!found && (index <= numberOfEntries))
   {
      if (anEntry.equals(list[index]))
         found = true;
      index++;
   } // end while

   return found;
} // end contains
```

This way of looking for a particular entry in an array is called a **sequential search**. Chapter 18 discusses this technique further and presents another algorithm that is generally faster.

## The Efficiency of Using an Array to Implement the ADT List

Before we look at another implementation of the ADT list, let's examine the time complexity of some of the methods in our class `AList`.

**13.14**   **Adding to the end of a list.** Let's begin with the operation that adds a new entry to the end of a list. Listing 13-1 provided the following definition for this operation:

```java
public void add(T newEntry)
{
   checkInitialization();
   list[numberOfEntries] = newEntry;
   numberOfEntries++;
   ensureCapacity();
} // end add
```

If the array of list entries is not full, each step in this method is an O(1) operation. By applying our knowledge of the material presented in Segments 4.16 and 4.17 of Chapter 4, we can show that this method is O(1), if the array is not resized. That is, we can add an entry to the end of a list independently of any other entries in the list.

As we have seen in previous chapters, resizing an array is an O($n$) operation. Thus, the method `ensureCapacity` would require O($n$) time if it encounters a full array. In this case, adding to the end of a list would be an O($n$) operation. If we continued to add to the end of the list, the operations would be O(1) again.

**13.15**   **Adding to a list at a given position.** The second add method adds a new entry to a list at a client-specified position. Let's recall its definition from Segment 13.8:

```java
public void add(int newPosition, T newEntry)
{
   checkInitialization();
   if ((newPosition >= 1) && (newPosition <= numberOfEntries + 1))
   {
```

```
      if (newPosition <= numberOfEntries)
         makeRoom(newPosition);
      list[newPosition] = newEntry;
      numberOfEntries++;
      ensureCapacity();
   }
   else
      throw new IndexOutOfBoundsException(
                "Given position of add's new entry is out of bounds.");
} // end add
```

This method differs from the previous add method because it usually calls the private method
makeRoom, whose definition appears in Segment 13.9, to make room in the array for the new entry.
The only time it does not call makeRoom is when the addition is at the end of the list.

After removing makeRoom's assert statement and comments, we are left with the following
code:

```
private void makeRoom(int newPosition)
{
   int newIndex = newPosition;
   int lastIndex = numberOfEntries;
   for (int index = lastIndex; index >= newIndex; index--)
      list[index + 1] = list[index];
} // end makeRoom
```

The method requires the most time when newPosition is 1, because it must shift all of the list
entries. If the list contains *n* entries, the body of the loop is repeated *n* times in this case. Therefore,
the method makeRoom is O(*n*) in the worst case.

We already know that ensureCapacity is either O(*n*) or O(1), according to whether or not
it resizes the array. Also, the other tasks in the add method, including the assignment of the new
entry to an array element, are O(1) operations. These observations imply that the method add is
also O(*n*) in the worst case. The best case occurs when the array is not resized and newPosition
is numberOfEntries + 1—that is, when we add to the end of the list—because we do not call
makeRoom. Thus, in the best case, add is O(1).

 **Note:** Adding to the beginning of an array-based list is an O(*n*) operation. Adding to the end
is O(1) if the underlying array is not resized; otherwise it is O(*n*). The time required to add at
other positions depends on the position. As the position number increases, the time needed for
an addition decreases.

 **Question 12** What is the Big Oh of the list method remove in the best case and the worst case?

**Question 13** Repeat Question 12 for the list method replace.

**Question 14** Repeat Question 12 for the list method getEntry.

**Question 15** Repeat Question 12 for the list method contains.

**Note:** In Chapter 6, we used a vector—that is, an instance of the class `java.util.Vector`—instead of an array to contain the entries in a stack. You can use a vector to contain the entries in a list. Since Java's class `Vector` uses an array in its implementation, a vector-based implementation of the ADT list will be array based. It, like `AList`, uses a resizable array to contain the list's entries, so that a list can grow in size as needed. We leave this new implementation to you as a programming project.

**Note:** The methods in a class `VectorList` that implements `ListInterface` and uses a vector to store a list's entries would function similarly to methods in Java's class `Vector`, but their specifications would differ. `VectorList` would simply invoke methods of the class `Vector`. `VectorList` is an example of an adapter class, which we described in Segment D.3 of Appendix D.

**Note:** When you use an array or a vector to implement the ADT list,
- Retrieving the entry at a given position is fast
- Adding an entry at the end of a list is fast
- Adding or removing an entry that is between other entries requires shifting them within the array
- Increasing the size of the array or vector requires copying entries

## CHAPTER SUMMARY

- The implementation of the ADT list in this chapter uses an array to store the items in a list.

- Using an array results in a straightforward implementation of the list, but it is somewhat more involved than the implementations of either the ADT bag or the ADT stack.

- An array provides direct access to any of its elements, so a method such as `getEntry` has a simple, efficient implementation.

- Adding an entry to or removing an entry from an array-based list typically requires that other entries shift by one position within the array. This data movement degrades the time efficiency of these operations, particularly when the list is long and the position of the addition or removal is near the beginning of the list.

- Expanding the size of an array adds to the time required by the affected `add` method, since doing so requires copying the contents of the array to a larger array.

## EXERCISES

1. Add a constructor to the class `AList` that creates a list from a given array of objects.

2. Suppose that you want an operation for the ADT list that returns the number of occurrences of a given object in the list. The header of the method could be as follows:

    ```
    public int getCount(T anObject)
    ```

    where `T` is the generic type of the objects in the list. Write an implementation of this method for the class `AList`.

3. Suppose that you want an operation for the ADT list that removes the last occurrence of a given object from the list. The header of the method could be as follows:

    ```
    public boolean removeLast(T anObject)
    ```

    where T is the generic type of the objects in the list. The method returns true if the list contained anObject and that object was removed. Write an implementation of this method for the class AList.

4. Suppose that you want an operation for the ADT list that moves the last item in the list to the front of the list. The header of the method could be as follows:

    ```
    public void moveToFront()
    ```

    Write an implementation of this method for the class AList.

5. Exercise 8 in the previous chapter asked you to write statements at the client level that replace an object in a given list. Write a method at the client level that performs such a replacement. How does your method compare with the method replace of the ADT list?

6. The method largest for the ADT list returns the largest object. Implement a method largest for the class AList that returns a boolean value.

7. Suppose that a list contains Comparable objects. Implement the following methods for the class AList:

    ```
    /** Returns the largest object in the list. */
    public T getMax()
    /** Removes and returns the largest object in the list. */
    public T removeMax()
    ```

8. Implement a smaller method for the ADT list that returns true when the entries in one list are smaller than the entries in a second list. In particular, add this method to the class AList.

9. Repeat the previous exercise, but have the smaller method call a private recursive method that detects smaller entries.

10. Consider the method getCount as described in Exercise 2. Revise the method's definition so that it calls a private recursive method to count the number of occurrences of a given object in the list.

11. The class AList has an array that can grow in size as objects are added to the list. Consider a similar class whose array also can shrink in size as objects are removed from the list. Accomplishing this task will require two new private methods.

    The first new method checks whether we should reduce the size of the array:

    ```
    private boolean isTooBig()
    ```

    This method returns true if the number of entries in the list is less than half the size of the array and the size of the array is greater than 20.

    The second new method creates a new array that is three quarters the size of the current array and then copies the objects in the list to the new array:

    ```
    private void reduceArray()
    ```

    Implement each of these two methods for our new class. Then use these methods in the definition of the method remove.

**12.** Consider the two private methods described in the previous exercise.

   **a.** The method isTooBig requires the size of the array to be greater than 20. What problem could occur if this requirement is dropped?

   **b.**  The method reduceArray is not analogous to the method ensureCapacity in that it does not reduce the size of the array by one half. What problem could occur if the size of the array is reduced by half instead of three quarters?

## PROJECTS

**1.** Write a program that thoroughly tests the class AList.

**2.** Define a class of bags by using an instance of the class AList to contain its entries. Then write a program that adequately demonstrates your new class.

**3.** Repeat Project 2, but define a class of stacks instead.

**4.** Repeat Project 2, but define a class of queues instead.

**5.** Repeat Project 2, but define a class of deques instead.

**6.** Repeat Project 2, but define a class of sets instead. Recall from Project 1 in Chapter 1 that a set is a bag whose entries are distinct.

**7.** By using an instance of the class java.util.Vector to contain a list's entries, define a class VectorList that implements ListInterface.

   **a.** What are the advantages and disadvantages of this implementation, and how do they compare with those of AList?

   **b.** Add to VectorList the methods described in Exercises 1, 2, 3, 4, 6, 7, 8, and 9.

**8.** Implement the interface ListInterface by using an array in which you do not ignore the first array location. Thus, you store the list's $i$th entry in the array location at index i - 1.

**9.** Using a fixed-size array to implement the ADT list limits the size of the list. Some applications can use a list that has a limited length. For example, the length of a list of airline passengers or a list of ticket holders to a movie should not exceed a known maximum.

   Define an interface FixedSizeListInterface that is similar to ListInterface, but adds the method isFull and revises the specifications of other methods as necessary to accommodate a fixed-size list. Consider whether your new interface should extend ListInterface. Then define and demonstrate a class that implements FixedSizeListInterface.

**10.** Implement as the class Shoe the ADT shoe that Project 4 of Chapter 1 describes. *Hint*: To shuffle the shoe, use two private lists of cards, a source list and a shuffled list. Put all the available cards into the source list. Initially, this will be every card. Later, only those cards not held by a player will be available. Use the class java.util.Random to repeatedly generate a random position in the source list, remove the card at that position, and put it at the end of the shuffled list.

   Write a program that adequately demonstrates the operation of the class Shoe.

**11.** Implement the collection of bids that Project 5 of Chapter 1 describes.

**12.** Implement the ADT for the objects in Santa's nice list that Project 8 of Chapter 12 describes. Then create some instances of your class and place them in the nice list.

**13.** Implement the ADT recipe that Project 9 of Chapter 12 describes.

**14.** Repeat Project 5 of Chapter 4, but use an instance of `AList` instead of a bag.

**15.** Revise `ListInterface`, as given in Listing 12-1 of the previous chapter, so that each of the methods `add`, `remove`, `replace`, and `getEntry` returns either `null` or false instead of throwing an exception if the position passed to it is out of range. Then revise the class `AList` so that it implements your revised interface.

**16.** The popular social network Facebook™ was founded by Mark Zuckerberg and his classmates at Harvard University in 2004. At the time, he was a sophomore studying computer science.

Design and implement an application that maintains the data for a simple social network. Each person in the network should have a profile that contains the person's name, optional image, current status, and a list of friends. Your application should allow a user to join the network, leave the network, create a profile, modify the profile, search for other profiles, and add friends.

## ANSWERS TO SELF-TEST QUESTIONS

**1.** When the name comes after the name of the student in the last occupied desk; the new student then sits at the desk after the last one that is currently occupied.

**2.** The students remain in consecutively numbered positions. You do not have to keep track of the locations of the empty desks.

**3.** Time is saved by not moving the students.

**4.**
```
public static void displayList(ListInterface<String> list)
{
    System.out.println("The list contains " + list.getLength() +
                        " entries, as follows:");
    Object[] listArray = list.toArray();
    for (int index = 0; index < listArray.length; index++)
    {
        System.out.print(listArray[index] + " ");
    } // end for

    System.out.println();
} // end displayList
```

**5.** Advantage: It is easier to implement this `add` method. Your code will more likely be correct if the other `add` method is correct.

Disadvantage: Invoking another method uses more execution time. Additionally, the second `add` method must decide not to invoke `makeRoom` when called by the first `add` method.

**6.**  **a.** a b c d w e
   **b.** a b c d e w
   **c.** The operation in Part *a*

**7.** `myList.add(newEntry)`, assuming that add is defined as in Listing 13-1.

**8.** If the list is empty, `numberOfEntries` is zero, so the boolean expression in the `if` statement is always false. Thus, the only way that the previous expression can be true is if the list is not empty.

**9.** By the reasoning given in the previous answer, if the list is empty, the `else` clause executes.

**10.** We could, but it is not necessary. After remove decrements `numberOfEntries`, `list[numberOfEntries]` is the array location that Haley originally occupied. So `list[numberOfEntries]` and `list[numberOfEntries - 1]` both reference Haley. Since we are not deallocating Haley, we do not have to set `list[numberOfEntries]` to `null`. We can simply ignore its contents.

11. The method `clear` could take one of the following actions to deallocate the objects currently in a list: (1) Set elements of the array `list` to `null`; (2) repeatedly remove the last entry in the list by repeatedly calling `remove(numberOfEntries)`; (3) reallocate the array `list`.

12. $O(1)$; $O(n)$.

13. $O(1)$; $O(1)$.

14. $O(1)$; $O(1)$.

15. $O(1)$ when the entry is found immediately in position 1. $O(n)$ when the entry is found in the last position or is not found at all.

# A List
# Implementation
# That Links Data

## Contents

## Prerequisites

## Objectives

After studying this chapter, you should be able to

- Describe a linked organization of data
- Implement the ADT list by using a linked chain of nodes
- Discuss the advantages and disadvantages of the implementation presented
- Compare and contrast the array-based and link-based implementations of the ADT list

Using an array to implement the ADT list has both advantages and disadvantages, as you saw in the previous chapter. An array can either have a fixed size or be moved to a larger array when it becomes full. Since a fixed-size array can lead to a full list, our class AList uses a resizable array to provide as much space as the list needs. This strategy, however, requires data to move each time the array expands. In addition, any array requires you to move data either to make room for a new entry or to close up a gap after a deletion.

This chapter describes a linked implementation of the list. Like our previous linked implementations, this one uses memory only as needed for a new entry and returns any unneeded memory to the system after an entry is removed. Moreover, it avoids moving data when adding or removing list entries. These features make this way of implementing a list an important alternative to array-based approaches.

## Operations on a Chain of Linked Nodes

We used a chain of linked nodes in Chapter 3 to implement the ADT bag and in Chapter 6 to implement the ADT stack. In both of those cases, we added a node to and removed a node from the beginning of the chain. We added a node to the end of a chain in Chapter 11 for one implementation of the ADT queue. While those operations are still needed for a list, we also must be able to add a node between existing nodes and to delete a node from positions other than the beginning or end. Let's talk about these operations. We use the same class, Node, that appears in Listing 3-4 of Chapter 3.

### Adding a Node at Various Positions

To add a node to a chain at a specified position, we must consider the following cases:

- Case 1: The chain is empty
- Case 2: Adding a node at the chain's beginning
- Case 3: Adding a node between adjacent nodes
- Case 4: Adding a node to the chain's end

As you will see, we will be able to combine these four cases into two. To that end, we examine each case, even though some of the detail will be familiar to you.

**14.1**    **Case 1: Adding a node to an empty chain.** Although we have added nodes to an empty chain before, let's recall the necessary steps. If firstNode is the head reference to the chain, it will contain null when the chain is empty. Figure 14-1a illustrates this state, along with a node that we want to add to the chain.

FIGURE 14-1    (a) An empty chain and a new node; (b) after adding the new
node to a chain that was empty

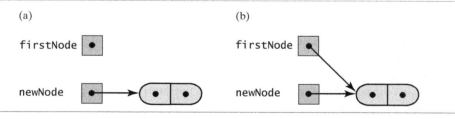

The following pseudocode establishes a new node for the given data—referenced by newEntry—and inserts it into the empty chain:

> newNode *references a new instance of* Node
> *Place* newEntry *in* newNode
> firstNode = *address of* newNode

Figure 14-1b shows the result of this operation. In Java, these steps appear as follows, where newEntry references the entry to be added to the list:

```
Node newNode = new Node(newEntry);
firstNode = newNode;
```

Notice that in Figure 14-1b, firstNode and newNode reference the same node. After the insertion of the new node is complete, only firstNode should reference it. We could set newNode to null, but as you will see, newNode will be a local variable of the method add. As such, newNode will not exist after add ends its execution.

**14.2**   **Case 2: Adding a node to the beginning of a chain.** This case should be familiar to you as well. The following pseudocode describes the steps needed to add a node to the beginning of a chain:

> newNode *references a new instance of* Node
> *Place* newEntry *in* newNode
> *Set* newNode's *link to* firstNode
> *Set* firstNode *to* newNode

The new node is now the first node. Figure 14-2 illustrates these steps, and the following Java statements implement them:

```
Node newNode = new Node(newEntry);
newNode.setNextNode(firstNode);
firstNode = newNode;
```

To simplify the figure, we have omitted the actual entries in the list. These entries are objects that the nodes reference.

---

**FIGURE 14-2**   A chain of nodes (a) just prior to adding a node at the beginning; (b) just after adding a node at the beginning

---

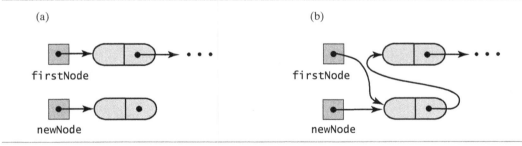

(a)

firstNode

newNode

(b)

firstNode

newNode

---

 **Note:** Recall that adding a node to an empty chain, as Figure 14-1 depicts, is actually the same as adding a node to the beginning of a chain.

**14.3**   **Case 3: Adding a node between adjacent nodes of a chain.** Because the ADT list allows additions between two existing entries, we must be able to add a node to a chain between two existing, consecutive nodes. The necessary steps for this task are described by the following pseudocode:

> newNode *references the new node*
> *Place* newEntry *in* newNode

> *Let* nodeBefore *reference the node that will be before the new node*
> *Set* nodeAfter *to* nodeBefore*'s link*
> *Set* newNode*'s link to* nodeAfter
> *Set* nodeBefore*'s link to* newNode

To indicate where in the chain the new node should be inserted, let's number the nodes, beginning with 1. We need to locate the node at a given position within the chain and get a reference to it. Suppose that the method getNodeAt performs this task for us. Since the method returns a reference to a node, and the class Node will be an inner class of a class of lists, getNodeAt is an implementation detail that we would not want a client to use. Thus, getNodeAt should be a private method. Let's specify getNodeAt as follows:

```
// Returns a reference to the node at a given position.
// Precondition: The chain is not empty;
//               1 <= givenPosition <= numberOfNodes.
private Node getNodeAt(int givenPosition)
```

We can define the method later.

In the meantime, knowing only what getNodeAt does, and not how it does it, we can use it in the implementation of the previous pseudocode. If newPosition is the number of the new node after its insertion, the following Java statements add the new node to the chain:

```
Node newNode = new Node(newEntry);
Node nodeBefore = getNodeAt(newPosition - 1);
Node nodeAfter = nodeBefore.getNextNode();
newNode.setNextNode(nodeAfter);
nodeBefore.setNextNode(newNode);
```

Figure 14-3a shows the chain after the first three statements execute, and Figure 14-3b shows it after the node has been added. In this figure, newPosition is 3.

---

**FIGURE 14-3**    A chain of nodes (a) just prior to adding a node between two
adjacent nodes; (b) just after adding a node between two
adjacent nodes

---

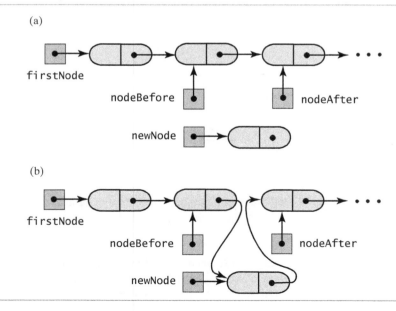

**Question 1** Describe the steps that the method `getNodeAt` must take to locate the node at a given position.

**14.4**   **Case 4: Adding a node to the end of a chain.** To add a node to the end of an existing chain, we can take the following steps:

> `newNode` *references a new instance of* `Node`
> *Place* `newEntry` *in* `newNode`
> *Locate the last node in the chain*
> *Place the address of* `newNode` *in this last node*

That is, we make the last node in the chain reference the new node. Using the same method, `getNodeAt`, that the previous segment described, we can implement these steps in Java as follows:

```
Node newNode = new Node(newEntry);
Node lastNode = getNodeAt(numberOfEntries);
lastNode.setNextNode(newNode);
```

Note that `numberOfEntries` is the current number of entries—and the current number of nodes—in the chain. Figure 14-4 illustrates this addition to the end of a chain of nodes.

**FIGURE 14-4**   A chain of nodes (a) prior to adding a node at the end; (b) after locating its last node; (c) after adding a node at the end

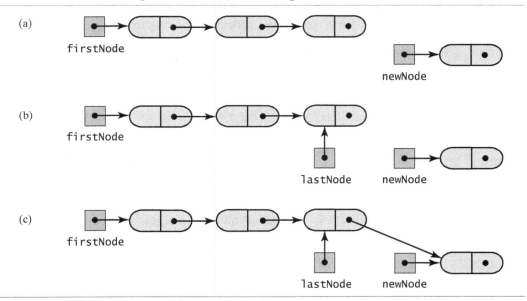

**Note:** Adding a new node to the end of a chain of *n* nodes can be thought of as adding the node at position *n* + 1.

**Question 2** The code that we developed in Segment 14.3 to add a node between two adjacent nodes of a chain is

```
Node newNode = new Node(newEntry);
Node nodeBefore = getNodeAt(newPosition - 1);
Node nodeAfter = nodeBefore.getNextNode();
newNode.setNextNode(nodeAfter);
nodeBefore.setNextNode(newNode);
```

Is it possible to use this code instead of the following code, which we just developed, to add a node to the end of a chain? Explain your answer.

```
Node newNode = new Node(newEntry);
Node lastNode = getNodeAt(numberOfNodes);
lastNode.setNextNode(newNode);
```

**Question 3** Adding a node to an empty chain could be thought of as adding a node to the end of a chain that is empty. Can you use the statements in Segment 14.4 instead of

```
Node newNode = new Node(newEntry);
firstNode = newNode;
```

which we developed in Segment 14.1 to add a node to an empty chain? Why or why not?

## Removing a Node from Various Positions

To remove a node at a specified position within a nonempty chain, we must consider two cases:

- Case 1: Removing the first node
- Case 2: Removing a node other than the first one

14.5   **Case 1: Removing the first node.** This case should be familiar to you, as we removed the first node in the linked implementations of the ADTs bag, stack, queue, deque, and priority queue. The steps to take are

*Set* firstNode *to the link in the first node.*
*Since all references to the first node no longer exist, the system automatically recycles the first node's memory.*

Figure 14-5 illustrates these steps, and the following Java statement implements them:

```
firstNode = firstNode.getNextNode();
```

---

**FIGURE 14-5**   A chain of nodes (a) just prior to removing the first node; (b) just after removing the first node

(a)

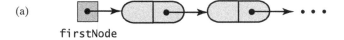

firstNode

(b)

firstNode

**14.6**    **Case 2: Removing a node other than the first one.** In the second case, we remove a node at a position other than the beginning of the chain. Here are the steps to take:

> *Let* nodeBefore *reference the node before the one to be removed.*
> *Set* nodeToRemove *to* nodeBefore*'s link;* nodeToRemove *now references the node to be removed.*
> *Set* nodeAfter *to* nodeToRemove*'s link;* nodeAfter *now references the node after the one to be removed.*
> *Set* nodeBefore*'s link to* nodeAfter. *(*nodeToRemove *is now disconnected from the chain.)*
> *Set* nodeToRemove *to* null.
> *Since all references to the disconnected node no longer exist, the system automatically recycles the node's memory.*

The following Java statements implement these steps, assuming that the node to remove is at position givenPosition:

```
Node nodeBefore = getNodeAt(givenPosition - 1);
Node nodeToRemove = nodeBefore.getNextNode();
Node nodeAfter = nodeToRemove.getNextNode();
nodeBefore.setNextNode(nodeAfter);
nodeToRemove = null;
```

Figure 14-6a illustrates the chain after the first three statements execute, and Figure 14-6b shows it after the node is removed.

FIGURE 14-6    A chain of nodes (a) just prior to removing an interior node;
(b) just after removing an interior node

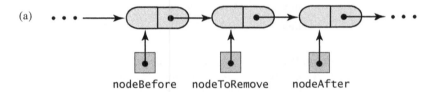

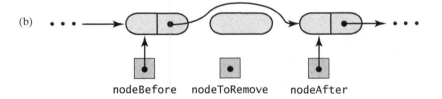

## The Private Method getNodeAt

**14.7**    The previous operations on a chain depended on the method getNodeAt, which returns a reference to the node at a given position within the chain. Recall the specifications for this method:

```
// Returns a reference to the node at a given position.
// Precondition: The chain is not empty;
//               1 <= givenPosition <= numberOfNodes.
private Node getNodeAt(int givenPosition)
```

To locate a particular node within a chain, we begin at the chain's first node and traverse the chain from one node to another. We know that firstNode contains a reference to the first node in the chain. That first node contains a reference to the second node in the chain, the second node contains a reference to the third node, and so on.

We can use a temporary variable, currentNode, to reference the nodes one at a time as we traverse the chain from the first node to the desired node. Initially, we set currentNode to firstNode so that it references the first node in the chain. If we are seeking the first node, we are done. Otherwise, we move to the next node by executing

```
currentNode = currentNode.getNextNode();
```

If we are seeking the second node, we are done. Otherwise, we move to the next node by executing

```
currentNode = currentNode.getNextNode();
```

once again. We continue in this manner until we locate the node at the desired position within the list.

The implementation for getNodeAt follows:

```
private Node getNodeAt(int givenPosition)
{
    assert (firstNode != null) &&
           (1 <= givenPosition) && (givenPosition <= numberOfNodes);
    Node currentNode = firstNode;

    // Traverse the chain to locate the desired node
    // (skipped if givenPosition is 1)
    for (int counter = 1; counter < givenPosition; counter++)
        currentNode = currentNode.getNextNode();

    assert currentNode != null;

    return currentNode;
} // end getNodeAt
```

Within the for loop, currentNode should never become null if the method's precondition is met. As a private method, getNodeAt can trust that its precondition will be honored. Thus, currentNode.getNextNode() never executes if currentNode is null. You can enable the assert statements during the testing of getNodeAt to verify these claims.

**Question 4** The statements in Segment 14.4 that add an entry to the end of a chain invoke the method getNodeAt. Suppose that you use these statements repeatedly to create a chain by adding entries to its end.

  a.   How efficient of time is this approach?
  b.   Is there a faster way to repeatedly add entries to the end of a chain? Explain.

**Question 5** How does getNodeAt's precondition prevent currentNode from becoming null?

# Beginning the Implementation

**Design Decision: How should we efficiently construct the chain of linked nodes?**
Imagine that we have a collection of data from which we will create a list. That is, our data will be the list's entries. If the data is in the order in which the entries will appear in the list, we create the list by repeatedly adding the next entry to the end of the list.

We could do this by using the list's first add method. However, if add contains the statements in Segment 14.4 that add an entry to the end of a list, the method getNodeAt will be invoked to locate the last node in the chain. To accomplish this task, getNodeAt must begin at the first node and traverse the chain until it locates the last node. Given a reference to the last node, add can insert the new entry at the end of the chain. If this reference is not retained when the method completes its task, adding another entry to the end of the list forces add to invoke getNodeAt again. The result is another traversal of the chain from its beginning. Since we plan to add entries repeatedly to the end of the list, many repetitious traversals will occur.

In such cases, maintaining a reference to the end of the chain—as well as a reference to the beginning of the chain—is advantageous. Such a reference to the end of a chain is called a tail reference, and was introduced in Chapter 11 for the linked implementation of a queue. Figure 14-7 illustrates two linked chains: one with a head reference and the other with both head and tail references.

Maintaining both head and tail references is somewhat more involved for a list than it was for a queue. Thus, our first class of lists using a linked implementation will not define a tail reference. After we successfully complete this simpler definition, we will modify it by adding a tail reference and thereby improve its time efficiency. Recall that solving a simpler problem first is often a reasonable strategy.

**FIGURE 14-7**    A linked chain with (a) a head reference; (b) both a head reference and a tail reference

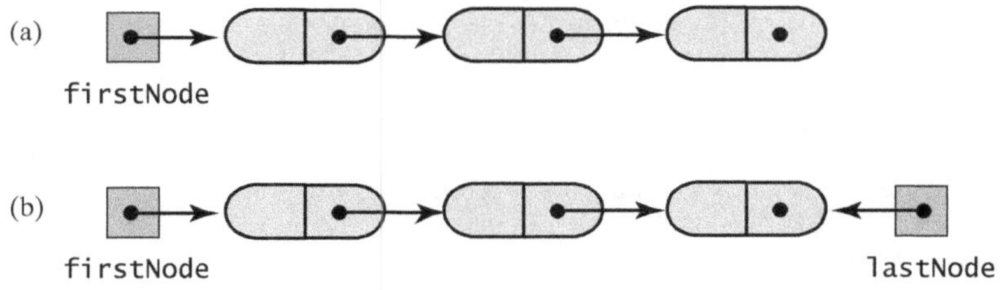

## The Data Fields and Constructor

**14.8**    Listing 14-1 contains an outline of the class LList[1] that implements the ADT list. Recall that Chapter 12 defined the interface ListInterface. It and the classes that implement it define a generic type T for the objects in the list. We plan to define a chain of linked nodes to contain the list's entries. Thus, we need the class Node, which we have used in our previous discussion, and so we define it as an inner class of LList. The generic type T that appears in LList's header is the same one that we use in the class Node.

**LISTING 14-1    An outline of the class LList**

```java
/**
   A linked implementation of the ADT list.
   @author Frank M. Carrano
*/
public class LList<T> implements ListInterface<T>
{
    private Node firstNode; // Reference to first node of chain
    private int numberOfEntries;
```

---

1. We named this class LList instead of LinkedList to avoid confusion with Java's class LinkedList in the package java.util. You will see Java's LinkedList at the end of this chapter.

```
 9
10      public LList()
11      {
12         initializeDataFields();
13      } // end default constructor
14
15      public void clear()
16      {
17         initializeDataFields();
18      } // end clear
19      < Implementations of the public methods add, remove, replace, getEntry, contains,
20        getLength, isEmpty, and toArray go here. >
21      . . .
22
23      // Initializes the class's data fields to indicate an empty list.
24      private void initializeDataFields()
25      {
26         firstNode = null;
27         numberOfEntries = 0;
28      } // end initializeDataFields
29
30      // Returns a reference to the node at a given position.
31      // Precondition: List is not empty;
32      //                1 <= givenPosition <= numberOfEntries.
33      private Node getNodeAt(int givenPosition)
34      {
35         < See Segment 14.7. >
36      } // end getNodeAt
37
38      private class Node // Private inner class
39      {
40         < See Listing 3-4 in Chapter 3. >
41      } // end Node
42  } // end LList
```

As we discussed earlier, this version of the class will maintain only a head reference to the chain of nodes. The data field firstNode is this head reference. Another data field, numberOfEntries, records the number of entries in the current list. Recall that this number is also the number of nodes in the chain. The default constructor simply initializes these data fields by calling the private method initializeDataFields. So initially, the list is empty, firstNode is null, and numberOfEntries is 0.

**Design Decision: What should be the relationship between LList's constructor and its method clear?**

LList's constructor and its method clear both set the class's data fields to the same initial values by calling a private method initializeDataFields. We could have used assignment statements in both the constructor and clear instead of calling a private method, as we did previously for classes such as LinkedStack in Chapter 6 and LinkedQueue and LinkedDeque in Chapter 11. Although both techniques adhere to the desirable guideline that the constructor's initialization of the class's data fields be obvious, LList also follows another desirable guideline: to reuse code when possible. Since the tasks of initializing and clearing are simple, either approach is acceptable. Later in this chapter, we will revise LList by giving a tail reference to the chain of linked nodes. We will have to change only the private method initializeDataFields, instead of changing both the constructor and the method clear.

Another way to avoid repeating the assignment statements in LList's constructor and method clear is to have the constructor call clear, and then to define clear as follows:

```
public final void clear() // Note the final method
{
   firstNode = null;
   numberOfEntries = 0;
} // end clear
```

As we note in Appendix D, when a constructor calls another public method such as clear, that method should be final so that no subclass can override it, thereby changing the effect of the constructor. Adding final to clear's header is an implementation detail that is not reflected in ListInterface. Recall from the Prelude that an interface cannot declare a method to be final. Having the constructor call clear, however, makes it less obvious that the constructor initializes the data fields. Moreover, we might want to modify the definition of clear within LList—even though a subclass cannot— and such a change can adversely affect the constructor.

The constructor should not call clear. Initializing an object and clearing its data are two different actions conceptually that should not be coupled. Subsequent modifications to clear should not affect the constructor. In the class AList in the previous chapter, note that the constructor is unrelated to the method clear, as they perform different actions.

## Adding to the End of the List

**14.9**    Let's choose the methods add and toArray as the core methods that we will implement first.

We begin with the first add method. This method adds a new entry to the end of the list. Like the statements in Segment 14.4, the following statements make this addition:

```
Node newNode = new Node(newEntry);
Node lastNode = getNodeAt(numberOfEntries);
lastNode.setNextNode(newNode);
```

Assuming that we have the private method getNodeAt, which we defined in Segment 14.7, we can complete the method add as follows:

```
public void add(T newEntry)
{
   Node newNode = new Node(newEntry);

   if (isEmpty())
      firstNode = newNode;
   else                              // Add to end of nonempty list
   {
      Node lastNode = getNodeAt(numberOfEntries);
      lastNode.setNextNode(newNode); // Make last node reference new node
   } // end if

   numberOfEntries++;
} // end add
```

This method first creates a new node for the new entry. If the list is empty, it adds the new node by making firstNode reference it. If the list is not empty, however, we must locate the end of the list. Because we have a reference only to the first node, we must traverse the list until we locate the last node and obtain a reference to it. We call the private method getNodeAt to accomplish this task. Since the data field numberOfEntries contains the size of the list, and since we identify list entries by their positions within the list beginning with 1, the last node is at position numberOfEntries. We need to pass this value to getNodeAt. Once getNodeAt gives us a reference to the last node, we can set the last node's link to reference the new node.

Note that we must define isEmpty, since add calls it, and so we add it to our core group of methods that we define first.

## Adding at a Given Position Within the List

**14.10**    The second add method adds a new entry at a specified position within the list. After creating a new node that newNode references, we see whether the existing list is empty. If it is, we add the new node to the list by writing firstNode = newNode, as we did in the first add method. If the list is not empty, we must consider two cases:

- Case 1: Adding the entry to the beginning of the list
- Case 2: Adding the entry at a position other than the beginning of the list

Segment 14.2 gives the following statements for an addition to the beginning of a list:

```
Node newNode = new Node(newEntry);
newNode.setNextNode(firstNode);
firstNode = newNode;
```

Recall that these statements apply whether the list is empty or not. Additions anywhere else are performed by the statements shown in Segment 14.3:

```
Node newNode = new Node(newEntry);
Node nodeBefore = getNodeAt(newPosition - 1);
Node nodeAfter = nodeBefore.getNextNode();
newNode.setNextNode(nodeAfter);
nodeBefore.setNextNode(newNode);
```

**14.11**    **The Java method.** The following implementation of the add method is based on the previous code fragments. We begin by checking the validity of the insertion position, newPosition. If it is within range, we create the new node. We then insert the new node into the chain according to its intended position, newPosition: The insertion is either at the beginning of the list or somewhere else in the list.

```
public void add(int newPosition, T newEntry)
{
   if ((newPosition >= 1) && (newPosition <= numberOfEntries + 1))
   {
      Node newNode = new Node(newEntry);
      if (newPosition == 1)                    // Case 1
      {
         newNode.setNextNode(firstNode);
         firstNode = newNode;
      }
      else                                     // Case 2: List is not empty
      {                                        // and newPosition > 1
         Node nodeBefore = getNodeAt(newPosition - 1);
         Node nodeAfter = nodeBefore.getNextNode();
         newNode.setNextNode(nodeAfter);
         nodeBefore.setNextNode(newNode);
      } // end if

      numberOfEntries++;
   }
   else
      throw new IndexOutOfBoundsException(
            "Illegal position given to add operation.");
} // end add
```

**Question 6** Consider the first else clause of the previous method add.

**a.**    What assert statement could you add to this clause?

**b.**    What call to getNodeAt could replace the value assigned to nodeAfter?

**c.**    Should we make the change suggested in Part *b*?

**Question 7** In the previous method add, the second if statement tests the value of newPosition. Should the boolean expression it tests be isEmpty() || (newPosition == 1)? Explain.

**Question 8** How do the add methods given in Segments 14.9 and 14.11 enforce the precondition of getNodeAt?

## The Methods isEmpty and toArray

14.12 **The method isEmpty and assertions.** The implementation of the method isEmpty could simply test that the length of the list is zero, as it did in the array-based implementations that you saw in the previous chapter. However, we have another criterion that we could use here. When a list is empty, the reference firstNode is null. If our implementation is correct, either criterion is fine, but what happens during development when some part of our class might contain an error in logic? We can use assert statements involving the second criterion to help us catch an error, as in the following version of isEmpty:

```java
public boolean isEmpty()
{
    boolean result;
    if (numberOfEntries == 0) // Or getLength() == 0
    {
        assert firstNode == null;
        result = true;
    }
    else
    {
        assert firstNode != null;
        result = false;
    } // end if

    return result;
} // end isEmpty
```

14.13 **Example.** Let's look at an example of how the previous implementation of isEmpty can help us find an error in logic. Consider the definition of the first add method given in Segment 14.9. If we had been concerned that we might forget to increment the data field numberOfEntries, we might have written numberOfEntries++ as the method's first action instead of as one of its last. This change would have caused an error. If the list was empty when the method was called, numberOfEntries would have been given the value 1, and isEmpty would have been invoked. Since firstNode would have been null, the second assertion within isEmpty would have produced an error message like the following one, assuming that we had enabled assertions:

```
Exception in thread "main" java.lang.AssertionError
        at LList.isEmpty(LList.java:175)
        at LList.add(LList.java:23)
        at Driver.main(driver.java:15);
```

This message indicates that the method add called isEmpty, which produced the assertion error. We could clarify this message by adding to the assert statements in isEmpty. For example, if the second assert statement is

**assert** firstNode != **null** : "numberOfEntries is not 0 but firstNode is null";

the previous error message would begin as follows:

```
Exception in thread "main" java.lang.AssertionError:
numberOfEntries is not 0 but firstNode is null
```

If we ran our program without enabling assertions, isEmpty would simply test numberOf-Entries. Since numberOfEntries would not be zero, isEmpty would return false, so add's else clause would execute. When add invoked getNodeAt(1), null would be returned—since firstNode would be null—and assigned to lastNode. As a result, lastNode.setNextNode(newNode) would cause an exception and would produce an error message such as

```
Exception in thread "main" java.lang.NullPointerException
        at LList$Node.access$102(LList.java:212)
        at LList.add(LList.java:28)
        at Driver.main(driver.java:15);
```

This message is not as clear as the previous one, so more effort would be needed to discover the problem.

**Question 9** Suppose that the body of the method isEmpty contains only the following single statement:

```
return (numberOfEntries == 0) && (firstNode == null);
```

If we make the error in the method add that is described in the previous segment, what happens when add is called and the list is empty? Assume that assertions are enabled.

14.14   **The method toArray.** By implementing the method toArray, we will be able to test the previous methods that we have written before we complete the rest of LList. The method must traverse the chain and copy the data in each node to an element within an array. Thus, it needs a local variable to reference each node in the chain. For example, currentNode could reference the node whose data we want to copy. That data is currentNode.getData().

   Initially, we want currentNode to reference the first node in the chain, so we set it to firstNode. To make currentNode reference the next node, we would execute the statement

```
currentNode = currentNode.getNextNode();
```

Thus, we can write a loop that iterates until currentNode becomes null.

   The following method toArray uses these ideas:

```
public T[] toArray()
{
    // The cast is safe because the new array contains null entries
    @SuppressWarnings("unchecked")
    T[] result = (T[])new Object[numberOfEntries];

    int index = 0;
    Node currentNode = firstNode;
    while ((index < numberOfEntries) && (currentNode != null))
    {
        result[index] = currentNode.getData();
        currentNode = currentNode.getNextNode();
        index++;
    } // end while

    return result;
} // end toArray
```

**Question 10** In the previous implementation of toArray, the while statement tests the values of both index and currentNode. Can you replace the while statement with

   **a.**   while (index < numberOfEntries)
   **b.**   while (currentNode != null)

Explain your responses.

SELF-TEST

**Question 11** Compare the work required by the loop in the previous method `toArray` with that required by the following version of the loop:

```
int index = 0;
Node currentNode = firstNode;
while ((index < numberOfEntries) && (currentNode != null))
{
    currentNode = getNodeAt(index + 1);
    result[index] = currentNode.getData();
    index++;
} // end while
```

## Testing the Core Methods

**14.15** Earlier, we realized that the add methods are fundamental to our class, so they are part of the core group of methods that we implement and test first. The method `toArray` lets us see whether add works correctly, so it too is in our core group. The constructor is also fundamental, and so is the method `initializeDataFields`, since the constructor calls it. Similarly, since add calls `isEmpty` and `getNodeAt`, they are among the core methods that we implement and test first. Although `clear` is not a core method, we have defined it, and so we will test it. Lastly, we define the method `getLength` as a check that the add methods correctly maintain the field `numberOfEntries`. Although it is not really an essential method right now, its definition is simple and is the same as for the array-based implementation that you saw in the previous chapter.

Now that we have implemented these core methods, we can test them. Since `LList` implements `ListInterface`, however, we first must write stubs for the remaining methods in the interface. We assume that we have completed that simple task.

Let's choose the add method that adds to the end of the list for our first tests. Listing 14-2 contains an example of a `main` method that we could use for this purpose. Notice how the descriptive output makes it easier to see whether our implementation is correct. The method `displayList` is the same as the one that we used in the previous chapter to test the partial implementation of the class `AList`. You can see it in the answer to Self-Test Question 4 in that chapter. Recall that this method calls the method `toArray`, thereby testing it.

---

**LISTING 14-2** A main method that tests part of the implementation of the ADT list

```
1  public static void main(String[] args)
2  {
3      System.out.println("Create an empty list.");
4      ListInterface<String> myList = new LList<>();
5      System.out.println("List should be empty; isEmpty returns " +
6                          myList.isEmpty() + ".");
7      System.out.println("\nTesting add to end:");
8      myList.add("15");
9      myList.add("25");
10     myList.add("35");
11     myList.add("45");
12     System.out.println("List should contain 15 25 35 45.");
13     displayList(myList);
14     System.out.println("List should not be empty; isEmpty() returns " +
15                         myList.isEmpty() + ".");
16     System.out.println("\nTesting clear():");
17     myList.clear();
```

```
18      System.out.println("List should be empty; isEmpty returns " +
19                          myList.isEmpty() + ".");
20  } // end main
```

**Output**
```
Create an empty list.
List should be empty; isEmpty returns true.

Testing add to end:
List should contain 15 25 35 45.
List contains 4 entries, as follows:
15 25 35 45
List should not be empty; isEmpty() returns false.

Testing clear():
List should be empty; isEmpty returns true.
```

**Question 12** Consider the method displayList, as given in the answer to Self-Test Question 4 of Chapter 13. What is the time efficiency of this method when the list is an instance of

    **a.**  AList, as given in the previous chapter?

    **b.**  LList, as given in this chapter?

# Continuing the Implementation

To complete the class LList, we now define the methods remove, replace, getEntry, and contains.

**14.16**   **The method remove.** To remove the first entry from our list, we execute the statement

```
firstNode = firstNode.getNextNode();
```

To remove an entry after the first one, we execute the following statements:

```
Node nodeBefore = getNodeAt(givenPosition - 1);
Node nodeToRemove = nodeBefore.getNextNode();
Node nodeAfter = nodeToRemove.getNextNode();
nodeBefore.setNextNode(nodeAfter);
nodeToRemove = null;
```

Recall that the remove method returns the entry that it deletes from the list. Although the node that contains this entry is recycled, the entry itself is not, as long as the client saves the reference to it.

VideoNote
Completing the class
LList

```
public T remove(int givenPosition)
{
   T result = null;                            // Return value
   if ((givenPosition >= 1) && (givenPosition <= numberOfEntries))
   {
      assert !isEmpty();
      if (givenPosition == 1)                  // Case 1: Remove first entry
      {
         result = firstNode.getData();         // Save entry to be removed
         firstNode = firstNode.getNextNode();  // Remove entry
      }
```

```
    else                                    // Case 2: Not first entry
    {
        Node nodeBefore = getNodeAt(givenPosition - 1);
        Node nodeToRemove = nodeBefore.getNextNode();
        result = nodeToRemove.getData();       // Save entry to be removed
        Node nodeAfter = nodeToRemove.getNextNode();
        nodeBefore.setNextNode(nodeAfter);    // Remove entry
    } // end if
    numberOfEntries--;                          // Update count
    return result;                              // Return removed entry
}
else
    throw new IndexOutOfBoundsException(
            "Illegal position given to remove operation.");
} // end remove
```

Notice that we use the private method getNodeAt, which we wrote originally for the add methods, to locate the node before the one to be removed. This method is called only when we remove an entry other than the first one. Thus, its argument givenPosition − 1 will always be greater than zero, as its precondition requires.

Also notice that we do not explicitly set nodeToRemove to null after disconnecting the node. This variable is local to the remove method and so does not exist after the method completes execution. Although we could set nodeToRemove to null, doing so is not necessary.

**Question 13** Why is the assertion in the previous method true?

**14.17**   **The method replace.** Replacing a list entry requires us to replace the data portion of a node with other data. We can use the private method getNodeAt to locate the node and then simply replace its data portion. Before calling getNodeAt, we check that the list is not empty and the given position is valid. The implementation appears as follows:

```
public T replace(int givenPosition, T newEntry)
{
    if ((givenPosition >= 1) && (givenPosition <= numberOfEntries))
    {
        assert !isEmpty();
        Node desiredNode = getNodeAt(givenPosition);
        T originalEntry = desiredNode.getData();
        desiredNode.setData(newEntry);
        return originalEntry;
    }
    else
        throw new IndexOutOfBoundsException(
                "Illegal position given to replace operation.");
} // end replace
```

**Note:** The method replace replaces the data in a node, but not the node itself.

**Question 14** Compare the time required to replace an entry in a list using the previous method replace with the time required for the array-based version given in Segment 13.12 of the previous chapter.

**14.18** **The method getEntry.** Retrieving a list entry is straightforward:

```
public T getEntry(int givenPosition)
{
   if ((givenPosition >= 1) && (givenPosition <= numberOfEntries))
   {
      assert !isEmpty();
      return getNodeAt(givenPosition).getData();
   }
   else
      throw new IndexOutOfBoundsException(
               "Illegal position given to getEntry operation.");
} // end getEntry
```

The method getNodeAt returns a reference to the desired node, so

```
getNodeAt(givenPosition).getData()
```

is the data portion of that node.

Although our implementations of getEntry and replace are easy to write, each does more work than if we had used an array to represent the list. Here, getNodeAt starts at the first node in the chain and moves from node to node until it reaches the desired one. In Segment 13.12, you saw that replace and getEntry can reference the desired array entry directly, without involving any other entry in the array.

**Question 15** Consider the method displayList, as given in Listing 12-2 of Chapter 12. What is the time efficiency of this method when the list is an instance of

**a.** AList, as given in the previous chapter?
**b.** LList, as given in this chapter?

**14.19** **The method contains.** The method contains for a list could have the same definition as the one given in Segment 3.17 of Chapter 3 for a bag. However, the inner class Node now has set and get methods, so contains can appear as follows:

```
public boolean contains(T anEntry)
{
   boolean found = false;
   Node currentNode = firstNode;
   while (!found && (currentNode != null))
   {
      if (anEntry.equals(currentNode.getData()))
         found = true;
      else
         currentNode = currentNode.getNextNode();
   } // end while

   return found;
} // end contains
```

Because the ADT bag has a remove method that removes a given entry, it must do the same search as contains. For that reason, we revised the definition of contains in Chapter 3 so that the search is performed by a private method that both contains and remove can call. Our version of the ADT list, however, removes entries by position, not by the value of the entry. Thus, the search that contains does is performed only by contains.

**Note: Test the class LList**
The class LList is now complete and should be thoroughly tested before we continue. We leave this test to you as an exercise. You will be able to use your program later when you test the improved version of LList that we are about to write.

# A Refined Implementation

Currently, the chain of linked nodes that contains a list's entries has only a head reference. When we began writing the class LList, we noted that the first add method, which adds a new entry at the end of the chain, must invoke the private method getNodeAt to locate the chain's last node. To do so, getNodeAt must traverse the chain from its beginning. We can improve the time efficiency of this add method by maintaining a reference to the end of the chain, as well as a reference to the beginning of the chain, as pictured earlier in Figure 14-7b and repeated here in Figure 14-8. In this way, we avoid a traversal of the entire chain each time that add is called.

FIGURE 14-8       A linked chain with both a head reference and a tail reference

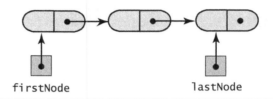

firstNode                          lastNode

**Question 16** Examine the implementation of the class LList given in this chapter. Which methods would require a new definition if you use both a head reference and a tail reference?

## The Tail Reference

**14.20**   The tail reference, like the head reference, is a private data field of the class. Thus, the private data fields of the revised class are now

```
private Node firstNode;      // Head reference to first node
private Node lastNode;       // Tail reference to last node
private int numberOfEntries; // Number of entries in list
```

By examining the class LList, as described earlier in this chapter, you should find that the two add methods and the methods remove and initializeDataFields are the ones that will involve the head and tail references and, thus, need to be revised. Although the private method getNodeAt can have the same definition as it does in LList, we can revise it to avoid traversing the chain when we need to access its last node. We should also revise the assertions in the method isEmpty. The rest of the original implementation, including the constructor, remains the same. Let's examine these revisions. We will name the revised class LListWithTail to distinguish it from the original one.

**14.21**   **The method initializeDataFields.** We begin with the method initializeDataFields, because the constructor calls it. It must initialize both the head and tail references as well as the field numberOfEntries:

```
private void initializeDataFields()
{
   firstNode = null;
   lastNode = null;
   numberOfEntries = 0;
} // end initializeDataFields
```

Here, and in the rest of the revision, changes to the original implementation are highlighted.

**14.22** **Adding to the end of the list.** The steps required to add an entry to the end of a list depend upon whether the list is empty or not. After an item is added to the end of an empty list, both the head and tail references must reference the new solitary node. Thus, after creating a new node that newNode references, the add method would execute

```
firstNode = newNode;
lastNode = newNode;
```

Adding to the end of a nonempty list no longer requires a traversal to locate the last entry: The tail reference lastNode provides this information. After the addition has been made, the tail reference must change to refer to the new last entry. The following statements perform these steps, as Figure 14-9 illustrates:

```
lastNode.setNextNode(newNode);
lastNode = newNode;
```

**FIGURE 14-9** Adding a node to the end of a nonempty chain that has a tail reference

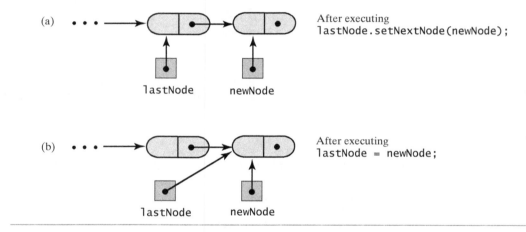

The following revision of the first add method reflects the previous comments:

```
public void add(T newEntry)
{
    Node newNode = new Node(newEntry);
    if (isEmpty())
        firstNode = newNode;
    else
        lastNode.setNextNode(newNode);
    lastNode = newNode;
    numberOfEntries++;
} // end add
```

Note that the method no longer calls getNodeAt to establish lastNode, as it did in Segment 14.9.

**14.23** **Adding to the list at a given position.** Adding to a list by position affects the tail reference only when we are adding to an empty list or adding to the end of a nonempty list. Other cases do not affect the tail reference, so we treat them as we did in Segment 14.11 when we did not have a tail reference.

Thus, the implementation of the method that adds by position is

```
public void add(int newPosition, T newEntry)
{
```

```
if ((newPosition >= 1) && (newPosition <= numberOfEntries + 1))
{
    Node newNode = new Node(newEntry);
    if (isEmpty())
    {
        firstNode = newNode;
        lastNode = newNode;
    }
    else if (newPosition == 1)
    {
        newNode.setNextNode(firstNode);
        firstNode = newNode;
    }
    else if (newPosition == numberOfEntries + 1)
    {
        lastNode.setNextNode(newNode);
        lastNode = newNode;
    }
    else
    {
        Node nodeBefore = getNodeAt(newPosition - 1);
        Node nodeAfter = nodeBefore.getNextNode();
        newNode.setNextNode(nodeAfter);
        nodeBefore.setNextNode(newNode);
    } // end if

    numberOfEntries++;
}
else
    throw new IndexOutOfBoundsException(
                "Illegal position given to add operation.");
} // end add
```

**14.24 Removing an entry from a list.** Removing an entry can affect the tail reference in two cases:

- Case 1: If the list contains one entry and we remove it, an empty list results, and we must set both the head and tail references to null.
- Case 2: If the list contains several entries and we remove the last one, we must change the tail reference so that it references the new last entry.

Figure 14-10 illustrates these two cases.

---

**FIGURE 14-10**    Removing the last node from a chain that has both head and tail references when the chain contains (a) one node; (b) more than one node

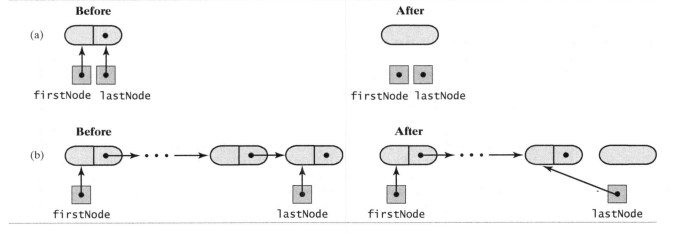

The following method considers the previous two cases in its implementation of the remove operation:

```java
public T remove(int givenPosition)
{
   T result = null;                             // Return value
   if ((givenPosition >= 1) && (givenPosition <= numberOfEntries))
   {
      assert !isEmpty();
      if (givenPosition == 1)                   // Case 1: Remove first entry
      {
         result = firstNode.getData();          // Save entry to be removed
         firstNode = firstNode.getNextNode();
         if (numberOfEntries == 1)
            lastNode = null;                     // Solitary entry was removed
      }
      else                                      // Case 2: Not first entry
      {
         Node nodeBefore = getNodeAt(givenPosition - 1);
         Node nodeToRemove = nodeBefore.getNextNode();
         Node nodeAfter = nodeToRemove.getNextNode();
         nodeBefore.setNextNode(nodeAfter);
         result = nodeToRemove.getData();        // Save entry to be removed

         if (givenPosition == numberOfEntries)
            lastNode = nodeBefore;               // Last node was removed
      } // end if
      numberOfEntries--;
   }
   else
      throw new IndexOutOfBoundsException(
              "Illegal position given to remove operation.");
   return result;                               // Return removed entry
} // end remove
```

 **Note:** Adding to the end of a chain of linked nodes requires less work when you maintain a tail reference because you avoid a traversal of the chain. Removing the last node from a chain requires a traversal to locate the next-to-last node, whether or not you have a tail reference.

 **Question 17** In light of the tail reference, what changes should you make to the assertions in the method isEmpty, as given in Segment 14.12?

## The Efficiency of Using a Chain to Implement the ADT List

Let's consider the time complexity of some of the methods in our classes LList and LListWithTail. Several of these methods call the private method getNodeAt, as given in Segment 14.7. The loop in getNodeAt cycles $i - 1$ times in its search for the $i^{th}$ node in the chain. Thus, getNodeAt is $O(n)$ in general, but $O(1)$ when the loop is skipped. We will use this observation in our analysis of the public methods.

14.25   **Adding to the end of the list.** Because the chain in the class LList does not have a tail reference, LList's add method, as described in Segment 14.9, must traverse the entire chain of linked nodes to locate the last one before it can add an entry at the end of the list. The method calls getNodeAt to locate this node. Since getNodeAt is $O(n)$ in this case, this add method is also $O(n)$.

The class LListWithTail, on the other hand, does maintain a tail reference for its chain of linked nodes. Thus, its add method, as given in Segment 14.22, does not call getNodeAt, and so is $O(1)$.

**14.26**   **Adding to a list at a given position.** The add method, as given in Segment 14.11, for the class LList can add an entry to the beginning of a list in O(1) time. Adding to a list at other positions depends on the position. As the position number increases, the time needed for an addition increases. In other words, add is O(*n*) when the addition is beyond the beginning of the list, because add calls getNodeAt in such cases, and getNodeAt is O(*n*).

The add method, as given in Segment 14.23, for the class LListWithTail can add an entry to either the beginning or the end of a list in O(1) time. Note that getNodeAt is not called in these cases. For other additions, getNodeAt requires O(*n*) time.

**Question 18** What is the Big Oh of the method toArray, as given in Segment 14.14?

**Question 19** What is the Big Oh of the method remove, as given in Segment 14.16?

**Question 20** What is the Big Oh of the method replace, as given in Segment 14.17?

**Question 21** What is the Big Oh of the method getEntry, as given in Segment 14.18?

**Question 22** What is the Big Oh of the method contains, as given in Segment 14.19?

**Question 23** In light of the tail reference, what changes can you make to the method getNodeAt, as given in Segment 14.7, to improve the time complexity of the methods replace, getEntry, and contains?

**14.27**   Using Big Oh notation, Figure 14-11 summarizes the time complexities of the operations of the ADT list for the implementations that use an array and a chain of linked nodes. For some operations, two or three complexities are given: The first one indicates the time requirement for an operation at the beginning of the list, the second is for operations at other positions within the list, and the third one, if it exists, is for operations at the end of the list.

**FIGURE 14-11**   The time efficiencies of the ADT list operations for three implementations, expressed in Big Oh notation

| Operation | Alist | LList | LListWithTail |
|---|---|---|---|
| add(newEntry) | O(1) | O(*n*) | O(1) |
| add(newPosition, newEntry) | O(*n*); O(*n*); O(1) | O(1); O(*n*) | O(1); O(*n*); O(1) |
| toArray() | O(*n*) | O(*n*) | O(*n*) |
| remove(givenPosition) | O(*n*); O(*n*); O(1) | O(1); O(*n*) | O(1); O(*n*) |
| replace(givenPosition, newEntry) | O(1) | O(1); O(*n*) | O(1); O(*n*); O(1) |
| getEntry(givenPosition) | O(1) | O(1); O(*n*) | O(1); O(*n*); O(1) |
| contains(anEntry) | O(*n*) | O(*n*) | O(*n*) |
| clear(), getLength(), isEmpty() | O(1) | O(1) | O(1) |

For example, the first add method in an array-based implementation is O(1), and the second add method is O(*n*), unless it adds at the end of the list, in which case it is O(1). The method toArray is always O(*n*), and getEntry is always O(1).

For the linked implementation LList, which maintains only a head reference to the chain of nodes, the first add method and toArray are each O(*n*). The second add method is O(*n*) unless it adds to the beginning of the list, in which case it is O(1).

For the linked implementation LListWithTail, which maintains both a head reference and a tail reference to the chain of nodes, the first add method is O(1), and toArray is O(n). The second add method is O(n), unless it adds to either the beginning or the end of the list, in which case it is O(1).

As you can see, some of the operations have the same time complexity for each implementation. However, operations that add to the end of a list, replace an entry, or retrieve an entry take less time when you use an array to represent a list than when you use a chain of linked nodes. If your application uses these particular operations frequently, an array-based implementation could be attractive.

The operations that add or remove an entry at a given position have time requirements that depend on this position regardless of their implementation. If your application primarily adds and removes entries at or near the beginning of a list, use a linked implementation. If these operations are mostly at or near the end of the list, use an array-based implementation. The operations that you use the most in an application should influence your choice of implementation for an ADT.

**Design Decision: Which implementation of an ADT should you use?**
Even small changes to an ADT's underlying data structure can increase or decrease the time efficiency of the ADT's operations. When choosing an implementation for an ADT, you should consider the operations that your application requires. If you use a particular operation frequently, you want its implementation to be efficient. Conversely, if you rarely use an operation, you can afford to use a class that has an inefficient implementation of that operation.

Like the linked implementations you have seen in previous chapters, the classes LList and LListWithTail enable their instances to grow as large as necessary. You can add as many nodes to a chain—and, therefore, entries to a list—as computer memory allows. Although resizing the array in an array-based implementation gives you the same advantage, it comes with the cost of copying data from one array to another. No such copying occurs in a linked implementation.

In addition, a chain enables you to add and remove nodes without moving any existing entries that are already in the list. With an array, adding and removing entries usually requires that other entries be moved within the array. However, you must traverse a chain from its beginning to determine where to make the addition or deletion.

Retrieving an existing entry from a chain requires a similar traversal to locate the desired entry. When you use an array instead of a chain, you can access any element directly by position, without searching the array. However, a method such as contains that does not have the position of an entry must perform a search regardless of whether an array or a chain represents the list.

Finally, as you have seen before, a chain stores additional references compared to an array. For each entry in a list, a chain stores two references, compared to an array's one. This additional memory requirement is somewhat offset by the fact that a chain uses memory only as needed for each list entry, whereas an array often is larger than necessary, thereby wasting memory.

Any implementation of an ADT has its advantages and disadvantages. You should choose the implementation that best suits your particular application.

# Java Class Library: The Class LinkedList

**14.28**    Recall from Chapter 12 that the Java Class Library contains the interface java.util.List. This interface is like our ListInterface, but it declares more methods. Also, some methods have different names or specifications, and the list entries begin at position 0 instead of 1. Segment 12.14 of Chapter 12 summarized these differences.

The same package java.util contains the class LinkedList. This class implements the interface List, as well as the interfaces Queue and Deque that are described in Chapter 10. Thus, LinkedList defines more methods than are in the interface List. Furthermore, you can use the class LinkedList as an implementation of the ADT queue, deque, or list.

CHAPTER SUMMARY

- When a chain has only a head reference, the following are true:
  - Adding a node to the chain's beginning is a special case.
  - Removing the first node from the chain is a special case.
  - Adding or removing a node that is last in the chain requires a traversal of the entire chain.
  - Adding a node anywhere within a chain requires a change of at most two references.
  - Removing any node from a chain requires a change of at most two references.

- When a chain has both head and tail references, the following are true:
  - Adding a node to an empty chain is a special case.
  - Adding a node to the chain's end is a special case, but does not require a traversal.
  - Removing the last node from a chain is a special case.

- Maintaining a reference to a chain's last node as well as to its first node eliminates the need for a traversal when adding a node at the end of the chain. Thus, adding to the end of a list is faster when the chain has both head and tail references than when it has only a head reference. For this reason, we have used a chain that has both head and tail references to implement the ADT list.

EXERCISES

1. Add a constructor to the class LList that creates a list of objects in a given array in the reverse order. Consider at least two different ways to implement such a constructor. Which way requires the least amount of work?

2. Write a program that tests the class LList.

3. Consider the definition of the add method that adds an entry to a list at a given position and appears in Segment 14.11. Replace the statements that execute in case 1 with the following ones:

```
if (isEmpty() || (newPosition == 1)) // Case 1
{
   firstNode = newNode;
   newNode.setNextNode(firstNode);
}
```

   a. What is displayed by the following statements in a client of the modified LList?

```
ListInterface<String> myList = new LList<>();
myList.add(1, "30");
myList.add(2, "40");
myList.add(3, "50");
myList.add(1, "10");
myList.add(5, "60");
myList.add(2, "20");
int numberOfEntries = myList.getLength();
for (int position = 1; position <= numberOfEntries; position++)
   System.out.print(myList.getEntry(position) + " ");
```

   b. What methods, if any, in LList could be affected by the change to the method add when they execute? Why?

4. Suppose that you want an operation for the ADT list that adds an array of items to the end of the list. The header of the method could be as follows:

    `public void addAll(T[] items)`

    Write an implementation of this method for the class LList.

5. Define the method getCount, as described in Exercise 2 of the previous chapter, for the class LList. Compare the execution time required by this method with the version of getCount defined in the class AList.

6. Implement a smaller method for the class LList that returns true when the entries in one list are smaller than the entries in a second list.

7. Implement the getCount method of Exercise 10 of the previous chapter, but use the class LList instead of AList.

8. Suppose that a list contains Comparable objects. Implement a method that returns a new list of items that are greater than some given item. The header of the method could be as follows:

    `public ListInterface<T> getAllGreaterThan(Comparable<T> anObject)`

    Write an implementation of this method for the class LList. Make sure that your method does not affect the state of the original list.

9. Define the method remove, as described in Exercise 3 of the previous chapter, for the class LList.

10. Repeat the previous exercise, but remove all occurrences of anObject from the list.

11. Define the method moveToFront, as described in Exercise 4 of the previous chapter, for the class LList.

12. Modify the method removeLast, as described in Exercise 3 of the previous chapter, to removeFirst for the class LList.

13. Suppose that a list contains Comparable objects. Define the methods getMax and removeMax, as described in Exercise 7 of the previous chapter, for the class LList.

14. Consider an instance arrayList of AList, as given in the previous chapter. Let the list have an initial size of 10. Also, consider an instance of LList called chainList.

    a. How large is the underlying array after adding 145 items to arrayList?
    b. How large is the underlying array after adding 20 more items to arrayList?
    c. How many nodes are in the chain after adding 145 items to chainList?
    d. How many nodes are in the chain after adding 20 more items to chainList?
    e. Each node in a chain has two references, so a chain of $n$ nodes has $2n$ references. An array of size $n$, on the other hand, has $n$ references. Count the number of references in each of the situations described in Parts $a$ through $d$.
    f. When will arrayList use fewer references than chainList?
    g. When will chainList use fewer references than arrayList?

15. A doubly linked chain, like the one described in Exercise 12 of Chapter 3, has nodes that each can reference a previous node and a next node. In Chapter 3, the doubly linked chain has only a head reference, but it can have both a head reference and a tail reference, as Figure 14-12 illustrates.
    List the steps necessary to add a node to a doubly linked chain when the new node is

    a. First in the chain
    b. Last in the chain
    c. Between existing nodes in the chain

**FIGURE 14-12**     A doubly linked chain for Exercises 15 and 16 and Project 8

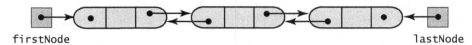

firstNode                                                                          lastNode

**16.** List the steps necessary to remove a node from the doubly linked chain shown in Figure 14-12 when the node is

    **a.** First in the chain
    **b.** Last in the chain
    **c.** Between existing nodes in the chain.

## PROJECTS

**1.** Write a program that thoroughly tests the class LListWithTail.

**2.** Listing 3-5 of Chapter 3 shows the class Node as part of a package. Create another package that contains Node, LList, and ListInterface. Revise LList to use this version of Node.

**3.** Create a Java interface that declares the following additional methods for a list:

```
/** Adds a new entry to the beginning of this list. */
public void addFirst(T newEntry)

/** Adds a new entry to the end of this list. */
public void addLast(T newEntry)

/** Removes and returns the first entry in this list. */
public T removeFirst()

/** Removes and returns the last entry in this list. */
public T removeLast()

/** Returns the first entry in this list. */
public T getFirst()

/** Returns the last entry in this list. */
public T getLast()

/** Moves the first entry in this list to the end of the list. */
public void moveToEnd()
```

Then define DoubleEndedListInterface by extending this interface and ListInterface. Write a class that implements DoubleEndedListInterface. Represent the list's entries by using a chain of nodes that has both a head reference and a tail reference. Write a program that thoroughly tests your class.

**4.** Repeat the previous project, but do not use a tail reference.

**5.** Adding nodes to or removing nodes from a linked chain requires a special case when the operation is at the beginning of the chain. To eliminate the special case, you can add a **dummy node** at the beginning of the chain. The dummy node is always present but does not contain a list entry. The chain, then, is never empty, and so the head reference is never null, even when the list is empty. Modify the class LList, as presented in this chapter, by adding a dummy node to the chain.

6.  In a circular linked chain, the last node references the first node. Commonly, only one external reference—to the last node—is maintained, since the first node is found easily from the last one. Figure 11-11 in Chapter 11 illustrates such a chain.

    Modify the class LList, as presented in this chapter, by using a circular linked chain and a tail reference.

7.  Implement as the class Ring the ADT ring that Project 3 of Chapter 1 described. Represent the ring as a chain of linked nodes. Consider using a circular linked chain, as described in the previous project.

8.  Implement and test a class of lists using a doubly linked chain, as shown in Figure 14-12, to represent the entries in the list. Use an inner class of nodes like the one that Exercise 12 of Chapter 3 asked you to define, but include set and get methods.

9.  You can add a dummy node, as Project 5 describes, to the beginning of a doubly linked chain. Modify the implementation of the ADT list described in the previous project by adding a dummy node to the beginning of the chain.

10. Define a class that is a linked implementation of the interface FixedSizeListInterface, as described in Project 9 of the previous chapter.

11. Repeat any of the projects 1 through 5 and 10 through 16 in the previous chapter by using the class LList instead of the class AList.

## ANSWERS TO SELF-TEST QUESTIONS

1.  To locate the $n^{th}$ node in a chain, getNodeAt starts at the first node and counts nodes as it traverses the chain from node to node, until it reaches the $n^{th}$ one. The following pseudocode describes the steps in more detail:

    ```
    currentNode = firstNode
    for (counter = 1 to n)
       currentNode = currentNode.getNextNode()
    ```
    *The desired node is at* currentNode

2.  Yes. With newPosition equal to numberOfNodes + 1, nodeBefore will reference the last node in the chain. Moreover, nodeAfter will be null, newNode's link field will be set to null, and the last node's link will reference the new node.

3.  No. The statements given in Segment 14.4 do not assign a new value to firstNode. Also, when the chain is empty, numberOfNodes is zero. The precondition of getNodeAt given in Segment 14.3 requires a positive argument. Even if you redesign getNodeAt, the empty chain will remain a special case.

4.  a. This approach is inefficient of time, since each addition causes getNodeAt to traverse the chain from its beginning until it locates the chain's last node. Thus, each addition depends on the length of the chain.
    b. Maintaining a tail reference would allow additions to the end of the chain to occur in O(1) time, that is, independently of the length of the chain.

5.  Since the chain is not empty, firstNode is not null. Thus, currentNode's initial value is not null. The loop in getNodeAt can iterate no more than numberOfNodes – 1 times. After the first iteration, currentNode references the second node. After the second iteration, it references the third node. If the loop were to iterate numberOfNodes – 1 times, currentNode would reference the last node. It would not be null.

6.  a. **assert** !isEmpty() && (newPosition > 1);
    b. getNodeAt(newPosition)
    c. No. Calling getNodeAt to get a reference to the node after the one that nodeBefore references results in another traversal of the chain from its beginning. The expression nodeBefore.getNextNode() provides a much faster way to get the required reference.

7. It could be, but testing for an empty list is unnecessary. The first `if` statement ensures that the value of `newPosition` ranges from 1 to `numberOfEntries` + 1. If the list is empty, `numberOfEntries` is 0, and therefore `newPosition` must be 1. Since adding to an empty list is the same as adding to the beginning of any list, we need not be concerned with empty lists.

8. The first method `add` invokes `getNodeAt` only if the list is not empty. Thus, the argument `numberOfEntries` passed to `getNodeAt` is ≥ 1 and ≤ itself. The second method `add` checks the validity of `newPosition` and then calls `getNodeAt` only if the list is not empty and `newPosition` > 1. It is possible for `newPosition` to equal `numberOfEntries` + 1, but since `getNodeAt`'s argument is `newPosition` − 1, the argument's value is ≤ `numberOfEntries` as required.

9. When the method `add` calls the method `isEmpty`, `isEmpty` will return false because `numberOfEntries` incorrectly is not zero. Thus, the method `getNodeAt` will be invoked. The second `assert` statement in `getNodeAt` will cause an `AssertionError`, because `currentNode` is `null`.

10. Either version of the `while` statement would control the loop in `toArray` correctly, assuming that the rest of the class is correct. Testing both `index` and `currentNode` in the `while` statement guards against a mistake somewhere else in the class.

11. The version of `toArray` that calls `getNodeAt` performs much more work than the original version. Each call to `getNodeAt` results in a traversal of the chain of nodes from its first node to the desired node. The original version of `toArray` traverses the chain only once.

12. The efficiency of `displayList` is directly related to the efficiency of the method `toArray`. For both `AList` and `LList`, `toArray` is O($n$). Thus, the efficiency of `displayList` is the same for both classes.

13. If the list is empty, `numberOfEntries` is zero. Thus, (`givenPosition >= 1`) && (`givenPosition <= 0`) is always false, and the method would then throw an exception. The only way the body of the first `if` statement can execute is if the list is not empty.

14. The method `replace` given in this chapter performs more work than an array-based `replace` because it must traverse the chain to locate the entry to replace. An array-based `replace` can locate the desired entry directly, given its array index.

15. The efficiency of `displayList` is directly related to the efficiency of the method `getEntry`. In the class `AList`, `getEntry` retrieves any entry from a list in O(1) time, because the list's entries are stored in an array. The corresponding method in `LList` must traverse a chain of linked nodes to retrieve a list entry. It is an O($n$) operation.

    **a.** For `AList`, `displayList` is O($n$).
    **b.** For `LList`, `displayList` is O($n^2$).

16. The methods `initializeDataFields`, both `add` methods, and the method `remove` would need to be revised to accommodate the addition of a tail reference.

17. The first assertion should be
    **assert** (firstNode == **null**) && (lastNode == **null**);
The second assertion should be
    **assert** (firstNode != **null**) && (lastNode != **null**);

18. O($n$).

19. O(1) when removing the first entry, or O($n$) otherwise.

20. O(1) when replacing the first entry, or O($n$) otherwise.

**21.** O(1) when retrieving the first entry, or O(*n*) otherwise.

**22.** O(*n*).

**23.**
```java
private Node getNodeAt(int givenPosition)
{
    assert (firstNode != null) && (1 <= givenPosition) && (givenPosition <= numberOfEntries);
    Node currentNode = firstNode;

    if (givenPosition == numberOfEntries)
        currentNode = lastNode;
    else if (givenPosition > 1) // Traverse the chain to locate the desired node
    {
        for (int counter = 1; counter < givenPosition; counter++)
            currentNode = currentNode.getNextNode();
    } // end if

    assert currentNode != null;
    return currentNode;
} // end getNodeAt
```

## Contents

## Prerequisites

**A**n iterator is an object that traverses a collection of data. During the traversal, you can look at the data entries, modify them, add entries, and remove entries. The Java Class Library contains two interfaces, Iterator and ListIterator, that specify methods for an iterator. While you could add these iterator methods to the operations of an ADT, you should instead implement them as a distinct class that interacts with the ADT. This iterator class can be outside of the ADT or hidden within its implementation. We will explore both of these approaches in this interlude and the next chapter.

## What Is an Iterator?

**JI5.1** How would you count the number of lines on this page? You could use your finger to point to each line as you counted it. Your finger would keep your place on the page. If you paused at a particular line, your finger would be on the current line, and there would be a previous line and a next line. If you think of this page as a list of lines, you would be traversing the list as you counted the lines.

An **iterator** is a program component that enables you to step through, or **traverse**, a collection of data such as a list, beginning with the first entry. During one complete traversal, or **iteration**, each data item is considered once. You control the progress of the iteration by repeatedly asking the iterator to give you a reference to the next entry in the collection. You also can modify the collection as you traverse it by adding, removing, or simply changing entries.

You are familiar with iteration because you have written loops. For example, if `nameList` is a list of strings, you can write the following `for` loop to display the entire list:

```java
int listSize = nameList.getLength();
for (int position = 1; position <= listSize; position++)
    System.out.println(nameList.getEntry(position));
```

Here the loop traverses, or **iterates**, through the entries in the list. Instead of simply displaying each entry, we could do other things to or with it.

**JI5.2**   Notice that the previous loop is at the client level, since it uses the ADT operation `getEntry` to access the list. For an array-based implementation of the list, `getEntry` can retrieve the desired array entry directly and quickly. But if a chain of linked nodes represents the list's entries, `getEntry` must move from node to node until it locates the desired one. For example, to retrieve the $n^{th}$ entry in the list, `getEntry` would begin at the first node in the chain and then move to the second node, the third node, and so on until it reached the $n^{th}$ node. At the next repetition of the loop, `getEntry` would retrieve the $n + 1^{st}$ entry in the list by beginning again at the first node in the chain and stepping from node to node until it reached the $n + 1^{st}$ node. This wastes time.

Iteration is such a common operation that we could include it as part of the ADT list. Doing so would enable a more efficient implementation than we can achieve at the client level. Notice that the operation `toArray` of the ADT list performs a traversal. It is an example of a traversal controlled by the ADT. A client can invoke `toArray` but cannot control its traversal once it begins.

But `toArray` only returns the list's entries. What if we want to do something else with them as we traverse them? We do not want to add another operation to the ADT each time we think of another way to use an iteration. We need a way for a client to step through a collection of data and retrieve or modify the entries. The traversal should keep track of its progress; that is, it should know where it is in the collection and whether it has accessed each entry. An iterator provides such a traversal.

**Note:** Iterators

An iterator is a program component that steps through, or traverses, a collection of data. The iterator keeps track of its progress during the traversal, or iteration. It can tell you whether a next entry exists and, if so, return a reference to it. During one cycle of the iteration, each data item is considered once.

The package `java.util` in the Java Class Library contains two standard interfaces—`Iterator` and `ListIterator`—that specify methods appropriate for an iterator. Let's begin by examining the interface `Iterator`.

# The Interface **Iterator**

**JI5.3**   Like many of the interfaces we have considered, Iterator, as given in Listing JI5-1, specifies a generic type to represent the data type of the entries involved in the iteration. It specifies only three methods—hasNext, next, and remove—that an iterator can have. These methods enable you to traverse a collection of data from its beginning.

---

**LISTING JI5-1**   Java's interface java.util.Iterator

```java
1  package java.util;
2  public interface Iterator<T>
3  {
4     /** Detects whether this iterator has completed its traversal
5         and gone beyond the last entry in the collection of data.
6         @return  True if the iterator has another entry to return. */
7     public boolean hasNext();
8
9     /** Retrieves the next entry in the collection and
10        advances this iterator by one position.
11        @return  A reference to the next entry in the iteration,
12                 if one exists.
13        @throws  NoSuchElementException if the iterator had reached the
14                 end already, that is, if hasNext() is false. */
15    public T next();
16
17    /** Removes from the collection of data the last entry that
18        next() returned. A subsequent call to next() will behave
19        as it would have before the removal.
20        Precondition: next() has been called, and remove() has not
21        been called since then. The collection has not been altered
22        during the iteration except by calls to this method.
23        @throws  IllegalStateException if next() has not been called, or
24                 if remove() was called already after the last call to next().
25        @throws  UnsupportedOperationException if the iterator does
26                 not permit a remove operation. */
27    public void remove(); // Optional method
28  } // end Iterator
```

---

**JI5.4**   An iterator marks its current position within a collection much as your finger can point to an entry in a list or to a line on this page. However, in Java, the position of an iterator is not *at* an entry. Instead, it is positioned either before the first entry in the collection, between two entries, or after the last entry, as Figure JI5-1 illustrates. For a collection of $n$ entries, the cursor has $n + 1$ possible positions. The **next entry** in an iteration is the one right after the position of the iterator's **cursor**. The method hasNext sees whether a next entry exists and returns true or false accordingly.

As long as hasNext returns true, the method next moves the iterator's cursor over the next entry and returns a reference to it, as Parts *a* and *b* of Figure JI5-2 illustrate. Repeated calls to next traverse through the collection. As the iteration progresses, the iterator returns entry after entry. Once next has returned the last entry in the collection, a subsequent call to it causes a NoSuchElementException.

**FIGURE JI5-1**   Possible positions of an iterator's cursor within a collection

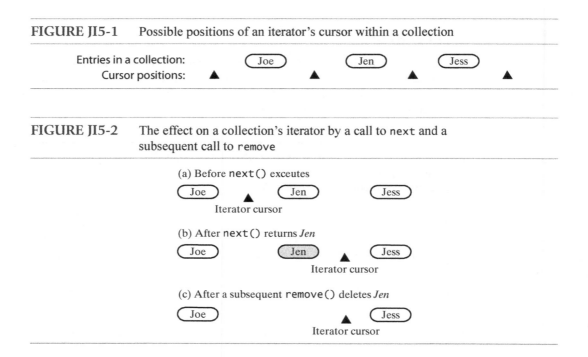

**FIGURE JI5-2**   The effect on a collection's iterator by a call to `next` and a
subsequent call to `remove`

The method `remove` removes the entry that `next` just returned, as shown in Part *c* of Figure JI5-2. Contrast this with, for example, the ADT list operation `remove`, which removes the entry at a given position within the list. When you implement the `Iterator` interface, you do not have to provide a `remove` operation—it is optional—but you do need to define a method `remove`, because it appears in the interface. Such a method should throw the exception `UnsupportedOperationException` if the client invoked it.

 **Note:** Java's interface `java.util.Iterator` specifies three methods: `hasNext`, `next`, and `remove`. The method `hasNext` sees whether the iterator has a next entry to return. If so, `next` returns a reference to it. The method `remove` can remove the entry last returned by a call to `next`, or it can simply throw an `UnsupportedOperationException` if you choose to disallow removals by the iterator.

 **Programming Tip:** All of the exceptions mentioned in the interface `Iterator` are runtime exceptions, so no `throws` clause is necessary in any of the methods' headers. In addition, you do not have to write `try` and `catch` blocks when you invoke these methods. However, you will need to import `NoSuchElementException` from the package `java.util`. The other exceptions are in `java.lang`, so no `import` statement is necessary for them.

## The Interface **Iterable**

**JI5.5** Different ways of obtaining an iterator for a given collection are possible. One way is for the collection itself to create and give you such an iterator. A class that implements the standard interface java.lang.Iterable—shown in Listing JI5-2—can do this. This interface declares only one method, iterator, which returns an iterator that adheres to the interface Iterator. We will use this method in the examples that follow.

---

**LISTING JI5-2** The interface java.lang.Iterable

```
1 package java.lang;
2 public interface Iterable<T>
3 {
4     /** @return  An iterator for a collection of objects of type T. */
5     Iterator<T> iterator();
6 } // end Iterable
```

---

## Using the Interface **Iterator**

Some details of using an iterator depend on the approach used to implement the iterator methods. The next chapter will explore these approaches. For now, we assume that the class that implements an ADT has a method that returns an iterator to the ADT's entries so that we can focus on how the methods in the interface Iterator behave.

**JI5.6**  **Example.** Let's look at an example of how the methods hasNext and next of the interface Iterator work with the ADT list. Suppose that our ListInterface extends the interface Iterable, and the class MyList implements ListInterface. The following statements create a list of names, which are simply strings:

```
ListInterface<String> nameList = new MyList<>();
nameList.add("Jamie");
nameList.add("Joey");
nameList.add("Rachel");
```

At this point, nameList contains the strings

Jamie
Joey
Rachel

To get an iterator for nameList, we call nameList's method iterator as follows:

```
Iterator<String> nameIterator = nameList.iterator();
```

The iterator nameIterator is positioned just before the first entry in the list. The following sequence of events demonstrates the iterator methods:

- nameIterator.hasNext() returns true because a next entry exists.
- nameIterator.next() returns the string *Jamie* and advances the iterator.
- nameIterator.next() returns the string *Joey* and advances the iterator.
- nameIterator.next() returns the string *Rachel* and advances the iterator.
- nameIterator.hasNext() returns false because the iterator is beyond the end of the list.
- nameIterator.next() causes a NoSuchElementException.

Figure JI5-3 illustrates these events.

**FIGURE JI5-3**    The effect of the iterator methods `hasNext` and `next` on a list

Iterator cursor ▶

| Jamie |
| Joey |
| Rachel |

`hasNext()` returns true

▶
| **Jamie** |
| Joey |
| Rachel |

`next()` returns *Jamie* and
advances the iterator

| Jamie |
▶ | **Joey** |
| Rachel |

`next()` returns *Joey* and
advances the iterator

| Jamie |
| Joey |
▶ | **Rachel** |

`next()` returns *Rachel* and
advances the iterator

| Jamie |
| Joey |
| Rachel |
▶

`hasNext()` returns false;
`next()` causes a `NoSuchElementException`

**JI5.7**    **Example.** We can use an iterator to display all the entries in a list. The following statements display the strings in the list `nameList`, one per line:

```
Iterator<String> nameIterator = nameList.iterator();
while (nameIterator.hasNext())
    System.out.println(nameIterator.next());
```

We first create an iterator object by invoking `nameList`'s method `iterator`. The resulting iterator
`nameIterator` is positioned just before the first entry in the list. Therefore, `nameIterator.next()`
will return that first entry and advance the iterator. As long as `hasNext` returns true, `next` returns
the next entry in the list and advances the iterator. Thus, every entry in the list is retrieved and
displayed.

**JI5.8**    **Example.** The interface `Iterator` provides an operation to remove an entry from a data collection. This entry is the one returned by the last call to the method `next`. Thus, you must invoke `next`
before you can call `remove`.
     If `nameList` contains the strings *Andy*, *Brittany*, and *Chris*, and `nameIterator` is defined as
in the previous example,

- `nameIterator.next()`  returns the string *Andy* and advances the iterator.
- `nameIterator.next()` returns the string *Brittany* and advances the iterator.
- `nameIterator.remove()` removes *Brittany* from the list.
- `nameIterator.next()` returns the string *Chris* and advances the iterator.

Figure JI5-4 shows the list during the previous iteration.

FIGURE JI5-4    The effect of the iterator methods next and remove on a list

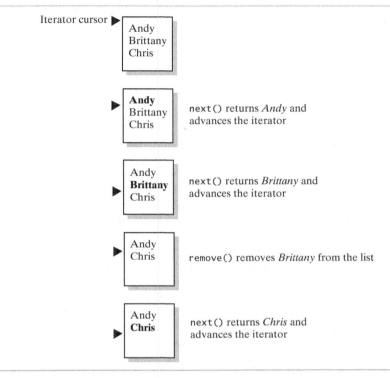

Iterator cursor ▶

| Andy<br>Brittany<br>Chris |

▶ | **Andy**<br>Brittany<br>Chris |    next() returns *Andy* and<br>advances the iterator

| Andy<br>**Brittany**<br>Chris |
▶                    next() returns *Brittany* and<br>advances the iterator

| Andy<br>Chris |
▶          remove() removes *Brittany* from the list

| Andy<br>**Chris** |
▶           next() returns *Chris* and<br>advances the iterator

**JI5.9**

**Example.** The requirement that you invoke next before you call remove results in two situations that cause the exception IllegalStateException. If nameList is defined as in the previous example, and we write

```
Iterator<String> nameIterator = namelist.iterator();
nameIterator.hasNext();
nameIterator.remove();
```

an IllegalStateException occurs because we did not call next before we called remove. Similarly, if we instead write

```
nameIterator.next();
nameIterator.remove();
nameIterator.remove();
```

the second remove causes an IllegalStateException because remove had been called already since the most recent call to next.

**Question 1** Assume that nameList contains the names Jamie, Joey, and Rachel, as it does in Segment JI5.6. What output is produced by the following Java statements?

```
Iterator<String> nameIterator = namelist.iterator();
nameIterator.next();
nameIterator.next();
nameIterator.remove();
System.out.println(nameIterator.hasNext());
System.out.println(nameIterator.next());
```

**Question 2** If `nameList` contains at least three strings, and `nameIterator` is defined as in the previous question, write Java statements that display the list's third entry.

**Question 3** Given `nameList` and `nameIterator` as described in the previous question, write statements that display the even-numbered entries in the list. That is, display the second entry, the fourth entry, and so on.

**Question 4** Given `nameList` and `nameIterator` as described in Question 2, write statements that remove all entries from the list.

**JI5.10 Multiple iterators.** Although the previous examples show one iterator traversing a collection, we can have several iterations of the same collection in progress simultaneously. For example, imagine a printed list of names that are not distinct and are in no particular order. Running one finger down that list to count the names is like having one iteration of a list. Now suppose that you want to count the number of times each name occurs in the printed list. You can use two fingers, as follows. With your left hand, use one finger to point to the first name in the list. With your right hand, use one finger to point to each of the names in the list, starting with the first one. As you traverse the list with your right hand, compare each name to the name that your left hand marks. In this way, you can count the number of times the first name occurs in the list. Now move your left-hand finger to the next name in the list and use your right hand to point to the beginning of the list. Repeat the previous process to count the number of times that the second name appears in the list. Try it with the names in Figure JI5-5. (Since your left hand will encounter *Jane* three times, you will repeat the computation needlessly unless you are careful. We consider this detail a bit later.)

Each of your two fingers can traverse the list independently of the other. They are like two independent iterators that traverse the same list, as you will see in the next example.

**FIGURE JI5-5**   Counting the number of times that *Jane* appears in a list of names

|  |  | **Number of times** *Jane* **appears in list** |
|---|---|---|
| Brad | Right hand as it | 0 |
| Left hand → Jane | advances | 1 |
| Bob | through the list | 1 |
| Jane |  | 2 |
| Bette |  | 2 |
| Brad |  | 2 |
| Jane |  | 3 |
| Brenda |  | 3 |

*Jane* **occurs 3 times**

**JI5.11**    **Example.** Let's write some code that counts the occurrences of each name shown in Figure JI5-5. Let nameIterator correspond to your left hand in the figure. Now we'll define a second iterator, countingIterator, that corresponds to your right hand. For each name that your left hand marks, your right hand traverses the entire list to count the occurrences of that name. Thus, we have the following nested loops, assuming that nameList is the list:

```java
Iterator<String> nameIterator = namelist.iterator();
while (nameIterator.hasNext())
{
    String currentName = nameIterator.next();
    int nameCount = 0;
    Iterator<String> countingIterator = namelist.iterator();
    while (countingIterator.hasNext())
    {
        String nextName = countingIterator.next();
        if (currentName.equals(nextName))
            nameCount++;
    } // end while
    System.out.println(currentName + " occurs " + nameCount + " times.");
} // end while
```

To reset countingIterator to the list's beginning, we call the the method iterator again, since the interface Iterator does not have a method for this purpose.

   With the names given in Figure JI5-5, these statements produce the following output:

```
Brad occurs 2 times.
Jane occurs 3 times.
Bob occurs 1 times.
Jane occurs 3 times.
Bette occurs 1 times.
Brad occurs 2 times.
Jane occurs 3 times.
Brenda occurs 1 times.
```

As you can see, since nameIterator (your left hand) encounters *Brad* twice and *Jane* three times, the computation in the inner loop is repeated needlessly. For example, we compute that *Brad* occurs twice each time nameIterator encounters *Brad*.

   If nameIterator supports a remove operation, and if we are allowed to destroy the list, we can remove the duplicate entries—and thereby prevent the repeated computations—by modifying the if statement as follows:

```java
if (currentName.equals(nextName))
{
    nameCount++;
    if (nameCount > 1)
        countingIterator.remove();
} // end if
```

When nameCount exceeds 1, nextName must be a name that the iterator countingIterator has retrieved from the list more than once. Thus, we remove that entry so that nameIterator will not encounter it. We do so by invoking countingIterator.remove(). The iterator countingIterator then continues with the next entry.

## Iterable and for-each loops

**JI5.12**  A class that implements the interface Iterable has a distinct advantage over classes that do not: You can use a for-each loop to traverse the objects in an instance of such a class. For example, suppose that nameList is a newly created instance of a class of lists, and the class implements Iterable. Let's add four strings to this empty list, as follows:

```java
nameList.add("Joe");
nameList.add("Jess");
```

```
92          @throws  IllegalStateException if next() or previous() has not
93                   been called, or if remove() or add() has been called
94                   already after the last call to next() or previous().
95          @throws  UnsupportedOperationException if the iterator does not
96                   permit a set operation. */
97     public void set(T newEntry); // Optional method
98  } // end ListIterator
```

**JI5.14 Observations.** Notice that `ListIterator` extends `Iterator`. Thus, `ListIterator` would include the methods `hasNext`, `next`, and `remove` from the interface `Iterator`, even if we did not write them explicitly. We have done so for your reference and to indicate `remove`'s additional behavior.

The methods `remove`, `add`, and `set` are optional in the sense that you can choose not to provide one or more of these operations. In that case, however, each such operation must have an implementation that throws the exception `UnsupportedOperationException` if the client invokes the operation. An iterator of type `ListIterator` that does not support `remove`, `add`, and `set` is still useful, since it enables you to traverse a list in both directions. It is also easier to implement without these operations.

The programming tip given in Segment JI5.4 for the interface `Iterator` applies here as well. We repeat it here in terms of `ListInterface`.

**Programming Tip:** All of the exceptions mentioned in the interface `ListIterator` are run-time exceptions, so no `throws` clause is necessary in any of the methods' headers. In addition, you do not have to write `try` and `catch` blocks when you invoke these methods. However, you will need to import `NoSuchElementException` from the package `java.util`. The other exceptions are in `java.lang`, so no `import` statement is necessary for them.

**JI5.15 The next entry.** Recall that the method `hasNext` sees whether a next entry exists after the iterator's position. If one exists, `next` returns a reference to it and advances the iterator's cursor by one position, as Figure JI5-2 illustrated. Repeated calls to `next` step through the list. So far, nothing is different from what you learned about the interface `Iterator` earlier in this chapter.

**JI5.16 The previous entry.** `ListIterator` also provides access to the entry just before the iterator's position—that is, to the previous entry. The method `hasPrevious` sees whether a previous entry exists. If so, the method `previous` returns a reference to it and moves the iterator's cursor back by one position. Figure JI5-6 shows the effect of `previous` on a list. Intermixing calls to `previous` and `next` enables you to move back and forth within the list. If you call `next` and then call `previous`, each method returns the same entry. Like `next`, `previous` throws an exception when called after it has completed its traversal of the list.

**Note:** The cursor position of an iterator of type `ListIterator` always is between the entry that `previous` will return and the entry that `next` will return.

**FIGURE JI5-6** The effect of a call to previous on a list

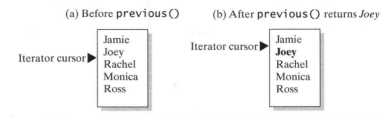

**JI5.17 The indices of the current and previous entries.** As Figure JI5-7 shows, the methods nextIndex and previousIndex each return the index of the entry that a subsequent call to next or previous, respectively, would return. Note that the iterator numbers the list's entries beginning with 0, instead of 1 as our ADT list operations do. If a call to next would throw an exception because the iterator is at the end of the list, nextIndex returns the size of the list. Similarly, if a call to previous would throw an exception because the iterator is at the beginning of the list, previousIndex returns -1.

**FIGURE JI5-7** The indices returned by the methods nextIndex and previousIndex

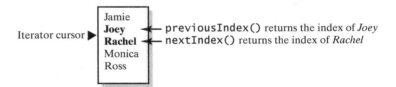

 **Note:** The interface ListIterator specifies nine methods, including the three methods that Iterator specifies. They are hasNext, hasPrevious, next, previous, nextIndex, previousIndex, add, remove, and set.

## The Interface List Revisited

**JI5.18** The interface java.util.List that we described in Segment 12.14 of Chapter 12 extends the interface Iterable, so it has the method iterator. Additionally, List declares the following methods related to iterators:

```
public ListIterator<T> listIterator(int index);
public ListIterator<T> listIterator();
```

Each of the listIterator methods returns an iterator whose methods are specified in the interface ListIterator. The iterator returned by the first version of listIterator begins at the list entry indicated by index, where zero indicates the first entry in the list. The second version of this method has the same effect as listIterator(0).

Since the standard classes ArrayList, LinkedList, and Vector of the package java.util implement the interface List, they have these two listIterator methods as well as the method iterator.

## Using the Interface `ListIterator`

**JI5.19 Example: Traversals.** Let's look at an example of the methods that work with the current and previous entries and then use it to describe the remaining methods in the interface. We make the following assumptions:

- The list `nameList` is of type `java.util.List` and contains the following names:

  Jess
  Jim
  Josh

- The iterator `traverse` is defined as

  ```
  ListIterator<String> traverse = nameList.listIterator();
  ```

  and includes the operations `add`, `remove`, and `set`.

Since `traverse` is at the beginning of the list, the Java statements

```
System.out.println("nextIndex      " + traverse.nextIndex());
System.out.println("hasNext        " + traverse.hasNext());
System.out.println("previousIndex  " + traverse.previousIndex());
System.out.println("hasPrevious    " + traverse.hasPrevious());
```

produce the output

```
nextIndex      0
hasNext        true
previousIndex -1
hasPrevious    false
```

If we then execute the statements

```
System.out.println("next       " + traverse.next());
System.out.println("nextIndex  " + traverse.nextIndex());
System.out.println("hasNext    " + traverse.hasNext());
```

the output is

```
next       Jess
nextIndex  1
hasNext    true
```

Finally, the statements

```
System.out.println("previousIndex  " + traverse.previousIndex());
System.out.println("hasPrevious    " + traverse.hasPrevious());
System.out.println("previous       " + traverse.previous());
System.out.println("nextIndex      " + traverse.nextIndex());
System.out.println("hasNext        " + traverse.hasNext());
System.out.println("next           " + traverse.next());
```

produce the output

```
previousIndex 0
hasPrevious    true
previous       Jess
nextIndex      0
hasNext        true
next           Jess
```

**Question 5** Suppose that `traverse` is an iterator as defined in the previous segment, but the contents of `nameList` are unknown. Write Java statements that display the names in `nameList` in reverse order, beginning at the end of the list.

**JI5.20**  **Example: The method** `set`. The method `set` replaces the entry that either `next` or `previous` just returned. At the end of the preceding segment, `next` had just returned *Jess*, so

```
traverse.set("Jen");
```

replaces *Jess* with *Jen*. Since *Jess* was the first entry in the list, the list now appears as

> Jen
> Jim
> Josh

Note that this replacement operation does not affect the position of the iterator within the list. Thus, calls to `nextIndex` and `previousIndex`, for example, are not affected. In this case, since the iterator is between *Jen* and *Jim*, `nextIndex` returns 1 and `previousIndex` returns 0. Also note that we can call `set` again; doing so here will replace *Jen*.

---

**Question 6** If the iterator's position is between the first two entries of the previous list, write Java statements that replace *Josh* with *Jon*.

---

**JI5.21**  **Example: The method** `add`. The method `add` inserts an entry into the list just before the iterator's current position. Thus, the insertion is made immediately before the entry, if any, that `next` would have returned before `add` was called and just after the entry, if any, that `previous` would have returned. Note that if the list is empty, `add` inserts a new entry as the only entry in the list.

If the iterator's position is currently between the first two entries of the previous list, the statement

```
traverse.add("Ashley");
```

adds *Ashley* to the list just before *Jim*—that is, at index 1 or, equivalently, at list position 2. After this addition, the list is as follows:

> Jen
> Ashley
> Jim
> Josh

A call to `next` at this point returns *Jim*, since `next` would have returned *Jim* had we not called `add`. If, however, we call `previous` instead of `next`, the new entry *Ashley* will be returned. Furthermore, the addition increases by 1 the values that `nextIndex` and `previousIndex` will return. Thus, immediately after the addition, `nextIndex` will return 2 and `previousIndex` will return 1.

---

**Question 7** If the iterator's position is between *Ashley* and *Jim*, write Java statements that add *Miguel* right after *Jim*.

---

**JI5.22** **Example: The method** `remove`. The behavior of the method `remove` is similar to that of `remove` in the interface `Iterator`, which you saw earlier in this chapter. But in the interface `ListIterator`, `remove` is affected by the method `previous` as well as by `next`. Thus, `remove` removes the list entry that the last call to either `next` or `previous` returned.

If the list contains

> Jen
> Ashley
> Jim
> Josh

and the iterator `traverse` is positioned between *Ashley* and *Jim*, the statements

```
traverse.previous();
traverse.remove();
```

remove *Ashley* from the list, since `previous` returns *Ashley*. The iterator's position remains just before *Jim*.

Notice that both `set` and `remove` will throw the exception `IllegalStateException` if neither `next` nor `previous` has been called, or if either `remove` or `add` has been called already since the last call to `next` or `previous`. As you will see in the next chapter, this behavior complicates the implementation somewhat.

## ANSWERS TO SELF-TEST QUESTIONS

1. The output is
   ```
   true
   Rachel
   ```

2. ```
   nameIterator.next();
   nameIterator.next();
   System.out.println(nameIterator.next());
   ```

3. ```
   nameIterator.next(); // Skip first entry; list has > 1 entry
   while (nameIterator.hasNext())
   {
      System.out.println(nameIterator.next()); // Display even-numbered entry
      if (nameIterator.hasNext())
         nameIterator.next();                  // Skip odd-numbered entry
   } // end while
   ```

4. ```
   while (nameIterator.hasNext())
   {
      nameIterator.next();
      nameIterator.remove();
   } // end while
   ```

5. ```
   while (traverse.hasNext())
      traverse.next();
   while (traverse.hasPrevious())
      System.out.println(traverse.previous());
   ```

6. ```
   traverse.next();       // Return Jim
   traverse.next();       // Return Josh
   traverse.set("Jon");   // Replace Josh
   ```

7. ```
   traverse.next();            // Return Jim
   traverse.add("Miguel");     // Add Miguel after Jim
   ```

# Iterators for the ADT List

## Contents

## Prerequisites

## Objectives

After studying this chapter, you should be able to

- Use an iterator to traverse or manipulate a list
- Implement in Java a separate class iterator and an inner class iterator for a list
- Describe the pros and cons of separate class iterators and inner class iterators

$\mathbf{A}$s you know from the previous Java interlude, an iterator is an object that enables you to traverse the entries in a data collection. The interlude gave some examples of using an iterator and introduced the standard interfaces Iterator, ListIterator, and Iterable. In this chapter, we will implement Iterator and ListIterator for the classes AList and LList that Chapters 13 and 14 defined. In doing so, we will describe several ways in which to define an iterator.

## Ways to Implement an Iterator

**15.1**   A possible, but not optimal, way to provide an ADT with traversal operations is to define them as ADT operations. For example, if `ListInterface` extends `Iterator`, a list object would have iterator methods as well as list methods. Although such an approach provides efficient traversals, it has disadvantages, as you will see.

A better way is to implement the iterator methods within their own class. In one approach, this class is public and separate from the class that implements the ADT in question. The two classes must, of course, interact in some way. We will call an instance of such an iterator class a **separate class iterator**. Alternatively, the iterator class can be a private inner class of the class that implements the ADT. We'll call an instance of this inner class an **inner class iterator**. As you will see, an inner class iterator is usually preferable. This chapter will discuss both approaches.

A separate class iterator of a list and an inner class iterator of a list are objects distinct from the list. You invoke the methods of both of these iterators in the same way.

## A Separate Class Iterator

**15.2**   Imagine that `nameList` is a list of strings that is an instance of either of the classes `AList` or `LList`, as given in Chapters 13 and 14, respectively. If the public class `SeparateIterator` implements the interface `java.util.Iterator`, we can create an iterator for `nameList` by writing

```
Iterator<String> nameIterator = new SeparateIterator<>(nameList);
```

`SeparateIterator`'s constructor connects the iterator `nameIterator` to the list `nameList` and positions the iterator just before the first entry in the list. Because `nameIterator` is an instance of an iterator class that is distinct from the class of lists, it is a separate class iterator. You can use `nameIterator` just as we did in Segments JI5.6 and JI5.8 of the previous Java interlude, since it has the methods declared by the interface `Iterator`.

Let's define the class `SeparateIterator`.

**15.3**   **An outline of the class `SeparateIterator`.** To enable us to connect an instance of the class `SeparateIterator` with an existing list by invoking the class's constructor, `SeparateIterator` needs a data field that references the list. As you can see in Listing 15-1, the constructor assigns this reference to the field. Also, notice that we make the definition of `SeparateIterator` independent of a particular implementation of the list, such as `AList` or `LList`, by defining the field `list` as an instance of `ListInterface`.

In addition to connecting the iterator to the list in question, the constructor initializes the iterator so it will begin at the first entry in the list. To enable this, the class has another data field `nextPosition` that tracks where we are in the iteration. This field is simply the integer position of the entry in the list that the method `next` last returned. It is convenient to initialize this field to zero.

---

**LISTING 15-1   An outline of the class `SeparateIterator`**

```java
1  import java.util.Iterator;
2  import java.util.NoSuchElementException;
3  public class SeparateIterator<T> implements Iterator<T>
4  {
5      private ListInterface<T> list;
6      private int nextPosition;      // Position of entry last returned by next()
7      private boolean wasNextCalled; // Needed by remove
8
```

```
 9      public SeparateIterator(ListInterface<T> myList)
10      {
11         list = myList;
12         nextPosition = 0;
13         wasNextCalled = false;
14      } // end constructor
15
16      < Implementations of the methods hasNext, next, and remove go here >
17      . . .
18  } // end SeparateIterator
```

Providing an iterator with a remove operation is optional; however, we shall do so here because the previous examples used one. This desire complicates our class somewhat, because the client must call the method next before each call to remove. This requirement isn't simply a precondition. The remove method must throw an exception if it isn't met. Therefore, we need an additional data field—a boolean flag—that enables remove to check whether next was called. We name this data field wasNextCalled. The constructor initializes this field to false.

**15.4**    **The method hasNext.** The class SeparateIterator has no special access to the private data fields of the class that implements the list. It is a client of the list and so can process the list only by using the list's ADT operations. Figure 15-1 shows a separate class iterator with a reference to a list but without knowledge of the list's implementation. The implementations of the iterator methods will use methods specified in ListInterface. The resulting implementations are rather straightforward but take longer to execute, in general, than the implementation of an inner class iterator. For example, the method hasNext calls the list's getLength method:

```
public boolean hasNext()
{
   return nextPosition < list.getLength();
} // end hasNext
```

**Question 1** What does the method hasNext return when the list is empty? Why?

FIGURE 15-1    A separate class iterator with a reference to an ADT, an indicator of its position within the iteration, and no knowledge of the ADT's implementation

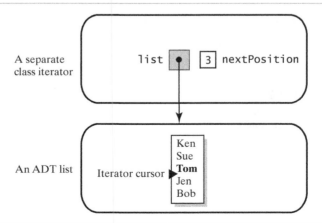

**15.5**    **The method next.** As long as the iteration has not ended—that is, as long as hasNext returns true—the method next retrieves the iteration's next entry by calling the list's getEntry method. If, however, the iteration has ended, next throws an exception.

```
public T next()
{
    if (hasNext())
    {
        wasNextCalled = true;
        nextPosition++;
        return list.getEntry(nextPosition);
    }
    else
        throw new NoSuchElementException("Illegal call to next(); " +
                                        "iterator is after end of list.");
} // end next
```

Since nextPosition begins at zero, we must increment it before passing it to getEntry. Doing so advances the iterator as required. Notice that we also set the field wasNextCalled to true so that the method remove can tell that next was called.

**Question 2** The work performed by the method next depends upon the implementation of the ADT list that is ultimately used. For which implementation of the list, array-based or linked, will next use the most execution time? Why?

**15.6**    **The method remove.** The iterator's method remove removes from the list the entry that the most recent call to next returned. If next was not called, or if remove has been called since the last call to next, remove throws an IllegalStateException. The class's data field wasNextCalled helps us to implement this aspect of the method. If the field is true, we know that next has been called. Then, by setting the field to false, we enable a subsequent invocation of remove to require another call to next.

The field nextPosition is the position of the entry just returned by next, so it is the position of the entry to be removed. Thus, we pass it to the list's remove method. Then, since a subsequent call to next must behave as it would have before the removal, we must decrement nextPosition.

Figure 15-2 shows a list and the field nextPosition just before the call to next, just after the call to next but before the call to remove, and just after the call to remove. Notice in Part *b* that next increments nextPosition and then returns a reference to *Chris*, the entry at that position and the next entry in the iteration. A call to remove in Part *c* removes the entry—*Chris*—at nextPosition. Afterwards, the next entry—*Dan* in the figure—moves to the next lower-numbered position in the list. Thus, remove must decrement nextPosition so that a subsequent call to next will return *Dan*.

**FIGURE 15-2**    Changes to a list and nextPosition when removing *Chris* from the list

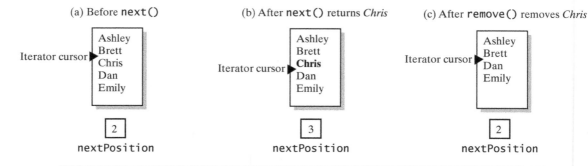

The following implementation of remove reflects this discussion.

```java
public void remove()
{
    if (wasNextCalled)
    {
        // nextPosition was incremented by the call to next(), so
        // it is the position number of the entry to be removed
        list.remove(nextPosition);
        nextPosition--;          // A subsequent call to next() must be
                                 // unaffected by this removal
        wasNextCalled = false; // Reset flag
    }
    else
        throw new IllegalStateException("Illegal call to remove(); " +
                                        "next() was not called.");
} // end remove
```

**Note:  Separate class iterators**
A separate class iterator must access an ADT's data by using the public methods of the ADT. However, certain ADTs, such as a stack, do not provide sufficient public access to their data to make such an iterator possible. In addition, the typical separate class iterator takes longer to perform its operations than do other kinds of iterators because of the indirect access to the ADT's data. On the other hand, the implementation of a separate class iterator is usually straightforward. You can also have several independent separate class iterators in existence at the same time for a given ADT.

To provide an iterator for an ADT's implementation that has none and cannot be altered, you might need to define a separate class iterator.

# An Inner Class Iterator

VideoNote

Alternative iterator
implementations

15.7    By using separate class iterators, you can have multiple and distinct iterations of a list exist simultaneously. However, separate class iterators belong to a public class, so they can access the list's data fields only indirectly via ADT operations. As a result, the iterations take more time than those performed by other kinds of iterators. For ADTs other than a list, a separate class iterator might have insufficient access to the data fields to perform an iteration.

A desirable alternative is to define the iterator class as an inner class of the ADT. Because the resulting iterator objects are distinct from the ADT, you can have multiple iterations in progress at the same time. Moreover, since the iterator belongs to an inner class, it has direct access to the ADT's data fields. For these reasons, an inner class iterator is usually preferable to a separate class iterator.

In this section, we will implement the interface Iterator by adding an inner class to each of two implementations of the ADT list. First, we will use a linked implementation of the list but will provide only the iterator operations hasNext and next. Then we will use an array-based list and support all three operations of Iterator.

**Programming Tip:**  A class that defines an inner class iterator should implement the interface Iterable. A client of the class then can use a for-each loop to traverse the objects in an instance of the class.

## A Linked Implementation

**15.8**    To achieve our goal, we must define the methods specified in `Iterator` within a new inner class of the class that implements the ADT list. We'll name this inner class `IteratorForLinkedList` and name the outer class `LinkedListWithIterator`. The outer class will be much like the class `LList` of Chapter 14. However, it needs another method that the client can use to create an iterator. As the previous Java interlude described, this method is `iterator` and is declared in the standard interface `java.lang.Iterable`. It returns an iterator that adheres to the interface `Iterator`. The method has the following simple implementation:

```java
public Iterator<T> iterator()
{
    return new IteratorForLinkedList();
} // end iterator
```

 **Note:** Although the method `iterator` has a standard name, you might confuse it with the interface `Iterator`. We like to provide an additional method, `getIterator`, that has the same purpose as `iterator`. Because both methods return the same iterator, the implementation of one should call the other. Since we have already defined `iterator`, `getIterator` will call `iterator`.

To accommodate the methods `iterator` and `getIterator`, we create a new interface—shown in Listing 15-2—that extends `ListInterface` instead of changing it. This interface has all the list methods of `ListInterface` and the methods `iterator` and `getIterator`.

---

**LISTING 15-2**    The interface `ListWithIteratorInterface`

```java
1  import java.util.Iterator;
2  public interface ListWithIteratorInterface<T> extends ListInterface<T>,
3                                                          Iterable<T>
4  {
5     public Iterator<T> getIterator();
6  } // end ListWithIteratorInterface
```

---

Declaring the method `iterator` explicitly within the interface is permissible but not necessary, because the interface extends `Iterable`. Since `Iterable` is in `java.lang`, no `import` statement is needed for it.

Because a class can implement several interfaces, we could define the class `LinkedList-WithIterator` without using our new interface. But having this interface enables us to declare an object of type `ListWithIteratorInterface` and know that the object will have the list methods as well as the methods `iterator` and `getIterator`.

**15.9**    **An outline of the class.** Listing 15-3 outlines the class `LinkedListWithIterator` with its inner classes `IteratorForLinkedList` and `Node`. We will define the methods declared in the interface `Iterator` within the inner class `IteratorForLinkedList`. However, we will not give the iterators the ability to remove entries from the data collection.

---

**LISTING 15-3**    An outline of the class `LinkedListWithIterator`

```java
1  import java.util.Iterator;
2  import java.util.NoSuchElementException;
3  public class LinkedListWithIterator<T> implements ListWithIteratorInterface<T>
4  {
5     private Node firstNode;
6     private int  numberOfEntries;
7
```

```
 8    public LinkedListWithIterator()
 9    {
10       initializeDataFields();
11    } // end default constructor
12
13    < Implementations of the methods of the ADT list go here;
14        you can see them in Chapter 14, beginning at Segment 14.7 >
15    . . .
16    public Iterator<T> iterator
17    {
18       return new IteratorForLinkedList();
19    } // end iterator
20
21    public Iterator<T> getIterator()
22    {
23       return iterator();
24    } // end getIterator
25
26    < Segment 15.10 begins a description of the following inner class.>
27    private class IteratorForLinkedList implements Iterator<T>
28    {
29       private Node nextNode;
30
31       private IteratorForLinkedList()
32       {
33          nextNode = firstNode;
34       } // end default constructor
35       < Implementations of the methods in the interface Iterator go here;
36           you can see them in Segments 15.11 through 15.13.>
37       . . .
38    } // end IteratorForLinkedList
39    < Implementation of the private class Node (Listing 3-4 of Chapter 3) goes here. >
40    . . .
41 } // end LinkedListWithIterator
```

**15.10**   **The inner class `IteratorForLinkedList`.** As you can see in Listing 15-3, the private inner class `IteratorForLinkedList` has a data field `nextNode` to track an iteration. The constructor initializes this field to `firstNode`, which is a data field of the outer class and references the first node in the chain that contains the list's entries. We cannot position the iterator between nodes, even though we imagine its position to be between entries. Nor can `nextNode` reference the node before the one that `next` will access, because the first node has no node before it. Thus, `nextNode` references the next node in the iteration, that is, the node that the method `next` must access to get the next entry.

**Note:** An inner class can refer to its outer class's data fields by name alone, if it does not also use the same names for its own definitions. For example, the constructor of the inner class `IteratorForLinkedList` references the field `firstNode` directly by name since no other `firstNode` exists. But we could have written `LinkedListWithIterator.this.firstNode` instead.

Figure 15-3 illustrates an inner class iterator. The iterator has direct access to the ADT's underlying data structure—a linked chain, in this example. Since the data field `nextNode` maintains the current position of the iteration, the iterator can quickly retrieve the next entry in the iteration without first returning to the beginning of the chain.

We now implement the methods of the interface `Iterator` within the inner class. These methods will be public, even though they appear within a private class, because they are public in `Iterator` and will be used by clients of `LinkedListWithIterator`.

FIGURE 15-3      An inner class iterator with direct access to the linked chain
                 that implements the ADT

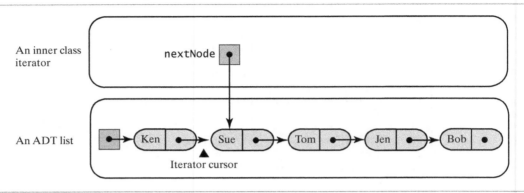

**15.11**   **The method next.** If the iteration has not ended, `nextNode` references the node containing the next entry in the iteration. Thus, `next` can easily get a reference to this entry. The method then must advance `nextNode` to the next node and return the retrieved list entry. However, `next` must throw an exception if the iteration has already ended.

```
public T next()
{
    if (hasNext())
    {
        Node returnNode = nextNode;             // Get next node
        nextNode = nextNode.getNextNode();      // Advance iterator

        return returnNode.getData();            // Return next entry in iteration
    }
    else
        throw new NoSuchElementException("Illegal call to next(); " +
                                         "iterator is after end of list.");
} // end next
```

**15.12**   **The method hasNext.** After the method `next` returns the last entry in the iteration, `nextNode` will be `null`, since `null` is in the link portion of the last node in the chain. The method `hasNext` can simply compare `nextNode` with `null` to see whether the iteration has ended:

```
public boolean hasNext()
{
    return nextNode != null;
} // end hasNext
```

**Question 3** What does the method `hasNext` return when the list is empty? Why?

**15.13**   **The method remove.** Even though we decided not to support a `remove` operation for this iterator, we must implement the method because it is declared in the interface `Iterator`. If the client invokes `remove`, the method simply throws the runtime exception `UnsupportedOperationException`. Here is an example of how you can define `remove`:

```
public void remove()
{
    throw new UnsupportedOperationException("remove() is not " +
                                            "supported by this iterator");
} // end remove
```

This exception is in the package java.lang and so is included automatically in every Java program. Thus, an import statement is unnecessary.

**Note:** **The remove method**
An iterator that does not allow the removal of items during a traversal is not unusual. In such cases, the remove method is defined, but it throws an exception if invoked.

**Note:** **Inner class iterators**
An inner class iterator has direct access to an ADT's data, so it typically can execute faster than a separate class iterator. Its implementation is usually more involved, however. Both of these iterators have another advantage: Several iterator objects can be in existence at the same time and traverse a list independently of one another.

**Question 4** Given the class LinkedListWithIterator, what Java statements create the iterators nameIterator and countingIterator mentioned in Segment JI5.11 of the previous Java interlude?

**Question 5** Revise the method displayList, as shown in Listing 12-2 of Chapter 12, for use in a client of the class LinkedListWithIterator by using iterator methods to display the list.

## An Array-Based Implementation

15.14 For the array-based implementation, our iterator will support the remove method. Let's begin with the array-based implementation of the ADT list, AList, as given in Chapter 13. Our new class, whose form is shown in Listing 15-4, has the same data fields and methods as the class AList. But since our new class implements the interface ListWithIteratorInterface, it also includes the methods iterator and getIterator. Our class also contains the inner class IteratorForArrayList, which implements the interface Iterator.

**LISTING 15-4** An outline of the class ArrayListWithIterator

```
1  import java.util.Arrays;
2  import java.util.Iterator;
3  import java.util.NoSuchElementException;
4  public class ArrayListWithIterator<T> implements ListWithIteratorInterface<T>
5  {
6      private T[] list; // Array of list entries; ignore list[0]
7      private int numberOfEntries;
8      private boolean initialized = false;
9      private static final int DEFAULT_CAPACITY = 25;
10     private static final int MAX_CAPACITY = 10000;
11
12     public ArrayListWithIterator()
13     {
14         this(DEFAULT_CAPACITY);
15     } // end default constructor
16
17     public ArrayListWithIterator(int initialCapacity)
18     {
19         // Is initialCapacity too small?
20         if (initialCapacity < DEFAULT_CAPACITY)
21             initialCapacity = DEFAULT_CAPACITY;
22         else // Is initialCapacity too big?
23             checkCapacity(initialCapacity);
```

```
24
25          // The cast is safe because the new array contains null entries
26          @SuppressWarnings("unchecked")
27          T[] tempList = (T[])new Object[initialCapacity + 1];
28          list = tempList;
29          numberOfEntries = 0;
30          initialized = true;
31      } // end constructor
32
33      < Implementations of the methods of the ADT list go here;
34        you can see them in Chapter 13, beginning at Segment 13.5.>
35      . . .
36      public Iterator<T> iterator()
37      {
38          return new IteratorForArrayList();
39      } // end iterator
40
41      public Iterator<T> getIterator()
42      {
43          return iterator();
44      } // end getIterator
45
46      < Segment 15.15 begins a description of the following inner class. >
47      private class IteratorForArrayList implements Iterator<T>
48      {
49          private int nextIndex;            // Index of next entry
50          private boolean wasNextCalled; // Needed by remove
51
52          private IteratorForArrayList()
53          {
54              nextIndex = 1; // Begin at list's first entry
55              wasNextCalled = false;
56          } // end default constructor
57
58          < Implementations of the methods in the interface Iterator go here;
59            you can see them in Segments 15.16 through 15.18. >
60          . . .
61      } // end IteratorForArrayList
62  } // end ArrayListWithIterator
```

**15.15**   **The inner class `IteratorForArrayList`.** Just as you can use your finger to keep track of your place on this page, our iterator implementation uses an index to keep track of the iterator's position within the array of list entries. This index, which we call `nextIndex`, is a data field of the private inner class `IteratorForArrayList`. It will be the index of the next entry in the iteration. The constructor initializes `nextIndex` to 1, as Listing 15-4 shows, because the array of list entries in our particular implementation of the ADT list uses indexes that begin at 1.

Just as you saw earlier in Segments 15.3 and 15.6, providing an iterator with a remove operation requires an additional data field that the `remove` method can use to see whether `next` was called. Again, we name this data field `wasNextCalled`, but here it is defined within the inner class. The constructor initializes this field to false.

**15.16**   **The method `hasNext`.** The iterator has a next entry to retrieve if `nextIndex` is less than or equal to the length of the list. Thus, `hasNext` has the following straightforward implementation:

```
public boolean hasNext()
{
    return nextIndex <= numberOfEntries;
} // end hasNext
```

Notice that `hasNext` returns false when the list is empty, that is, when `numberOfEntries` is zero.

**15.17** **The method next.** The implementation of the method `next` has the same general form as the version given in Segment 15.5 for the separate class iterator. If `hasNext` returns true, `next` returns the next entry in the iteration. Here, the next entry is `list[nextIndex]`. The method also advances the iteration by incrementing `nextIndex` and sets the flag `wasNextCalled` to true. On the other hand, if `hasNext` returns false, `next` throws an exception.

```
public T next()
{
   if (hasNext())
   {
      wasNextCalled = true;
      T nextEntry = list[nextIndex];
      nextIndex++; // Advance iterator
      return nextEntry;
   }
   else
      throw new NoSuchElementException("Illegal call to next(); " +
                                      "iterator is after end of list.");
} // end next
```

**15.18** **The `remove` method.** Removing an entry from the list involves shifting entries within the array `list`. Since we have already developed that code for the list's `remove` method, we will call it instead of accessing the array `list` directly. To do that, we need the position number of the list entry to be removed. Recall from Segment 12.1 that the position number of an entry in a list begins at 1, so it is the same as the corresponding array index for this implementation.

Figure 15-4 illustrates how to use `nextIndex` in this implementation. The figure shows the array of list entries and the index `nextIndex` just before the call to `next`, just after the call to `next` but before the call to `remove`, and just after the call to `remove`. Part *b* shows that `next` returns a reference to the next entry, *Chris*, in the iteration and then increments `nextIndex`. The method `remove` must remove this entry from the list. Since `nextIndex` is now 1 larger than the index of *Chris*, it is 1 larger than the position number of the list entry that must be removed. After *Chris* is removed in Part *c*, the next entry—*Deb*—moves to the next lower-numbered position in the array. Thus, `remove` decrements `nextIndex` so that it remains the index of the next entry in the iteration.

**FIGURE 15-4** Changes to the array of list entries and `nextIndex` when removing *Chris* from the list

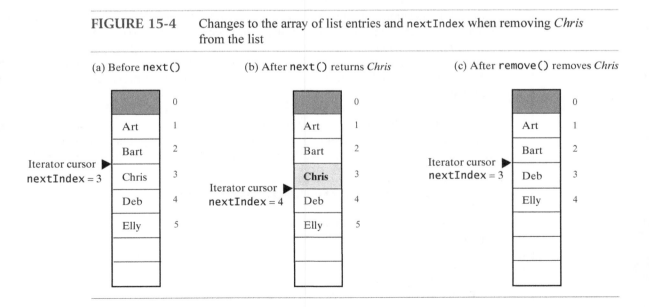

The method `remove` within the inner class `IteratorForArrayList` has the following definition:

```java
public void remove()
{
   if (wasNextCalled)
   {
      // nextIndex was incremented by the call to next, so it is
      // 1 larger than the position number of the entry to be removed
      ArrayListWithIterator.this.remove(nextIndex - 1);
      nextIndex--;               // Index of next entry in iteration
      wasNextCalled = false;     // Reset flag
   }
   else
      throw new IllegalStateException("Illegal call to remove(); " +
                                      "next() was not called.");
} // end remove
```

To call the list's method `remove`, which is defined in the outer class, from within the iterator's `remove`, we must precede the name of the list's method with `ArrayListWithIterator.this`.

**Question 6** Consider the list and the calls to `next` and `remove` in Figure 15-4.

    **a.** What would a call to `next` return if it occurred after the call to `remove` in Figure 15-4c?

    **b.** What would a call to `next` return if it occurred after the call to `next` in Figure 15-4b?

**Question 7** What changes would be necessary to the methods in the inner class `Iterator-ForArrayList` if its constructor set `nextIndex` to 0 instead of 1?

## Why Are Iterator Methods in Their Own Class?

15.19    Both separate class iterators and inner class iterators enable us to have several distinct iterations of a data collection in progress at the same time. Because inner class iterators have direct access to the structure containing the ADT's data, they can execute faster than separate class iterators, and so are usually preferable.

    Why didn't we simply consider the iterator operations as additional ADT operations? To answer this question, let's modify the linked implementation of the list given in the previous chapter by including the methods specified in Java's interface `Iterator`. To keep this implementation simple, we will not provide the remove operation specified in `Iterator`. The resulting class, outlined in Listing 15-5, is actually quite similar to the class `LinkedListWithIterator`, described in Segment 15.9, which implements an inner class iterator. The differences between these classes are highlighted.

    The inner class `IteratorForLinkedList` shown in Segment 15.9 does not appear in our new class, but its data field `nextNode` and its iterator methods `hasNext`, `next`, and `remove` do appear unchanged. Instead of the inner class's constructor, we have the public method `resetTraversal`, which sets `nextNode` to `firstNode`. We'll call this method before we begin a traversal.

---

**LISTING 15-5**   An outline of the class `ListWithTraversal`

```java
1 import java.util.Iterator;
2 import java.util.NoSuchElementException;
3 public class ListWithTraversal<T> implements ListInterface<T>,
4                                              Iterator<T>
5 {
6    private Node firstNode;
7    private int  numberOfEntries;
```

```
 8     private Node nextNode; // Node containing next entry in iteration
 9
10     public ListWithTraversal()
11     {
12        initializeDataFields();
13     } // end default constructor
14
15     < Implementations of the remaining methods of the ADT list go here;
16        you can see them in Chapter 14, beginning at Segment 14.7.>
17     . . .
18     private void initializeDataFields()
19     {
20        firstNode = null;
21        numberOfEntries = 0;
22        nextNode = null;
23     } // end initializeDataFields
24
25     < Implementations of the methods in the interface Iterator go here;
26        you can see them in Segments 15.11 through 15.13.>
27     . . .
28     public void resetTraversal()
29     {
30        nextNode = firstNode;
31     } // end resetTraversal
32
33     < Implementation of the private class Node (Listing 3-4 of Chapter 3) goes here.>
34 } // end ListWithTraversal
```

**15.20**   **Example: Traversing a list.** If myList is an instance of the previous class ListWithTraversal, it has methods of the ADT list as well as the methods in Iterator. Thus, if we add strings to myList using invocations such as myList.add("Chris"), we can display the list as follows:

```
myList.resetTraversal();
while (myList.hasNext())
    System.out.println(myList.next());
```

Invoking resetTraversal is essential to set the traversal to the beginning of the list. Notice that you use the list myList instead of an iterator object to invoke the Iterator methods. The reverse was true in Segment 15.2.

**Question 8** Revise the method displayList, as shown in Listing 12-2 of Chapter 12, for use in a client of the class ListWithTraversal by using the approach of the previous example to display the list. Is there any disadvantage to this implementation? Explain.

**Question 9** Suppose that you want to omit the method resetTraversal.

    **a.**  Could the default constructor initialize nextNode to firstNode? Explain.

    **b.**  Could the add methods initialize nextNode to firstNode? Explain.

**15.21**   **What's wrong with this approach?** Although these traversal methods can execute quickly because they have direct access to the underlying data structure of the list, including them as list operations has disadvantages. Only one traversal can be in progress at a time. Moreover, an operation like resetTraversal, which is not in the interface Iterator, is necessary to initialize the traversal. The resulting ADT has too many operations; it suffers from **interface bloat**. More importantly, mixing the functionality of a list with that of an iterator is a poor design. Conceptually, when you point to the lines on a book's page, your finger is not a part of the book. It is a separate object used to track a characteristic of the book.

With a little additional programming effort, you can organize the iterator methods as an inner class. In doing so, you retain the speed of execution and suffer none of the disadvantages.

## An Array-Based Implementation of the Interface `ListIterator`

**15.22**   As we did for the interface `Iterator` earlier in this chapter, we will implement the interface `ListIterator` as an inner class of a class that uses an array to represent the ADT list. First, we define an interface in Listing 15-6 that declares the operations of the ADT list implicitly and the method `getIterator` explicitly. In this case, the `getIterator`'s return type is `ListIterator<T>` instead of `Iterator<T>`. Since our interface also extends `Iterable`, it implicitly declares the method `iterator` whose return type is `Iterator<T>`.

---

**LISTING 15-6**   The interface `ListWithListIteratorInterface`

```
1  import java.util.ListIterator;
2  public interface ListWithListIteratorInterface<T> extends Iterable<T>,
3                                                    ListInterface<T>
4  {
5     public ListIterator<T> getIterator();
6  } // end ListWithListIteratorInterface
```

---

**15.23**   **The class that implements the ADT list.** Our class has the same data fields and methods as the class `AList` given in Chapter 13, and includes the methods `iterator` and `getIterator`. The class also contains the inner class `ListIteratorForArrayList`, which implements the interface `ListIterator`. Listing 15-7 shows the form of our new class of lists.

---

**LISTING 15-7**   An outline of the class `ArrayListWithListIterator`

```
1  import java.util.Arrays;
2  import java.util.Iterator;
3  import java.util.ListIterator;
4  import java.util.NoSuchElementException;
5  public class ArrayListWithListIterator<T>
6             implements ListWithListIteratorInterface<T>
7  {
8     private T[] list; // Array of list entries; ignore list[0]
9     private int numberOfEntries;
10    private boolean initialized = false;
11    private static final int DEFAULT_CAPACITY = 25;
12    private static final int MAX_CAPACITY = 10000;
13
14    public ArrayListWithListIterator()
15    {
16       this(DEFAULT_CAPACITY);
17    } // end default constructor
18
19    public ArrayListWithListIterator(int initialCapacity)
20    {
21       // Is initialCapacity too small?
22       if (initialCapacity < DEFAULT_CAPACITY)
23          initialCapacity = DEFAULT_CAPACITY;
24       else // Is initialCapacity too big?
25          checkCapacity(initialCapacity);
26
```

---

```
27          // The cast is safe because the new array contains null entries
28          @SuppressWarnings("unchecked")
29          T[] tempList = (T[])new Object[initialCapacity + 1];
30          list = tempList;
31          numberOfEntries = 0;
32          initialized = true;
33      } // end constructor
34
35      < Implementations of the public methods of the ADT list go here;
36        you can see them in Chapter 13, beginning at Segment 13.5.>
37      . . .
38      public ListIterator<T> getIterator()
39      {
40          return new ListIteratorForArrayList();
41      } // end getIterator
42
43      public Iterator<T> iterator()
44      {
45          return getIterator();
46      } // end iterator
47      . . .
48      private class ListIteratorForArrayList implements ListIterator<T>
49      {
50          < The description of this implementation begins with Segment 15.24. >
51          . . .
52      } // end ListIteratorForArrayList
53  } // end ArrayListWithListIterator
```

## The Inner Class

**15.24**   **The data fields and constructor.** We begin implementing the inner class `ListIteratorForArrayList` by thinking about how the methods `remove` and `set` will throw the exception `IllegalStateException`. Both of these methods throw this exception for the same reasons, that is, if either

- `next` or `previous` was not called or
- `remove` or `add` has been called since the last call to `next` or `previous`

Figure 15-5 shows calls to `remove` in various contexts that cause an `IllegalStateException`.
This aspect of the implementation might be intimidating at first, but it need not be difficult. When we implemented `Iterator`'s `remove` method in Segment 15.18, we tested the boolean data field `wasNextCalled` to see whether `next` had been called. We could do that here and define analogous fields for the methods `previous` and `add`, but the logic would be more involved than necessary. Instead, let's define a boolean field to indicate whether a call to either `remove` or `set` is legal:

> `private boolean isRemoveOrSetLegal;`

If either `remove` or `set` finds this field to be false, it should throw an `IllegalStateException`. This field should be initialized to false by the constructor. The methods `next` and `previous` should set it to true, and the methods `add` and `remove` should set it to false.

Both `remove` and `set` must know which of `next` or `previous` was called so that they can access the correct list entry. Thus, we define a data field to track the last call to these methods and an enumeration to provide values for the field. The following enumeration will suffice:

> `private enum Move {NEXT, PREVIOUS}`

Since an enumeration is really a class, we define it outside of the inner class `ListIterator-ForArrayList`, but within `ArrayListWithListIterator`. The data field then is simply

> `private Move lastMove;`

FIGURE 15-5    Possible contexts in which the method remove of the iterator
traverse throws an exception when called

(a)  `traverse.remove();`   ←— Causes an exception; neither next nor previous
has been called

(b)  `traverse.next();`

`traverse.remove();`   ←— Legal

`traverse.remove();`   ←— Causes an exception

(c)  `traverse.previous();`

`traverse.remove();`   ←— Legal

`traverse.remove();`   ←— Causes an exception

(d)  `traverse.next();`

`traverse.add(...);`

`traverse.remove();`   ←— Causes an exception

(e)  `traverse.previous();`

`traverse.add(...);`

`traverse.remove();`   ←— Causes an exception

In addition to these two data fields, we need a field nextIndex to track the index of the next entry in the iteration. This field is just like the one we described earlier in Segment 15.15. Thus, the inner class begins as follows:

```java
private class ListIteratorForArrayList implements ListIterator<T>
{
   private int nextIndex;            // Index of next entry in the iteration
   private boolean isRemoveOrSetLegal;
   private Move lastMove;

   private ListIteratorForArrayList()
   {
      nextIndex = 1;                 // Iteration begins at list's first entry
      isRemoveOrSetLegal = false;
      lastMove = null;
   } // end default constructor
   . . .
```

**15.25   The method hasNext.** The method hasNext has the same implementation that it had earlier in Segment 15.16. Recall that it returns true if the iterator has not reached the end of the list.

```java
public boolean hasNext()
{
   return nextIndex <= numberOfEntries;
} // end hasNext
```

**15.26   The method next.** The implementation of next is similar to the one given in Segment 15.17. Here, however, it has different fields to set. We set lastMove to Move.NEXT and isRemoveOrSetLegal to true.

```java
public T next()
{
   if (hasNext())
   {
      lastMove = Move.NEXT;
      isRemoveOrSetLegal = true;

      T nextEntry = list[nextIndex];
      nextIndex++; // Advance iterator

      return nextEntry;
   }
   else
      throw new NoSuchElementException("Illegal call to next(); " +
                                       "iterator is after end of list.");
} // end next
```

**15.27**  **The methods hasPrevious and previous.** The methods hasPrevious and previous have implementations that are analogous to those of hasNext and next, respectively.

```java
public boolean hasPrevious()
{
   return (nextIndex > 1) && (nextIndex <= numberOfEntries + 1);
} // end hasPrevious

public T previous()
{
   if (hasPrevious())
   {
      lastMove = Move.PREVIOUS;
      isRemoveOrSetLegal = true;

      T previousEntry = list[nextIndex - 1];
      nextIndex--; // Move iterator back
      return previousEntry;
   }
   else
      throw new NoSuchElementException("Illegal call to previous(); " +
                                       "iterator is before beginning of list.");
} // end previous
```

**15.28**  **The methods nextIndex and previousIndex.** The method nextIndex returns either the index of
the entry that the method next would return if called or the size of the list if the iterator is after the
end of the list. Even though our variable nextIndex counts from 1, remember that a ListIterator
object counts from 0.

```java
public int nextIndex()
{
   int result;
   if (hasNext())
      result = nextIndex - 1;    // Change to zero-based numbering of iterator
   else
      result = numberOfEntries; // End-of-list flag

   return result;
} // end nextIndex
```

The method previousIndex returns either the index of the entry that the method previous
would return if called or -1 if the iterator is before the beginning of the list.

```java
public int previousIndex()
{
   int result;
   if (hasPrevious())
      result = nextIndex - 2; // Change to zero-based numbering of iterator
```

```
        else
            result = -1;              // Beginning-of-list flag
        return result;
    } // end previousIndex
```

**15.29**    **The method add.** The method add inserts an entry into the list just before the iterator's current position, that is, immediately before the entry in list[nextIndex], as Figure 15-6 illustrates. To avoid duplicate code and effort, we call the list's add method to add an entry at position nextIndex within the list. Recall that entries after the new entry will be shifted and renumbered. Therefore, we need to increment nextIndex so that it will continue to mark the entry that a subsequent call to next would return. Thus, add has the following implementation:

```
    public void add(T newEntry)
    {
        isRemoveOrSetLegal = false;

        // Insert newEntry immediately before the the iterator's current position
        ArrayListWithListIterator.this.add(nextIndex, newEntry);
        nextIndex++;
    } // end add
```

FIGURE 15-6    Changes to the array of list entries and nextIndex when adding *Ben* to the list

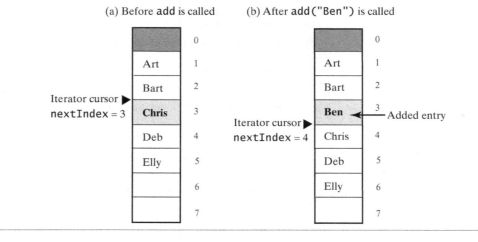

**15.30**    **The method remove.** The logic for the remove method when a call to next precedes its call is somewhat like the logic for the remove method in the interface Iterator, which you saw in Segment 15.18. Recall that Figure 15-4 illustrated the array of list entries and the index nextIndex before and after the calls to next and remove. Figure 15-7 provides a similar illustration, showing what happens when a call to previous precedes the call to remove. In Part *b*, previous returns a reference to the previous entry—*Bart*—in the iteration and decrements nextIndex. The method remove must remove this entry from the list. After the entry *Bart* has been removed in Figure 15-7c, the next entry—*Chris*—moves to the next lower-numbered position in the array. Thus, nextIndex remains the index of the next entry in the iteration and so is unchanged.

**FIGURE 15-7**     Changes to the array of list entries and `nextIndex` when
removing *Chris* from the list

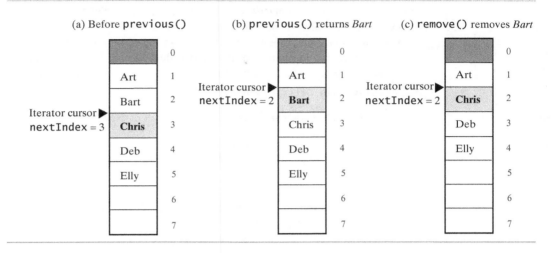

Remember, `remove` must throw an exception if the field `isRemoveOrSetLegal` is false. If the field is true, the method must set it to false. An implementation of `remove` follows:

```
public void remove()
{
    if (isRemoveOrSetLegal)
    {
        isRemoveOrSetLegal = false;

        if (lastMove.equals(Move.NEXT))
        {
            // next() called, but neither add() nor remove() has been
            // called since

            // Remove entry last returned by next()

            // nextIndex is 1 more than the index of the entry returned
            // by next()
            ArrayListWithListIterator.this.remove(nextIndex - 1);
            nextIndex--; // Move iterator back
        }
        else
        {
            // previous() called, but neither add() nor remove() has been
            // called since
            assert lastMove.equals(Move.PREVIOUS);

            // Remove entry last returned by previous()

            // nextIndex is the index of the entry returned by previous()
            ArrayListWithListIterator.this.remove(nextIndex);
        } // end if
    }
    else
        throw new IllegalStateException("Illegal call to remove(); " +
                                "next() or previous() was not called, OR " +
                                "add() or remove() called since then.");
} // end remove
```

**15.31**   **The method set.** The method set replaces the entry in the list that the last call to either next or previous has returned. It uses nextIndex, as updated by either of the methods next or previous. Since the method next returns the list entry at position nextIndex and then increments nextIndex, the method set would replace the entry at position nextIndex - 1 after a call to next. Likewise, since previous returns the list entry at position nextIndex - 1 and then decrements nextIndex, the method set would replace the list entry at position nextIndex after a call to previous.

The following implementation of set reflects these observations and uses the same logic that we used in remove to see whether to throw IllegalStateException:

```java
public void set(T newEntry)
{
   if (isRemoveOrSetLegal)
   {
      if (lastMove.equals(Move.NEXT))
         list[nextIndex - 1] = newEntry; // Replace entry last returned by
                                         // next()
      else
      {
         assert lastMove.equals(Move.PREVIOUS);
         list[nextIndex] = newEntry; // Replace entry last returned by
                                     // previous()
      } // end if
   }
   else
      throw new IllegalStateException("Illegal call to set(); " +
                               "next() or previous() was not called, OR " +
                               "add() or remove() called since then.");
} // end set
```

**Design Decision:** **When defining the method set, should we favor clarity or efficiency?**
Clarity versus efficiency is a tradeoff that you will often face during programming. We encounter this situation with the previous method set. The method's definition likely would be clearer—that is, easier to understand—if we called the ADT list method replace instead of assigning values to array elements. However, doing so would have the same degradation of efficiency as a separate class iterator. Since we are defining an inner class iterator, time efficiency is our goal.

**Note:** Implementing the entire interface ListIterator as an inner class is easier when the associated ADT has an array-based implementation rather than a linked implementation. (See Exercise 17.)

**Note:** An iterator of type ListIterator is simpler to implement when it does not support the operations add, remove, and set. Such an iterator is useful, as it enables you to traverse a list in both directions. We leave this implementation as an exercise.

## CHAPTER SUMMARY

- The interface Iterator specifies three methods: hasNext, next, and remove. An iterator that implements this interface need not provide a remove operation. Instead, the method remove would throw the exception UnsupportedOperationException.

- The interface `ListIterator` specifies nine methods, including the three methods that `Iterator` specifies. They are `hasNext`, `next`, `hasPrevious`, `previous`, `nextIndex`, `previousIndex`, `add`, `remove`, and `set`. The methods `add`, `remove`, and `set` are optional in the sense that they can throw the exception `UnsupportedOperationException` instead of affecting the list.

- You can implement each of the interfaces `Iterator` and `ListIterator` as its own class. This class could be an inner class of the class that implements the ADT in question, or it could be public and separate from the ADT's class.

- An inner class iterator enables you to have several independent iterators that traverse a collection. It also allows the iterator direct access to the underlying data structure, so its implementation can be efficient.

- A separate class iterator also allows multiple and distinct iterations to exist simultaneously. However, since the iterator can access the list's data fields only indirectly via ADT operations, the iteration takes more time than one performed by an inner class iterator. On the other hand, the implementation is usually straightforward.

- Certain ADTs do not provide sufficient public access to their data to make a separate class iterator possible. However, to provide an iterator for an ADT's implementation that already exists and cannot be altered, you might need to define a separate class iterator.

## PROGRAMMING TIP

- A class that defines an inner class iterator should implement the interface `Iterable`. A client of the class can then use a for-each loop to traverse the objects in an instance of the class.

## EXERCISES

1. Suppose that `nameList` is a list that contains the following strings: *Kyle, Cathy, Sam, Austin, Sara.* What output is produced by the following sequence of statements?

   ```
   Iterator<String> nameIterator = nameList.getIterator();
   System.out.println(nameIterator.next());
   nameIterator.next();
   System.out.println(nameIterator.next());
   nameIterator.remove();
   System.out.println(nameIterator.next());
   displayList(nameList);
   ```

2. Repeat Exercise 1, but instead use the following statements:

   ```
   Iterator<String> nameIterator = nameList.getIterator();
   nameIterator.next();
   nameIterator.remove();
   nameIterator.next();
   nameIterator.next();
   nameIterator.remove();
   System.out.println(nameIterator.next());
   displayList(nameList);
   System.out.println(nameIterator.next());
   System.out.println(nameIterator.next());
   ```

3.  Suppose that nameList is a list of at least two strings and that nameIterator is defined as follows:

    ```
    Iterator<String> nameIterator = nameList.getIterator();
    ```

    Write Java statements that use nameIterator to display only the second last string in the list.

4.  Given nameList and nameIterator as described in Exercise 3, write statements that display all strings in the list from last to first.

5.  Given nameList and nameIterator as described in Exercise 3, write statements that use nameIterator to remove all the entries from the list.

6.  Given nameList and nameIterator as described in Exercise 3, write statements that remove all occurrences of the string *CANCEL* from the list.

7.  Given nameList and nameIterator as described in Exercise 3, write statements that remove any duplicates in the list.

8.  Given nameList and nameIterator as described in Exercise 3, write statements that count the number of times each string occurs in the list, without altering the list and without repeating the computations.

9.  Suppose that aList and bList are instances of java.util.ArrayList. Use two iterators to find and display the smallest values in both the lists. Do not alter the contents of either list.

10. Assume that aList and bList are instances of java.util.ArrayList that contain Comparable objects in order from largest to smallest. Use two iterators to move the objects from bList to the appropriate locations in aList. When you are done, the objects in aList should be in order, and bList should be empty.

11. Revise the class SeparateIterator outlined in Segment 15.3 so that it does not support a remove operation. Simplify the class as much as possible.

12. Imagine a class that implements the interface ListWithIteratorInterface, as given in Listing 15-2 of Segment 15.8. Suppose that aList is an instance of this class and contains Comparable objects in no particular order. Using an iterator, implement the following two methods within the class:

    a.  getMin returns the smallest object in the list
    b.  removeMin removes and returns the smallest object in the list

13. Repeat the previous exercise, but use a for-each loop instead of an iterator.

14. Suppose that nameList is a list that contains the following strings: *Smith, Jason, Miller, Jones, Brown*. What output is produced by the following sequence of statements?

    ```
    ListIterator<String> nameIterator = nameList.getIterator();
    System.out.println(nameIterator.next());
    nameIterator.next();
    System.out.println(nameIterator.next());
    nameIterator.remove();
    nameIterator.set("Sam");
    nameIterator.previous();
    nameIterator.remove();
    System.out.println(nameIterator.next());
    displayList(nameList);
    ```

15. Repeat the previous exercise, but instead use the following statements:

```
ListIterator<String> nameIterator = nameList.getIterator();
nameIterator.next();
nameIterator.remove();
nameIterator.next();
nameIterator.previous();
nameIterator.remove();
System.out.println(nameIterator.next());
nameIterator.next();
nameIterator.set("Sam");
System.out.println("Revised list:");
displayList(nameList);
System.out.println(nameIterator.previous());
System.out.println(nameIterator.next());
```

16. Given a list of strings and an iterator nameIterator whose data type is ListIterator, write statements that add the string *Bob* before the first occurrence of the string *Sam*.

17. If you wanted to implement the interface ListIterator as an inner class iterator by using a linked implementation, what difficulties would you face?

## PROJECTS

1. Revise the class LinkedListWithIterator described in Segment 15.9 so that the inner class Iterator-ForLinkedList provides a remove operation. You will need another data field priorNode to reference the node before the next one.

2. Implement all of the methods in the interface ListIterator as a separate class iterator.

3. Implement the interface ListIterator as an inner class of the class LList—as given in Chapter 14—but do not support the operations add, remove, and set.

4. Implement an iterator that includes a remove operation as an inner class of a class of bags whose implementation is

   a. Array-based.
   b. Linked.

5. If you were to add an iterator to the ADT stack, should the iterator support a remove operation?

   a. Implement an iterator for the linked implementation of a stack, using an inner class.
   b. Implement an iterator for the array-based implementation of a stack, using an inner class.

6. Consider a solitaire matching game in which you have a list of random integer values between 10 and 99. You remove from the list any pair of consecutive integers whose first or second digits match. If all values are removed, then you win.

   For example, consider the following sequence of 10 integers:

   10 82 43 23 89 12 43 84 23 32

The integers in the pair 10 and 82 do not match in either digit and so cannot be removed. However, the integers in the pair 43 and 23 match in the second digit and are removed, leaving the following sequence:

10 82 89 12 43 84 23 32

Continue checking for pairs from 89, the value after the removed pair. No other pairs have matching integers. Now return to the beginning of the list and check the pairs. The integers in the pair 82 and 89 match in the first digit and can be removed:

10 12 43 84 23 32

No other pairs can be removed, so we lose.

Write a program that simulates this game. It should generate 40 random two-digit integers and place them in an instance of java.util.ArrayList, using an instance of ListIterator. Then, using this iterator, scan the list and remove matching pairs of values. After each pair is removed, use an iterator to display the values remaining in the list.

7. One statistical operation that is sometimes performed on a set of data values is to remove values that are far from the average. Write a program that reads real values from a text file, one per line. Store the data values as Double objects in an instance of the class java.util.ArrayList. Then

   - Use an iterator to compute the average and standard deviation of the values. Display these results.
   - Use a second iterator to remove any value that is more than two standard deviations away from the average.
   - Use a for-each loop to display the remaining values and compute the new average. Display the new average.

   If the data values are $x_1$, $x_2$, ..., $x_n$, their average $\mu$ is their sum divided by $n$, and their standard deviation is

   $$\sigma = \sqrt{\frac{1}{n}\sum_{i=1}^{n}(x_i - \mu)^2}$$

8. Consider the following situation. You create a list, and then you add 10 items to it. You get an iterator to the list and call next twice to advance it. You remove the first five items from the list, using the list's remove method. You then call the iterator's remove method, expecting to remove the item last returned by the method next. However, this entry has already been removed from the list. Changing the state of the list while using the iterator, as you have done here, may result in unpredictable behavior of the iterator.

   Modify the interface Iterator so that the methods will throw the exception StateChangedException if the state of the list is changed after the iterator was created but before the method is called. Modify the implementation of LinkedListWithIterator that Project 1 describes to accommodate the changes to Iterator.

9. Revise the class ArrayListWithIterator outlined in Segment 15.14 so that it extends the class AList, as discussed in Chapter 13.

10. Repeat Projects 9 and 10 of Chapter 12, adding an iterator to the ADT recipe.

## ANSWERS TO SELF-TEST QUESTIONS

1.  False. When the list is empty, both `nextPosition` and `list.getLength()` are zero.

2.  Linked. The particular implementation of the list affects the amount of work that the method `getEntry` must perform. For an array-based implementation, `getEntry` accesses the required entry directly and immediately. For a linked implementation, `getEntry` must traverse a chain of nodes to find the desired entry. This takes more time to accomplish than accessing an array entry.

3.  False. When the list is empty, `firstNode`, and therefore `nextNode`, is `null`.

4.  Create the iterators by writing either the same statements as given in Segment JI5.11 or the following ones:

    ```
    Iterator<String> nameIterator = nameList.getIterator();
    Iterator<String> countingIterator = nameList.getIterator();
    ```

5.  ```
    public static void displayListQ5(ListWithIteratorInterface<String> list)
    {
        int numberOfEntries = list.getLength();
        System.out.println("The list contains " + numberOfEntries +
                            " entries, as follows:");
        Iterator<String> traverser = list.getIterator(); // Or list.iterator()
        int position = 0;
        while (traverser.hasNext())
        {
            position++;
            System.out.println(traverser.next() + " is entry " + position);
        } // end while

        System.out.println();
    } // end displayListQ5
    ```

6.  a. Deb.
    b. Deb.

7.  Originally, `nextIndex` is the index of the next entry that `next` will return. The change makes `nextIndex` 1 less than the index of the next entry that `next` will return. Thus, the following changes are needed:

    - The comparison in `hasNext` should be `nextIndex < numberOfEntries` instead of `nextIndex <= numberOfEntries`
    - `next` should return the entry in `list[nextIndex + 1]` instead of the entry in `list[nextIndex]`
    - `remove` should remove the entry in `list[nextIndex]` instead of the entry in `list[nextIndex - 1]`

8.  ```
    public static void displayListQ8(ListWithTraversal<String> list)
    {
        int numberOfEntries = list.getLength();
        System.out.println("The list contains " + numberOfEntries +
                            " entries, as follows:");
        list.resetTraversal();
        int position = 0;
    ```

```
      while (list.hasNext())
      {
         position++;
         System.out.println(list.next() + " is entry " + position);
      } // end while

      System.out.println();
} // end displayListQ8
```

A disadvantage is that if you have an iteration in progress, and you pause it to call displayListQ8, you will not be able to resume your iteration.

9.  **a.** No. The default constructor creates an empty list. If it sets nextNode to firstNode, nextNode would be set to null.
    **b.** Yes, but with a disadvantage. Each addition to the list would set nextNode to firstNode. After creating a list, you could traverse it. However, the only way you could reset the traversal to the list's beginning would be to add another entry to the list.

# Mutable and Immutable Objects

## Contents

## Prerequisites

## Objectives

After studying this chapter, you should be able to
- Distinguish among mutable and immutable objects
- Define a class of immutable objects
- Define companion classes, one of immutable objects and the other of mutable objects

When a class has public mutator, or set, methods, a client can use these methods to alter objects of that class. Although this ability seems reasonable, it is unreasonable if another class organizes those objects in a particular way. For example, the next chapter describes the ADT sorted list, which maintains its entries in sorted order according to any criterion you want—alphabetical order, for instance. If a client can alter a name in the sorted list, it can destroy the order of the list.

This interlude looks at one strategy to prevent this problem. It simply requires a client to place into a collection only objects that cannot be altered. Java Interlude 9 will present a second strategy, which requires the collection to make a copy, or *clone*, of any object that a client adds to it. With this technique, the client has no reference to the copy in the collection and so cannot change it.

## Mutable Objects

**JI6.1**   Many of the classes you have studied so far have private data fields and public methods that either look at or change these fields. As you know, such methods are called accessor methods and mutator methods—or, alternatively, get and set methods. An object that belongs to a class that has public mutator methods is said to be *mutable*—as we mentioned in Chapter 10—because the client can use the set methods to change the values of the object's data fields. For example, you saw the class Name of two-part names in Segment C.16 of Appendix C. It has the following two data fields:

```
private String first; // First name
private String last;  // Last name
```

To enable the client to change the values of these fields, we give the class the mutator methods setFirst and setLast. To look at the fields, it has the accessor methods getFirst and getLast.

 **Note:**   A mutable object belongs to a class that has mutator (set) methods for its data fields.

**JI6.2**   Let's use this class to create an object for *Chris Coffee* by writing the following Java statement:

```
Name chris = new Name("Chris", "Coffee");
```

Figure JI6-1 illustrates this object and the reference variable chris.

---

**FIGURE JI6-1**   An object and its reference variable chris

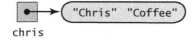

chris

---

Now suppose we create a list and then add chris to the list by writing

```
ListInterface<Name> nameList = new LList<>();
nameList.add(1, chris);
```

Since chris is a mutable object, we can change its data fields by writing, for example,

```
chris.setLast("Smith");
```

After this change, the object chris represents the name *Chris Smith*. Nothing is surprising here. What might be surprising, however, is that the list has changed! That's right: If we retrieve the first item in the list by writing, for instance,

```
System.out.println(nameList.getEntry(1));
```

we will get *Chris Smith* instead of *Chris Coffee*.

**JI6.3**   How can it be that the list, which we created before changing the name, contains the changed name? Remember that in Java, the list contains references to the actual objects that the client places in it. So the list has a reference to its first item, but so does the client, since it has the variable chris, as Figure JI6-2a shows.

**FIGURE JI6-2**     An object in the list `nameList` (a) initially; (b) after the
reference variable `chris` is used to change it

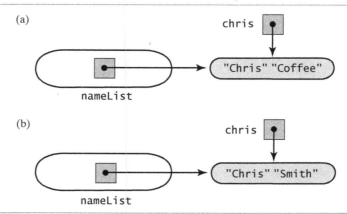

When we altered the object by executing

```
chris.setLast("Smith");
```

we changed the one and only copy of the object, as Figure JI6-2b shows. Since the list still references that object, `nameList.getEntry(1)` returns a reference to the object. This aspect of Java can be a convenient way for the client to alter the objects it has placed in a list.

 **Note:** When a client creates a mutable object and adds it to an ADT list, only one copy of the object ordinarily exists. Thus, if the client alters the object, the list changes. Ideally, the client will use the `replace` operation to revise an entry in the list, but we cannot force the client to do so.

**JI6.4**   The ability to alter mutable objects in a collection can permit a client to destroy the collection's integrity. For example, suppose that we create a list of names in alphabetical order. If we write

```
Name jesse = new Name("Jesse", "Java");
Name rob = new Name("Rob", "Bean");
ListInterface<Name> alphaList = new AList<>();
alphaList.add(jesse);
alphaList.add(1, rob);
```

we would get the alphabetized list

    Rob Bean
    Jesse Java

Now if we write

```
rob.setLast("Smith");
```

the list changes to

    Rob Smith
    Jesse Java

This list is no longer alphabetical. One solution to this problem is to require the client to use immutable objects, as the next segment describes.

# Immutable Objects

**JI6.5**   As Chapter 10 indicated, an immutable object is one whose data fields cannot be altered by a client. The class to which an immutable object belongs has no public mutator (set) methods, so once you create the object, you cannot change its data fields. If you need to change them, you will have to discard the object and create a new one with the revised fields. Such a class is said to be **read only**. A client that places immutable objects into a sorted list cannot alter those objects and thus cannot destroy the sorted order of the list.

**Note:**  An immutable object belongs to a read-only class. Such an object prevents a client from changing the values of its data fields.

**Note:**  When a collection—such as a sorted list—organizes objects in a certain way, a client should not destroy this organization by altering the objects directly. Yet if the client retains references to the objects, that is exactly what a client could do. You can prevent this problem by adding only immutable objects to the collection.

**JI6.6**   **Mutable or immutable?** Most classes have set methods, so their instances are mutable. Being able to change an object's data is convenient and efficient, particularly when an object's state must change often during the course of a program's execution. For example, a bank must regularly update the object that represents your checking account. If that object were immutable, it would be discarded and a new object representing the updated data would be created each time there was a change. But replacing an object takes more time than revising it.

On the other hand, sharing a mutable object can be dangerous. Suppose that you have two references, x and y, to the same object. If you use x to modify the object, you might get confused when you use y to reference it. But sharing immutable objects is safe, since no matter how you reference them, they remain unchanged.

**Programming Tip:**  Use an immutable object if it will be shared or added to a collection that can be corrupted by changes to the object. Use a mutable object if its data will change frequently.

## Creating a Read-Only Class

**JI6.7**   To convert the previous class Name into a read-only class, we can change the access modifiers of the methods setFirst, setLast, and setName from public to private to prevent a client from invoking them. (We could instead omit these methods altogether, modifying the other methods that invoke them.) We also omit Name's method giveLastNameTo.

Let's call the resulting class ImmutableName. If we place instances of ImmutableName in a list or a sorted list, we will not be able to change these objects by using any references that we might have retained to them. Of course, we can use the replace operation of the ADT list to replace a particular item in a list, but as you will see in the next chapter, no such operation exists for a sorted list. To change an entry in a sorted list, we would have to remove the entry and add a new one. In this way, the sorted list maintains its sorted order.

Suppose that `ImmutableName` had protected mutator methods such as `setFirst` and `setLast`. A programmer could use inheritance to alter the behavior of the class. Imagine deriving a class of mutable objects from `ImmutableName`. You then could add instances of this new class to a sorted list of `ImmutableName` objects. Since these entries would be mutable, you could change them and destroy the order of the sorted list. To prevent this from happening, we can make the class final, as described in the Security Note at the end of Segment 2.15 in Chapter 2.

**JI6.8**  Listing JI6-1 defines `ImmutableName` as a final class. Since the class has no set methods, we did not define a default constructor. You could define one, even though its use is unnecessary.

---

**LISTING JI6-1**  The read-only class `ImmutableName`

```java
1  public final class ImmutableName
2  {
3     private String first; // First name
4     private String last;  // Last name
5
6     public ImmutableName(String firstName, String lastName)
7     {
8        first = firstName;
9        last = lastName;
10    } // end constructor
11
12    public String getFirst()
13    {
14       return first;
15    } // end getFirst
16
17    public String getLast()
18    {
19       return last;
20    } // end getLast
21
22    public String getName()
23    {
24       return toString();
25    } // end getName
26
27    public String toString()
28    {
29       return first + " " + last;
30    } // end toString
31 } // end ImmutableName
```

---

**JI6.9**  We have one more concern. Imagine a class that has a `Name` object as a data field. The class has accessor methods, including one that returns the `Name` field, but has no mutator methods. However, a client of this class can access the `Name` field and then use `Name`'s set methods to alter the field's value. In other words, the class is not read only. To make it read only, we can define the field as final. Note that the fields of `ImmutableName` are strings, which are immutable, so we need not make them final.

---

**Note:  Design guidelines for a read-only class**

- The class should be final.
- Data fields should be private.
- Data fields that are mutable objects should be final.
- The class should not have public set methods.

**Question 1** Define a constructor for ImmutableName that has a Name object as a parameter.

## Companion Classes

**JI6.10** Although immutable objects are desirable for certain applications, mutable objects have their place. Sometimes we will want to represent an object in both immutable and mutable forms. In such cases, a pair of **companion classes** can be convenient. The classes ImmutableName and Name are examples of two such companion classes. The objects in both classes represent names, but one type of object cannot be altered, while the other can be.

To make the classes even more convenient, you could include constructors and/or methods that convert an object from one type to the other. For example, we might add the following constructor and method to the class ImmutableName:

```
// Add to the class ImmutableName:
public ImmutableName(Name aName)
{
   first = aName.getFirst();
   last = aName.getLast();
} // end constructor

public Name getMutable()
{
   return new Name(first, last);
} // end getMutable
```

Similarly, we could add the following constructor and method to the class Name:

```
// Add to the class Name
public Name(ImmutableName aName)
{
   first = aName.getFirst();
   last = aName.getLast();
} // end constructor

public ImmutableName getImmutable()
{
   return new ImmutableName(first, last);
} // end getMutable
```

Figure JI6-3 illustrates the two classes Name and ImmutableName.

---

**FIGURE JI6-3**    The classes Name and ImmutableName

| Name |
| --- |
| first<br>last |
| getFirst()<br>getLast()<br>getName()<br>setFirst(firstName)<br>setLast(lastName)<br>setName(firstName, lastName)<br>giveLastNameTo(aName)<br>toString()<br>getImmutable() |

| ImmutableName |
| --- |
| first<br>last |
| getFirst()<br>getLast()<br>getName()<br>toString()<br>getMutable() |

**JI6.11**  **Example:** Let's see how we can use the previous additions to our companion classes. If we have a Name object such as flexibleName in the statement

```
Name flexibleName = new Name("Maria", "Mocha");
```

and we no longer need the capability to change it, we can use ImmutableName's constructor, as follows:

```
ImmutableName fixedName = new ImmutableName(flexibleName);
```

The new object fixedName has the same data fields as flexibleName, but it is immutable. Alternatively, we could have invoked Name's method getImmutable, as follows:

```
ImmutableName fixedName = flexibleName.getImmutable();
```

Similarly, if we have another instance of ImmutableName, such as

```
ImmutableName persistent = new ImmutableName("Jesse", "Java");
```

and we find that we need to alter it, we can define a new mutable object as either

```
Name transient = new Name(persistent);
```

or

```
Name transient = persistent.getMutable();
```

The new object transient has the same data fields as persistent, but it also has set methods to change them.

 **Note:** If you do not want anyone to use the class Name as a base class, you can declare it as final.

 **Question 2** Write Java statements that take the following steps:
- Create an object of the class Name.
- Convert the object to an immutable object without changing its data fields.
- Add the immutable object to the list nameList.

**Question 3** Write Java statements that take the following steps:
- Create an object of the class ImmutableName.
- Convert the object to a mutable object without changing its data fields.
- Change the last name of the new object.
- Convert the revised mutable object to an immutable object.

 **Note:** Java's class String is a read-only class. That is, instances of String are immutable. Once you create a string, you cannot change it. Frequently, however, string applications require that you either remove a portion of a string or join two strings together. For such applications, Java provides the class StringBuilder of mutable strings. StringBuilder provides several methods that modify a string by adding, removing, or replacing substrings. Appendix B describes some of the methods that belong to these two classes.

String and StringBuilder are a pair of companion classes. String has a constructor that takes an instance of StringBuilder as an argument and produces an immutable string with the same value. StringBuilder has an analogous constructor that creates mutable strings from immutable ones. StringBuilder also has the methods substring and toString that return instances of String.

## ANSWERS TO SELF-TEST QUESTIONS

1.
```java
public ImmutableName(Name aName)
{
   first = aName.getFirst();
   last = aName.getLast();
} // end constructor
```

2.
```java
// Create an object of the class Name
Name derek = new Name("Derek", "Greene");
// Convert the object to an immutable object; don't change its data fields
ImmutableName derekI = derek.getImmutable();
// Add the immutable object to the list nameList
ListInterface<ImmutableName> nameList = new AList<>();
nameList.add(derekI);
```

3.
```java
// Create an object of the class ImmutableName
ImmutableName lila = new ImmutableName("Lila", "Bleu");
// Convert the object to a mutable object; don't change its data fields
Name changer = lila.getMutable();
// Change the last name of the new object
changer.setLast("Greene");
// Convert the revised mutable object to an immutable object
ImmutableName unchanger = changer.getImmutable();
```

# Sorted Lists

## Contents

## Prerequisites

## Objectives

After studying this chapter, you should be able to
- Use a sorted list in a program
- Describe the differences between the ADT list and the ADT sorted list
- Implement the ADT sorted list by using a chain of linked nodes
- Implement the ADT sorted list by using the operations of the ADT list

Chapter 12 introduced you to the ADT list. The entries in a list are ordered simply by their positions within the list. Thus, a list has a first entry, a second entry, and so on. This ADT enables you to order entries according to any criterion you want—alphabetical or chronological, for instance. In fact, Chapter 12 showed you an example that used a list to organize names in alphabetical order. To do so, the client had to determine where in the list a particular entry belonged.

If your application creates a list and then at some point needs to sort the list's entries into numerical or alphabetical order, for example, you can add a sort operation to the ADT list. You can use one of the algorithms given in Chapters 8 and 9 to implement this operation. But when your application requires only sorted data, having an ADT that orders the data for you would be more convenient than the ADT list. The sorted list is such an ADT.

When you either add an entry to or remove an entry from a sorted list, you provide only the entry. You do not specify where in the list the entry belongs or exists. The ADT determines this for you.

This chapter describes the operations of the ADT sorted list, provides examples of using a sorted list, and presents two possible Java implementations. One of these implementations uses the ADT list, but it is not especially efficient. Chapter 17 addresses the reuse of a class and provides a more efficient implementation of the sorted list as it discusses the use of inheritance.

## Specifications for the ADT Sorted List

**16.1**   The ADT list leaves it up to the client to arrange the objects in a given collection. The client can maintain the objects in any order that meets its needs. Suppose that you want a list of names or other strings that are in alphabetical order. You could certainly use the ADT list for this task, but you would have to determine the position that each string should have within the list. Wouldn't it be more convenient if the list itself alphabetized the entries as you added them? What you need is a different ADT, namely the **sorted list**.

Recall that to use the add operations of the ADT list, you specify the new entry and then must add it either to the end of the list or at a desired position within the list. Such operations are not desirable for the ADT sorted list, since the sorted list is responsible for organizing its entries. If you were allowed to specify a new entry's position, you might destroy the order of the sorted list's entries. Instead, the add operation of the ADT sorted list requires only the new entry. The operation compares the new entry to other entries in the sorted list to determine the new entry's position. Thus, the entries in a sorted list must be objects that can be compared with one another.

What, then, can you place in a sorted list? One possibility is strings, since the class String provides a compareTo method for comparing two strings. In general, you can have a sorted list of any objects of a class that has a compareTo method. As you saw at the beginning of Java Interlude 3, such classes implement the interface Comparable. Since Java's wrapper classes, such as Integer and Double, implement the Comparable interface, you can place instances of them into a sorted list.

**16.2**   Let's examine the possible operations for this ADT. For simplicity, we will allow the sorted list to contain duplicate items. Insisting that the sorted list contain only unique items is somewhat more complicated, and we will leave this variation as an exercise.

We've already mentioned that you can add an entry to the sorted list. Since the sorted list determines the position of a new entry, you could ask the ADT for this position. That is, you could ask for the position of an existing entry or for the position in which a proposed entry would occur if you added it to the list. You could also ask the ADT whether it contained a particular entry. And clearly you should be able to remove an entry.

Let's specify these operations more carefully.

| | ABSTRACT DATA TYPE: SORTED LIST | |
|---|---|---|

**DATA**

- A collection of objects in sorted order and having the same data type
- The number of objects in the collection

**OPERATIONS**

| PSEUDOCODE | UML | DESCRIPTION |
|---|---|---|
| add(newEntry) | +add(newEntry: T): void | Task: Adds newEntry to the sorted list so that the list remains sorted.<br>Input: newEntry is the object to be added.<br>Output: None. |
| remove(anEntry) | +remove(anEntry: T): boolean | Task: Removes the first or only occurrence of anEntry from the sorted list.<br>Input: anEntry is the object to be removed.<br>Output: Returns true if anEntry was located and removed, or false if not. In the latter case, the list remains unchanged. |
| getPosition(anEntry) | +getPosition(anEntry: T): integer | Task: Gets the position of the first or only occurrence of anEntry.<br>Input: anEntry is the object to be found.<br>Output: Returns the position of anEntry if it occurs in the list. Otherwise, returns the position where anEntry would occur in the list, but as a negative integer. |

The following operations behave as they do for the ADT list and are described in Chapter 12:

```
getEntry(givenPosition)
contains(anEntry)
remove(givenPosition)
clear()
getLength()
isEmpty()
toArray()
```

**16.3**    The first two methods are straightforward, but getPosition deserves some comment. Given an entry in the sorted list, the method getPosition returns the entry's position number within the list, as you would expect. We number the entries beginning with 1, just as we do for the ADT list. But what if the given entry is not in the sorted list? In this case, getPosition returns the position number where the entry belongs in the list. The returned number is negative, however, to signal that the entry is not in the list. For example, if missingObject is not in the sorted list sList but belongs at position 3, sList.getPosition(missingObject) would return -3. Note that getPosition deals with an empty list by returning -1 to indicate that any given entry belongs at position 1.

The sorted list also has some, but not all, of the operations of an ADT list. We have already mentioned that adding an entry at a given position is not possible, because otherwise the client could destroy the order of the sorted list. For the same reason, the list's replace method is not available to a sorted list. The other operations of the ADT list, however, are useful for a sorted list as well, including the ones that retrieve or remove the entry at a given position. The methods getEntry and remove each have a position number as a parameter, but they will not alter the relative order of the entries in the sorted list.

Although the list's remove method returns the object removed from the list, it is not necessary for the sorted list's remove method to do so. The client already has at least a copy of this entry to enable it to invoke the sorted list's remove.

**16.4**    The Java interface in Listing 16-1 specifies these operations in more detail. The notation ? super T, which Segment JI3.13 of Java Interlude 3 introduced, means any superclass of the generic type T.

---

**LISTING 16-1**    The interface SortedListInterface

```java
1   /** An interface for the ADT sorted list.
2       Entries in the list have positions that begin with 1.
3       @author Frank M. Carrano
4   /*
5   public interface SortedListInterface<T extends Comparable<? super T>>
6   {
7       /** Adds a new entry to this sorted list in its proper order.
8           The list's size is increased by 1.
9           @param newEntry  The object to be added as a new entry. */
10      public void add(T newEntry);
11
12      /** Removes the first or only occurrence of a specified entry
13          from this sorted list.
14          @param anEntry  The object to be removed.
15          @return  True if anEntry was located and removed; */
16              otherwise returns false. */
17      public boolean remove(T anEntry);
18
19      /** Gets the position of an entry in this sorted list.
20          @param anEntry  The object to be found.
21          @return  The position of the first or only occurrence of anEntry
22                   if it occurs in the list; otherwise returns the position
23                   where anEntry would occur in the list, but as a negative
24                   integer. */
25      public int getPosition(T anEntry);
26
27      // The following methods are described in Segment 12.9 of Chapter 12
28      // as part of the ADT list:
29
30      public T getEntry(int givenPosition);
31      public boolean contains(T anEntry);
```

```
32      public T remove(int givenPosition);
33      public void clear();
34      public int getLength();
35      public boolean isEmpty();
36      public T[] toArray();
37  } // end SortedListInterface
```

**Note:** The ADT sorted list can add, remove, or locate an entry, given the entry as an argument. The sorted list has several operations that are the same as ADT list operations, namely getEntry, contains, remove (by position), clear, getLength, isEmpty, and toArray. However, a sorted list will not let you add or replace an entry by position.

**Note:** The ADT sorted list compares its entries to determine their order. Thus, as discussed in the Design Decision in Segment 10.19 of Chapter 10, a sorted list cannot contain null entries.

**Note: The method remove(givenPosition) versus the method remove(anEntry)**
The ADT sorted list has two methods that remove an entry, but the functionalities of these two methods differ. The method that removes a given entry from a sorted list returns either true or false according to its success or failure. Here, failure simply means that the entry was not found in the list. A client can use this method to search a sorted list for a given entry and, if it is found, to remove it. On the other hand, the method that removes an entry at a given position from a sorted list either returns that entry or throws an exception if the position is out of range. The exception is necessary because an out-of-range position can have more severe consequences and a different meaning than not finding an item.

**Note: Naming the methods that add or remove an entry from a sorted list**
Both the method that removes a given entry from a sorted list and the method that removes an entry at a given position have the same name, remove. To avoid confusion between these methods, you could name the former method removeEntry. And if you like, you could change the name of the method add to addEntry.

## Using the ADT Sorted List

**16.5**    **Example.** To demonstrate the operations of the ADT sorted list that the previous section specifies, we first create a sorted list of strings. We begin by declaring and allocating the list nameList, where we assume that SortedList is an implementation of the ADT operations specified by the interface SortedListInterface:

```
SortedListInterface<String> nameList = new SortedList<>();
```

Next, we add names in an arbitrary order, realizing that the ADT will organize them alphabetically:

```
nameList.add("Jamie");
nameList.add("Brenda");
nameList.add("Sarah");
nameList.add("Tom");
nameList.add("Carlos");
```

The sorted list now contains the following entries:

> Brenda
> Carlos
> Jamie
> Sarah
> Tom

**16.6**   Assuming the list just given, here are some examples of the ADT operations on the sorted list:

> `nameList.getPosition("Jamie")` returns 3, the position of *Jamie* in the list
> `nameList.contains("Jill")` returns false, because *Jill* is not in the list
> `nameList.getPosition("Jill")` returns –4, because *Jill* belongs at position 4 in the list
> `nameList.getEntry(2)` returns *Carlos*, because he is at position 2 in the list

Now remove *Tom* and the first name in the list by writing

```
nameList.remove("Tom");
nameList.remove(1);
```

The list now contains

> Carlos
> Jamie
> Sarah

Removing the last entry, *Tom*, did not change the positions of the other entries in the list, but removing the first entry did. *Carlos* is now at position 1, instead of 2.

**Question 1** Suppose that `wordList` is an unsorted list of words. Using the operations of the ADT list and the ADT sorted list, create a sorted list of these words.

**Question 2** Assuming that the sorted list you created in the previous question is not empty, write Java statements that

**a.** Display the last entry in the sorted list.

**b.** Without removing the sorted list's first entry, add it to the sorted list again.

# A Linked Implementation

**VideoNote**
**The class LinkedSortedList**

As with all ADTs, you have a choice of several ways in which to implement the sorted list. You could store a sorted list's entries in, for example, an array, a chain of linked nodes, an instance of a vector, or an instance of an ADT list. In this chapter, we will consider a chain of linked nodes and an instance of an ADT list. In Chapter 17, we will use inheritance and the ADT list to develop a completely different implementation.

**16.7**   **An outline of the class.** An implementation that uses a chain of linked nodes to store the entries in a sorted list has several details in common with the linked implementation of the ADT list that you studied in Chapter 14. In particular, it has the same data fields, similar constructors, the same implementations for several of its methods, and the same definition of the inner class `Node`. Thus, we outline in Listing 16-2 a class definition that implements the ADT sorted list.

LISTING 16-2    An outline of a linked implementation of the ADT sorted list

```
1  public class LinkedSortedList<T extends Comparable<? super T>>
2              implements SortedListInterface<T>
3  {
4     private Node firstNode; // Reference to first node of chain
5     private int  numberOfEntries;
6
7     public LinkedSortedList()
8     {
9        firstNode = null;
10       numberOfEntries = 0;
11    } // end default constructor
12
13    < Implementations of the sorted list operations go here.>
14    . . .
15    private class Node
16    {
17       private T    data;
18       private Node next;
19       < Constructors >
20       . . .
21       < Accessor and mutator methods: getData, setData, getNextNode, setNextNode >
22       . . .
23    } // end Node
24 } // end LinkedSortedList
```

## The Method add

**16.8**    **Locating the insertion point.** Adding an entry to a sorted list requires that you find where in the list the new entry belongs. Since the entries are sorted, you compare the new entry with the entries in the sorted list until you reach an entry that is not smaller than the new entry. Figure 16-1 depicts a chain of linked nodes, each containing a name, sorted alphabetically. The figure shows where the additional names *Ally*, *Cathy*, *Luke*, *Sue*, and *Tom* would be inserted into the chain and the last comparisons that would have to occur to arrive at those locations.

FIGURE 16-1    Places to insert additional names into a sorted chain of
                linked nodes

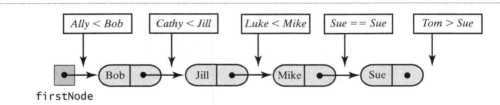

You can see from the figure that, in a string comparison, *Ally* is less than *Bob*, and so it would be inserted at the beginning of the chain. To see where to insert *Luke*, you would find that *Luke* is greater than both *Bob* and *Jill* but less than *Mike*. Thus, *Luke* belongs before *Mike* in the chain. *Sue*, on the other hand, is already in one of the nodes. You would discover that *Sue* is greater than *Bob*, *Jill*, and *Mike* but not greater than *Sue*. So you would insert the new entry *Sue* just before the existing entry *Sue*. Finally, *Tom* is greater than all the current names in the list, so you would add it to the end of the chain.

**Note:** Given a sorted list with entries in ascending order, you insert a new entry just before the first entry that is not smaller than the new entry.

**16.9** **The algorithm.** Recall from Segment 14.10 of Chapter 14 that you handle the addition of a new node to the beginning of a chain differently from an addition at other points in the chain. Adding to the beginning is easy, since firstNode references the first node in the chain. To add anywhere else, you need a reference to the node that will ultimately occur before the new node. Thus, while you traverse the chain of linked nodes to discover where the new entry belongs, you must retain a reference to the node prior to the one under consideration.

A high-level algorithm that describes our strategy follows:

*Algorithm* add(newEntry)
*// Adds a new entry to the sorted list.*

*Allocate a new node containing* newEntry
*Search the chain until either you find a node containing* newEntry *or you pass the point*
*where it should be*
*Let* nodeBefore *reference the node before the insertion point*
**if** (*the chain is empty or the new node belongs at the beginning of the chain*)
*Add the new node to the beginning of the chain*
**else**
*Insert the new node after the node referenced by* nodeBefore

*Increment the length of the sorted list*

**16.10** **An iterative implementation of add.** A Java implementation of the previous algorithm follows. We use a private method, getNodeBefore, to search the chain for the node before the insertion point.

```java
public void add(T newEntry)
{
    Node newNode = new Node(newEntry);
    Node nodeBefore = getNodeBefore(newEntry);

    if (isEmpty() || (nodeBefore == null))
    {
        // Add at beginning
        newNode.setNextNode(firstNode);
        firstNode = newNode;
    }
    else
    {
        // Add after nodeBefore
        Node nodeAfter = nodeBefore.getNextNode();
        newNode.setNextNode(nodeAfter);
        nodeBefore.setNextNode(newNode);
    } // end if

    numberOfEntries++;
} // end add
```

**16.11** **The private method getNodeBefore.** We still need to implement the private method getNode-Before. We will need two references as we traverse the list. Clearly we need a reference to the current node so we can compare its entry to the desired entry. But we also must retain a reference to the previous node, because it is this reference that the method returns. In the following implementation, these references are currentNode and nodeBefore:

```java
// Finds the node that is before the node that should or does
// contain a given entry.
// Returns either a reference to the node that is before the node
```

```
// that does or should contain anEntry, or null if no prior node exists
// (that is, if anEntry is or belongs at the beginning of the list).
private Node getNodeBefore(T anEntry)
{
   Node currentNode = firstNode;
   Node nodeBefore = null;

   while ( (currentNode != null) &&
           (anEntry.compareTo(currentNode.getData()) > 0) )
   {
      nodeBefore = currentNode;
      currentNode = currentNode.getNextNode();
   } // end while

   return nodeBefore;
} // end getNodeBefore
```

Recall that the method `compareTo` returns a negative, zero, or positive integer according to whether the comparison is, respectively, less than, equal to, or greater than.

**Question 3** In the `while` statement of the method `getNodeBefore`, how important is the order of the two boolean expressions that the operator `&&` joins? Explain.

**Question 4** What does `getNodeBefore` return if the sorted list is empty? How can you use this fact to simplify the implementation of the method add given in Segment 16.10?

**Question 5** Suppose that you use the previous method add to add an entry to a sorted list. If the entry is already in the list, where in the list will add insert it: Before the first occurrence of the entry, after the first occurrence of the entry, after the last occurrence of the entry, or somewhere else?

**Question 6** What would be the answer to the previous question if you changed > to >= in the `while` statement of the method `getNodeBefore`?

16.12    **Thinking recursively.** Using recursion to process a chain of linked nodes can be an attractive alternative to an iterative approach. The basic concept is easy, but, as you will see, the implementation is more involved, since Java passes objects to methods as references.

Recall from Segment 7.20 of Chapter 7 that you can process the chain's first node and then recursively process the rest of the chain. Thus, to add a new node to a sorted chain of linked nodes, you use the following logic:

**if** (*the chain is empty or the new node belongs at the beginning of the chain*)
    *Add the new node to the beginning of the chain*
**else**
    *Ignore the first node and add the new node to the rest of the chain*

Figure 16-2 illustrates the logic needed to recursively add the name *Luke* to a sorted chain of names. Since *Luke* is greater than *Bob*, you recursively consider the subchain that begins at *Jill*. *Luke* is also greater than *Jill*, so you now consider the subchain beginning at *Mike*. Finally, *Luke* is less than *Mike*, so you make the actual addition at the beginning of this subchain—that is, before *Mike*. Adding to the beginning of a chain—or subchain—is the base case of this recursion. Happily, the beginning of a chain is the easiest place to make an addition.

If `currentNode` initially references the chain and later references the rest of the chain, we can add some detail to the previous logic, as follows:

**if** ( (currentNode == **null**) *or* (newEntry <= currentNode.getData()) )
    currentNode = **new** Node(newEntry, currentNode)
**else**
    *Recursively add* newEntry *to the chain beginning at* currentNode.getNextNode()

FIGURE 16-2    Recursively adding *Luke* to a sorted chain of names

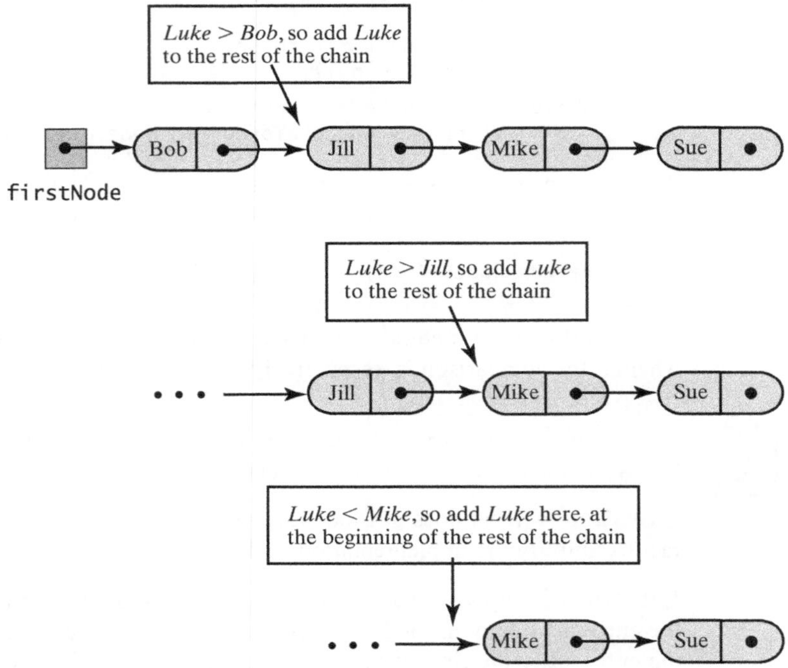

16.13    **A recursive implementation of add.** The example in Segment 7.20 displayed the contents of a chain. Since that operation does not alter the chain, its recursive formulation was straightforward. Obviously, in our present situation, the method add does alter the chain. Getting the recursive method to make these changes is the challenge in Java.

Let's look at the recursive implementation of the method add before we describe why it works. You learned in Segment 7.19 that you write a private method to perform the recursion and you write a public method—typically the one that implements the ADT operation—to invoke this private method. Thus, we have the following method definitions:

```java
public void add(T newEntry)
{
   firstNode = add(newEntry, firstNode);
   numberOfEntries++;
} // end add

private Node add(T newEntry, Node currentNode)
{
   if ( (currentNode == null) ||
        (newEntry.compareTo(currentNode.getData()) <= 0) )
   {
      currentNode = new Node(newEntry, currentNode);
   }
   else
   {
      Node nodeAfter = add(newEntry, currentNode.getNextNode());
      currentNode.setNextNode(nodeAfter);
   } // end if
   return currentNode;
} // end add
```

The private method add adds newEntry to the subchain that begins at currentNode. We will trace and explain its logic in a moment.

**Question 7** Repeat Question 5, using the method add that was just given.

**16.14**  **Tracing an addition to the list's beginning.** Suppose that nameList is the sorted list that the chain in Figure 16-3a represents. Let's invoke nameList.add("Ally") to add *Ally* to this list. This addition will occur at the beginning of the chain. The public method add will call the private method add with the invocation add("Ally", firstNode). The reference in the argument firstNode is copied to the parameter currentNode, and so it also references the first node in the chain, as Figure 16-3b illustrates.

**FIGURE 16-3**    Recursively adding a node at the beginning of a chain

(a) The list before any additions

(b) As add("Ally", firstNode) begins execution

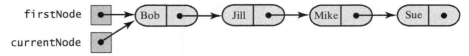

(c) After a new node is created (the base case)

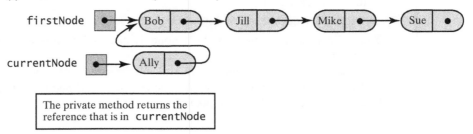

The private method returns the reference that is in currentNode

(d) After the public add assigns the returned reference to firstNode

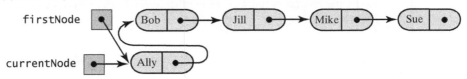

Since *Ally* will be added to the beginning of the chain, the statement

```
currentNode = new Node("Ally", currentNode);
```

executes and creates a new node for *Ally*. This node is linked to the original chain, as Figure 16-3c shows. Notice that firstNode is unchanged, even though it is the argument that corresponds to the parameter currentNode.

The private method now returns the value of currentNode, and the public method add assigns that value to firstNode. Thus, the chain with the completed addition appears as in Figure 16-3d.

**16.15** **Tracing an addition to the list's interior: the recursive calls.** What happens when the addition is not at the beginning of the original chain? Let's trace what happens when we add *Luke* to the chain in Figure 16-4a. The public method add calls the private method add with the invocation add("Luke", firstNode). As in the previous segment, the reference in firstNode is copied to the parameter currentNode, and so it also references the first node in the chain, as Figure 16-4a illustrates.

Since *Luke* comes after *Bob*, another recursive call occurs:

```
add("Luke", currentNode.getNextNode())
```

The second argument is a reference to the chain's second node, the one containing *Jill*. This reference is copied to the parameter currentNode, as Figure 16-4b depicts.

*Luke* comes after *Jill*, so the recursive process is repeated again, and currentNode references the chain's third node—*Mike*'s node—as shown in Figure 16-4c. *Luke* is less than *Mike*, so no recursive call occurs. We are at the base case. A new node is created that contains *Luke* and references *Mike*'s node, as Figure 16-4d illustrates.

**16.16** **Tracing the returns from the recursive method.** Having just created a new node, the private method add returns a reference to it, as Figure 16-4d indicates. The statement that invoked add now resumes execution:

```
nodeAfter = add("Luke", currentNode.getNextNode());
```

Thus, nodeAfter is assigned a reference to the new node containing *Luke*, as Figure 16-4e illustrates.

At this point, currentNode references *Jill*'s node, as it did in Part *b* of the figure. The next statement to execute is

```
currentNode.setNextNode(nodeAfter);
```

Thus, the data field next in *Jill*'s node is changed to reference *Luke*'s node, as shown in Figure 16-4f.

The private method add now returns a reference to *Jill*'s node. If we continue the trace, we will make *Bob*'s node reference *Jill*'s node and firstNode reference *Bob*'s node, even though these references are already in place.

**Note:** A recursive addition to a chain of nodes locates and remembers the nodes prior to the insertion point. After the portion of the chain that follows the insertion point is linked to the new node, the recursion links the remembered nodes back into the chain.

**FIGURE 16-4**   Recursively adding a node between existing nodes in a chain

(a) As `add("Luke", firstNode)` begins execution

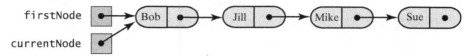

(b) As the recursive call `add("Luke", currentNode.getNextNode())` begins execution

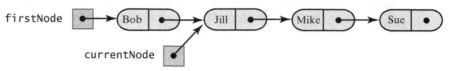

(c) As the recursive call `add("Luke", currentNode.getNextNode())` begins execution

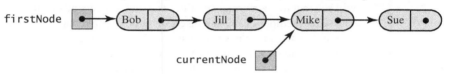

(d) After a new node is created (the base case)

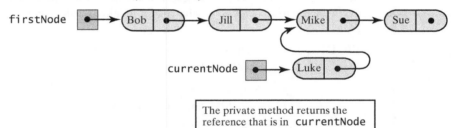

The private method returns the reference that is in `currentNode`

(e) After the returned reference is assigned to `nodeAfter`

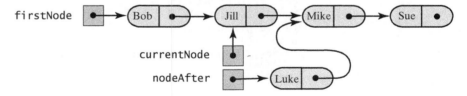

(f) After `currentNode.setNextNode(nodeAfter)` executes

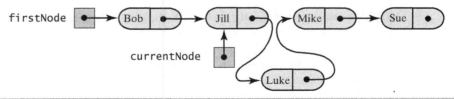

**16.17**    Projects 1 and 2 at the end of this chapter ask you to complete the iterative and recursive implementations of the sorted list. Notice that many of the sorted list operations are the same as operations of the ADT list and so would have implementations like those you saw in Chapter 14.

**Note:** Since the ADTs sorted list and list share many of the same operations, portions of their implementations are identical.

**Question 8** The linked implementation of the ADT sorted list, as given in this chapter, does not maintain a tail reference. Why is a tail reference more significant for a linked implementation of the ADT list than it is for a sorted list?

## The Efficiency of the Linked Implementation

**16.18**    If you consider the analysis of the linked implementation of the ADT list given in Chapter 14, you will see that the performance of the add method depends on the efficiency of the method getNodeAt. The latter method locates the insertion point by traversing the chain of nodes. It is an $O(n)$ operation. The add method for the sorted list does its own traversal of the list to locate where to make the addition. This traversal is also $O(n)$, making the addition to a sorted list an $O(n)$ operation.

VideoNote
An array-based sorted list

Figure 16-5 summarizes the performance of the sorted list operations. Deriving these results is left as an exercise. When comparing implementations, you should realize that the worst cases can occur under different circumstances. For example, a worst-case addition to an array-based sorted list occurs at the list's beginning, whereas for a linked implementation, it occurs at the list's end.

**FIGURE 16-5**    The worst-case efficiencies of the operations on the ADT sorted list for two implementations

| ADT Sorted List Operation | Array | Linked |
|---|---|---|
| add(newEntry) | O(n) | O(n) |
| remove(anEntry) | O(n) | O(n) |
| getPosition(anEntry) | O(n) | O(n) |
| getEntry(givenPosition) | O(1) | O(n) |
| contains(anEntry) | O(n) | O(n) |
| remove(givenPosition) | O(n) | O(n) |
| display() | O(n) | O(n) |
| clear(), getLength(), isEmpty(), isFull() | O(1) | O(1) |

# An Implementation That Uses the ADT List

**16.19**    As we noted in Segment 16.17, the linked implementation of the ADT sorted list repeats much of the corresponding implementation of the ADT list. Can we avoid this duplication of effort and reuse portions of the list's implementation? The answer to this question is yes, as you will soon see.

You can certainly use the ADT list to create and maintain an alphabetical list of strings. It is natural, then, to consider using the ADT list when implementing the ADT sorted list. Basically, you can do this in one of two ways. Here we will use a list as a data field within the class that implements the sorted list. Figure 16-6 shows an instance of such a sorted list. Recall from Segment D.1 of Appendix D that this approach is called composition and illustrates the *has-a* relationship between two classes. Chapter 17 considers the second approach, using inheritance to derive the sorted list from the list.

FIGURE 16-6    An instance of a sorted list that contains a list of its entries

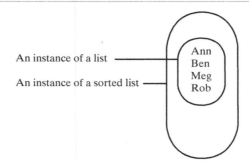

An instance of a list ——————

An instance of a sorted list ——————

Ann
Ben
Meg
Rob

**16.20**  Our class SortedList will implement the interface SortedListInterface. We begin this class by declaring a list as a data field and defining a default constructor. We assume that the class LList, as discussed in Chapter 14, is an implementation of the interface ListInterface for the ADT list. Thus, our class begins as follows:

```
public class SortedList<T extends Comparable<? super T>>
               implements SortedListInterface<T>
{
    private ListInterface<T> list;
    public SortedList()
    {
       list = new LList<>();
    } // end default constructor
       . . .
} // end SortedList
```

Note our use of the generic type T when we declare the data field list.

**16.21**  **The method add.** The implementations of the operations of the ADT sorted list are brief, as the list does most of the work. To add a new entry to the sorted list, we first use the method getPosition, which is an operation of the sorted list. We assume that it is already implemented, even though we have not written it yet. Recall that getPosition finds the position of an existing entry within a sorted list, or the position at which we should insert a new entry that does not occur in the sorted list. The method sets the sign of the integer it returns to indicate whether the entry exists in the list already. When adding an entry to a sorted list that can contain duplicate entries, it does not matter whether the entry exists in the sorted list already. Thus, we can ignore the sign of the integer that getPosition returns. Notice that the following implementation uses the method abs of the class Math to discard this sign. It also uses the add operation of the ADT list. (In this section, calls to ADT list operations are highlighted.)

```
public void add(T newEntry)
{
    int newPosition = Math.abs(getPosition(newEntry));
    list.add(newPosition, newEntry);
} // end add
```

**Question 9** Repeat Question 5, using the method add that was just given.

**Question 10** Can a client of SortedList invoke the operation add(position, entry) of the ADT list? Explain.

**16.22** **The method remove.** We also use getPosition when removing an object from a sorted list. This time, however, we do need to know whether the given entry exists in the sorted list. If it does not exist, we cannot remove it. In such cases, remove returns false. Also notice that the method uses the operation remove of the ADT list to make the deletion. Thus, the method has the following implementation:

```
public boolean remove(T anEntry)
{
    boolean result = false;
    int position = getPosition(anEntry);
    if (position > 0)
    {
        list.remove(position);
        result = true;
    } // end if
    return result;
} // end remove
```

**Question 11** If a sorted list contains five duplicate objects, and you use the previous method remove to remove one of them, what will be removed from the list: the first occurrence of the object, the last occurrence of the object, or all occurrences of the object?

**Question 12** The previous method remove for the sorted list calls the list's method remove to remove an entry at a given position. The list's method can throw an exception, but we do not catch it. Why is catching an exception unnecessary here?

**16.23** **The logic for getPosition.** Implementing getPosition is somewhat harder than implementing the previous two methods. To decide where in the list anEntry is or belongs, we need to compare anEntry to the entries already in the list, beginning with the first one. If anEntry is in the list, we obviously compare entries until we find a match. However, if anEntry is not in the list, we want to stop the search at the point where it belongs in the sorted list. We take advantage of the sorted order of the objects by using logic similar to that described in Segment 16.8.

For example, suppose that the sorted list contains the four names *Brenda*, *Carlos*, *Sarah*, and *Tom*. If we want to see where *Jamie* belongs in the sorted list, we discover that, as strings,

    Jamie > Brenda
    Jamie > Carlos
    Jamie < Sarah

Thus, *Jamie* belongs after *Carlos* but before *Sarah*—that is, at position 3 in the sorted list, as Figure 16-7 illustrates.

To compare anEntry to an entry in the sorted list, we first use the list operation getEntry to return the entry at a given position within the sorted list. Then the expression

    anEntry.compareTo(list.getEntry(position))

makes the comparison.

**FIGURE 16-7**     A sorted list in which *Jamie* belongs after *Carlos* but before *Sarah*

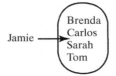

**16.24** **The implementation of getPosition.** In the following implementation of getPosition, the while loop finds anEntry's position in the sorted list, and the if statement sees whether anEntry is in the list.

```java
public int getPosition(T anEntry)
{
    int position = 1;
    int length = list.getLength();
    // Find position of anEntry
    while ( (position <= length) &&
            (anEntry.compareTo(list.getEntry(position)) > 0) )
    {
        position++;
    } // end while
    // See whether anEntry is in list
    if ( (position > length) ||
         (anEntry.compareTo(list.getEntry(position)) != 0) )
    {
        position = -position; // anEntry is not in list
    } // end if

    return position;
} // end getPosition
```

**Question 13** Assume that the sorted list nameList contains the four names *Brenda*, *Carlos*, *Sarah*, and *Tom* as strings. By tracing the code for getPosition, see what getPosition returns when anEntry represents

**a.** *Carlos*   **b.** *Alan*   **c.** *Wendy*   **d.** *Tom*   **e.** *Jamie*

**Question 14** Since you can decide whether a given entry is in a particular sorted list by testing the sign of the integer that getPosition returns, you can use getPosition to implement the method contains. Write such an implementation.

**16.25** Each of the remaining methods—contains, remove, getEntry, clear, getLength, isEmpty, and toArray—has the same specifications as in the ADT list. Each can simply invoke the corresponding list method. For example, the method getEntry has the following implementation in SortedList:

```java
public T getEntry(int givenPosition)
{
    return list.getEntry(givenPosition);
} // end getEntry
```

**Question 15** You can implement the method contains by invoking either getPosition, as Question 14 suggests, or the ADT list's contains method. Which of these implementations will execute faster when the entry sought is not present in the sorted list? Why?

## Efficiency Issues

Except perhaps for some subtle logic in getPosition, you can write the previous implementation quickly and with few, if any, errors. Saving human time is an attractive feature of using an existing class to build another. But does the implementation use computer time efficiently? In this particular implementation, several methods invoke getPosition, so their efficiency depends on getPosition's efficiency.

**16.26   The efficiency of `getPosition`.** As we examine `getPosition`, as given in Segment 16.24, we note that the list method `getLength` is an O(1) operation. Therefore, we need not be concerned with it. On the other hand, a loop examines the entries in the list one at a time by invoking `getEntry` until the desired entry is located. Thus, the efficiency of `getPosition` depends in part on the efficiency of `getEntry`. However, the efficiency of `getEntry` depends upon which implementation of the ADT list you use. We will examine two list implementations that lead to rather different efficiencies for `getPosition`.

Chapter 14 discussed the efficiencies of the ADT list operations. Figure 16-8 recalls the worstcase performance of the list operations that we need to complete our analysis of the sorted list. If you use an array to represent the entries in a list, `getEntry` is always an O(1) operation. The loop in `getPosition` is therefore O($n$) in the worst case, and so `getPosition` is O($n$) when the list has an array-based implementation.

If you use a chain of linked nodes to contain the entries in a list, the method `getEntry` is O($n$). Since `getPosition`'s loop invokes `getEntry`, we see that `getPosition` is O($n^2$) in the worst case. Each time `getEntry` retrieves the next entry in the list, it starts its search at the beginning of the chain. This fact is the cause of `getPosition`'s inefficiency.

**FIGURE 16-8**   The worst-case efficiencies of selected ADT list operations
for array-based and linked implementations

| ADT List Operation | Array | Linked |
|---|---|---|
| `getEntry(givenPosition)` | O(1) | O($n$) |
| `add(newPosition, newEntry)` | O($n$) | O($n$) |
| `remove(givenPosition)` | O($n$) | O($n$) |
| `contains(anEntry)` | O($n$) | O($n$) |
| `display()` | O($n$) | O($n$) |
| `clear(), getLength(), isEmpty(), isFull()` | O(1) | O(1) |

**16.27   The efficiency of `add`.** The implementation of the sorted list method `add` given in Segment 16.21 contains the following statements:

```
int newPosition = Math.abs(getPosition(newEntry));
list.add(newPosition, newEntry);
```

For an array-based implementation of the ADT list, both `getPosition` and the list operation `add` are O($n$) operations. Thus, the sorted list operation `add` is O($n$) in the worst case. For a linked implementation of the list, `getPosition`'s worst-case behavior is O($n^2$) and dominates the list operation `add`, which is only O($n$). Thus, the sorted list operation `add` is O($n^2$) in the worst case.

**16.28**   Figure 16-9 summarizes the efficiencies of the sorted list operations for array-based and linked implementations of the ADT list. Confirmation of these results is left as an exercise. As you can see, the implementation of the sorted list given in this section is easy to write but is not very efficient if the underlying list uses a chain of linked nodes. Chapter 17 will show you how you can reuse the ADT list in the implementation of the sorted list without sacrificing efficiency.

**Question 16** Give an advantage and a disadvantage of using composition in the implementation of the class `SortedList`.

FIGURE 16-9    The worst-case efficiencies of the ADT sorted list operations when implemented using an instance of the ADT list

| ADT Sorted List Operation | List Implementation | |
| --- | --- | --- |
| | Array | Linked |
| add(newEntry) | $O(n)$ | $O(n^2)$ |
| remove(anEntry) | $O(n)$ | $O(n^2)$ |
| getPosition(anEntry) | $O(n)$ | $O(n^2)$ |
| getEntry(givenPosition) | $O(1)$ | $O(n)$ |
| contains(anEntry) | $O(n)$ | $O(n)$ |
| remove(givenPosition) | $O(n)$ | $O(n)$ |
| display() | $O(n)$ | $O(n)$ |
| clear(), getLength(), isEmpty(), isFull() | $O(1)$ | $O(1)$ |

**Note:  Using composition to implement the ADT sorted list**
When you use an instance of an ADT list to represent the entries in the ADT sorted list, you must use the list's operations to access the sorted list's entries, instead of accessing them directly. Such an implementation of the sorted list is easy to write but is inefficient when the underlying list uses a chain of linked nodes to store its entries.

## CHAPTER SUMMARY

- The ADT sorted list maintains its entries in sorted order. It, not the client, determines where to place an entry.

- The ADT sorted list can add, remove, or locate an entry, given the entry as an argument.

- The sorted list has several operations that are the same as the corresponding operations of the ADT list. However, a sorted list will not let you add or replace an entry by position.

- A chain of linked nodes provides a reasonably efficient implementation of the sorted list.

- An implementation of the sorted list that uses an ADT list as a data field is easy to write. However, depending upon how the ADT list is implemented, its efficiency can suffer.

## EXERCISES

1. Suppose that nameList is a sorted list of names. Using the operations of the ADT list and the ADT sorted list, create a list of these names in the reverse order.

2. As specified in this chapter, the sorted list can contain duplicate entries. Specify a sorted list of unique items.

3. The *mode* of a list of values is the value having the greatest frequency.
   a. Write an algorithm to find the mode of a sorted list using only methods of the ADT sorted list.
   b. What is the Big Oh of the algorithm if the sorted list has an array-based implementation?
   c. What is the Big Oh of the algorithm if the sorted list has a linked implementation?

4. The schedule of activities for a room consists of an *activity list*. Each activity has a description, a start time, and an end time. You can add activities to the list, but they must be compatible with the other activities. Two activities are incompatible if their time intervals overlap. Specify the ADT activity list.

5. Imagine you are working for a geologist who has records for earthquakes that occurred during the past 50 years. Each record includes a date, location, strength, and duration. Design and specify an ADT for this collection of data.

6. Explain how you can use the ADT sorted list in the implementations of the ADTs described in Exercises 4 and 5.

7. Consider an array-based implementation of the sorted list. To implement the method `delete`, you must delete an entry from a sorted array so that the array remains sorted.

    a. Describe the steps in this implementation.
    b. On which sort have you based your logic?
    c. Analyze the worst-case efficiency of this implementation of `delete`.

8. Figure 16-5 tabulates the worst-case efficiencies of the sorted list operations for both array-based and linked implementations. Derive these Big Oh expressions.

9. Figure 16-9 tabulates the worst-case efficiencies of the sorted list operations when implemented using an instance of the ADT list. Derive these Big Oh expressions.

10. Consider an array-based implementation of the sorted list. Let the array `list` be the data field that represents the list's entries. If a constructor is given an array of unsorted list entries, the constructor must place them into `list` in sorted order. To do so, it could repeatedly use the sorted list's `add` method to add the entries to the sorted list (and hence to the array `list`) in their proper order. Or it could copy the entries to `list` and sort them by using a sort algorithm from Chapters 8 and 9.

    a. For the first approach, what will be the best-case and the worst-case efficiencies?
    b. For the second approach, which sort algorithm will be the best suited?

11. Consider the implementation of the sorted list that uses an instance of the ADT list. In particular, consider the method `contains`. One implementation of `contains` could invoke `getPosition` (see Question 14 at the end of Segment 16.24). Another implementation could simply invoke `list.contains`. Compare the efficiencies of these two implementations.

12. Write a linked implementation of the sorted list method `contains`. Your search of the chain should end when it either locates the desired entry or passes the point at which the entry should have occurred.

13. Compare the efficiency of the method `contains` that Exercise 12 describes with that of the list's version of `contains`.

14. Segment 9.2 of Chapter 9 described how to merge two sorted arrays into one sorted array. Add an operation to the ADT sorted list that merges two sorted lists. Implement the merge in three ways, as follows:

    a. Use only sorted list operations.
    b. Assume an array-based implementation.
    c. Assume a linked implementation.

## PROJECTS

1. Complete the linked implementation of the ADT sorted list that was begun in this chapter. Use iteration instead of recursion.

2. Repeat Project 1, but use recursion wherever possible.

3. Implement the ADT sorted list by using an array to represent the ADT's entries. Use array resizing so that the sorted list can grow as large as necessary.

4. Implement the ADT sorted list by using an instance of `Vector` to represent the ADT's entries. Project 7 of Chapter 13 asked you to create a similar implementation for the ADT list.

5. Exercise 2 asked you to specify an ADT sorted list of unique items. Implement such an ADT.

**6.** Add an iterator to the ADT sorted list by defining an inner class within the class that implements the ADT.

**7.** A *polynomial* in $x$ is an algebraic expression that involves integer powers of $x$, as follows:

$$P(x) = a_n x^n + a_{n-1} x^{n-1} + \ldots + a_1 x + a_0$$

The $a$'s are called *coefficients*. The *degree* of the polynomial is $n$, the highest exponent of $x$ that appears in $P(x)$. Although $a_n$ cannot be zero in a degree $n$ polynomial, any other coefficient can be zero.

Specify an ADT polynomial that includes operations such as `getDegree`, `getCoefficient`, `setCoefficient`, `add`, and `subtract`. Implement this ADT by using a sorted list. The sorted list should not contain any coefficients that are zero.

**8.** Exercise 3 asked you to create an algorithm to find the mode of a sorted list. Let's add a method to the implementation of a sorted list that finds the list's mode. The header of such a method could be

```
public T getMode()
```

Implement this method in three ways, as follows:

    **a.** Use only sorted list operations.
    **b.** Assume an array-based implementation.
    **c.** Assume a linked implementation.

**9.** You can use a *substitution code* to encode a message. In this scheme, a *key* maps each letter to another letter. Each letter in the *plain-text* message is replaced according to the key to produce the encoded message, or *cipher text*.

Suppose you are given some cipher text, but not the key. One method of breaking such a code is to count the frequency of letters in the cipher text and then make guesses about the mapping based on the frequencies of letters in typical English text. Write a program that reads characters from a file and uses a sorted list to find the frequency of each letter.

**10.** Implement the ADT priority queue by using a sorted list to contain the priority queue's entries.

**11.** Segment 1.21 of Chapter 1 defines a set as a bag that does not allow duplicate entries. Implement the ADT set by using a sorted list to contain its entries. Include the operations union, intersection, and difference, as described respectively in Exercises 5, 6, and 7 of Chapter 1.

**12.** In certain computer networks, a message is not sent as a continuous stream of data. Instead, it is divided into pieces, called *packets*, and sent a packet at a time. The packets might not arrive at their destination in the same order as the one in which they were sent. To enable the receiver to assemble the packets in their correct order, each packet contains a sequence number.

For example, to send the message "Meet me at 6 o'clock" three characters at a time, the packets would appear as follows:

```
1 Mee
2 t m
3 e a
4 t 6
5 o'
6 clo
7 ck
```

Regardless of when the packets arrive, the receiver can order the packets by their sequence numbers to determine the message.

Given a text file containing the packets of data in the order they were received, write an application that reads the file and extracts the message by using a sorted list. Design and create auxiliary classes such as `Packet` and `Message`.

## ANSWERS TO SELF-TEST QUESTIONS

**1.**
```
SortedListInterface<String> sortedWordList = new SortedList<>();
int numberOfWords = wordList.getLength();
for (int position = 1; position <= numberOfWords; position++)
   sortedWordList.add(wordList.getEntry(position));
```

**2.**
**a.**
```
int length = sortedWordList.getLength();
String lastEntry = sortedWordList.getEntry(length);
System.out.println(lastEntry);
```

**b.** `sortedList.add(sortedList.getEntry(1));`

**3.** The order is critical. When `currentNode` is `null`, `currentNode != null` is false. Thus, the entire expression in the `while` statement is false without executing the call `currentNode.getData()`. If the latter call were to execute first when `currentNode` was `null`, an exception would occur. Thus, the `while` statement should remain as written.

**4.** When the sorted list is empty, `getNodeBefore` returns `null`. Thus, in the definition of `add`, you can omit the call to `isEmpty` in the `if` statement.

**5.** Before the first occurrence of the entry.

**6.** After the last occurrence of the entry.

**7.** Before the first occurrence of the entry.

**8.** The method `add(newEntry)` for a list adds a new entry at the end of the list. A tail reference makes this method O(1) instead of O(n). For a sorted list, `add(newEntry)` must traverse the chain to locate the point of insertion. If the insertion is at the end of the chain, the traversal will give you a reference to the last node. A separate tail reference is not needed.

**9.** Before the first occurrence of the entry. Note that `getPosition` returns the position of the first occurrence of the entry within the list.

**10.** No. The field `list` is private, so its methods are unavailable to a client of `SortedList`.

**11.** The first occurrence of the object. Note that `getPosition` returns the position of the first occurrence of the entry within the list.

**12.** The list's `remove` method will never throw an `IndexOutOfBoundsException`, because we verify that the list contains the given entry by calling `getPosition` and checking its return value. As a runtime exception that will not occur, we need not catch it.

**13.** **a.** 2; **b.** –1; **c.** –5; **d.** 4; **e.** –3.

**14.**
```
public boolean contains(T anEntry)
{
    return getPosition(anEntry) > 0;
} // end contains
```

**15.** The implementation that invokes `getPosition` will execute faster. Because the list is sorted, the method `getPosition` does not always search the entire list when the entry is not present. However, the list's method `contains` always searches the entire list in this case.

**16.** Advantage: The implementation is easy to write.
Disadvantage: The implementation is not efficient when the implementation of the underlying list is linked.

# Inheritance and Polymorphism

## Contents

## Prerequisites

This interlude expands our discussion of inheritance that we began in Appendix D and develops the concept of polymorphism. We will use these aspects of Java in the next chapter when we examine other ways to implement the ADT list.

## Further Aspects of Inheritance

So far, this book has used inheritance in a basic, somewhat intuitive, way. For example, we wrote our own exception classes in Java Interlude 4 that extend one of the standard exception classes available to us in the Java Class Library. Although Appendix D presents the mechanics of inheritance in detail, it does not consider fully the implications of and appropriateness of inheritance. We consider these points next.

### When to Use Inheritance

**JI7.1**     **Example: Should `VectorStack` extend `Vector`?** When Chapter 6 implemented the ADT stack by storing the stack's entries in an instance of the standard class `Vector`, it used composition to define the class `VectorStack`. This class, as given in Listing 6-3, begins as follows:

```java
public class VectorStack<T> implements StackInterface<T>
{
    private Vector<T> stack;
    . . .
```

Thus, an instance of `VectorStack` contains an instance of `Vector`.

Suppose that we instead used inheritance to derive `VectorStack` from `Vector` as follows:

```java
public class VectorStack<T> extends Vector<T> implements StackInterface<T>
{ . . .
```

The resulting class would have all the methods of `Vector` in addition to those in `StackInterface`. However, these `Vector` methods enable a client to add or remove entries anywhere within the stack, thus violating the premise of the ADT stack. Instead of a stack, we would have an enhanced vector. But a stack is not a vector. Since we do not have an *is-a* relationship between stacks and vectors, we should not use inheritance to define `VectorStack`.

The class `java.util.Stack` in the Java Class Library that we introduced in Segment 5.23 of Chapter 5 does extend `Vector`. Thus, an instance of this class is not really a stack.

**Security Note:** **Limit your use of inheritance**
Either design a class specifically for its future use as a base class (superclass) or prevent such use by declaring it as a final class. A final class is easier to define and to verify that it is secure. A class that is not final can have its nonfinal methods maliciously overridden by an attacker.
Prefer composition to inheritance.

**Security Note:** **Realize that a superclass can affect the behavior of a subclass**
A subclass cannot maintain absolute control over its own behavior. After a subclass is written, its superclass can be revised, thereby affecting the behavior of the subclass. For example, an attacker could change the definition of a superclass's method that is inherited but not overridden by the subclass. Even if a subclass overrides all of the inherited methods—thereby defeating the purpose of inheritance—revisions to its superclass can still affect the subclass's behavior. Possible modifications include adding new public methods or altering the private methods called by existing public methods. Such changes to a superclass can intentionally or unintentionally break the assumptions made in a subclass and lead to subtle security vulnerabilities.

## Protected Access

VideoNote
Inheritance

**JI7.2**   You know that you control access to a class's data fields and methods by using an access modifier like `public` or `private`. As Appendix C shows, you can omit the access modifier entirely when the class is within a package and you want the class to be available only to other classes in the package. You also have one other choice for controlling access: You can use the access modifier `protected` for methods and data fields.

A method or data field that is modified by `protected` can be accessed by name only within

- Its own class definition `C`
- Any class derived from `C`
- Any class within the same package as `C`

That is, if a method is marked `protected` in class `C`, you can invoke it from within any method definition in a class derived from class `C`. However, with classes that are not derived from `C` or that are not in the same package as `C`, a protected method behaves as if it were private.

You should continue to declare all data fields as private. If you want a subclass to have access to a data field in the superclass, define protected accessor or mutator methods within the superclass.

Note that package access is more restricted than protected access and gives more control to the programmer defining the classes. If you control the package directory, you control who is allowed package access.

Figure JI7-1 illustrates the various kinds of access modifiers.

**FIGURE JI7-1**   Public, private, protected, and package access of the data fields and methods of class C

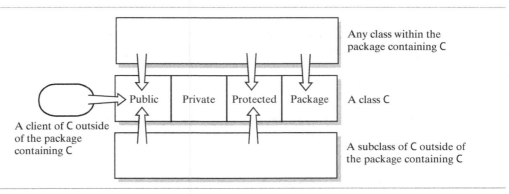

## Abstract Classes and Methods

**JI7.3**   The class Student defined in Listing D-1 of Appendix D is a superclass for other classes such as CollegeStudent, as given in Listing D-3. We really do not need to create objects of type Student, although it is certainly legal to do so. We might, however, want to prevent a client from creating objects of type Student. To do so, we can declare the class to be an **abstract class** by including the reserved word abstract in the header of the class definition, as follows:

```
public abstract class Student
{
    . . .
```

 **Note:**  An abstract class will be the superclass of another class. Thus, an abstract class is sometimes called an **abstract superclass**.

Often when programmers define an abstract class, they declare one or more methods that have no body. The intention in doing so is to require that every subclass implement such methods in an appropriate way for the subclass. For example, we might want every subclass of Student to implement a method display. We certainly cannot write such a method for a future class that is not yet defined, but we can require one. To do so, we declare display as an **abstract method** by including the reserved word abstract in the header of the method, as follows:

```
public abstract void display();
```

Note that the method header is followed by a semicolon; the method has no body.

 **Note:**  An abstract method declaration within an abstract class consists of the method's header followed by a semicolon. The header must include the reserved word abstract. An abstract method cannot be private, static, or final.

**JI7.4** If a class has at least one abstract method, Java requires that you declare the class itself as abstract. This makes sense, for otherwise you could create an object of an incomplete class. In our example, the object would have a method `display` without an implementation.

What if the subclass of an abstract class does not implement all of the abstract methods? Java will treat the subclass as abstract and prevent you from creating an object of its type. For example, if the class `CollegeStudent`, which is derived from `Student`, did not implement `display`, `CollegeStudent` would have to be abstract.

 **Note:** A class with at least one abstract method must be declared as an abstract class. Thus, abstract methods can appear only within an abstract class.

Even after we've made the class `Student` abstract by adding the abstract method `display`, not all of its methods are abstract. All the method definitions, except for the method `display`, are exactly the same as in our original definition. They are full definitions that do not use the reserved word `abstract`. When it makes sense to implement a method in an abstract class, you should do so. In this way, you include as much detail as possible in the abstract class, detail that need not be repeated in subclasses.

 **Note: Constructors cannot be abstract**
Since a class cannot override a constructor in its superclass, if the constructor were abstract, it could not be implemented. Thus, constructors are never abstract.

**JI7.5**  **Example.** Let's add another method to the class `Student`, one that invokes the abstract method `display`. Before you complain about invoking a method that has no body, remember that `Student` is an abstract class. When we finally derive a class from `Student` that is not abstract, `display` will be implemented.

The method we have in mind serves mainly as an example, rather than doing anything useful. It simply skips the specified number of lines before displaying an object:

```java
/** Displays the object after skipping numberOfLines lines. */
public void displayAt(int numberOfLines)
{
   for (int count = 0; count < numberOfLines; count++)
      System.out.println();
   display();
} // end displayAt
```

The method `displayAt` invokes the abstract method `display`. Here the abstract method serves as a placeholder for a method that will be defined in a future subclass. If `display` were not abstract, we would have to give it a body that really would be useless, since every subclass would override it.

 **Question 1** Suppose that you change the name of the previous method `displayAt` to `display`. Does the resulting method overload or override the method `display`? Why?

## Interfaces Versus Abstract Classes

**JI7.6**   **Example: Abstract classes versus interfaces.** Segment P.45 of the Prelude defined the following interface:

```java
public interface Circular
{
    public void setRadius(double newRadius);
    public double getRadius();
} // end Circular
```

Despite being unable to provide a field for the radius, this interface declares both set and get methods in anticipation that the class implementing the interface will do so. In fact, the class `Circle` in Segment P.45 implements this interface, declares a field for the radius, and defines the methods `setRadius` and `getRadius`. It also defines a third method, `getArea`.

Instead of defining the interface `Circular`, let's define an abstract class:

```java
public abstract class CircularBase
{
    private double radius;
    public void setRadius(double newRadius)
    {
        radius = newRadius;
    } // end setRadius
    public double getRadius()
    {
        return radius;
    } // end getRadius
    public abstract double getArea();
} // end CircularBase
```

This class declares the data field `radius` that descendant classes will inherit. Since the data field `radius` is private, the class `CircularBase` must implement set and get methods so that its descendant classes can access it. If `CircularBase` simply declared `setRadius` and `getRadius` as abstract—omitting their implementations—a descendant class would be unable to define them because it would be unable to access `radius`. If the definition of `CircularBase` stopped here, it would not need to be abstract, but it still would be a useful base class. However, this class also declares the abstract method `getArea`, which its descendant classes must implement in their own way.

The following class is derived from the class `CircularBase`. It implements the abstract method `getArea`, invoking the inherited method `getRadius` to access the inherited data field `radius`. `Circle` cannot reference the data field `radius` by name.

```java
public class Circle extends CircularBase
{
    public double getArea()
    {
        double radius = getRadius();
        return Math.PI * radius * radius;
    } // end getArea
} // end Circle
```

In this method, `radius` is simply a local variable.

 **Programming Tip:** If you want to define a method or declare a private data field that your classes will have in common, use an abstract class. Otherwise, use an interface.

# Polymorphism

**JI7.7** The term "polymorphism" comes from a Greek word meaning "many forms." Polymorphism as a concept is actually common in English. For example, the English instruction "Play your favorite sport" means different things to different people. To one person it means to play baseball. To another person it means to play soccer. In Java, **polymorphism** allows the same program instruction to mean different things in different contexts. In particular, one method name, used as an instruction, can cause different actions depending on the kind of object performing the action.

Originally, overloading a method name was considered polymorphism. However, the modern usage of the term refers to an object determining at execution time which action of a method it will use for a method name that is overridden either directly or indirectly.

> **Note: Polymorphism**
> One method name in an instruction can cause different actions according to the kinds of objects that receive the method invocation.

**JI7.8** **Example.** For example, a method named `display` can display the data in an object. But the data it displays and how much it displays depend on the kind of object that you use to invoke the method. Let's add the method `display` to the class `Student` in Listing D-1 of Appendix D and assume that neither the method nor the class is abstract. Thus, `display` has an implementation within the class `Student`. Now add to the class the method `displayAt` as it appears in Segment JI7.5.

If the only class around were `Student`, these changes would not be exciting. But we derived the class `UndergradStudent` from the class `CollegeStudent`, which we derived from the class `Student`. The class `UndergradStudent` inherits the method `displayAt` from the class `Student`. In addition, `UndergradStudent` overrides the method `display` defined in `Student` by providing its own implementation. So what? you might be wondering.

Well, look at the poor compiler's job when it encounters the following Java statements (we are ignoring the constructor's arguments):

```java
UndergradStudent ug = new UndergradStudent(. . .);
ug.displayAt(2);
```

The method `displayAt` was defined in the class `Student`, but it calls the method `display` that is defined in the class `UndergradStudent`, as Figure JI7-2 illustrates. The code for `displayAt` could have been compiled with the class `Student` *before* the class `UndergradStudent` was even written. In other words, this compiled code could use a definition of the method `display` that was not even written at the time that `displayAt` was compiled. How can that be?

When the code for `displayAt` is compiled, the call to `display` produces an annotation that says, "use the appropriate definition of `display`." Then, when we invoke `ug.displayAt(2)`, the compiled code for `displayAt` reaches this annotation and replaces it with an invocation of the version of `display` that goes with `ug`. Because in this case `ug` is of type `UndergradStudent`, the version of `display` that is used will be the definition in the class `UndergradStudent`.

**FIGURE JI7-2** The method displayAt calls the correct version of display

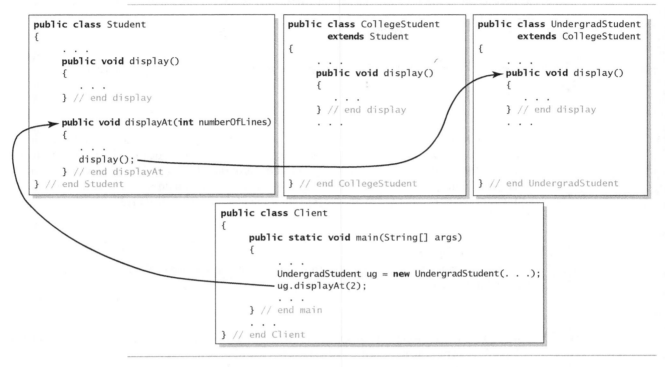

**JI7.9** The decision as to which method definition to use depends on the receiving object's place in the inheritance chain, not on the type of the variable naming the object. For example, consider the following code:

```
UndergradStudent ug = new UndergradStudent(. . .);
Student s = ug;
s.displayAt(2);
```

As we noted in Segment D.21 of Appendix D, assigning an object of the class Undergrad-student to a variable of type Student is perfectly legal. Here, the variable s is just another name for the object that ug references. That is, s and ug are aliases. But the object still remembers that it was created as an UndergradStudent. In this case, s.displayAt(2) ultimately will use the definition of display given in UndergradStudent, not the definition of display given in Student.

A variable's **static type** is the type that appears in its declaration. For example, the static type of the variable s is Student. The static type is fixed and determined when the code is compiled. The type of object that a variable references at a point in time during execution is called its **dynamic type**. A variable's dynamic type can change as execution progresses. When the assignment s = ug executes in the previous code, the dynamic type of s is UndergradStudent. A variable of a reference type is called a **polymorphic variable**, since its dynamic type can differ from its static type and change during execution.

For our example, Java decides which definition of display to use by seeing which constructor created the object. That is, Java uses the dynamic type of the variable s to make this determination.

 **Note:** Java uses an object's dynamic type, not its name, to see which method to invoke.

This way of handling a call to a method that might be overridden later is called **dynamic binding** or **late binding**, because the *meaning* of the method invocation is not bound to the *location* of the method invocation until you run the program. If Java did not use dynamic binding when you ran the preceding code, you would not see the data for an undergraduate student. Instead you would see only what the method display of the class Student provided.

 **Note: Dynamic binding**
Dynamic binding is the process that enables different objects to use different method actions for the same method name.

**JI7.10**  Java is so good at figuring out which definition of a method to use that even a type cast will not fool it. Recall that you use a type cast to change the type of a value to some other type. The meaning of s.displayAt(2) in the previous segment will always be appropriate for an UndergradStudent, even if we use a type cast to change the type of ug to the type Student, as in the following statements:

```
UndergradStudent ug = new UndergradStudent(. . .);
Student s = (Student)ug;
s.displayAt(2);
```

Despite the type cast, s.displayAt(2) will use the definition of display given in UndergradStudent, not the definition of display given in Student. An object's dynamic type, not its name, is the determining factor in choosing the correct method to invoke.

To see that dynamic binding really is a big deal, consider the following code:

```
UndergradStudent ug = new UndergradStudent(. . .);
Student s = ug;
s.displayAt(2);
GradStudent g = new GradStudent(. . .);
s = g;
s.displayAt(2);
```

The two highlighted lines are identical, yet each one invokes a different version of display. The first line displays an UndergradStudent and the second displays a GradStudent, as Figure JI7-3 illustrates. An object remembers what method definitions it had when the new operator created it. You can place the object in a variable of a different (but ancestor) class type, but that has no effect on which method definition the object uses for an overridden method.

Let's pursue this process a bit more to see that it is even more dramatic than it may appear at first glance. Note that objects of the classes UndergradStudent and GradStudent inherit the method displayAt from the class Student and do not override it. Thus, the text of the method definition is even the same for objects of the classes UndergradStudent and GradStudent. It is the method display, invoked in the definition of displayAt, that is overridden.

---

FIGURE JI7-3      An object, not its name, determines its behavior

---

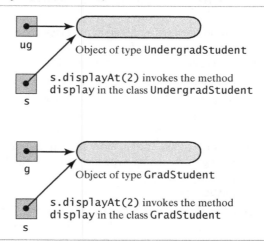

ug      Object of type UndergradStudent

s.displayAt(2) invokes the method
display in the class UndergradStudent

s

g       Object of type GradStudent

s.displayAt(2) invokes the method
display in the class GradStudent

s

---

**Note:  Objects know how they are supposed to act**
When an object receives a call to either an overridden method or a method that calls an overridden method, the action of that method is the one defined in the class whose constructor created the object. The choice of action is not affected by the static type of the variable naming the object. A variable of any ancestor class can reference an object of a descendant class, but the object always remembers which method actions to use for every method name, because Java uses dynamic binding.

---

**JI7.11   Type checking and dynamic binding.** You need to be aware of how dynamic binding interacts with Java's type checking. For example, if UndergradStudent is a subclass of the class Student, we can assign an object of type UndergradStudent to a variable of type Student, as in

```
Student s = new UndergradStudent();
```

But that is not the end of the story.

Although we can assign an object of type UndergradStudent to a variable s of type Student, we cannot use s to invoke a method that is only in the class UndergradStudent. However, if the method is overridden in the definition of the class UndergradStudent, the version of the method defined in UndergradStudent will be used. In other words, the variable determines what method names can be used, but the object determines which definition of the method name will be used. If we want to use a method name that was first introduced in the class UndergradStudent with the object named by the variable s of type Student, we must use a type cast.

**JI7.12  Example.** For example, recall that Student is not abstract and implements the method display. Also remember that UndergradStudent is a subclass of Student. The following statements are legal:

```
Student s = new UndergradStudent(. . .);
s.setName(new Name("Jamie", "Jones"));
s.display();
```

The definition of display given in the class UndergradStudent is used. *Remember, the object, not the variable, determines which definition of a method will be used.*

On the other hand, the following is illegal:

```
s.setDegree("B.A."); // ILLEGAL
```

because setDegree is not the name of a method in the class Student. *Remember, the variable determines which method names can be used.*

The variable s is of type Student, but it references an object of type UndergradStudent. That object can still invoke the method setDegree, but the compiler does not know this. To make the invocation legal, we need a type cast, such as the following:

```
UndergradStudent ug = (UndergradStudent)s;
ug.setDegree("B.A."); // LEGAL
```

You may think this is all just a silly exercise, because you would never assign an object of type UndergradStudent to a variable of type Student. Not so. You might not often make such an assignment directly, but you frequently will do so unwittingly. Recall that we can have an argument of type UndergradStudent for a method parameter of type Student and that a parameter behaves like a local variable that is assigned the value of its corresponding argument. In this case an object of type UndergradStudent (the argument in the method invocation) is assigned to a variable of type Student (the parameter in the method definition).

**JI7.13  Example.** Since each of the classes Student and Name has an appropriate version of the method toString, we can display an object of this class as follows:

```
Name joe = new Name("Joe", "Student");
Student s = new Student(joe, "5555");
System.out.println(s.toString());
```

But thanks to dynamic binding, we do not even need to write toString in our invocation of System.out.println. The method invocation System.out.println(s) will work just as well and will produce exactly the same output. Let's see why.

The object System.out has the method println. One definition of the method println has a single parameter of type Object. The definition is equivalent to the following:

```
public void println(Object theObject)
{
   System.out.println(theObject.toString());
} // end println
```

The method `println` invoked inside the braces is a different, overloaded definition of the method `println` that has a parameter of type `String`, not `Object`.

These definitions of `println` existed before the class `Student` was defined. Yet the invocation

```
System.out.println(s);
```

with an object `s` of type `Student`—and hence also of type `Object`—uses `Student`'s `toString`, not `Object`'s `toString`. Dynamic binding is what makes this work.

**JI7.14**  **Example: Interfaces.** You have seen that if class `B` is a subclass of class `A`, you can write

```
A item = new B();
```

The variable `item` is polymorphic, since its dynamic type can differ from its static type. Polymorphism also occurs when we use interfaces. For example, Segment P.48 of the Prelude talks about the classes `Name` and `AnotherName`, both of which implement the interface `NameInterface`. If we write

```
NameInterface myName = new Name("Jose", "Mendez");
```

the variable `myName` is polymorphic. Its data type is the interface `NameInterface`; `myName` has all of the methods in `NameInterface`. For instance, `myName.getFirst()` returns the string `"Jose"`. Furthermore, if we now write

```
myName = AnotherName("Maria", "Lopez");
```

`myName.getFirst()` will return the string `"Maria"`. Thus, polymorphic variables can occur as a result of using either inheritance or interfaces.

---

**Question 2** Is a method `display` with no parameters that is defined explicitly in each of the classes `Student`, `CollegeStudent`, and `UndergradStudent` an example of overloading or overriding? Why?

**Question 3** Is overloading a method name an example of polymorphism?

**Question 4** In the following code, will the two invocations of `displayAt` produce the same output?

```
Student s = new UndergradStudent(. . .);
s.displayAt(2);
s = new GradStudent(. . .);
s.displayAt(2);
```

---

**ANSWERS TO SELF-TEST QUESTIONS**

1. Overload. The two methods have the same name but different signatures: One has a parameter, one does not.

2. Overriding. The methods have the same signatures and return types.

3. At one time, overloading was an example of polymorphism. Today, polymorphism describes a situation in which an object determines at execution time which action of a method it will use for a method name that is overridden either directly or indirectly.

4. No. Each call to `displayAt` will invoke the correct version of `display`. The first invocation calls `display` in `UndergradStudent`; the second invocation calls `display` in `GradStudent`.

# Inheritance and Lists

## Contents

## Prerequisites

## Objectives

After studying this chapter, you should be able to

- Design a class that contains protected methods to make it suitable for use as a base class
- Design and use an abstract base class
- Write an efficient implementation of a sorted list by using inheritance

Chapter 16 introduced you to the ADT sorted list, which maintains its entries in a sorted order. As with many other ADTs, you can implement the sorted list by using either an array or a chain of linked nodes. The advantage of such implementations is their time efficiency. However, they require you to repeat a portion of the implementation of the ADT list, since the ADTs sorted list and list have several operations in common.

    In an attempt to avoid this duplication of effort, Chapter 16 used an instance of the ADT list to contain the entries of the sorted list. This list was a data field of the class implementing the sorted list. The result was an implementation that you could write quickly, because the implementation of the list had done most of the work. But since the sorted list operations used the list in the same way that a client would, these operations were inefficient of time when the ADT list had a linked implementation.

But what if, instead of using composition, as we did in Chapter 16, we use inheritance? This chapter looks at the implications of deriving a sorted list from a list. In doing so we'll find that a subclass (derived class) can be more efficient if it can access the underlying data structures of its superclass (base class). This is possible if the superclass includes methods that enable future subclasses to examine or modify its data fields. A class designer should plan for the future use of a class as well as the present need.

## Using Inheritance to Implement a Sorted List

**17.1**

VideoNote
Inheritance and ADT
implementations

Recall the implementation of the class `SortedList` that we developed in Chapter 16 beginning at Segment 16.20. `SortedList` has an instance of another class, `LList` in this case, as a data field. `SortedList` and `LList` have a *has-a* relationship. Several of `SortedList`'s methods—namely `remove` (by position), `getEntry`, `contains`, `clear`, `getLength`, `isEmpty`, and `toArray`—behave like `LList`'s methods. If `SortedList` inherited these methods from `LList`, we would not have to implement them again, as we did in the previous chapter. Thus, we could revise `SortedList` as follows:

```
public class SortedList<T extends Comparable<? super T>>
              extends LList<T> implements SortedListInterface<T>
{
   public void add(T newEntry)
   {
      int newPosition = Math.abs(getPosition(newEntry));
      super.add(newPosition, newEntry);
   } // end add

   < Implementations of remove(anEntry) and getPosition(anEntry) go here. >
   . . .
} // end SortedList
```

The notation `T extends Comparable<? super T>`, introduced in Java Interlude 3, defines the generic type `T`. The class that `T` represents must implement the interface `Comparable`. Writing `? super T`, which means any superclass of `T`, allows some flexibility in the type of objects that a sorted list can contain.

You can see that `SortedList` is derived from `LList`. Also notice that we have omitted the data field `list` and the default constructor that appeared in Segment 16.20. To revise the add method given in Segment 16.21, we simply replaced `list` with `super`. That is, we wrote

```
super.add(newPosition, newEntry);
```

to invoke the add operation of the ADT list, instead of

```
list.add(newPosition, newEntry);
```

Coincidentally, `SortedList`'s add method overrides the other add method in `LList` that adds to the end of a list.

We would make similar changes to the methods `remove` and `getPosition`. The remaining methods of the sorted list are inherited from `LList`, and so they do not appear explicitly in `SortedList`.

**Question 1** Although `SortedList` inherits the method `contains` from `LList`, the method is not as efficient as it could be. Why? Show how you could override `contains` with a more efficient version.

**17.2**   **A pitfall.** This implementation contains a pitfall that is the direct result of using inheritance. Although SortedList conveniently inherits methods such as isEmpty from LList, it also inherits two methods that a client can use to destroy the order of a sorted list. These two methods appear in ListInterface as follows:

```
/** Adds newEntry to the list at position newPosition. */
public void add(int newPosition, T newEntry);

/** Replaces the entry at givenPosition with newEntry. */
public T replace(int givenPosition, T newEntry);
```

If a client writes

```
SortedList<String> sList = new SortedList<>();
```

for example, it can use sList to invoke any method declared in either SortedListInterface or ListInterface, including the previous methods add and replace. Thus, a client could destroy the order of the entries in a sorted list either by adding an entry out of order or by replacing an entry.

**17.3**   **Possible ways to avoid the pitfall.** What can we do to avoid this pitfall? Here are three possibilities:

- Use SortedListInterface in the client's declaration of the sorted list. For example, if the client contains

```
SortedListInterface<String> sList = new SortedList<>();
```

it can use sList to invoke only methods declared within SortedListInterface. Notice that the list operations add and replace do not appear in SortedListInterface. Although using SortedListInterface in this way can be a good programming practice, that is all it is. A client need only ignore this practice and define the data type of sList as SortedList to have all operations of the ADT list available to it. You have already seen how a client can sabotage the sorted list in this case.

- Implement the list's add and replace methods within the class SortedList, and give them empty bodies. However, a client that calls either method would be unaware that the method did not do anything.

- Implement the list's add and replace methods within the class SortedList and have them throw an exception when invoked. For example, add could appear as follows:

```
public void add(int newPosition, T newEntry)
{
    throw new UnsupportedOperationException("Illegal attempt to add " +
                            "at a specified position within a sorted list.");
} // end add
```

This version of add also overrides the version that LList implements. If the client invokes this method, an exception occurs. This approach is a common practice, and it is the one we prefer.

**Note:** If SortedList overrides the list's method add, the class's implementation still can invoke the method, as happens in Segment 17.1. The use of super in the call indicates that we are invoking the list's version of the method, not the overriding version in SortedList.

**Question 2** As a variation of the second possibility just given, you could implement the ADT list's two add methods within SortedList so that each one calls the add method specified in SortedListInterface. In this way, the new entry is added in its correct position within the sorted list. Why is this not a good idea?

**Question 3** The method `toArray` that `SortedList` inherits from its base class `LList` is inappropriate for a sorted list.

    **a.**    Why is the previous statement true?

    **b.**    Write the method `toArray` in `SortedList` so that it overrides `toArray` in `LList`.

**Programming Tip:** If your class inherits methods that are inappropriate, you can override them with methods that throw an exception when invoked. In such a case, examine your design and consider whether inheritance was the right choice. Do the benefits of inheritance outweigh the inconvenience of overriding the inappropriate methods, or would composition provide a cleaner design?

**17.4**    **Efficiency.** The implementation of `SortedList` given here has the same efficiency—or inefficiency in this case—as the version that uses composition given in the previous chapter. If `LList` had been designed with inheritance in mind, `SortedList` could access `LList`'s underlying data structure and provide faster operations. To this end, we revise the class `LList` in the next section.

**Note:** The implementation of the sorted list that extends the class `LList` is as inefficient as the implementation that uses composition given in Chapter 16.

**Question 4** Give at least one advantage and one disadvantage of using inheritance in the way shown in this section to implement the class `SortedList`.

## Designing a Base Class

**17.5**    Let's examine the class `LList` that we developed in Chapter 14 as a linked implementation of the ADT list. Recall that the class places each of the list's entries into its own node. These nodes are linked so that the first entry's node references the node of the second entry, and so on. A data field `firstNode` of the class references the first node, and another data field `numberOfEntries` counts the number of entries in the list.

    Like most classes, `LList` has data fields that are private. The client cannot access these fields directly by name. The class designer must decide whether to provide public methods that give the client indirect access to the data fields. In the case of `LList`, the public method `getLength` enables the client to get the length of the list. The client, however, cannot directly change the list's length. Only other member methods, such as `add` and `remove`, can alter the length. In addition, `LList` denies the client access to the field `firstNode` by not providing public accessor or mutator methods for this field. This design is appropriate, as `firstNode` is an implementation detail that should be hidden from the client.

**17.6**    The excerpt of the class `LList` given in Listing 17-1 shows aspects of the class that are relevant to this discussion. Each node is represented by the private class `Node`, which is defined within `LList` and hidden from the client. The method `getNodeAt` facilitates the implementation of other member methods by returning a reference to the node at a given position. We do not want the client to have access to this node, since it is part of the underlying representation of the list, so we make the method private.

LISTING 17-1   Relevant aspects of the class LList

```java
 1  public class LList<T> implements ListInterface<T>
 2  {
 3     private Node firstNode; // Reference to first node
 4     private int numberOfEntries;
 5
 6     public LList()
 7     {
 8        initializeDataFields();
 9     } // end default constructor
10
11     public int getLength()
12     {
13        return numberOfEntries;
14     } // end getLength
15
16     < Implementations of the public methods add, remove, clear, replace, getEntry,
17       contains, isEmpty, and toArray go here. >
18        . . .
19     // Initializes the class's data fields to indicate an empty list.
20     private void initializeDataFields()
21     {
22        firstNode = null;
23        numberOfEntries = 0;
24     }  // end initializeDataFields
25
26     // Returns a reference to the node at a given position.
27     private Node getNodeAt(int givenPosition)
28     {
29
30        . . .
31
32     }  // end getNodeAt
33
34     private class Node
35     {
36        private T data;
37        private Node next;
38
39        . . .
40
41     } // end Node
42  } // end LList
```

17.7    So far, nothing should be new to you. Now imagine that we want LList to serve as a base class for another class that you are developing. You saw in the previous section of this chapter that a sub-class of LList—just like a client of LList—cannot access by name anything declared as private within LList. That is, a subclass cannot access the data field firstNode, the method getNodeAt, or the class Node, as Figure 17-1 illustrates. If we want to extend the capability of LList and do so efficiently, the subclass will need access to these aspects of the class—in other words, to the underlying data structure.

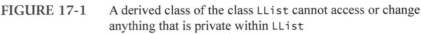

FIGURE 17-1    A derived class of the class LList cannot access or change
                anything that is private within LList

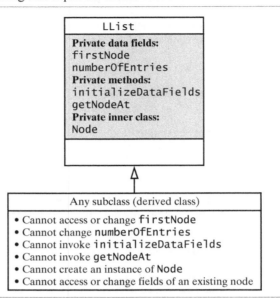

We can revise LList to make it more suitable as a base class by providing its subclasses controlled access to items that are hidden from a client. First, let's recall protected access, which we discussed in Segment JI7.2 of Java Interlude 7:

**Note:  Protected access**
You can access a protected method or data field by name only within its own class definition C, within any subclass of C, or within any class in the same package as C.

Our goal, then, is to give a subclass protected—but limited—access to the underlying chain of nodes. The subclass should be able to traverse or modify the chain efficiently. However, modifications to the chain must be done in a way that helps to maintain its integrity.

**17.8**    To enable a subclass to access the data fields by name without giving this access to the client, we could declare firstNode and numberOfEntries as protected. It is more typical, however, to keep them private and to provide protected methods for only the access we desire. The subclass will need to access the head reference firstNode, so we provide a protected get method to do this. Since getLength is public, the subclass can get the value of numberOfEntries.

A subclass likely will need to change firstNode and numberOfEntries, so we could provide protected methods that do so. But while we want an efficient subclass, we also want to keep our data structure intact. So we will not allow a subclass to change these fields directly. Instead, we can provide protected methods that modify our chain of nodes in a way that can satisfy both of our desires. For example, protected methods can add or delete nodes, updating the chain's length in the process. To prevent a subclass from overriding these protected methods, we declare them as final. No mutators will be available to directly change either the field numberOfEntries or a node's link. Thus, the subclass can alter the chain efficiently, but we are assured that the nodes will be linked correctly and the chain's length will be accurate.

**17.9** As a result of this discussion, we make the following changes to LList:

1. We define a protected method getFirstNode, enabling the subclass to access the head reference firstNode:

```
protected final Node getFirstNode()
{
    return firstNode;
} // end getFirstNode
```

2. We define protected methods to add and remove nodes, changing firstNode and numberOfEntries as necessary. Ensuring that these methods cannot be overridden by making them final is essential to preserving the integrity of the underlying data structure and hence the list.

```
/** Adds a node to the beginning of a chain. */
protected final void addFirstNode(Node newNode)

/** Adds a node to a chain after a given node. */
protected final void addAfterNode(Node nodeBefore, Node newNode)

/** Removes a chain's first node. */
protected final T removeFirstNode()

/** Removes the node after a given one. */
protected final T removeAfterNode(Node nodeBefore)
```

The implementations of these methods use the techniques presented in Chapter 14. For example, addFirstNode has the following definition, assuming that newNode is not null and the inner class Node has set and get methods:

```
protected final void addFirstNode(Node newNode)
{
    assert newNode != null : "null argument in addFirstNode";
    newNode.setNextNode(firstNode);
    firstNode = newNode;
    numberOfEntries++;
} // end addFirstNode
```

3. The public methods of LList and its subclasses can call the previous methods, and thereby reduce the chance of error. For example, we can revise LList's method remove as follows:

```
public T remove(int givenPosition)
{
    T result = null;
    if ((givenPosition >= 1) && (givenPosition <= getLength()))
    {
        assert !isEmpty();
        if (givenPosition == 1)          // Case 1: Remove first entry
            result = removeFirstNode();
        else                             // Case 2: givenPosition > 1
        {
            Node nodeBefore = getNodeAt(givenPosition - 1);
            result = removeAfterNode(nodeBefore);
        } // end if
        return result;                   // Return removed entry
    }
    else
        throw new IndexOutOfBoundsException(
                    "Illegal position given to remove operation.");
} // end remove
```

4. Next, we make getNodeAt protected and final instead of private. The client still cannot use this method, but the implementations of the class and any subclass can. They cannot, however, change the method by overriding it.

**5.** We also make the class Node protected and final instead of private. Node will remain hidden from the client but will be available to any subclass of LList. We could make Node's data fields data and next protected instead of private, but just as we did for LList, we instead make them private and provide protected accessor methods. We also provide a protected set method for a node's data. To ensure the integrity of our chain, we do not allow a subclass to alter the link portion of a node, and so we make that set method private. Thus, Node has the following four methods:

```
protected final T getData()
protected final void setData(T newData)
protected final Node getNextNode()
private final void setNextNode(Node nextNode)
```

Finally, we make Node's first constructor protected but leave its second constructor private, since it sets a node's link portion.

Making these changes to the class LList results in a new class, which we will name LListRevised. Figure 17-2 illustrates this class and the access that a derived class has to it.

**Programming Tip:  Planning for the future**

When designing a class, you should plan for its future use as well as the present need. If public accessor methods are not already in your design, provide protected accessor methods. Decide whether you want any future subclass to manipulate your class's data fields. If you do, provide protected methods that enable a subclass to make changes to the data fields both efficiently and safely.

**FIGURE 17-2**   Access available to a class derived from the class LListRevised

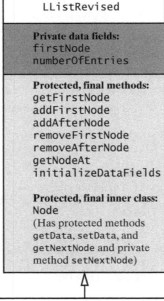

**Question 5** Imagine a subclass of the class `LListRevised`.

    **a.** Implement a method within the subclass that adds an entry to the beginning of the list.

    **b.** Implement a method within the subclass that adds an entry right after the entry at the midpoint of the list. If the list contains *n* entries, the entry at the midpoint is at position *n* / 2, where the division is truncated to an integer.

## Creating an Abstract Base Class

**VideoNote**

**Creating a base class**

**17.10**    We can simplify the previous class `LListRevised` by organizing the portion of it that deals with the chain of linked nodes into an abstract base class. Listing 17-2 outlines such a class, `LinkedChainBase`. Note that this class is abstract by virtue of the keyword `abstract`. All of its methods are implemented, but we do not allow instances of this class.

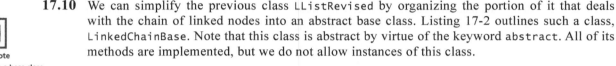

**LISTING 17-2**   The abstract base class `LinkedChainBase`

```
1  public abstract class LinkedChainBase<T>
2  {
3     private Node firstNode; // Reference to first node
4     private int numberOfEntries;
5
6     public LinkedChainBase()
7     {
8        initializeDataFields();
9     } // end default constructor
10
11    < Implementations of the public methods clear, getLength, isEmpty, and toArray go here. >
12    . . .
13    < Implementations of the protected, final methods getNodeAt, getFirstNode, addFirstNode,
14      addAfterNode, removeFirstNode, removeAfterNode, and initializeDataFields
15      go here. >
16    . . .
17    protected final class Node
18    {
19       private T data;     // Entry in list
20       private Node next; // Link to next node
21
22       protected Node(T dataPortion)
23       {
24          data = dataPortion;
25          next = null;
26       } // end constructor
27
28       private Node(T dataPortion, Node nextNode)
29       {
30          data = dataPortion;
31          next = nextNode;
32       } // end constructor
33       < Implementations of the protected methods getData, setData, and getNextNode go here. >
34       . . .
35       < Implementation of the private method setNextNode goes here. >
36       . . .
37    } // end Node
38 } // end LinkedChainBase
```

**Security Note:** To protect the integrity of any list that is an object of a subclass of LinkedChainBase, we do not allow the subclass to directly make additions to or deletions from the underlying chain of linked nodes. Moreover, the subclass cannot directly change the field numberOfEntries. As a result, any subclass of LinkedChainBase cannot damage the integrity of our data structure by failing to synchronize the value of numberOfEntries with the current number of nodes in the chain. Realize that such damage might be malicious, but could be accidental.

**17.11**   We can now extend LinkedChainBase and use what remains of LListRevised to form the class LinkedChainList, as shown in Listing 17-3.

---

LISTING 17-3   A revision of LListRevised that extends LinkedChainBase

```
1  public class LinkedChainList<T> extends LinkedChainBase<T>
2                                  implements ListInterface<T>
3  {
4     public LinkedChainList()
5     {
6        super(); // Initializes the linked chain
7     } // end default constructor
8
9     < Implementations of the public methods add, remove, replace, getEntry, and contains
10       go here. >
11       . . .
12  } // end LinkedChainList
```

---

The base class LinkedChainBase can be useful in other contexts as well. You can use it to define an efficient implementation of the ADT sorted list, as you will see next.

 **Note:** LListRevised, as Figure 17-2 illustrates, is a complicated class. It tries to describe a list, while providing managed access for subclasses to its underlying linked chain of nodes. Dividing these tasks between classes as we have done is a common approach. As a result, LinkedChainList can be concerned only with the list, while LinkedChainBase manages the linked-chain tasks safely.

---

 **Question 6** Some public methods of LinkedChainList cannot have definitions identical to the ones in the class LList.

   **a.** Which methods are these?
   **b.** Why must the method definitions in LinkedChainList differ from those in LList?
   **c.** What changes are necessary to the methods in LList to make them appropriate for LinkedChainList?

---

# An Efficient Implementation of a Sorted List

**17.12**   Instead of calling ADT list operations to perform operations on an ADT sorted list, our implementation will execute faster if it can be similar to the linked implementation that we wrote in Chapter 16, beginning at Segment 16.7. The protected methods defined in the class LinkedChainBase will enable us to manipulate the list's underlying data structure faster than if we had to rely solely on the operations of the ADT list to do so. Thus, we want our class to extend LinkedChainBase. We begin it by writing

```java
public class LinkedSortedList<T extends Comparable<? super T>>
                  extends LinkedChainBase<T>
                  implements SortedListInterface<T>
```

As before, we will implement a sorted list of Comparable objects.

## The Method add

**17.13**   The add method in our new class is quite similar to the one given in Segment 16.10 for the class LinkedSortedList. However, the details of that previous addition now are hidden within the protected methods addFirstNode and addAfterNode of LinkedChainBase. Thus, our revised method appears as follows (changes to the add method of Segment 16.10 are highlighted):

```java
public void add(T newEntry)
{
    Node newNode = new Node(newEntry);
    Node nodeBefore = getNodeBefore(newEntry);
    if (nodeBefore == null) // No need to call isEmpty
        addFirstNode(newNode);
    else
        addAfterNode(nodeBefore, newNode);
} // end add
```

Preceding each of the protected methods with super is optional, since no other methods have their names.

Question 4 in Segment 16.11 of Chapter 16 suggested the simplification for empty lists that we made here. When a list is empty, getNodeBefore returns null. Thus, we can omit a call to isEmpty in the if statement.

**17.14**   **The private method getNodeBefore.** We still need to implement the private method getNodeBefore. The implementation is like the one given in Segment 16.11, but it uses getFirstNode() instead of firstNode:

```java
private Node getNodeBefore(T anEntry)
{
    Node currentNode = getFirstNode();
    Node nodeBefore = null;

    while ((currentNode != null) &&
           (anEntry.compareTo(currentNode.getData()) > 0))
    {
        nodeBefore = currentNode;
        currentNode = currentNode.getNextNode();
    } // end while

    return nodeBefore;
} // end getNodeBefore
```

**17.15** **Efficiency.** This version of the method add executes faster than the versions given in Segments 17.1 and 16.21. Those earlier versions can use only the operations of the ADT list—that is, the public methods of the class LList. Recall that those add methods first invoke getPosition to find where in the list the new entry belongs, and then they invoke the list's add method. The implementation of getPosition given in Segment 16.24 traverses the sorted list to determine the position for the new entry. Within the $O(n)$ loop that performs this traversal is an invocation of the method getEntry. When getEntry has a linked implementation, it also traverses the sorted list, and so it is $O(n)$. Thus, getPosition is $O(n^2)$. It follows that the add methods in Segment 17.1 and Segment 16.21 are each $O(n^2)$.

Our improved add method in Segment 17.13 adds a new node in its proper location by traversing the chain of nodes at most once. Even though the method must use the protected methods to alter the chain of linked nodes, it can add the new node as soon as it finds its proper location, without traversing the chain repeatedly. Thus, it is an $O(n)$ operation.

**17.16** **The rest of the class.** To implement remove and getPosition, we would make similar changes to their linked implementations. Recall that Chapter 16 left these implementations as an exercise. We also need to implement the remaining operations of the ADT list that are common to the ADT sorted list but not inherited from LinkedChainBase. They are getEntry, contains, and remove (by position). Finally, we must override the inherited method toArray because it allocates an array of objects that cannot be cast to Comparable objects.

**Note:** You can use inheritance *and* maintain efficiency if your base class provides protected access to its underlying data structure.

**Note:** More than one implementation of an ADT is often possible. When choosing a particular implementation for a given application, you should consider all of the factors relevant to your situation. Execution time, memory use, and extensibility are just some of the issues that you should weigh. These same considerations should also be examined when you implement an ADT.

## CHAPTER SUMMARY

- This chapter demonstrated the difference between implementations that use composition and those that use inheritance. The basic ideas are the same as those described in Appendix D. With composition, a class has an object as a data field. The class's methods must act as clients of the object, so they use only the object's public methods. With inheritance, a class inherits all the public methods of its base class. Its implementation, as well as its client, can use these public methods.

- A base class can provide protected methods that enable its subclasses to manipulate its data fields in ways that its client cannot. In this way, a subclass's methods can be more efficient than if they had to use only public methods, as the client must.

- You can derive the sorted list from a base class that has appropriate protected methods and still have an efficient implementation.

## PROGRAMMING TIPS

- If your class inherits methods that are inappropriate, you can override them with methods that throw an exception when invoked. In such cases, examine your design and consider whether inheritance was the right choice. Do the benefits of inheritance outweigh the inconvenience of overriding the inappropriate methods, or would composition provide a cleaner design?

- When designing a class, you should plan for its future use as well as the present need. If public accessor methods are not already in your design, provide protected accessor methods. Decide whether you want any future subclass to manipulate your class's data fields. If you do, provide protected methods that enable a subclass to make changes to the data fields both efficiently and safely.

## EXERCISES

1. Implement the method contains for the class LinkedSortedList, as described in Segment 17.12. Take advantage of the list's sorted nature.

2. Write a constructor for the class LinkedSortedList, as described in Segment 17.12, that has as a parameter an instance of a class that implements ListInterface. The new sorted list should contain all the entries in the list, but in sorted order.

3. Write an equals method for the class LinkedSortedList, as described in Segment 17.12, that overrides the method equals inherited from the class Object. Assuming that objects in the list have an appropriate implementation of equals, your new method should return true if each entry in one list equals the corresponding entry in a second list.

4. Repeat Exercise 3 for the class LinkedChainList, as described in Segment 17.11, instead of the class LinkedSortedList.

5. If the class LinkedChainBase had the method iterator, as described in Segment 15.8 of Chapter 15, what would you need to do to define an iterator for the class LinkedSortedList?

6. Compare the time efficiency of the sorted list method
   ```
   public void delete(T newEntry)
   ```
   with that of the list method
   ```
   public void delete(int newPosition, T newEntry)
   ```

7. Exercise 5 in Chapter 16 asked you to design an ADT for a list of earthquake records. Can you implement this ADT by using inheritance, with LinkedChainBase as the base class? Which methods would you need to override? Is containment more appropriate?

8. Repeat Exercise 7, but consider the class LinkedSortedList, as described in Segment 17.12, instead of LinkedChainBase.

9. Suppose that the class LinkedChainBase, as given in Segment 17.10, implements the interface java.util.ListIterator, as described in Segment JI5.13 of Java Interlude 5. If LinkedChainBase is a base class of LinkedSortedList, which of the iterator methods are appropriate for a sorted list?

## Projects

1. Complete the implementation of the class `LinkedSortedList` that Segment 17.12 began.

2. Derive the class `LinkedSortedList` from the class `LListRevised`, as described in Segment 17.11. What is the disadvantage of this approach?

3. Exercise 4 in Chapter 16 asked you to design the ADT activity list. Show how you would implement such a class by using inheritance with the base class

   a. `LinkedChainBase`.
   b. `LinkedChainList`.

4. Project 8 in Chapter 16 asked you to implement the method `getMode`. Show how you would implement this method for the class `LinkedSortedList`, as described in Segment 17.12.

5. Using inheritance, derive the class `LinkedListWithIterator`, as described in Chapter 15 in Segment 15.9, from the class `LinkedChainList`.

6. Define a class of bags that implements the interface `BagInterface`, as given in Listing 1-1 of Chapter 1, and is a subclass of `LinkedChainBase`, as given in Listing 17-2.

7. Stacks, queues, and deques are similar in operation in many ways. Suppose that we wanted to create an abstract base class `QueueBase` and then use it and inheritance to implement each of the three ADTs.

   a. Design the class `QueueBase`. Indicate whether each field and method should be public, protected, or private, and explain why.
   b. Implement each of the ADTs stack, queue, and deque as a class that extends the base class `QueueBase`.

8. Segment 17.3 considered three ways to avoid the pitfall of a sorted list inheriting the add-by-position and replace-by-position operations from the ADT list. Revise the class `SortedList` that Segment 17.1 describes by overriding `add` and `replace` and changing their behaviors as follows:

   ```
   /** Adds newEntry to this sorted list in its correct sorted order, ignoring the
       value of newPosition. */
   public void add(int newPosition, T newEntry);

   /** Removes the entry at givenPosition from this sorted list and
       then adds newEntry in its correct sorted order. */
   public T replace(int givenPosition, T newEntry);
   ```

## ANSWERS TO SELF-TEST QUESTIONS

1. The list's method `contains` searches the entire list when the desired entry is not present. By calling `getPosition`, `contains` can take advantage of the sorted order of the entries. The answer to Question 14 of Chapter 16 gives such a method. By adding this method to `SortedList`, you can override `LList`'s `contains`.

2. The client will be unaware of what has happened and will not know where in the sorted list the addition was made.

3. a. The method `toArray` in `LList` allocates an array of objects of type `Object`. The client cannot cast these objects to `Comparable` objects, as required by a sorted list.

   b.
```java
public T[] toArray()
{
    int numberOfEntries = getLength();

    // The cast is safe because the new array contains null entries
    @SuppressWarnings("unchecked")
    T[] result = (T[])new Comparable[numberOfEntries]; // Warning: [unchecked]
                                                       // unchecked cast

    for (int index = 0; index < numberOfEntries; index++)
        result[index] = super.getEntry(index + 1);

    return result;
} // end toArray
```

4. Advantages: The implementation is easy to write. You inherit methods such as `isEmpty` that you do not have to implement.
   Disadvantages: The implementation is not efficient, especially when the implementation of the underlying list is linked. Using inheritance in this way is as inefficient as using composition. You inherit methods (add and replace by position) that you do not want. Moreover, since inheritance implies an *is a* relationship between the sorted list and the list, type compatibility dictates that the sorted list be able to behave like a list. This clearly is not the case, since you cannot insert or replace entries at any given position. Thus, a sorted list is not really a list.

5. a.
```java
public void addToBeginning(T newEntry)
{
    addFirstNode(new Node(newEntry));
} // end addToBeginning
```

   b.
```java
public void addAfterMidpoint(T newEntry)
{
    Node nodeBefore = getNodeAt(getLength() / 2);
    addNodeAfter(nodeBefore, new Node(newEntry));
} // end addAfterMidpoint
```

6. a. add, add, remove, replace, getEntry, contains.
   b. The methods in `LList` reference the private data fields `firstNode` and `numberOfEntries`. Since these fields are now private in `LinkedChainBase`, `LinkedChainList` cannot reference them directly by name.
   c. Replace occurrences of `numberOfEntries` with `getLength()`, and replace occurrences of `firstNode` with `getFirstNode()`.

# Chapter

# 18

# Searching

## Contents

## Prerequisites

## Objectives

After studying this chapter, you should be able to

- Search an array by using a sequential search
- Search an array by using a binary search
- Search a chain of linked nodes sequentially
- Describe the time efficiency of a search

**Question 1** Revise the previous method inArray so that it returns the index of the first array entry that equals anEntry. If the array does not contain such an entry, return −1.

**Question 2** Write a static method inList that performs an iterative sequential search of a list by using only operations of the ADT list. The method should return true if a given item is in a given list.

## A Recursive Sequential Search of an Unsorted Array

18.4   We begin a sequential search of an array by looking at the first entry in the array. If that entry is the desired one, we end the search. Otherwise we search the rest of the array. Since this new search is also sequential, and since the rest of the array is smaller than the original array, we have a recursive description of a solution to our problem. Well, almost. We need a base case. An empty array could be the base case because it never contains the desired item.

For the array a, we search the n elements a[0] through a[n - 1] by beginning with the first element, a[0]. If it is not the one we seek, we need to search the rest of the array—that is, we search array elements a[1] through a[n - 1]. In general, we search the array elements a[first] through a[n - 1]. To be even more general, we can search array elements a[first] through a[last], where first ≤ last.

18.5   The following pseudocode describes the logic of our recursive algorithm:

> *Algorithm to search* a[first] *through* a[last] *for* desiredItem
> **if** (*there are no elements to search*)
>     **return false**
> **else if** (desiredItem *equals* a[first])
>     **return true**
> **else**
>     **return** *the result of searching* a[first + 1] *through* a[last]

Figure 18-3 illustrates a recursive search of an array.

18.6   The method that implements this algorithm will need parameters first and last. To spare the client the detail of providing values for these parameters, and to allow the method inArray to have the same header as it did in Segment 18.3, we implement the algorithm as a private method search that inArray invokes.

```
/** Searches an array for anEntry. */
public static <T> boolean inArray(T[] anArray, T anEntry)
{
    return search(anArray, 0, anArray.length - 1, anEntry);
} // end inArray

// Searches anArray[first] through anArray[last] for desiredItem.
// first >= 0 and < anArray.length.
// last >= 0 and < anArray.length.
```

```
private static <T> boolean search(T[] anArray, int first, int last,
                                  T desiredItem)
{
    boolean found;
    if (first > last)
        found = false; // No elements to search
    else if (desiredItem.equals(anArray[first]))
        found = true;
    else
        found = search(anArray, first + 1, last, desiredItem);

    return found;
} // end search
```

**FIGURE 18-3**     A recursive sequential search of an array that (a) finds its
target; (b) does not find its target

**(a) A successful search for 8**

Look at the first entry, 9:

| 9 | 5 | 8 | 4 | 7 |

$8 \neq 9$, so search the next subarray.

Look at the first entry, 5:

| 5 | 8 | 4 | 7 |

$8 \neq 5$, so search the next subarray.

Look at the first entry, 8:

| 8 | 4 | 7 |

$8 = 8$, so the search has found 8.

**(b) An unsuccessful search for 6**

Look at the first entry, 9:

| 9 | 5 | 8 | 4 | 7 |

$6 \neq 9$, so search the next subarray.

Look at the first entry, 5:

| 5 | 8 | 4 | 7 |

$6 \neq 5$, so search the next subarray.

Look at the first entry, 8:

| 8 | 4 | 7 |

$6 \neq 8$, so search the next subarray.

Look at the first entry, 4:

| 4 | 7 |

$6 \neq 4$, so search the next subarray.

Look at the first entry, 7:

| 7 |

$6 \neq 7$, so search an empty array.

No entries are left to consider, so the
search ends. 6 is not in the array.

**Question 3** List the comparisons that the previous method `search` makes while searching for the object o in the following array of objects. Assume that the object is not found.

o1    o2    o3    o4    o5

**Question 4** Implement at the client level a recursive method `search` that searches a list of objects. Use only operations of the ADT list. The method should return true if a given item is in a given list.

## The Efficiency of a Sequential Search of an Array

18.7    Whether you implement a sequential search iteratively or recursively, the number of comparisons will be the same. In the best case, you will locate the desired item first in the array. You will have made only one comparison, and so the search will be O(1). In the worst case, you will search the entire array. Either you will find the desired item at the end of the array or you will not find it at all. In either event, you will have made *n* comparisons for an array of *n* entries. The sequential search in the worst case is therefore O(*n*). Typically, you will look at about one-half of the entries in the array. Thus, the average case is O(*n*/2), which is just O(*n*).

**Note:** **The time efficiency of a sequential search of an array**
Best case:    O(1)
Worst case:   O(*n*)
Average case: O(*n*)

# Searching a Sorted Array

A sequential search of an unsorted array is rather easy to understand and to implement. When the array contains relatively few entries, the search is efficient enough to be practical. However, when the array contains many entries, a sequential search can be time-consuming. For example, imagine that you are looking through a jar of coins for one minted during the year of your birth. A sequential search of 10 coins is not a problem. With 1000 coins, the search could be lengthy; with 1 million coins, it is overwhelming. A faster search method would be welcome. Fortunately, faster searches are possible.

### A Sequential Search of a Sorted Array

18.8    Suppose that before you begin searching your coins, someone arranges them in sorted order by their dates. If you search the sorted coins in Figure 18-4 sequentially for the date 1997, you would look at the coins dated 1990, 1992, 1993, and 1995 before arriving at 1997. If, instead, you look for the date 1996, you would look at the first five coins without finding it. Should you keep looking? If the coins are sorted into ascending order and you have reached the one dated 1997, you will not find 1996 beyond it. If the coins were not sorted, you would have to examine all of them to see that 1996 was not present.

**Note:** A sequential search can be more efficient if the data is sorted.

FIGURE 18-4    Coins sorted by their mint dates

If our array is sorted into either ascending or descending order, we can use the previous ideas to revise the sequential search. This modified search can tell whether an item does not occur in an array faster than a sequential search of an unsorted array. The latter search always examines the entire array in this case. With a sorted array, however, the modified sequential search often makes far fewer comparisons to make the same determination. Exercise 2 at the end of this chapter asks you to implement a sequential search of a sorted array.

After expending the effort to sort an array, you often can search it even faster by using the method that we discuss next.

## A Binary Search of a Sorted Array

**18.9**    Think of a number between 1 and 1 million. When I guess at your number, tell me whether my guess is correct, too high, or too low. At most, how many attempts will I need before I guess correctly? You should be able to answer this question by the time you reach the end of this section!

If you had to find a new friend's telephone number in a printed directory, what would you do? Typically you would open the book to a page near its middle, glance at the entries, and quickly see whether you were on the correct page. If you were not, you would decide whether you had to look at earlier pages—those in the left "half" of the book—or later pages—those in the right "half." What aspect of a telephone directory enables you to make this decision? The alphabetical order of the names does.

If you decided to look in the left half, you could ignore the entire right half. In fact, you could tear off the right half and discard it, as Figure 18-5 illustrates. You have reduced the size of the search problem dramatically, as you have only half of the book left to search. You then would repeat the process on this half. Eventually you would either find the telephone number or discover that it is not there. This approach—called a **binary search**—sounds suspiciously recursive.

**18.10**    Let's adapt these ideas to searching an array a of n integers that are sorted into ascending order. (Descending order would also work with a simple change in our algorithm.) We know that

$$a[0] \leq a[1] \leq a[2] \leq \ldots \leq a[n-1]$$

Because the array is sorted, we can rule out whole sections of the array that could not possibly contain the number we are looking for—just as you ruled out an entire half of the telephone directory.

For example, if we are looking for the number 7 and we know that a[5] is equal to 9, then, of course, we know that 7 is less than a[5]. But we also know that 7 cannot appear after a[5] in the array, because the array is sorted. That is,

$$7 < a[5] \leq a[6] \leq \ldots \leq a[n-1]$$

FIGURE 18-5    Ignoring one half of the data when the data is sorted

*I don't need this half of the book. I'll just throw it away.*

We know this without looking at the elements beyond a[5]. We therefore can ignore these elements as well as a[5]. Similarly, if the sought-after number were greater than a[5] (for example, if we were looking for 10), we could ignore a[5] and all the elements before it.

Replacing the index 5 in the preceding example with whatever index is in the middle of the array leads to a first draft of an algorithm for a binary search of an array:

> *Algorithm to search* a[0] *through* a[n - 1] *for* desiredItem
> mid = *approximate midpoint between* 0 *and* n - 1
> **if** (desiredItem *equals* a[mid])
>     **return true**
> **else if** (desiredItem < a[mid])
>     **return** *the result of searching* a[0] *through* a[mid - 1]
> **else if** (desiredItem > a[mid])
>     **return** *the result of searching* a[mid + 1] *through* a[n - 1]

Notice that to

> *Search* a[0] *through* a[n - 1]

you have to either

> *Search* a[0] *through* a[mid - 1]

or

> *Search* a[mid + 1] *through* a[n - 1]

These two searches of a portion of the array are smaller versions of the very problem we are solving, and so can be accomplished by calling the algorithm itself recursively.

**18.11**  One complication arises, however, when we write the recursive calls in the previous pseudocode. Each call searches a subrange of the array. In the first case, it is the elements indexed by 0 through `mid - 1`. In the second case, it is the elements indexed by `mid + 1` through `n - 1`. Thus, we need two extra parameters—`first` and `last`—to specify the first and last indices of the subrange of the array that is to be searched. That is, we search `a[first]` through `a[last]` for `desiredItem`.

Using these parameters and making the recursive calls look more like Java, we can express the pseudocode as follows:

> *Algorithm* binarySearch(a, first, last, desiredItem)
> mid = *approximate midpoint between* first *and* last
> **if** (desiredItem *equals* a[mid])
>    **return true**
> **else if** (desiredItem < a[mid])
>    **return** binarySearch(a, first, mid - 1, desiredItem)
> **else if** (desiredItem > a[mid])
>    **return** binarySearch(a, mid + 1, last, desiredItem)

To search the entire array, we initially set `first` to 0 and `last` to `n - 1`. Each recursive call will then use some other values for `first` and `last`. For example, the recursive call that appears first would set `first` to 0 and `last` to `mid - 1`.

When you write any recursive algorithm, you should always check that the recursion is not infinite. Let's check whether every possible invocation of the algorithm will lead to a base case. Consider the three cases in the nested `if` statement in the previous pseudocode. In the first case, the sought-after item is found in the array, so there is no recursive call, and the process terminates. In each of the other two cases, a smaller portion of the array is searched by a recursive call. If the sought-after item is in the array, the algorithm uses smaller and smaller portions of the array until it finds the item. But what if the item is not anywhere in the array? Will the resulting series of recursive calls eventually lead to a base case? Unfortunately not, but that is not hard to fix.

**18.12**  Note that in each recursive call, either the value of `first` is increased or the value of `last` is decreased. If they ever pass each other and `first` actually becomes larger than `last`, we will have run out of array elements to check. In that case, `desiredItem` is not in the array. If we add this test to our pseudocode and refine the logic a bit, we get the following more complete algorithm:

> *Algorithm* binarySearch(a, first, last, desiredItem)
> mid = (first + last) / 2 // *Approximate midpoint*
> **if** (first > last)
>    **return false**
> **else if** (desiredItem *equals* a[mid])
>    **return true**
> **else if** (desiredItem < a[mid])
>    **return** binarySearch(a, first, mid - 1, desiredItem)
> **else** // *desiredItem > a[mid]*
>    **return** binarySearch(a, mid + 1, last, desiredItem)

Figure 18-6 provides an example of a binary search.

---

**Question 5** When the previous binary search algorithm searches the array in Figure 18-6 for 8 and for 16, how many comparisons to an array entry are necessary in each case?

FIGURE 18-6    A recursive binary search of a sorted array that (a) finds its
target; (b) does not find its target

**(a) A successful search for 8**

Look at the middle entry, 10:

| 2 | 4 | 5 | 7 | 8 | **10** | 12 | 15 | 18 | 21 | 24 | 26 |
|---|---|---|---|---|---|---|---|---|---|---|---|
| 0 | 1 | 2 | 3 | 4 | 5 | 6 | 7 | 8 | 9 | 10 | 11 |

8 < 10, so search the left half of the array.

Look at the middle entry, 5:

| 2 | 4 | **5** | 7 | 8 |
|---|---|---|---|---|
| 0 | 1 | 2 | 3 | 4 |

8 > 5, so search the right half of the array.

Look at the middle entry, 7:

| **7** | 8 |
|---|---|
| 3 | 4 |

8 > 7,  so search the right half of the array.

Look at the middle entry, 8:

| **8** |
|---|
| 4 |

8 = 8, so the search ends. 8 is in the array.

**(b) An unsuccessful search for 16**

Look at the middle entry, 10:

| 2 | 4 | 5 | 7 | 8 | **10** | 12 | 15 | 18 | 21 | 24 | 26 |
|---|---|---|---|---|---|---|---|---|---|---|---|
| 0 | 1 | 2 | 3 | 4 | 5 | 6 | 7 | 8 | 9 | 10 | 11 |

16 > 10, so search the right half of the array.

Look at the middle entry, 18:

| 12 | 15 | **18** | 21 | 24 | 26 |
|---|---|---|---|---|---|
| 6 | 7 | 8 | 9 | 10 | 11 |

16 < 18, so search the left half of the array.

Look at the middle entry, 12:

| **12** | 15 |
|---|---|
| 6 | 7 |

16 > 12,  so search the right half of the array.

Look at the middle entry, 15:

| **15** |
|---|
| 7 |

16 > 15, so search the right half of the array.

The next subarray is empty, so the search ends. 16 is not in the array.

**18.13**  Although the implementations of the sequential search that were given in Segments 18.3 and 18.6 use the method `equals` to make the necessary comparisons, the binary search requires more than a test for equality. To make the necessary comparisons, we need the method `compareTo`. Since all classes inherit `equals` from the class `Object` and can override it, all objects have the method `equals`. But for an object to have `compareTo`, it must belong to a class that implements the interface `Comparable`. Such is the case for objects in a sorted list, as Segment 16.1 of Chapter 16 indicates, and for objects in a sorted array.

The method `binarySearch` can have the following implementation:

```java
private static <T extends Comparable<? super T>>
        boolean binarySearch(T[] anArray, int first, int last, T desiredItem)
{
    boolean found;
    int mid = first + (last - first) / 2;

    if (first > last)
        found = false;
    else if (desiredItem.equals(anArray[mid]))
        found = true;
    else if (desiredItem.compareTo(anArray[mid]) < 0)
        found = binarySearch(anArray, first, mid - 1, desiredItem);
    else
        found = binarySearch(anArray, mid + 1, last, desiredItem);

    return found;
} // end binarySearch
```

Now the public method `inArray` appears as follows:

```java
public static <T extends Comparable<? super T>> boolean inArray(T anEntry)
{
    return binarySearch(anArray, 0, anArray.length - 1, anEntry);
} // end contains
```

> **Note:**  Notice that the Java computation of the midpoint `mid` is
>
> ```java
> int mid = first + (last - first) / 2;
> ```
>
> instead of
>
> ```java
> int mid = (first + last) / 2;
> ```
>
> as discussed in the Note at the end of Segment 7.18 in Chapter 7.

> **Programming Tip:**  Classes that implement the `Comparable` interface must define a `compareTo` method. Such classes should also define an `equals` method that overrides the `equals` method inherited from `Object`. Both `compareTo` and `equals` should use the same test for equality. The previous method `binarySearch` calls both the method `equals` and the method `compareTo`. If the objects in the array did not have an appropriate `equals` method, `binarySearch` would not execute correctly. Note, however, that you could use `compareTo` instead of `equals` to test for equality.

**Question 6** During a binary search, which entries in the array

4  8  12  14  20  24

are compared to the target when the target is **a.** 2; **b.** 8; **c.** 15.

**Question 7** Modify the previous method `inArray` so that it returns the index of the first array entry that equals `anEntry`. If the array does not contain such an entry, return -1. You will have to modify `binarySearch` also.

**Question 8** What changes to the binary search algorithm are necessary when the array is sorted in descending order (from largest down to smallest) instead of ascending order, as we have assumed during our discussion?

## Java Class Library: The Method `binarySearch`

**18.14** The class `Arrays` in the package `java.util` defines several versions of a static method `binarySearch` with the following specification:

```
/** Searches an entire array for a given item.
    @param array       An array sorted in ascending order.
    @param desiredItem The item to be found in the array.
    @return  Index of the array entry that equals desiredItem;
             otherwise returns -belongsAt - 1, where belongsAt is
             the index of the array element that should contain
             desiredItem. */
public static int binarySearch(type[] array, type desiredItem);
```

Here, both occurrences of *type* must be the same; *type* can be `Object` or any of the primitive types `byte`, `char`, `double`, `float`, `int`, `long`, or `short`.

## The Efficiency of a Binary Search of an Array

**18.15** The binary search algorithm eliminates about half of the array from consideration after examining only one element. It then eliminates another quarter of the array, and then another eighth, and so on. Thus, most of the array is not searched at all, saving much time. Intuitively, the binary search algorithm is very fast.

But just how fast is it? Counting the comparisons that occur will provide a measure of the algorithm's efficiency. To see the algorithm's worst-case behavior, you count the maximum number of comparisons that can occur when searching an array of $n$ items. Comparisons are made each time the algorithm divides the array in half. After each division, half of the items are left to search. That is, beginning with $n$ items, we would be left with $n/2$ items, then $n/4$ items, and so on. In the worst case, the search would continue until only one item was left. That is, $n/2^k$ would equal 1 for some integer value of $k$. This value of $k$ gives us the number of times the array is divided in half, or the number of recursive calls to `binarySearch`.

If $n$ is a power of 2, $n$ is $2^k$ for some positive $k$. By the definition of a logarithm, $k$ is $\log_2 n$. If $n$ is not a power of 2, you can find a positive integer $k$ so that $n$ lies between $2^{k-1}$ and $2^k$. For example, if $n$ is 14, $2^3 < 14 < 2^4$. Thus, we have for some $k \geq 1$,

$$2^{k-1} < n < 2^k$$
$$k - 1 < \log_2 n < k$$
$$k = 1 + \log_2 n \text{ rounded down}$$
$$= \log_2 n \text{ rounded up}$$

To summarize,

$k = \log_2 n$ when $n$ is a power of 2

$k = \lceil \log_2 n \rceil$ when $n$ is not a power of 2

In general, $k$—the number of recursive calls to binarySearch—is $\lceil \log_2 n \rceil$.

**Note: Ceiling and floors**

The *ceiling* of a number $x$, denoted as $\lceil x \rceil$, is the smallest integer greater than or equal to $x$. For example, $\lceil 4.1 \rceil$ is 5. The *floor* of a number $x$, denoted as $\lfloor x \rfloor$, is the largest integer less than or equal to $x$. For example, $\lfloor 4.9 \rfloor$ is 4. When you *truncate* a positive real number to an integer, you actually are computing the number's floor by discarding any fractional portion.

Each call to binarySearch, with the possible exception of the last one, makes two comparisons between the target and the middle entry in the array: One tests for equality and one for less than or greater than. Thus, the binary search performs at most $2 \times \lceil \log_2 n \rceil$ comparisons, and so in the worst case is O(log $n$).

To search an array of 1000 elements, the binary search will compare the target to about 10 array entries in the worst case. In contrast, a simple sequential search could compare the target to as many as all 1000 array entries, and on average will compare it to about 500 array entries.

**Note:** **The time efficiency of a binary search of an array**

Best case:  O(1)

Worst case:  O(log $n$)

Average case: O(log $n$)

**Question 9** Think of a number between 1 and 1 million. When I guess at your number, tell me whether my guess is correct, too high, or too low. At most, how many attempts will I need before I guess correctly? *Hint*: You are counting guesses, not comparisons.

**18.16**  **Alternate analysis of efficiency.** The binary search makes comparisons each time it locates the midpoint of the array. Thus, to search $n$ items, the binary search looks at the middle item and then searches $n/2$ items. If we let $t(n)$ represent the time requirement for searching $n$ items, we find that at worst

$t(n) = 1 + t(n/2)$ for $n > 1$

$t(1) = 1$

We encountered this recurrence relation in Segment 7.25 of Chapter 7. There, we showed that

$t(n) = 1 + \log_2 n$

Thus, the binary search is O(log $n$) in the worst case.

# Searching an Unsorted Chain

**18.17**  Within a linked implementation of either the ADT list or the ADT sorted list, the method contains would search a chain of linked nodes for the target. As you will see, a sequential search is really the only practical choice. We begin with a chain whose data is unsorted, as typically would be the case for the ADT list.

VideoNote
Searching a linked chain

Regardless of a list's implementation, a sequential search of the list looks at consecutive entries in the list, beginning with the first one, until either it finds the desired entry or it looks at all entries without success. When the implementation is linked, however, moving from node to node is not as simple as moving from one array location to another. Despite this fact, you can implement a sequential search of a chain of linked nodes either iteratively or recursively and with the same efficiency as that of a sequential search of an array.

## An Iterative Sequential Search of an Unsorted Chain

**18.18** Figure 18-7 illustrates a chain of linked nodes that contain the list's entries. Recall from Segment 14.8 of Chapter 14 that `firstNode` is a data field of the class that implements the list. While it is clear that a method can access the first node in this chain by using the reference `firstNode`, how can it access the subsequent nodes? Since `firstNode` is a data field that always references the first node in the chain, we would not want our search to alter it or any other aspect of the list. Thus, an iterative method `contains` should use a local reference variable `currentNode` that initially contains the same reference as `firstNode`. To make `currentNode` reference the next node, we would execute the statement

```
currentNode = currentNode.getNextNode();
```

**FIGURE 18-7**    A chain of linked nodes that contain the entries in a list

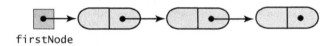

firstNode

The iterative sequential search has the following straightforward implementation:

```java
public boolean contains(T anEntry)
{
   boolean found = false;
   Node currentNode = firstNode;

   while (!found && (currentNode != null))
   {
      if (anEntry.equals(currentNode.getData()))
         found = true;
      else
         currentNode = currentNode.getNextNode();
   } // end while

   return found;
} // end contains
```

This implementation is like the one given in Segment 14.19 of Chapter 14.

## A Recursive Sequential Search of an Unsorted Chain

**18.19** When done recursively, a sequential search looks at the first entry in the list and, if it is not the desired entry, searches the rest of the list. This recursive approach is the same regardless of whether you implement the search at the client level by using only the list's ADT operations—as you did in Question 4—or as a public method of an array-based implementation of the list—much as we did in Segment 18.6. We use the same approach for a linked implementation of the list, as follows.

How would you implement the step *search the rest of the list* when the list's entries are in a chain of linked nodes? The iterative method `contains` that you saw in the previous segment uses a local variable `currentNode` to move from node to node. A recursive method could not have `currentNode` as a local variable, since `currentNode` would get reset to an initial value at each recursive call. Instead, such a method needs `currentNode` as a parameter. But then we would have a method whose parameter depends on the list's implementation, making it unsuitable as a public method. Just as we did earlier in Segments 18.6 and 18.13, we would make this search method private and call it from a public method.

**18.20**   The private recursive method `search` examines the list entry in the node that its parameter `currentNode` references. If the entry is not the desired one, the method recursively calls itself with an argument that references the next node in the chain. Thus, the method `search` has the following implementation:

```
// Recursively searches a chain of nodes for desiredItem,
// beginning with the node that currentNode references.
private boolean search(Node currentNode, T desiredItem)
{
   boolean found;

   if (currentNode == null)
      found = false;
   else if (desiredItem.equals(currentNode.getData()))
      found = true;
   else
      found = search(currentNode.getNextNode(), desiredItem);

   return found;
} // end search
```

Now we write the public method `contains` as follows:

```
public boolean contains(T anEntry)
{
   return search(firstNode, anEntry);
} // end contains
```

Notice that the call to the method `search` initializes the parameter `currentNode` to `firstNode`, much as an iterative method initializes its local variable `currentNode` to `firstNode`.

## The Efficiency of a Sequential Search of a Chain

**18.21**   The efficiency of a sequential search of a chain is really the same as that of a sequential search of an array. In the best case, the desired item will be first in the chain. Thus, at best the search will be O(1), since you will have made only one comparison. In the worst case, you will search the entire chain, making $n$ comparisons for a chain of $n$ nodes. Therefore, the sequential search in the worst case is O($n$). Typically, you will look at about half of the nodes in the chain. Thus, the average-case search is O($n/2$), which is just O($n$).

 **Note:**   **The time efficiency of a sequential search of a chain of linked nodes**
Best case:      O(1)
Worst case:    O($n$)
Average case: O($n$)

# Searching a Sorted Chain

We now search a chain whose data is sorted. Such a chain would occur in a linked implementation of the ADT sorted list.

## A Sequential Search of a Sorted Chain

**18.22**   Searching a chain of linked nodes whose data is sorted is similar to sequentially searching a sorted array, as described in Segment 18.8. Here, we incorporate that logic into the following implementation of `contains`:

```
public boolean contains(T anEntry)
{
   Node currentNode = firstNode;
```

```
    while ( (currentNode != null) &&
            (anEntry.compareTo(currentNode.getData()) > 0) )
    {
       currentNode = currentNode.getNextNode();
    } // end while
    return (currentNode != null) &&
            anEntry.equals(currentNode.getData());
} // end contains
```

The method traverses the chain until it either reaches a node that could contain the desired object or examines all nodes without success. Following the traversal, a final test is necessary to arrive at a conclusion. Because the data is sorted, determining that `anEntry` is not in the chain takes less time than it would if the data were not sorted.

## A Binary Search of a Sorted Chain

**18.23**   A binary search of an array looks first at the element that is at or near the middle of the array. It is easy to determine the index `mid` of this element by computing `first + (last - first) / 2`, where `first` and `last` are the indices of the first and last elements, respectively, in the array. Accessing this middle element is also easy: For an array a, it is simply `a[mid]`.

Now consider searching a chain of linked nodes, such as the one you saw earlier in Figure 18-7, whose nodes are sorted. How would you access the entry in the middle node? Since this chain has only three nodes, you can get to the middle node quickly, but what if the chain contained 1000 nodes? In general, you need to traverse the chain, beginning at the first node, until you reach the middle node. How will you know when you get there? If you know the length of the chain, you can divide the length in half and count nodes as you traverse. The details are not as important as a realization that it takes a bit of work to access the middle node.

After looking at the entry in the middle node, you probably need to ignore half of the chain and search the other half. Do not change the chain when ignoring part of it. Remember that you want to search the chain, not destroy it. Once you know which half to search, you must find its middle node, again by traversing the chain. It should be clear to you that a binary search of a linked chain of nodes would be challenging to implement and less efficient than a sequential search.

 **Note:** A binary search of a chain of linked nodes is impractical.

# Choosing a Search Method

**18.24**   **Choosing between a sequential search and a binary search.** You just saw that you should use a sequential search to search a chain of linked nodes. But if you want to search an array of objects, you need to know which algorithms are applicable. To use a sequential search, the objects must have a method `equals` that ascertains whether two distinct objects are equal in some sense. Since all objects inherit `equals` from the class `Object`, you must ensure that the objects you search have overridden `equals` with an appropriate version. To perform a binary search on an array of objects, on the other hand, the objects must have a `compareTo` method and the array must be sorted. If these conditions are not met, you must use a sequential search.

If both search algorithms are applicable to your array, what search should you use? If the array is small, you can simply use a sequential search. If the array is large and already sorted, a binary search is typically much faster than a sequential search. But if the array is not sorted, should you sort it and then use a binary search? The answer depends on how often you plan to search the array. Sorting takes time, typically more time than a sequential search would. If you plan to search an unsorted array only a few times, sorting the array so that you can use a binary search likely will not save you time; use a sequential search instead.

Figure 18-8 summarizes the time efficiencies of the sequential search and the binary search. Only the sequential search is applicable to unsorted data. The efficiencies given for the binary search are for a sorted array. For a large, sorted array, the binary search is typically much faster than a sequential search.

**FIGURE 18-8**    The time efficiency of searching, expressed in Big Oh notation

|  | Best Case | Average Case | Worst Case |
|---|---|---|---|
| Sequential search (unsorted data) | $O(1)$ | $O(n)$ | $O(n)$ |
| Sequential search (sorted data) | $O(1)$ | $O(n)$ | $O(n)$ |
| Binary search (sorted array) | $O(1)$ | $O(\log n)$ | $O(\log n)$ |

18.25 **Choosing between an iterative search and a recursive search.** Since the recursive sequential search is tail recursive, you can save some time and space by using the iterative version of the search. The binary search is fast, so using recursion will not require much additional space for the recursive calls. Also, coding the binary search recursively is somewhat easier than coding it iteratively. To convince yourself of this, try to code an iterative version of the binary search. (See Exercise 6 at the end of this chapter.)

## CHAPTER SUMMARY

- A sequential search of either a list, an array, or a chain looks at the first item, the second item, and so on until it either finds a particular item or discovers that the item does not occur in the group.

- The average-case performance of a sequential search is $O(n)$.

- Typically, you perform a sequential search iteratively, although a simple recursive approach is also possible.

- A binary search of an array requires that the array be sorted. It looks first to see whether the desired item is at the middle of the array. If it is not, the search decides in which half of the array the item can occur and repeats this strategy on only this half.

- A binary search is $O(\log n)$ in the worst case.

- Typically, you perform a binary search recursively, although an iterative approach is also possible.

- A binary search of a linked chain of nodes is impractical.

## PROGRAMMING TIP

- Classes that implement the Comparable interface must define a compareTo method. Such classes should also define an equals method that overrides the equals method inherited from Object. Both compareTo and equals should use the same test for equality. The method binarySearch in Segment 18.13 calls both the method equals and the method compareTo. If the objects in the array did not have an appropriate equals method, binarySearch would not execute correctly. Note, however, that you could use compareTo instead of equals to test for equality.

## Exercises

1. Revise the recursive method `search`, as given in Segment 18.6, so that it looks at the last entry in the array instead of the first one.

2. When searching a sorted array sequentially, you can ascertain that a given item does not appear in the array without searching the entire array. For example, if you search the array

   2 5 7 9

   for 6, you can use the approach described in Segment 18.8. That is, you compare 6 to 2, then to 5, and finally to 7. Since you did not find 6 after comparing it to 7, you do not have to look further, because the other entries in the array are greater than 7 and therefore cannot equal 6. Thus, you do not simply ask whether 6 equals an array entry, you also ask whether it is greater than the entry. Since 6 is greater than 2, you continue the search. Likewise for 5. Since 6 is less than 7, you have passed the point in the array where 6 would have had to occur, so 6 is not in the array.

   a. Write an iterative method `inArray` to take advantage of these observations when searching a sorted array sequentially.
   b. Write a recursive method `search` that a method `inArray` can call to take advantage of these observations when searching a sorted array sequentially.

3. How many comparisons are made by the recursive method `search` described in Part *b* of the previous exercise when searching the array in Figure 18-6 for 8 and for 16?

4. Trace the method `binarySearch`, as given in Segment 18.13, when searching for 4 in the following array of values:

   5 8 10 13 15 20 22 26 30 31 34 40

   Repeat the trace when searching for 34.

5. Modify the method `binarySearch` in Segment 18.13 so that it returns the index of the first array entry that equals `desiredItem`. If the array does not contain such an entry, return `-(belongsAt + 1)`, where `belongsAt` is the index of the array location that should contain `desiredItem`. At the end of Segment 18.13, Question 7 asked you to return -1 in this case. Notice that both versions of the method return a negative integer if and only if `desiredItem` is not found.

6. Implement a binary search of an array iteratively. Model your methods after the ones given in Segment 18.13.

7. Write a recursive method to find the smallest object in an array of `Comparable` objects. Like the binary search, your method should divide the array into halves. Unlike the binary search, your method should search both halves for the smallest object. The smallest object in the array will then be the smaller of these two smallest objects.

8. Suppose that you are searching an unsorted array of objects that might contain duplicates. Devise an algorithm that returns a list of the indices of all objects in the array that match a given object. If the desired object is not in the list, return an empty list.

9. Repeat the previous exercise for a sorted array. Your algorithm should be recursive and efficient.

10. Assume a linked implementation of the ADT sorted list.

    a. Implement the method `contains` that calls a private method to perform binary search.
    b. Revise this private method to search for duplicate entries.

11. Consider the number $f(n)$ of comparisons that a binary search makes in the worst case.

    a. Write a recurrence relation for $f(n)$.
    b. Prove by induction on $n$ that $f(n) = n$.

**12.** At the end of Segment 18.3, Question 2 asked you to write a method that performs an iterative sequential search of a list by using only operations of the ADT list. Compare the time efficiency of this method with the ADT operation `contains`.

**13.** In Segment 18.7, we said that a sequential search of an array will examine on average about half of the $n$ entries. Let's look a little more carefully at this computation. A sequential search is either successful or not. Let $\alpha$ be the probability that we will find the desired value in the array and $1 - \alpha$ be the probability that we will not. We further assume that the value, if found, is equally likely to be in each of the locations of the array. We need to consider each possibility.

For each case, we count the comparisons and determine its probability of occurrence. To find the average number of comparisons made by the search, we first multiply each probability by the number of comparisons in each case. The following table summarizes these results:

|  | Probability | Number of Comparisons | Product |
|---|---|---|---|
| Found at index 0 | $\alpha/n$ | 1 | $\alpha/n$ |
| Found at index 1 | $\alpha/n$ | 2 | $2\alpha/n$ |
| Found at index 2 | $\alpha/n$ | 3 | $3\alpha/n$ |
| ... | ... | ... | ... |
| Found at index $n-2$ | $\alpha/n$ | $n-1$ | $(n-1)\alpha/n$ |
| Found at index $n-1$ | $\alpha/n$ | $n$ | $\alpha$ |
| Not found | $1-\alpha$ | $n$ | $(1-\alpha)n$ |

**a.** Compute the average number of comparisons by adding all the products in the last column of the table.
**b.** What is the average number of comparisons if the search is guaranteed to be successful ($\alpha = 1$)?
**c.** What is the average number of comparisons if the search is guaranteed to be unsuccessful ($\alpha = 0$)?
**d.** What is the average number of comparisons if the search is successful half of the time ($\alpha = 0.5$)?

**14.** Repeat Part $a$ of the previous exercise, but now assume that we are not equally likely to search for each value in the array. We could arrange the $n$ items in the array such that the ones we are more likely to search for occur first. Suppose that we search for the first item one half of the time, the second item one quarter of the time, the third item one eighth of the time, and so on. We will search for the last two items $1/2^{n-1}$ of the time. Revise the table in the previous exercise accordingly.

## PROJECTS

**1.** When an object does not occur in an array, a sequential search for it must examine the entire array. If the array is sorted, you can improve the search by using the approach described in Exercise 2. A **jump search** is an attempt to reduce the number of comparisons even further.

Instead of examining the $n$ objects in the array $a$ sequentially, you look at the elements $a[j]$, $a[2j]$, $a[3j]$, and so on, for some positive $j < n$. If the target $t$ is less than one of these objects, you need to search only the portion of the array between the current object and the previous object. For example, if $t$ is less than $a[3j]$ but is greater than $a[2j]$, you search the elements $a[2j+1]$, $a[2j+2]$, ..., $a[3j-1]$ by using the method in Exercise 2. What should you do when $t > a[k \times j]$, but $(k+1) \times j > n$?

Devise an algorithm for performing a jump search. Then, using $\lceil \sqrt{n} \rceil$ as the value of $j$, implement the jump search.

**2.** An **interpolation search** assumes that the data in an array is sorted and uniformly distributed. Whereas a binary search always looks at the middle item in an array, an interpolation search looks where the sought-for item is more likely to occur. For example, if you searched your telephone book for Victoria Appleseed, you probably would look near its beginning rather than its middle. And if you discovered many Appleseeds, you would look near the last Appleseed.

Instead of looking at the element a[mid] of an array a, as the binary search would, an interpolation search examines a[index], where

```
p = (desiredElement - a[first])/(a[last] - a[first])
index = first + [(last − first) × p]
```

Implement an interpolation search of an array. For particular arrays, compare the outcomes of an interpolation search and of a binary search. Consider arrays that have uniformly distributed entries and arrays that do not.

**3.** Suppose that you have numerical data stored in a two-dimensional array, such as the one in Figure 18-9. The data in each row and in each column is sorted in increasing order.

**a.** Devise an efficient search algorithm for an array of this type.
**b.** If the array has $m$ rows and $n$ columns, what is the Big Oh performance of your algorithm?
**c.** Implement and test your algorithm.

FIGURE 18-9   A two-dimensional array for Project 3

| 1 | 4 | 55 | 88 |
|---|---|----|----|
| 7 | 15 | 61 | 91 |
| 14 | 89 | 90 | 99 |

**4.** Consider an array data of $n$ numerical values in sorted order and a list of numerical target values. Your goal is to compute the smallest range of array indices that contains all of the target values. If a target value is smaller than data[0], the range should start with -1. If a target value is larger than data[n - 1], the range should end with $n$.

For example, given the array in Figure 18-10 and the target values (8, 2, 9, 17), the range is -1 to 5.

**a.** Devise an efficient algorithm that solves this problem.
**b.** If you have $n$ data values in the array and $m$ target values in the list, what is the Big Oh performance of your algorithm?
**c.** Implement and test your algorithm.

FIGURE 18-10   An array for Project 4

| 5 | 8 | 10 | 13 | 15 | 20 | 22 | 26 |
|---|---|----|----|----|----|----|----|
| 0 | 1 | 2 | 3 | 4 | 5 | 6 | 7 |

**5.** One way to organize a collection of words is to use an array of sorted lists. The array contains one sorted list for each letter of the alphabet. To add a word to this data structure, you add it to the sorted list that corresponds to the word's first letter. Design an ADT for such a collection, including the operations add and contains. Define a Java interface for your ADT. Then implement your interface as a class and test it. Use a text file of words to populate your data structure.

6 Write a program that reads a Java program from a text file and performs the following tasks.

    **a.** Display a list in alphabetical order of the unique Java keywords used in the program.

    **b.** Repeat Part *a*, but add the number of times each keyword occurs in the program.

    **c.** Repeat either Part *a* or Part *b*, but add the line number of each line that contains the keyword.

## ANSWERS TO SELF-TEST QUESTIONS

1.
```java
public static <T> int inArray(T[] anArray, T anEntry)
{
   boolean found = false;
   int result = -1;
   int index = 0;
   while (!found && (index < anArray.length))
   {
      if (anEntry.equals(anArray[index]))
      {
         found = true;
         result = index;
      } // end if
      index++;
   } // end while

   return result;
} // end contains
```

2.
```java
public static <T> boolean inList(AList<T> theList, T anEntry)
{
   boolean found = false;
   int length = theList.getLength();
   int position = 1;
   while (!found && (position <= length))
   {
      if (anEntry.equals(theList.getEntry(position)))
         found = true;
      position++;
   } // end while
   return found;
} // end inList
```

3. The object o is compared with o1, then o2, o3, o4, and o5.

4.
```java
public static <T> boolean inArray(AList<T> theList, T anEntry)
{
   return search(theList, 1, theList.getLength(), anEntry);
} // end inArray

private static <T> boolean search(AList<T> theList, int first, int last, T desiredItem)
{
   boolean found;

   if (first > last)
      found = false;
   else if (desiredItem.equals(theList.getEntry(first)))
      found = true;
   else
      found = search(theList, first + 1, last, desiredItem);
   return found;
} // end search
```

5. Searching for 8 requires seven comparisons, as follows:
8 == 10?
8 < 10?
8 == 5?
8 < 5?
8 == 7?
8 < 7?
8 == 8?

Searching for 16 requires eight comparisons, as follows:
16 == 10?
16 < 10?
16 == 18?
16 < 18?
16 == 12?
16 < 12?
16 == 15?
16 < 15?

6. a. 12 and 4.
   b. 12, 4, and 8.
   c. 12, 20, and 14.

7.
```java
public static <T extends Comparable<? super T>> int inArray(T[] anArray, T anEntry)
{
    return binarySearch(anArray, 0, anArray.length - 1, anEntry);
} // end contains

private static <T extends Comparable<? super T>> int binarySearch(T[] anArray, int first,
                                                                   int last, T desiredItem)
{
    int result;
    int mid = first + (last - first) / 2;

    if (first > last)
        result = -1;
    else if (desiredItem.equals(anArray[mid]))
        result = mid;
    else if (desiredItem.compareTo(anArray[mid]) < 0)
        result = binarySearch(anArray, first, mid - 1, desiredItem);
    else
        result = binarySearch(anArray, mid + 1, last, desiredItem);
    return result;
} // end binarySearch
```

8. In the second else if, change < to >.

9. 20 (log 1,000,000 rounded up).

# Generics Once Again

## Contents

More Than One Generic Type

## Prerequisites

$T$his brief interlude describes how to define and use more than one generic data type within a class or interface. This topic is essential to our discussion of the ADT dictionary, which we begin in the next chapter.

## More Than One Generic Type

**JI8.1**  Recall the class `OrderedPair` in Listing JI1-2 of Java Interlude 1:

```java
public class OrderedPair<T> implements Pairable<T>
{
    private T first, second;

    < The constructor and the methods getFirst, getSecond, toString, and changeOrder
      are here. >
    . . .
} // end OrderedPair
```

VideoNote
Multitype generics

The two paired objects in an instance of `OrderedPair` have either the same data type or data types related by inheritance. For example, the following statement pairs two strings by creating an object of `OrderedPair`:

```java
OrderedPair<String> fruit = new OrderedPair<>("apples", "oranges");
```

**JI8.2**  You can define more than one generic type within a class definition by writing their identifiers, separated by commas, within the angle brackets after the class's name, as in the class `Pair` shown in Listing JI8-1. In this example, `S` and `T` are the generic data types. Each one represents an actual data type that is specified by the client when it instantiates an object of the class.

```
LISTING JI8-1   The class Pair
1  public class Pair<S, T>
2  {
3     private S first;
4     private T second;
5
6     public Pair(S firstItem, T secondItem)
7     {
8        first = firstItem;
9        second = secondItem;
10    } // end constructor
11
12    public String toString()
13    {
14       return "(" + first + ", " + second + ")";
15    } // end toString
16 } // end Pair
```

For example, you can use the class `Pair` to pair a name and a telephone number by writing the following statements, where the class `Name` is given in Listing C-1 of Appendix C:

```
Name joe = new Name("Joe", "Java");
String joePhone = "(401) 555-1234";
Pair<Name, String> joeEntry = new Pair<>(joe, joePhone);
System.out.println(joeEntry);
```

The output displayed is

```
(Joe Java, (401) 555-1234)
```

**Question 1** Can you use the class `OrderedPair`, as defined in Listing JI1-2, to pair two objects having different and unrelated data types? Why or why not?

**Question 2** Can you use the class `Pair`, as defined in the previous segment, to pair two objects having the same data type? Why or why not?

**Question 3** Using the class `Name`, as defined in Appendix C, write statements that pair two students as lab partners.

**Question 4** Using the class `Name`, as defined in Appendix C, write statements that pair your name with the random sequence number given in the `int` variable `number`.

### Answers to Self-Test Questions

1. No. The class defines only one generic type.

2. Yes. You can write the same data type twice to correspond to both `S` and `T`.

3. 
```
Name kristen = new Name("Kristen", "Doe");
Name luci = new Name("Luci", "Lei");
OrderedPair<Name> labPartners = new OrderedPair<>(kristen, luci);
```

4. 
```
Name kristen = new Name("Kristen", "Doe");
Integer seqN = number;
Pair<Name, Integer> aPair = new Pair<>(kristen, seqN);
```

# Dictionaries

## Contents

## Prerequisites

## Objectives

After studying this chapter, you should be able to

- Describe the operations of the ADT dictionary
- Distinguish between a dictionary and a list
- Use a dictionary in a program

If you need to check the meaning of a word, you look it up in a dictionary. If you need a friend's address, you consult your address book. If you need someone's telephone number, you check your list of contacts on your cell phone, use a telephone directory, or search for it online.

Each of these examples involves a kind of dictionary. This chapter describes and uses an abstract data type that generalizes our everyday notion of a dictionary. Subsequent chapters will examine implementations of this ADT.

The previous examples—finding a word's definition, a friend's address, or someone's telephone number—are all examples of searching a dictionary. Chapter 18 examined how to search an array, a chain of linked nodes, and ultimately a list. You will see that a dictionary provides a more powerful way to organize searchable data than a list.

## Specifications for the ADT Dictionary

**19.1**   The ADT **dictionary**—also called a **map**, **table**, or **associative array**—contains entries that each have two parts:

- A keyword—usually called a **search key**—such as an English word or a person's name
- A value—such as a definition, an address, or a telephone number—associated with that key

**VideoNote**
**The ADT dictionary**

The search key enables you to locate the desired entry.

Figure 19-1 illustrates an everyday English dictionary. Each entry has a word as the search key and the word's definition as the value associated with the key. In general, the search keys and values in an ADT dictionary are objects, as shown in Figure 19-2. Each search key is paired with a corresponding value.

The ADT dictionary organizes and identifies its entries by their search keys, rather than by another criterion such as position. Thus, you can retrieve or remove an entry from a dictionary given only the entry's search key. The fact that every entry in a dictionary has a search key distinguishes the dictionary from other ADTs such as a list. Although you certainly could put an entry that has a search key in a list, a list's data is organized by position, not by search key.

**FIGURE 19-1**    An English dictionary

**computer** A device for the processing and storage of information.

FIGURE 19-2    An instance of the ADT dictionary has search keys paired
with corresponding values

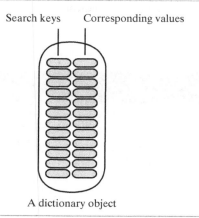

Some dictionaries have distinct search keys, but others allow two or more entries to have the same search key. For example, a dictionary of student records organized by student identification number has distinct search keys, since those numbers are unique. On the other hand, an English-language dictionary has duplicate search keys, since it often has several meanings for a word. For example, my dictionary has three entries for the word "book": One is a noun, one is a verb, and one is an adjective.

Printed versions of a natural-language dictionary, a telephone directory, a library catalog, and a thesaurus all have entries sorted by their search keys. These databases are dictionaries, but the ADT dictionary does not require sorted entries. Some dictionaries do sort their entries by search key, while other dictionaries have unsorted entries. Why do our examples of printed dictionaries sort their entries? Because sorting makes it easier for the reader to find a particular entry. In contrast, if you searched a computerized thesaurus for a word, you would not be aware of the order of its entries. Nor would you care, as long as you could retrieve a particular entry. Thus, whether a dictionary has sorted or unsorted search keys is more of an implementation detail than a necessary characteristic of the dictionary. But remember that the details of any implementation affect the efficiencies of the ADT operations in various ways.

**19.2**    The ADT dictionary has the same major operations—insert, delete, retrieve, search, and traverse—that are common to most databases and other ADTs, even if a particular implementation sorts its entries or allows duplicate search keys. In particular, these operations are

- Add a new entry to the dictionary, given a search key and associated value
- Remove an entry, given its associated search key
- Retrieve a value associated with a given search key
- See whether the dictionary contains a given search key
- Traverse all the search keys in the dictionary
- Traverse all the values in the dictionary

In addition, the ADT dictionary has the following basic operations that are often included in an ADT:

- Detect whether a dictionary is empty
- Get the number of entries in the dictionary
- Remove all entries from the dictionary

**Note:** The ADT dictionary contains entries that are key-value pairs organized by their search keys. You can add a new entry, and you can locate, retrieve, or remove an entry, given its search key. In addition, you can traverse a dictionary's search keys or values.

The following specifications define a set of possible operations for the ADT dictionary:

---

### ABSTRACT DATA TYPE: DICTIONARY

**DATA**

- A collection of pairs $(k, v)$ of objects $k$ and $v$, where $k$ is the search key and $v$ is the corresponding value
- The number of pairs in the collection

**OPERATIONS**

| PSEUDOCODE | UML | DESCRIPTION |
|---|---|---|
| add(key, value) | +add(key : K, value : V) : void | Task: Adds the pair (key, value) to the dictionary.<br>Input: key is an object search key, value is an associated object.<br>Output: None. |
| remove(key) | +remove(key : K) : V | Task: Removes from the dictionary the entry that corresponds to a given search key.<br>Input: key is an object search key.<br>Output: Returns either the value that was associated with the search key or null if no such object exists. |
| getValue(key) | +getValue(key : K) : V | Task: Retrieves from the dictionary the value that corresponds to a given search key.<br>Input: key is an object search key.<br>Output: Returns either the value associated with the search key or null if no such object exists. |
| contains(key) | +contains(key : K) : boolean | Task: Sees whether any entry in the dictionary has a given search key.<br>Input: key is an object search key.<br>Output: Returns true if an entry in the dictionary has key as its search key. |
| getKeyIterator() | +getKeyIterator() : Iterator<K> | Task: Creates an iterator that traverses all search keys in the dictionary.<br>Input: None.<br>Output: Returns an iterator that provides sequential access to the search keys in the dictionary. |

| | | |
|---|---|---|
| getValueIterator() | +getValueIterator() : Iterator<V> | Task: Creates an iterator that traverses all values in the dictionary.<br>Input: None.<br>Output: Returns an iterator that provides sequential access to the values in the dictionary. |
| isEmpty() | +isEmpty() : boolean | Task: Sees whether the dictionary is empty.<br>Input: None.<br>Output: Returns true if the dictionary is empty. |
| getSize() | +getSize() : integer | Task: Gets the size of the dictionary.<br>Input: None.<br>Output: Returns the number of entries (key-value pairs) currently in the dictionary. |
| clear() | +clear() : void | Task: Removes all entries from the dictionary.<br>Input: None.<br>Output: None. |

 **Note:** So far, most of our ADTs have permitted null entries. The ADT list, for example, is position based, and so a null entry could serve as a placeholder for an item that will be either inserted later or left empty. With this approach, the positions of the other entries in the list will not change. For instance, suppose that 20 horses enter a race and are assigned post positions 1 through 20. If one horse fails to enter the starting gate and is disqualified, the other horses do not change positions. In a similar manner, stacks, queues and deques can have null values that act as placeholders in time.

A dictionary is quite different from a position-based ADT. It stores key-value pairs. If a key has no value associated with it, it would not appear in the dictionary. That is, we do not store a key-null pair. Finding such a pair would have the same meaning as not finding the key at all: The key has no associated value. Because we disallow key-null pairs, the dictionary methods remove and getValue are free to return null to signal the failure of finding a given search key. The Design Decisions in Segment 5.2 of Chapter 5 and Segment 10.19 of Chapter 10 discuss the use of null in these situations.

**19.3** **Refining the specifications.** Even though all dictionaries can have this common set of operations, you do need to refine some of the specifications according to whether a dictionary's search keys are distinct:

- **Distinct search keys.** The method add can ensure that the search keys in a dictionary are distinct. If key is already in the dictionary, the operation add(key, value) could either refuse to add another key-value entry or change the existing value associated with key to value. In the latter case, the method could return the old replaced value instead of not having an output, as indicated earlier.

    Regardless of how add guarantees distinct search keys, the remaining methods can have simpler implementations than if duplicate search keys are allowed. For example, the methods remove and getValue will either find the one value associated with a given search key or discover that no such entry exists.

- **Duplicate search keys.** If the method add adds every given key-value entry to a dictionary, the methods remove and getValue must deal with multiple entries that have the same search key. Which entry should be removed or returned? The method remove could either remove the first value it finds or remove all values associated with the given search key. If getValue returns an object, it could return the first value it finds. Or you could modify getValue to return a list of values, for example.

    Another possibility is to have a secondary search key that is used only when several entries have the same primary search key. For example, if you call directory assistance for a common name like John Smith, you most certainly will be asked for John's address.

For simplicity, we will assume distinct search keys and consider duplicate search keys in the exercises and projects at the end of this chapter.

## A Java Interface

**19.4**    Listing 19-1 contains a Java interface for the ADT dictionary that specifies distinct search keys. The add method replaces the value associated with any search key that is already in the dictionary. Note that this method is not a void method as indicated in our initial specifications.

Like the interfaces for the ADTs list and sorted list, this interface specifies the data type of its entries generically. Since the search keys can have a data type that differs from the type of the associated values, we use two generic type parameters, K and V. K represents the data type of the search keys, and V is the type of the associated values.

**LISTING 19-1    An interface for the ADT dictionary**

```java
1  import java.util.Iterator;
2  /**
3      An interface for a dictionary with distinct search keys.
4      @author Frank M. Carrano
5  */
6  public interface DictionaryInterface<K, V>
7  {
8      /** Adds a new entry to this dictionary. If the given search key already
9          exists in the dictionary, replaces the corresponding value.
10         @param key    An object search key of the new entry.
11         @param value  An object associated with the search key.
12         @return   Either null if the new entry was added to the dictionary
13                   or the value that was associated with key if that value
14                   was replaced. */
15     public V add(K key, V value);
16
17     /** Removes a specific entry from this dictionary.
18         @param key  An object search key of the entry to be removed.
19         @return   Either the value that was associated with the search key
20                   or null if no such object exists. */
21     public V remove(K key);
22
23     /** Retrieves from this dictionary the value associated with a given
24         search key.
25         @param key  An object search key of the entry to be retrieved.
26         @return   Either the value that is associated with the search key
27                   or null if no such object exists. */
28     public V getValue(K key);
29
30     /** Sees whether a specific entry is in this dictionary.
31         @param key  An object search key of the desired entry.
32         @return   True if key is associated with an entry in the dictionary. */
33     public boolean contains(K key);
```

```
34
35     /** Creates an iterator that traverses all search keys in this dictionary.
36         @return  An iterator that provides sequential access to the search
37                  keys in the dictionary. */
38     public Iterator<K> getKeyIterator();
39
40     /** Creates an iterator that traverses all values in this dictionary.
41         @return  An iterator that provides sequential access to the values
42                  in this dictionary. */
43     public Iterator<V> getValueIterator();
44
45     /** Sees whether this dictionary is empty.
46         @return  True if the dictionary is empty. */
47     public boolean isEmpty();
48
49     /** Gets the size of this dictionary.
50         @return  The number of entries (key-value pairs) currently
51                  in the dictionary. */
52     public int getSize();
53
54     /** Removes all entries from this dictionary. */
55     public void clear();
56 } // end DictionaryInterface
```

**19.5**   Let's see how to create an instance of a class `Dictionary` that implements `DictionaryInterface`. This dictionary will contain data about the students at your school. Assume that student numbers are the search keys and that we have the class `Student` to represent the student data. The following statement creates the instance `dataBase`:

```
DictionaryInterface<String, Student> dataBase = new Dictionary<>();
```

`String` corresponds to the parameter `K` in `DictionaryInterface`, so each occurrence of `K` in the interface is replaced by `String`. Similarly, `Student` replaces every occurrence of `V` in the interface. The same correspondence occurs between these actual types and the generic types of the class `Dictionary`.

We will examine several examples of dictionaries in more detail later in this chapter.

## Iterators

**19.6**   The methods `getKeyIterator` and `getValueIterator` each return an iterator that conforms to the interface `java.util.Iterator` that we discussed in Java Interlude 5. You can create iterators for the dictionary `dataBase` that we instantiated in the previous segment by writing

```
Iterator<String> keyIterator = dataBase.getKeyIterator();
Iterator<Student> valueIterator = dataBase.getValueIterator();
```

Recall that `Iterator` specifies a generic type in its definition. Here we have defined an iterator for the `String` search keys and another for the `Student` values.

You can use each of these iterators either separately or together. That is, you can traverse

- All of the search keys in a dictionary without traversing the values
- All of the values without traversing the search keys
- All the search keys and all the values in parallel

In the last case, the $i^{th}$ search key returned by keyIterator corresponds to the $i^{th}$ dictionary value returned by valueIterator, as Figure 19-3 illustrates. Clearly, the two iterations have the same length, since the number of search keys in a dictionary must be the same as the number of values.

**FIGURE 19-3**     Two iterators that traverse a dictionary's keys and values in parallel

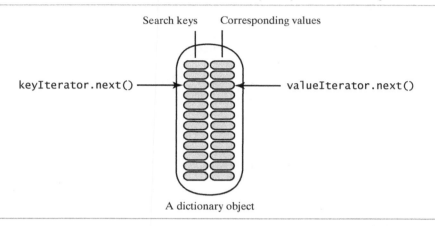

The following loop displays each entry in the dictionary as a key-value pair:

```java
while (keyIterator.hasNext())
    System.out.println(keyIterator.next() + ", " + valueIterator.next());
```

For a sorted dictionary, keyIterator traverses the search keys in sorted order. For an unsorted dictionary, this traversal order is not specified. The examples in the next section demonstrate these iterators in several contexts.

 **Note:** An iteration of a dictionary's values corresponds to an iteration of its search keys. That is, the $i^{th}$ value in one iteration is associated in the dictionary with the $i^{th}$ search key in the second iteration.

 **Question 1** If the class Dictionary implements DictionaryInterface, write a Java statement that creates an empty dictionary myDictionary. This dictionary will contain the names and telephone numbers of your friends. Assume that the names are the search keys, and you have the class Name to represent them. Let each telephone number be a string.

**Question 2** Write a Java statement that adds your name and telephone number to the dictionary that you created in Question 1.

**Question 3** Write Java statements that display either Britney Storm's telephone number, if she is in the dictionary described in Question 1, or an error message if she is not.

## Using the ADT Dictionary

The three examples in this section demonstrate how to use the ADT dictionary in a program. We begin by creating a telephone directory.

VideoNote
**Using the ADT dictionary**

## A Problem Solved: A Directory of Telephone Numbers

A telephone directory contains the names and telephone numbers of the people who live in a given geographical region. Implement software that defines such a directory.

**19.7**   The most frequent operation performed on a telephone directory is the retrieval of a telephone number, given a person's name. Thus, using the ADT dictionary to represent a telephone directory is a good choice. Clearly, the name should be the search key, and the telephone number should be the corresponding value. Often, but not always, retrieval is more efficient when the dictionary is sorted. Additionally, a sorted dictionary would make it easier to create a printed directory with entries alphabetized by name. To simplify this example, we assume that the directory will contain distinct names with no duplicates.

A major task, at least initially, is to create the directory from the available names and telephone numbers. Having this data in a text file will make this task convenient. After the telephone directory is created, operations on the directory, such as adding an entry, removing an entry, or changing a telephone number, will be used less often than searching for a given name. Traversing the directory is important to create either a hard copy or a text file of the data, but this operation too is not done frequently. As we noted in Chapter 4, you should choose an implementation of an ADT based on the efficiency of its expected use.

**19.8**   **Design and use of the class TelephoneDirectory.** Our next step is to design a class to represent the telephone directory. A sorted dictionary will represent the data, which consists of name-number pairs. Each person's name can be an instance of the class Name that we first encountered in Appendix C, and the telephone number can be a string without embedded blanks. Figure 19-4 shows a class diagram for our design. The class TelephoneDirectory contains an instance phoneBook of a dictionary. The class has the method readFile, which reads the data from the file and adds it to phoneBook. It also has the method getPhoneNumber to retrieve a telephone number, given a name. For simplicity, we are ignoring any other operations mentioned in the previous segment.

FIGURE 19-4    A class diagram for a telephone directory

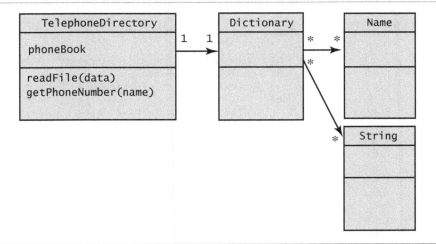

Before we implement the class TelephoneDirectory, let's consider its use. A client would create an instance of TelephoneDirectory and read the data file by invoking the method readFile.

The first two highlighted lines in the main method of Listing 19-2 perform these steps. Given the name data.txt of the text file, main creates a scanner for the file and passes it to readFile. Note the exception that might occur in creating the scanner. If you need more information about either exceptions or files, consult Java Interlude 2 and Appendix E, respectively.

After the file is read, main interacts with the user via the private method getName. Each name read from the user is passed to the method getPhoneNumber, where it will be the key in a search of the telephone directory. Notice how getName uses Scanner to both read the user's input and then process it.

LISTING 19-2    A client of the class TelephoneDirectory

```java
import java.util.Scanner;
import java.io.File;
import java.io.FileNotFoundException;
public class Driver
{
   private static final Name INPUT_ERROR = new Name("error", "error");
   private static final Name QUIT = new Name("quit", "quit");

   public static void main(String[] args)
   {
      TelephoneDirectory directory = new TelephoneDirectory();
      String fileName = "data.txt"; // Or file name could be read

      try
      {
         Scanner data = new Scanner(new File(fileName));
         directory.readFile(data);
      }
      catch (FileNotFoundException e)
      {
         System.out.println("File not found: " + e.getMessage());
      }

      Name nextName = getName();    // Get name for search from user
      while (!nextName.equals(QUIT))
      {
         if (nextName.equals(INPUT_ERROR))
            System.out.println("Error in entering name. Try again.");
         else
         {
            String phoneNumber = directory.getPhoneNumber(nextName);
            if (phoneNumber == null)
               System.out.println(nextName + "  is not in the directory.");
            else
               System.out.println("The phone number for " + nextName +
                                  " is " + phoneNumber);
         } // end if

         nextName = getName();
      } // end while
      System.out.println("Bye!");
   } // end main

   // Returns either the name read from user, INPUT_ERROR, or QUIT.
   private static Name getName()
   {
      Name result = null;
      Scanner keyboard = new Scanner(System.in);
```

```
49
50        System.out.print("Enter first name and last name, " +
51                          "or quit to end: ");
52        String line = keyboard.nextLine();
53
54        if (line.trim().toLowerCase().equals("quit"))
55           result = QUIT;
56        else
57        {
58           String firstName = null;
59           String lastName = null;
60           Scanner scan = new Scanner(line);
61
62           if (scan.hasNext())
63           {
64              firstName = scan.next();
65              if (scan.hasNext())
66                 lastName = scan.next();
67              else
68                 result = INPUT_ERROR;
69           }
70           else
71              result = INPUT_ERROR;
72
73           if (result == null)
74              // First and last names have been read
75              result = new Name(firstName, lastName);
76        } // end if
77
78        return result;
79     } // end getName
80  } // end Driver
```

**Output**

```
Enter first name and last name or quit to end: Maria Lopez
The phone number for Maria Lopez is 401-555-1234
Enter first name and last name or quit to end: Hunter
Error in entering name. Try again.
Enter first name and last name or quit to end: Hunter Smith
Hunter Smith is not in the directory.
Enter first name and last name or quit to end: quit
Bye!
```

**19.9** **Beginning the implementation.** The class `TelephoneDirectory` begins as shown in Listing 19-3. We assume that the class `SortedDictionary` implements a sorted version of the ADT dictionary having distinct search keys. A sorted dictionary requires its search keys to belong to a class that implements the interface `Comparable`. We assume that `Name` does so.

LISTING 19-3    An outline of the class `TelephoneDirectory`

```
1  import java.util.Iterator;
2  import java.util.Scanner;
3  public class TelephoneDirectory
4  {
5     private DictionaryInterface<Name, String> phoneBook;
6
```

```
7     public TelephoneDirectory()
8     {
9        phoneBook = new SortedDictionary<>();
10    } // end default constructor
11
12    /** Reads a text file of names and telephone numbers.
13        @param data   A text scanner for the text file of data. */
14    public void readFile(Scanner data)
15    {
16
17       . . . < See Segment 19.10. >
18
19    } // end readFile
20
21    /** Gets the phone number of a given person. */
22    public String getPhoneNumber(Name personName)
23    {
24
25       . . . < See Segment 19.11. >
26
27    } // end getPhoneNumber
28    . . .
```

**19.10**    To implement the method `readFile`, you need to know what the data file looks like. Suppose that each line in the file contains three strings—a first name, a last name, and a telephone number—separated by blanks. Thus, a typical line might appear as

Suzanne Nouveaux 401-555-1234

The method `readFile` must read each of these strings. Recall that the `main` method in Listing 19-2 in Segment 19.8 creates a scanner for the file and passes it to `readFile`. Using `Scanner`'s method `next`, `readFile` can read each string in a line of data and assign them, respectively, to the variables `firstName`, `lastName`, and `phoneNumber`. The following Java statements, then, will add the desired entry to the dictionary `phoneBook`:

```
Name fullName = new Name(firstName, lastName);
phoneBook.add(fullName, phoneNumber);
```

We assume that the text file contains distinct names.

Here is the definition of `readFile`:

```
public void readFile(Scanner data)
{
   while (data.hasNext())
   {
      String firstName   = data.next();
      String lastName    = data.next();
      String phoneNumber = data.next();

      Name fullName = new Name(firstName, lastName);
      phoneBook.add(fullName, phoneNumber);
   } // end while

   data.close();
} // end readFile
```

Using `Scanner`'s methods `hasNext` and `next`, we extract each name and telephone number as strings from the text file. Then, using the two statements we examined earlier, we create a `Name` object and add it and the telephone number to the dictionary.

**Programming Tip: java.util.Scanner**
The class Scanner enables you to break a string into substrings, or **tokens**, that are separated by characters called **delimiters**. By default, white-space characters are the delimiters. You pass to Scanner's constructor either the string to be **parsed** or a text file represented as an instance of the class java.io.File.

The following methods in the class Scanner enable you to extract the tokens from any string:

```
public String next();
public boolean hasNext();
```

Appendix B discusses Scanner in more detail, beginning at Segment B.81.

---

**Question 4** Although the statement

```
directory.readFile(data);
```

is inside a try block near the beginning of the method main in Listing 19-2, it need not be. Explain its present location, why it can appear outside of a try block, and what you can do to move it.

---

**19.11** **A method that searches.** The class TelephoneDirectory has a method to find a person's telephone number. This method needs the person's name, and the user must supply it. If we assume that the client will interact with the user and provide the desired name to the method—as does the client in Listing 19-2—we could define the method as follows:

```
public String getPhoneNumber(Name personName)
{
    return phoneBook.getValue(personName);
} // end getPhoneNumber
```

The method either returns a string that contains the desired telephone number or returns null if the number is not found.

We could define a similar method instead of or in addition to the previous method, as follows:

```
public String getPhoneNumber(String firstName, String lastName)
{
    Name fullName = new Name(firstName, lastName);
    return phoneBook.getValue(fullName);
} // end getPhoneNumber
```

Additional methods to add or remove a person or to change a person's telephone number are straightforward and are left as exercises.

---

**Question 5** Implement a method for the class TelephoneDirectory that removes an entry from the directory. Given the person's name, the method should return either the person's telephone number or null if the person is not in the directory.

**Question 6** Implement a method for the class TelephoneDirectory that changes a person's telephone number. Given the person's name, the method should return either the person's old telephone number or null if the person was not in the directory but has been added to it.

---

## A Problem Solved: The Frequency of Words

 Some word processors provide a count of the number of times each word occurs in a document. Create a class FrequencyCounter that provides this capability.

**19.12** This class is somewhat like the one in the previous example, so we will omit some of the design details. Basically, the class needs to count each occurrence of a word as it reads the document from a text file. It then needs to display the results. For example, if the text file contains

row, row, row your boat

the desired output would be

    boat 1
    row   3
    your 1

The class will have a constructor and the methods readFile and display. As in the previous example, readFile will read the input text from a file. Then display will write the output. Listing 19-4 shows a client of FrequencyCounter. It is similar to the beginning of the client in the previous example.

---

**LISTING 19-4    A client of the class FrequencyCounter**

```
1  import java.util.Scanner;
2  import java.io.File;
3  import java.io.FileNotFoundException;
4
5  public class Driver
6  {
7     public static void main(String[] args)
8     {
9        FrequencyCounter wordCounter = new FrequencyCounter();
10       String fileName = "Data.txt"; // Or file name could be read
11
12       try
13       {
14          Scanner data = new Scanner(new File(fileName));
15          wordCounter.readFile(data);
16       }
17       catch (FileNotFoundException e)
18       {
19          System.out.println("File not found: " + e.getMessage());
20       }
21
22       wordCounter.display();
23    } // end main
24 } // end Driver
```

**Output**

    boat 1
    row   3
    your 1

**19.13**   Is the ADT dictionary the right one to use for this problem? A word and its frequency of occurrence in the document form a pair that is suitable as an entry in a dictionary. If we want to know a given word's frequency, the word should be the search key. Also, the words in the dictionary must be distinct, and if they are sorted, we can display them in alphabetical order. Thus, a sorted dictionary with distinct search keys is an appropriate choice for this problem. As in the previous example, we assume SortedDictionary is such an implementation.

The dictionary will be a data field of a new class FrequencyCounter, which will begin much like the class TelephoneDirectory in the previous example. Let's call the dictionary for this example wordTable. Since the value portion of any dictionary entry is an object, we use the wrapper class Integer to represent each frequency. Thus, our class can begin as shown in Listing 19-5.

---

**LISTING 19-5      An outline of the class FrequencyCounter**

```
1  import java.util.Iterator;
2  import java.util.Scanner;
3  public class FrequencyCounter
4  {
5     private DictionaryInterface<String, Integer> wordTable;
6
7     public FrequencyCounter()
8     {
9        wordTable = new SortedDictionary<>();
10    } // end default constructor
11
12    /** Reads a text file of words; counts their frequencies of occurrence.
13        @param data  A text scanner for the text file of data. */
14    public void readFile(Scanner data)
15    {
16
17       . . . < See Segment 19.16. >
18
19    } // end readFile
20
21    /** Displays words and their frequencies of occurrence. */
22    public void display()
23    {
24
25       . . . < See Segment 19.17. >
26
27    } // end display
28 } // end FrequencyCounter
```

---

**19.14   Creating the dictionary.** Now let's look at the method readFile, which creates the dictionary from the text file. We invoke this method as we did earlier in Listing 19-4 of Segment 19.12. That is, the client passes to readFile a Scanner object associated with the text file. The method then can process the text file by using the Scanner methods hasNext and next, in the same way that readFile processed the file in Segment 19.10.

After extracting the next word from the file, readFile checks whether the word is in the dictionary. If it is not, we add it with an associated value of 1. That is, this word has occurred once so far. However, if the word is in the dictionary already, we retrieve its associated value—its count—increment it, and store it back into the dictionary. To avoid issues of case, readFile can change all the words it reads to lowercase.

**19.15**   **Delimiters.** The programming tip at the end of Segment 19.10 mentioned that, by default, Scanner uses white-space characters as delimiters. But as in the example given in Segment 19.12, our data can contain punctuation, so those characters must also be delimiters. You can use the Scanner method useDelimiter to specify the delimiters. You represent them by using the notation shown in Figure B-6 of Appendix B. (See Segment B.83.) You then pass a string of the delimiters to useDelimiter.

The simplest way to specify white space and punctuation as delimiters is to use the notation \W, since it represents any character other than a letter, digit, or underscore. We then write useDelimiter's argument as "\\W+". Remember that we must duplicate the backslash to distinguish the notation from an escape character. The plus sign means *one or more occurrences of.* Thus, the statement

```
dataFile.useDelimiter("\\W+");
```

sets the delimiters to one or more occurrences of punctuation, white-space characters, and some other characters that will not occur in our data.

 **Programming Tip:**  When using a Scanner object to process text, any character can be a delimiter if it does not occur in any desired token. You create a string of these delimiters using a special notation and give it to the Scanner method useDelimiter. Consult Segment B.82 of Appendix B for more details.

**19.16**   The following implementation of the method readFile reflects the previous discussion:

```
/** Reads a text file of words and counts their frequencies of occurrence.
    @param data   A text scanner for the text file of data. */
public void readFile(Scanner data)
{
   data.useDelimiter("\\W+");
   while (data.hasNext())
   {
      String nextWord = data.next();
      nextWord = nextWord.toLowerCase();
      Integer frequency = wordTable.getValue(nextWord);

      if (frequency == null)
      {  // Add new word to table
         wordTable.add(nextWord, new Integer(1));
      }
      else
      {  // Increment count of existing word; replace wordTable entry
         frequency++;
         wordTable.add(nextWord, frequency);
      } // end if
   } // end while

   data.close();
} // end readFile
```

 **Question 7** The previous method readFile does not call contains to see whether a word is already in the dictionary, but instead calls getValue. Why did we do this?

19.17    **Displaying the dictionary.** Now that we have created the dictionary, we need to display the results. An iteration of the search keys will produce the words in alphabetical order. A parallel iteration of the values provides the corresponding frequencies. The following method is a possible solution for this task:

```
public void display()
{
    Iterator<String>  keyIterator = wordTable.getKeyIterator();
    Iterator<Integer> valueIterator = wordTable.getValueIterator();

    while (keyIterator.hasNext())
    {
        System.out.println(keyIterator.next() + "  " + valueIterator.next());
    } // end while
} // end display
```

**Question 8**  Implement a second method display for the class FrequencyCounter that displays only words that occur with a frequency given as the method's sole parameter.

## A Problem Solved: A Concordance of Words

An *index* provides a way to locate the occurrence of certain words within a larger document. For example, the index to this book is an alphabetical listing of words paired with the page numbers on which the words occur. For this problem, we will create a simpler kind of index—called a *concordance*—to all the words in a text file. Instead of page numbers, a concordance provides the line numbers that contain a particular word.

19.18    Let's begin by looking at an example of a concordance. Suppose that a text file contains only these lines:

Learning without thought is labor lost;
thought without learning is perilous.

The following concordance of all the words in the file indicates the line numbers in which the words occur:

is 1 2
labor 1
learning 1 2
lost 1
perilous 2
thought 1 2
without 1 2

Although a word can appear in several lines of the file, it appears only once in the concordance. Like the previous word-frequency example, this feature of the concordance suggests that we use a dictionary whose search keys are the words in the concordance. But unlike the word-frequency example, the value associated with each of these words is a list of line numbers. Since the line numbers are sorted, we could use the ADT sorted list. However, by processing the lines in the file in order, we can add the line numbers to the end of an ordinary unsorted list and achieve a sorted order.

**19.19**   A class `Concordance` to represent the concordance and the class `FrequencyCounter` from the previous example are quite similar in their design and implementation. In fact, the use of these classes is virtually identical. By replacing `FrequencyCounter` with `Concordance` in Listing 19-4, you will have a client for `Concordance`.

Listing 19-6 contains an outline of the class `Concordance`. Note the similarities to the outline of `FrequencyCounter` given in Listing 19-5 of Segment 19.13. The major difference, other than the implementations of the methods, is the data type of the value of each dictionary entry. Since the value is a list of `Integer` objects, and since we will want to traverse each list to display the line numbers, we give the value a data type of `ListWithIteratorInterface<Integer>`. Segment 15.8 of Chapter 15 defined this interface as having the methods `iterator` and `getIterator` as well as the methods of `ListInterface`.

---

**LISTING 19-6**      An outline of the class Concordance

```
1  import java.util.Iterator;
2  import java.util.Scanner;
3
4  public class Concordance
5  {
6     private DictionaryInterface<String, ListWithIteratorInterface<Integer>>
7                                                            wordTable;
8
9     public Concordance()
10    {
11       wordTable = new SortedDictionary<>();
12    } // end default constructor
13
14    /** Reads a text file of words and creates a concordance.
15        @param data  A text scanner for the text file of data. */
16    public void readFile(Scanner data)
17    {
18
19       . . . < See Segment 19.20. >
20
21    } // end readFile
22
23    /** Displays words and the lines in which they occur. */
24    public void display()
25    {
26
27       . . . < See Segment 19.21. >
28
29    } // end display
30 } // end Concordance
```

---

**19.20**   **The method readFile.** The method `readFile` reads the text file and uses the dictionary `wordTable` to create the concordance. Since we must record the line number of each word, we read the file a line at a time. We process all the words in a line before moving on to the next line. Thus, the following definition of `readFile` contains two loops that are nested. The outer loop reads lines from the file using the `Scanner` object that was passed as an argument. The inner loop uses another scanner to extract the words from a line as soon as it is read. The class `LinkedListWithIterator` from Segment 15.9 of Chapter 15 is used to form each list of line numbers.

```
public void readFile(Scanner data)
{
    int lineNumber = 1;
    while (data.hasNext())
    {
        String line = data.nextLine();
        line = line.toLowerCase();

        Scanner lineProcessor = new Scanner(line);
        lineProcessor.useDelimiter("\\W+");
        while (lineProcessor.hasNext())
        {
            String nextWord = lineProcessor.next();
            ListWithIteratorInterface<Integer> lineList =
                                    wordTable.getValue(nextWord);

            if (lineList == null)
            { // Create new list for new word; add list and word to index
                lineList = new LinkedListWithIterator<>();
                wordTable.add(nextWord, lineList);
            } // end if

            // Add line number to end of list so list is sorted
            lineList.add(lineNumber);
        } // end while

        lineNumber++;
    } // end while
    data.close();
} // end readFile
```

The most interesting part of this method is the list of line numbers as the value associated with a search key. Since we have chosen a linked implementation of the list, we need to be concerned with the efficiency of adding to the end of the list. If the underlying chain of nodes has only a reference to the first node—as is true of LinkedListWithIterator—each such addition requires a traversal to reach the end of the chain. Choosing a list implementation that maintains a reference to the last node in the chain would make the addition to the end of the list quite efficient. We discussed such tail references at the beginning of Chapter 11. We should make this adjustment to our class of lists for this application.

19.21    **The method display.** Earlier, we chose a list implementation that included an iterator so that the following method display could display the line numbers in the concordance efficiently. Notice that we use the dictionary iterators, just as we did in the analogous method display given in Segment 19.17 for the previous example. But here each value is a list with its own iterator, which we use to traverse the list's line numbers.

```
public void display()
{
    Iterator<String> keyIterator = wordTable.getKeyIterator();
    Iterator<ListWithIteratorInterface<Integer>> valueIterator =
                                    wordTable.getValueIterator();

    while (keyIterator.hasNext())
    {
        // Display the word
        System.out.print(keyIterator.next() + "  ");

        // Get line numbers and iterator
        ListWithIteratorInterface<Integer> lineList = valueIterator.next();
        Iterator<Integer> listIterator = lineList.getIterator();
```

```
                         // Display line numbers
                         while (listIterator.hasNext())
                         {
                             System.out.print(listIterator.next() + "  ");
                         } // end while

                         System.out.println();
                     } // end while
                 } // end display
```

**Question 9** Write a method `getLineNumbers` for the class `Concordance` that returns a list of the numbers of the lines that contain a given word.

## Java Class Library: The Interface `Map`

**19.22**    The standard package `java.util` contains the interface `Map<K, V>` that is similar to our interface for the ADT dictionary. The following method headers are for a selection of methods in `Map` that are like the ones you have seen in this chapter. We have highlighted where they differ from our methods.

```
public V put(K key, V value);
public V remove (Object key);
public V get(Object key);
public boolean containsKey(Object key);
public boolean containsValue(Object value);
public Set<K> keySet();
public Collection<V> values();
public boolean isEmpty();
public int size();
public void clear();
```

Notice the differences in the names of the methods. `Map` uses the method names `put`, `get`, `containsKey`, and `size` instead of our names `add`, `getValue`, `contains`, and `getSize`. `Map` also has the additional method `containsValue` that finds out whether a dictionary contains a given value.

Instead of our methods `getKeyIterator` and `getValueIterator` that return iterators to a dictionary's keys and values, respectively, `Map` specifies the method `keySet`, which returns a set of keys, and the method `values`, which returns a collection of values. The Java Class Library contains the interfaces `Set` and `Collection`, and each of these interfaces has a method `iterator` that returns an iterator to the values in the corresponding ADT.

Duplicate search keys are not permitted in a dictionary that conforms to the `Map` interface. Each key must correspond to only one value. Also, some of `Map`'s methods use `Object` as the data type of the search key, whereas we use the more specific generic data type `K`.

## Chapter Summary

- The entries in the ADT dictionary each contain two parts: a search key and a value associated with that key. The dictionary identifies its entries by their search keys.

- An English dictionary, a directory of telephone numbers, an address book, and a library catalog are common examples of dictionaries.

- You can add an entry to a dictionary given its search key and value. You can retrieve or remove an entry given only its search key. By using an iterator, you can traverse all the keys or all the values in a dictionary.

- Dictionaries can organize their search keys in either sorted or unsorted order. The search keys can be either distinct or duplicate.

- Whether a dictionary has sorted or unsorted search keys is an implementation detail that can affect the efficiency of its operations.
- The Java Class Library contains the interface Map, which is similar to our DictionaryInterface.

## PROGRAMMING TIPS

- The class Scanner enables you to break a string into substrings, or tokens, that are separated by characters called delimiters. By default, white-space characters are the delimiters. You pass to Scanner's constructor either the string to be parsed or a text file represented as an instance of the class java.io.File.

- The following methods in the class Scanner enable you to extract the tokens from any string:

```
public String next();
public boolean hasNext();
```

Appendix B discusses Scanner in more detail beginning at Segment B.81.

- When using a Scanner object to process text, any character can be a delimiter, if it does not occur in any desired token. You create a string of these delimiters using a special notation and give it to the Scanner method useDelimiter. Consult Segment B.82 of Appendix B for more details.

## EXERCISES

1. How does a dictionary differ from a position-based ADT?

2. Implement a method for the class TelephoneDirectory—described in Segment 19.9—that adds an entry to the directory, given the person's name and telephone number. The method should return true if the entry was added. If the person is already in the directory, the method should replace the person's telephone number and return false.

3. Implement a method for the telephone directory problem of Segment 19.9 to display everyone's name and telephone number.

4. In the telephone directory problem of Segment 19.9, the case of the letters in a name affects the name's order in the dictionary. What steps can you take so that case variations in the input file do not affect this order?

5. In the telephone directory problem of Segment 19.9, suppose that the text file of names and telephone numbers is sorted by name.

   a. What impact would this aspect of the file have on the efficiency of the method readFile for various implementations of the dictionary?
   b. Would it matter whether the file was in reverse alphabetical order?

6. A *reverse directory* allows one to search for the name corresponding to a given telephone number. Modify the class TelephoneDirectory of Segment 19.9 to give it this capability. Use a second dictionary as the reverse directory. Add a query method and modify the method readFile accordingly.

7. Draw a class diagram for the class FrequencyCounter, as outlined in Segment 19.13, that is analogous to the diagram in Figure 19-4 of Segment 19.8.

8. The word-frequency problem of Segment 19.12 finds the frequency with which each distinct word occurs within some given text. Describe the changes that you could make to the class FrequencyCounter if you wanted to list the words that occur for each frequency.

**9.** Repeat Exercise 7 for the class Concordance, as outlined in Segment 19.19.

**10.** In the concordance problem of Segment 19.18, if a word occurs more than once in a single line, the number of that line appears more than once in the concordance. Revise the method readFile given in Segment 19.20 so that the line numbers associated with a given word are distinct.

**11.** Design an ADT that stores the lists of students registered for various courses. Provide a method that returns the list of registered students for a given course. Then use a dictionary to implement the class CourseRegisteredStudents.

**12.** Consider a look-up service for monorail timings on a given date. A file contains information about these timings. Each monorail's data appears on two lines. The first line gives the arrival time, the departure time, and the route number. These entries are separated by tildes (~), and the times are in 24-hour notation (for example, 1 p.m. is 13:00). The second line briefly describes the route of the monorail.

Implement a method with the header

```
public void readFile(Scanner data)
```

to read the file into a dictionary that will be searched. Decide what data should be the search key and what should be the associated value. Design any classes needed for the key and the value.

**13.** The ADT dictionary that we discussed in this chapter assumes distinct search keys. Revise the specifications of the dictionary to remove this restriction. Consider each of the following possibilities:

   **a.** The method add adds an entry whose search key is already in the dictionary but whose value is not. The remove method deletes all entries with a given search key. The method getValue retrieves all values associated with a given search key.
   **b.** The methods behave as Part *a* describes, but a secondary search key enables remove and getValue to delete or retrieve a single entry.

## PROJECTS

**1.** To simplify the telephone directory problem of Segment 19.7, we assumed that the text file contained distinct names. Remove this assumption, with and without a secondary search key. (See Exercise 13.)

**2.** Discovering the authorship of certain famous pieces of literature is an interesting problem. Comparisons are made between pieces whose authorship is disputed and those of known authorship. One approach is to compare the frequency of pairs of letters. There are 26 x 26 different pairs of letters. Not all of them will appear in a piece of writing. For example, "qz" is unlikely to appear, while "th" is likely to appear often. Design a program, similar to the frequency counter of Segments 19.12 through 19.17, that counts all the pairs of letters that appear in a given piece of text.

**3.** A compiler must examine tokens in a program and decide whether or not they are reserved words or identifiers defined by the user. Design a program that reads a Java program and makes a list of all the identifiers. To do this, you should make use of two dictionaries. The first dictionary should hold all the Java reserved words. The second dictionary should hold all the identifiers that you find. Whenever you encounter a token, you first should search the dictionary of reserved words. If the token is not a reserved word, you then should search the dictionary of identifiers. If the token is not in either dictionary, you should add it to the dictionary of identifiers.

**4.** Suppose that we want to implement the ADT set. Recall from Project 1 of Chapter 1 that a set is an unordered collection of objects in which duplicates are not allowed. The operations that a set should support are

- Add a given object to the set
- Remove a given object from the set
- See whether the set contains a given object
- Clear all objects from the set
- Get the number of objects in the set
- Return an iterator to the set
- Return a set that combines the items in two sets (the union)
- Return a set of those items that occur in both of two sets (the intersection)

Define a class `DictionarySet` that uses a dictionary internally to implement these operations.

**5.** Suppose that we want to help physicians to diagnose illnesses. A physician observes a patient's symptoms and considers the illnesses that could be associated with those symptoms. Design and implement a class `PhysiciansHelper` that provides a list of those illnesses.

   `PhysiciansHelper` should contain a dictionary of illnesses and symptoms. A method should read a text file of illnesses with their symptoms into the dictionary. Each line in the file will contain the name of an illness followed by a colon and a comma-separated list of symptoms. For example, one line could be

```
head cold: nasal stuffiness, sneezing, runny nose
```

   `PhysiciansHelper` should maintain a list of symptoms for the current patient. A method should add a symptom to this list and return a list of illnesses that are associated with those symptoms. Another method should remove a given symptom from the list, and a method should clear the patient symptom list.

**6.** Write a program that plays the game tic-tac-toe. Represent the game board by an array of nine values. Each location in the array contains either an X, an O, or a blank. The total number of possible board configurations is $3^9$, or approximately 20,000. Associated with every possible configuration is a best move.

   Generate all possible board configurations, and let them be search keys in a dictionary. For each search key, let the next best move be its associated value. Once you have created the dictionary, use it to decide the moves for a computer-based player in a game of tic-tac-toe.

**7.** A *picture dictionary* is a collection of images, each of which is identified by a descriptive word. Form a picture dictionary from the data in external files, which you can create from royalty-free images found online. Design and implement a user interface that provides search and display functions.

### ANSWERS TO SELF-TEST QUESTIONS

**1.**
```
DictionaryInterface<Name, String> myDictionary = new Dictionary<>();
```

**2.**
```
myDictionary.add(new Name("Joe", "Java"), "555-1234");
```

**3.**
```
Name britney = new Name("Britney", "Storm");
if (myDictionary.contains(britney))
   System.out.println("Britney's phone number is " + myDictionary.getValue(britney));
else
   System.out.println("Britney is not in the dictionary");
```
*or*
```
String phoneNumber = myDictionary.getValue(new Name("Britney", " Storm"));
if (phoneNumber == null)
   System.out.println("Britney is not in the dictionary");
else
   System.out.println("Britney's phone number is " +  phoneNumber);
```

4. The Scanner methods hasNext and next that readFile calls throw only runtime exceptions, which need not be caught. So although the call to readFile can be outside of a try block, it is inside the try block because its argument—the Scanner object data—is local to the try block. By declaring data outside of the try block, you could move the call to readFile after the last catch block.

5.
```java
public String remove(Name personName)
{
   return phoneBook.remove(personName);
} // end remove
```

6.
```java
public String changePhoneNumber(Name personName, String newPhoneNumber)
{
   return phoneBook.add(personName, newPhoneNumber);
} // end changePhoneNumber
```

7. We called getValue instead of contains to simplify the logic. If we called contains and found that the current word was already in the dictionary, we would need to call getValue to get its frequency. But we can use the result of getValue to see whether the word is in the dictionary.

8.
```java
/** Displays only the words that occur with a given frequency.
    @param frequency  An integer count of the desired frequency. */
public void display(int frequency)
{
   Iterator<String> keyIterator = wordTable.getKeyIterator();
   Iterator<Integer> valueIterator = wordTable.getValueIterator();

   System.out.println("Words that occur " +  frequency + "  times:");
   boolean atLeastOneWord = false;
   while (keyIterator.hasNext())
   {
      String word = keyIterator.next();
      Integer count = valueIterator.next();

      if (count.equals(frequency))
      {
         atLeastOneWord = true;
         System.out.println(word);
      } // end if
   } // end while

   if (atLeastOneWord == false)
      System.out.println("(There are none.)");
} // end display
```

9.
```java
public ListWithIteratorInterface<Integer> getLineNumbers(String word)
{
   return wordTable.getValue(word);
} // end getLineNumbers
```

# Dictionary Implementations

## Contents

Array-Based Implementations
>   An Unsorted Array-Based Dictionary
>   A Sorted Array-Based Dictionary

Linked Implementations
>   An Unsorted Linked Dictionary
>   A Sorted Linked Dictionary

## Prerequisites

## Objectives

After studying this chapter, you should be able to

- Implement the ADT dictionary by using either an array or a chain of linked nodes

The implementations of the ADT dictionary that we present in this chapter employ techniques like the ones we used to implement the ADT list. We will store the dictionary's entries in either an array or a chain of linked nodes. In doing so, we will consider both sorted and unsorted dictionaries with distinct search keys. Later chapters will present more-sophisticated implementations of the ADT dictionary.

# Array-Based Implementations

**20.1**   The ability to resize an array, as introduced in Segment 2.35 of Chapter 2, means that an array can provide as much storage as necessary for the entries in a dictionary. Remember that each entry consists of two parts—a search key and a value. You can encapsulate the two parts into an object, as Figure 20-1a illustrates. With this approach, you define a class Entry to represent the entries. A second, less attractive approach uses two arrays, as shown in Figure 20-1b. One array represents the search keys and a second, **parallel array** represents the corresponding values. We will discuss the first approach and leave the exploration of the second as an exercise. At that time, you will see that parallel arrays can be awkward to manage.

FIGURE 20-1   Two possible ways to use arrays to represent the entries in a dictionary: (a) an array of objects that encapsulate each search key and corresponding value; (b) parallel arrays of search keys and values

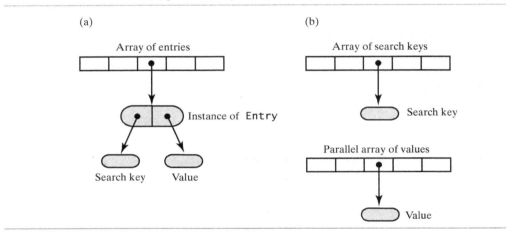

**Question 1** Figure 20-1 shows two ways to represent an array-based dictionary. How do the memory requirements for the two representations compare?

## An Unsorted Array-Based Dictionary

**20.2**   **Beginning the implementation.** Our implementation uses one array, as pictured in Figure 20-1a, to represent the dictionary. Each entry in the dictionary, and therefore the array, is an instance of a class Entry that we must define. We can make this class either public, part of a package, or private and internal to the dictionary class. We chose the latter approach in defining the private class Entry shown in Listing 20-1. Note that its constructor disallows null keys and values.

The outer class ArrayDictionary begins with its data fields and constructors stated in terms of type parameters K and V. These parameters represent the data types of the search keys and their associated values, respectively.

LISTING 20-1   The class `ArrayDictionary` and its private inner class `Entry`

```java
1  import java.util.Arrays;
2  import java.util.Iterator;
3  import java.util.NoSuchElementException;
4  /**
5      A class that implements a dictionary by using a resizable array.
6      The dictionary is unsorted and has distinct search keys.
7      @author Frank M. Carrano
8  */
9  public class ArrayDictionary<K, V> implements DictionaryInterface<K, V>
10 {
11     private Entry<K, V>[] dictionary; // Array of unsorted entries
12     private int numberOfEntries;
13     private boolean initialized = false;
14     private final static int DEFAULT_CAPACITY = 25;
15     private static final int MAX_CAPACITY = 10000;
16
17     public ArrayDictionary()
18     {
19        this(DEFAULT_CAPACITY);         // Call next constructor
20     } // end default constructor
21
22     public ArrayDictionary(int initialCapacity)
23     {
24        checkCapacity(initialCapacity);
25        // The cast is safe because the new array contains null entries
26        @SuppressWarnings("unchecked")
27        Entry<K, V>[] tempDictionary = (Entry<K, V>[])new Entry[initialCapacity];
28        dictionary = tempDictionary;
29        numberOfEntries = 0;
30        initialized = true;
31     } // end constructor
32
33     <Implementations of methods in DictionaryInterface. >
34     . . .
35
36     private class Entry<S, T>
37     {
38        private S key;
39        private T value;
40
41        private Entry(S searchKey, T dataValue)
42        {
43           key = searchKey;
44           value = dataValue;
45        } // end constructor
46
47        private S getKey()
48        {
49           return key;
50        } // end getKey
51
52        private T getValue()
53        {
54           return value;
55        } // end getValue
56
```

```
57      private void setValue(T newValue)
58      {
59         value = newValue;
60      } // end setValue
61   } // end Entry
62 } // end ArrayDictionary
```

Notice that the inner class `Entry` has no method `setKey` to set or change the search key. Even though `setValue` can be useful in the implementation of `add`, you never need to change the search key. Without `setKey`, a default constructor would be useless, so none is defined.

**Note:  Compiler warning**

The constructor for `ArrayDictionary`, as shown in Listing 20-1, allocates memory for the array dictionary using the expression **new** `Entry[initialCapacity]`. The compiler sees an array whose elements have type `Entry`. When the constructor assigns this array to an array whose elements are of type `Entry<K, V>`, the compiler warns us of an unchecked conversion. An attempt to cast the new array to `Entry<K, V>[]` results in a similar warning. In either event, all should be well despite the compiler's concern. Thus, we suppress the warning as we have done in the past when our constructors cast instances of `Object` to a generic type.

**20.3**    **Some private methods.** One problem with array-based implementations of an ADT is the finite size of the array. To avoid a full dictionary, we double the array's size as necessary, just as we did in earlier chapters. We will use a private method, as we did then. Its specification is as follows:

```
// Doubles the size of the array of entries if it is full.
private void ensureCapacity()
```

Adding, removing, or retrieving an entry requires a sequential search, since the search keys are not sorted. A sequential search must look at all the search keys in the array to conclude that an entry is not present in the dictionary. Implementing this search as the following private method will simplify the definitions of these three dictionary operations:

```
// Returns the index of the entry that contains key or
// returns numberOfEntries if no such entry exists.
private int locateIndex(K key)
```

Finally, to enhance the security of our code, we also define the private methods `checkCapacity` and `checkInitialization`, just as we have done for previous array-based implementations.

**20.4**    **Adding an entry.** Another potential problem with array-based implementations is the shifting of array entries that often occurs. When a dictionary's search keys are unsorted, however, we can add or remove an entry without shifting other entries. Thus, when adding a new key-value entry, we can insert it after the last entry in the array, as Figure 20-2 shows. In this case, `add` returns `null`. However, if the search key was in the dictionary already, we replace its corresponding value with the new value and return the original value. The following algorithm performs these steps:

*Algorithm* add(key, value)
*// Adds a new key-value entry to the dictionary and returns* null. *If* key *already exists*
*// in the dictionary, returns the corresponding value and replaces it with* value.
    result = **null**
    *Search the array for an entry containing* key
    **if** (*an entry containing* key *is found in the array*)
    {
        result = *value currently associated with* key

> *Replace* key*'s associated value with* value
> }
> **else** *// Insert new entry*
> {
>     **if** (*array is full*)
>         *Double size of array*
>     *Insert a new entry containing* key *and* value *after the last entry in the array*
>     *Increment the size of the dictionary*
> }
> **return** result

---

**FIGURE 20-2**    Adding a new entry to an unsorted array-based dictionary

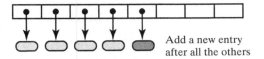

Add a new entry
after all the others

---

**20.5**  **The method** add. The following implementation of the method add invokes the private methods locateIndex and ensureCapacity, as specified in Segment 20.3, as well as the private method checkInitialization:

```java
public V add(K key, V value)
{
    checkInitialization();
    if ((key == null) || (value == null))
        throw new IllegalArgumentException();
    else
    {
        V result = null;

        int keyIndex = locateIndex(key);

        if (keyIndex < numberOfEntries)
        {
            // Key found; return and replace entry's value
            result = dictionary[keyIndex].getValue(); // Get old value
            dictionary[keyIndex].setValue(value);       // Replace value
        }
        else // Key not found; add new entry to dictionary
        {
            // Add at end of array
            dictionary[numberOfEntries] = new Entry<>(key, value);
            numberOfEntries++;
            ensureCapacity(); // Ensure enough room for next add
        } // end if
        return result;
    } // end if
} // end add
```

To search an unsorted array, locateIndex has the following definition:

```java
private int locateIndex(K key)
{
    int index = 0;
    while ( (index < numberOfEntries) &&
            !key.equals(dictionary[index].getKey()))
        index++;

    return index;
} // end locateIndex
```

**20.6** **Removing an entry.** To remove an entry from an unsorted array-based dictionary, we first locate the entry and then replace it with the last entry in the dictionary, as Figure 20-3 illustrates. Thus, we can fill the "hole" in the array without shifting the other entries. Since the size of the dictionary is reduced by 1, the extra reference remaining after the current entries will be ignored. However, for security reasons, we will set that reference to null.

**FIGURE 20-3** Removing an entry from an unsorted array-based dictionary

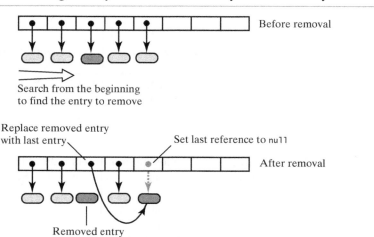

The following algorithm describes the remove operation:

*Algorithm* remove(key)
*// Removes an entry from the dictionary, given its search key, and returns its value.*
*// If no such entry exists in the dictionary, returns* null.

result = **null**
*Search the array for an entry containing* key

**if** (*an entry containing* key *is found in the array*)
{
    result = *value currently associated with* key
    *Replace the entry with the last entry in the array*
    *Decrement the size of the dictionary*
}
*// Else* result *is* null

**return** result

This logic can be implemented as follows:

```java
public V remove(K key)
{
    checkInitialization();
    V result = null;
    int keyIndex = locateIndex(key);
    if (keyIndex < numberOfEntries)
    {
        // Key found; remove entry and return its value
        result = dictionary[keyIndex].getValue();
        dictionary[keyIndex] = dictionary[numberOfEntries - 1];
        dictionary[numberOfEntries - 1] = null;
        numberOfEntries--;
    } // end if
    // Else result is null
```

```
        return result;
    } // end remove
```

**20.7 The remaining methods.** We leave the rest of the dictionary implementation to you as an exercise, since it is not difficult once you have reached this point. Note that an iteration, or traversal, of the dictionary entries simply moves from location to location within the array. Since the search keys are not sorted, the order of the iteration is not specified. Whatever order is easy to implement is fine. Typically, you start with the first entry in the array and move sequentially through the remaining entries.

**20.8 Efficiency.** For this implementation, the worst-case efficiencies of the operations are as follows:

Addition O($n$)
Removal O($n$)
Retrieval O($n$)
Traversal O($n$)

Even though additions occur after the last entry in the array dictionary without shifting any data, the search necessary to prevent duplicate search keys in the dictionary makes the overall operation O($n$). Removals and retrievals use a similar search of the array, making them O($n$) as well. Finally, traversing an array is an O($n$) operation.

Realize that if you fill the array of dictionary entries, you must allocate a new, larger array and copy entries from the original array to the new array. This requirement adds overhead to any array-based implementation that the previous analysis does not reflect. In Java, the array entries are references to objects, so copying the array is fast. Ideally, you want to choose a sufficiently large array, but not one that wastes space because it is overly large.

## A Sorted Array-Based Dictionary

**20.9** Some of the implementation for an unsorted dictionary, as shown in Segment 20.2, is independent of the order of the dictionary's entries, and so can be used for a sorted dictionary. However, the search keys now must belong to a class that implements the interface Comparable so that we can order them. An outline for an implementation of a sorted dictionary appears in Listing 20-2. The notation K extends Comparable<? super K>, which was first introduced in Segment JI3.13 of Java Interlude 3, defines the generic type K. It allows us to compare objects of type K with either objects of type K or objects of any superclass of K.

---

**LISTING 20-2**   An outline of the class SortedArrayDictionary

```
1  import java.util.Arrays;
2  import java.util.Iterator;
3  import java.util.NoSuchElementException;
4  /**
5      A class that implements a dictionary by using a resizable sorted array.
6      @author Frank M. Carrano
7  */
8  public class SortedArrayDictionary<K extends Comparable<? super K>, V>
9              implements DictionaryInterface<K, V>
10
11     < Data fields as shown in Listing 20-1 of Segment 20.2. >
12     . . .
13     < Constructors analogous to those in Listing 20-1. >
```

```
14      . . .
15
16      public V add(K key, V value)
17      {
18          . . . < See Segment 20.11. >
19      } // end add
20
21      < Implementations of other methods in DictionaryInterface. >
22      . . .
23
24      < The private class Entry, as shown in Listing 20-1. >
25  } // end SortedArrayDictionary
```

**20.10  Adding an entry.** When the dictionary's key-value entries are sorted by their search keys, adding a new entry requires a search of the array of entries to see where the new entry belongs. After you determine the correct position for the new entry, you must make room for it in the array. You do this by shifting subsequent array entries up by one position, beginning at the last entry, as Figure 20-4 shows. You then insert the new entry into the array so it is in its proper order by search key.

The following algorithm for adding an entry has similarities to the one given in Segment 20.4 for an unsorted dictionary:

*Algorithm* add(key, value)
*// Adds a new key-value entry to the dictionary and returns* null. *If key already exists*
*// in the dictionary, returns the corresponding value and replaces it with* value.

result = null
*Search the array until you either find an entry containing* key *or locate the point where it
    should be*
if (*an entry containing* key *is found in the array*)
{
    result = *value currently associated with* key
    *Replace* key's *associated value with* value
}
else // *Insert new entry*
{
    *Make room in the array for a new entry at the index determined by the previous search*
    *Insert a new entry containing* key *and* value *into the vacated location of the array*
    *Increment the size of the dictionary*

    if (*array is full*)
    *Double size of array*
}
return result

---

**Question 2** Describe how the previous algorithm differs from the one given in Segment 20.4 for an unsorted dictionary.

FIGURE 20-4    Adding an entry to a sorted array-based dictionary: (a) search;
(b) make room; (c) insert

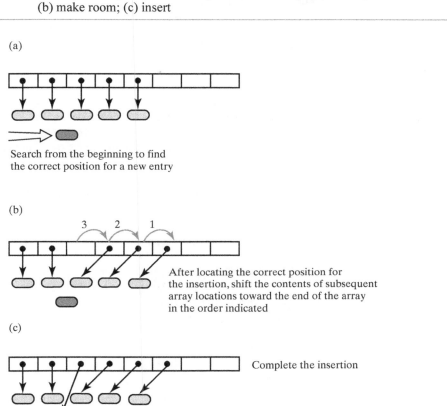

(a)

Search from the beginning to find
the correct position for a new entry

(b)

After locating the correct position for
the insertion, shift the contents of subsequent
array locations toward the end of the array
in the order indicated

(c)

Complete the insertion

**20.11    The method** add. We can implement this algorithm by using the private methods described in
Segment 20.3, but we need to use a different implementation for `locateIndex`. When the dictionary is unsorted, `locateIndex` simply detects whether the dictionary contains a given search key.
But here, `locateIndex` must also determine where in the array to make the insertion. Thus, we
revise the method's specification as follows:

```
// Returns the index of either the entry that contains key or
// the location that should contain key, if no such entry exists.
private int locateIndex(K key)
```

The following additional method will also be helpful in the implementation:

```
// Makes room for a new entry at a given index by shifting
// array entries towards the end of the array.
private void makeRoom(int keyIndex)
```

Using these methods, we can implement the method add as follows:

```java
public V add(K key, V value)
{
   checkInitialization();
   if ((key == null) || (value == null))
      throw new IllegalArgumentException();
   else
   {
      V result = null;
      int keyIndex = locateIndex(key);
      if ( (keyIndex < numberOfEntries) &&
            key.equals(dictionary[keyIndex].getKey()) )
      {
         // Key found; return and replace entry's value
         result = dictionary[keyIndex].getValue(); // Get old value
         dictionary[keyIndex].setValue(value);      // Replace value
      }
      else // Key not found; add new entry to dictionary
      {
         makeRoom(keyIndex);
         dictionary[keyIndex] = new Entry<>(key, value);
         numberOfEntries++;
         ensureCapacity(); // Ensure enough room for next add
      } // end if
      return result;
   } // end if
} // end add
```

The differences between this method and the one given in Segment 20.5 for an unsorted dictionary are highlighted.

**20.12**    **The method locateIndex.** Since the array is sorted, locateIndex can generally search it in less time than it could search an unsorted array. Recall from Segment 18.8 of Chapter 18 that a sequential search can detect when an entry is not in a sorted array without searching the entire array. Using that technique, we define the private method locateIndex as follows:

```java
private int locateIndex(K key)
{
   // Search until you either find an entry containing key or
   // pass the point where it should be
   int index = 0;
   while ( (index < numberOfEntries) &&
            key.compareTo(dictionary[index].getKey()) > 0 )
      index++;

   return index;
} // end locateIndex
```

The difference between this method and the one given in Segment 20.5 for an unsorted dictionary is highlighted.

**Question 3** A binary search would be faster, in general, than the modified sequential search just given—particularly when the dictionary is large. Implement the private method locateIndex for a sorted dictionary using a binary search.

**20.13**  **Removing an entry.** To remove an entry from a sorted array-based dictionary, we first locate the entry by calling the method `locateIndex` that we used in the previous segment for the `add` method. Since the entries are sorted, we must maintain their order. Thus, any entries after the one to be removed must shift to the next lower position in the array. Figure 20-5 illustrates these two steps.

FIGURE 20-5    Removing an entry from a sorted array-based dictionary: (a) search; (b) shift entries

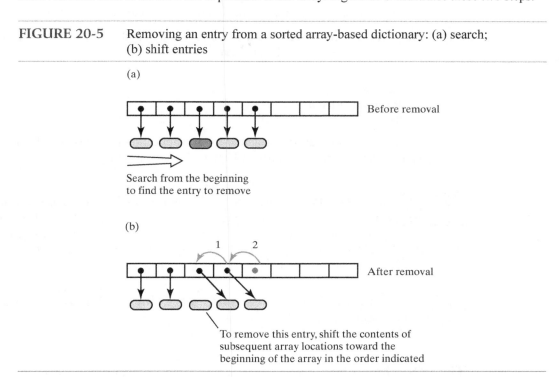

(a)

Before removal

Search from the beginning
to find the entry to remove

(b)

1    2

After removal

To remove this entry, shift the contents of
subsequent array locations toward the
beginning of the array in the order indicated

The following algorithm describes the remove operation:

*Algorithm* `remove(key)`
*// Removes an entry from the dictionary, given its search key, and returns its value.*
*// If no such entry exists in the dictionary, returns* `null`.

`result = null`
*Search the array for an entry containing* `key`

`if` (*an entry containing* `key` *is found in the array*)
`{`
     `result = ` *value currently associated with* `key`
     *Shift any entries that are after the located one to the next lower position in the array*
     *Decrement the size of the dictionary*
`}`
`return result`

We leave the implementation of this algorithm as an exercise. Defining the following private method will be helpful:

```
// Removes an entry at a given index by shifting array
// entries toward the entry to be removed.
private void removeArrayEntry(int keyIndex)
```

**20.14**  **The remaining methods.** At the heart of the method `getValue`, which retrieves the value in an existing entry given its search key, is the method `locateIndex`, as described earlier. Since the array of entries is sorted, `locateIndex` can use a binary search, as Question 3 indicated.

An iteration, or traversal, of the entries in the dictionary starts with the first entry in the array and moves sequentially through the remaining entries. This part of the implementation can be the same as for an unsorted dictionary. But here, since the array is sorted, the iteration will traverse the dictionary in sorted search-key order.

We leave the completion of this implementation to you as an exercise.

**20.15** **Efficiency.** When `locateIndex` uses a binary search in the sorted array-based implementation, the worst-case efficiencies of the dictionary operations are as follows:

Addition $O(n)$
Removal $O(n)$
Retrieval $O(\log n)$
Traversal $O(n)$

This implementation is suitable for an application that creates a dictionary and then makes many retrievals. This point from Chapter 14 bears repeating here:

 **Programming Tip:** When choosing an implementation for an ADT, you should consider the operations that your application requires. If you use a particular ADT operation frequently, you want its implementation to be efficient. Conversely, if you rarely use an operation, you can afford to use a class that has an inefficient implementation of that operation.

 **Programming Tip:** Include comments in a class's implementation that advertise the efficiencies of its methods.

 **Question 4** When the sorted array-based implementation of a dictionary uses a binary search, its retrieval operation is $O(\log n)$. Since add and remove use a similar search, why are they not $O(\log n)$ as well?

# Linked Implementations

**20.16** The last implementations of the ADT dictionary that we will consider in this chapter store the dictionary's entries in a chain of linked nodes. As presented in Chapter 3, for example, a chain can provide as much storage as necessary for the entries. You can encapsulate the two parts of an entry into an object, as Figure 20-6a illustrates, just as you did for an array. If you choose this option, your dictionary class can use the classes Node from Segment 3.25 and Entry from Listing 20-1.

Another option does not use the class Entry. You could use two chains, as in Figure 20-6b, but a simpler approach is to revise the definition of a node to include both parts of the entry, as Figure 20-6c illustrates. The private inner class Node, defined within the dictionary class, would then contain the data fields.

**VideoNote**
Linked-chain dictionaries

```
private K key;
private V value;
private Node next;
```

The generic types K and V are defined by the outer class. In addition to constructors, the class Node would contain the methods getKey, getValue, setValue, getNextNode, and setNextNode. Since changing the search key is not necessary and, in fact, could destroy the order of a sorted dictionary, no setKey method is provided.

**FIGURE 20-6**   Three possible ways to use linked nodes to represent the entries in a dictionary: (a) a chain of nodes that each reference an entry object; (b) parallel chains of search keys and values; (c) a chain of nodes that each reference a search key and a value

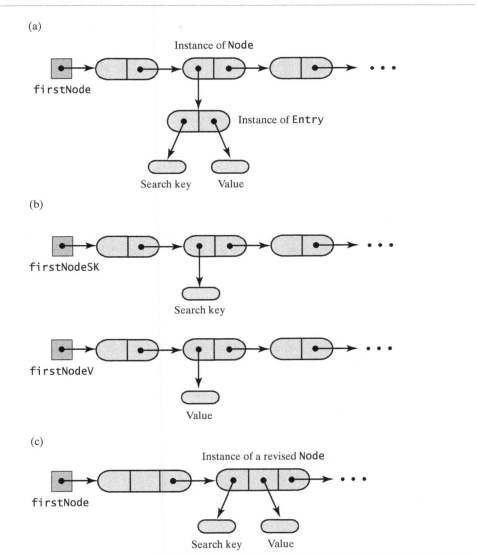

## An Unsorted Linked Dictionary

**20.17**   Since the entries in an unsorted dictionary are in no particular order, you add a new entry in the most efficient manner. When the entries are in a linked chain, such as the one in Figure 20-6c, the fastest addition is at the beginning of the chain, as Figure 20-7 shows. (If the class also maintains a tail reference to the last node of the chain, adding an entry after the last node would be equally fast.) While this aspect of an addition is O(1), preventing duplicate search keys would require a sequential search from the beginning of the chain. Just as you would for an array, you would have to look at all the search keys in the chain to learn that a particular entry was not present.

**FIGURE 20-7**     Adding to an unsorted linked dictionary

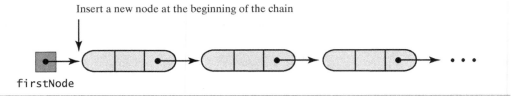

Removing or retrieving an entry uses a similar search. A traversal of either the search keys or the values involves the entire chain. Thus, for this implementation, the worst-case efficiencies of the operations are as follows:

Addition O($n$)
Removal O($n$)
Retrieval O($n$)
Traversal O($n$)

**Question 5** To remove an entry from an unsorted array-based dictionary, we replaced the removed entry with the last entry in the array (see Segment 20.6). Should we use the same strategy to remove an entry from an unsorted linked dictionary? Explain.

## A Sorted Linked Dictionary

**20.18**   **Adding an entry.** When the nodes in a chain are sorted by their search keys, adding a new entry to the dictionary requires a sequential search of the chain from its beginning to determine the correct location for the new node. Since the search keys are sorted, you can detect that a desired search key does not exist in the chain as soon as you pass the node that should have contained it. That is, you do not have to look at the entire chain, as you would if the search keys were unsorted. Segments 18.8 and 18.22 in Chapter 18 describe this variation of a sequential search.

The following algorithm adds a new entry to a sorted linked dictionary:

*Algorithm* add(key, value)
*// Adds a new key-value entry to the dictionary and returns* null. *If* key *already exists*
*// in the dictionary, returns the corresponding value and replaces that value with* value.

result = **null**
*Search the chain until either you find a node containing* key *or you pass the point where*
    *it should be*
**if** (*a node containing* key *is found in the chain*)
{
    result = *value currently associated with* key
    *Replace* key's *associated value with* value
}
**else**
{
    *Allocate a new node containing* key *and* value
    **if** (*the chain is empty or the new entry belongs at the beginning of the chain*)
    *Add the new node to the beginning of the chain*
    **else**
        *Insert the new node before the last node that was examined during the search*
    *Increment the size of the dictionary*
}
**return** result

**20.19**   Listing 20-3 shows the beginning of the class `SortedLinkedDictionary` and the implementation of the method `add`. Implementations for the methods `remove` and `getValue` are similar to the implementation for `add`, but are a bit simpler. We leave them as exercises.

LISTING 20-3      The class `SortedLinkedDictionary`

```java
 1  import java.util.Iterator;
 2  import java.util.NoSuchElementException;
 3  /**
 4     A class that implements a dictionary by using a sorted linked chain.
 5     The dictionary has distinct search keys.
 6     @author Frank M. Carrano
 7  */
 8  public class SortedLinkedDictionary<K extends Comparable<? super K>, V>
 9             implements DictionaryInterface<K, V>
10  {
11     private Node firstNode; // Reference to first node of chain
12     private int  numberOfEntries;
13
14     public SortedLinkedDictionary()
15     {
16        initializeDataFields();
17     } // end default constructor
18
19     public V add(K key, V value)
20     {
21        V result = null;
22
23        // Search chain until you either find a node containing key
24        // or locate where it should be
25        Node currentNode = firstNode;
26        Node nodeBefore = null;
27        while ((currentNode != null) && key.compareTo(currentNode.getKey()) > 0)
28        {
29           nodeBefore = currentNode;
30           currentNode = currentNode.getNextNode();
31        } // end while
32
33        if ( (currentNode != null) && key.equals(currentNode.getKey()) )
34        {
35           result = currentNode.getValue();      // Get old value
36           currentNode.setValue(value);          // Replace value
37        }
38        else
39        {
40           Node newNode = new Node(key, value); // Create new node
41           if (nodeBefore == null)
42           { // Add at beginning (includes empty chain)
43              newNode.setNextNode(firstNode);
44              firstNode = newNode;
45           }
46           else // Add elsewhere in non-empty chain
47           {
48              newNode.setNextNode(currentNode); // currentNode is after new node
49              nodeBefore.setNextNode(newNode);  // nodeBefore is before new node
50           } // end if
51
52           numberOfEntries++; // Increase length for both cases
53        } // end if
```

```
54
55        return result;
56     } // end add
57
58     < Implementations of the other methods in DictionaryInterface. >
59     . . .
60
61     < Private classes KeyIterator and ValueIterator (see Segment 20.20). >
62     . . .
63
64     < The private class Node. >
65     . . .
66
67  } // end SortedLinkedDictionary
```

**20.20**   **Iterators.** Iterators provide the client with an easy way to traverse a dictionary's search keys and their corresponding values. The public methods getKeyIterator and getValueIterator have the same implementations here as they do in the other dictionary implementations. The private inner classes KeyIterator and ValueIterator, however, differ. Each has a data field nextNode to mark an iteration's place in the chain as the traversal progresses. Listing 20-4 shows the private class KeyIterator. ValueIterator has a similar definition. Both of these classes are like the inner class IteratorForLinkedList that appears in Segments 15.9 through 15.13 of Chapter 15.

---

**LISTING 20-4**   SortedLinkedDictionary's private inner class KeyIterator

```java
1  private class KeyIterator implements Iterator<K>
2  {
3     private Node nextNode; // Node containing next entry in iteration
4
5     private KeyIterator()
6     {
7        nextNode = firstNode;
8     } // end default constructor
9
10    public boolean hasNext()
11    {
12       return nextNode != null;
13    } // end hasNext
14
15    public K next()
16    {
17       K result;
18       if (hasNext())
19       {
20          result = nextNode.getKey();
21          nextNode = nextNode.getNextNode();
22       }
23       else
24          throw new NoSuchElementException();
25       return result;
26    } // end next
27
28    public void remove()
29    {
30       throw new UnsupportedOperationException();
31    } // end remove
32 } // end KeyIterator
```

**20.21** **Efficiency.** Like adding an entry, removing or retrieving an entry requires a sequential search of the chain. Traversal of a sorted chain proceeds just as it would for an unsorted chain. Thus, the worstcase efficiencies of the dictionary operations for a sorted linked implementation are as follows:

Addition $O(n)$
Removal $O(n)$
Retrieval $O(n)$
Traversal $O(n)$

The addition or removal of an entry is an $O(n)$ operation regardless of whether you use an array or a chain to implement a dictionary. Realize, however, that an array requires you to shift its entries, whereas a linked chain does not. Also, the preceding linked implementation does not require a good estimate of the dictionary's ultimate size. When you use an array that is too small, you can expand it by copying its entries to a new, larger array, but this takes time. If you use an array that is larger than necessary, you waste space. Neither of these situations occur with a linked implementation.

## CHAPTER SUMMARY

- You can implement a dictionary by using either an array or a chain of linked nodes. A linked implementation does not require a good estimate of the dictionary's ultimate size. When you use an array that is too small, you need to copy its entries to a new, larger array. If you use an array that is larger than necessary, you waste space. Neither of these situations occur with a linked implementation.

- The worst-case efficiencies of the dictionary operations for array-based and linked implementations are as follows:

| | Array-Based | | Linked | |
|---|---|---|---|---|
| | Unsorted | Sorted | Unsorted | Sorted |
| Addition | $O(n)$ | $O(n)$ | $O(n)$ | $O(n)$ |
| Removal | $O(n)$ | $O(n)$ | $O(n)$ | $O(n)$ |
| Retrieval | $O(n)$ | $O(\log n)$ | $O(n)$ | $O(n)$ |
| Traversal | $O(n)$ | $O(n)$ | $O(n)$ | $O(n)$ |

- For a sorted or unsorted dictionary, the addition or removal of an entry is an $O(n)$ operation regardless of whether you use an array or a chain to implement it. Realize, however, that an array requires the shifting of its entries, whereas a linked chain does not.

- Using an array to implement a sorted dictionary allows for an efficient retrieval operation because you can use a binary search.

- To implement the method `getKeyIterator` or `getValueIterator`, define a private inner class for the dictionary class. This private class should implement the interface `java.util.Iterator`.

## PROGRAMMING TIP

- When choosing an implementation for an ADT, you should consider the operations that your application requires. If you use a particular ADT operation frequently, you want its implementation to be efficient. Conversely, if you rarely use an operation, you can afford to use a class that has an inefficient implementation of that operation.

- Include comments in a class's implementation that advertise the efficiencies of its methods.

## EXERCISES

1. Begin an array-based implementation of the ADT dictionary according to the data structure illustrated in Figure 20-1b. Declare the data fields, define the constructors, and define the method add for unsorted data. Use arrays that you can resize during execution.

2. Begin two linked implementations of the ADT dictionary according to the two data structures illustrated in Parts *a* and *b* of Figure 20-6. Declare the data fields, define the constructors, and define the method add for unsorted data.

3. Using Big Oh notation, indicate the time requirement of the method locateIndex in the worst case.

4. An array-based implementation of a dictionary requires shifting of array entries when a new entry is added. Is shifting required for unsorted search keys?

5. Segment 20.20 defines the class KeyIterator. An instance of this class is an iterator that traverses the search keys in the dictionary. In a similar fashion, define a class ValueIterator to provide a way to traverse the dictionary's values.

6. Suppose that in an array-based implementation of a dictionary, the search keys are unsorted. Describe the steps required to remove an entry from this array. Indicate the time requirement of this method using Big Oh notation.

7. Consider adding operations to the ADT dictionary to form the union and intersection of two given dictionaries. Each operation returns a new dictionary. The union should combine the entries in both dictionaries into a third dictionary. The intersection should be a dictionary of the entries common to both of the two dictionaries.

   Within each given dictionary, search keys are not repeated. However, an entry in one dictionary could have the same search key as an entry in the second dictionary. Propose and discuss ways to specify these two operations for this case.

8. Implement the union and intersection operations that Exercise 7 describes for an unsorted array-based dictionary.

9. Repeat Exercise 8 for a sorted array-based dictionary.

10. Repeat Exercise 8 for a sorted linked dictionary.

## PROJECTS

1. Implement an unsorted array-based dictionary. Allow the array to expand as necessary during execution.

2. Repeat the previous project, but maintain the search keys in sorted order.

3. Implement an unsorted dictionary by using an instance of Vector or ArrayList to contain the dictionary entries. You can use one or two vectors or lists, much like the one or two arrays pictured in Parts *a* and *b* of Figure 20-1. Since the underlying implementation of either Vector or ArrayList is array based, the algorithms for the dictionary operations and their efficiencies are essentially the same whether you use an array, a list, or a vector.

   Note that the classes Vector and ArrayList are introduced in Segment 6.14 of Chapter 6 and Segment 12.15 of Chapter 12, respectively.

4. Repeat the previous project, but maintain the search keys in sorted order. Use a binary search instead of a sequential search when searching the dictionary for a key.

5. Implement an unsorted dictionary by using a chain of linked nodes.

6. Implement a sorted dictionary by using a chain of linked nodes.

7. In this chapter, the ADT dictionary has distinct search keys. Implement a dictionary that removes this restriction. Choose one of the possibilities given in Exercise 13 of the previous chapter.

8. Segment 19.7 of the previous chapter began a discussion of a telephone directory. Use your dictionary implementation from Project 7 in a revision of the telephone directory that allows duplicate names.

9. Figure 20-1b illustrates how you can use parallel arrays to represent the entries in a dictionary. Implement the ADT dictionary by using this approach.

10. Revise the class `Entry` given in Listing 20-1 of Segment 20.2 as a public class that implements the interface `Comparable`. You compare two `Entry` objects by comparing their search keys. Using this class and an implementation of the ADT sorted list, write an implementation for a sorted dictionary. The classes, including `Entry`, should belong to the same package.

11. Repeat the previous project, but instead of a sorted list, use an array of `Entry` objects.

12. Repeat Project 10, but instead of a sorted list, use a chain of linked nodes that each reference an instance of `Entry`.

13. Implement the interface `DictionaryInterface<String, String>` to create a class of glossaries. A *glossary* is a dictionary of specialized terms and their corresponding definitions. Represent the glossary as a collection of 26 sorted lists, one list for each letter of the alphabet. Each entry—which consists of a term and its definition—in a glossary is stored in the sorted list corresponding to the term's first letter. Thoroughly test your class using a text file of terms and definitions as data for your glossary.

## ANSWERS TO SELF-TEST QUESTIONS

1. The memory requirements for the search keys and the values are the same for each representation, so let's ignore them. The memory requirement for the representation shown in Figure 20-1a uses three references for each entry in the dictionary: one in the array and two in the `Entry` object. The parallel arrays in Figure 20-1b require only two references for each dictionary entry. Thus, for $n$ entries in the dictionary, the representation in Part $a$ requires $3n$ references, but the representation in Part $b$ requires only $2n$ references. However, if each array has a length of $m$, where $m$ is greater than $n$, Part $a$ has $m - n$ unused locations and Part $b$ has twice that number.

2. The initial search determines the insertion point when the dictionary is sorted, whereas the insertion point for an unsorted dictionary is always right after the last entry in the array. Insertion into a sorted dictionary generally requires shifting other entries in the array. No shifting is necessary for an unsorted dictionary.

3.
```java
private int locateIndex(K key)
{
   return binarySearch(0, numberOfEntries - 1, key);
} // end locateIndex

private int binarySearch(int first, int last, K key)
{
   int result;

   if (first > last)
      result = first;
   else

   {
      int mid = first + (last - first) / 2;
      K midKey = dictionary[mid].getKey();

      if (key.equals(midKey))
         result = mid;
      else if (key.compareTo(midKey) < 0)
         result = binarySearch(first, mid - 1, key);
      else
         result = binarySearch(mid + 1, last, key);
   } // end if

   return result;
} // end binarySearch
```

4. Typically, add must shift array entries to make room for a new entry, and remove must shift array entries to avoid a vacancy within the array. These shifts of data are O(*n*) operations in the worst case. The best case occurs when the addition or removal is at the end of the array. These operations are O(1).

5. No. Replacing the entry to be removed with the last entry in a chain would require a traversal of the chain. We would need references to both the last node and the next-to-last node so that we could delete the last node. Although we can ignore the last entry in an array, we should shorten the chain by setting the link portion of the next-to-last node to null. Note that having a tail reference does not eliminate the need for a traversal, since we need but do not have a reference to the next-to-last node. The strategy for an unsorted array-based dictionary avoids shifting any of the other entries. No shifting is needed in a linked implementation. After locating the node to delete, you simply adjust either the head reference or the reference in the preceding node.

# Chapter 21

# Introducing Hashing

## Contents

## Prerequisites

## Objectives

After studying this chapter, you should be able to

- Describe the basic idea of hashing
- Describe the purpose of a hash table, a hash function, and a perfect hash function
- Explain why you should override the method hashCode for objects used as search keys
- Describe how a hash function compresses a hash code into an index to the hash table
- Describe collisions and explain why they occur
- Describe open addressing as a method to resolve collisions
- Describe linear probing, quadratic probing, and double hashing as particular open addressing schemes
- Describe algorithms for the dictionary operations getValue, add, and remove when open addressing resolves collisions
- Describe separate chaining as a method to resolve collisions
- Describe algorithms for the dictionary operations getValue, add, and remove when separate chaining resolves collisions
- Describe clustering and the problems it causes

**B**ecause searching databases is such a widespread application of computers, the dictionary is an important abstract data type. The implementations that we discussed in the previous chapter are fine for certain applications, but for others they are inadequate. For example, if locating data is critical, even an O(log *n*) search can be too slow. Such is the case for the emergency telephone (911) system. If you call 911 from a land line, your telephone number is the key in a search of a dictionary of street addresses. Obviously, you want this search to find your location immediately!

This chapter introduces a technique called hashing that ideally can result in O(1) search times. We will complete our exploration of this topic in the next chapter. Hashing can be an excellent choice for implementing a dictionary when searching is the primary task. But as good as hashing can be, it is not always appropriate. For example, hashing cannot provide a traversal of the search keys in sorted order. Later in this book we will consider other implementations of the ADT dictionary.

# What Is Hashing?

VideoNote
Hashing

**21.1**    **A place for everything; everything in its place.** Do you spend time looking for your keys in the morning? Or do you know exactly where they are? Some of us spend too much time sequentially searching our unsorted possessions. Others have a special place for things and know just where to find each one.

An array can provide a place for a dictionary's entries. Admittedly, arrays have their disadvantages, but you can access any entry in an array directly if you know its index. No other array entry need be involved. **Hashing** is a technique that determines this index using only an entry's search key, without searching. The array itself is called a **hash table**.

A **hash function** takes a search key and produces the integer index of an element in the hash table. This array element is where you would either store or look for the value associated with a search key. For example, the 911 emergency system can take your telephone number, convert it to a suitable integer *i*, and store a reference to your street address in the array element a[i]. We say that the telephone number—that is, the search key—**maps**, or **hashes**, to the index i. This index is called a **hash index**. Sometimes we will say that the search key maps, or hashes, into the table location at the index i.

**21.2**    **Ideal hashing.** Consider an emergency system for a small town where everyone's telephone number begins with 555. Let the hash function *h* convert a telephone number to its last four digits. For example,

$$h(555\text{-}1214) = 1214$$

If hashTable is the hash table, we would place a reference to the street address associated with this telephone number in hashTable[1214], as Figure 21-1 illustrates. If the cost of evaluating the hash function is low, adding an entry to the array hashTable is an O(1) operation.

**FIGURE 21-1**    A hash function indexes its hash table

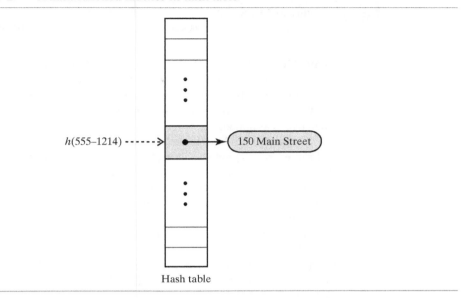

Hash table

To later find the street address associated with the number 555-1214, we once again compute $h$(555-1214) and use the result to index `hashTable`. Thus, from `hashTable[1214]`, we get the desired street address. This operation also is O(1). Notice that we did not search the array `hashTable`.

**21.3**    Let's summarize what we know so far by writing simple algorithms for the dictionary operations that add or retrieve entries:

*Algorithm* **add(key, value)**
```
index = h(key)
hashTable[index] = value
```

*Algorithm* **getValue(key)**
```
index = h(key)
return hashTable[index]
```

Will these algorithms always work? We can make them work if we know all the possible search keys. In this example, the search keys range from 555-0000 to 555-9999, so the hash function will produce indices from 0 to 9999. If the array `hashTable` has 10,000 elements, each telephone number will correspond to one unique element in `hashTable`. That element references the appropriate street address. This scenario describes the ideal case for hashing, and the hash function here is a **perfect hash function**.

**Note:** A perfect hash function maps each search key into a different integer that is suitable as an index to the hash table.

21.4  **Typical hashing.** Because we need a database of all street addresses in the previous example, we must have one entry in the hash table for each telephone number. Our perfect hash function needs a hash table this large because it produces 10,000 different indices between 0 and 9999 from the 10,000 possible search keys. This hash table is always full if every telephone number in the 555 exchange is assigned.

Although a full hash table is quite reasonable for this application, most hash tables are not full and can even be **sparse**—that is, have only a few of their elements actually in use. For example, if our small town required only 700 telephone numbers, most of the 10,000-location hash table would be unused. We would waste most of the space allocated to the hash table. If the 700 numbers were not sequential, we would need a different hash function if we wanted to use a smaller hash table.

We might develop this different hash function as follows. Given a nonnegative integer $i$ and a hash table with $n$ locations, the value of $i$ modulo $n$ ranges from 0 to $n - 1$. Since $i$ is nonnegative, $i$ modulo $n$ is the integer remainder after dividing $i$ by $n$. This value is a valid index for the hash table. So a hash function $h$ for a telephone number could have the following algorithm:

*Algorithm* `getHashIndex(phoneNumber)`
*// Returns an index to an array of* `tableSize` *elements.*

$i$ = *last four digits of* `phoneNumber`
**return** `i % tableSize`

This hash function—like typical hash functions—performs two steps:

1. Convert the search key to an integer called the **hash code**.
2. **Compress** the hash code into the range of indices for the hash table.

Often the search key is not an integer, and frequently it is a string. So a hash function first converts the key to an integer hash code. Next it transforms that integer into one that is suitable as an index to the particular hash table.

The hash function that the algorithm `getHashIndex` describes is not a perfect hash function when `tableSize` is less than 10,000. Since 10,000 telephone numbers map into `tableSize` indices, some telephone numbers will map into the same index. We call such an occurrence a **collision**. For example, if `tableSize` is 101, `getHashIndex("555-1214")` and `getHashIndex("555-8132")` each map into 52. If we have already stored the street address for 555-1214 in `hashTable[52]`, as Figure 21-2 shows, what will we do with the address for 555-8132? Handling such collisions is called **collision resolution**. Before we look at collision resolution, we will explore hash functions a bit further.

 **Note:** Typical hash functions are not perfect, because they can allow more than one search key to map into a single index, causing a collision in the hash table.

FIGURE 21-2    A collision caused by the hash function *h*

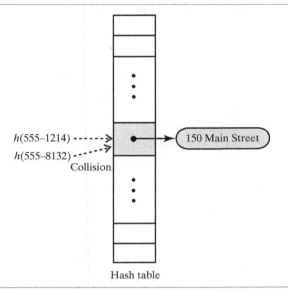

Hash table

## Hash Functions

**21.5**  **General characteristics.** Any function can be a hash function if it produces an integer that is suitable as an array index. But not every such function is a *good* hash function. Our previous discussions suggest that a good hash function should

- Minimize collisions
- Be fast to compute

Recall that a typical hash function first converts a search key to an integer hash code. The hash function then compresses the hash code into an integer that is suitable as an index to the particular hash table.

 **Note:** To reduce the chance of a collision, choose a hash function that distributes entries uniformly throughout the hash table.

First, consider how to convert a search key to an `int`. Realize that a search key can be either a primitive type or an instance of a class.

### Computing Hash Codes

**21.6**  **The hash code for a class type.** Java's base class `Object` has a method `hashCode` that returns an integer hash code. Since every class is a subclass of `Object`, all classes inherit this method. But unless a class overrides `hashCode`, the method will return an `int` value based on the memory address of the object used to invoke it. This default hash code usually is not appropriate for hashing, because equal but distinct objects will have different hash codes. To be useful as a dictionary implementation, hashing must map equal objects into the same location in a hash table. Thus, a class should define its own version of hashCode that adheres to the following guidelines.

**Note:  Guidelines for the method hashCode**
- If a class overrides the method equals, it should override hashCode.
- If the method equals considers two objects equal, hashCode must return the same value for both objects.
- If you call an object's hashCode more than once during the execution of a program, and if the object's data remains the same during this time, hashCode must return the same hash code.
- An object's hash code during one execution of a program can differ from its hash code during another execution of the same program.

A perfect hash function would require that unequal objects have distinct hash codes. In general, however, unequal objects might have the same hash codes. Since duplicate hash codes lead to collisions, you want to avoid this situation when possible.

**21.7**   **A hash code for a string.** Search keys are often strings, so generating a good hash code from a string is important. Typically, you begin by assigning an integer to each character in the string. For example, you could assign the integers 1 through 26 to the letters "A" through "Z" and the integers 27 through 52 to the letters "a" through "z." However, using a character's Unicode integer is more common and actually easier to do.

Suppose that the search keys for a telephone directory are names such as *Brett*, *Carol*, *Gail*, and *Josh*. You can compute hash codes for these names in several ways. For example, you could take the Unicode value of the first letter in each name and get distinct hash codes. But if several names begin with the same letter, their hash codes will be the same if you use this scheme. Since the letters that occur in any one position of a name do not occur with equal probability, a hash function that uses any particular letter will not distribute the names uniformly throughout the hash table.

Suppose that you sum the Unicode values for each letter in the search key. In an application where two different search keys never contain the same letters, this approach can work. But search keys that consist of different arrangements of the same letters—as in the airport codes *DUB* and *BUD*, for example—would have the same hash code. This approach also can restrict the range of the hash codes, since the Unicode values for letters lie between 65 and 122. Thus, three-letter words would map into values between 195 and 366 under this plan.

**Note:**  Real-world data is not uniformly distributed.

**21.8**   **A better hash code for a string.** A better approach to generating a hash code for a string involves multiplying the Unicode value of each character by a factor based on the character's position within the string. The hash code is then the sum of these products. Specifically, if the string *s* has

$n$ characters, let $u_i$ be the Unicode value for the $i^{th}$ character in $s$ ($i$ is zero for the first character). Then the hash code can have the form

$$u_0 g^{n-1} + u_1 g^{n-2} + \ldots + u_{n-2} g + u_{n-1}$$

for some positive constant $g$. This expression is a polynomial in $g$. To minimize the number of arithmetic operations, write the polynomial in the following algebraically equivalent form:

$$( \ldots ((u_0 g + u_1) g + u_2) g + \ldots + u_{n-2}) g + u_{n-1}$$

This way of evaluating a polynomial is called *Horner's method.*

The following Java statements perform this computation for the string s and the int constant g:

```
int hash = 0;
int n = s.length();
for (int i = 0; i < n; i++)
    hash = g * hash + s.charAt(i);
```

The $i^{th}$ character of the string is s.charAt(i). Adding this character to the product g * hash actually adds the character's Unicode value. An explicit cast of s.charAt(i) to int is not necessary and would not affect the result.

This computation can cause an overflow, particularly for long strings. Java ignores these overflows and, for an appropriate choice of g, the result will be a reasonable hash code. Current implementations of the method hashCode in Java's class String use this computation with 31 as the value of g. Realize, however, that the overflows can produce a negative result. You can deal with that when you compress the hash code into an appropriate index for the hash table.

---

**Question 1** Calculate the hash code for the string *Java* when $g$ is 31. Compare your result with the value of the expression "Java".hashCode().

---

**21.9** **The hash code for a primitive type.** This segment contains Java operations that might be unfamiliar to you. However, they are not essential to the rest of this chapter.

If the search key's data type is int, you can use the key itself as the hash code. If the search key is an instance of either byte, short, or char, you can cast it to an int to get a hash code. Thus, casting to an int is one way to generate a hash code.

For other primitive types, you manipulate their internal binary representations. If the search key is an integer of type long, it contains 64 bits. An int has 32 bits. Simply casting the 64-bit search key to an int—or performing a modulo $2^{32}$—would lose its first 32 bits. As a result, all keys that differ in only their first 32 bits will have the same hash code and collide. For this reason, ignoring part of a search key can be a problem.

**Note:** Derive the hash code from the *entire* search key. Do not ignore part of it.

Instead of ignoring a part of a long search key, divide it into several pieces. Then combine the pieces by using either addition or a bit-wise boolean operation such as **exclusive or**. This process is called **folding**.

For example, let's divide a long search key into two 32-bit halves. To get the left half, we can shift the search key to the right by a certain number of bits, or places. For example, if we shift the 8-bit binary number 10101100 to the right by 4 bits, we will get 00001010. We have isolated the number's left half and discarded its right half. If we now combine 00001010 with the original value and ignore the left half of the result, we will effectively have combined the left and right halves of the original key.

Now let's see how to do this in Java. The expression key >> 32 shifts the 64-bit key to the right by 32 bits, in effect eliminating its right half. Java's exclusive-or operator is ^ and has the following effect on 1-bit quantities:

0 ^ 0 is 0
1 ^ 1 is 0
0 ^ 1 is 1
1 ^ 0 is 1

For two multibit quantities, the operator combines pairs of corresponding bits. So

1100 ^ 1010 is 0110

Thus, the expression key ^ (key >> 32) uses an exclusive-or operation to combine the halves of a 64-bit key. Although the result has 64 bits, the rightmost 32 bits contain the combined halves of key. We discard the leftmost 32 bits by casting the result to an int. Thus, the necessary computation is

(int)(key ^ (key >> 32))

We can perform a similar computation for a search key of type double. Since key is a real value, we cannot use it in the previous expression. Instead, we must get key's bit pattern by calling Double.doubleToLongBits(key). Thus, the following statements produce the desired hash code:

```
long bits = Double.doubleToLongBits(key);
int hashCode = (int)(bits ^ (bits >> 32));
```

Why not simply cast the search key from double to int? Since the search key is a real value, casting it to an int will simply give us the integral portion of the value. For example, if the key's value is 32.98, casting it to int results in the integer 32. While we could use 32 as the hash code, all search keys that have 32 as their integer portion also would have a hash code of 32. Unless you know that your real values have distinct integral portions, casting them to int values can cause many collisions.

The hash code of a search key of type float can be simply its 32 bits. You get these by calling Float.floatToIntBits(key).

These computations of hash codes for the primitives types are actually used by the corresponding wrapper classes in their implementations of the method hashCode.

## Compressing a Hash Code into an Index for the Hash Table

**21.10**    The most common way to scale an integer so that it lies within a given range of values is to use Java's % operator. For a positive hash code $c$ and a positive integer $n$, $c \% n$ divides $c$ by $n$ and takes the remainder as the result. This remainder lies between 0 and $n - 1$. Thus, $c \% n$ is ideal for the index of a hash table that has $n$ locations.

So $n$ should equal the size of the hash table, but not any $n$ will do. For example, if $n$ is even, $c \% n$ has the same **parity** as $c$—that is, if $c$ is even, $c \% n$ is even; if $c$ is odd, $c \% n$ is odd. If the hash codes are biased toward either even or odd values (and note that hash codes based on memory addresses are typically even), the indices to the hash table will have the same bias. Instead of a uniform distribution of indices, you will leave out the indices of many table locations if $n$ is even. Thus, $n$—the size of the hash table—always should be an odd number.

When $n$ is a **prime number**—one that is divisible only by 1 and itself—$c \% n$ provides values that are distributed throughout the index range 0 through $n - 1$. Prime numbers—with the exception of 2—are odd.

**Note:** The size of a hash table should be a prime number *n* greater than 2. Then, if you compress a positive hash code *c* into an index for the table by using *c* % *n*, the indices will be distributed uniformly between 0 and *n* - 1.

One final detail remains. You saw earlier that the method `hashCode` might return a negative integer, so you need to be a bit careful. If *c* is negative, *c* % *n* lies between 1 - *n* and 0. A zero result is fine, but if *c* % *n* is negative, add *n* to it so that it lies between 1 and *n* - 1.

**21.11**   We now can implement a hash function for the ADT dictionary. The following method computes the hash index for a given search key whose data type is the generic object type K. The data field `hashTable` is the array that serves as the hash table. Realize that `hashTable.length` is the size of the array, not the number of current entries in the hash table. We assume that this size is a prime number and that the method `hashCode` returns a hash code consistent with the previous discussion.

```
private int getHashIndex(K key)
{
    int hashIndex = key.hashCode() % hashTable.length;
    if (hashIndex < 0)
        hashIndex = hashIndex + hashTable.length;

    return hashIndex;
} // end getHashIndex
```

**Question 2**   Question 1 in Segment 21.8 asked you to compute the hash code for the string *Java*. Use that value to calculate what `getHashIndex("Java")` returns when the length of the hash table is 101.

**Question 3**   What one-character string, when passed to `getHashIndex`, will cause the method to return the same value as in the previous question?

# Resolving Collisions

**21.12**   When adding to a dictionary, if your hash function maps a search key into a location in the hash table that is already in use, you need to find another spot for the search key's value. You have two fundamental choices:

- Use another location in the hash table
- Change the structure of the hash table so that each array element can represent more than one value

VideoNote
Resolving collisions

Finding an unused, or open, location in the hash table is called **open addressing**. This choice sounds simple, but it can lead to several complications. Changing the structure of the hash table is not as difficult as it might sound and can be a better choice for resolving collisions than using an open addressing scheme. We will examine both approaches, beginning with several variations of open addressing.

## Open Addressing with Linear Probing

**21.13**   When a collision occurs during the addition of an entry to a hash table, an open addressing scheme locates an alternate location in the hash table that is available, or open. You then use this location to reference the new entry.

Locating an open location in the hash table is called **probing**, and various probing techniques are possible. With **linear probing**, if a collision occurs at hashTable[k], we see whether hashTable[k + 1] is available. If not, we look at hashTable[k + 2], and so on. The table locations that we consider in this search make up the **probe sequence**. If a probe sequence reaches the end of the hash table, it continues at the beginning of the table. Thus, we treat the hash table as if it were circular: The first location in the table comes immediately after the last location.

 **Note:** **Linear probing** resolves a collision during hashing by examining consecutive locations in the hash table—beginning at the original hash index—to find the next available one.

**21.14** **Additions that collide.** Recall the example illustrated in Figure 21-2. The search keys 555-1214 and 555-8132 both mapped into the index 52. Suppose that 555-4294 and 555-2072 also map into that same index, and we make the following additions to an empty dictionary addressBook:

```
addressBook.add("555-1214", "150 Main Street");
addressBook.add("555-8132", "75 Center Court");
addressBook.add("555-4294", "205 Ocean Road");
addressBook.add("555-2072", "82 Campus Way");
```

The first addition would use hashTable[52]. The second addition would find hashTable[52] occupied, so it would probe ahead and use hashTable[53]. The third addition would find both hashTable[52] and hashTable[53] occupied, so it would probe ahead and use hashTable[54]. Finally, the fourth addition would probe the locations at indices 52, 53, and 54 before using hashTable[55] for the addition. Figure 21-3 shows the result of these additions to the hash table.

FIGURE 21-3    The effect of linear probing after adding four entries whose search keys hash to the same index

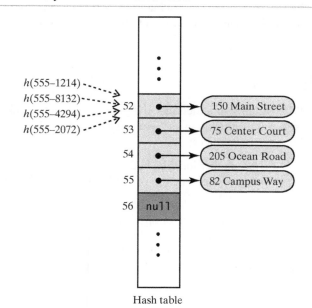

Hash table

 **Note:** Linear probing can examine every location in a hash table. As a result, this type of probing ensures the success of the add operation as long as the hash table is not full.

**21.15**    **Retrievals.** Now that we've used linear probing to resolve collisions while adding our four entries, how do we retrieve the street address associated with the last search key we added, 555-2072? That is, if the statement

```
String streetAddress = addressBook.getValue("555-2072");
```

is executed, what will getValue do? Since getHashIndex("555-2072") is 52, getValue will search consecutive elements in the array beginning at hashTable[52] until it finds the street address associated with the search key 555-2072. But wait! How can we tell which street address is the right one? We can't, unless we package a search key with its value. Segment 20.2 of Chapter 20 provided a class Entry that we could use for this purpose. Figure 21-4 shows the hash table given in Figure 21-3 after we make this revision.

**FIGURE 21-4**    A revision of the hash table shown in Figure 21-3 when
linear probing resolves collisions; each entry contains a
search key and its associated value

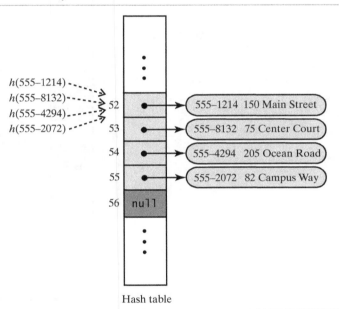

Hash table

Now the search for 555-2072 can follow the same probe sequence that was used to add this search key and its value to the hash table. This fact will be useful later when we assess the efficiency of hashing.

 **Note:** A successful search for an entry that corresponds to a given search key follows the same probe sequence used to add the entry to the hash table.

What happens if the search key is not in the hash table? The search of the probe sequence would encounter a null location, indicating an unsuccessful search. But before we can reach this conclusion, we need to know what the remove method does, because it has the potential to adversely affect subsequent retrievals.

**21.16**   **Removals.** Suppose that after the four additions illustrated in Figure 21-4, we removed two entries by executing the following code:

```
addressBook.remove("555-8132");
addressBook.remove("555-4294");
```

The simplest way to remove an entry from a table location is to place `null` in the location. Figure 21-5 shows the hash table after `remove` places `null` into the array elements `hashTable[53]` and `hashTable[54]`. But now an attempt to find the search key 555-2072 will terminate unsuccessfully at `hashTable[53]`. Although a location in the hash table that was never used should end a search, a location that had been used and is now available again for use should not.

FIGURE 21-5     A hash table if `remove` used `null` to remove entries

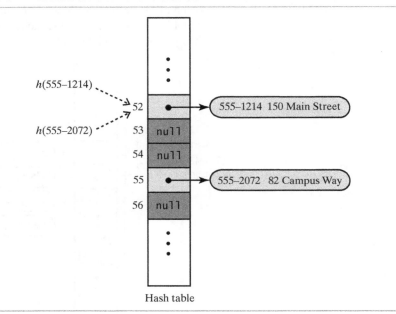

Hash table

Thus, we need to distinguish among three kinds of locations in the hash table:

- Occupied—the location references an entry in the dictionary
- Empty—the location contains `null` and always has
- Available—the location's entry was removed from the dictionary

Accordingly, the method `remove` should not place `null` into the hash table, but instead should encode the location as available. The search during a retrieval should then continue if it encounters an available location and should stop only if it is successful or reaches a `null` location. A search during a removal behaves in the same way.

**Question 4** Suggest ways to implement the three states of a location in a hash table. Should this state be a responsibility of the location or of the dictionary entry that it references?

**21.17**   **Reusing locations in the hash table during an addition.** Recall the hash table pictured in Figure 21-4. The entry whose search key is 555-2072 mapped into `hashTable[52]` but was added to the hash table at `hashTable[55]` due to collisions. Figure 21-6a shows this hash table again, but in a simpler form.

The four occupied locations constitute a probe sequence; the other locations contain null. Since the search key 555-2072 maps into the first location of the probe sequence but actually occurs in the fourth location, a brief sequential search will find it.

Now let's try removing the middle two entries of the probe sequence, as Figure 21-6b shows. A search for 555-2072 starts at the beginning of the probe sequence, must continue beyond the removed entries, and stops successfully at the last location in the probe sequence. If 555-2072 does not occur in this last location, the search will end unsuccessfully at the next location, since it contains null. Figure 21-6c illustrates these searches.

**FIGURE 21-6**  A linear probe sequence (a) after adding an entry; (b) after removing two entries; (c) after a search; (d) during the search while adding an entry; (e) after an addition to a formerly occupied location

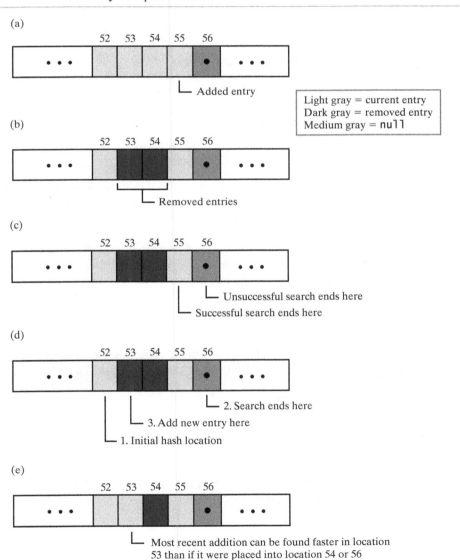

Finally, consider what happens when we add an entry that maps into this probe sequence. For example, the search key 555-1062 maps into hashTable[52]. The add operation first must see whether this search key is in the hash table already. To do so, it searches the probe sequence. It has to search the entire probe sequence and reach a null location to discover that 555-1062 is not in the table. Figure 21-6d shows that this search ends at hashTable[56]. Should add place the new entry in this location? It could, but that would fill the hash table faster than if add reused a location that is presently in the available state. Two such locations are at the indices 53 and 54. We should place the new entry at hashTable[53]—that is, closest to the beginning of the probe sequence—so we can find it more quickly later. Figure 21-6e illustrates the hash table after this addition.

**Note:** **Searches that dictionary operations require when open addressing resolves collisions**

- To retrieve an entry, getValue(key) searches the probe sequence for key. It examines entries that are present and ignores locations that are in the available state. The search stops when either key is found or null is reached.
- The operation remove(key) searches the probe sequence using the same logic as a retrieval. If it finds key, it marks the location as available.
- The operation add(key, value) searches the probe sequence using logic like that of a retrieval, but it also notes the index of the first location encountered that is either in the available state or contains null. The operation uses this location for a new entry if key is not found.

21.18 **Clustering.** Collisions that are resolved with linear probing cause groups of consecutive locations in the hash table to be occupied. Each group is called a **cluster**, and the phenomenon is known as **primary clustering**. Each cluster is actually a probe sequence that you must search when adding, removing, or retrieving a table entry. When few collisions occur, probe sequences remain short and can be searched rapidly. But during an addition, any collision within a cluster increases the size of the cluster. Bigger clusters mean longer search times following a collision. As the clusters grow in size, they can merge into even larger clusters, compounding the problem. This occurrence can place many entries in one part of the hash table while another part is relatively empty.

**Note:** Linear probing is apt to cause primary clustering. Each cluster is a group of consecutive and occupied locations in the hash table. During an addition, any collision with any location within a cluster causes the cluster to get larger.

## Open Addressing with Quadratic Probing

21.19 You can avoid primary clustering by changing the probe sequence that you use to resolve a collision. As we discussed in the previous section, if a given search key hashes to index $k$, linear probing looks at the consecutive locations beginning at index $k$. **Quadratic probing**, on the other hand, considers the locations at indices $k + j^2$ for $j \geq 0$—that is, it uses the indices $k$, $k + 1$, $k + 4$, $k + 9$, and so on. As before, if the probe sequence reaches the end of the hash table, it wraps around to the beginning of the table. This open addressing scheme separates the entries in the probe sequence, after the first two. In fact, this separation increases as the sequence grows in length. Figure 21-7 highlights the locations in a hash table that form one such probe sequence of five entries.

**FIGURE 21-7**    A probe sequence of length five using quadratic probing

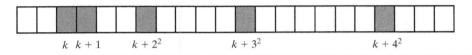

$k\ \ k+1\qquad k+2^2\qquad\qquad k+3^2\qquad\qquad\qquad k+4^2$

Except for the change in probe sequence, quadratic probing is like linear probing. It uses the three states that Segment 21.16 describes: occupied, empty, and available. Additionally, it reuses table locations in the available state, as described in Segment 21.17.

Although quadratic probing avoids primary clustering, entries that collide with an existing table entry use the same probe sequence, thereby increasing the probe sequence's length. This phenomenon—called **secondary clustering**—is usually not a serious problem, but it increases search times.

An advantage of linear probing is that it can reach every location in the hash table. As we mentioned earlier, this property is important since it guarantees the success of the add operation when the hash table is not full. Quadratic probing can also guarantee a successful add operation, as long as the hash table is at most half full and its size is a prime number. (See Exercise 8 at the end of this chapter.)

Quadratic probing requires more effort to compute the indices for the probe sequence than does linear probing. Exercise 2 at the end of this chapter shows how to compute these indices efficiently.

 **Note:  Quadratic probing**
- Resolves a collision during hashing by examining locations in the hash table at the original hash index plus $j^2$, for $j \geq 0$
- Reaches half of the locations in the hash table if the size of the table is a prime number
- Avoids primary clustering but can lead to secondary clustering

## Open Addressing with Double Hashing

**21.20**    Beginning at the original hash index $k$, both linear probing and quadratic probing add increments to $k$ to define a probe sequence. These increments—1 for linear probing and $j^2$ for quadratic probing—are independent of the search key. **Double hashing** uses a second hash function to compute these increments in a key-dependent way. In this way, double hashing avoids both primary and secondary clustering.

Double hashing, like other open addressing schemes, should produce a probe sequence that reaches the entire table. Such will be the case if the size of the hash table is a prime number. (See Exercise 9 at the end of this chapter.) The second hash function must be different from the original hash function and must never have a zero value, since zero is not an appropriate increment.

**21.21**    **Example.** For example, consider the following pair of hash functions for a hash table whose size is 7:

$$h_1(key) = key \text{ modulo } 7$$
$$h_2(key) = 5 - key \text{ modulo } 5$$

This hash table is unusually small, but it allows us to study the behavior of the probe sequence. For a search key of 16, we have

$$h_1(16) = 2$$
$$h_2(16) = 4$$

The probe sequence begins at 2 and probes locations at increments of 4, as Figure 21-8 illustrates. Remember that when probing reaches the end of the table, it continues at the table's beginning. The table locations in the probe sequence then have the following indices: 2, 6, 3, 0, 4, 1, 5, 2, .... This sequence reaches all locations in the table and then repeats itself. Notice that the table size, 7, is a prime number.

**FIGURE 21-8**      The first three locations in a probe sequence generated by double hashing for the search key 16

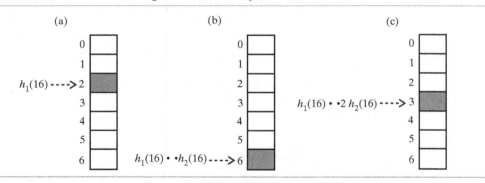

What happens if we change the size of the table to 6 and use the hash functions

$$h_1(key) = key \text{ modulo } 6$$
$$h_2(key) = 5 - key \text{ modulo } 5$$

For a search key of 16, we have

$$h_1(16) = 4$$
$$h_2(16) = 4$$

The probe sequence begins at 4 and probes locations at increments of 4. The sequence's indices are then 4, 2, 0, 4, 2, 0, .... The probe sequence does not reach all table locations before it begins to repeat. Notice that the table size, 6, is not prime.

**Note: Double hashing**

- Resolves a collision during hashing by examining locations in the hash table at the original hash index plus an increment defined by a second hash function. The second hash function should
  - Differ from the first hash function
  - Depend on the search key
  - Have a nonzero value
- Reaches every location in the hash table, if the size of the table is a prime number
- Avoids both primary clustering and secondary clustering

**Question 5** What size hash table should you use with double hashing when the hash functions are

$h_1(key) = key$ modulo 13
$h_2(key) = 7 - key$ modulo 7

Why?

**Question 6** What probe sequence is defined by the hash functions given in the previous question when the search key is 16?

## A Potential Problem with Open Addressing

**21.22** The previous three open addressing schemes for collision resolution assume that each table location is in one of three states: occupied, empty, or available. Recall that only empty locations contain null. Frequent additions and removals can cause every location in the hash table to reference either a current entry or a former entry. That is, a hash table might have no location that contains null, regardless of how many or how few entries are actually in the dictionary. If this happens, our approach to searching a probe sequence will not work. Instead, every unsuccessful search can end only after considering every location in the hash table. Also, detecting the end of the search will be somewhat more involved and costly than simply looking for null.

You should safeguard your implementation against this failure. Increasing the size of the hash table (see Segment 22.7 in the next chapter) can correct the problem, if you act in time. Separate chaining—which we consider next—does not have this problem.

**Note:** Open addressing can be simplified when an application does not require removals. Such is the case, for example, when a compiler builds a symbol table. It can use a dictionary that does not permit removals. Locations in the hash table will either reference a dictionary entry or contain null. Defining the three states given in Segment 21.16 is not needed. Project 1 at the end of this chapter asks you to develop this implementation.

## Separate Chaining

**21.23**  A second general approach to collision resolution alters the structure of the hash table so that each location can represent more than one value. Such a location is called a **bucket**. Anytime a new search key maps into a particular location, you simply place the key and its associated value in the bucket, much as we did with open addressing. To find a value, you hash the search key, locate the bucket, and look through the key-value pairs in it. In all likelihood, the bucket contains few values, so this mini-search will be fast. When you remove an entry, you find it in its bucket and delete it. Thus, the entry no longer exists in the hash table.

What can you use to represent a bucket? A list, a sorted list, a chain of linked nodes, an array, or a vector are some possibilities with which you are familiar. Anything that involves an array or vector will cause a substantial memory overhead, since each location in the hash table will have a fixed amount of memory allocated to it. Much of this memory will be unused. Either a linked implementation of a list or a chain of linked nodes is a reasonable choice for a bucket, since memory is allocated to the bucket only as needed. Figure 21-9 illustrates a hash table with linked chains as buckets. In this arrangement, each location in the hash table is a head reference to a chain of linked nodes that make up the bucket. Each node contains references to a search key, to the key's associated value, and to the next node in the chain. Notice that a node must reference the search key so that you can locate it later when you search the chain. Resolving collisions by using buckets that are linked chains is called **separate chaining**.

**FIGURE 21-9**      A hash table for use with separate chaining; each bucket is a
chain of linked nodes

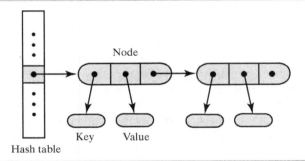

**21.24**  If your dictionary allows duplicate search keys, adding a new entry to the beginning of the appropriate chain is fastest, as Figure 21-10a indicates. However, if you want distinct search keys, adding a new entry requires you to search a chain for the search key. If you do not find it, you will be at the end of the chain, where you can add the new entry. Figure 21-10b illustrates this case. But since you have to search the chain anyway, you could maintain the chain in sorted order by search key, as Figure 21-10c shows. Subsequent searches would then be a little faster. As you will see, however, typical chains are short, so this refinement might not be worth the effort.

**Question 7**  Consider search keys that are distinct integers. If the hash function is

$h(key) = key$ modulo 5

and separate chaining resolves collisions, where in the hash table do the following search keys appear after being added? 4, 6, 20, 14, 31, 29

**FIGURE 21-10**   Where to insert a new entry into a linked bucket when the
integer search keys are (a) unsorted and possibly duplicate;
(b) unsorted and distinct; (c) sorted and distinct

(a) Duplicate, unsorted keys

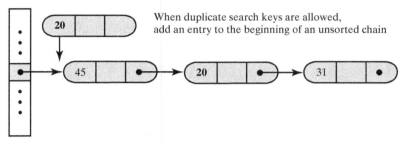

Hash table

(b) Distinct, unsorted keys

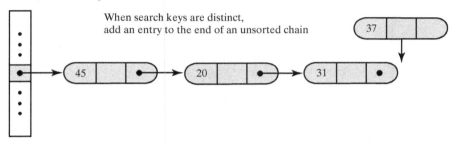

Hash table

(c) Distinct, sorted keys

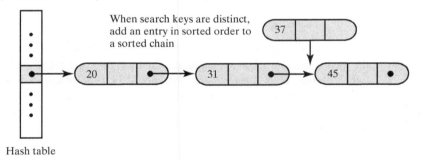

Hash table

**21.25**   With distinct search keys and unsorted chains, the algorithms for the dictionary's add, remove, and
getValue methods are as follows:

```
Algorithm add(key, value)
index = getHashIndex(key)
if (hashTable[index] == null)
{
    hashTable[index] = new Node(key, value)
    numberOfEntries++
    return null
}
else
{
```

*Search the chain that begins at* hashTable[index] *for a node that contains* key
```
if (key is found)
{ // Assume currentNode references the node that contains key
    oldValue = currentNode.getValue()
    currentNode.setValue(value)
    return oldValue
}
else // Add new node to end of chain
{ // Assume nodeBefore references the last node
    newNode = new Node(key, value)
    nodeBefore.setNextNode(newNode)
    numberOfEntries++
    return null
}
}
```

*Algorithm* remove(key)
```
index = getHashIndex(key)
```
*Search the chain that begins at* hashTable[index] *for a node that contains* key
```
if (key is found)
{
    Remove the node that contains key from the chain
    numberOfEntries--
    return value in removed node
}
else
    return null
```

*Algorithm* getValue(key)
```
index = getHashIndex(key)
```
*Search the chain that begins at* hashTable[index] *for a node that contains* key
```
if (key is found)
    return value in found node
else
    return null
```

All three operations search a chain of nodes. Each chain should contain only a few entries, if the hash table is sufficiently large and the hash function distributes the entries uniformly throughout the table. Thus, these operations should be time efficient. For a dictionary of *n* entries, the operations certainly are faster than O(*n*). In the worst case, however, all entries are in one chain, so the efficiency degenerates to O(*n*). We will discuss the efficiency of hashing in more detail in the next chapter.

**Note:** **Separate chaining** provides an efficient and simple way to resolve collisions. Because the structure of the hash table is altered, however, separate chaining requires more memory than open addressing.

**Question 8** With distinct search keys and separate chaining with sorted chains, write an algorithm for the dictionary's add method.

**Question 9** Can you define an iteration of a dictionary's search keys in sorted order when you use hashing in its implementation? Explain.

## CHAPTER SUMMARY

- Hashing is a dictionary implementation that stores entries into an array called the hash table. A hash function transforms an entry's search key into the index of the array element that will contain the entry.

- All classes have a method `hashCode` that returns an integer hash code. If a class's instances are to be search keys, you should override `hashCode` to produce suitable hash codes. A hash code should depend on the entire search key.

- A hash function uses `hashCode` to compute a hash code from a search key and then compresses that hash code into an index to the hash table. A typical way to compress the hash code $c$ is to compute $c$ modulo $n$, where $n$ is a prime number and the size of the hash table. This computation produces an index whose magnitude lies between 0 and $n - 1$.

- A perfect hash function maps each search key into a distinct location in the hash table. You can find such a function if you know all possible search keys. Using a perfect hash function makes possible $O(1)$ implementations of the dictionary operations.

- With a typical hash function, more than one search key can map into the same location in the hash table. This occurrence is called a collision.

- Various methods are available to deal with collisions. Among them are open addressing and separate chaining.

- With open addressing, all entries that map into the same location are ultimately stored within the hash table. These entries are in a sequence of locations called the probe sequence. Several different versions of open addressing are common. Linear probing uses consecutive locations. Quadratic probing spaces the locations in a probe sequence at increasing increments. These increments are 1, 4, 9, and so on—that is, the squares of the integers 1, 2, 3, . . . . Double hashing uses a fixed increment that depends on the search key. A second hash function provides this increment.

- With open addressing, you remove an entry by placing it into a removed state. You do not set its table location to `null`, because that would terminate subsequent searches prematurely. You retrieve an entry by searching its probe sequence, ignoring removed entries, until you either find the desired entry or encounter `null`. You perform the same search when you add a new entry, but while searching, you note the first location—if any—that references a removed entry. You use this location for the added entry. If no such location exists, the addition extends the probe sequence by using the `null` location encountered after searching the entire sequence.

- A disadvantage of linear probing and quadratic probing is clustering. Clustering lengthens a probe sequence and so increases the time to search it. Double hashing avoids this problem.

- With separate chaining, the hash table is an array of buckets. All entries that map into the same array element are stored in the bucket that the location references. Each bucket can be a chain of linked nodes, for example. That is, each location in the hash table can reference the beginning of a chain.

- You can add new entries to a bucket's chain in sorted search-key order. Although sorted chains can improve search time somewhat, they usually are unnecessary, as typical chains are short. You add new entries to an unsorted chain either at the beginning, if duplicates are allowed, or at the end if not.

- With separate chaining, you retrieve or remove an entry by mapping its search key into a table location. You then search the bucket that the location references.

- An iteration of the entire hash table will not be in sorted order even if separate chaining with sorted buckets is used to resolve collisions.

## EXERCISES

1. Define a hashCode method for the class Name, as given in Segment C.16 of Appendix C.

2. Quadratic probing uses the following indices to define a probe sequence:

   $(k + j^2)$ modulo $n$ for $j \geq 0$

   where $k$ is the hash index and $n$ is the size of the hash table.

   a. If the hash table contains 17 locations and the hash index is 3, what are the first six indices of the array elements in the probe sequence that quadratic probing defines?

   b. You can compute the indices for the probe sequence more efficiently by using the recurrence relation

   $k_{i+1} = (k_i + 2i + 1)$ modulo $n$ for $i \geq 0$ and $k_0 = k$

   Derive this recurrence relation.

   c. Demonstrate that you can replace the modulo operation in Part *b* with one comparison and an occasional subtraction.

3. Project 10 in Chapter 20 revised the class Entry, which is in Listing 20-1, to make it public, and then used it in an implementation of a dictionary. Consider a hash table of Entry objects. Without further changes to the definition of Entry, how could you indicate a removed entry?

4. Suppose that the size of your hash table is 31, that you use the hash code described in Segment 21.8, and that you use separate chaining to resolve collisions. List five different names that would hash to the same location in the table.

5. Assume the hash table and hash function described in Exercise 4, but use open addressing with linear probing to resolve collisions. List five different names that do not all hash to the same location in the table yet would nonetheless result in collisions and clustering.

6. Repeat Exercise 5, but instead use open addressing with quadratic probing to resolve collisions.

7. Give an example of a probe sequence produced by quadratic probing that does not reach the entire hash table, even if the size of the table is a prime number.

8. Demonstrate that quadratic probing will guarantee a successful addition if the hash table is at most half full and its size is a prime number.

9. Demonstrate that double hashing will produce a probe sequence that reaches the entire table if the size of the hash table is a prime number. *Hint*: Show that this is true if the increment and the table size are relatively prime. Then, if the table size is prime, all increments will be relatively prime to it.

10. Imagine that you alter the linear probing scheme of Segment 21.13 as follows. When a collision occurs at hashTable[k], you check hashTable[k + c], hashTable[k + 2 * c], hashTable[k + 3 * c], and so on, where c is a constant. Does this scheme eliminate primary clustering?

11. Consider data whose search key consists of two floating-point values (longitude and latitude, for example). Suggest at least two possible hash functions for this data.

12. You have approximately 900 thumbnail images that you want to store in a dictionary that uses hashing in its implementation. Each image is 25 pixels wide by 25 pixels high, and each pixel is one of 512 colors. Suggest some possible hash functions that you could use.

## PROJECTS

1.  The note at the end of Segment 21.22 describes a dictionary that does not support a remove operation. Implement this dictionary by using open addressing with linear probing to resolve collisions.

2.  Consider records for patients at a medical facility. Each record contains an integer identification for a patient and strings for the date, the reason for the visit, and the treatment prescribed. Design and implement the class PatientRecord so that it overrides the method hashCode. Write a program that tests your new class.

3.  Design a class PatientDataBase that stores instances of PatientRecord, as described in the previous project. The class should provide at least three query operations, as follows. Given a patient identification and date, the first operation should return the reason for the visit, and the second operation should return the treatment. The third query operation should return a list of dates, given a patient identification.

4.  The following experiment compares the performance of linear probing and quadratic probing. You will need a list of 500 names or user names that can be obtained from your instructor or from a system administrator. Implement a hash table of size 1000, and use the hash code described in Segment 21.8. Count the number of collisions that occur for both linear probing and quadratic probing when 500 names are added to the table. Repeat the experiment for tables of size 950, 900, 850, 800, 750, 700, 650, and 600.

5.  Design an experiment similar to the one in Project 4, but instead of comparing linear probing and quadratic probing, compare two different hash functions.

6.  Write a program that uses hashing to guess which of two choices a user has made. The following sample output demonstrates an interaction between computer and user:

    ```
    Choose either A or B, and I will guess your choice.
    Press Return when you are ready.
    I guess that you chose A; am I right? no
    Score: 0 correct, 1 incorrect

    Choose either A or B, and I will guess your choice.
    Press Return when you are ready.
    I guess that you chose A; am I right? yes
    Score: 1 correct, 1 incorrect

    Choose either A or B, and I will guess your choice.
    Press Return when you are ready.
    I guess that you chose B; am I right? yes
    Score: 2 correct, 1 incorrect

        . . .
    ```

    Initially, your program will make random guesses. After the user makes five choices, your program should begin to build a hash table that it can use to predict future choices. The last four user choices form a key to the hash table. The value stored in the table at the hash address represents how many times the user's next choice was A and how many times it was B. The program uses these counts to make its guess.

    For example, if AAAB hashes to an object containing the counts 5 and 2, where 5 is the number of times the user has chosen A after having chosen A, A, A, and B, the program would predict A as the user's next choice. The specifics of how your program makes its prediction based on these counts are up to you.

**ANSWERS TO SELF-TEST QUESTIONS**

**1.** 2301506. `"Java".hashCode()` has the same value.

**2.** 19

**3.** `"x"`

**4.** Since the implementation defines both the hash table and the dictionary entry, you have a choice as to where to add a field to indicate the state of a location in a hash table. You could add a field having three states to each table location, but you really need only two states, since a `null` location is empty. You could use a boolean-valued field: If the field is true, the location is occupied; if it is false, it is available. Alternatively, you can use an enumeration to define the states.

   Adding a similar data field to the dictionary entry instead of to the hash table leads to a cleaner implementation. Note that the implementation that appears in the next chapter uses this scheme.

**5.** 13. Since 13 is both prime and the modulo base in $h_1$, the probe sequence can reach all locations in the table before it repeats.

**6.** 3, 8, 0, 5, 10, 2, 7, 12, 4, 9, 1, 6, 11, 3, ...

**7.**
```
hashTable[0]    20
hashTable[1]     6    31
hashTable[2] is null
hashTable[3] is null
hashTable[4]     4    14    29
```

**8.** The add algorithm is the same as the one given in Segment 21.25, but it uses a different search of a chain. Regardless of whether the chain is sorted, you stop the search as soon as you find the desired search key. However, if the key is not in the chain, you have to search an entire unsorted chain to learn this. If the chain is sorted, you can stop the search when you reach the point where the key should have occurred if it were present.

**9.** No. Suppose that *a*, *b*, *c*, and *d* are search keys in sorted order in the hash table. With separate chaining, *b* and *d* might appear in one chain while the other keys appear in another. Traversing the chains in order will not visit the keys in sorted order. The same is true of open addressing when traversing the occupied array elements.

# Hashing as a Dictionary Implementation

Chapter

22

## Contents

The Efficiency of Hashing
    The Load Factor
    The Cost of Open Addressing
    The Cost of Separate Chaining
Rehashing
Comparing Schemes for Collision Resolution
A Dictionary Implementation That Uses Hashing
    Entries in the Hash Table
    Data Fields and Constructors
    The Methods `getValue`, `remove`, and `add`
    Iterators
Java Class Library: The Class `HashMap`
Java Class Library: The Class `HashSet`

## Prerequisites

## Objectives

After studying this chapter, you should be able to
- Describe the relative efficiencies of the various collision resolution techniques
- Describe a hash table's load factor
- Describe rehashing and why it is necessary
- Use hashing to implement the ADT dictionary

The previous chapter described hashing as a technique for implementing a dictionary when searching is the primary task. We now study hashing's performance and examine the details of its implementation in Java.

# The Efficiency of Hashing

VideoNote
Hashing efficiency

**21.1**  As you saw in the previous chapter, implementations of the ADT dictionary depend on whether the dictionary requires distinct search keys. In this section, we consider only dictionaries with distinct search keys. Recall that the add method for such a dictionary must ensure that duplicate search keys do not occur.

Each of the dictionary operations getValue, remove, and add searches the hash table for a given search key. The success or failure of a search for a given key directly affects the success or failure of the retrieval and removal operations. The successful addition of a new entry occurs after a search for a given key fails. An unsuccessful addition replaces the value of an existing entry instead of adding a new entry. This operation occurs after a successful search for a given key. Thus, we have the following observations about the time efficiency of these operations:

- A successful retrieval or removal has the same efficiency as a successful search
- An unsuccessful retrieval or removal has the same efficiency as an unsuccessful search
- A successful addition has the same efficiency as an unsuccessful search
- An unsuccessful addition has the same efficiency as a successful search

So it is sufficient to analyze the time efficiency of searching the hash table for a given search key.

 **Note:** A successful search for an entry searches the same chain or probe sequence that was searched when the entry was first added to the hash table. Thus, the cost of a successful search for an entry is the same as the cost of inserting that entry.

## The Load Factor

**22.2**  We began our discussion of hashing in the previous chapter with a perfect hash function that caused no collisions. If you can find a perfect hash function for your particular set of search keys, using it to implement the ADT dictionary will provide operations that are each O(1). Such an implementation is ideal. The good news is that finding a perfect hash function is quite feasible in certain situations. Unfortunately, using a perfect hash function is not always possible or practical. In those situations, collisions are likely to occur.

Resolving a collision takes time and thus causes the dictionary operations to be slower than an O(1) operation. As a hash table fills, collisions occur more often, decreasing performance even further. Since collision resolution takes considerably more time than evaluating the hash function, it is the prime contributor to the cost of hashing.

To help us express this cost, we define a measure of how full a hash table is. This measure—the **load factor** $\lambda$—is the ratio of the size of the dictionary to the size of the hash table. That is,

$$\lambda = \frac{Number\ of\ entries\ in\ the\ dictionary}{Number\ of\ locations\ in\ the\ hash\ table}$$

Notice that λ is zero when the dictionary—and hence the hash table—is empty. The maximum value of λ depends on the type of collision resolution you use. For open addressing schemes, λ's maximum value is 1 when the hash table is full. In that case, each entry in the dictionary uses one location in the hash table. Notice that the number of locations in the available state does not affect λ. For separate chaining, the number of entries in the dictionary can exceed the size of the hash table, so λ has no maximum value.

**Note:  The load factor**
The load factor λ is a measure of the cost of collision resolution. It is the ratio of the number of entries in the dictionary to the size of the hash table. λ is never negative. For open addressing, λ does not exceed 1. For separate chaining, λ has no maximum value. As you will see, restricting the size of λ improves the performance of hashing.

**Question 1**  When λ is 0.5 with open addressing, how many locations in the hash table contain dictionary entries?

**Question 2**  With separate chaining, does λ indicate how many buckets in the hash table are not empty? Explain.

## The Cost of Open Addressing

**22.3**    Recall that all open addressing schemes use one location in the hash table per entry in the dictionary. The dictionary operations `getValue`, `remove`, and `add` each require a search of the probe sequence indicated by both the search key and the collision resolution scheme in effect. Analyzing the efficiency of these searches is sufficient.

For each open addressing scheme that we considered earlier, we will state the number of comparisons necessary to locate a search key in the hash table. We will express these numbers in terms of the load factor λ. The derivations of these numbers are messy at best and in some cases difficult, so we omit them. Interpreting the results, however, is straightforward. Recall that for open addressing, λ ranges from 0, when the table is empty, to 1 when it is full.

**22.4**    **Linear probing.** When you use linear probing, more collisions will likely occur as the hash table fills. After a collision, you search a probe sequence that forms a cluster. If you add a new entry, the cluster grows in size. So you would expect the probe sequences to grow and, therefore, require longer search times. In fact, the average number of comparisons needed to search the probe sequence for a given search key is about

$$\frac{1}{2}\left\{1 + \frac{1}{(1 - \lambda)^2}\right\} \text{ for an unsuccessful search and}$$

$$\frac{1}{2}\left\{1 + \frac{1}{(1 - \lambda)}\right\} \text{ for a successful search}$$

After evaluating these expressions for a few values of λ, we get the results in Figure 22-1. As λ increases—that is, as the hash table fills—the number of comparisons for these searches increases. This result satisfies our initial intuition. For example, when the hash table is half full— that is, when λ is 0.5—an average unsuccessful search requires about 2.5 comparisons and an average successful search requires about 1.5 comparisons. As λ increases beyond 0.5, the number of comparisons for an unsuccessful search increases much more rapidly than for a successful search. Thus, performance degrades rapidly when the hash table is more than half full. Should this happen, you'd need to define a larger hash table, as we describe a bit later in this chapter in the section "Rehashing."

 **Note:** The performance of hashing with linear probing degrades significantly as the load factor λ increases. To maintain reasonable efficiency, the hash table should be less than half full. That is, keep λ < 0.5.

**FIGURE 22-1**      The average number of comparisons required by a search of the hash table for given values of the load factor λ when using linear probing

| λ | Unsuccessful Search | Successful Search |
|-----|-----|-----|
| 0.1 | 1.1 | 1.1 |
| 0.3 | 1.5 | 1.2 |
| 0.5 | 2.5 | 1.5 |
| 0.7 | 6.1 | 2.2 |
| 0.9 | 50.5 | 5.5 |

**22.5**   **Quadratic probing and double hashing.** Secondary clustering as a result of quadratic probing is not as serious as the primary clustering that occurs when you use linear probing. Here, the average number of comparisons needed to search the probe sequence for a given search key is about

$$\frac{1}{(1-\lambda)} \text{ for an unsuccessful search and}$$

$$\frac{1}{\lambda}\log\left(\frac{1}{1-\lambda}\right) \text{ for a successful search}$$

Figure 22-2 evaluates these expressions for the same values of λ that we used for linear probing. Notice that the number of comparisons for an unsuccessful search grows with λ more rapidly than for a successful search. Although, the degradation in performance as λ increases is not as severe as with linear probing, you still want λ < 0.5 to maintain efficiency.

Even though double hashing avoids the clustering of linear probing and quadratic probing, the estimate of its efficiency is the same as for quadratic probing.

 **Note:** If you use quadratic probing or double hashing, the hash table should be less than half full. That is, λ should be less than 0.5.

FIGURE 22-2    The average number of comparisons required by a search
of the hash table for given values of the load factor λ when
using either quadratic probing or double hashing

| λ | Unsuccessful Search | Successful Search |
|---|---|---|
| 0.1 | 1.1 | 1.1 |
| 0.3 | 1.4 | 1.2 |
| 0.5 | 2.0 | 1.4 |
| 0.7 | 3.3 | 1.7 |
| 0.9 | 10.0 | 2.6 |

## The Cost of Separate Chaining

**22.6**   With separate chaining as the collision resolution strategy, each entry in the hash table can reference a chain of linked nodes. The number of such chains, including empty ones, is then the size of
the hash table. Thus, the load factor λ is the number of dictionary entries divided by the number
of chains. That is, λ is the average number of dictionary entries per chain. Since this number is
an average, we expect some chains to contain fewer than λ entries—or even none—and some to
have more. We assume that the chains are not sorted and that the search keys in the dictionary
are distinct.

The dictionary operations getValue, remove, and add each require a search of the chain indicated by the search key. As was the case for open addressing, analyzing the efficiency of these
searches is sufficient. Again, we will state the number of comparisons necessary to locate a search
key in the hash table in terms of the load factor λ.

An unsuccessful search of a hash table sometimes will encounter an empty chain, and so that
operation is O(1) and would be the best case. But for the average case when the chains are not
sorted, searching for an entry in the hash table without success examines λ nodes. In contrast, a
successful search always inspects a chain that is not empty. In addition to seeing that the table
location at the hash index is not null, an average successful search considers a chain of λ nodes
and locates the desired entry after looking at λ/2 of them. Thus, the average number of comparisons during a search when separate chaining is used is about

λ              for an unsuccessful search
1 + λ/2    for a successful search

After evaluating these expressions for a few values of λ, we get the results in Figure 22-3.
The number of comparisons for these searches increases only slightly as λ increases—that is, as
the hash table fills. A typical upper bound for λ is 1, as smaller values do not provide significantly
better performance. Notice the unusual result: Successful searches take more time than unsuccessful searches when λ < 2.

Remember that these results are for the average case. In the worst case, all search keys map
into the same table location. Thus, all entries occur in the same chain of nodes. The worst-case
search time, then, is O(n), where n is the number of entries.

**Note:** The average performance of hashing with separate chaining does not degrade significantly as the load factor λ increases. To maintain reasonable efficiency, you should keep λ < 1.

FIGURE 22-3    The average number of comparisons required by a search
of the hash table for given values of the load factor λ when
using separate chaining

| λ | Unsuccessful Search | Successful Search |
|---|---|---|
| 0.1 | 0.1 | 1.1 |
| 0.3 | 0.3 | 1.2 |
| 0.5 | 0.5 | 1.3 |
| 0.7 | 0.7 | 1.4 |
| 0.9 | 0.9 | 1.5 |
| 1.1 | 1.1 | 1.6 |
| 1.3 | 1.3 | 1.7 |
| 1.5 | 1.5 | 1.8 |
| 1.7 | 1.7 | 1.9 |
| 1.9 | 1.9 | 2.0 |
| 2.0 | 2.0 | 2.0 |

**Note:  Maintaining the performance of hashing**
Collisions and their resolution typically cause the load factor λ to increase and the efficiency
of the dictionary operations to decrease. To maintain efficiency, you should restrict the size of
λ as follows:

> λ < 0.5 for open addressing
> λ < 1.0 for separate chaining

Should the load factor exceed these bounds, you must increase the size of the hash table, as the
next section describes.

# Rehashing

**22.7**    The previous section discussed the efficiency of hashing as a dictionary implementation when
using various ways of resolving collisions. As you saw, to ensure an efficient implementation, you
must not let the load factor λ get too large. You can readily compute λ and see whether it exceeds
the upper limit for the particular collision resolution scheme, as given in the previous note.

So what do you do when λ reaches its limit? First, you can resize the array that serves as
the hash table, as described in Chapter 2. Typically, you double the size of an ordinary array, but
here you need to ensure that the array's size is a prime number. Expanding the array's size to a
prime number that is at least twice its previous size is not too difficult.

Ordinarily, when you expand an array, the next step is to copy the contents of the original array
into corresponding locations of the new array. This is not the case for a hash table, however. Since
you have changed the size $n$ of the hash table, the compression function $c \% n$ will compute different indices than it did for the original hash table. For example, if the hash table originally contained
101 locations, the function $c \% 101$ compresses the hash code 505 to the index 0. The new hash
table will contain 211 locations, since 211 is the smallest prime number greater than 2 times 101. But
now $c \% 211$ compresses 505 to the index 83. You cannot simply copy the contents of the location at

index 0 from the original table to the location at index 0 in the new table. And you cannot copy it to the location at index 83 in the new table, because you also need to consider collisions.

After creating a new, larger hash table of an appropriate size, you use the dictionary method add to add each item in the original hash table to the new table. The method computes the hash index using the size of the new table and handles any collisions. This process of enlarging a hash table and computing new hash indices for its contents is called **rehashing**. You can see that increasing the size of a hash table requires considerably more work than increasing the size of an ordinary array. Rehashing is a task that you should not do often.

**Note: Rehashing**
When the load factor λ becomes too large, resize the hash table. To compute the table's new size, first double its present size and then increase the result to the next prime number. Use the method add to add the current entries in the dictionary to the new hash table.

**Question 3** Consider a hash table of size 5. The function $c \% 5$ places the entries whose hash codes are 20, 6, 18, and 14 into locations at indices 0, 1, 3, and 4, respectively. Show the effects of rehashing on this hash table when linear probing resolves collisions.

**Note: Dynamic hashing** allows a hash table to grow or shrink in size without the expense of rehashing. This technique, which we will not cover, is particularly useful in database management environments when the database is stored in external files.

## Comparing Schemes for Collision Resolution

**22.8** In previous segments, you saw how the load factor λ affects the average number of comparisons required by a search of a hash table for various ways to resolve collisions. The graphs in Figure 22-4 illustrate this effect for various collision resolution schemes. When λ is less than 0.5, the average number of comparisons for a successful search is about the same regardless of the process used to resolve collisions. For unsuccessful searches, the three open addressing schemes have about the same efficiency when λ is less than 0.5. However, separate chaining is somewhat more efficient in this case.

As λ exceeds 0.5, the efficiency of open addressing degrades rapidly, with linear probing the least efficient. Separate chaining, on the other hand, remains efficient for values of λ up to 1. In fact, the tabulated data in Figure 22-3 shows that its efficiency degrades only slightly for λ between 1 and 2.

Separate chaining certainly appears to be the fastest approach. But separate chaining can require more memory than open addressing, since each location in the hash table can reference a chain of linked nodes. On the other hand, the hash table itself can be smaller than when you use an open addressing scheme, since λ can be larger. Thus, space need not be a deciding factor in how you resolve collisions.

If all of these collision resolution schemes used hash tables of equal size, open addressing would be more likely to lead to rehashing than separate chaining would. To reduce the likelihood of rehashing, an open addressing strategy could use a large hash table.

Among open addressing schemes, double hashing is a good choice. It uses fewer comparisons than linear probing. Additionally, its probe sequence can reach the entire table, whereas quadratic probing cannot.

---

**FIGURE 22-4**   The average number of comparisons required by a search of the hash table versus the load factor λ for four collision resolution techniques when the search is (a) successful; (b) unsuccessful

---

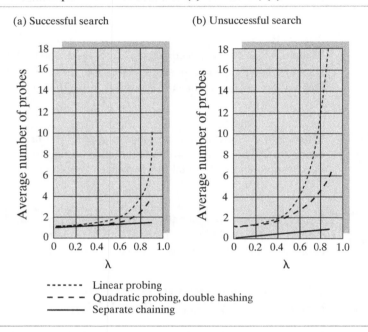

---

# A Dictionary Implementation That Uses Hashing

**VideoNote**
**Implementing a dictionary**

The efficiency of separate chaining makes it a desirable method for resolving collisions that occur during hashing. Because its implementation is relatively straightforward, we leave it to you to implement. Instead, we will implement the linear probing method of open addressing. Most of this dictionary implementation is independent of the particular open addressing technique that you use. Adapting it to use quadratic probing or double hashing involves few changes.

### Entries in the Hash Table

**22.9**   Our hash table will be like the array in Figure 20-1a of Chapter 20 that we used to implement the dictionary. Each array location can reference an object that contains a search key and an associated value.

However, with open addressing, each location in the hash table is in one of three states: occupied, empty, or available. (See Segment 21.16 of the previous chapter.) An empty location contains null. Rather than altering the structure of the hash table to indicate the other states, we make the entry objects indicate whether they are currently in the table or have been removed from it. Hence, we add another data field to the class of entry objects. Although this field could be a boolean flag that is true if the entry is in the dictionary or false if it has been removed, we will define it as an enumeration that names the states. Figure 22-5 illustrates the hash table and one dictionary entry.

**FIGURE 22-5**   A hash table and one of its entry objects

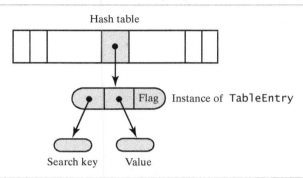

Thus, we create the private class `TableEntry` and make it internal to the dictionary class. `TableEntry` begins as follows:

```
private static class TableEntry<S, T>
{
   private S key;
   private T value;
   private States state; // Flags whether this entry is in the hash table
   private enum States {CURRENT, REMOVED} // Possible values of state

   private TableEntry(S searchKey, T dataValue)
   {
      key = searchKey;
      value = dataValue;
      state = States.CURRENT;
   } // end constructor
   . . .
```

This class is similar to the class `Entry` that you saw in Segment 20.2 of Chapter 20. However, in addition to the methods `getKey`, `getValue`, and `setValue`, this class has the methods `isIn`, `isRemoved`, `setToIn`, and `setToRemoved` to either interrogate or set the value of the flag `state`. Moreover, since the enum is like a class within the inner class `TableEntry`, `TableEntry` must be a static class. The alternative is to define the enum outside of `TableEntry` but within the class `HashedDictionary`.

 **Note:** A location in the hash table that is in the available state contains an entry in the removed state.

## Data Fields and Constructors

**22.10**  If you do not use a perfect hash function, you must expect collisions. All open addressing methods for resolving collisions become less efficient as the hash table fills, so you need to increase the size of the table. As Segment 21.22 mentioned, increasing the size of the table can also ensure that it will contain a `null` entry—a necessity for ending the search of a probe sequence. Since our hash table is an array, we expand it and rehash the dictionary entries, as described in Segment 22.7. However, we modify the definition of the load factor $\lambda$ by replacing the number of dictionary entries with the number of table locations in either the occupied or available state. This change increases $\lambda$ so that rehashing occurs before the table loses its last `null` entry. Thus, the class begins as shown in Listing 22-1.

**LISTING 22-1** An outline of the class `HashedDictionary`

```java
import java.util.Iterator;
import java.util.NoSuchElementException;
/**
   A class that implements the ADT dictionary by using hashing and
   linear probing to resolve collisions.
   The dictionary is unsorted and has distinct search keys.
   @author Frank M. Carrano
*/
public class HashedDictionary<K, V> implements DictionaryInterface<K, V>
{
   // The dictionary:
   private int numberOfEntries;
   private static final int DEFAULT_CAPACITY = 5; // Must be prime
   private static final int MAX_CAPACITY = 10000;

   // The hash table:
   private TableEntry<K, V>[] hashTable;
   private int tableSize;                          // Must be prime
   private static final int MAX_SIZE = 2 * MAX_CAPACITY;
   private boolean initialized = false;
   private static final double MAX_LOAD_FACTOR = 0.5; // Fraction of hash table
                                                      // that can be filled

   public HashedDictionary()
   {
      this(DEFAULT_CAPACITY); // Call next constructor
   } // end default constructor

   public HashedDictionary(int initialCapacity)
   {
      checkCapacity(initialCapacity);
      numberOfEntries = 0; // Dictionary is empty

      // Set up hash table:
      // Initial size of hash table is same as initialCapacity if it is prime;
      // otherwise increase it until it is prime size
      int tableSize = getNextPrime(initialCapacity);
      checkSize(tableSize); // Check for max array size

      // The cast is safe because the new array contains null entries
      @SuppressWarnings("unchecked")
      TableEntry<K, V>[] temp = (TableEntry<K, V>[])new TableEntry[tableSize];
      hashTable = temp;
      initialized = true;
   } // end constructor

   < Implementations of methods in DictionaryInterface are here.>
   . . .
   < Implementations of private methods are here.>
   . . .
   private class TableEntry<S, T>
   {
      < See Segment 22.9 >
   } // end TableEntry
} // end HashedDictionary
```

The field numberOfEntries counts the number of entries currently in the dictionary. Thus, it is incremented when an entry is added to the dictionary but decremented when an entry is removed. We distinguish between the capacity of the dictionary and the size of the hash table, since the client's concern is the dictionary and not its implementation. By calling one of the constructors, the client can create a dictionary whose initial capacity is either a default value or one it chooses. We base the initial size of the hash table on this initial capacity. However, to ensure that the table's size is prime and at least as big as necessary, the second constructor calls the private method getNextPrime to find the first prime number that is greater than or equal to a given integer. The default constructor invokes the second constructor, giving it a default initial capacity for the dictionary.

 **Programming Tip:** To implement getNextPrime(anInteger), first see whether anInteger is even. If it is, it cannot be prime, so add 1 to make it odd. Then use a private method isPrime to find the first prime number among the parameter anInteger and subsequent odd integers.

To implement isPrime, note that 2 and 3 are prime but 1 and even integers are not. An odd integer 5 or greater is prime if it is not divisible by every odd integer up to its square root.

## The Methods getValue, remove, and add

We now consider the major operations of the dictionary: getValue, remove, and add. The note at the end of Segment 21.17 in the previous chapter summarized what these operations need to do.

**22.11   The method getValue.** We begin with an algorithm for the retrieval method getValue:

*Algorithm* getValue(key)
*// Returns the value associated with the given search key, if it is in the dictionary.*
*// Otherwise, returns* null.

index = getHashIndex(key)
*Search the probe sequence that begins at* hashTable[index] *for* key
**if** (key *is found*)
    **return** *value in found entry*
**else**
    **return null**

In addition to the private method getHashIndex, which you saw in Segment 21.11, this algorithm suggests another private method that searches the probe sequence. We name this method locate and specify it informally as follows:

locate(index, key)
Searches the probe sequence that begins at index (key's hash index) and returns either the index of the entry containing key or -1, if no such entry exists.

We'll implement locate in Segment 22.13.
The method getValue then has the following implementation:

```
public V getValue(K key)
{
   checkInitialization();
   V result = null;

   int index = getHashIndex(key);
   index = locate(index, key);

   if (index != -1)
      result = hashTable[index].getValue(); // Key found; get value
   // Else key not found; return null

   return result;
} // end getValue
```

**22.12**   **The method remove.** Removing an entry from the hash table, like retrieving an entry, involves locating the search key. If found, the entry is flagged as removed. The following pseudocode describes the necessary steps for this operation:

*Algorithm* remove(key)
// *Removes a specific entry from the dictionary, given its search key.*
// *Returns either the value that was associated with the search key or* null *if no such object*
// *exists.*

index = getHashIndex(key)
*Search the probe sequence that begins at* hashTable[index] *for* key
**if** (key *is found*)
{
    *Flag entry as removed*
    numberOfEntries--
    **return** *value in removed entry*
}
**else**
    **return null**

As the following implementation shows, you call the private method locate to locate the desired entry. If you find it, you change its state to removed and return its value. Otherwise, you return null.

```
public V remove(K key)
{
    checkInitialization();
    V removedValue = null;

    int index = getHashIndex(key);
    index = locate(index, key);

    if (index != -1)
    { // Key found; flag entry as removed and return its value
        removedValue = hashTable[index].getValue();
        hashTable[index].setToRemoved();
        numberOfEntries--;
    } // end if
    // Else key not found; return null

    return removedValue;
} // end remove
```

**22.13**   **The private method locate.** Before we look at add, let's implement the method locate that both getValue and remove invoke. The method looks for the given search key along the probe sequence that begins at hashTable[index], where index is the key's hash index. Recall that the search must ignore entries that are in the removed state. The search continues until it locates either key or null.

To follow the probe sequence, locate must implement a particular open addressing scheme to resolve collisions. For simplicity, we will implement linear probing. The following algorithm summarizes our approach:

*Algorithm* locate(index, key)
// *Returns either the index of the entry containing key or -1 if no such entry is found.*

**while** (key *is not found and* hashTable[index] *is not* null)
{
    **if** (hashTable[index] *references an entry that is in the dictionary and contains* key)
        *Exit loop*
    **else**
        index = *next probe index*
}

**if** (key *is found*)
    **return** index
**else**
    **return** -1

The implementation of locate now follows from this pseudocode:

```
// Precondition: checkInitialization has been called.
private int locate(int index, K key)
{
    boolean found = false;
    while ( !found && (hashTable[index] != null) )
    {
        if ( hashTable[index].isIn() &&
             key.equals(hashTable[index].getKey()) )
            found = true; // Key found
        else              // Follow probe sequence
            index = (index + 1) % hashTable.length; // Linear probing
    } // end while
    // Assertion: Either key or null is found at hashTable[index]

    int result = -1;
    if (found)
        result = index;

    return result;
} // end locate
```

You can change from linear probing to another open addressing scheme for collision resolution by replacing the highlighted assignment statement in the previous method.

**22.14    The method add.** We begin with the algorithm for adding a new entry:

> *Algorithm* add(key, value)
> // *Adds a new key-value entry to the dictionary. If key is already in the dictionary,*
> // *returns its corresponding value and replaces it in the dictionary with* value.
>
> **if** (*hash table is too full*)
>     rehash()
>
> index = getHashIndex(key)
> *Check for collision and resolve it (this step can alter* index)
> **if** (key *is not found* )
> { // *Add entry to hash table*
>     hashTable[index] = **new** TableEntry(key, value)
>     numberOfEntries++
>     locationsUsed++
>     **return null**
> }
> **else** // *Search key is in table; return and replace entry's value*
> {
>     oldValue = hashTable[index].getValue()
>     hashTable[index].setValue(value)
>     **return** oldValue
> }

This algorithm suggests that you write several more private methods. We specify them informally as follows:

isHashTableTooFull()
Returns true if the hash table's load factor is greater than or equal to MAX_LOAD_FACTOR. Here we define the load factor as the ratio of locationsUsed to hashTable.length.

enlargeHashTable()
Expands the hash table to a size that is both prime and at least double its current size, and then adds the current entries in the dictionary to the new hash table. In doing so, this method must rehash the table entries.

probe(index, key)

Detects whether key collides with hashTable[index] and resolves it by following a probe sequence. Returns the index of either an available location along the probe sequence or the entry containing key. This index is always legal, since the probe sequence stays within the hash table.

Using these private methods, we implement the method add as follows:

```java
public V add(K key, V value)
{
    checkInitialization();
    if ((key == null) || (value == null))
        throw new IllegalArgumentException();
    else
    {
        V oldValue;                    // Value to return

        int index = getHashIndex(key);
        index = probe(index, key); // Check for and resolve collision

        // Assertion: index is within legal range for hashTable
        assert (index >= 0) && (index < hashTable.length);

        if ( (hashTable[index] == null) || hashTable[index].isRemoved())
        { // Key not found, so insert new entry
            hashTable[index] = new TableEntry<>(key, value);
            numberOfEntries++;
            oldValue = null;
        }
        else
        { // Key found; get old value for return and then replace it
            oldValue = hashTable[index].getValue();
            hashTable[index].setValue(value);
        } // end if

        // Ensure that hash table is large enough for another add
        if (isHashTableTooFull())
            enlargeHashTable();

        return oldValue;
    } // end if
} // end add
```

**22.15    The private method probe.** The method probe(key, index) is similar to the method locate in that it looks for key along the probe sequence that begins at hashTable[index]. The search ignores entries that are in the removed state and continues until it locates either key or null. During this search, the method records the index of the first location, if any, that references an entry that has been removed from the table. This additional task is what distinguishes probe from locate. Thus, probe returns the index of a table location that either references an entry containing key or is available for an addition to the table.

Notice that probe returns the index of the removed entry that it *first* encounters along the probe sequence. Since add will insert a new entry into this location, a subsequent search for this entry will encounter it sooner than if add had inserted it in a location further along the probe sequence.

The following pseudocode summarizes the logic of probe:

*Algorithm* probe(index, key)
// *Searches the probe sequence that begins at* index. *Returns either the index of the entry*
// *containing* key *or the index of an available location in the hash table.*

**while** (key *is not found and* hashTable[index] *is not* null)
{
    **if** (hashTable[index] *references an entry in the dictionary*)

```
      {
         if (the entry in hashTable[index] contains key)
            Exit loop
         else
            index = next probe index
      }
      else // hashTable[index] references a removed entry
      {
         if (this is the first removed entry encountered)
            removedStateIndex = index

         index = next probe index
      }
}
if (key is found or a removed entry was not encountered)
   return index
else
   return removedStateIndex // Index of first entry removed
```

The following method implements this algorithm:

```
// Precondition: checkInitialization has been called.
private int probe(int index, K key)
{
   boolean found = false;
   int removedStateIndex = -1; // Index of first location in removed state
   while ( !found && (hashTable[index] != null) )
   {
      if (hashTable[index].isIn())
      {
         if (key.equals(hashTable[index].getKey()))
            found = true; // Key found
         else          // Follow probe sequence
            index = (index + 1) % hashTable.length; // Linear probing
      }
      else // Skip entries that were removed
      {
         // Save index of first location in removed state
         if (removedStateIndex == -1)
            removedStateIndex = index;

         index = (index + 1) % hashTable.length;    // Linear probing
      } // end if
   } // end while
   // Assertion: Either key or null is found at hashTable[index]

   if (found || (removedStateIndex == -1) )
      return index;                 // Index of either key or null
   else
      return removedStateIndex; // Index of an available location
} // end probe
```

The methods probe and locate are so similar that you can omit locate and use probe instead. To do so, you must change the implementations of remove and getValue slightly. The following question asks you to make this change.

**Question 4** What changes to the methods remove and getValue are necessary so they can call probe instead of locate?

22.16   **The private method enlargeHashTable.** Recall that the method enlargeHashTable expands the hash table to a size that is both prime and at least double its current size. Since the hash function depends on the size of the table, you cannot copy entries from the old array and put them into the same positions in the new array. You need to apply the revised hash function to each entry to determine its proper position in the new table. But doing so can lead to collisions that need to be resolved. Thus, you should use the method add to add the existing entries to the new and larger hash table. Since add increments the data field numberOfEntries, you must remember to set this field to zero before adding the entries.

The method has the following implementation:

```java
// Precondition: checkInitialization has been called.
private void enlargeHashTable()
{
    TableEntry<K, V>[] oldTable = hashTable;
    int oldSize = hashTable.length;
    int newSize = getNextPrime(oldSize + oldSize);

    // The cast is safe because the new array contains null entries
    @SuppressWarnings("unchecked")
    TableEntry<K, V>[] temp = (TableEntry<K, V>[])new TableEntry[newSize];
    hashTable = temp;
    numberOfEntries = 0; // Reset number of dictionary entries, since
                         // it will be incremented by add during rehash

    // Rehash dictionary entries from old array to the new and bigger
    // array; skip both null locations and removed entries
    for (int index = 0; index < oldSize; index++)
    {
        if ( (oldTable[index] != null) && oldTable[index].isIn() )
            add(oldTable[index].getKey(), oldTable[index].getValue());
    } // end for
} // end enlargeHashTable
```

As we traverse the old hash table, notice that we skip both the null locations and the entries that have been removed from the dictionary but are still in the hash table.

This method does not retain the instances of TableEntry that were in the old hash table. Instead, it uses an entry's key and value to create a new entry. You can avoid this reallocation of entries; Exercise 4 at the end of this chapter asks you to investigate this possibility.

**Question 5** When the method add calls enlargeHashTable, enlargeHashTable calls add. But when enlargeHashTable calls add, does add call enlargeHashTable? Explain.

## Iterators

22.17   Finally, we provide iterators for the dictionary, much as we did in Chapter 20. For example, we can implement an internal class KeyIterator to define an iteration of the search keys. The iteration must traverse the hash table, ignoring cells that either contain null or reference removed entries. Figure 22-6 shows a sample hash table. Cells in light gray reference the dictionary entries, dark gray cells reference removed entries, and medium gray cells contain null. As we traverse this table, we skip cells that are medium gray or dark gray. The only real concern in this implementation is detecting when the iteration ends—that is, when the method hasNext should return false. The status of a cell and the size of the hash table are not the proper criteria for this determination. Instead, you simply count backward from currentSize each time the method next returns the next search key.

**FIGURE 22-6**   A hash table containing dictionary entries, removed entries, and null values

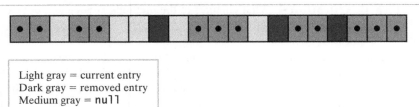

Light gray = current entry
Dark gray = removed entry
Medium gray = null

The implementation of KeyIterator follows. A class that defines an iteration of values would have a similar implementation.

```java
private class KeyIterator implements Iterator<K>
{
    private int currentIndex; // Current position in hash table
    private int NumberLeft;    // Number of entries left in iteration

    private KeyIterator()
    {
        currentIndex = 0;
        numberLeft = numberOfEntries;
    } // end default constructor

    public boolean hasNext()
    {
        return numberLeft > 0;
    } // end hasNext

    public K next()
    {
        K result = null;

        if (hasNext())
        {
            // Skip table locations that do not contain a current entry
            while ( (hashTable[currentIndex] == null) ||
                        hashTable[currentIndex].isRemoved() )
            {
                currentIndex++;
            } // end while

            result = hashTable[currentIndex].getKey();
            numberLeft--;
            currentIndex++;
        }
        else
            throw new NoSuchElementException();

        return result;
    } // end next

    public void remove()
    {
        throw new UnsupportedOperationException();
    } // end remove
} // end KeyIterator
```

 **Note:** Hashing as an implementation of the ADT dictionary does not provide the ability to sort its entries. Such an implementation is not suitable for any application that requires a sorted iteration of the entries.

## Java Class Library: The Class **HashMap**

**22.18**    The standard package java.util contains the class HashMap<K, V>. This class implements the interface java.util.Map that we mentioned in Segment 19.22 of Chapter 19. Recall that this interface is similar to our DictionaryInterface. HashMap assumes that the search-key objects belong to a class that overrides the methods hashCode and equals. Its hash table is a collection of buckets, with each bucket able to contain several entries. As you know, a hash table's load factor $\lambda$ is a measure of how full the table is. The constructors for HashMap enable you to specify the initial number of buckets and the maximum load factor $\lambda_{max}$. These constructors are as follows:

**public** HashMap()
Creates an empty map (dictionary) with a default initial capacity of 16 and a default maximum load factor of 0.75.

**public** HashMap(**int** initialCapacity)
Creates an empty map (dictionary) with a given initial capacity and a default maximum load factor of 0.75.

**public** HashMap(**int** initialCapacity, **float** maxLoadFactor)
Creates an empty map (dictionary) with a given initial capacity and a given maximum load factor.

**public** HashMap(Map<? **extends** K, ? **extends** V> map)
Creates a map (dictionary) with the same entries as map.

The authors of HashMap chose a default maximum load factor of 0.75 to provide a balance between time and memory requirements. Even though higher values of the load factor permit smaller hash tables, they cause higher search times, which in turn reduce the efficiency of the get, put, and remove methods.

When the number of entries in the hash table exceeds $\lambda_{max}$ times the number of buckets, the size of the hash table is increased by using rehashing. But rehashing takes time. You can avoid rehashing if you choose

$$Number\ of\ buckets > \frac{Maximum\ number\ of\ entries\ in\ the\ dictionary}{\lambda_{max}}$$

Of course, too large a hash table wastes space.

## Java Class Library: The Class **HashSet**

**22.19**    The package java.util of the Java Class Library also contains the class HashSet<T>. This class implements the interface java.util.Set that we presented in Segment 1.22 of Chapter 1. Recall that a set is a collection that does not contain duplicate entries, but otherwise is similar to a bag. HashSet uses an instance of the class HashMap, as introduced in the previous segment, to contain the entries in a set.

Among the constructors defined in HashSet are the following:

**public** HashSet()
Creates an empty set having a default initial capacity of 16. The underlying instance of HashMap uses a load factor of 0.75.

**public** HashSet(**int** initialCapacity)
Creates an empty set having the given initial capacity. The underlying instance of HashMap uses a load factor of 0.75.

**public** HashSet(**int** initialCapacity, **float** loadFactor)
Creates an empty set having the given initial capacity. The underlying instance of HashMap uses the specified load factor.

**CHAPTER SUMMARY**

- Hashing is efficient as long as the ratio of dictionary size to hash-table size remains small. This ratio is called the load factor. The load factor should be less than 1 for separate chaining and less than 0.5 for open addressing. If the load factor exceeds these bounds, you must rehash the table.

- Rehashing is the process that increases the size of a hash table to a prime number that is greater than twice the table's current size. Since the hash function depends on the table size, you cannot simply copy entries from the old table to the new one. Instead, you use the method add to add all current entries to the new table.

- Separate chaining, as compared to open addressing, provides faster dictionary operations on average, can use a smaller hash table, and needs rehashing less frequently. If both approaches have the same size array for a hash table, separate chaining uses more memory due to its linked chains.

- Hashing as a dictionary implementation does not support operations that involve sorted search keys. For example, you cannot easily traverse the keys in sorted order, find keys that lie within a given range, or identify the largest or smallest search key.

- The package java.util contains both the class HashMap<K, V>, which implements the interface Map<K, V>, and the class HashSet<T>, which implements the interface Set<T>.

## EXERCISES

1. Suppose that you use open addressing to resolve collisions. Now imagine that the entries in the hash table are increasing.

   a. Which method implicitly checks whether the hash table is full?
   b. Does a nearly full or full hash table lead to any performance issues? If so, what may be the solution?

2. To guarantee that the average number of probes is less than or equal to 5, what is the maximum load factor that a hash table can have if it uses

   a. Linear probing
   b. Double hashing
   c. Separate chaining

3. Revise the method add given in Segment 22.14 to allow duplicate search keys in the dictionary.

4. The method rehash does not retain the instances of TableEntry that were in the old hash table. It could if the method add had an entry as its parameter instead of the search key and value. Write such a method as an additional but public add method, and then revise rehash so it retains the instances of TableEntry that were in the old hash table.

5. Imagine a collection of names that are instances of the class Name, as modified in Exercise 1 of Chapter 21. For each name, imagine a string that represents a nickname. Suppose that each nickname is a search key, and you plan to add nickname-name pairs to a dictionary that is an instance of the class HashMap, as described in Segment 22.18.

   a. Suppose that you plan to add 1000 entries to this dictionary. Create an instance of the class HashMap that can accommodate the 1000 entries without rehashing.
   b. Write statements that add four nickname-name pairs to your dictionary. Then write statements that retrieve and display the name that corresponds to a nickname of your choice.

6. Can you use a hash table to implement a priority queue? Explain.

## PROJECTS

1. Implement the ADT dictionary by using hashing and separate chaining. Use a chain of linked nodes as each bucket. The dictionary's entries should have distinct search keys.

2. Repeat Project 1, but use the ADT list for each bucket instead of a chain of linked nodes. What implementation of the list would be reasonable?

3. Implement the class PatientDataBase, that you designed in Project 3 of the previous chapter. Use a hash table to store the patient records. Write a program that demonstrates and tests this class.

4. Even though two implementations of a hash table may require the same average number of comparisons, their distributions may be different. The following experiment will examine this possibility for linear probing and double hashing. You will need two disjoint lists of names: one with at least 1000 names and the other with at least 10,000 names.

   a. For both of the collision resolution schemes linear probing and double hashing, determine the load factor that results in an average of 1.5 comparisons for an unsuccessful search of a hash table holding 100 objects. From the load factor, determine the size of the table required.

   b. Create two hash tables of the appropriate size and two corresponding empty lists, which will hold counts. Use linear probing for one table and double hashing for the other. Inside a loop that iterates 1000 times, do the following:

   - Clear the hash tables.
   - Randomly choose 100 names from the list of 1000 and insert them into the tables.
   - Randomly choose 100 names from the list of 10,000 and search the tables for each name. (Each search will be unsuccessful because the two lists have no names in common.)
   - Count the number of comparisons made in each table for the 100 searches and record the count in the list corresponding to the table.

   After the iteration is complete, each list should contain 1000 values. Each of these values is the total number of comparisons required to search for 100 names. Compute and display the average and standard deviation of each list. We expect the average number of comparisons for both hash tables to be equal to 150 (1.5 times 100).

5. Modify the previous project as follows:

   - Let the user enter the desired average number of comparisons.
   - Display a histogram of the results. A histogram shows the frequency of data values in given intervals of the same length. Use the floor of the average number of comparisons as the interval length.

6. Chapter 1 defined a set as a bag that does not permit duplicate entries. Define a class of sets that uses a hash table to store a set's entries.

## ANSWERS TO SELF-TEST QUESTIONS

1. Half of them.

2. No. Even when $\lambda$ is large, all entries could be in one bucket.

3. After expanding the table to 11 locations (11 is the prime number larger than twice the current table size of 5), the function $c \% 11$ places the entry whose hash code is 20 at index 9, 6 at index 6, and 14 at index 3. The hash code 18 causes a collision at index 9, so we probe ahead and place it at index 10.

4. In each method, replace the statements

   ```
   index = locate(index, key);
   if (index != -1)
   ```

   with

   ```
   index = probe(index, key);
   if ((hashTable[index] != null) && hashTable[index].isIn())
   ```

5. No. The table size has increased, so rehashing is not necessary.

## Contents

## Prerequisites

## Objectives

After studying this chapter, you should be able to

- Describe binary trees and general trees, using standard terminology
- Traverse a tree in one of four ways: preorder, postorder, inorder, or level order
- Give examples of binary trees, including expression trees, decision trees, binary search trees, and heaps
- Give examples of general trees, including parse trees and game trees

**A**s a plant, a tree is well known. As a way to organize data, the tree is more familiar than you might think. A family tree or a chart of players in a tournament are two common examples of a tree. A tree provides a hierarchical organization in which data items have ancestors and descendants. The organization is richer and more varied than any you have seen previously.

This chapter explores the ADT tree in its two forms—binary and general—and provides several examples of how such trees are used.

## Tree Concepts

**23.1**     The data organizations that you have seen so far have placed data in a linear order. Objects in a stack, queue, list, or dictionary appear one after the other. As useful as these organizations are, you often must categorize data into groups and subgroups. Such a classification is **hierarchical**, or **nonlinear**, since the data items appear at various levels within the organization.

We begin by looking at several familiar examples of hierarchical data. Each example will be illustrated by a diagram that represents a tree.

### Hierarchical Organizations

**23.2**     **Example: Family trees.** Your relatives can be arranged hierarchically in more than one way. Figure 23-1 shows Carole's children and grandchildren. Her son Brett has one daughter, Susan. Carole's daughter, Jennifer, has two children—Jared and Jamie.

Using a different arrangement, Figure 23-2 shows Jared's parents and grandparents. Jared's father is John and his mother is Jennifer. John's father and mother are James and Mary; Jennifer's parents are Robert and Carole.

**FIGURE 23-1**     Carole's children and grandchildren

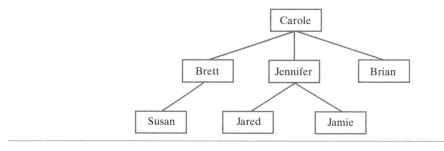

**FIGURE 23-2**     Jared's parents and grandparents

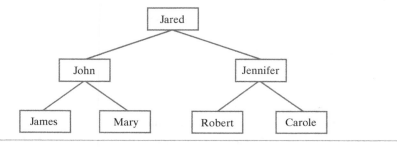

**23.3**     **Example: A university's organization.** Corporations, schools, churches, and governments all organize their staff hierarchically. For example, Figure 23-3 shows a portion of the administrative structure of a typical university. All offices ultimately report to the president. Immediately beneath the president are three vice presidents. The Vice President for Academic Affairs, for example, oversees the deans of the colleges. The deans in turn supervise the chairs of the various academic departments, such as computer science and accounting.

FIGURE 23-3    A portion of a university's administrative structure

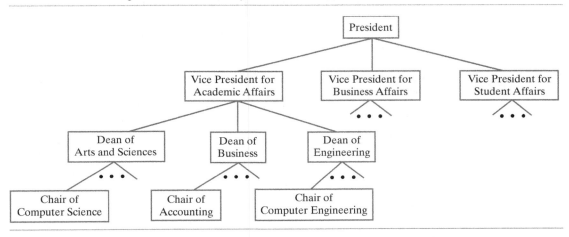

**23.4**     **Example: File directories.** Typically, you organize the files on your computer into folders, or directories. Each folder contains several other folders and/or files. Figure 23-4 shows the organization of the folders and files on Paul's computer. This organization is hierarchical. That is, all of Paul's files are organized within folders that are ultimately within the folder myStuff. For example, to look at his budget, Paul would start with the folder myStuff, find the folder home, and finally locate the file budget.txt.

FIGURE 23-4    Computer files organized into folders

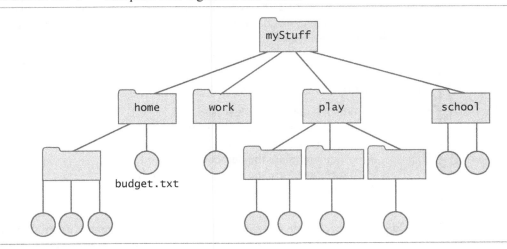

## Tree Terminology

**23.5**    Each of the previous figures is an example of a tree. A **tree** is a set of **nodes** connected by **edges** that indicate the relationships among the nodes. The nodes are arranged in **levels** that indicate the nodes' hierarchy. At the top level is a single node called the root. Figure 23-5 shows a tree that, except for the names of the nodes, is identical to the tree in Figure 23-4. In Figure 23-4, the root of the tree is the folder myStuff; in Figure 23-5, the root is node *A*.

---

**FIGURE 23-5**    A tree equivalent to the tree in Figure 23-4

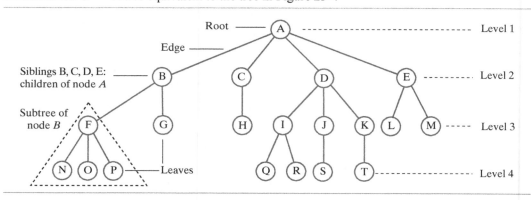

The nodes at each successive level of a tree are the **children** of the nodes at the previous level. A node that has children is the **parent** of those children. In Figure 23-5, node *A* is the parent of nodes *B*, *C*, *D*, and *E*. Since these children have the same parent, they are called **siblings**. They also are the **descendants** of node *A*, and node *A* is their **ancestor**. Furthermore, node *P* is a descendant of *A*, and *A* is an ancestor of *P*. Notice that node *P* has no children. Such a node is called a **leaf**. A node that is not a leaf—that is, one that has children—is called either an **interior node** or a **nonleaf**. Such a node is also a parent.

**Note: Trees**
While the roots of most plants are firmly in the ground, the root of an ADT tree is at the tree's top; it is the origin of a hierarchical organization. Each node can have children. A node with children is a parent; a node without children is a leaf. The root is the only node that has no parent; all other nodes have one parent each.

---

**Question 1** Consider the tree in Figure 23-5.

    **a.** Which nodes are the leaves?
    **b.** Which nodes are the siblings of node *K*?
    **c.** Which nodes are the children of node *B*?
    **d.** Which nodes are the descendants of node *B*?
    **e.** Which nodes are the ancestors of node *N*?
    **f.** Which nodes are parents?

---

**23.6**    In general, each node in a tree can have an arbitrary number of children. We sometimes call such a tree a **general tree**. If each node has no more than *n* children, the tree is called an *n*-ary tree. Realize that not every general tree is an *n*-ary tree. If each node has at most two children, the tree is called a **binary tree**. The tree in Figure 23-2 is a binary tree, but the trees in the other previous figures are general trees.

**Note: Can a tree be empty?**
We allow any of our trees to be empty. Some people allow empty binary trees but require that general trees contain at least one node. While the reasons for doing so are quite valid, we will avoid confusion here by not making this subtle distinction between binary and general trees.

Any node and its descendants form a **subtree** of the original tree. A **subtree of a node** is a tree rooted at a child of that node. For example, one subtree of node *B* in Figure 23-5 is the tree rooted at *F*. A **subtree of a tree** is a subtree of the tree's root. It is rooted at a child of the tree's root.

**Question 2** This book has a hierarchical organization that you can represent by using a tree. Sketch a portion of this tree and indicate whether it is a general tree or a binary tree.

**23.7** The **height** of a tree is the number of levels in the tree. We number the levels in a tree beginning with the root at level 1. The tree in Figure 23-5 has four levels, and so its height is 4. The height of a one-node tree is 1, and the height of an empty tree is 0.

We can express the height of a nonempty tree recursively by considering its subtrees:

Height of tree $T$ = 1 + height of the tallest subtree of $T$

The root of the tree in Figure 23-5 has four subtrees of heights 3, 2, 3, and 2. Since the tallest of these subtrees has height 3, the tree has height 4.

We can reach any node in a tree by following a **path** that begins at the root and goes from node to node along the edges that join them. The path between the root and any other node is unique. The **length of a path** is the number of edges that compose it. For example, in Figure 23-5, the path that passes through the nodes *A*, *B*, *F*, and *N* has length 3. No other path from the root to a leaf is longer than this particular path. This tree has height 4, which is 1 more than the length of this longest path. In general, the height of a tree is 1 more than the length of the longest of the paths between its root and its leaves. Alternatively, the height of a tree is the number of nodes along the longest path between the root and a leaf.

**Note:** The path between a tree's root and any other node is unique.

**Note:** The **height of a tree** is the number of levels in the tree. The height also equals the number of nodes along the longest path between the root and a leaf.

**Note: Alternate definitions of height and level**
Some people define both the height of a tree and its levels to be 1 less than those we will use in this book. For example, a one-node tree would have height 0 instead of 1. Also, the root of a tree would be at level 0 instead of 1.

**Question 3** What are the heights of the trees in Figures 23-1, 23-2, and 23-4?

**23.8**   **Binary trees.** As we mentioned earlier, each node in a binary tree has at most two children. They are called the **left child** and the **right child**. For example, each tree in Figure 23-6 is a binary tree. In Figure 23-6a, nodes *B*, *D*, and *F* are left children, and nodes *C*, *E*, and *G* are right children. The root of this binary tree has two subtrees. The **left subtree** is rooted at *B* and the **right subtree** is rooted at *C*. Thus, the left subtree of a binary tree is the left subtree of its root; likewise for the right subtree.

Every subtree in a binary tree is also a binary tree. In fact, we can think of a binary tree recursively, as follows:

 **Note:** A binary tree either is empty or has the following form:

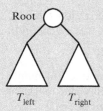

where $T_{\text{left}}$ and $T_{\text{right}}$ are binary trees.

**23.9**   **Full and complete binary trees.** When a binary tree of height *h* has all of its leaves at level *h* and every nonleaf (parent) has exactly two children, the tree is said to be **full**. Figure 23-6a shows a full binary tree. If all levels of a binary tree but the last contain as many nodes as possible, and the nodes on the last level are filled in from left to right—as in Figure 23-6b—the tree is **complete**. The binary tree in Figure 23-6c is neither full nor complete. In this case, a node can have a left child but no right child (for example, node *S*), or a right child but no left child (for example, node *U*).

 **Note:** All leaves in a full binary tree are on the same level and every nonleaf has exactly two children. A complete binary tree is full to its next-to-last level, and its leaves on the last level are filled from left to right. Binary trees are used extensively, and these special trees will be important to our later discussions.

**FIGURE 23-6**   Three binary trees

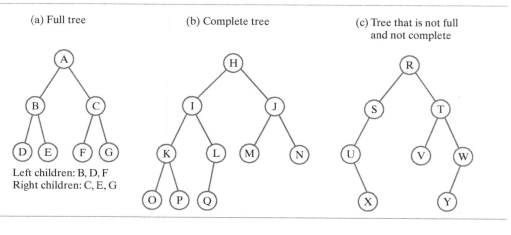

(a) Full tree

(b) Complete tree

(c) Tree that is not full and not complete

Left children: B, D, F
Right children: C, E, G

**23.10** **Balanced binary trees.** When each node in a binary tree has two subtrees whose heights are exactly the same, the tree is said to be **completely balanced**. The only completely balanced binary trees are full. For example, the full tree in Figure 23-6a is completely balanced. Other trees are said to be **height balanced**, or simply **balanced**, if the subtrees of each node in the tree differ in height by no more than 1. A complete binary tree—such as the one in Figure 23-6b—is height balanced, but so are some trees that are not complete, as Figure 23-7 shows. Moreover, the concept of balance applies to all trees, not just binary trees.

   A node in a binary tree whose subtrees differ in height by no more than 1 is known as a **balanced node**. Thus, all nodes in a balanced binary tree are balanced.

**FIGURE 23-7**   Some binary trees that are height balanced

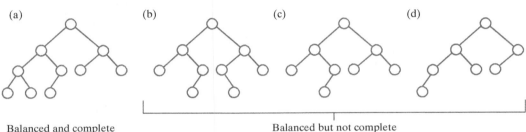

(a)   (b)   (c)   (d)

Balanced and complete              Balanced but not complete

**23.11** **The height of full or complete trees.** In later chapters, the height of trees that are either full or complete will be important in our discussions of efficiency. Figure 23-8 shows some full trees that get progressively taller. We can compute the number of nodes that each tree contains as a function of its height. Beginning at the root of each tree in the figure, we can see that the number of nodes at each level doubles as we move toward the leaves. The total number of nodes in the tallest tree in the figure is $1 + 2 + 4 + 8 + 16$, or, $31$. In general, the number of nodes in a full binary tree is

$$\sum_{i=0}^{h-1} 2^i$$

where $h$ is the tree's height. This sum is equal to $2^h - 1$. You can convince yourself that this result is true by examining Figure 23-8, and you can prove it as an exercise by using mathematical induction.

   Now, if $n$ is the number of nodes in a full tree, we have the following results:

$n = 2^h - 1$
$2^h = n + 1$
$h = \log_2 (n + 1)$

That is, the height of a full tree that has $n$ nodes is $\log_2 (n + 1)$.

   We leave it to you as an exercise to prove that the height of a complete tree having $n$ nodes is $\log_2 (n + 1)$ rounded up.

**Note:** The height of a binary tree with $n$ nodes that is either complete or full is $\log_2 (n + 1)$ rounded up.

**Programming Tip:** To compute $\log_2 x$ in Java, first observe that $\log_a x = \log_b x / \log_b a$. In Java, `Math.log(x)` returns the natural logarithm of x. So `Math.log(x) / Math.log(2.0)` computes the base 2 logarithm of x.

FIGURE 23-8    The number of nodes in a full binary tree as a function of the
tree's height

| Full Tree | Height | Number of Nodes |
|:---:|:---:|:---:|
| | 1 | $1 = 2^1 - 1$ |
| | 2 | $3 = 2^2 - 1$ |
| | 3 | $7 = 2^3 - 1$ |
| | 4 | $15 = 2^4 - 1$ |
| | 5 | $31 = 2^5 - 1$ |

Number of
nodes per level
1
2
4
8
16

**Question 4** Show that the relationship between a tree's height and its number of nodes is true for the binary trees in Parts *a* and *b* of Figure 23-6.

**Question 5** How many nodes are in a full binary tree of height 6?

**Question 6** What is the height of a complete tree that contains 14 nodes?

## Traversals of a Tree

23.12    Until now, we treated the contents of the nodes in a tree simply as labels for identification. Because the tree is an ADT, however, its nodes contain data that we process. We now consider the nodes in this way.

Traversing the items in a data collection is a common operation that we have seen in previous chapters. In those cases, data was arranged linearly, so the sequence of the items in the traversal was clear. Such is not the case for a tree.

VideoNote
The ADT Tree

In defining a traversal, or iteration, of a tree, we must **visit**, or process, each data item exactly once. However, the order in which we visit items is not unique. We can choose an order suitable to our application. Because traversals of a binary tree are somewhat easier to understand than traversals of a general tree, we begin there. To simplify our discussion, we will use the phrase "visit a node" to mean "process the data within a node."

 **Note:** "Visiting a node" means "processing the data within a node." It is an action that we perform during a traversal of a tree. A traversal can pass through a node without visiting it at that moment. Realize that traversals of a tree are based on the positions of its nodes, but not on the nodes' data values.

## Traversals of a Binary Tree

**23.13**   We know that the subtrees of the root of a binary tree are themselves binary trees. Using this recursive nature of a binary tree in the definition of its traversal is natural. To visit all the nodes in a binary tree, we must

> Visit the root
> Visit all the nodes in the root's left subtree
> Visit all the nodes in the root's right subtree

Visiting the nodes in the left subtree before visiting those in the right subtree is simply a convention, but we must follow it consistently throughout each traversal. Whether we visit the root before, between, or after visiting these two subtrees, however, defines three common orders for a traversal. A fourth traversal order uses a completely different approach.

In a **preorder traversal**, we visit the root *before* we visit the root's subtrees. We then visit all the nodes in the root's left subtree before we visit the nodes in the right subtree. Figure 23-9 numbers the nodes in a binary tree in the order in which a preorder traversal visits them. After first visiting the root, we visit the nodes in the root's left subtree. Since this subtree is a binary tree, visiting its nodes in preorder means that we visit its root before visiting its left subtree. The traversal continues in this recursive manner until all nodes are visited.

**FIGURE 23-9**    The visitation order of a preorder traversal

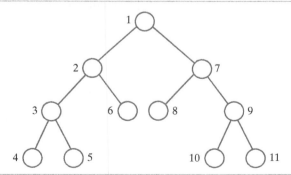

**23.14**   An **inorder traversal** visits the root of a binary tree *between* visiting the nodes in the root's subtrees. In particular, it visits nodes in the following order:

> Visit all the nodes in the root's left subtree
> Visit the root
> Visit all the nodes in the root's right subtree

Figure 23-10 numbers the nodes in a binary tree in the order in which an inorder traversal visits them. Recursively visiting the nodes in the left subtree results in visiting the leftmost leaf first. We visit that leaf's parent next and then the parent's right child. We visit the tree's root after we have visited all of the nodes in the root's left subtree. Finally, we visit the nodes in the root's right subtree in this recursive manner.

**FIGURE 23-10** The visitation order of an inorder traversal

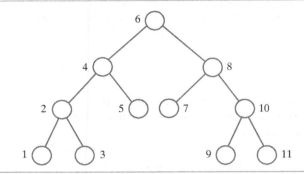

**23.15** A **postorder traversal** visits the root of a binary tree *after* visiting the nodes in the root's subtrees. In particular, it visits nodes in the following order:

Visit all the nodes in the root's left subtree
Visit all the nodes in the root's right subtree
Visit the root

Figure 23-11 numbers the nodes in a binary tree in the order in which a postorder traversal visits them. Recursively visiting the nodes in the left subtree results in visiting the leftmost leaf first. We then visit that leaf's sibling and then their parent. After visiting all the nodes in the root's left subtree, we visit the nodes in the root's right subtree in this recursive manner. Finally we visit the root.

**FIGURE 23-11** The visitation order of a postorder traversal

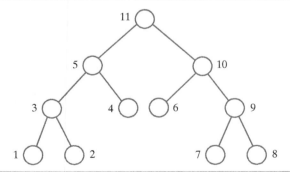

**23.16** A **level-order traversal**—the last traversal we will consider—begins at the root and visits nodes one level at a time. Within a level, it visits nodes from left to right. Figure 23-12 numbers the nodes in a binary tree in the order in which a level-order traversal visits them.

FIGURE 23-12   The visitation order of a level-order traversal

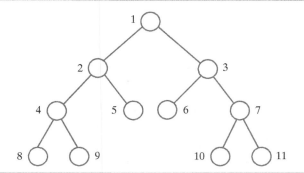

The level-order traversal is an example of a **breadth-first traversal**. It follows a path that explores an entire level before moving to the next level. The preorder traversal is an example of a **depth-first traversal**. This kind of traversal fully explores one subtree before exploring another. That is, the traversal follows a path that descends the levels of a tree as deeply as possible until it reaches a leaf.

**Note:  Traversals of a binary tree**
A preorder traversal visits the root of a binary tree before visiting the nodes in its two subtrees.
An inorder traversal visits the root between visiting the nodes in its two subtrees.
A postorder traversal visits the root after visiting the nodes in its two subtrees.
A level-order traversal visits nodes from left to right within each level of the tree, beginning with the root.

**Question 7** Suppose that visiting a node means simply displaying the data in the node. What are the results of each of the following traversals of the binary tree in Figure 23-2? Preorder, postorder, inorder, and level order.

## Traversals of a General Tree

**23.17**   A general tree has traversals that are in level order, preorder, and postorder. An inorder traversal is not well defined for a general tree.

A level-order traversal visits nodes level by level, beginning at the root. This traversal is just like a level-order traversal of a binary tree, except that nodes in a general tree can have more than two children each.

A preorder traversal visits the root and then visits the nodes in each of the root's subtrees. A postorder traversal first visits the nodes in each of the root's subtrees and then visits the root last. Figure 23-13 gives an example of a preorder traversal and a postorder traversal for a general tree.

**Question 8** In what order will a level-order traversal visit the nodes of the tree in Figure 23-13?

FIGURE 23-13    The visitation order of two traversals of a general tree

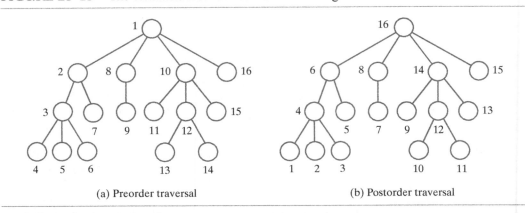

(a) Preorder traversal                                    (b) Postorder traversal

# Java Interfaces for Trees

Trees come in many shapes and have varied applications. Writing one Java interface for an ADT tree that satisfies every use would be an unwieldy task. Instead we will write several interfaces that we can combine as needed for a particular application. We will include these interfaces in a package that also will contain the classes that implement them. In this way, the package can contain implementation details, such as a class of nodes, that we want to hide from the trees' clients. The next chapter will examine these implementations.

## Interfaces for All Trees

**23.18    Fundamental operations.** We begin with an interface that specifies operations common to all trees. The interface in Listing 23-1 uses the generic type T as the type of data in the nodes of the tree.

LISTING 23-1    An interface of methods common to all trees

```
1  package TreePackage;
2  public interface TreeInterface<T>
3  {
4     public T getRootData();
5     public int getHeight();
6     public int getNumberOfNodes();
7     public boolean isEmpty();
8     public void clear();
9  } // end TreeInterface
```

This interface is quite basic. It does not include operations to add or remove nodes, as even the specification of these operations depends on the kind of tree. We also did not include traversal operations in this interface, since not every application uses them. Instead we will provide a separate interface for traversals.

**23.19    Traversals.** One way to traverse a tree is to use an iterator that has the methods hasNext and next, as given in the interface java.util.Iterator. As in previous chapters, we can define a method that returns such an iterator. Since we can have several kinds of traversals, a tree class could have several methods that each return a different kind of iterator. Listing 23-2 defines an interface for these methods. A tree class can implement this interface and define as many of the methods as are needed.

---

**LISTING 23-2    An interface of traversal methods for a tree**

```
1  package TreePackage;
2  import java.util.Iterator;
3  public interface TreeIteratorInterface<T>
4  {
5     public Iterator<T> getPreorderIterator();
6     public Iterator<T> getPostorderIterator();
7     public Iterator<T> getInorderIterator();
8     public Iterator<T> getLevelOrderIterator();
9  } // end TreeIteratorInterface
```

---

## An Interface for Binary Trees

**23.20**    Many applications of trees in fact use binary trees. We could use a Java class of general trees for such an application, but using a special class of binary trees is more convenient and efficient. Because binary trees occur so frequently, developing special Java classes for them is worthwhile.

We can define an interface for a basic binary tree by adding methods to those already in the interfaces `TreeInterface` and `TreeIteratorInterface`. Since a Java interface can extend more than one interface, we can write the interface shown in Listing 23-3 for a class of binary trees.

---

**LISTING 23-3    An interface for a binary tree**

```
1  package TreePackage;
2  public interface BinaryTreeInterface<T> extends TreeInterface<T>,
3                                         TreeIteratorInterface<T>
4  {
5     /** Sets this binary tree to a new one-node binary tree.
6        @param rootData  The object that is the data for the new tree's root.
7     */
8     public void setTree(T rootData);
9
10    /** Sets this binary tree to a new binary tree.
11       @param rootData  The object that is the data for the new tree's root.
12       @param leftTree  The left subtree of the new tree.
13       @param rightTree The right subtree of the new tree. */
14    public void setTree(T rootData, BinaryTreeInterface<T> leftTree,
15                                    BinaryTreeInterface<T> rightTree);
16 } // end BinaryTreeInterface
```

---

The two `setTree` methods transform an existing binary tree object into a new tree composed of given arguments. The first method forms a one-node tree from a given data object. The second method forms a tree whose root node contains a given data object and has as its subtrees the two given binary trees. A class that implements this interface certainly could have constructors that perform the same tasks as these two methods. However, since an interface cannot contain constructors, we have no way to force an implementor to provide them.

**23.21**    **Example.** Suppose that the class `BinaryTree` implements the interface `BinaryTreeInterface`. To  construct the binary tree in Figure 23-14, we first represent each of its leaves as a one-node tree. Notice that each node in this tree contains a one-letter string. Moving up the tree from its leaves, we use `setTree` to form larger and larger subtrees until we have the desired tree. Here are some Java statements that build the tree and then display some of its characteristics:

```
// Represent each leaf as a one-node tree
BinaryTreeInterface<String> dTree = new BinaryTree<>();
dTree.setTree("D");
BinaryTreeInterface<String> fTree = new BinaryTree<>();
fTree.setTree("F");
BinaryTreeInterface<String> gTree = new BinaryTree<>();
gTree.setTree("G");
BinaryTreeInterface<String> hTree = new BinaryTree<>();
hTree.setTree("H");
BinaryTreeInterface<String> emptyTree = new BinaryTree<>();

// Form larger subtrees
BinaryTreeInterface<String> eTree = new BinaryTree<>();
eTree.setTree("E", fTree, gTree);       // Subtree rooted at E

BinaryTreeInterface<String> bTree = new BinaryTree<>();
bTree.setTree("B", dTree, eTree);       // Subtree rooted at B

BinaryTreeInterface<String> cTree = new BinaryTree<>();
cTree.setTree("C", emptyTree, hTree);   // Subtree rooted at C

BinaryTreeInterface<String> aTree = new BinaryTree<>();
aTree.setTree("A", bTree, cTree);       // Desired tree rooted at A

// Display root, height, number of nodes
System.out.println("Root of tree contains " + aTree.getRootData());
System.out.println("Height of tree is " + aTree.getHeight());
System.out.println("Tree has " + aTree.getNumberOfNodes() + " nodes");

// Display nodes in preorder
System.out.println("A preorder traversal visits nodes in this order:");
Iterator<String> preorder = aTree.getPreorderIterator();
while (preorder.hasNext())
   System.out.print(preorder.next() + " ");
System.out.println();
```

---

**FIGURE 23-14** A binary tree whose nodes contain one-letter strings

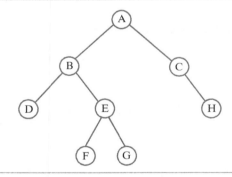

---

**Question 9** What output is produced by the Java code shown in the previous segment?

---

## Examples of Binary Trees

We now look at some examples that use trees to organize data, leaving details of the implementations for the next chapter. Our first example includes a demonstration of some of the traversals introduced earlier in this chapter.

## Expression Trees

**23.22** We can use a binary tree to represent an algebraic expression whose operators are binary. Recall from Segment 5.5 in Chapter 5 that a binary operator has two operands. For example, we can represent the expression *a* / *b* as the binary tree in Figure 23-15a. The root of the tree contains the operator / and the root's children contain the operands for the operator. Notice that the order of the children matches the order of the operands. Such a binary tree is called an **expression tree**. Figure 23-15 also contains other examples of expression trees. Notice that any parentheses in an expression do not appear in its tree. The tree in fact captures the order of the expression's operations without the need for parentheses.

**FIGURE 23-15** Expression trees for four algebraic expressions

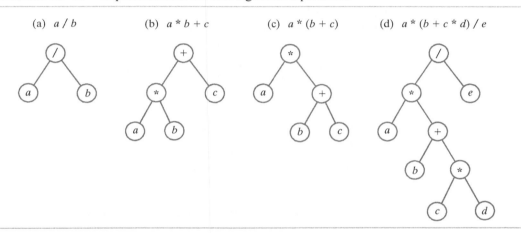

**23.23** Segment 5.5 mentioned that we can write an algebraic expression in several ways. The expressions that we normally write, in which each binary operator appears between its two operands, are called infix expressions. A prefix expression places each operator before its two operands, and a postfix expression places each operator after its two operands. Various traversals of an expression tree are related to these forms of an expression.

An inorder traversal of an expression tree visits the variables and operators in the tree in the order in which they appear in the original infix expression. If we were to write each node's contents when we visited it, we would get the infix expression, but without any parentheses.

A preorder traversal produces a prefix expression that is equivalent to the original infix expression. For example, a preorder traversal of the tree in Figure 23-15b visits nodes in this order: + * *a b c*. This result is the prefix form of the infix expression *a* * *b* + *c*. Recall that, like an expression tree, a prefix expression never contains parentheses.

A postorder traversal produces a postfix expression that is equivalent to the original expression. A postfix expression also has no parentheses, so the traversal produces the correct result. For example, a postorder traversal of the tree in Figure 23-15b visits nodes in the following order: *a b* * *c* +. This result is the postfix form of the infix expression *a* * *b* + *c*.

**Question 10** Write an expression tree for each of these algebraic expressions.

**a.** *a* + *b* * *c*

**b.** (*a* + *b*) * *c*

**Question 11** In what order are nodes visited by a preorder, inorder, and postorder traversal of the trees in Parts *a*, *c*, and *d* of Figure 23-15?

**Question 12** Which trees, if any, in Figure 23-15 are full? Which are complete? Which are balanced?

23.24   **Evaluating an algebraic expression.** Since an expression tree represents the order of an expression's operations, we can use it to evaluate the expression. The root of an expression tree is always an operator whose operands are represented by the root's left and right subtrees. If we can evaluate the subexpressions that these subtrees represent, we can evaluate the entire expression. Notice that such is the case for each expression tree in Figure 23-15, if we know the values of the variables.

A postorder traversal of an expression tree visits the root's left subtree, then the root's right subtree, and finally the root. If during the visits to the subtrees we evaluate their expressions, we can combine the results with the operator in the root and get the value of the original expression. Thus, the value of an expression tree is given by the following recursive algorithm:

```
Algorithm evaluate(expressionTree)
if (expressionTree is empty)
    return 0
else
{
    firstOperand = evaluate(left subtree of expressionTree)
    secondOperand = evaluate(right subtree of expressionTree)
    operator = the root of expressionTree
    return the result of the operation operator and its operands firstOperand
        and secondOperand
}
```

We will implement an expression tree in the next chapter.

**Question 13** What value does the previous algorithm return for the expression tree in Figure 23-15b? Assume that *a* is 3, *b* is 4, and *c* is 5.

## Decision Trees

23.25   **Example: Expert systems.** An **expert system** helps its users solve problems or make decisions. Such a program might help you pick a major or apply for financial aid. It reaches a conclusion based upon your answers to a series of questions.

A **decision tree** can be the basis of an expert system. Each parent (nonleaf) in a decision tree is a question that has a finite number of responses. For example, we might use questions whose answers are true or false, yes or no, or multiple choice. Each possible answer to the question corresponds to a child of that node. Each child might be an additional question or a conclusion. Nodes that are conclusions would have no children, and so they would be leaves.

In general, a decision tree is an *n*-ary tree so that it can accommodate multiple-choice questions. Often, however, a decision tree is a binary tree. For example, the decision tree in Figure 23-16 shows part of a binary tree of yes-or-no questions that diagnose a problem with a television. To use this decision tree, we first would display the question in the root, which is the **current node**. According to the user's answer, we would move to the appropriate child—the new current node—and display its contents. Thus, we move along a path in a decision tree from the root to a leaf according to responses made by the user. At each nonleaf, we display a question. When we reach a leaf, we provide a conclusion. Notice that each node in a binary decision tree either has two children or is a leaf.

A decision tree provides operations that move us along a path through the tree and access the current node. Listing 23-4 contains a possible Java interface for a binary decision tree.

**FIGURE 23-16**   A portion of a binary decision tree

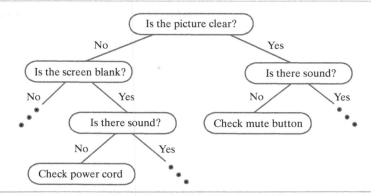

---

LISTING 23-4     An interface for a binary decision tree

```
1   package TreePackage;
2   public interface DecisionTreeInterface<T> extends BinaryTreeInterface<T>
3   {
4      /** Gets the data in the current node.
5          @return  The data object in the current node, or
6                   null if the current node is null. */
7      public T getCurrentData();
8
9      /** Sets the data in the current node.
10        Precondition: The current node is not null.
11        @param newData  The new data object. */
12     public void setCurrentData(T newData);
13
14     /** Sets the data in the children of the current node,
15        creating them if they do not exist.
16        Precondition: The current node is not null.
17        @param responseForNo   The new data object for the left child.
18        @param responseForYes  The new data object for the right child. */
19     public void setResponses(T responseForNo, T responseForYes);
20
21     /** Sees whether the current node contains an answer.
22        @return  True if the current node is a leaf, or
23                 false if it is a nonleaf. */
24     public boolean isAnswer();
25
26     /** Sets the current node to its left child.
27        If the child does not exist, sets the current node to null.
28        Precondition: The current node is not null. */
29     public void advanceToNo();
30
31     /** Sets the current node to its right child.
32        If the child does not exist, sets the current node to null.
33        Precondition: The current node is not null. */
34     public void advanceToYes();
35
36     /** Makes the root of the tree the current node.*/
37     public void resetCurrentNode();
38  } // end DecisionTreeInterface
```

**23.26**  **Example: Guessing game.** In a guessing game, you think of something and I have to guess what it is by asking you questions that have a yes or no answer. Suppose that a program asks the questions for me. This program uses a binary decision tree that grows as the game progresses. Instead of creating the tree before it is used, the program acquires facts from the user and adds them to the decision tree. Thus, the program learns by playing the game and becomes more proficient over time.

To simplify the problem, let's restrict your choice of things. For example, suppose that you think of a country. The program could begin with the simple three-node tree pictured in Figure 23-17.

FIGURE 23-17    An initial decision tree for a guessing game

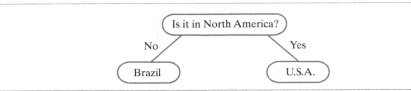

With this tree, the program asks the question in the root and makes one of two guesses, depending on the answer to the question. Here is one possible exchange between the program and the user (user replies are bold):

```
Is it in North America?
> yes
My guess is U.S.A. Am I right?
> yes
I win.
Play again?
```

The program has guessed correctly; the tree remains unchanged.

**23.27**  **Augmenting the tree in the guessing game.** Suppose the user is thinking of something else. The exchange might go like this:

```
Is it in North America?
> no
My guess is Brazil. Am I right?
> no
I give up; what are you thinking of?
> England
Give me a question whose answer is yes for England and no for Brazil.
> Is it in Europe?
Play again?
```

With this new information, we augment the tree, as in Figure 23-18. We replace the contents of the leaf that contained the wrong answer—Brazil in this case—with the new question provided by the user. We then give the leaf two children. One child contains the guess that was in the former leaf (Brazil), and the other contains the user's answer (England) as a new guess. The program now can distinguish between Brazil and England.

**23.28**  **A class for the guessing game.** We demonstrate some of the methods declared in the interface `DecisionTreeInterface` by implementing part of a class `GuessingGame`. This class, as shown in Listing 23-5, begins with a decision tree as a data field and a constructor that creates an initial tree. The tree has one yes-or-no question as its root and two guesses as children, one guess for each possible answer to the question. We assume that `DecisionTree` will have the constructors that we used here.

**FIGURE 23-18**   The decision tree for a guessing game after acquiring another fact

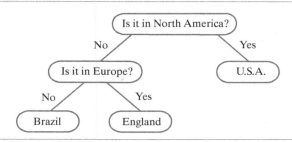

**LISTING 23-5**   The class GuessingGame

```java
1  import TreePackage.DecisionTreeInterface;
2  import TreePackage.DecisionTree;
3  public class GuessingGame
4  {
5      private DecisionTreeInterface<String> tree;
6
7      public GuessingGame(String question, String noAnswer, String yesAnswer)
8      {
9         DecisionTree<String> no = new DecisionTree<>(noAnswer);
10        DecisionTree<String> yes = new DecisionTree<>(yesAnswer);
11        tree = new DecisionTree<>(question, no, yes);
12     } // end default constructor
13
14     public void play()
15     {
16        tree.reset(); // Initialize current node to root
17        while (!tree.isAnswer())
18        {
19           // Ask current question
20           System.out.println(tree.getCurrentData());
21           if (Client.isUserResponseYes())
22              tree.advanceToYes();
23           else
24              tree.advanceToNo();
25        } // end while
26        assert tree.isAnswer(); // Assertion: Leaf is reached
27
28        // Make guess
29        System.out.println("My guess is " + tree.getCurrentData() +
30                          ". Am I right?");
31        if (Client.isUserResponseYes())
32           System.out.println("I win.");
33        else
34           learn();
35     } // end play
36
37     private void learn()
38     {
39        < Implementation left as a project in the next chapter. >
40        . . .
41     } // end learn
42  } // end GuessingGame
```

The public method play uses methods of DecisionTree to maintain the tree. Since the game requires user interaction, we assume that the client of GuessingGame provides methods that communicate with the user. In particular, we assume that a class Client has a static method isUserResponseYes that returns true if the user responds "yes" to a question.

The private method learn asks the user for a question that distinguishes between two guesses. Using this information, the method adds nodes to the decision tree, as described earlier in Segment 23.27. The next chapter will give you the tools to implement this method.

**Question 14** Why should the method learn be private within the class GuessingGame?

## Binary Search Trees

**23.29** Earlier chapters have already discussed the importance of searching for data. Since we can traverse the nodes in any tree, searching a tree for a specific piece of data is certainly feasible. Doing so, however, can be as inefficient as performing a sequential search of an array. A **search tree**, on the other hand, organizes its data so that a search can be more efficient. In this chapter, we present the simplest kind of search tree, the binary search tree. Chapter 27 will look at other search trees.

A **binary search tree** is a binary tree whose nodes contain Comparable objects and are organized as follows:

**Note:** For each node in a binary search tree,
- The node's data is greater than all the data in the node's left subtree
- The node's data is less than all the data in the node's right subtree

For example, Figure 23-19 shows a binary search tree of names. As a string, *Jared* is greater than all the names in *Jared*'s left subtree but less than all names in *Jared*'s right subtree. These characteristics are true for every node in the tree, not only for the root. Notice that each of *Jared*'s subtrees is itself a binary search tree.

**Note:** Every node in a binary search tree is the root of a binary search tree.

The previous definition of a binary search tree implies that the tree's entries are distinct. We have imposed this restriction to make our discussion simpler, but we could revise our definition to allow duplicate entries. Chapter 25 considers this possibility.

FIGURE 23-19    A binary search tree of names

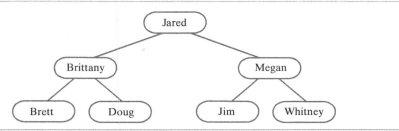

**23.30**    The configuration of a binary search tree is not unique. That is, we can form several different binary search trees from the same set of data. For example, Figure 23-20 shows two binary search trees containing the same names that are in Figure 23-19; other binary search trees are possible.

FIGURE 23-20    Two binary search trees containing the same data as the tree in Figure 23-19

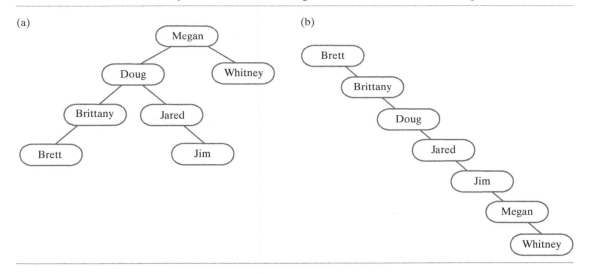

**Question 15** How many different binary search trees can you form from the strings *a*, *b*, and *c*?

**Question 16** What are the heights of the shortest and tallest trees that you formed in Question 15?

**23.31**    **Searching a binary search tree.** The organization of the nodes in a binary search tree enables us to search the tree for a particular data object, given its search key. For example, suppose that we search the tree in Figure 23-19 for the string *Jim*. Beginning at the root of the tree, we compare *Jim* with *Jared*. Since the string *Jim* is greater than the string *Jared*, we search the right subtree of the root. Comparing *Jim* to *Megan*, we find that *Jim* is less than *Megan*. We search *Megan*'s left subtree next and find *Jim*.

To search for *Laura*, we would compare *Laura* with *Jared*, then with *Megan*, and then with *Jim*. Since *Laura* is greater than *Jim*, we would search *Jim*'s right subtree. But this subtree is empty, so we conclude that *Laura* does not occur in the tree.

We can express our search algorithm recursively: To search a binary search tree, we search one of its two subtrees. The search ends when either we find the item we seek or we encounter an empty subtree. We can formalize this search by writing the following pseudocode:

*Algorithm* `bstSearch(binarySearchTree, desiredObject)`
*// Searches a binary search tree for a given object.*
*// Returns true if the object is found.*

`if` (`binarySearchTree` *is empty*)
    `return false`
`else if` (`desiredObject ==` *object in the root of* `binarySearchTree`)
    `return true`
`else if` (`desiredObject` < *object in the root of* `binarySearchTree`)
    `return bstSearch(`*left subtree of* `binarySearchTree, desiredObject)`
`else`
    `return bstSearch(`*right subtree of* `binarySearchTree, desiredObject)`

This algorithm is somewhat like a binary search of an array. Here we search one of two subtrees; a binary search searches one half of an array. You will see how to implement this algorithm in Chapter 25.

If you think that you could implement the ADT dictionary by using a binary search tree, you would be right. Chapter 25 will show you how.

**23.32**   **The efficiency of a search.** The algorithm `bstSearch` examines nodes along a path through a binary search tree, beginning at the tree's root. The path ends at either the node that contains the desired object or some other node that is a leaf. In the previous segment, the search for *Jim* in Figure 23-19 examined the three nodes containing *Jared*, *Megan*, and *Jim*. In general, the number of comparisons that a successful search requires is the number of nodes along the path from the root to the node that contains the desired item.

Searching for *Jim* in Figure 23-20a requires four comparisons; searching Figure 23-20b for *Jim* requires five comparisons. Both trees in Figure 23-20 are taller than the tree in Figure 23-19. As you can see, the height of a tree directly affects the length of the longest path from the root to a leaf and hence affects the efficiency of a worst-case search. Thus, searching a binary search tree of height $h$ is O($h$).

Note that the tree in Figure 23-20b is as tall as a tree containing seven nodes can be. A search of this tree has the performance of a sequential search of either a sorted array or a sorted linked chain. Each of these searches has an efficiency of O($n$).

To make searching a binary search tree as efficient as possible, the tree must be as short as possible. The tree in Figure 23-19 is full and is the shortest possible binary search tree that we can form with this data. As you will see in Chapter 25, inserting or deleting nodes can change the shape of a binary search tree. Thus, such operations can decrease the time efficiency of a search. Chapter 27 will show you strategies for maintaining the search's efficiency.

## Heaps

**23.33**   **Definitions.** A **heap** is a complete binary tree whose nodes contain `Comparable` objects and are organized as follows. Each node contains an object that is no smaller (or no larger) than the objects in its descendants. In a **maxheap**, the object in a node is greater than or equal to its descendant objects. In a **minheap**, the relation is less than or equal to. Figure 23-21 gives an example of a maxheap and a minheap. For simplicity, we use integers instead of objects in our illustrations.

FIGURE 23-21    (a) A maxheap and (b) a minheap that contain the same values

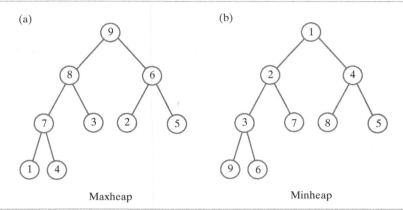

The root of a maxheap contains the largest object in the heap. Notice that the subtrees of any node in a maxheap are also maxheaps. Although we will focus on maxheaps, minheaps behave in an analogous fashion.

 **Note:** A maxheap is a complete binary tree such that each node in the tree contains a `Comparable` object that is greater than or equal to the objects in the node's descendants. Unlike a binary search tree, however, no relationship exists between the subtrees of a node in a heap.

**23.34 Operations.** In addition to typical ADT operations such as `add`, `isEmpty`, `getSize`, and `clear`, a heap has operations that retrieve and remove the object in its root. This object is either the largest or the smallest object in the heap, depending on whether we have a maxheap or a minheap. This characteristic enables us to use a heap to implement the ADT priority queue, as you will see in the next segment.

The Java interface in Listing 23-6 specifies operations for a maxheap.

LISTING 23-6    An interface for a maxheap

```
 1  public interface MaxHeapInterface<T extends Comparable<? super T>>
 2  {
 3      /** Adds a new entry to this heap.
 4          @param newEntry  An object to be added. */
 5      public void add(T newEntry);
 6
 7      /** Removes and returns the largest item in this heap.
 8          @return  Either the largest object in the heap or,
 9                   if the heap is empty before the operation, null. */
10      public T removeMax();
11
```

```
12      /** Retrieves the largest item in this heap.
13          @return  Either the largest object in the heap or,
14                   if the heap is empty, null. */
15      public T getMax();
16
17      /** Detects whether this heap is empty.
18          @return  True if the heap is empty, or false otherwise. */
19      public boolean isEmpty();
20
21      /** Gets the size of this heap.
22          @return  The number of entries currently in the heap. */
23      public int getSize();
24
25      /** Removes all entries from this heap. */
26      public void clear();
27 } // end MaxHeapInterface
```

If you place items into a maxheap and then remove them, you will get the items in descending order. Thus, we can use a heap to sort an array, as you will see in Chapter 26.

**Question 17** Does a maxheap that contains a given set of objects have a unique root? Justify your answer by using the maxheap in Figure 23-21a as an example.

**Question 18** Is a maxheap that contains a given set of objects unique? Justify your answer by using the maxheap in Figure 23-21a as an example.

**23.35 Priority queues.** We can use a heap to implement the ADT priority queue. Assuming that the class MaxHeap implements MaxHeapInterface, a class that implements the priority queue as an adapter class begins as given in Listing 23-7. Recall that we defined PriorityQueueInterface in Segment 10.19 of Chapter 10.

---

**LISTING 23-7   The beginning of the class PriorityQueue**

```
1  public final class HeapPriorityQueue<T extends Comparable<? super T>>
2                    implements PriorityQueueInterface<T>
3  {
4     private MaxHeapInterface<T> pq;
5
6     public HeapPriorityQueue()
7     {
8        pq = new MaxHeap<>();
9     } // end default constructor
10
11    public void add(T newEntry)
12    {
13       pq.add(newEntry);
14    } // end add
15    < Implementations of remove, peek, isEmpty, getSize, and clear are here. >
16    . . .
17 } // end HeapPriorityQueue
```

---

Alternatively, the class MaxHeap could implement PriorityQueueInterface. We then could define a priority queue of strings, as follows:

```
PriorityQueueInterface<String> pq = new MaxHeap<>();
```

# Examples of General Trees

We conclude this chapter with two examples of general trees. A parse tree is useful in the construction of a compiler; a game tree is a generalization of the decision tree that Segment 23.25 described.

## Parse Trees

**23.36**  Segment 7.44 in Chapter 7 gave the following rules to describe strings that are valid algebraic expressions:

- An algebraic expression is either a term or two terms separated by a + or - operator.
- A term is either a factor or two factors separated by a * or / operator.
- A factor is either a variable or an algebraic expression enclosed in parentheses.
- A variable is a single letter.

These rules form a **grammar** for algebraic expressions, much like the grammar that describes the English language. In fact, every programming language has a grammar.

Typically, computer scientists use a notation to write the rules of a grammar. For example, the rules just given for algebraic expressions could appear as follows, where the symbol | means "or":

*<expression>* ::= *<term>* | *<term>* + *<term>* | *<term>* - *<term>*
*<term>* ::= *<factor>* | *<factor>* * *<factor>* | *<factor>* / *<factor>*
*<factor>* ::= *<variable>* | ( *<expression>* )
*<variable>* ::= a | b | ... | z | A | B ... | Z

To see whether a string is a valid algebraic expression—that is, to check its syntax—we must see whether we can derive the string from *<expression>* by applying these rules. If we can, the derivation can be given as a **parse tree** with *<expression>* as its root and the variables and operators of the algebraic expression as its leaves. A parse tree for the expression *a* * (*b* + *c*) is shown in Figure 23-22. Beginning at the tree's root, we see that an expression is a term. A term is the product of two factors. The first factor is a variable, in particular, *a*. The second factor is an expression enclosed in parentheses. That expression is the sum of two terms. Each of those terms is a factor; each of those factors is a variable. The first variable is *b*; the second is *c*. Since we are able to form this parse tree, the string *a* * (*b* + *c*) is a valid algebraic expression.

A parse tree must be a general tree so that it can accommodate any expression. In fact, we are not restricted to algebraic expressions. We can use a parse tree to check the validity of any string according to any grammar. Since programming languages have grammars, compilers use parse trees both to check the syntax of a program and to produce executable code.

**Question 19** Draw a parse tree for the algebraic expression *a* * *b* + *c*.

## Game Trees

**23.37.**  For a two-person game such as tic-tac-toe, we can use a general decision tree to represent the possible moves in any situation. Such a decision tree is called a **game tree**. If a given node in the tree represents the state of the game after one player has made a move, the node's children represent the states possible after the second player makes a move. Figure 23-23 shows a portion of a game tree for tic-tac-toe.

We can use a game tree like the one shown in the figure in a program that plays tic-tac-toe. We could create the tree ahead of time or have the program build the tree as it plays. In either case, the program could ensure that poor moves do not remain in the tree. In this way, the program could use a game tree to improve its play.

**FIGURE 23-22** A parse tree for the algebraic expression $a * (b + c)$

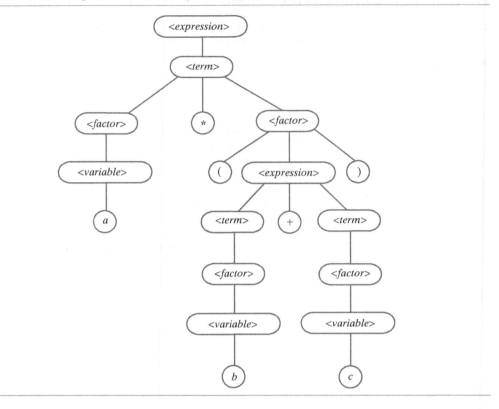

**FIGURE 23-23** A portion of a game tree for tic-tac-toe

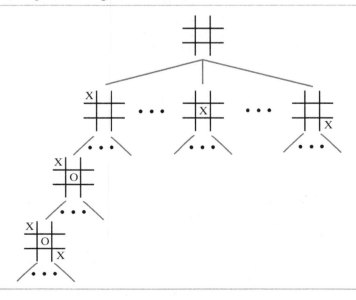

## CHAPTER SUMMARY

- A tree is a set of nodes connected by edges that indicate the relationships among the nodes. The nodes are arranged in levels that denote their hierarchy. At the top level is a single node called the root.

- At each successive level of a tree are nodes that are the children of the nodes at the previous level. A node with no children is called a leaf. A node that has children is the parent of those children. The root is the only node with no parent. All other nodes have one parent each.

- A node in a binary tree has at most two children. In an *n*-ary tree, a node can have up to *n* children. In a general tree, a node can have any number of children.

- The height of a tree is the number of levels in the tree. The height also equals the number of nodes along the longest path between the root and a leaf.

- All leaves in a full binary tree are on the same level, and every nonleaf has exactly two children.

- A full tree of height $h$ has $2^h - 1$ nodes, which is as many as it can contain.

- A complete binary tree is full to its next-to-last level. Its leaves on the last level are filled from left to right.

- The height of a binary tree with $n$ nodes that is either complete or full is $\log_2 (n + 1)$ rounded up.

- In a completely balanced binary tree, the subtrees of each node have exactly the same height. Such trees must be full. Other binary trees are said to be height balanced if the subtrees of each node in the tree differ in height by no more than 1.

- You can traverse the nodes in a tree by visiting each node exactly once. Several traversal orders are possible. A level-order traversal begins at the root and visits nodes from left to right, one level at a time. In a preorder traversal, you visit the root before you visit nodes in the root's subtrees. In a postorder traversal, you visit the root after you visit the root's subtrees. For a binary tree, an inorder traversal visits the nodes in the left subtree, then the root, and finally the nodes in the right subtree. For a general tree, an inorder traversal is not well defined.

- An expression tree is a binary tree that represents an algebraic expression whose operators are binary. The operands of the expression appear in the tree's leaves. Any parentheses in an expression do not appear in the tree. You can use an expression tree to evaluate an algebraic expression.

- A decision tree contains a question in each nonleaf. Each child of the nonleaf corresponds to one possible response to the question. Within each of these children is either an additional question or a conclusion. Nodes that are conclusions have no children, and so they are leaves. You can use a decision tree to create an expert system.

- A binary search tree is a binary tree whose nodes contain `Comparable` objects that are organized as follows:
  - The data in a node is greater than the data in the node's left subtree.
  - The data in a node is less than the data in the node's right subtree.

- A search of a binary search tree can be as fast as O(log $n$) or as slow as O($n$). The performance of the search depends on the shape of the tree.

- A heap is a complete binary tree whose nodes contain `Comparable` objects. The data in each node is no smaller (or no larger) than the data in the node's descendants.

- You can use a heap to implement a priority queue.

- Certain rules form a grammar that describes an algebraic expression. A parse tree is a general tree that pictures how these rules apply to a specific expression. You can use a parse tree to check the syntax of a given expression.

- A game tree is a general decision tree that contains the possible moves for a game such as tic-tac-toe.

## EXERCISES

1. In Chapter 7, Figure 7-10a shows the recursive computation of the term $F_6$ in the Fibonacci sequence. Recall that this sequence is defined as follows:

   $$F_0 = 1, F_1 = 1, F_n = F_{n-1} + F_{n-2} \text{ when } n \geq 2$$

   The root of the tree is the value for $F_6$. The children of $F_6$ are $F_5$ and $F_4$, the two values necessary to compute $F_6$. Notice that the leaves of the tree contain the base-case values $F_0$ and $F_1$.

   Using Figure 7-10a as an example, draw a binary tree that represents the recursive calls in the algorithm mergeSort, as given in Segment 9.3 of Chapter 9. Assume an array of 20 entries.

2. What is the maximum number of nodes in the shortest binary tree with height 5? What is the maximum number of leaf nodes?

3. Consider a complete binary tree that has 21 nodes.

   **a.** What is the height of the tree?
   **b.** How many nodes are there at the highest level?
   **c.** Answer the previous two questions for a complete binary tree with 100 nodes.

4. Write a recursive algorithm to calculate the height of a binary tree.

5. Assume that you have been given a binary search tree and that this tree is to be traversed in the ascending order. Which traversal algorithm would you select for this task? Explain.

6. Consider a traversal of a binary tree. Suppose that visiting a node means to simply display the data in the node. What are the results of each of the following traversals of the tree in Figure 23-24a?

   **a.** Preorder
   **b.** Postorder
   **c.** Inorder
   **d.** Level order

---

**FIGURE 23-24** Two trees for Exercises 6, 7, and 8

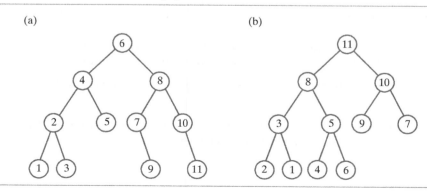

7. Repeat Exercise 6, but instead traverse the tree in Figure 23-24b.

8. The two trees in Figure 23-24 contain integer data.

    a. Is the tree in Part *a* a binary search tree? Why or why not?
    b. Is the tree in Part *b* a maxheap? Why or why not?

9. Draw the shortest possible binary search tree from the following strings: *Ann, Ben, Chad, Drew, Ella, Jenn, Jess, Kip, Luis, Pat, Rico, Scott, Tracy, Zak*. Is your tree unique?

10. Suppose we know that the inorder traversal of a binary tree is

    D B E A F C

    and the preorder traversal of the tree is

    A B D E C F

    What is the postorder traversal of the tree?

11. Which traversal methods are used to traverse a tree in breadth-first order and depth-first order? Explain.

12. Which data structure can be used for a level-order traversal? Give the pseudocode.

13. Prove that the sum

$$\sum_{i=0}^{h-1} 2^i$$

is equal to $2^h - 1$. Use mathematical induction.

14. At least, how many nodes can a complete binary tree have with height *h*? Use mathematical induction to prove your answer.

15. What is the time complexity to search an element in a binary search tree with *n* nodes?

16. Suppose that you number the nodes of a complete binary tree in the order in which a level-order traversal would visit them. The tree's root would then be node 1. Figure 23-25 shows an example of such a tree. What number, in terms of *i*, is node *i*'s

    a. Sibling, if any
    b. Left child, if any
    c. Right child, if any
    d. Parent, if any

**FIGURE 23-25**   A complete binary tree with its nodes numbered in level order (Exercise 16)

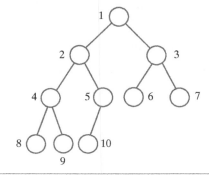

17. Consider a full $n$-ary tree of height $h$.
   a. What is the total number of nodes?
   b. How many nodes are there at height $h$?
   c. Is inorder traversal possible?

18. Suppose that you have $n$ values to put into an empty binary search tree.

   a. In how many different orders can you add the $n$ values to the tree? This is not the same as the number of possible binary search trees for $n$ values. Explain why.
   b. Figure 23-20b shows a binary search tree that effectively acts like a sorted list. In how many different orders can you add the $n$ values to the tree such that every parent has only one child? Such a tree has worst-case performance.
   c. What is the probability that a randomly constructed binary search tree has worst-case performance? *Hint*: Compute the fraction of the total number of possible orders that results in the worst case.

19. What fraction of time is spent in reading the maximum number of elements from maxheap?

20. What value does the algorithm given in Segment 23.24 return for the expression tree in Figure 23-15c? Assume that $a$ is 3, $b$ is 4, and $c$ is 5.

21. Draw a parse tree for each of the following algebraic expressions:

   a. $a + b * c$
   b. $(a + b) * (c - d)$

## PROJECTS

1. Draw a class diagram for the guessing game described in Segments 23.26 through 23.28.

   *For each of the following projects, assume that you have a class that implements* `BinaryTreeInterface`, *given in Segment 23.20. The next chapter will discuss such implementations.*

2. Write Java code like the code in Segment 23.21 that creates a binary tree whose eight nodes contain the strings $A$, $B$, . . ., $H$, such that the inorder traversal of the tree visits the nodes in alphabetical order. Write one version that creates a full tree and one version that creates a tree of maximum height. The inorder traversals of both trees should produce the same result.

3. Given an array `wordList` of 15 strings in any order, write Java code that creates a full binary tree whose inorder traversal returns the strings in alphabetical order. *Hint*: Sort the list of strings and then use the eighth string as the root.

4. Design an algorithm that produces a binary expression tree from a given postfix expression. You can assume that the postfix expression is a string that has only binary operators and one-letter operands.

5. Repeat the previous project, but begin with an infix expression instead of a postfix expression.

6. Develop an interface `GeneralTreeInterface` for a general tree.

7. Given a class `GeneralTree` that implements the `GeneralTreeInterface` from Project 6, implement a program that will read a fully parenthesized Lisp expression, as described in Projects 7 and 8 of Chapter 5, and create an expression tree. For example, the expression

```
(+ (- height)
   (* 3 3 4)
   (/ 3 width length)
   (* radius radius)
)
```

has the expression tree shown in Figure 23-26.

FIGURE 23-26　An expression tree for Project 7

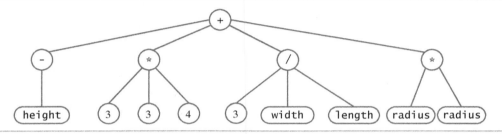

8. Design algorithms for a spelling checker that has at least the following methods:

- **void** add(String word)—Adds a word to a spelling checker's collection of correctly spelled words
- **boolean** check(String word)—Returns true if the given word is spelled correctly

Store the collection of correctly spelled words in a 26-ary tree. Each node in this tree has a child corresponding to a letter in the alphabet. Each node also indicates whether the word represented by the path between the root and the node is spelled correctly. For example, the tree shown in Figure 23-27 depicts this indication as a filled-in node. This tree stores the words "boa," "boar," "boat," "board," "hi," "hip," "hit," "hop," "hot," "trek," and "tram."

To check whether a given word is spelled correctly, you begin at the tree's root and follow the reference associated with the first letter in the word. If the reference is `null`, the word is not in the tree. Otherwise, you follow the reference associated with the second letter in the word, and so on. If you finally arrive at a node, you check whether it indicates a correctly spelled word. For example, the tree in Figure 23-27 indicates that "t," "tr," and "tre" are spelling mistakes, but "trek" is spelled correctly.

FIGURE 23-27　A general tree for Project 8

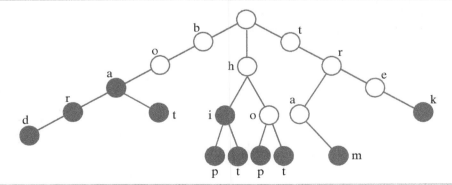

**ANSWERS TO SELF-TEST QUESTIONS**

1.  **a.** N, O, P, G, H, Q, R, S, T, L, M.

    **b.** I, J.

    **c.** F, G.

    **d.** F, G, N, O, P.

    **e.** F, B, A.

    **f.** A, B, C, D, E, F, I, J, K

2.  A tree that represents the organization of this book is a general tree, such as the following:

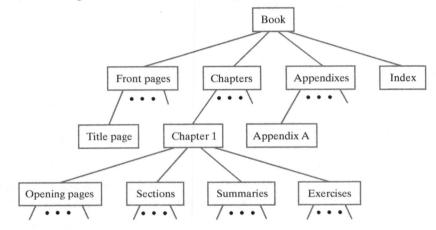

3.  3, 3, and 4, respectively.

4.  **a.** For the tree in Figure 23-6a, $n$ is 7 and $h$ is 3. Since the tree is full and $7 = 2^3 - 1$, the relationship $n = 2^h - 1$ is true. Also, $3 = \log_2 (7 + 1)$, so the relationship $h = \log_2 (n + 1)$ is true.

    **b.** For the tree in Figure 23-6b, $n$ is 10 and $h$ is 4. The tree is complete, and $\log_2 (10 + 1)$ is approximately 3.5, which rounded up is 4. Thus, the relationship $h = \log_2 (n + 1)$ rounded up is true.

5.  $2^6 - 1$, or 63.

6.  $\log_2 (14 + 1)$ is approximately 3.9. When rounded up, we get 4.

7.  Preorder: Jared, John, James, Mary, Jennifer, Robert, Carole
    Postorder: James, Mary, John, Robert, Carole, Jennifer, Jared
    Inorder: James, John, Mary, Jared, Robert, Jennifer, Carole
    Level order: Jared, John, Jennifer, James, Mary, Robert, Carole

8.

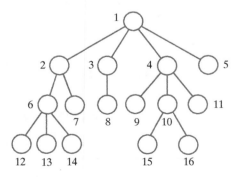

**9.**
```
Root of tree contains A
Height of tree is 4
Tree has 8 nodes
A preorder traversal visits nodes in this order:
A B D E F G C H
```

**10.**

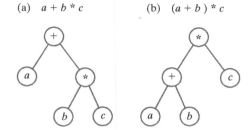

(a)  $a + b * c$    (b)  $(a + b) * c$

**11.** Figure 23-15a
Preorder: $/ a b$
Inorder: $a / b$
Postorder: $a b /$

Figure 23-15c
Preorder: $* a + b c$
Inorder: $a * b + c$
Postorder: $a b c + *$

Figure 23-15d
Preorder: $/ * a + b * c d e$
Inorder: $a * b + c * d / e$
Postorder: $a b c d * + * e /$

**12.** In Figure 23-15, the tree in Part *a* is full, the tree in Part *b* is complete, and the trees in Parts *a*, *b*, and *c* are balanced.

**13.** 17.

**14.** The method `learn` augments the tree under conditions that the class `GuessingGame` must control. It would be inappropriate for a client to invoke this method.

**15.** 5.

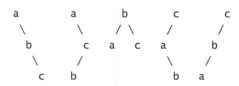

**16.** The shortest tree has height 2; the tallest tree has height 3.

**17.** The root of a maxheap contains the object with the largest value. If this object is unique in the set of objects, the root is unique. If another object has the same value, it would be a child of the root. In Figure 23-21a, only 9 can be the root.

**18.** No. The order of siblings is not specified in a heap, so several different heaps can contain the same data. For example, in Figure 23-21a, you could exchange 2 and 5, or you could exchange the root's two subtrees, and still have a maxheap.

**19.**

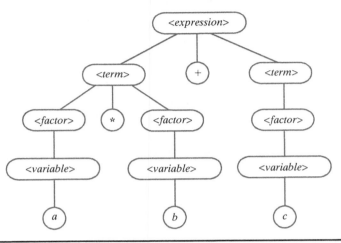

# Tree Implementations

## Contents

## Prerequisites

## Objectives

After studying this chapter, you should be able to

- Describe the necessary operations on a node within a binary tree
- Implement a class of nodes for a binary tree
- Implement a class of binary trees
- Implement an expression tree
- Describe the necessary operations on a node within a general tree
- Use a binary tree to represent a general tree

The most common implementation of a tree uses a linked structure. Nodes, analogous to the nodes we used in a linked chain, represent each element in the tree. Each node can reference its children, which are other nodes in the tree. This chapter emphasizes binary trees, although it concludes with a brief discussion of general trees. We do not cover binary search trees here, as the entire next chapter is devoted to them.

Although we could use either an array or a vector to implement a tree, we will not do so in this chapter. These implementations are attractive only when the tree is complete. In such cases, the link between a parent and child is not stored explicitly, so the data structure is simpler than if the tree is not complete. In Chapter 26, we will encounter a use for a complete tree, so we will postpone until then any other implementation of the tree.

## The Nodes in a Binary Tree

**24.1**   The elements in a tree are called nodes, as are the Java objects in a linked chain. We will use similar objects to represent a tree's nodes and call them nodes as well. The distinction between a node in a tree that you draw and the Java node that represents it usually is not essential.

A node object that represents a node in a tree references both data and the node's children. We could define one class of nodes for all trees, regardless of how many children a node has. But such a class would not be convenient or efficient for a node in a binary tree, since it has at most two children. Figure 24-1 illustrates a node for a binary tree. It contains a reference to a data object and references to its left child and right child, which are other nodes in the tree. Either reference to a child could be null. If both of them are null, the node is a leaf node.

---

**FIGURE 24-1**     A node in a binary tree

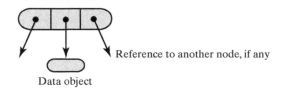

Reference to another node, if any

Data object

---

Although the nodes in a linked chain belong to a private class Node that is internal to classes such as LinkedStack and LList, our class of tree nodes will not be internal to the class of binary trees. Since any class that extends our fundamental class of binary trees might need to manipulate nodes, we will define our class of tree nodes outside of our binary tree class. But we will not make this class of nodes public. Instead, we will give it package access within a package that contains the classes of the various trees and their interfaces. In this way the node remains an implementation detail that is not available to any of the tree's clients.

---

 **Note:** A node object in a linked chain references another node in the chain. Although we can process the chain recursively, a node does not reference a chain. Likewise, a node object in a binary tree references other nodes in the tree. Although we often think of a binary tree recursively, as Segment 23.8 of the previous chapter describes, a tree node does not reference another tree.

## A Class of Binary Nodes

24.2    Listing 24-1 contains a portion of a class of nodes suitable for a binary tree. We place the class in the package TreePackage and omit its access modifier. Without this modifier, the class is accessible only by other classes within TreePackage. These nodes have more responsibilities than the nodes in a linked chain. Soon you will see how the last three methods in this class simplify the implementation of the binary tree.

**LISTING 24-1**    The class BinaryNode

```java
1  package TreePackage;
2  class BinaryNode<T>
3  {
4     private T data;
5     private BinaryNode<T> leftChild;
6     private BinaryNode<T> rightChild;
7
8     public BinaryNode()
9     {
10        this(null); // Call next constructor
11    } // end default constructor
12
13    public BinaryNode(T dataPortion)
14    {
15       this(dataPortion, null, null); // Call next constructor
16    } // end constructor
17
18    public BinaryNode(T dataPortion, BinaryNode<T> newLeftChild,
19                                     BinaryNode<T> newRightChild)
20    {
21       data = dataPortion;
22       leftChild = newLeftChild;
23       rightChild = newRightChild;
24    } // end constructor
25
26    /** Retrieves the data portion of this node.
27        @return  The object in the data portion of the node. */
28    public T getData()
29    {
30       return data;
31    } // end getData
32
33    /** Sets the data portion of this node.
34        @param newData  The data object. */
35    public void setData(T newData)
36    {
37       data = newData;
38    } // end setData
39
40    /** Retrieves the left child of this node.
41        @return  The node that is this node's left child. */
42    public BinaryNode<T> getLeftChild()
43    {
44       return leftChild;
45    } // end getLeftChild
46
47    /** Sets this node's left child to a given node.
48        @param newLeftChild  A node that will be the left child. */
```

```
49      public void setLeftChild(BinaryNode<T> newLeftChild)
50      {
51         leftChild = newLeftChild;
52      } // end setLeftChild
53
54      /** Detects whether this node has a left child.
55          @return   True if the node has a left child. */
56      public boolean hasLeftChild()
57      {
58         return leftChild != null;
59      } // end hasLeftChild
60
61      /** Detects whether this node is a leaf.
62          @return   True if the node is a leaf. */
63      public boolean isLeaf()
64      {
65         return (leftChild == null) && (rightChild == null);
66      } // end isLeaf
67
68         < Implementations of getRightChild, setRightChild, and hasRightChild are
69           analogous to their left-child counterparts. >
70
71      /** Counts the nodes in the subtree rooted at this node.
72          @return   The number of nodes in the subtree rooted at this node. */
73      public int getNumberOfNodes()
74      {
75         < See Segment 24.10 >
76      } // end getNumberOfNodes
77
78      /** Computes the height of the subtree rooted at this node.
79          @return   The height of the subtree rooted at this node. */
80      public int getHeight()
81      {
82         < See Segment 24.10 >
83      } // end getHeight
84
85      /** Copies the subtree rooted at this node.
86          @return   The root of a copy of the subtree rooted at this node. */
87      public BinaryNode<T> copy()
88      {
89         < See Segment 24.5 >
90      } // end copy
91      . . .
92   } // end BinaryNode
```

 **Note:**  Typically, the class that represents a node in a tree is a detail that you hide from the client. Omitting its access modifier and placing it within a package of classes that implement trees makes it available only to other classes in the package.

## An Implementation of the ADT Binary Tree

The previous chapter described several variations of a binary tree. The expression tree and decision tree, for example, each include operations that augment the basic operations of a binary tree. We will define a class of binary trees that can be the superclass of other classes, such as the class of expression trees.

## Creating a Basic Binary Tree

**24.3**    Segment 23.20 of the previous chapter defines the following interface for a class of binary trees:

```
public interface BinaryTreeInterface<T>
        extends TreeInterface<T>, TreeIteratorInterface<T>
{
   public void setTree(T rootData);

   public void setTree(T rootData, BinaryTreeInterface<T> leftTree,
                                   BinaryTreeInterface<T> rightTree);

} // end BinaryTreeInterface
```

**VideoNote**
Creating a binary tree

Recall that TreeInterface in Segment 23.18 specifies basic operations—getRootData, getHeight, getNumberOfNodes, isEmpty, and clear—common to all trees, and TreeIteratorInterface in Segment 23.19 specifies operations for traversals of a tree. These three interfaces are in our package TreePackage.

We begin our implementation of a binary tree with constructors and the setTree methods, as given in Listing 24-2. The private method privateSetTree has parameters of type BinaryTree, whereas the public setTree that the interface specifies has parameters of type BinaryTreeInterface. We use this private method in the implementation of setTree to simplify the casts from BinaryTreeInterface to BinaryTree.

The third constructor—which has parameters of type BinaryTree—also calls privateSetTree. If it called setTree, we would declare setTree as a final method so that no subclass could override it and thereby change the effect of the constructor. Note as well that we could have named the private method setTree instead of privateSetTree.

---

**LISTING 24-2    A first draft of the class BinaryTree**

```
 1  package TreePackage;
 2  import java.util.Iterator;
 3  import java.util.NoSuchElementException;
 4  import StackAndQueuePackage.*; // Needed by tree iterators
 5  /**
 6     A class that implements the ADT binary tree.
 7     @author Frank M. Carrano.
 8  */
 9  public class BinaryTree<T> implements BinaryTreeInterface<T>
10  {
11     private BinaryNode<T> root;
12
13     public BinaryTree()
14     {
15        root = null;
16     } // end default constructor
17
18     public BinaryTree(T rootData)
19     {
20        root = new BinaryNode<>(rootData);
21     } // end constructor
22
23     public BinaryTree(T rootData, BinaryTree<T> leftTree, BinaryTree<T> rightTree)
24     {
25        privateSetTree(rootData, leftTree, rightTree);
26     } // end constructor
27
28     public void setTree(T rootData)
29     {
30        root = new BinaryNode<>(rootData);
31     } // end setTree
```

```
32
33    public void setTree(T rootData, BinaryTreeInterface<T> leftTree,
34                                    BinaryTreeInterface<T> rightTree)
35    {
36       privateSetTree(rootData, (BinaryTree<T>)leftTree,
37                                (BinaryTree<T>)rightTree);
38    } // end setTree
39
40    private void privateSetTree(T rootData, BinaryTree<T> leftTree,
41                                            BinaryTree<T> rightTree)
42    {
43       < FIRST DRAFT - See Segments 24.4 - 24.7 for improvements. >
44       root = new BinaryNode<>(rootData);
45
46       if (leftTree != null)
47          root.setLeftChild(leftTree.root);
48
49       if (rightTree != null)
50          root.setRightChild(rightTree.root);
51    } // end privateSetTree
52
53    < Implementations of getRootData, getHeight, getNumberOfNodes, isEmpty, clear,
54      and the methods specified in TreeIteratorInterface are here. >
55
56    . . .
57 } // end BinaryTree
```

**Programming Tip:** No cast is needed when you pass an instance of `BinaryTree` to a method whose parameter has the type `BinaryTreeInterface`. The converse, however, requires a cast.

## The Method `privateSetTree`

**24.4** **A problem.** The implementation of `privateSetTree` just given is really not sufficient to handle all possible uses of the method. Suppose that the client defines three distinct instances of the class `BinaryTree`—`treeA`, `treeB`, and `treeC`—and executes the statement

    treeA.setTree(a, treeB, treeC);

Since `setTree` calls `privateSetTree`, `treeA` shares nodes with `treeB` and `treeC`, as Figure 24-2 illustrates. If the client now changes `treeB`, for example, `treeA` also changes. This result generally is undesirable.

---

**FIGURE 24-2**     The binary tree `treeA` shares nodes with `treeB` and `treeC`

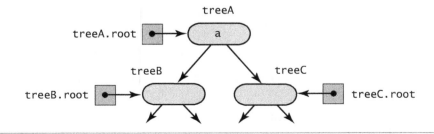

---

**Question 1** We stated that it is undesirable to have treeA change as a result of a client changing treeB. Why would this situation be dangerous?

**24.5    One solution.** One solution is for privateSetTree to copy the nodes in treeB and treeC. Then treeA will be separate and distinct from treeB and treeC. Any subsequent changes to either treeB or treeC will not affect treeA. Let's explore this approach.

Since we are copying nodes, we use the method copy as defined in the class BinaryNode. To copy a node, we actually must copy the subtree rooted at the node. Beginning with the node, we copy it and then copy the nodes in its left and right subtrees. Thus, we perform a preorder traversal of the subtree. For simplicity, we will not copy the data in the nodes.

We define the method copy in the class BinaryNode as follows:

```
public BinaryNode<T> copy()
{
    BinaryNode<T> newRoot = new BinaryNode<>(data);

    if (leftChild != null)
        newRoot.setLeftChild(leftChild.copy());

    if (rightChild != null)
        newRoot.setRightChild(rightChild.copy());

    return newRoot;
} // end copy
```

Now privateSetTree can invoke copy to copy the nodes from the two given subtrees:

```
private void privateSetTree(T rootData, BinaryTree<T> leftTree,
                                        BinaryTree<T> rightTree)
{
    root = new BinaryNode<>(rootData);

    if ((leftTree != null) && !leftTree.isEmpty())
        root.setLeftChild(leftTree.root.copy());

    if ((rightTree != null) && !rightTree.isEmpty())
        root.setRightChild(rightTree.root.copy());
} // end privateSetTree
```

Since copying nodes is expensive, we could consider other implementations of this method. As you will see next, we must copy at least some nodes in certain situations.

**24.6    Another approach, more problems.** Instead of always copying nodes, privateSetTree could behave as follows. Returning to our earlier example,

```
treeA.setTree(a, treeB, treeC);
```

privateSetTree first could link the root node of treeA to the root nodes of treeB and treeC. It then could set treeB.root and treeC.root to null. This approach solves the problem of a node appearing in more than one tree, but it makes the trees that the client passed as arguments empty. As a result, two other difficulties can occur.

Suppose that the client executes

```
treeA.setTree(a, treeA, treeB);
```

If privateSetTree makes the subtrees empty, setTree will destroy the new treeA!

Another problem occurs if the client executes

```
treeA.setTree(a, treeB, treeB);
```

In this case, the left and right subtrees of treeA's root will be identical, as Figure 24-3 illustrates. The solution to this dilemma is to copy the nodes of treeB so that the subtrees are distinct. Thus, the general case cannot avoid copying nodes, but such copying will be infrequent.

We now implement a solution to these difficulties.

FIGURE 24-3    treeA has identical subtrees

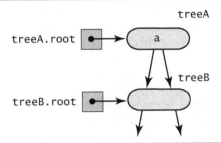

**24.7**    **The second solution.** To summarize, the method `privateSetTree` should take the following steps:

1. Create a root node $r$ containing the given data.
2. If the left subtree exists and is not empty, attach its root node to $r$ as a left child.
3. If the right subtree exists, is not empty, and is distinct from the left subtree, attach its root node to $r$ as a right child. But if the right and left subtrees are the same, attach a copy of the right subtree to $r$ instead.
4. If the left subtree exists and differs from the tree object used to call `privateSetTree`, set the subtree's data field `root` to `null`.
5. If the right subtree exists and differs from the tree object used to call `privateSetTree`, set the subtree's data field `root` to `null`.

An implementation of `privateSetTree` follows:

```
private void privateSetTree(T rootData, BinaryTree<T> leftTree,
                                        BinaryTree<T> rightTree)
{
   root = new BinaryNode<>(rootData);
   if ((leftTree != null) && !leftTree.isEmpty())
      root.setLeftChild(leftTree.root);
   if ((rightTree != null) && !rightTree.isEmpty())
   {
      if (rightTree != leftTree)
         root.setRightChild(rightTree.root);
      else
         root.setRightChild(rightTree.root.copy());
   } // end if
   if ((leftTree != null) && (leftTree != this))
      leftTree.clear();
   if ((rightTree != null) && (rightTree != this))
      rightTree.clear();
} // end privateSetTree
```

**Question 2** At the end of the implementation of `privateSetTree`, can you set `rightTree` to `null` instead of invoking `clear`? Explain.

## Accessor and Mutator Methods

**24.8**    The public methods getRootData, isEmpty, and clear are easy to implement. In addition to these methods, we define several protected methods—setRootData, setRootNode, and getRootNode—that will be useful in the implementation of a subclass. The implementations of these methods follow. EmptyTreeException is a class of runtime exceptions that we define.

**VideoNote**

**Binary tree operations**

```
public T getRootData()
{
    if (isEmpty())
        throw new EmptyTreeException();
    else
        return root.getData()
} // end getRootData

public boolean isEmpty()
{
    return root == null;
} // end isEmpty

public void clear()
{
    root = null;
} // end clear

protected void setRootData(T rootData)
{
    root.setData(rootData);
} // end setRootData

protected void setRootNode(BinaryNode<T> rootNode)
{
    root = rootNode;
} // end setRootNode

protected BinaryNode<T> getRootNode()
{
    return root;
} // end getRootNode
```

## Computing the Height and Counting Nodes

**24.9**    **Methods within BinaryTree.** The methods getHeight and getNumberOfNodes are more interesting than the methods given in the previous segment. Although we could perform the necessary computations within the class BinaryTree, performing them within the class BinaryNode is easier. Thus, the following methods of BinaryTree invoke analogous methods of BinaryNode:

```
public int getHeight()
{
    return root.getHeight();
} // end getHeight

public int getNumberOfNodes()
{
    return root.getNumberOfNodes();
} // end getNumberOfNodes
```

We now complete the methods getHeight and getNumberOfNodes within BinaryNode.

**24.10**    **Methods within BinaryNode.** Within BinaryNode, the method getHeight returns the height of the subtree rooted at the node used to invoke the method. Likewise, getNumberOfNodes returns the number of nodes within that same subtree.

The public method `getHeight` can call a private recursive method `getHeight` that has a node as its parameter. The height of the tree rooted at a node is 1—for the node itself—plus the height of the node's tallest subtree. Thus, we have the following implementation:

```java
public int getHeight()
{
   return getHeight(this); // Call private getHeight
} // end getHeight

private int getHeight(BinaryNode<T> node)
{
   int height = 0;
   if (node != null)
      height = 1 + Math.max(getHeight(node.getLeftChild()),
                            getHeight(node.getRightChild()));

   return height;
} // end getHeight
```

We could implement `getNumberOfNodes` by using the same approach, but instead we will show you another way. The number of nodes in a tree rooted at a given node is 1—for the node itself—plus the number of nodes in both the left and right subtrees. Thus, we have the following recursive implementation:

```java
public int getNumberOfNodes()
{
   int leftNumber = 0;
   int rightNumber = 0;
   if (leftChild != null)
      leftNumber = leftChild.getNumberOfNodes();

   if (rightChild != null)
      rightNumber = rightChild.getNumberOfNodes();

   return 1 + leftNumber + rightNumber;
} // end getNumberOfNodes
```

## Traversals

**24.11  Traversing a binary tree recursively.** The previous chapter described four orders in which we could traverse all the nodes in a binary tree: inorder, preorder, postorder, and level order. An inorder traversal, for example, visits all nodes in the root's left subtree, then visits the root, and finally visits all nodes in the root's right subtree. Since an inorder traversal visits the nodes in the subtrees by using an inorder traversal, its description is recursive.

We could add a recursive method to the class `BinaryTree` to perform an inorder traversal. Such a method, however, must do something specific to or with the data in each node that it visits. For simplicity, we will display the data, even though a class that implements an ADT generally should not perform input or output.

For the method to process the subtrees recursively, it needs the root of a subtree as a parameter. To hide this detail from the client, we make the recursive method private and call it from a public method that has no parameters. Thus, we have the following result:

```java
public void inorderTraverse()
{
   inorderTraverse(root);
} // end inorderTraverse

private void inorderTraverse(BinaryNode<T> node)
{
   if (node != null)
   {
      inorderTraverse(node.getLeftChild());
      System.out.println(node.getData());
```

```
        inorderTraverse(node.getRightChild());
    } // end if
} // end inorderTraverse
```

We could implement similar methods for preorder and postorder traversals.

**Question 3** Trace the method `inorderTraverse` with the binary tree in Figure 24-4. What data is displayed?

**Question 4** Implement a recursive method `preorderTraverse` that displays the data in a binary tree in preorder.

**Note:** Generally, the methods in a class that implements an ADT should not perform input and output. We are doing so here to simplify the method. However, instead of actually displaying the data in the tree, a method like `inorderTraverse` could return a string composed of the data. The client that uses the tree could display this string by using a statement such as

```
System.out.println(myTree.inorderTraverse());
```

**FIGURE 24-4**     A binary tree

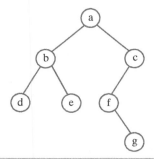

**24.12   Traversals that use an iterator.** A method such as `inorderTraverse` is not hard to implement, but this method only displays the data during the traversal. In addition, the entire traversal takes place once the method is invoked. To provide the client with more flexibility, we should define the traversals as iterators. In this way, the client can do more than simply display data during a visit and can control when each visit takes place.

Recall that Java's interface `Iterator` declares the methods `hasNext` and `next`. These methods enable a client to retrieve the data from the current node in the traversal at any time. That is, the client can retrieve a node's data, do something with it, perhaps do something else, and then retrieve the data in the next node in the iteration.

If we look at `BinaryTreeInterface` in Segment 23.20 of the previous chapter, we see that the class `BinaryTree` must implement the methods in the interface `TreeIteratorInterface`. For example, the method `get-InorderIterator` can be implemented within `BinaryTree` as follows:

```
public Iterator<T> getInorderIterator()
{
    return new InorderIterator();
} // end getInorderIterator
```

As we did in earlier chapters, we define the class `InorderIterator` as a private inner class of `BinaryTree`.

An iterator must be able to pause during a traversal. This suggests that we not use recursion in its implementation. Chapter 7 showed how to use a stack instead of recursion. That is what we will do here.

**24.13**    **An iterative version of an inorder traversal.** Before we define an iterator, let's consider an iterative method that performs an inorder traversal. This method will be a little easier to construct than the iterator, yet it will take similar steps.

Figure 24-5 shows the tree in Figure 24-4 and the result of using a stack to perform its inorder traversal. We begin by pushing the root, *a*, onto the stack. We then traverse to the left as far as possible, pushing each node onto the stack. We then pop the *d* from the stack and display it. Since *d* has no children, we pop the stack again and display *b*. Now *b* has a right child, *e*, which we push onto the stack. Since *e* has no children, we pop it from the stack and display it. The process continues until we have visited all the nodes—that is, until both the stack is empty and the current node is null.

**FIGURE 24-5**    Using a stack to perform an inorder traversal of a binary tree

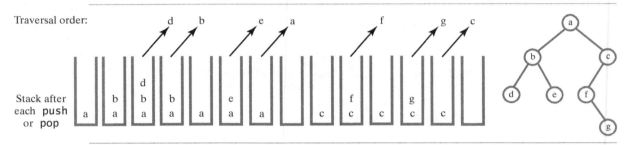

Here is an iterative method that performs an inorder traversal:

```java
public void iterativeInorderTraverse()
{
    StackInterface<BinaryNodeInterface<T>> nodeStack = new LinkedStack<>();
    BinaryNode<T> currentNode = root;

    while (!nodeStack.isEmpty() || (currentNode != null))
    {
        // Find leftmost node with no left child
        while (currentNode != null)
        {
            nodeStack.push(currentNode);
            currentNode = currentNode.getLeftChild();
        } // end while

        // Visit leftmost node, then traverse its right subtree
        if (!nodeStack.isEmpty())
        {
            BinaryNode<T> nextNode = nodeStack.pop();
            assert nextNode != null;   // Since nodeStack was not empty
                                       // before the pop

            System.out.println(nextNode.getData());
            currentNode = nextNode.getRightChild();
        } // end if
    } // end while
} // end iterativeInorderTraverse
```

**Question 5** Trace the previous method with the binary tree shown in Figure 23-14 of the previous chapter.

**24.14**    **The private class** InorderIterator. Now let's implement an inorder traversal as an iterator. We distribute the logic of the previous method iterativeInorderTraverse among the iterator's constructor and the methods hasNext and next. The stack and the variable currentNode are data fields in the iterator class. The method next advances currentNode, adds to the stack as necessary, and eventually pops the stack to return the data in the node that is next in the iteration. Thus, the implementation of the private inner class InorderIterator appears as given in Listing 24-3.

---

**LISTING 24-3** The private inner class InorderIterator

```java
private class InorderIterator implements Iterator<T>
{
   private StackInterface<BinaryNode<T>> nodeStack;
   private BinaryNode<T> currentNode;

   public InorderIterator()
   {
      nodeStack = new LinkedStack<>();
      currentNode = root;
   } // end default constructor

   public boolean hasNext()
   {
      return !nodeStack.isEmpty() || (currentNode != null);
   } // end hasNext

   public T next()
   {
      BinaryNode<T> nextNode = null;

      // Find leftmost node with no left child
      while (currentNode != null)
      {
         nodeStack.push(currentNode);
         currentNode = currentNode.getLeftChild();
      } // end while

      // Get leftmost node, then move to its right subtree
      if (!nodeStack.isEmpty())
      {
         nextNode = nodeStack.pop();
         assert nextNode != null; // Since nodeStack was not empty
                                  // before the pop
         currentNode = nextNode.getRightChild();
      }
      else
         throw new NoSuchElementException();

      return nextNode.getData();
   } // end next

   public void remove()
   {
      throw new UnsupportedOperationException();
   } // end remove
} // end InorderIterator
```

---

**24.15 Iterative preorder, postorder, and level-order traversals.** Figure 24-6 shows the result of using a stack to perform a preorder traversal and a postorder traversal of the tree in Figure 24-4. The iterative postorder traversal—like the previous iterative inorder traversal—replaces each recursive call in its recursive counterpart with a push operation and replaces each visit with a pop. However, the iterative preorder traversal pushes a node's children onto the stack in the opposite order of the recursive calls in a recursive preorder traversal, so that nodes are visited in the correct order. Finally, the iterative level-order traversal uses a queue instead of a stack. The traversal first enqueues the root. While the queue is not empty, the traversal dequeues a node, visits the node, and enqueue's the node's children. Figure 24-7 shows the result of using a queue to perform a level-order traversal of the same tree. We leave the implementation of the necessary iterator classes for you as an exercise.

---

**FIGURE 24-6**     Using a stack to traverse a binary tree in (a) preorder; (b) postorder

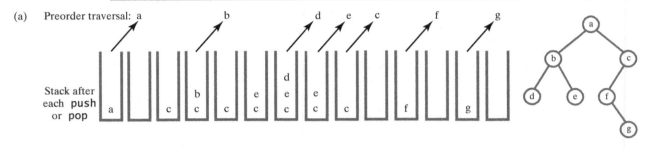

(a)     Preorder traversal: a

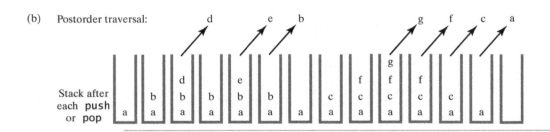

(b)     Postorder traversal:

---

**FIGURE 24-7**     Using a queue to traverse a binary tree in level order

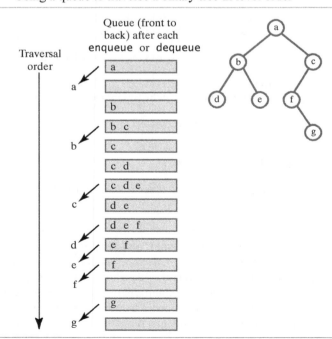

**Programming Tip:** An iterator object that has not traversed the entire binary tree can be adversely affected by changes to the tree.

 **Note:** A complete traversal of an *n*-node binary tree is an O(*n*) operation, if visiting a node is O(1), for both recursive and iterative implementations.

## An Implementation of an Expression Tree

**24.16** In the previous chapter, you saw that an expression tree is a binary tree that represents an algebraic expression. Figure 23-15 provided some examples of these trees. By using the algorithm given in Segment 23.24, we can evaluate the expression in this type of tree.

We can define an interface for an expression tree by extending the interface for a binary tree and adding a declaration for the method `evaluate`, as shown in Listing 24-4. Since you can treat the components of an expression as strings, we assume that an expression tree contains strings as its data.

---

**LISTING 24-4   An interface for an expression tree**

```
1  package TreePackage;
2  public interface ExpressionTreeInterface
3                  extends BinaryTreeInterface<String>
4  {
5     /** Computes the value of the expression in this tree.
6         @return  The value of the expression. */
7     public double evaluate();
8  } // end ExpressionTreeInterface
```

---

**24.17** An expression tree is a binary tree, so we can derive a class of expression trees from `BinaryTree`. We define the method `evaluate` within the derived class. A portion of the class `ExpressionTree` appears in Listing 24-5.

---

**LISTING 24-5   The class ExpressionTree**

```
1  package TreePackage;
2  public class ExpressionTree extends BinaryTree<String>
3                              implements ExpressionTreeInterface
4  {
5     public ExpressionTree()
6     {
7     } // end default constructor
8
9     public double evaluate()
10    {
11       return evaluate(getRootNode());
12    } // end evaluate
13
14    private double evaluate(BinaryNode<String> rootNode)
15    {
16       double result;
17       if (rootNode == null)
18          result = 0;
```

```
19      else if (rootNode.isLeaf())
20      {
21         String variable = rootNode.getData();
22         result = getValueOf(variable);
23      }
24      else
25      {
26         double firstOperand = evaluate(rootNode.getLeftChild());
27         double secondOperand = evaluate(rootNode.getRightChild());
28         String operator = rootNode.getData();
29         result = compute(operator, firstOperand, secondOperand);
30      } // end if
31
32      return result;
33   } // end evaluate
34
35   private double getValueOf(String variable)
36   {
37      . . .
38   } // end getValueOf
39
40   private double compute(String operator, double firstOperand,
41                                            double secondOperand)
42   {
43      . . .
44   } // end compute
45 } // end ExpressionTree
```

The public method `evaluate` calls a private method `evaluate` that is recursive. This private method calls the private methods `getValueOf` and `compute` as well as methods defined in `BinaryNode`. The method `getValueOf` returns the numeric value of a given variable in the expression, and `compute` returns the result of a given arithmetic operation and two given operands.

Notice how important the methods of the class `BinaryNode` are to the implementation of `evaluate`. For this reason, we do not want `BinaryNode` to be hidden within `BinaryTree`. Rather, it should be part of a package.

**Question 6** Trace the method `evaluate` for the expression tree in Figure 23-15c of the previous chapter. What value is returned? Assume that *a* is 3, *b* is 4, and *c* is 5.

# General Trees

To wrap up our discussion of tree implementations, we will consider one way to represent a node for a general tree. Rather than developing an implementation of a general tree that uses this node, we will see that we can use a binary tree to represent a general tree.

## A Node for a General Tree

**24.18** Since a node in a binary tree can have only two children, it is reasonable for each node to contain two references to these children. In addition, the number of node operations that test for, set, or get each child is reasonable. But dealing with more children per node in this way quickly becomes unwieldy.

We can define a node for a general tree that accommodates any number of children by referencing an object, such as a list or a vector, that contains the children. For example, the node in Figure 24-8 contains two references. One reference is to the data object, and the other is to a list of child nodes. An iterator for the list enables us to access these children.

**FIGURE 24-8**    A node for a general tree

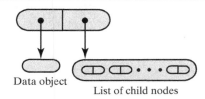

Data object

List of child nodes

In the interface for a general node given in Listing 24-6, getChildrenIterator returns an iterator to the node's children. A separate operation adds a child to the node, assuming that the children are in no particular order. If the order of the children is important, the iterator could provide an operation to insert a new child at the current position within the iteration.

**LISTING 24-6**   An interface for a node in a general tree

```
 1  package TreePackage;
 2  import java.util.Iterator;
 3  interface GeneralNodeInterface<T>
 4  {
 5      public T getData();
 6      public void setData(T newData);
 7      public boolean isLeaf();
 8      public Iterator<GeneralNodeInterface<T>> getChildrenIterator();
 9      public void addChild(GeneralNodeInterface<T> newChild);
10  } // end GeneralNodeInterface
```

 **Note:** Algorithms for the operations on a general tree are more complex than those for a binary tree due to the flexible number of children per node in a general tree. For this reason, general trees are sometimes represented by binary trees. Note that many file systems use a general tree in their design to expedite searches for directories and files on a disk. The next section discusses how to transform a general tree into an equivalent binary tree.

## Using a Binary Tree to Represent a General Tree

**24.19**  Instead of the implementation just suggested, we can use a binary tree to represent any general tree. For example, let's represent the general tree in Figure 24-9a as a binary tree. As an intermediate step, we connect the nodes with new edges, as follows. We give the root *A* one of its original children—*B* in this case—as a left child. We then draw an edge from *B* to its sibling *C* and from *C* to another sibling *D*, as Figure 24-9b shows. Likewise, we give each parent in the general tree one of its original children as a left child in the binary tree, and link these children by edges.

If we consider each node in Figure 24-9b that is to the right of its sibling as the right child of that sibling, we will have a binary tree that has an unorthodox form. We can move the nodes in the drawing without disconnecting them to get the familiar look of a binary tree, as Figure 24-9c shows.

**24.20**   **Traversals.** Let's examine the various traversals of the general tree in Figure 24-9a and compare them with traversals of the equivalent binary tree pictured in Figure 24-9c. The general tree has the following traversals:

Preorder:    A, B, E, F, C, G, H, I, D, J
Postorder:   E, F, B, G, H, I, C, J, D, A
Level order: A, B, C, D, E, F, G, H, I, J

The traversals of the binary tree are as follows:

Preorder:    A, B, E, F, C, G, H, I, D, J
Postorder:   F, E, I, H, G, J, D, C, B, A
Level order: A, B, E, C, F, G, D, H, J, I
Inorder:     E, F, B, G, H, I, C, J, D, A

The preorder traversals of the two trees are the same. The postorder traversal of the general tree is the same as the inorder traversal of the binary tree. We must invent a new kind of traversal of the binary tree to get the same results as a level-order traversal of the general tree. We leave that task to you as an exercise.

FIGURE 24-9    (a) A general tree; (b) an equivalent binary tree; (c) a more conventional view of the same binary tree

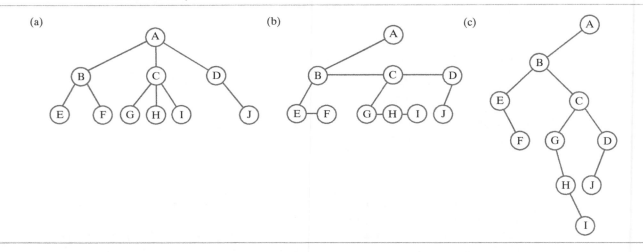

**Question 7** What binary tree can represent the general tree in Figure 23-1 of the previous chapter?

## CHAPTER SUMMARY

- A node in a binary tree is an object that references a data object and two child nodes in the tree.

- A basic class of binary trees contains methods common to all trees: getRootData, getHeight, getNumberOfNodes, isEmpty, clear, and various traversals. The basic class also has a method that sets the root and subtrees of an existing binary tree to given values.

- The implementation of getHeight and getNumberOfNodes is easier if the class of nodes has similar methods.

- Preorder, postorder, and inorder traversals have simple recursive implementations. But to implement a traversal as an iterator, you must use an iterative approach, since an iterator needs to be able to pause during the traversal. You use a stack for preorder, postorder, and inorder traversals; you use a queue for a level-order traversal.

- You can derive a particular binary tree, such as an expression tree, from the class of basic binary trees.

- A node in a general tree is an object that references its children and a data object. To accommodate any number of children, the node can reference a list or a vector, for example. An iterator can provide access to the children. In this way, the node contains only two references.

- Instead of creating a general node for a general tree, you can use a binary tree to represent a general tree.

## PROGRAMMING TIPS

- No cast is needed when you pass an instance of BinaryTree to a method whose parameter has the type BinaryTreeInterface. The converse, however, requires a cast.

- An iterator object that has not traversed the entire binary tree can be adversely affected by changes to the tree.

## EXERCISES

1. Implement the method getHeight in the class BinaryNode, using the approach that Segment 24.10 uses for the method getNumberOfNodes. That is, getHeight should not call a private method.

2. Implement the method getNumberOfNodes in the class BinaryNode, using the approach that Segment 24.10 uses for the method getHeight. That is, getNumberOfNodes should call a private method.

3. In Segment 24.11, Question 4 asked you to implement a recursive preorder traversal of a binary tree. Implement a recursive method postorderTraverse that displays the data in a binary tree in postorder.

4. Trace the iterative method iterativeInorderTraverse given in Segment 24.13 as it traverses the binary tree in Figure 24-10. Show the contents of the stack after each push and pop.

FIGURE 24-10   A binary tree for Exercises 4, 5, 6, and 17

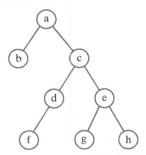

**5.** Show the contents of the stack after each `push` and `pop` during a preorder traversal of the binary tree in Figure 24-10. Repeat for a postorder traversal.

**6.** Show the contents of the queue after each `enqueue` and `dequeue` during a level-order traversal of the binary tree in Figure 24-10.

**7.** Suppose we want to create a method for the class `BinaryTree` that counts the number of times an object occurs in the tree. The header of the method could be as follows:

```
public int count(T anObject)
```

   **a.** Write this method using a private recursive method of the same name.
   **b.** Write the method using one of the iterators of the binary tree.
   **c.** Compare the efficiencies of the previous two versions of the method.

**8.** Trace the method `evaluate` given in Segment 24.17 for the expression tree in Figure 23-15d of the previous chapter. What value is returned? Assume that $a$ is 2, $b$ is 4, $c$ is 5, $d$ is 6, and $e$ is 4.

**9.** Write a method to print all the nodes falling between 'low' and 'high'. The method could have the following prototype:

```
void printTNodes(int low, int high)
```

**10.** What binary tree represents the general tree in each of the following figures from the previous chapter?

   **a.** Figure 23-5
   **b.** Figure 23-22

**11.** Given a general tree, consider an equivalent binary tree. Define a traversal of this binary tree that is equivalent to a level-order traversal of the general tree.

**12.** Knowing the preorder and inorder traversals of a binary tree will enable you to uniquely define the tree. The same is true for the postorder and inorder traversals.

   **a.** Is it possible to construct a unique tree using the following sets of traversals?

   inorder and level-order
   preorder and level-order
   postorder and level-order

   **b.** Write a code in Java to construct a tree when the inorder and postorder traversals are given.

**13.** There may be many paths, each consisting of several nodes, between any two leaf nodes of a binary tree. But the width of the tree is determined by counting the number of nodes on the longest path between two leaf nodes of the tree. What is the width of the binary tree shown in Figure 24-10?

**14.** Suppose we want to create a method for the class `BinaryTree` that traverses and prints the boundary of the tree. It traverses the leftmost nodes from top to bottom, then the leaf nodes from left to right, and, lastly, the rightmost nodes from bottom to top. The prototype could be as follows:

```
public void traverseBoundary(BinaryNode<T> tree)
```

Write this method, using a recursive method of the same name.

**15.** As mentioned in Exercise 13, the width of a binary tree is determined by counting the number of nodes on the longest path between two leaf nodes. Write the recursive method to find the width.

**16.** Sometimes you need to move from a tree node to its parent. To do this, you would need to provide a binary tree node with a reference to its parent. You then would be able to traverse a path from a leaf to the root. Redesign the node used in a binary tree so that each one has a reference to its parent as well as to its left child and right child. What methods will need to be changed?

**17.** Another way of representing a binary tree is to use an array. The items in the tree are assigned to locations in the array in a level-order fashion. For example, Figure 24-11 shows an array that represents the binary tree in Figure 24-10. Notice that gaps in the array correspond to missing nodes in the tree. The array is sufficiently large to represent any binary tree up to height 4.

   **a.** What are the indices of the children of the node stored at index $i$?
   **b.** What is the parent of the node stored at index $i$?
   **c.** What are the advantages and disadvantages of this representation?

**FIGURE 24-11**    An array for Exercise 17 that represents the binary tree in Figure 24-10

| a | b | c |   |   | d | e |   |   |   |    |    | f  |    | g  | h  |
|---|---|---|---|---|---|---|---|---|---|----|----|----|----|----|----|
| 0 | 1 | 2 | 3 | 4 | 5 | 6 | 7 | 8 | 9 | 10 | 11 | 12 | 13 | 14 |

**18.** Add a method to the class `BinaryTree` to delete a tree. The prototype of the method could be as follows:

```
public void deleteTree()
```

**19.** Implement the method `toString` for the class `BinaryTree`. The method should return a string that, when displayed, shows the shape of the tree in two dimensions. Ignore the data in each node. For example a tree might appear as follows:

## PROJECTS

**1.** Using the examples in Figures 24-6 and 24-7 to suggest algorithms, implement iterator classes for preorder, postorder, and level-order traversals of a binary tree. Begin by writing iterative versions of the traversals similar to the method `iterativeInorderTraverse` given in Segment 24.13.

**2.** Write a Java program that distinguishes among 10 different animals. The program should play a guessing game similar to the one described in Segment 23.26 of the previous chapter. The user thinks of one of the 10 animals, and the program asks a sequence of questions until it can guess the animal.

   Your program should learn from the user. If the program makes an incorrect guess, it asks the user to enter a new question that can distinguish between the correct animal and the program's incorrect guess. The decision tree should be updated with this new question.

**3.** Complete the implementation of an expression tree that was begun in Segment 24.17. Add two constructors that create an expression tree given either a postfix expression or an infix expression. Projects 4 and 5 in the previous chapter asked you to design algorithms for these two tasks. To simplify the method `getValueOf`, you can restrict the choice of variables and give them specific values.

**4.** Consider the redesigned node for a binary tree that Exercise 16 describes. Add an additional data field to the node to record the height of the subtree tree rooted at the node. Modify all the methods in the implementation of the binary tree so that the height field is updated anytime the structure of the tree changes.

**5.** Project 6 in the previous chapter asked you to develop an interface `GeneralTreeInterface` for a general tree. Write the class `GeneralTree` that implements `GeneralTreeInterface`. Use a binary tree to represent the general tree, as described in Segment 24.19. Implement iterators for the preorder and postorder traversals. As an extra challenge, implement an iterator for the level-order traversal.

**6.** Some implementations of a binary tree do not use `null` to indicate the absence of a child. Instead, they use references to a single dummy node. The reference to an empty tree is to this same dummy node. Modify the implementation of `BinaryTree` in this way.

**7.** Implement the class `ArrayBinaryTree` that uses an array representation of the tree, as described in Exercise 17.

**8.** Create a dictionary for a glossary of terms, as described in Project 13 of Chapter 20. Instead of an array of sorted lists, use a 26-ary tree to represent the glossary. Figure 23-27 in Project 8 of the previous chapter illustrates such a tree, but one that is used for a spelling checker. To adapt that tree for this project, place a term's definition in the filled-in node instead of an indicator of the term's spelling.

**9.** *Huffman coding* is a technique that compresses the size of data. For example, a .zip file of a text document is a compressed version of the original document. This so-called lossless data compression is a result of Huffman coding.

Although ASCII and Unicode use bit strings having a fixed length—8 and 16, respectively—to represent symbols, Huffman codes have variable lengths. These codes are based on the frequency of occurrence of a symbol in a given data set. Symbols that occur frequently have shorter codes than those occurring less frequently. A binary tree—called a **Huffman tree**—is used to generate these codes.

For example, let's encode some text composed only of the letters A through E. Suppose these letters occur with the following frequencies: A, 12 times; B, 3 times; C, 1 time; D, 9 times; and E, 15 times. We need to arrange these letters by their frequencies in increasing order. To do so, we associate each letter with its frequency of occurrence and add these pairs to a collection, such as a sorted list or a priority queue. The result is shown in Figure 24-12a. Now we remove the two entries having the lowest frequencies and make them leaves in a binary tree. The parent of these leaves is a node containing the sum of the frequencies in the leaves, as illustrated in Figure 24-12b. Since the parent contains only a frequency, the letter portion of the node is `null`, which is shown as • in the figure. We now add the contents of the parent to our list or queue, as shown to the right of the tree in Figure 24-12b.

When we remove the next two entries from the list, we create a new leaf containing D 9 and join it to the existing tree with a new root containing the sum of the frequencies in its two children. The result is given in Figure 24-12c. Note that we then place the contents of this new root in its correct order within the remaining data. Parts *d* and *e* of the figure show the remaining steps in this process.

Figure 24-12f shows the resulting binary tree with its left links and right links labeled with 0 and 1, respectively. To encode a character, you begin at a leaf and traverse the tree to its root, recording 0s and 1s in reverse order according to the left and right branches that you take. The Huffman codes for our example are as follows: A is 10, B is 1101, C is 1100, D is 111, and E is 0. To decode a Huffman code, you traverse the tree from its root to a leaf by taking a left branch for each 0 encountered and a right branch for each 1 encountered.

Write a program that reads a text file of alphabetic data, creates a Huffman tree, and uses the tree to compress the file. Your program should then take the compressed file and, using your tree, decode it.

FIGURE 24-12    The steps in creating a binary tree for Huffman coding

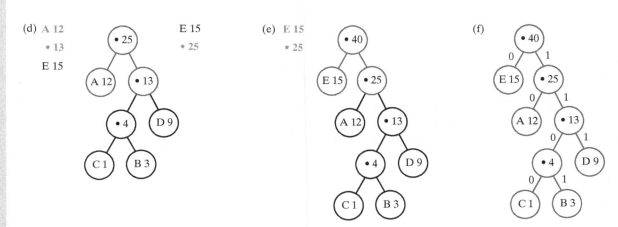

10.  Java Interlude 9, which follows this chapter, introduces the *clone* of an object. A clone is an exact duplicate, or copy. The class `BinaryNode`, as defined in this chapter, defines the method `copy` to make a copy of a node. (See Segment 24.5.) This method is needed by the class `BinaryTree` in Segment 24.7 for the method `privateSetTree`. Java Interlude 9 describes how to replace the method `copy` with the method `clone`. This method makes a duplicate copy of a node. Revise the method `privateSetTree` in `BinaryTree` so that it calls `clone` instead of `copy`. Then add a `clone` method to the class `BinaryTree`.

## ANSWERS TO SELF-TEST QUESTIONS

1.  The client builds `treeA` from `treeB` and `treeC`. The programmer could be unaware—or could easily forget—that `treeA` shares nodes with `treeB` and `treeC`, and treat them as distinct trees. Thus, the modification of `treeA` by intentional changes to `treeB` would be unexpected and could cause difficult-to-find errors in logic.

2.  No. Setting `rightTree` to `null` affects only the local copy of the reference argument `rightTree`. An analogous comment applies to `leftTree`.

3.  The data in the objects *d*, *b*, *e*, *a*, *f*, *g*, and *c* is displayed on separate lines.

4.
```java
public void preorderTraverse()
{
    preorderTraverse(root);
} // end preorderTraverse

private void preorderTraverse(BinaryNode<T> node)
{
    if (node != null)
    {
        System.out.println(node.getData());
        preorderTraverse(node.getLeftChild());
        preorderTraverse(node.getRightChild());
    } // end if
} // end preorderTraverse
```

5.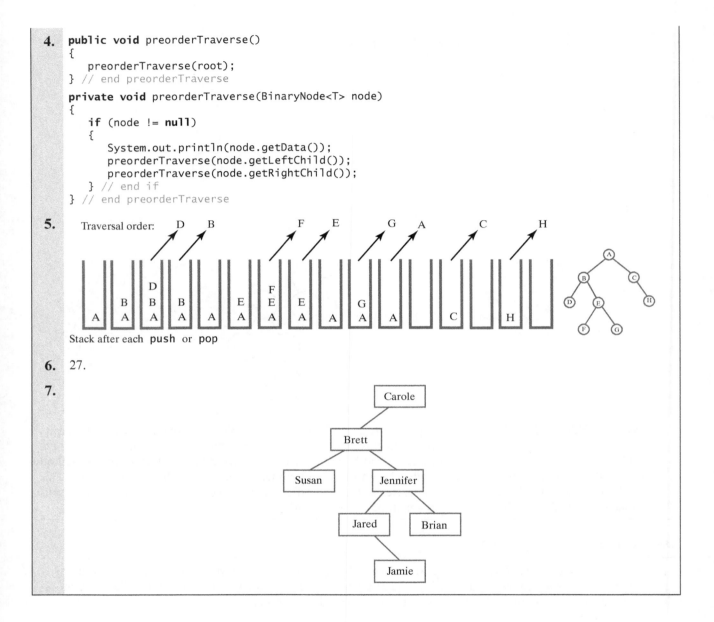

6. 27.

7.

# Cloning

## Contents

Segment JI6.4 of Java Interlude 6 created a list of mutable objects in sorted order. Unfortunately, the client of this list could modify the objects so that they are no longer sorted. As you saw then, one solution is to always place immutable objects in a sorted list. A more involved solution has the list copy the client's objects. The list then can control what the client can and cannot do to the copies. This interlude examines how to make a copy, or **clone**, of an object.

## Cloneable Objects

**JI9.1**   In Java, a clone is a copy of an object. Typically, we clone only mutable objects. Since sharing an immutable object is safe, cloning it is usually unnecessary.

The class Object contains a protected method clone that returns a copy of an object. The method has the following header:

VideoNote
Cloneable objects

```
protected Object clone() throws CloneNotSupportedException
```

Since clone is protected, and since Object is the superclass of all other classes, the implementation of any method can contain the invocation

```
super.clone()
```

But clients of a class cannot invoke `clone` unless the class overrides it and declares it public. Making copies of objects can be expensive, so it might be something you do not want a class to do. By making `clone` a protected method, the designers of Java force you to think twice about cloning.

**Programming Tip:** Not all classes should have a public `clone` method. In fact, most classes, including read-only classes, do not have one.

**JI9.2**   If you want your class to contain a public method `clone`, the class needs to state this fact by implementing the Java interface `Cloneable`, which is in the package `java.lang` of the Java Class Library. Such a class would begin as follows:

```
public class MyClass implements Cloneable
{ . . .
```

The interface `Cloneable` is simply

```
public interface Cloneable
{
} // end Cloneable
```

As you can see, the interface is empty. It declares no methods and serves only as a way for a class to indicate that it implements `clone`. If you forget to write `implements Cloneable` in your class definition, and you use an instance of your class to invoke `clone`, the exception `CloneNotSupportedException` will occur. This result can be confusing at first, particularly if you did implement `clone`.

**Programming Tip:** If your program produces the exception `CloneNotSupportedException` even though you implemented a method `clone` in your class, you probably forgot to write `implements Cloneable` in your class definition.

**Note:** **The `Cloneable` interface**
The empty `Cloneable` interface is not a typical interface. A class implements it to indicate that it will provide a public `clone` method. Since the designers of Java wanted to provide a default implementation of the method `clone`, they included it in the class `Object` and not in the interface `Cloneable`. But because the designers did not want every class to automatically have a public `clone` method, they made `clone` a protected method.

**Note:** **Cloning**
Cloning is not an operation that every class should be able to do. If you want your class to have this ability, you must

- Declare that your class implements the `Cloneable` interface
- Override the protected method `clone` that your class inherits from the class `Object` with a public version

**JI9.3**   **Example: Cloning a `Name` object.** Let's add a method `clone` to the class `Name` of Segment C.16 in Appendix C. Before we begin, we should add `implements Cloneable` to the first line of the class definition, as follows:

```
public class Name implements Cloneable
```

The public method `clone` within `Name` must invoke the method `clone` of its superclass by executing `super.clone()`. Because `Name`'s superclass is `Object`, `super.clone()` invokes `Object`'s protected method `clone`. `Object`'s version of `clone` can throw an exception, so we must enclose each call to it in a `try` block and write a `catch` block to handle the exception. The method's final action should return the cloned object.

Thus, `Name`'s method `clone` could appear as follows:

```
public Object clone()
{
    Name theCopy = null;
    try
    {
        theCopy = (Name)super.clone(); // Object can throw an exception
    }
    catch (CloneNotSupportedException e)
    {
        System.err.println("Name cannot clone: " + e.toString());
    }
    return theCopy;
} // end clone
```

Since `super.clone()` returns an instance of `Object`, we cast this instance to `Name`. After all, we are creating a `Name` object as the clone. The `return` statement will implicitly cast `theCopy` to `Object`, as required. But why not declare `theCopy`'s data type as `Object` and avoid the cast? Doing so would prevent us from using `theCopy` to invoke `Name` methods within the `clone` method. Since `theCopy` is not used this way here, its data type could be `Object`. Declaring `theCopy` as `Object`, however, is discouraged. We have written this `clone` method in a more general way.

The exception that `Object`'s method `clone` can throw is `CloneNotSupportedException`. Since we are writing a `clone` method for our class `Name`, this exception will never occur. Even so, we still must use `try` and `catch` blocks when invoking `Object`'s `clone` method. Instead of the `println` statement in the `catch` block, we could write the simpler statement

```
throw new Error(e.toString());
```

**Programming Tip:** Every public `clone` method must invoke the method `clone` of the base class by executing `super.clone`. Ultimately, `Object`'s protected `clone` method will be invoked. That invocation must appear in a `try` block, even though a `CloneNotSupportedException` will never occur.

**Programming Tip:** When `Name`'s `clone` method invokes `Object`'s protected `clone` method, an instance of `Object` is returned. By casting that instance to `Name`, you can be sure that, even though `Name`'s `clone` method will return an instance of `Object`, the client will be able to cast the return value back into a `Name` object. Realize that if the return value cannot be cast into a `Name` object, Java will throw a `ClassCastException`.

**Programming Tip:** Just as you should call a person by name instead of by shouting "Hey object!" you should declare a Java object as its actual or generic data type instead of as an `Object`.

**JI9.4** **Two ways to copy.** What does this method `clone` actually do? You want it to make copies of the data fields associated with the receiving object. When a data field is an object, you can copy it in one of two ways:

- You can copy the reference to the object and share the object with the clone, as illustrated in Figure JI9-1a. This copy is called a **shallow copy**; the clone is a **shallow clone**.
- You can copy the object itself, as illustrated in Figure JI9-1b. This copy is called a **deep copy**; the clone is a **deep clone**.

**Note:** Object's `clone` method returns a shallow clone.

---

**FIGURE JI9-1**   (a) A shallow clone; (b) a deep clone

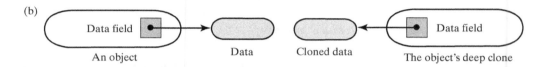

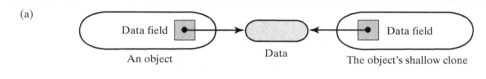

---

**JI9.5**  **Name's clone is shallow.** The class `Name` has the data fields `first` and `last`, which are instances of `String`. Each field contains a reference to a string. It is these references that are copied when `clone` invokes `super.clone()`. For example, Figure JI9-2 illustrates the objects that the following statements create:

```
Name april = new Name("April", "Jones");
Name twin = (Name)april.clone();
```

The clone `twin` is a shallow clone because the strings that are the first and last names are not copied.

---

**FIGURE JI9-2**    An instance of `Name` and its shallow clone

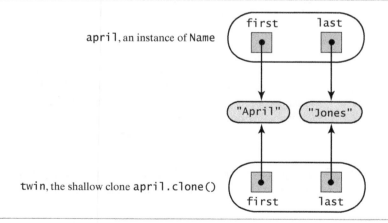

---

A shallow clone is good enough for the class `Name`. Recall that instances of `String` are immutable. Having an instance of `Name` and its clone share the same strings is not a problem because no one can change the strings. This is good news since, like many classes that Java provides, `String` has no method `clone`. Thus, if we change the clone's last name by writing

```
twin.setLast("Smith");
```

twin's last name will be *Smith*, but april's will still be *Jones*, as Figure JI9-3 shows. That is, setLast changes twin's data field last so that it references another string *Smith*. It does not change april's data field last, so it still references *Jones*.

**FIGURE JI9-3**    The clone twin, after the statement twin.setLast("Smith") changes one of its data fields

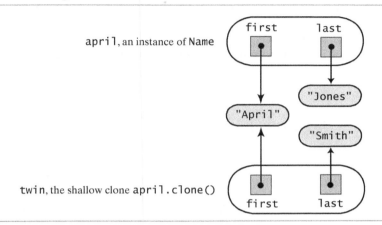

> **Programming Tip:** Shallow copies of data fields that reference immutable objects are typically sufficient for a clone. Sharing an immutable object is usually safe.

**JI9.6**    **Example: Creating a deep clone of a single field.** Sometimes a shallow clone is unsuitable. If a class has mutable objects as data fields, you must clone the objects and not simply copy their references. For example, let's add a method clone to the class Student that we encountered in Segment D.2 of Appendix D. The class has the following form after we add the required implements clause:

```
public class Student implements Cloneable
{
    private Name    fullName;
    private String id;
    < Constructors and the methods setStudent, setName, setId, getName, getId, and
       toString go here. >
    . . .
} // end Student
```

Since the class Name has set methods, the data field fullName is a mutable object. Therefore, we should be sure to clone fullName within the definition of Student's clone method. We can do that because we added a clone method to Name in Segment JI9.3. Since String is a read-only class, id is immutable, and so cloning it is unnecessary. Thus, we can define a clone method for the class Student as follows:

```
public Object clone()
{
    Student theCopy = null;
    try
    {
        theCopy = (Student)super.clone(); // Object can throw an exception
    }
```

```
        catch (CloneNotSupportedException e)
        {
            throw new Error(e.toString());
        }
        theCopy.fullName = (Name)fullName.clone();
        return theCopy;
    } // end clone
```

After invoking super.clone(), we clone the mutable data field fullName by calling Name's public clone method. This latter invocation need not be within a try block. Only Object's clone method contains a throws clause.

Figure JI9-4 illustrates an instance of Student and the clone that this method returns. As you can see, the Name object that represents the student's full name is copied, but the strings that represent the first and last names, as well as the ID number, are not.

**FIGURE JI9-4**   An instance of Student and its clone, including a deep copy of fullName

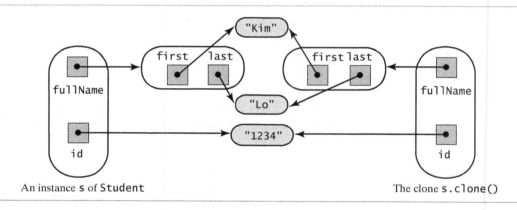

An instance s of Student                    The clone s.clone()

Had we failed to clone the data field fullName—that is, had we omitted the statement

```
    theCopy.fullName = (Name)fullName.clone();
```

the student's full name would be shared by the original instance and its clone. Figure JI9-5 illustrates this situation.

**FIGURE JI9-5**   An instance of Student and its clone, including a shallow copy of fullName

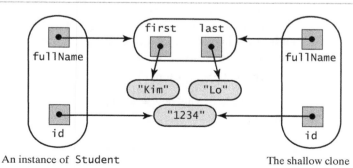

An instance of Student                    The shallow clone

**Question 1** Suppose that x is an instance of Student and y is its clone; that is,

```
Student y = (Student)x.clone();
```

a.   If you change x's last name by executing

```
Name xName = x.getName();
xName.setLast("Smith");
```

does y's last name change? Explain.

b.   If you fail to clone fullName within Student's clone method, will changing x's last name change y's last name as well? Explain.

> **Note:**  Within each public clone method, you typically perform the following tasks:
> - Invoke the clone method of the superclass by writing super.clone().
> - Enclose this call to clone in a try block, and write a catch block to handle the possible exception CloneNotSupportedException. You can skip this step if super.clone() invokes a public clone method.
> - Clone the mutable data fields of the object that super.clone() returns, when possible.
> - Return the clone.

**JI9.7**   **Example: Cloning a CollegeStudent object.** Now let's add a clone method to a subclass of Student. Segment D.8 of Appendix D defines such a subclass, namely the class CollegeStudent. Adding an implements clause to its definition is optional, since we are extending a cloneable class:

```
public class CollegeStudent extends Student implements Cloneable
{
    private int    year;   // Year of graduation
    private String degree; // Degree sought
    < Constructors and the methods setStudent, setYear, getYear, setDegree, getDegree,
      toString, and clone go here. >
    . . .
} // end CollegeStudent
```

The data fields of a CollegeStudent object are a primitive value and an immutable object, and so they do not need to be cloned. Thus, the definition of clone that we add to CollegeStudent is as follows:

```
public Object clone()
{
    CollegeStudent theCopy = (CollegeStudent)super.clone();
    return theCopy;
} // end clone
```

The method must call Student's clone method, and it does so with the invocation super.clone(). Note that since Student's clone method does not throw an exception, no try block is necessary when we call it. Had CollegeStudent defined fields that needed to be cloned, we would clone them right before the return statement.

## Cloning an Array

**JI9.8**   The class AList that you saw in Chapter 13 uses an array to implement the ADT list. Suppose that we want to add a clone method to this class.

While making a copy of the list, clone needs to copy the array and all the objects in it. Thus, the objects in the list must have a clone method as well. Recall that AList defines a generic type T for the objects it contains. Beginning AList as

```
public class AList<T extends Cloneable> . . . // Incorrect
```

will not work correctly, since the interface Cloneable is empty.

Instead, we define a new interface that declares a public method clone to override Object's protected version of the method:

```java
public interface Copyable extends Cloneable
{
   public Object clone();
} // end Copyable
```

We then can begin AList with any one of the following statements:

- **public class** AList<T **extends** Copyable> **implements** ListInterface<T>, Cloneable
- **public class** AList<T **extends** Copyable> **implements** ListInterface<T>, Copyable
- **public class** AList<T **extends** Copyable> **implements** CloneableListInterface<T>

where CloneableListInterface is defined as follows:

```java
public interface CloneableListInterface<T>
                  extends ListInterface<T>, Copyable // Or Cloneable
{
} // end CloneableListInterface
```

The notation

```java
AList<T extends Copyable>
```

requires the objects in the list to belong to a class that implements our interface Copyable.

Note that CloneableListInterface extends two interfaces, ListInterface and either Copyable or Cloneable. As noted in Segment P.46 of the Prelude, an interface can extend more than one interface, even though a class can extend only one other class.

 **Programming Tip:** When bounding generic types, use an interface that declares a public method clone instead of using Cloneable. The new interface must extend Cloneable, however.

**JI9.9**    Using Copyable as a bound for T requires us to change the implementation of AList's constructor. Recall from Listing 13-1 in Chapter 13 that one field of AList is an array of list entries:

```java
private T[] list;
```

Writing

```java
T[] tempList = (T[]) new Object[initialCapacity + 1];
```

in the constructor causes a ClassCastException. Instead, we write

```java
T[] tempList = (T[]) new Copyable[initialCapacity + 1]; // Change Object to
                                                        // Copyable
```

**JI9.10**    Now we can implement clone. We will invoke super.clone() within a try block but perform the rest of the tasks after the catch block. Thus, we have the following outline for AList's method clone:

```java
public Object clone()
{
   AList<T> theCopy = null;

   try
   {
      @SuppressWarnings("unchecked")
      AList<T> temp = (AList<T>)super.clone();
      theCopy = temp;
   }
```

```
      catch (CloneNotSupportedException e)
      {
          throw new Error(e.toString());
      }
      < For a deep copy, we need to do more here, as you will see. >
          . . .
      return theCopy;
  } // end clone
```

The method first invokes `super.clone` and casts the returned object to `AList<T>`. To perform a deep copy, we need to clone the data fields that are or could be mutable objects. Thus, we need to clone the array `list`.

**JI9.11** Arrays in Java have a public `clone` method; in other words, they implement `Cloneable`. So we can add the following statement to the list's `clone` method:

```
      theCopy.list = (T[])list.clone();
```

No `try` and `catch` blocks are necessary here because `clone` is public.

An array's `clone` method creates a shallow copy of each object in the array. For our deep copy, we need to clone each array entry. Since we insisted that the list's entries have a public `clone` method, we can write a loop whose body contains the following statements:

```
      @SuppressWarnings("unchecked")
      T temp = (T)list[index].clone();
      theCopy.list[index] = temp;
```

We can control the loop by using `index` and `AList`'s data field `numberOfEntries`, which records the number of entries in the list.

Thus, we have the following definition of `clone` for the class `AList`:

```
      public Object clone()
      {
          AList<T> theCopy = null;
          // Clone the list
          try
          {
              @SuppressWarnings("unchecked")
              AList<T> temp = (AList<T>)super.clone();
              theCopy = temp;
          }
          catch (CloneNotSupportedException e)
          {
              throw new Error(e.toString());
          }
          // Clone the list's array
          theCopy.list = list.clone();
          // Clone the entries in the array (list[0] is unused and ignored)
          for (int index = 1; index <= numberOfEntries; index++)
          {
              @SuppressWarnings("unchecked")
              T temp = (T)list[index].clone();
              theCopy.list[index] = temp;
          } // end for
          return theCopy;
      } // end clone
```

**Note:**  To make a deep clone of an array x of cloneable objects, you invoke x.clone() and then clone each object in the array. For example, if myArray is an array of Thing objects, and Thing implements Cloneable, you would write

```
Thing[] clonedArray = (Thing[])myArray.clone();
for (int index = 0; index < myArray.length; index++)
    clonedArray[index] = (Thing)myArray[index].clone();
```

## Cloning a Chain

**JI9.12**  Now suppose that we want to add a clone method to a linked implementation of the ADT list, such as the class LList of Chapter 14 or the class LinkedChainBase of Chapter 17. (The clone methods for these classes are virtually identical.) Given the interface Copyable, we can begin the class in one of the ways given in Segment JI9.8. Ultimately, the class and the objects in the list must implement the interface Cloneable. Thus, LList, for example, could begin as follows:

```
public class LList<T extends Copyable> implements CloneableListInterface<T>
{
    private Node firstNode; // Reference to first node of chain
    private int  numberOfEntries;
    . . .
```

The first part of the clone method would be like the code that you saw in Segment JI9.10, except that we would replace AList with LList. If we invoked only super.clone(), our method would produce a shallow copy of the list, as Figure JI9-6 illustrates. In other words, both the original list and its clone would reference the same chain of nodes, and these nodes would reference one set of data.

As before, clone needs to do more to perform a deep copy. It needs to clone the chain of nodes as well as the data that the nodes reference. Figure JI9-7 shows a list with its deep clone.

**FIGURE JI9-6**     A list and its shallow clone: linked implementation

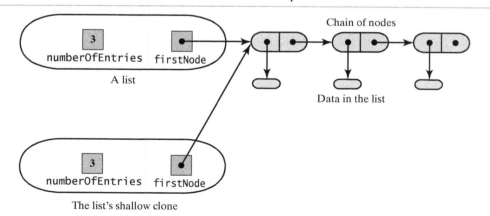

**FIGURE JI9-7** A list and its deep clone: linked implementation

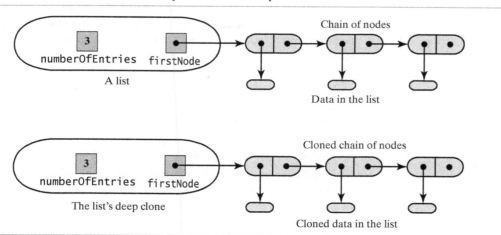

JI9.13 **Cloning a node.** To clone the nodes in the chain, we need to add a method clone to the inner class Node. First, we add implements Cloneable to the declaration of the class Node. Note that Node is private in LList but protected in LinkedChainBase. Node's clone method begins like other clone methods, but then it goes on to clone the data portion of the node. We do not bother cloning the link, since the list's clone method will set it. With these changes, the revised class Node appears in LList as follows (changes are highlighted):

```java
private class Node implements Cloneable
{
    private T    data;
    private Node next;

    < Constructors >
    . . .
    < Accessor and mutator methods getData, setData, getNextNode, and setNextNode. >
    . . .
    protected Object clone()
    {
        Node theCopy = null;
        try
        {
            @SuppressWarnings("unchecked")
            Node temp = (Node)super.clone();
            theCopy = temp;
        }
        catch (CloneNotSupportedException e)
        {
            throw new Error(e.toString());
        }
        @SuppressWarnings("unchecked")
        T temp = (T)data.clone();
        theCopy.data = temp;
        theCopy.next = null; // Don't clone link; it's set later

        return theCopy;
    } // end clone
} // end Node
```

Remember that data invokes a public method clone that does not throw an exception, and so data.clone() can appear outside of a try block.

**JI9.14** **Cloning the chain.** LList's clone method invokes super.clone() in statements equivalent to

```
LList<T> theCopy = (LList<T>)super.clone();
```

The method then must clone the chain of nodes that stores the list's data. To do so, the method needs to traverse the chain, clone each node, and link the cloned nodes appropriately. We begin by cloning the first node so that we can set the data field firstNode correctly:

```
// Make a copy of the first node
theCopy.firstNode = (Node)firstNode.clone();
```

Next, we traverse the rest of the chain. A reference newRef references the last node that we have added to the new chain, while the reference oldRef keeps track of where we are in the traversal of the original chain. The statement

```
newRef.setNextNode((Node)oldRef.clone()); // Attach cloned node
```

clones the current node in the original chain, along with its data, and then links the clone to the end of the new chain. Recall that Node's clone method also clones the data that a node references.

The following statements incorporate the previous ideas and clone the rest of the chain:

```
Node newRef = theCopy.firstNode;         // Last node in new chain
Node oldRef = firstNode.getNextNode();   // Next node in old chain

for (int count = 2; count <= numberOfEntries; count++)
{
   newRef.setNextNode((Node)oldRef.clone()); // Attach cloned node
   newRef = newRef.getNextNode();            // Update references
   oldRef = oldRef.getNextNode();
} // end for
```

**JI9.15** The code in the previous segment assumes a nonempty chain of nodes. The complete clone method that follows checks for an empty chain and suppresses warnings about unchecked casts.

```
public Object clone()
{
   LList<T> theCopy = null;
   try
   {
      @SuppressWarnings("unchecked")
      LList<T> temp = (LList<T>)super.clone();
      theCopy = temp;
   }
   catch (CloneNotSupportedException e)
   {
      throw new Error(e.toString());
   }

   // Copy underlying chain of nodes
   if (firstNode == null) // If chain is empty
   {
      theCopy.firstNode = null;
   }
   else
   {
      // Make a copy of the first node
      @SuppressWarnings("unchecked")
      Node temp = (Node)firstNode.clone();
      theCopy.firstNode = temp;

      // Make a copy of the rest of chain
      Node newRef = theCopy.firstNode;
      Node oldRef = firstNode.getNextNode();
```

```
        for (int count = 2; count <= numberOfEntries; count++)
        {
            // Clone node and its data; link clone to new chain
            @SuppressWarnings("unchecked")
            Node temp2 = (Node)oldRef.clone();
            newRef.setNextNode(temp2);
            newRef = newRef.getNextNode();
            oldRef = oldRef.getNextNode();
        } // end for
    } // end if

    return theCopy;
} // end clone
```

 **Note:** To make a deep clone of a chain of linked nodes that reference cloneable objects, you must clone the nodes as well as the objects.

 **Question 2** The for loop in Segment JI9.15 is controlled by the number of nodes in the chain. Revise this loop so that it is controlled by oldRef.

## A Sorted List of Clones

**JI9.16** Segment JI6.4 of Java Interlude 6 talked about the danger of placing mutable objects in a collection such as a list whose entries are sorted. If the client retains a reference to any of the objects, it could alter those objects and destroy the integrity of the collection. Similarly for an instance of the ADT sorted list, the client could destroy the sorted order of the objects.

Segment JI6.5 offered one solution to this problem, namely to place only immutable objects in the collection. We now offer another solution that enables you to place mutable objects in the collection.

Suppose that a client adds an object to a collection. Imagine that the collection clones the object before adding it to its data. The client then would be able to access or change the collection's data only by using ADT operations. It would not have a reference to the clone that it could use to alter the clone. Of course, this scenario requires that the added object be Cloneable. Let's examine the details of such an implementation of the ADT sorted list.

**JI9.17** Segment 16.1 of Chapter 16 noted that objects in a sorted list must be Comparable—that is, they must have a compareTo method. In this case, we also want the objects to be Cloneable. Segment JI9.8 defined an interface Copyable that declares a public method clone. Using that interface, let's create another one:

```
public interface ComparableAndCopyable<T> extends Comparable<T>, Copyable
{
} // end ComparableAndCopyable
```

This interface will enable us to bound the generic type of the objects we place into the sorted list, as the next segment will show.

A class that implements ComparableAndCopyable must define the methods compareTo and clone. For example, the class Name mentioned in Segment JI9.3 could be revised by adding the method compareTo in addition to the method clone and by beginning it as follows:

```
public class ComparableCopyableName
             implements ComparableAndCopyable<ComparableCopyableName>
```

The method clone is given in Segment JI9.3, and you wrote compareTo when you answered Question 1 in Java Interlude 3.

**JI9.18** Since we want the sorted list to contain only objects that are both `Comparable` and `Copyable`, we can revise our interface for a sorted list by beginning it as follows:

```
public interface SortedListOfClonesInterface
                 <T extends ComparableAndCopyable<? super T>>
```

and then use it in the definition of a class `LinkedSortedListOfClones`:

```
public class LinkedSortedListOfClones
             <T extends ComparableAndCopyable<? super T>>
             implements SortedListOfClonesInterface<T>
```

**JI9.19** With these logistics out of the way, we propose the following changes to the implementation of the ADT sorted list. You can apply these changes to the implementations discussed in Chapters 16 and 17:

- In add, place a clone of the desired entry into the sorted list instead of the entry itself. That is, place `newEntry.clone()` into the list instead of `newEntry`. Thus, the body of the method could begin with

  ```
  Node newNode = new Node((T)newEntry.clone());
  ```

  Since `clone` returns an instance of `Object`, the cast to the generic type `T` is necessary.

- In getEntry, return a clone of the desired entry instead of the entry itself. For example, you could return `(T)result.clone()` instead of `result`.

Let's examine these changes more closely. Suppose that a client has a reference, `newEntry`, to an object, and that it adds the object to a collection. The collection clones the object and adds the clone instead of the original object, as Figure JI9-8 illustrates. The client has no reference to the collection's data. If the client modifies the object that `newEntry` references, the collection is not changed.

What if getEntry did not return a clone of the desired entry but instead returned a reference to the desired entry in the collection? As Figure JI9-9 illustrates, the client would be able to change the entry within the collection. So even though the collection contains a clone of the client's original object, getEntry would give the client access to the clone. With the ability to change this clone, the client could damage the integrity of the collection. Thus, it is necessary for getEntry to return a clone of the desired entry. This is a clone of the clone of the client's original object, as Figure JI9-10 shows.

**FIGURE JI9-8**   A collection and its client after the clone of an object is added to the collection

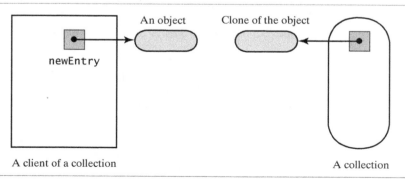

An object   Clone of the object

newEntry

A client of a collection          A collection

FIGURE JI9-9    The effect of `getEntry` if it did not return a clone

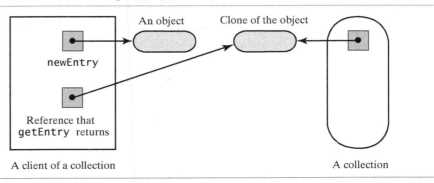

FIGURE JI9-10    The effect of `getEntry` when it returns a clone

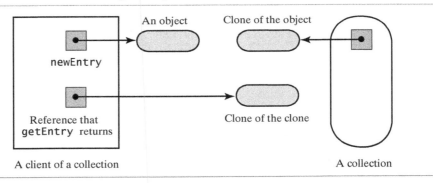

> ♩ **Note:** A collection can clone the objects that a client adds to it, but you will have duplicates of each entry in the collection. For complex objects, the time and memory needed to make each copy can be substantial.

## Cloning a Binary Node

**JI9.20** The class `BinaryNode` given in Chapter 24 defines the method `copy` in Segment 24.5 to make a copy of a node. This method is needed by the class `BinaryTree` in Segment 24.7 for the method `privateSetTree`. You should now realize that we really should have defined the method `clone` instead of `copy`.

To do so, BinaryNode's clone method must invoke Object's clone method, since Object is BinaryNode's superclass. It then must clone the node's data portion and finally clone the node's two children. Here is the resulting method:

```java
/** Makes a clone of this node and its subtrees.
    @return  The clone of the subtree rooted at this node. */
public Object clone()
{
    BinaryNode<T> theCopy = null;
    try
    {
        @SuppressWarnings("unchecked")
        BinaryNode<T> temp = (BinaryNode<T>)super.clone();
        theCopy = temp;
    }
    catch (CloneNotSupportedException e)
    {
        throw new Error("BinaryNode cannot clone: " + e.toString());
    }

    theCopy.data = (T)data.clone();

    if (left != null)
        theCopy.left = (BinaryNode<T>)left.clone();

    if (right != null)
        theCopy.right = (BinaryNode<T>)right.clone();

    return theCopy;
} // end clone
```

## ANSWERS TO SELF-TEST QUESTIONS

1. **a.** No. The clone y has a Name object that is distinct from x's Name object, because a deep copy was made. (See Figure JI9-4.)
   **b.** Yes. Both objects share one Name object. (See Figure JI9-5.)

2. 
```java
Node newRef = theCopy.firstNode;
Node oldRef = firstNode.getNextNode();
while (oldRef != null)
{
    @SuppressWarnings("unchecked")
    Node temp2 = (Node)oldRef.clone();
    newRef.setNextNode(temp2);
    newRef = newRef.getNextNode();
    oldRef = oldRef.getNextNode();
} // end while
```

# A Binary Search Tree Implementation

## Contents

## Prerequisites

## Objectives

After studying this chapter, you should be able to

- Decide whether a binary tree is a binary search tree
- Locate a given entry in a binary search tree using the fewest comparisons
- Traverse the entries in a binary search tree in sorted order
- Add a new entry to a binary search tree
- Remove an entry from a binary search tree
- Describe the efficiency of operations on a binary search tree
- Use a binary search tree to implement the ADT dictionary

Recall from Chapter 23 that a search tree stores data in a way that facilitates searching. In particular, we saw the binary search tree, which is both a binary tree and a search tree. The nature of a binary search tree enables us to search it by using a simple recursive algorithm. This algorithm is similar in spirit to a binary search of an array and can be just as efficient. However, the shape of a binary search tree affects the efficiency of this algorithm. Since we can create several different binary search trees from the same data, we want to pick the tree whose shape provides the most efficient search.

For a database that remains stable, a binary search tree provides a relatively simple way to achieve an efficient search. Most databases, however, change to remain current. Thus, we must add nodes to and remove nodes from the binary search tree. Unfortunately, these operations change the shape of the tree, often making a search less efficient.

This chapter implements the binary search tree and, in doing so, describes the algorithms for adding and removing entries. Chapter 27 looks at ways that a search tree can provide an efficient search despite additions and removals.

## Getting Started

**25.1**   A **binary search tree** is a binary tree whose nodes contain Comparable objects and are organized as follows. For each node in the tree,

- The data in a node is greater than the data in the node's left subtree
- The data in a node is less than the data in the node's right subtree

Figure 25-1 shows the binary search tree that you saw in Chapter 23.

---

**FIGURE 25-1**   A binary search tree of names

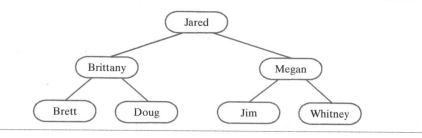

---

Recall that a Comparable object belongs to a class that implements the interface Comparable. We use the class's method compareTo to compare such objects. The basis for this comparison varies from class to class, depending on the data fields compareTo examines.

## An Interface for the Binary Search Tree

**25.2**    **The operations.** In addition to the common operations of a tree, as given in the interface `TreeInterface`, a binary search tree has basic database operations that search, retrieve, add, remove, and traverse its entries. We can design an interface for a binary search tree, as well as for other search trees that you will see in Chapter 27. Listing 25-1 provides such an interface. Note that we do not allow `null` values in a search tree; thus, methods can return `null` to indicate failure. To simplify our discussion, the entries in a search tree must be distinct.

---

**LISTING 25-1    An interface for a search tree**

```
1   package TreePackage;
2   import java.util.Iterator;
3   public interface SearchTreeInterface<T extends Comparable<? super T>>
4          extends TreeInterface<T>
5   {
6      /** Searches for a specific entry in this tree.
7          @param entry  An object to be found.
8          @return  True if the object was found in the tree. */
9      public boolean contains(T entry);
10
11     /** Retrieves a specific entry in this tree.
12         @param entry  An object to be found.
13         @return  Either the object that was found in the tree or
14                  null if no such object exists. */
15     public T getEntry(T entry);
16
17     /** Adds a new entry to this tree, if it does not match an existing
18         object in the tree. Otherwise, replaces the existing object with
19         the new entry.
20         @param newEntry  An object to be added to the tree.
21         @return  Either null if newEntry was not in the tree already, or
22                  the existing entry that matched the parameter newEntry
23                  and has been replaced in the tree. */
24     public T add(T newEntry);
25
26     /** Removes a specific entry from this tree.
27         @param entry  An object to be removed.
28         @return  Either the object that was removed from the tree or
29                  null if no such object exists. */
30     public T remove(T entry);
31
32     /** Creates an iterator that traverses all entries in this tree.
33         @return  An iterator that provides sequential and ordered access
34                  to the entries in the tree. */
35     public Iterator<T> getInorderIterator();
36   } // end SearchTreeInterface
```

---

**25.3**    **Understanding the specifications.** These specifications allow us to use a binary search tree in the implementation of the ADT dictionary, as you will see later in this chapter. The methods use return values instead of exceptions to indicate whether an operation has failed. The return value for a successful retrieve, add, or remove operation, however, might seem strange at first. For example, it appears that the retrieve operation, `getEntry`, returns the same entry it is given to find. In fact, `getEntry` returns an object that is in the tree and that matches the given entry according to the entry's `compareTo` method. Let's look at an example that adds entries and then retrieves them.

Imagine a class `Person` that has two strings as data fields representing the person's name and identification number. The class implements the `Comparable` interface, and so has a `compareTo` method. Suppose that `compareTo` bases its comparison only on the name field. Consider the following statements that create and add to a binary search tree:

```
SearchTreeInterface<Person> myTree = new BinarySearchTree<>();
Person whitney = new Person("Whitney", "111223333");
Person returnValue = myTree.add(whitney);
```

Following the add operation, `returnValue` is `null`, since `whitney` was not in the tree already. Now suppose we try to add another *Whitney*, who has a different identification number:

```
Person whitney2 = new Person("Whitney", "444556666");
returnValue = myTree.add(whitney2);
```

Since `whitney` and `whitney2` have the same names, they are equal. That is, the expression `whitney.compareTo(whitney2)` is zero. Therefore, the add method will not simply add `whitney2` to the tree. Instead it replaces `whitney` with `whitney2` and returns `whitney`, the original object in the tree, as Figure 25-2 illustrates. We can think of this as a way to change the identification number of a person named *Whitney*.

**FIGURE 25-2** Adding an entry that matches an entry already in a binary search tree

(a) Before `myTree.add(whitney2)` executes

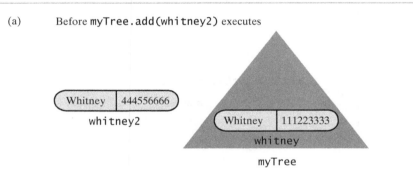

(b) After `myTree.add(whitney2)` executes

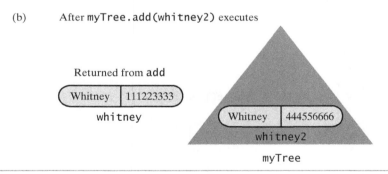

Now the statement

```
returnValue = myTree.getEntry(whitney);
```

sets `returnValue` to `whitney2`, since it is in the tree and matches `whitney`. Similarly,

```
returnValue = myTree.remove(whitney);
```

returns and removes `whitney2`.

Now imagine that the method `compareTo` uses both the name and identification fields of a `Person` object to make a comparison. Since `whitney` and `whitney2` would not be equal according to this `compareTo`, we could add both objects to the tree. Then `getEntry(whitney)` would return `whitney`, and `remove(whitney)` would remove and return `whitney`.

## Duplicate Entries

**25.4**   Notice that the add method, as specified in `SearchTreeInterface`, ensures that duplicates are never added to the tree. In practice, this restriction can be desirable for many applications, but sometimes it is not. By making a small change to our definition of a binary search tree, we can allow duplicate entries, that is, multiple entries that are equal according to `compareTo`.

Figure 25-3 shows a binary search tree in which *Jared* occurs twice. If we are at the root of this tree and want to know whether *Jared* occurs again, it would help to know in which subtree we should look. Thus, if any entry *e* has a duplicate entry *d*, we arbitrarily require that *d* occur in the right subtree of *e*'s node. Accordingly, we modify our definition as follows:

For each node in a binary search tree,

- The data in a node is greater than the data in the node's left subtree
- The data in a node is less than *or equal to* the data in the node's right subtree

Notice that an inorder traversal of the tree in Figure 25-3 visits the duplicate entry *Jared* immediately after visiting the original *Jared*.

---

**FIGURE 25-3**   A binary search tree with duplicate entries

---

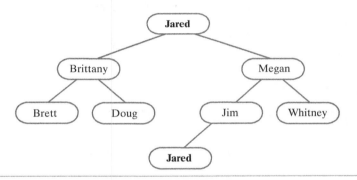

---

With duplicate entries permitted, the add method has less to do. But which entry will `getEntry` retrieve? Will the method `remove` delete the first occurrence of an entry or all occurrences? Exactly what happens is up to the class designer, but these questions should indicate the complications that duplicate entries cause. We will not consider duplicate entries any further, and will leave this issue to you as a programming project. (See Project 1 at the end of this chapter.)

 **Note:  Duplicate entries**
If you permit duplicate entries in a binary search tree, you can arbitrarily place the duplicate of an entry in the entry's right subtree. Once you choose the right subtree, you must be consistent. Project 2 at the end of this chapter suggests another strategy for handling duplicates.

---

 **Question 1** If you add a duplicate entry *Megan* to the binary search tree in Figure 25-3 as a leaf, where should you place the new node?

---

## Beginning the Class Definition

**25.5** **An outline of the class.** Let's begin the definition of a class of binary search trees. Since a binary search tree is a binary tree, we derive our new class from the class `BinaryTree` that we defined in the previous chapter. Thus, we begin our class as indicated in Listing 25-2. Note the call by the constructor to the protected method `setRootNode`, which the class inherits from `BinaryTree`. Segment 24.8 of Chapter 24 contains a definition of `setRootNode`.

---

**LISTING 25-2** An outline of the class `BinarySearchTree`

```
1  package TreePackage;
2  import java.util.Iterator;
3  public class BinarySearchTree<T extends Comparable<? super T>>
4              extends BinaryTree<T>
5              implements SearchTreeInterface<T>
6  {
7     public BinarySearchTree()
8     {
9        super();
10    } // end default constructor
11
12    public BinarySearchTree(T rootEntry)
13    {
14       super();
15       setRootNode(new BinaryNode<T>(rootEntry));
16    } // end constructor
17
18    public void setTree(T rootData) // Disable setTree (see Segment 25.6)
19    {
20       throw new UnsupportedOperationException();
21    } // end setTree
22
23    public void setTree(T rootData, BinaryTreeInterface<T> leftTree,
24                                    BinaryTreeInterface<T> rightTree)
25    {
26       throw new UnsupportedOperationException();
27    } // end setTree
28
29    < Implementations of contains, getEntry, add, and remove are here. Their definitions appear
30      in subsequent sections of this chapter. Other methods in SearchTreeInterface are inherited
31      from BinaryTree. >
32    . . .
33 } // end BinarySearchTree
```

---

 **Note:** The class `BinarySearchTree` is not a final class. We declared it that way so that we can use it as a base class.

**25.6** **Disable `setTree`.** Before we go any further, consider the two `setTree` methods that our class inherits from `BinaryTree`. The client could use these methods to create a tree that, unfortunately, is not a binary search tree. This outcome would be impossible if the client used `SearchTreeInterface` to declare an instance of the tree. For example, if we wrote

```
SearchTreeInterface<String> dataSet = new BinarySearchTree<String>();
```

`dataSet` would not have either of the `setTree` methods, since they are not in `SearchTreeInterface`. But if we wrote

```
BinarySearchTree<String> dataSet = new BinarySearchTree<String>();
```

`dataSet` would have the `setTree` methods.

To prevent a client from using either version of setTree, we override these two methods so that they throw an exception if called. Listing 25-2 shows definitions for these methods that do just that.

**Question 2** The second constructor in the class BinarySearchTree calls the method setRootNode. Is it possible to replace this call with the call setRootData(rootEntry)? Explain.

**Question 3** Is it necessary to define the methods isEmpty and clear within the class Binary-SearchTree? Explain.

# Searching and Retrieving

**25.7**  **The search algorithm.** Segment 23.31 of Chapter 23 presented the following recursive algorithm to search a binary search tree:

> *Algorithm* **bstSearch(binarySearchTree, desiredObject)**
> // *Searches a binary search tree for a given object.*
> // *Returns true if the object is found.*
>
> **if** (binarySearchTree *is empty*)
>     **return false**
> **else if** (desiredObject == *object in the root of* binarySearchTree)
>     **return true**
> **else if** (desiredObject < *object in the root of* binarySearchTree)
>     **return** bstSearch(*left subtree of* binarySearchTree, desiredObject)
> **else**
>     **return** bstSearch(*right subtree of* binarySearchTree, desiredObject)

This algorithm is the basis of the method getEntry.

**Note:**  Searching a binary search tree is like performing a binary search of an array: You search one of two subtrees of the binary search tree instead of searching one of two halves of an array.

**25.8**  While it is convenient to express our recursive algorithm in terms of trees and subtrees, our implementation of a binary tree in the previous chapter suggests that we use root nodes instead. The root node of a tree or subtree provides a way for us to search or manipulate its descendant nodes.

The following algorithm is equivalent to the one just given, but describes our actual implementation more closely:

> *Algorithm* **bstSearch(binarySearchTreeRoot, desiredObject)**
> // *Searches a binary search tree for a given object.*
> // *Returns true if the object is found.*
>
> **if** (binarySearchTreeRoot *is* **null**)
>     **return false**
> **else if** (desiredObject == *object in* binarySearchTreeRoot)
>     **return true**
> **else if** (desiredObject < *object in* binarySearchTreeRoot)
>     **return** bstSearch(*left child of* binarySearchTreeRoot, desiredObject)
> **else**
>     **return** bstSearch(*right child of* binarySearchTreeRoot, desiredObject)

We will continue to express subsequent algorithms in terms of trees and subtrees, but will use root nodes in our implementations without explicitly mentioning it.

**25.9**    **The method getEntry.** As is often the case with recursive algorithms, we implement the actual search as a private method findEntry that the public method getEntry invokes. Although the algorithm returns a boolean value, our implementation will return the located data object. Thus, we have the following methods:

```java
public T getEntry(T entry)
{
   return findEntry(getRootNode(), entry);
} // end getEntry

private T findEntry(BinaryNode<T> rootNode, T entry)
{
   T result = null;

   if (rootNode != null)
   {
      T rootEntry = rootNode.getData();

      if (entry.equals(rootEntry))
         result = rootEntry;
      else if (entry.compareTo(rootEntry) < 0)
         result = findEntry(rootNode.getLeftChild(), entry);
      else
         result = findEntry(rootNode.getRightChild(), entry);
   } // end if

   return result;
} // end findEntry
```

We use the methods compareTo and equals to compare the given entry with the existing entries in the tree. Also, notice our use of methods from the class BinaryNode. We assume that we have at least package access to this class.

You can implement getEntry iteratively as well, with or without the use of a private method such as findEntry. We leave this implementation as an exercise.

**25.10**    **The method contains.** The method contains can simply call getEntry to see whether a given entry is in the tree:

```java
public boolean contains(T entry)
{
   return getEntry(entry) != null;
} // end contains
```

# Traversing

**25.11**    SearchTreeInterface provides the method getInorderIterator, which returns an inorder iterator. Since our class is a subclass of BinaryTree, it inherits getInorderIterator. For a binary search tree, this iterator traverses the entries in ascending order, as defined by the entries' method compareTo.

**Question 4** How would you declare a reference to an object of BinarySearchTree to be able to call the other methods in TreeIteratorInterface?

# Adding an Entry

VideoNote

Binary search tree additions
and removals

**25.12** Adding entries to a binary search tree is an essential operation, since that is how we build one initially. So suppose that we have a binary search tree and we want to add a new entry to it. We cannot add it just anywhere in the tree, because we must retain the relationships among the nodes. That is, the tree must still be a binary search tree after the addition. Also, the method `getEntry` must be able to locate the new entry. For example, if we wanted to add the entry *Chad* to the tree in Figure 25-4a, we could not add the new node to *Jared*'s right subtree. Since *Chad* comes before *Jared*, *Chad* must be in *Jared*'s left subtree. Since *Brittany* is the root of this left subtree, we compare *Chad* with *Brittany* and find that *Chad* is larger. Thus, *Chad* belongs in *Brittany*'s right subtree. Continuing, we compare *Chad* with *Doug* and find that *Chad* belongs in *Doug*'s left subtree. But this subtree is empty. That is, *Doug* has no left child.

If we make *Chad* the left child of *Doug*, we will get the binary search tree in Figure 25-4b. Now `getEntry` will be able to locate *Chad* by making the same comparisons we just described. That is, `getEntry` will compare *Chad* with *Jared*, *Brittany*, and *Doug* before locating *Chad*. Notice that the new node is a leaf.

 **Note:** Every addition to a binary search tree adds a new leaf to the tree.

**FIGURE 25-4**    (a) A binary search tree; (b) the same tree after adding *Chad*

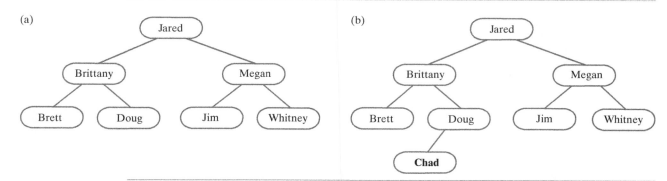

**Question 5** Add the names *Chris*, *Jason*, and *Kelley* to the binary search tree in Figure 25-4b.

**Question 6** Add the name *Miguel* to the binary search tree in Figure 25-4a, and then add *Nancy*. Now go back to the original tree and add *Nancy* and then add *Miguel*. Does the order in which you add the two names affect the tree that results?

## A Recursive Implementation

**25.13**    The method add has an elegant recursive implementation. Consider again the example given in the previous segment. If we want to add *Chad* to the binary search tree in Figure 25-4a, we take the following steps:

- To add *Chad* to the binary search tree whose root is *Jared*:

  Observe that *Chad* is less than *Jared*.
  Add *Chad* to *Jared*'s left subtree, whose root is *Brittany*.

- To add *Chad* to the binary search tree whose root is *Brittany*:

  Observe that *Chad* is greater than *Brittany*.
  Add *Chad* to *Brittany*'s right subtree, whose root is *Doug*.

- To add *Chad* to the binary search tree whose root is *Doug*:

  Observe that *Chad* is less than *Doug*.
  Since *Doug* has no left subtree, make *Chad* the left child of *Doug*.

We can see that adding an entry to the tree rooted at *Jared* depends upon adding to progressively smaller subtrees, as Figure 25-5 shows.

**FIGURE 25-5**    Recursively adding *Chad* to smaller subtrees of a binary search tree

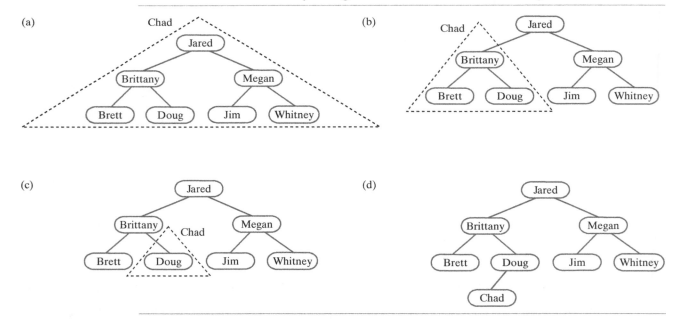

**25.14    A recursive algorithm for adding a new entry.** The following recursive algorithm formalizes this approach, in accordance with the specifications of the method add in SearchTreeInterface. Recall that we decided to have only distinct entries in the binary search tree. If we try to add an entry to a tree that matches an entry already in the tree, we replace that entry with the new entry and return the old entry.

To simplify our algorithm, let's assume for the moment that the binary search tree is not empty:

*Algorithm* `addEntry(binarySearchTree, newEntry)`
*// Adds a new entry to a binary search tree that is not empty.*
*// Returns* `null` *if* `newEntry` *did not exist already in the tree. Otherwise, returns the*
*// tree entry that matched and was replaced by* `newEntry`.

```
result = null
if (newEntry matches the entry in the root of binarySearchTree)
{
    result = entry in the root
    Replace entry in the root with newEntry
}
else if (newEntry < entry in the root of binarySearchTree)
{
    if (the root of binarySearchTree has a left child)
        result = addEntry(left subtree of binarySearchTree, newEntry)
    else
        Give the root a left child containing newEntry
}
else // newEntry > entry in the root of binarySearchTree
{
    if (the root of binarySearchTree has a right child)
        result = addEntry(right subtree of binarySearchTree, newEntry)
    else
        Give the root a right child containing newEntry
}

return result
```

We can handle the addition to an empty binary search tree as a special case within another algorithm that invokes `addEntry`, as follows:

*Algorithm* `add(binarySearchTree, newEntry)`
*// Adds a new entry to a binary search tree.*
*// Returns* `null` *if* `newEntry` *did not exist already in the tree. Otherwise, returns the*
*// tree entry that matched and was replaced by* `newEntry`.

```
result = null
if (binarySearchTree is empty)
    Create a node containing newEntry and make it the root of binarySearchTree
else
    result = addEntry(binarySearchTree, newEntry)

return result;
```

**25.15** **The private recursive method `addEntry`.** Recall the recursive search algorithm given in Segment 25.7. The public method `getEntry` in Segment 25.9 invokes a private recursive method `findEntry` that implements the search algorithm. We have a similar organization here. The public method `add` calls a private recursive method `addEntry`, if the tree is not empty. Like `findEntry`, `addEntry` has a node as a parameter that is initially the root node of the tree. When `addEntry` is called recursively, this parameter is either the left child or the right child of the current root.

Remember where we place a new node into a binary search tree. As Figures 25-4 and 25-5 illustrate, a new node always becomes a leaf in the tree. Now imagine the recursive calls to `addEntry` when adding *Chad* to the tree in Figure 25-5a. Eventually, the node containing *Doug* is passed to `addEntry` as its argument (Figure 25-5c). Since *Chad* is less than *Doug*, and *Doug*'s node has no left child, `addEntry` creates one containing *Chad* (Figure 25-5d).

The following implementation of addEntry closely follows the pseudocode given in Segment 25.14:

```java
// Adds newEntry to the nonempty subtree rooted at rootNode.
private T addEntry(BinaryNode<T> rootNode, T newEntry)
{
    assert rootNode != null;
    T result = null;
    int comparison = newEntry.compareTo(rootNode.getData());

    if (comparison == 0)
    {
        result = rootNode.getData();
        rootNode.setData(newEntry);
    }
    else if (comparison < 0)
    {
        if (rootNode.hasLeftChild())
            result = addEntry(rootNode.getLeftChild(), newEntry);
        else
            rootNode.setLeftChild(new BinaryNode<>(newEntry));
    }
    else
    {
        assert comparison > 0;

        if (rootNode.hasRightChild())
            result = addEntry(rootNode.getRightChild(), newEntry);
        else
            rootNode.setRightChild(new BinaryNode<>(newEntry));
    } // end if

    return result;
} // end addEntry
```

We begin by comparing the new entry with the entry in the root. If the entries match, we replace and return the original entry in the root. If the comparison is "less than," and the root has a left child, we pass that child to addEntry. Remember that when we are coding a recursive method such as addEntry, we assume that it works when we write the recursive call. Thus, addEntry places a new node containing newEntry into the root's left subtree. If the root has no left child, we give it one containing the new entry. Analogous code handles the case when the new entry is greater than the entry in the root.

**25.16**    **The public method add.** The public method add not only invokes the recursive addEntry, it ensures that the tree it passes to addEntry is not empty. Accordingly, add deals with empty trees itself. The following implementation of add adheres to the algorithm given in Segment 25.14. Note the use of the protected methods setRootNode and getRootNode that are inherited from BinaryTree.

```java
public T add(T newEntry)
{
    T result = null;

    if (isEmpty())
        setRootNode(new BinaryNode<>(newEntry));
    else
        result = addEntry(getRootNode(), newEntry);

    return result;
} // end add
```

## An Iterative Implementation

You can implement the method addEntry iteratively. We will mimic the logic of the recursive version of addEntry given earlier, so you can compare the two approaches. Exercise 12 at the end of this chapter suggests another iterative algorithm.

**25.17**    **An iterative algorithm for adding a new entry.** The following iterative algorithm adds a new entry to a binary search tree that is not empty:

```
Algorithm addEntry(binarySearchTree, newEntry)
// Adds a new entry to a binary search tree that is not empty.
// Returns null if newEntry did not exist already in the tree. Otherwise, returns the
// tree entry that matched and was replaced by newEntry.

result = null
currentNode = root node of binarySearchTree
found = false

while (found is false)
{
    if (newEntry matches the entry in currentNode)
    {
        found = true
        result = entry in currentNode
        Replace entry in currentNode with newEntry
    }
    else if (newEntry < entry in currentNode)
    {
        if (currentNode has a left child)
            currentNode = left child of currentNode
        else
        {
            found = true
            Give currentNode a left child containing newEntry
        }
    }
    else // newEntry > entry in currentNode
    {
        if (currentNode has a right child)
            currentNode = right child of currentNode
        else
        {
            found = true
            Give currentNode a right child containing newEntry
        }
    }
}

return result
```

The while loop tries to match the new entry with an existing entry in the tree. If the new entry is not in the tree already, the search for it ends at a node's null child reference. This is where a new node belongs. But if the new entry matches an entry in the tree, we return the existing entry and replace it in the tree with the new entry.

**25.18**    **An iterative implementation of the method addEntry.** The Java implementation of the previous algorithm closely follows the algorithm's logic. Note the use of the protected method getRootNode that is inherited from BinaryTree.

```java
private T addEntry(T newEntry)
{
    BinaryNode<T> currentNode = getRootNode();
    assert currentNode != null;
```

```
      T result = null;
      boolean found = false;
      while (!found)
      {
         T currentEntry = currentNode.getData();
         int comparison = newEntry.compareTo(currentEntry);

         if (comparison == 0)
         {  // newEntry matches currentEntry;
            // return and replace currentEntry
            found = true;
            result = currentEntry;
            currentNode.setData(newEntry);
         }
         else if (comparison < 0)
         {
            if (currentNode.hasLeftChild())
               currentNode = currentNode.getLeftChild();
            else
            {
               found = true;
               currentNode.setLeftChild(new BinaryNode<>(newEntry));
            } // end if
         }
         else
         {
            assert comparison > 0;
            if (currentNode.hasRightChild())
               currentNode = currentNode.getRightChild();
            else
            {
               found = true;
               currentNode.setRightChild(new BinaryNode<>(newEntry));
            } // end if
         } // end if
      } // end while

   return result;
} // end addEntry
```

The method add that calls this iterative addEntry is like the one given in Segment 25.16, except for the actual invocation of addEntry. Since the iterative addEntry has one parameter instead of two, the invocation is addEntry(newEntry) instead of addEntry(getRootNode(), newEntry).

 **Programming Tip:** Whether you use this iterative addEntry method, the one suggested in Exercise 12, or the recursive version given earlier depends in part on which approach is clearest to you. You'll spend less time debugging if you really understand your algorithm.

## Removing an Entry

25.19   To remove an entry from a binary search tree, we pass a matching entry to the method remove. The desired entry is then removed from the tree and returned to the client. If no such entry exists, the method returns null and the tree remains unchanged.

Removing an entry is somewhat more involved than adding an entry, as the required logic depends upon how many children belong to the node containing the entry. We have three possibilities:

- The node has no children—it is a leaf
- The node has one child
- The node has two children

We now consider these three cases.

## Removing an Entry Whose Node Is a Leaf

**25.20**   The simplest case in removing an entry is when its node is a leaf, that is, has no children. For example, suppose that node $N$ contains the entry to be removed from the binary search tree. Figure 25-6a shows two possibilities for node $N$: It could be either the left child or the right child of its parent node $P$. Since $N$ is a leaf, we can delete it by setting the appropriate child reference in node $P$ to `null`. Figure 25-6b shows the result of this operation.

FIGURE 25-6    Removing a leaf node $N$ from its parent node $P$ when $N$ is
(a) a left child; (b) a right child

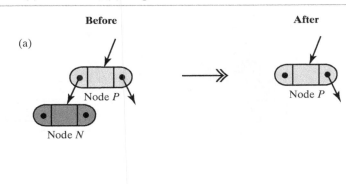

## Removing an Entry Whose Node Has One Child

**25.21**   Now imagine that the entry to be removed is in a node $N$ that has exactly one child $C$. Figure 25-7a shows the four possibilities for node $N$ and its parent $P$. $N$ is either a left child or a right child of $P$, and $C$ is either a left child or a right child of $N$. To remove the entry in $N$, we remove $N$ from the tree. We do this by making $C$ a child of $P$ instead of $N$. As Figure 25-7b shows, if $N$ was a left child of $P$, we make $C$ be the left child of $P$. Likewise, if $N$ was a right child of $P$, we make $C$ be the right child of $P$.

Is the resulting tree a binary search tree? If $N$ is the left child of $P$, for example, the entry in $P$ is greater than all entries in $P$'s left subtree. After we remove $N$, this relationship is still true, and so our tree is still a binary search tree. Analogous reasoning applies when $N$ is the right child of $P$.

FIGURE 25-7    Removing a node *N* from its parent node *P* when *N* has one
child and is itself (a) a left child; (b) a right child

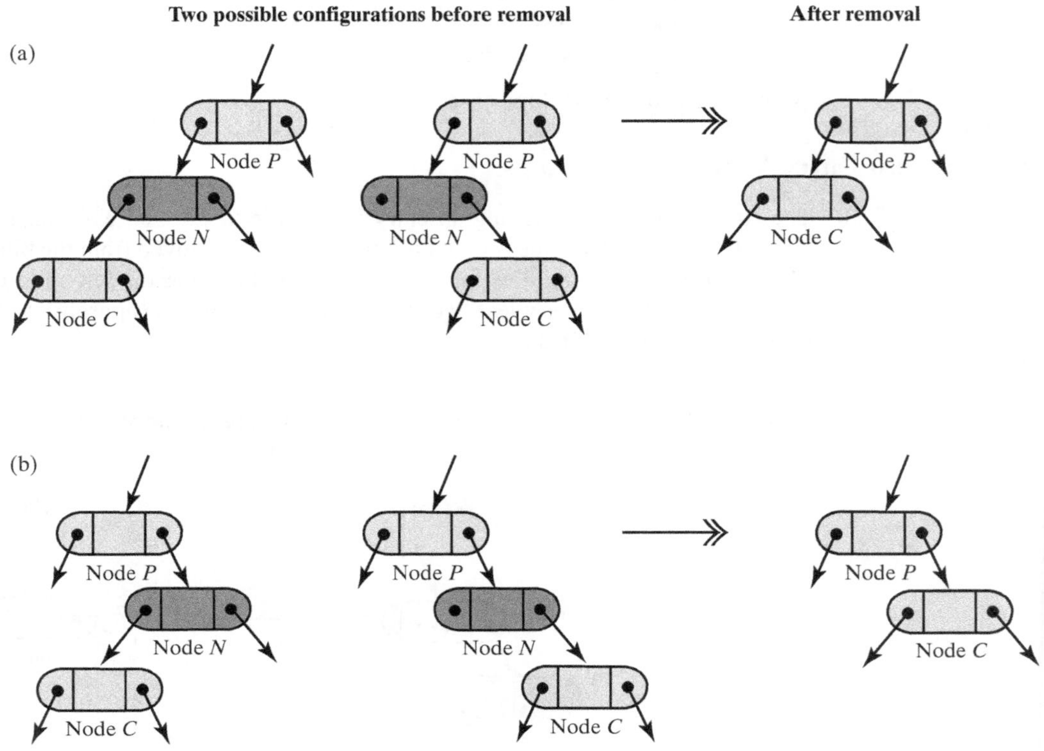

## Removing an Entry Whose Node Has Two Children

**25.22**    The previous two cases are really not too difficult, conceptually or in practice. But this last case is a bit involved. Once again, suppose that the entry to be removed is in a node *N*, but now *N* has two children. Figure 25-8 shows two possible configurations for *N*. If we try to remove node *N*, we will leave its two children without a parent. Although node *P* could reference one of them, it hasn't room for both. Thus, removing node *N* is not an option.

Remember that our goal is to remove an entry from the tree. We do not actually have to remove node *N* to remove its entry. Let's find a node *X* that is easy to remove—it would have no more than one child—and replace *N*'s entry with the entry now in *X*. We then can remove node *X* and still have the correct entries in the tree. But will the tree still be a binary search tree? Clearly, node *X* cannot be just any node; it must contain an entry in the tree that legally can be in node *N*.

FIGURE 25-8    Two possible configurations of a node $N$ that has two children

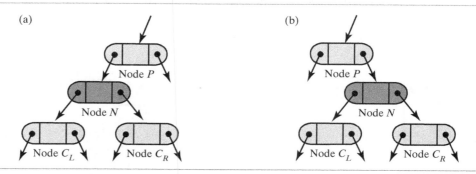

**25.23**    We know that the entries in the tree are distinct. Let $e$ be the entry in node $N$. Since node $N$ has two children, $e$ is larger than the entry in $N$'s left child and smaller than the entry in $N$'s right child. Thus, $e$ cannot be the smallest entry in the tree, nor can it be the largest. So, if we imagine the tree's entries in ascending order, we can write

$$... a < e < b ...$$

Here, $a$ is the entry that is immediately before $e$, and $b$ is the one that is immediately after. An in-order traversal of the tree would visit these entries in this same order. Thus, $a$ is called the **inorder predecessor** of $e$, and $b$ is the **inorder successor** of $e$.

The entry $a$ must occur in a node in $N$'s left subtree; $b$ is in a node in $N$'s right subtree, as Figure 25-9a illustrates. Moreover, $a$ is the largest entry in $N$'s left subtree, since $a$ is the entry that is immediately before $e$. Suppose that we are able to delete the node that contains $a$ and replace $e$ with $a$, as Figure 25-9b shows. Now all of the remaining entries in $N$'s left subtree are less than $a$, as needed. All of the entries in $N$'s right subtree are greater than $e$ and so are greater than $a$. Thus, we still have a binary search tree.

FIGURE 25-9    Node $N$ and its subtrees: (a) the entry $a$ is immediately before the entry $e$, and $b$ is immediately after $e$; (b) after deleting the node that contained $a$ and replacing $e$ with $a$

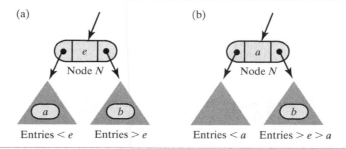

**25.24    Locating the entry $a$.** The previous segment assumed that we could find the appropriate entry $a$ and delete its node. So, let's locate the node that contains $a$ and verify that it does not have two children. Consider again the original tree in Figure 25-9a. We already know that $a$ must be in $N$'s left subtree, and that $a$ is the largest entry in that subtree. To find an entry larger than the one in any given node, we look at the node's right child. Thus, $a$ occurs in the subtree's rightmost node $R$, as Figure 25-10 illustrates. Node $R$ cannot have a right child, because if it did, the child's entry would be greater than $a$. Therefore, node $R$ has no more than one child and so can be removed from the tree easily.

FIGURE 25-10    The largest entry *a* in node *N*'s left subtree occurs in the subtree's rightmost
node *R*

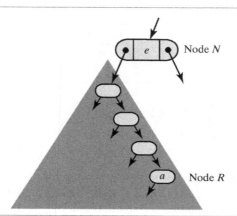

**25.25**   The following pseudocode summarizes this discussion:

> ***Algorithm Remove the entry e from a node N that has two children***
> *Find the rightmost node R in N's left subtree*
> *Replace the entry in node N with the entry that is in node R*
> *Delete node R*

An alternate approach involves *b*, the entry in Figure 25-9a that is immediately after *e* in sorted order. We have already noted that *b* occurs in *N*'s right subtree. It would have to be the smallest entry in that subtree, so it would occur in the leftmost node in the subtree. Thus, we have the following alternate pseudocode:

> ***Algorithm Remove the entry e from a node N that has two children***
> *Find the leftmost node L in N's right subtree*
> *Replace the entry in node N with the entry that is in node L*
> *Delete node L*

Both approaches work equally well.

 **Note:** To remove an entry whose node has two children, you first replace the entry with another whose node has no more than one child. You then remove the second node from the binary search tree.

**25.26**    **Example.** Figure 25-11 shows several consecutive removals from a binary search tree of names. The first algorithm given in the previous segment is used. To remove *Chad* from the tree in Figure 25-11a, we replace it with its inorder predecessor *Brittany*. We then remove the node that contained *Brittany* to get the tree in Figure 25-11b. To remove *Sean* from this new tree, we replace it with its inorder predecessor *Reba* and remove *Reba*'s original node. This gives us the tree in Figure 25-11c. Finally, to remove *Kathy* from this tree, we replace it with its inorder predecessor *Doug* and remove *Doug*'s original node, to get the tree in Figure 25-11d.

**FIGURE 25-11** (a) A binary search tree; (b) after removing *Chad*; (c) after removing *Sean*; (d) after removing *Kathy*

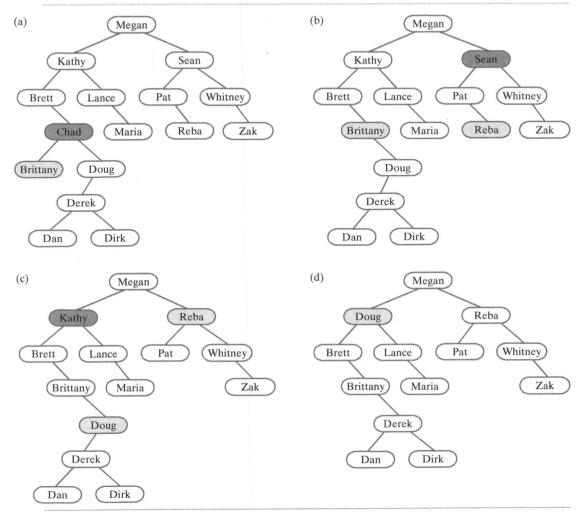

**Question 7** The second algorithm described in Segment 25.25 involves the inorder successor. Using this algorithm, remove *Sean* and *Chad* from the tree in Figure 25-11a.

**Question 8** Remove *Megan* from the tree in Figure 25-11a in two different ways.

## Removing an Entry in the Root

**25.27** Removing an entry that is in the root of the tree is a special case only if we actually remove the root node. That will occur when the root has at most one child. If the root has two children, the previous segment shows that we would replace the root's entry and delete a different node.

If the root is a leaf, the tree has only one node. Deleting it results in an empty tree. If the root has one child, as Figure 25-12 illustrates, the child is either a right child or a left child. In either case, we simply delete the root node by making the child node *C* the root of the tree.

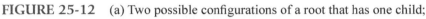

FIGURE 25-12    (a) Two possible configurations of a root that has one child;
(b) after removing the root

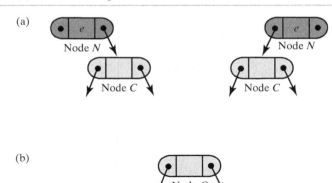

## A Recursive Implementation

**25.28**    **The algorithm.** The entry to be removed from the tree is the one that matches the object passed
to the method remove as its argument. The method returns the removed entry. The following
recursive algorithm describes the method's logic at a high level:

```
Algorithm remove(binarySearchTree, entry)
oldEntry = null
if (binarySearchTree is not empty)
{
    if (entry matches the entry in the root of binarySearchTree)
    {
        oldEntry = entry in root
        removeFromRoot(root of binarySearchTree)
    }
    else if (entry < entry in root)
        oldEntry = remove(left subtree of binarySearchTree, entry)
    else // entry > entry in root
        oldEntry = remove(right subtree of binarySearchTree, entry)
}
return oldEntry
```

The method removeFromRoot will remove the entry in the root of a given subtree based on how
many children belong to the root.

**25.29**    **The public method remove.** We have several details to consider before implementing the previous algorithm. The public method remove should have only one parameter—entry—so just as
the method add calls the private recursive method addEntry, remove will call a private recursive
method removeEntry.

As we mentioned in Segment 25.8, we will pass the root of the tree, instead of the tree itself,
to removeEntry. Since the method might remove the root node from the tree, we must be careful
to always retain a reference to the tree's root. As a result, we make removeEntry return a reference
to the root of the revised tree, which remove can save. But removeEntry must also give to remove
the entry it removes. A solution is to pass another parameter—oldEntry—to removeEntry and
have the method change its value to the removed entry. Thus, the header for removeEntry will be

```
private BinaryNode<T> removeEntry(BinaryNode<T> rootNode, T entry,
                                  ReturnObject oldEntry)
```

ReturnObject is an inner class that has a single data field and simple methods set and get to manipulate it. Initially, oldEntry's data field is null, since remove returns null when the entry is not found in the tree.

Thus, the public remove has the following implementation:

```java
public T remove(T entry)
{
    ReturnObject oldEntry = new ReturnObject(null);
    BinaryNode<T> newRoot = removeEntry(getRootNode(), entry, oldEntry);
    setRootNode(newRoot);

    return oldEntry.get();
} // end remove
```

**25.30**  **The private method removeEntry.** Since remove handles the communication with removeEntry, most of the algorithm of Segment 25.28 is left for removeEntry. If the entry to be removed is in the root, removeEntry calls the yet-to-be-written method removeFromRoot to remove it. If the entry is in either of the root's subtrees, removeEntry calls itself recursively. The implementation of removeEntry follows:

```java
// Removes an entry from the tree rooted at a given node.
// rootNode is a reference to the root of a tree.
// entry is the object to be removed.
// oldEntry is an object whose data field is null.
// Returns the root node of the resulting tree; if entry matches
//          an entry in the tree, oldEntry's data field is the entry
//          that was removed from the tree; otherwise it is null.
private BinaryNode<T> removeEntry(BinaryNode<T> rootNode, T entry,
                                  ReturnObject oldEntry)
{
    if (rootNode != null)
    {
        T rootData = rootNode.getData();
        int comparison = entry.compareTo(rootData);

        if (comparison == 0)      // entry == root entry
        {
            oldEntry.set(rootData);
            rootNode = removeFromRoot(rootNode);
        }
        else if (comparison < 0) // entry < root entry
        {
            BinaryNode<T> leftChild = rootNode.getLeftChild();
            BinaryNode<T> subtreeRoot = removeEntry(leftChild, entry, oldEntry);
            rootNode.setLeftChild(subtreeRoot);
        }
        else                      // entry > root entry
        {
            BinaryNode<T> rightChild = rootNode.getRightChild();
            rootNode.setRightChild(removeEntry(rightChild, entry, oldEntry));
        } // end if
    } // end if

    return rootNode;
} // end removeEntry
```

**25.31**  **The algorithm removeFromRoot.** The previous method removeEntry removes the entry in the root of a given subtree by calling the method removeFromRoot. In that method, we see whether the root node has zero, one, or two children and then proceed according to the discussion in Segments 25.20 through 25.27. If the given node has at most one child, we delete the node and its entry. To remove the entry in a node having two children, we must find the largest entry in the node's left subtree. We remove the node containing this largest entry. The largest entry then replaces the entry to be removed.

The following algorithm summarizes these steps:

*Algorithm* `removeFromRoot(rootNode)`
*// Removes the entry in a given root node of a subtree.*

`if` (rootNode *has two children*)
{
    `largestNode` = *node with the largest entry in the left subtree of* rootNode
    *Replace the entry in* rootNode *with the entry in* largestNode
    *Remove* largestNode *from the tree*
}
`else if` (rootNode *has a right child*)
    rootNode = rootNode*'s right child*
`else`
    rootNode = rootNode*'s left child* // *Possibly* null
*// Assertion: If* rootNode *was a leaf, it is now* null

`return` rootNode

**25.32**   **The private method `removeFromRoot`.** The implementation of the previous algorithm calls the private methods `findLargest` and `removeLargest`, which we will write shortly. Although `removeFromRoot` is not recursive, both `findLargest` and `removeLargest` are.

Given the root of a subtree, `removeFromRoot` returns the root of the subtree after a node is removed.

```
// Removes the entry in a given root node of a subtree.
// rootNode is the root node of the subtree.
// Returns the root node of the revised subtree.
private BinaryNode<T> removeFromRoot(BinaryNode<T> rootNode)
{
    // Case 1: rootNode has two children
    if (rootNode.hasLeftChild() && rootNode.hasRightChild())
    {
        // Find node with largest entry in left subtree
        BinaryNode<T> leftSubtreeRoot = rootNode.getLeftChild();
        BinaryNode<T> largestNode = findLargest(leftSubtreeRoot);

        // Replace entry in root
        rootNode.setData(largestNode.getData());

        // Remove node with largest entry in left subtree
        rootNode.setLeftChild(removeLargest(leftSubtreeRoot));
    } // end if

    // Case 2: rootNode has at most one child
    else if (rootNode.hasRightChild())
        rootNode = rootNode.getRightChild();
    else
        rootNode = rootNode.getLeftChild();

    // Assertion: If rootNode was a leaf, it is now null

    return rootNode;
} // end removeEntry
```

**25.33**   **The private method `findLargest`.** The node with the largest entry will occur in the rightmost node of a binary search tree. Thus, as long as a node has a right child, we search the subtree rooted at that child. The following recursive method performs this search, given the tree:

```
// Finds the node containing the largest entry in a given tree.
// rootNode is the root node of the tree.
// Returns the node containing the largest entry in the tree.
```

```java
private BinaryNode<T> findLargest(BinaryNode<T> rootNode)
{
    if (rootNode.hasRightChild())
        rootNode = findLargest(rootNode.getRightChild());

    return rootNode;
} // end findLargest
```

**25.34   The private method `removeLargest`.** To remove the node with the largest entry, we cannot simply call `findLargest` and then remove the returned node. We cannot remove a node from a tree knowing only its reference. We must have a reference to its parent as well. The following recursive method removes the node with the largest entry—that is, the rightmost node—but unfortunately it must repeat the search that `findLargest` just performed.

```java
// Removes the node containing the largest entry in a given tree.
// rootNode is the root node of the tree.
// Returns the root node of the revised tree.
private BinaryNode<T> removeLargest(BinaryNode<T> rootNode)
{
    if (rootNode.hasRightChild())
    {
        BinaryNode<T> rightChild = rootNode.getRightChild();
        rightChild = removeLargest(rightChild);
        rootNode.setRightChild(rightChild);
    }
    else
        rootNode = rootNode.getLeftChild();

    return rootNode;
} // end removeLargest
```

The method begins much like `findLargest`. To remove the rightmost node from the given tree, we remove the rightmost node from the tree's right subtree. The recursive call returns the root of the revised subtree. This root must become the right child of the original tree's root.

When a tree's root has no right child, the left child is returned, effectively deleting the root. Notice that this recursive method does not explicitly keep track of the parent of the current right child. Rather, a reference to this parent is retained in the implicit stack of the recursion.

**Note:** The previous recursive approach to removing an entry from a binary search tree is typical. A language, such as Java, that uses only call-by-value to pass arguments tends to complicate this recursive implementation by forcing methods to return references to root nodes. You might find the following iterative approach somewhat easier to understand. Since it deletes the node containing the inorder predecessor without repeating the search for it, the iterative remove is more efficient than the recursive version.

## An Iterative Implementation

**25.35   The algorithm.** Recall that the method `remove` is given an entry that matches the entry to be removed from the tree. So `remove`'s first step is to search the tree. We locate the node whose data matches the given entry, and we note the node's parent, if any. Whether we delete the node we've found or another one depends on how many children it has. Although Segment 25.19 listed three possibilities, we can collapse them into two cases:

1. The node has two children
2. The node has at most one child

In the second case, we delete the node itself. But if the node has two children, we delete another node that has at most one child. That is, we transform Case 1 into Case 2.

The following pseudocode describes what remove must do:

*Algorithm* remove(entry)
```
result = null
currentNode = node that contains a match for entry
parentNode = currentNode's parent

if (currentNode != null) // That is, if entry is found
{
    result = currentNode's data (the entry to be removed from the tree)

    // Case 1
    if (currentNode has two children)
    {
        // Get node to remove and its parent
        nodeToRemove = node containing entry's inorder predecessor; it has at most one child
        parentNode = nodeToRemove's parent

        Copy entry from nodeToRemove to currentNode
        currentNode = nodeToRemove
        // Assertion: currentNode is the node to be removed; it has at most one child
        // Assertion: Case 1 has been transformed to Case 2
    }

    // Case 2: currentNode has at most one child
    Delete currentNode from the tree
}

return result
```

**25.36  The public method remove.** We will implement the major steps of the previous algorithm as private methods that remove can call. The private method findNode locates the node that contains a match for the given entry. Since we need a reference to that node as well as one to its parent, we make findNode return a pair of nodes. To that end, we design a private class NodePair that has constructors and the accessor methods getFirst and getSecond. NodePair will be an inner class of our class BinarySearchTree.

The private method getNodeToRemove finds the node containing the inorder predecessor of the entry in a given node. Since we also need that node's parent, the method returns a pair of nodes as an instance of the class NodePair.

Finally, the private method removeNode deletes a node that has at most one child. We give the method references to the node and its parent, if any.

Using these private methods, we can implement remove as follows:

```java
public T remove(T entry)
{
    T result = null;

    // Locate node (and its parent) that contains a match for entry
    NodePair pair = findNode(entry);
    BinaryNode<T> currentNode = pair.getFirst();
    BinaryNode<T> parentNode = pair.getSecond();

    if (currentNode != null) // Entry is found
    {
        result = currentNode.getData(); // Get entry to be removed

        // Case 1: currentNode has two children
        if (currentNode.hasLeftChild() && currentNode.hasRightChild())
        {
            // Replace entry in currentNode with the entry in another node
            // that has at most one child; that node can be deleted
```

```
                         // Get node to remove (contains inorder predecessor; has at
                         // most one child) and its parent
                         pair = getNodeToRemove(currentNode);
                         BinaryNode<T> nodeToRemove = pair.getFirst();
                         parentNode = pair.getSecond();

                         // Copy entry from nodeToRemove to currentNode
                         currentNode.setData(nodeToRemove.getData());

                         currentNode = nodeToRemove;
                         // Assertion: currentNode is the node to be removed; it has at
                         //            most one child
                         // Assertion: Case 1 has been transformed to Case 2
                      } // end if

                      // Case 2: currentNode has at most one child; delete it
                      removeNode(currentNode, parentNode);
                   } // end if

                   return result;
                } // end remove
```

**25.37 The private method findNode.** To find the node that contains a match for a given entry, we use the compareTo method within a loop to compare the given entry with the other entries in the tree. The method returns a pair of references to the desired node and its parent as an instance of the class NodePair. Thus, findNode has the following form:

```
       private NodePair findNode(T entry)
       {
          NodePair result = new NodePair();
          boolean found = false;
          . . .
          if (found)
             result = new NodePair(currentNode, parentNode);
             // Located entry is currentNode.getData()

          return result;
       } // end findNode
```

The details of the implementation of findNode are left as an exercise.

**Question 9** Complete the implementation of the method findNode.

**25.38 The private method getNodeToRemove.** After remove locates the node that contains the entry to be removed from the tree, it proceeds according the number of the node's children. If the node has two children, remove must remove another node that has no more than one child. The private method getNodeToRemove finds this node. In particular, the method implements the first step of the pseudocode given in Segment 25.25:

*Find the rightmost node R in N's left subtree*

Here, node $N$ is currentNode and node $R$ is rightChild.

The details of this step are described by the following pseudocode:

```
       // Find the inorder predecessor by searching the left subtree; it will be the largest
       // entry in the subtree, occurring in the node as far right as possible
       leftSubtreeRoot = left child of currentNode
       rightChild = leftSubtreeRoot
       priorNode = currentNode
```

```
while (rightChild has a right child )
{
   priorNode = rightChild
   rightChild = right child of rightChild
}
// Assertion: rightChild is the node to be removed and has no more than one child
```

The following Java code implements getNodeToRemove:

```
private NodePair getNodeToRemove(BinaryNode<T> currentNode)
{
   // Find node with largest entry in left subtree by
   // moving as far right in the subtree as possible
   BinaryNode<T> leftSubtreeRoot = currentNode.getLeftChild();
   BinaryNode<T> rightChild = leftSubtreeRoot;
   BinaryNode<T> priorNode = currentNode;

   while (rightChild.hasRightChild())
   {
      priorNode = rightChild;
      rightChild = rightChild.getRightChild();
   } // end while

   // rightChild contains the inorder predecessor and is the node to
   // remove; priorNode is its parent

   return new NodePair(rightChild, priorNode);
} // end getNodeToRemove
```

**25.39 The private method removeNode.** Our last method assumes that the node to remove—call it nodeToRemove—has at most one child. If nodeToRemove is not the root, parentNode is its parent.

The method begins by setting childNode to the child, if any, of nodeToRemove. If nodeToRemove is a leaf, childNode is set to null. Then the method removes nodeToRemove, accounting for the case when the node is the root as follows:

```
if (nodeToRemove is the root of the tree)
   Set the root of the tree to childNode
else
   Link parentNode to childNode, thereby deleting nodeToRemove
```

If we set the root of the tree to childNode, realize that we will correctly set the root to null if nodeToRemove is a leaf.

The implementation of removeNode follows:

```
private void removeNode(BinaryNode<T> nodeToRemove, BinaryNode<T> parentNode)
{
   BinaryNode<T> childNode;

   if (nodeToRemove.hasLeftChild())
      childNode = nodeToRemove.getLeftChild();
   else
      childNode = nodeToRemove.getRightChild();

   // Assertion: If nodeToRemove is a leaf, childNode is null
   assert (nodeToRemove.isLeaf() && childNode == null) ||
          !nodeToRemove.isLeaf();

   if (nodeToRemove == getRootNode())
      setRootNode(childNode);
   else if (parentNode.getLeftChild() == nodeToRemove)
      parentNode.setLeftChild(childNode);
   else
      parentNode.setRightChild(childNode);
} // end removeNode
```

## The Efficiency of Operations

**25.40** Each of the operations add, remove, and getEntry requires a search that begins at the root of the tree. When adding an entry, the search ends at a leaf if the entry is not already in the tree; otherwise, the search can end sooner. When removing or retrieving an entry, the search ends at a leaf if it is unsuccessful; a successful search can end sooner. So in the worst case, these searches begin at the root and examine each node on a path that ends at a leaf. The longest path from the root to a leaf has a length that equals the height of the tree. Thus, the maximum number of comparisons that each operation requires is directly proportional to the height $h$ of the tree. That is, the operations add, remove, and getEntry are O($h$).

Recall that several different binary search trees can contain the same data. Figure 25-13 contains two such trees. Figure 25-13a is the shortest binary search tree that we can form from this data; Figure 25-13b is the tallest such tree.

The tallest tree has height $n$ if it contains $n$ nodes. In fact, this tree looks like a linked chain, and searching it is like searching a linked chain. It is an O($n$) operation. Thus, add, remove, and getEntry for this tree are also O($n$) operations.

In contrast, the shortest tree is full. Searching this tree will be as efficient as possible. In Chapter 23, we saw that the height of a full tree containing $n$ nodes is $\log_2 (n + 1)$. Thus, in the worst case, searching a full binary search tree is an O(log $n$) operation. So add, remove, and getEntry are O(log $n$) operations in this case.

**Question 10** Using Big Oh notation, what is the time complexity of the method contains?

**Question 11** Using Big Oh notation, what is the time complexity of the method isEmpty?

**FIGURE 25-13**   Two binary search trees that contain the same data

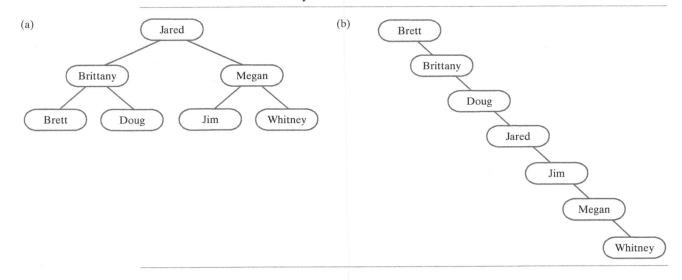

## The Importance of Balance

**25.41**    We do not need a full binary search tree to get O(log $n$) performance from the addition, removal, and retrieval operations. For example, if we remove some of the leaves from a full tree, we will not change the performance of these operations. In particular, a complete tree will also give us O(log $n$) performance.

It happens that the concept of balance, as introduced in Segment 23.10 of Chapter 23, affects the performance of a particular search tree. In fact, the addition, removal, and retrieval operations of a binary search tree will have O(log $n$) performance if the tree is height balanced. Certainly when we create a binary search tree, we want it to be height balanced. Unfortunately, we can disturb the balance of a binary search tree by adding or removing entries, since these operations affect the shape of the tree.

## The Order in Which Nodes Are Added

**25.42**    If you answered Question 6 in Segment 25.12 correctly, you realized that the order in which you add entries to a binary search tree affects the shape of the tree. This observation is most important when you create a binary search tree by making additions to an initially empty tree.

For example, suppose that we want to create the full binary search tree in Figure 25-13a from a given set of data. Often such data sets are sorted, so it is reasonable to assume that we have the names in alphabetical order. Now imagine that we define an empty binary search tree and then add the names to it in alphabetical order as follows: *Brett*, *Brittany*, *Doug*, *Jared*, *Jim*, *Megan*, *Whitney*. Figure 25-13b shows the tree that results from these additions. It is as tall as possible and has the least efficient operations among the trees that we could build.

 **Note:** If you add entries into an initially empty binary search tree, do not add them in sorted order.

**25.43**    In what order should we add the entries? *Jared* is the root of the tree in Figure 25-13a, so let's add *Jared* first. Next add *Brittany* and then *Brett* and *Doug*. Finally, add *Megan*, *Jim*, and *Whitney*. While it should be clear that by using this order we get the tree in Figure 25-13a, how do we determine the order ahead of time? Looking at our alphabetical set of names, notice that *Jared* is exactly in the middle. We add *Jared* first. *Brittany* is in the middle of the left half of the data set, so we add *Brittany* next. The halves that *Brittany* defines each contain only one name, so we add them next. We repeat this process with the names that occur after *Jared*—that is, the right half of the data set.

We shouldn't have to do this much work! In fact, if we add data to a binary search tree in random order, we can expect a tree whose operations are O(log $n$). It probably will not be the shortest tree we could create, but it will be close.

The operations of a binary search tree ensure that the tree remains a binary search tree. Unfortunately, they do not ensure that the tree remains balanced. Chapter 27 looks at search trees that are responsible for maintaining their balance, and hence their efficiency.

# An Implementation of the ADT Dictionary

**25.44**    We can use the ideas developed thus far in this chapter to implement the ADT dictionary. Recall from Chapter 19 that a dictionary stores search keys and their associated values. For example, suppose that you want a dictionary of names and telephone numbers. In terms of the ADT dictionary, the name could be the search key and the telephone number could be the corresponding value. To retrieve a telephone number, we would provide a name, and the dictionary would return its value.

Here is the interface for a dictionary as given in Segment 19.4, but without the comments:

```
import java.util.Iterator;
public interface DictionaryInterface<K, V>
{
    public V add(K key, V value);
    public V remove(K key);
    public V getValue(K key);
    public boolean contains(K key);
    public Iterator<K> getKeyIterator();
    public Iterator<V> getValueIterator();
    public boolean isEmpty();
    public int getSize();
    public void clear();
} // end DictionaryInterface
```

Chapter 20 suggested several implementations of the ADT dictionary. A dictionary implementation that uses a balanced search tree to store its entries can be an attractive alternative to these implementations. As an example of such an implementation, we will use a binary search tree here, even though it might not remain balanced after additions or removals. Chapter 27 presents search trees that are always balanced and could be used instead to implement the dictionary.

**25.45**    **The data entries.** We need a class of data objects that will contain both a search key and an associated value. A class `Entry`—similar to the class we used in the array-based implementation of the ADT dictionary in Chapter 20—is suitable for our purpose. Here we make the class `Comparable` by defining the method `compareTo`. This method compares two instances of `Entry` by comparing their search keys. Thus, the search keys of this dictionary must belong to a `Comparable` class.

The class `Entry` can be private and internal to the class `Dictionary`, as Listing 25-3 shows. This listing also shows `Dictionary`'s data field—a binary search tree—as well as the constructor that allocates the tree. Notice how `Entry` is used in both the declaration and allocation of the tree.

LISTING 25-3    An outline of an implementation of the ADT dictionary that uses a binary search tree

```
 1  import TreePackage.SearchTreeInterface;
 2  import TreePackage.BinarySearchTree;
 3  import java.util.Iterator;
 4  public class BstDictionary<K extends Comparable<? super K>, V>
 5          implements DictionaryInterface<K, V>
 6  {
 7      private SearchTreeInterface<Entry<K, V>> bst;
 8
 9      public BstDictionary()
10      {
11          bst = new BinarySearchTree<>();
12      } // end default constructor
13
14      < Methods that implement dictionary operations are here. >
15      . . .
16
17      private class Entry<S extends Comparable<? super S>, T>
18              implements Comparable<Entry<S, T>>
19      {
20          private S key;
21          private T value;
22
23          private Entry(S searchKey, T dataValue)
24          {
```

```
25       key = searchKey;
26       value = dataValue;
27    } // end constructor
28
29    public int compareTo(Entry<S, T> other)
30    {
31       return key.compareTo(other.key);
32    } // end compareTo
33
34    < The class Entry also defines the methods equals, toString, getKey, getValue,
35      and setValue; no setKey method is provided. >
36    . . .
37    } // end Entry
38 } // end BstDictionary
```

**25.46**    **The BstDictionary methods.** The method add encapsulates the given search key and value into an instance of Entry that it passes to BinarySearchTree's add method. It then uses the entry that this method returns to form its own return value. BstDictionary's add method has the following implementation:

```
public V add(K key, V value)
{
   Entry<K, V> newEntry = new Entry<>(key, value);
   Entry<K, V> returnedEntry = bst.add(newEntry);

   V result = null;
   if (returnedEntry != null)
      result = returnedEntry.getValue();

   return result;
} // end add
```

Both remove and getValue have implementations that are similar to add's. Since these methods have only a search key as a parameter, the instances of Entry that they form encapsulate the key and a null value. For example, remove begins as

```
public V remove(K key)
{
   Entry<K, V> findEntry = new Entry<>(key, null);
   Entry<K, V> returnedEntry = bst.remove(findEntry);
```

and ends just like the method add. The implementation of the method getValue is identical to that of remove, except that it calls getEntry from BinarySearchTree instead of remove.

We can implement the methods getSize, isEmpty, contains, and clear by calling appropriate methods of BinarySearchTree. We leave these to you as exercises.

**Question 12** Implement each of the BstDictionary methods getSize, isEmpty, contains, and clear by calling methods of BinarySearchTree.

**Question 13** Write another implementation of the method contains by invoking BstDictionary's method getValue.

**25.47**    **The iterators.** DictionaryInterface specifies two methods that return iterators. The method getKeyIterator returns an iterator that accesses the search keys in sorted order; getValueIterator returns an iterator that provides the values belonging to these search keys.

For example, getKeyIterator has the following implementation:

```
public Iterator<K> getKeyIterator()
{
    return new KeyIterator();
} // end getKeyIterator
```

The class KeyIterator is internal to BstDictionary and uses the method getInorderIterator from BinarySearchTree. It has the following implementation:

```
private class KeyIterator implements Iterator<K>
{
    Iterator<Entry<K, V>> localIterator;

    public KeyIterator()
    {
        localIterator = bst.getInorderIterator();
    } // end default constructor

    public boolean hasNext()
    {
        return localIterator.hasNext();
    } // end hasNext

    public K next()
    {
        Entry<K, V> nextEntry = localIterator.next();
        return nextEntry.getKey();
    } // end next

    public void remove()
    {
        throw new UnsupportedOperationException();
    } // end remove
} // end KeyIterator
```

You implement getValueIterator in a similar manner.

**25.48 Comments.** This implementation of the ADT dictionary is as time efficient as the underlying search tree. When the binary search tree is balanced, the operations are O(log $n$). But a binary search tree can lose its balance, and so the efficiency of the dictionary operations can degrade to O($n$) as entries are added or removed. A search tree that stays balanced, such as those you will see in Chapter 27, would provide a better implementation of the dictionary than the one shown here.

Also, notice that a binary search tree maintains the dictionary entries in sorted order by their search keys. As a result, getKeyIterator enables us to traverse the search keys in sorted order. In contrast, other dictionary implementations—hashing, for example—traverse the search keys in unsorted order.

## CHAPTER SUMMARY

- A binary search tree is a binary tree whose nodes contain Comparable objects. For each node in the tree,

  - The data in a node is greater than the data in the node's left subtree
  - The data in a node is less than (or equal to) the data in the node's right subtree

- A search tree has the operations contains, getEntry, add, remove, and getInorderIterator, in addition to the operations common to all trees.

- The class BinarySearchTree can be a subclass of BinaryTree, but it must disallow setTree. To avoid changing the order of the nodes in the tree, a client must create a binary search tree by using only the add method.

- The search algorithm to locate an entry in a binary search tree forms the basis of the methods getEntry, add, and remove. These methods each have reasonable iterative and recursive implementations.

- Each addition of an entry to a binary search tree adds a leaf to the tree. The new entry is placed where the search algorithm will find it.

- Removing an entry from a binary search tree depends on the number of children that belong to the node containing the entry. When the node is a leaf or has one child, you remove the node itself. The node's parent can adopt a solitary child when it exists. However, when the node $N$ has two children, you replace the node's entry with another one $r$ whose node is easy to remove. To maintain the order of the binary search tree, this entry $r$ can be either the largest entry in $N$'s left subtree or the smallest entry in $N$'s right subtree. It follows that $r$'s node is either a leaf or a node with one child.

- The retrieve, add, and remove operations on a binary search tree can be as fast as $O(\log n)$ or as slow as $O(n)$. The performance of the search depends on the shape of the tree. When the tree is height balanced, the operations on a binary search tree are $O(\log n)$.

- The order in which you add entries to a binary search tree affects the tree's shape and hence its balance. Random additions, as opposed to sorted ones, tend to result in a balanced tree.

- You can implement the ADT dictionary by using a binary search tree. Although the implementation is not difficult to write, its efficiency can suffer if additions and removals destroy the balance of the tree.

## Exercises

1. Show the results of adding the following search keys to an initially empty binary search tree: 10, 5, 6, 13, 15, 8, 14, 7, 12, 4.

2. What ordering of the search keys 25, 63, 41, 13, 72, 18, 32, 59, 67 would result in the most balanced tree if they were added to an initially empty binary search tree?

3. Give four different orderings of the search keys 25, 63, 41, 13, 72, 18, 32, 59, 67 that would result in the least balanced tree if they were added to an initially empty binary search tree.

4. Write a recursive method that would find the mirror image of a binary search tree. The root of the given tree is passed as an input parameter.

5. Implement the method getEntry iteratively.

6. Remove *Doug* from the binary search tree pictured in Figure 25-11a. Then remove *Chad* in two different ways.

7. Write an algorithm that returns the largest key in a binary search tree.

8. Suppose that a node with two children contains an entry $e$, as Figure 25-9a illustrates. Show that you will have a binary search tree if you replace $e$ with its inorder successor $b$ and remove the node that contains $b$.

9. Why does an inorder traversal of a binary search tree visit the nodes in sorted search-key order? Use the definition of a binary search tree given in Segment 25.1.

10. Consider the full binary search tree pictured in Figure 25-13a. Now imagine that you traverse the tree and save its data in a file. If you then read the file and add the data to an initially empty binary search tree, what tree will you get if the traversal was

     **a.** Preorder          **b.** Inorder          **c.** Level order          **d.** Postorder

11. Imagine that you traverse a binary search tree and save its data in a file. If you then read the file and add the data to an initially empty binary search tree, what traversal should you use when writing the file so that the new tree is

    **a.** As tall as possible
    **b.** Identical to the original binary search tree

12. Segment 25.17 gave an iterative algorithm for the method `addEntry`. Implement the following alternate algorithm for this method:

```
Algorithm addEntry(binarySearchTree, newEntry)

result = null
currentNode = root node of binarySearchTree
parentNode = null

while (newEntry is not found and currentNode is not null)
{
    if (newEntry matches entry in currentNode)
    {
        result = entry in currentNode
        Replace entry in currentNode with newEntry
    }
    else if (newEntry < entry in currentNode)
    {
        parentNode = currentNode
        currentNode = the left child of currentNode
    }
    else // newEntry > entry in currentNode
    {
        parentNode = currentNode
        currentNode = the right child of currentNode
    }
}

if (newEntry is not found in the tree)
{
    Create a new node and place newEntry into it

    if (newEntry < entry in parentNode)
        Make the new node the left child of parentNode
    else
        Make the new node the right child of parentNode
}

return result
```

13. The methods `remove` and the recursive `removeEntry`, as described in Segments 25.28 through 25.30, use the inner class `ReturnObject`. In this way, `removeEntry` can convey to `remove` both the root of the revised tree and the entry it removed. Revise these methods to instead use a class `Pair<T1, T2>`, like the one given in Java Interlude 8. `Pair` will need accessor methods for its fields. The method `removeEntry` can then return the root and the removed entry as a `Pair` object.

14. Segment 25.43 builds a balanced binary search tree from one particular group of search keys. Generalize this approach, and write a recursive algorithm that creates a balanced binary search tree from a sorted collection of *n* items.

15. Write an algorithm that returns the smallest search key in a binary search tree.

16. Beginning with Segment 25.23, you saw how to find the inorder predecessor or the inorder successor of a node with two children. Unfortunately, this approach will not work for a leaf node. For a node with one child, the technique will find either the predecessor or the successor, but not both. Discuss how the structure of a node might be modified so that the inorder predecessor or the inorder successor can be found for any node.

17. Write an algorithm that returns the $k^{\text{th}}$ smallest value in a binary search tree containing at least two nodes.

18. Write a method for a binary search tree that receives a node as an input and returns the successor node.

19. Consider a method for a binary search tree that decides whether the tree is height balanced, as Segment 23.10 of Chapter 23 describes. The header of the method could be as follows:

    ```
    public boolean isBalanced()
    ```

    Write this method for the class BinarySearchTree. It should call a private recursive method of the same name.

20. Write a static method that accepts as its argument a BinaryTree object and returns true if the argument tree is a binary search tree. Examine each node in the given tree only once.

21. Consider two empty binary search trees that allow duplicate entries with the same search key. To one of the trees, add $m$ unique entries, each with a different search key. To the other, add each of these $m$ entries $k$ times for a total of $m \times k$ entries. Assuming that each entry is stored in a single node, compare the heights of the two trees. Discuss how the order in which entries are added to the second tree affects its height. Give the addition orders that lead to the tallest tree and the shortest tree.

22. Segment 25.4 describes a binary search tree that allows duplicates. You place the duplicate of an entry in the entry's right subtree.

    a. What is an advantage and a disadvantage of this scheme?
    b. Suppose that we change the definition of a binary search tree so that the duplicate of an entry can be in either the entry's right subtree or its left subtree. If we choose the subtree randomly, what is an advantage and a disadvantage of this scheme?

## PROJECTS

1. Specify and implement a class of binary search trees in which duplicate entries are allowed. Place the duplicate of an entry in the entry's right subtree, as suggested in Segment 25.4. Provide a method that searches the tree for a given entry and returns the first one it finds. Also, provide a similar method that returns a list of all entries that match the given one.

2. Repeat the previous project, but instead randomly place the duplicate of an entry in the entry's left or right subtree. Thus, we modify the definition of a binary search tree as follows:
   For each node in a binary search tree,

   • The data in a node is greater than *or equal to* the data in the node's left subtree
   • The data in a node is less than *or equal to* the data in the node's right subtree

   Searching for a duplicate must allow a search of both subtrees.

3. Implement the ADT sorted list by using a binary search tree.

4. Devise an algorithm that uses a binary search tree to sort an array of objects. Such a sort is called **tree sort**. Implement and test your algorithm. Discuss the time efficiency of your tree sort in both the average and worst cases.

5. Implement a binary search tree that includes the following methods based on Exercises 15 and 16:

```
/** @return  The entry with the smallest search key. */
public T getMin();

/** @return  The entry with the largest search key. */
public T getMax();

/** @return  Either the inorder predecessor of entry, or
             entry if it's the smallest item in the tree, or
             null if entry is not in the tree. */
public T getPredecessor(T entry);

/** @return  Either the inorder successor of entry, or
             entry if it's the largest item in the tree, or
             null if entry is not in the tree. */
public T getSuccessor(T entry);
```

6. Implement the class `ArrayBinarySearchTree` that extends `ArrayBinaryTree`, as described in Project 7 of Chapter 24.

7. Write Java code that creates a binary search tree from $n$ random integer values and returns the height of the search tree. Run the code for $n = 2^h - 1$, where $h$ ranges from 4 to 12. Compare the height of the randomly built search tree with $h$, the height of the shortest binary search tree.

8. Chapter 1 defined a set as a bag that does not permit duplicate entries. Define a class of sets that uses a binary search tree to store a set's entries.

9. Repeat Project 3 of Chapter 19, but use binary search trees to implement the two dictionaries. Write Java code that will create a balanced binary search tree within the first dictionary of the reserved words in the Java language. Why is it important that the search tree containing Java reserved words be balanced? Can you guarantee that the search tree of user-defined identifiers is also balanced?

10. Repeat Project 8 of Chapter 24, but use a binary search tree instead of a 26-ary tree.

11. Compare the performance of two binary search trees as more objects are added to them. Initially, one tree is balanced and the other is not.

    First modify `BinarySearchTreeInterface` and `BinarySearchTree` so that the add method returns the number of comparisons used. Then write a program that uses the new version of `BinarySearchTree`, as follows. Create two empty binary search trees. Associate two variables with each tree. One variable sums the number of comparisons used in adding values to a tree, and the other sums the heights of a tree at certain times following the insertion of several values. Name these variables `comparisonSum1`, `comparisonSum2`, `heightSum1`, and `heightSum2`.

    In a loop that executes 100 times, do the following:

    - Add the values 1000, 2000, 3000, 4000, 5000, 6000, and 7000 to both trees. In the first tree, add them in increasing order. In the second, add them in an order that forms a complete tree. Your first tree will be unbalanced, while the second tree will be balanced.
    - Generate 10 random values between 0 and 8000. Add these values to each tree in the same order. After each of these additions, update each tree's `comparisonSum` variable by the number of comparisons performed for the insertion.
    - Add each tree's height to its `heightSum` variable.
    - Clear the two trees.

After the loop ends, compute the average number of comparisons needed to insert values into each tree. (For each tree, divide its comparisonSum by 1000. Note that 1000 is 100—the number of iterations— multiplied by 10—the number of values inserted in one iteration.) Also compute the average height of each tree after the insertions. (Divide each heightSum variable by 100.) Display and record your results.

Run the program a second time, but instead add 100 random values between 0 and 8000 during each iteration of the loop. Run it a third time, but instead add 1000 random values. Discuss your results and draw a conclusion.

12. A *k*d-tree, or *k*-dimensional tree, is a binary tree that organizes points in *k*-dimensional space. Every node contains and represents a *k*-dimensional point. Every node *N* that is not a leaf corresponds to a hyperplane[1] that divides the space into two portions. Points to the left of the hyperplane are in *N*'s left subtree, and points to the right of the hyperplane are in *N*'s right subtree. The relationship between the *k*-dimensional space and a *k*d-tree enables you to use the tree to find all points within a given range—a *range search*—or to find the closest point to a given point—a *nearest-neighbor search*.

In this project, we will choose *k* to be 2 and consider two-dimensional space and a **2d-tree** whose nodes contain points in that space. In an attempt to avoid any confusion that the term "2d-tree" might cause, computer scientists commonly would describe the tree as a "2-dimensional *k*d-tree." We, however, will use the shorter name "2d-tree" here.

A 2d-tree generalizes a binary search tree in that it positions each node according to either the *x* or *y* coordinate of its data point. The coordinate choice depends on the level at which the node is inserted into the tree. The first point you insert into an empty tree is placed into a node that becomes the tree's root. If the next point to be inserted has an *x*-coordinate that is less than the *x*-coordinate of the point in the root, you place the new point into the left child of the root. Otherwise, you place it into the root's right child. Insertions at the next level—level 3—compare *y*-coordinates; insertions at level 4 compare *x*-coordinates, and so on.

For example, let's insert the points (50, 40), (40, 70), (80, 20), (90, 10), and (60, 30) into an initially empty 2d-tree. Figure 25-14 traces the construction of this tree. Part *a* shows the root containing the first point, (50, 40). (For the moment, ignore the drawings beneath the trees.) To insert (40, 70) into a child of the root, you compare 40, the point's *x*-coordinate, with 50, the *x*-coordinate of the point in the root. Since 40 is less than 50, the new point goes into the left child of the root, as Figure 25-14b shows. Similarly, since 80 is greater than 50, you place the next point, (80, 20), into the right child of the root (Figure 25-14c). To insert (90, 10), you begin at the tree's root and compare *x*-coordinates. Since 90 is greater than 50, you move to the root's right child and compare *y*-coordinates. We find that 10 is less than 20, so (90, 10) goes into the left child of the root's right child, as shown in Figure 25-14d. The final point, (60, 30), is positioned using similar steps to obtain the tree in Figure 25-14e.

The graphical significance of a 2d-tree is illustrated beneath the trees shown in Figure 25-14. We begin with a square that contains all of the points in the tree. For example, a 100 by 100 square, as shown in Figure 25-14a, will contain the five points in our example. By passing a vertical line through the *x*-coordinate of the point in the root, we divide the square into two regions. Any points in the root's left subtree will be to the left of this line, while points in the root's right subtree will lie to the right of the line. Figure 25-14b shows a horizontal line through the point (40, 70). Points in the left subtree of the node containing (40, 70) lie above this horizontal line and to the left of the vertical line; that is, they lie within the upper-left rectangle within the original square.

---

1.  A *hyperplane* in *k*-dimensional space is a ($k$ − 1)-dimensional surface, described by a single linear equation in *k* variables, that divides the space into two regions. For example, in 2-dimensional space, a straight line divides the space and is described by a linear equation in the variables *x* and *y*. In 3-dimensional space, a plane divides the space and is described by a linear equation in the variables *x* , *y*, and *z*.

Implement a 2d-tree, providing at least a method to insert a new point and a method to test whether a given point is in the tree.

FIGURE 25-14    The steps in creating a 2d-tree for five given points

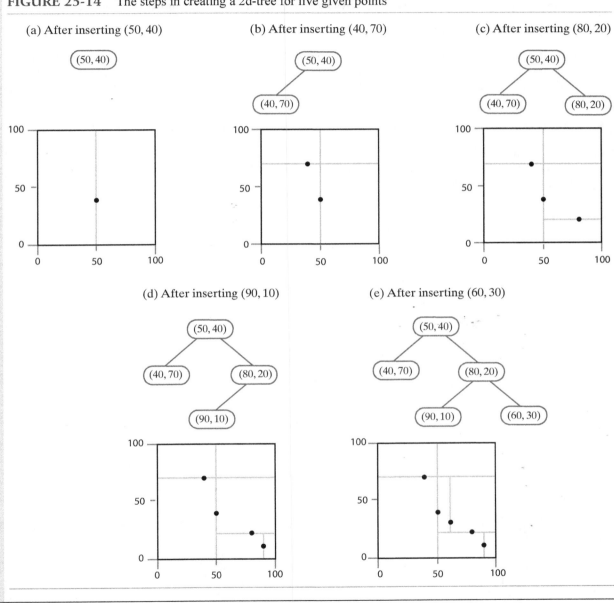

## ANSWERS TO SELF-TEST QUESTIONS

1. As the left child of the node that contains *Whitney*.

2. No. The constructor first calls the default constructor of `BinaryTree`, which sets `root` to `null`. The method `setRootData` contains the call `root.setData(rootData)`, which would cause an exception.

3. No; `BinarySearchTree` inherits these methods from `BinaryTree`.

4. The situation is like that described for `setTree` in Segment 25.6. `BinarySearchTree` inherits the methods declared in `TreeIteratorInterface` from `BinaryTree`. A client of `BinarySearchTree` can use an object whose static type is `BinarySearchTree` to invoke these methods, but it cannot use an object whose static type is `SearchTreeInterface` to do so.

5. *Chris* is the right child of *Chad*. *Jason* is the left child of *Jim*. *Kelley* is the right child of *Jim*.

6. When you add *Miguel* first, *Miguel* is the left child of *Whitney*, and *Nancy* is the right child of *Miguel*. When you add *Nancy* first, *Nancy* is the left child of *Whitney*, and *Miguel* is the left child of *Nancy*. Thus, the order of the additions does affect the tree that results.

7.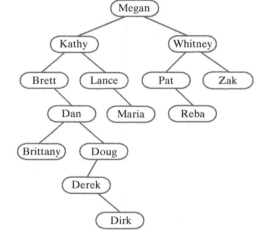

8.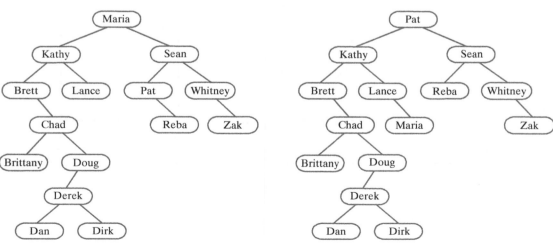

**9.**
```java
private NodePair findNode(T entry)
{
    NodePair result = new NodePair();
    boolean found = false;

    BinaryNode<T> currentNode = getRootNode();
    BinaryNode<T> parentNode = null;
    while (!found && (currentNode != null) )
    {
        T currentEntry = currentNode.getData();
        int comparison = entry.compareTo(currentEntry);

        if (comparison < 0)
        {
            parentNode = currentNode;
            currentNode = currentNode.getLeftChild();
        }
        else if (comparison > 0)
        {
            parentNode = currentNode;
            currentNode = currentNode.getRightChild();
        }
        else // comparison == 0
            found = true;
    } // end while

    if (found)
        result = new NodePair(currentNode, parentNode);
        // Located entry is currentNode.getData()
    return result;
} // end findNode
```

**10.** Since the method contains invokes getEntry, the efficiency of these methods is the same. So if the tree's height is as small as possible, the efficiency is $O(\log n)$. If the tree's height is as large as possible, the efficiency is $O(n)$.

**11.** $O(1)$.

**12.**
```java
public int getSize()
{
    return bst.getNumberOfNodes();
} // end getSize

public boolean isEmpty()
{
    return bst.isEmpty();
} // end isEmpty

public boolean contains(K key)
{
    Entry<K, V> findEntry = new Entry<>(key, null);

    return bst.contains(findEntry);
} // end contains
```

```java
public void clear()
{
   bst.clear();
} // end clear

public boolean contains(K key)
{
   return getValue(key) != null;
} // end contains
```

13.
```java
public boolean contains(K key)
{
   return getValue(key) != null;
} // end contains
```

# A Heap Implementation

## Contents

## Prerequisites

## Objectives

After studying this chapter, you should be able to

- Use an array to represent a heap
- Add an entry to an array-based heap
- Remove the root of an array-based heap
- Create a heap from given entries
- Sort an array by using a heap sort

**R**ecall from Chapter 23 that a heap is a complete binary tree whose nodes are ordered in a certain manner. When a binary tree is complete, you can use an array to represent it in an efficient and elegant way. The most common implementation of a heap uses an array, and that is the one we will describe in this chapter.

As you saw in Chapter 23, you can use a heap as an efficient implementation of the ADT priority queue. Later, this chapter will show you how to sort an array by using a heap.

## Reprise: The ADT Heap

26.1    A heap is a complete binary tree whose nodes contain `Comparable` objects. In a maxheap, the object in each node is greater than or equal to the objects in the node's descendants. Segment 23.34 provided the following interface for the maxheap:

```
public interface MaxHeapInterface<T extends Comparable<? super T>>
{
    public void add(T newEntry);
    public T removeMax();
    public T getMax();
    public boolean isEmpty();
    public int getSize();
    public void clear();
} // end MaxHeapInterface
```

We will use this interface in our implementation of a maxheap.

 **Note:** You may also have heard the word "heap" used to refer to the collection of memory cells that are available for allocation to your program when the `new` operator executes. But that heap is not an instance of the ADT heap that we will discuss in this chapter. It would be covered, however, in a book about programming languages.

## Using an Array to Represent a Heap

26.2    **Representing a complete binary tree.** We begin by using an array to represent a complete binary tree. A complete tree is full to its next-to-last level, and its leaves on the last level are filled in from left to right. Thus, until we get to the last leaf, a complete tree has no holes.

Suppose that we number the nodes in a complete binary tree in the order in which a level-order traversal would visit them, beginning with 1. Figure 26-1a shows such a tree numbered in this way. Now suppose that we place the result of this tree's level-order traversal into consecutive array locations beginning at index 1, as Figure 26-1b shows. This representation of the data in the tree enables us to implement any needed tree operations. By beginning at index 1 instead of 0, we can simplify the implementation somewhat, as you will see.

VideoNote
Implementing the ADT heap

26.3    Since the tree is complete, we can locate either the children or the parent of any node by performing a simple computation on the node's number. This number is the same as the node's corresponding array index. Thus, the children of the node $i$—if they exist—are stored in the array at indices $2i$ and $2i + 1$. The parent of this node is at array index $i/2$, unless, of course, the node is the root. In that case, $i/2$ is 0, since the root is at index 1. To detect the root, we can watch for either this index or a special value—called a **sentinel**—that we could place at index 0.

 **Note:** When a binary tree is complete, using an array instead of linked nodes is desirable. You can use a level-order traversal to store the tree's data into consecutive locations of an array. This representation enables you to quickly locate the data in a node's parent or children. If you begin storing the tree at index 1 of the array—that is, if you skip the array's first element—the node at array index $i$

- Has a parent at index $i/2$, unless the node is the root ($i$ is 1)
- Has any children at indices $2i$ and $2i + 1$

FIGURE 26-1    (a) A complete binary tree with its nodes numbered in level
order; (b) its representation as an array

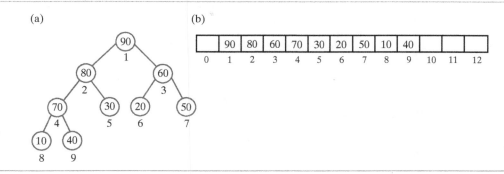

The complete binary tree in Figure 26-1a is actually a maxheap. We will now use its array
representation—as shown in Figure 26-1b—in our implementation of a maxheap.

**Question 1** If an array contains the entries of a heap in level order beginning at index 0, what
array entries represent a node's parent, left child, and right child?

26.4    **Beginning the class** MaxHeap. As Listing 26-1 shows, our class begins with the following data
fields: an array of Comparable heap entries, the index of the last entry in the array, and a constant
for the default capacity of the heap. If lastIndex is less than 1, the heap is empty, since we begin
the heap at index 1. Two constructors are similar to constructors we have seen before in array-
based implementations. We allocate one extra array location, since we will not use the first one.
The methods getMax, isEmpty, getSize, and clear have simple implementations that are shown
in this listing. We consider the methods add and removeMax next.

LISTING 26-1    The class MaxHeap, partially completed

```
1  import java.util.Arrays;
2  public final class MaxHeap<T extends Comparable<? super T>>
3              implements MaxHeapInterface<T>
4  {
5     private T[] heap;        // Array of heap entries
6     private int lastIndex; // Index of last entry
7     private boolean initialized = false;
8     private static final int DEFAULT_CAPACITY = 25;
9     private static final int MAX_CAPACITY = 10000;
10
11    public MaxHeap()
12    {
13       this(DEFAULT_CAPACITY); // Call next constructor
14    } // end default constructor
15
```

```java
public MaxHeap(int initialCapacity)
{
   // Is initialCapacity too small?
   if (initialCapacity < DEFAULT_CAPACITY)
      initialCapacity = DEFAULT_CAPACITY;
   else // Is initialCapacity too big?
      checkCapacity(initialCapacity);

   // The cast is safe because the new array contains all null entries
   @SuppressWarnings("unchecked")
   T[] tempHeap = (T[]) new Comparable[initialCapacity + 1];
   heap = tempHeap;
   lastIndex = 0;
   initialized = true;
} // end constructor

public void add(T newEntry)
{
   < See Segment 26.8. >
} // end add

public T removeMax()
{
   < See Segment 26.12. >
} // end removeMax

public T getMax()
{
   checkInitialization();
   T root = null;
   if (!isEmpty())
      root = heap[1];
   return root;
} // end getMax

public boolean isEmpty()
{
   return lastIndex < 1;
} // end isEmpty

public int getSize()
{
   return lastIndex;
} // end getSize

public void clear()
{
   checkInitialization();
   while (lastIndex > -1)
   {
      heap[lastIndex] = null;
      lastIndex--;
   } // end while
   lastIndex = 0;
} // end clear
< Private methods >
   . . .
} // end MaxHeap
```

# Adding an Entry

**26.5** **The basic algorithm.** The algorithm to add an entry to a heap is not difficult. Recall that in a maxheap, the object in a node is greater than or equal to its descendant objects. Suppose that we want to add 85 to the maxheap in Figure 26-1. We first would place the new entry as the next leaf in the tree. Figure 26-2a shows that we add 85 as a left child of the 30. Notice that we actually would place 85 at index 10 of the array in Figure 26-1b.

Figure 26-2a is no longer a heap, since 85 is out of place. To transform the tree into a heap, we let 85 *float up* to its correct location. Since 85 is larger than its parent, 30, we swap it with the parent, as Figure 26-2b shows. The 85 is still larger than its new parent, 80, so we swap again (Figure 26-2c). Now 85 is less than its parent, so we have transformed the tree in Figure 26-2a into a maxheap.

**FIGURE 26-2**    The steps in adding 85 to the maxheap in Figure 26-1a

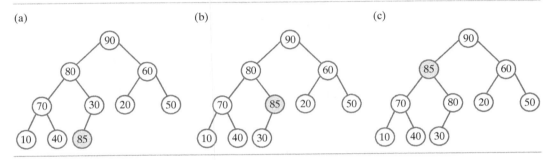

Question 2 What steps are necessary to add 100 to the heap in Figure 26-2c?

**26.6** **Avoiding swaps.** Although the swaps mentioned in the previous segment make the algorithm easier to understand and to describe, they require more work than is actually necessary. Instead of placing the new entry in the next available position within the tree, as we did in Figure 26-2a, we need only reserve space for it. In an array-based implementation, we simply check that the array is not full. Figure 26-3a shows the new child as an empty circle.

We then compare the new entry—the 85 in this example—with the parent of the new child. Since 85 is larger than 30, we move the 30 to the new child, as Figure 26-3b shows. We treat the node that originally contained 30 as if it were empty. We now compare 85 with the parent, 80, of the empty node. Since 85 is larger than 80, we move the 80 to the empty node, as Figure 26-3c shows. Since 85 is not larger than the next parent, 90, we place the new entry into the empty node, as Figure 26-3d shows.

> **Note:** To add a new entry to a heap, you begin at the next available position for a leaf. You follow a path from this leaf toward the root until you find the correct position for the new entry. As you do, you move entries from parent to child to ultimately make room for the new entry.

FIGURE 26-3    A revision of the steps to add 85, as shown in Figure 26-2, to
avoid swaps

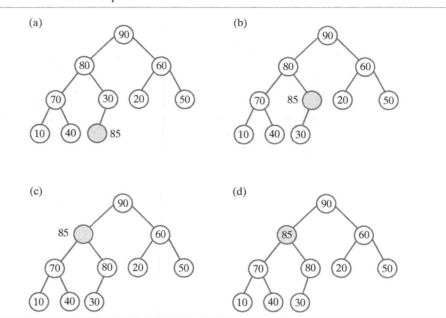

Figure 26-4 shows these same steps from the viewpoint of the array that represents the heap.
In Part *a*, which is analogous to Figure 26-3a, we note that we have room for a new entry at
index 10. The parent of this location is at location 10/2, or 5. We thus compare the new entry
85 to 30, the contents of the location at index 5. Since 85 > 30, we move 30 to the location at
index 10 (Figures 26-4b and 26-3b.) The remaining steps proceed in a similar fashion. Note that
Figure 26-4d corresponds to Figure 26-3c, and Figure 26-4f corresponds to Figure 26-3d.

26.7    **The refined algorithm.** The following algorithm summarizes the steps that add a new entry to a
heap. To ignore the first location of the array, we simply ensure that parentIndex is greater than 0.
Notice that the size of the array is expanded as necessary after the addition, as we did for AList's
add method in Chapter 13.

*Algorithm* **add(newEntry)**
*// Precondition: The array heap has room for another entry.*

```
newIndex = index of next available array location
parentIndex = newIndex/2                    // Index of parent of available location
while (parentIndex > 0 and newEntry > heap[parentIndex])
{
    heap[newIndex] = heap[parentIndex]    // Move parent to available location

    // Update indices
    newIndex = parentIndex
    parentIndex = newIndex/2
}

heap[newIndex] = newEntry                   // Place new entry in correct location
if (the array heap is full)
    Double the size of the array
```

FIGURE 26-4    An array representation of the steps in Figure 26-3

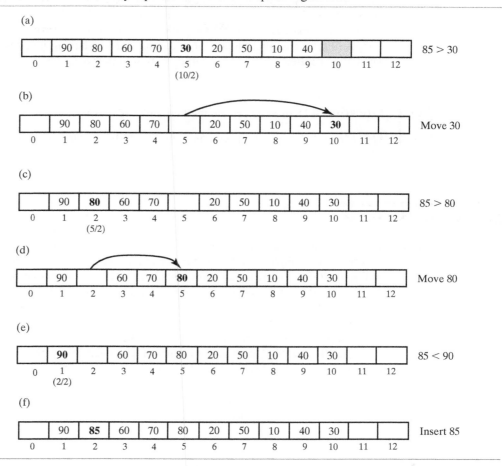

(a)

| | 90 | 80 | 60 | 70 | **30** | 20 | 50 | 10 | 40 | | | | 85 > 30 |
| 0 | 1 | 2 | 3 | 4 | 5 | 6 | 7 | 8 | 9 | 10 | 11 | 12 | |

(10/2)

(b)

| | 90 | 80 | 60 | 70 | | 20 | 50 | 10 | 40 | **30** | | | Move 30 |
| 0 | 1 | 2 | 3 | 4 | 5 | 6 | 7 | 8 | 9 | 10 | 11 | 12 | |

(c)

| | 90 | **80** | 60 | 70 | | 20 | 50 | 10 | 40 | 30 | | | 85 > 80 |
| 0 | 1 | 2 | 3 | 4 | 5 | 6 | 7 | 8 | 9 | 10 | 11 | 12 | |

(5/2)

(d)

| | 90 | | 60 | 70 | **80** | 20 | 50 | 10 | 40 | 30 | | | Move 80 |
| 0 | 1 | 2 | 3 | 4 | 5 | 6 | 7 | 8 | 9 | 10 | 11 | 12 | |

(e)

| | **90** | | 60 | 70 | 80 | 20 | 50 | 10 | 40 | 30 | | | 85 < 90 |
| 0 | 1 | 2 | 3 | 4 | 5 | 6 | 7 | 8 | 9 | 10 | 11 | 12 | |

(2/2)

(f)

| | 90 | **85** | 60 | 70 | 80 | 20 | 50 | 10 | 40 | 30 | | | Insert 85 |
| 0 | 1 | 2 | 3 | 4 | 5 | 6 | 7 | 8 | 9 | 10 | 11 | 12 | |

**Question 3** Repeat Question 2 using the previous algorithm without swaps. Show the heap at each step as a tree and as an array.

**26.8**    **The method add.** We now closely follow the previous algorithm to implement the method add.

```java
public void add(T newEntry)
{
   checkInitialization();          // Ensure initialization of data fields
   int newIndex = lastIndex + 1;
   int parentIndex = newIndex / 2;
   while ( (parentIndex > 0) && newEntry.compareTo(heap[parentIndex]) > 0)
   {
      heap[newIndex] = heap[parentIndex];
      newIndex = parentIndex;
      parentIndex = newIndex / 2;
   } // end while

   heap[newIndex] = newEntry;
   lastIndex++;
   ensureCapacity();
} // end add
```

We can omit the test of parentIndex in the while statement if we place a sentinel value in the unused array location at index 0. We can use newEntry as this sentinel. You should answer Question 5 and convince yourself that this change will work.

In the worst case, this method follows a path from a leaf to the root. In Segment 23.11 of Chapter 23, we saw that the height of a complete tree having $n$ nodes is $\log_2 (n + 1)$ rounded up. Thus, the add method is an $O(\log n)$ operation in the worst case.

**Question 4** Define the private method ensureCapacity.

**Question 5** Revise the previous method add by placing newEntry as a sentinel value in the unused array location at index 0. You then can omit the test of parentIndex in the while statement.

# Removing the Root

**26.9**    **The basic algorithm.** The removeMax method for a maxheap removes and returns the heap's largest object. This object is in the root of the maxheap. Let's remove the entry in the root of the heap in Figure 26-3d. Figure 26-5a shows this heap as if its root was empty.

We do not want to rip the root node out of the heap, as this will leave two disjoint subtrees. Instead we remove a leaf, namely the last one in the heap. To do so, we copy the leaf's data—30—to the root and then remove the leaf from the tree, as Figure 26-5b illustrates. Of course, in the array-based implementation, removing this leaf simply means adjusting lastIndex.

The 30 is out of place, so we no longer have a heap. We let the 30 *sink down* to its correct location. As long as 30 is less than its children, we swap it with its larger child. Thus, in Figure 26-5c, we have swapped 30 and 85. Continuing, we swap 30 and 80, as Figure 26-5d shows. In this case the 30 has settled at a leaf. In general, the out-of-place entry will settle at a node whose children are not greater than the entry.

**Question 6** What steps are necessary to remove the root from the heap in Figure 26-5d?

**26.10**    **Transforming a semiheap into a heap.** The tree in Figure 26-5b is called a **semiheap**. Except for the root, the objects in a semiheap are ordered as they are in a heap. In removing the root of the heap, we formed a semiheap and then transformed it back into a heap. As in the method add, we can save time by not swapping entries. Figure 26-6 shows the semiheap from Figure 26-5b and the steps that transform it into a heap without the swaps.

**FIGURE 26-5**     The steps to remove the entry in the root of the maxheap in
Figure 26-3d

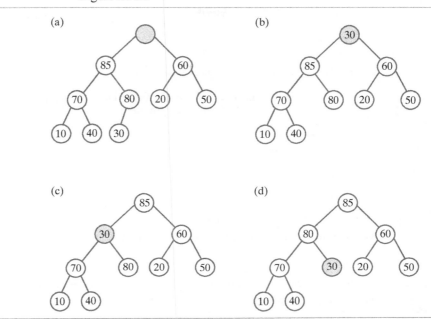

**FIGURE 26-6**     The steps that transform a semiheap into a heap without swaps

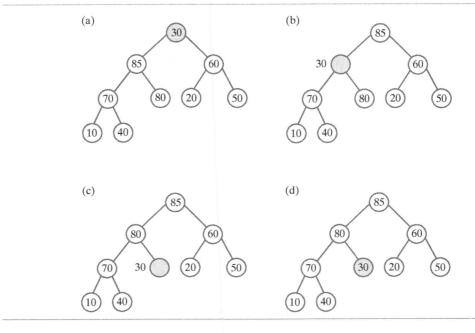

The following algorithm transforms a semiheap to a heap. To make the algorithm more general, we assume that the root of the semiheap is at a given index instead of at index 1.

*Algorithm* `reheap(rootIndex)`
*// Transforms the semiheap rooted at* `rootIndex` *into a heap*

```
done = false
orphan = heap[rootIndex]

while (!done and heap[rootIndex] has a child)
{
    largerChildIndex = index of the larger child of heap[rootIndex]
    if (orphan < heap[largerChildIndex])
    {
        heap[rootIndex] = heap[largerChildIndex]
        rootIndex = largerChildIndex
    }
    else
        done = true
}

heap[rootIndex] = orphan
```

As you will see, this algorithm has several uses.

**Question 7** Show the contents of the array `heap` as you trace the steps of the algorithm `reheap` that correspond to those pictured in Figure 26-6.

26.11 **The method reheap.** The implementation of the `reheap` algorithm as a private method follows:

```
private void reheap(int rootIndex)
{
    boolean done = false;
    T orphan = heap[rootIndex];
    int leftChildIndex = 2 * rootIndex;
    while (!done && (leftChildIndex <= lastIndex) )
    {
        int largerChildIndex = leftChildIndex; // Assume larger
        int rightChildIndex = leftChildIndex + 1;
        if ( (rightChildIndex <= lastIndex) &&
            heap[rightChildIndex].compareTo(heap[largerChildIndex]) > 0)
        {
            largerChildIndex = rightChildIndex;
        } // end if

        if (orphan.compareTo(heap[largerChildIndex]) < 0)
        {
            heap[rootIndex] = heap[largerChildIndex];
            rootIndex = largerChildIndex;
            leftChildIndex = 2 * rootIndex;
        }
```

```
        else
            done = true;
    } // end while
    heap[rootIndex] = orphan;
} // end reheap
```

In the worst case, the method reheap follows a path from the root to a leaf. The number of nodes along this path is less than or equal to the height $h$ of the heap. Thus, reheap is O($h$). Recall that the height of a complete $n$-node tree is $\log_2 (n + 1)$ rounded up, so reheap is an O(log $n$) operation.

**26.12**  **The method removeMax.** The method removeMax replaces the heap's root with its last leaf to form a semiheap like the one in Figure 26-6a. The method then calls reheap to transform the semiheap back into a heap. Thus, removeMax has the following implementation:

```
public T removeMax()
{
    checkInitialization();             // Ensure initialization of data fields
    T root = null;

    if (!isEmpty())
    {
        root = heap[1];                // Return value
        heap[1] = heap[lastIndex];     // Form a semiheap
        lastIndex--;                   // Decrease size
        reheap(1);                     // Transform to a heap
    } // end if

    return root;
} // end removeMax
```

Since reheap is an O(log $n$) operation in the worst case, so is removeMax.

**Note:** To remove a heap's root, you first replace the root with the heap's last leaf. This step forms a semiheap, so you use the method reheap to transform the semiheap to a heap.

# Creating a Heap

**26.13**  **Using add.** We could create a heap from a collection of objects by using the add method to add each object to an initially empty heap. Figure 26-7 shows the steps that this approach would take to add 20, 40, 30, 10, 90, and 70 to a heap. Since add is an O(log $n$) operation, creating the heap in this manner would be O($n$ log $n$).

Notice that we have a heap after each addition. This process does more than we really need. With less work, we can create one heap from a collection of objects without maintaining a heap at each intermediate step, as the next segment shows.

**26.16**   **Another constructor.** We can use the technique described in Segment 26.14 to implement another constructor for the class MaxHeap. Suppose that *n* entries for our heap are given in an array of exactly *n* locations. The following constructor takes this array, copies it into the data field heap, and uses reheap to create a heap. Although the entries in the given array begin at index 0, we place them into the array heap beginning at index 1. Note that this constructor calls MaxHeap's second constructor, thereby verifying the required capacity and allocating the array heap.

```java
public MaxHeap(T[] entries)
{
    this(entries.length); // Call other constructor
    assert initialized = true;

    // Copy given array to data field
    for (int index = 0; index < entries.length; index++)
        heap[index + 1] = entries[index];

    // Create heap
    for (int rootIndex = lastIndex / 2; rootIndex > 0; rootIndex--)
        reheap(rootIndex);
} // end constructor
```

## Heap Sort

**26.17**   We can use a heap to sort an array. If we place the array items into a maxheap and then remove them one at a time, we will get the items in descending order. We saw in Segments 26.13 and 26.14 that using reheap instead of add is a more efficient way to create a heap from an array of items. In fact, we wrote a constructor in the previous segment that invoked reheap for this purpose. So if myArray is the array of items—strings, for example—we could use this constructor to create the heap, as follows:

VideoNote
The heap sort

```java
MaxHeapInterface<String> myHeap = new MaxHeap<>(myArray);
```

As we remove the items from myHeap, we could place them in order back into myArray. The problem with this approach is the additional memory required, since the heap uses an array besides the given array. However, by mimicking the heap's array-based implementation, we can make this approach more efficient without using the class MaxHeap. The resulting algorithm is called a **heap sort**.

**26.18**   To create an initial heap from the given array, we call reheap repeatedly, as we did in the constructor given in Segment 26.16. Parts *a* and *b* of Figure 26-9 show an array and the heap that results after this step. Since the array to be sorted begins at index 0, but in the constructor the heap begins at index 1, we must adjust reheap, as you will see.

The largest item in the array of Figure 26-9b is now first in the array, so we swap it with the last item in the array, as Figure 26-9c shows. The array is now partitioned into a tree region and a sorted region.

Following this swap, we call reheap on the tree portion—transforming it into a heap—and perform another swap, as Figures 26-9d and 26-9e illustrate. We repeat these operations until the tree region consists of one item (Figure 26-9k). The array is now sorted into ascending order. Notice that the array actually is sorted in Figure 26-9g, but the algorithm does not detect this fact.

**FIGURE 26-9**   A trace of heap sort

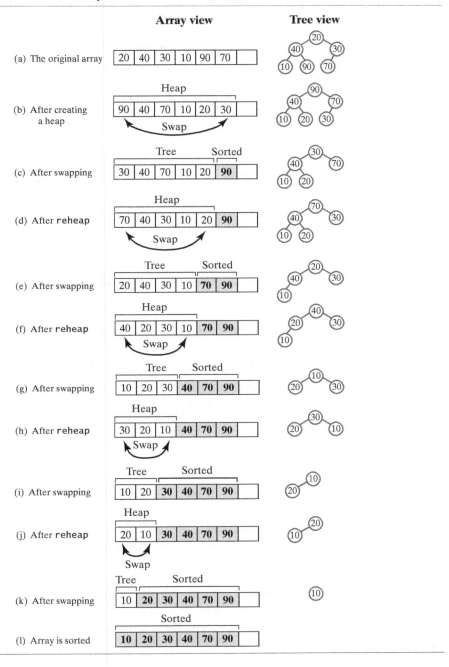

**26.19**    **Adjusting reheap.** We must revise the method reheap so that it is suitable for our sorting algorithm. The original method in Segment 26.11 uses the data fields heap and lastIndex of the class MaxHeap. Here, we make them parameters of the method. Thus, we change the method's header, as follows:

```
private static <T extends Comparable<? super T>>
        void reheap(T[] heap, int rootIndex, int lastIndex)
```

The portion of the array heap that represents the heap ranges from the index 0 to the index lastIndex. The semiheap is rooted at the index rootIndex.

Since the heap begins at index 0 instead of 1, as it did in Segment 26.11, the left child of the node at index $i$ is at index $2i + 1$ instead of $2i$. Recall that Question 1 asked you to find this index. This change affects the two statements within reheap that determine leftChildIndex.

The revised reheap appears as follows:

```
private static <T extends Comparable<? super T>>
        void reheap(T[] heap, int rootIndex, int lastIndex)
{
   boolean done = false;
   T orphan = heap[rootIndex];
   int leftChildIndex = 2 * rootIndex + 1;

   while (!done && (leftChildIndex <= lastIndex))
   {
      int largerChildIndex = leftChildIndex;
      int rightChildIndex = leftChildIndex + 1;
      if ( (rightChildIndex <= lastIndex) &&
            heap[rightChildIndex].compareTo(heap[largerChildIndex]) > 0)
      {
         largerChildIndex = rightChildIndex;
      } // end if

      if (orphan.compareTo(heap[largerChildIndex]) < 0)
      {
         heap[rootIndex] = heap[largerChildIndex];
         rootIndex = largerChildIndex;
         leftChildIndex = 2 * rootIndex + 1;
      }
      else
         done = true;
   } // end while

   heap[rootIndex] = orphan;
} // end reheap
```

**26.20**    **The method heapSort.** The implementation of heap sort begins by calling reheap repeatedly, as we did in the constructor given in Segment 26.16, to create an initial heap from the given array. However, since the heap begins at index 0 instead of 1, we must adjust the loop somewhat:

```
for (int rootIndex = n / 2 - 1; rootIndex >= 0; rootIndex--)
   reheap(heap, rootIndex, n - 1);
```

This loop assumes $n$ entries in the array heap, beginning at index 0. Exercise 3 at the end of this chapter asks you to verify the starting value of rootIndex.

The complete method appears as follows:

```
public static <T extends Comparable<? super T>> void heapSort(T[] array, int n)
{
   // Create first heap
   for (int rootIndex = n / 2 - 1; rootIndex >= 0; rootIndex--)
      reheap(array, rootIndex, n - 1);
   swap(array, 0, n - 1);

   for (int lastIndex = n - 2; lastIndex > 0; lastIndex--)
```

```
        {
            reheap(array, 0, lastIndex);
            swap(array, 0, lastIndex);
        } // end for
    } // end heapSort
```

Like merge sort and quick sort, heap sort is an O($n \log n$) algorithm. As implemented here, heap sort does not require a second array, but merge sort does. Recall from Chapter 9 that quick sort is O($n \log n$) most of the time, but is O($n^2$) in its worst case. Since we usually can avoid quick sort's worst case by choosing appropriate pivots, it generally is the preferred sorting method.

 **Note:  The time efficiency of heap sort**
Although heap sort is O($n \log n$) in the average case, quick sort usually is the sorting method of choice.

 **Question 9** Trace the steps that the method `heapSort` takes when sorting the following array into ascending order: 9 6 2 4 8 7 5 3.

## CHAPTER SUMMARY

- Since a heap is a complete binary tree, it has an efficient array-based implementation.

- You add a new entry to a heap as the next leaf in a complete binary tree. You then make the entry float up to its proper location within the heap.

- You begin to remove the root entry of a heap by replacing it with the entry in the last leaf and then removing the leaf. The result is a semiheap. You transform the semiheap into a heap by making the new root entry sink down to its proper location within the heap.

- You could create a heap from a given array of entries by adding each entry to the heap. A more efficient approach considers the complete tree that the array represents and treats each nonleaf as a semiheap. You transform each such semiheap into a heap by using the same technique that you use when removing the root of the heap.

- A heap sort uses a heap to sort the entries in a given array.

## EXERCISES

1. Trace the formation of a maxheap by the constructor given in Segment 26.16 for each of the following arrays:

   **a.** 10 20 30 40 50
   **b.** 10 20 30 40 50 60 70 80 90 100

2. Trace the addition of each of the following values to an initially empty maxheap:
   10 20 30 40 50

   Compare your trace with the results of Exercise 1a.

3. The method `heapSort` given in Segment 26.20 contains a loop that creates an initial heap from an array of $n$ values. The loop variable `rootIndex` begins at n/2 - 1. Derive this starting value and show that the loop executes the same number of times as the corresponding loop in the constructor given in Segment 26.16.

4. Trace the steps of a heap sort on each of the following arrays:

    **a.** 11 25 33 24 55 68
    **b.** 2 9 7 6 5 8
    **c.** 20 55 40 5 65 35

5. Specify a constructor that can be used to create a heap. Discuss the problems that may occur if constructors of this kind are used in the program.

6. Segment 26.15 showed that the complexity of creating a heap by using reheap is

$$O\left( \sum_{l=1}^{h-1} (h - l + 1) \times 2^{l-1} \right)$$

Show that this expression is equivalent to $O(2^h)$, which is $O(n)$. *Hint*: First, change the summation variable from $l$ to $j$, where $j = h - l + 1$. Then show by induction that

$$\sum_{j=2}^{h} j/2^j = 3/2 - \frac{h + 2}{2^h}$$

7. Consider the loop in a heap sort that creates the initial heap from an array of $n$ values (see Segment 26.20):

```
// Create first heap
for (int rootIndex = n / 2 - 1; rootIndex >= 0; rootIndex--)
    reheap(array, rootIndex, n - 1);
```

Show that the actual number of calls to the method compareTo during the execution of this loop is no less than $n - 1$.

8. Consider again the loop mentioned in the previous exercise. Show that the actual number of calls to the method compareTo during the execution of this loop is no greater than $n \log_2 n$.

9. Heap sort is not the only way to sort an array using a heap. In this exercise you will explore a less efficient algorithm. After building an initial heap, as you would in the first step of a heap sort, the largest value will be in the first position of the array. If you leave this value in place and then build a new heap using the remaining values, you will get the next largest value in the entire array. By continuing in this manner, you can sort the array into descending order. If you use a minheap instead of a maxheap, you will sort the array into ascending order.

    **a.** Implement one of these sorts as the method newSortUsingAHeap.
    **b.** What is the Big Oh performance of this method?

## PROJECTS

1. Recall from Segment 23.33 of Chapter 23 that in a minheap, the object in each node is less than or equal to the objects in the node's descendants. While a maxheap has the method getMax, a minheap has the method getMin instead. Use an array to implement a minheap.

2. Compare the execution times of heap sort, merge sort, and quick sort on various arrays chosen at random. The "Projects" section of Chapter 4 described one way to time the execution of code.

3. Use a binary search tree in the implementation of MaxHeapInterface. Where in the tree will the largest entry occur? How efficient is this implementation?

**4.** Consider the problem of combining two heaps together into a single heap.

    **a.** Write an efficient algorithm for combining two heaps, one with size $n$ and the other with size 1. What is the Big Oh performance of your algorithm?

    **b.** Write an efficient algorithm for combining two heaps of equal size $n$. What is the Big Oh performance of your algorithm?

    **c.** Write an efficient algorithm for combining two arbitrary-sized heaps into one heap. What is the Big Oh performance of your algorithm?

    **d.** Implement the algorithm that you wrote in Part $c$.

**5.** You can study the average performance of the first step in a heap sort—building the initial heap—by taking the following steps:

- Modify the method `reheap` so that it returns the number of calls made to `compareTo`.
- Write a program that will iterate 1000 times. During each iteration, generate $n$ random values and place them into an array. Count the number of comparisons needed by the code given in Exercise 7 to convert the array into a heap. Add the number of comparisons in each iteration into a total. After the loop has ended, compute the average number of comparisons needed to build the heap by dividing the number of comparisons by 1000.
- In the previous step, let $n = 10, 20, 30, 40, 50, 60, 70, 80, 90, 100, 200, 400$, and $800$. For each $n$, see whether the average number of calls to `compareTo` is greater than or equal to the lower bound $n - 1$ (see Exercise 7) and less than or equal to the upper bound $n \log_2 n$ (see Exercise 8).

**6.** Statisticians often are interested in the *median* value in a collection of data. In a collection, about the same number of values are greater than the median value as are less than the median value. When the data is sorted, the median value occurs at the midpoint of the collection. But when the data is not sorted, the median is not as easy to find.

    A problem more general than finding the median is to find the $k^{th}$ smallest value in a collection of $n$ values, where $0 < k < n$. To find the median, $k$ would be $\lceil n/2 \rceil$—that is, the smallest integer greater than or equal to $n/2$. For example, the median value of 11 items is the $6^{th}$ smallest one.

    Design an algorithm that uses a minheap to find the $k^{th}$ smallest value in a collection of $n$ values. Using the class of minheaps defined in Project 1, implement your algorithm as a method at the client level.

## Answers to Self-Test Questions

**1.** The node at array index $i$

- Has a parent at index $(i - 1)/2$, unless the node is the root ($i$ is 0).
- Has any children at indices $2i + 1$ and $2i + 2$.

**2.** Place 100 as a right child of 80. Then swap 100 with 80, swap 100 with 85, and finally swap 100 with 90.

**3.**

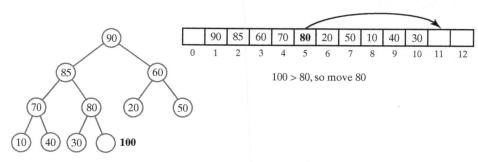

100 > 80, so move 80

*(continues on next page)*

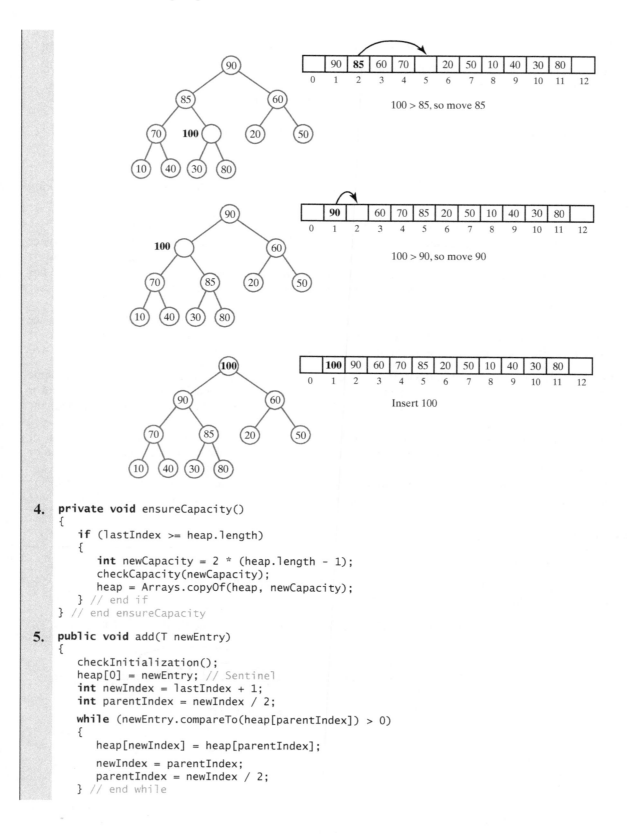

4.
```java
private void ensureCapacity()
{
    if (lastIndex >= heap.length)
    {
        int newCapacity = 2 * (heap.length - 1);
        checkCapacity(newCapacity);
        heap = Arrays.copyOf(heap, newCapacity);
    } // end if
} // end ensureCapacity
```

5.
```java
public void add(T newEntry)
{
    checkInitialization();
    heap[0] = newEntry; // Sentinel
    int newIndex = lastIndex + 1;
    int parentIndex = newIndex / 2;

    while (newEntry.compareTo(heap[parentIndex]) > 0)
    {
        heap[newIndex] = heap[parentIndex];

        newIndex = parentIndex;
        parentIndex = newIndex / 2;
    } // end while
```

```
        heap[newIndex] = newEntry;
        lastIndex++;
        ensureCapacity();
} // end add
```

**6.**

(a)

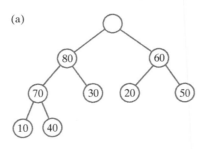

(b)

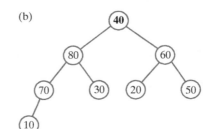

(c)

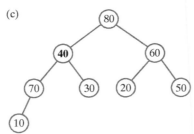

(d)

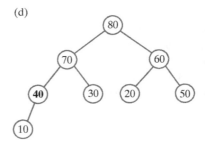

**7.** (a)

85 is larger child of 30; 30 < 85, so move 85

| | 30 | **85** | 60 | 70 | 80 | 20 | 50 | 10 | 40 | |
|---|---|---|---|---|---|---|---|---|---|---|
| 0 | 1 | 2 | 3 | 4 | 5 | 6 | 7 | 8 | 9 | 10 |

(b)    80 is larger child of vacated node; 30 < 80, so move 80

| | 85 | | 60 | 70 | **80** | 20 | 50 | 10 | 40 | |
|---|---|---|---|---|---|---|---|---|---|---|
| 0 | 1 | 2 | 3 | 4 | 5 | 6 | 7 | 8 | 9 | 10 |

(c)

Reached leaf

| | 85 | 80 | 60 | 70 | | 20 | 50 | 10 | 40 | |
|---|---|---|---|---|---|---|---|---|---|---|
| 0 | 1 | 2 | 3 | 4 | 5 | 6 | 7 | 8 | 9 | 10 |

(d)

Insert 30

| | 85 | 80 | 60 | 70 | **30** | 20 | 50 | 10 | 40 | |
|---|---|---|---|---|---|---|---|---|---|---|
| 0 | 1 | 2 | 3 | 4 | 5 | 6 | 7 | 8 | 9 | 10 |

8. If a node at index *i* has children, they are at indices 2*i* and 2*i* + 1. The node at `lastIndex/2` then has a child at `lastIndex`. Since this child is the last leaf, any nodes beyond the one at `lastIndex/2` cannot have children and so must be leaves. Thus, the node at `lastIndex/2` must be the nonleaf closest to the end of the array.

   Alternatively, examine some complete trees and notice that the desired nonleaf is the parent of the last child. This child is at index `lastIndex` of the array representation, so its parent has index `lastIndex/2`.

9. 
   | | | | | | | | | |
   |---|---|---|---|---|---|---|---|---|
   | 9 | 6 | 2 | 4 | 8 | 7 | 5 | 3 | Original array |

   9 6 2 4 8 7 5 3   Original array
   9 8 7 4 6 2 5 3   After repeated calls to reheap
   3 8 7 4 6 2 5 **9**   After swap
   8 6 7 4 3 2 5 **9**   After reheap
   5 6 7 4 3 2 **8 9**   After swap
   7 6 5 4 3 2 **8 9**   After reheap
   2 6 5 4 3 **7 8 9**   After swap
   6 4 5 2 3 **7 8 9**   After reheap
   3 4 5 2 **6 7 8 9**   After swap
   5 4 3 2 **6 7 8 9**   After reheap
   2 4 3 **5 6 7 8 9**   After swap
   4 2 3 **5 6 7 8 9**   After reheap
   3 2 **4 5 6 7 8 9**   After swap
   3 2 **4 5 6 7 8 9**   After reheap
   2 **3 4 5 6 7 8 9**   After swap
   **2 3 4 5 6 7 8 9**   Done

# Balanced Search Trees

## Contents

## Prerequisites

## Objectives

After studying this chapter, you should be able to

- Perform a rotation to restore the balance of an AVL tree after an addition
- Search for or add an entry to a 2-3 tree
- Search for or add an entry to a 2-4 tree
- Form a red-black tree from a given 2-4 tree
- Search for or add an entry to a red-black tree
- Describe the purpose of a B-tree

In Chapter 25, you saw that the operations on a binary search tree are O(log *n*) if the tree is balanced. Unfortunately, the add and remove operations do not ensure that a binary search tree remains balanced. This chapter will consider search trees that maintain their balance, and hence their efficiency.

Our goal is to introduce you to several types of balanced search trees and compare them. We will discuss the algorithms that add entries to a search tree while retaining its balance. We also will show you how to search the trees. We will not, however, cover the algorithms that remove entries, leaving this topic for a future course.

The entries in a tree are usually objects, but to make the pictures of trees clear and concise, we will show the entries as integers.

# AVL Trees

VideoNote
AVL trees

27.1   Segment 23.30 in Chapter 23 showed that you can form several differently shaped binary search trees from the same collection of data. Some of these trees will be balanced and some will not. You could take an unbalanced binary search tree and rearrange its nodes to get a balanced binary search tree. Recall that every node in a balanced binary tree has subtrees whose heights differ by no more than 1.

This idea of rearranging nodes to balance a tree was first developed in 1962 by two mathematicians, Adel'son-Vel'skii and Landis. Named after them, the **AVL tree** is a binary search tree that rearranges its nodes whenever it becomes unbalanced. The balance of a binary search tree is upset only when you add or remove a node. Thus, during these operations, the AVL tree rearranges nodes as necessary to maintain its balance.

For example, Parts *a*, *b*, and *c* of Figure 27-1 show a binary search tree as we add 60, 50, and 20 to it. After the third addition, the tree is not balanced. An AVL tree would rearrange its nodes to restore balance, as shown in Figure 27-1d. This particular reorganization is called a **right rotation**, since you can imagine the nodes rotating about 50. If we now add 80 to the tree, it remains balanced, as Figure 27-2a shows. Adding 90 disrupts the balance (Figure 27-2b), but a **left rotation** restores it (Figure 27-2c). Here the rotation is about 80. Notice that after each rotation, the tree is still a binary search tree.

In discussing balance, we sometimes will mention a **balanced node**. A node is balanced if it is the root of a balanced tree, that is, if its two subtrees differ in height by no more than 1.

## Single Rotations

27.2   **Right rotations.** Let's examine the previous rotations in more detail. Figure 27-3a shows a subtree of an AVL tree that is balanced. The heights of the subtrees $T_1$, $T_2$, and $T_3$ are the same. An addition that occurs in the left subtree $T_1$ of node *C* will add a leaf to $T_1$. Suppose that such an addition increases the height of $T_1$ by 1, as Figure 27-3b shows. The subtree rooted at node *N* is now unbalanced.

FIGURE 27-1   After inserting (a) 60; (b) 50; and (c) 20 into an initially empty binary search tree, the tree is not balanced; (d) a corresponding AVL tree rotates its nodes to restore balance

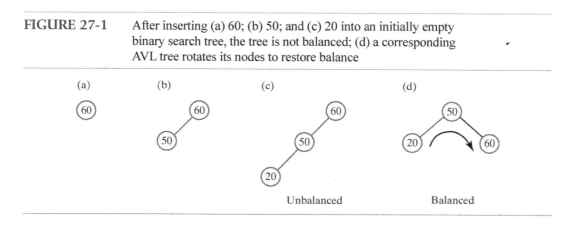

**FIGURE 27-2** (a) Adding 80 to the tree in Figure 27-1d does not change the balance of the tree; (b) a subsequent addition of 90 makes the tree unbalanced ; (c) a left rotation restores its balance

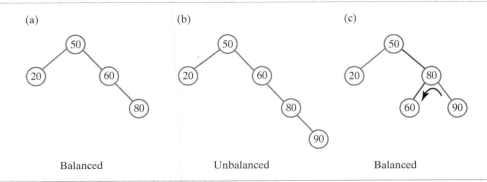

$N$ is the first node that is unbalanced along the path between the inserted leaf and $N$. A right rotation about node $C$ restores the balance of the tree, as Figure 27-3c shows. After the rotation, $C$ is above $N$, and the tree has the same height as it did before the addition of a node.

Since we had a binary search tree before the rotation (Figure 27-3b), the value in node $N$ is greater than the value in node $C$ and all the values in $T_2$. Moreover, all values in $T_2$ are greater than the value in node $C$. These relationships are maintained after the rotation (Figure 27-3c), since node $N$ is a right child of node $C$, and $T_2$ is a left subtree of node $N$. Finally, the subtrees $T_1$ and $T_3$ have their original parents in the new tree. Thus, the resulting tree is still a binary search tree.

Figure 27-4 provides a specific instance of the right rotation depicted in Figure 27-3. Part $a$ of the figure shows an imbalance at node $N$ after 4 was added to the tree. A right rotation restores the tree's balance, as Part $b$ illustrates. To simplify the figure, we have labeled only the roots of the subtrees $T_1$, $T_2$, and $T_3$. Here, node $N$ was the root of the AVL tree, and node $C$ became the root. However if node $N$ had a parent before the rotation, we would make node $C$ a child of that parent after the rotation.

**FIGURE 27-3** Before and after an addition to an AVL subtree that requires a right rotation to maintain its balance

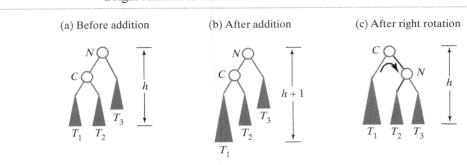

FIGURE 27-4    Before and after a right rotation restores balance to an AVL tree

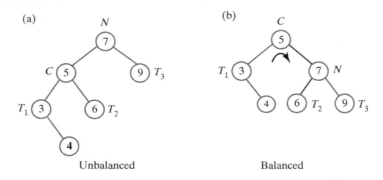

(a)                                                    (b)

Unbalanced                          Balanced

The following algorithm performs the right rotation illustrated in Figures 27-3 and 27-4:

*Algorithm* `rotateRight(nodeN)`
*// Corrects an imbalance at a given node* nodeN *due to an addition*
*// in the left subtree of* nodeN*'s left child.*

nodeC = *left child of* nodeN
*Set* nodeN*'s left child to* nodeC*'s right child*
*Set* nodeC*'s right child to* nodeN
**return** nodeC

**Question 1** Using the notation of Figure 27-3, label nodes $N$ and $C$, and subtrees $T_1$, $T_2$, and $T_3$, in Parts $c$ and $d$ of Figure 27-1.

**27.3**    **Left rotations.** Figure 27-5 shows a left rotation in a mirror image of Figure 27-3. The following algorithm performs this left rotation:

*Algorithm* `rotateLeft(nodeN)`
*// Corrects an imbalance at a given node* nodeN *due to an addition*
*// in the right subtree of* nodeN*'s right child.*

nodeC = *right child of* nodeN
*Set* nodeN*'s right child to* nodeC*'s left child*
*Set* nodeC*'s left child to* nodeN
**return** nodeC

FIGURE 27-5    Before and after an addition to an AVL subtree that requires
a left rotation to maintain its balance

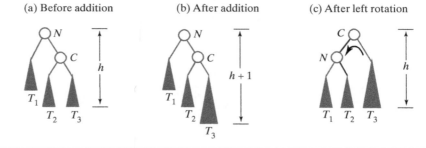

(a) Before addition          (b) After addition          (c) After left rotation

**Question 2** Why is the tree in Figure 27-5c a binary search tree?

**Question 3** Using the notation of Figure 27-5, label nodes $N$ and $C$, and subtrees $T_1$, $T_2$, and $T_3$, in Parts *b* and *c* of Figure 27-2.

**Question 4** Just as Figure 27-4 gave an example of a right rotation, provide a specific example of the left rotation illustrated in Figure 27-5.

**Note:** An imbalance at node $N$ of an AVL tree due to an addition to the tree can be corrected by a single rotation if

- The addition occurred in the left subtree of $N$'s left child $C$ (right rotation), or
- The addition occurred in the right subtree of $N$'s right child $C$ (left rotation)

In both cases, we can imagine node $C$ rotating above node $N$.

## Double Rotations

**27.4**    **Right-left double rotations.** Now we add 70 to the AVL tree in Figure 27-2c. An imbalance occurs at the tree's root, as Figure 27-6a shows. A right rotation about the node containing 60 results in the tree in Figure 27-6b. The mechanics of this rotation are the same as the one in Figure 27-3, where the rotation is about node $C$. The subtree heights differ in these two figures, however.

Unfortunately, this rotation does not balance the tree. A subsequent left rotation about the node containing 60—corresponding to node $C$ in Figure 27-5b—is necessary to restore the balance (Figure 27-6c). Together, these two rotations are called a **right-left double rotation**. First, 60 rotates above 80 and then it rotates above 50. Again, notice that after each rotation, the tree is still a binary search tree.

**FIGURE 27-6**    (a) Adding 70 to the tree in Figure 27-2c destroys its balance; to restore the balance, perform both (b) a right rotation and (c) a left rotation

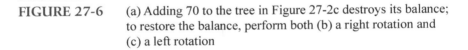

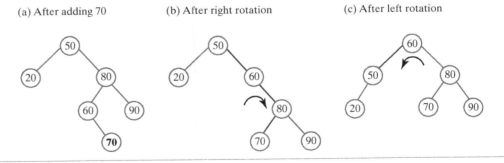

Let's look at the general case. Figure 27-7a shows a subtree of an AVL tree that is height balanced. Node $N$ has a child $C$ and a grandchild $G$. An addition that occurs in the right subtree $T_3$ of node $G$ adds a leaf to $T_3$. When such an addition increases the height of $T_3$, as Figure 27-7b shows, the subtree rooted at $N$ becomes unbalanced. Notice that nodes $N$, $C$, and $G$ correspond to the nodes in Figure 27-6a that contain 50, 80, and 60, respectively.

Node $N$ is the first node that is unbalanced along the path between the inserted leaf and $N$. After a right rotation about node $G$, the subtree rooted at $G$ is unbalanced, as Figure 27-7c shows.

Figure 27-9 shows a left-right double rotation in general. It is a mirror image of the right-left double rotation pictured in Figure 27-7. Both left-right and right-left double rotations cause node *G* to rotate first above node *C* and then above node *N*.

The following algorithm performs the left-right double rotation illustrated in Figure 27-9:

***Algorithm*** `rotateLeftRight(nodeN)`
*// Corrects an imbalance at a given node* `nodeN` *due to an addition*
*// in the right subtree of* `nodeN`*'s left child.*

`nodeC` = *left child of* `nodeN`
*Set* `nodeN`*'s left child to the node returned by* `rotateLeft(nodeC)`
**return** `rotateRight(nodeN)`

**Question 6** Using the notation of Figure 27-9, label nodes *N*, *C*, and *G*, and subtrees $T_1$, $T_2$, $T_3$, and $T_4$ in Figure 27-8.

**Note:** A double rotation is accomplished by performing two single rotations:

1. A rotation about node *N*'s grandchild *G* (its child's child)
2. A rotation about node *N*'s new child

We can imagine *G* rotating first above *N*'s original child *C* and then above *N*.

**Note:** An imbalance at node *N* of an AVL tree can be corrected by a double rotation if

- The addition occurred in the left subtree of *N*'s right child (right-left rotation), or
- The addition occurred in the right subtree of *N*'s left child (left-right rotation)

**27.6** **Summary comments about rotation after an addition.** Following an addition to an AVL tree, a temporary imbalance might occur. Let *N* be an unbalanced node that is closest to the new leaf. Either a single or double rotation will restore the tree's balance. No other rotations are necessary. To see this, remember that before the addition, the tree was balanced; after all, it is an AVL tree. After an addition that causes a rotation, the tree has the same height as it did before the addition. Therefore, no node above *N* can be unbalanced now if it was balanced before the addition. Moreover, the four rotations cover the only four possibilities for the cause of the imbalance at node *N*:

- The addition occurred in the left subtree of *N*'s left child (right rotation)
- The addition occurred in the right subtree of *N*'s left child (left-right rotation)
- The addition occurred in the left subtree of *N*'s right child (right-left rotation)
- The addition occurred in the right subtree of *N*'s right child (left rotation)

Removing an entry from a binary search tree results in the removal of a node, but not necessarily the node that contained the entry. Thus, removing an entry from an AVL tree can lead to a temporary imbalance. We restore the tree's balance by using single or double rotations as described previously for addition. We leave the details for you to develop in Project 1.

**Note:** One single or double rotation during the addition of an entry will restore the balance of an AVL tree.

**Question 7** What AVL tree results when you make the following additions to an initially empty AVL tree? 70, 80, 90, 20, 10, 50, 60, 40, 30

**Question 8** What tree results when you make the same additions given in the previous question to an initially empty binary search tree? How does this tree compare to the AVL tree you created in the previous question?

**Question 9** Why is the tree shown in Figure 27-7d a binary search tree?

**Question 10** Why is the tree shown in Figure 27-9d a binary search tree?

27.7 **An AVL tree versus a binary search tree.** We created the AVL tree in Figure 27-8d by adding 60, 50, 20, 80, 90, 70, 55, 10, 40, and 35 to an initially empty AVL tree. Figure 27-10a shows that tree again. If we make the same additions to an initially empty binary search tree, we get the tree in Figure 27-10b. This tree is unbalanced and is taller than the AVL tree.

**FIGURE 27-10** The result of adding 60, 50, 20, 80, 90, 70, 55, 10, 40, and 35 to an initially empty (a) AVL tree; (b) binary search tree

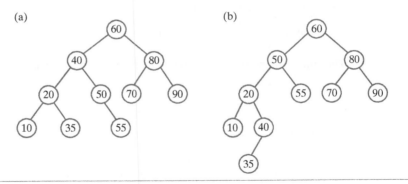

## Implementation Details

27.8 **An outline of the class.** Listing 27-1 outlines our class of AVL trees. Since an AVL tree is also a binary search tree, we will derive the class AVLTree from the class BinarySearchTree, which we discussed in Chapter 25. The methods add and remove are like those in BinarySearchTree but require logic to detect and correct any imbalance that might occur. Thus, we need to override these methods. The other methods specified in SearchTreeInterface are inherited from BinarySearchTree.

**LISTING 27-1** An outline of the class AVLTree

```
1  package TreePackage;
2  public class AVLTree<T extends Comparable<? super T>>
3                extends BinarySearchTree<T> implements SearchTreeInterface<T>
4  {
5     public AVLTree()
6     {
7        super();
8     } // end default constructor
```

```
9
10      public AVLTree(T rootEntry)
11      {
12         super(rootEntry);
13      } // end constructor
14
15      < Implementations of add and remove are here. A definition of add appears in Segment 27.12 of
16         this chapter. Other methods in SearchTreeInterface are inherited. >
17      . . .
18      < Implementations of private methods to rebalance the tree using rotations are here. >
19      . . .
20   } // end AVLTree
```

**27.9**    **Rotations.** As we discussed earlier, an AVL tree uses rotations to maintain its balance following the addition or removal of a node. The methods that perform these rotations closely follow the pseudocode given in the previous segments.

For example, consider the algorithm for a single right rotation, as given in Segment 27.2:

*Algorithm* **rotateRight(nodeN)**
*// Corrects an imbalance at a given node* nodeN *due to an addition*
*// in the left subtree of* nodeN*'s left child.*

nodeC = *left child of* nodeN
*Set* nodeN*'s left child to* nodeC*'s right child*
*Set* nodeC*'s right child to* nodeN
**return** nodeC

The following method implements this pseudocode as a private method of the class AVLTree:

```
// Corrects an imbalance at the node closest to a structural
// change in the left subtree of the node's left child.
// nodeN is a node, closest to the newly added leaf, at which
// an imbalance occurs and that has a left child.
private BinaryNode<T> rotateRight(BinaryNode<T> nodeN)
{
   BinaryNode<T> nodeC = nodeN.getLeftChild();
   nodeN.setLeftChild(nodeC.getRightChild());
   nodeC.setRightChild(nodeN);
   return nodeC;
} // end rotateRight
```

The method rotateLeft has a similar implementation and is left as an exercise.

Since a double rotation is equivalent to two single rotations, the methods that perform double rotations each call the methods that perform single rotations. For example, the algorithm for a right-left double rotation, as it appeared in Segment 27.4, is

*Algorithm* **rotateRightLeft(nodeN)**
*// Corrects an imbalance at a given node* nodeN *due to an addition*
*// in the left subtree of* nodeN*'s right child.*

nodeC = *right child of* nodeN
*Set* nodeN*'s right child to the node returned by* rotateRight(nodeC)
**return** rotateLeft(nodeN)

An implementation of this pseudocode follows:

```
// Corrects an imbalance at the node closest to a structural
// change in the left subtree of the node's right child.
// nodeN is a node, closest to the newly added leaf, at which
// an imbalance occurs and that has a right child.
```

```
private BinaryNode<T> rotateRightLeft(BinaryNode<T> nodeN)
{
    BinaryNode<T> nodeC = nodeN.getRightChild();
    nodeN.setRightChild(rotateRight(nodeC));
    return rotateLeft(nodeN);
} // end rotateRightLeft
```

The method `rotateLeftRight` has a similar implementation and is left as an exercise.

**Question 11** Implement the algorithm given in Segment 27.3 for a single left rotation.

27.10 **Rebalancing.** As you saw previously, you can correct an imbalance at node $N$ of an AVL tree caused by the addition of a node by performing only one of the following rotations, according to where in the tree the change to its structure occurred:

- Right rotation if the addition occurred in the left subtree of $N$'s left child
- Left-right rotation if the addition occurred in the right subtree of $N$'s left child
- Left rotation if the addition occurred in the right subtree of $N$'s right child
- Right-left rotation if the addition occurred in the left subtree of $N$'s right child

The following pseudocode uses these criteria and the rotation methods to rebalance the tree:

*Algorithm* **rebalance(nodeN)**
**if** (nodeN's *left subtree is taller than its right subtree by more than 1*)
{    *// Addition was in* nodeN's *left subtree*
    **if** (*the left child of* nodeN *has a left subtree that is taller than its right subtree*)
        rotateRight(nodeN)        *// Addition was in left subtree of left child*
    **else**
        rotateLeftRight(nodeN) *// Addition was in right subtree of left child*
}
**else if** (nodeN's *right subtree is taller than its left subtree by more than 1*)
{    *// Addition was in* nodeN's *right subtree*
    **if** (*the right child of* nodeN *has a right subtree that is taller than its left subtree*)
        rotateLeft(nodeN)        *// Addition was in right subtree of right child*
    **else**
        rotateRightLeft(nodeN) *// Addition was in left subtree of right child*
}

No rebalancing is needed if the heights of node $N$'s two subtrees either are the same or differ by 1.

27.11 **The method** `rebalance`. A method `getHeightDifference` that returns the difference in the heights of a node's left and right subtrees would help us to implement the previous algorithm. By giving a sign to the height difference it returns, `getHeightDifference` can indicate which subtree is taller. This method can be defined within either the class `AVLTree` or the class `BinaryNode`. The latter choice would be more efficient if each node maintained height information as one or more data fields instead of recomputing it each time the method is called. (See Project 4.)

A node is unbalanced if its two subtrees differ in height by more than 1, that is, if `getHeightDifference` returns a value either greater than 1 or less than -1. If this return value is greater than 1, the left subtree is taller; if it is less than -1, the right subtree is taller.

Using the method `getHeightDifference`, we can implement the previous pseudocode for `rebalance` within the class `AVLTree` as follows:

```java
private BinaryNode<T> rebalance(BinaryNode<T> nodeN)
{
   int heightDifference = getHeightDifference(nodeN);

   if (heightDifference > 1)
   { // Left subtree is taller by more than 1,
      // so addition was in left subtree
      if (getHeightDifference(nodeN.getLeftChild()) > 0)
         // Addition was in left subtree of left child
         nodeN = rotateRight(nodeN);
      else
         // Addition was in right subtree of left child
         nodeN = rotateLeftRight(nodeN);
   }
   else if (heightDifference < -1)
   { // Right subtree is taller by more than 1,
      // so addition was in right subtree
      if (getHeightDifference(nodeN.getRightChild()) < 0)
         // Addition was in right subtree of right child
         nodeN = rotateLeft(nodeN);
      else
         // Addition was in left subtree of right child
         nodeN = rotateRightLeft(nodeN);
   } // end if
   // Else nodeN is balanced

   return nodeN;
} // end rebalance
```

**27.12**  **The method add.** Adding to an AVL tree is just like adding to a binary search tree, but with a rebalancing step. For example, we can begin with the recursive implementations of the methods add and addEntry of BinarySearchTree (Segments 25.15 and 25.16 in Chapter 25) and revise them by inserting calls to rebalance. The resulting methods in AVLTree are as follows:

```java
public T add(T newEntry)
{
   T result = null;

   if (isEmpty())
      setRootNode(new BinaryNode<>(newEntry));
   else
   {
      BinaryNode<T> rootNode = getRootNode();
      result = addEntry(rootNode, newEntry);
      setRootNode(rebalance(rootNode));
   } // end if

   return result;
} // end add

private T addEntry(BinaryNode<T> rootNode, T newEntry)
{
   assert rootNode != null;
   T result = null;
   int comparison = newEntry.compareTo(rootNode.getData());
   if (comparison == 0)
   {
      result = rootNode.getData();
      rootNode.setData(newEntry);
   }
```

```
    else if (comparison < 0)
    {
        if (rootNode.hasLeftChild())
        {
            BinaryNode<T> leftChild = rootNode.getLeftChild();
            result = addEntry(leftChild, newEntry);
            rootNode.setLeftChild(rebalance(leftChild));
        }
        else
            rootNode.setLeftChild(new BinaryNode<>(newEntry));
    }
    else
    {
        assert comparison > 0;

        if (rootNode.hasRightChild())
        {
            BinaryNode<T> rightChild = rootNode.getRightChild();
            result = addEntry(rightChild, newEntry);
            rootNode.setRightChild(rebalance(rightChild));
        }
        else
            rootNode.setRightChild(new BinaryNode<>(newEntry));
    } // end if

    return result;
} // end addEntry
```

Although `rebalance` is called several times during the course of executing these methods, a rebalancing of the tree occurs at most once. Most calls to `rebalance` simply check whether a rebalancing is needed.

As attractive as an AVL tree might seem, better search trees have been developed, as you will now see.

## 2-3 Trees

VideoNote
2-3 trees

**27.13** A **2-3 tree** is a general search tree whose interior nodes must have either two or three children. A **2-node** contains one data item *s* and has two children, like the nodes in a binary search tree. This data *s* is greater than any data in the node's left subtree and less than any data in the right subtree. That is, the data in the node's left subtree is less than *s*, and any data in the right subtree is greater than *s*, as Figure 27-11a shows.

A **3-node** contains two data items, *s* and *l*, and has three children. Data that is less than the smaller data item *s* occurs in the node's left subtree. Data that is greater than the larger data item *l* occurs in the node's right subtree. Data that is between *s* and *l* occurs in the node's middle subtree. Figure 27-11b shows a typical 3-node.

Because it can contain 3-nodes, a 2-3 tree tends to be shorter than a binary search tree. To make the 2-3 tree balanced, we require that all leaves occur on the same level. Thus, a 2-3 tree is completely balanced.

 **Note:** A 2-3 tree is a general search tree whose interior nodes must have either two or three children and whose leaves occur on the same level. A 2-3 tree is completely balanced.

FIGURE 27-11    Nodes in a 2-3 tree

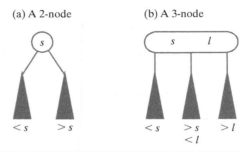

(a) A 2-node                     (b) A 3-node

## Searching a 2-3 Tree

**27.14**    If we had a 2-3 tree, such as the one in Figure 27-12, how would we search it? Notice that each 2-node adheres to the ordering of a binary search tree. The 3-node leaf <35 40> contains values that are between the values in its parent. Knowing this, we can search for the 40, for example, by first comparing 40 with the root value 60. We then move to 60's left subtree and compare 40 with the values in the root of this subtree. Since 40 lies between 20 and 50, it would occur in the middle subtree, if it appears at all. While searching the middle subtree, we compare 40 with 35 and then finally with 40.

FIGURE 27-12    A 2-3 tree

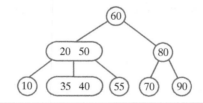

The search algorithm is an extension of the search algorithm for a binary search tree:

*Algorithm* `search23Tree(23Tree, desiredObject)`
*// Searches a 2-3 tree for a given object.*
*// Returns true if the object is found.*

**if** (`23Tree` *is empty*)
    **return false**
**else if** (`desiredObject` *is in the root of* `23Tree`)
    **return true**
**else if** (*the root of* `23Tree` *contains two entries*)
{
    **if** (`desiredObject` < *smaller object in the root*)
        **return** `search23Tree`(*left subtree of* `23Tree`, `desiredObject`)

    **else if** (`desiredObject` > *larger object in the root*)
        **return** `search23Tree`(*right subtree of* `23Tree`, `desiredObject`)
    **else**
        **return** `search23Tree`(*middle subtree of* `23Tree`, `desiredObject`)
}

```
else if (desiredObject < object in the root)
    return search23Tree(left subtree of 23Tree, desiredObject)
else
    return search23Tree(right subtree of 23Tree, desiredObject)
```

**Question 12** What comparisons are made while searching the 2-3 tree in Figure 27-12 for each of the following values?

**a.** 5     **b.** 55     **c.** 41     **d.** 30

## Adding Entries to a 2-3 Tree

**27.15** Using an example, we will describe how to add an entry to a 2-3 tree. As we did when adding to a binary search tree, we add an entry to a 2-3 tree at a leaf. We locate this leaf by using the search algorithm that we described in the previous segment. Thus, once we make the addition, the search algorithm will be able to locate the new entry.

So that we can compare our results with an AVL tree, we will make the same sequence of additions to an initially empty 2-3 tree that we made when forming the AVL tree in Figure 27-10a: 60, 50, 20, 80, 90, 70, 55, 10, 40, and 35.

**27.16** **Adding 60, 50, and 20.** After we add 60, the 2-3 tree consists of a single 2-node. After we add 50, the tree is a single 3-node. Figures 27-13a and 27-13b show the tree after each of these additions.

Now we add 20. To facilitate our description of this addition, we show the 20 in Figure 27-13c within the only node in the tree. This is an imaginary placement, since a 3-node can contain only two data items. We would not actually place more data in this node. Since the node cannot accommodate the 20, we **split** it into three nodes, moving the middle value 50 up one level. In this case, we are splitting a leaf that is also the tree's root. Moving the 50 up requires that we create a new node that becomes the new root of the tree. This step increases the height of the tree by 1, as Figure 27-13d shows.

**FIGURE 27-13**    An initially empty 2-3 tree after adding (a) 60 and (b) 50;
(c), (d) adding 20 causes the 3-node to split

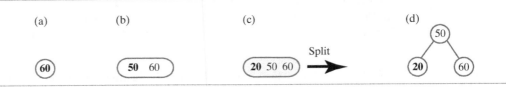

**27.17** **Adding 80, 90, and 70.** To add 80, we note that the search algorithm would look for 80 in the tree's rightmost leaf. Since this leaf has room for another data entry, that is where we should add 80. Figure 27-14a shows the result of this addition.

The search algorithm would look for 90 in the leaf to which we just added 80. Although the leaf has no room for another entry, we imagine that we have added 90 there. We then move the middle value—the 80—up a level and split the leaf into two nodes for the 60 and 90, as Figure 27-14b shows. Since the root can accept the 80, the addition is complete.

The entry 70 belongs in the root's middle subtree, and since this leaf can accept another entry, we add 70 there. Figure 27-14c shows the tree after this addition.

**FIGURE 27-14**   The 2-3 tree after adding (a) 80; (b) 90; (c) 70

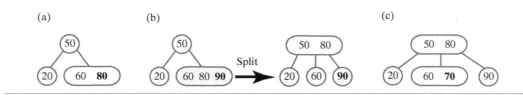

**27.18**   **Adding 55.** When we add 55 to the tree in Figure 27-14c, the search algorithm terminates at the root's middle subtree—a leaf—as Figure 27-15a indicates. Since this leaf cannot accommodate another entry, we split the leaf and move 60 up a level to the root, as shown in Figure 27-15b. Moving the 60 causes the root to split, and 60 moves up another level to a new node that becomes the new root. Figure 27-15c shows the result of this addition.

**FIGURE 27-15**   Adding 55 to the 2-3 tree in Figure 27-14c causes a leaf and then the root to split

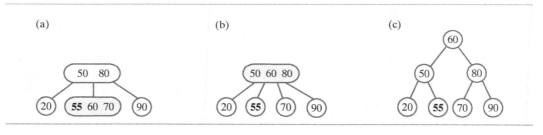

**27.19**   **Adding 10, 40, and 35.** The leaf of the tree in Figure 27-15c that contains 20 has room for 10 as an additional entry, as Figure 27-16a shows. An additional entry, 40, belongs in the same leaf. Since the leaf already contains two entries, we split it and move 20 up a level to the node that contains 50. Figures 27-16b and 27-16c show this result. Finally, Figure 27-17 shows the result of adding 35 to the tree. The leaf that contains 40 accommodates this new entry.

**FIGURE 27-16**   The 2-3 tree in Figure 27-15c after adding (a) 10; (b), (c) 40

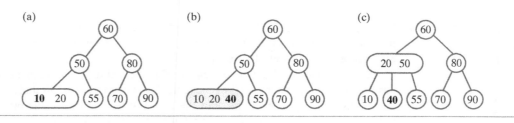

FIGURE 27-17    The 2-3 tree in Figure 27-16c after adding 35

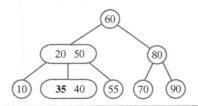

Compare the final 2-3 tree in Figure 27-17 with the AVL tree in Figure 27-10a. We used the same sequence of additions to form both trees. The 2-3 tree is completely balanced and shorter than the balanced AVL tree. Later, we will compare these trees with the 2-4 tree in the next section and draw some conclusions.

## Splitting Nodes During Addition

**27.20**    **Splitting a leaf.** During the addition of a new entry to a 2-3 tree, the first node that splits is a leaf that already contains two entries. Figure 27-18a shows a leaf that would need to accommodate three entries. These entries are shown in ascending order as *s*, *m*, and *l*: *s* is the smallest entry in the node, *m* is the middle entry, and *l* is the largest. The node splits into two nodes that contain *s* and *l*, respectively, and the middle entry *m* moves up a level. If the parent of the leaf has room for *m*, no further action is necessary. This is the case in Figure 27-18a. But in Figure 27-18b, the parent already contains two entries, so we must split it as well. We consider that case next.

Although Figure 27-18 shows the leaf as a right child of its parent, other analogous configurations are possible.

FIGURE 27-18    Splitting a leaf to accommodate a new entry when the leaf's
                parent contains (a) one entry; (b) two entries

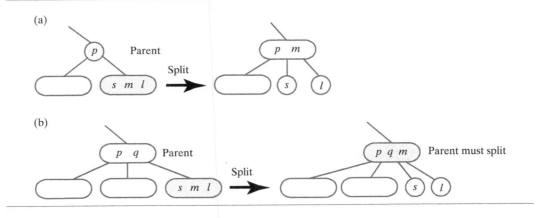

**27.21**    **Splitting an internal node.** You just saw that splitting a leaf can cause the leaf's parent to have too many entries. This parent also has too many children, as illustrated in Figure 27-18b. Figure 27-19 shows such an internal node in general. This node must accommodate three entries *s*, *m*, and *l*, given in ascending order, and four children that are the roots of the subtrees $T_1$ through $T_4$.

Thus, we split the node, move the middle entry *m* up to the node's parent, place *s* and *l* into their own nodes, and distribute the original node's subtrees between *s* and *l*. If the parent has room for *m*, no further splitting is necessary. If not, we split the parent as just described.

Other analogous configurations for an internal node are possible.

FIGURE 27-19   Splitting an internal node to accommodate a new entry

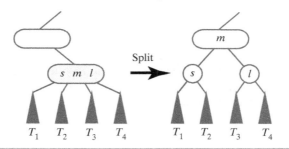

**27.22** **Splitting the root.** Splitting a root proceeds just like the previous cases, except that when we move an entry up a level, we allocate a new node for the entry. This new node becomes the root of the tree, as Figure 27-20 illustrates. Notice that only this case increases the height of a 2-3 tree.

FIGURE 27-20   Splitting the root to accommodate a new entry

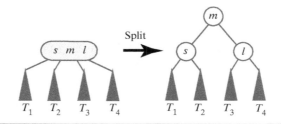

**Question 13**  What tree results when you add 30 to the 2-3 tree in Figure 27-17?

**Question 14**  What 2-3 tree results when you make the following additions to an initially empty 2-3 tree? 70, 80, 90, 20, 10, 50, 60, 40, 30

**Question 15**  How does the tree that you created in the previous question compare to the AVL tree you created in Question 7?

# 2-4 Trees

**27.23** A **2-4 tree**, sometimes called a **2-3-4 tree**, is a general search tree whose interior nodes must have either two, three, or four children and whose leaves occur on the same level. In addition to 2-nodes and 3-nodes, as we described in the previous section, this tree also contains 4-nodes. A **4-node** contains three data items *s*, *m*, and *l* and has four children. Data that is less than the smallest data item *s* occurs in the node's left subtree. Data that is greater than the largest data item *l* occurs in the node's right subtree. Data that is between *s* and the middle data item *m* or between *m* and *l* occurs in the node's middle subtrees. Figure 27-21 illustrates a typical 4-node.

**FIGURE 27-21**    A 4-node

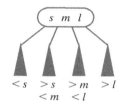

 **Note:** A 2-4 tree is a general search tree whose interior nodes must have two, three, or four children and whose leaves occur on the same level. A 2-4 tree is completely balanced.

Searching a 2-4 tree is like searching a 2-3 tree, but with additional logic to handle the 4-nodes. This search forms the basis of an algorithm to add entries to a 2-4 tree.

## Adding Entries to a 2-4 Tree

**27.24** Recall how we add a new entry to a 2-3 tree. We make comparisons along a path that begins at the root and ends at a leaf. At this point, if the leaf is a 3-node, it already contains two data entries, and so we must split it. Since an entry would now move up a level, this split could require splits in nodes above the leaf. Thus, adding to a 2-3 tree can require us to retrace the path from the leaf back to the root.

In a 2-4 tree, we avoid this retrace by splitting each 4-node as soon as we first consider it during the search from root to leaf. After a split, the next node along the comparison path is the result of the split, and so is not a 4-node. If this node has a 4-node child that we consider next, it has room for the entry that moves up from this child. No other splits occur, as would happen in a 2-3 tree. You will see an example of this shortly.

As in the previous section, we will use an example to demonstrate how to add entries to a 2-4 tree. So that we can compare our results with previous trees, we will use the same sequence of additions—namely, 60, 50, 20, 80, 90, 70, 55, 10, 40, and 35—that we used earlier.

**27.25** **Adding 60, 50, and 20.** Figure 27-22 shows the effect of adding 60, 50, and 20 to an initially empty 2-4 tree. The resulting tree consists of a single 4-node.

**FIGURE 27-22**    An initially empty 2-4 tree after adding (a) 60; (b) 50; (c) 20

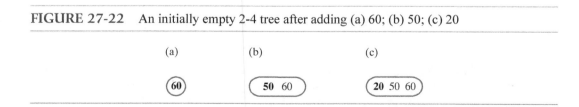

**27.26    Adding 80 and 90.** To add an entry to the 2-4 tree in Figure 27-22c, we find that the root is a 4-node. We split it by moving the middle entry, 50, up. Since we are at a root, we create a new node for the 50. That node becomes the new root of the tree, as shown in Figure 27-23a. We now can add 80 and 90 to the root's right leaf, as Figures 27-23b and 27-23c illustrate.

**FIGURE 27-23**    The 2-4 tree in Figure 27-22c after (a) splitting the root; (b) adding 80; (c) adding 90

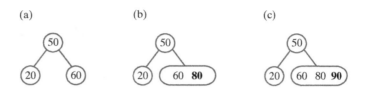

**27.27    Adding 70.** While searching the 2-4 tree in Figure 27-23c for a place to add 70, we encounter the 4-node that is the root's right child. We split this node into two nodes and move the middle entry 80 up to the root. The result of this split is shown in Figure 27-24a. We now have room to add 70 to the root's middle child, as Figure 27-24b shows.

**FIGURE 27-24**    The 2-4 tree in Figure 27-23c after (a) splitting a 4-node; (b) adding 70

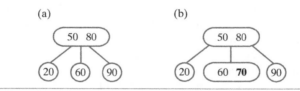

**27.28    Adding 55, 10, and 40.** The 2-4 tree in Figure 27-24b can accommodate the addition of 55, 10, and 40 without splitting nodes. Figure 27-25 shows the results of these additions.

**FIGURE 27-25**    The 2-4 tree in Figure 27-24b after adding (a) 55; (b) 10; (c) 40

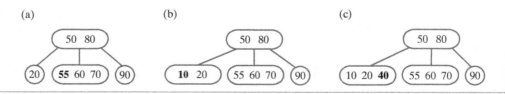

**27.29    Adding 35.** While adding 35 to the 2-4 tree in Figure 27-25c, our search encounters the root's left child, which is a 4-node. We split this node into two nodes and move the middle entry, 20, up to the root, as shown in Figure 27-26a. We now can add 35 to the root's middle left child, as Figure 27-26b shows. This is the final addition that we will make.

FIGURE 27-26 The 2-4 tree in Figure 27-25c after (a) splitting the leftmost 4-node; (b) adding 35

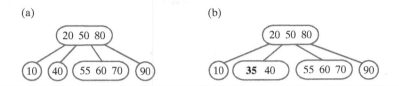

(a)

(b)

**Note:** When adding a new entry to a 2-4 tree, you split any 4-node as soon as you encounter it during the search for the new entry's position in the tree. The addition is complete right after this search ends. Thus, adding to a 2-4 tree is more efficient than adding to a 2-3 tree.

**Question 16** What comparisons are made while searching the 2-4 tree in Figure 27-26b for each of the following values?

    **a.** 5     **b.** 56     **c.** 41     **d.** 30

**Question 17** What tree results when you add 30 to the 2-4 tree in Figure 27-26b?

**Question 18** What 2-4 tree results when you make the following additions to an initially empty 2-4 tree? 70, 80, 90, 20, 10, 50, 60, 40, 30

**Question 19** How does the tree that you created in the previous question compare to the 2-3 tree you created in Question 14?

## Comparing AVL, 2-3, and 2-4 Trees

**27.30** Figure 27-27 compares the AVL tree in Figure 27-10a, the final 2-3 tree in Figure 27-17, and the 2-4 tree that we just constructed. The AVL tree is a balanced binary search tree of height 4. The other trees are completely balanced general search trees. The height of the 2-3 tree is 3; the height of the 2-4 tree is 2. In general, 2-4 trees are shorter than 2-3 trees, which are shorter than AVL trees.

FIGURE 27-27 Three balanced search trees obtained by adding 60, 50, 20, 80, 90, 70, 55, 10, 40, and 35

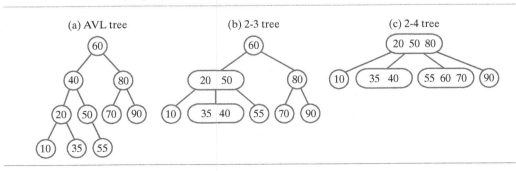

You saw in Segment 25.41 of Chapter 25 that searching a balanced binary search tree, such as an AVL tree, is an O(log *n*) operation. Since 2-3 and 2-4 trees are no taller than a corresponding AVL tree, we usually can search them by examining fewer nodes. However, 3-nodes and 4-nodes contain more entries than 2-nodes, and so they require a longer search time. In general, searching an AVL, 2-3, or 2-4 tree is an O(log *n*) operation.

A 2-3 tree is appealing because maintaining its balance is easier than for an AVL tree. Maintaining the balance of a 2-4 tree is even easier. But defining search trees whose nodes contain more than three data items is usually counterproductive, because the number of comparisons per node increases. As you will see later in this chapter, such a search tree is attractive when it is maintained in external storage, such as a disk, instead of internal memory.

## Red-Black Trees

**27.31**   You just saw that maintaining the balance of a 2-4 tree is easier than maintaining either an AVL tree or a 2-3 tree. While a 2-4 tree is a general tree, a **red-black tree** is a binary tree that is equivalent to a 2-4 tree. Adding an entry to a red-black tree is like adding an entry to a 2-4 tree, in that only one pass from root to leaf is necessary. But a red-black tree is a binary tree, so it uses simpler operations to maintain its balance than does a 2-4 tree. Additionally, the implementation of a red-black tree uses only 2-nodes, whereas a 2-4 tree requires 2-nodes, 3-nodes, and 4-nodes. This added requirement of a 2-4 tree makes it less desirable than a red-black tree.

 **Note:** A red-black tree is a binary tree that is equivalent to a 2-4 tree. Conceptually, a red-black tree is more involved than a 2-4 tree, but its implementation uses only 2-nodes and so is easier to implement.

**27.32**   When designing a node for the 2-4 tree, you need to decide how to represent the entries that are in the node. Since you must order these entries, you could use an ADT such as the sorted list for the entries. You might also use a binary search tree. For example, consider the 2-4 tree in Figure 27-27c. The entries in the root of this tree are 20, 50, and 80. We can represent these entries as a binary search tree whose root is 50 and whose subtrees are 20 and 80. Likewise, the entries in the 3-node leaf of this 2-4 tree are 35 and 40. We can represent these entries as one of two binary search trees: One has 35 as its root and 40 as its right subtree; the other has 40 as its root and 35 as its left subtree. Thus, we can convert all 3-nodes and 4-nodes to 2-nodes. The result is a binary search tree instead of a 2-4 tree.

Each time we convert a 3-node or a 4-node to a 2-node, we increase the height of the tree. We use color to highlight the new nodes that cause this increase in height. We use black for all the nodes in the original 2-4 tree. Since we do not change the 2-nodes, they remain black in the new tree.

Figure 27-28a shows how to represent a 4-node by using 2-nodes. The root of the resulting subtree remains black, but we color its children. The traditional color is red. Our figures use white instead of red. Similarly, Figure 27-28b shows how to represent a 3-node by using one of two different subtrees, each having a black root and a red child.

With this notation, we can draw the 2-4 tree in Figure 27-27c as the balanced binary search tree in Figure 27-29. This binary search tree is called a red-black tree.

 **Question 20** What comparisons are made while searching the 2-4 tree in Figure 27-27c and the equivalent red-black tree in Figure 27-29 for

**a.**   60      **b.**   55

**FIGURE 27-28**   Using 2-nodes to represent (a) a 4-node; (b) a 3-node

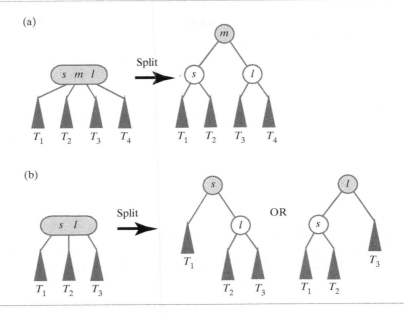

**FIGURE 27-29**   A red-black tree that is equivalent to the 2-4 tree in
Figure 27-27c

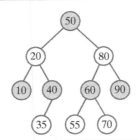

## Properties of a Red-Black Tree

**27.33**   The root of every red-black tree is black. If the original 2-4 tree had a 2-node as its root, the 2-node would be black. And if its root was either a 3-node or a 4-node, we would replace it with a subtree whose root is black, as shown in Figure 27-28.

Since we create red nodes only when we convert 3-nodes and 4-nodes to 2-nodes, every red node has a black parent, as you can see in Figure 27-29. It follows that a red node cannot have red children. If it did, a red child would have a red parent, and this contradicts our previous conclusion that every red node has a black parent.

When we formed a red-black tree equivalent to a 2-4 tree, 2-nodes stayed black and the representation of any other node contained one black node. Thus, every node in a 2-4 tree produced exactly one black node in the equivalent red-black tree. Since a 2-4 tree is completely balanced, all paths from its root to a leaf connect the same number of nodes. So every path from the root to a leaf in a red-black tree must contain the same number of black nodes.

**Note: Properties of a red-black tree**

1. The root is black.
2. Every red node has a black parent.
3. Any children of a red node are black; that is, a red node cannot have red children.
4. Every path from the root to a leaf contains the same number of black nodes.

**Question 21**  Show that the red-black tree in Figure 27-29 satisfies the four properties just given.

**Question 22**  What red-black tree is equivalent to the 2-4 tree in Figure 27-25c?

**Question 23**  Show that the red-black tree that answers Question 22 satisfies the four properties given previously.

**Note:  Creating a red-black tree**
In practice, you do not convert 2-4 trees into red-black trees. You create a red-black tree by adding entries to an initially empty red-black tree according to the steps described in the following section. These steps consider both the balance of the tree and the color of its nodes.

## Adding Entries to a Red-Black Tree

**27.34**  **Adding a leaf.** What color should we assign to a new node that we add to a red-black tree? If the tree is empty, the new node will be the tree's root, and so must be black. An addition to a nonempty binary search tree always occurs at a leaf, so the same is true for a red-black tree. If we use black for a new leaf, we will increase the number of black nodes on the paths to that leaf. This increase violates the fourth property of a red-black tree. Thus, any new node that is added to a nonempty red-black tree must be red. However, do not assume that all the leaves in a red-black tree are red. Adding or removing entries can change the color of various nodes, including that of leaves added earlier.

**Note:  The color of nodes added to a red-black tree**
If we add a node to an empty red-black tree, the node must be black because it is the root. Adding an entry to a nonempty red-black tree results in a new red leaf. The color of this leaf can change later when other entries are added or removed.

Consider some simple cases of adding to a red-black tree. A one-node red-black tree has one black node, its root. Figure 27-30 shows two possibilities when we add a new entry *e* to this tree. In each case, the new red node maintains the properties of a red-black tree, so it is legal.

FIGURE 27-30    The result of adding a new entry *e* to a one-node red-black tree

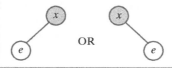

Now suppose that the red-black tree had two nodes before we added the new entry $e$. Figure 27-31a shows this original tree when it consists of a root $x$ and right child $y$. Also pictured is the 2-4 tree that is equivalent to the original red-black tree. The rest of the figure shows the possible outcomes of the addition, depending on how $e$ compares with $x$ and $y$. In Part $b$, $e$ is the left child of the root, and we are done. In Part $c$, a red node has a red child. These two consecutive red nodes are illegal in a red-black tree (properties 2 and 3). To understand what further action is necessary, consider the equivalent 2-4 tree. The original 2-node red-black tree is equivalent to the 2-4 tree that contains the one node $<x\ y>$ (Figure 27-31a). If we add an entry $e$ that is larger than $y$, the 2-4 tree becomes the single node $<x\ y\ e>$ (Figure 27-31c). Notice the red-black tree that is equivalent to this 3-node. This tree is the one we need as the result of adding $e$. We can get it from the first red-black tree shown in Part $c$ by first performing a single left rotation about the node containing $y$. You have seen this rotation before in Figures 27-5b and 27-5c when we talked about AVL trees. After the rotation, we need to reverse the colors of the nodes containing $x$ and $y$—that is, the original parent and grandparent of the new node. We call this step a **color flip**.

---

**FIGURE 27-31**  The possible results of adding a new entry $e$ to a two-node red-black tree

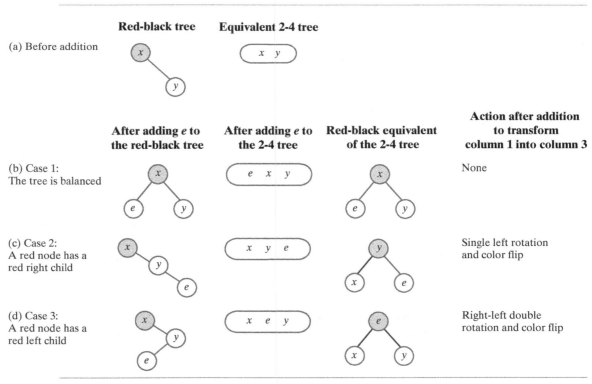

---

Figure 27-31d shows the last possible result of adding $e$ to the two-node red-black tree. Here, a right-left double rotation followed by a color flip of the new node and its original grandparent are necessary to avoid two consecutive red nodes. Figures 27-7b, 27-7c, and 27-7d show the rotation in general in the context of an AVL tree.

Figure 27-32 shows mirror images of the cases in Figure 27-31.

FIGURE 27-32    The possible results of adding a new entry *e* to a two-node
red-black tree: mirror images of Figure 27-31

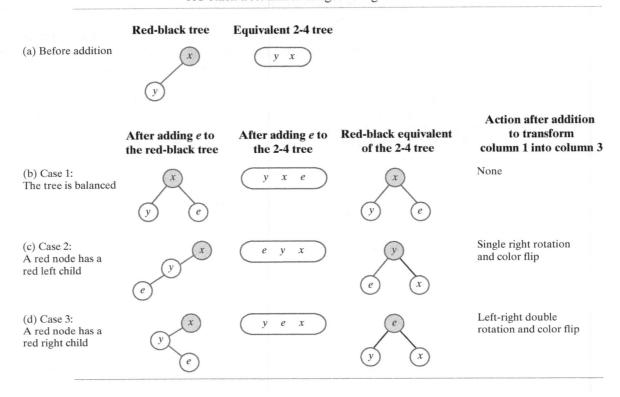

**27.35    Splitting a 4-node whose parent is black.** During an addition to a 2-4 tree, we split any 4-nodes that we encounter as we move along the path from the root to the eventual insertion point. We must perform an equivalent action during an addition to a red-black tree. Figure 27-28a shows that when a black node has two red children, we have encountered the red-black representation of a 4-node. We will call this configuration a red-black 4-node, or simply a 4-node.

**Note:  A red-black 4-node**
A red-black 4-node consists of a black node and two red children.

Figure 27-33a recalls how to split a 4-node when its parent in the 2-4 tree is a 2-node. The middle entry *m* moves up to the node's parent, and the other entries *s* and *l* are given their own nodes as replacement children of the parent. Figure 27-33b shows the corresponding red-black trees. Notice that the three nodes in the subtree rooted at *m* reverse colors. Thus, we split the red-black representation of a 4-node by performing a color flip.

A color flip is all that is necessary when a red-black 4-node has a black parent. As you can see in Figure 27-33, a black parent corresponds to a 2-node in the 2-4 tree. If a 4-node in a 2-4 tree has a 3-node as its parent, the red-black 4-node will have a red parent. We examine this situation in the next segment.

---

**FIGURE 27-33**   Splitting a 4-node whose parent is a 2-node

---

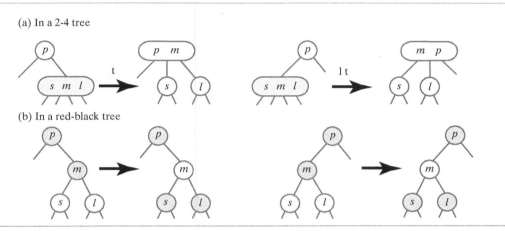

(a) In a 2-4 tree

(b) In a red-black tree

**27.36**   **Splitting a 4-node whose parent is red: Case 1.** Figure 27-34a shows the splitting of a 4-node that has a 3-node parent within a 2-4 tree. Here, the 4-node is the right child of its parent. Figure 27-34b shows the red-black representations of the two trees in Part *a*. How can we transform the first red-black tree into the second? Figure 27-35 shows the necessary steps. In Part *a*, we detect a 4-node at *m*, since this black node has two red children. A color flip results in two adjacent red nodes, as shown in Figure 27-35b. Earlier, in Figure 27-31c, we saw this configuration of a black node and two consecutive right descendants that are red. As we did then, we perform a left rotation about *p*, as Figure 27-35c shows, and then we reverse the colors of the nodes containing *p* and *g*. This color flip, together with the rotation, resolves the illegal red nodes. The result in Figure 27-35d is the desired red-black tree that we saw in Figure 27-34b.

Since a 3-node has two different red-black representations, we can replace Figure 27-35a with a different red-black tree. We leave it to you to show that the final result will be the same, but with less work. (See Exercise 13.)

**27.37**   **Splitting a 4-node whose parent is red: Case 2.** The 4-node in Figure 27-34a is a right child of its parent. If it were a left child, the red-black representation would be as in Figure 27-36a. The rest of this figure shows that both color flips and a right rotation are necessary to split the 4-node.

As before, we can use a different red-black representation of a 3-node and replace Figure 27-36a with a different red-black tree to get the same final result. Again we leave the details to you as an exercise. (See Exercise 14.)

**FIGURE 27-34**   Splitting a 4-node whose parent is a 3-node

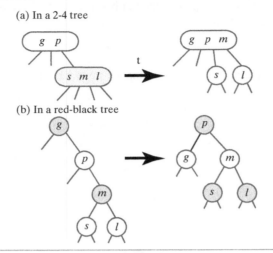

(a) In a 2-4 tree

(b) In a red-black tree

**FIGURE 27-35**   Splitting a 4-node that has a red parent within a red-black tree: Case 1

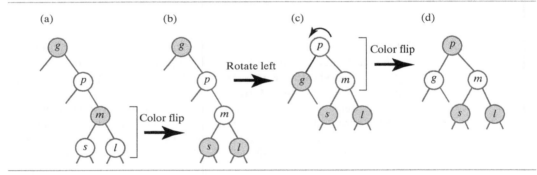

(a)          (b)          (c)          (d)

**FIGURE 27-36**   Splitting a 4-node that has a red parent within a red-black tree: Case 2

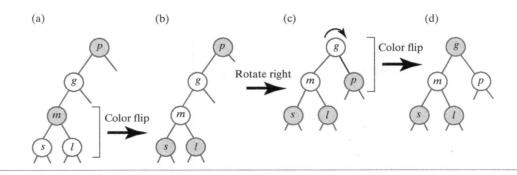

(a)          (b)          (c)          (d)

**27.38** **Splitting a 4-node whose parent is red: Cases 3 and 4.** Now consider the case in which the 4-node is the middle child of its 3-node parent. This time, we look at both red-black representations that the 3-node parent produces. Figure 27-37a shows one possible red-black tree. After the color flip in Part *b*, we resolve the consecutive red nodes as we did in Figure 27-31d. A right-left double rotation followed by a color flip produces the desired results, as you can see in the rest of Figure 27-37.

Figure 27-38a shows the second possible red-black tree. After the color flip in Part *b*, we resolve the consecutive red nodes as we did in Figure 27-32d. A left-right double rotation followed by a color flip is necessary, as the rest of Figure 27-38 shows. Notice that the tree in Figure 27-38e is the same as the one in Figure 27-37e.

**FIGURE 27-37**   Splitting a 4-node that has a red parent within a red-black tree: Case 3

(a)        (b)        (c)        (d)        (e)

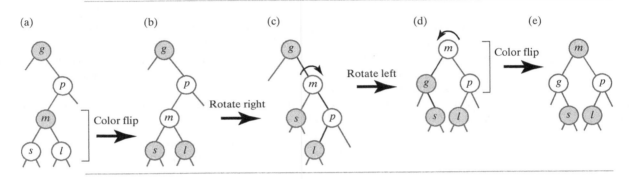

**FIGURE 27-38**   Splitting a 4-node that has a red parent within a red-black tree: Case 4

(a)        (b)        (c)        (d)        (e)

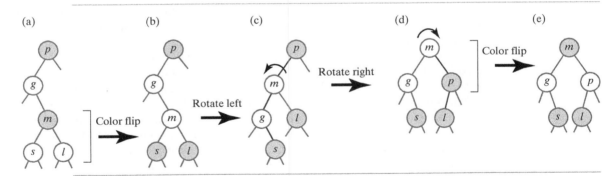

**Note:  Splitting a red-black 4-node**
When splitting a red-black 4-node, the color of its parent determines the necessary operations. If the parent is black, a color flip is sufficient. But if the parent is red, a color flip, a rotation, and another color flip are necessary.

## Java Class Library: The Class TreeMap

27.39    The package java.util contains the class TreeMap<K, V>. This class uses a red-black tree to implement the methods in the interface SortedMap<K, V> in the same package. SortedMap extends the interface Map<K, V>, which we described in Segment 19.22 of Chapter 19. Recall that the interface Map is similar to our interface for the ADT dictionary. SortedMap specifies a sorted dictionary in which the search keys are maintained in ascending order. Because TreeMap uses a red-black tree, methods such as get, put, remove, and containsKey are each an O(log $n$) operation.

# B-Trees

27.40    A **multiway search tree of order $m$**—or sometimes an **$m$-way search tree**—is a general tree whose nodes have up to $m$ children each. A node that has $k$ - 1 data items and $k$ children is called a **$k$-node**. An order $m$ multiway search tree can contain $k$-nodes for values of $k$ ranging from 2 to $m$.

A binary search tree is a multiway search tree of order 2. You know that not all binary search trees are balanced; likewise, not all multiway search trees are balanced. However, 2-3 trees and 2-4 trees are balanced multiway search trees of orders 3 and 4, respectively. We maintained the balance of a 2-3 tree, for example, by insisting that every interior node have two or three children and that all leaves occur on the same level.

A **B-tree of order $m$** is a balanced multiway search tree of order $m$ that has the following additional properties to maintain its balance:

- The root has either no children or between 2 and $m$ children.
- Other interior nodes (nonleaves) have between [$m/2$] and $m$ children each.
- All leaves are on the same level.

2-3 and 2-4 trees satisfy these constraints, and so are examples of B-trees.

27.41    The search trees that you have seen so far maintain their data within the main memory of a computer. At some point, we probably will save this data in external memory, such as a disk. As long as we can read the data back into internal memory, we can use any of the previous search trees. But what happens when your database becomes too large to be retained entirely within internal memory? Typically, you use a B-tree.

Accessing data in external memory is much slower than accessing data in main memory. When reading external data, the major cost is locating it on the storage device. Data on a disk, for example, is organized sequentially into **blocks**, whose size depends on the physical characteristics of the disk. When you read data from a disk, an entire block is read. Locating the block takes much more time than reading the data. If each block contains the data for at least one node, you can reduce the access time by placing numerous data items in each node. Although many comparisons per node could be necessary, their cost is much less than the cost of accessing external data.

Since increasing the number of data items per node decreases the tree's height, you decrease the number of nodes that you must search and hence the number of disk accesses. A high-order B-tree fits these requirements. You would choose the order $m$ so that $m$ - 1 data items fit into a block on the disk.

 **Note:** Although a high-order B-tree is usually counterproductive for an internal database because the number of comparisons per node increases, it is attractive when it is maintained in external storage such as a disk.

## CHAPTER SUMMARY

- An AVL tree is a balanced binary search tree that rearranges its nodes whenever it becomes unbalanced. If adding a node causes an imbalance, one single or double rotation restores the tree's balance.

- A 2-node is a node that has two children and one data item. A 3-node has three children and two data items.

- A 2-3 tree is a balanced search tree that contains 2-nodes and 3-nodes. When an addition to the tree would cause a leaf to have three data items, the leaf splits into two 2-nodes. These nodes contain the smallest and largest of the three data items and become the children of the former leaf's parent. The middle data item moves up to this parent node, possibly causing the node to split.

- A disadvantage of the 2-3 tree is that the addition algorithm follows a path from the root to a leaf and then returns along that path as nodes split.

- A 4-node has four children and three data items.

- A 2-4 (or 2-3-4) tree is a balanced search tree that contains 2-nodes, 3-nodes, and 4-nodes. During an addition to the tree, each 4-node is split as it is considered during the search from root to leaf. Thus, returning along the path to the root is unnecessary.

- A red-black tree is a binary search tree that is logically equivalent to a 2-4 tree. Conceptually, a red-black tree is more involved than a 2-4 tree, but its implementation is more efficient because it uses only 2-nodes.

- Additions to a red-black tree maintain the tree's balance and status as a red-black tree by using color flips as well as rotations like those used for an AVL tree.

- A $k$-node is a node that has $k$ children and $k-1$ data items.

- A multiway search tree of order $m$ is a general tree that contains $k$-nodes for values of $k$ ranging from 2 to $m$. A B-tree of order $m$ is a balanced multiway search tree of order $m$. To maintain its balance, a B-tree requires every interior node to have a certain number of children and has all its leaves on the same level.

- A 2-3 tree is a B-tree of order 3; a 2-4 tree is a B-tree of order 4.

- A B-tree is useful when data is maintained in external storage, such as a disk.

## EXERCISES

1. Implement the algorithm for a left-right double rotation, as given in Segment 27.5.

2. Add 62 and 65 to the AVL tree in Figure 27-27a.

3. Add 62 and 65 to the 2-3 tree in Figure 27-27b.

4. Add 62 and 65 to the 2-4 tree in Figure 27-27c.

5. Add 62 and 65 to the red-black tree in Figure 27-29.

6. Each of the trees in Figures 27-27 and 27-29 contains the same values. Exercises 2 through 5 asked you to add 62 and 65 to each of them. Describe the effect that these additions had on each tree.

7. What red-black tree is equivalent to the 2-4 tree in Figure 27-25b?

**8.** What tree results when you add the values 10, 20, 30, 40, 50, 60, 70, 80, 90, and 100 to each of the following initially empty trees?

  **a.** An AVL tree       **b.** A 2-3 tree       **c.** A 2-4 tree       **d.** A red-black tree

**9.** Add the values given in Exercise 8 to an initially empty binary search tree. Compare the resulting tree with the trees you created in Exercise 8. Which tree could you search most efficiently?

**10.** Give an example of the smallest possible tree that contains two levels for each of the following kinds of trees:

  **a.** An AVL tree       **b.** A 2-3 tree       **c.** A 2-4 tree       **d.** A red-black tree

**11.** Give an example of the largest possible tree that contains two levels for each of the following kinds of trees:

  **a.** An AVL tree       **b.** A 2-3 tree       **c.** A 2-4 tree       **d.** A red-black tree

**12.** Using pseudocode, describe a preorder traversal of

  **a.** A 2-3 tree       **b.** A 2-4 tree

**13.** Figure 27-34a shows a 4-node within a 2-4 tree that is the right child of a 3-node parent containing data items $g$ and $p$. When converting these nodes to red-black notation, make $p$ be the parent of $g$. Revise Figure 27-35 to show that a color flip is all that is necessary to get the desired red-black tree.

**14.** Repeat Exercise 13, but this time assume that the 4-node is a left child.

**15.** Color the nodes in each tree in Figure 27-39 so that it is a red-black tree.

**FIGURE 27-39**   Three binary trees for Exercise 15

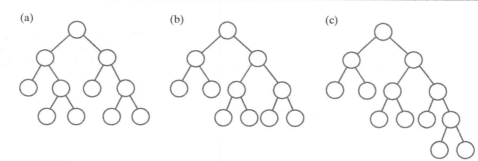

**16.** Compare the implementation of a priority queue using an AVL tree with that using a red-black tree.

**17.** How efficiently could a red-black tree or an AVL tree implement the add and remove methods of a priority queue?

**18.** What are the worst-case time complexities for search, insert, and delete operations in a general array and in a binary search tree?

## PROJECTS

**1.** You remove an entry from an AVL tree in the same way that you remove an entry from a binary search tree. However, after you remove the appropriate node from the tree, an imbalance can occur that you must correct by performing single or double rotations. Develop an algorithm that removes a node from an AVL tree.

**2.** Implement a class of AVL trees.

3. Consider the implementation of the method `rebalance` for an AVL tree, as given in Segment 27.11. The performance of this method depends on the cost of a rotation and the cost of the method `getHeightDifference`.

 a. Assume that the tree has height $h$ and that `nodeN` is at height $k$. What is the cost, using Big O notation, of each of the following tasks?

 - A rotation
 - Executing the method `getHeightDifference`
 - Executing the method `rebalance`

 b. Suppose that a node is added at the bottom of the tree by the method `add`. How many times will `rebalance` be called? Give a Big Oh expression for the cost of adding a node.

4. Design and implement a class of nodes that you can use in the implementation of an AVL tree. You can derive this class from `BinaryNode`. Each node, as the root of a subtree, should contain the height of this subtree. Implement a class of AVL trees using your new class of nodes.

5. Design a class of nodes that you can use in the implementation of a 2-4 tree. Is one class enough, or will you need several?

6. Implement a class of 2-4 trees in which only additions and retrievals are permitted.

7. Implement a class of red-black trees that permit only additions and retrievals.

8. Implement a class of sets that stores its entries in a red-black tree that is an instance of the class defined in the previous project. You can omit the methods `remove` and `clear` from your class. Recall that Chapter 1 defined a set as a bag that does not permit duplicate entries.

9. Design and carry out an experiment to compare the heights of ordinary binary search trees with the heights of either AVL trees or red-black trees. You first will need to complete either Project 2 or Project 7.

10. Design a class `BTreeNode` of nodes for a B-tree of order $m$. Consider operations that allow you to

 - Get a particular value from the node
 - Insert a value into the node while maintaining the links to subtrees (remember that the B-tree is a search tree)
 - Get a count of the number of values in the node
 - Replace a value in the node, if the search tree is maintained
 - Replace a subtree
 - Split a node into two nodes, each containing half the values

 Give an algorithm for adding a new value to a B-tree whose implementation uses your definition of `BTreeNode`.

11. Implement a priority queue by using one of the balanced search trees in this chapter.

## ANSWERS TO SELF-TEST QUESTIONS

1. Node $N$ contains 60, and node $C$ contains 50. $T_1$ is the one-node subtree containing 20. $T_2$ and $T_3$ are empty.

2. Since we had a binary search tree before the rotation, the value in node $N$ is less than the value in node $C$ and all the values in $T_2$. Moreover, all values in $T_2$ are less than the value in node $C$. These relationships are maintained after the rotation, since node $N$ is a left child of node $C$, and $T_2$ is a right subtree of node $N$. Also, the subtrees $T_1$ and $T_3$ have their original parents in the new tree. Thus, the resulting tree is a binary search tree.

3. Node $N$ contains 60, and node $C$ contains 80. $T_3$ is the one-node subtree containing 90. $T_1$ and $T_2$ are empty.

**4.** Part *a* of the following figure shows an imbalance at node *N* after 10 was added to the tree. A left rotation restores the tree's balance, as Part *b* illustrates.

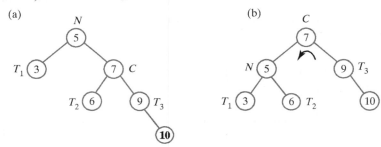

**5.** Node *N* contains 50, node *C* contains 80, and node G contains 60. $T_1$, $T_3$, and $T_4$ are one-node subtrees: $T_1$ contains 20, $T_3$ contains 70, and $T_4$ contains 90. $T_2$ is empty. In Parts *a* and *b*, $T_2$ is the left subtree of 60. In Part *c*, it is the right subtree of 50.

**6.** Node *N* contains 50, node *C* contains 20, and node G contains 40. $T_1$, $T_2$, and $T_4$ are one-node subtrees: $T_1$ contains 10, $T_2$ contains 35, and $T_4$ contains 55. $T_3$ is empty. In Parts *a*, *b* and *c*, $T_3$ is the right subtree of 40. In Part *d*, it is the left subtree of 50.

**7.**

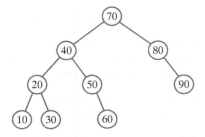

**8.** The following binary search tree is taller than the previous AVL tree, and it is not balanced:

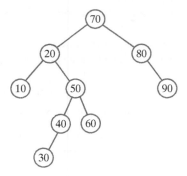

**9.** Since we had a binary search tree before the rotation, the value in node *N* is less than the values in nodes *C* and *G* and all the values in $T_2$ and $T_3$. The value in node *C* is greater than the value in node *G*, and each of these two values is greater than all values in $T_2$. Moreover, all values in $T_3$ are less than the value in node *C* but greater than the value in node *G*. These relationships are maintained after the rotation: Node *G* has node *N* as its left child and node *C* as its right child; $T_2$ is a right subtree of node *N*, and $T_3$ is a left subtree of node *C*. The subtrees $T_1$ and $T_4$ have their original parents in the new tree. Thus, the resulting tree is a binary search tree.

**10.** Since we had a binary search tree before the rotation, the value in node $N$ is greater than the values in nodes $C$ and $G$ and all the values in $T_2$ and $T_3$. The value in node $C$ is less than the value in node $G$, and each of these two values is less than all values in $T_3$. Moreover, all values in $T_2$ are less than the value in node $G$ but greater than the value in node $C$. These relationships are maintained after the rotation: Node $G$ has node $C$ as its left child and node $N$ as its right child; $T_2$ is a right subtree of node $C$, and $T_3$ is a left subtree of node $N$. The subtrees $T_1$ and $T_4$ have their original parents in the new tree. Thus, the resulting tree is a binary search tree.

**11.**
```java
private BinaryNode<T> rotateLeft(BinaryNode<T> nodeN)
{
    BinaryNode<T> nodeC = nodeN.getRightChild();
    nodeN.setRightChild(nodeC.getLeftChild());
    nodeC.setLeftChild(nodeN);
    return nodeC;
} // end rotateLeft
```

**12.** 60, 20, 10.
60, 20, 50, 55.
60, 20, 50, 35, 40.
60, 20, 50, 35.

**13.**

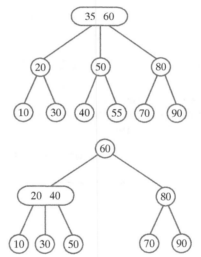

**14.**

**15.** The 2-3 tree is shorter than the AVL tree. Both trees are balanced.

**16.** **a.** 20, 10.
**b.** 20, 50, 80, 55, 60.
**c.** 20, 50, 35, 40.
**d.** 20, 50, 35.

**17.**

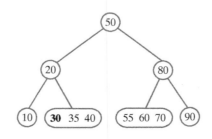

**18.**

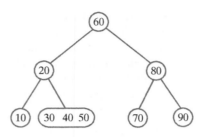

**19.** Both trees are completely balanced, and they have the same height. The 2-4 tree has fewer nodes.

**20.** **a.** 2-4: 20, 50, 80, 55, 60; Red-black: 50, 80, 60.
**b.** 2-4: 20, 50, 80, 55; Red-black: 50, 80, 60, 55.

**21.** The first three properties follow immediately by observing the tree. Every path from the root to a leaf contains two black nodes.

**22.**

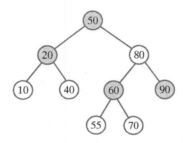

If you tried to form a red-black tree whose root is 80, you would find that the tree was not balanced and so could not be a red-black tree. (You normally do not convert 2-4 trees into red-black trees, but doing so as an exercise should give you some insight into the rationale of red-black trees.)

**23.** The first three properties follow immediately by observing the tree. Every path from the root to a leaf contains two black nodes.

# Graphs

## Contents

## Prerequisites

## Objectives

After studying this chapter, you should be able to

- Describe the characteristics of a graph, including its vertices, edges, and paths
- Give examples of graphs, including those that are undirected, directed, unweighted, and weighted
- Give examples of vertices that are adjacent and that are not adjacent for both directed and undirected graphs
- Give examples of paths, simple paths, cycles, and simple cycles
- Give examples of connected graphs, disconnected graphs, and complete graphs
- Perform a depth-first traversal and a breadth-first traversal on a given graph
- List a topological order for the vertices of a directed graph without cycles

- Detect whether a path exists between two given vertices of a graph
- Find the path with the fewest edges that joins one vertex to another
- Find the path with the lowest cost that joins one vertex to another in a weighted graph
- Describe the operations for the ADT graph

The news media often use line graphs, pie charts, and bar graphs to help us visualize certain statistics. But these common graphs are *not* examples of the kind of graph that we will study in this chapter. The graphs that computer scientists and mathematicians use include the trees that you saw in Chapter 23. In fact, a tree is a special kind of graph. These graphs represent the relationships among data elements. This chapter will present the terminology we use when discussing graphs, the operations on them, and some typical applications.

## Some Examples and Terminology

Although the graphs you have drawn in the past likely are not the kind of graph we will discuss here, the examples in this section will be familiar. But you probably have never called them graphs!

### Road Maps

28.1   Figure 28-1 contains a portion of a road map for Cape Cod, Massachusetts. Small circles represent the towns, and the lines that join them represent the roads. A road map is a graph. In a graph, the circles are called **vertices**, or **nodes**, and the lines are called **edges**. A **graph**, then, is a collection of distinct vertices and distinct edges. A **subgraph** is a portion of a graph that is itself a graph, just as the road map in Figure 28-1 actually is a part of a larger map.

FIGURE 28-1    A portion of a road map

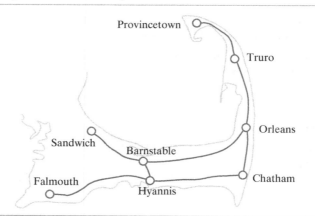

Since you can travel in both directions along the roads in Figure 28-1, the corresponding graph and its edges are said to be **undirected**. But cities often have one-way streets. The graph in Figure 28-2 has a vertex for each intersection in a city's street map. The edges each have a direction and are called **directed edges**. A graph with directed edges is called a **directed graph**, or **digraph**. You can transform an undirected graph into a directed graph by replacing each undirected edge with two directed edges that have opposite directions.

VideoNote
Graph concepts and
terminology

FIGURE 28-2    A directed graph representing a portion of a city's street map

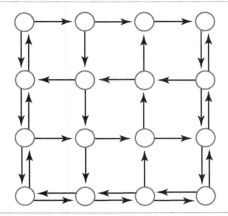

**28.2**   **Paths.** A **path** between two vertices in a graph is a sequence of edges. A path in a directed graph must consider the direction of the edges, and is called a **directed path**. The **length** of a path is the number of edges that it comprises. If the path does not pass through any vertex more than once, it is a **simple path**. Figure 28-1 contains a simple path from Provincetown to Orleans of length 2.

A **cycle** is a path that begins and ends at the same vertex. A **simple cycle** passes through other vertices only once each. In Figure 28-1, the cycle Chatham-Hyannis-Barnstable-Orleans-Chatham is a simple cycle. A graph that has no cycles is **acyclic**.

You use a road or street map to see how to get from point A to point B. The path you choose between these points will usually be a simple path. In doing so, you avoid retracing your steps or going around in circles. People who take a ride to view the autumn leaves, however, would follow a cycle that begins and ends at home.

**28.3**   **Weights.** You might be happy just to get from one place to another, but you often have a choice of several paths. You could choose the shortest, the fastest, or the cheapest path, for example. To do so, you use a **weighted graph**, which has values on its edges. These values are called either **weights** or **costs**. For example, Figure 28-3 shows the road map from Figure 28-1 as a weighted graph. In this version, each weight represents the distance in miles between two towns. Other types of weights you might use could represent the driving time or the cost of traveling by taxi.

A path in a weighted graph also has a weight, or cost, that is the sum of its edge weights. For example, the weight of the path from Provincetown to Orleans in Figure 28-3 is 27.

FIGURE 28-3    A weighted graph

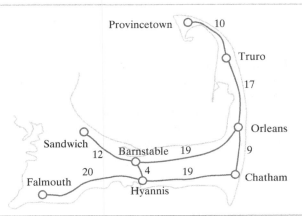

**Question 1** Consider the graph in Figure 28-3.

    **a.** What is the length of the path that begins in Provincetown, passes through Truro and Orleans, and ends in Chatham?

    **b.** What is the weight of the path just described?

    **c.** Consider all paths from Truro to Sandwich that do not have cycles. Which path has the shortest length?

    **d.** Of the paths you considered in Part *c*, which one has the smallest weight?

**28.4**    **Connected graphs.** The towns on a road map are connected by roads in a way that enables you to go from any town to any other town. That is, you can get from here to there. A graph that has a path between every pair of distinct vertices is **connected**. A **complete graph** goes even further; it has an edge between every pair of distinct vertices. Figure 28-4 provides examples of undirected graphs that are connected, complete, or **disconnected**—that is, not connected. Notice the simple path in Part *a* and the simple cycle in Part *c*.

**FIGURE 28-4**    Undirected graphs

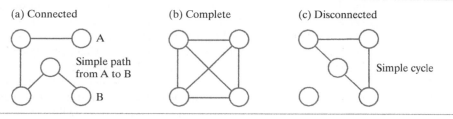

**28.5**    **Adjacent vertices.** Two vertices are **adjacent** in an undirected graph if they are joined by an edge. In Figure 28-3, Orleans and Chatham are adjacent, but Orleans and Sandwich are not. Adjacent vertices are called **neighbors**. In a directed graph, vertex *i* is adjacent to vertex *j* if a directed edge begins at *j* and ends at *i*. In Figure 28-5, vertex *A* is adjacent to vertex *B*, but vertex *B* is not adjacent to vertex *A*. That is, vertex *A* is vertex *B*'s neighbor, but the converse is not true.

    When convenient, we will place vertex labels within the circles that represent the vertices, as in Figure 28-5. But sometimes, the vertex labels will appear next to the circles, as in Figure 28-3.

**FIGURE 28-5**    Vertex *A* is adjacent to vertex *B*, but *B* is not adjacent to *A*

**28.6**    **The number of edges.** If a directed graph has *n* vertices, how many edges can it have? If the graph is complete, each vertex is a neighbor of all the other vertices. Thus, each vertex ends *n* - 1 directed edges. Consequently, the graph has $n \times (n - 1)$ edges. A complete undirected graph has half that number of edges. For example, the graph in Figure 28-4b has 4 vertices and (4 × 3) / 2, or 6, edges. To make the graph directed and complete, we would replace each edge with two directed edges, which results in a graph having 12 edges.

**Note:** If a graph has $n$ vertices, it can have at most
- $n \times (n - 1)$ edges if the graph is directed
- $n \times (n - 1) / 2$ edges if the graph is undirected

A graph is **sparse** if it has relatively few edges. It is **dense** if it has many edges. While these terms have no precise definition, we will say that a sparse graph has $O(n)$ edges, and a dense graph has $O(n^2)$ edges. The graph in Figure 28-1 has eight vertices and eight edges. It is sparse.

 **Note:** Typical graphs are sparse.

## Airline Routes

**28.7**  A graph that represents the routes that an airline flies is similar to one that represents a road map. They are different, however, because not every city has an airport, and not every airline flies to or from every airport. For example, the graph in Figure 28-6 shows the flights for a small airline on the East Coast of the United States. The graph is undirected and consists of two subgraphs that are each connected. The entire graph, however, is disconnected.

Notice that you can fly from Boston to Provincetown, but not from Boston to Key West. Algorithms exist that see whether a flight between given cities is possible.

 **Note:** Figure 28-6 contains one graph that consists of two distinct subgraphs. Although each subgraph is connected, the entire graph is disconnected.

**FIGURE 28-6**   Airline routes

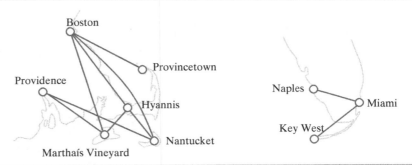

## Mazes

**28.8**  Mazes have been constructed in Victorian English gardens and modern-day cornfields. A typical maze, like the one in Figure 28-7a, has a path from its entrance to its exit. Other paths begin at the entrance, but some lead to dead ends, rather than to the exit. Can you find your way through the maze?

We can represent this maze as a graph by placing a vertex at the entrance and exit, at each turn in the path, and at each dead end, as Figure 28-7b shows. This graph, like the road map in Figure 28-1, is connected. For such graphs, we can find a path between any two vertices, as you will see later in this chapter.

FIGURE 28-7    (a) A maze; (b) its representation as a graph

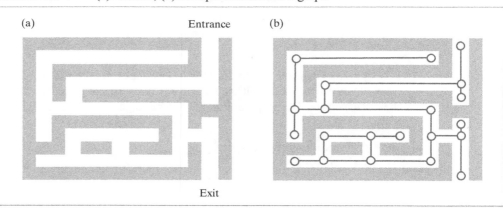

## Course Prerequisites

**28.9**    As a college student, you must take a sequence of courses in your major. Each course has certain prerequisite courses that you must complete first. In what order can you take the required courses and satisfy the prerequisites?

To answer this question, we first create a directed graph to represent the courses and their prerequisites. Figure 28-8 is an example of such a graph. Each vertex represents a course, and each directed edge begins at a course that is a prerequisite to another. Notice, for example, that you must complete cs1, cs2, cs4, cs7, cs9, *and* cs5 before you can take cs10.

This graph has no cycles. In a directed graph without cycles, we can arrange the vertices so that vertex *a* precedes vertex *b* whenever a directed edge exists from *a* to *b*. The order of the vertices in this arrangement is called a **topological order**. Later in this chapter, you will see how to find this order and, therefore, the order in which you should complete your course requirements.

FIGURE 28-8    The prerequisite structure for a selection of courses as a
directed graph without cycles

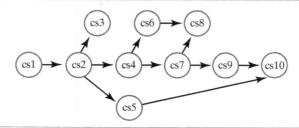

## Trees

**28.10**    The ADT tree is a kind of graph that uses parent-child relationships to organize its nodes in a hierarchical fashion. One particular node, the root, is the ancestor of all other nodes in the tree. But not all graphs have a hierarchical organization, and so not all graphs are trees.

**Note:** All trees are graphs, but not all graphs are trees. A tree is a connected graph without cycles.

**Question 2** What physical systems in a typical house could you represent as a graph?

**Question 3** Is the graph in Figure 28-1 connected? Is it complete?

**Question 4** Is the graph in Figure 28-8 a tree? Explain.

**Question 5** For the graph in Figure 28-8,

    **a.**  Is cs1 adjacent to cs2?    **c.**  Is cs1 adjacent to cs4?

    **b.**  Is cs2 adjacent to cs1?    **d.**  Is cs4 adjacent to cs1?

## Traversals

**VideoNote**
Graph operations

**28.11**  As you learned in earlier chapters, you usually search a tree for a node that contains a particular value. Graph applications, however, focus on the connections between vertices, rather than the contents of vertices. These applications often are based on a traversal of the graph's vertices.

    In Chapter 23, we examined several orders in which we could visit the nodes of a tree. The preorder, inorder, and postorder traversals are examples of a depth-first traversal. This kind of traversal follows a path that descends the levels of a tree as deeply as possible until it reaches a leaf, as Figure 28-9a shows. More generally, a depth-first traversal of a graph follows a path that goes as deeply into the graph as possible before following other paths. After visiting a vertex, this traversal visits the vertex's neighbor, the neighbor's neighbor, and so on.

    The level-order traversal of a tree is an example of a breadth-first traversal. It follows a path that explores an entire level before moving to the next level, as Figure 28-9b shows. In a graph, a breadth-first traversal visits all neighbors of a node before visiting the neighbors' neighbors.

**FIGURE 28-9**    The visitation order of two traversals

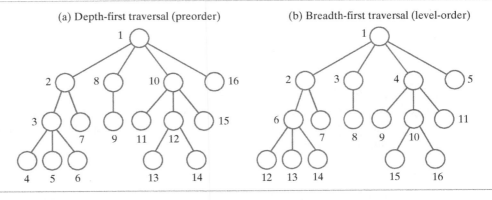

**Note:** Visiting a node in either a tree or a graph is an action that we perform during a traversal. In a tree, "visit a node" means to "process the node's data." In a graph, "visit a node" means simply to "mark the node as visited."

A traversal of a tree visits all of the tree's nodes beginning with the root. However, a graph traversal begins at any vertex—called the **origin vertex**—and visits only the vertices that it can reach. Only when a graph is connected can such a traversal visit all the vertices.

## Breadth-First Traversal

**28.12** Given an origin vertex, a breadth-first traversal visits the origin and the origin's neighbors. It then considers each of these neighbors and visits their neighbors. The traversal uses a queue to hold the visited vertices. When we remove a vertex from this queue, we visit and enqueue the vertex's unvisited neighbors. The traversal order is then the order in which vertices are added to the queue. We can retain this traversal order in a second queue.

The following algorithm performs a breadth-first traversal of a nonempty graph beginning at a given vertex.

```
Algorithm getBreadthFirstTraversal(originVertex)
traversalOrder = a new queue for the resulting traversal order
vertexQueue = a new queue to hold vertices as they are visited
Mark originVertex as visited
traversalOrder.enqueue(originVertex)
vertexQueue.enqueue(originVertex)

while (!vertexQueue.isEmpty())
{
    frontVertex = vertexQueue.dequeue()
    while (frontVertex has a neighbor)
    {
        nextNeighbor = next neighbor of frontVertex
        if (nextNeighbor is not visited)
        {
            Mark nextNeighbor as visited
            traversalOrder.enqueue(nextNeighbor)
            vertexQueue.enqueue(nextNeighbor)
        }
    }
}
return traversalOrder
```

Figure 28-10 traces this algorithm for a directed graph.

 **Note: Breadth-first traversal**
A breadth-first traversal visits a vertex and then each of the vertex's neighbors before advancing. The order in which these neighbors are visited is not specified and can depend on the graph's implementation.

 **Question 6** In what order does a breadth-first traversal visit the vertices in the graph shown in Figure 28-10 when you begin at vertex *E* and visit neighbors in alphabetic order?

**FIGURE 28-10** A trace of a breadth-first traversal beginning at vertex *A* of a directed graph

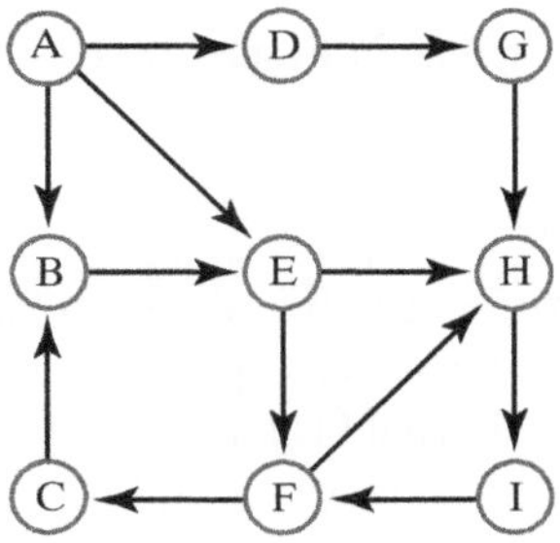

| frontVertex | nextNeighbor | Visited vertex | vertexQueue (front to back) | traversalOrder (front to back) |
|---|---|---|---|---|
| | | A | A | A |
| A | | | *empty* | |
| | B | B | B | AB |
| | D | D | BD | ABD |
| | E | E | BDE | ABDE |
| B | | | DE | |
| D | | | E | |
| | G | G | EG | ABDEG |
| E | | | G | |
| | F | F | GF | ABDEGF |
| | H | H | GFH | ABDEGFH |
| G | | | FH | |
| F | | | H | |
| | C | C | HC | ABDEGFHC |
| H | | | C | |
| | I | I | CI | ABDEGFHCI |
| C | | | I | |
| I | | | *empty* | |

## Depth-First Traversal

**28.13** Given an origin vertex, a depth-first traversal visits the origin, then a neighbor of the origin, and a neighbor of the neighbor. It continues in this fashion until it finds no unvisited neighbor. Backing up by one vertex, it considers another neighbor. This traversal has a recursive feel, since traversing from the origin leads to a traversal from the origin's neighbor. It should not surprise you, then, that we use a stack in the iterative description of this traversal.

We begin by pushing the origin vertex into the stack. When the vertex at the top of the stack has an unvisited neighbor, we visit and push that neighbor onto the stack. If no such neighbor exists, we pop the stack. The traversal order is the order in which vertices are added to the stack. We can maintain this traversal order in a queue.

The following algorithm performs a depth-first traversal of a nonempty graph, beginning at a given vertex:

*Algorithm* `getDepthFirstTraversal(originVertex)`
`traversalOrder` = *a new queue for the resulting traversal order*
`vertexStack` = *a new stack to hold vertices as they are visited*

*Mark* `originVertex` *as visited*
`traversalOrder.enqueue(originVertex)`
`vertexStack.push(originVertex)`

`while (!vertexStack.isEmpty())`
`{`
    `topVertex = vertexStack.peek()`
    `if (topVertex` *has an unvisited neighbor*`)`
    `{`
        `nextNeighbor =` *next unvisited neighbor of* `topVertex`
        *Mark* `nextNeighbor` *as visited*
        `traversalOrder.enqueue(nextNeighbor)`

```
            vertexStack.push(nextNeighbor)
      }
      else // All neighbors are visited
          vertexStack.pop()
}
return traversalOrder
```

Figure 28-11 traces this algorithm for the same directed graph as in Figure 28-10.

**Note:  Depth-first traversal**
A depth-first traversal visits a vertex, then a neighbor of the vertex, a neighbor of the neighbor, and so on, advancing as far as possible from the original vertex. It then backs up by one vertex and considers another neighbor. The order in which these neighbors are visited is not specified and can depend on the graph's implementation.

**Question 7** In what order does a depth-first traversal visit the vertices in the graph shown in Figure 28-11 when you begin at vertex *E* and visit neighbors in alphabetic order?

**FIGURE 28-11**   A trace of a depth-first traversal beginning at vertex *A* of a directed graph

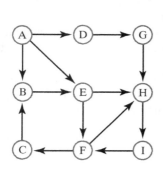

| topVertex | nextNeighbor | Visited vertex | vertexStack (top to bottom) | traversalOrder (front to back) |
|---|---|---|---|---|
|  |  | A | A | A |
| A |  |  | A |  |
|  | B | B | BA | AB |
| B |  |  | BA |  |
|  | E | E | EBA | ABE |
| E |  |  | EBA |  |
|  | F | F | FEBA | ABEF |
| F |  |  | FEBA |  |
|  | C | C | CFEBA | ABEFC |
| C |  |  | FEBA |  |
| F |  |  | FEBA |  |
|  | H | H | HFEBA | ABEFCH |
| H |  |  | HFEBA |  |
|  | I | I | IHFEBA | ABEFCHI |
| I |  |  | HFEBA |  |
| H |  |  | FEBA |  |
| F |  |  | EBA |  |
| E |  |  | BA |  |
| B |  |  | A |  |
| A |  |  | A |  |
|  | D | D | DA | ABEFCHID |
| D |  |  | DA |  |
|  | G | G | GDA | ABEFCHIDG |
| G |  |  | DA |  |
| D |  |  | A |  |
| A |  |  | *empty* | ABEFCHIDG |

# Topological Order

**28.14**   Figure 28-8 shows a graph that represents the prerequisite structure of a group of computer science courses. This graph is a directed graph without cycles. Recall that you can place the vertices of such a graph in a topological order.

 **Note:** In a topological order of the vertices in a directed graph without cycles, vertex *a* precedes vertex *b* whenever a directed edge exists from *a* to *b*.

The vertices in a graph can have several different topological orders. For example, one such order for the graph in Figure 28-8 is cs1, cs2, cs5, cs4, cs7, cs9, cs10, cs6, cs8, cs3. That is, if you complete the courses in this order, you will satisfy all prerequisites. Suppose that you can move the vertices in the graph so that they align in this order, stretching the edges as needed. The result will be like the graph in Figure 28-12a. Each edge points toward a node that comes after the edge's origin node. You will be able to find at least one such arrangement for every directed graph, if the graph has no cycles. Figure 28-12 shows two other topological orders for the graph in Figure 28-8 as well. As is true for this example, any one topological order is usually sufficient to solve a given problem.

**FIGURE 28-12**   Three topological orders for the graph in Figure 28-8

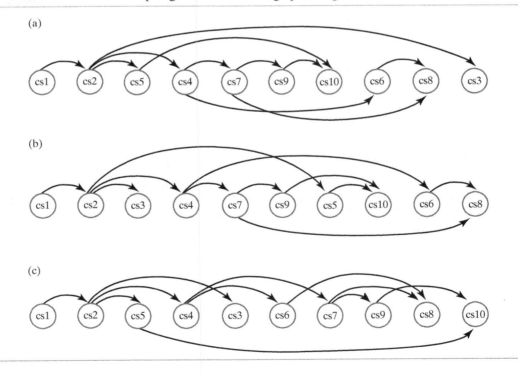

A topological order is not possible for a graph that has a cycle. If vertices *a* and *b* are on the cycle, a path exists from *a* to *b* and from *b* to *a*. One of these paths will contradict any order that we choose for *a* and *b*. For example, the graph in Figure 28-13 contains a cycle. You need to complete cs15 and cs20 before taking cs30. But you need to complete cs30 before taking cs20. This circular logic is caused by the cycle and creates an impossible situation.

**FIGURE 28-13**    An impossible prerequisite structure for three courses, as a directed graph with a cycle

    **Question 8** What is another topological order of the vertices in the graph in Figure 28-8?

**28.15**    The process that discovers a topological order for the vertices in a graph is called a **topological sort**. Several algorithms for this process are possible. We can begin a topological sort by locating a vertex that has no successor, that is, no adjacent vertex. Finding this vertex is possible because the graph has no cycles. We mark the vertex as visited and push it onto a stack. We continue by finding another vertex *u* that is unvisited and whose neighbors, if any, are visited. We mark *u* as visited and push it onto the stack. We proceed in this way until we have visited all the vertices. At that time, the stack contains the vertices in topological order, beginning at the top of the stack.

The following algorithm describes this topological sort:

```
Algorithm getTopologicalOrder()
vertexStack = a new stack to hold vertices as they are visited
numberOfVertices = number of vertices in the graph
for (counter = 1 to numberOfVertices)
{
    nextVertex = an unvisited vertex whose neighbors, if any, are all visited
    Mark nextVertex as visited
    vertexStack.push(nextVertex)
}
return vertexStack
```

Figure 28-14 traces this algorithm for the graph in Figure 28-8. At each iteration of the algorithm's loop, the next unvisited vertex (nextVertex) becomes shaded in the figure as it is visited. The topological order is the opposite of the order in which this shading occurs. In this example, the topological order is the one pictured in Figure 28-12a.

**FIGURE 28-14**   Finding a topological order for the graph in Figure 28-8

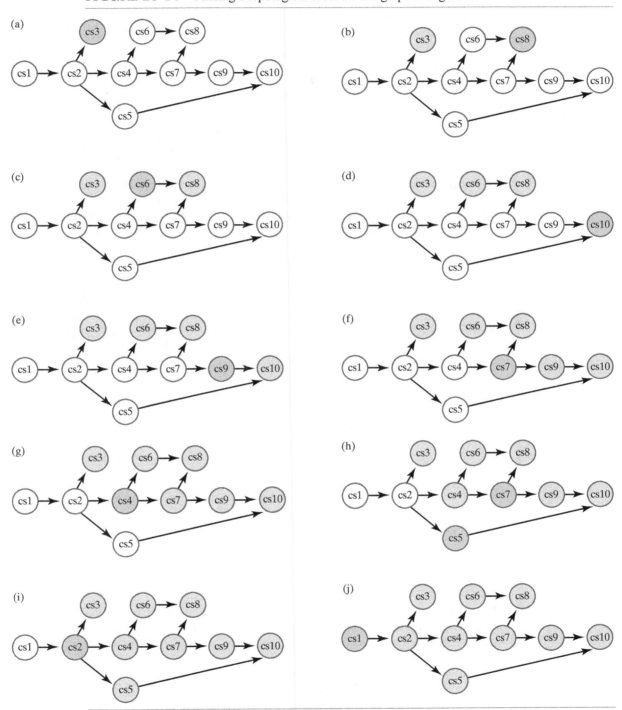

# Paths

Learning whether a particular airline flies between two given cities is important to the average traveler. We can obtain this information by using a graph—such as the one in Figure 28-6—to represent the airline's routes and testing whether a path exists from vertex *a* to vertex *b*. If a path exists, we can also find out what it is. If not any path will do, we can find the one that is shortest or cheapest.

## Finding a Path

**28.16**   For the moment we are content to find any path, not necessarily the best one. A depth-first traversal—discussed in Segment 28.13—stays on a path through the graph as it visits as many vertices as possible. We can easily modify this traversal to locate a path between two vertices. We begin at the origin vertex. Each time we visit another vertex, we see whether that vertex is the desired destination. If so, we are done and the resulting stack contains the path. Otherwise, we continue the traversal until either we are successful or the traversal ends. We leave the development of this algorithm as an exercise.

## The Shortest Path in an Unweighted Graph

**28.17**   **Example.** A graph can have several different paths between the same two vertices. In an unweighted graph, we can find the path with the shortest length, that is, the path that has the fewest edges. For example, consider the unweighted graph in Figure 28-15a. Suppose that we want to know the shortest path from vertex *A* to vertex *H*. By inspecting the graph, we can see that several simple paths—shown in Part *b* of the figure—are possible between these two vertices. The path from *A* to *E* to *H* has length 2 and is the shortest.

**FIGURE 28-15**   (a) An unweighted graph and (b) the possible paths from vertex *A* to vertex *H*

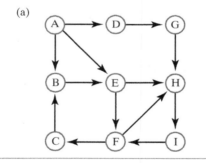

**28.18**   **Developing the algorithm.** The algorithm to find the shortest path between two given vertices in an unweighted graph is based on a breadth-first traversal. Recall that this traversal visits the origin vertex, then the origin's neighbors, the neighbors of each of these neighbors, and so on. Each vertex is placed into a queue as it is visited.

   To find the shortest path, we enhance the breadth-first traversal as follows. When we visit a vertex *v* and mark it as visited, we note the vertex *p* that we just left to reach *v*. That is, *p* precedes *v* in the graph. We also note the length of the path that the traversal followed to reach *v*. This length is 1 more than the length of the path to vertex *p*. We place both the length of the path to *v* and a reference to *p* into vertex *v*. At the end of the traversal, we will use this data in the vertices to construct the shortest path. Let's jump ahead to that part of the algorithm.

Figure 28-16a shows the state of the graph in Figure 28-15a after the algorithm has traversed from vertex *A* to vertex *H*. Each vertex contains its label, the length of the path to it, and the vertex that precedes it on this path, as shown in Figure 28-16b. Although a vertex also contains other data fields, we have ignored them in this figure.

**FIGURE 28-16**  (a) The graph in Figure 28-15a after the shortest-path algorithm has traversed from vertex *A* to vertex *H*; (b) the data in a vertex

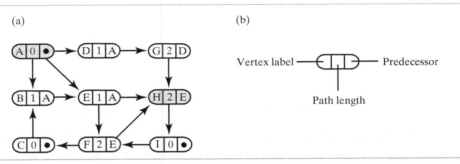

(a)

(b)

Now, by examining the destination vertex—*H*—we find that the length of the shortest path from *A* to *H* is 2. We also find that *H*'s predecessor along this shortest path is vertex *E*. From vertex *E* we see that its predecessor is vertex *A*. Thus, the desired shortest path from vertex *A* to vertex *H* is *A* → *E* → *H*. Our algorithm has discovered what we of course already knew to be true by inspecting this simple graph.

 **Note:** In an unweighted graph, the shortest path between two given vertices has the shortest length—that is, it has the fewest edges. The algorithm to find this path is based on a breadth-first traversal. If several paths have the same shortest length, the algorithm will find only one of them.

**28.19  The algorithm.** The following algorithm finds the shortest path in an unweighted graph between the vertices `originVertex` and `endVertex`. Like the breath-first traversal in Segment 28.12, the algorithm uses a queue to hold the vertices as they are visited. It then uses the given, initially empty stack `path` to construct the shortest path.

```
Algorithm getShortestPath(originVertex, endVertex, path)
done = false
vertexQueue = a new queue to hold vertices as they are visited
Mark originVertex as visited
vertexQueue.enqueue(originVertex)

while (!done && !vertexQueue.isEmpty())
{
    frontVertex = vertexQueue.dequeue()

    while (!done && frontVertex has a neighbor)
    {
        nextNeighbor = next neighbor of frontVertex
        if (nextNeighbor is not visited)
        {
            Mark nextNeighbor as visited
            Set the length of the path to nextNeighbor to 1 + length of path to frontVertex
            Set the predecessor of nextNeighbor to frontVertex
            vertexQueue.enqueue(nextNeighbor)
        }
```

```
            if (nextNeighbor equals endVertex)
                done = true
        }
    }
    // Traversal ends; construct shortest path
    pathLength = length of path to endVertex
    path.push(endVertex)

    vertex = endVertex
    while (vertex has a predecessor)
    {
        vertex = predecessor of vertex
        path.push(vertex)
    }
    return pathLength
```

When the algorithm ends, the stack path contains the vertices along the shortest path, with the origin at the top of the stack. The value returned is the length of this shortest path.

**28.20** **Tracing the algorithm.** Figure 28-17 traces the steps that the algorithm takes to produce the path information shown in Figure 28-16a for the unweighted graph in Figure 28-15a. After adding the origin—vertex $A$—to the queue, we visit the origin's three neighbors—$B$, $D$, and $E$—and enqueue them.

**FIGURE 28-17** A trace of the traversal in the algorithm to find the shortest path from vertex $A$ to vertex $H$ in an unweighted graph

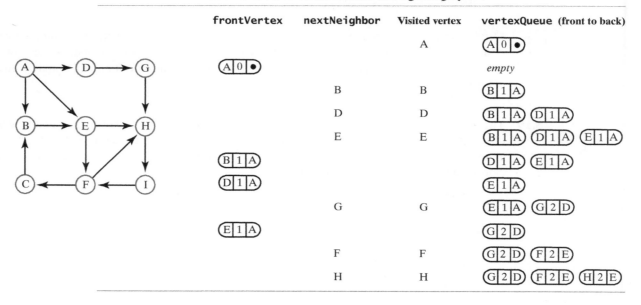

The length of each path from $A$ to these neighbors is 1. Since vertex $A$ has no more neighbors, we remove vertex $B$ from the queue. This vertex has vertex $E$ as a neighbor, but $E$ has been visited already. This implies that we can get to $E$ from $A$ without first going through $B$. That is, $B$ is not on any shortest path that begins at $A$ and goes through $E$. Indeed, the path $A \rightarrow B \rightarrow E$ is longer than the path $A \rightarrow E$. We do not know whether our final path involves $E$, but if it does, it will not pass through $B$.

The algorithm now removes vertex $D$ from the queue. Its neighbor $G$ is unvisited, so we set $G$'s path-length field to 2 and its predecessor to $D$. We then enqueue $G$. The algorithm continues in this manner and eventually encounters the destination vertex, $H$. After $H$ is updated, the outer loop ends. We then construct the path by working back from $H$, as we did earlier in Segment 28.18.

**Question 9** Continue the trace begun in Figure 28-17 to find the shortest path from vertex $A$ to vertex $C$.

## The Shortest Path in a Weighted Graph

**28.21** **Example.** In a weighted graph, the shortest path is not necessarily the one with the fewest edges. Rather, it is the one with the smallest edge-weight sum. Figure 28-18a shows a weighted graph obtained by adding weights to the graph in Figure 28-15a. The possible paths from vertex $A$ to vertex $H$ are the same as you saw in Figure 28-15b. This time, however, we list each path with its weight—that is, the sum of the weights of its edges—in Figure 28-18b.

We can see that the smallest path weight is 8, so the shortest path is $A \to D \to G \to H$. When the weights are distances, the term "shortest" is appropriate. When the weights represent costs, we might think of this path as the "cheapest" path.

**FIGURE 28-18** (a) A weighted graph and (b) the possible paths from vertex $A$ to vertex $H$, with their weights

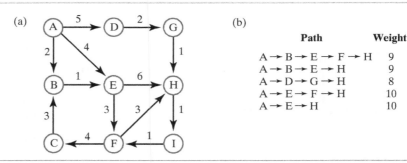

**28.22** **Developing the algorithm.** The algorithm to find the shortest, or cheapest, path between two given vertices in a weighted graph is based on a breadth-first traversal. It is similar to the algorithm we developed for an unweighted graph. In that algorithm, we noted the number of edges in the path that led to the vertex under consideration. Here, we compute the sum of the edge weights in the path leading to a vertex. In addition, we must record the cheapest of the possible paths. Whereas before we used a queue to order vertices, this algorithm uses a priority queue.

**Note:** In a weighted graph, the shortest path between two given vertices has the smallest edge-weight sum. The algorithm to find this path is based on a breadth-first traversal. Several paths in a weighted graph might share the same minimum edge-weight sum. Our algorithm will find only one of these paths.

Each entry in the priority queue is an object that contains a vertex, the cost of the path to that vertex from the origin vertex, and the previous vertex on that path. The priority value is the cost of the path, with the smallest value having the highest priority. Thus, the cheapest path is at the front of the priority queue, and it is thus the first one removed. Note that several entries in the priority queue might contain the same vertex but different costs.

At the conclusion of the algorithm, the vertices in the graph contain predecessors and costs that enable us to construct the cheapest path, much as we constructed the path with the fewest edges from the graph in Figure 28-16a.

**28.23 Tracing the algorithm.** Figure 28-19 traces the traversal portion of the algorithm for the weighted graph in Figure 28-18a when vertex *A* is the origin. Initially, an object containing *A*, zero, and null is placed in the priority queue. We begin a loop by removing the front entry from the priority queue. We use the contents of this entry to change the state of the indicated vertex—*A* in this case—in the graph. Thus, we store a path length of zero and a null predecessor into *A*. We also mark *A* as visited.

Vertex *A* has three unvisited neighbors, *B*, *D*, and *E*. The costs of the paths from *A* to each of these neighbors is 2, 5, and 4, respectively. These costs, along with *A* as the previous vertex,

**FIGURE 28-19** A trace of the traversal in the algorithm to find the cheapest path from vertex *A* to vertex *H* in a weighted graph

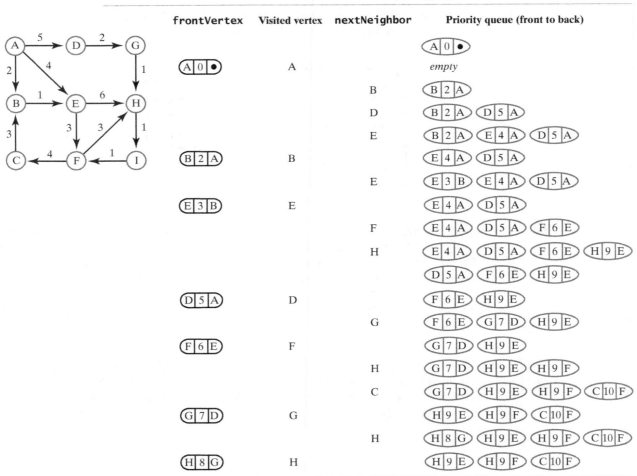

are used to create objects that are placed into the priority queue. The priority queue orders these objects so that the cheapest path is first.

We remove the front entry from the priority queue. The entry contains vertex *B*, so we visit *B*. We also store within vertex *B* the path cost 2 and its predecessor *A*. Now *B* has vertex *E* as its sole unvisited neighbor. The cost of the path $A \rightarrow B \rightarrow E$ is the cost of the path $A \rightarrow B$ plus the weight of the edge from *B* to *E*. This total cost is 3. We encapsulate *E*, the cost 3, and the predecessor *B* into an object that we add to the priority queue. Notice that two objects in the priority queue involve vertex *E*, but the most recent one has the cheapest path.

We again remove the front entry from the priority queue. The entry contains vertex *E*, so we visit it and store into *E* the path cost 3 and *E*'s predecessor *B*. Vertex *E* has two unvisited neighbors, *F* and *H*. The cost of each path to a neighbor is the cost of the path to *E* plus the weight of the edge to the neighbor. Two new objects are added to the priority queue.

The next object removed from the priority queue contains the vertex *E*, but since *E* has been visited, we ignore it. We then remove the next object from the priority queue. The algorithm continues until the destination vertex *H* is visited.

Figure 28-20 shows the state of the graph at the conclusion of the trace given in Figure 28-19. By looking at the destination vertex *H*, we can see that the weight of the cheapest path from *A* to *H* is 8. Tracing back from *H* to *A*, we see that this path is $A \rightarrow D \rightarrow G \rightarrow H$, as we noted in Segment 28.21.

**FIGURE 28-20** The graph in Figure 28-18a after finding the cheapest path from vertex *A* to vertex *H*

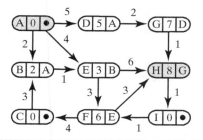

28.24 **The algorithm.** The pseudocode for the algorithm we just described follows. Objects in the priority queue are instances of a private class `EntryPQ`. Following the traversal, the algorithm pushes the vertices that occur along the cheapest path from `originVertex` to `endVertex` into a given, initially empty stack `path`.

```
Algorithm getCheapestPath(originVertex, endVertex, path)
done = false
priorityQueue = a new priority queue

priorityQueue.add(new EntryPQ(originVertex, 0, null))

while (!done && !priorityQueue.isEmpty())
{
    frontEntry = priorityQueue.remove()
    frontVertex = vertex in frontEntry

    if (frontVertex is not visited)
    {
        Mark frontVertex as visited
        Set the cost of the path to frontVertex to the cost recorded in frontEntry
        Set the predecessor of frontVertex to the predecessor recorded in frontEntry

        if (frontVertex equals endVertex)
```

```
            done = true
        else
        {
            while (frontVertex has a neighbor)
            {
                nextNeighbor = next neighbor of frontVertex
                weightOfEdgeToNeighbor = weight of edge to nextNeighbor

                if (nextNeighbor is not visited)
                {
                    nextCost = weightOfEdgeToNeighbor + cost of path to frontVertex
                    priorityQueue.add(new EntryPQ(nextNeighbor, nextCost,
                                                  frontVertex))
                }
            }
        }
    }
}
// Traversal ends; construct cheapest path
pathCost = cost of path to endVertex
path.push(endVertex)

vertex = endVertex
while (vertex has a predecessor)
{
    vertex = predecessor of vertex
    path.push(vertex)
}
return pathCost
```

The origin of the cheapest path will be at the top of the stack `path`. At the bottom of the stack is the destination vertex. The cost of the path is returned by the algorithm.

This algorithm is based on Dijkstra's algorithm, which finds the shortest paths from an origin to all other vertices.

**Question 10** Adapt the trace begun in Figure 28-19 to find the shortest (cheapest) path from vertex *A* to vertex *C*.

**Question 11** Why do we place instances of `EntryPQ` into the priority queue, instead of placing vertices?

# Java Interfaces for the ADT Graph

**28.25**   The ADT graph is a bit different from other ADTs in that, once you create it, you do not add, remove, or retrieve components. Instead, you use a graph to answer questions based on the relationships among its vertices.

We will divide the graph operations into two Java interfaces. You use the operations in the first interface to create the graph and to obtain basic information such as the number of vertices. The second interface specifies operations such as the traversals and path searches that we discussed earlier in this chapter. For convenience, we define a third interface, `GraphInterface`, that combines the first two interfaces.

To make these interfaces as general as possible, we have them specify graphs that are either directed or undirected, and weighted or unweighted. The first interface appears in Listing 28-1. The generic type T represents the data type of the objects that label the graph's vertices.

**LISTING 28-1    An interface of basic graph operations**

```java
package GraphPackage;
/** An interface of methods providing basic operations for directed
    and undirected graphs that are either weighted or unweighted. */
public interface BasicGraphInterface<T>
{
    /** Adds a given vertex to this graph.
        @param vertexLabel  An object that labels the new vertex and is
                            distinct from the labels of current vertices.
        @return  True if the vertex is added, or false if not. */
    public boolean addVertex(T vertexLabel);

    /** Adds a weighted edge between two given distinct vertices that
        are currently in this graph. The desired edge must not already
        be in the graph. In a directed graph, the edge points toward
        the second vertex given.
        @param begin  An object that labels the origin vertex of the edge.
        @param end    An object, distinct from begin, that labels the end
                      vertex of the edge.
        @param edgeWeight  The real value of the edge's weight.
        @return  True if the edge is added, or false if not. */
    public boolean addEdge(T begin, T end, double edgeWeight);

    /** Adds an unweighted edge between two given distinct vertices
        that are currently in this graph. The desired edge must not
        already be in the graph. In a directed graph, the edge points
        toward the second vertex given.
        @param begin  An object that labels the origin vertex of the edge.
        @param end    An object, distinct from begin, that labels the end
                      vertex of the edge.
        @return  True if the edge is added, or false if not. */
    public boolean addEdge(T begin, T end);

    /** Sees whether an edge exists between two given vertices.
        @param begin  An object that labels the origin vertex of the edge.
        @param end    An object that labels the end vertex of the edge.
        @return  True if an edge exists. */
    public boolean hasEdge(T begin, T end);

    /** Sees whether this graph is empty.
        @return  True if the graph is empty. */
    public boolean isEmpty();

    /** Gets the number of vertices in this graph.
        @return  The number of vertices in the graph. */
    public int getNumberOfVertices();

    /** Gets the number of edges in this graph.
        @return  The number of edges in the graph. */
    public int getNumberOfEdges();

    /** Removes all vertices and edges from this graph. */
    public void clear();
} // end BasicGraphInterface
```

**28.26** **Example.** Suppose that the class `UndirectedGraph` implements the interface `BasicGraphInterface`, as given in Listing 28-1, and is in the package `GraphPackage`. The following statements create the graph shown in Figure 28-21, which is a portion of the graph in Figure 28-6:

```java
BasicGraphInterface<String> airMap = new UndirectedGraph<>();
airMap.addVertex("Boston");
airMap.addVertex("Provincetown");
airMap.addVertex("Nantucket");
airMap.addEdge("Boston", "Provincetown");
airMap.addEdge("Boston", "Nantucket");
```

At this point,

```java
airMap.getNumberOfVertices()
```

returns 3, and

```java
airMap.getNumberOfEdges()
```

returns 2.

---

FIGURE 28-21    A portion of the flight map in Figure 28-6

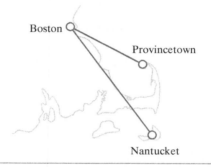

---

**Question 12** What revisions to the previous Java statements are necessary to make `airMap` a weighted graph?

**28.27** The algorithms discussed earlier in this chapter use graph operations that are not specified in the previous interface. Although we could add these operations to the interface so the client could implement various algorithms, such as the topological sort, we choose not to do so. Instead, methods that implement the graph algorithms will be a part of the graph class. The interface in Listing 28-2 specifies these methods. Again, the data type of the objects that label the graph's vertices are represented by the generic type T.

---

LISTING 28-2   An interface of operations on an existing graph

```java
1  package GraphPackage;
2  import ADTPackage.*; // Classes that implement various ADTs
3  /** An interface of methods that process an existing graph. */
4  public interface GraphAlgorithmsInterface<T>
5  {
6     /** Performs a breadth-first traversal of this graph.
7        @param origin  An object that labels the origin vertex of the traversal.
```

```
 8        @return   A queue of labels of the vertices in the traversal, with
 9                     the label of the origin vertex at the queue's front. */
10    public QueueInterface<T> getBreadthFirstTraversal(T origin);
11
12    /** Performs a depth-first traversal of this graph.
13        @param origin  An object that labels the origin vertex of the
14                     traversal.
15        @return   A queue of labels of the vertices in the traversal, with
16                     the label of the origin vertex at the queue's front. */
17    public QueueInterface<T> getDepthFirstTraversal(T origin);
18
19    /** Performs a topological sort of the vertices in a graph without cycles.
20        @return   A stack of vertex labels in topological order, beginning
21                     with the stack's top. */
22    public StackInterface<T> getTopologicalOrder();
23
24    /** Finds the path between two given vertices that has the shortest length.
25        @param begin  An object that labels the path's origin vertex.
26        @param end    An object that labels the path's destination vertex.
27        @param path   A stack of labels that is empty initially;
28                     at the completion of the method, this stack contains
29                     the labels of the vertices along the shortest path;
30                     the label of the origin vertex is at the top, and
31                     the label of the destination vertex is at the bottom.
32        @return   The length of the shortest path. */
33    public int getShortestPath(T begin, T end, StackInterface<T> path);
34
35    /** Finds the least-cost path between two given vertices.
36        @param begin  An object that labels the path's origin vertex.
37        @param end    An object that labels the path's destination vertex.
38        @param path   A stack of labels that is empty initially;
39                     at the completion of the method, this stack contains
40                     the labels of the vertices along the cheapest path;
41                     the label of the origin vertex is at the top, and
42                     the label of the destination vertex is at the bottom.
43        @return   The cost of the cheapest path. */
44    public double getCheapestPath(T begin, T end, StackInterface<T> path);
45 } // end GraphAlgorithmsInterface
```

The interface in Listing 28-3 combines BasicGraphInterface and GraphAlgorithmsInterface.

**LISTING 28-3   An interface for the ADT graph**

```
1 package GraphPackage;
2 public interface GraphInterface<T> extends BasicGraphInterface<T>,
3                                             GraphAlgorithmsInterface<T>
4 {
5 } // end GraphInterface
```

**28.28   Example.** Imagine that we want to find the shortest route between the towns of Truro and Falmouth. By "shortest route" we mean the route with the least number of miles, not the path with the fewest edges. We first could create the graph in Figure 28-3, using statements much like those in Segment 28.26. We then could use the method getCheapestPath to answer our question. The following statements indicate how to perform these steps and to display the names of the cities along the shortest route:

```
GraphInterface<String> roadMap = new UndirectedGraph<>();
roadMap.addVertex("Provincetown");
roadMap.addVertex("Truro");
   . . .
roadMap.addVertex("Falmouth");

roadMap.addEdge("Provincetown", "Truro", 10);
   . . .
roadMap.addEdge("Hyannis", "Falmouth", 20);

StackInterface<String> bestRoute = new LinkedStack<>();
double distance = roadMap.getCheapestPath("Truro", "Falmouth", bestRoute);
System.out.println("The shortest route from Truro to Falmouth is " +
                    distance + " miles long and " +
                    "passes through the following towns:");
while (!bestRoute.isEmpty())
    System.out.println(bestRoute.pop());
```

 **Note:** The operations of the ADT graph enable you to create a graph and answer questions about the relationships among its vertices.

 **Question 13** The previous example finds the shortest route between two towns. Why did we invoke the method `getCheapestPath` instead of `getShortestPath`?

## CHAPTER SUMMARY

- A graph is a collection of distinct vertices and distinct edges. Each edge joins two vertices. A subgraph is a portion of a graph that is itself a graph.

- A tree is a special graph that has a hierarchical order and a root that is the ancestor of all other nodes—that is, vertices—in the tree.

- Each edge in a directed graph has a direction from one vertex to another. The edges in an undirected graph are bidirectional.

- A path from one vertex to another is a sequence of edges. The length of the path is the number of these edges. A simple path passes through each of its vertices once. A cycle is a path that begins and ends at the same vertex. A simple cycle passes through its other vertices once.

- The edges in a weighted graph have values called weights or costs. A path in a weighted graph has a weight, or cost, that is the sum of its edge weights.

- A graph that has a path between every pair of distinct vertices is connected. A complete graph has an edge between every pair of distinct vertices.

- Two vertices in an undirected graph are adjacent if they are joined by an edge. In a directed graph, vertex $i$ is adjacent to vertex $j$ if a directed edge begins at $j$ and ends at $i$. Adjacent vertices are called neighbors.

- You can traverse the vertices in a graph by using either a depth-first traversal or a breadth-first traversal. A depth-first traversal follows a path that goes as deeply into the graph as possible before following other paths. A breadth-first traversal visits all neighbors of a vertex before visiting the neighbors' neighbors.

- A directed graph without cycles imposes an order on its vertices called a topological order. This order is not unique. You use a topological sort to discover these orders.

- You can use a depth-first traversal of a graph to see whether a path exists between two given vertices.

- You can modify the breadth-first traversal of a graph to find the path between two given vertices that has the fewest edges.

- You can modify the breadth-first traversal of a weighted graph to find the path between two given vertices that has the lowest cost.

## EXERCISES

**1.** Suppose that five vertices are arranged at the corners of an imaginary pentagon. Draw a connected graph that contains these vertices.

**2.** Describe each graph in Figure 28-22, using the terms introduced in Segments 28.1 through 28.4.

FIGURE 28-22    Graphs for Exercise 2

<table>
<tr><td>(a)</td><td>(b)</td><td>(c)</td></tr>
</table>

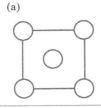
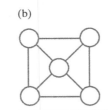
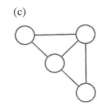

**3.** Consider a graph that represents acquaintances among people. Each vertex represents a person. Each edge represents an acquaintance between two people.

    **a.** Is this graph directed or undirected?
    **b.** Consider all vertices adjacent to a given vertex $x$. What does this set of vertices represent?
    **c.** What does a path in this graph represent?
    **d.** In what circumstance might one want to know the shortest path between two vertices in this graph?
    **e.** Is the graph associated with all the people alive on January 1, 1995, connected? Justify your answer.

**4.** In what order does a breadth-first traversal visit the vertices in the graph in Figure 28-10 when you begin at

    **a.** Vertex $G$
    **b.** Vertex $F$

**5.** Repeat the previous exercise, but perform a depth-first traversal instead.

**6.** Consider the directed graph that appears in Figure 28-10, and remove the edge between vertices $E$ and $F$, and the edge between vertices $F$ and $H$.

    **a.** In what order will a breadth-first traversal visit the vertices when you begin at vertex $A$?
    **b.** Repeat Part $a$, but perform a depth-first traversal instead.

**7.** Draw a directed graph that depicts the prerequisite structure of the courses required for your major. Find a topological order for these courses.

**8.** Construct the topological ordering for the weighted, directed, acyclic graph in Figure 28-23.

**FIGURE 28-23**   A graph for Exercises 8, 10, and 22

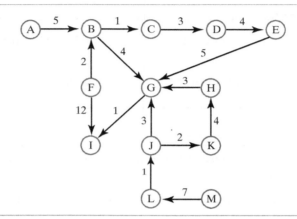

**9.** A computer network such as the Internet or a local area network can be represented as a graph. Each computer is a vertex in the graph. An edge between two vertices represents a direct connection between two computers. Explain when and why you would be interested in each of the following tasks:

    **a.** Finding a path in this graph
    **b.** Finding multiple paths from one particular vertex to another
    **c.** Finding the shortest path from one particular vertex to another
    **d.** Seeing whether the graph is connected

**10.** Find a path for the weighted graph in Figure 28-23 from vertex *A* to vertex *I*, and also find the cheapest path using the getCheapestPath algorithm.

**11.** A tree is a connected graph without cycles.

    **a.** What is the smallest number of edges that could be removed from the graph in Figure 28-1 to make it a tree?
    **b.** Give one example of such a set of edges.

**12.** Figure 28-7b shows a graph that represents a maze. Label the vertices of this graph, with the uppermost vertex labeled *S* (the entrance to the maze) and the lowest vertex labeled *T* (the exit from the maze).

    **a.** Is this graph a tree?
    **b.** What is the shortest path from *S* to *T*?
    **c.** What is the longest simple path in this graph?

**13.** Revise the unweighted, directed graph in Figure 28-15a by adding a directed edge from *D* to *H*. The resulting graph has two paths from *A* to *H* that are shortest among all paths between these two vertices. Which of these two paths will the algorithm getShortestPath in Segment 28.19 find?

**14.** Consider the unweighted graph in Figure 28-15. Find the path from vertex *A* to vertex *I*, and also find the shortest path using the getShortestPath algorithm.

**15.** Revise the weighted, directed graph in Figure 28-18a by adding a directed edge from $D$ to $H$. Let the weight of this new edge be 3. The resulting graph has two paths from $A$ to $H$ that are cheapest among all paths between these two vertices. Which of these two paths will the algorithm getCheapestPath in Segment 28.24 find?

**16.** Find a map of the routes of a major U. S. airline. Such maps are usually printed at the back of in-flight magazines. You could also search the Internet for one. The map is a graph like the one in Figure 28-6. Consider the following pairs of cities:

> Providence (RI) and San Diego (CA)
> Albany (NY) and Phoenix (AZ)
> Boston (MA) and Baltimore (MD)
> Dallas (TX) and Detroit (MI)
> Charlotte (NC) and Chicago (IL)
> Portland (ME) and Portland (OR)

    **a.** Which pairs of cities in this list have edges (nonstop flights) between them?
    **b.** Which pairs are not connected by any path?
    **c.** For each of the remaining pairs, find the path with the fewest edges.

**17.** Find the trail map of a cross-country ski area. Represent the trail map as an undirected graph, where each intersection of trails is a vertex, and each section of trail between intersections is an edge. Consider a cross-country skier who wishes to take the longest tour possible, but does not want to ski on any trail more than once. What is the longest path that starts and ends at the ski lodge and does not traverse any section of trail more than once? (Intersections may be passed through more than once, and some sections of trail may be left unskied.)

**18.** Find the trail map of a downhill ski area. Represent the trail map as a graph, where each intersection of trails is a vertex, and each section of trail between intersections is an edge.

    **a.** Is the graph directed or undirected?
    **b.** Does the graph have cycles?
    **c.** Find the longest path possible that begins at the top of the mountain and ends at the ski lodge.

**19.** Write statements appropriate for the client of the class UndirectedGraph that create the graph in Figure 28-3. Assume that UndirectedGraph implements GraphInterface.

**20.** Write statements appropriate for the client of the class DirectedGraph that create the graph in Figure 28-8. Assume that DirectedGraph implements GraphInterface. Then write statements to find and display a topological order for this graph.

**21.** A graph is said to be **biconnected** if two paths that do not share edges or vertices exist between every pair of vertices.

    **a.** Which graphs in Figures 28-1 and 28-4 are biconnected?
    **b.** What are some applications that would use a biconnected graph?

**22.** A **critical path** in a weighted, directed, acyclic graph is the path with the greatest weight. Let's assume that all edge weights are positive. Give each vertex a value equal to the weight of a path to that vertex. Initially, each vertex's value is zero.

    We can find the critical path by considering the vertices one at a time in topological order. For each vertex, consider all the edges that leave the vertex. For each of these edges, add the weight of the edge and the value of the edge's source vertex. Compare the sum with the value of the edge's destination vertex. Make the larger of these values the value of the destination vertex. After all vertices have been visited, the largest value stored in a vertex will be the weight of the critical path.

    Find the critical path for the graph in Figure 28-23.

## PROJECTS

1. In a search tree, it is easy to search for any value. For other trees in which the children of a node are not ordered in any particular way, you can use a breadth-first traversal, as described for graphs, to find a path from the root to some other node (vertex) $v$. Implement such a method for a general tree.

2. Write Java code that creates the graph given in Figure 28-1. Find the shortest path from Sandwich to Falmouth. Do the same for the weighted graph in Figure 28-3. (See Exercise 19.)

3. Write Java code that creates the graph in Figure 28-10. Perform a breadth-first traversal of the graph, beginning at the node labeled $A$.

4. In the game of Nim, an arbitrary number of chips are divided into an arbitrary number of piles. Each player can remove as many chips as desired from any single pile. The last player to remove a chip wins.

    Consider a limited version of this game, in which three piles contain 3, 5, and 8 chips, respectively. You can represent this game as a directed graph. Each vertex in this graph is a possible configuration of the piles (chips in each pile). The initial configuration, for example, is (3, 5, 8). Each edge in the graph represents a legal move in the game.

    **a.** Write Java statements that will construct this directed graph.
    **b.** Discuss how a computer program might use this graph to play Nim.

5. The **diameter** of an unweighted graph is the maximum of all the shortest distances between pairs of vertices in the graph.

    **a.** Give an algorithm for computing the diameter of a graph.
    **b.** What is the Big Oh performance of your algorithm in terms of the number of vertices and edges in the graph?
    **c.** Implement your algorithm.
    **d.** Discuss possible ways that you can improve the performance of the algorithm.

6. Exercise 22 described how to find the critical path in a weighted, directed, acyclic graph. Write a method that will find the critical path. You may assume the existence of a method that tests whether a graph is acyclic.

7. The $n$-puzzle is a one-person game that involves a square or rectangular frame that can contain exactly $n +$ 1 square tiles. The game begins with $n$ tiles numbered from 1 to $n$ positioned randomly in the frame. With one empty space in the frame, the objective is to slide the tiles—one at a time and either horizontally or vertically—until they appear in numerical order, as shown in Figure 28-24a. This solved configuration is for a 15-puzzle using a 4-by-4 frame.

**FIGURE 28-24**   (a) A solved 15-puzzle; (b) an unsolvable 15-puzzle

Not all initial configurations of an *n*-puzzle can be solved. For example, if the initial configuration of a 15-puzzle were as pictured in Figure 28-24b, with only the 14 and 15 tiles interchanged, no solution would be possible. A solvable 15-puzzle can take up to 80 moves to reach the solution; an 8-puzzle using a 3 × 3 frame will take at most 31 moves to solve, if it has a solution. To reduce our effort even further, we will consider 5-puzzles in 2 × 3 frames. Figure 28-25 shows two such puzzles with their solutions. Note that the empty space in a solution can be either before the 1 or after the 5.

Figure 23-23 in Chapter 23 showed a game tree for tic-tac-toe. A game tree, which is a kind of graph, contains the possible moves for a particular game. Because you cannot change a move made in tic-tac-toe, the game tree is a directed graph. Such is not the case for the *n*-puzzle, as you can change your mind about any move. Thus, an undirected graph can represent all of the possible moves.

Write Java code that creates an undirected graph of the possible board configurations for the 5-puzzle. Using a shortest-path search, find a solution to any given initial configuration.

**FIGURE 28-25**   The initial and final configurations of two 5-puzzles

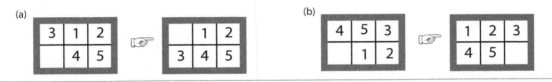

## ANSWERS TO SELF-TEST QUESTIONS

1. **a.** 3.
   **b.** 36.
   **c.** Truro-Orleans-Barnstable-Sandwich, with a length of 3.
   **d.** Truro-Orleans-Barnstable-Sandwich, with a weight of 48.

2. Electrical (or telephone or TV) wires, plumbing, hallways or other connections between rooms.

3. The graph is connected but not complete.

4. No; cs8 and cs10 each would have 2 parents.

5. **a.** No; **b.** Yes; **c.** No; **d.** No.

6. *E, F, H, C, I, B.*

7. *E, F, C, B, H, I.*

8. cs1, cs2, cs4, cs7, cs9, cs5, cs10, cs6, cs8, cs3; or cs1, cs2, cs3, cs4, cs5, cs6, cs7, cs8, cs9, cs10.

9. Remove vertex *G* from the queue. *G*'s neighbor *H* has been visited already. Now remove *F* from the queue. *F*'s neighbor *C* is unvisited. Set *C*'s predecessor to *F* and its path-length field to 3 (1 + the length recorded in *F*). Add *C* to the queue. Since *C* is the destination, construct the path by working backward from *C*, as we did in Segment 28.18. The shortest path is $A \rightarrow E \rightarrow F \rightarrow C$, with a length of 3.

10. Vertex *H* has one unvisited neighbor, *I*. The cost of the path to *I* is the cost of the path to *H* plus the weight of the edge from *H* to *I*. This total cost is 9. Encapsulate vertex *I*, the cost 9, and the predecessor *H* into an object and add it to the priority queue.
    Now remove the front entry from the priority queue. The entry contains *H*, and since *H* is visited already, ignore the entry. Remove the next entry. This entry also contains *H*, which is visited, so ignore it and remove the next entry. This entry contains *I*, which is unvisited. Visit *I*. *I*'s neighbor *F* is visited, so remove the next entry from the priority queue. This entry contains *C*, so visit *C*.

Since $C$ is the destination, construct the path by working backward from $C$, as we did in Segment 28.18. The shortest (cheapest) path is $A \rightarrow B \rightarrow E \rightarrow F \rightarrow C$, with a weight (cost) of 10.

11. Two or more entries in the priority queue can record data about the same vertex. For example, consider the trace in Figure 28-19. After we visit vertex $B$, the first two entries in the priority queue record data about vertex $E$. The first entry involves the path from $B$ to $E$, while the second entry involves the path from $A$ to $E$. While vertex $E$ can record similar data for one path, it cannot do so for multiple paths.

12. In the two calls to addEdge, you would add an edge weight as a third argument.

13. The method getCheapestPath finds the path with the smallest weight sum, which gives us the shortest route when measured in miles; getShortestPath finds the path that contains the fewest number of edges.

# Graph Implementations

## Contents

## Prerequisites

## Objectives

After studying this chapter, you should be able to

- Describe an adjacency matrix
- Describe an adjacency list
- Specify and implement the classes that represent the vertices and edges of a graph
- Implement the ADT graph by using adjacency lists

Like the ADTs you have seen previously, graphs have several implementations. Each implementation must represent the vertices in the graph and the edges between the vertices. In general, you use either a list or a dictionary to hold the vertices, and an array or a list to represent the edges. Each representation of the edges has its own advantages, but the list representation is most typical.

## An Overview of Two Implementations

Two common implementations of the ADT graph use either an array or a list to represent the graph's edges. The array is typically a two-dimensional array called an **adjacency matrix**. The list is called an **adjacency list**. Each of these constructs represents the connections—that is, the edges—among the vertices in the graph.

### The Adjacency Matrix

**29.1** The adjacency matrix for a graph of $n$ vertices has $n$ rows and $n$ columns. Each row and each column corresponds to a vertex in the graph. You number the vertices from 0 through $n - 1$ to match the row indices and the column indices. If $a_{ij}$ is the element in row $i$ and column $j$ of the matrix, $a_{ij}$ indicates whether an edge exists between vertex $i$ and vertex $j$. For an unweighted graph, you can use boolean values in the matrix. For a weighted graph, you can use edge weights when edges exist and a representation of infinity otherwise.

Figure 29-1 provides an example of an unweighted, directed graph and its adjacency matrix. Let's consider vertex $A$ of the graph, which we have numbered as vertex 0. Since directed edges exist from vertex $A$ to each of the vertices $B$, $D$, and $E$, the matrix elements $a_{01}$, $a_{03}$, and $a_{04}$ are true. We have used a "T" in the figure to represent true. The other entries in the first row are false (blank in the figure).

Although a directed edge exists from vertex $A$ to vertex $B$, the converse is not true. Therefore, $a_{10}$ is false, even though $a_{01}$ is true. The adjacency matrix for an undirected graph, however, is **symmetric**; that is, $a_{ij}$ and $a_{ji}$ have the same value. When an undirected graph has an edge from vertex $i$ to vertex $j$, it also has an edge from vertex $j$ to vertex $i$.

**FIGURE 29-1** (a) An unweighted, directed graph and (b) its adjacency matrix

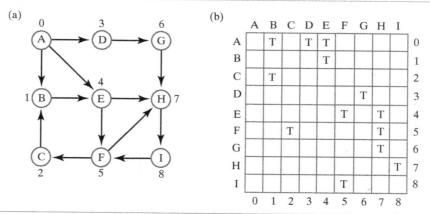

| | A | B | C | D | E | F | G | H | I | |
|---|---|---|---|---|---|---|---|---|---|---|
| A | | T | | T | T | | | | | 0 |
| B | | | | | T | | | | | 1 |
| C | T | | | | | | | | | 2 |
| D | | | | | | | T | | | 3 |
| E | | | | | | T | | T | | 4 |
| F | | | T | | | | | T | | 5 |
| G | | | | | | | | T | | 6 |
| H | | | | | | | | | T | 7 |
| I | | | | | | T | | | | 8 |
| | 0 | 1 | 2 | 3 | 4 | 5 | 6 | 7 | 8 | |

**29.2**   From an adjacency matrix, you quickly can see whether an edge exists between any two given vertices. This operation is O(1). But if you want to know all the neighbors of a particular vertex, you need to scan an entire row of the matrix, an O(*n*) task. Additionally, the matrix occupies a considerable, fixed amount of space that depends on the number of vertices but not on the number of edges. In fact, an adjacency matrix represents every possible edge in a graph, regardless of whether the edges actually exist. However, most graphs have relatively few of the many edges possible—that is, they are sparse. For such graphs, an adjacency list uses less space, as you will now see.

**Note:** An adjacency matrix uses a fixed amount of space that depends on the number of vertices, but not the number of edges, in a graph. The adjacency matrix for a sparse graph wastes space, because the graph has relatively few edges.

**Note:** Seeing whether an edge exists between any two given vertices of a graph can be done quickly when you use an adjacency matrix. But you need to scan an entire row of the matrix if you want to know all the neighbors of a particular vertex.

**Question 1** Consider the graph in Figure 28-4b of the previous chapter. Number the vertices from 0 through 3, starting at the vertex in the upper left corner and moving in a clockwise direction. What adjacency matrix represents this graph?

## The Adjacency List

**29.3**   An adjacency list for a given vertex represents only those edges that originate from the vertex. In Figure 29-2, each vertex of the graph in Figure 29-1a references a list of adjacent vertices. Space is not reserved for edges that do not exist. Thus, the adjacency lists, taken together, use less memory than the corresponding adjacency matrix in Figure 29-1b. For this reason, implementations of sparse graphs use adjacency lists. The implementation that we present in this chapter will do so also, since typical graphs are sparse.

   Although the adjacency lists in our diagram contain vertices, they will actually contain edges in our implementation. Each of these edges, however, will contain the illustrated vertex as its terminal vertex.

**Note:** An adjacency list for a given vertex represents only those edges that originate from the vertex. For a sparse graph, an adjacency list uses less memory than an adjacency matrix. For a dense graph, an adjacency matrix can be the better choice.

**Note:** Using adjacency lists, you can find all the neighbors of a particular vertex by traversing a list. If you want to know whether an edge exists between any two given vertices, you need to search a list. If the graph contains *n* vertices, each of these operations is O(*n*) at worst, but is faster on average.

**FIGURE 29-2**   Adjacency lists for the directed graph in Figure 29-1a

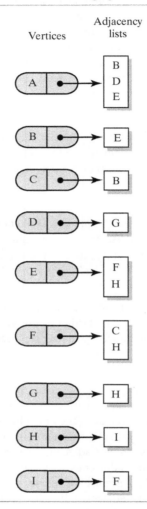

**Question 2** What adjacency lists represent the graph described in Question 1?

## Vertices and Edges

**29.4**   While designing a class that implements the ADT graph, we encounter two other types of objects, the vertex and the edge. These objects are interrelated: A vertex has edges that leave it, and an edge is defined by the vertices at its ends.

A vertex in a graph is somewhat like a node in a tree. Both vertices and nodes are implementation details that we hide from the client. In the implementation of a binary tree, we used a package-friendly class BinaryNode. (See Segment 24.2 of Chapter 24.) Here, a graph will have package access to the class Vertex. Previously, we simplified the implementation of a binary tree by giving BinaryNode more than simple accessor and mutator operations. The same is true now for the implementation of the ADT graph. In fact, the specifications of the ADT graph that you saw in the previous chapter (Segment 28.25) omit the operations necessary to implement various graph algorithms. We assign these operations to the vertices.

The structure of a vertex is more like the structure of a node in a general tree than the structure of a node in a binary tree. Both the general node in Figure 24-8 and a vertex reference a list that you use to address other nodes or vertices.

## Specifying the Class Vertex

**29.5**   **Identifying vertices.** First, we need a way to identify the vertices in a graph. One simple way is to use either integers or strings. A more general approach—the one we used in the previous chapter—labels each vertex with an object. This label will be a data field of the class Vertex. One operation of Vertex, then, is to retrieve a vertex's label. We'll use the constructor to set the label, omitting a mutator method for this field.

**29.6**   **Visiting vertices.** The algorithms that we discussed in the previous chapter required us to mark certain vertices when they were visited. We therefore give operations to Vertex that mark a vertex as visited, test whether a vertex has been visited, and remove the mark.

**29.7**   **The adjacency list.** As we mentioned earlier in this chapter, a vertex's adjacency list indicates its neighbors. Rather than placing this list within the class of graphs, it is more convenient to make it a part of the class Vertex. Soon we will define a simple class Edge whose instances we will place in these adjacency lists. Thus, a particular vertex's adjacency list contains the edges that leave the vertex. Each edge indicates its weight, if any, and references the vertex that ends the edge. Vertex then needs methods to add edges to the adjacency list. These methods essentially connect a vertex to its neighbors.

In addition, we must have access to the adjacency list for a given vertex. Thus, we define an iterator that returns a vertex's neighbors, as well as an iterator that returns the weights of the edges to those neighbors. For convenience, we also include a method to test whether a vertex has at least one neighbor.

As you will see, the adjacency list is the only place where we need instances of Edge. Thus, Edge is an implementation detail that we can hide within Vertex as an inner class.

**29.8**   **Path operations.** While finding a path through a graph, we must be able to locate the vertex that comes before a given vertex on the path—in other words, the vertex's predecessor. Thus, we need set, get, and test operations for a vertex's predecessor. Certain algorithms find the path with the shortest length or the path that has the smallest weight, or cost. A vertex can record either the length or the weight of the path from the origin to itself. Thus, we have operations that set and get this recorded value.

**29.9**   **The Java interface.** The interface in Listing 29-1 specifies the vertex operations that we have just introduced. The generic type T represents the data type of the object that labels a vertex.

---

LISTING 29-1   An interface for the vertices in a graph

```
1  package GraphPackage;
2  import java.util.Iterator;
3  public interface VertexInterface<T>
4  {
5     /** Gets this vertex's label.
6         @return  The object that labels the vertex. */
7     public T getLabel();
8
```

```java
9    /** Marks this vertex as visited. */
10   public void visit();
11
12   /** Removes this vertex's visited mark. */
13   public void unvisit();
14
15   /** Sees whether this vertex is marked as visited.
16       @return  True if the vertex is visited. */
17   public boolean isVisited();
18
19   /** Connects this vertex and a given vertex with a weighted edge.
20       The two vertices cannot be the same, and must not already
21       have this edge between them. In a directed graph, the edge
22       points toward the given vertex.
23       @param endVertex    A vertex in the graph that ends the edge.
24       @param edgeWeight   A real-valued edge weight, if any.
25       @return  True if the edge is added, or false if not. */
26   public boolean connect(VertexInterface<T> endVertex, double edgeWeight);
27
28   /** Connects this vertex and a given vertex with an unweighted
29       edge. The two vertices cannot be the same, and must not
30       already have this edge between them. In a directed graph,
31       the edge points toward the given vertex.
32       @param endVertex    A vertex in the graph that ends the edge.
33       @return  True if the edge is added, or false if not. */
34   public boolean connect(VertexInterface<T> endVertex);
35
36   /** Creates an iterator of this vertex's neighbors by following
37       all edges that begin at this vertex.
38       @return  An iterator of the neighboring vertices of this vertex. */
39   public Iterator<VertexInterface<T>> getNeighborIterator();
40
41   /** Creates an iterator of the weights of the edges to this
42       vertex's neighbors.
43       @return  An iterator of edge weights for edges to neighbors of this
44                vertex. */
45   public Iterator<Double> getWeightIterator();
46
47   /** Sees whether this vertex has at least one neighbor.
48       @return  True if the vertex has a neighbor. */
49   public boolean hasNeighbor();
50
51   /** Gets an unvisited neighbor, if any, of this vertex.
52       @return  Either a vertex that is an unvisited neighbor or null
53                if no such neighbor exists. */
54   public VertexInterface<T> getUnvisitedNeighbor();
55
56   /** Records the previous vertex on a path to this vertex.
57       @param predecessor  The vertex previous to this one along a path. */
58   public void setPredecessor(VertexInterface<T> predecessor);
59
60   /** Gets the recorded predecessor of this vertex.
61       @return  Either this vertex's predecessor or null if no predecessor
62                was recorded. */
63   public VertexInterface<T> getPredecessor();
64
```

```
65      /** Sees whether a predecessor was recorded for this vertex.
66          @return  True if a predecessor was recorded. */
67   public boolean hasPredecessor();
68
69      /** Records the cost of a path to this vertex.
70          @param newCost  The cost of the path. */
71   public void setCost(double newCost);
72
73      /** Gets the recorded cost of the path to this vertex.
74          @return  The cost of the path. */
75   public double getCost();
76 } // end VertexInterface
```

## The Inner Class Edge

**29.10**  As we mentioned, we will place instances of the class Edge in a vertex's adjacency list to indicate the edges that originate at the vertex. Thus, each edge must record both the vertex that ends it and the edge's weight, if any. Recording an edge weight is the only reason we need a class of edges. For unweighted graphs, we could simply place vertices in the adjacency list. Using edge objects, however, allows us to use one class of vertices for both weighted and unweighted graphs.

Since Vertex is the only class that uses Edge, we make Edge an inner class of Vertex. Listing 29-2 shows an implementation of Edge. We provide a data field for an edge's weight, if any. For unweighted graphs, we will set this field to zero rather than creating a class of unweighted edges.

---

**LISTING 29-2**   The protected class Edge, as an inner class of Vertex

```
1  protected class Edge
2  {
3     private VertexInterface<T> vertex; // Vertex at end of edge
4     private double weight;
5
6     protected Edge(VertexInterface<T> endVertex, double edgeWeight)
7     {
8        vertex = endVertex;
9        weight = edgeWeight;
10    } // end constructor
11
12    protected VertexInterface<T> getEndVertex()
13    {
14       return vertex;
15    } // end getEndVertex
16
17    protected double getWeight()
18    {
19       return weight;
20    } // end getWeight
21 } // end Edge
```

---

**Note:** An instance of the inner class Edge contains both the vertex that ends it and the edge's weight, if any. Although not necessary for unweighted graphs, Edge allows us to use one class of vertices for both weighted and unweighted graphs.

## Implementing the Class Vertex

**29.11    An outline of the class.** To hide Vertex from the clients of the graph, we place it within the package GraphPackage that we introduced in the previous chapter. Listing 29-3 outlines the class and shows its data fields and constructor. An ADT list that has an iterator serves as the adjacency list edgeList. We have chosen the linked implementation LinkedListWithIterator discussed in Segment 15.9 of Chapter 15.

---

**LISTING 29-3    An outline of the class Vertex**

```java
1  package GraphPackage;
2  import java.util.Iterator;
3  import java.util.NoSuchElementException;
4  import ADTPackage.*; // Classes that implement various ADTs
5  class Vertex<T> implements VertexInterface<T>
6  {
7     private T label;
8     private ListWithIteratorInterface<Edge> edgeList; // Edges to neighbors
9     private boolean visited;                          // True if visited
10    private VertexInterface<T> previousVertex;        // On path to this vertex
11    private double cost;                              // Of path to this vertex
12
13    public Vertex(T vertexLabel)
14    {
15       label = vertexLabel;
16       edgeList = new LinkedListWithIterator<>();
17       visited = false;
18       previousVertex = null;
19       cost = 0;
20    } // end constructor
21
22    < Implementations of the vertex operations go here. >
23    . . .
24
25    protected class Edge
26    {
27       < See Listing 29-2. >
28    } // end Edge
29 } // end Vertex
```

---

 **Note:** The data fields of the class Vertex facilitate the implementation of the algorithms presented in the previous chapter. For example, the fields previousVertex and cost are useful in a breadth-first search for the cheapest path from one vertex to another.

**29.12    The two connect methods.** Each method connect, as specified by VertexInterface in Listing 29-1, places an edge into a vertex's adjacency list. We first implement the method for weighted graphs and then use it to implement the method for unweighted graphs. Preventing the addition of an edge that either exists in the graph already or connects a vertex with itself consumes most of the method's effort. Once those details are complete, connect simply calls the ADT list's add method to add the edge.

```java
public boolean connect(VertexInterface<T> endVertex, double edgeWeight)
{
   boolean result = false;
```

```
      if (!this.equals(endVertex))
      {  // Vertices are distinct
         Iterator<VertexInterface<T>> neighbors = getNeighborIterator();
         boolean duplicateEdge = false;

         while (!duplicateEdge && neighbors.hasNext())
         {
            VertexInterface<T> nextNeighbor = neighbors.next();
            if (endVertex.equals(nextNeighbor))
               duplicateEdge = true;
         } // end while

         if (!duplicateEdge)
         {
            edgeList.add(new Edge(endVertex, edgeWeight));
            result = true;
         } // end if
      } // end if

      return result;
   } // end connect

   public boolean connect(VertexInterface<T> endVertex)
   {
      return connect(endVertex, 0);
   } // end connect
```

Although adding to a list can be done in O(1) time, scanning the list to prevent duplicate edges takes more time. Since each vertex in a graph of $n$ vertices can be the origin of at most $n - 1$ edges, connect is an O($n$) operation. For a sparse graph, however, the number of edges originating at any vertex is much less than $n$. In this case, connect is significantly faster than O($n$).

29.13   **The iterators.** The method getNeighborIterator returns an iterator to a vertex's adjacent vertices, that is, its neighbors. We define a private inner class—NeighborIterator—within Vertex that implements Java's interface Iterator. Thus, getNeighborIterator has the following implementation:

```
   public Iterator<VertexInterface<T>> getNeighborIterator()
   {
      return new NeighborIterator();
   } // end getNeighborIterator
```

The class NeighborIterator appears in Listing 29-4. Its constructor establishes an instance of the iterator defined in LinkedListWithIterator. The method next uses this iterator to traverse the edges in the vertex's adjacency list. Then, using Edge's method getEndVertex, next accesses the neighboring vertex and returns it.

LISTING 29-4   The private class NeighborIterator, as an inner class of Vertex

```
 1  private class NeighborIterator implements Iterator<VertexInterface<T>>
 2  {
 3     private Iterator<Edge> edges;
 4
 5     private NeighborIterator()
 6     {
 7        edges = edgeList.getIterator();
 8     } // end default constructor
 9
10     public boolean hasNext()
11     {
12        return edges.hasNext();
13     } // end hasNext
14
```

```
15      public VertexInterface<T> next()
16      {
17         VertexInterface<T> nextNeighbor = null;
18         if (edges.hasNext())
19         {
20            Edge edgeToNextNeighbor = edges.next();
21            nextNeighbor = edgeToNextNeighbor.getEndVertex();
22         }
23         else
24            throw new NoSuchElementException();
25
26         return nextNeighbor;
27      } // end next
28
29      public void remove()
30      {
31         throw new UnsupportedOperationException();
32      } // end remove
33   } // end NeighborIterator
```

In a similar manner, the method getWeightIterator returns an instance of a private inner class WeightIterator. This class is similar to the class NeighborIterator.

**29.14** **The methods hasNeighbor and getUnvisitedNeighbor.** The method hasNeighbor uses the method isEmpty of LinkedListWithIterator to test whether edgeList is empty:

```
public boolean hasNeighbor()
{
   return !edgeList.isEmpty();
} // end hasNeighbor
```

Using the iterator returned by getNeighborIterator, the method getUnvisitedNeighbor returns an adjacent vertex that is unvisited. This task is necessary in a topological sort.

```
public VertexInterface<T> getUnvisitedNeighbor()
{
   VertexInterface<T> result = null;

   Iterator<VertexInterface<T>> neighbors = getNeighborIterator();
   while ( neighbors.hasNext() && (result == null) )
   {
      VertexInterface<T> nextNeighbor = neighbors.next();
      if (!nextNeighbor.isVisited())
         result = nextNeighbor;
   } // end while

   return result;
} // end getUnvisitedNeighbor
```

**29.15** **The remaining methods.** Vertex should override the method equals. Two vertices are equal if their labels are equal.

```
public boolean equals(Object other)
{
   boolean result;

   if ((other == null) || (getClass() != other.getClass()))
      result = false;
   else
   {  // The cast is safe within this else clause
      @SuppressWarnings("unchecked")
      Vertex<T> otherVertex = (Vertex<T>)other;
      result = label.equals(otherVertex.label);
   } // end if
```

```
    return result;
} // end equals
```

The remaining methods of Vertex have uncomplicated implementations and are left as exercises.

**Question 3** Given the interface VertexInterface and the class Vertex, write Java statements that create the vertices and edges for the following directed, weighted graph. This graph contains three vertices—*A*, *B*, and *C*—and four edges, as follows: $A \rightarrow B$, $B \rightarrow C$, $C \rightarrow A$, $A \rightarrow C$. These edges have the weights 2, 3, 4, and 5, respectively.

# An Implementation of the ADT Graph

We now consider how to use Vertex in an implementation of a directed graph that can be either weighted or unweighted.

## Basic Operations

**29.16** **Beginning the class.** Whether our implementation uses an adjacency list—as it will here—or an adjacency matrix, it must have a container for the graph's vertices. If we use integers to identify the vertices, a list would be a natural choice for this container, since each integer could correspond to a position within the list. If we use an object such as a string to identify them, a dictionary is a better choice. That is what we will do here.

**Note:** Regardless of the kind of graph or how you implement it, you need a container such as a dictionary for the graph's vertices.

VideoNote
Implementing graph
operations

Figure 29-3 illustrates a dictionary of vertices for a small directed graph. Each of the vertices *A* and *D* has an adjacency list of the edges that originate at that vertex. The letters within these edges represent references to corresponding vertices within the dictionary. Since the ADT dictionary consists of key-value pairs, we can use the vertex labels as the search keys and the vertices themselves as the corresponding values. This organization allows us to quickly locate a particular vertex, given its label.

**FIGURE 29-3**    (a) A directed graph and (b) its implementation using adjacency lists

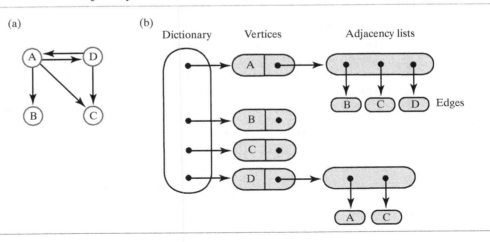

Our class begins as shown in Listing 29-5. Recall that the generic type T represents the data type of the objects that label the graph's vertices. The class's first data field is a dictionary of vertices. A count of vertices is not necessary, since the dictionary will count the vertices for us.

Since each vertex maintains its own adjacency list, the edges in the graph are not easily counted. Thus, we should maintain an edge count as a data field within the graph class.

---

**LISTING 29-5    An outline of the class `DirectedGraph`**

```
 1  package GraphPackage;
 2  import java.util.Iterator;
 3  import ADTPackage.*; // Classes that implement various ADTs
 4  public class DirectedGraph<T> implements GraphInterface<T>
 5  {
 6      private DictionaryInterface<T, VertexInterface<T>> vertices;
 7      private int edgeCount;
 8
 9      public DirectedGraph()
10      {
11          vertices = new LinkedDictionary<>();
12          edgeCount = 0;
13      } // end default constructor
14
15      < Implementations of the graph operations go here. >
16      . . .
17
18  } // end DirectedGraph
```

---

**29.17    Adding vertices.** The method addVertex uses Vertex's constructor to create a new vertex. It then adds the vertex to the dictionary by invoking the dictionary's method add:

```
public boolean addVertex(T vertexLabel)
{
    VertexInterface<T> addOutcome =
                vertices.add(vertexLabel, new Vertex<>(vertexLabel));
    return addOutcome == null; // Was addition to dictionary successful?
} // end addVertex
```

Notice that vertexLabel is the search key for the dictionary entry, and the new vertex is the associated value. Recall from the interface in Segment 19.4 of Chapter 19 that add returns null if the addition to the dictionary is successful. We use this fact to determine the return value for addVertex.

**29.18    Adding edges.** Methods such as addEdge that identify an existing vertex by its label must locate the vertex within the dictionary vertices. To do this, they invoke the dictionary method getValue, using the vertex label as the search key. Having located the two vertices that delineate the edge to be added, addEdge adds an edge to the adjacency list of the origin vertex. It does this by invoking Vertex's connect method. If the edge is added successfully, edgeCount is incremented. Thus, our graph's addEdge methods have the following definitions, one for weighted graphs and one for unweighted graphs:

```
public boolean addEdge(T begin, T end, double edgeWeight)
{
    boolean result = false;
    VertexInterface<T> beginVertex = vertices.getValue(begin);
    VertexInterface<T> endVertex = vertices.getValue(end);
    if ( (beginVertex != null) && (endVertex != null) )
        result = beginVertex.connect(endVertex, edgeWeight);
    if (result)
        edgeCount++;
```

```java
        return result;
    } // end addEdge

    public boolean addEdge(T begin, T end)
    {
        return addEdge(begin, end, 0);
    } // end addEdge
```

**29.19** **Testing for an edge.** The method `hasEdge` begins like `addEdge`, by locating the two vertices that define the desired edge. With the origin vertex in hand, `hasEdge` invokes `Vertex`'s method `getNeighborIterator` and searches the origin's adjacency list for the desired edge. In the following implementation, you can see why defining the `equals` method in `Vertex` is important.

```java
    public boolean hasEdge(T begin, T end)
    {
        boolean found = false;
        VertexInterface<T> beginVertex = vertices.getValue(begin);
        VertexInterface<T> endVertex = vertices.getValue(end);
        if ( (beginVertex != null) && (endVertex != null) )
        {
            Iterator<VertexInterface<T>> neighbors =
                                    beginVertex.getNeighborIterator();
            while (!found && neighbors.hasNext())
            {
                VertexInterface<T> nextNeighbor = neighbors.next();
                if (endVertex.equals(nextNeighbor))
                    found = true;
            } // end while
        } // end if

        return found;
    } // end hasEdge
```

**29.20** **Miscellaneous methods.** The methods `isEmpty`, `clear`, `getNumberOfVertices`, and `getNumberOfEdges` have the following simple implementations:

```java
    public boolean isEmpty()
    {
        return vertices.isEmpty();
    } // end isEmpty

    public void clear()
    {
        vertices.clear();
        edgeCount = 0;
    } // end clear

    public int getNumberOfVertices()
    {
        return vertices.getSize();
    } // end getNumberOfVertices

    public int getNumberOfEdges()
    {
        return edgeCount;
    } // end getNumberOfEdges
```

**29.21** **Resetting vertices.** You saw in Segment 29.11 that the class `Vertex` has the data fields `visited`, `previousVertex`, and `cost`. These fields are necessary for the implementation of the graph algorithms that we introduced in the previous chapter. Once you have searched a graph for a shortest path, for example, many of the vertices will have been visited and marked accordingly. Before you could perform a topological sort on the same graph, you would have to reset the field `visited` for each vertex in the graph.

The following method resetVertices sets the fields visited, previousVertex, and cost to their initial values. To do so, the method uses one of the iterators declared in the interface DictionaryInterface. The method is not public, as we will call it only from methods declared in GraphAlgorithmsInterface.

```
protected void resetVertices()
{
   Iterator<VertexInterface<T>> vertexIterator = vertices.getValueIterator();
   while (vertexIterator.hasNext())
   {
      VertexInterface<T> nextVertex = VertexIterator.next();
      nextVertex.unvisit();
      nextVertex.setCost(0);
      nextVertex.setPredecessor(null);
   } // end while
} // end resetVertices
```

**Question 4** Create an instance of the class DirectedGraph for the graph described in Question 3.

**29.22** **Efficiency.** Adding a vertex to a graph is an O($n$) operation, since the vertex is added to a linked dictionary. Adding an edge involves retrieving two vertices from the dictionary and then calling Vertex's method connect. Thus, the method addEdge is also O($n$). Likewise, hasEdge is O($n$), as it first retrieves two vertices from the dictionary. It then iterates through the edges that leave the first vertex to see whether one of them ends at the second vertex. As you can see, the performance of these three graph operations depends on the number of vertices in the graph. The remaining methods in BasicGraphInterface are each O(1). Figure 29-4 summarizes these observations.

**FIGURE 29-4**   The performance of basic operations of the ADT graph when implemented by using adjacency lists

| | |
|---|---|
| addVertex | O($n$) |
| addEdge | O($n$) |
| hasEdge | O($n$) |
| isEmpty | O(1) |
| getNumberOfVertices | O(1) |
| getNumberOfEdges | O(1) |
| clear | O(1) |

## Graph Algorithms

**29.23** **Breadth-first traversal.** Segment 28.12 of the previous chapter presented an algorithm for a breadth-first traversal of a nonempty graph, beginning at a given origin vertex. Recall that the traversal first visits the origin and the origin's neighbors. It then visits each neighbor of the origin's neighbors. The traversal uses a queue to hold the vertices as they are visited. The traversal order is the order in which vertices are added to this queue. But since the algorithm must remove vertices from this queue, we maintain the traversal order in a second queue. Since this second queue is returned to the client, we enqueue vertex labels instead of vertices. Remember that the class Vertex is unavailable to the client.

The following implementation of the method getBreadthFirstTraversal closely follows the pseudocode given in the previous chapter. The parameter origin is an object that labels the origin vertex of the traversal.

```java
public QueueInterface<T> getBreadthFirstTraversal(T origin)
{
    resetVertices();
    QueueInterface<T> traversalOrder = new LinkedQueue<>();
    QueueInterface<VertexInterface<T>> vertexQueue = new LinkedQueue<>();

    VertexInterface<T> originVertex = vertices.getValue(origin);
    originVertex.visit();
    traversalOrder.enqueue(origin);       // Enqueue vertex label
    vertexQueue.enqueue(originVertex);    // Enqueue vertex

    while (!vertexQueue.isEmpty())
    {
        VertexInterface<T> frontVertex = vertexQueue.dequeue();

        Iterator<VertexInterface<T>> neighbors =
                             frontVertex.getNeighborIterator();

        while (neighbors.hasNext())
        {
            VertexInterface<T> nextNeighbor = neighbors.next();
            if (!nextNeighbor.isVisited())
            {
                nextNeighbor.visit();
                traversalOrder.enqueue(nextNeighbor.getLabel());
                vertexQueue.enqueue(nextNeighbor);
            } // end if
        } // end while
    } // end while

    return traversalOrder;
} // end getBreadthFirstTraversal
```

The implementation of a similar method to perform a depth-first traversal is left as an exercise.

**Question 5** Write Java statements that display the vertices in a breadth-first traversal of the graph that you created in Question 4, beginning with vertex *A*.

29.24  **Shortest path.** The shortest path of all paths from one vertex to another in an unweighted graph is the path that has the fewest edges. The algorithm that finds this path—as you saw in Segment 28.19 of the previous chapter—is based on a breadth-first traversal. When we visit a vertex *v*, we mark it as visited, note the vertex *p* that precedes *v* in the graph, and note the length of the path that the traversal followed to reach *v*. We place both this path length and a reference to *p* into the vertex *v*. When the traversal reaches the desired destination, we can construct the shortest path from this data in the vertices.

The implementation of the method getShortestPath closely follows the pseudocode given in the previous chapter. The parameters begin and end are objects that label the origin and destination vertices of the path. The third parameter path is an initially empty stack. At the conclusion of the method, this stack contains the labels of the vertices along the shortest path. The method returns the length of this path.

```java
public int getShortestPath(T begin, T end, StackInterface<T> path)
{
    resetVertices();
    boolean done = false;
    QueueInterface<VertexInterface<T>> vertexQueue = new LinkedQueue<>();
```

```java
        VertexInterface<T> originVertex = vertices.getValue(begin);
        VertexInterface<T> endVertex = vertices.getValue(end);

        originVertex.visit();
        // Assertion: resetVertices() has executed setCost(0)
        // and setPredecessor(null) for originVertex

        vertexQueue.enqueue(originVertex);

        while (!done && !vertexQueue.isEmpty())
        {
            VertexInterface<T> frontVertex = vertexQueue.dequeue();

            Iterator<VertexInterface<T>> neighbors =
                                    frontVertex.getNeighborIterator();

            while (!done && neighbors.hasNext())
            {
                VertexInterface<T> nextNeighbor = neighbors.next();

                if (!nextNeighbor.isVisited())
                {
                    nextNeighbor.visit();
                    nextNeighbor.setCost(1 + frontVertex.getCost());
                    nextNeighbor.setPredecessor(frontVertex);
                    vertexQueue.enqueue(nextNeighbor);
                } // end if

                if (nextNeighbor.equals(endVertex))
                    done = true;
            } // end while
        } // end while

        // Traversal ends; construct shortest path
        int pathLength = (int)endVertex.getCost();
        path.push(endVertex.getLabel());

        VertexInterface<T> vertex = endVertex;
        while (vertex.hasPredecessor())
        {
            vertex = vertex.getPredecessor();
            path.push(vertex.getLabel());
        } // end while

        return pathLength;
    } // end getShortestPath
```

The implementation of the method getCheapestPath for a weighted graph is left as an exercise.

**Question 6** Write Java statements that display the vertices in the shortest path from vertex *A* to vertex *C* for the graph that you created in Question 4. Also, display the length of this path.

## CHAPTER SUMMARY

- An adjacency list for a given vertex contains references to the vertex's neighbors.

- Using an adjacency list, you can quickly find all the neighbors of a particular vertex. But if you want to know whether an edge exists between any two given vertices, you need to search a list.

- An adjacency matrix is a two-dimensional array that represents the edges in a graph. If you number the vertices from 0 through *n* - 1, the entry in row *i* and column *j* of the matrix indicates whether an edge exists between vertex *i* and vertex *j*. For an unweighted graph, you can use boolean values in the matrix. For a weighted graph, you can use edge weights when edges exist and a representation of infinity otherwise.

- Using an adjacency matrix, you can quickly discover whether an edge exists between any two given vertices. But if you want to know all the neighbors of a particular vertex, you need to scan an entire row of the matrix.

- Each adjacency list represents only those edges that originate from a vertex, but an adjacency matrix reserves space for every possible edge in a graph. Thus, when a graph is sparse, adjacency lists use less memory than a corresponding adjacency matrix. For this reason, typical graph implementations use adjacency lists.

- One way to implement an adjacency list is to make it a data field of a class Vertex. So that you can represent weighted graphs as well as unweighted graphs, you place instances of a class Edge in the adjacency list. Edge's data fields include the terminal vertex of an edge and the edge weight. Vertex is accessed from within a package instead of publicly. Edge is an inner class of Vertex. Thus, both Vertex and Edge are hidden from the graph's client.

- To facilitate the implementation of various graph algorithms, an instance of the class Vertex can indicate whether it has been visited. It also can record data about a path to it, such as the previous vertex and the path's cost.

## EXERCISES

1. What adjacency matrix represents the graph in Figure 28-15a of the previous chapter?

2. What adjacency matrix represents the graph in Figure 28-18a of the previous chapter?

3. What adjacency lists represent the graph in Figure 28-15a of the previous chapter?

4. What adjacency lists represent the graph in Figure 28-18a of the previous chapter?

5. Why is an adjacency matrix not space-efficient for sparse graphs?

6. Suppose that you want only to test whether an edge exists between two particular vertices. Does an adjacency matrix or an adjacency list provide a more efficient way of doing this?

7. Suppose that you want only to find all vertices that are adjacent to some particular vertex. Does an adjacency matrix or an adjacency list provide a more efficient way of doing this with respect to time?

8. Complete the implementation of the class Vertex that was begun in Segment 29.11.

9. What is the Big Oh of the methods getBreadthFirstTraversal and getShortestPath, as given in Segments 29.23 and 29.24?

10. The out degree of a vertex is the number of edges that originate at the vertex. How is the adjacency matrix used to find the out degree of a directed graph?

11. The in degree of a vertex is the number of edges that terminate at the vertex. How is the adjacency matrix useful for finding the in degree of a directed graph?

12. If a depth-first traversal is done on an $n$ vertex that is represented by using an adjacency matrix, then what is its Big Oh? Explain.

13. Modify the class DirectedGraph so that it can compute the in degree and out degree of any of its vertices.

**14.** Suppose that you have a weighted, directed graph in which the out degree and in degree of every vertex is at most 4. (See the previous exercise.) If the graph has $n$ vertices, you could represent it by using an array that has $n$ rows and 4 columns. Each of the $n$ rows is associated with a different vertex in the graph. The entries in a row associated with vertex $v$ are the vertices at the ends of the edges that begin at $v$. Since the out degree of a vertex can be less than 4, some entries in a row might be `null`.

What is the Big Oh of each of the following operations?

**a.** Testing whether two given vertices are adjacent
**b.** Finding all vertices adjacent to a given vertex

**15.** A graph is said to be **bipartite** if the vertices can be divided into two groups such that every edge goes from a vertex in one group to a vertex in the other group. Figure 28-1 of the previous chapter contains a bipartite graph. We could put Sandwich, Hyannis, Orleans, and Provincetown in group $A$, and Barnstable, Falmouth, Chatham, and Truro in group $B$. Every edge goes from a vertex of group $A$ to a vertex of group $B$.

**a.** Which of the graphs in Figures 28-4, 28-6, and 28-7b are bipartite?
**b.** How might the implementation of a bipartite graph differ from that of a regular graph to take advantage of its bipartite nature?

**16.** Consider a directed graph that has $n$ nodes and $e$ edges, where $0 \le e \le n^2$.

**a.** What is the time complexity, using Big Oh notation, for each of the following operations when an adjacency matrix is used to represent the graph?

- Testing whether two vertices are joined by an edge
- Finding the successors of a given vertex
- Finding the predecessors of a given vertex

**b.** Repeat part $a$, but assume that the graph uses an adjacency list in its implementation instead of an adjacency matrix.

**17.** A **loop** in a graph is an edge that starts and ends at the same vertex. Figure 29-5 shows an example of a loop in a directed, weighted graph.

**a.** Give an example of a problem where allowing loops would be useful.
**b.** Can the adjacency matrix and adjacency list representations of a graph support loops?

---

**FIGURE 29-5** A graph for Exercise 17

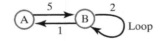

---

**18.** A **multiple edge** in a graph occurs when two vertices are joined by two or more edges in the same direction. Figure 29-6 shows a directed, weighted graph that has a multiple edge from $D$ to $B$.

**a.** Give an example of a problem in which allowing multiple edges would be useful.
**b.** Can an adjacency matrix represent an unweighted graph that has multiple edges?
**c.** Can an adjacency matrix represent a weighted graph that has multiple edges?
**d.** Can adjacency lists represent an unweighted graph that has multiple edges?
**e.** Can adjacency lists represent a weighted graph that has multiple edges?

FIGURE 29-6    A graph for Exercise 18

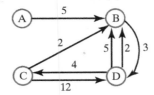

## PROJECTS

**1.** Complete the implementation of the class DirectedGraph that was begun in Segment 29.16 of this chapter.

**2.** Implement a class of undirected graphs by extending the class DirectedGraph. What methods should you override? What methods, if any, in DirectedGraph do not apply to an undirected graph? If such methods exist, what should you do in your new class? Note that the method getNumberOfEdges is the only accessor method to a data field of DirectedGraph.

**3.** Revise the class DirectedGraph by defining protected mutator methods for the data fields vertices and edgeCount. Also, define a protected accessor method for vertices. Then repeat Project 2, using your revised DirectedGraph. Compare the performance of the addEdge methods in this implementation of an undirected graph versus the implementation possible under the assumptions of Project 2.

**4.** Implement the classes Vertex and DirectedGraph by using an adjacency matrix.

**5.** Assuming an implementation of a class of undirected graphs, implement a method that detects whether an undirected graph is acyclic. You can look for cycles during either a breadth-first traversal or a depth-first traversal by discovering an edge to a vertex that is not the predecessor and has already been visited. To simplify the problem initially, you can assume that the graph is connected. Then remove this assumption.

**6.** Implement a method that detects whether a graph is connected.

**7.** Create the classes LimitedVertex and LimitedDirectedGraph that use the representation described in Exercise 14.

**8.** A **graph coloring** assigns a color to every vertex in a graph, with the restriction that two vertices of the same color cannot be adjacent. A graph is said to be **k-colorable** if it can be colored in $k$ or fewer colors.

  - Give an algorithm that will return true if a graph is 2-colorable and false otherwise.
  - Exercise 15 defined a bipartite graph. Show that a graph is bipartite if and only if it is 2-colorable. Then, using this fact, implement a method that detects whether a graph is bipartite.

**9.** Repeat Project 16 in Chapter 13 to create a simple social network. Use a graph to track the friend relationships among members of the network. Add a feature to enable people to see a list of their friends' friends.

## Answers to Self-Test Questions

**1.**

|   | 0 | 1 | 2 | 3 |
|---|---|---|---|---|
| 0 |   | T | T | T |
| 1 | T |   | T | T |
| 2 | T | T |   | T |
| 3 | T | T | T |   |

**2.**  Vertex 0 references the list 1, 2, 3.
Vertex 1 references the list 0, 2, 3.
Vertex 2 references the list 0, 1, 3.
Vertex 3 references the list 0, 1, 2.

**3.**
```
VertexInterface<String> vertexA = new Vertex<>("A");
VertexInterface<String> vertexB = new Vertex<>("B");
VertexInterface<String> vertexC = new Vertex<>("C");
vertexA.addEdge(vertexB, 2.0);
vertexB.addEdge(vertexC, 3.0);
vertexC.addEdge(vertexA, 4.0);
vertexA.addEdge(vertexC, 5.0);
```

**4.**
```
DirectedGraph<String> myGraph = new DirectedGraph<>();
myGraph.addVertex("A");
myGraph.addVertex("B");
myGraph.addVertex("C");
myGraph.addEdge("A", "B", 2.0);
myGraph.addEdge("B", "C", 3.0);
myGraph.addEdge("C", "A", 4.0);
myGraph.addEdge("A", "C", 5.0);
```

**5.**
```
QueueInterface<String> bfs = myGraph.getBreadthFirstTraversal("A");
while (!bfs.isEmpty())
   System.out.print(bfs.dequeue() + " ");
System.out.println();
```

**6.**
```
StackInterface<String> path = new LinkedStack<>();
int pathLength = myGraph.getShortestPath("A", "C", path);
System.out.println("The shortest path from A to C has length " + pathLength +
                   " and passes through the following vertices:");
while (!path.isEmpty())
   System.out.print(path.pop() + " ");
System.out.println();
```

# Documentation and Programming Style

## Contents

## Prerequisite

Some knowledge of Java

Most programs are used many times and are changed either to fix bugs or to accommodate new demands by the user. If the program is not easy to read and to understand, it will not be easy to change. It might even be impossible to change without heroic efforts. Even if you use your program only once, you should pay some attention to its readability. After all, you will have to read the program to debug it.

In this appendix, we discuss three techniques that can help make your program more readable: meaningful names, indenting, and comments.

## Naming Variables and Classes

**A.1** Names without meaning are almost never good variable names. The name you give to a variable should suggest what the variable is used for. If the variable holds a count of something, you might name it count. If the variable holds a tax rate, you might name it taxRate.

In addition to choosing names that are meaningful and legal in Java, you should follow the normal practice of other programmers. That way it will be easier for them to read your code and to combine your code with their code, when you work on a project with more than one person. By convention, each variable name begins with a lowercase letter, and each class name begins with an uppercase letter. If the name consists of more than one word, use a capital letter at the beginning of each word, as in the variable numberOfTries and the class StringBuffer.

Use all uppercase letters for named constants to distinguish them from other variables. Use the underscore character to separate words, if necessary, as in INCHES_PER_FOOT.

# Indenting

**A.2**  A program has a structure: Smaller parts are within larger parts. You use indentation to indicate this structure and thereby make your program easier to read. Although Java ignores any indentation you use, indenting consistently is essential to good programming style.

Each class begins at the left margin and uses braces to enclose its definition. For example, you might write

```
public class CircleCalculation
{
   . . .
} // end CircleCalculation
```

The data fields and methods appear indented within these braces, as illustrated in the following simple program:

```
public class CircleCalculation
{
   public static final double PI = Math.PI;

   public static void main(String[] args)
   {
      double radius; // In inches
      double area;   // In square inches
      . . .
   } // end main
} // end CircleCalculation
```

Within each method, you indent the statements that form the method's body. These statements in turn might contain compound statements that are indented further. Thus, the program has statements nested within statements.

Each level of nesting should be indented from the previous level to show the nesting more clearly. The outermost structure is not indented at all. The next level is indented. The structure nested within that is double indented, and so on. Typically, you should indent two or three spaces at each level of indentation. You want to see the indentation clearly, but you want to be able to use most of the line for the Java statement.

If a statement does not fit on one line, you can write it on two or more lines. However, when you write a single statement on more than one line, you should indent the successive lines more than the first line, as in the following example:

```
System.out.println("The volume of a sphere whose radius is " +
                   radius + " inches is " + volume +
                   " cubic inches.");
```

Ultimately, you need to follow the rules for indenting—and for programming style in general—given by your instructor or project manager. In any event, you should indent consistently within any one program.

# Comments

**A.3**  The documentation for a program describes what the program does and how it does it. The best programs are **self-documenting**. That is, their clean style and well-chosen names make the program's purpose and logic clear to any programmer who reads the program. Although you should strive for such self-documenting programs, your programs will also need a bit of explanation to make them completely clear. This explanation can be given in the form of **comments**.

Comments are notations in your program that help a person understand the program, but that are ignored by the compiler. Many text editors automatically highlight comments in some way, such as showing them in color. In Java, there are several ways of forming comments.

## Single-Line Comments

**A.4**    To write a comment on a single line, begin the comment with two slashes //. Everything after the slashes until the end of the line is treated as a comment and is ignored by the compiler. This form is handy for short comments, such as

```
String sentence; // Spanish version
```

If you want a comment of this kind to span several lines, each line must contain the symbols //.

## Comment Blocks

**A.5**    Anything written between the matching pair of symbols /* and */ is a comment and is ignored by the compiler. This form is not typically used to document a program, however. Instead, it is handy during debugging to temporarily disable a group of Java statements. Java programmers do use the pair /** and */ to delimit comments written in a certain form, as you will see in Segment A.7.

## When to Write Comments

**A.6**    It is difficult to explain just when you should write a comment. Too many comments can be as bad as too few. Too many comments can hide the really important ones. Too few comments can leave a reader baffled by things that were obvious to you. Just remember that you also will read your program. If you read it next week, will you remember what you did just now?

Every program file should begin with an explanatory comment. This comment should give all the important information about the file: what the program does, the name of the author, how to contact the author, the date that the file was last changed, and in a course, what the assignment is. Every method should begin with a comment that explains the method.

Within methods, you need comments to explain any nonobvious details. Notice the poor comments on the following declarations of the variables radius and area:

```
double radius; // The radius
double area;   // The area
```

Because we chose descriptive variable names, these comments are obvious. But rather than simply omitting these comments, can we write something that is not obvious? What units are used for the radius? Inches? Feet? Meters? Centimeters? We will add a comment that gives this information, as follows:

```
double radius; // In inches
double area;   // In square inches
```

## Java Documentation Comments

**A.7**    The Java language comes with a utility program named **javadoc** that will generate HTML documents that describe your classes. These documents tell people who use your program or class how to use it, but they omit all the implementation details.

The program javadoc extracts the header for your class, the headers for all public methods, and comments that are written in a certain form. No method bodies and no private items are extracted.

For javadoc to extract a comment, the comment must satisfy two conditions:

- The comment must occur immediately before a public class definition or the header of a public method.
- The comment must begin with /** and end with */.

Segment A.12 contains an example of a comment in this style.

You can insert HTML commands in your comments so that you gain more control over javadoc, but that is not necessary and we have not done so in this book.

**A.8** **Tags.** Comments written for javadoc usually contain special **tags** that identify such things as the programmer and a method's parameters and return value. Tags begin with the symbol @. We will describe only four tags in this appendix.

The tag @author identifies the programmer's name and is required of all classes and interfaces. The other tags of interest to us are used with methods. They must appear in the following order within a comment that precedes a method's header:

```
@param
@return
@throws
```

We will describe each of these tags next.

**A.9** **The @param tag.** You must write a @param tag for every parameter in a method. You should list these tags in the order in which the parameters appear in the method's header. After the @param tag, you give the name and description of the parameter. Typically, you use a phrase instead of a sentence to describe the parameter, and you mention the parameter's data type first. Do not use punctuation between the parameter name and its description, as javadoc inserts one dash when creating its documentation.

For example, the comments

```
@param code     The character code of the ticket category.
@param customer  The string that names the customer.
```

will produce the following lines in the documentation:

```
code - The character code of the ticket category.
customer - The string that names the customer.
```

**A.10** **The @return tag.** You must write a @return tag for every method that returns a value, even if you have already described the value in the method's description. Try to say something more specific about this value here. This tag must come after any @param tags in the comment. Do not use this tag for void methods and constructors.

**A.11** **The @throws tag.** Next, if a method can throw a checked exception, you name it by using a @throws tag, even if the exception also appears in a throws clause in the method's header. You can list unchecked exceptions if a client might reasonably catch them. Include a @throws tag for each exception, and list them alphabetically by name.

**A.12** **Example.** Here is a sample javadoc comment for a method. We usually begin such comments with a brief description of the method's purpose. This is our convention; javadoc has no tag for it.

```
/** Adds a new entry to a roster.
    @param newEntry     The object to be added to the roster.
    @param newPosition  The position of newEntry within the roster.
    @return  True if the addition is successful.
    @throws  RosterException if newPosition < 1 or newPosition > 1 + the length
             of the roster. */
public boolean add(Object newEntry, int newPosition) throws RosterException
```

The documentation that javadoc prepares from the previous comment appears as follows:

**add**

```
public boolean add(java.lang.Object newEntry,
                   int newPosition)
            throws RosterException
```

Adds a new entry to a roster.

**Parameters:**

> `newEntry` - The object to be added to the roster.
> `newPosition` - The position of newEntry within the roster.

**Returns:**

> True if the addition is successful.

**Throws:**

> `RosterException` - if newPosition < 1 or newPosition > 1 + the length of the
> roster.

To save space in this book, we sometimes omit portions of a comment that we would include in our actual programs. For example, some methods might have only a description of their purpose, and some might have only a @return tag. Note that javadoc accepts these abbreviated comments.

Further details about javadoc are available at docs.oracle.com/javase/8/docs/technotes/tools/unix/javadoc.html.

# Java Basics

(online at www.pearsonglobaleditions.com/Carrano)

# Appendix C

# Classes

(online at www.pearsonglobaleditions.com/Carrano)

# Creating Classes from Other Classes

## Contents

## Prerequisites

A major advantage of object-oriented programming is the ability to use existing classes when defining new classes. That is, you use classes that you or someone else has written to create new classes, rather than reinventing everything yourself. We begin this appendix with two ways to accomplish this feat.

In the first way, you simply declare an instance of an existing class as a data field of your new class. In fact, you have done this already if you have ever defined a class that had a string as a data field. Since your class is composed of objects, this technique is called composition.

The second way is to use inheritance, whereby your new class inherits properties and behaviors from an existing class, augmenting or modifying them as desired. This technique is more complicated than composition, so we will devote more time to it. As important as inheritance is in Java, you should not ignore composition as a valid and desirable technique in many situations, because inheritance can be used to violate the integrity of an ADT.

Both composition and inheritance define a relationship between two classes. These relationships are often called, respectively, *has a* and *is a* relationships. You will see why when we discuss them in this appendix.

# Composition

**D.1**    Appendix C introduces you to the class Name to represent a person's name. It defines constructors, accessor methods, and mutator methods that involve the person's first and last names. The data fields in Name are instances of the class String. A class uses **composition** when it has a data field that is an instance of another class. And since the class Name has an instance of the class String as a data field, the relationship between Name and String is called a *has a* relationship.

Let's create another class that uses composition. Consider a class of students, each of whom has a name and an identification number. Thus, the class Student contains two objects as data fields: an instance of the class Name and an instance of the class String:

```
private Name    fullName;
private String id;
```

Figure D-1 shows an object of type Student and its data fields. Notice that the Name object has two String objects as its data fields. It is important to realize that these data fields actually contain references to objects, not the objects themselves.

For methods, we give the class Student constructors, accessors, mutators, and toString. Recall that toString is invoked when you use System.out.println to display an object, so it is a handy method to include in your class definitions.

**FIGURE D-1**    A Student object is composed of other objects

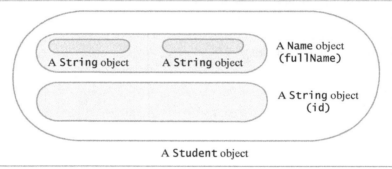

A Student object

**Note: Composition (*has a*)**
A class uses composition when it has objects as data fields. The class's implementation has no special access to such objects and must behave as a client would. That is, the class must use an object's methods to manipulate the object's data. Since the class "has a," or contains, an instance (object) of another class, the classes are said to have a *has a* relationship.

**D.2**    Look at the definition of the class Student in Listing D-1, and then we will make a few more observations.

LISTING D-1    The class Student

```
1  public class Student
2  {
3      private Name    fullName;
4      private String id;        // Identification number
5
```

```
6      public Student()
7      {
8         fullName = new Name();
9         id = "";
10     } // end default constructor
11
12     public Student(Name studentName, String studentId)
13     {
14        fullName = studentName;
15        id = studentId;
16     } // end constructor
17
18     public void setStudent(Name studentName, String studentId)
19     {
20        setName(studentName); // Or fullName = studentName;
21        setId(studentId);     // Or id = studentId;
22     } // end setStudent
23
24     public void setName(Name studentName)
25     {
26        fullName = studentName;
27     } // end setName
28
29     public Name getName()
30     {
31        return fullName;
32     } // end getName
33
34     public void setId(String studentId)
35     {
36        id = studentId;
37     } // end setId
38
39     public String getId()
40     {
41        return id;
42     } // end getId
43
44     public String toString()
45     {
46        return id + " " + fullName.toString();
47     } // end toString
48  } // end Student
```

The method setStudent is useful when we create a student object by using the default constructor or if we want to change both the name and identification number that we gave to a student object earlier. Notice that the method invokes the other set methods from this class to initialize the data fields. For example, to set the field fullName to the parameter studentName, setStudent uses the statement

```
setName(studentName);
```

We could also write this statement as

```
this.setName(studentName);
```

where this refers to the instance of Student that receives the call to the method setStudent. Or we could write the assignment statement

```
fullName = studentName;
```

Implementing methods in terms of other methods is usually desirable.

Suppose that we want `toString` to return a string composed of the student's identification number and name. It must use methods in the class `Name` to access the name as a string. For example, `toString` could return the desired string by using either

```
return id + " " + fullName.getFirst() + " " + fullName.getLast();
```

or, more simply,

```
return id + " " + fullName.toString();
```

The data field `fullName` references a `Name` object whose private fields are not accessible by name in the implementation of the class `Student`. We can access them indirectly via the accessor methods `getFirst` and `getLast` or by invoking `Name`'s `toString` method.

**Question 1** What data fields would you use in the definition of a class `Address` to represent a student's address?

**Question 2** Add a data field to the class `Student` to represent a student's address. What new methods should you define?

**Question 3** What existing methods need to be changed in the class `Student` as a result of the added field that Question 2 described?

**Question 4** What is another implementation for the default constructor that uses `this`, as described in Segment C.25 of Appendix C?

## Adapters

**D.3**   Suppose that you have a class, but the names of its methods do not suit your application. Or maybe you want to simplify some methods or eliminate others. You can use composition to write a new class that has an instance of your existing class as a data field and defines the methods that you want. Such a new class is called an **adapter class**.

For example, suppose that instead of using objects of the class `Name` to name people, we want to use simple nicknames. We could use strings for nicknames, but like `Name`, the class `String` has more methods than we need. The class `NickName` in Listing D-2 has an instance of the class `Name` as a data field, a default constructor, and set and get methods. Arbitrarily, we use the first-name field of the class `Name` to store the nickname.

---

**LISTING D-2**   The class `NickName`

```
 1  public class NickName
 2  {
 3     private Name nick;
 4
 5     public NickName()
 6     {
 7        nick = new Name();
 8     } // end default constructor
 9
10     public void setNickName(String nickName)
11     {
12        nick.setFirst(nickName);
13     } // end setNickName
14
15     public String getNickName()
16     {
```

```
17        return nick.getFirst();
18    } // end getNickName
19 } // end NickName
```

Notice how this class uses the methods of the class Name to implement its methods. A NickName object now has only NickName's methods, and not the methods of Name.

**Question 5** Write statements that define bob as an instance of NickName to represent the nickname *Bob*. Then, using bob, write a statement that displays *Bob*.

# Inheritance

**D.4**   **Inheritance** is an aspect of object-oriented programming that enables you to organize classes. The name comes from the notion of inherited traits like eye color, hair color, and so forth, but it is perhaps clearer to think of inheritance as a classification system. Inheritance allows you to define a general class and then later to define more specialized classes that add to or revise the details of the older, more general class definition. This saves work, because the specialized class inherits all the properties of the general class and you need only program the new or revised features.

For example, you might define a class for vehicles and then define more specific classes for particular types of vehicles, such as automobiles, wagons, and boats. Similarly, the class of automobiles includes the classes of cars and trucks. Figure D-2 illustrates this hierarchy of classes. The Vehicle class is the superclass for the subclasses, such as Automobile. The Automobile class is the superclass for the subclasses Car and Truck. Another term for superclass is base class, and another term for subclass is derived class.

**FIGURE D-2**      A hierarchy of classes

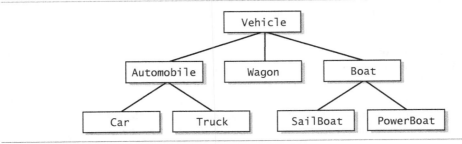

As you move up in the diagram, the classes are more general. A car is an automobile and therefore is also a vehicle. However, a vehicle is not necessarily a car. A sailboat is a boat and is also a vehicle, but a vehicle is not necessarily a sailboat.

**D.5**   Java and other programming languages use inheritance to organize classes in this hierarchical way. A programmer can then use an existing class to write a new one that has more features. For example, the class of vehicles has certain properties—like miles traveled—that its data fields record. The class also has certain behaviors—like going forward—that its methods define. The classes Automobile, Wagon, and Boat have these properties and behaviors as well. Everything that is true of all Vehicle objects, such as the ability to go forward, is described only once and inherited by the classes Automobile, Wagon, and Boat. The subclasses then add to or revise the properties and behaviors that they inherit. Without inheritance, descriptions of behaviors like going forward would have to be repeated for each of the subclasses Automobile, Wagon, Boat, Car, Truck, and so on.

**Note:** **Inheritance**
Inheritance is a way of organizing classes so that common properties and behaviors can be defined only once for all the classes involved. Using inheritance, you can define a general class and then later define more specialized classes that add to or revise the details of the older, more general class definition.

Since the Automobile class is derived from the Vehicle class, it inherits all the data fields and public methods of that class. The Automobile class would have additional fields for such things as the amount of fuel in the fuel tank, and it would also have some added methods. Such fields and methods are not in the Vehicle class, because they do not apply to all vehicles. For example, wagons have no fuel tank.

Inheritance gives an instance of a subclass all the behaviors of the superclass. For example, an automobile will be able to do everything that a vehicle can do; after all, an automobile *is a* vehicle. In fact, inheritance is known as an *is a* relationship between classes. Since the subclass and the superclass share properties, you should use inheritance only when it makes sense to think of an instance of the subclass as also being an instance of the superclass.

**Note:** **An *is a* relationship**
With inheritance, an instance of a subclass is also an instance of the superclass. Thus, you should use inheritance only when the *is a* relationship between classes is meaningful.

**Question 6** Some vehicles have wheels and some do not. Revise Figure D-2 to organize vehicles according to whether they have wheels.

**D.6**  **Example.** Let's construct an example of inheritance within Java. Suppose we are designing a program that maintains records about students, including those in grade school, high school, and college. We can organize the records for the various kinds of students by using a natural hierarchy that begins with students. College students are then one subclass of students. College students divide into two smaller subclasses: undergraduate students and graduate students. These subclasses might further subdivide into still smaller subclasses. Figure D-3 diagrams this hierarchical arrangement.

A common way to describe subclasses is in terms of family relationships. For example, the class of students is said to be an **ancestor** of the class of undergraduate students. Conversely, the class of undergraduate students is a **descendant** of the class of students.

Although our program may not need any class corresponding to students in general, thinking in terms of such classes can be useful. For example, all students have names, and the methods of initializing, changing, and displaying a name will be the same for all students. In Java, we can define a class that includes data fields for the properties that belong to all subclasses of students. The class likewise will have methods for the behaviors of all students, including methods that manipulate the class's data fields. In fact, we have already defined such a class—Student—in Segment D.2.

FIGURE D-3    A hierarchy of student classes

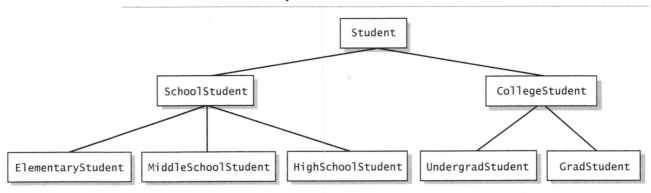

**D.7**    Now consider a class for college students. A college student is a student, so we use inheritance to derive the class `CollegeStudent` from the class `Student`. Here, `Student` is the existing superclass and `CollegeStudent` is the new subclass. The subclass inherits—and therefore has—all the data fields and methods of the superclass. In addition, the subclass defines whatever data fields and methods we wish to add.

To indicate that `CollegeStudent` is a subclass of `Student`, we write the phrase `extends Student` on the first line of the class definition. Thus, the class definition of `CollegeStudent` begins

```
public class CollegeStudent extends Student
```

When we create a subclass, we define only the added data fields and the added methods. For example, the class `CollegeStudent` has all the data fields and methods of the class `Student`, but we do not mention them in the definition of `CollegeStudent`. In particular, every object of the class `CollegeStudent` has a data field called `fullName`, but we do not declare the data field `fullName` in the definition of the class `CollegeStudent`. The data field is there, however. But because `fullName` is a private data field of the class `Student`, we cannot reference `fullName` directly by name within `CollegeStudent`. We can, however, access and change this data field by using `Student`'s methods, since the class `CollegeStudent` inherits all of the public methods in the superclass `Student`.

For example, if `cs` is an instance of `CollegeStudent`, we can write

```
cs.setName(new Name("Joe", "Java"));
```

even though `setName` is a method of the superclass `Student`. Since we have used inheritance to construct `CollegeStudent` from the class `Student`, every college student *is a* student. That is, a `CollegeStudent` object "knows" how to perform `Student` behaviors.

**D.8**    A subclass, like `CollegeStudent`, can also add some data fields and/or methods to those it inherits from its superclass. For example, `CollegeStudent` adds the data field `year` and the methods `setYear` and `getYear`. We can set the graduation year of the object `cs` by writing

```
cs.setYear(2019);
```

Suppose that we also add a data field that represents the degree sought and the methods to access and change it. We could also add fields for an address and grades, but to keep it simple, we will not. Let's look at the class as given in Listing D-3 and focus on the constructors first.

**LISTING D-3**   The class `CollegeStudent`

```
1  public class CollegeStudent extends Student
2  {
3     private int    year;   // Year of graduation
4     private String degree; // Degree sought
5
6     public CollegeStudent()
7     {
8        super();        // Must be first statement in constructor
9        year = 0;
10       degree = "";
11    } // end default constructor
12
13    public CollegeStudent(Name studentName, String studentId,
14                          int graduationYear, String degreeSought)
15    {
16       super(studentName, studentId); // Must be first
17       year = graduationYear;
18       degree = degreeSought;
19    } // end constructor
20
21    public void setStudent(Name studentName, String studentId,
22                           int graduationYear, String degreeSought)
23    {
24       setName(studentName); // NOT fullName = studentName;
25       setId(studentId);     // NOT id = studentId;
26 // Or setStudent(studentName, studentId); (see Segment D.16)
27
28       year = graduationYear;
29       degree = degreeSought;
30    } // end setStudent
31    < The methods setYear, getYear, setDegree, and getDegree go here. >
32    . . .
33    public String toString()
34    {
35       return super.toString() + ", " + degree + ", " + year;
36    } // end toString
37 } // end CollegeStudent
```

## Invoking Constructors from Within Constructors

**D.9**   **Calling the superclass's constructor.** Constructors typically initialize a class's data fields. In a subclass, how can the constructor initialize data fields inherited from the superclass? One way is to call the superclass's constructor. The subclass's constructor can use the reserved word super as a name for the constructor of the superclass.

Notice that the default constructor in the class `CollegeStudent` begins with the statement

`super();`

This statement invokes the default constructor of the superclass. Our new default constructor must invoke the superclass's default constructor to properly initialize the data fields that are inherited from the superclass. Actually, if you do not invoke super, Java will do it for you. In this book, we will always invoke super explicitly, to make the action a bit clearer. Note that the call to super must occur first in the constructor. You can use super to invoke a constructor only from within another constructor.

In like fashion, the second constructor invokes a corresponding constructor in the superclass by executing the statement

**super**(studentName, studentId);

If you omit this statement, Java will invoke the default constructor, which is *not* what you want.

**Note: Calling the constructor of the superclass**
You can use super within the definition of a constructor of a subclass to call a constructor of the superclass explicitly. When you do, super always must be the first action taken in the constructor definition. You cannot use the name of the constructor instead of super. If you omit super, each constructor of a subclass automatically calls the default constructor of the superclass. Sometimes this action is what you want, but sometimes it is not.

**Note: Constructors are not inherited**
A constructor of a class C creates an object whose type is C. It wouldn't make sense for this class to have a constructor named anything other than C. But that is what would happen if a class like CollegeStudent inherited Student's constructors: CollegeStudent would have a constructor named Student.

Even though CollegeStudent does not inherit Student's constructors, its constructors do call Student's constructors, as you have just seen.

**D.10** **Reprise: Using this to invoke a constructor.** As you saw in Segment C.25 of Appendix C, you use the reserved word this much as we used super here, except that it calls a constructor of the same class instead of a constructor of the superclass. For example, consider the following definition of a constructor that we might add to the class CollegeStudent in Segment D.8:

```
public CollegeStudent(Name studentName, String studentId)
{
   this(studentName, studentId, 0, "");
} // end constructor
```

The one statement in the body of this constructor definition is a call to the constructor whose definition begins

```
public CollegeStudent(Name studentName, String studentId,
                      int graduationYear, String degreeSought)
```

As with super, any use of this must be the first action in a constructor definition. Thus, a constructor definition cannot both a call using super and a call using this. What if you want both a call with super and a call with this? In that case, you would use this to call a constructor that has super as its first action.

## Private Fields and Methods of the Superclass

**D.11** **Accessing inherited data fields.** The class CollegeStudent has a setStudent method with four parameters, studentName, studentId, graduationYear, and degreeSought. To initialize the inherited data fields fullName and id, the method invokes the inherited methods setName and setId:

```
setName(studentName); // NOT fullName = studentName
setId(studentId);     // NOT id = studentId
```

Recall that `fullName` and `id` are private data fields defined in the superclass `Student`. Only a method in the class `Student` can access `fullName` and `id` directly by name from within its definition. Although the class `CollegeStudent` inherits these data fields, none of its methods can access them by name. Thus, `setStudent` cannot use an assignment statement such as

```
id = studentId; // ILLEGAL in CollegeStudent's setStudent
```

to initialize the data field `id`. Instead it must use some public mutator method such as `setId`.

 **Note:** A data field that is private in a superclass is not accessible by name within the definition of a method for any other class, including a subclass. Even so, a subclass inherits the data fields of its superclass.

The fact that you cannot access a private data field of a superclass from within the definition of a method of a subclass seems wrong to people. To do otherwise, however, would make the access modifier `private` pointless: Anytime you wanted to access a private data field, you could simply create a subclass and access it in a method of that class. Thus, all private data fields would be accessible to anybody who was willing to put in a little extra effort.

**D.12**   **Private methods of the superclass.** A subclass cannot invoke a superclass's private methods directly. This should not be a problem, since you should use private methods only as helpers within the class in which they are defined. That is, a class's private methods do not define behaviors. Thus, we say that a subclass does not inherit the private methods of its superclass. If you want to use a superclass's method in a subclass, you should make the method either protected or public. We discuss protected methods in Java Interlude 7.

Suppose that superclass `B` has a public method `m` that calls a private method `p`. A class `D` derived from `B` inherits the public method `m`, but not `p`. Even so, when a client of `D` invokes `m`, `m` calls `p`. Thus, a private method in a superclass still exists and is available for use, but a subclass cannot call it directly by name.

 **Note:** A subclass does not inherit and cannot invoke by name a private method of the superclass.

## Overriding and Overloading Methods

**D.13**   The set and get methods of the class `CollegeStudent` are straightforward, so we will not bother to look at them. However, we have provided the class with a method `toString`. Why did we do this, when our new class inherits a `toString` method from its superclass `Student`? Clearly, the string that the superclass's `toString` method returns can include the student's name and identification number, but it cannot include the year and degree that are associated with the subclass. Thus, we need to write a new method `toString`.

But why not have the new method invoke the inherited method? We can do this, but we'll need to distinguish between the method that we are defining for `CollegeStudent` and the method inherited from `Student`. As you can see from the class definition in Segment D.8, the new method `toString` contains the statement

```
return super.toString() + ", " + degree + ", " + year;
```

Since `Student` is the superclass, we write

```
super.toString()
```

to indicate that we are invoking the superclass's `toString`. If we omitted `super`, our new version of `toString` would invoke itself. Here we are using `super` as if it were an object. In contrast, we used `super` with parentheses as if it were a method within the constructor definitions.

If you glance back at Segment D.2, you will see that `Student`'s `toString` method appears as follows:

```java
public String toString()
{
    return id + " " + fullName.toString();
} // end toString
```

This method calls the `toString` method defined in the class `Name`, since the object `fullName` is an instance of the class `Name`.

**D.14**   **Overriding a method.** In the previous segment, you saw that the class `CollegeStudent` defines a method `toString` and also inherits a method `toString` from its superclass `Student`. Both of these methods have no parameters. The class, then, has two methods with the same name, the same parameters, and the same return type.

When a subclass defines a method with the same name, the same number and types of parameters, and the same return type as a method in the superclass, the definition in the subclass is said to **override** the definition in the superclass. Objects of the subclass that invoke the method will use the definition in the subclass. For example, if `cs` is an instance of the class `CollegeStudent`,

```java
cs.toString()
```

uses the definition of the method `toString` in the class `CollegeStudent`, not the definition of `toString` in the class `Student`, as Figure D-4 illustrates. As you've already seen, however, the definition of `toString` in the subclass can invoke the definition of `toString` in the superclass by using `super`.

**FIGURE D-4**     The method `toString` in `CollegeStudent` overrides the method `toString` in `Student`

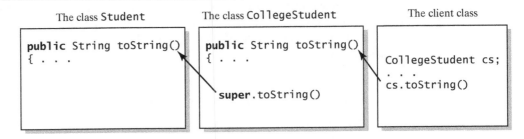

**Note:  Overriding a method definition**
A method in a subclass overrides a method in the superclass when both methods have the same name, the same number and types of parameters, and the same return type. Since a method's signature is its name and parameters, a method in a subclass overrides a method in the superclass when both methods have the same signature and return type.

**Note: Overriding and access**
An overriding method in a subclass can have either public, protected, or package access according to the access of the overridden method in the superclass, as follows:

| Access of the overridden method in the superclass | Access of the overriding method in the subclass |
| --- | --- |
| public | public |
| protected | protected or public |
| package | package, protected, or public |

A private method in a superclass cannot be overridden by a method in a subclass.

Note that Segment JI7.2 in Java Interlude 7 discusses protected access, and Segment C.34 of Appendix C describes package access.

**Note:** You can use super in a subclass to call an overridden method of the superclass.

**Question 7** Question 5 asked you to create an instance of NickName to represent the nickname *Bob*. If that object is named bob, do the following statements produce the same output? Explain.

```
System.out.println(bob.getNickName());
System.out.println(bob);
```

**D.15   Covariant return types (Optional).** A class cannot define two methods that have different return types but the same signatures—that is, the same name and parameters. However, if the two methods are in different classes, and one class is a subclass of the other, this can be possible. In particular, when a method in a subclass overrides a method in the superclass, their signatures are the same. But the return type of the method in the subclass can be a subclass of the return type of the method in the superclass. Such return types are said to be **covariant**.

For example, in Segment D.8 the class CollegeStudent was derived from the class Student defined in Segment D.2. Now imagine a class School that maintains a collection of Student objects. (This book will give you the tools to actually do this.) The class has a method getStudent that returns a student given his or her ID number. The class might appear as follows:

```
public class School
{
   . . .
   public Student getStudent(String studentId)
   {
      . . .
   } // end getStudent
} // end School
```

Now, consider a class College that has a collection of college students. We can derive College from School and override the method getStudent, as follows:

```
public class College extends School
{
   . . .
   public CollegeStudent getStudent(String studentId)
   {
      . . .
   } // end getStudent
} // end College
```

The method getStudent has the same signature as getStudent in School, but the return types of the two methods differ. In fact, the return types are covariant—and therefore legal—because CollegeStudent is a subclass of Student.

**D.16**    **Reprise: Overloading a method.** Segment C.29 of Appendix C discussed overloaded methods within the same class. Such methods have the same name but different signatures. Java is able to distinguish between these methods since their parameters are not identical.

Suppose that a subclass has a method with the same name as a method in its superclass, but the methods' parameters differ in number or data type. The subclass would have both methods—the one it defines and the one it inherits from the superclass. The method in the subclass overloads the method in the superclass.

For example, the superclass Student and the subclass CollegeStudent each have a method named setStudent. The methods are not exactly the same, however, as they have a different number of parameters. In Student, the method's header is

```
public void setStudent(Name studentName, String studentId)
```

whereas in CollegeStudent it is

```
public void setStudent(Name studentName, String studentId,
                       int graduationYear, String degreeSought)
```

An instance of the class Student can invoke only Student's version of the method, but an instance of CollegeStudent can invoke either method. Again, Java can distinguish between the two methods because they have different parameters.

Within the class CollegeStudent, the implementation of setStudent can invoke Student's setStudent to initialize the fields fullName and id by including the statement

```
setStudent(studentName, studentId);
```

instead of making calls to the methods setName and setId, as we did in Segment D.8. Since the two versions of setStudent have different parameter lists, we do not need to preface the call with super to distinguish the two methods. However, we are free to do so by writing

```
super.setStudent(studentName, studentId);
```

**Note: Overloading a method definition**
A method in a class overloads another method in either the same class or its superclass when both methods have the same name but differ in the number or types of parameters. Thus, overloaded methods have the same name but different signatures.

Although the terms "overloading" and "overriding" are easy to confuse, you should distinguish between the concepts, as they both are important.

**D.17**    **Multiple use of super.** As we have already noted, within the definition of a method of a subclass, you can call an overridden method of the superclass by prefacing the method name with super and a dot. However, if the superclass is itself derived from some other superclass, you cannot repeat the use of super to invoke a method from that superclass.

For example, suppose that the class UndergradStudent is derived from the class CollegeStudent, which is derived from the class Student. You might think that you can invoke a method of the class Student within the definition of the class Undergraduate, by using super.super, as in

```
super.super.toString(); // ILLEGAL!
```

As the comment indicates, this repeated use of super is not allowed in Java.

**Note: super**
Although a method in a subclass can invoke an overridden method defined in the superclass by using super, the method cannot invoke an overridden method that is defined in the superclass's superclass. That is, the construct super.super is illegal.

**Question 8** Are the two definitions of the constructors for the class Student (Segment D.2) an example of overloading or overriding? Why?

**Question 9** If you add the method

```
public void setStudent(Name studentName, String studentId)
```

to the class CollegeStudent and let it give some default values to the fields year and degree, are you overloading or overriding setStudent in the class Student? Why?

D.18   **The final modifier.** Suppose that a constructor calls a public method m. For simplicity, imagine that this method is in the same class C as the constructor, as follows:

```
public class C
{
    . . .
    public C()
    {
        m();
        . . .
    } // end default constructor
    public void m()
    {
        . . .
    } // end m
    . . .
```

Now imagine that we derive a new class from C and we override the method m. If we invoke the constructor of our new class, it will call the superclass's constructor, which will call our overridden version of the method m. This method might use data fields that the constructor has not yet initialized, causing an error. Even if no error occurs, we will, in effect, have altered the behavior of the superclass's constructor.

To specify that a method definition cannot be overridden with a new definition in a subclass, you make it a **final method** by adding the final modifier to the method header. For example, you can write

```
public final void m()
```

Note that private methods are automatically final methods, since you cannot override them in a subclass.

**Programming Tip:** If a constructor invokes a public method in its class, declare that method to be final so that no subclass can override the method and hence change the behavior of the constructor.

Constructors cannot be final. Since a subclass does not inherit, and therefore cannot override, a constructor in the base case, final constructors are unnecessary.

You can declare an entire class as a **final class**, in which case you cannot use it as superclass to derive any other class from it. Java's String class is an example of a final class.

**Note:** String cannot be the superclass for any other class because it is a final class.

 **Programming Tip:** When you design a class, consider the classes derived from it, either now or in the future. They might need access to your class's data fields. If your class does not have public accessor or mutator methods, provide protected versions of such methods. Keep the data fields private. Protected access is discussed in Java Interlude 7.

### Multiple Inheritance

**D.19** Some programming languages allow one class to be derived from two different superclasses. That is, you can derive class C from classes A and B. This feature, known as **multiple inheritance**, is not allowed in Java. In Java, a subclass can have only one superclass. You can, however, derive class B from class A and then derive class C from class B, since this is not multiple inheritance.

A subclass can implement any number of interfaces—which we describe in the prelude to this book—in addition to extending any one superclass. This capability gives Java an approximation to multiple inheritance without the complications that arise with multiple superclasses.

## Type Compatibility and Superclasses

**D.20** **Object types of a subclass.** Previously, you saw the class CollegeStudent, which was derived from the class Student. In the real world, every college student is also a student. This relationship holds in Java as well. Every object of the class CollegeStudent is also an object of the class Student. Thus, if we have a method that has a parameter of type Student, the argument in an invocation of this method can be an object of type CollegeStudent.

Specifically, suppose that the method in question is in some class and begins as follows:

```
public void someMethod(Student scholar)
```

Within the body of someMethod, the object scholar can invoke public methods that are defined in the class Student. For example, the definition of someMethod could contain the expression scholar.getId(). That is, scholar has Student behaviors.

Now consider an object joe of CollegeStudent. Since the class CollegeStudent inherits all the public methods of the class Student, joe can invoke those inherited methods. That is, joe can behave like an object of Student. (It happens that joe can do more, since it is an object of CollegeStudent, but that is not relevant right now.) Therefore, joe can be the argument of someMethod. That is, for some object o, we can write

```
o.someMethod(joe);
```

No automatic type casting[1] has occurred here. As an object of the class CollegeStudent, joe is also of type Student. The object joe need not be, and is not, type-cast to an object of the class Student.

We can take this idea further. Suppose that we derive the class UndergradStudent from the class CollegeStudent. In the real world, every undergraduate is a college student, and every college student is also a student. Once again, this relationship holds for our Java classes. Every object of the class UndergradStudent is also an object of the class CollegeStudent and so is also an object of the class Student. Thus, if we have a method whose parameter is of type Student, the argument in an invocation of this method can be an object of type UndergradStudent. Thus, an object can actually have several types as a result of inheritance.

---

1. Segment B.21 of Appendix B reviews type casts.

**Note:** An object of a subclass has more than one data type. Everything that works for objects of an ancestor class also works for objects of any descendant class.

**D.21**   Because an object of a subclass also has the types of all of its ancestor classes, you can assign an object of a class to a variable of any ancestor type, but not the other way around. For example, since the class `UndergradStudent` is derived from the class `CollegeStudent`, which is derived from the class `Student`, the following are legal:

```
Student amy = new CollegeStudent();
Student brad = new UndergradStudent();
CollegeStudent jess = new UndergradStudent();
```

However, the following statements are all illegal:

```
CollegeStudent cs = new Student();          // ILLEGAL!
UndergradStudent ug = new Student();        // ILLEGAL!
UndergradStudent ug2 = new CollegeStudent(); // ILLEGAL!
```

This makes perfectly good sense. For example, a college student is a student, but a student is not necessarily a college student. Some programmers find the phrase "is a" to be useful in deciding what types an object can have and what assignments to variables are legal.

 **Programming Tip:** Because an object of a subclass is also an object of the superclass, do not use inheritance when an *is a* relationship does not exist between your proposed class and an existing class. Even if you want class C to have some of the methods of class B, use composition if these classes do not have an *is a* relationship.

 **Question 10** If `HighSchoolStudent` is a subclass of `Student`, can you assign an object of `HighSchoolStudent` to a variable of type `Student`? Why or why not?

**Question 11** Can you assign an object of `Student` to a variable of type `HighSchoolStudent`? Why or why not?

## The Class `Object`

**D.22**   As you have already seen, if you have a class A and you derive class B from it, and then you derive class C from B, an object of class C is of type C, type B, and type A. This works for any chain of subclasses no matter how long the chain is.

Java has a class—named `Object`—that is at the beginning of every chain of subclasses. This class is an ancestor of every other class, even those that you define yourself. Every object of every class is of type `Object`, as well as being of the type of its class and also of the types of all the other ancestor classes. If you do not derive your class from some other class, Java acts as if you had derived it from the class `Object`.

 **Note:** Every class is a descendant class of the class `Object`.

The class `Object` contains certain methods, among which are `toString`, `equals`, and `clone`. Every class inherits these methods, either from `Object` directly or from some other ancestor class that ultimately inherited the methods from the class `Object`.

The inherited methods toString, equals, and clone, however, will almost never work correctly in the classes you define. Typically, you need to override the inherited method definitions with new, more appropriate definitions. Thus, whenever you define the method toString in a class, for example, you are actually overriding Object's method toString.

**D.23** **The toString method.** The method toString takes no arguments and is supposed to return all the data in an object as a String. However, you will not automatically get a nice string representation of the data. The inherited version of toString returns a value based upon the invoking object's memory address. You need to override the definition of toString to cause it to produce an appropriate string for the data in the class being defined. You might want to look again at the toString methods in Segments D.2 and D.8.

**D.24** **The equals method.** Consider the following objects of the class Name that we defined in Appendix C:

```java
Name joyce1 = new Name("Joyce", "Jones");
Name joyce2 = new Name("Joyce", "Jones");
Name derek = new Name("Derek", "Dodd");
```

Now joyce1 and joyce2 are two distinct objects that contain the same name. Typically, we would consider these objects to be equal, but in fact joyce1.equals(joyce2) is false. Since Name does not define its own equals method, it uses the one it inherits from Object. Object's equals method compares the addresses of the objects joyce1 and joyce2. Because we have two distinct objects, these addresses are not equal. However, joyce1.equals(joyce1) is true, since we are comparing an object with itself. This comparison is an **identity**. Notice that identity and equality are different concepts.

The method equals has the following definition in the class Object:

```java
public boolean equals(Object other)
{
   return (this == other);
} // end equals
```

Thus, the expression x.equals(y) is true if x and y reference the same object. We must override equals in the class Name if we want it to behave more appropriately.

As you will recall, Name has two data fields, first and last, that are instances of String. We could decide that two Name objects are equal if they have equal first names and equal last names. The following method, when added to the class Name, detects whether two Name objects are equal by comparing their data fields:

```java
public boolean equals(Object other)
{
   boolean result = false;

   if (other instanceof Name)
   {
      Name otherName = (Name)other;
      result = first.equals(otherName.first) &&
               last.equals(otherName.last);
   } // end if

   return result;
} // end equals
```

To ensure that the argument passed to the method equals is a Name object, you use the Java operator instanceof. For example, the expression

```java
other instanceof Name
```

is true if other references an object of either the class Name or a class derived from Name. If other references an object of any other class, or if other is null, the expression will be false.

Given an appropriate argument, the method equals compares the data fields of the two objects. Notice that we first must cast the type of the parameter other from Object to Name so that we can access Name's data fields. To compare two strings, we use String's equals method. The class String defines its own version of equals that overrides the equals method inherited from Object.

**Question 12** If sue and susan are two instances of the class Name, what if statement can decide whether they represent the same name?

**D.25**   **The clone method.** Another method inherited from the class Object is the method clone. This method takes no arguments and returns a copy of the receiving object. The returned object is supposed to have data identical to that of the receiving object, but it is a different object (an identical twin or a "clone"). As with other methods inherited from the class Object, we need to override the method clone before it can behave properly in our class. However, in the case of the method clone, there are other things we must do as well. A discussion of the method clone appears in Java Interlude 9.

## ANSWERS TO SELF-TEST QUESTIONS

**1.** Some possibilities are roomNumber and dorm, or street, city, state, zip.

**2.** `private` Address residence;
Add the methods setAddress and getAddress.

**3.** The constructors, setStudent, and toString.

**4.**
```
public Student()
{
    this(new Name(), "");
} // end default constructor
```

**5.**
```
NickName bob = new NickName();
bob.setNickName("Bob");
System.out.println(bob.getNickName());
```

**6.** The Vehicle class has two subclasses, WheeledVehicle and WheellessVehicle. The subclasses of WheeledVehicle are Automobile and Wagon. Boat is a subclass of WheellessVehicle. The remaining subclasses are the same as given in the figure.

**7.** No. Since getNickName returns a string, the first statement implicitly calls the method toString defined in the class String. Thus, *Bob* is displayed. Since the class NickName does not define its own version of toString, the second statement invokes Object's toString. The output involves the memory address of the object referenced by bob.

**8.** Overloading. The constructors have the same name but different signatures.

**9.** Overriding. The revised version of setStudent in CollegeStudent has the same signature and return type as the version in the superclass Student.

**10.** Yes. You can assign an object of a class to a variable of any ancestor type. An object of type HighSchoolStudent can do anything that an object of type Student can do.

**11.** No. The Student object does not have all the behaviors expected of a HighSchoolStudent object.

**12.** `if (sue.equals(susan))`

# Appendix E

# File Input and Output

(online at www.pearsonglobaleditions.com/Carrano)

# Index

# Reserved Words

Reserved words are also called **keywords**. You may not redefine any of these reserved words. Their meanings are determined by the Java language and cannot be changed. In particular, you cannot use any of these reserved words for variable names, method names, or class names.

| | | | |
|---|---|---|---|
| abstract | false | package | void |
| assert | final | private | volatile |
| | finally | protected | |
| boolean | float | public | while |
| break | for | | |
| byte | | return | |
| | goto | | |
| case | | short | |
| catch | if | static | |
| char | implements | strictfp | |
| class | import | super | |
| const | instanceof | switch | |
| continue | int | synchronized | |
| | interface | | |
| default | | this | |
| do | long | throw | |
| double | | throws | |
| | native | transient | |
| else | new | true | |
| enum | null | try | |
| extends | | | |

# Operator Precedence

In the following list, operators on the same line are of equal precedence. As you move down the list, each line is of lower precedence. When the order of operations is not dictated by parentheses, the operator of higher precedence executes before an operator of lower precedence. When operators have equal precedence, binary operators execute in left-to-right order, and unary operators execute in right-to-left order.

**Highest Precedence**
The unary operators +, -, ++, --, !, ~
The unary operators new and (*type*)
The binary operators *, /, %
The binary operators +, -
The binary (shift) operators <<, >>, >>>
The binary operators <, >, <=, >=
The binary operators ==, !=
The binary operator &
The binary operator ^
The binary operator |
The binary operator &&
The binary operator ||
The ternary (conditional) operator ? :
Assignment operators =, *=, /=, %=, +=, -=, <<=, >>=, >>>=, &=, ^=, |=
**Lowest Precedence**

---

# Primitive Data Types

| Type | Size | Values |
|------|------|--------|
| **Integer** | | |
| byte | 1 byte | -128 to 127 |
| short | 2 bytes | -32,768 to 32,767 |
| int | 4 bytes | -2,147,483,648 to 2,147,483,647 |
| long | 8 bytes | -9,223,372,036,854,775,808 to 9,223,372,036,854,775,807 |
| **Real** | | |
| float | 4 bytes | $-3.402824 \times 10^{38}$ to $3.402824 \times 10^{38}$ |
| double | 8 bytes | $-1.79769313486232 \times 10^{308}$ to $1.79769313486232 \times 10^{308}$ |
| **Character (Unicode)** | | |
| char | 2 bytes | All Unicode values between 0 and 65,535 |
| **Boolean** | | |
| boolean | 1 bit | true, false |

# Unicode Character Codes

The printable characters shown are a subset of the Unicode character set known as the ASCII character set. The numbering is the same whether the characters are considered to be members of the Unicode character set or members of the ASCII character set. (Character number 32 is the blank.)

| | | | | | | | |
|---|---|---|---|---|---|---|---|
| 32 | | 56 | 8 | 80 | P | 104 | h |
| 33 | ! | 57 | 9 | 81 | Q | 105 | i |
| 34 | " | 58 | : | 82 | R | 106 | j |
| 35 | # | 59 | ; | 83 | S | 107 | k |
| 36 | $ | 60 | < | 84 | T | 108 | l |
| 37 | % | 61 | = | 85 | U | 109 | m |
| 38 | & | 62 | > | 86 | V | 110 | n |
| 39 | ' | 63 | ? | 87 | W | 111 | o |
| 40 | ( | 64 | @ | 88 | X | 112 | p |
| 41 | ) | 65 | A | 89 | Y | 113 | q |
| 42 | * | 66 | B | 90 | Z | 114 | r |
| 43 | + | 67 | C | 91 | [ | 115 | s |
| 44 | , | 68 | D | 92 | \ | 116 | t |
| 45 | - | 69 | E | 93 | ] | 117 | u |
| 46 | . | 70 | F | 94 | ^ | 118 | v |
| 47 | / | 71 | G | 95 | _ | 119 | w |
| 48 | 0 | 72 | H | 96 | ` | 120 | x |
| 49 | 1 | 73 | I | 97 | a | 121 | y |
| 50 | 2 | 74 | J | 98 | b | 122 | z |
| 51 | 3 | 75 | K | 99 | c | 123 | { |
| 52 | 4 | 76 | L | 100 | d | 124 | | |
| 53 | 5 | 77 | M | 101 | e | 125 | } |
| 54 | 6 | 78 | N | 102 | f | 126 | ~ |
| 55 | 7 | 79 | O | 103 | g | | |